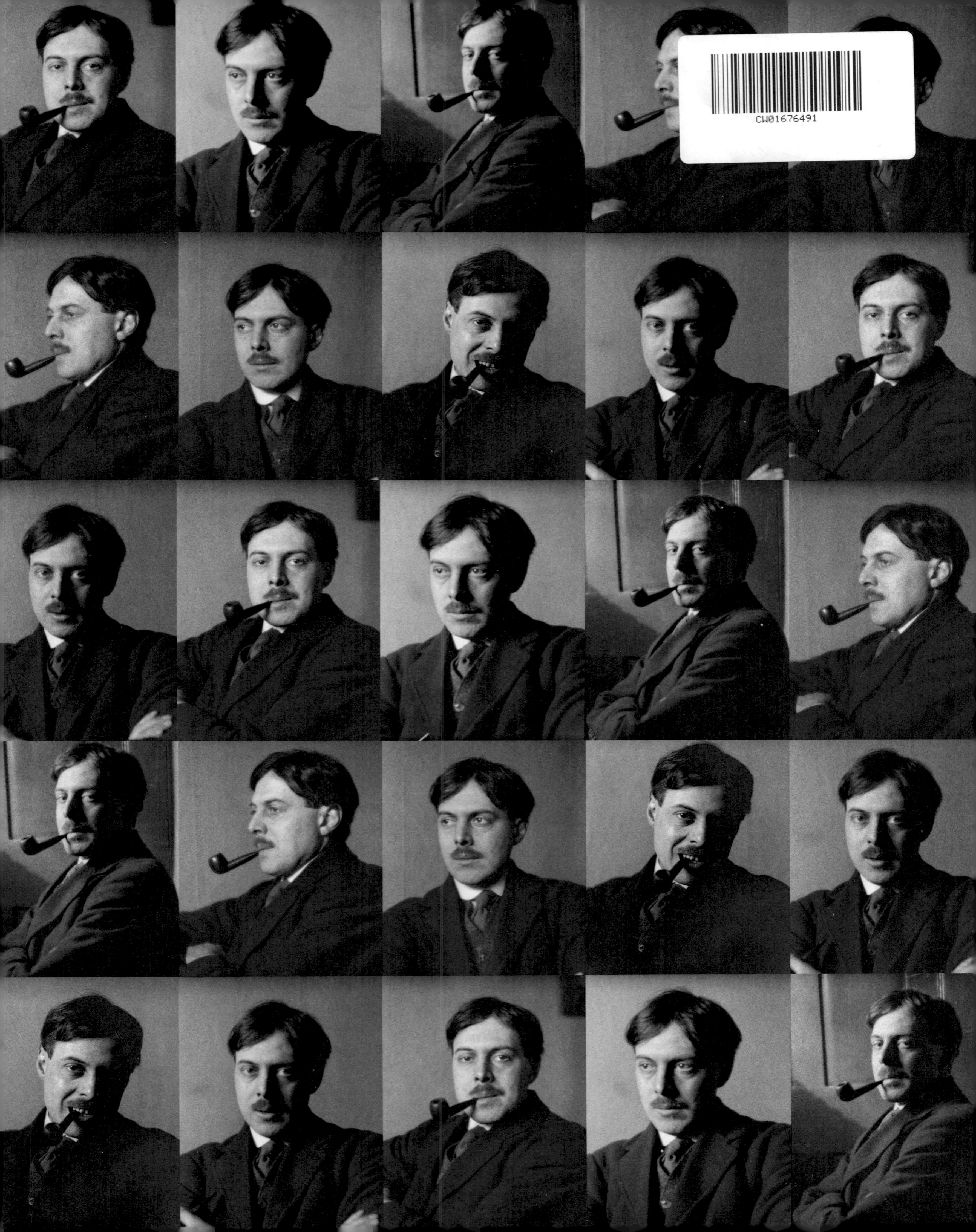

WYN DHAM LEWIS

(1882-1957)

FUNDACIÓN JUAN MARCH

This catalogue, and its Spanish edition, are published on the occasion of the exhibition

WYNDHAM LEWIS (1882-1957)

Fundación Juan March
Madrid

5 February - 16 May 2010

ACKNOWLEDGMENTS

The Fundación Juan March would like to express their gratitude to the following individuals and institutions whose generous loans have made this exhibition possible:

Aberdeen Art Gallery & Museums Collections
Aberystwyth University, School of Art Museum and Galleries
Art Gallery of Ontario, Toronto
Arts Council Collection, Southbank Centre, London
Austin/Desmond Fine Art, London
The Barber Institute of Fine Arts, The University of Birmingham
Collection of BNY Mellon, New York
The Courtauld Gallery, London
The Courtauld Institute of Art, London
George Eastman House, International Museum of Photography and Film, Rochester
Durban Art Gallery, KwaZulu-Natal
Ferens Art Gallery, Hull Museums, Kingston-upon-Hull
Fred L. Emerson Gallery, Hamilton College, Clinton
Imperial War Museum, London
Leeds Museums and Galleries (City Art Gallery)
Manchester City Galleries
The Metropolitan Museum of Art, New York
Middlesbrough Institute of Modern Art
The Museum of Modern Art, New York
National Gallery of Canada, Ottawa
National Portrait Gallery, London
Pembroke College. Oxford Junior Common Room Art Collection, Cambridge
The Potteries Museum & Art Gallery, Stoke-on-Kent
Rugby Art Gallery and Museum
Rugby School, Warwickshire
San Francisco Museum of Modern Art
Santa Barbara Museum of Art
Scottish National Gallery of Modern Art, Edinburgh
Scottish National Portrait Gallery, Edinburgh
Southampton City Art Gallery
Tate, London
Trustees of the British Museum, London
UCL Art Collections, University College, London
Victoria and Albert Museum, London
The Warden and Scholars of New College, Oxford

Wyndham Lewis Memorial Trust, London
Wyndham Lewis Memorial Trust, London. G. and V. Lane Collection
Wyndham Lewis Memorial Trust, London. J. Dolman Collection

Hugh Anson-Cartwright Collection
David Bowie Collection
Ivor Braka Ltd Collection
C.J. Fox Collection
Mark McLean Collection
O'Keeffe Collection
Brian Sewell Collection
Bobbie and Mike Wilsey Collection
YMJB Collection

Our thanks also go to those lenders who have chosen to remain anonymous.

We would also like to express our appreciation to the following individuals for their valuable help and collaboration:

Peter Appleton, Juan Ignacio Arias, Alison Beckett, Ian Berry, Julia Blanks, Juan Bonilla, Dr Michael Burden, Thomas Campbell, Laure Cavalié, Catherine Clement, Caroline Collier, Alix Collingwood, Jill Constantine, Tim Craven , Patrick Derham, Stephen Deuchar, Caroline Douglas, Paul Edwards, Patrick Elliott, Peter Ellis, Dr Mark Evans, Larry J. Feinberg, Erica Foden-Lenahan, Paloma Galante, Andrzej Gasiorek, Margherita Gatt, Jaime Gil-Delgado, Beth Greenacre (Rokeby), A.V. Griffiths, James Halloway, Lynne Henderson, Rebecca Herman, Henry Hillgarth, Neil Holland, Richard Humphreys, Cynthia Iavarone, Mark Jones, Robert P. Kelly, Philippa Kirkham, Dana L. Krueger, Brian J. Lang, Diane Lees, John Leighton, Glenn D. Lowry, Neil MacGregor, Rusty MacLean, Ceridwen Maycock, Marc Mayer, Monika McConnell, Sally McIntosh, David McNeff, Gill Metcalfe, Robert Meyrick , Jean Milton, Yolanda Morató, Jessica Morgan, Timothy Morgan-Owen, Alan Munton, Sandy Nairne, Wataru Okada, Sophie Olivier, Dr Nina Pearlman, Christine Rew, Holly Robbins, John Roles, Kirsten Simister, Nicole Simões da Silva, Ulrike Smalley, Dr P. Spencer-Longhurst, Chanté St Clair Inglis, Chris Stephens, Jell Sterrett, Moira Stevenson, Jenny Stretton, Cherie Summers, Ann Sumner , Matthew Teitelbaum, Gary Tinterow, Vicente Todolí, Ernst Vegelin, Jenny Wood, Phillippa Wood, Dr Barnaby Wright and José-Francisco Yvars.

LENDERS (Institutions)

Country	Town and institution	Cat. and B&M Cat.
SOUTH AFRICA	KwaZulu-Natal, Durban Art Gallery	123, 147
CANADA	Ottawa, National Gallery of Canada	189, 196
	Toronto, Art Gallery of Ontario	175, 195
SPAIN	Madrid, Fundación Juan March	**B&M:** 56, 59
UNITED KINGDOM	Aberdeen, Aberdeen Art Gallery & Museums Collections	155
	Aberystwyth, Aberystwyth University, School of Art Museum and Galleries	85
	Birmingham,The Barber Institute of Fine Arts, The University of Birmingham	172
	Edinburgh, Scottish National Gallery of Modern Art	95, 98
	Edinburgh, Scottish National Portrait Gallery	210
	Hanley, The Potteries Museum & Art Gallery	148
	Kingston-upon-Hull, Ferens Art Gallery, Hull Museums	99
	Leeds, Leeds Museums and Galleries (City Art Gallery)	72, 153
	London, Arts Council Collection, Southbank Centre	15, 156
	London, Book Library, The Courtauld Institute of Art	**B&M:** 63
	London, Imperial War Museum	63, 71
	London, National Portrait Gallery	139, 140, 206, 209, 212
	London, Tate	46, 48, 58, 59, 76, 77, 105, 124, 128, 149, 161, 162, 208
	London, Trustees of the British Museum	24, 142
	London, UCL Art Collections, University College	1
	London, Victoria and Albert Museum	6, 12, 13, 17, 23, 41, 43, 51, 52, 60, 61
	London, Wyndham Lewis Memorial Trust	2, 3, 14, 129, 152, 163, 167, 178, 190, 192, 193 **B&M:** 2, 3, 4, 5, 8, 9, 11, 14, 15, 16, 18, 19, 21, 24, 28, 29, 30, 31, 32, 33, 34, 36, 37, 39, 40, 41, 43, 44, 47, 48, 49, 53, 57, 58, 59, 61, 62, 204
	London, Wyndham Lewis Memorial Trust. G. and V. Lane Collection	18, 22, 30, 31, 32, 34, 35, 36, 37, 39, 40, 89, 91, 106, 112, 141, 143, 176
	London, Wyndham Lewis Memorial Trust. J. Dolman Collection	205
	Manchester, Manchester City Galleries	8, 67, 84,92
	Middlesbrough, Collection of Middlesbrough Institute of Modern Art	173
	Oxford, Pembroke College Oxford Junior Common Room Art Collection	82
	Oxford, The Warden and Scholars of New College	164
	Rugby, Rugby Art Gallery and Museum	151
	Rugby, Rugby School	114
	Southampton, Southampton City Art Gallery	25, 66
USA	Clinton, Fred L. Emerson Gallery, Hamilton College	169
	New York, Collection of BNY Mellon	111
	New York, The Metropolitan Museum of Art	101, 127
	New York, The Museum of Modern Art	118, 158, 168
	Rochester, George Eastman House, International Museum of Photography and Film	211 (a-h)
	San Fransisco, San Francisco Museum of Modern Art	53, 54, 110
	Santa Barbara, Santa Barbara Museum of Art	159, 200

LENDERS (Collections)

Country	Collection	Cat. and B&M Cat.
CANADA	Hugh Anson-Cartwright	180, 181, 183, 191
	C.J. Fox	9, 136, 179
	Mark McLean	197, 199
	Private collection	27, 32, 33, 40, 45, 47, 50, 57, 64, 70, 193, 203
SPAIN	YMJB	**B&M:**1, 2, 7, 10, 12, 13, 17, 20, 21, 23, 25, 26, 27, 30, 31, 32, 35, 40, 42, 43, 45, 50, 51, 52, 54, 55, 57, 60, 69
UNITED KINGDOM	David Bowie	26, 44
	Ivor Braka Ltd	10, 75
	O'Keeffe	86
	Brian Sewell	4
	Private collections	7, 10, 11, 16, 17, 20, 21, 25, 29, 45, 63, 65, 67, 71, 74, 78-81, 83, 84, 88, 90, 97, 98, 103, 107, 109, 113, 115, 124-26, 130-32, 137, 138, 143 145, 150, 151, 157, 165, 180, 192, 202, 206, 207
USA	Bobbie and Mike Wilsey	53, 54, 110
	Private collections	49, 64, 92-94, 102, 120-22, 133, 146, 160, 194

A

ESSAYS

B

WYNDHAM LEWIS: THE ARTIST

FOREWORD

Wyndham Lewis (1882-1957), the exhibition that this catalogue accompanies, conceived of and organised by the Fundación Juan March with the assistance of some of the most noted specialists in Lewis's work, seeks to interrupt the thundering silence that has surrounded and still surrounds one of the most vigorous pictorial and literary bodies of work of the first half of the twentieth century. Lewis himself was aware of this and at times described himself as "a skeleton in a cupboard."

To this end, the exhibition reveals, in all its complex simplicity, with its shadowy angles and luminous outlines, the work of Wyndham Lewis to the interested viewer and reader, allowing them the opportunity to prove that the "skeleton in a cupboard" is actually – to paraphrase the title of another of his works – *A Dragon in a Cage*, still unfamiliar but with a volcanic creative energy.

This is the first exhibition in Spain dedicated to the artist and the most complete display of his work since *Wyndham Lewis and Vorticism*, the retrospective organised by the Tate Gallery, London, in 1956, a year before Lewis's death. In its wake, there have been few monographic exhibitions, the most recent being the 2008 exhibition dedicated to his portraits at London's National Portrait Gallery. Our exhibition presents Lewis's life and artistic and literary work through more than 150 paintings and drawings and over 60 books, magazines and manifestos, with loans from museums, institutions and private collections in England and throughout the world.

The publication ***Wyndham Lewis (1882-1957)*** constitutes a complete presentation, for the broader public, of Lewis and his work – the catalogue of works is organised chronologically and thematically and features more than 200 catalogue entries, followed by a section analysing Lewis's output as a writer with entries on each of the more than 40 books included. In addition to a large number of illustrations and articles, there is a selected anthology of texts by and about Lewis, an extensive bibliography, an illustrated biography, a comprehensive listing of his exhibitions and, in particular, illuminating essays by Richard Humphreys, Alan Munton, Andrzej Gąsiorek, Yolanda Morató and Juan Bonilla, preceded by a thorough introduction to Lewis by Paul Edwards. It should be pointed out that, given the almost complete lack of publications on Lewis, we have chosen to unite the exacting nature of this catalogue with the aspects of a monograph: this is the reason for the extent of this book and also why the reader will find more catalogue entries than there are works in the exhibition (as noted in each entry).

In conjunction with the exhibition, the Fundación Juan March has published two supplementary books: a semi-facsimile Spanish edition of the magazine *Blast* (1914), the "enormous puce coloured periodical" that was, in Lewis's own words, "the verbal expression" of Vorticism; and a bilingual edition of Shakespeare's *Timon of Athens* with illustrations by Lewis that were meant to accompany a 1912 English edition of the text, which was never published. With the latter publication this situation has been remedied and Lewis's illustrations now accompany a text in whose first act the protagonist declares: "Painting is welcome."

The acknowledgements section of this catalogue is sufficiently extensive to make clear that this project could not have been realised without the help of many individuals and institutions. In addition to this list, the Fundación Juan March would like to express its special appreciation to the Wyndham Lewis Memorial Trust, as well as to the senior members of that generation of "Lewisians" who, through their collections and publications, have kept the memory of Lewis alive and have encouraged and assisted in this project: Walter Michel, C.J. Fox and Graham Lane, among others. We would also like to express our sincere gratitude to the Tate Gallery – holder of a large number of works by Wyndham Lewis – and, in particular, to Chris Stephens and to the director, Sir Nicholas Serota, for the many critical loans granted. Our thanks also go to Alan Munton, Andrzej Gasiorek, Yolanda Morató, Juan Bonilla and Kevin Power (the last for his biographies of the Vorticists in the Spanish edition of *Blast*) for enthusiastically accepting our invitation to write the essays herein and providing enlightening contributions on various and essential aspects on the life and work of Lewis. We are grateful to Yolanda Morató for her prudent and dedicated translations, particularly those of Lewis's own writings.

Lastly, if this exhibition would have been difficult to realise without the participation of the aforementioned individuals and institutions, there are others without whom it would have been virtually impossible. The Fundación Juan March would like to express its appreciation to the exhibition's guest curator, Paul Edwards, who – together with the sure judgement and knowledge (and humour) of Richard Humphreys – has given us a memorable model of team work, helping to "translate" his vast and detailed knowledge of Wyndham Lewis into the practices of curating and installing an exhibition.

Fundación Juan March
Madrid, Februrary 2010

WYNDHAM LEWIS: AS UNKNOWN AS THE FUTURE

As unknown as the future from whence he continues to reach out to us, Wyndham Lewis (Amherst, Nova Scotia, 1882 – London, 1957) was the consummate artist who founded Vorticism ("this strange synthesis of cultures and times," as he called it) and created a fascinating body of work full of energetic variety in which he simultaneously combined cubo-futurist, Vorticist and abstract compositions with the most significant of portraits. As he wrote, "I wished the reader … to see what could be done by burying Euclid deep in the living flesh – that of Mr Eliot or of Mr Pound – rather than, at this time of day, displaying the astral geometries of those gentlemen." However, in addition to being a pioneering abstract artist, portraitist and war painter, Lewis was a prolific and varied writer. He wrote manifestos, published magazines – such as *Blast* and *The Enemy* – and wrote hundreds of articles on art and literature, as well as more than 40 books, ranging from novels to plays, literary and art criticism, poetry, and philosophical and political essays with astute and controversial analyses of his time and world. In short, he was a "one-man avant-garde."

Lewis has been considered "the most fascinating personality of our time … in whose work we recognise the thought of the modern and energy of the cave-man," (T.S. Eliot); "the great portraitist of this or any other time," (Walter Sickert); the writer "with enough talent to set up dozens of ordinary writers," (George Orwell); one of "Ezra Pound's artists," (Richard Humphreys); the person who, due to his numerous speculations about and intellectual references to such figures as Nietzsche, Rousseau,

Mallarmé, Bergson, Kant, Dostoyevsky, and Le Bon, has been classified as a "One-Man *Frankfurter Schule*" (Paul Edwards).

The exhibition's objective is to present Lewis in the most comprehensive way possible. However, neither the exhibition nor its catalogue is intended as some sort of "rescue operation" for an artist comparatively disdained and forgotten along the margins of twentieth-century art and culture. The thesis at the heart of the exhibition is that Lewis is a major figure in the history of modern art, literature and culture, whose pictorial work warrants – as one of his definitions of "beauty" reads – "an immense predilection." Also, the idea that Lewis is not as extensively known as he should be is not only due to the reasons usually put forward to explain (and justify) his obscurity, but also to the fact that the artist (and above all his work) perhaps poses a challenge to the usual way we organise our memory of art and historicise art, ideas and culture.

Lewis's work does not require a rescue operation to save it from presumed obscurity, from the past, but it does need to be considered as something that comes to us from the future and obliges us to understand the realities of modern art and culture beyond the classifying categories currently in use. "The future," as he wrote in 1922, "possesses its history as well as the past …. *All living art is the history of the future*. The greatest artists, men of science and political thinkers, come to us from the future – from the opposite direction to the past."

The "future" from which Lewis reaches out to us (like the "Diogenes of our time," as he called himself in the second issue of *The Enemy*) is, chronologically, that of the first half of the twentieth century. Intellectually, however, Lewis's work, with all of its light and shade, anticipates contemporary artistic, social, political and cultural reality, aspects of which were rarely glimpsed at the time. Such is the case with his ideas on the entropic character of modern art, his spatial and non-temporal understanding of reality, his analysis of the corruptions of totalitarianism (and of democracy) and the cult of the child and the adolescent in modern culture, the dialectic between the new in art and fashion, his theory on laughter, the mechanical and the external, his diatribes against modern philosophy of the time and against psychology, his opinions on the relationships between art and war and art and politics (he defined the uproar caused by *Blast* as "art behaving like politics") and on the luck of art in a mechanised and globalised world. It is not a coincidence that Lewis had such a great influence on someone such as Marshall McLuhan and that he has come to the attention of analysts such as Frederic Jameson and Hal Foster.

Therefore, how is it possible that Lewis could remain almost completely unknown by the majority of the public? This situation has not been remedied, not even when – as has been the case for several decades now – alternatives to the historical art canon have been attempted. These have reviewed its so-called ethnocentric dependencies or have resolved the venerable history of art in the form of histories that humanity recounts to itself from the fragmentary perspectives of *mille plateaux*, from a thousand platforms and through different, multiple and, it would appear, legitimately simultaneous discourses. For some figures, eras and places, this flourishing of micro-histories has already meant a first step towards an inescapable canonisation or revaluation of what was previously considered peripheral, secondary or marginal.

Wyndham Lewis continues to retain the authentic status of a truly marginal figure: one whom we are unaware is a marginal figure because he is unknown to us. If the history of the first twentieth-century vanguards is a bellicose one – that of new against old, rupture against tradition – then Lewis is perhaps its most illustrious figure, missing in combat. And the initial practical consequence of this is that paying him attention – as with this exhibition – tends to always begin with justifications that also sound like self-justifications. It seems that one must start by explaining why Lewis is *somebody*, in order to justify why we should consider an unknown figure.

Basically, there are three reasons why so many people would be relatively ignorant of an artist and his work. The first is that both went unnoticed in the artist's own day; the second, that they have remained forgotten in the past; and the third, that they then belonged – and continue to belong – more to the future. We have to imagine what the future may be like. Only with difficulty can we anticipate it so as to articulate it along with that which is already known, and then domesticate it by understanding it. The past is a domestic animal, the present is an animal in the process of domestication, and the future is a savage creature, with *The Wild Body* (the title of one of Lewis's books) full of possibilities, flashes of light, foreboding and surprises.

While Lewis is still a comparatively unknown artist – and perhaps he has never been completely familiar – it is certainly not because he was unnoticed in his own day. In 1914 in London, Lewis was a controversial celebrity who was responsible for the explosion (*Blast!*) of the first and only English avant-garde movement: Vorticism. It emerged in the midst of the anaemic *post-Cézannisme* of the Bloomsbury Group and the somewhat post-Impressionist decorativism of Roger Fry's Omega Workshops. Soon after, in 1918, Lewis reaped success as a writer (with his first novel, *Tarr*, an incisive *Künstlerroman*). Therefore, the second reason for his obscurity – obscurity itself – does address the issue and the question naturally becomes: why is he not as well known as he deserves to be? This question assumes greater urgency when one examines Lewis in detail and, above all, the polyhedral and impressive variety of his work, beginning with the fact – almost unparalleled in history to the extent practised by Lewis – of his fascinating status as a double agent: both painter and writer.

The reasons normally employed to explain Lewis's relative obscurity – a subject addressed by some of the essays in this catalogue – tend to allude to his status as an eccentric British artist within an England already eccentric in the context of modern art (Richard Humphreys). Or they refer to his character, at once harsh (his entry in *The Concise Dictionary of National Biography* defines him as "a towering, undisciplined and quarrelsome egotist, his greatest enemy was himself") and complex (he was once described as "an untalented genius"). Lewis apparently had a great capacity for having a point of view about everything with something to offend everybody. This, of course, was also true of some of his satirical and, particularly, his political gambles (Andrzej Gasiorek), the latter of which were naive and flawed and uselessly submitted to subsequent retractions; after *The Apes of God* and *Hitler*, his fame remained in tatters.

Nevertheless, perhaps the main reason that Wyndham Lewis does not form part of the traditional art canon to an extent proportional to his unquestionable importance – and the point from which this exhibition departs – is perhaps that he embodied avant-garde logic so radically that one is hard pressed to find parallels with other artists (there are exceptions, such as the less popularised Kazimir Malevich or Pavel Filonov, among others). Lewis took to its final consequences – in life and in art – the logic of the modern avant-garde, which is the belligerent, paradoxical and contradictory logic of historicism. In fact, to a certain extent, taking avant-garde logic to its final consequences consists in simultaneously maintaining the dual status of avant-garde and anti-avant-garde artist, without synthesizing it, leaving it open to contradiction. That is the meaning behind the title of *The Enemy*, which Lewis imposed on himself, making it as interesting as it is uncomfortable and untameable in attempting to understand him. The work and the artist escape us when one tries to understand the logic of the cultural narratives of modernity from the simplicity of the binary pair, "or tradition or rupture," still common today.

The work of Wyndham Lewis will undoubtedly remain a presence in the art, literature and culture of the present day and the future; and this exhibition and its catalogue will hopefully contribute to bringing awareness to one of the most stimulating and eccentric artists of the twentieth century.

No small task, as Lewis himself put forth in *After Abstract Art* (1940): "To imitate what is under our eyes, to develop these imitations into generalized (super-natural – but not super-real) realities; and beyond that, and in a more general way, to care for, and to influence people to observe, the visual amenities, and to banish as far as possible from the visual field all that is degrading or stupid, all that is of trivial or slovenly design and texture: these are great human functions, surely, that people neglect to their cost."

Manuel Fontán del Junco
Director of Exhibitions
Fundación Juan March

"A PORTRAIT OF THE ARTIST AS AN ENEMY"

WYNDHAM LEWIS (1882–1957): ILLUSTRATED BIOGRAPHY

▸ "The mother and the father of the author," in *Blasting and Bombardiering: Autobiography* (1914–1926), 1937.
▾ Percy Wyndham Lewis, in an Eastbourne photographic studio, aged about 6. Division of Rare and Manuscript Collections, Cornell University Library, Ithaca, NY.
▾▸ Stallard House, Rugby House, 1898. Burser of Rugby School.

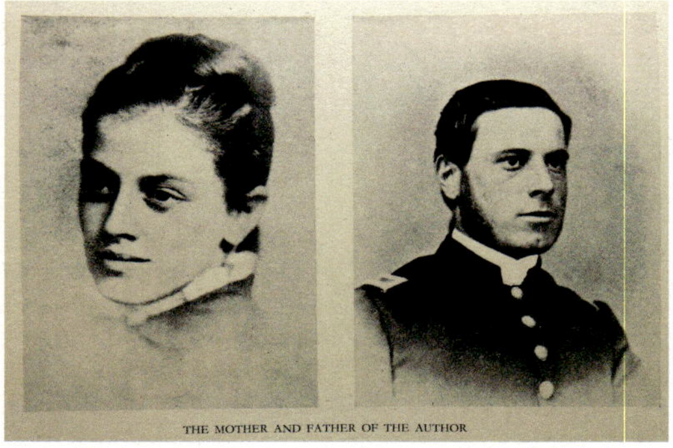

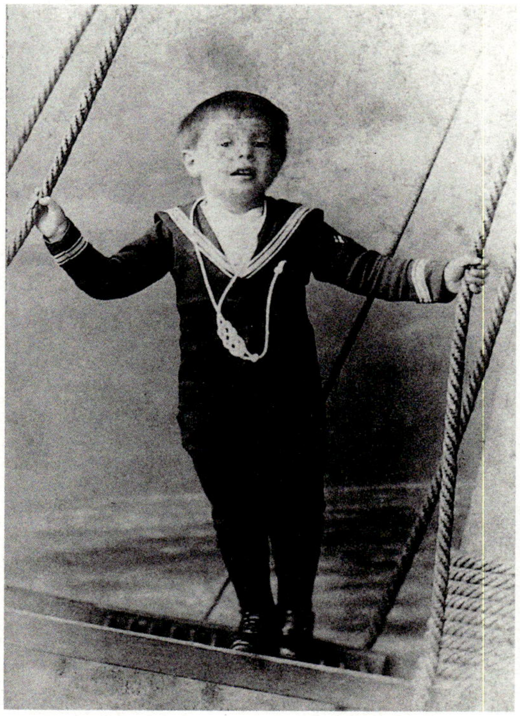

1882

* Percy Wyndham Lewis is born on 18 November in Amherst, Nova Scotia, Canada, on board his father's boat. He is the only child of American father, Charles Edward Lewis, and English mother, Anne Stuart Prickett. Spends his early years in Maryland.

1888

* The family moves to the Isle of Wight, England.

1893

* Following his parents' separation, Lewis and his mother settle in London.

1897–98

* Attends Rugby School, England.

1898–1901

* Studies at Slade School of Fine Art, London. Expelled in 1901.
* Becomes acquainted with a group of older artists and writers. He is introduced to the art of Gustave Flaubert by Thomas Sturge Moore, and Laurence Binyon initiates him into oriental art. In addition to non-European art, his work is influenced by painter and writer William Blake and the great eighteenth-century English caricaturists.
* Painter Augustus John becomes his teacher and mentor.

1902

* Travels to Europe to complete his artistic training and acquires an in-depth knowledge of continental art and culture. Lives in Paris for four years, during which he goes on study trips to Holland, Germany and Spain.
* Visits Madrid with artist Spencer Gore; copies paintings by Goya at the Museo del Prado.

1903

* Discovers the bohemian life of Montparnasse, satirically depicted in his first novel *Tarr* (1918).
* Meets Ida Vendel ("Bertha" in *Tarr*) and begins a relationship that will last until 1907.

1908

* Second trip to Spain; visits León, San Sebastián and Vigo. Holiday in Brittany with his mother. In December, he settles permanently in London.

1909

* First published writing, "The 'Pole'," appears in *The English Review* edited by Ford Hermann Hueffer, and subsequently in *The Tramp*. A revision of these stories is published in *The Wild Body* in 1927.

1910

* Meets poet Ezra Pound at the Vienna Café on New Oxford Street; however, their friendship does not develop until 1913.
* Spends summer in Brittany with painter Henry Lamb.

1911

* Member of Camden Town Group, London, a group of artists who gather around Walter Sickert. Members of the group include Gore and Harold Gilman. The Group holds its first exhibition. Lucien Pissarro is repulsed by Lewis's paintings. Until 1922, his work features a deliberately provocative combination of grotesque and strange shapes, primitive and caricature-like figures, loud and bizarre acid colours, and an unusual narrative.
* Draws Cubist self-portraits and begins to experiment with Futurism.
* Has a son, Hoel, with lover Olivia Johnson.

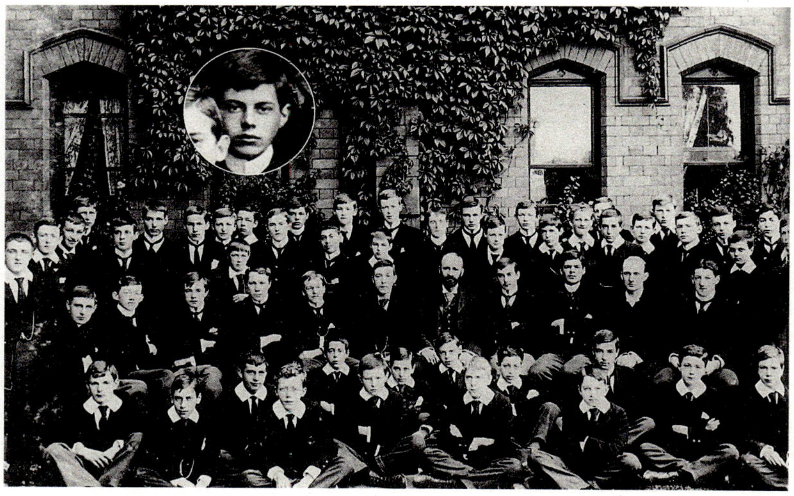

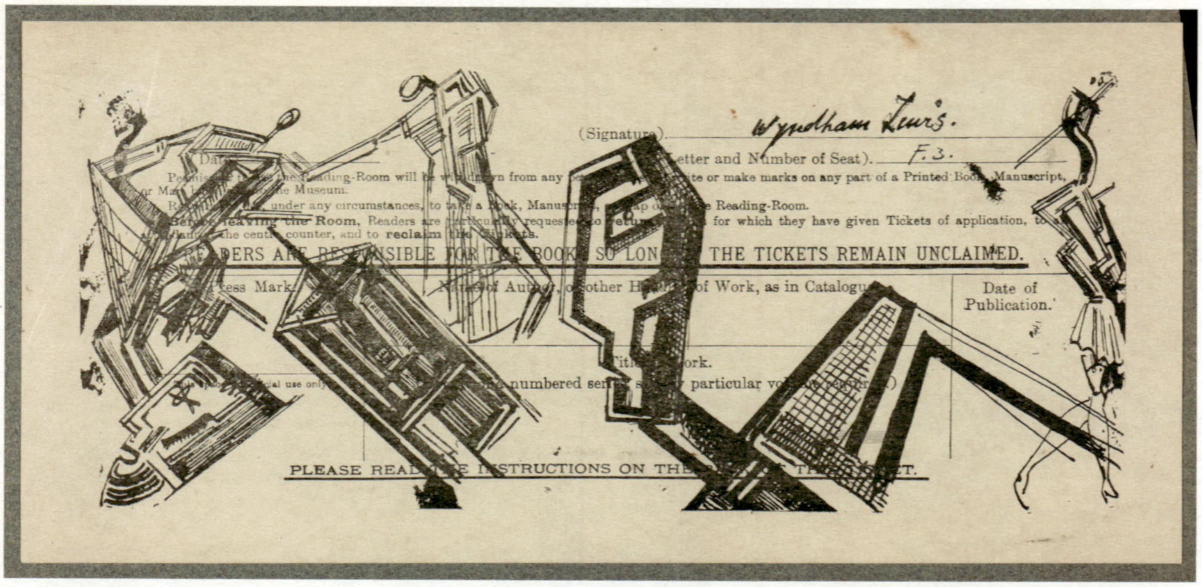

* Unsuccessfully submits *The Man of the World*, "the book of 500,000 words," to various publishers. Later publishes a revised and extended version in separate books.

1926

* Lewis re-launches his career as a writer and devotes himself entirely to this task until 1931. For several years, he immerses himself in writing and the study of political theory, anthropology and philosophy, which drives him to a somewhat clandestine existence, "burying himself in the Reading Room at the British Museum or hiding in a secret workshop."
* Publishes his first non-fiction book, *The Art of Being Ruled*, a work of political theory and analysis that attempts to distinguish sources of revolutionary change in society.

1927

* Launches *The Enemy*, a new magazine largely written by him. In the first issue, he carries out a critique of the literary avant-garde (including Pound and Joyce) for the political and philosophical naivety of their work. He presents himself as "the enemy," a soldier fighting on his own for a much-needed revolution. In *The Enemy*, No. 2, he examines the cult of the "primitive" in the work of writers D.H. Lawrence and Sherwood Anderson.
* Publishes *Time and Western Man*, which reprints articles published in *The Enemy* and extends its critique to cover contemporary metaphysical theory; also publishes *The Lion and the Fox*, a study of Shakespeare's characters, and *The Wild Body*, revisions of early short stories set in Brittany and Spain.

1928

* His drawings show Surrealist and metaphysical influences.
* Publishes *The Childermass: Section I*, a fantasy about the posthumous existence "outside Heaven," and also a revised version of *Tarr*.

1929

* Publishes *Paleface: The Philosophy of the Melting Pot*, which reprints and revises essays published in *The Enemy*, No. 2. Publishes *The Enemy*, No. 3, a critique of Paris avant-garde.
* Meets poets W.H. Auden and Stephen Spender.

1930

* Publishes a limited and signed edition of *The Apes of God*. It is a satirical novel describing the London art world of the 1920s, including his patrons and so-called friends Sitwell and Schiff.
* Marries one of his models, Gladys Anne ("Froanna") Hoskyns, with whom he will spend the rest of his life. She becomes one of his main models and a source of inspiration for his literary characters.
* Meets writer Naomi Mitchison; he will paint several portraits of her.

1931

* In *Hitler* (articles written for *Time and Tide* upon his return from Berlin in 1930), Lewis states Hitler is a "man of peace" and defends certain aspects of Fascism against Communism. In spite of subsequent attempts to clarify these opinions, his reputation is permanently damaged.
* Following a serious illness, visits Morocco with his wife and later travels to Harvard, Cambridge, Massachusetts.

1932

* Resumes his artistic career, in particular oil painting. His compositions are increasingly metaphysical and enigmatic. They are inspired by literary, historical and mythological sources, which fascinated him.
* Publishes the portfolio *Thirty Personalities and a Self-Portrait* and organises an exhibition under the same name at The Lefevre Galleries, London.
* Publishes *Filibusters in Barbary*, a travel book based on his experiences in Morocco, and *The Doom of Youth*, a study of "youth politics." Both are prohibited after libel action. Furthermore, the comic novel *Snooty Baronet* – a sharp satire of behaviourism – is banned by Smiths and Boots lending libraries.

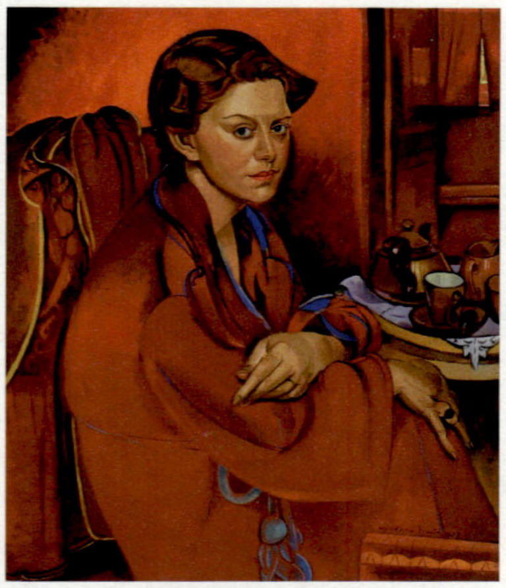

▲▲ Drawing on the face of a book requisition slip from the Reading Room of the British Museum, London (Porfolio *Fifteen Drawings: Reading Room*, 1915). Wyndham Lewis Memorial Trust, London.
▲ *Froanna (Portrait of the Artist's Wife)*, 1937. Glasgow Museums (Cat. 144).

1933

* Publishes *One-Way Song*, a collection of poems.

1934

* Bladder operation.
* Critique of Eliot, Virginia Woolf, William Faulkner and Ernest Hemingway in *Men Without Art*.

1935

* Collaborates with Mitchison, illustrating her fantasy *Beyond This Limit*.

1936

* Second and third operations.
* Publishes *Left Wings Over Europe*, an anti-war book.

1937

* Publishes *The Revenge for Love*, a tragic novel regarding the left wing's naive political commitments prior to the Spanish Civil War; *Count Your Dead: They are Alive!*, an anti-war text on the Spanish Civil War, sympathetic to the Fascist side; and *Blasting and Bombardiering*, his first autobiography.
* Paints *The Armada* and *The Surrender of Barcelona*.
* First major solo exhibition since 1921, at The Leicester Galleries: exhibits portraits, drawings and paintings on metaphysical and historical themes. It is a critical success, but a commercial failure. A letter signed by Henry Moore – among others – is addressed to the Tate Gallery and other institutions urging them to recognise Lewis's importance and to purchase his work.
* Visits Berlin and Warsaw. Change of views regarding Nazism.
* In the special "Wyndham Lewis" issue of *Twentieth Century Verse* (edited by Julian Symons), he declares that he feels "much deceived in politicians."

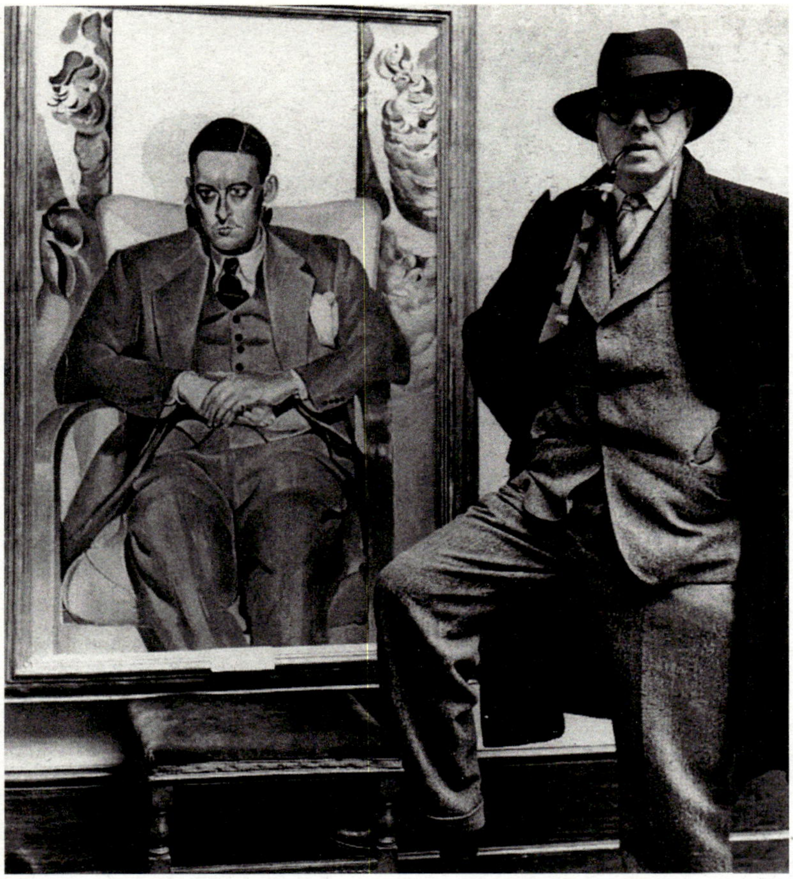

◀ Wyndham Lewis with his rejected portrait of T.S. Eliot at the Royal Academy, 21 April 1938, London.
▼ *John Macleod*, 1938. Yale Center for British Art, New Haven, Conn.
▼▼ *Hedwig (Portrait of Mrs. Meyrick Booth)*, 1938. Herbert F. Johnson Museum of Art, Cornell University, Ithaca, NY.

1938

* Paints a large portrait of T.S. Eliot. On account of its rejection by the Royal Academy in London, he briefly returns to the headlines in art publications.
* The painting of Eliot belongs to an outstanding series of portraits produced between 1937 and 1939, among them stand out those of the "men of 1914" and of his wife Froanna (*Ezra Pound*, *Froanna*, *Naomi Mitchinson*, *Stephen Spender*, *Julian Symons*, *Hedwig*). These works, along with his portraits from the early 1920s and his portfolio of 1932, prove he was the greatest British portraitist of the twentieth century.
* Donates a painting for auction in aid of republican Spain.
* Exhibition at Beaux Arts Gallery in London.
* Publishes *The Mysterious Mr Bull*, a historical study of the British character, praised by George Orwell.
* Pound visits London; Lewis begins a portrait of him.

1939

* Publishes *The Jews: Are they Human?*, a fervent defence of the Jews, and *The Hitler Cult*, which attacks Nazism and predicts that the war will end in six years.
* *Wyndham Lewis the Artist* brings together writings on art, including a new essay advocating the return to nature (though not to naturalism).
* In September, Lewis and Froanna leave for the United States and Canada in search of their roots; they stay for six years. Lewis believes his career, especially as a portraitist, will be more successful here. Also, he did not want to witness once more the destruction that would befall Europe after the Second World War. They live in Buffalo, New York, throughout October and November. Paints Chancellor of the University at Buffalo, Samuel Capen.
* They live in New York for nearly a year, but Lewis is not able to sell his work or receive commissions. Lectures on art and literature at Harvard and Columbia Universities.

1940

* Lewis and his wife move into Hotel Tudor, Shelbourne Street, in Toronto. The paintings and drawings from this period reflect their economic hardships, also described in the novel Self Condemned.
* Publishes *America, I Presume*, an extraordinary satirical account of American society.

1941

* Begins a marvellous and imaginative series of watercolours on themes of creation, gestation and crucifixion; also a series of bathing scenes.
* The entire stock of "The Role of Line in Art" – an illustrated essay published by Lord Carlow, Lewis's patron – is destroyed during an air raid on London.
* *Anglosaxony: A League that Works* is published by Ryerson Press. Also published is *The Vulgar Streak*, a critique of the prejudices of English society.
* A tumour causes serious deterioration in Lewis's eyesight.

1943

* Lewis and his wife move to Windsor, Ontario. Gives a series of lectures on "The Philosophical Roots of Art and Modern Literature" and "The Concept of Liberty in American History" at Assumption College.
* Meets Marshall McLuhan, whose ideas on global culture have a great impact on him.

The Armada, 1937. Collection of the Vancouver Art Gallery.

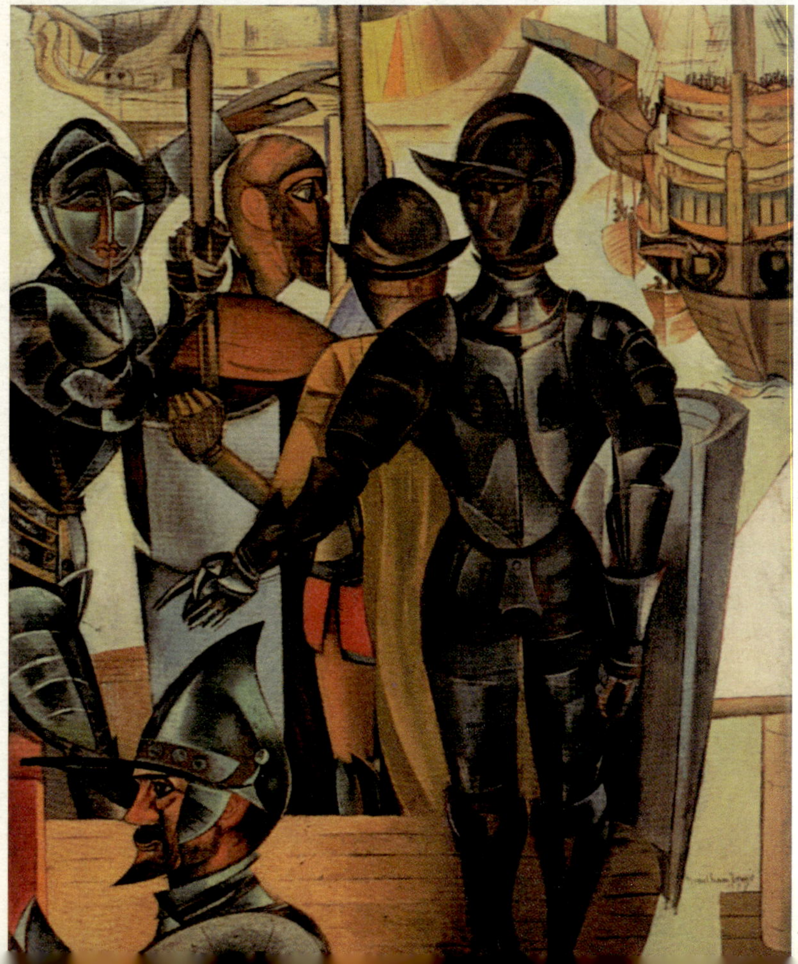

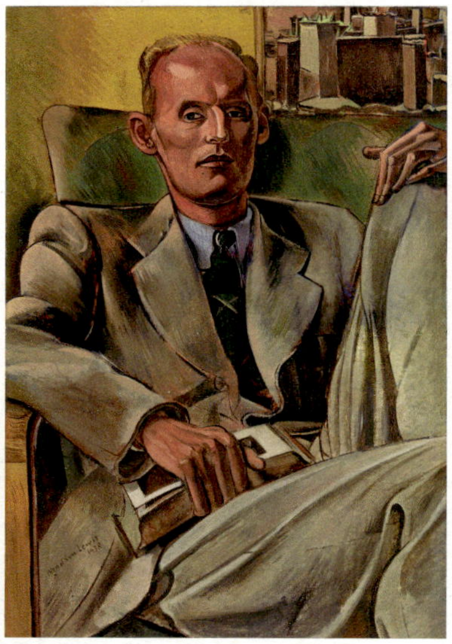

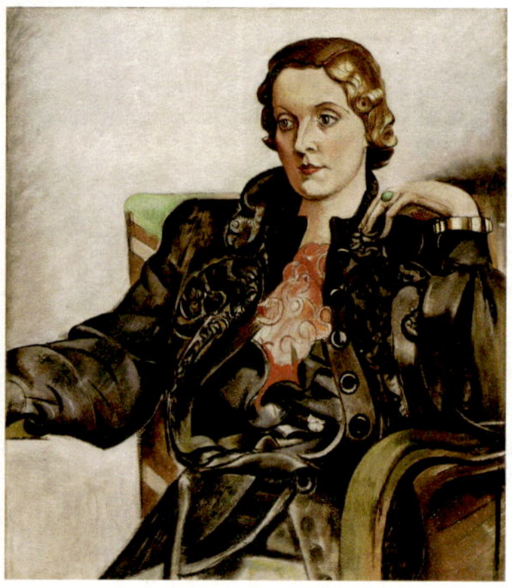

1944

* Lewis and his wife live temporarily in St Louis and Ottawa. Lewis is commissioned to produce various portraits of important American and Canadian figures, such as Joseph Erlanger, Nobel Prize Winner in Medicine, and the wife of Ernest Stix, President of Rice-Stix Dry Goods Company, St Louis.

1945

* Lewis and Froanna return to London with financial assistance from Malcolm MacDonald, politician and diplomat (High Commissioner to Canada during Second World War), and settle in Notting Hill, where Lewis lives until his death.

1946

* Employed as art critic for the weekly BBC programme, *The Listener*; praises the work of young British artists such as Michael Ayrton, Francis Bacon and Robert Colquhoun.

1948

* Publishes *America and Cosmic Man*, a study of American history and society as a model for international politics.

1949

* Works on a portrait of T.S. Eliot, his last oil painting before losing his sight.
* Retrospective exhibition at the Redfern Gallery, London.

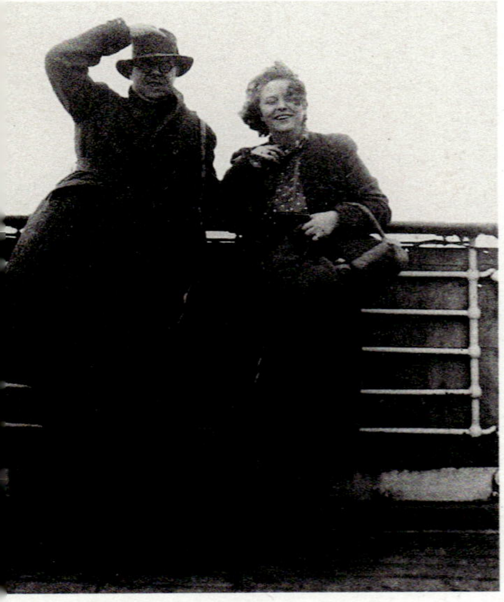

Lewis and Gladys aboard SS Empress of Britain, September 1939. Division of Rare and Manuscript Collections, Cornell University Library, Ithaca, NY.

1950

* Publishes *Rude Assignment*, an autobiography.

1951

* Announces his blindness in "The Sea-Mists of the Winter," his final article as art critic for the *The Listener*. He then abandoned his career as a painter and drawer, but not as a writer. He wrote seven more books.
* Publishes *Rotting Hill*, a collection of short stories on life in England during the period of "austerity" presided over by Chancellor of the Exchequer, Sir Stafford Cripps.

1952

* Publishes *The Writer and the Absolute*, containing essays on Jean Paul Sartre, André Malraux, Albert Camus and Orwell.
* Receives an honorary doctorate from the University of Leeds.

1954

* Publishes *The Demon of Progress in the Arts*.

1955

* The BBC broadcast *The Childermass*, published as *The Human Age, Book Two: Monstre Gai* and *Book Three: Malign Fiesta*.

1956

* Publishes he novel *The Red Priest*, in which the main character is a boxing high churchman who murders his curate.
* Sir John Rothenstein organises the retrospective *Wyndham Lewis and Vorticism* at the Tate Gallery, a travelling exhibition touring several venues in the UK. A frail and blind Lewis, who had written the introduction to the catalogue, attends the opening.

1957

* Lewis dies on 7 March at the Westminster Hospital as a result of a brain tumour.

The above chronology is based on Paul Edwards's chronology for the *Wyndham Lewis: Portraits* exhibition held at the National Portrait Gallery, London in 2008. Other sources reviewed: Jeffrey Meyers, *The Enemy. A Biography of Wyndham Lewis* (Boston/London/Melbourne: Routledge & Kegan Paul, 1980); Paul O'Keeffe, *Some Sort of Genius. A Life of Wyndham Lewis* (London: Jonathan Cape, 2000).

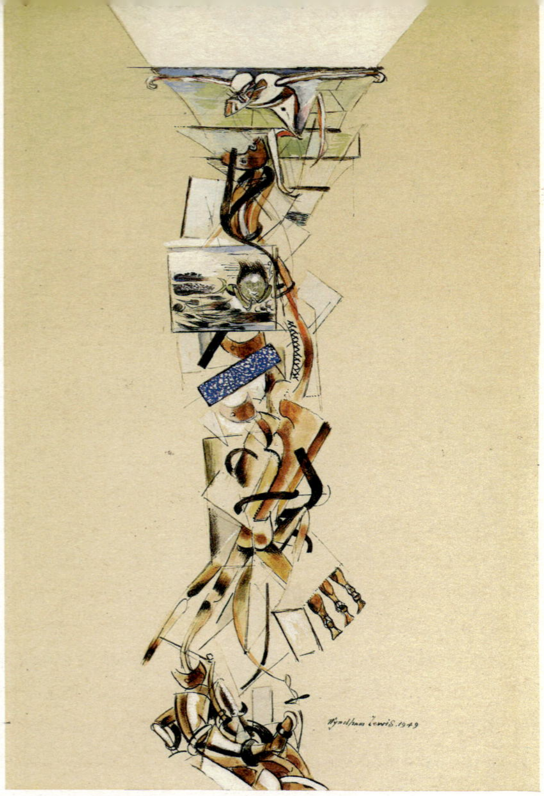

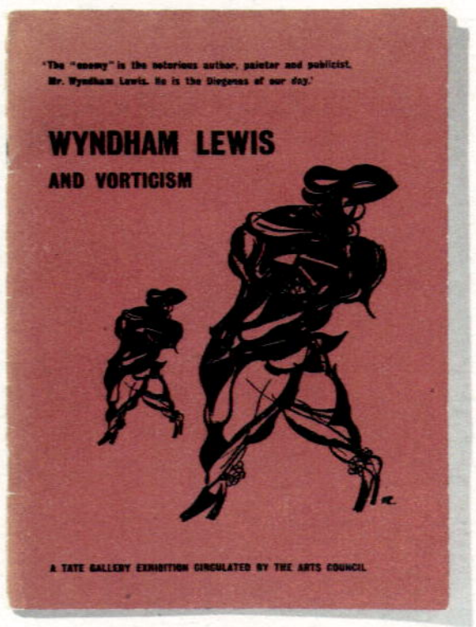

▲ *The Ascent*, 1949. Private collection (Cat. 203).
▶ *Wyndham Lewis and Vorticism* Exhibition Catalogue, Tate Gallery, London, 1956.

▼ Lewis writing when blind. Division of Rare and Manuscript Collections, Cornell University Library, Ithaca, NY.

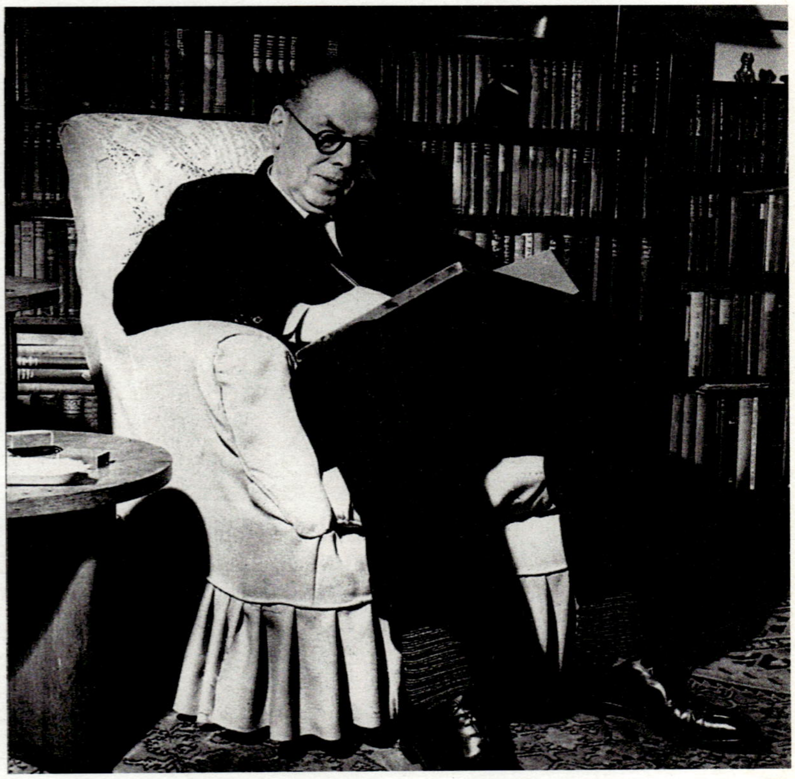

“The future possesses its history as well as the past… All living art is the history of the future. The greatest artists, men of science and political thinkers, come to us from the future–from the opposite direction to the past.”

Wyndham Lewis,
Essay on the Objective of Plastic Art in our Time, 1922

A

ESSAYS

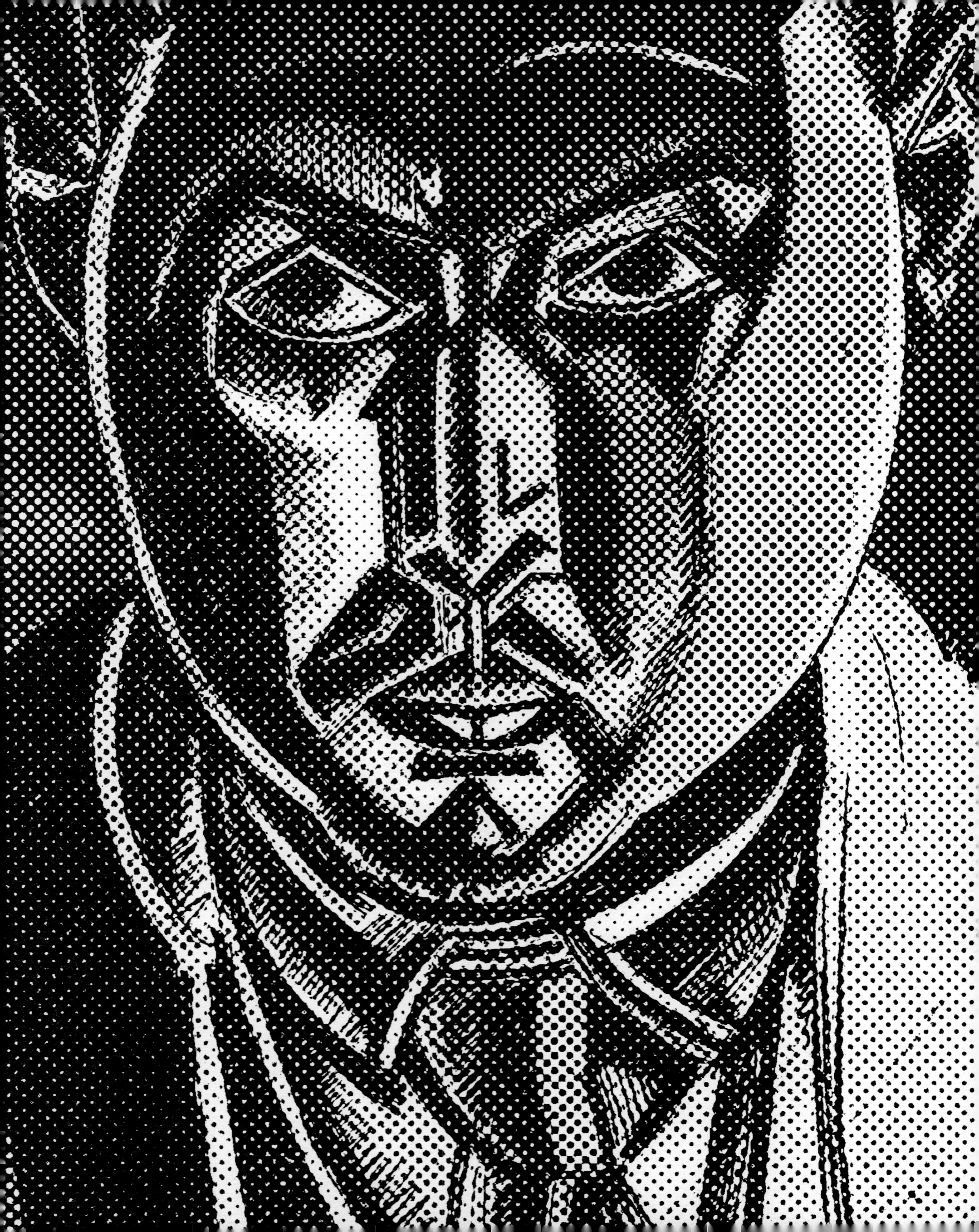

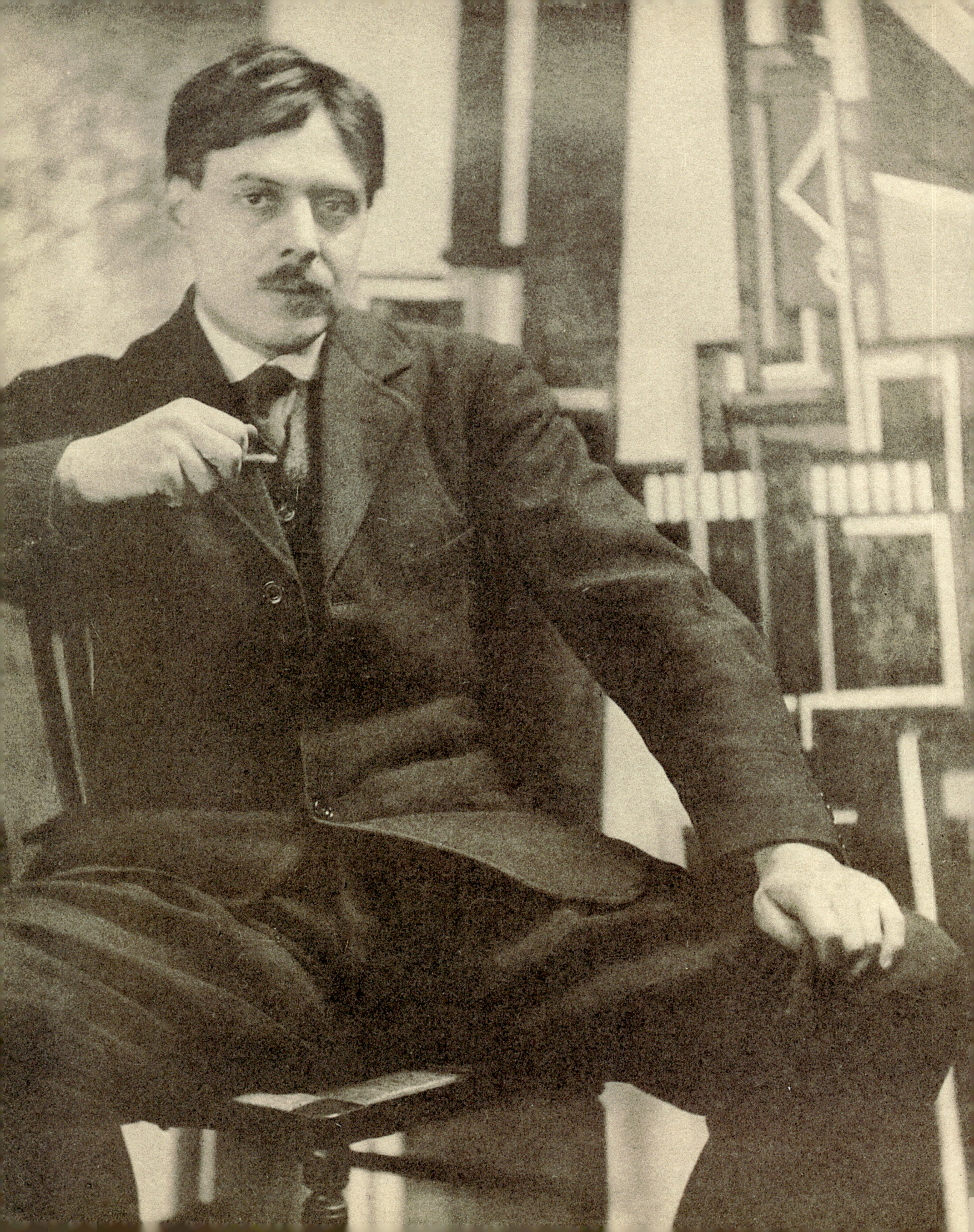

"CREATION MYTH": THE ART AND WRITING OF WYNDHAM LEWIS

Paul Edwards

Contradict yourself.
In order to live,
you must remain broken up.[1]

Alvin Langdon Coburn,
Wyndham Lewis, 1916.
Scottish National Portrait
Gallery, Edinburgh (Cat. 210)

HOW TO INTRODUCE WYNDHAM LEWIS TO A WORLDWIDE AUDIENCE

when in truth he still needs introducing to the Anglo-Saxon world? Few artists since the Renaissance have conceived so comprehensively a series of roles for themselves: Lewis wished to be a master in the visual arts, a political, social and cultural analyst, a novelist, and a philosophical and aesthetic critic. He is England's most important and most fertile modernist, and his achievement in each of these fields is among the highest, though exactly how high in each field remains disputed. In 2008, the prominent American literary and legal theorist Stanley Fish had occasion to sketch out a syllabus covering the "high points" of conservative political thought. Beginning with Plato (ca. 428–ca. 348BC) and Aristotle (384–322BC), his list continued with "Hooker, Hobbes, Adam Smith, Burke, Schmitt, Wyndham Lewis, Oakeshott, Strauss, Kirk, Bork et al."[2] Yet, it is questionable whether Lewis should be classified as politically conservative at all. In the field of painting, his activities as the vital driving force in England's most significant avant-garde movement, Vorticism, have given him a secure place in the history of British art. He was the inventor of a kind of geometrical abstraction that, through reproduction in the Vorticist magazine he edited, *Blast* (B&M Cats. 2 and 3), influenced the development of abstraction in Russia and elsewhere. But he abandoned this form of abstraction and his later work is virtually ignored in the histories. The English painter Walter Sickert (1860–42), Lewis's near-contemporary, called him "the greatest portraitist of this or any other time,"[3] yet when an exhibition of his portraits was held at the National Portrait Gallery in London in 2008, at least two critics questioned whether what Lewis produced in this line were – however impressive as paintings – properly portraits at all. As a writer of fiction, Lewis features in critical surveys such as *The Cambridge Companion to the Modernist Novel* (2007); modernist novels are supposed to focus on the flows of internal consciousness and on transcendent epiphanic moments, but Lewis's are dogmatically external and satirical, and his first novel, *Tarr* (1918) (B&M Cat. 5), has even been described as "anti-modernist." During a productive career of nearly 50 years, Lewis wrote, painted and engaged in public controversy as if England were a full participant in the culture of mainland Europe, and this assumption made him look eccentric to the English; yet to a foreign eye he is likely to resemble no one so much as his great English predecessor, the painter and writer, William Blake (1757–1827). Like Blake, he was an enemy of what was tame, acceptable and compromised, and, like Blake, a visionary master of line who rejected all that was cloudy and ill defined.

Confronted by the sheer range of Lewis's *oeuvre*, a totality that apparently lacks a centre, the simplest strategy is to accept its variety and appreciate whatever fractions of the whole happen to please; it is one of the triumphs of this particular exhibition that enough has been gathered in one place for this to be possible, especially in the case of his visual work. This option is open to the visitor to the exhibition or to the viewer of the reproductions and literary extracts contained in this book. As an introduction for those who hope to understand something more of the totality of his work and the relations between its parts, however, this essay attempts to provide something like a loose genealogy, though an ideal, non-chronological one that claims less for its developing argument than for the incidental light that it aims to throw on various aspects of Lewis's work as it proceeds.

> There is nothing so impressive as the number TWO.
> You must be a duet in everything.
> For, the Individual, the single object, and the isolated, is, you will admit, an absurdity.[4]

Fig. 1.
Seated Lady (Woman with a Sash), 1920. Trustees of The British Museum, London

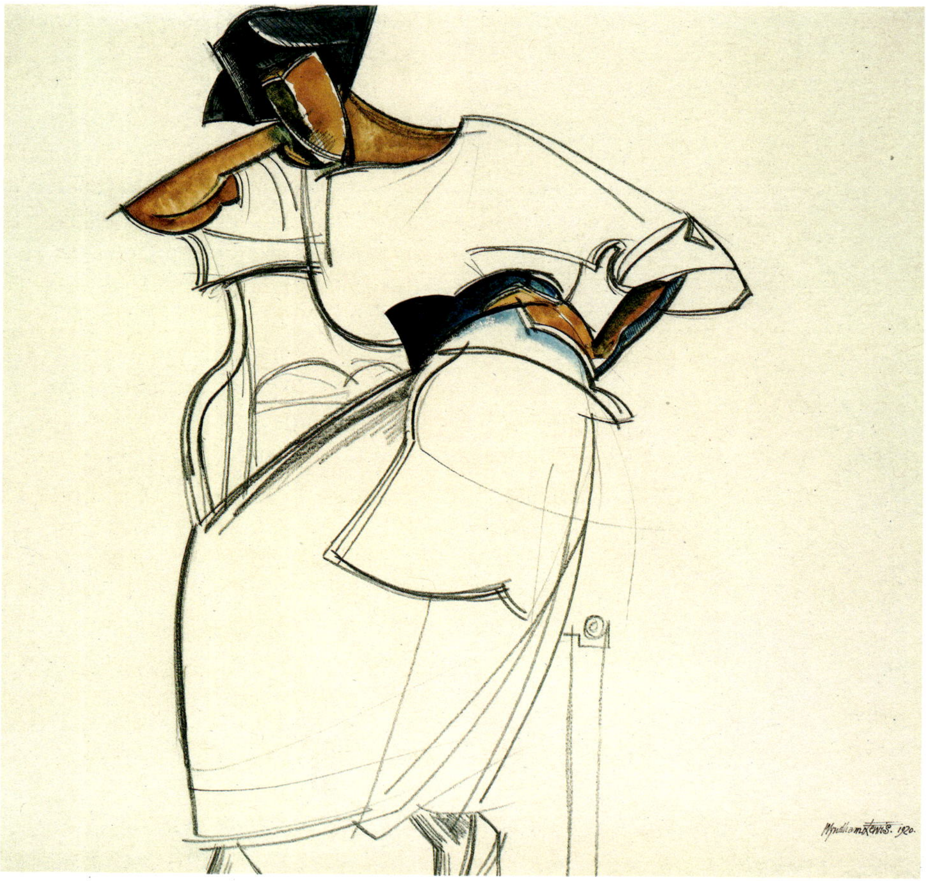

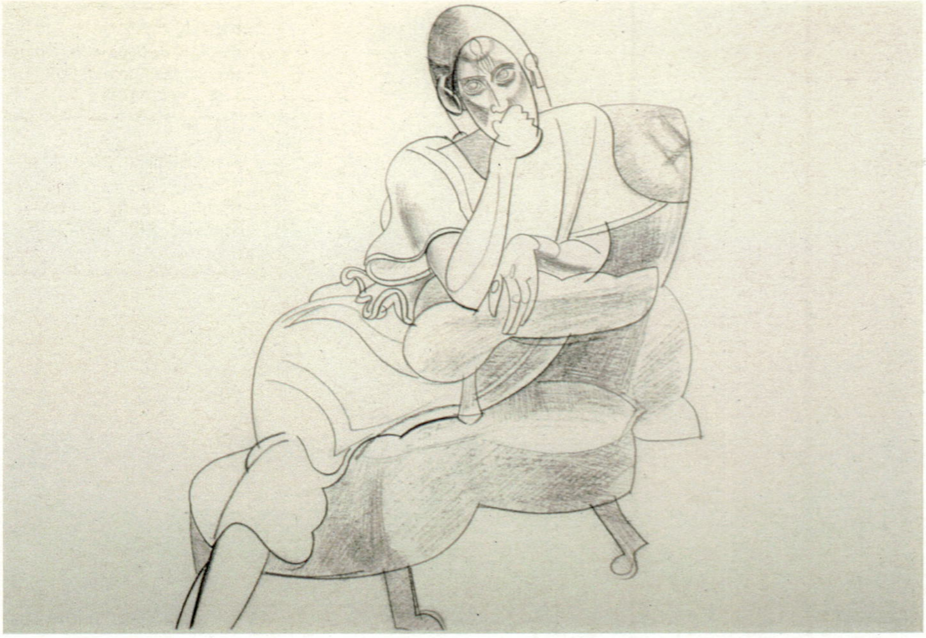

Fig. 2.
Miss "E," 1920.
Manchester City Galleries

With this injunction in his "Wyndham Lewis Vortex No. 1: Art Vortex" in 1915, Wyndham Lewis provided one key to his own unparalleled productivity as a painter and writer throughout his long career. The initial splitting of "No. 1" into two recurs repeatedly at almost any moment at which he might be thought to have reached a settled unity in his work. It is like the multiplication of cells by division of the original "blast" cell[5] of an organism; or the furnishing of a world with all its forms in some theogony; or like the confrontation of being and non-being, self and not-self, in a Hegelian or Fichtean dialectic. James Joyce (1881–1941), whose artistic procedure was the reverse of Lewis's, wittily summed up this strategy of division in *Finnegans Wake* (1939) (at the same time taking a swipe at Lewis's dogmatic critical habits) in the words, "you must, how, in undivided reawlity draw the line somewhawre."[6] Joyce's reality is "undivided," a single object. In terms of creation, for Lewis the primal act is to draw a line on the blank sheet of paper. On either side of the line, a different symbolic function is then assigned to the paper (void or solid), which is confirmed or complicated by further lines intersecting or joining the first. In Lewis's Vorticist abstractions, such as *Abstract Composition III* (1914–15) (Cat. 53), the reality thus created is "virtual" and irreconcilable with the three-dimensional manifold of the real world; it is supported by a different use of line hatching to symbolise solid, and wash to suggest that this is (like ours) a world with light in it. A work like *Woman with a Sash* (1920) (**Fig. 1**) is not so different, calling on us to recognise not a figure so much as the creation of the figure out of these same pictorial elements. It hovers slightly uncomfortably between a flat planar design and a three-dimensional solid. Again wash and some hatching bring plasticity into the world of the drawing, and by doing so make the figure a "human" body constrained by a chair and under the pressure of its own uncomfortable torsion; but these sculpted wash-filled forms are also, from a human point of view, the parts of the drawing most resistant to our empathy: hewn roughly, it would seem, from wood. It has no eyes, but lines suggest the bony ridges above the eye sockets with their fringing of hair.

The eye sockets of the *Lady in a Windsor Chair* (1920) (Cat. 84) are drawn in beneath similar double lines, but it is up to us to fill them in our imagination with eyes that return our gaze. But our attention is elsewhere, on the astonishing interplay of precisely incised line. We are almost persuaded that these lines are governed by the haphazard creases and folds of drapery, shaped by the posture of a seated figure, but we recognise that their primary motivating force is in a certain predilection of the artist himself for "the great line, the creative line; the fine, exultant mass; the gaiety that snaps and clacks like a fine gut string."[7] To assemble these into a structure as monumental and coherent as this seated figure is an intellectual feat of a high order. The same can be said of a drawing of yet another seated female figure of 1920, *Miss "E"* (**Fig. 2**). A simple addition here, of eyes that appear to answer our gaze, now transforms our experience of the drawing so that it becomes an encounter with a raw, intense and perhaps fearful personality – maybe a little disturbed by the artist's attention to curves. Finally, we may contrast *Cabby* (1920) (Cat. 87), a forceful personality despite the absence of eyes, emerging and solidifying from the paper like a genie emanating from a bottle.

Meanwhile, we may say, the other part of the "duet" that is Wyndham Lewis is born out of a different relationship with its "other" and out of another kind of signifying medium. The austerity or purity of the painter's vision was, according to Lewis, achieved thanks to a filtering process. He describes how, when painting a beggar in Brittany,

> **a lot of discarded matter collected there, as I was painting or drawing, in the back of my mind – in the back of my consciousness. As I squeezed out *everything* that smacked of literature from my vision of the beggar, it collected at the back of my mind. It imposed itself upon me as a complementary creation.**

Lewis claims that in this case the complementary creation was a short story, "The Death of the Ankou."[8] He is referring here to content, the material that provided the subject matter of his writing; but in some ways more important is a doubling of the way he creates an "other" through line by the way he does so through words. He commented on the two alternative "languages," visual and verbal:

> **Painting as much as Writing is a speech. [...] Writing, of course, involves a far more elaborate mental apparatus: it is far more complex, and it is, in its nature, artificial and allusive, a juggling with symbols in themselves neither valid nor of any significance nor value. Regarding them as two tongues, the visual arts are the 'purer' language.[9]**

The visual artist invents at every moment of his activity the signs from which a signified may be inferred; the writer has to make do with the ready-made language that his culture supplies. Both as a writer and as a painter Lewis foregrounds (in typical modernist fashion) the fact that he is constructing with signs, arranging "sentences." The alternative (which may draw just as much attention for its artfulness, of course) would be to efface as far as possible the mediation of either language, so that they seem mere unmediating transparency through which the represented object itself shines clearly. Lewis's objects have clarity and brilliance, but only at those points where the chosen signifiers create it, and they are assembled according to Lewisian predilection rather than by the contours of the object or the dictates of conventional grammar:

At the ferry-station there is a frail figure planted on the discoloured stones facing the stream. Hatless, feet thrust into old leather slippers, the brown vamp prolonged up the instep by a japanned tongue of black, it might be a morning in the breezy popular summer, a visitor halted on the quay of the holiday-port, to watch the early morning catch. Sandy-grey hair in dejected spandrils strays in rusty wisps: a thin rank moustache is pressed by the wind, bearing first from one direction then another, back against the small self-possessed mouth. Shoulders high and studious, the right arm hugs, as a paradoxical ally, a humble limb of nature, an oaken sapling Wicklow-bred.[10]

The figure is assembled, and the words and associations used are given an artificial value by their sudden relationships. As Hugh Kenner (1923–2003), one of Lewis's earliest (and still one of his best) critics, pointed out, these relationships seem to be governed by aural qualities rather than by the visual ones of their subject – unexpectedly, given Lewis's declared visual bias.[11] "Sandy-grey hair in dejected spandrils strays in rusty wisps": the shortness of most of the vowel sounds of the last five words of the clause compresses them, so that the plosive consonants are crowded in, and the alternation of the *s*s, *r*s, *t*s and *p*s produces an alliterative effect, though not one that would be at home in verse.

Just as in Lewis's virtuosity as a draughtsman there is a point where the motif becomes, first "real," and eventually living, with its own identity, so in his writing a similar process occurs. He propounded his own "externalist" aesthetic – based on a "philosophy of the *eye*" in justification of working in this direction. The other direction, of assuming that showing a character's mind at work in a novel would persuade readers to endow that character in their minds' eye with "a body, a local habitation and a name," was Henry James's (1843–1916).[12] Lewis asserts that the opposite is true, and that readers or viewers will indeed read life into a character (or a drawn figure) that in fact is ontologically devoid of consciousness: an arrangement of words or visual effects. Indeed, he goes so far as to claim that it is in this direction that art by its nature works:

[...] art consists among other things in a *mechanizing* of the natural. It bestows its delightful disciplines upon our aimless emotions: it puts its gentle order in the place of natural chaos: it substitutes for the direct image a picture. And, ultimately, and analysed far enough, it substitutes a *thing* for a *person* every time – and this is as true of the book as of the painted picture.[13]

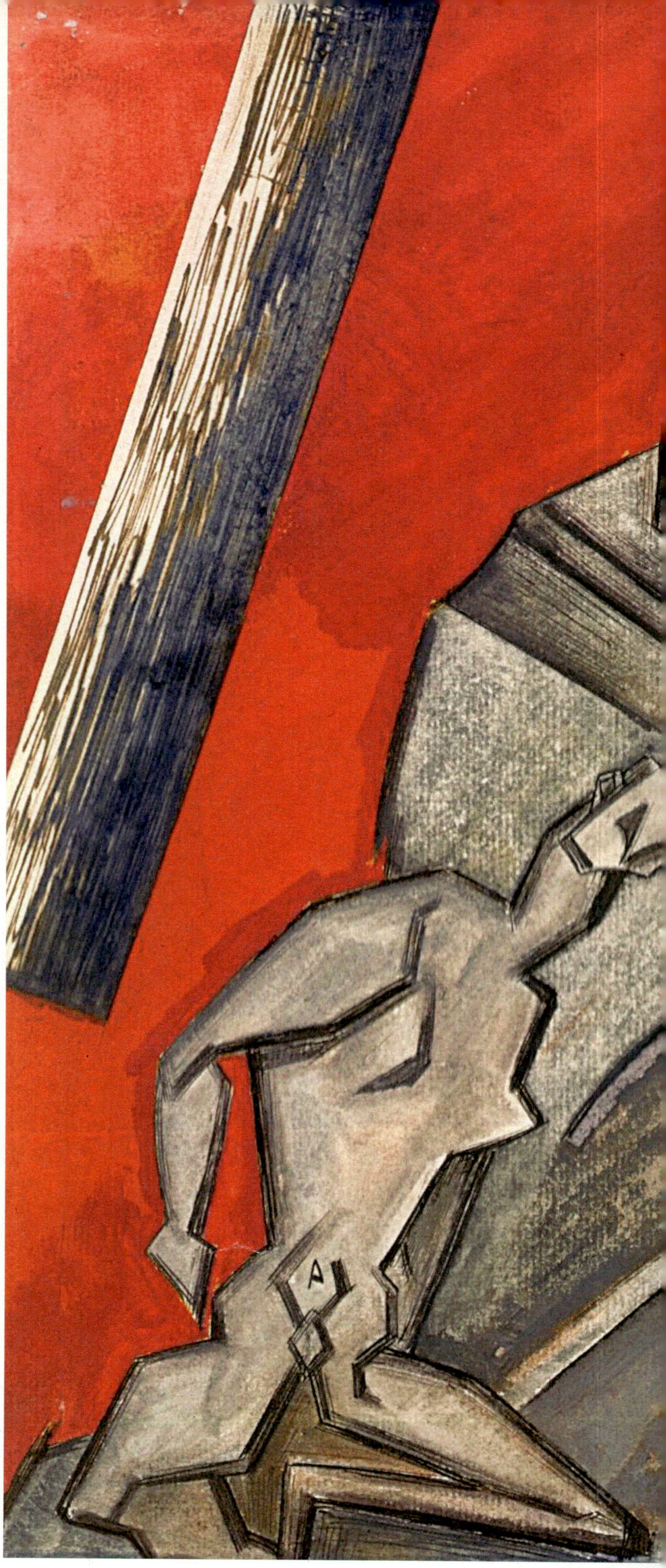

Sunset among the Michelangelos, 1912. Victoria and Albert Museum, London

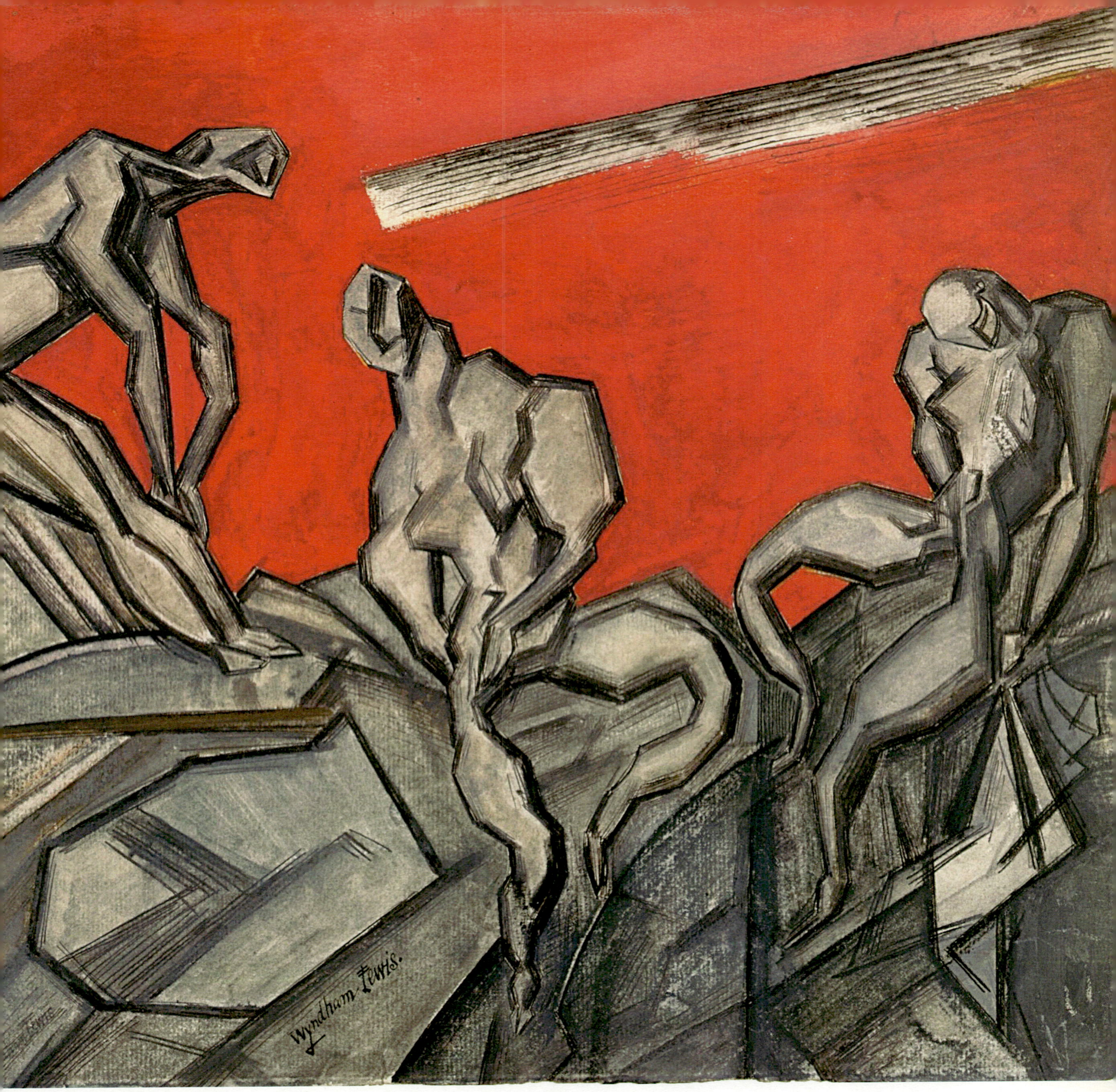
Wyndham Lewis.

What Lewis's art does (though his aesthetic has not a great deal to say about this) is create these "things," yet enable us to be simultaneously external to them and mysteriously empathetic with them. Characters in his novels, which are apparently no more than predictable mechanical contrivances (such as the character Val, in the 1932 novel *Snooty Baronet* (B&M Cat. 33)[14]), win our sympathy despite the narrator's evident hostility to them, or despite the obvious artifice involved in their construction. The point is that the "other" created through the deployment of signs corresponds to some reality that is not merely the projection of a division in the artist's self. In "Vortex No. 1," Lewis recognises the relation of that other to something outside the artist's self:

> **There is Yourself: and there is the Exterior World, that fat mass you browse on.**
> **You knead it into an amorphous imitation of yourself inside yourself.**[15]

If we do not respond empathetically to some aspect of the work in front of us, either the work has failed or we have. But we must be prepared to accept that our response may be self-contradictory: a delight, corresponding to the artist's delight in his own mechanical efficiency in his use of one of his "languages," but also an emotional reaction in favour of the human reality that such efficiency often slights. This dilemma is the source of one of the critical cruces concerning Lewis's work – judgement based on an assumption that it is only the inhuman mechanical efficiency that is to be attributed to Lewis, while the human sympathies all belong to us. Thus, Hal Foster states: "for Lewis a person is nothing but such a mechanistic thing."[16] Lewis's dualism is collapsed by the critic back into an empty monism or solipsism. And it must be admitted that Lewis riskily invites this judgement. In his fiction he delights in deploying narrators to whom it definitely applies. The narrator of *Snooty Baronet*, Sir Michael Kell-Imrie, confronted with an automaton in a shop window, doffing its hat to advertise the shop's wares, finds it impossible to see the difference between this machine and a human being:

> **There was something *absolute* in this distinction, recognised by everybody there excepting myself. I alone did not see it. What exactly was the difference however? [...]**
>
> **He was *one of us*, as much as the people at my side, about whom I knew no more than I knew of him, indeed rather less.**[17]

Another of Lewis's narrators, Ker-Orr, in *The Wild Body* (1927) (B&M Cat. 17), confesses, "I simply cannot help converting everything into burlesque patterns. And I admit that I am disposed to forget that people are real – that they are, that is, not subjective patterns belonging specifically to me [. . .] ."[18] But what is here raised to a level of explicitness by the invention of a dramatised narrator often remains implicit simply in style and technique itself. In narrative theory it is virtually axiomatic that narrative voice should not be identified with the voice or personality of the (biographical) author; a similar distinction has not been thought necessary for the visual arts, probably because their basis in a specialised technical skill (instead of a personality with a voice and language that are part of everyday life) has always been clear. But Lewis's drawings and paintings are also the products of a kind of persona: one that embodies a version of the self as a mechanical, technical power of observation and translation into linear patterns and then acts in accordance with that compulsion. Lewis "himself," meanwhile, knows that such a compulsion has no ultimate authority. It is what he calls an "inferior religion," a kind of superstition: "In a painting certain forms MUST be SO; in the same meticulous, profound manner that your pen and book must lie on the table at a certain angle, your clothes at night be arranged in a set personal symmetry, certain birds be voided, a set of railings tapped with your hand as you pass, without missing one."[19] Different painters, Lewis recognises, have different compulsions. The concluding section of the essay, "Inferior Religions" (1914–15), provides brief poetic evocations of how, in the case of great painters like Paulo Uccello (1397–1475), Ogata Kōrin (1658–1716), John Constable (1776–1837) or Paul Cézanne (1839–1906), such compulsions are visible in their work.[20]

If one of the compulsions that Lewis followed at certain periods of his output was the assembling of quasi-mechanical lines into patterns, those patterns are by no means always "burlesque" (as Ker-Orr's verbal ones tend to be), but sometimes they are, as in the case of the caricatural "Tyros" Lewis produced in 1921. The self-portrait, Mr Wyndham Lewis as a Tyro (1920–21) (Cat. 99), is an object lesson in the self-reflexive dialectical effect of technique and "subject." The subject – a living, breathing being – is traduced by this reductive mechanised technique; but in this case it is precisely such a limited subjectivity (reduced to a capacity to translate reality to this repertoire of lines and sour colours) that we are told by the title has produced the "portrait." The solipsism of technique – attributable to the compulsions of "Mr Wyndham Lewis" rather than to any larger personality the artist may possess – seems here to allow no room for an "other": we grin back, just as Kell-Imrie doffs his hat in response to the polite gesture of the automaton before him. And where Lewis's writing is concerned, Fredric Jameson (b. 1934), in a brilliant analysis of his style in the story, "Cantelman's Spring-Mate," also identifies a capacity that has "mechanised" itself as the origin of the style: "a veritable self-generating image- and sentence-producing machine comes into view behind the dextrous and imperceptible substitutions of literal and figural levels for one another."[21]

This flirting with a mechanisation of the self ("Any machine then, that you like: but become mechanical by fundamental dual repetition"[22]) is not purely the result of what "Inferior Religions" calls "an immense predilection."[23] It is, of course, also historically and culturally conditioned, as Lewis himself knew perfectly well. To produce an art that is shaped out of an ethos of mechanical efficiency and control is necessarily to say something about an ethos that pervades the modern world. In the case of a minor artist or writer (and, perhaps, also in the case of the very greatest of all), the material of a latent critique of their time is discoverable by the superior hindsight of a later critic. But with Lewis it is a good rule of thumb to proceed on the assumption that he knew exactly what he was doing. Despite what looks like an enthusiastic, almost Futurist, embrace of the machine, Lewis was always aware of its potential cost. Even his earliest mechanomorphic works, such as *Timon* (1913) (Cat. 38), which shows the painful imbrication of humanity in the mechanised manifold of modernity, or *The Vorticist* (1912) (Cat. 25), which depicts a screaming figure apparently enclosed and confined by its mechanical armour, resist Futurist romanticisation of the machine. Nevertheless, Lewis, particularly in the period 1913 to 1919, was more positive than negative in his attitudes to modernity and mechanism. Curiously, but characteristically, it was after what he had seen of the terrible effects of machinery in the First World War (and been appalled by them) that his embrace of the beneficial possibilities of the technological transformation of life in modernity was at its most positive. His 1919 pamphlet, *The Caliph's Design* (B&M Cat. 7), is representative of the moment when the avant-garde abandons the carnival atmosphere of pre-war festivity (expressed in the playful aggression of *Blast*) and takes on the seriousness of the post-war need for reconstruction. It calls for the rebuilding of London and the renovation of industrial design using the forms developed in Vorticist painting (the architectural dimension of many of which works was already quite obvious). In doing so, it provides an English theoretical equivalent to such projects as Tony Garnier's *Une Cité Industrielle* (1918), Bruno Taut's *Die Stadtkröne* (1919) and Le Corbusier's *Une Ville Contemporaine* (1921–22). Lewis joyfully envisaged, as well, a transformation and expansion of consciousness, enabled by industrial technique:

Let us substitute ourselves everywhere for the animal world; replace the tiger and the cormorant with some invention of our mind, so that we can intimately control this new Creation. [...]

It is not a bird-like act for a man to set himself coldly to solve the riddle of the bird and understand it; as it is human to humanise it. So we do not wish to become a vulture or a swallow. We want to enjoy our consciousness, but to enjoy it in all forms of life, and use all modes and processes for our satisfaction. [...]

What is [man's] synthesis going to be? So far it has been endless imitation; he has done nothing with his machinery but that. Will he arrive where there is no power, enjoyment or organisation of which other living beings have been capable of which he will not, in his turn, and by a huge mechanical effort, possess the means?[24]

The idea here is that new techniques could make us not (like machines themselves) less than human, but by transforming the experiences available to us make us more than what humanism (in art and other forms of thought) has made thinkable for us. It is not in itself a political vision, but without political organisation of the right kind the vision will not be realised. Lewis's 1926 book of political analysis and theory, *The Art of Being Ruled* (B&M Cat. 10), was partly intended to show the range of modern political techniques by which this might be managed. Politics, too, had been transformed by industrial technique and the mass-society that went with modernity, resulting in, among other things, the two variant forms of anti-liberal authoritarianism, Fascism and Bolshevism, to both of which Lewis was initially attracted. Real transformation of people's lives, though, would come through intellectual and material culture, for Lewis considered that the state or any form of political organisation was too constricting and barren a vehicle for an adequate expression of a full or extended "humanity."[25]

There is an art that could begin to model such an expression, however, containing not only some of the mechanised forms and lines that Lewis deployed in his figurative drawings of the early 1920s, but also going beyond humanism (or a critique of it). It would do so by incorporating a range of invented forms suggested by nature and synthesised with the art and myths of cultures (of the East, of Oceania, America and Africa) that had a profound vision of realities beyond the horizons of European art. This was the "world-art" of which (Lewis maintained) Vorticism had been one of the pioneers.[26] The strange abstractions and semi-abstractions that he began to create from around 1921, so different formally from the abstractions of Vorticism, were Lewis's fullest development of such a world-art. Works like *Archimedes Reconnoitring the Enemy Fleet* (1922) (Cat. 113), the three totemic *Abstract Compositions* of 1926 (Cats. 120–22) and their large-scale counterpart *Bagdad* (1927–28) (Cat. 128), *Manhattan* (1927) (Cat. 126) or *Bathing Scene* (1938) (Cat. 167), to choose a few at random, show Lewis as still among the most advanced painters in Europe. But it must be understood that this achievement went virtually unrecognised in England and received no exposure elsewhere.[27]

Lewis's celebration, in *The Caliph's Design*, of the potential of technology to transform life and consciousness was not unshadowed by a dark "other." Accompanying it was this caveat: "The danger, as it would appear at present, and in our first flight of substitution and remounting, is evidently that we should become overpowered by our creation, and become as mechanical as a tremendous insect world, all our awakened reason entirely disappeared."[28] The warning is also threaded through the political analysis in *The Art of Being Ruled*. It applies not only to the body politic, however, but also to the person, as Lewis points out in an essay, "The Meaning of the Wild Body," published in 1927 as a commentary on the stories collected in *The Wild Body*. Lewis insists here on the necessity of dualism, of spirit and matter (or "machine") in the human. Without a relatively emancipated "Cartesian" (though in keeping with Lewis's cosmopolitanism, here Upanishadic) self to accompany and observe the functional bias of the human machine,

men sink to the level of insects. [...] the 'lord of the past and future, he who is the same today and tomorrow' – that 'person of the size of a thumb that stands in the middle of the Self' – departs. So the 'Self' ceases, necessarily. The conditions of an insect communism are achieved.[29]

As with all of Lewis's apparently secure positions, this one, too, turns out to have two dichotomous offshoots. First, the dualistic condition is to be celebrated, precisely because it does emancipate us from mere functionality. And even the failure of our "mechanical" side to match up to the perfect functionality of the truly efficient machine is a sign of the happiness of our condition, for "the art impulse reposes upon a conviction that the state of limitation of the human being is more desirable than the state of the automaton; or a feeling of the gain and significance residing in this human fallibility for us."[30] Art, in this view, is like a game (like other sports), in which we pit ourselves against our vision of total mechanical efficiency. Since "mechanical perfection will not tally with the human thing," "the game consists in seeing how near you can get, without the sudden extinction and neutralization that awaits you as matter, or as the machine."[31] Hence the "persona" that produces the *almost* inhuman line of some of Lewis's drawings.

The second "offshoot" of this dualism comes from the judgement of the observing self on the imperfect machine that is the body, or, by extension, the body politic. The disparity between what our souls conceive of and what we are is the source of our sense of the absurd, and it leads to the other great mode of Lewis's creative achievement; that is, *satire*. There is a (sometimes only slight) satirical edge to much of Lewis's work, enhancing the sense that it is withholding a more absolute non-human judgement of the realities with which it deals. But also, in the 1930 novel set in the London art world, *The Apes of God* (B&M Cat. 21), Lewis produced one of the most devastating satires in the English language, containing some of his most brilliant virtuoso prose. It focuses an aggressive eye on the body and on the body politic; the possessor of that eye masquerades precisely as a non-human "absolute" judging the lamentable imperfections of the personnel and social institutions of the novel. The London it depicts is a huge machine, like the "tremendous insect world" that Lewis warned against in *The Caliph's Design*. But it is also running out of energy, a vortex reducing to a placid calm that is lifeless and cannot be revivified even by the Sorelian disruption of a General Strike (with which the novel concludes). The strike, explicitly a depiction of the actual General Strike held in England in May 1926, only confirms the incipient paralysis of a body politic still entrenched in its Victorian past. The revolution in culture and the political organisation needed to allow it to take effect had not happened. And individual bodies are in a similar state, or, where vitalised by energy, only emptily so, discharging it to no purpose beyond the petty competition of ordinary social life. The pointless convolutions of these characters, many of whom are caricatural versions of actual people prominent in the culture of the period (the famous family of poets, the Sitwells, for example, and members of the Bloomsbury Group, such as Lytton Strachey (1880–1932)) are depicted as low farce in some of the novel's funniest chapters. But Lewis's virtuosity itself has a hint of the emptily mechanical about it, reminding us of the paradox he put forward in "Essay on the Objective of Plastic Art in our Time" (1922):

In a great deal of art you find its motive in the assertion of the beauty and significance of the human as opposed to the mechanical; a virtuoso display of its opposite. But this virtuosity, in its precision even in being imprecise, is not so removed from a mechanical perfection as would at first sight appear.[32]

The paradox involves Lewis in his own critique; though relatively superior to his apes, like them he is finally only a shadow of some ultimate perfection, an imitator of a hidden God, and (from any absolute perspective) as absurd as they.

Because one thing seems to turn into its opposite in the manner described, Lewis knows that his "duets" are not clear-cut and Cartesian, but (in a more Hegelian manner) interdependent, each side liable suddenly to take on characteristics of what it projects as its other. It was a lesson learnt early and expounded in one of his most obscure but important literary works, *Enemy of the Stars*, a Vorticist-Expressionist "play" first published in *Blast*, No. 1, in 1914.[33] Its protagonist and antagonist are two Beckett-like clowns or fetishes whose mutual violence results in shared destruction. The play's complexities defy summary but it has an allegorical dimension that may be isolated. In "Vortex No. 1," Lewis recommends an accommodation of the two principles (whatever they are): "You can establish yourself as a Machine of two similar fraternal surfaces overlapping."[34] But the original self is wounded by its own division, and the two characters that result from it in *Enemy of the Stars*, Arghol and Hanp, are more fratricidal than fraternal: difference negates uniqueness by begetting imitation. Arghol seems to represent the spiritual self, Hanp the material or mechanical. The motivating force of the play's psychological narrative is partly determined through a version of Nietzschean *ressentiment*. Its dialectic is also influenced by the anti-left-Hegelian author Max Stirner (1806–1856), whose *Der Einzige und sein Eigentum* (1844) Arghol throws out of a window in a fit of disgust.[35] In accordance with his *ressentiment*, Arghol wishes to return to the pristine state that precedes material existence, but is dogged by the poodle version of himself that he has induced Hanp to become:

I talk to you for an hour and get more disgusted with myself.
I find I wanted to make a naïf yapping Poodle-parasite of you. – I shall always be a prostitute.
I wanted to make you my self; you understand?
Every man who wants to make another HIMSELF, is seeking a companion for his detached ailment of a self.
You are an unclean little beast, crept gloomily out of my ego. You are the world, brother, with its family objections to me.[36]

Through a doubly self-replicating dialectic, Hanp reflects Arghol's disgust with himself in his own disillusion with Arghol's pretensions to unique self-sufficiency. There is no such self-sufficiency, and the two cannot finally be separated. But they can negate their difference through violence: Hanp kills Arghol and, with no spirit informing his own body any longer, consigns himself decisively to matter by jumping into

Creation Myth, 1920-33. Withworth Art Gallery, University of Manchester

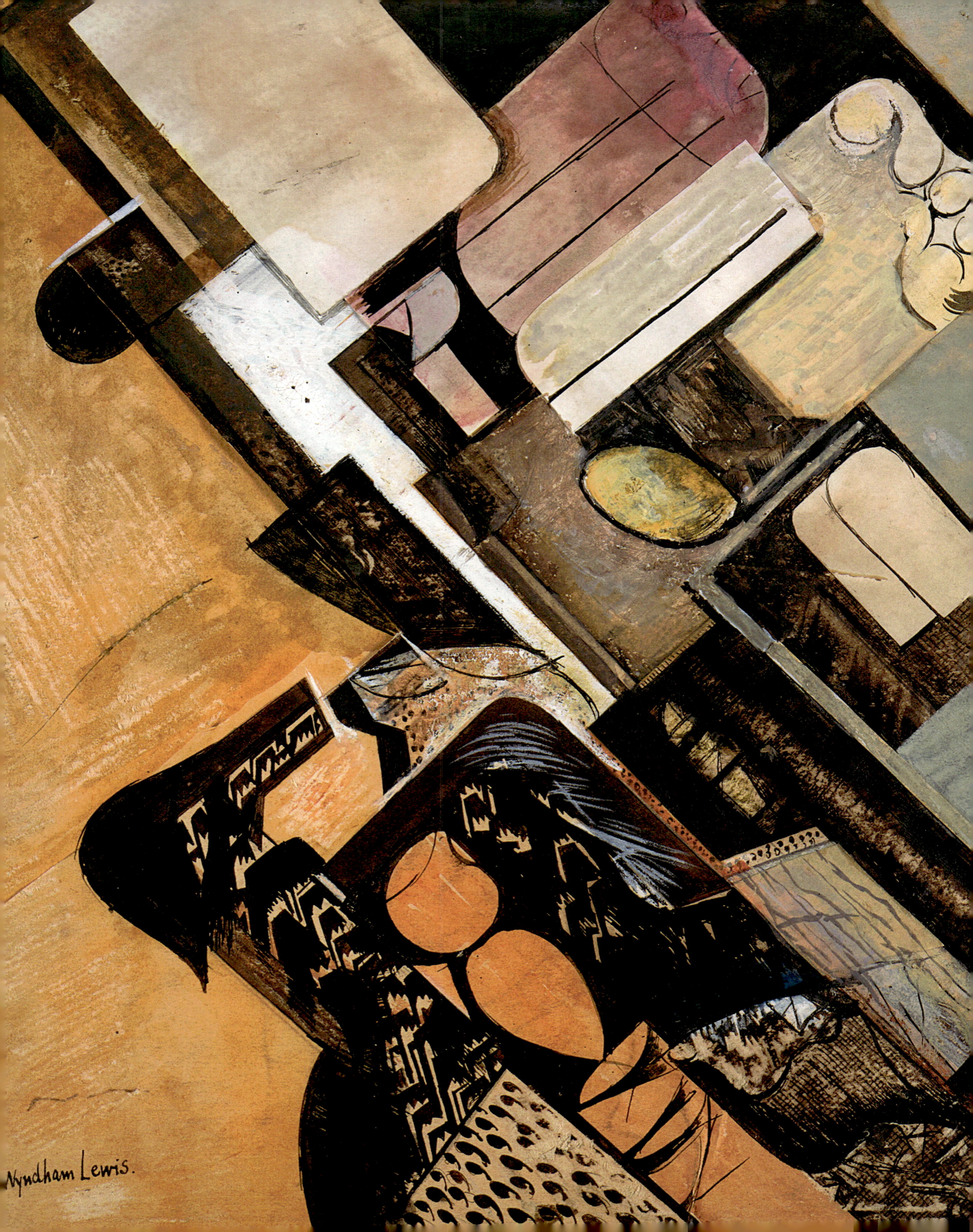
Wyndham Lewis.

a canal and drowning. What remains (according to the final, revised version of the play) is "no sound in particular and only the blackness of a moonless and unstarlit night."[37] *Enemy of the Stars* provides an object lesson in the importance of remaining divided without allowing a continuously productive dialectic to implode into nothingness. An antithetical, positive depiction of the successful organisation of a division that can never be as pure as the drawn line is in the versions of *Red Duet* that Lewis produced in 1915 (**Fig. 3**), the most impressive of which he appears to be sitting in front of in Alvin Langdon Coburn's (1882–1966) two portrait photos taken in 1916 (**Fig. 4**).

As a positive strategy it is summed up in "Vortex No. 1" as "You must talk with two tongues, if you do not wish to cause confusion,"[38] and is reflected in the organisation of some of Lewis's most ambitious books, particularly *The Art of Being Ruled*. In later life, he realised that confusion was precisely what the strategy could cause:

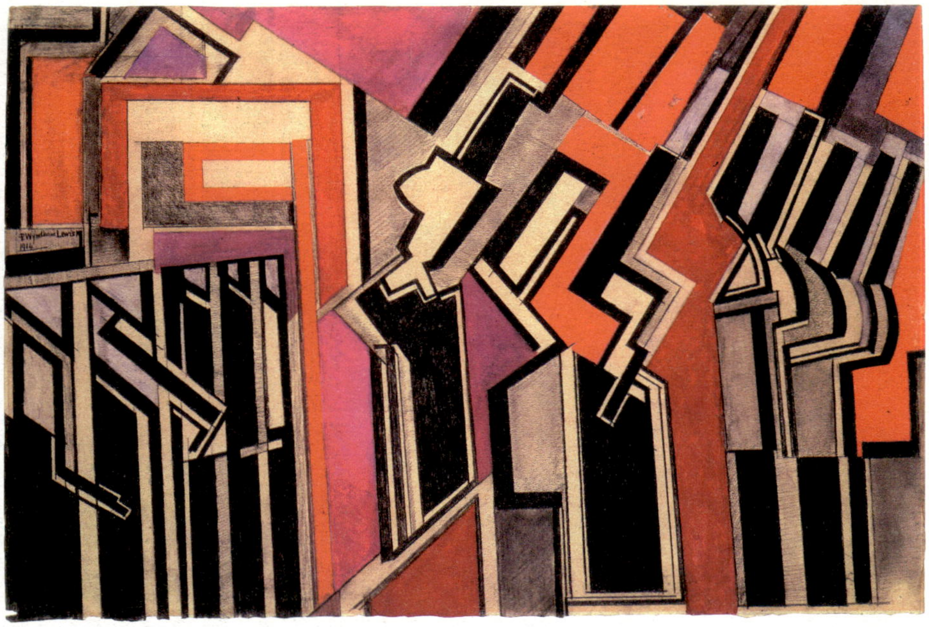

Fig. 3.
Red Duet, 1914. Private collection, Ivor Braka Ltd

It is not an easy book to write about, because its argument bursts out into manifold byways. There is a further complication. It was my idea at the outset – inspired by the Hegelian dialectic, with its thesis and antithesis – to state, here and there, both sides of the question to be debated, and allow these opposites to struggle in the reader's mind to find their synthesis.[39]

The strategy, dramatised, also provides the organising principle of the narrative of Lewis's strange fantasy novel depicting the preliminary judgement of the dead, *The Childermass* (1928) (B&M Cat. 19), set in the afterworld "outside Heaven," where a debate between two powerful protagonists, the Bailiff (in charge of proceedings) and the rebellious Hyperides, takes place about what the standard of judgement should actually be. For in place of traditional theological or ethical considerations, the Bailiff uses the concepts of reality developed in the "time" philosophies of Alfred North Whitehead (1861–1947), Bertrand Russell (1872–1970) or Henri Bergson (1859–1941) to establish whether the ghosts before him have attained sufficient fixity to cross the river Styx to an uncertain heaven. Hyperides and his followers reply with an ideological critique of the Bailiff's motives and of the disempowering effects of the versions of reality and identity that he promotes, deploying more classical idealist concepts in their own response. But the Bailiff has all the vitality of what Hugh Kenner called an "incarnate Zeitgeist."

The same competitive argument had taken place in Lewis's 1927 study of modern philosophy and culture, *Time and Western Man* (B&M Cat. 12). What Lewis objected to in what he called "time-philosophy" was what he saw as the removal of the relative independence of the human mind (or spirit) from the material world (or the mechanical world – by now the machine and nature were almost synonymous for him) in which it exists.[40] The self was merging again into its other, culture was becoming a slavish *product* of historical process, art was becoming identified with life; the individual was becoming a powerless and negligible aspect of a political, metaphysical and theological Absolute. Because of its philosophical naivety, the avant-garde (including those writers with whom Lewis had been particularly associated, such as James Joyce and Ezra Pound (1885–1972)) was inadvertently complicit with this process and was therefore the object of some of Lewis's most devastatingly witty criticism. Lewis explained how he had developed the "self" from which he made his attacks, acknowledging what should not, by now, surprise the reader, that he had another side to that self which felt quite differently about these matters:

Well, the way I have gone about it is generally as follows. I have allowed these contradictory things to struggle together, and the group that has proved the most powerful I have fixed on as my most essential ME. This decision has not, naturally, suppressed or banished the contrary faction, almost equal in strength, and even sometimes in the ascendant. [...] All I have said to myself is that always, when it comes to the pinch, I will side and identify myself with the powerfullest Me, and in its interests I will work.[41]

The same tactic underlies his simultaneous and related intervention into avant-garde practice, the magazine, *The Enemy* (1927–29) (B&M Cats. 14–16), in which an "Enemy" persona uses the form of the avant-garde magazine to question the revolutionary pretensions of arts that for him did not really act in the service of the kind of transformation he had outlined in *The Caliph's Design*.[42]

In *The Childermass*, on the other hand, although Lewis's satire is clearly working primarily for the cause espoused in the non-fictional works of the time, the balance of argument between the Bailiff and his antagonist is allowed to swing back and forth until the full extent to which they mirror each other becomes abundantly clear, and the need for difference comes to seem more important than the actual substance of the difference. As the Bailiff says to his antagonist, " [...] these myrmidons will whirl about and my particles will agitate and collide, vortex within vortex, mine and thine, with a buzzing of meum and tuum, a fine angry senseless music, it will be an unintelligible beating of the air if we go on just as if we do not." To which Hyperides replies, "In that case let us go on!"[43] Yet it is ultimately the subject of the argument that is important (even if a conclusion cannot be reached), and it is partly through argument that the subject emerges: the mystery of Being, the question of the ultimate ground of our own being, how we emerge from it, what happens when we return to it, and what the purpose of our existence can be. The strange deformation of our world that Lewis's imagination brings about in his descriptions of life in the no man's land of posthumous existence, as the innocents await judgement in their dugouts and makeshift shelters, brings such questions to our consciousness. They are usually hidden from us by the normality of our everyday existence, but for Lewis they should always be pressing. "For what the artist's public also has to be brought to do is to see its world, and the people in it, as a *stranger* would."[44] Naturalism, in art or writing, cannot bring this about, or raise such questions. In Lewis's visual art the figure–ground relationship (which Cubism had taught him could be mysterious) always suggests, too, these ultimate questions. They are made explicit in such works as the 1927 *ΑΘΑΝΑΤΟΝ ΑΡΑ Ἡ ΨΥΧΗ* ("*Immortal Therefore the Soul*") (Cat. 127), or the 1933 *ΑΘΑΝΑΤΟΝ* (**Fig. 5**), which depicts the journey of the soul to some form of eternal order of which classical architecture is proposed as the closest analogy.

The most concerted, substantial effort that Lewis made in his painting, the series of oil paintings (some related to *ΑΘΑΝΑΤΟΝ*) produced during a period of severe illness for Lewis personally, and of political turbulence more generally, also attempts to provide a sense of such ultimate metaphysical questions. The paintings do so using contexts of ritual (*Group of Three Veiled Figures* (1933) (Cat. 153), for example), illness (*The Mud Clinic* (1937) (**Fig. 6**)), cyclical history (*The Surrender of Barcelona* (1936–37) (Cat. 162)) and, as in *The Childermass*, of a strange afterworld (*One of the Stations of the Dead* (1933) (Cat. 155)). These paintings, which Lewis said formed "some sort of series,"[45] are Lewis's equivalent of such studies of universal history and its relation to eternity as Pound's *The Cantos*, Joyce's *Finnegans Wake* or W.B. Yeats's (1865–1939) *A Vision*. And they transcend (in a way that

Fig. 4. ▸▸
Alvin Langdon Coburn, *Untitled* (8 Photographs of Wyndham Lewis), ca. 1916. George Eastman House, Rochester, NY

Fig. 5. ▸
AOANATON (Immortality), 1933. Private collection

Fig. 6. ▾
The Mud Clinic, 1937. Beaverbrook Art Gallery, New Brunswick

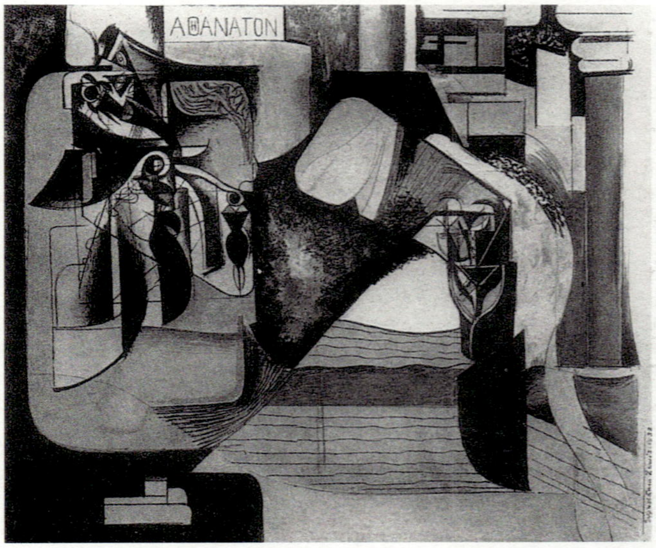

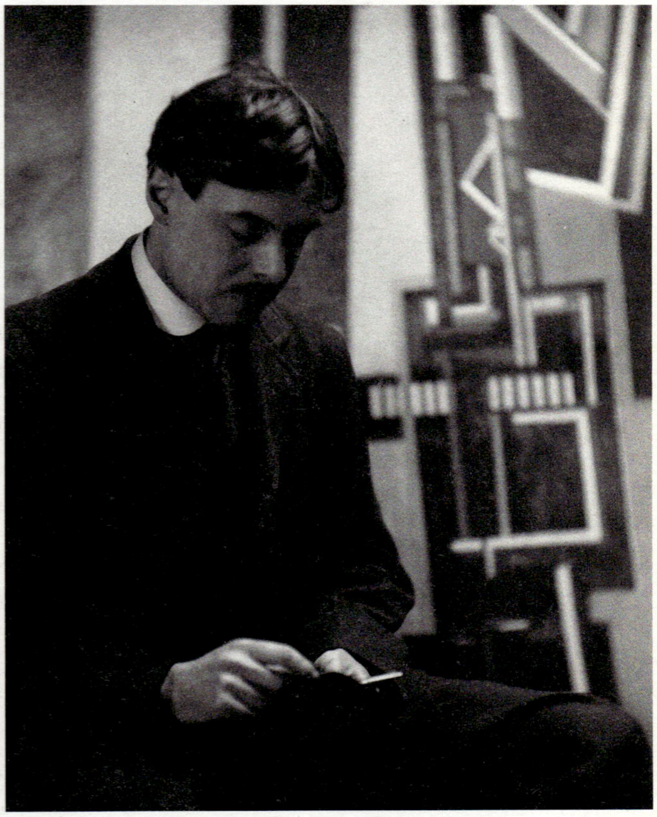

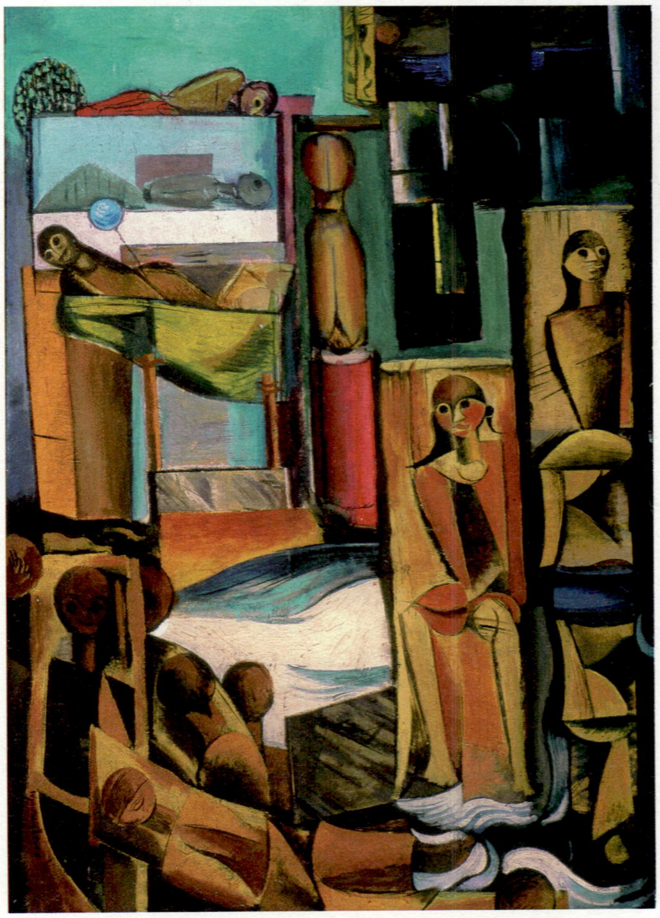

The Cantos do not) the pragmatic political alignments – with National Socialism, with the Falangist side in the Spanish Civil War – that Lewis took up during the same years but renounced when he realised that they were not the guarantee of peace that he naively hoped they were. The same themes and questions are taken up in a minor key, but often with even more intensity, in the fantastic watercolours that Lewis produced in the 1940s in North America, in a final flowering of his visual genius before blindness descended on him in 1951. The strangeness of creation (an abiding preoccupation since his early days in Paris),[46] scenes of bathers immersed in the material delights of water (joyful "other" to Hanp's dismal extinction in the same substance), tragic delineations of the maimed, the sacrificed and the dead; these are works that of all other English artists only William Blake could have conceived, but only Wyndham Lewis could have executed.

Especially in the period following the First World War, when Lewis was at his prime as a virtuoso draughtsman and literary stylist expending all his artistic and critical energy in an effort to hold off nothingness, his work has the slightly inhuman quality proper to his ambition to go beyond the human to an enjoyment of "our consciousness [...] in all forms of life." Our human values seemed to him at times then "*Menschliches, Allzumenschliches*": "life is in itself not important. Our values make it so: but they are mostly, the important ones, non-human values, although the intenser they are the more they imply a supreme, vital connotation."[47] Love, the feminine, ethics, nature and natural attachment to others all seem to be slighted. This is partly a consequence of his aesthetic decision that art is life's "other," not its copy. It has also a psychological origin too, no doubt. But, particularly as he suffered more of the imperfections and ills our flesh is heir to, the art–life boundary that insulated art from natural and ethical humanity seemed less necessary to him and was breached increasingly frequently. Indeed, even in the early 1920s, such drawings as *Head of a Girl* (1922) (Cat. 101) (a portrait of his future wife) are less concerned with virtuoso linear control than they are with the delicate emergence of a personality valued for its own sake. Sensitivity in Lewis's drawing is actually as common as his pitiless "whiplash" line; it is just less immediately striking (see the 1923 portrait drawing of Edith Sitwell, for example (Cat. 104); a sitter whom Lewis was elsewhere inclined to satirise). The full expression of his respect for others as more than "subjective patterns" constructed out of his own predilection is in his portraiture, notably the series of drawings and paintings of his wife. *Red Portrait* (1937) (Cat. 143), in particular, translates the gentleness of *Head of a Girl* into a full-scale meditation on a loved identity. And faced by the portraits of his artistic peers, Pound, Joyce and T.S. Eliot (1888–1965), we encounter the greatness of the sitters, not the competitive ego of the rival who subjected their work to such searching criticism in his writing.

A similar humanity is also revealed in Lewis's later novels, starting with sympathy for Margot, in *The Revenge for Love* (1937) (B&M Cat. 39), as she is victimised by ideologues and swindlers; sympathy with Hester, in the 1954 novel based on the Lewises' years in Toronto during the Second World War, *Self Condemned* (B&M Cat. 54). In some ways this novel is a celebration of simple love and domestic companionship in trying circumstances – the last thing we would expect from this scorner of bourgeois values and lifestyles. The culmination of this tendency in Lewis's work is his continuation (in a quite new key) of *The Childermass* in 1955 in two further parts, *Monstre Gai* and *Malign Fiesta* (*The Human Age, Books Two and Three*) (B&M Cat. 57). In these, the erring intellectual, Pullman, faces judgement by God for his political alignments with evil, and judgement is no longer based on the minutiae of competing metaphysics, as it had been in the Bailiff's court in *The Childermass*. Far greater values, human and divine, are now brought into play. The application to Lewis's own career of the 1930s is obvious. But the fiction actually covers all such political alignments, all compromises of artistic truth for worldly advantage. T.S. Eliot recognised *The Human Age* (along with *Self Condemned*) as a book of "unbearable spiritual agony," but Lewis has not received credit for it, or for the self-assessment it contains. It seems as if, in the Anglo-Saxon world, alignments with the authoritarian right, however temporary, must be evidence of some hidden (and perhaps infectious) poison,[48] whereas, increasingly since 1989, alignments with the authoritarian left have become more pardonable – commendable even, as a sign of humanitarian commitment.

In these Anglo-Saxon cultures, Lewis remains not much more than an abrasive and an irritant, mistrusted and not comprehended. And it is certainly right to reject some of Lewis's ideas and prejudices.[49] It could be argued that an oppositional, outsider, role is the proper one for him, the one he made for himself when he "drew the line" and became the "Enemy." But in the end, our cultures are impoverished by their puritanical recoil from most of his work. Here, at last, is an opportunity for a European culture in which Lewis felt "the fundamentals of life are still accessible" to see what it can make of the art of this incomparably and variously gifted man.[50]

NOTES

1. Wyndham Lewis, "The Code of a Herdsman," *The Little Review* 4, no. 3 (July 1917), p. 7.
2. Stanley Fish, "More Colorado Follies," *New York Times* (25 May 2008). Rprt. "Think Again." http://tinyourl.com/yfetd [accessed 21 October 2009].
3. Walter Sickert made this comment in a telegram to the publisher of Lewis's portfolio, *Thirty Personalities and a Self-Portrait* (1932) (manuscript in Lewis archive at Cornell University). The statement is quoted in John Rothenstein, "Great British Masters – 26: Wyndham Lewis," *Picture Post* (25 March 1939), n.p.
4. Wyndham Lewis, "Wyndham Lewis Vortex No. 1: Art Vortex," *Blast*, No. 2 (July 1915), p. 91.
5. Lewis is said to have liked the coincidence of this homonym for the germ cell of an organism and for an explosive force, encapsulated in the title of the Vorticist magazine.
6. James Joyce, *Finnegans Wake* (New York: Viking, 1966), p. 292. Joyce is also mocking Lewis's hostility to going beyond a certain limit in artistic experiment, presciently anticipating the argument of his last writing on art, *The Demon of Progress in the Arts* (London: Methuen, 1954). Chapter 8 is entitled, "There is a Limit, beyond which there is Nothing."
7. Wyndham Lewis, *The Caliph's Design: Architects! Where is Your Vortex?* (1919). Rprt. ed. Paul Edwards (Santa Barbara: Black Sparrow Press, 1986), p. 25.
8. Wyndham Lewis, "Beginning" (1935). Rprt. *Creatures of Habit and Creatures of Change: Essays on Art, Literature and Society*. Ed. Paul Edwards (Santa Rosa: Black Sparrow Press, 1989), p. 266. Lewis's account is not literally true. For an analysis of (and alternative to) this idealised version, see Paul Edwards, "Wyndham Lewis's Narrative of Origins: 'The Death of the Ankou'," *The Modern Language Review* 92, no. 1 (January 1997), pp. 22–35.
9. Wyndham Lewis, "The Vita of Wyndham Lewis" (1949). Rprt. ed. Bernard Lafourcade, *Enemy News*, no. 20 (Winter 1984), p. 13.
10. Wyndham Lewis, *The Childermass: Section I* (London: Chatto and Windus, 1928), p. 2.
11. 'New York's "shabby baskers saluting the sun with many a caustic blink" (*America, I Presume*) are fixed to the page by a pattern of k's and flat a's.' Hugh Kenner, *Wyndham Lewis* (London: Methuen, 1954), p. 106. And, earlier, "the words don't matter so much as the abrupt gestures of their consonants and phrasal intervals" (pp. 103–4).
12. Henry James, quoted in Wyndham Lewis, *Men Without Art* (1934). Rprt. ed. Seamus Cooney (Santa Rosa: Black Sparrow Press, 1987), p. 122.
13. Ibid., p. 129.
14. Wyndham Lewis, *Snooty Baronet* (1932). Rprt. ed. Bernard Lafourcade (Santa Barbara: Black Sparrow Press, 1984).
15. "Vortex No. 1," p. 91.
16. Hal Foster, "Prosthetic Gods," *Modernism/Modernity* 4, no. 2 (April 1997), p. 28.
17. *Snooty Baronet*, pp. 136–37.
18. Wyndham Lewis, "A Soldier of Humour" (1927). Rprt. *The Complete Wild Body* (1927). Ed. Bernard Lafourcade (Santa Barbara: Black Sparrow Press, 1982), p. 17.
19. Wyndham Lewis, "Fêng Shui and Contemporary Form," *Blast*, No. 1 (June 1914), p. 138.
20. See Anthology, p. 357. The first version of "Inferior Religions" is dated by Lafourcade to 1917 (*The Complete Wild Body*, p. 314). It actually dates from 1914–15.
21. Fredric Jameson, *Fables of Aggression: Wyndham Lewis, the Modernist as Fascist* (Berkeley: University of California Press, 1979), p. 28.
22. "Vortex No. 1," p. 91.
23. *The Complete Wild Body*, p. 154.
24. *The Caliph's Design*, pp. 76–78.
25. It is perhaps this limitation on the role of politics that causes Stanley Fish to place him with Hobbes as a conservative theorist.
26. See Wyndham Lewis, "A World Art and Tradition" (1929). Rprt. *Wyndham Lewis on Art: Collected Writings 1913–1956*. Eds. Walter Michel and C.J. Fox (London: Thames and Hudson, 1969), pp. 255–59. "What has fact on its side is still this strange synthesis of cultures and times (which we named Vorticism in England) and which is the first projection of a world-art, and also I think the clearest trail promising us delivery from the mechanical impasse" (p. 259).
27. This was partly Lewis's fault; invited to exhibit at *L'Effort moderne* gallery in Paris in the early 1920s, he failed to assemble sufficient work, and the show never materialised. The problem may have been economic; as C.J. Fox (most tireless campaigner on behalf of "the Enemy") once remarked in conversation, Lewis never knew where his next glass of champagne was coming from.
28. *The Caliph's Design*, pp. 74–76.
29. Wyndham Lewis, "The Meaning of the Wild Body" (1927). *The Complete Wild Body*, p. 158. See Anthology, pp. 356–57. The quoted phrases are from the Katha Upanishad, IV, 12–13 (*The Sacred Books of the East*, vol. 15, *The Upanishads, Part Two*. Trans. Max Müller (Oxford: Oxford University Press, 1884), p. 16).
30. Wyndham Lewis, "Essay on the Objective of Plastic Art in our Time" (1922). *Wyndham Lewis on Art*, p. 204.
31. Ibid., p. 205.
32. Ibid.
33. It was later revised and reissued: Wyndham Lewis, *Enemy of the Stars* (London: Desmond Harmsworth, 1932). Both versions are included in Wyndham Lewis, *Collected Poems and Plays*. Ed. Alan Munton (Manchester: Carcanet, 1979).
34. "Vortex No. 1," p. 91.
35. The gesture is doubled in Lewis's 1954 novel, *Self Condemned* (London: Methuen), when the protagonist throws George Eliot's *Middlemarch* (1874) into the ocean.
36. Wyndham Lewis, *Enemy of the Stars*, *Blast*, No. 1 (June 1914), p. 73.
37. *Collected Poems and Plays*, p. 191.
38. "Vortex No. 1," p. 91.
39. Wyndham Lewis, *Rude Assignment: A Narrative of my Career Up-to-date* (London: Hutchinson, 1950), p. 169.
40. Lewis makes much of the fact, for instance, that Alfred North Whitehead calls his philosophy a philosophy of "organic mechanism."
41. Wyndham Lewis, *Time and Western Man* (1927). Rprt. ed. Paul Edwards (Santa Rosa: Black Sparrow Press, 1993), pp. 132–33.
42. See Tyrus Miller, "No Man's Land: Wyndham Lewis and the Cultural Revolution," *Wyndham Lewis Annual* 12 (2005), pp. 12–28.
43. *The Childermass*, p. 291.
44. "Essay on the Objective of Plastic Art" (1922). *Wyndham Lewis on Art*, p. 210.
45. Wyndham Lewis, "Foreword," in *Paintings and Drawings by Wyndham Lewis* [exh. cat. The Leicester Galleries, London]. London: The Leicester Galleries, December 1937. Rprt. *Wyndham Lewis on Art*, p. 301.
46. "I'm installing myself [in a studio] today, and begin a series of paintings and drawings of the Creation of the World"; Wyndham Lewis, letter to his mother (n.d.: Paris, ca. 1903) in Wyndham Lewis, *The Letters of Wyndham Lewis*. Ed. W.K. Rose (London: Methuen, 1963), p. 10.
47. Wyndham Lewis, *The Art of Being Ruled* (1926). Rprt. ed. Reed Way Dasenbrock (Santa Rosa: Black Sparrow Press, 1989), p. 59.
48. The critical reception of an exhibition of Lewis's portraits (*Wyndham Lewis Portraits*, National Portrait Gallery, London, 3 July–19 October 2008) provides evidence for this. In many reviews, it was only after a denunciation of Lewis's supposed politics (and sometimes of nearly all his other work) that anything like an appreciation of the work on show – seen as uncharacteristic of him – could begin.
49. Particularly his recurrent anti-Semitism. It should be realised, however, that Lewis himself rejected this. After Germany's state-sponsored pogrom, *Kristallnacht*, of November 1938, he wrote a pro-Semitic study, *The Jews: Are they Human?* (London: George Allen and Unwin, 1939), pointing out that it was the Christian nations who "degraded the Jew, and then mocked at him for being degraded. We must give all people of Jewish race a new deal among us" (p. 111).
50. Lewis's phrase refers directly to the French peasants of Brittany that he encountered before the First World War, but his numerous writings on Spain (and his paintings) show that he felt something similar about that country.

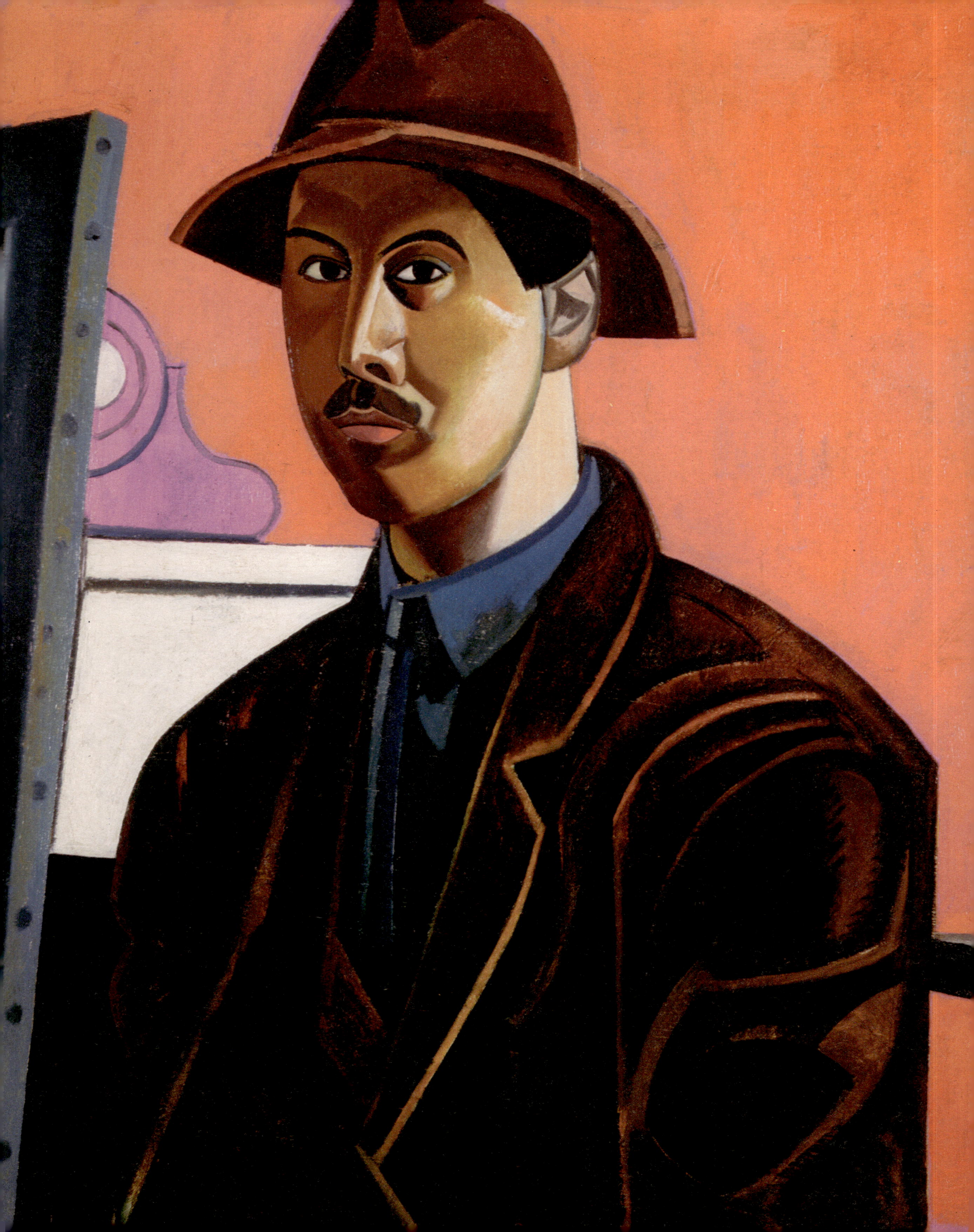

"A STRANGE SYNTHESIS": LEWIS, BRITISH ART AND A WORLD TRADITION

Richard Humphreys

Portrait of the Artist as the Painter Raphael, 1921. Manchester City Galleries (Cat. 97)

IN FEBRUARY 1929, WYNDHAM LEWIS

wrote an article, "A World Art and Tradition,"[1] in which he proposed for contemporary artists a greatly extended cultural sphere and a matching cosmopolitan aesthetic. This new culture and its aesthetic would be catholic in both space and time: artists would draw on all the possibilities of the visual cultures around them, whether European or from further afield, or whether of the present or the distant and not-so-distant past. The result would be "a strange synthesis of cultures and times."[2] The article was in part a response to the conditions of the art scene as Lewis saw them at the time, encouraging the expanded range of visual sources that the Surrealists were exploring, but also seeking a genuine interaction of cultures in a rapidly shrinking world. The article pointed out something Lewis felt not enough artists had understood: "the Earth has become one place, instead of a romantic tribal patchwork of places."[3] The Canadian cultural theorist Marshall McLuhan (1911–80) later acknowledged his debt to these ideas of Lewis for the development of his concept of the "global village."[4] Lewis referred to himself and a minority of western artists, in Europe and America, as the buried heroes of a "submerged civilisation."[5] Working in opposition to the commercial compromises of capitalist societies and the oppressive directions of Soviet cultural policy, this vanguard of artists could herald a new world of invention and liberation. Artists such as Max Ernst (1891–1976), Paul Klee (1879–1940) and, of course, Lewis himself, were already creating a "complete world, with its aqueducts, its drains, its courts, private dwellings, personal ornaments, almost its religion with its theurgic implements which have never existed."[6]

While at the Slade School of Art, London from 1899 to 1901, Lewis was looking not only at the various forms of Realist, post-Impressionist and late Symbolist art that were the dominant forms of contemporary practice at the time, but also at what would become the ingredients of the "world-art" he favoured by the time he published his 1929 essay. His frequent visits to the British Museum with its great collections of African, Oceanic, Oriental and other non-European art and artefacts, planted the seed of his ambitious vision to develop an art without boundaries. He was himself a "bohemian" at the time, but even in his early admiration of the artist Augustus John (1878–1961), who was a teacher and mentor in artistic and sexual matters, Lewis saw beyond what he saw as the "cul-de-sac" of the romantic gypsy life John followed. Lewis wanted more than the freedom of personal expression and sexual liberation his bearded friend desired. Known at art school as "the poet," Lewis's imagination was fuelled by a far wider range of imaginative and intellectual sources than John's, or indeed most contemporaries in the British art world. In this he was encouraged above all by another early mentor, the now fairly obscure figure of the poet and artist Thomas Sturge Moore (1878–1944), who had nurtured in his young protégé a taste for abstract and dialectical thought. Following a fairly brief spell at the Slade School of Art, he set off in 1902 on a number of journeys of self-education and self-discovery across Europe, living in cities such as Paris, Munich, and Madrid and more remote corners such as Brittany.

By the time Lewis settled for good in London in 1908, he had acquired considerable language skills and a deep knowledge of the art and culture of continental Europe. He had seen Cubist and Expressionist art at first hand and had also imbibed much of the literary, political and philosophical culture out of which they had grown: Henri Bergson (1859–1941), Arthur Schopenhauer (1788–1860), Friedrich Nietzsche (1844–1900), Karl Marx (1818–83), Pierre-Joseph Proudhon (1809–65), Georges Sorel (1847–1922), Arthur Rimbaud (1854–91), are just a few of the writers with whose works he was familiar and to whom his ideas refer and react against. There was also an important theological dimension to Lewis's interests that is less obvious at this

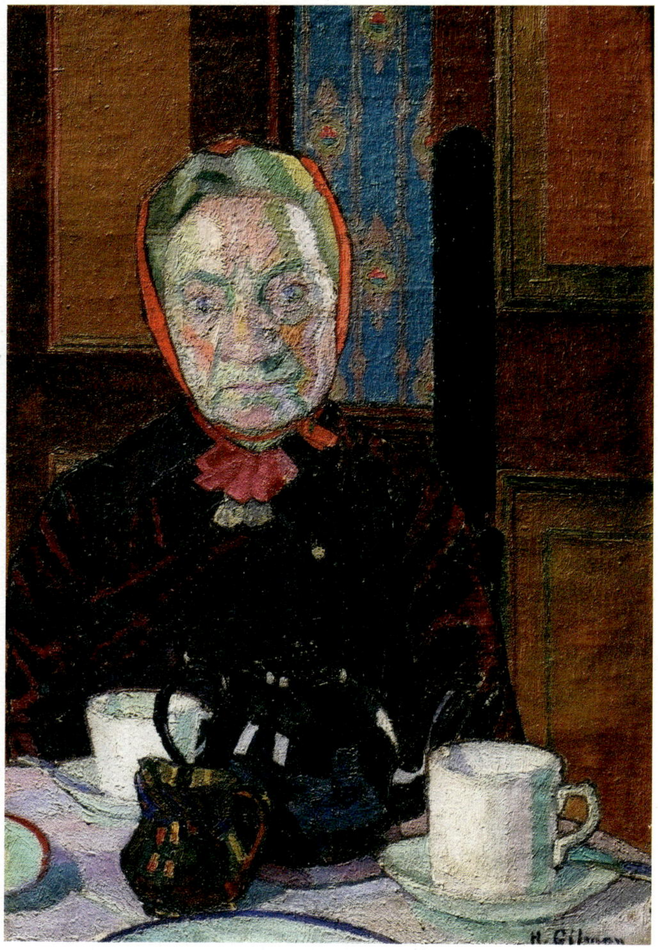

Fig. 1.
Harold Gilman, *Mrs. Mounter at the Breakfast Table*, exhibited 1917. Tate, London

stage but which grows stronger after 1920. At this point, it is indicated by a fascination with occult and mystical matters, often seemingly at odds with the hard, satirical tone of much of his art and writing. Nevertheless, the "hardness" itself has roots in Lewis's deep interest in dualistic philosophies and religious traditions, as we shall see.

In 1909 Lewis was a member of the Camden Town Group, a body of artists in London under the leadership of Walter Sickert (1860–1942). These artists, including Lewis's friends Spencer Gore (1878–1914) and Harold Gilman (1876–1919) (**Fig. 1**), worked in a mode characterised by broadly social Realist subject matter and experimentation with a strongly coloured post-Impressionist style. Typical imagery included the seedy bed-sit rooms in which such artists and their models would have lived in central and north London, cheap working-class cafés, and the rowdy Victorian music halls that before cinema were the main venues of popular entertainment. Oil paint was applied with an emphasis on "facture" and with a colour range that could, by contemporary standards, lapse into vulgarity. Lewis, however, was the odd man out in the group and far exceeded them in their tendency to shock. A writer of short stories that were beginning to gain him notoriety on account of their grotesque characters and dark satirical vision, Lewis exhibited works in pen and ink and watercolour, rather than oil, which were as much an affront to many of his avant-garde colleagues as to the wider public. In 1911, at the Camden Town Group's first exhibition,[7] Lewis exhibited works that so repulsed Lucien Pissarro (1863–1944) that he threatened to withdraw his own works from the display. "The pictures of Lewis are quite impossible," he wrote to Spencer Gore.[8] Surely, Lewis could not be serious with this puerile stuff.

Lewis was always suspicious of the potential tyranny of good taste and polite culture and much of his painting, at least before 1922, is informed by a deliberately provocative combination of awkward or grotesque form, strident or acidically strange colour and unusual subject matter or narrative. *The Theatre Manager* (1909) (Cat. 6) was exactly the kind of work Pissarro would have been offended by. It also shows, on a modest scale, what was so original about Lewis's art and the direction much of his work was to take in the future. A group of 12 actors in a frieze-like composition surround the seated and exasperated looking theatre manager. His profile's reflection can be seen in a mirror at the centre of the image. The figures are highly caricatural and primitive with their phallic noses and distorted bodies. Lewis is clearly aware at this point of the early Cubist work of Pablo Picasso (1881–1973) and the deliberately primitivising styles of other European artists of the time. It has been suggested, indeed, that Lewis saw Picasso's *Les Desmoiselles d'Avignon* (1907) in the artist's studio and this small work may well bear out this claim.

There is another visual source at work, however. It is the art of the great English caricaturists of the eighteenth century that Lewis would have seen in abundance in the Department of Prints and Drawings at the British Museum, the treasure store that so greatly informed his visual imagination: William Hogarth (1697–1764), Thomas Rowlandson (1765–1827) and, perhaps above all, James Gillray (1757–1815). Throughout his career, Lewis wrote satire and looked to the great satirists of the past such as Gillray and the writer Jonathan Swift (1667–1745) for inspiration. So, with an eye on Picasso, non-European art and the English satirical tradition, Lewis presented himself to the Edwardian London art world as a man with a unique and disturbing voice. Where his Camden Town contemporaries painted the performers on the stage, or the audience watching them, Lewis went behind the scenes to show, as it were, the mechanics of the spectacle.

The Theatre Manager looks grotesque, but it is also about themes that Lewis dwelt upon throughout his career: the individual and the crowd, and the personality and its enigmatic constituents. The manager seems collapsed under the weight of his responsibilities, surrounded by creatures that he has to organise into performance and life, and uncertain whether they are separate individuals or aspects of his imagination. The book he stares at seems to be of little help to him; in a number of Lewis's later works, a text, actual or implied, is often a significant element. From 1909, therefore, Lewis staked out a path for himself that took him far from most of his British contemporaries, pursuing formal risks and investigating a range of themes and concepts that made him, along with his powerful urge towards satire, a controversial and quite unclassifiable figure.

If Lewis deliberately created a highly original kind of narrative at a time when many British artists shunned anything suggestive of story-telling in the name of formal purity, his response to his European peers was equally dialectical and provocative. Lewis was the most enthusiastic and intelligent of the British artists who were drawn to Filippo Tommaso Marinetti's (1876–1944) Futurist movement after the Italians' first exhibition in London in 1912.[9] He saw the intellectual, dramatic and formal possibilities of Futurism, but from these he created an art that was in effect a critique of its sources. Lewis opposed what he saw as the imitative and impressionist attempt to capture moving form with which Giacomo Balla (1871–1958) and his colleagues had experimented, with an art of implicit energy, a classical sense of contained power. The dynamism he sought would be in the rigorous organisation of line and form, rather than in the repetition of lines suggestive of perceived movement. Lewis admired the Futurists' inventive and often iconoclastic attitude and their ambition to extend the subject matter and narrative possibilities of art in the modern world; however, for him, "modernity" did not simply mean mechanisation and speed, cities and radical politics.

It was probably a belief that significant content in contemporary art, paradoxically, might be drawn from historical sources, which led Lewis, in 1912, to make a series of remarkable drawings for an edition of one of William Shakespeare's least well-known plays, *Timon of Athens*. In these drawings, it looks as though Lewis has been studying Umberto Boccioni's (1882–1916) most recent work, yet

Willian Roberts, The Vorticists at the Restaurant de la Tour Eiffel: Spring, 1915, 1961-62, Tate, London (Cat. 208)

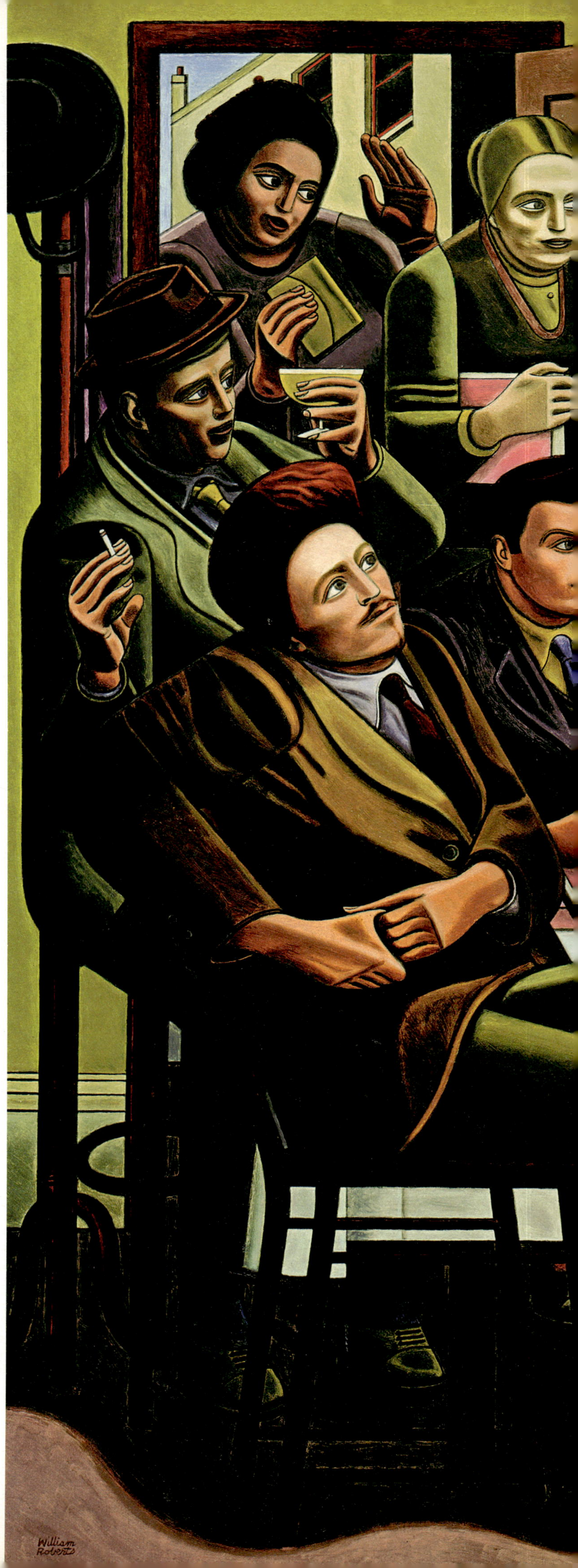

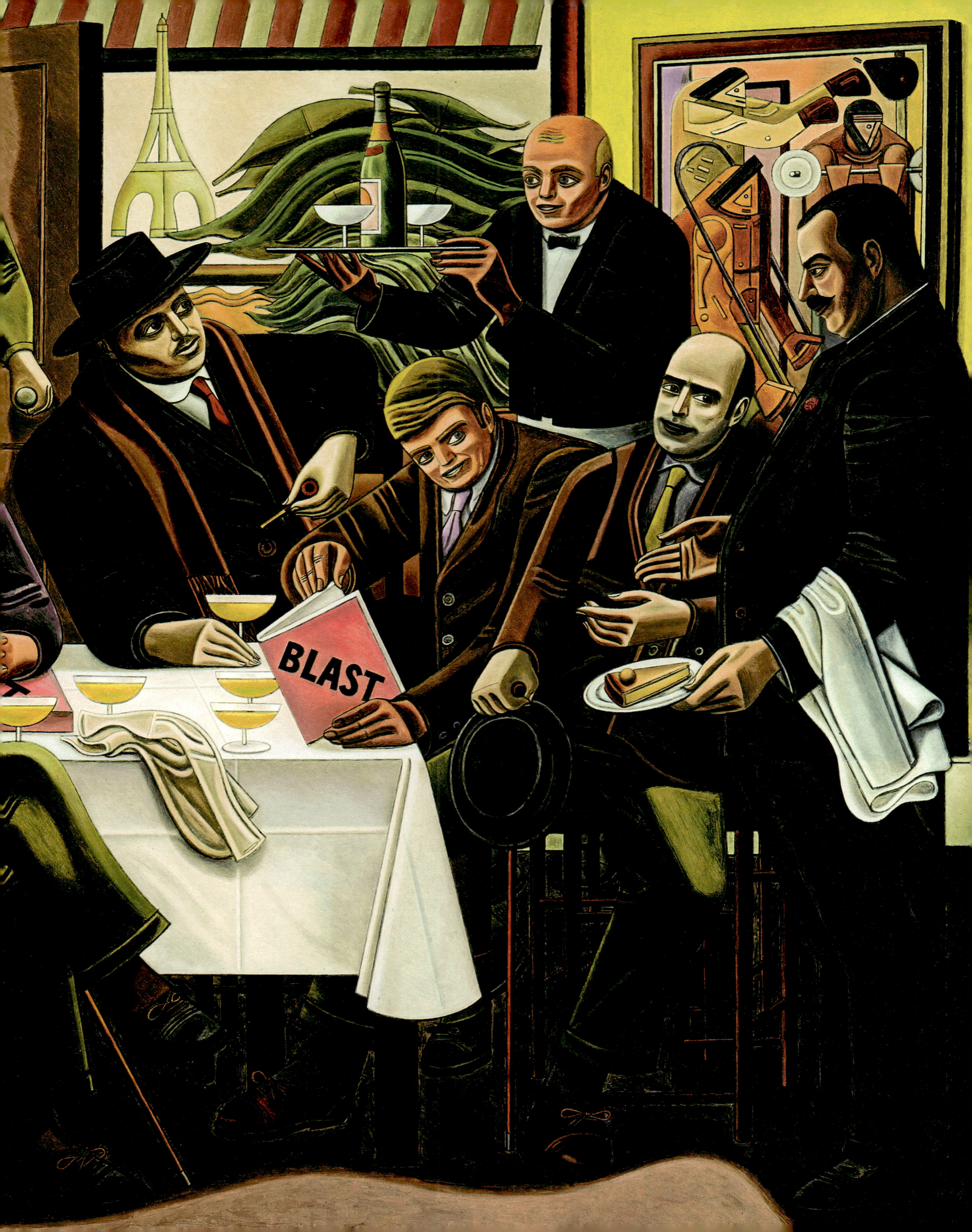
BLAST

he has absorbed the Italian artist's visual vocabulary and made of it a language entirely his own. There are echoes of Japanese art throughout his work between 1912 and 1914, and in general an oriental aesthetic that favours asymmetry and with the possibilities of large areas of empty space on the surface. Furthermore, rather than make complex images of people leaving modern railway stations or riding bicycles, Lewis presents the key episodes of a classical tragedy. The effect, however, is stunningly of its time; it is as if Shakespeare's Greek characters had become part of a science fiction drama on an alien planet. Lewis's interest in the figure of Timon continued into the 1920s as he pondered the nature of human generosity, action and detachment. In 1912, it seems likely he was particularly interested in Marx's ideas about the "cash-nexus" as expressed in a discussion of *Timon of Athens*, and the passage in the play where two characters debate the relative merits of poetry and painting.

By 1914, Lewis was acknowledged as the leading figure among a group of artists who were interested in developing the more radical aspects of contemporary European art. In this venture, they parted company with both Camden Town painters and those associated with the Bloomsbury Group. These latter, while experimenting with abstract form, had no interest in the kind of modernity that Lewis and his artists wished to engage with. This group, including Edward Wadsworth (1888–1949) and Henri Gaudier-Brzeska (1891–1915) and supported by the American poet Ezra Pound ((1885–1972), coalesced into a movement called Vorticism that produced two issues of the celebrated magazine *Blast* (B&M Cats. 2 and 3), in 1914 and 1915, and exhibited work at the Doré Galleries in 1915. Lewis was the editor of, and dominant contributor to, *Blast*, and used its pages to broadcast his views on the art of his times as well as to publish his extraordinary drama, *Enemy of the Stars*, as well as his ideas about matters such as feng shui and contemporary psychology. Although a reasonable number of his watercolours and drawings of this phase survive, there are only two extant Vorticist oil paintings, *Workshop* (1915) (Cat. 58) and *The Crowd* (1914–15) (Cat. 59). *The Crowd* is a grand statement of the political realities of the time. Various massed groups of human units are shown trapped in an urban landscape of diagrammatic terror. Lewis has moved from the crudely drawn group of grotesques around his theatre manager to a full-scale map of the forces he saw shaping future civilisation: an anonymous, uniform crowd controlled by equally anonymous powers signified by robotic figures in the foreground. These latter echo the figure in the London-based American sculptor Jacob Epstein's (1880–1959) iconic *Rock Drill* sculpture of 1913–15. With the Timon drawings and *The Crowd*, Lewis had established much of his art's future direction.

After service as an artillery officer and then as an official war artist during the First World War, Lewis returned to London in 1919 hoping to reinvigorate the art scene and to carry on the pre-war Vorticist movement, albeit in a new guise to suit new conditions. His war art had again distinguished Lewis from his British contemporaries, neither moving towards a melancholy landscape art as Paul Nash (1889–1946), nor a lurid Realism in the fashion, for instance, of William Orpen (1878–1931). Lewis rejected any kind of sentimentality or bogus heroism and created his wartime masterpiece, *A Battery Shelled* (1919) (Cat. 71), after working on some brilliantly muscular drawings of men at work and in combat on the Western Front. The insect-like soldiers in the foreground in the oil painting now in the Imperial War Museum stand in relation to the larger figures as his masonry-like masses do to the controlling presences in *The Crowd*. Lewis was essentially a figurative artist but was always keen to use the possibilities developed in his more abstract and conceptual pieces. Thus between 1919 and 1922 he embarked on a prolonged effort at modernist invention alongside the refinement of his very considerable skills as a traditional draughtsman. The results are among the most compelling works produced anywhere in Europe at the time. Lewis was in regular touch with the developments in France, Germany and elsewhere and at one point earmarked as the London correspondent for the *De Stijl* magazine under Theo van Doesburg (1883–1931). His combative essay, *The Caliph's Design* (1919) (B&M Cat. 7), was a

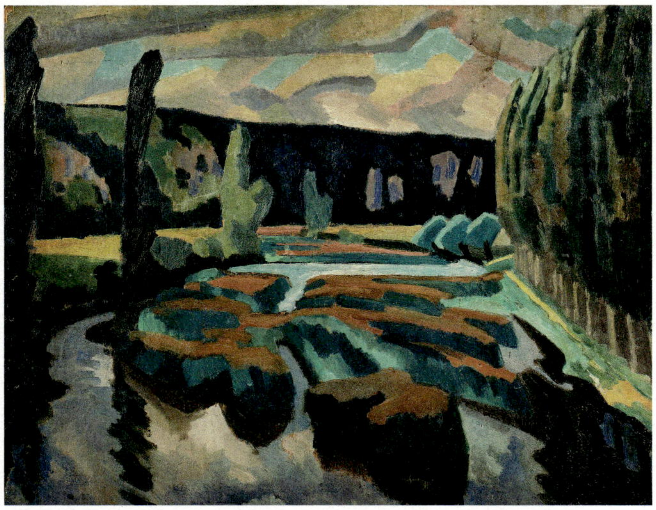

Fig. 2.
Roger Fry, *River with Poplars*, ca. 1912. Tate, London

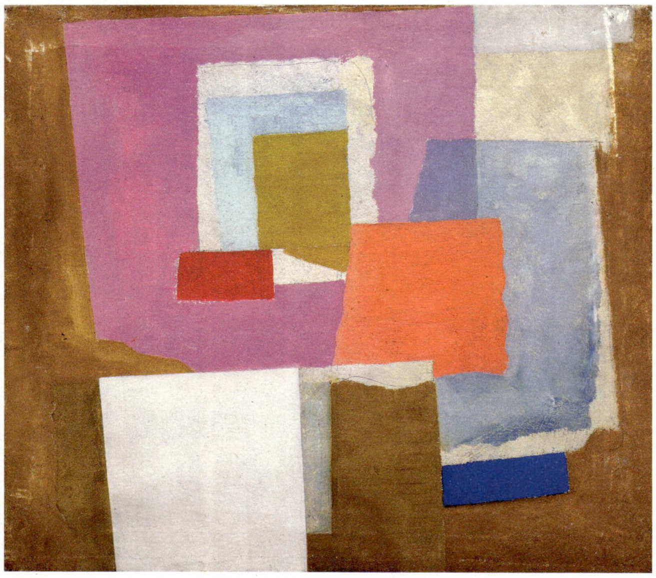

Fig. 3.
Ben Nicholson, 1924 (First Abstract Painting, Chelsea), ca. 1923–24. Tate, London

clarion call to architects and artists to develop a modernist aesthetic for the post-war period. Lewis's own work shows that he could compete with Picasso's portrait and figure drawing and sustain a modernist visual project as inventive as Constructivist, Dadaist and other artists. Although "Group X," an attempt to regroup the Vorticists failed, and his magazine *The Tyro* (B&M Cats. 8 and 9) and the related paintings and drawings proved a short-lived enterprise, they represent a one-man and heroic effort to keep a thorough-going experimental avant-garde alive in unpromising circumstances. British art was largely confined to more timid retrenchments in traditional and Realist modes, characterised by Lewis as the "ugly and untidy kitchen-garden that is a London Group exhibition."[10] That comment was aimed at his great *bête noire*, the fine critic but mediocre painter Roger (1866–1934), who Lewis believed was in control of most possibilities in London for much of the 1920s (**Fig. 2**).

Although by 1924 some younger artists, such as Ben Nicholson (1894–1982) **Fig. 3**) for example, and some old colleagues such as Wadsworth, were venturing out into more demanding areas and taking note of the modernist scene abroad, Lewis was by then convinced that no amount of organised activity among like-minded artists would achieve the progress he was after. In a work such as *Archimedes Reconnoitring the Fleet* (1922) (Cat. 113), we have a fine example of why Lewis felt so isolated. An extraordinary frieze of almost emblematic complex forms is organised within a delicate envelope of fine encompassing lines. The colours are delicate pastel shades. By this time, Lewis was deeply fascinated by Egyptian art as well as by the recent work of Purists such as Fernand Leger (1881–1955) and the humorous and enigmatic narratives and conceits of Dada and Constructivist art. Visually there was nothing remotely like this being made in Britain and the debts to Synthetic Cubism and other European examples are gathered into a wholly new idiom. The subject matter, as ever with Lewis, is highly individual and original and tells us much about his interests and development at this stage. Lewis was fascinated by the history of science, but even more so by the possibilities and limits of the intellect's capacities. Many of his works are concerned with visualising a mind at work in the world and among its own constructions. Archimedes was an aristocratic mathematical genius who, according to Plutarch, defended King Hiero's magnificent city of Syracuse against the Roman fleet commanded by Marcellus. His brilliantly conceived war machines, somewhat like the bizarre imaginary contraptions of Lewis's contemporaries Francis Picabia (1879–1953) and Ernst, seem to be part human and part inanimate. In Archimedes' case they included fire-ball catapults, rock-dropping and ship-lifting machinery and, most legendary of all, a vast mirrored shield with which the Carthaginians reflected the sun's light to set alight the Roman ships' sails. These machines, the ships, Archimedes and other concealed forms are deeply buried in Lewis's composition. The tragic element in the story, which like that of Timon would have interested Lewis, was Archimedes' pride and vagueness, which led to his death at the hands of a Roman soldier.

After 1923, having produced not only these brilliantly innovative works and his figure drawings, but also some of the finest portraits in twentieth century British art, such as *Praxitella* (1920–21) (Cat. 96) and *Edith Sitwell* (1923–36) (Cat. 105), Lewis took to a lengthy period of writing and a kind of underground existence away from the distractions of the London art and literary scenes. The motivations for this were as complex as the outcomes: his concern to define a political and cultural context for art of the highest creativity and quality; his engagement with the philosophical tendencies of the time; and his desire to continue the fictional work of his early short stories and his first novel *Tarr* (1918) (B&M Cat. 5). Lewis kept an alert eye on the artistic currents around him between 1923 and 1933 and undertook some important commissions and personal projects, many of which built on the achievements of the early 1920s. Such work was typically on a small scale and mostly on paper, probably his preferred support as an artist. His magazine *The Enemy* (B&M Cats. 14–16), three issues of which appeared in 1927–29, carried various pieces on the visual arts and illustrations of his own and other painting, such as that of Giorgio de Chirico (1888–1978), which he admired.

Nevertheless, it was not until 1933 that Lewis began to paint seriously again, hoping to produce a sequence of works within a relatively short period to show to the wider world what he could do. Illness and literary projects prevented this from happening until December 1937, when he held his first major exhibition since 1921 at The Leicester Galleries, London. By then, British art had become far more international in outlook with groups such as Unit One, led by Nash, investigating the possibilities of abstraction and Surrealism and seeking, as Lewis had when he prophetically wrote *The Caliph's Design* in 1919, to bring modernist art into fruitful partnership with the most advanced forms of architecture and design. Lewis by then, however, was probably regarded more as a writer than a painter and although still a highly respected voice in British visual arts was no longer seen as a leader-figure. The main critical exponent for the new tendencies was Herbert Read (1893–1968), a man, like Fry who had died in 1934, Lewis regarded with suspicion, dubbing him "committee-man" and seeing him as a weakly principled mouthpiece for anything "new" that was passing by.[11] Lewis continued, however, to support the modernist tendency in articles published throughout the decade. His own work of the period strikes a typically original and unorthodox stance, although the sculptor Henry Moore (1898–1986) (**Fig. 4**) thought of Lewis as "our only great man," showing that in spite of the older artist's unpopular political opinions he was still a figure of almost totemic power among a younger generation. Moore and others signed a letter in 1937 demanding the Tate Gallery and other institutions recognise Lewis's importance by acquiring works from The Leicester Galleries exhibition.[12]

In a sense, the 1937 show was Lewis's opportunity to show what he had meant in his 1929 article, "A World Art and Tradition." What might this large claim to bring together so many sources into a truly international art actually amount to? The 24 oil paintings and 30 drawings constitute a sadly overlooked achievement, their invisibility in many histories of twentieth-century British art no doubt reflecting hostility to Lewis's politics and the difficulty that their subject matter and form pose to categorisation. Lewis was sympathetic to the abstract efforts of his contemporaries at a general level, but was at heart convinced that no significant art could be created outside figuration and the traditions of "history painting." The narrative content of his 1930s paintings, as ever, is complex and drawn from a variety of often arcane sources. Formally Lewis had drawn, true to his word, on sources as diverse as Cubism and Metaphysical Art, and Renaissance, Chinese and Egyptian painting. Lewis's remarkable novel *The Childermass* (1928) (B&M Cat. 19), set in the after-life, is one source for a number of linked images such as *The Inferno* (1937) (Cat. 166) (**Fig. 5**), *One of the Stations of the Dead* (1933) (Cat. 155), and *Red Scene* (1933–36) (Cat. 161), and reminds us that from an early age he was a great admirer of William Blake (1757–1827), like himself an artist who worked as a writer and painter. Like Blake, Lewis needed a deep mythology within which to work and believed in the reality of the metaphysical regions opened up by the imagination. There are also far more personal images that have a strong metaphysical aspect and a sense of some sphere between mind and body, demanding enquiry, such as *The Convalescent* (1933) (Cat. 154) (**Fig. 6**) and *The Tank in the Clinic* (1937) (Cat. 163), which are concerned with the trials of the body in ill health and the mind's stoical resistance to pain. There are also directly humorous and satirical images, such as *The Betrothal of the Matador* (1933) (Cat. 152), *Two Beach Babies* (1933) (Cat. 151) and *Cubist Museum* (1936) (Cat. 160), the latter an ironic commentary on modernism and its audience, yet also a warm tribute to the recently founded Museum of Modern Art, New York, which he so greatly admired. Lewis wanted humour in art as much as serious content and, in fact, many of the 1930s' works continue the satirical impulse found in earlier paintings.

Perhaps most interestingly, Lewis also roamed widely across time and space to create some major historical images: *Inca and the Birds* (1933) (Cat. 156), *The Surrender of Barcelona* (1936–37) (Cat. 162), and *Landscape with Northmen* (1936–37) (Cat. 165). The first two are meditations on texts by the great American Romantic historian, William H. Prescott (1796–1859), a blind man who worked entirely from written sources read out to him. Lewis was deeply moved and inspired it seems by these products of a mind without eyes dependent on inner vision and intellect to achieve a special version of truth. *Inca and the Birds* is concerned with ancient rites of passage, leadership and the passing of empire. It is also a satirical image in its implicit commentary on the political and cultural decay that Lewis was recording in his own fiction and criticism. A young Inca might as easily be a bogus artist of recent times. *The Surrender of Barcelona* was Lewis's most explicitly historical image, with its obvious reference to the tragedy unfolding in Spain at the time. While the narrative concerns the 1472 siege of Barcelona, it is also a meditation on the circularities of history. The events of 1472 led to Spain's rapid growth as a world empire, of course; *Landscape with Northmen* is similarly concerned with a moment of imperial triumph, in this case of the Vikings.

Hell, Purgatory, Spain, Peru, New York – these are just a few of the regions that Lewis inhabited imaginatively, travelling in time and seeking to turn the expectations and habits of his contemporaries on their heads. There is a sense of surface and hollowness in many of his forms that paradoxically is played off against a sense of great depth and richness, both of space and time. He stages his narratives with enormous and almost clairvoyant skill. Often one feels that Lewis is offering many more points of view and moments in time

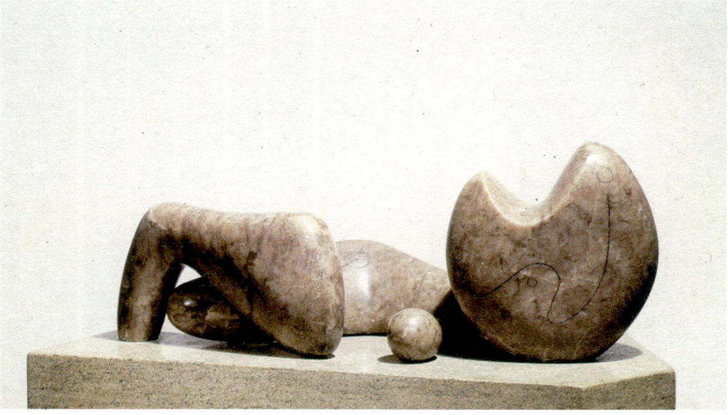

Fig. 4.
Henry Moore, *Four-Piece Composition: Reclining Figure*, 1934. Tate, London

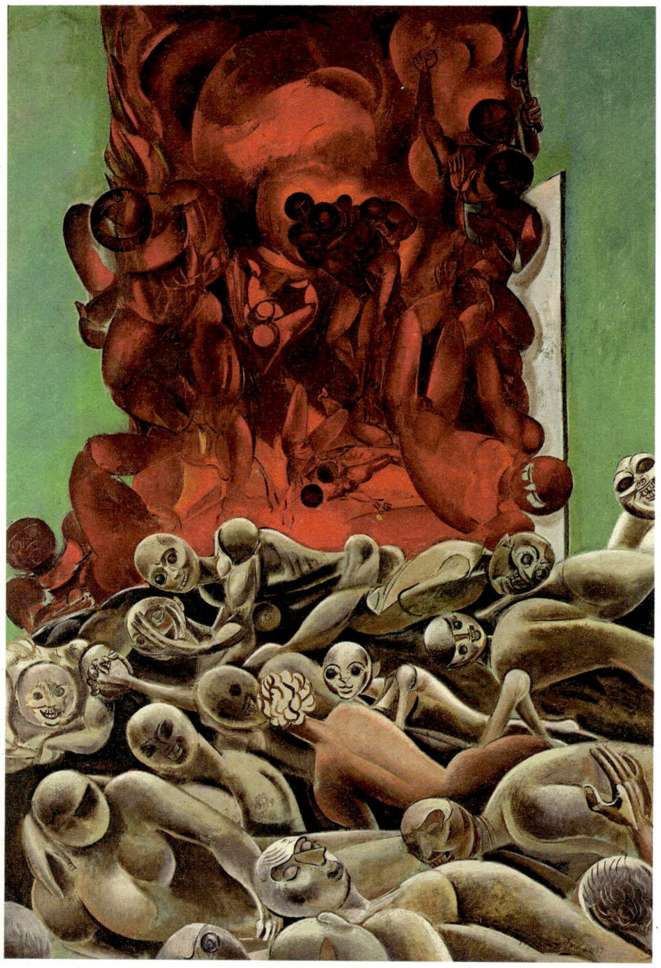

Fig. 5.
Inferno, 1937. National Gallery of Victoria, Melbourne (Cat. 166)

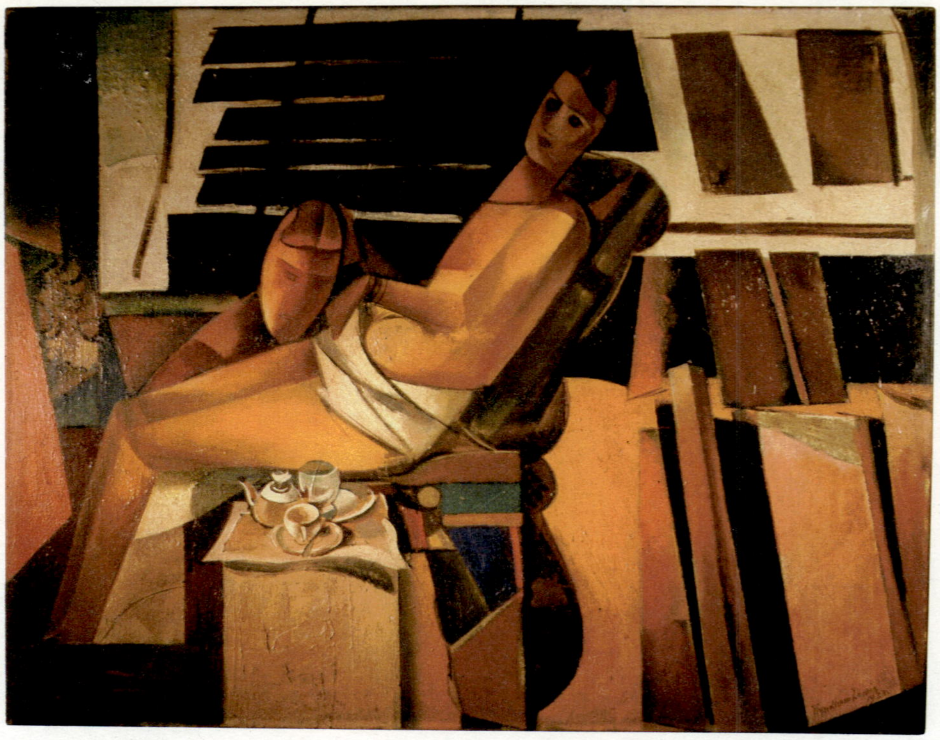

Fig. 6.
The Convalescent, 1933.
Glynn Vivian Art Gallery, Swansea (Cat. 144)

than is really possible. While Lewis still demanded strong structural composition, like a good Cubist or Egyptian tomb artist, his actual touch as a painter is extraordinarily delicate, as if a rococo artist has joined forces with a Chinese one of the Sung Dynasty. There are wonderful passages of colour, which is always unexpected in its combinations, deftly suggesting a sail, the curve of a body or a glimpse of sky. Tonally, Lewis moves from a light to a dark palette, and the 1930s' paintings as a whole create an almost symphonic scope when seen in sufficient numbers.

Lewis was clearly delighted with the critical reception he received from his most discerning critics and from admirers such as Henry Moore for The Leicester Galleries exhibition. Few works were sold, however, but in 1938, no doubt emboldened by a sense of achievement, he painted his great portrait of T.S. Eliot (1888–1965), which was rejected by the Royal Academy and briefly put him back in the forefront of artistic news in Britain, returning him to the notoriety that he had enjoyed as a Vorticist a quarter of a century before. Lewis saw himself as the skeleton in the nation's artistic cupboard and took enormous pleasure in the furore in the press and on newsreels that for a while enlivened London's summertime gossip. The painting of Eliot was one of a number of major portraits that he executed in 1938–39, which, with those of the early 1920s and the 1932 portfolio of drawings, established him as arguably Britain's greatest portraitist of the last century. Lewis was soon to leave England for North America where in 1941–42 he produced a stunning series of imaginative watercolours that show him in touch, or at least in sympathy, with the most recent developments of the New York School. This was to be his last major effort as a painter. Writing and illness steered him in a different direction and when he returned to London after the Second World War his most significant contribution to Britain's art scene was as a critic in exhibition reviews and a fierce opponent of what he believed was the nihilism of extreme abstraction in his book *The Demon of Progress in the Arts* (1954) (B&M Cat. 55). Throughout his life, Lewis had engaged with British, European and "world-art," in search of a new tradition, with an astonishing intelligence, imagination and energy. He is still something of a skeleton in the cupboard, but continues to rattle vigorously and is constantly being resurrected, each time exhibiting more life than ever before.

NOTES

1. Wyndham Lewis, "A World Art and Tradition," in *Drawing and Design* 5, no. 32 (February 1929), pp. 29–30. Rprt. *Wyndham Lewis on Art: Collected Writings 1913–1956*. Eds. Walter Michel and C.J. Fox (London: Thames and Hudson, 1969), p. 258.
2. Ibid, p. 259.
3. Ibid.
4. Marshall McLuhan, *Understanding Media* (1964). Rprt. (Berkeley, California: Gingko Press, 2003), p. 6.
5. Wyndham Lewis, "A World Art and Tradition" (1929), p. 258.
6. Ibid.
7. The Camden Town Group's first exhibition was held at the Carfax Gallery, London in June 1911.
8. Lucien Pissarro letter to Spencer Gore, n.d., Ashmolean Museum, Oxford.
9. The Italian Futurists' first exhibition in London was held at the Sackville Galleries in 1912.
10. Wyndham Lewis, "A World Art and Tradition" (1929), p. 256.
11. Wyndham Lewis letter to Herbert Read, 17 November 1950. *The Letters of Wyndham Lewis*. Ed. W.K. Rose (London: Methuen, 1963), p. 527.
12. Henry Moore et al., letter to the editor: "Mr Wyndham Lewis's Works," *The Times*, no. 47874 (22 December 1937), p. 8.

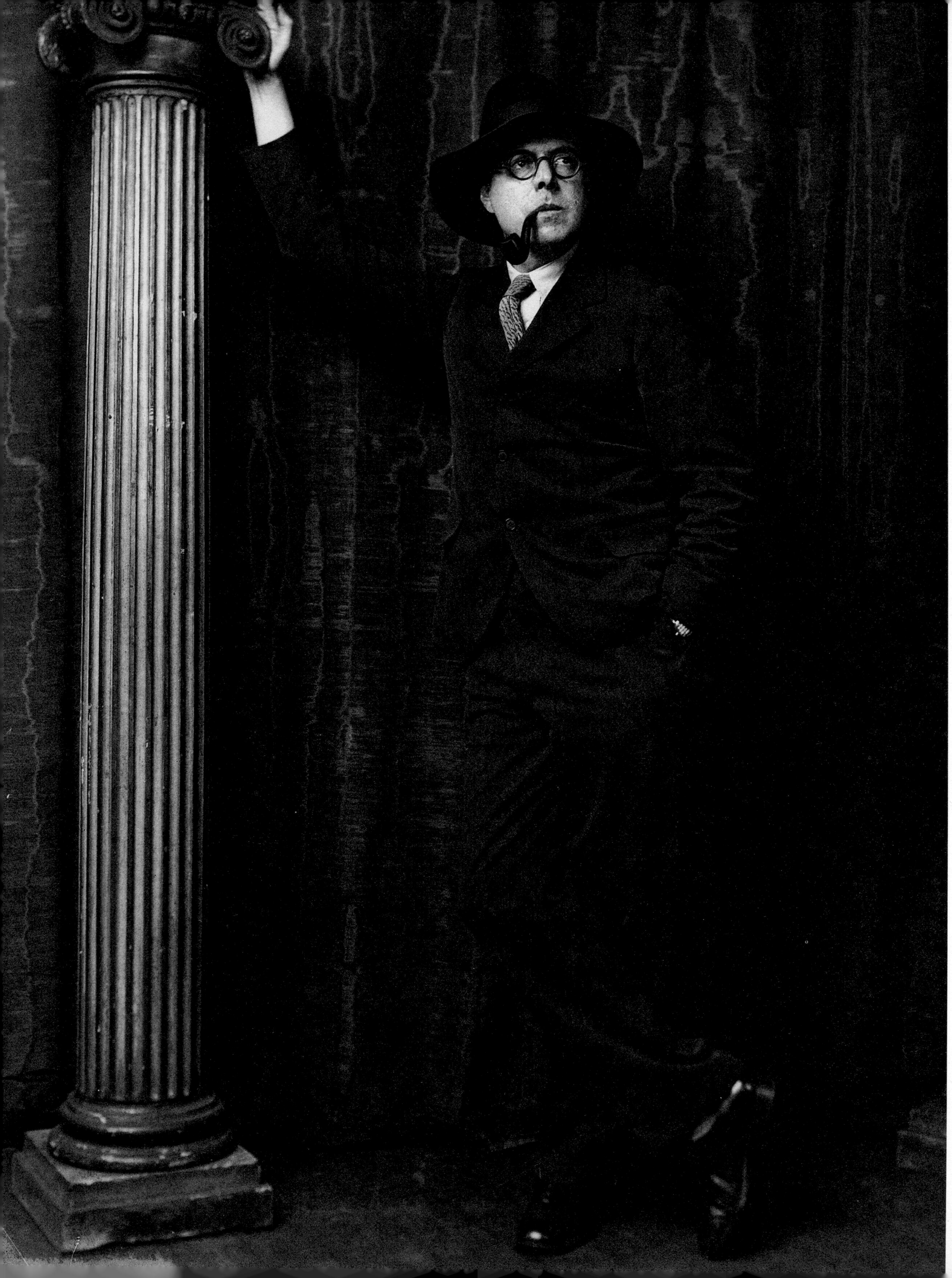

WYNDHAM LEWIS: A TWENTIETH-CENTURY EUROPEAN INTELLECTUAL IN CHIAROSCURO

Yolanda Morató

G.C. Beresford, *Wyndham Lewis*, 1929. National Portrait Gallery, London (Cat. 212)

ANYONE WHO HAS THE CHANCE TO READ

Wyndham Lewis's essays will rapidly appreciate that his sagacity with regard to aesthetic, literary and philosophical issues made him an intellectual of European standing, as well as understand a little better the errors that led his work to disappear from the shelves of many bookshops. In addition, the reader of these essays will be a privileged witness to the splendour and squalor of half a century of art and politics, on the streets and in the drawing rooms of the wealthiest classes. That reader will smile at Lewis's black humour and will be horrified by some little-known facts.

However, this only applies to those who have actually had the chance to read his essays.

Wyndham Lewis's reputation as an author was obscured for a variety of reasons throughout his life as well as after it and he became one of the least acknowledged and most criticised figures within English-speaking modernism. Most of his works have been out of print for decades – with the exception of an impressive collection of scholarly editions reprinted by Black Sparrow Press in the 1980s and 1990s – while in a country such as Spain, with a long-established tradition of translations of modernist authors, Lewis was not published until 2005. The legend that he himself created through the persona of "the Enemy" accompanied him beyond the grave. The constant criticisms of his life and work by various influential critics and historians with regard to their meaning or what they were thought to mean is explicable up to the 1960s when the wounds inflicted by the Second World War had still not totally healed. Everything after that date, however, is a matter of different trends of criticism, many of them based on Fredric Jameson's (b. 1934) influential study, *Fables of Aggression: Wyndham Lewis, the Modernist as Fascist* (1979).

Many of the interpretations that were published in the second half of the twentieth century specifically arise from this error: that of wishing to interpret an author's complete *oeuvre* on the basis of the first part, using the wisdom and experience that history has offered those of us who have lived in the second half. Others, however, have used Lewis as a scapegoat in a more literal sense. The prestigious academic John Carey (b. 1934), author of monographs on a wide range of subjects (including John Donne, Charles Dickens, a history of Utopia and another of Science), is a good example of this type of biased usage. In *The Intellectuals and the Masses* (1992),[1] republished several times, Carey compared Lewis to Adolf Hitler (1889–1945) to such an extent that he devoted almost half of the chapter supposedly on Lewis to the Nazi leader. It is clear that the figure who really interested Carey was Hitler, otherwise it is difficult to understand why he entitled the longest section of his essay on Lewis "Adolf Hitler's intellectual Programme." Carey was particularly keen on quoting passages from *Mein Kampf* (1925) in the same way that Jameson could not help seeing everything from a Marxist viewpoint.[2] Historians who read with ideological glasses on are like surgeons in a butcher's shop, finding it easy to take things out of context.

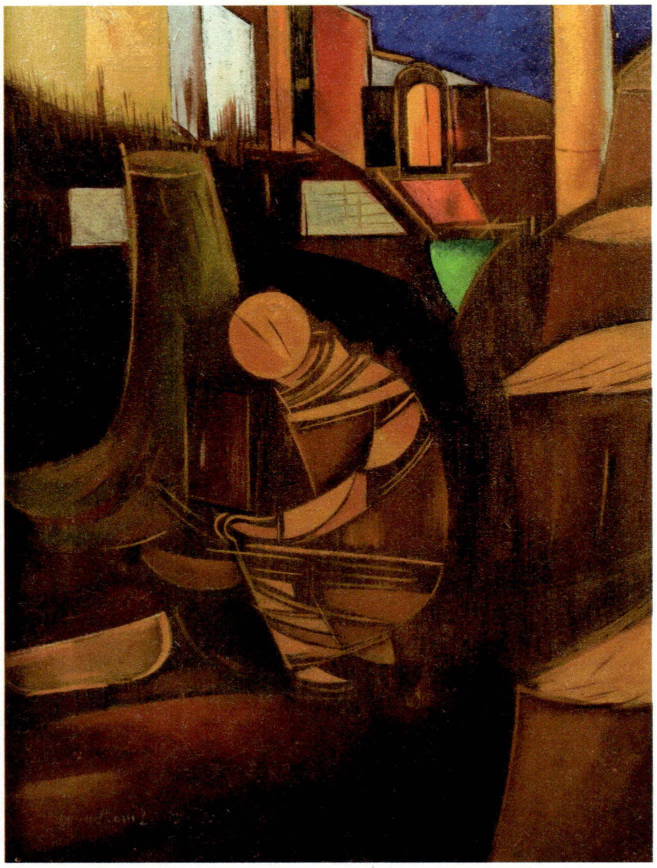

Abstract, 1932. Manor House Museum & Alfred East Art Gallery, Kettering

Lewis was an intellectual who was ill served by the uncertainties of his times, giving himself over to speculation on too many occasions in his works and often arriving at mistaken conclusions. In this desire to lead from the front – in the sense of the term "avant-garde" – Lewis located himself on the front line and was consequently hit by more than one bullet. He was rejected by publishing houses (including Chatto and Windus, who had previously published much of his work in an exceptionally fine manner), writers filed suits against him, literary circles closed their doors to him and Lewis, the "Enemy of the Stars," was shut out, exiled to another galaxy. This exile seems to have had no limits: England did not provide him with a living, the USA did not work out as he had hoped and finally, at the other end of the world, Lewis and his wife, Gladys Anne, were reduced to living in a series of rooms in different houses in Windsor (Canada) before ending up, victims of cold, poverty and oblivion, in an hotel room in Toronto. As if his life story required yet one more episode, the hotel burned down.[3]

As Paul Edwards has stated, it was not that Lewis's ideology shifted at the start of the 1930s; rather, it was history that changed.[4] Even before the years when his writings were definitively buried and forgotten, it is possible to appreciate Lewis's growing weariness with the apathy of English society, which he blamed for the lamentable state of its democracy. In the philosophical-literary treatise, *Time and Western Man* (1927) (B&M Cat. 12), he stated:

It is clear that we cannot go on for ever [*sic*] making revolutions which are returns merely to some former period of history [...] Victorian England had piled up a scientific materialism, a mercantile spirit and a nonconformist humbug of such dimensions, that it was a target no artist-attack could miss. [...] nothing new can be invented, it seemed to say, or, if invented, it could not be swallowed by the Publics degraded by the last phases of the democratic régime.[5]

Naomi Mitchison, 1930-33. City Art Centre: City of Edinburgh Museums and Galleries

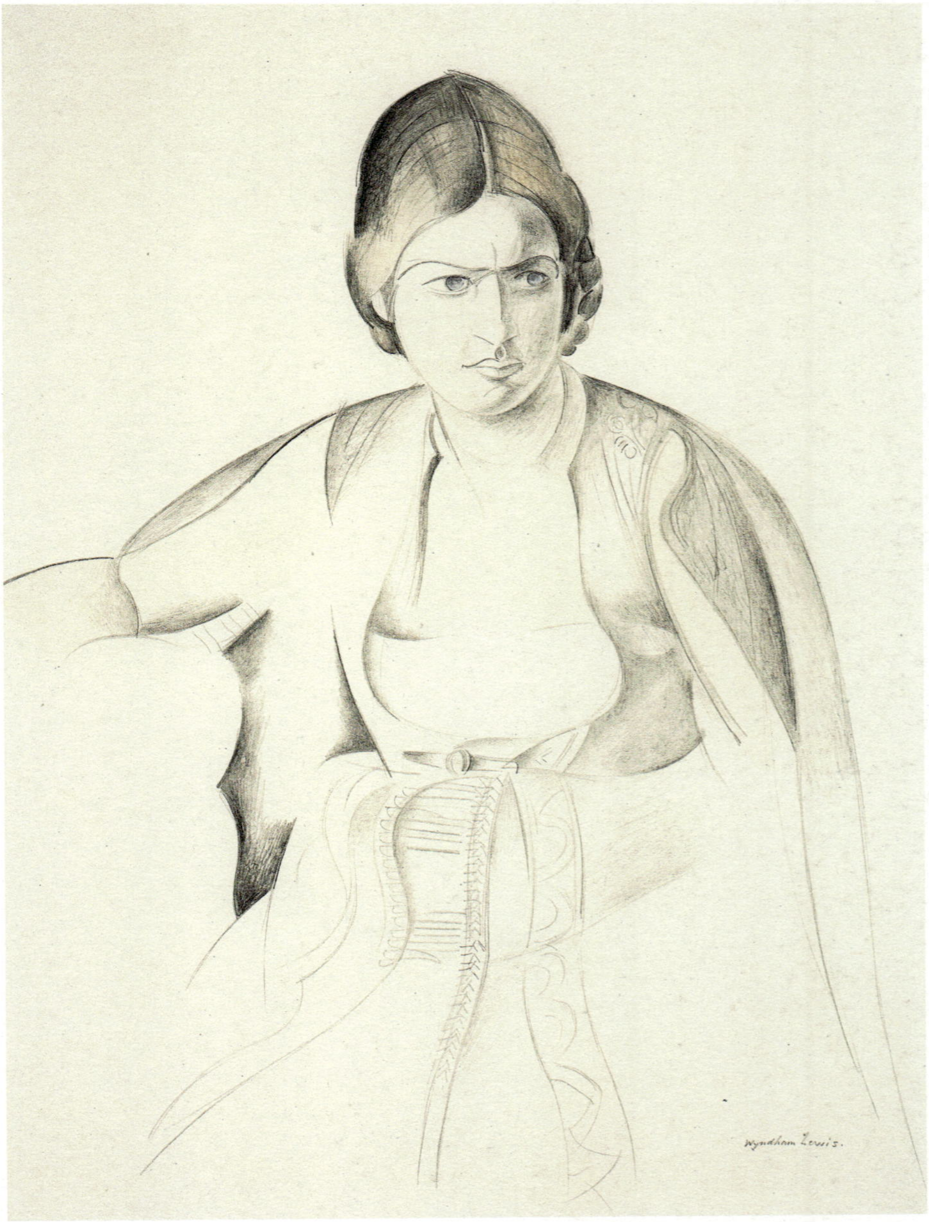

The Public – or less politely put, the insufferable and dangerous mob – was one of the targets against which Lewis inveighed with most ferocity. On numerous occasions he attacked this collective which was, paradoxically, the one that, without any academic or artistic education, without previous wisdom or experience, could determine the manner in which a country's culture was expressed, allowing itself to be swept along by a single voice. From a politically correct viewpoint, Lewis's disdain for the collective, characterless voice has been criticised as signifying a disdain for the normal citizen. This could not be further from the truth. Before José Ortega y Gasset's (1883–1955) celebrated *The Revolt of the Masses* (1929), Lewis criticised the mediocrity of all those who were guided by the opinion of others without questioning how this opinion affected them as individuals. He attacked popular critics and writers for their use of mechanisms that reduced the individual and converted him or her into a sort of animal that is fed pre-masticated food. Lewis thus started a debate that continues to be hotly contested today: that of high-brow and low-brow literature in relation to the reading public's book-buying habits.

Before getting bogged down in the *querelle* over whether the term "bestseller" necessarily implies low literary quality in quest of high financial remuneration, the English had already resolved this problem with the use of the colloquial term "potboiler."[6] Lewis, harassed by debts that he had run up during his European travels, wrote one between 1909 and 1910 entitled *Mrs Dukes' Million* (B&M Cat. 1). It enjoyed so little success that the original manuscript of this story about a rich woman who is the victim of fraud and an innovative company of actors whose street shows are Performance Art *avant la lettre* (Lewis at his finest), passed from one owner to another and eventually ended up in one of those charity shops in England where one occasionally finds a treasure for little or nothing. The manuscript – with corrections written by his devoted mother, Anne – is now in the archives of Cornell University along with numerous other items sold to that institution, which declined to employ Lewis when he was in need of a salary. It is an entertaining novel, with some marvellous touches of humour, and demonstrates how even custom-made books need correct marketing to reach the masses.

Some would say that Wyndham Lewis deserved what he got and that anyone who calls himself "The Enemy" cannot expect much charity in exchange. This is true, but why in the case of other writers and artists do we put their works before their more dubious deeds? Lewis has been called a misogynist when just a few of Pablo Picasso's (1881–1973) or Albert Einstein's (1879–1955) opinions would make any by Lewis pale in comparison. Furthermore, Lewis had two women in his Vorticist movement, Helen Saunders (1885–1963) and Jessica Dismorr (1885–1939), whom decades later he described as "very gifted women."[7] Lewis regularly praised the work of women such as Rebecca West (1892–1983), Nancy Cunard (1896–1965) and Naomi Mitchison (1897–1999) (the three figureheads of feminism and socialism), but he criticised Virginia Woolf (1882–1941), not for being a woman, but for being elitist and for favouring a type of sentimentality that, as a reader, I find twee and sanctimonious. It is thus not surprising that Woolf criticised West or was extremely displeased every time she was visited by Cunard, whose works were published by the Woolfs' own press, the Hogarth Press, on the insistence of Leonard Woolf (1880–1969). These women were too liberated for a middle-class woman with traditional values.

The real complications arrive when we get to Fascism. During a number of years – 1931, 1936 and 1937 – Lewis was categorically wrong, publishing treatises that have served to cancel out the other 30 or so works written during his prolific career as an author. Lewis was neither Martin Heidegger (1889–1976) nor Gottfried Benn (1886–1956) nor, obviously, Louis-Ferdinand Céline (1894–1961). He never joined a political party or attended as a militant any of the eccentric demonstrations held in England at that period. While it is true that his essays that dealt with politics are full of mistakes, they are in general the result of rashness rather than political conviction, particularly in his desire to avoid at all costs the spectre of war, a spectre he knew well and which he had condemned in a thousand different ways in his first autobiography, *Blasting and Bombardiering* (1937) (B&M Cat. 40). This dread becomes evident if we look at the extremist statements to be found in his books such as *Left Wings Over Europe: Or, How to Make a War about Nothing* (1936) (B&M Cat. 37) and *Count Your Dead: They are Alive!* (1937) (B&M Cat. 38) as well as the personal confessions found in his autobiography (1937).

Lewis's extreme individualism is synonymous with furious opinion rather than with any formal appeal to collectivity, which he hated; there is no evidence that he was member of any official political affiliation. What we must not lose sight of, and this is a most delicate matter that is ignored or neglected by some scholars, is the date on which Lewis published his works. *Hitler* (B&M Cat. 26), a collection of articles previously serialised in the magazine *Time and Tide* between January and February, was launched in March 1931, together with some new essays. Hitler had won 107 seats in the elections to the Reichstag in September 1930 and he did not come to power until 1933. The truth is that critics continue to judge Lewis's Fascism on his pre-war books, while in the year the Second World War began, he published his recantation, *The Hitler Cult* (1939) (B&M Cat. 44), in which he attacks Hitlerism for having brought war back to Europe. After all, Lewis's two main concerns were to avoid the slaughter that he had witnessed on the Western Front from 1916 to 1918, and to be able to live in a Europe that had a prosperous economy, was politically stable and culturally rich. It is obvious that Lewis – in common with the rest of Europe – could not have ever imagined the horrors that war against Hitler would bring.

The proof of just how difficult it is to state with conviction that Lewis was a Fascist is to be found in the numerous texts still being written on this subject. During the 10 years that I have devoted to reading over 40 works by Lewis, I have faced many obstacles when trying to obtain copies of some of them. I have pursued them in auctions, second-hand bookshops and English-speaking libraries where records indicate that they were last requested for loan in the 1970s. Dates are always

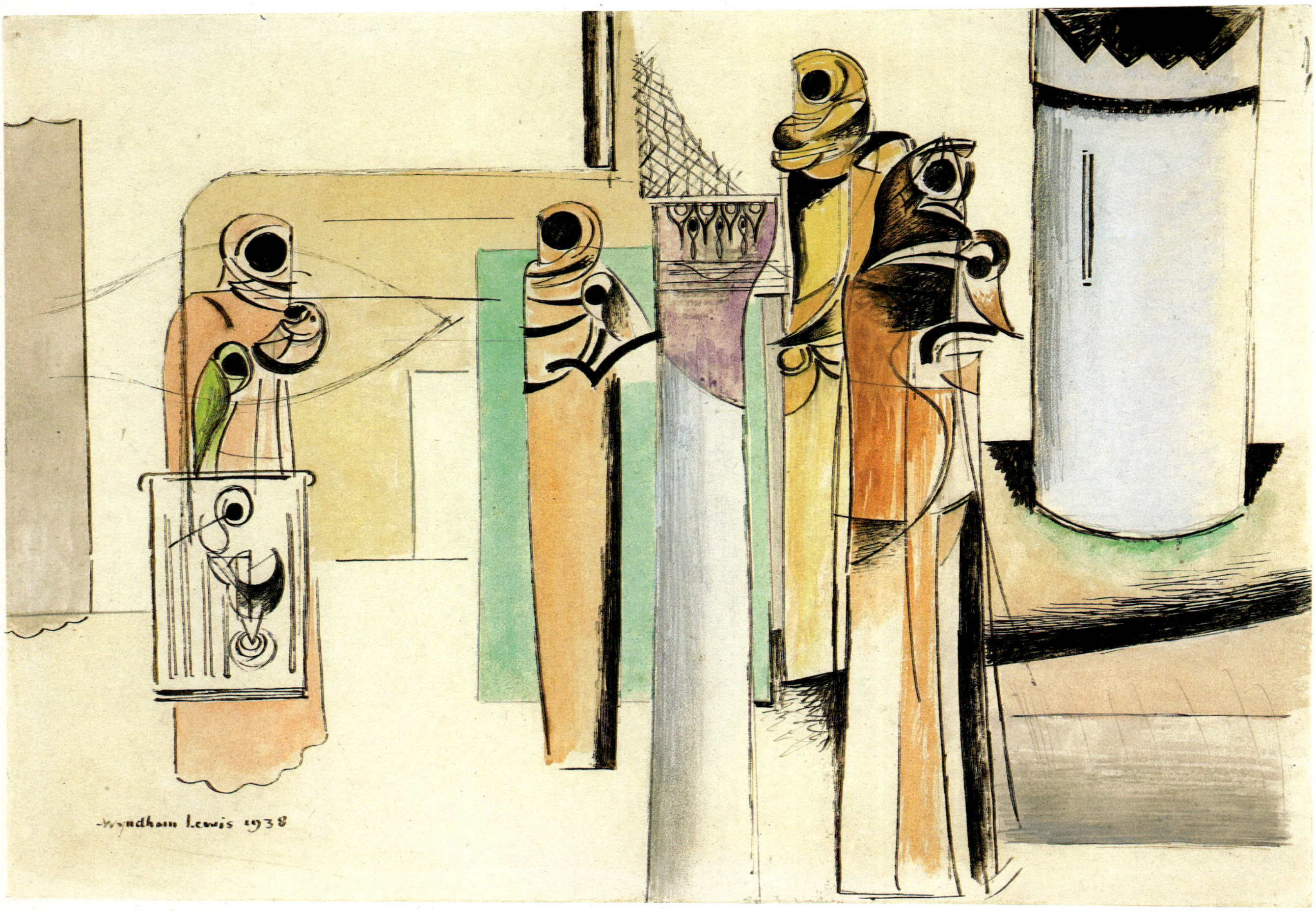

◀ *Meeting of Sheiks*, 1938. Wyndham Lewis Memorial Trust

▶ *Three Sisters*, 1927. Wyndham Lewis Memorial Trust. G. and V. Lane Collection

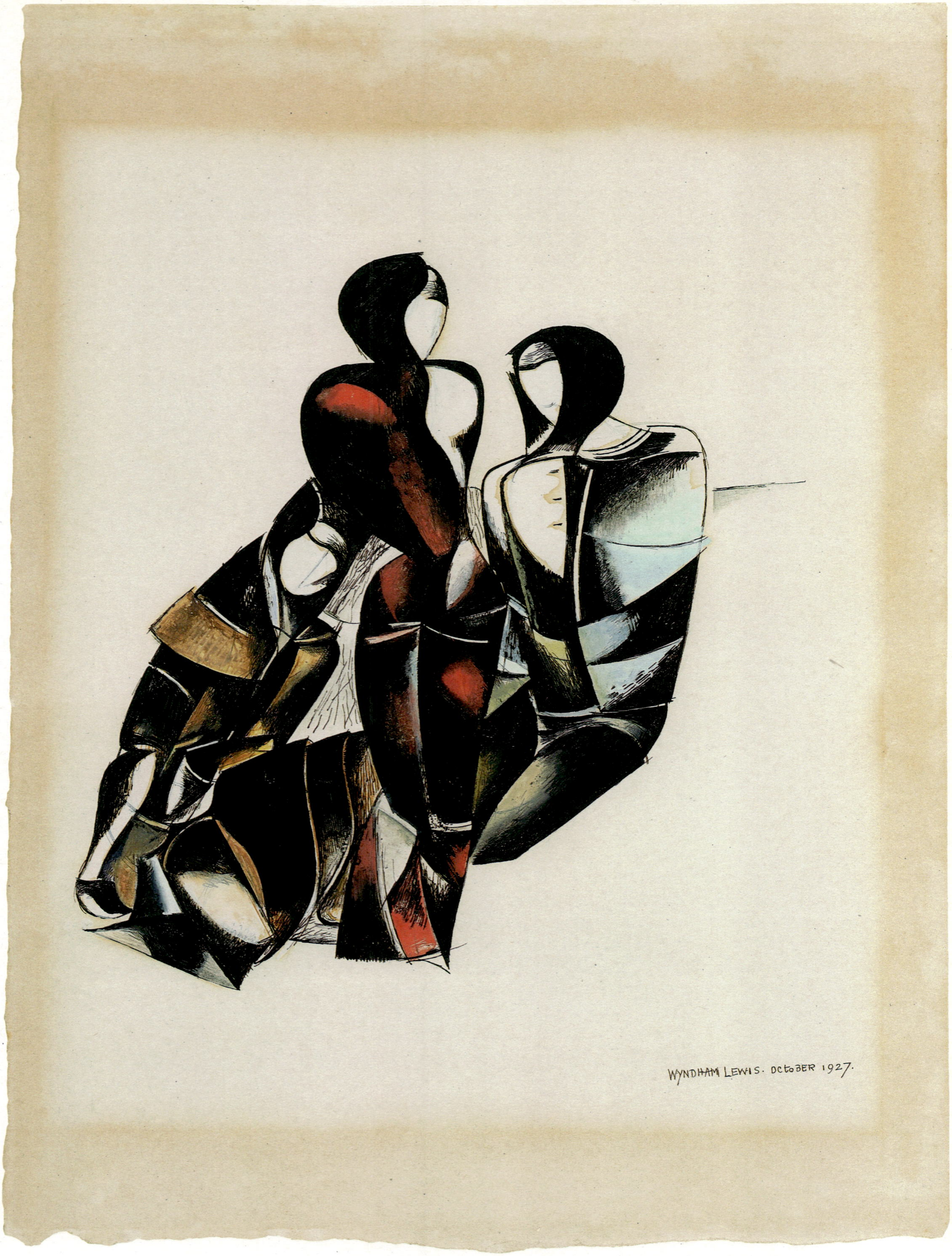
WYNDHAM LEWIS. October 1927.

give-aways and in the case of Lewis they are of crucial importance. Even Oxford emeritus professor, John Carey, has been mistaken with regard to the dates of two key works: *Time and Western Man* (1927, not 1928, which is the date of the New York edition) and *The Apes of God* (1930, not 1932, which is again the US edition) (B&M Cat. 21). This lack of scholarly rigour, possibly the result of wishing to write too much without having read sufficiently beforehand, is unpardonable in the context of Carey's accusation of racism to be found in his book.[8] When Carey objects to Lewis's ideas about black people as found in *Paleface: The Philosophy of the "Melting-Pot"* (1929) (B&M Cat. 20), he quotes passages from *The Apes of God*, Lewis's great satirical novel, as if they were part of the book that he is discussing in that paragraph; in fact, these last excerpts are acknowledged only in endnote 44.

Such instances are not as uncommon as might be thought. Some critics even allow themselves to feel an ironic sort of pity for those of us who actually read the complete works before discussing them, rather than taking quotations out of context or making use of a quotation that was originally ironic in tone without taking this into account. One such person is Professor Jessica Burstein who has said that being an expert on Wyndham Lewis "means constantly apologizing."[9] The particular case of the aversion felt towards Lewis is certainly an extremely strange one. All writers have their enemies. Furthermore, the great writers are pursued by scholars whose aim is to destroy their reputation for having overshadowed less highly esteemed authors (as in the case of Jorge Luis Borges (1899–1986) and his circle). Lewis, however, has not overshadowed anyone. Quite the opposite, in fact: he was overshadowed by declarations made by those who found him troubling – Woolf, F.R. Leavis (1895–1978), Ernest Hemingway (1899–1961) (who eventually helped him) – while during the second part of the twentieth century and into the twenty-first century a group of scholars and journalists has been determined to bury him once and for all.[10] Why is this the case?

The explanation is that Lewis continues to be a dangerous thinker, even in our own time. He said things that many would like to be able to say but which cannot be said out of political correctness, good manners or excessive prudishness. In addition, Lewis was able to formally retract his earlier beliefs, which does not suit those who use his declarations to make a big effect. A statement by Lewis generally tends to have its counter-statement. Anyone referring to what he said in *Hitler* (1931) should bear in mind that *The Hitler Cult* (1939) is a recantation, while *Rude Assignment: A Narrative of my Career Up-to-date* (1950) (B&M Cat. 50) is a reflection on both texts. Critics generally refer to Lewis's taste for Nietzsche's views but forget the crucial maxim, point 16 in one of his texts that comes closest to Nietzsche, the early "The Code of a Herdsman": "Contradict yourself. In order to live you must remain broken up."[11] This was probably the only piece of advice that Lewis adhered to for the rest of his life. Like the good Cartesian that he was, he divided body and soul, instinct and intellect, public and private life, to the desperation of those who have delved so deeply into the rumours surrounding his life. Why have some described him as disagreeable, coarse and unsociable, when those who knew him described him as being an excellent conversationalist, amusing and having excellent manners? "In order to live, you must remain broken up."

Perhaps the greatest dividing line in Lewis's life was a trench. It is easy to imagine what he saw in the years that he spent swallowed up by the First World War in France (we need only to read his chilling portraits of mud and death in *Blasting and Bombardiering*), and consequently appreciate that however much he armed himself with a breastplate of black humour the war left him incurably wounded in body (he was gassed) and mind, a recurring theme, either direct or indirect, in his fiction and essays. In fact, from the time of his return to England until the publication of *Hitler*, Lewis's work became a mammoth reflection on the human condition and existence, a body of work that he intended to entitle *The Man of the World*.[12] The result was to anticipate Jean-Paul Sartre (1905–80).

Art was also affected by this new world created by the Great War. In an article published in early 1919 and entitled "The Men who will Paint Hell: Modern War as a Theme for the Artist,"[13] Lewis pointed at this early date to the appearance of modern war in the world of art. Less than four months after the Armistice, he was already describing the "modern" nature of this war, and foreseeing the repercussions that it would have on the future of the art world and the horror that awaited the citizens of the twentieth century. On the publication of the second issue of Lewis's magazine *The Tyro* (B&M Cat. 9) in 1922, the painter Walter Sickert (1860–1942) lamented that an individual as influential as Lewis had not received the admiration he deserved:

If there were in this country an alert and active body of criticism, a magazine which succeeds in publishing, in one number, nine such items as 'Recent Painting in London,' 'The Essay on the Objective of Plastic Art in Our Time,' the 'Tyronic Dialogues X and F,' the story 'Bestre,' and five drawings by the same hand, would be gladly and generously hailed as an intellectual achievement not only astounding, but of first-rate importance.[14]

Sickert's words emphasise British critics' indifference to the "intellectual achievements" of an artist such as Lewis. The term "intellectual" has a particular connotation in this context, as it is important to remember that even at this early date the idea of belonging to a group of intellectuals was viewed negatively. Lewis made frequent use of a term of Russian origins, "intelligentsia," which had entered the English language in the early nineteenth century with equally negative connotations and which was used to differentiate and separate the lone intellectual from those who associated with the upper-class social circles so criticised by Lewis. While the members of these elite groups defended each other (each artistic group in London had seven or eight tame writers), the solitary thinker was exposed to the judgement of the publications controlled by these very groups. Lewis referred to

▶ *Rebecca West*, 1932. National Portrait Gallery, London (Cat. 139)

▶▶ *Study for Portrait of T.S. Eliot*, 1938. Private collection (Cat. 146)

▼ *Potfolio Fifteen Drawings: Ezra Pound, 1919.* Tate, London

▼▼ *James Joyce*, 1921. Collection National Gallery of Ireland, Dublin

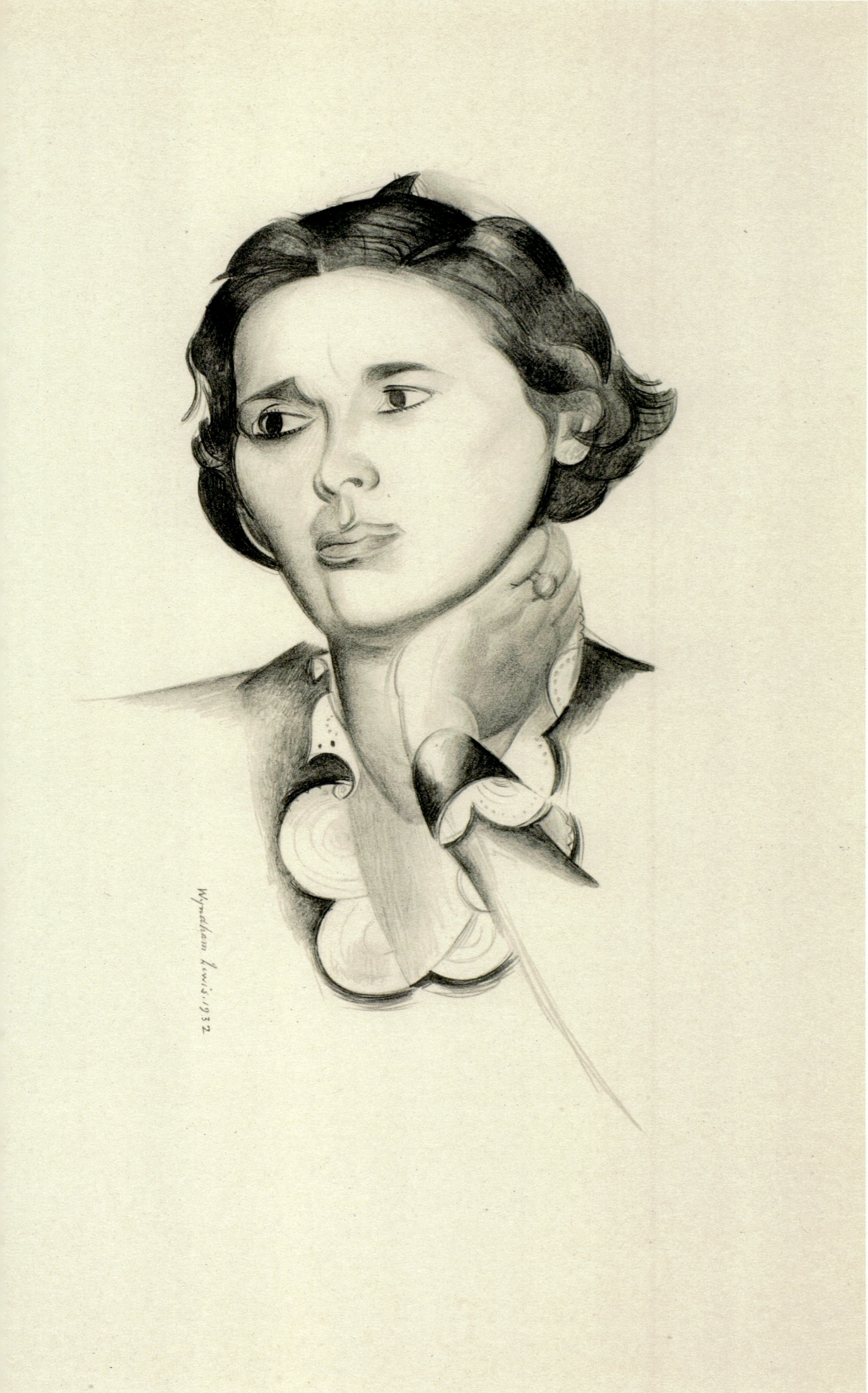
Wyndham Lewis 1932

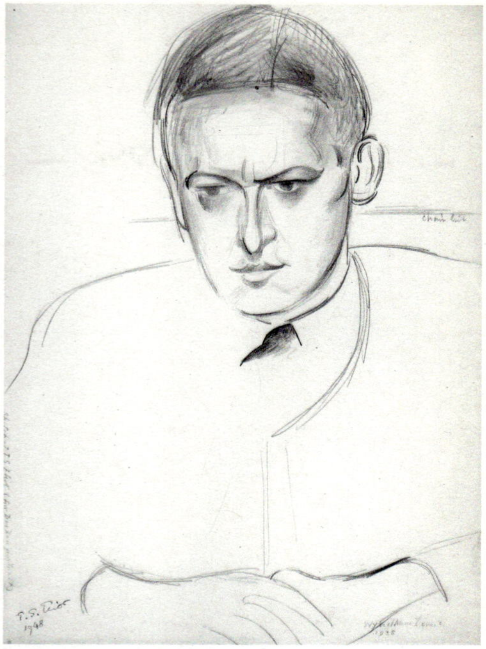

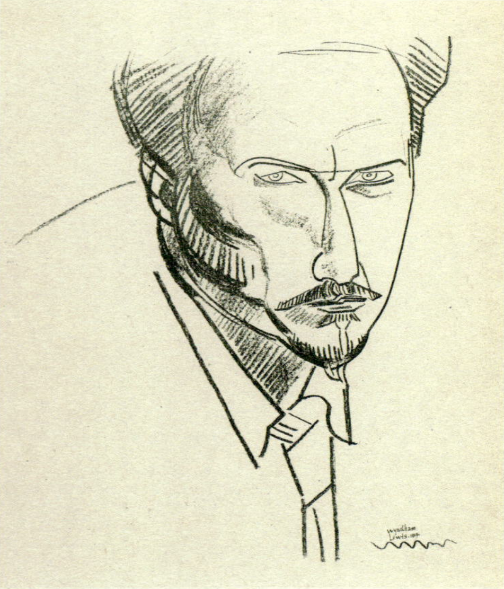

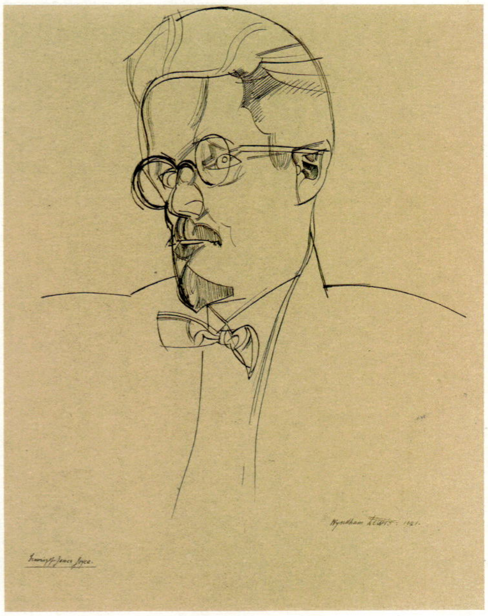
Wyndham Lewis 1921.

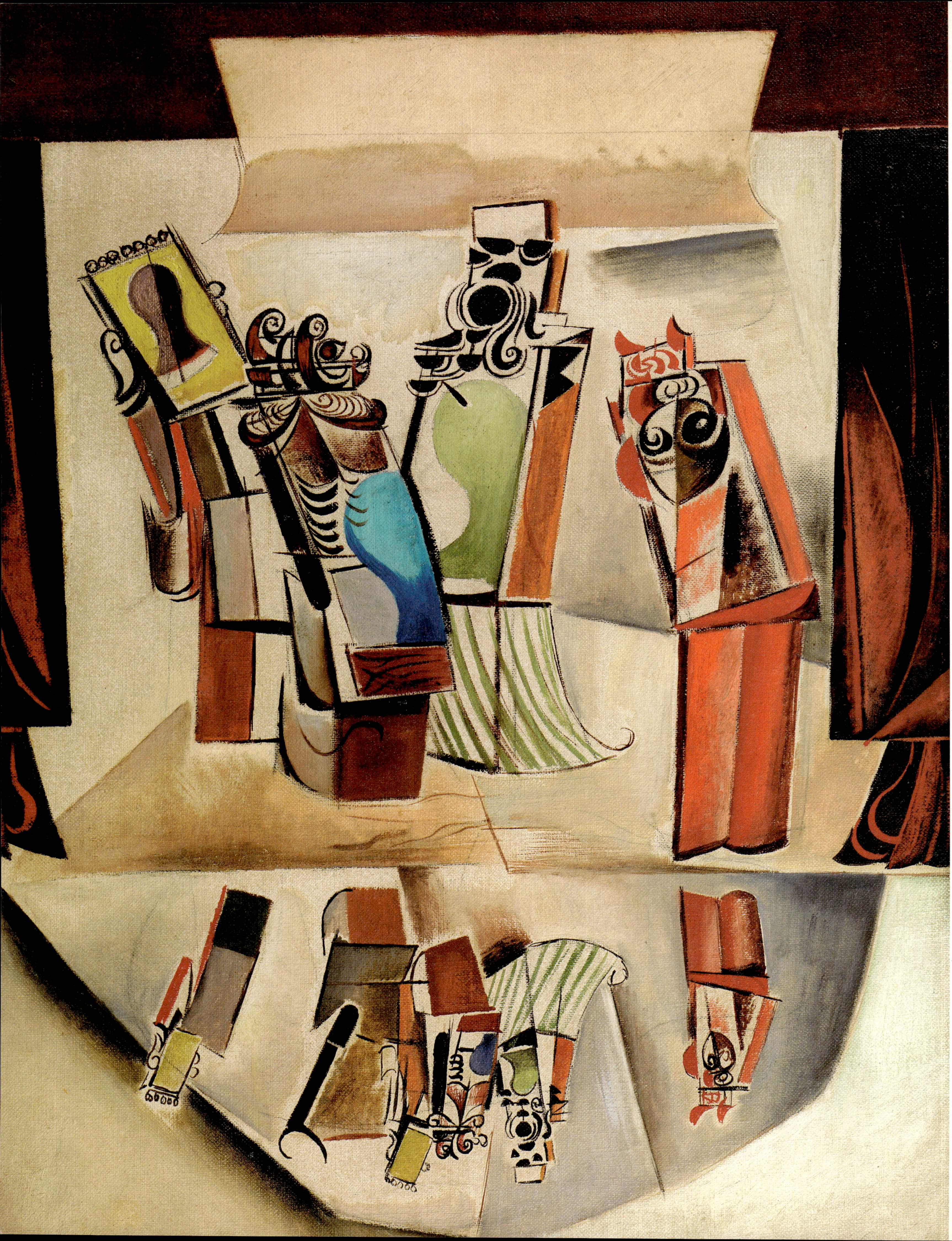

Players upon a Stage, 1936-37. Wyndham Lewis Memorial Trust, London

this in 1914 in the first issue of *Blast* (B&M Cat. 2) when he compared the situation in England with that of France ("You can't be too intelligent here!") ("It is the only place in Europe where that is the case.").[15]

The fact of belonging to a "class" of intellectuals whom Lewis himself called "The men of 1914" (Ezra Pound (1885–1972), T.S. Eliot (1888–1965), James Joyce (1882–1941), and Lewis himself) brought him more problems than advantages. While it is true that in the first decades of the century these figures mutually supported each other, the passing of the years and Pound's tragic destiny resulted in a barrier that particularly affected Lewis, given that the shadow of Fascism became more evident when linked with the name of Pound. Not by chance was the first section of Lewis's second autobiography, *Rude Assignment* (1950) entitled "Three Fatalities." Among these three misfortunes, the first was his facet as an intellectual (while the other two, not surprisingly, were satire and politics). While Eliot and Joyce were active members of intellectual circles, Lewis's social rejection by a society in which he moved but which he had criticised provided the substance for one of his finest novels, *The Apes of God* (1930). This lengthy, biting satire on highbrows, middlebrows and lowbrows that revealed the importance of class sentiment within English society fulfilled almost all the author's expectations (Lewis had dreamed of writing a sort of *Ulysses* in his own style), but it also made people aware of the impact that these "portraits" could have. Two years later, Alec Waugh (1898–1981), author of *The Loom of Youth*, brought Lewis to the High Court of Justice (King's Bench Division, August 1932) on alleged libellous charges of homosexuality in *The Doom of Youth*. In the making since 1926, Lewis was unable to find a publisher for his project, which he eventually published himself under his own imprint of the Arthur Press.

In 2001, John Richardson focused on this famous satire when analysing Lewis's position in relation to English society:

> **Feelings of social inferiority have generated some of the finest works of fiction produced in England (and not just those by Evelyn Waugh), but illusions of social superiority also on occasions condemn the work of a writer to those unreachable top shelves of the library where total neglect lies in wait.**[16]

These class issues are also evident in "The Highbrow, and the two Publics," chapter 2 in Lewis's second autobiog-

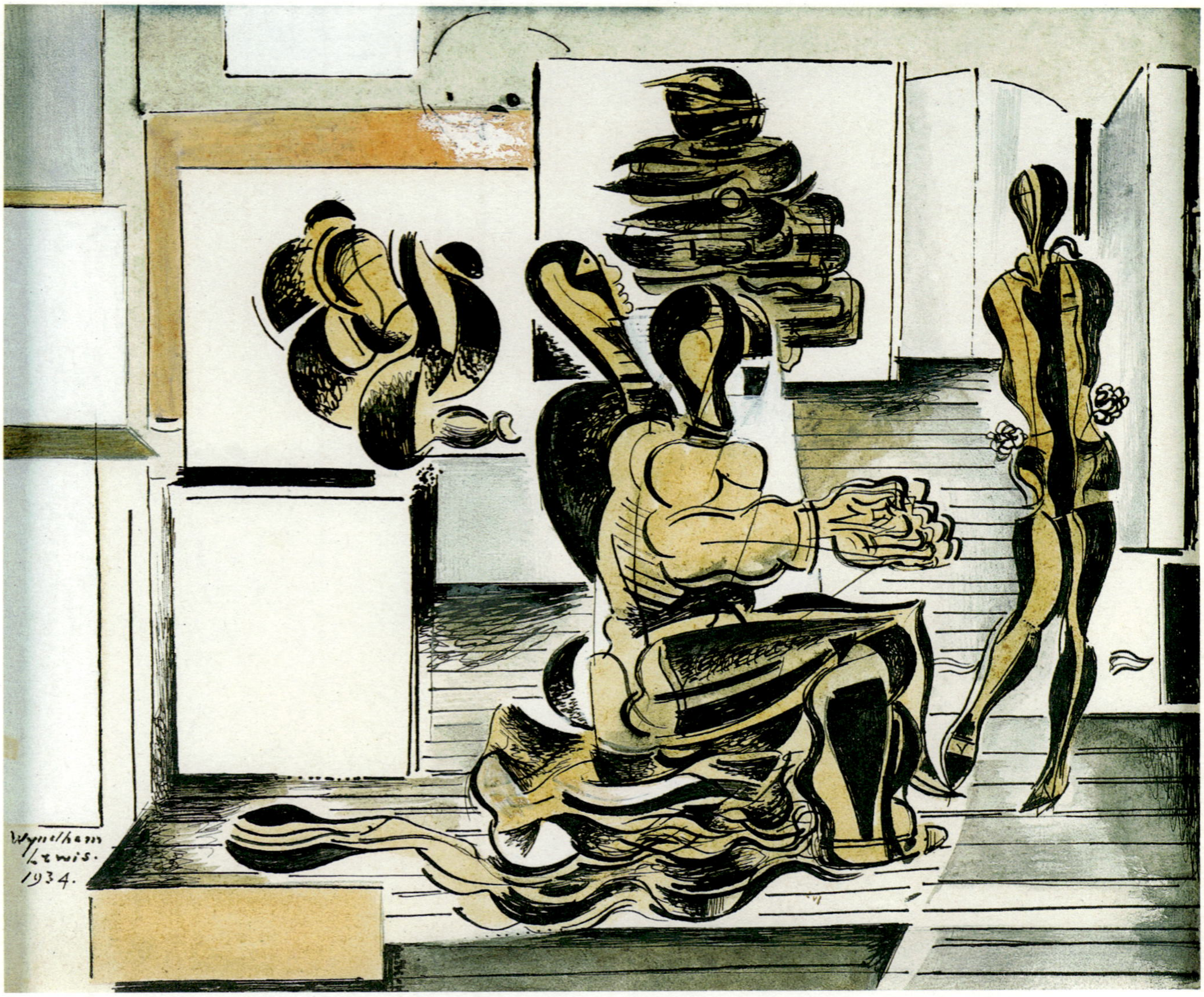

Composition (Figures in an Interior), 1934. Pallant House Gallery, Chichester

raphy, *Rude Assignment*. Interestingly, the colloquial terms "highbrow," "lowbrow," and "middlebrow" originated in the USA and in the case of "highbrow" did not appear in England until 1908.[17] They were rapidly accepted but were phrases created by and for the more elevated social classes and were not used by the rest of the population. The idea of the two Publics thus excludes the working class. As Lewis noted critically: "This classification does not extend beyond the bourgeoisie. The working class of course do not count. The typical 'lowbrow' would not like to think he shared his brow with *them*. They might, if it came to the point, be described as the 'no-brows'."[18] Lewis's opinions are frequently revealing given his position as an intellectual on the margins and as an individual who did not share the bourgeois origins of those around him, but who nonetheless moved among these groups, was acquainted with them and criticised them from his vantage point.

The importance of Lewis as an intellectual should not be measured by the number of criticisms that he has received in studies on Fascism, feminism and the war, but from the wealth of references to the contribution made by his work that are to be found in the writings of other prestigious authors. From Marshall McLuhan (1911–80) to Martin Amis (b. 1949), Lewis has left very few indifferent and all have been able to salvage some original aspect of his work to add to their own. In 1981, during the annual lecture on human values held at Oxford University, Saul Bellow (1915–2005) observed that if there was one figure who could explain the situation of American cities from a modern and accurate perspective, it was Wyndham Lewis.[19] Bellow, himself a Nobel prizewinner, quoted a lengthy passage from *America and Cosmic Man* (1948) (B&M Cat. 48), a book that he considered "invaluable."

Lewis was unrivalled in his ability to foresee trends and concepts. However, he had the defect of impatience. Were it not for the rapidity of his mind and the slowness of his prose, the ideas that remained only sketched out and which others subsequently developed would have raised him to the level of a visionary. A consideration of the problems arising from the clash between science and the arts, for which C.P. Snow (1905–80) earned so much prestige in the 1950s, is already to be found in *Blast*, presented in a totally positive manner: "Engineer or artist might conceivably become transposable terms, or one, at least, imply the other."[20] This is a statement that clearly brings to mind Walter Benjamin's (1892–1940) figure of the aesthetic engineer in *One-Way Street* (1928), an idea that Benjamin fully developed in *The Arcades Project*. In *The Caliph's Design* (1919) (B&M Cat. 7), Lewis had again examined this idea. In the "Parable of the Caliph's Design" and in other essays in that volume, he considered the idea that the artist's and architect's creativity should be placed at the service of the engineer, who is by nature scientific, and vice versa. He saw this as the only solution for remedying the disasters of a society in which two worlds (science and art) had been separated when in fact they should be working closely together.

At heart, and beneath his tireless energy, Lewis was profoundly pessimistic regarding the twentieth century's destiny; a destiny that he know he would see nothing of, since, like Ortega y Gasset, he considered that he was simply a member of the present, part of "a Future that has not materialised."[21] Nonetheless, this did not prevent him from discerning the horizon and seeing that the young Francis Bacon (1909–92) was a great talent in the making,[22] or that the media were the key to a not so distant globalisation:

> **An even more powerful agency of intellectual confusion, however, than the antinomies of the social scene outlined above, can be shown to exist. I refer to the more comprehensive revolution brought about by those great twentieth-century techniques, of flying, radio, cinematography, rotary photogravure, and so forth, unifying the nations in spite of themselves.**[23]

Despite all of this and despite having anticipated Benjamin, Sartre and McLuhan in numerous ways, we may still read opinions as categorical as those of John Carey, who continues to declare that Lewis was a man of "relatively few" ideas.[24] Furthermore, we have not even looked at other aspects of his activities as a journalist, poet, playwright and philosopher, the last of which is particularly interesting. In his work *Time and Western Man* (1927), Lewis chose to adopt a more restrained and reflective approach when criticising the three great cults of the modern age: the cult of youth (and the "Peter Pan syndrome"),[25] the cult of intuition and sentimentality, and the cult of time per se. Space does not permit a discussion of these ideas but they once again reveal the intellectual richness of a natural, bold and incisive observer. The fact that his style and many of his ideas remain relevant today is ample proof of this.

NOTES

1. John Carey, *The Intellectuals and the Masses. Pride and Prejudice among the Literary Intelligentsia, 1880–1939* (London: Faber and Faber, 1992).
2. As Alan Munton stated, Fredric Jameson in *Fables of Aggression: Wyndham Lewis, the Modernist as Fascist* (Berkeley: University of California Press, 1979, p.27) was "unable to define Lewis as a fascist, and was forced to invent the elusive but nevertheless damaging term 'proto-fascist'(p. 15) in order to ensure Lewis's political exclusion as a modernist of the right," in "Wyndham Lewis: from Proudhon to Hitler (and back): the Strange Political Journey of Wyndham Lewis," *EREA* 4.2 [online journal] (autumn 2006), pp. 28–33. www.e-rea.org [last accessed 27 October 2009].
3. Paul O'Keeffe states that the fire did not reach the Lewises' room and that he exaggerated their losses. *Some Sort of Genius. A Life of Wyndham Lewis* (London: Jonathan Cape, 2000), pp. 460–61.
4. Paul Edwards, "'It's time for another war': The Historical Unconscious and the Failure of Modernism," in *Wyndham Lewis and the Art of Modern War*. Ed. David Peters Corbett (Cambridge: Cambridge University Press, 1998), pp. 124–53.
5. Wyndham Lewis, *Time and Western Man* (London: Chatto and Windus, 1927), p. 51.
6. From the English expression "boiling the pot," meaning to make a living. The *Oxford English Dictionary* dates the first appearance of the term to 1783 and in its second usage defines a "potboiler" as "a book, film, etc. produced purely to make the writer or artist a living by catering to popular taste." *OED*, www.oed.com [last revision of the term 2007, last consultation 6 September 2009]. Works of this type are similar to modern bestsellers with thriller-type plots that

involve issues of interest to contemporary society. Fashionable from Romanticism onwards, these themes still include medieval subjects, codes, secret buildings and ruins. In recent years, we have also witnessed the revival of another nineteenth-century phenomenon, that of Gothic literature with castles, vampires and underworlds.

7. "The Vorticists," *Vogue* (London, September 1956). Rprt. *Wyndham Lewis on Art: Collected Writings 1913–1956.* Eds. Walter Michel and C.J. Fox (New York: Funk & Wagnalls, 1969), p. 457.
8. Carey 1992, p. 232.
9. Jessica Burstein, "Being Wyndham Lewis means never having to say you're sorry. Being a Lewis critic, on the other hand, means constantly apologizing" (p.172), in the "Review of Vincent B. Sherry, *Ezra Pound, Wyndham Lewis, and Radical Modernism*," *Modernism/Modernity* 1, no. 2 (1994), pp. 172–74.
10. Iain Sinclair (*Guardian* Review, 12 July 2008) gave an account of the current critical situation: "The English art-noticing classes, a voluble minority, have never had much time for Percy Wyndham Lewis. But they do know one thing, they prefer to dislike him as a writer (racist, misogynist, premature Hitler enthusiast) than as a painter. [...] The literary works are anathematised, allowed to drift, harmlessly, out of print. The paintings, for the most part, are confined to provincial museums, private collections, Texas depositories." http://www.guardian.co.uk/books/2008/jul/12/art [last accessed 10 November 2009].
11. Wyndham Lewis, "The Code of a Herdsman," *The Little Review* 4, no. 3, (July 1917), p. 7.
12. Paul Edwards devotes a splendid chapter entitled "'The Enemy' versus 'The Man of the World'. Defending a Future that has not materialised, 1924–1937" to the birth, growth and break-up into shorter essays (of around 300–400 pages each) of this monumental project. In *Wyndham Lewis. Painter and Writer* (London/New Haven: Yale University Press, 2000), pp. 285–316.
13. Article published on 10 February 1919 in the *Daily Express*, included in *Wyndham Lewis on Art*, p. 107.
14. Walter Sickert, "*The Tyro* (review) (The Egoist Press, 2 Robert St, Adelphi)," *The Burlington Magazine for Connoisseurs* 41, no. 232–37 (July–December 1922), p. 200. Sickert's review ends with a piece of advice: "Qua painter, he should follow the rule of the wise old lady who said, 'Never explain, never apologise'." Perhaps all the explanations that Lewis offered over the course of his life encouraged him to entitle one of his autobiographical novels *Self Condemned* (1954).
15. Wyndham Lewis, "Policeman and the Artist," *Blast*, No. 1 (June 1914), p. 137.
16. John Richardson, *Sacred Monsters, Sacred Masters* (2001). Spanish edition, *Maestros sagrados, sagrados monstruos.* Trans. Miguel Martinez-Lage (Madrid: Alianza editorial, 2003), p. 145.
17. In the *Saturday Evening Post* of 29 August 1908. See "highbrow." *OED*, www.oed.com [last revision of the term 1989, last consultation 6 September 2009].
18. Wyndham Lewis, "The Highbrow, and the Two Publics," *Rude Assignment: A Narrative of my Career Up-to-date* (London: Hutchinson, 1950), p. 13.
19. "A Writer from Chicago," lecture by Saul Bellow for The Tanner Lectures on Human Values, Brasenose College, Oxford University (18 and 25 May 1981). Although in Bellow's opinion the USA no longer has industrial cities that lack space for creative life (one of the ideas championed by Lewis following his unproductive time there in the late 1930s), his talk referred on various occasions to ideas proposed by Lewis during the second quarter of the century.
20. *Blast*, No. 1 (June 1914), p. 135.
21. Wyndham Lewis, *Blasting and Bombardiering: Autobiography (1914–1926)* (London: Eyre & Spottiswoode, 1937), p. 258.
22. Wyndham Lewis, "Explanatory Note on the Plates," in *The Demon of Progress in the Arts* (London: Methuen, 1954), n.p. (between p. 51 and p. 52)..
23. Wyndham Lewis, "Towards an Earth Culture. The Eclectic Culture of the Transition" (1946). Rprt. *Wyndham Lewis on Art*. Eds. Walter Michel and C.J. Fox 1969, p. 381.
24. Carey 1992, p. 219.
25. This still notably relevant issue interested Lewis from an early date. Two good starting points are "A brief explanation of the cult of the child" (Book 1, chapter 11 of *Time and Western Man*, 1927), and *The Doom of Youth* (1932).

ANTWERP

BY FORD MADOX HUEFFER

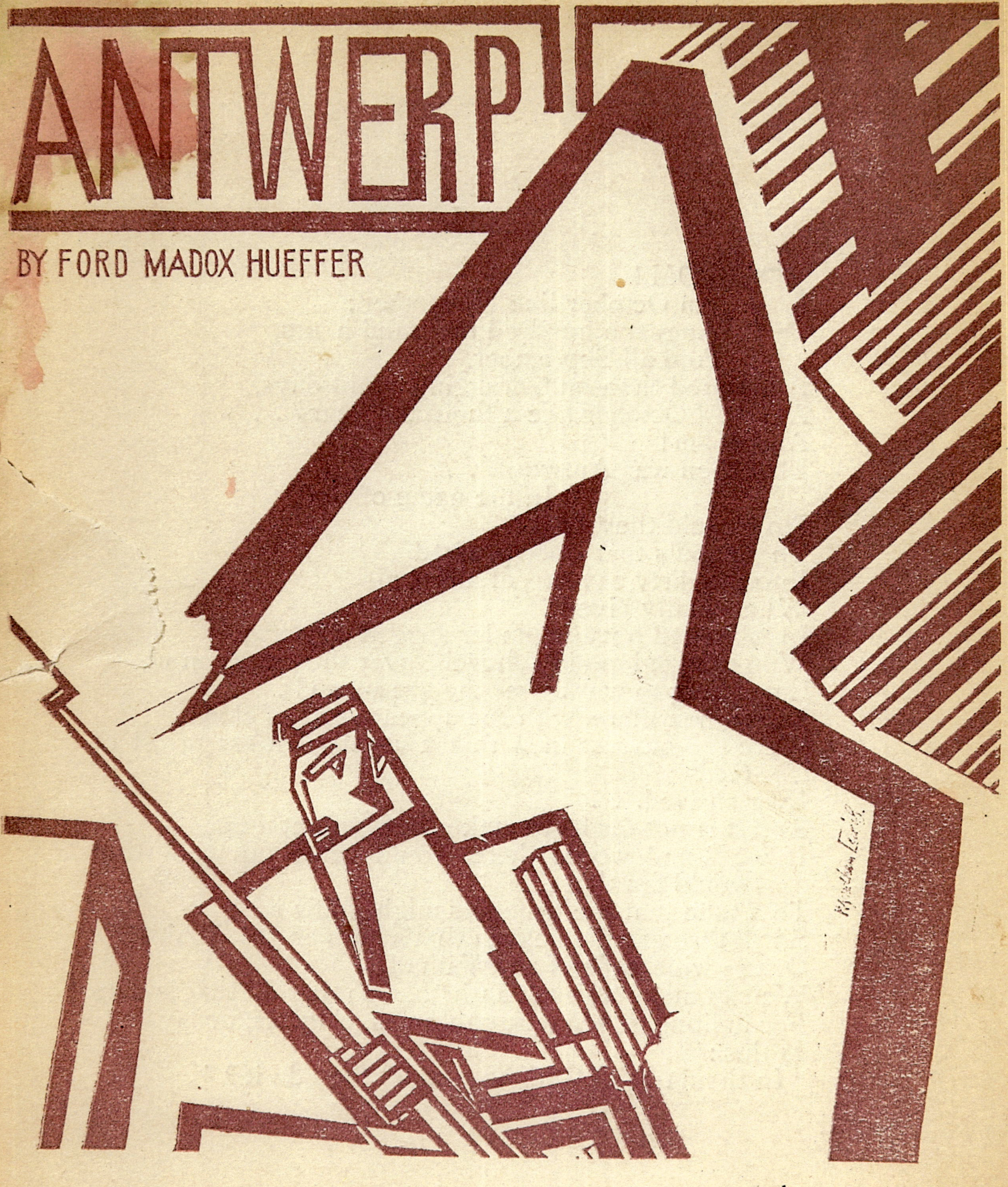

THE POETRY BOOKSHOP

3D. net

WYNDHAM LEWIS AND MODERN WAR

Juan Bonilla

Cover designed by Wyndham Lewis for *Antwerp* by Ford Madox Hueffer. Private collection YMJB (B&M Cat. 69)

WHAT FOLLOWS IS A DECIDEDLY EMPHATIC PARAGRAPH

from *Blasting and Bombardiering* (1937) (B&M Cat. 40), a book filled with decidedly emphatic paragraphs:

> **My attitude to War is complex. Per se, I neither hate it nor love it. War I only came to know gradually, it is true. War takes some getting to know. I know it intimately. And what's more, I know all about war's gestation and antecedents, and I have savoured its aftermaths. What I don't know about War is not worth knowing.**
>
> **When first I met War face to face I brought no moral judgements with me at all. I have never been able to regard war – modern war – as good or bad. Only supremely stupid.[1]**

Prior to this paragraph, at the start of his autobiography where he explains to the reader why he wrote it, Lewis confessed: "I wish I could get away from war. This book is perhaps an attempt to do so. Writing about war may be the best way to shake the accursed thing off, by putting it in its place, as an unseemly joke."[2]

Naturally, he did not succeed. War runs through Wyndham Lewis's *oeuvre* from start to finish and was a subject from which he could not distance himself, nor did he know how or wish to. This is simply because it functioned as the perfect mirror of the time in which he happened to live; a war that, just like modern war itself, was simply and fundamentally stupid. It could be said that not being able to distance himself entirely from the shadow of war suited him, as there was nothing better than an enemy of such splendid proportions for a writer endowed with Lewis's excellent satirical gifts. There, where we least expect war, it appears with its sinister smile and its bold-faced ability to make the Mass a creature so hysterical and impassioned, so fond of its screaming headlines on the front pages of newspapers, and so forgetful of its tragedies.

A character gets out of a taxi on a New York street in Lewis's novel *Snooty Baronet* (1932) (B&M Cat. 33).[3] The author describes his face in minute detail. And suddenly, the narrator is obliged to make a confession to his readers: the face is mine, he says, and he asks forgiveness, acknowledging that he is a writer and thus could not have started off by saying: "The taxi stopped, I crawled out. I have a wooden leg," as this would have had the immediate effect of putting off readers, who on reading the scene and coming across a character with a wooden leg, would have said: "Is the War not over yet?" before rushing off to find a different book. Just a few short years ago, such readers would have only opened books about the war, not read them. Lewis knew that his readers were tired of the war and would rather forget that there had been one (despite having most enthusiastically and emotionally supported it). They preferred not to think about the fact that the world was being rushed along on a toboggan of threats and idiocies towards another still more technological and bloody one. Despite all this, however, Lewis could not put the war completely to one side. It obliged him to act; it made him, in his own words, into a political animal, and it constantly lay in wait for him. It was not by chance that during the First World War, and in other later conflicts (the Spanish Civil War and the Second World War), he was "the anti-war war artist" in art historian Tom Normand's memorable phrase.[4]

The Futurists had glorified war, which was the only way of cleaning up the planet, according to the famous and sinister slogan that is point 9 in the first *Futurist Manifesto* published by Filippo Tommaso Marinetti (1876–1944) in 1909. They understood it as a great spectacle that provided the world with the emotion, visual impact and intensity with which to crush bourgeois routine (and we might consider the last link in the chain of this macabre celebration of war as spectacle to be the musician Karlheinz Stockhausen's (1928–2007) declaration at the sight of planes smashing into the Twin Towers of the World Trade Center, New York City on 11 September 2001 that the attack was "the greatest work of art imaginable for the whole cosmos"[5]). Lewis, however, from an early date and before he had any first-hand experience of it, considered war to be the most telltale expression of the human desire to make stupidity its most highly-prized characteristic. There are many reasons for exculpating the Vorticists and their leader Lewis from the accusation of being merely the Futurist branch in Great Britain and Lewis's radical opposition to the celebration of war as a great, photogenic spectacle is by no means the least important of them. Lewis was, in fact, very far from the Futurists' enthusiastic clamouring for war. He was also far from considering war, as Guillaume Apollinaire (1880–1918) did in his famous letter to Ardengo Soffici (1879–1964), as "the grandiose and marvellous spectacle, night and day, the terrible incessant din, the deep-set plain that every now and then is sown with the metal of death from which new life will have to spring."[6]

The first group of texts that we should consider in order to assess Lewis's relationship with war is undoubtedly "War Notes." It comprises five verbal broadsides ("The God of Sport and Blood," "Constantinople our Star," "Mr Shaw's effect on my Friend," "A Super-Krupp or War's End" and "The European War and Great Communities") and was published in the second issue of the journal *Blast* (B&M Cat. 3),[7] whose legendary first issue (B&M Cat. 2)[8] had brought Lewis an

Portfolio *Fifteen Drawings: Drawing for Timon of Athens* I, 1919. Tate, London

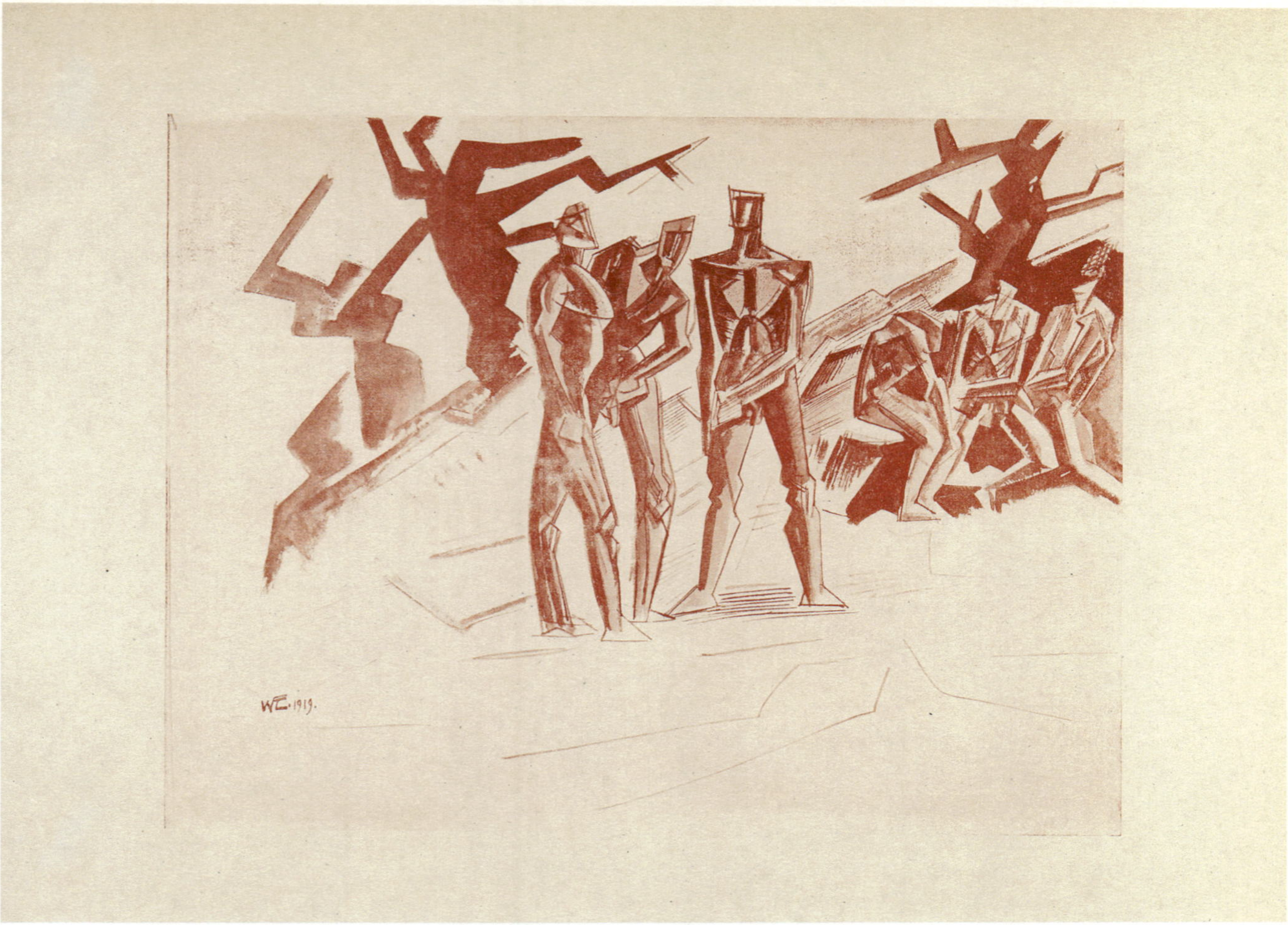

Portfolio *Fifteen Drawings: Drawing for Timon of Athens* II, 1919. Tate, London

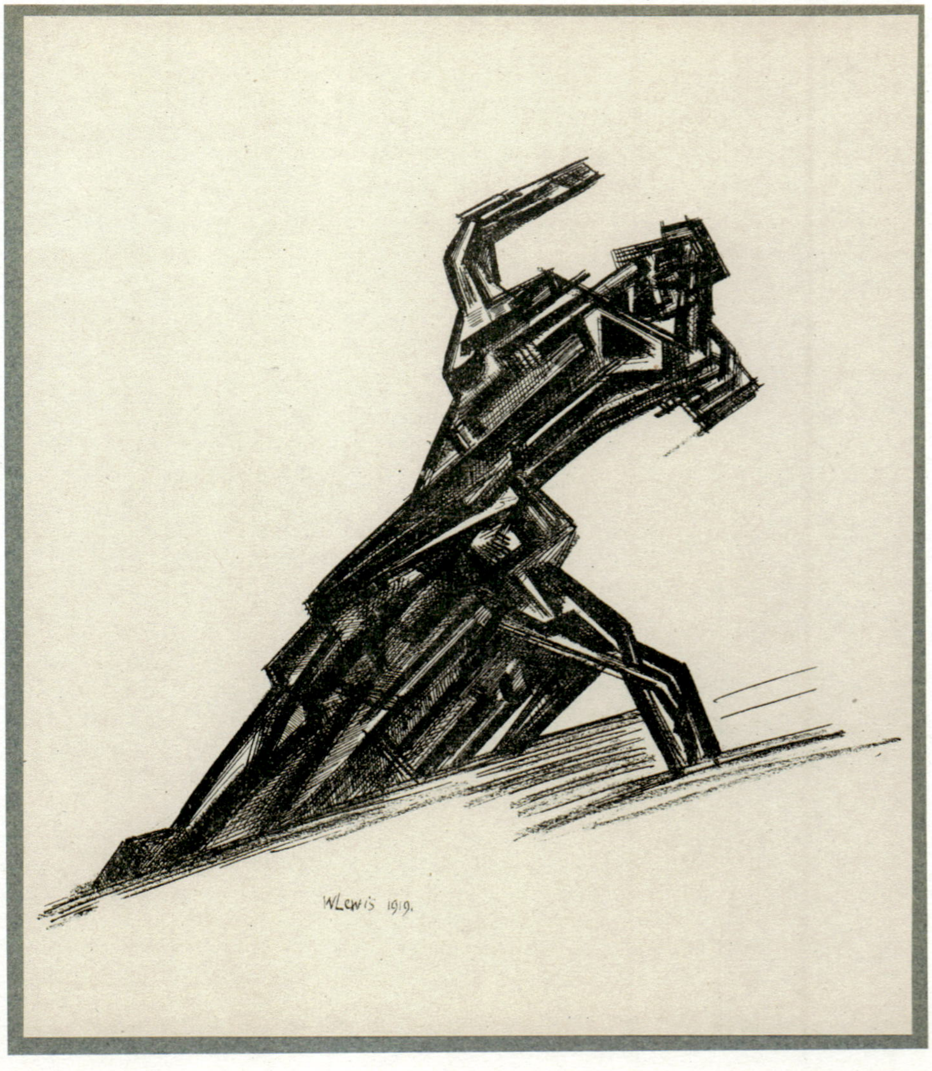

instant celebrity that involved a combination of caustically insulting opinions (the *Morning Post* wrote: "The first futurist quarterly is a vast folio in pink paper covers, full of irrepressible imbecility which is not easily distinguished from the words and works of Marinetti's disciple"[9]) accompanied by other enthusiastic plaudits (the *Sunday Times* ventured to write: "What the yellow book did for the artistic movement of its decade BLAST aims at doing for the arts and literature of today"[10]). The fame achieved by *Blast* was certainly well merited if we bear in mind that it included the publications of authors of the stature of T.S. Eliot (1888–1965), Rebecca West (1892–1983) and Ford Madox Ford (1873–1939), and there is no denying Lewis's talent for recruiting writers from among the troop of unknown names who milled about London at that period. A striking note in the editorial of the second issue of July 1915 is his statement that "we will continue to talk about Culture when the War ends."[11]

Even more surprising is the question, written in capital letters, to be found in one of the "War Notes" that runs: "IS THIS THE WAR THAT WILL END WAR?."[12] It is an important question as, thanks to it, Lewis provides a reply that is utterly prophetic: "Perpetual War may well be our next civilisation."[13] The idea that what was starting with the First World War (this technological war that could be considered the first modern war) was a state of permanent war – and thus it was not that "this war" was going to end wars but that "war" was going to impose itself as a natural, everyday state – would soon

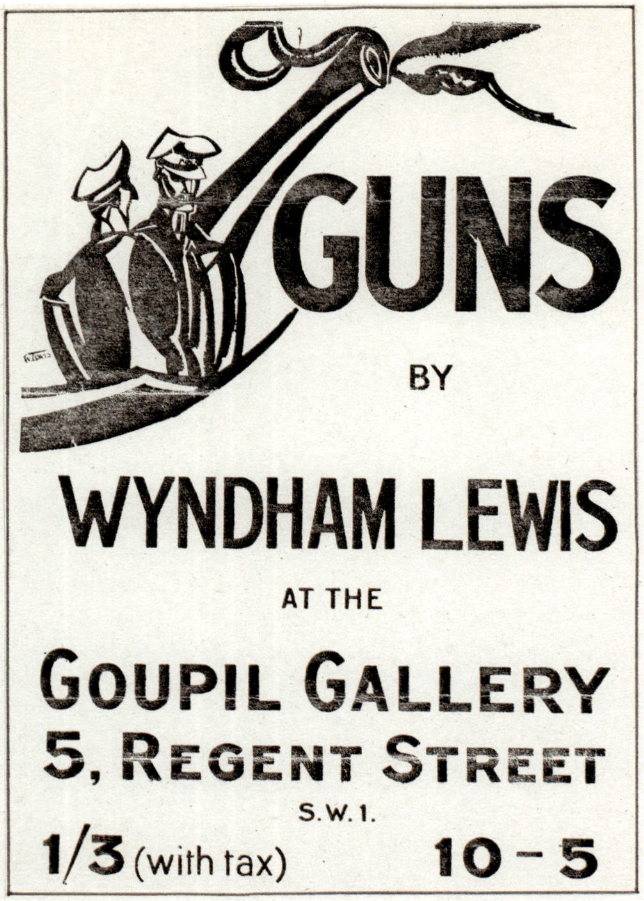

Guns by Wyndham Lewis
Exhibition Poster, 1919.
Wyndham Lewis Memorial Trust, London (Cat. 62)

be the matter of investigation by various authors who are crucial for a knowledge of "totalitarian thought." By these I refer, of course, to Ernst Jünger (1895–1998) in *Storm of Steel*[14] but above all to Carl Schmitt (1888–1985), the Nazi jurist, who suggested that this state of permanent war was the all-important base on which any system must lay its foundations.[15] In addition, we cannot forget the Futurist Vladimir Mayakovsky's (1893–1930) cry of "war everyday."[16]

My intention is not to relate Lewis to those writers; in fact, rather the opposite, as what was enthusiasm in Schmitt, Jünger and Mayakovsky was disapproval and criticism in Lewis or mere acknowledgement of the level of monstrousness that was about to assail contemporary man. Of course, in relation to Nazi thinkers it would be easy to mention here Lewis's polemical book *Hitler* of 1931 (B&M Cat. 26),[17] in which he went so far as to state that the Nazi leader was a man of peace. I will make no attempt to excuse Lewis and in fact he acknowledged his own error in the form of a recantation entitled *The Hitler Cult* (1939) (B&M Cat. 44). That publication was not, however, enough to save him from the attacks of his left-wing enemies who were ever ready to shout "Fascist" when his name was heard. We should, however, bear in mind the date of the book's publication and the fact that this book (as little read as it was constantly referred to) comprises articles published in the press to which Wyndham Lewis added comments. We should also remember the fact (important although not an excuse) that when the German edition was published a year after the first edition (with an impressive collage on the cover, whether or not by Lewis the present author is not certain), the volume was soon added to the list of books banned by Joseph Goebbels (1897–1945) and his followers as being pernicious. "No one except Marinetti, the Kaiser and professional soldiers DESIRE war. And from this short list we could possibly cross out the Kaiser," wrote Lewis in "War Notes."[18] These "Notes" are written with his characteristically agitated prose, an impatient prose that seems to record a process of thought much faster than the writing that expresses it, as if the author knew beforehand that however fast he went he could only step on the shadow of the idea behind his writings. In these "Notes," what Lewis is attacking is precisely the enthusiasm for the war that seemed to have gripped the entire world, when in fact only a few had aesthetic or financial reasons for maintaining this enthusiasm (and his criticism of Marinetti seems immediately to make clear that what some saw as *Blast*'s Futurist affiliations were nothing more than the usual misunderstandings of the type Lewis would frequently have to endure). Artists could be seen as a group that might benefit from the war: at the very least, it offered them a completely new subject, given that Lewis did not tire of repeating the idea that war as a subject for artists had nothing to do with *modern* war as a subject for artists.

It is true that in these "War Notes" Lewis goes over the top on occasions in the manner of his finest satirical style, which is particularly splendid in *The Apes of God* (1930) (B&M Cat. 21), with, for example, the memorable aphorism: "The English 'Sense of Humour' is the greatest enemy of England: far worse than poor Germany."[19] It could not be said, however, that Lewis's sense of humour was his worst enemy, even when dealing with a subject as sinister as war: over the years, rather than losing it, he made it more brutal. Lewis was never a humorist (his ambitions were far from those of Evelyn Waugh (1903–66)), but there is a great deal of humour in all his books, a humour that he high-handedly used to deflate the stature of almost everything: war, of course, as well as love, art and loyalty to an ideal. Put succinctly, he was never afraid of his humour being offensive, tasteless and, of course, very un-English.

Although they do not appear in the index of *Blast*, No. 2 as "War Notes," there are other texts in that issue that can undoubtedly be considered commentaries on the war. Among them, the most important (along with the habitual ticking-off of Marinetti) is "Artists and the War."[20] The title refers to a matter to which Lewis would devote some major considerations after the war had ended. The text in *Blast*, No. 2 is still light, even superficial, in tone and the author limits himself to saying that the war would naturally affect the art world for the simple reason that it affected our pockets, there being an inevitable relationship between money and art. However, Lewis never believed in the concept of a war artist, or in the miracle that war made someone an artist. In fact, in the text that he devoted to Marinetti, he went as far as to acknowledge the grandeur of some of the Futurist painters, or, more specifically, of artists who were great in peacetime. But the war would not make any artist great who was not so beforehand. It could, however, achieve the opposite: reduce some figures through the drastic method of removing them from the face of the earth. In fact, the most moving page in *Blast*, No. 2 is the one that includes Henri Gaudier-Brzeska's (1891–1915) obituary notice, alongside a ferocious Vorticist text by that young sculptor.[21] Lewis would include a succinct and moving recollection of Gaudier-Brzeska in *Blasting and Bombardiering* (becoming emotional was one of the things that Wyndham Lewis seems to have forbidden himself).[22]

The "War Notes" that Lewis published after the end of the conflict (albeit not with that title) are more substantial than the ones published in his journal. Notable among them is the "Foreword" he wrote for the catalogue of his exhibition *Guns* (B&M Cat. 6), held at the Goupil Gallery in London in February 1919;[23] "The Men who will Paint Hell," written for the *Daily Express* on 10 February 1919 and subtitled "Modern War as a Theme for the Artist";[24] and "What Art Now?," published in *The English Review* in April 1919.[25] These texts are particularly interesting as they allow us to come close to a Lewis who had already been in the war, that is, someone who could place experience above theory. However, he did not make use of that method and it would seem that he had devoted the time between the publication of the "War Notes" in *Blast*, No. 2 and that of these newspaper, magazine and catalogue articles to compiling documentation that would prove his arguments. He was barely able to mention a single truly important work of art that was the product of the recent war and he had no option but to look to the past to encounter the names of artists who painted the horrors and conveyed the visual power of war. Paulo Uccello (1397–1475) is one of his key names and we need only to look at Lewis's own compositions that he entitled *Combat* (1914) (see Cat. 52) to understand how he had been inspired by the chilly tone of the Italian painter. In addition, however, Lewis does not fail to mention the other side of the artistic coin; the powerful, passionate Francisco Goya (1746–1828). Although we need to make a sizeable jump in time, it is worth recalling that in 1940 Lewis returned to Goya (whom he had studied in the early years of the century in the Museo del Prado) for the purposes of his study of the work and importance of Pablo Picasso (1881–1973) published in *The Kenyon Review*. In that exceptional text, Lewis was unenthusiastic about *Guernica* (1937), considering it a highly intellectual poster and totally unrelated to the historical event that inspired it. He contrasted it with Goya's *Disasters of War* (1810–15), in which the artist had

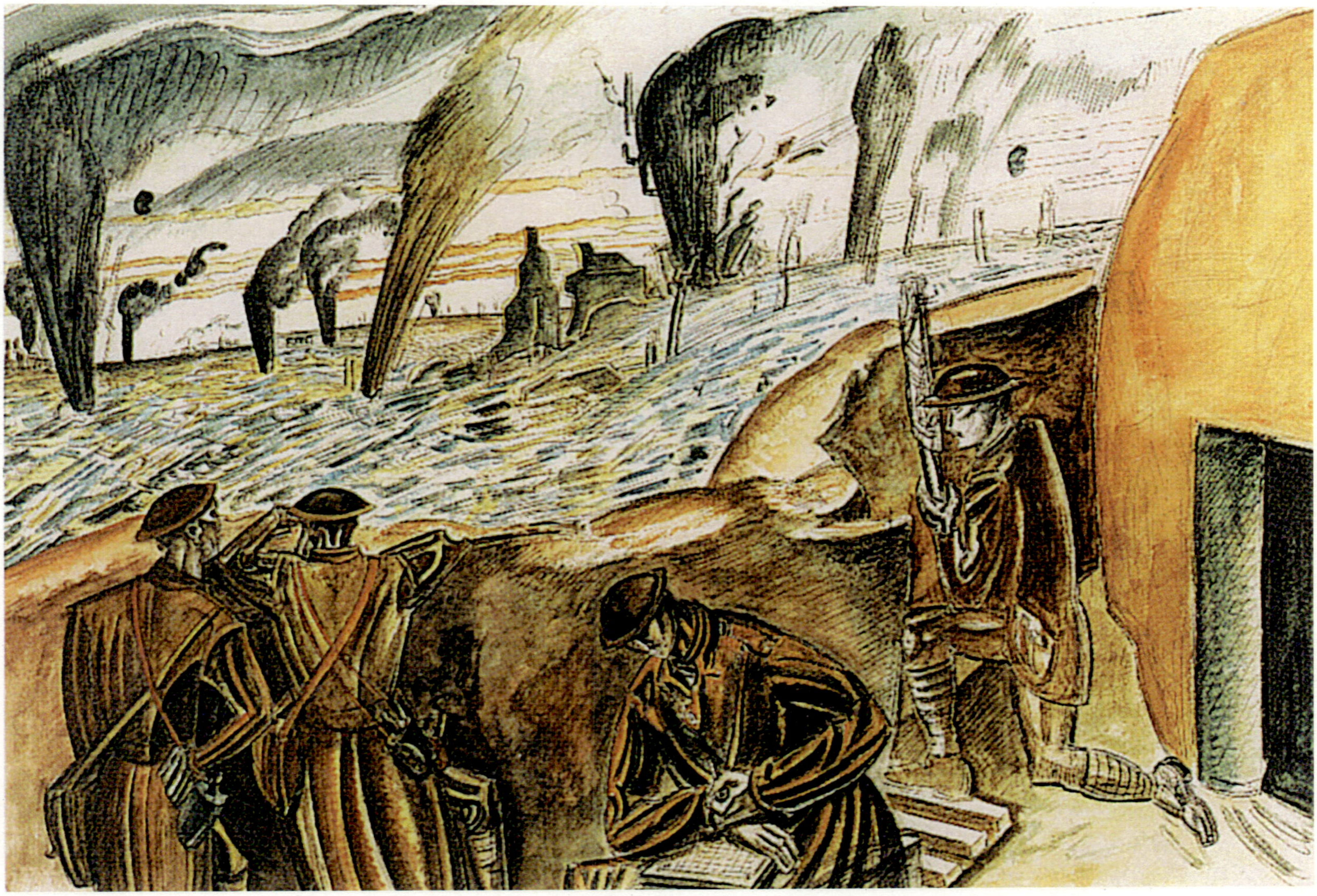

Great War Drawing No. 2, 1918. Southampton City Art Gallery (Cat. 66)

recorded his feelings of disillusionment and rage at the sight of Spain's destruction. It is here, Lewis says, that the artist creates a work that is more than a photogenic depiction: it is flesh and blood, pure truth, and not a cartoon.[26] This does not, however, prevent Lewis in his text for the exhibition *Guns* from singling out Uccello and his coldness. He considers that he "[...] does not borrow from the fact of War any emotion, any disturbing or dislocating violence, terror or compassion – any of the psychology that is proper to the events of War. Goya is as passionate as Uccello is cold, but both are equally great as war artists."[27] For Lewis, it was perfectly possible to imagine what an artist would see in the war by looking at that artist's work: "You know Van Gogh's scene in a prison yard? Then you know how he would treat war."[28]

As Javier Arnaldo has commented: "When Lewis noted that the war being depicted was not just any war but modern war, his aim was to draw his readers' attention to the correspondence between the pictorial language promoted in his exhibition *Guns* and the technological violence that the Great War had unleashed."[29] Years later, when Lewis decided to undertake his second autobiographical volume, *Rude Assignment* (1950) (B&M Cat. 50), he quoted various sentences from the introduction to his exhibition of 1919, including them in the following statements:

Where I am saying that in the midst of war 'serious interpretation' is not possible, I have a good saying – expressing something that is echoed everywhere in what I have written at all periods. It is 'Truth has no place in action.'

Later on I assert that the Man of Action has his counterpart in the works of the mind. 'Another comes to pictorial expression with one or other of the attendant genii of passion at his elbow.' These 'genii of passion' may lead him to the truth: that of passion. But in the moment of passion, or the moment of action, there is no truth. – And even the truth of passion, it seems to follow – although I do not say this here – is an inferior truth: just as the man of action is an inferior man to the man of the mind.[30]

As he also noted in *Rude Assignment*, the principal reason for writing that catalogue text was not to remind himself who had been his masters when painting modern war but rather to forewarn the bewildered public, who would visit the gallery expecting to see an exhibition of abstract art and not expecting to come face to face with "traditional war scenes and figures of soldiers." The following paragraph must be quoted in its entirety:

It will be remarked that I repudiate a fanaticism in the past for the 'abstract'. It is open to the same artist, I suggest, to undertake, on the one hand, any experiment, however far it may lead him from the accepted canons of visual expression, or, on the other hand, to 'tell a story' which the simplest could understand. This he has as much right to do as the literary man, a Dickens, or a Tchekhov, or a Stendhal – or, for that matter, as earlier artists, who without exception showed no squeamishness about literary subject matter.

From this position I never departed. It is as much my position today as it was then. Had it not been for the war I should not have arrived at it so quickly. War, and specially those miles of hideous desert known as 'the Line' in Flanders and France, presented me with a subject matter so consonant with the austerity of that 'abstract' vision I had developed, that it was an easy transition.[31]

Lewis would subsequently define war as a profound, animal dream in which images that belonged to a new order appeared to him. On awakening, he came face to face with a completely different world, while he himself had also changed a great deal, as he says: "The geometrics which had interested me so exclusively before, I now felt were bleak and empty [...] I can never feel any respect for a picture that cannot be reduced, at will, to a fine formal abstraction. But I now busied myself for some years acquiring a maximum of skill in work from nature."[32] Lewis's sympathy for the man of thought as opposed to the man of action (in the true sense of sympathy: that of having shared interests) is evident throughout almost all his writings and it is also there that we have to look for his mistrust of epic and his much written-about disdain for romance. And what could be more romantic than war? If, in the heat of the action and movement, truth can be nothing more than a mirage, then epic is made up of mere illusions, sentimentality and grandiose nothings. It is easy to imagine Lewis's scornful expression every time he encountered a trivial epic scene that championed the war, and he would have had frequent opportunities to assume this expression during the legendary years of the avant-garde movements. He also had the chance to appreciate that, however much he tried to stand on the shoulders of his own era in order to make out the future, he always ended tangled up on the floor of the age in which he had by chance been born. In his own words in *Blasting and Bombardiering*: "It is somewhat depressing to consider how as an artist one is always holding the mirror up to politics without knowing it [...] A prophet is a most unoriginal person: all he is doing is imitating something that is not there, but soon will be. With me war and art have been mixed up from the start. It is still."[33] In this book, Lewis presents himself as a bombardier, a non-commissioned soldier in the Royal Artillery, in order to subsequently remove his uniform: first, the man of war, then the man of peace. The difference between the two lies merely in the uniform. This is because Lewis passed through the war in the same way that Fabricio del Dongo passed through the Battle of Waterloo: without noticing. The attitude was the same although the information available to the two men was very different: Lewis had enough information but nonetheless seems not to have wanted to take on board more than could be captured through the eye. This may have been because he knew that there was nothing to notice in a pigsty and that there was nothing worthy of respect in the effusive tales of war that would provide the basis for the exquisite fiction of a conflict that he had had to live through. If there is one really moving aspect (albeit well concealed) of *Blasting and Bombardiering*, it is the author's decision to deny the status of history to what he had lived through. If Lewis decided not to undertake an

Blast, No. 2, 1915. Wyndham Lewis Memorial Trust, London (B&M Cat. 3)

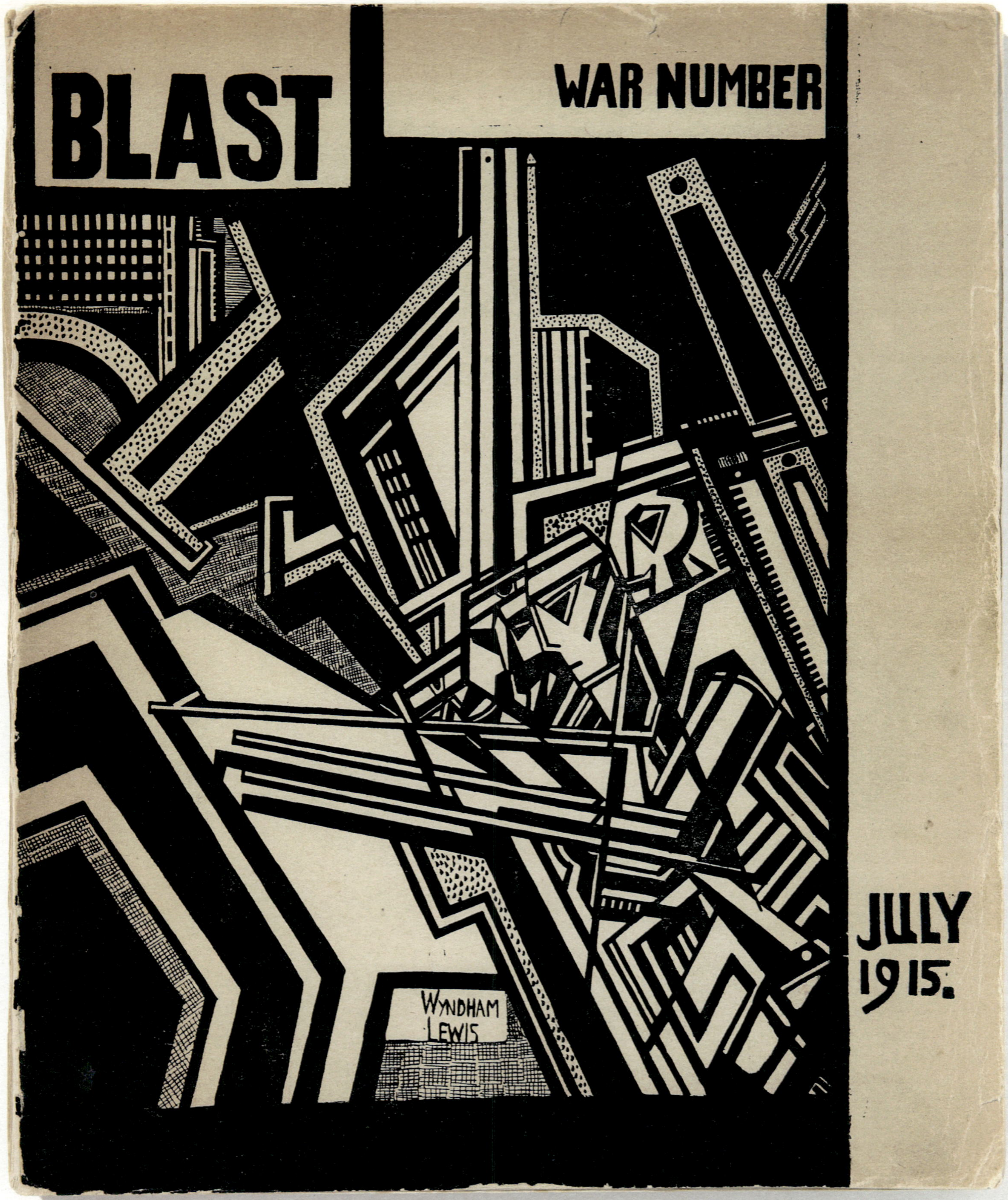
BLAST
WAR NUMBER
WYNDHAM
LEWIS
JULY
1915.

exemplary account of everything that he experienced at the Front, and if he refused to reveal to us any edifying aspect of war and described himself as a "masterpiece of conformity," it is because he decided at a particular moment that the only way to endure it all and to survive was to live it as if he had been an extra, placed there (like so many others) to fill out numbers by a sinister director who had only one idea in mind: that the public likes massacres.

Lewis says elsewhere in *Blasting and Bombardiering*,

All that I know is that I moved hither and thither over this sea of mud and have since been told that it was a fool who was moving me. However, had it been the greatest Captain in the world it would have been all one to me. I am not interested in Great Captains. 'Every thing bores me except the philosophic man.' There is for me no good war (*la bonne guerre*) and bad war.

There is only bad war. Ours, then, was an epic of mud.[34]

As we have seen, this epic of mud inspired Lewis the reflective thinker and Lewis the painter, the most combative side of him but also the most satirical. He found an excellent target for his broadsides in all those intellectuals who dared to speak of the war from the comfort of their cool, shady gardens. The numerous reasons that Lewis encountered for declaring his own particular war on the "bloomsburies" were assisted by the attitude of these individuals, encouraging him to use them as targets for his satirical skills, in the manner of Jonathan Swift (1667–1745). *The Apes of God* (1930 (B&M Cat. 21), widely regarded as Lewis's most important narrative work, is a novel in which he portrayed London intellectuals with masterly ability. His animosity was personal here, even though Lewis was sufficiently distanced to be able to limit himself to expiating his personal ghosts and scoring a mighty hit against the role of the intellectual in society. Speaking with Ford Madox Ford in *Blasting and Bombardiering*, Lewis asks him if it is really fair that Gaudier died while so many five o'clock tea drinking intellectuals with their little fingers stuck out offered lessons in morality in the press, having spent all morning trimming a rose bush. Not even here does Lewis lose his characteristic coolness, and he is more convincing as a result, given that the effectiveness of his chosen genre, satire, is increased by the use of this tone.

"What I don't know about war isn't worth knowing," Lewis wrote in the paragraph that opens this text.[35] In some of his books (his journalistic writings, which are possibly the least important within his *oeuvre* as in them he was unable to control that wretched coolness of his), it seems that Lewis knew more than most about war: enough, in fact, to make significant mistakes. His anti-war books (to which he devoted a harshly critical chapter in *Rude Assignment*, acknowledging that he found it difficult to agree with what he had written in them) are furious outbursts in which he commits the very error that he had criticised in so many writers on the war: that of playing the prophet. He was notably unsuccessful, and in *Count Your Dead* (1937) (B&M Cat. 38)[36] (which Paul Edwards rightly considers Lewis's worst book) and *Left Wings Over Europe* (1936) (B&M Cat. 37)[37] we encounter rare examples of how an intelligent man can be kidnapped by his convictions. The two books are crashing failures of which his enemies – already well trained for the task after the publication of his book on Hitler – would make full use. It is difficult to offer Lewis's hatred of war as an excuse for his tolerance of Adolf Hitler (1889–1945) and Benito Mussolini (1883–1945) acting as they pleased, the one in Europe and the other in Abyssinia. It continues to be odd that a person who so perceptively warned of the inevitable ills of the war machine, which disguised the epic beneath Romantic sentimentality, was unable to perceive the Romantic component within the Imperial nationalist forces that did not limit themselves to loving their own mother countries but also felt the need to expand into everyone else's. It is consequently depressing to read these books in which Lewis, who would very soon afterwards criticise his own hasty conclusions, reveals that being a prophet is not as easy as he thought: in fact, when he set about being one, he stumbled as never before. However, the wrong-headed analysis that Lewis proposed of Germany's right to recover its former grandeur and his subsequent retraction do not prevent us from acknowledging him as a lucid analyst of the monstrous nature of modern war. In fact, we might ask what made him enter this mire and only one answer seems possible: he simply decided to adopt the opposite opinion to that of his declared enemies, and given that the British Left was clear that the mainland European dictatorships had to be held back as far as possible, Lewis was left with the only option of expressing the opposite opinion, simply in order to do so rather than because he really believed his own arguments.

In this brief survey we have seen Lewis sketching out ideas, describing situations, and restraining his disgust so that the idea of epic that was so indissolubly associated with war should not win out, strengthened by its association with the new technology. At the end we must return to the emphatically expressed pages of his great book *Blasting and Bombardiering* and to his encounter with the ever sensible Ford Madox Ford, with whom he discussed the fact that the "bloomsburies" had remained out of it as they had the money to do so:

[...] ultimately it was to keep them fat and prosperous – or thin and prosperous which is even worse – that other people were to risk their skins. Then there were the tales of how a certain famous artist, of military age and militant bearing, would sit in the Café Royal and addressing an admiring group back from the Front, would exclaim: 'We are the civilization for which you are fighting!'.[38]

For Lewis the issue is a very simple one: he had no emotional aversion to war, but in a civilised era there must have been a good reason for that concerted failure of our civilised manners. What was it? Or, to ask the question in his own words,

Who was proposing to kill or maim me? [...] I saw clearly that it was not my German opposite number. He, like myself, was an instrument. That we were all on a fool's errand had become plain to many of us,

for, beyond a certain point, victory becomes at the best a Pyrrhic victory [...]

Nor could I obtain much comfort from cursing my mother and father, grandmother and grandfather, as Mr Aldington or the Sitwells did. For it was not quite certain that we were not just as big fools as our not very farsighted forebears. There was not much sense in blaming the ancestors of the community to which I belonged for the murderous nonsense in which I found myself, up to the neck, it seemed to me [...]

Where was I then? If you have a little politics you will say, perhaps, is *any* society worth being killed, or ruined for? Is the Sovereign State to be taken seriously? Are any merely national institutions so valuable, so morally or intellectually valid, that we should lay down our lives for them, as a matter of course?

I could not answer that question by a mere yes or no. Naturally I can imagine a State that it would be your duty to die for. There are many principles also, which *might* find themselves in a State, which I personally consider matters of life and death. But whether the machine-age has left any State intact in such a way as to put men under a moral or emotional compulsion to die for it, is a matter I am unable to discuss.[39]

Like the great philosophers, in the matter of war Lewis does not teach us to come up with feeble, satisfactory answers (like those of a catechism), answers that are painkillers for a troubled conscience. Rather, he teaches us to ponder the questions that he asks until we are obliged to come face to face with the impossibility of being satisfied with any answer.

NOTES

1. Wyndham Lewis, *Blasting and Bombardiering: Autobiography (1914–1926)* (London: Eyre & Spottiswoode, 1937), p. 90.
2. Ibid., p. 4.
3. Wyndham Lewis, *Snooty Baronet* (London: Cassell, 1932), p. 2.
4. Tom Normand, "Wyndham Lewis, the Anti-War War Artist," *Wyndham Lewis and the Art of Modern War*. Ed. David Peters Corbett (Cambridge: Cambridge University Press, 1998), p. 104.
5. Karlheinz Stockhausen, quoted in Julia Spinola, "Monstrous Art," *Frankfurter Allgemeine Zeitung* (25 September 2001).
6. Letter from Apollinaire to Soffici, in *European Friends of Apollinaire*, 16th Symposium of Stavelot, 1–3 September 1993. Ed. Michel Décaudin (Paris: Presses Sorbonne Nouvelle, 1995), p. 85.
7. *Blast*, No. 2 (July 1915).
8. *Blast*, No. 1 (June 1914).
9. *Morning Post*, quoted in the advertisements included at the end of *Blast*, No. 2 (July 1915), p. 104.
10. *Sunday Times*, quoted ibid.
11. *Blast*, No. 2 (July 1915), p. 5.
12. Ibid., p. 13.
13. Ibid.
14. Ernst Jünger, *Storm of Steel*. Trans. Basil Creighton (London: Chatto and Windus, 1929).
15. Carl Schmitt, *Political Theology* (1922). Spanish edition: *Estudios Politicos* (Madrid: Cultura Española, 1941), pp. 35–39.
16. Vladimir Mayakovsky, *Vladimir Ilyich Lenin* (1924) (Moscow: Progress Publishers, 1970), p. 80.
17. Wyndham Lewis, *Hitler* (London: Chatto and Windus, 1931).
18. *Blast*, No. 2 (July 1915), pp. 9–16.
19. Wyndham Lewis, "Constantinople Our Star," *Blast*, No. 2 (July 1915), p. 11.
20. *Blast*, No. 2 (July 1915), p. 23.
21. Ibid., p. 34.
22. *Blasting and Bombardiering*, pp. 114–15.
23. Wyndham Lewis, "Foreword," in *Guns* [exh. cat. Goupil Gallery, London]. London: Goupil Gallery, 1919, n.p.
24. Wyndham Lewis, "The Men who will Paint Hell. Modern War as a Theme for the Artist," *Daily Express*, no. 5877 (10 February 1919), p. 4.
25. Wyndham Lewis, "What Art Now?," *The English Review* 28 (April 1919), pp. 334–38.
26. Wyndham Lewis, "Picasso," *The Kenyon Review* 2, no. 2 (Spring 1940), pp. 196–211.
27. "Foreword," in *Guns*, n.p.
28. Ibid.
29. Javier Arnaldo, in *¡1914! La Vanguardia y la Gran Guerra* [exh. cat. Museo Thyssen-Bornemisza and Fundación Caja, Madrid]. Madrid: Fundación Colección Thyssen-Bornemisza, 2008, p. 256.
30. Wyndham Lewis, *Rude Assignment: A Narrative of my Career Up-to-date* (London: Hutchinson, 1950), p. 128.
31. Ibid., p. 129.
32. Ibid.
33. *Blasting and Bombardiering*, p. 4.
34. Ibid., p. 161.
35. Ibid., p. 182.
36. Wyndham Lewis, *Count Your Dead: They are Alive! Or, A New War in the Making* (London: Lovat Dickson, 1937).
37. Wyndham Lewis, *Left Wings Over Europe: Or, How to Make a War about Nothing* (London: Jonathan Cape, 1936).
38. *Blasting and Bombardiering*, p. 183.
39. Ibid., pp. 185–86.

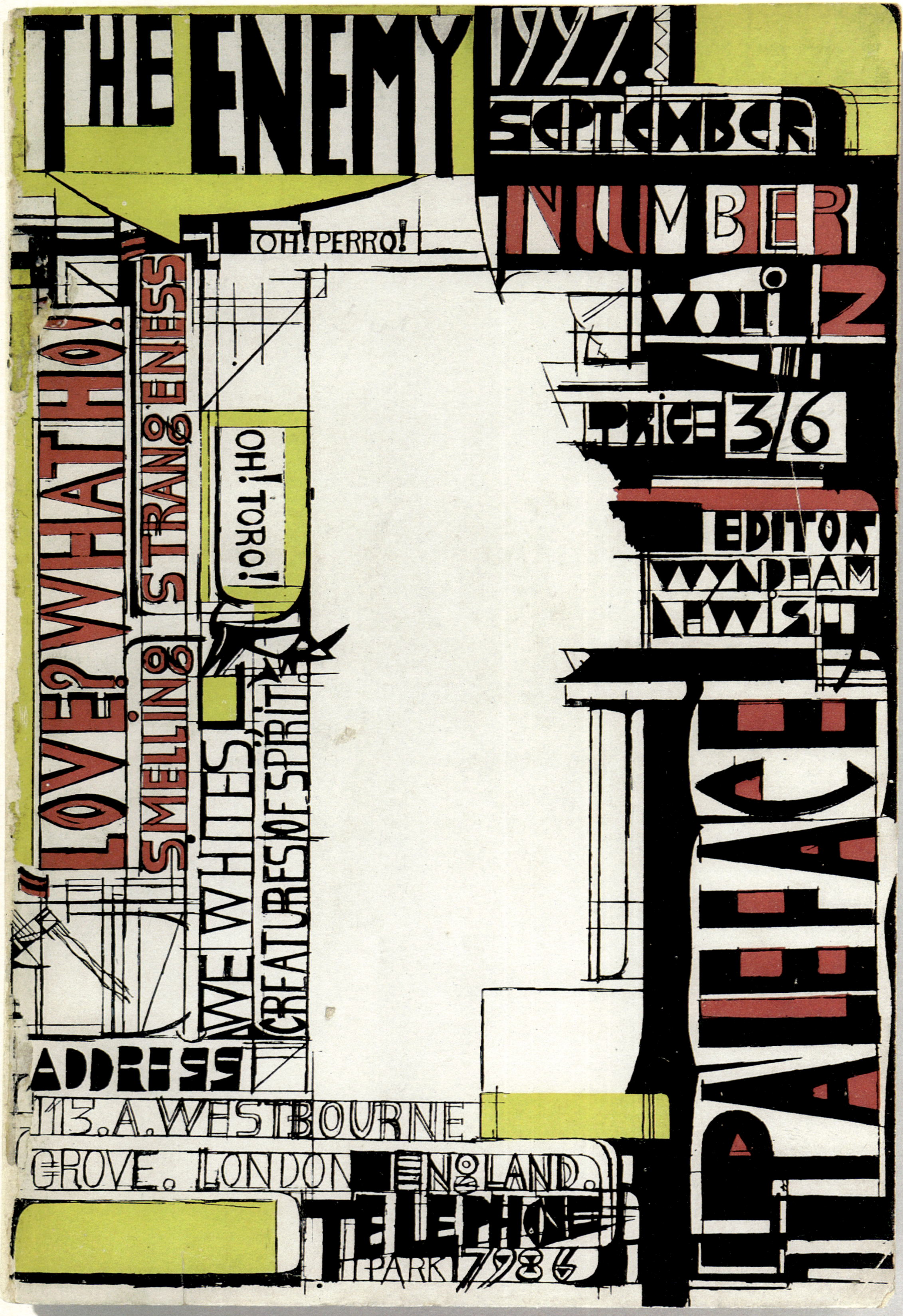
THE ENEMY
1927.
SEPTEMBER NUMBER
VOL 2
PRICE 3/6
EDITOR WYNDHAM LEWIS
OH! PERRO!
"LOVE? WHAT HO! SMELLING OF STRANGENESS"
OH! TORO! HO! TORO!
WE WHITES, CREATURES OF SPIRIT
PALEFACE
ADDRESS
113. A. WESTBOURNE GROVE. LONDON ENGLAND.
TELEPHONE PARK 7986

WYNDHAM LEWIS AND POLITICS

Andrzej Gąsiorek

The Enemy, No. 2, 1927.
Wyndham Lewis Memorial Trust,
London (B&M Cat. 15)

WYNDHAM LEWIS, IT SEEMS, WILL NEVER BE FREE

from certain political associations. He was aware of this discomfiting fate, as he made clear in his interim autobiography *Blasting and Bombardiering* (1937) (B&M Cat. 40): "in 1926 I began writing about politics, not because I like politics but everything was getting bogged in them and before you could do anything you had to deal with the politics with which it is encrusted. And I've got so bepoliticked myself in the process that in order to get at *me*, to-day, you have to get the politics off me first."[1] This is a revealing description. Lewis implies that politics should be seen as an extrinsic concern, an organisational activity outside of society and the self. He reiterated this conviction in the 1950s when, following the Italian philosopher Benedetto Croce (1866–1952), he argued that politics should be seen as "a department of life *below* the more humane and virtuous levels of our nature as men" and that it was "a region governed by laws of its own, and distinct from all the other activities of our existence."[2] In *Blasting and Bombardiering* he suggested that he was forced to engage with politics because everything that mattered to him – the arts, culture, human values – was in the 1920s becoming suffused with political considerations, which in his view were of secondary importance. The ensuing paradox was this: by challenging the belief that politics was the most important feature of contemporary life Lewis was embroiling himself in the domain from which he wanted to extricate art and the individuals who created it. He was so "bepoliticked" as a result that the "self" he sought to preserve beyond the political arena became harder to maintain. Two years before the outbreak of the Second World War he admitted: "no one in 1937 can help being other than political. We are in politics up to our necks."[3]

Blasting and Bombardiering offers a revisionist account of Lewis's career from the days of *Blast* and Vorticism to the late 1930s. It is not entirely accurate in its claim that Lewis became involved in politics in 1926, the year he published *The Art of Being Ruled* (B&M Cat. 10). This was at that time the most overtly political of Lewis's books, but it would be a mistake to ignore the political implications of earlier texts, most notably the two issues of *Blast* (the avant-garde "little magazine" Lewis edited in 1914 and 1915 (B&M Cats. 2 and 3)) and his post-First World War pamphlet *The Caliph's Design: Architects! Where is Your Vortex?* (1919) (B&M Cat. 7).

Two features of Vorticism are key to any consideration of Lewis's politics: firstly, its commitment to the representation of industrial modernity in a style that belonged to modernity; secondly, its desire, by means of this style, to explore contemporary life in a manner that differed from "academic" or "realist" treatments. Vorticism drew on Cubism and Futurism to create a stylised geometric art that rejected the Kandinskyan path to abstraction. Vorticist art aimed to grasp the inner truth of modern life through form as well as subject matter; in form and content it challenged conventional and familiar responses to daily reality. Vorticism attempted "a geometrical and condensed translation of the perceived world," as Richard Humphreys puts it.[4] Implicit in this geometrisation of forms was a desire to envisage how contemporary reality might be transformed. Industry, urbanisation and technology were accepted as the artist's primary data, but they were not celebrated after the manner of the Italian Futurists. *Blast* enjoined the Vorticist painter to engage critically with the modern world by abstracting its most significant features from it and articulating in paint its latent potentialities. When Lewis argued that all "revolutionary painting to-day has in common the rigid reflections of steel and stone in the spirit of the artist" and that people were being invited "to change entirely their idea of the painter's mission, and penetrate, deferentially, with him into a transposed universe as abstract as, though different from, the musician's," he was suggesting that modernist art was providing visionary templates for the future creation of an alternative society.[5] Lewis was explicit about this aspect of Vorticism in his later accounts of the movement:

> **It was, after all, a new civilisation that I – and a few other people – was making the blueprints for: these things never being more than that. A rough design for a way of seeing for men who as yet were not there [...] It was more than just picture-making: one was manufacturing fresh eyes for people, and fresh souls to go with the eyes.**[6]

More than just picture-making. This is the salient point. Vorticism was not solely an aesthetic project but also a utopian enterprise that conceived avant-garde art as the progenitor of as yet unrealised forms of social life.

What did this mean? It did not mean that the arts were to intervene directly in social or political spheres. Nor did it mean that Vorticism aimed to fuse art and life through social praxis. Based on the segregation of "life" and "art" – also a central concern of Lewis's novel *Tarr* (1918) (B&M Cat. 5) – Vorticism resisted the premature closing of the gap between them. Vorticism aimed rather to make patterns in the here-and-now for a future life that might follow in the wake of avant-garde creativity. Lewis articulated this position in the second issue of *Blast*: "If the material world were not empirical and matter simply for science, but were organized as in the imagination, we should live as though we were dreaming. Art's business is to show how, then, life would be."[7]

Blast identified a "moment" in 1914 when the chance for a transformation of art and culture seemed briefly to present

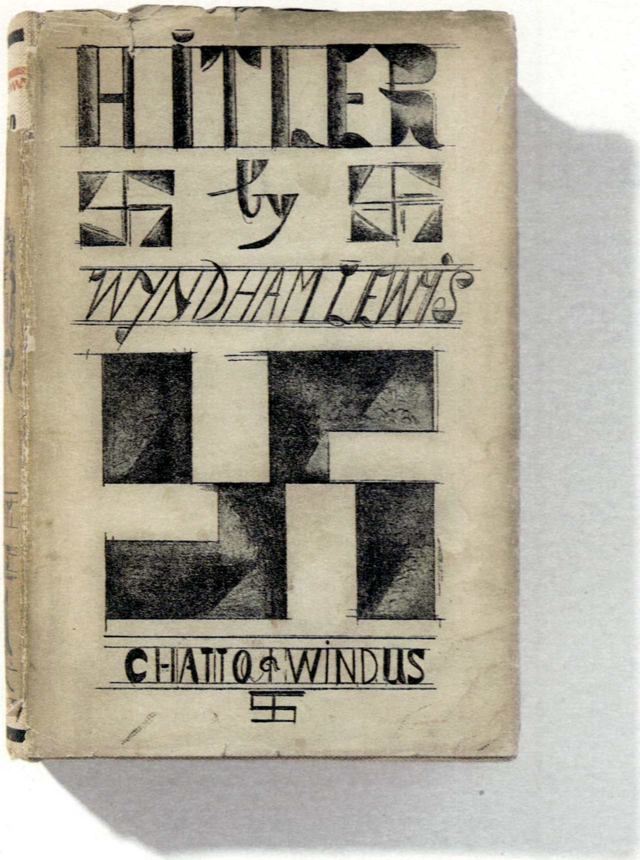

Hitler, 1931. Private collection YMJB (B&M Cat. 26)

itself. In association with the American poet Ezra Pound (1885–1972), who collaborated with him on *Blast*, Lewis galvanised a group of artists and writers into action, arguing that the adversity of the conditions obtaining in England, if exploited along the lines urged by the Vorticists, could give birth to an unexpected explosion of creative energy. But the First World War broke out just as Vorticism seemed to be on the verge of making an impact on English cultural life. A second issue of *Blast* – the "War Number" – appeared in 1915, but Vorticism had been overtaken by events and no further issues were published.

Putting it like this might suggest that Vorticism was destroyed by the war. There is a degree of truth to this assumption, but the reality was more complex. Lewis did not immediately abandon Vorticism but made various attempts to regroup and to continue the Vorticist project under other guises. *The Caliph's Design*, Lewis's intervention in debates about architecture in the aftermath of the First World War, is an important document because it developed arguments that were implicit in *Blast*. Although Lewis was in 1914–15 principally concerned with painting and writing, he had no interest in sealing them off from society. On the contrary, modernist art was for Lewis in the vanguard of the social changes it both desired and sought to predict. *The Caliph's Design* took this one step further. Lewis now insisted that art must be taken out of the studios and the galleries so that it could participate in ordinary daily life, where it might play a role in the transformation of social reality. In the first major restatement of his views after the war he wrote: "*You must get Painting, Sculpture, and Design out of the studio and into life* [...] if you are not going to see this new vitality desiccated in a Pocket of inorganic experimentation."[8] Lewis, in short, sought nothing less than the transfiguration of the everyday. He argued that architecture and design should bestow significance on all aspects of the material environment. If the modern city were "rebuilt on a more conscious pattern," he maintained, then architects and engineers would together "make a new form-content for our everyday vision."[9]

An emancipatory view of politics informed this position, though it was not couched in party political or policy terms. The artist's duty, Lewis argued, was "to desire equity, mansuetude, in human relations, fight against violence, and work for formal beauty, significance and so forth, in the arrangement and aspect of life."[10] The technological age was no less important to Lewis's thinking in 1919 than it had been in 1914. Indeed, *The Caliph's Design* upheld Lewis's Vorticist commitment to a machine-inflected geometric art, treating technology as a resource to be reworked and redeployed. By being "absorbed into the aesthetic consciousness," machinery could be "put to different uses than those for which it was originally intended," and this artistic transformation of its original functions would force it to serve different human purposes and needs.[11] The alternative (which Lewis associated with Italian Futurism) was an uncritical acceptance of the machine age that subordinated individuals to the technology they were supposed to control and thus denied them agency. Stranded in "the indiscriminate, mechanical and unprogressive world," the individual was turned into a product of technical processes: "The danger, as it would appear at present, and in our first flight of substitution and remounting, is evidently that we should become overpowered by our creation, and become as mechanical as a tremendous insect world, all our awakened reason entirely disappeared."[12]

These words offer a proleptic commentary on the issues with which Lewis would be preoccupied in the 1920s and 1930s. He increasingly turned his attention to what he saw as a machining of subjectivity that in his view was a key feature of social life in the inter-war years. Between 1926 and 1938, Lewis was deeply critical of democracy and strongly drawn to authoritarian politics. He associated democracy with weakness and with hypocrisy. Democracies were feeble in comparison with centralised states, such as those of the Soviet Union or Fascist Italy, and they were dishonest because they lauded the virtues of participatory politics but subjugated individuals through various techniques of thought control. Lewis's anger at the coercive nature of what in *The Art of Being Ruled* he described as an "*educationalist state*," led him to analyse and to resist the ideologies that were being imposed on citizens by means of political propaganda, the mass media and what Theodor Adorno (1903–69) and Max Horkheimer (1895–1973) would later describe as the "culture industry."[13] The "awakened reason" was under threat in this situation. This is why *The Art of Being Ruled* was conceived as the first of a "series of books devoted to the work of radical analysis of the ideas by which our society has been taught to live."[14]

There are many contradictions in Lewis's thinking in the 1920s and 1930s. Among the most significant of these is his inconsistent view of why individuals were enslaved by certain ideologies and how they might resist them. Lewis oscillated between two accounts of subjectivity. On the one hand he maintained that most people were innately predisposed to unthinking servitude and actively desired to pass their lives as standardised "mass" units of a structured social order, but on the other hand he argued that individuals were unwitting victims of interest groups that kept them in a tutelage of which they were largely unaware. The first view implied that the majority deserved their fate and in a strange sense courted it, while the second view suggested that this fate was imposed on them by the social manufacturing of identity. Drawing on Goethe's (1749–1832) distinction between "natures" (autonomous individuals with the capacity for independent thought and action) and "puppets" (manipulable ciphers whose every waking moment was controlled by extrinsic forces), Lewis made the politically objectionable claim that the majority actually wanted to be puppets because the effort required to be self-directed agents was beyond them: "in the mass people wish to be *automata*: they wish to be *conventional*: they hate you teaching them or forcing them into 'freedom': they wish to be obedient, hard-working machines, as near dead as possible."[15] This view sanctioned a hierarchical conception of human types and led Lewis to argue that the "division into *natural* men and *mechanical* men [...] answers to the solution advocated" in *The Art of Being Ruled*.

This aspect of Lewis's thinking is radically anti-democratic. But as is often the case with Lewis, progressive views vie with elitist sentiments in his work. *The Art of Being Ruled* was, after all, written as a warning to the victims of entrenched economic and political interests and as an encouragement to them to resist the blandishments of ideology. It concludes with a fragment from Parmenides (ca. 520–ca. 450BCE): "*I wish to communicate this view of the world to you exactly as it manifests itself: and so no human opinion will ever be able to get the better of you.*"[16] In *Men Without Art* (1934) (B&M Cat. 36), Lewis made it clear that in his view the majority of people suffered at the hands of an inequitable social system. When he wrote about unemployed workers in Belfast, for example, he applauded their rebelliousness and asked: "What can these people do but band together against those discredited masters of theirs, who cannot even manage their own affairs, let alone other people's!"[17] Lewis was at all times aware that the English class system kept the majority in servitude and impeded their efforts to educate themselves and thus to grasp the truth of contemporary politics and of their position within a stratified society. (His novel *The Vulgar Streak* (1941) (B&M Cat. 47) focused on this issue at length.) The critical books Lewis wrote were part of a campaign of enlightenment that embraced a form of ideology critique that was articulated not from a leftist standpoint (as in the work of Adorno and Horkheimer) but from a position of aggressive scepticism.

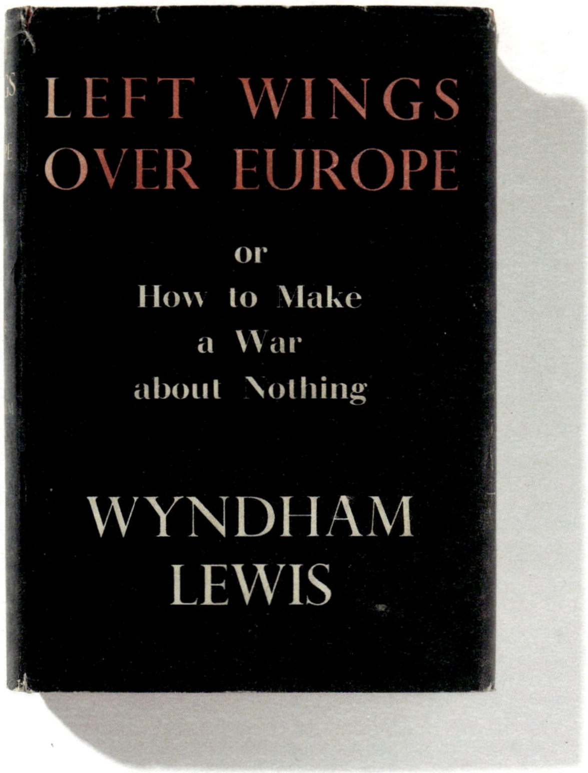

Left Wings Over Europe: Or, How to Make a War about Nothing, 1936. Wyndham Lewis Memorial Trust, London (B&M Cat. 37)

Lewis was explicit about the need for all individuals to wake from their uncritical slumbers:

> everyone, I think [...] has this alternative. Either he must be prepared to sink to the level of chronic tutelage and slavery, dependent for all he is to live by upon a world of ideas, and its manipulators, about which he knows nothing: or he must get hold as best he can of the abstract principles involved in the very 'intellectual' machinery set up to control and change him.[18]

Lewis's response to this situation was to argue that writers and artists should interpret and criticise society, without offering premature solutions to the problems they diagnosed. Alan Munton suggests that for Lewis the intellectual was characterised by "the potential capacity for a detached and dispassionate analysis of his society" and was to be seen as "the source of suggestions and definitions of human possibility," not as a participant in practical political affairs.[19] This is a fair summary. Lewis wrote that it was imperative to distinguish "on the one hand between (1) *political* revolution [...] and (2) upon the other, all thought and activity that is certainly revolutionary, and so disturbing to the comfortable average, but not committed to any particular *political* doctrine – that is to say to any practical programme of change."[20] For Lewis, in other words, art's power resided in its speculative freedom and its refusal of doctrinaire (read "false") closures. Art was a quintessentially radical endeavour that had the capacity to liberate individuals from ideological servitude, though not from political systems or circumstances. It was "a breaker-down of walls, a dissolvent of nations, factions, and protective freemasonries, a radio-active something in the midst of more conservative aggregations."[21]

If writers and artists were to aspire to independence of thought and impartiality, which for Lewis represented an ideal, then it followed that they could not be completely apolitical. Lewis recognised this. Writers, he argued, might try to be as detached and as fair-minded as possible but this did not mean they could "stand above the *mêlée*, and [...] function as an instrument of impartial truth, or anything of that sort."[22] What, then, of his own politics, which have gained him so much notoriety among those who know little of his work? The first point that needs to be made is that Lewis's politics underwent a number of changes over time and cannot easily be pinned down. As he himself put it: "Politics are something flexible, vivid, various, not cut and dried."[23] During his Vorticist phase, he was committed to an emancipatory utopian politics that viewed aesthetic renewal as the precursor of wider social change. A decade later, *The Art of Being Ruled* argued for an amalgamation of Communism and Fascism, a stance that derived from Lewis's desire to centralise political power and thus (so he hoped) to leave artists free to concentrate on their creative work. Lewis wrote in positive terms of both the Soviet Union and Fascist Italy in *The Art of Being Ruled*, arguing that a moribund British society could be revivified by a similar approach to the exercise of political power. He suggested that "when these *one*-party states are centrally organised" they are immediately effective, and he considered that, despite their flaws, what "they have done in a short time in the way of organisation must be the admiration of the world."[24] England, in contrast, was stuck in a pre-war "liberal" time-warp and was unable to transform its society after the manner of Communism and Fascism.

A key premise of *The Art of Being Ruled* was Lewis's belief that adequate rule requires the state to wield power. Liberal democracies were afraid to acknowledge this cold fact and thus pretended that all citizens participated in their own governance. Lewis was interested in Communism and Fascism because they were prepared to be authoritarian, even despotic, and this enabled them to get things done. It is easy to see with hindsight how naive and impractical his thinking was on these issues. He hardly differentiated Fascism from Communism, for example, identifying both with the centralisation of power that attracted him. When he tentatively endorsed Fascism in *The Art of Being Ruled*, he described it as an outgrowth of Communism. In "the abstract," Lewis thought "the sovietic system to be the best" because of its "desire to alleviate the lot of the poor and outcast, and not merely to set up a cast-iron, militarist-looking state," but he claimed that in practice, "for anglo-saxon countries as they are constituted today some modified form of fascism would probably be best."[25]

This is confusing enough. It is made more so when we consider that Lewis drew on Michael Farbman's sympathetic account of the Soviet Union in *After Lenin: The New Phase in Russia* (1924) to argue that Farbmann's conclusions about the Bolshevik view of power corresponded "with those I am expressing throughout this essay."[26] For Lewis, the principal connection between Fascism and Communism was that they were *étatiste*; by concentrating power in the hands of ruling cadres, they supposedly freed individuals to follow various non-political pursuits within a "stable" social order. Lewis was concerned above all with finding the means by which cultural labour could be undertaken without political interference. Describing Benito Mussolini's (1883–1945) Fascism as a development of Marxism, Lewis put his case as follows:

> And that is the sort of socialism that this essay would indicate as the most suitable for anglo-saxon countries or colonies, with as much of sovietic proletarian sentiment as could be got into it without impairing its discipline, and as little coercion as is compatible with good sense. In short, to get some sort of peace to enable us to work, we should naturally seek the most powerful and stable authority that can be devised.[27]

He went on to describe a situation in which "political standardization, with the suppression of the last vestiges of the party system, will rescue masses of energy otherwise wasted in politics for more productive ends."[28]

Lewis's inability to grasp that the delegation of political power to unelected groups was more likely than anything else to result in political interference in the artistic realm and in the suppression of individuality led him to make one mistake after another in ensuing years. His politics in the late 1920s and early 1930s were authoritarian and illiberal. If he never fully endorsed Fascism, he was certainly sympathetic to it, and as he became more critical of Communism his appreciation of Fascism grew.[29] In 1930, following a visit to Germany, he wrote the first book in English devoted to Hitler. Although he was sceptical about national socialism,

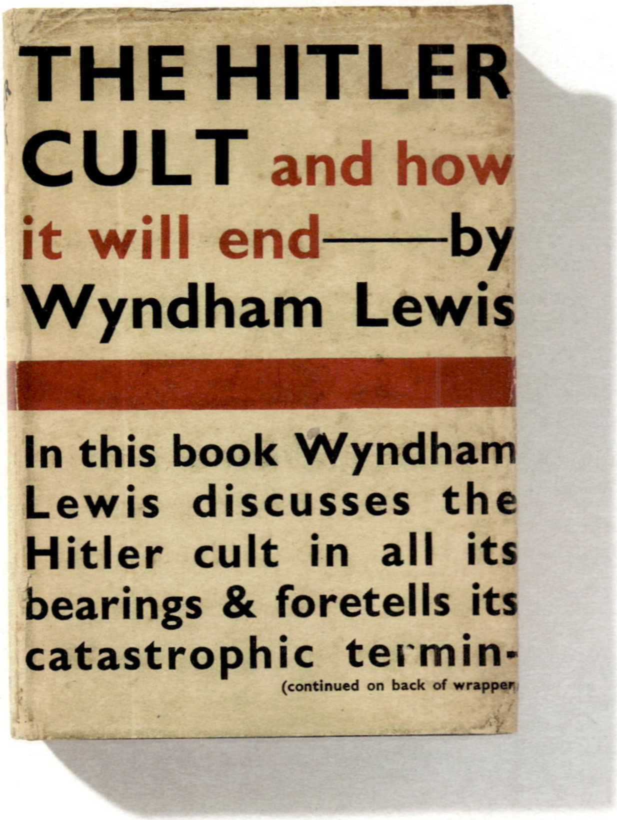

The Hitler Cult, 1939.
Wyndham Lewis Memorial Trust, London (B&M Cat. 44)

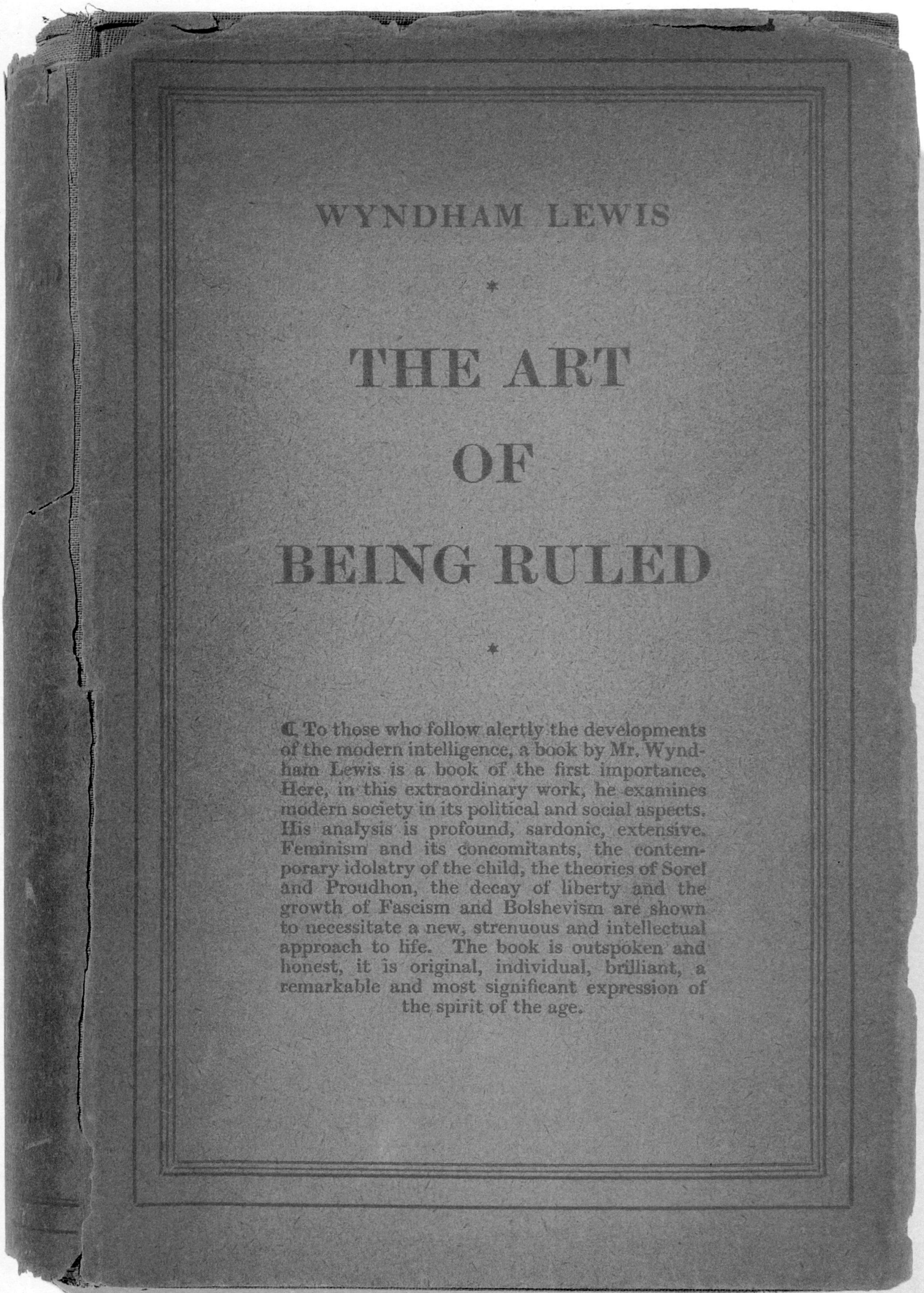
WYNDHAM LEWIS
THE ART OF BEING RULED
To those who follow alertly the developments of the modern intelligence, a book by Mr. Wyndham Lewis is a book of the first importance. Here, in this extraordinary work, he examines modern society in its political and social aspects. His analysis is profound, sardonic, extensive. Feminism and its concomitants, the contemporary idolatry of the child, the theories of Sorel and Proudhon, the decay of liberty and the growth of Fascism and Bolshevism are shown to necessitate a new, strenuous and intellectual approach to life. The book is outspoken and honest, it is original, individual, brilliant, a remarkable and most significant expression of the spirit of the age.

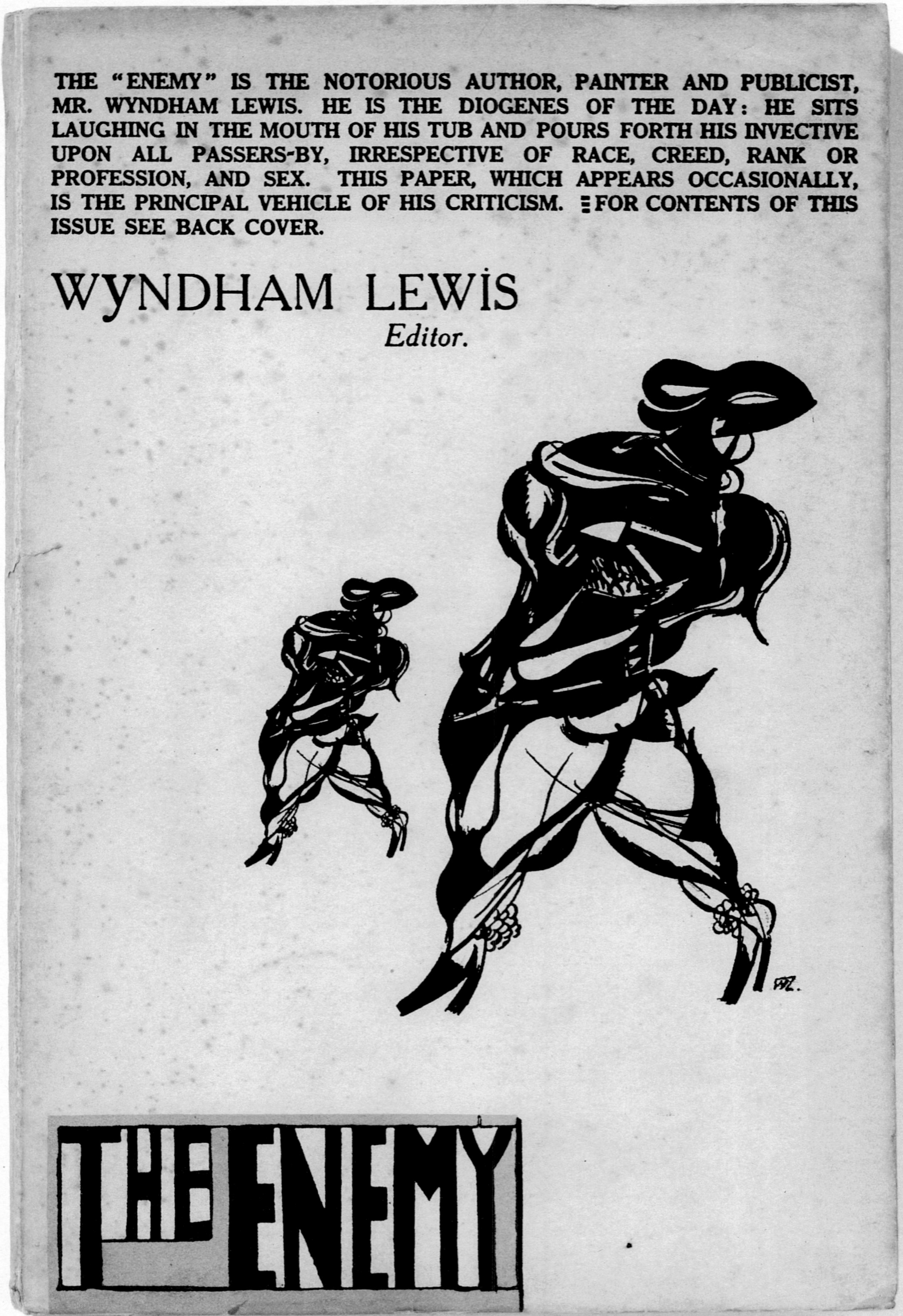

THE "ENEMY" IS THE NOTORIOUS AUTHOR, PAINTER AND PUBLICIST, MR. WYNDHAM LEWIS. HE IS THE DIOGENES OF THE DAY: HE SITS LAUGHING IN THE MOUTH OF HIS TUB AND POURS FORTH HIS INVECTIVE UPON ALL PASSERS-BY, IRRESPECTIVE OF RACE, CREED, RANK OR PROFESSION, AND SEX. THIS PAPER, WHICH APPEARS OCCASIONALLY, IS THE PRINCIPAL VEHICLE OF HIS CRITICISM. FOR CONTENTS OF THIS ISSUE SEE BACK COVER.

WYNDHAM LEWIS
Editor.

THE ENEMY

◂◂ *The Art of Being Ruled*, 1926. Private collection YMJB (B&M Cat. 10)

◂ *The Enemy*, No. 3, 1929. Wyndham Lewis Memorial Trust (B&M Cat. 16)

especially its racial doctrines, he argued in *Hitler* (1931) (B&M Cat. 26) that these doctrines promised "political unity" and by so doing tended to "secure greater social efficiency"; he further suggested that there was "a great deal of political àpropos and sagacity" in the national socialist "plan to *draw in* and to *concentrate*, rather than to diffuse, disperse and mix."[30] Claiming to be "a detached exponent" of what he had witnessed in Germany, Lewis worried that some of what he had written might "sound too much like criticism"; he insisted that it was because of his "sympathy with this great german party" that he was "concerned to see these difficulties brought out into the light, and, it is to be hoped, overcome."[31] Why, exactly? Lewis's answer was clear:

The Hitler Movement has done wonders inside the frontiers of Germany, and its leaders should, I think, extend their message – which also would be a message of peace – to other countries of a similar culture [...] It is to them that we must look for a great movement of political *concentration* – to call a halt to the growing stagnation and diffusion elsewhere.[32]

The arguments advanced in *Hitler* meld with those put forward in *The Art of Being Ruled*. Lewis's desire to centralise political power in order to free up other areas of human activity blinded him to the real implications of Hitlerism and led him to undervalue the freedoms preserved within and defended by liberal democracies. By the time he wrote *The Hitler Cult* (1939) (B&M Cat. 44) – a recantation of his earlier views – he had grasped that whatever the limitations of English society, it was preferable to the political despotism and racial hatred of Nazi Germany.[33] He insisted that individuals must choose "between the French and Celtic culture generally, allied to the genius for tolerance of the Anglo-Saxon, on the one hand, and the most efficient exponents of machine-age barbarism [...] on the other."[34] He had long regarded Communism and Fascism as commutative, in that both were motivated by the desire to centralise power. But whereas he had initially applauded this as political realism and had foolishly believed such centralisation would safeguard the arts, he now decisively rejected this line of thinking and suggested that he had in the 1930s been too concerned to protect his "tribe" of artists and had not thought enough "about 'le genre humain' of the revolutionary song."[35]

Why, though, was Lewis unable to understand the true nature of National Socialism for so long? This is partly because he knew little about what was taking place in Germany in the mid-1930s and partly because his political thinking was so abstract, so severed from real events, movements and policies. At the same time, we should note that events seemed always to force Lewis to make choices that would in his view avert war; hypnotised by his conviction that Hitler was a man of peace, he was an appeaser for much of the 1930s. But Lewis was preoccupied above all with the fate of the arts and wanted to live in a society in which they could flourish. Frustrated at the failure of the pre-war avant-gardes to have the cultural impact he had dreamed they might have, he was looking for a political order that would allow the arts to play an active role in the remaking of social life. If a ramshackle liberal democracy was incapable of valuing and making use of modernist artists, then liberal democracy had to go. Lewis's thinking was here influenced by such figures as Mikhail Bakunin (1814–76), Pierre-Joseph Proudhon (1809–65), and Georges Sorel (1847–1922), all of whom argued that democratic systems practised deception on a gigantic scale, fooling citizens into thinking they participated in the political process when in reality they were merely its pawns. Convinced that liberalism was a sham and that the only viable alternatives to it were the *étatiste* systems of Fascism and Communism, Lewis made the disastrous mistake of concluding that politics could simply be left to those who made it their profession, allowing artistically inclined individuals to pursue their supposedly more important *métier*. Lewis wrote: "For since to-day the political intelligence is (both upon Left and Right) far too perfectly organised to allow any effective interference on the part of a too dangerously intelligent man, it is possible for such a man to recognise the second-rate character of all that is in its essence 'political,' and without regret to leave such activities to those for whom they are the breath of life."[36] It was not until the mid-1930s that Lewis was able to see how ignorant he had been about the real significance of Fascism's and Communism's insistence on control of all political processes. *Left Wings Over Europe* (1936) (B&M Cat. 37) was, he wrote, "from cover to cover, one long plea against the centralization of power [...] Centralized power – when it is human power – is for me, politically, the greatest evil it is possible to imagine."[37]

The change that occurred in Lewis's thinking from the late 1930s onwards can be traced in such key texts as *The Vulgar Streak* (1941) (B&M Cat. 47), *Anglosaxony: A League that Works* (1941) (B&M Cat. 46), *America and Cosmic Man* (1948) (B&M Cat. 48), *Rude Assignment* (1950) (B&M Cat. 50), and *The Writer and the Absolute* (1952) (B&M Cat. 53). Lewis became a convinced democrat, supported the post-war Labour government's plans for nationalisation, and urged the creation of a loose federalist world-state that would do away with class distinctions and would erode racial differences. Despite democracy's imperfections, it was the best political system available and was to be defended against the "religion" of Fascism, with its worship of soil and nation, and its predilection for violent geographical expansionism. Lewis argued that democracy was central to the Anglo-Saxon heritage and was connected to England's seafaring past. In contrast to the Fascist emphasis on land, democracy should celebrate the ocean-wave, "with all that [it] takes with it of elasticity and freedom, of intangibility and in a sense rootlessness."[38]

This argument took Lewis back to views he had already put forward in the first issue of *Blast*. By suggesting that democracy was cosmopolitan and internationalist, Lewis was linking it to his earliest account of abstraction and universalism:

The English character is based on the Sea.

The particular qualities and characteristics that
The sea always engenders in men are those
That are, among the many diagnostics of our
Race, the most fundamentally English.

That unexpected universality as well, found in
The completest English artists, is due to this.[39]

Lewis held that, although artists could never be fully detached, they had the ability to combine personal vision with a paradoxical self-effacement that permitted them to attain something very like a "universal" standpoint. This depended on the artist's "remarkable capacity for non-identity, or abstraction," an ability to go beyond the self, which then enabled the artist to act as "a sort of guardian of the public stock of truth, of the purest objectivity."[40] Towards the end of his life, Lewis was perhaps above all concerned with what he saw as the etiolation of the public sphere. In keeping with his belief that writers and artists should always be politically non-aligned, he insisted on the need for society to "strengthen the organization of what used to be called the 'Republic of Letters'," which he saw as "the last precarious refuge of the civilized intelligence."[41] This was a worthy aim, but one that was closely bound up with a sense of defeat. The modernist arts of which Lewis had been such a powerful exponent had failed to deliver on their emancipatory promises, as had radical political solutions to the problems of twentieth-century modernity. Lewis's defence of a republic of letters with a vibrant role to play in the public sphere was in keeping with his view of the artist's necessary autonomy, but it was also an admission that artists were powerless to intervene in or to mould political life. If modernist artists had been the prophets of "a 'great age' that has not 'come off'," then it is scarcely surprising that Lewis in the 1950s came to stress his "growing indifference as to those events upon which I can exercise no more influence than a fly by its buzzing."[42]

NOTES

1. Wyndham Lewis, *Blasting and Bombardiering: Autobiography (1914–1926)* (1937) (London: John Calder, 1982), p. 339.
2. Wyndham Lewis, *Rude Assignment: A Narrative of my Career Up-to-date* (London: Hutchinson: 1950), p. 61.
3. *Blasting and Bombardiering*, p. 15.
4. Richard Humphreys, *Futurism* (London: Tate Gallery, 2003), p. 56.
5. Wyndham Lewis, "The Cubist Room," *The Egoist* (1 January 1914), pp. 8–9, p. 9.
6. *Rude Assignment*, p. 125.
7. Wyndham Lewis, "A Review of Contemporary Art," *Blast*, No. 2 (July 1915), p. 45.
8. Wyndham Lewis, *The Caliph's Design: Architects! Where is Your Vortex?* (1919). Rprt. ed. Paul Edwards (Santa Barbara: Black Sparrow Press, 1986), p. 12.
9. Ibid., pp. 33 and 34.
10. Ibid., p. 25.
11. Ibid., p. 57.
12. Ibid., p. 77 and pp. 75–6.
13. Wyndham Lewis, *The Art of Being Ruled* (1926). Rprt. ed. Reed Way Dasenbrock (Santa Rosa: Black Sparrow Press, 1989), p. 106. See also Theodor Adorno and Max Horkheimer, *Dialectic of Enlightenment*. Trans. John Cumming (London: Verso, 1979).
14. Wyndham Lewis, *The Diabolical Principle and the Dithyrambic Spectator* (London: Chatto and Windus, 1931), pp. 82–83
15. *The Art of Being Ruled*, p. 125.
16. Ibid., p. 375.
17. Wyndham Lewis, *Men Without Art* (1934). Rprt. ed. Seamus Cooney (Santa Rosa: Black Sparrow Press, 1987), p. 204.
18. Wyndham Lewis, *Time and Western Man* (1927). Rprt. ed. Paul Edwards (Santa Rosa: Black Sparrow Press, 1993), p. xi.
19. Alan Munton, "The Politics of Wyndham Lewis," *PN Review* 1 (March 1976), pp. 34–39, p. 38.
20. *The Diabolical Principle and the Dithyrambic Spectator*, p. 134.
21. Wyndham Lewis, "Physics of the Not Self" (1932). *Collected Poems and Plays*. Ed. Alan Munton (Manchester: Carcanet, 1979), p. 198.
22. Wyndham Lewis, "'Detachment' and the Fictionist" (1934). Rprt. *Creatures of Habit and Creatures of Change: Essays on Art, Literature and Society 1914–1956*. Ed. Paul Edwards (Santa Rosa: Black Sparrow Press, 1989): pp. 214–30, p. 227. For further reflections on the implications of "detachment," a term Lewis accepted only in a qualified way, see Lewis, *Rude Assignment*, pp. 69–72.
23. *Rude Assignment*, p. 91.
24. *The Art of Being Ruled*, p. 75.
25. Ibid., p. 320 and p. 321.
26. Ibid., p. 89.
27. Ibid., p. 321.
28. Ibid.
29. See his claim that "Marx, with his dreadful plan for helot states, is *not* the only solution [...] Fascism is at least a better solution than that [...] Fascism might be a very good solution indeed. But *any* solution would be better than Marx." Wyndham Lewis, *Count Your Dead: They Are Alive! Or, A New War in the Making* (London: Chatto and Windus, 1937), p. 83.
30. Wyndham Lewis, *Hitler* (London: Chatto and Windus, 1931), p. 85 and p. 108.
31. Ibid., p. 143. Lewis introduced the book by remarking that he offered his articles on the subject "as an exponent – not as critic nor yet as advocate – of German Nationalsocialism, or Hitlerism" (p. 4).
32. Ibid., p. 143.
33. Wyndham Lewis, *The Hitler Cult* (London: Dent, 1939), p. 254.
34. Ibid., p. 255.
35. Letter to Eric Kennington, June 1942, in Wyndham Lewis, *The Letters of Wyndham Lewis*. Ed. W.K. Rose (London: Methuen, 1963), p. 324. The phrase "le genre humain" comes from the "Internationale."
36. Wyndham Lewis, *The Enemy*, No. 3 (1929), p. 82.
37. Wyndham Lewis, *Left Wings Over Europe: Or, How to Make a War about Nothing* (London: Jonathan Cape, 1936), p. 16.
38. Wyndham Lewis, *Anglosaxony: A League that Works* (Toronto: Ryerson Press, 1941), p. 50.
39. Wyndham Lewis, *Blast*, No. 1 (June 1914), p. 35.
40. Wyndham Lewis, *The Writer and the Absolute* (London: Methuen, 1952), p. 20 and p. 12. See also Lewis, *Letters*, p. 289 and p. 310.
41. *The Writer and the Absolute*, pp. 52–53.
42. *Blasting and Bombardiering*, p. 256; *Rude Assignment*, p. 81.

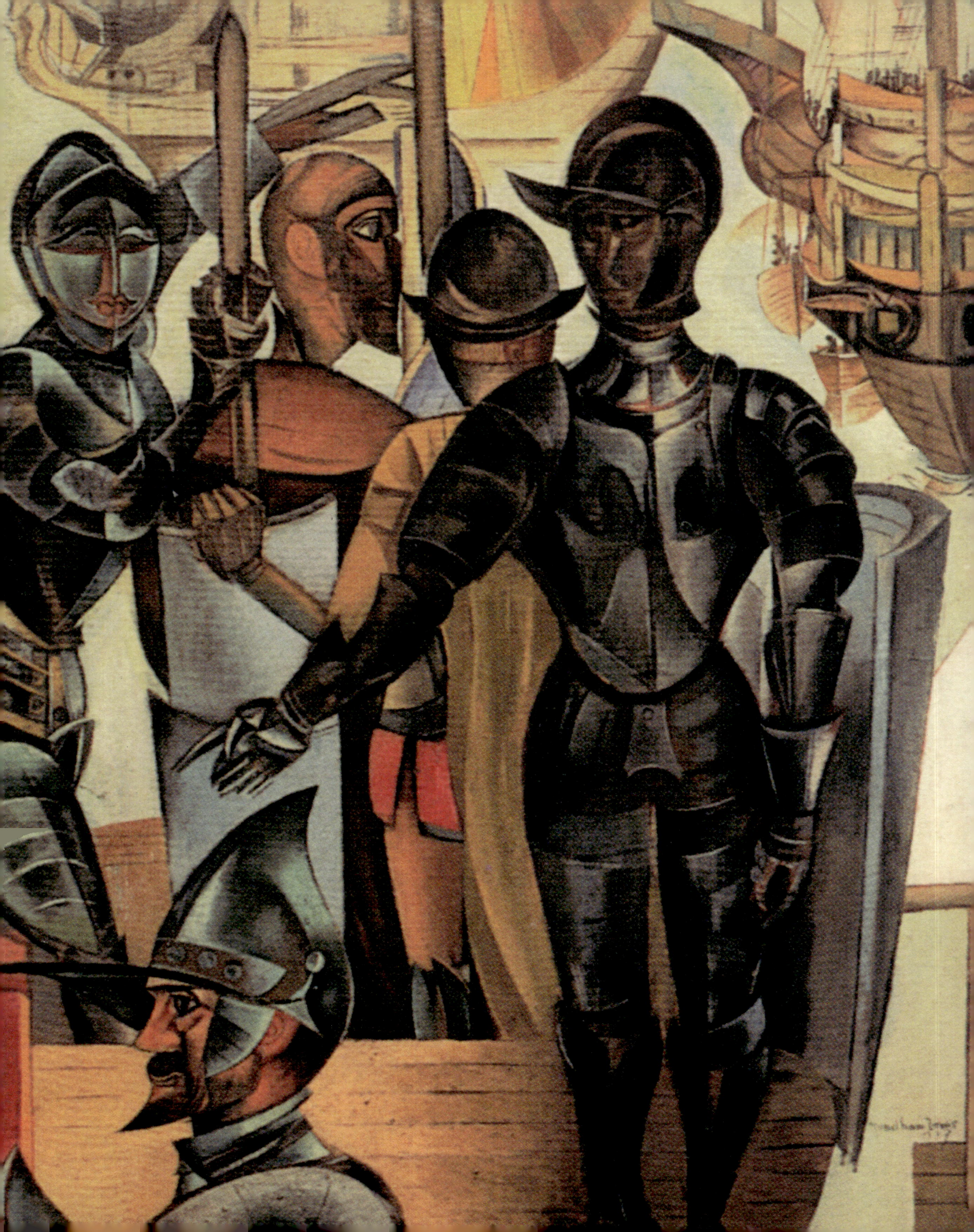

WYNDHAM LEWIS AND SPAIN: ANARCHISM, CLICHÉ, IMAGE

Alan Munton

The Armada, 1937.
Vancouver Art Gallery

IN 1903, AGED 20, WYNDHAM LEWIS TRAVELLED TO MADRID

and went to the Prado, where he copied the work of Goya. His admiration for Francisco Goya (1746–1828) never left him, and in later decades *The Disasters of War* (1810–15) became for him a powerful representation of the folly of war; he accepted entirely Goya's satire upon "this jagged horror."[1] In 1908, Lewis again visited Spain, but on this occasion he travelled to the margins rather than to the centre – to Vigo, by way of San Sebastián and León. There he found a room in the Calle Real, where the owner Doña Elvira was, in Lewis's vivid description, "a small, stone woman with dark red arms and face, and, in some way, like one of Velazquez' dwarfs."[2] Here, the young Lewis sees the actual in terms of the painterly, and brings with him, no doubt from *Las Meninas* (1656) by Diego Velázquez, a memory of the Prado. In this report of travel, entitled "A Spanish Household," he includes a lengthy account of a Castilian painter called Don Ramiro who is really no painter at all. He is a commercial illustrator of plates, palettes and tambourines who repeats three pictures endlessly: a Moorish palace reflected in a stream, boats on the sea, and a water-mill in the mountains. Yet Lewis shows affection for this absurd figure, animating him comically as he jerks about to look at the work from a new angle, in order to "startle himself into a freshness of vision."[3] Lewis published this report on Spain in 1910, at the moment when he was about to engage with Cubism and Futurism, and create for British art a freshness of vision that would contribute significantly to European modernism.

For Lewis, sexuality and Spain are mixed up in significant ways. In his travel sketch about Vigo, he gives the name La Flora to Doña Elvira's servant, "a tall, lithe and handsome fisher-girl" who – it is very likely – passed to Lewis the gonorrhoea that was to trouble him for decades. He told his friend the painter Augustus John (1878–1961), who wrote ironically in reply: "Is this Spanish frankness?"[4] In 1936 he wrote: "*All* my juvenile inattentiveness to the dictates of sex hygiene came home to roost" at that time.[5] In July 1934, Lewis took a holiday in France and Spain in order to recover from operations necessary to deal with the long-term consequences of this early gonorrhoeal infection. He went to the Pyrénées-Orientales, just to the east of Andorra, and visited Bourg-Madame and Font-Romeu in France, and Puigcerdá just over the border in Spain. All these places turn up, lightly disguised as Bourg-le-Comte, Pont-Romeu, and Puigmoro, in the concluding Part VII of *The Revenge for Love* (1937) (B&M Cat. 39).[6] Some 40 years after his first visit, Lewis told the American art critic James Johnson Sweeney (1900–86): "I know that when I was in Spain as a student some priests in my pension discussed very learnedly about the local brothels and, unsolicited, strongly recommended one as being the cleanest. That seems the healthy attitude."[7]

On that second visit, Lewis left Vigo on 18 June 1910, and travelled by sea to Cherbourg and from there into Brittany, where he "lived in a state of copulation with a wandering Spanish romi," according to John.[8] Lewis had left his German mistress, Ida Vendel, in Paris, so that out of the three known relationships entered into between 1905 and 1908, two were with Spanish women. By his own admission, Lewis was deeply naive during his 20s, and wrote in his late autobiography *Rude Assignment* (1950) (B&M Cat. 50) that he remained "congealed in a kind of cryptic immaturity," his social relations "primitive."[9] It is an amusing aspect of Lewis's "primitive" personal relations that on an unused part of a letter from John, he should have written out, in columns, "the complete conjugation of the Spanish verb AMAR: to love."[10]

Nevertheless, Lewis was becoming a European at this time, and Spain was only a part of his experience. This Canadian, who had already lived in the USA as a child, made extended visits to Paris and Germany, and shorter ones to Holland. Back in Paris in 1908, he ended his relationship with Ida Vendel, and in December returned more or less permanently to London. This story may explain a remark that the American poet Ezra Pound (1885–1972) made about Lewis in 1918: that he was "a collection of races."[11] Here, "race" means nationality, and one of the available "races," evidently, was Spanish. This in turn may explain why in 1905 John could make a *Portrait of Percy Wyndham Lewis* (**Fig. 1**) that showed him as a Spaniard. The picture is dramatic and Lewis's long hair is painted a very deliberate black. The supposed Spanish attributes of a dark and smouldering intensity, allied with a well-judged narrow moustache, are present to tell us that this is "a Castilian man." Yet it is also recognisably the detached and immature Lewis. With a coat over his arm (and the arm painted "wrong"), he is about to move away, the traveller that he was in these years. John has imposed upon Lewis's de-nationalised identity what other images told him were the supposed national characteristics of a Spanish male. He has concocted around Lewis a mixture of personal reality and Spanish cliché that will soon recur in Lewis's own work.

The Spanish Anarchist

"'*Mi novia es mas bonita que la tuya*" – thus La Flora, quoting to the narrator of "A Spanish Household" the words that concluded an argument that caused the death of a young

Fig. 1.
Augustus Edwin John, *Wyndham Lewis,* 1905. Private collection (Cat. 207)

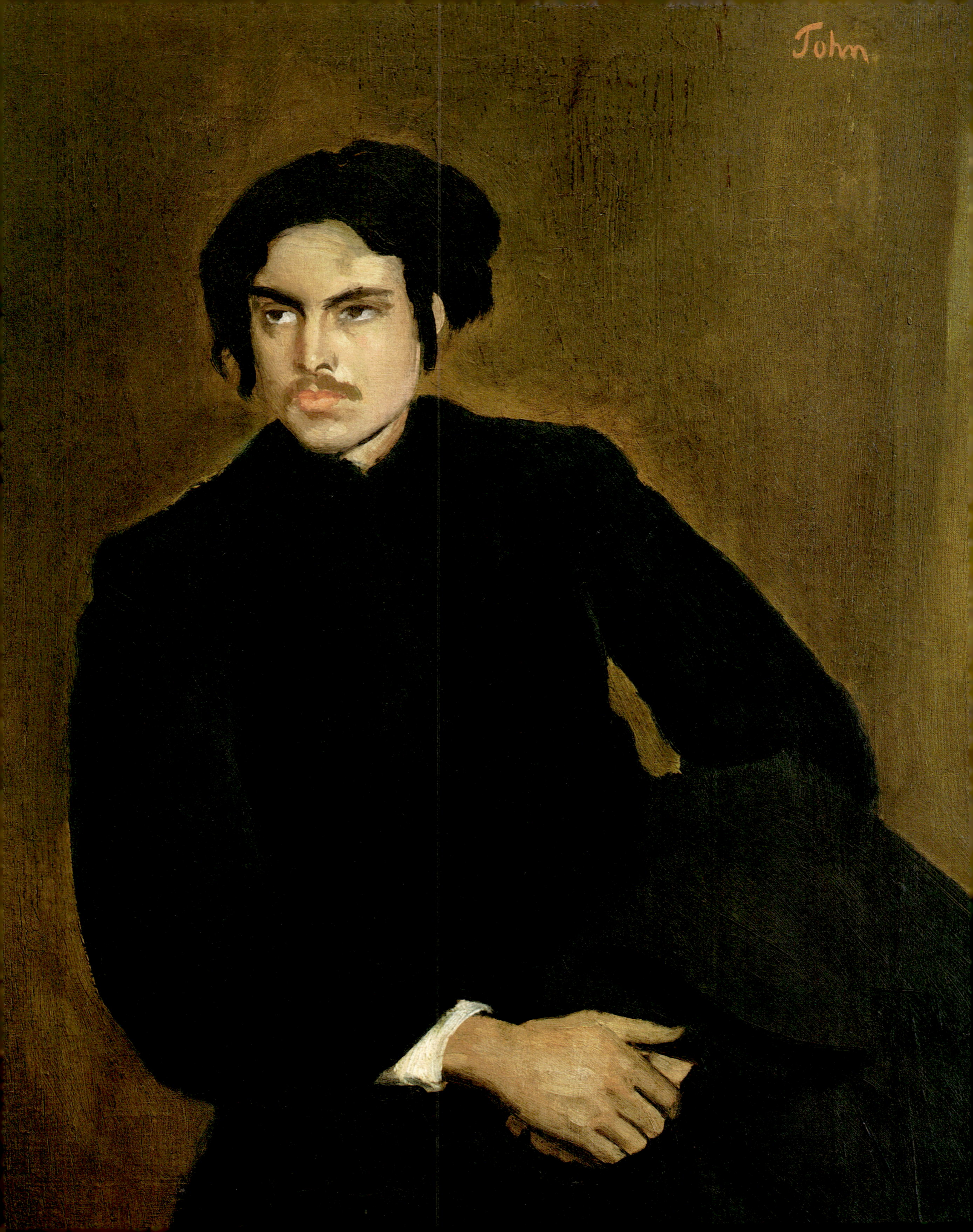
John.

man, probably at the hands of her own *novio*. The *carabineros* (Lewis's word) have taken him to prison, "his elbows tied behind his back and his shirt blood-stained."[12] The same incident recurs in another Spanish story of about 1910, "Crossing the Frontier." The narrator crosses into Spain by train at Hendaye and talks with a young man who appears not to have a ticket. At San Sebastián, the narrator alights, but the young Spaniard has disappeared. Later in the day, he encounters him in the street, "conducted [...] by a man in plain clothes with a large stick."[13] The narrator notices that "Neither of them was very explicit about his crime,"[14] and this leads to a double reflection:

As I returned to my hotel, I thought at first that he had been merely crossing the frontier without a ticket. But he may have been a young man who had exiled himself after some unlawful proceeding or other, and was now entering his country again to give himself up.[15]

This political interpretation is plausible. On the train the young man had discussed the Ley de Terrorismo proposed in January 1908 by Antonio Maura (1853–1925), the conservative prime minister. This law – which was not passed – was specifically directed against anarchists, and would have allowed the authorities to close anarchist centres and newspapers, and deport anarchists. Lewis's narrator reports the young man as saying "that if this law were passed the whole country would be in revolt on the following day."[16] Only an anarchist, I suggest, would offer such an argument.

This incident provoked Lewis's earliest political thought. That anarchism should be the political theory he first encounters is significant, for this is a decentralist politics experienced from below, and quite different from the authoritarian politics he later adopted for a period in the 1930s. We are not, of course, concerned with bomb-throwing anarchism, though the proposed Ley de Terrorismo attempted to make this connection; Maura's primary purpose was to prevent the circulation of dissident ideas in political organisations and in newspapers. Anarchism remained of permanent interest to Lewis until the end of his career, and its next manifestation was the extensive reading of Pierre-Joseph Proudhon's (1809–65) work that he began during the First World War, and which emerged most fully in *The Art of Being Ruled* (B&M Cat. 10), published in 1926. Lewis understood well the decentralist federal structures that Proudhon proposed in order to counter the centralism of a nascent capitalism. Lewis also understood the opposition between Karl Marx (1818–83) and Proudhon when in 1939 he wrote that he "favour[ed] always Proudhon rather than Marx, as a political thinker."[17] Yet it is Spain, not France, that gave Lewis his first intimation of anarchism.

Lewis also experienced daily life as anarchic. He describes his earliest experiences among exiled Russian students in Paris, and "alcoholic fishermen" in Brittany, as "an anarchist material." But there is some control, for "the ring-master of this circus" is a fictional character called Ker-Orr,[18] who is the protagonist of another story set in Spain, the seminal "A Soldier of Humour," which (like the other stories) although it existed by 1911, was not published until 1917, and was then revised for *The Wild Body* collection of 1927 (B&M Cat. 17).[19] "A Soldier of Humour" shows the narrator taking Lewis's 1908 route into Spain, by train from Bayonne to Venta de Baños, then to Palencia and León, and finally to "Pontaisandra," which is Vigo, attracting part of the name of Pontevedra, a little to the north. Here a psychological drama takes place. Pine (or Ker-Orr in the later version) is humiliated by M. de Valmore, a Frenchman from the Midi who thinks of himself as an American – he has visited New York and picked up the accent – but who is angered by the narrator's refusal to play his American game: this Englishman insists upon speaking French. In revenge, the narrator recruits three American friends to first make friends with M. de Valmore at the café Pelayo, encourage him in his "American" delusion, and then invite Ker-Orr to join them as a friend. De Valmore shakes physically and collapses psychologically: "[A]s the scope of my victory dawned upon him, his personal mortification assumed the proportions of a national calamity."[20] This is the text of origin for the complex encounters involving psychological warfare that will mark all Lewis's important work, from *Tarr* in 1918 (B&M Cat. 5), through *The Revenge for Love* in 1937, to *Self Condemned* (B&M Cat. 54) in 1954. Spain, again, is the place and the provocation.

"A Soldier of Humour" is also where Lewis begins to generalise about Spain: "Spain is an overflow of sombreness. 'Africa commences at the Pyrenees'." These are the first words of the story and they define Spain as Other, as excessive, as not-Europe. The quotation –variously attributed to Napoleon Bonaparte (1769–1821) or to Alexandre Dumas (1802–70) – is a cultural insult with a racial component whose history of (mis)use extends to the present. Spain is also the site of invasion, where "primitive gallic chivalry" was enacted, so that only with the death at Ronscevalles of Roland (one of Charlemagne's invading commanders) in 778 does the Spanish landscape become "historic." Into this dependent landscape bursts Ker-Orr, a barbarian who specialises in laughter, "uncivilized [...] laughter,"[21] and who will engage in "a *quarrel of humour*" with M. de Valmore that takes place in hotel restaurants and on café terraces no different from those of Paris.[22] Ker-Orr brings to Spain a contemporary psychology of comic opposition and adroit self-recovery that dissolves any remaining "sombreness" into triumphant laughter. Lewis's story first adopts, and then adapts, and finally rejects, the clichés about Spain.

After this, it is some decades before the anarchist theme returns. Lewis's great political novel *The Revenge for Love* concerns the years *preceding* the Spanish Civil War. Begun in 1934, it was published on 20 May 1937, just over three weeks after the bombing of Guernica on 27 April. This was not good timing for a satire upon Communism and anarchism, but the novel's reputation has risen in recent years as it becomes apparent that it is about the *way* in which ideas are held, and – with regard to the character Margot, the woman who loves too much – that it is feminist. The novel begins and ends in different Spanish prisons, with the five intervening parts set in London, amongst young Communists and artistic bohemians. The opening section shows an English Communist, plump Percy Hardcaster, awaiting trial in a prison in Andalusia, in the company of a dozen Spanish *sindicalistas*. The atmosphere is electric with tension, since their jailer, a shrewd ex-Civil Guard called Alvaro, has discovered that Hardcaster intends to escape. A peasant girl has brought a message in a basket of food with a false bottom, and this shows that the Catalan guard, Serafín, has been bribed to assist. When the attempt takes place, Alvaro follows, shoots Hardcaster in the leg and kills Serafín. Back in London, his amputated leg evidence of political commitment, Hardcaster becomes an object of veneration for the young Communists.

This narrative is energised politically by the conversation between Alvaro and Percy, and the exchanges between the Spanish Communists and the Englishman whom they admire: "'Percy, chico, ven acá!'."[23] For Alvaro, Percy and the Communists are "*Mala gente* of the pestiferous Red Syndics";[24] to the Communist prisoners Percy is the "courteous communist from the land of Wellington and foster-land of Karl Marx, established among the dago descendants of Ferrer."[25] That is what Alvaro might be expected to think, but the second example (with its attempt to neutralise "dago") is more complex. Wellington helped remove the French from Spain, and held Madrid in 1812, when Goya painted him: this takes us back to Lewis's admiration for Goya, which began at the Prado in 1902. The allusion to the anarchist Francisco Ferrer (1859–1909), cruelly executed in 1909 as a consequence of the Tragic Week (la Semana Trágica) and Maura's anti-anarchist policy, returns us to the story of the young anarchist on the train. But each allusion also has a political content valid for the mid-1930s. If Wellington could free Spain, why should not a later generation of British arrivals be welcomed? (This is an ironic prolepsis of the International Brigades.) To mention Ferrer as an antecedent of Spanish Communism suggests how socialist politics in Spain was influenced by its anarchist antecedents.

In the latter sections of this Spanish episode, Lewis satirises the divisions that arise between Communists, who are part of a movement ostensibly unified, but notoriously fractious –particularly when Trotskyists are involved. During a hospital ward conversation with Virgilio Muntán, a Basque Communist, differences open up on several fronts. Class causes problems, for Hardcaster recognises an administrative caste within Soviet Communism, whereas Virgilio wants no classes at all. Virgilio declares that the English are essentially bourgeois and a nation of shopkeepers, and draws the conclusion: "You cannot understand the Spanish,"[26] and so nationalism breaks into the debate. Miguel de Cervantes (1547–1616) is invoked when Hardcaster alleges Virgilio is "climbing up on to our Rozinante, are we not?," in what he implies is a nationalist – not internationalist – strategy. Virgilio suddenly accuses Hardcaster of being a Fascist: "You have not the communist mind,"[27] for his idea of revolution is "Administrative."[28] Percy is unsettled by this barrage and replies by invoking anarchism: "'You are an Anarchist at bottom, Virgilio,' said Percy at last in a palpably lame counter-attack. 'That is what you are. It is the old, old Spanish difficulty – you can never get away from it. The Spaniard spoils his socialism with his anarchism'."[29] Virgilio replies: "The Spaniard desires freedom. Not a new sort of slavery. He has had enough masters."[30] We are back at the opening of "A Soldier of Humour," where Spain was the site "on which primitive gallic chivalry played its most brilliant games,"[31] and when only the invasion of Charlemagne brought Spain into history. But we are also very much beyond those introductory simplicities, because Virgilio's defence is valid for the present in which he speaks. After all, what exactly is Hardcaster doing there? (He is based on Ralph Bates (1899–2000), the English novelist and author of *Lean Men: An Episode in A Life* (1934), who was a bilingual English Communist active in Spain long before the Civil War – and Lewis knew Bates.) In this case, the proleptic irony is the arrival during the Civil War of Italian soldiers and German bombers, regrettably effective foreign "masters." The exchanges between Percy and Virgilio show the decay of radical political discourse into "the desiccated paths of communist controversy."[32] Lewis calls these Communists *sindicalistas*, a term that reminds the reader of syndics, meaning political organisation around the workplace, or in a trade, and an example of the decentralised forms of organisation favoured by anarchist theory. The only point that Percy can make successfully against Virgilio is to accuse him of being an anarchist. In Lewis's Spain it always comes back to that.

Getting Spain Wrong

Lewis took care to make sure that the Spanish spoken in *The Revenge for Love* was accurate;[33] equally, the politics are substantially real, if satirically presented. The same cannot be said of the politics in Lewis's anti-war polemic, *Count Your Dead: They Are Alive!* (B&M Cat. 38), published on 26 April 1937, just under a month before *The Revenge for Love*, but conceived and begun much later, in 1936. Here, Lewis uses a ponderous irony to undermine support for the elected Spanish government. He settles on the claim that in the February election of 1936, which brought Manuel Azaña's (1880–1940) republican government to power, a majority actually voted against the republic: "still a majority of the Spanish people voted for the principles so vilely upheld by the unmentionable Franco."[34] This is untrue. As Anthony Beevor has written, "the Popular Front had won by over 150,000 votes," and the Falangists (who were, or were to be, closest to Franco, and achieved no seats) "received only 42,000 votes out of nearly ten million throughout Spain."[35] Not only were the figures much disputed by the right, but also Lewis failed to recognise that Spain's electoral system favoured not individual parties but alliances and coalitions, such as the Popular Front or the National Front. As Hugh Thomas points out, "votes cast [for individual parties within a coalition] cannot be given," only the seats gained.[36] Lewis

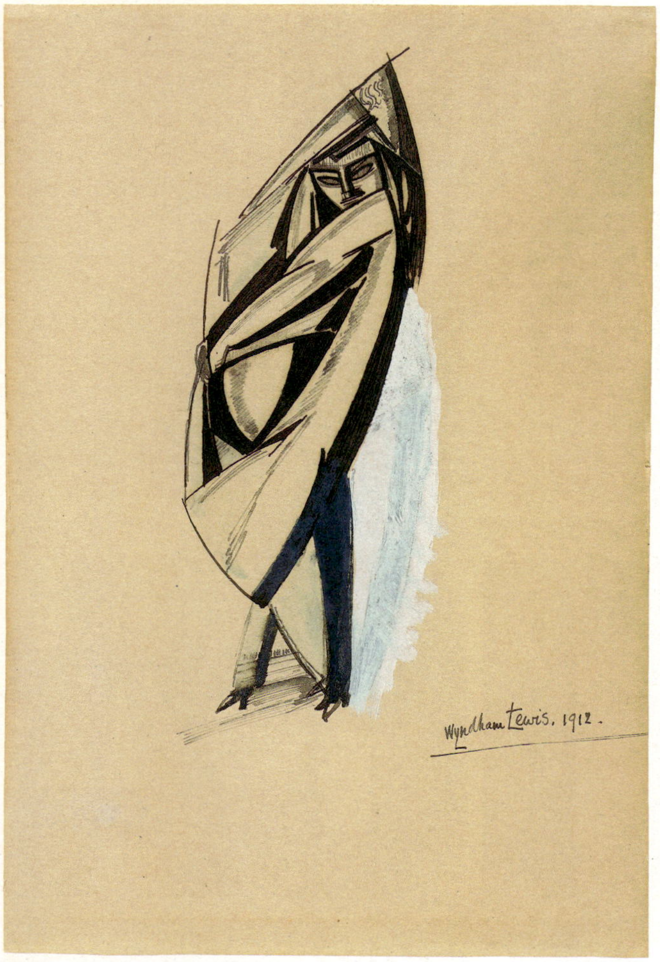

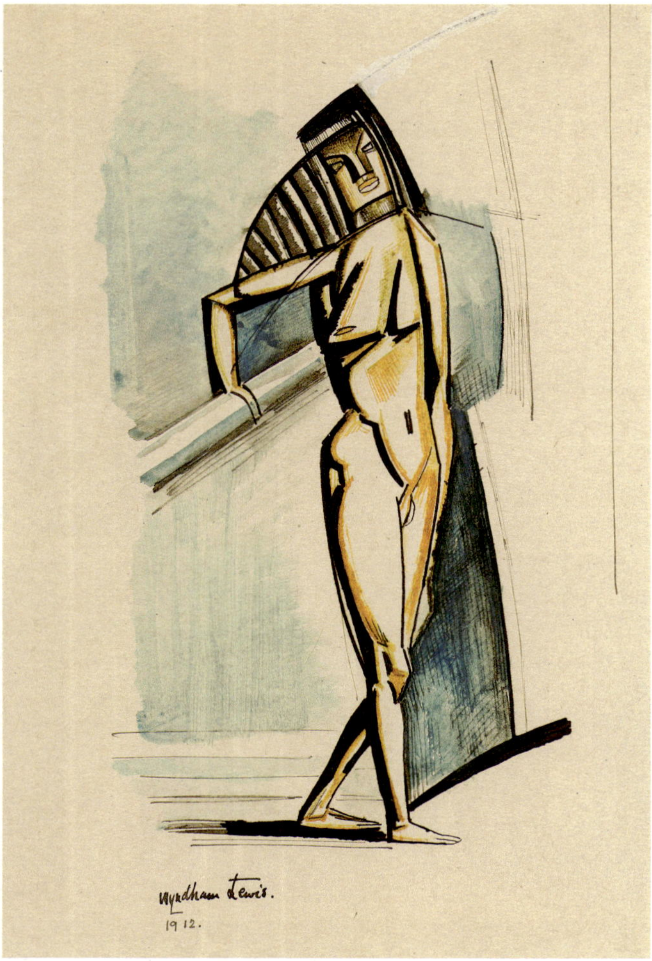

Fig. 2.
Figure (Spanish Woman), 1912. Wyndham Lewis Memorial Trust, London. G. and V. Lane Collection (Cat. 22)

Fig. 3.
Standing Figure, 1912. The Museum of Modern Art, NY

could not have known what he claims to know about the voting and no doubt he got his "information" from a right-wing newspaper, perhaps J.L. Garvin's (1868–1947) *Observer*.

Lewis's thinking was characteristically dualist, but Spain was not a two-party state, as he seems to believe. Unfortunately, he makes this assertion about actual votes repeatedly in *Count Your Dead*. Lewis works through a spokesman called Launcelot Nidwit (*nitwit* in English is equivalent to *tonto* in Spanish), whom he can keep at an ironic distance yet still partly endorse. So Nidwit can write both that "Franco is a dastardly rebel. [...] I hold no brief for Franco,"[37] and on the next page, "In spite of all this Franco *has* a case."[38] But there was no such electoral case. Lewis's confusing ironies are not to his credit. One feels that he knows very well the truth of the situation, yet is impelled to use irony to destabilise it. He cannot accept the legitimacy of the elected government,[39] and jeers at the International Brigades.[40] The only creditable aspect of his attitude towards Spain is that he eventually repudiated it. His general position on the dictators changed sharply in 1938 and in 1939 he acknowledged that force should have been used against Franco, which had from the outset been the position of the political Left .[41] In 1944 he wrote to a friend indicating that he had changed his mind. Mary Campbell was the Catholic wife of Lewis's long-time friend Roy Campbell (1901–57), the poet. Campbell associated himself with the *requetés*, or authoritarian Carlists, and wrote a vicious

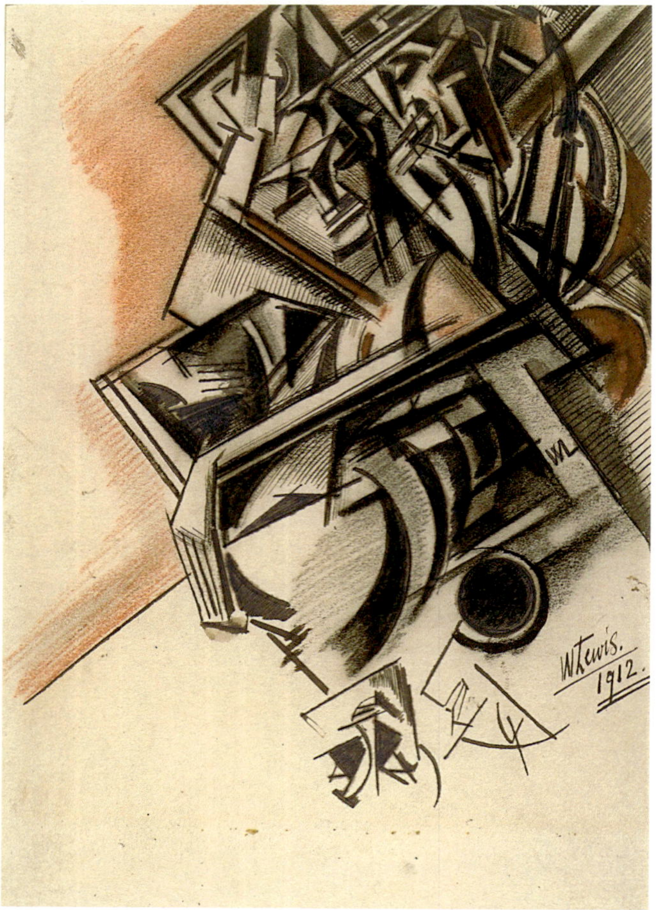

Fig. 4.
The Courtesan, 1912. Victoria and Albert Museum, London (Cat. 23)

pro-Franco and anti-Republican satirical poem entitled *Flowering Rifle* (1939). From Canada, Lewis wrote to Mary: "The best Catholic opinion now – and I speak from very near the horses [*sic*] mouth – is that the requetés were on the wrong side in the land of the flowering rifle."[42] This is heavily coded, but it means that Campbell was wrong to support Franco. The "horses mouth" refers to the Basilian Fathers at Assumption College in Windsor, Ontario, where Lewis was teaching. It was these liberal Catholics who at last confirmed to Lewis that he was wrong about Franco.

From Spain to Vorticism

Lewis executed four drawings between 1912 and 1914 that are distinctively Spanish in content. The clue to the Spanishness of *Figure (Spanish Woman)* of 1912 (Cat. 22) (**Fig. 2**) is the hint of a mantilla above the head, but it also has other characteristics, notably the tiny feet and the hint of floor and skirting board, that are shared by other drawings in this group. Also of 1912 is *The Courtesan* (Cat. 23) (**Fig. 4**), in which the seated woman turns to her pimp, who whispers in her ear. An elaborate hat, or headdress, identifies her as Spanish. From 1914 comes *Spanish Dance* (**Fig. 3**), in which the woman's headdress has become strangely elaborate, but is not sufficiently intimidating to put off the man, who takes the first step in the dance. Finally, there is the mis-named *Abstract Composition*, usually assigned to ca. 1914. It too shows a figure with tiny feet and again there is an elaborate headdress, heavily abstracted, but clearly Spanish. All these figures are noticeably static. The *Spanish Woman* (Cat. 22) may be a dancer, but she has not yet moved (in fact she may be pushing forward her stomach, or pregnant), and in *Spanish Dance* the woman stands still. The headdress in *Abstract Composition* is so highly developed that one feels the figure might fall over backwards. *The Courtesan* confirms something implicit in all these designs: a tension that precedes the sexual moment. These works express the sexualised Spain that Lewis had experienced in 1903 and 1908.

The Spanish drawings show Lewis taking the route towards his greatest early success, Vorticism. The visual characteristics of this movement were stasis, tension and detachment. There is no Futurist flow in them, or lines of force; instead, Vorticist energy is internalised in the diagonals that actually constitute the image. If we compare the Spanish drawings with those based on Lewis's visits to Brittany, we find explicit sexual violence in the staring male eyes and passionate embrace of the *Study for Kermesse* (1912) (Cat. 19), while the couples embracing in *Lovers* (1912) (Cat. 20) may, as Lisa Tickner has argued, derive from the aggressive Apache dances (expressing *voyou* Parisian street violence) popular at the time.[43] We can say that the wild and psychologically-disturbed Breton world is post-Futurist, while the sexualised Spanish drawings are post-Cubist and pre-Vorticist. The vital French image was superseded by the static Spanish image and it was the latter that led directly to Vorticism.

The 1930s: Politics and Imagination

The next substantial Spanish reference in Lewis's work occurs nearly 20 years later, in 1933, when he paints *The Betrothal of the Matador* (Cat. 152) (**Fig. 5**). It is difficult to understand why he should turn to such an improbable subject, except that in the 1930s his work entered a phase of unexpected imaginative structures. Here, the diffident matador stands between a figure that Paul Edwards identifies as "his agent,"[44] and the fiancée he (the agent) has brought in from the local brothel – the red light is conspicuous on the right. Edwards's reading is persuasive: the matador has a hat of the kind Lewis wore, so that "this painting imagines Lewis as a heroic naïf in a different life."[45] Significantly, the figures are superimposed on an "intricate 'Vorticist' design" of buildings whose flat planes make no architectural sense.[46] This Spain is post-Vorticist, as the early Spanish drawings had been pre-Vorticist. If we consider an earlier state of the painting, in which the fiancée (or prostitute) has realistically rendered naked breasts, then we have further evidence that in Lewis's imagination Spain was the site of the erotic, of what precedes the sexual moment.

The painting entitled *The Surrender of Barcelona* (1936–37) (Cat. 162) (**Fig. 6**) is Lewis's final and most important visual statement about Spain. It is political and obscurely so. "I set out," he said, "to paint a Fourteenth Century [*sic*] scene as I should do it could I be transported there, without too great a change in the time adjustment involved."[47] Lewis means fifteenth century, since the painting refers to a significant event of 1472, when King John II of Aragon (1397–1479) negotiated the surrender of Barcelona after a siege. (His son, Ferdinand (1452–1516), had married Isabella of Castile (1451–1504)

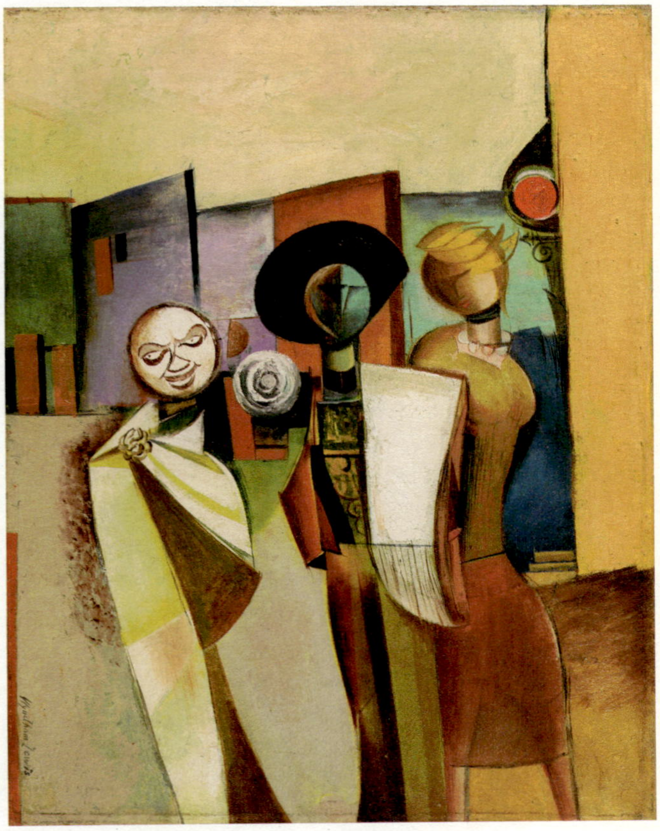

Fig. 5.
The Betrothal of the Matador, 1933. Wyndham Lewis Memorial Trust, London (Cat. 152)

in 1469, so this was an event in the eventual unification of Spain.) Lewis's source was William H. Prescott's (1796–1859) *History of the Reign of Ferdinand and Isabella the Catholic*, and when he read Prescott's conclusion that "Thus ended this long, disastrous civil war," he would have been reminded of another civil war that had broken out in July 1936, the year in which he began the painting. Prescott describes how King John II "made his entrance to the city by the gate of St Anthony, mounted on a white charger" and how he encountered "so many pallid countenances and emaciated figures" suffering from famine.[48]

In Lewis's picture, the hindquarters of a bay horse can be seen entering the scene from the centre right, accompanied by lancers on foot. The head of its rider is a blank, but has a confident tilt: this, surely, is the city's new ruler. But we do not see any starving inhabitants; rather, the city is populated by military figures, on foot and on horseback, who casually occupy the city. They have hanged a man from a structure that rather resembles a sculpture by Richard Serra (b. 1939), and certainly an object as unimaginable in 1472 as are the "Vorticist" buildings of *The Betrothal of the Matador*. The two works are related, therefore, in being what Lewis called "realist fantasies."[49] The later painting was first entitled *The Siege of Barcelona*, although it fantasises and modernises the immediate aftermath of the surrender of 1472. It became *The Surrender of Barcelona* after the Nationalists occupied Barcelona on 26 January 1939. A massacre ensued in the city.

Writing in "the early months of the year 1939,"[50] Lewis declared that "as the Catalan sun sets – in human blood, alas! As Barcelona falls, and the phalangist standard is unfurled there, we can all see that that is the end of a chapter – of painting, among other things."[51] The artists of Barcelona (and Lewis always mistook Picasso for a Catalan) would no longer be able to fertilise that greater artistic centre, Paris. Worse still, the "highly experimental" art advocated by Lewis since 1914 – Vorticism, Cubism, and Expressionism in particular – were finished. They had "presupposed a new human ethos" that had not emerged, though had it done so it would not have been a feeling "of a merely national order".[52] The fall of Barcelona was, in political terms, a victory for nationalism of the most brutal kind, but what it also signified for Lewis was the failure of the modern movement in art and design.

What, finally, do we see when looking at *The Surrender of Barcelona*? We see a remarkable number of verticals – mostly in buildings that resemble the towers of Bologna more than they do Barcelona – and no diagonals. This is not a post-Vorticist work, but something new emerging from a modernist representation of something old. As Andrew Causey perceptively observed, at the square window halfway up the central tower there sits an artist at his easel.[53] Consider what this artist sees: the casual, assured occupation by an enemy, a hanged man opposite, and – his distance, our foreground – a line of armoured figures. These we have met before, in *The Revenge for Love*. As Victor, Percy and Margot stare across from France into Spain, they see the police post lit from within, so that "the cloaked figures of the frontier guards had become portentous medieval silhouettes."[54] Similarly, the armoured men in the painting portend no good for the artist in his tower, which is so far from being an ivory tower that it gives him a unique vantage-point from which to observe the violent, arrogant, casual, but power-laden occupation that is being organised around him.

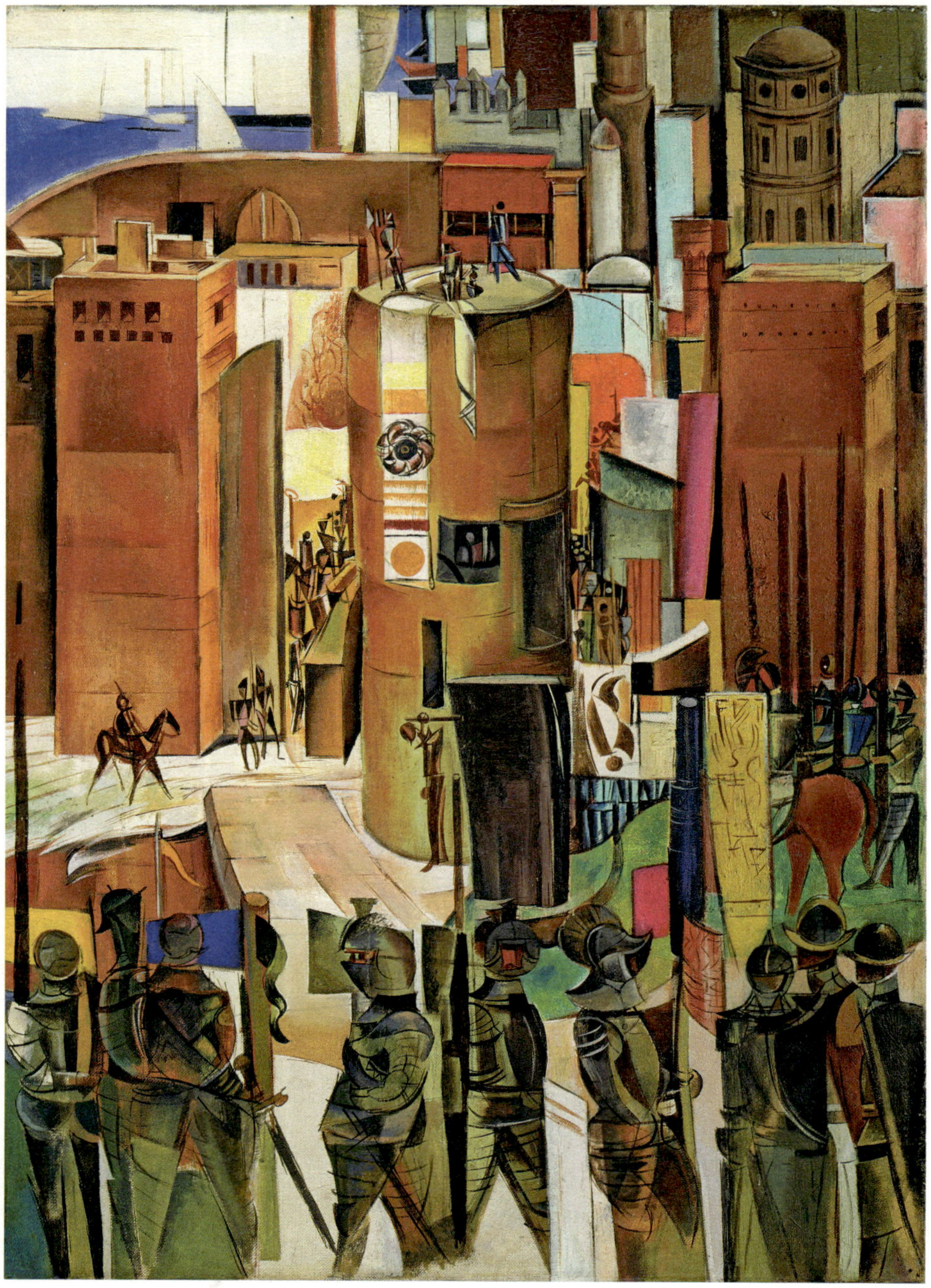

Fig. 6.
The Surrender of Barcelona, 1936–37.
Tate, London (Cat. 162)

This image has two titles and two meanings. As *The Siege of Barcelona*, it *predicted* the defeat of certain values and was more medieval (or early Renaissance) than it was modern. As *The Surrender of Barcelona*, it represented the *fact* of defeat, of both the Spanish Republic and of Lewis's hopes for the transformative possibilities of visual modernism. Under that title, it was more modern than medieval. Spain finally took its revenge upon Lewis, providing him with the image by which he measured the loss of what he most valued (modernism) and – in the same image – forced him to recognise something that he took too long to acknowledge: the suffering and humanity of the politically defeated. From this date (1939–40) he begins to move towards an internationalist attitude and in that welcome development an image of Spain is crucial.[55]

A final tribute to Spain occurs in *Malign Fiesta* (B&M Cat. 57), a novel published in 1955 that is effectively Lewis's last achievement (he died in 1957). At the fiesta, organised by angels in a world after death, a "brilliantly handsome Spanish woman" comes forward to dance. The passage is evocative, and seems to avoid cliché, even if the event itself is a commonplace evocation of "Spain":

> **[S]he raised the castanets, and, to the rolling and hammering of the instruments, began a slow dance, in which the ability of the centre of her body to simulate the slowly heaving motion of the most professional love, drew the solemn attention of the audience. [...] A big fellow in black tights, and black silken Spanish hat, with a strap beneath the tip of the chin, stamped and assumed attitudes reminiscent of the dancers of Badajos [*sic*] or of Valencia, rigid and awkward-looking, ritualistic. The girl intensified the act, in front of the stiff and stamping black monster, until in the wildest manner she ended that dance, stomach forward and quivering, eyes closed.[56]**

Even in old age, Lewis never forgot his earliest experiences in Spain.

NOTES

1. Wyndham Lewis, "Foreword," *Guns* [exh. cat. Goupil Gallery, London, 1919]. Rprt. *Wyndham Lewis on Art: Collected Writings 1913–1956*. Eds. Walter Michel and C.J. Fox (London: Thames and Hudson, 1969), p. 106.
2. Wyndham Lewis, "A Spanish Household" (1910). Rprt. *The Complete Wild Body* (1927). Ed. Bernard Lafourcade (Santa Barbara: Black Sparrow Press, 1982), p. 259.
3. Ibid., p. 261.
4. Paul O'Keeffe, *Some Sort of Genius: A Life of Wyndham Lewis* (London: Cape, 2000), p. 87.
5. Peter Alexander, *Roy Campbell: A Critical Biography* (Oxford: Oxford University Press, 1982), p. 154.
6. Wyndham Lewis, *La Rançon de L'Amour* [*The Revenge for Love*]. Trans. Bernard Lafourcade (Lausanne: L'Age d'Homme, 1980), p. 347.
7. Wyndham Lewis, *The Letters of Wyndham Lewis*. Ed. W.K. Rose (London: Methuen, 1963), p. 342.
8. O'Keeffe 2000, p. 86.
9. Wyndham Lewis, *Rude Assignment: An Intellectual Autobiography*. Ed. Toby Foshay (Santa Barbara: Black Sparrow Press, 1984), p. 126. First published as *Rude Assignment: A Narrative of my Career Up-to-date* (London: Hutchinson, 1950).
10. O'Keeffe 2000, p. 87.
11. Paul Edwards, *Wyndham Lewis: Painter and Writer* (New Haven/London: Yale University Press, 2000), p. 194.
12. *The Complete Wild Body*, p. 264.
13. Ibid., p. 204.
14. Ibid., p. 205.
15. Ibid.
16. Ibid., p. 203.
17. Wyndham Lewis, *The Hitler Cult* (London: Dent, 1939), p. 21; see Alan Munton, "From Proudhon to Hitler (and back): The Strange Political Journey of Wyndham Lewis," in *Right / Left / Right: Revolving Commitments: France and Britain 1929–1950*. Eds. Jennifer Birkett and Stan Smith (Newcastle: Cambridge Scholars Publishing, 2008), pp. 47–60.
18. *Rude Assignment*, p. 126.
19. *The Complete Wild Body*, p. 16.
20. Ibid., pp. 45, 349.
21. Ibid., p. 17.
22. Ibid., p. 19.
23. Wyndham Lewis, *The Revenge for Love* (1937). Rprt. ed. Reed Way Dasenbrock (Santa Rosa: Black Sparrow Press, 1991), p. 29.
24. Ibid., p. 17.
25. Ibid., p. 30.
26. Ibid., p. 59.
27. Ibid., p. 57.
28. Ibid., p. 58.
29. Ibid.
30. Ibid.
31. Wyndham Lewis, "A Soldier of Humour" (1927). Rprt. *The Complete Wild Body*, p. 17.
32. *The Revenge for Love*, p. 59.
33. Ibid., p. 352.
34. Wyndham Lewis, *Count Your Dead: They are Alive! Or, A New War in the Making* (London: Lovat Dickson, 1937), p. 113.
35. Anthony Beevor, *The Battle for Spain: The Spanish Civil War 1936–1939* (London: Phoenix, 2007), p. 42.
36. Hugh Thomas, *The Spanish Civil War* (Harmondsworth: Penguin Books, 1977), p. 156.
37. Ibid., p. 112.
38. Ibid., p. 113.
39. Ibid.
40. Ibid., p. 265.
41. *The Hitler Cult*, p. 182.
42. *The Letters of Wyndham Lewis*, p. 374.
43. Lisa Tickner, *Modern Life and Modern Subjects: British Art in the Early Twentieth Century* (New Haven/London: Yale University Press, 2000), pp. 84–85.
44. Edwards 2000, p. 415.
45. Ibid., p. 417.
46. Ibid., p. 416.
47. *Rude Assignment*, p. 140.
48. William H. Prescott, *History of the Reign of Ferdinand and Isabella the Catholic* (n.d.). Ed. John Foster Kirk (London: Swan Sonnenschein, 1841).
49. *Rude Assignment*, p. 140.
50. *The Hitler Cult*, p. 18.
51. Ibid., p. 19.
52. Ibid.
53. Andrew Causey, "Wyndham Lewis and History Painting in the Later 1930s," in *Wyndham Lewis and the Art of Modern War*. Ed. David Peters Corbett (Cambridge: Cambridge University Press, 1998), pp. 155–80, p. 167.
54. *The Revenge for Love* (1991), p. 290 and Wyndham Lewis, *Dobles Fondos* [*The Revenge for Love*]. Trans. Miguel Temprano García (Madrid: Alfaguara, 2005), p. 430.
55. In 2009, *The Surrender of Barcelona* was shown in the influential exhibition *The Discovery of Spain*; this confirmed Lewis's significant place in the British understanding of Spain in visual art. See Paul Stirton, "British Artists and the Spanish Civil War," in *The Discovery of Spain: British Artists and Collectors: Goya to Picasso*. Eds. Christopher Baker et al. [exh. cat. National Galleries of Scotland, Edinburgh]. Edinburgh: National Galleries of Scotland, 2009, p. 137.
56. Wyndham Lewis, *The Human Age, Book Two: Monstre Gai*; *Book Three: Malign Fiesta* (London: Methuen, 1955), pp. 506–7.

"The artist goes back to the fish. […] The creation of a work of art is an act of the same description as the evolution of wings on the sides of a fish, the feathering of its fins; or the invention of a weapon within the body of a hymenopter to enable it to meet the terrible needs of its life."

Wyndham Lewis,
The Caliph's Design, 1919

WYNDHAM LEWIS:
THE ARTIST

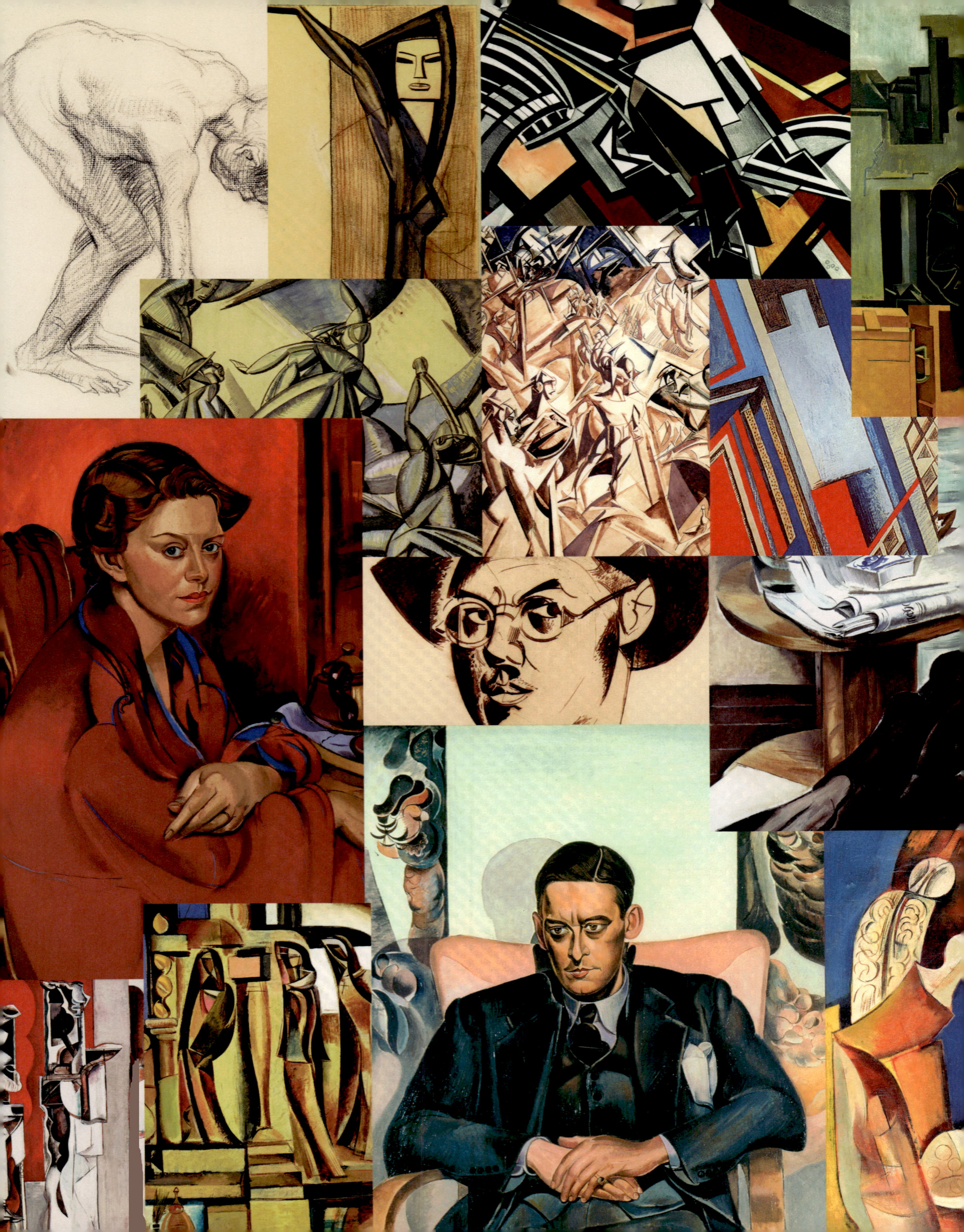

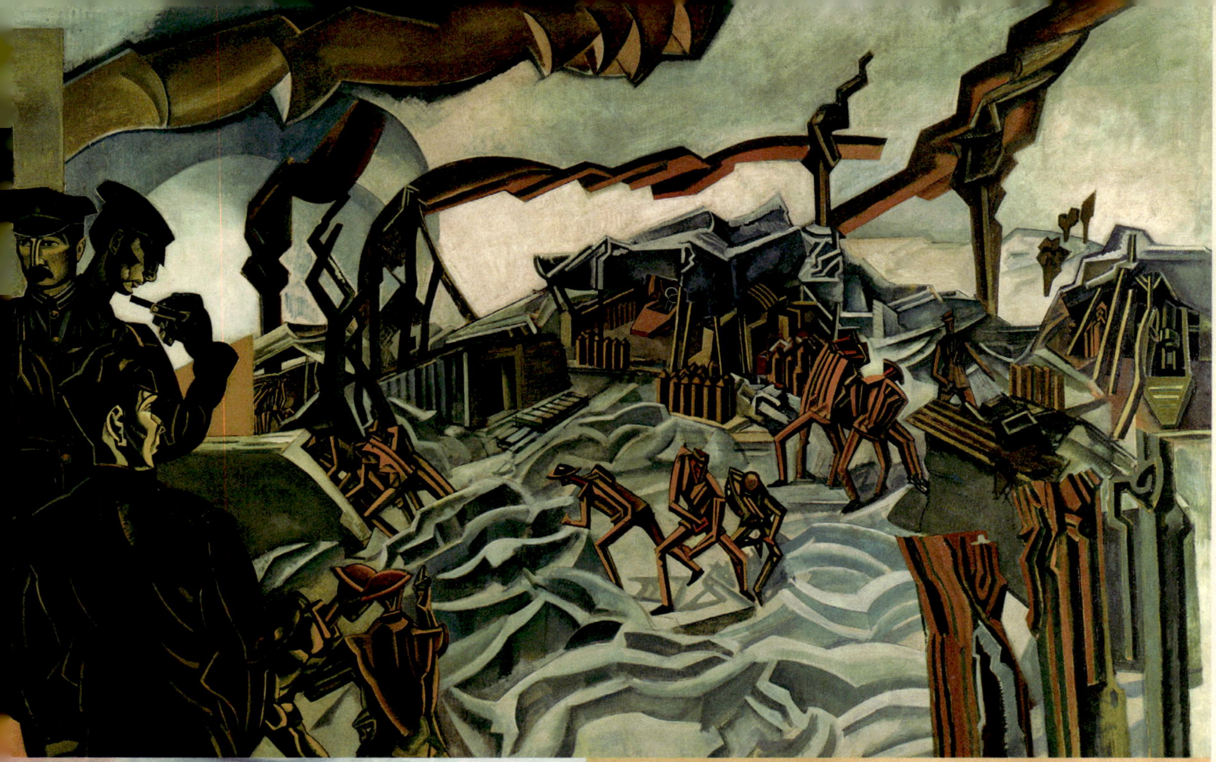
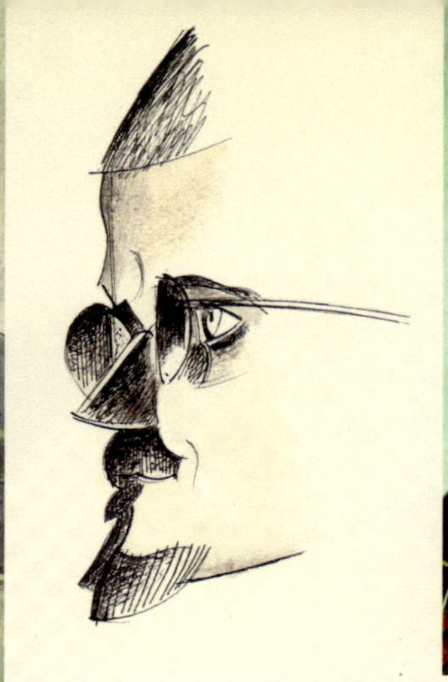

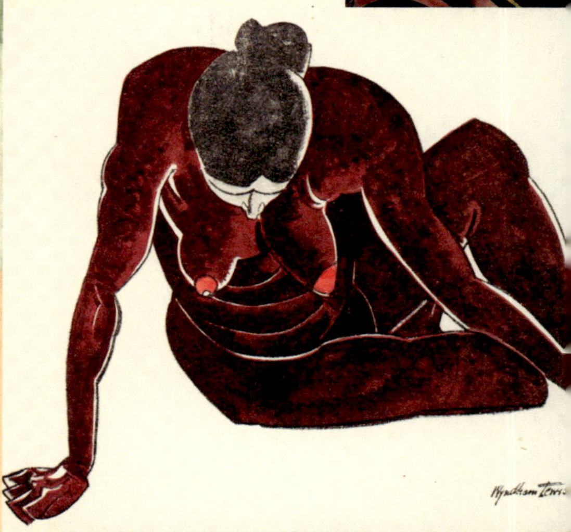
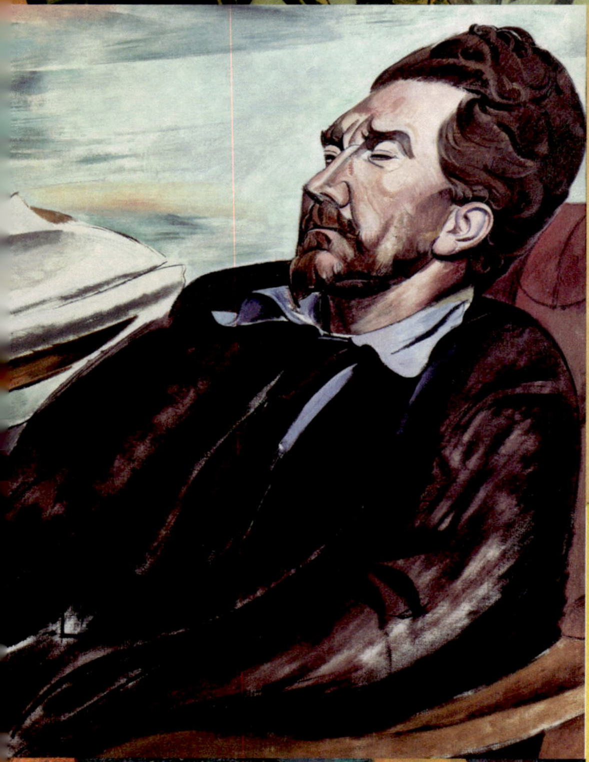
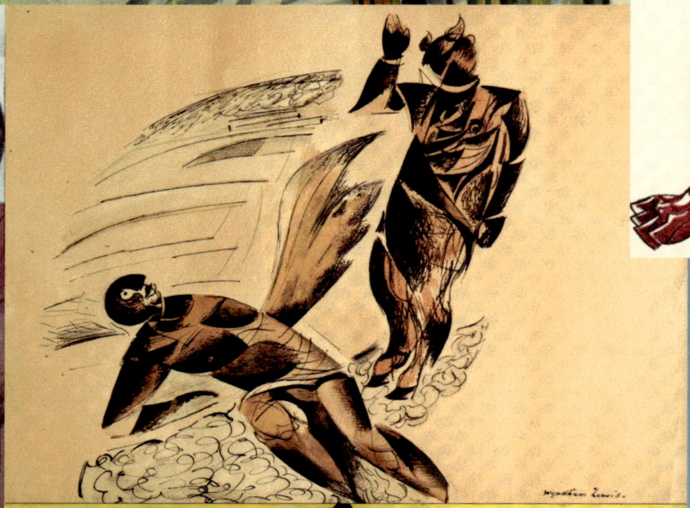
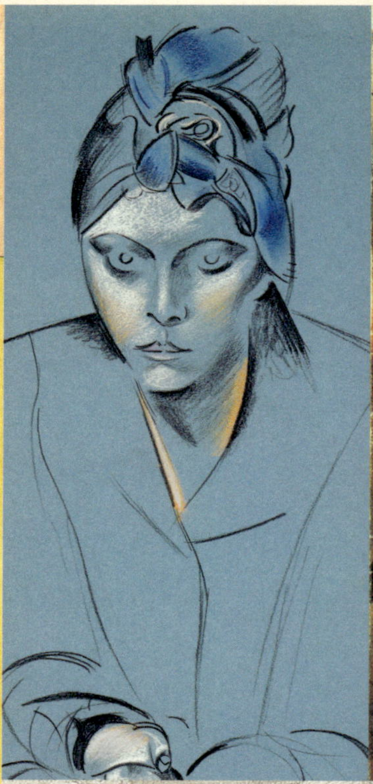
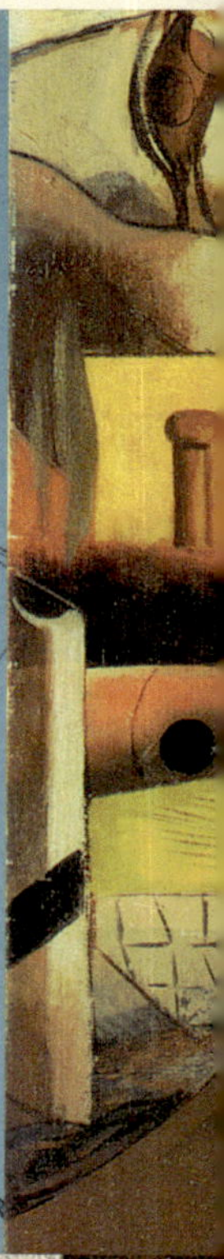
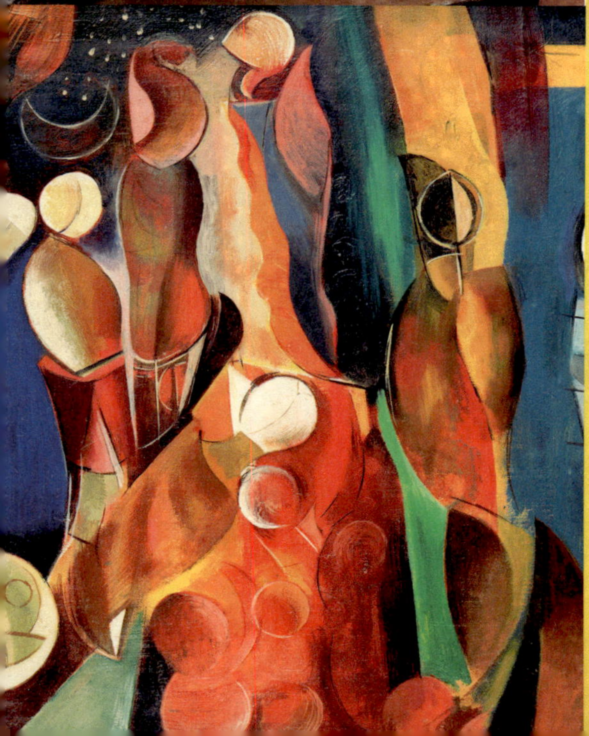
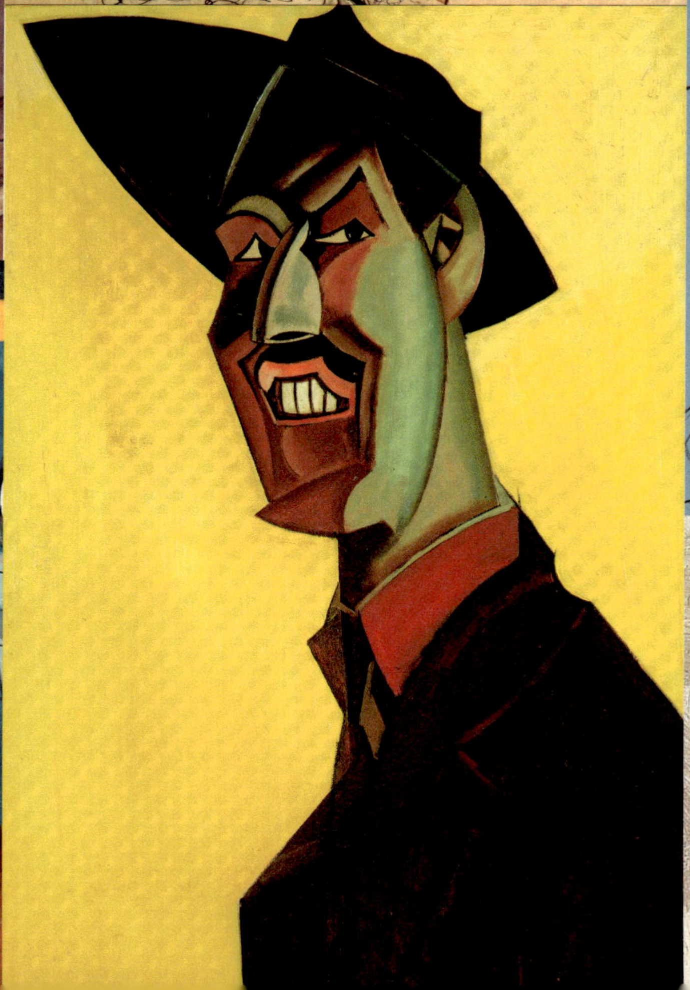
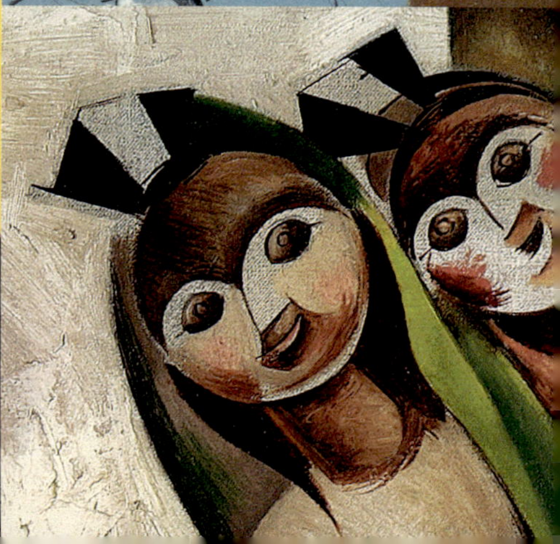

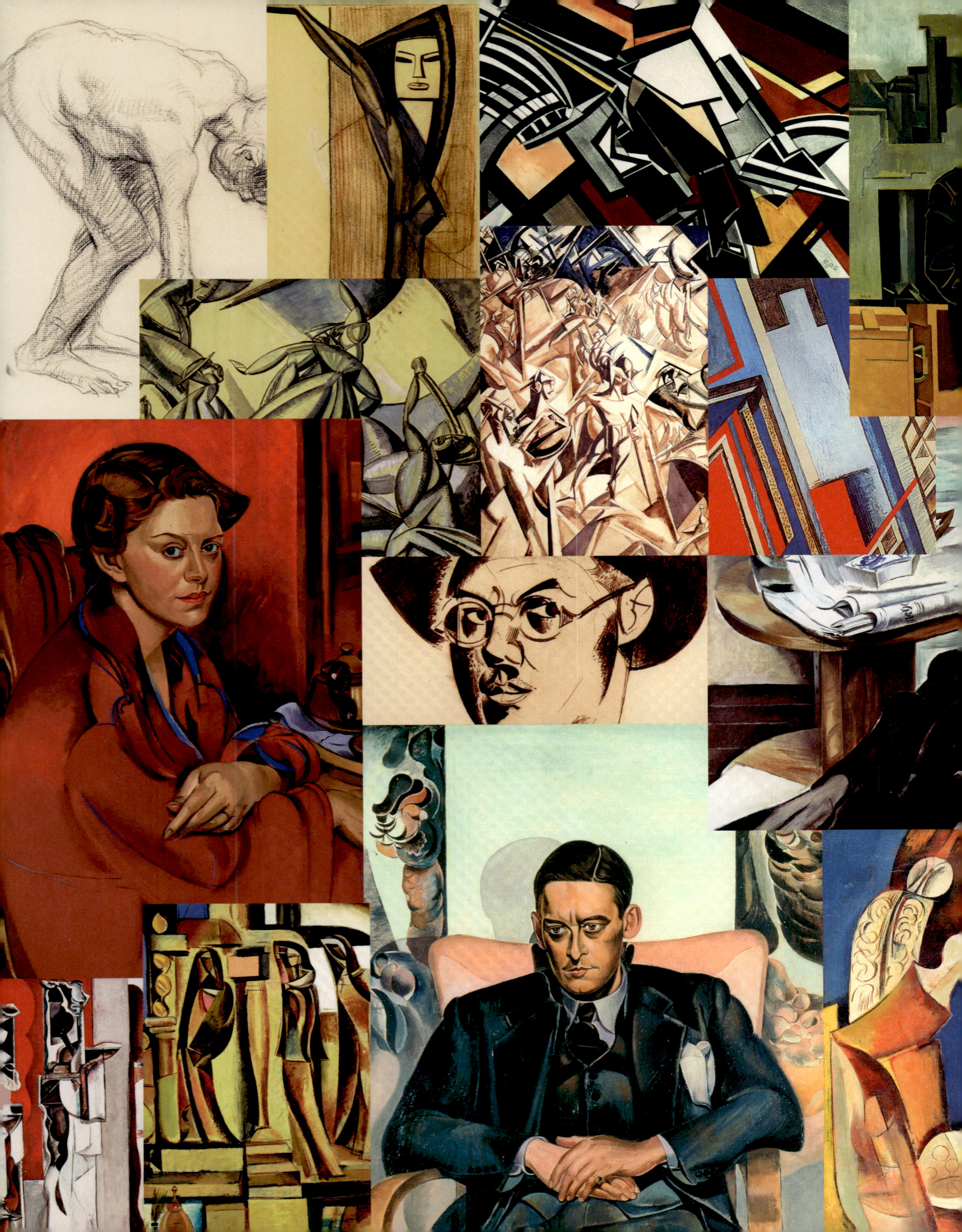

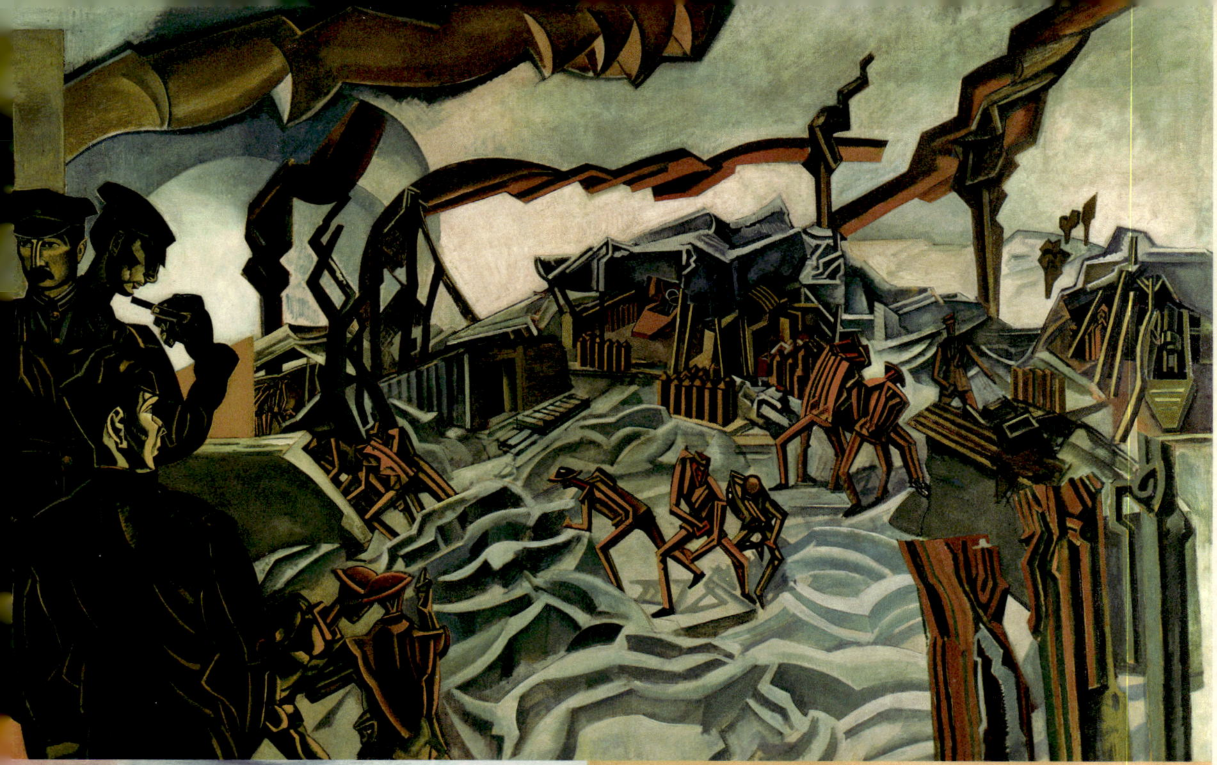
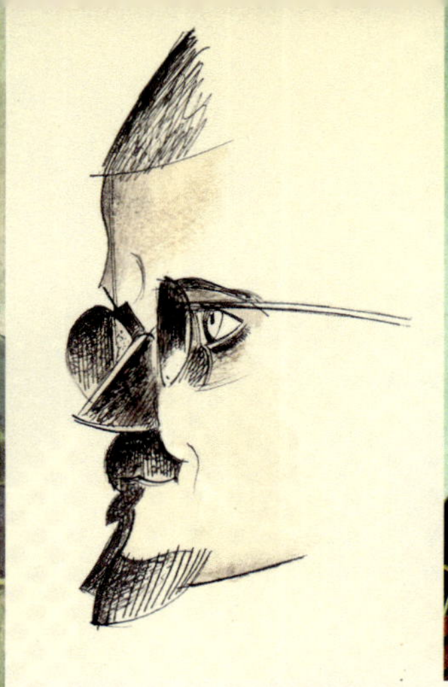

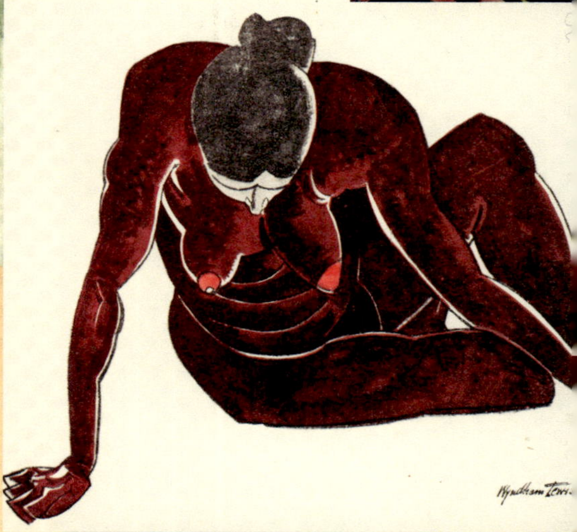
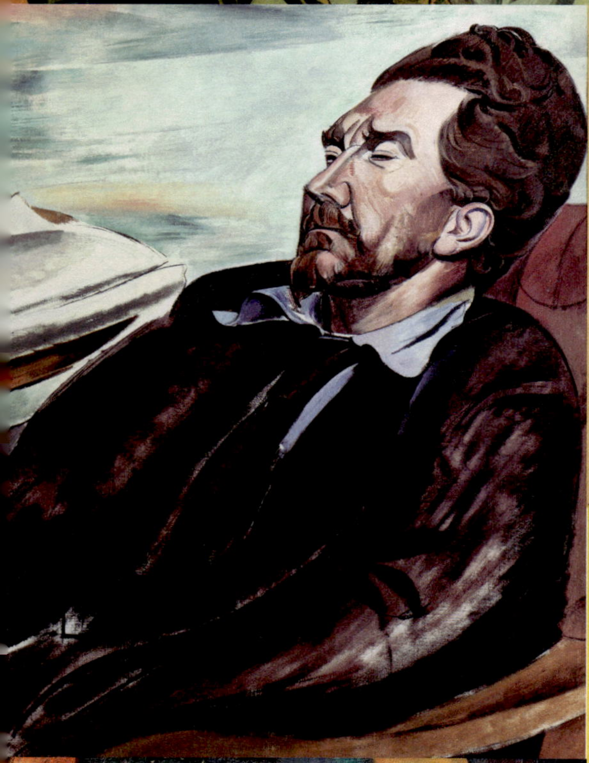
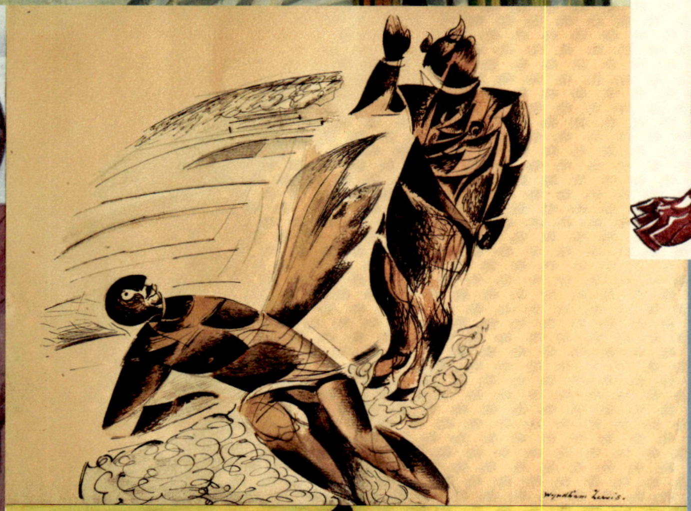
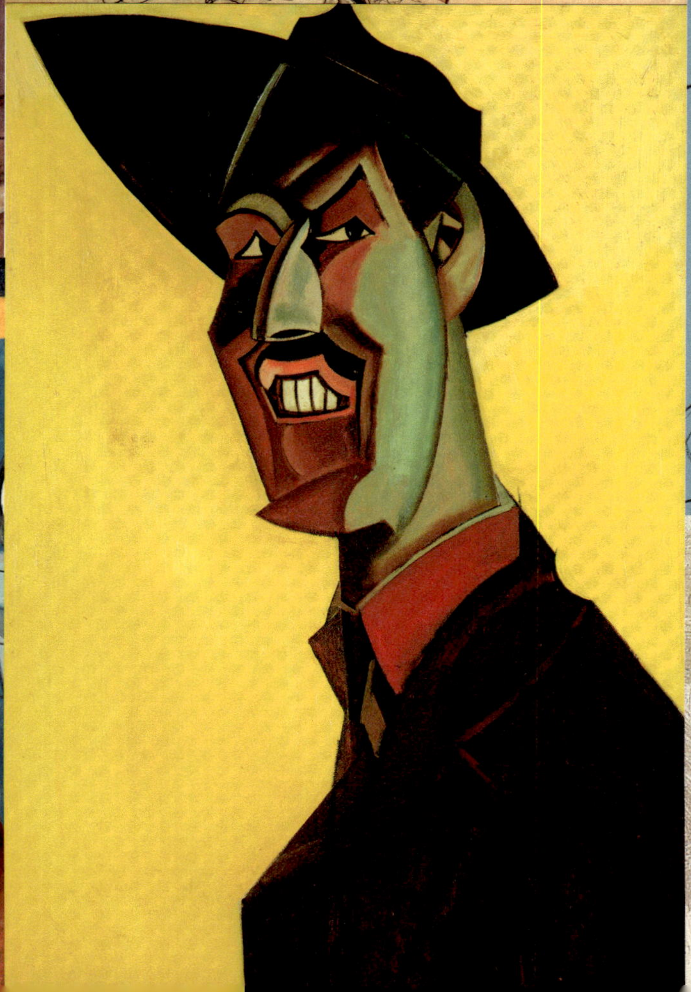
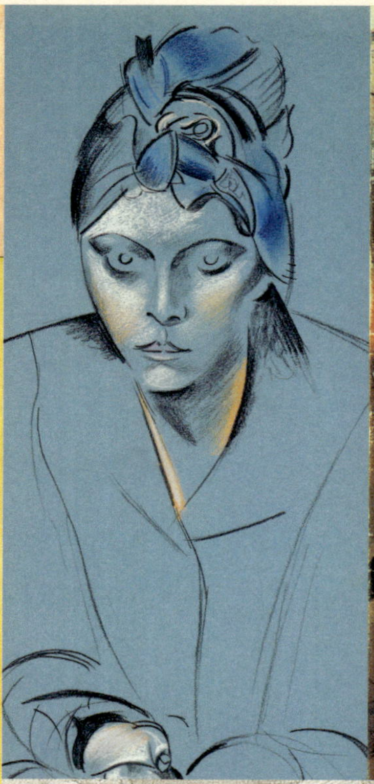
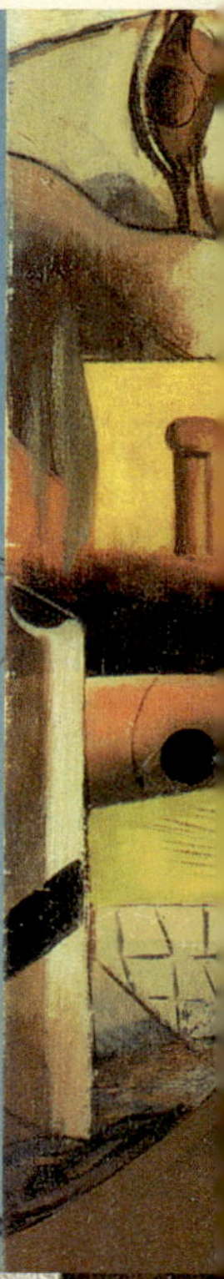
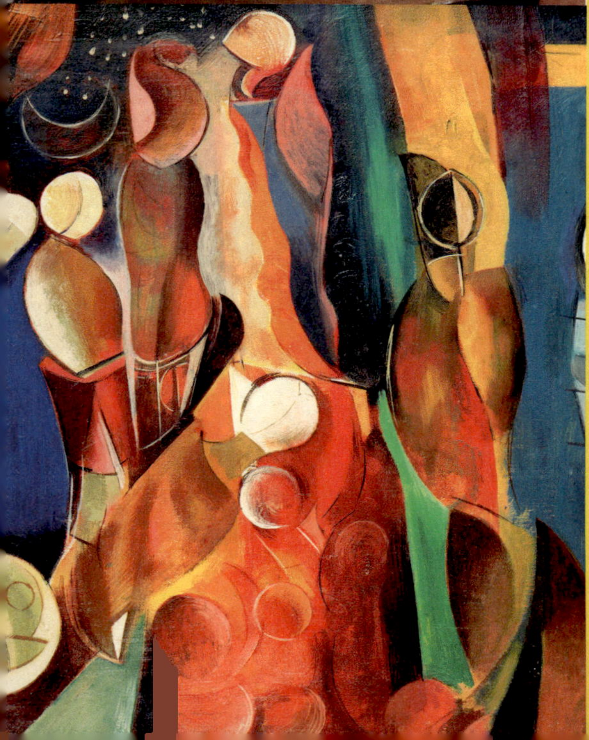
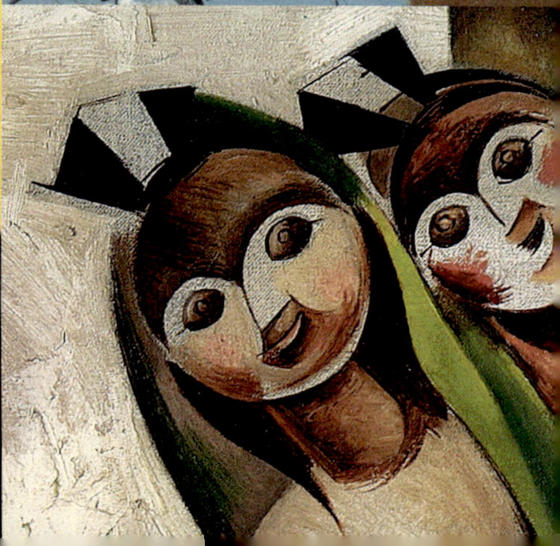

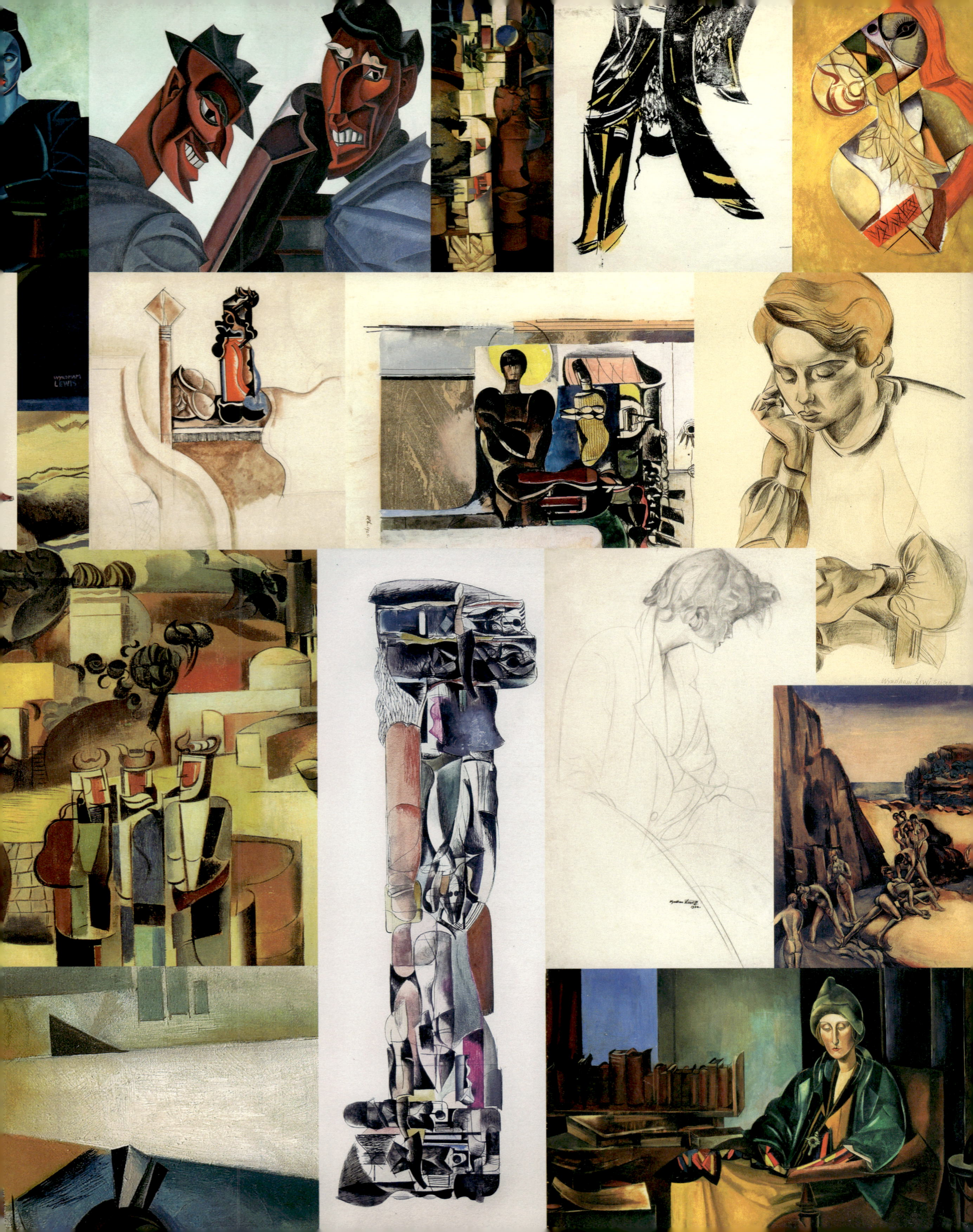
WYNDHAM LEWIS

1900-

-1919

From
Great London Vortex
to the
Western Front

Lewis's ejection from the Slade School of Art in 1901 marked the end of his formal education. He was already a master of the traditional draughtsmanship taught there, but was known as "the poet" on the strength of the obscure and convoluted philosophical verse that he wrote at the time. His broader education began with his friendship with a group of older writers and artists at the British Museum (at this time not separate from the British Library). From Thomas Sturge Moore (1870–1944) he learned of William Blake (1757–1827) and Gustave Flaubert (1821–80); from Laurence Binyon (1869–1943) he learnt about oriental art. In 1904, he moved to Paris to finish his training as an artist, and began to live the Bohemian life he described in his first novel, *Tarr* (B&M Cat. 5), which he started writing as early as 1909, though it was not finished until 1915.

Remarkably little of Lewis's early work survives. His letters tell of his travels in France, Holland, Spain and Germany, and of his turbulent personal life, but no confirmed pictures remain, and he did not become a published writer until after his return to England in 1908. His subject then was the life he had observed as he moved between boarding houses and hotels on his continental travels, especially the life of the Breton people. He followed the Pont Aven School in admiring their "primitive" qualities, but in his representations of them they are both wilder and more calculating than in earlier idealisations. His vision combines comedy (as in *Café* (1910–11) (Cat. 7) with awe at the sheer energy of their dances. A lost painting of 1912, *Kermesse*, depicted the intensity of this outpouring of energy, which is also seen in *Lovers* (1912) (Cat. 20). He was conscious, too, of a tragic dimension to existence and expressed it in such works as *Russian Madonna* (1912) (Cat. 17) and *Man and Woman* (1912) (Cat. 18), but often undercut pathos with a satirical edge (for example, in *Figure Holding a Flower* (1912) (Cat. 14)). Observing the manners of people different from the middle-class English among whom he had been brought up made the young Lewis conscious of incongruities and (as he saw it) irrational compulsions in people's behaviour.

Modern art came belatedly but suddenly to England in the four years leading up to the First World War. Lewis's *The Theatre Manager* (1909) (Cat. 6) may be the first English picture to show knowledge of Pablo Picasso's (1881–1973) *Les Demoiselles d'Avignon*; in 1911 he was experimenting with Cubism, and in 1912 he began to enliven his Cubist style with the energies of Futurism. Lewis was a founder member of the Camden Town Group of painters, whose leader was Walter Sickert (1860–1942). They were Realists concerned with unglamorous aspects of urban life and valued a kind of "honesty" in the handling of oil paint. Lewis's primitivism, his sardonic attitude and his emphasis on line made him an unwelcome member of the group. He was impressed by Filippo Tommaso Marinetti (1876–1944), who criticised the reserved and traditional English in a "Futurist Address to the English" in 1910. Lewis's exaltation of primitive energy now had a critical edge. But it was for its purely formal qualities that his paintings were admired by the Bloomsbury critic Roger Fry (1866–1934) in 1912. In Fry's *Second Post-Impressionist Exhibition*, at the Grafton Galleries in London, Lewis showed several paintings and watercolour drawings in his Futurist-inspired version of energised Cubism. The most important surviving works from the exhibition are the illustrations for a projected edition of William Shakespeare's play, *Timon of Athens*. For some reason the play text was printed without any provision having been made for the placement of plates and smaller decorations, and the images were issued instead as a portfolio without the text.

Why was Lewis so fascinated by this play? Perhaps because it embodied his own personal myth. Timon begins as open-hearted, generous and trusting, willing to give or lend his "friends" whatever they desire. He finds that when he faces a temporary hardship they do not reciprocate and his realisation of this truth about human nature drives him to the opposite extreme of misanthropy. It is the satirist's justification – that his jaundiced view of humanity is forced on him. Lewis's sympathy with Timon's rage is more profound than this, however, and it is related to the fantasies of escape from our material condition that were fostered by the philosophy of Henri Bergson (1859–1941) (and to some extent also by that of Friedrich Nietzsche (1844–1900)) and found expression in the Futurist enthusiasm for the transformation of life through technology. Lewis had been a student of both philosophers since his sojourn in Paris. His early work seems to show the influence of a discipleship (later violently repudiated) of Bergson, whose evolutionary system Lewis said that he had followed for a while. We could say that Timon's rage is an outburst of energy that seeks to break through human limits, to a world as spiritual as he has imagined it to be, and as Bergson imagined it might become. But matter remains recalcitrant, and the Nietzschean "Overman" is "human, all too human": brutal and voracious in animal fashion, rather (as seen in *A Feast of Overmen* (1913) (Cat. 32)). Some of the *Timon* works reproduced in the portfolio no longer survive, particularly the ones executed in black ink, such as the title pages of some of the acts, and the blue ink(?) mechanomorphic *Timon* (1912) (Cat. 38). No doubt Lewis restricted his visual means in these works mainly with printing in mind. But with their unyielding geometry and restricted visual vocabulary, they mark a transition to the next, and historically the most recognised and important phase of Lewis's visual art, that of the avant-garde style of abstraction known as Vorticism.

Fry's inclusion of Lewis in the *Second Post-Impressionist Exhibition* put him in a brief but tense alliance with Bloomsbury. He joined Fry's Omega Workshops, helping design interior decor, furniture and other artefacts for the fashionable London bourgeoisie (*Design for a Folding Screen* (1913) (Cat. 41)). Bloomsbury painting comprised mainly tentative imitations of Paul Cézanne (1839–1906) or Henri Matisse (1869–1954), while Lewis was by now a master of much more advanced modernist styles. His association with Omega would have seemed to him like an act of generosity. It was repaid (as he saw it) by treachery, as Fry appropriated in entirety a commission for Omega, half of which had been intended for Lewis personally. When he discovered the cheat, Lewis walked out in a rage, taking other painters who would help him as founder members of their own group, based at a new "Rebel Art Centre" with Lewis at its head. It was from here that Vorticism was launched (after one more quarrel, this time with Marinetti and his English follower C.R.W. Nevinson (1889–1946)) in June 1914.

The stark geometric forms of *Timon* were now supplemented by colour and varied textures to create a new style of geometrical abstraction that showed a world transformed by technology, and the human figure subsumed or redistributed into its urban networks. It is a futurist vision, with vibrant colours and clashing dynamic "perspectives" clearly showing excitement at this transformation. But at its heart is a realisation that life remains limited and its embrace of the machine is, as Lewis wrote, "stoic." *The Crowd* (1914–15) (Cat. 59), Lewis's answer to Luigi Russolo's (1885–1947) *La Rivolta* (1911), contains both an anarchist joy in revolution and a sober sense of the enclosing structures of modernity that make real transcendence of our condition in a Sorelian revolution almost impossible.

Lewis edited the Vorticist magazine, *Blast* (B&M Cats. 2 and 3), and was also responsible for its stunning typography and design. By now he had become close friends with the American poet Ezra Pound (1885–1972), who was pleased to be able at last to take a leading part in an avant-garde movement bent on modernising all the arts. But his "imagism" was too pallid and tasteful for Lewis, who felt that he would have to supply personally a truly modern Vorticist literature that would be a worthy equivalent of Vorticist painting. This he did both in the vivid sections of the Vorticist Manifesto itself and in a "play" unprecedented in English, *Enemy of the Stars*. It reads like notes towards a screenplay of an Expressionist film. Its two protagonists, Hanp and Arghol, act out the contest of spirit and matter, each contaminated by the other until both expire in an outburst of mutual violence.

In retrospect, *Blast* and Vorticism, like so much of the apocalyptic art of Europe in these years, can be seen as prophetic of the First World War. Without great enthusiasm, Lewis decided to enlist, but was delayed by a long period of intermittent illness. In the interval he prepared another issue of *Blast*, held an exhibition of the Vorticists at the Doré Galleries in London and set about completing the novel, *Tarr*, which he had begun several years previously. Now it came in for some of the benefits of the modernist stylist of *Blast* and was enlisted in Lewis's avant-garde aim to overcome British complacency. One of its characters, who is subject to a withering verbal assault from the (semi-autobiographical) hero, Frederick Tarr, is modelled on Fry. But in the pseudo-artist, Otto Kreisler, a German of Dostoyevskian wildness and psychological complexity, Lewis also provided a critique of the warped Romanticism that he saw as underlying German aggression in 1914.

Lewis trained as a gunner, then as an officer, finally reaching France in June 1917. His short story, "Cantelman's Spring-Mate," is based on his experience in training. Cantelman expresses a Timon-like disillusion with nature and humanity for failing to live up to the ideals he had envisaged for them. Spring is, for him, simply a part of the same explosive machinery that leads to mechanised war, and he takes his revenge by seducing and abandoning a girl from the nearby village. A similar mood is discernible in *Moonlight* (1914) (Cat. 51), which transposes Matissean pastoral to a mechanised, post-Vorticist mode. After serving at the front as a second-lieutenant in charge of heavy guns at the Third Battle of Ypres (one of the most terrible and intense of the war), Lewis returned to England and took up a position as a war artist, painting for the Canadian and British governments. As part of these projects, he also produced a series of mainly ink and watercolour works that he exhibited in 1919 in his first one-man show, *Guns*. The works adapted the vocabulary of Vorticism even more thoroughly and they can pass as a particularly formalised realism. But the Vorticist kinship is clear in such works as *The No. 2* (1918) (Cat. 64). Lewis's war paintings measure the cost of mechanisation on human life, showing the adaptations men have to make, sometimes to almost sub-human inertia, in order to cope with the inhuman landscape of war. The culmination is the immense *A Battery Shelled* (1919) (Cat. 71), in which the three figures in the foreground show different reactions – numb refusal to look, distraction or apparent indifference – to the scene of destruction behind them. It is one of the most complete statements about war in twentieth-century art. There could be no return to the tactics of the avant-garde in England after the First World War, though it took Lewis some time to realise it fully.

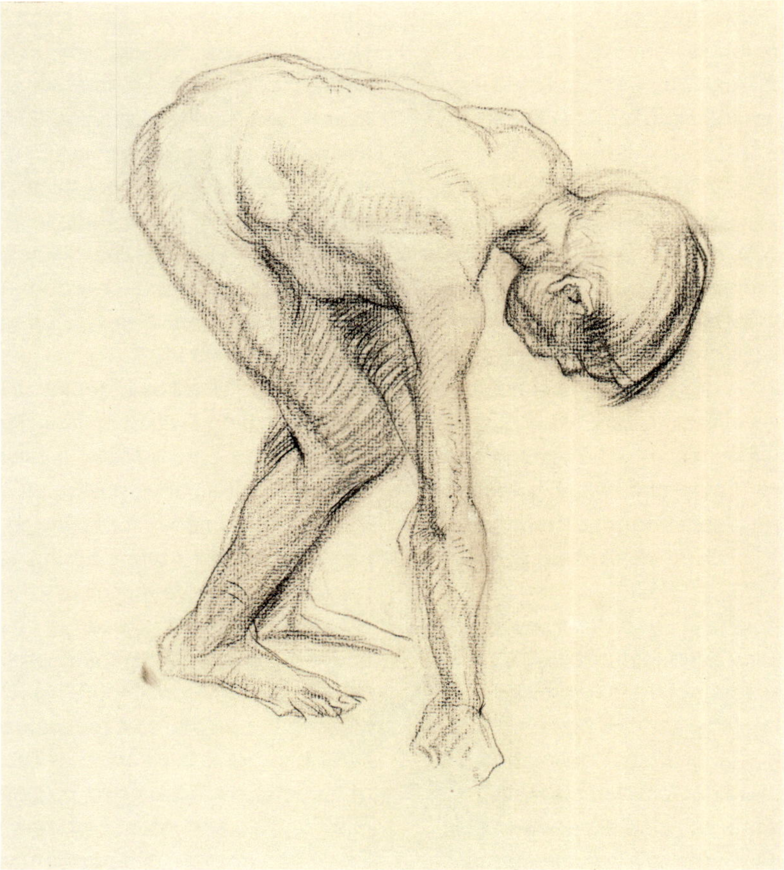

Cat. 1.
***Nude Boy Bending (Stooping Nude Boy)*, 1900. Pencil on paper. 34.5 x 29 cm. UCL Art Collections, University College London (SDC6003). M 2**

Lewis won a scholarship to the Slade School of Art at the age of 16, after coming bottom of his class at Rugby School. The main teacher of draughtsmanship was Henry Tonks, who insisted on a traditional Renaissance-based style. Some of the best draughtsmen of English twentieth-century art learnt their skills under Tonks (Augustus John, William Orpen, Stanley Spencer). Lewis felt that the Impressionist-derived style of painting in oils inculcated by Frederick Brown (professor of painting) was completely at variance with Tonks's teaching. Although Lewis's draughtsmanship pleased the authorities – as the retention of this drawing by them testifies – his attitude did not, and he was expelled. In 1914, he retaliated by "blasting" Tonks in the Vorticist manifesto.

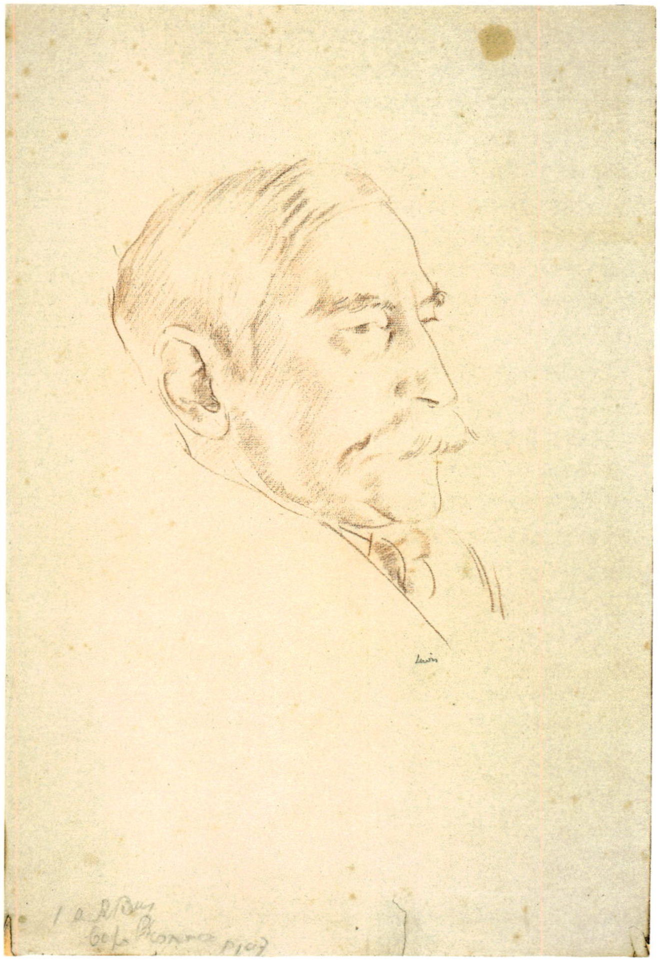

Cat. 2.
***Alfred de Pass*, ca. 1903. Red chalk on paper. 46.8 x 31 cm. Wyndham Lewis Memorial Trust (LD.2004.XX.1)**

Lewis uses the sanguine chalk of the Italian masters he had been taught to emulate. It is believed that the sitter was a South African businessman who was friendly with Augustus John. Lewis had become friends with John in 1902. Andrew Brighton has argued that the seeds of Lewis's later "visio-tactile" epistemology were sown by his training in draughtsmanship at the Slade.[1] While Lewis's mature draughtsmanship tends to be more obedient to his own visual predilections than to the detail of the forms he describes, he remained capable of the sensitivity displayed in this drawing. The treatment of the collar and tie looks forward to some of the more daring "shorthand" of his later drawing.

1. See Andrew Brighton, "Post-War Establishment Distaste for Wyndham Lewis: Some Origins," in *Volcanic Heaven: Essays on Wyndham Lewis's Painting and Writing*. Ed. Paul Edwards (Santa Rosa: Black Sparrow Press, 1996), pp. 170–73.

Cat. 3.
Two Nudes, 1903. Pen and ink, and ink wash on paper. 24.4 x 39.5 cm. Wyndham Lewis Memorial Trust (LD.2004.XX.2). M 6

This work shows an influence from Augustus John. In his autobiography Lewis recalls how John renounced temporarily the Italian ideal of drawing promulgated at the Slade, and arrived at a life class there one day and produced some squat Rembrandtesque drawings of the model. This led to a sudden fashion among the students for this style of drawing, to the disgust of their teachers.[1] This drawing perhaps shows the influence of this phase of John's work. But the humour, and the ability to convey a "dramatic" or narrative relationship between a couple, were Lewis's own.

1. Wyndham Lewis, *Rude Assignment: A Narrative of my Career Up-to-date* (London: Hutchinson, 1950), pp. 119–20.

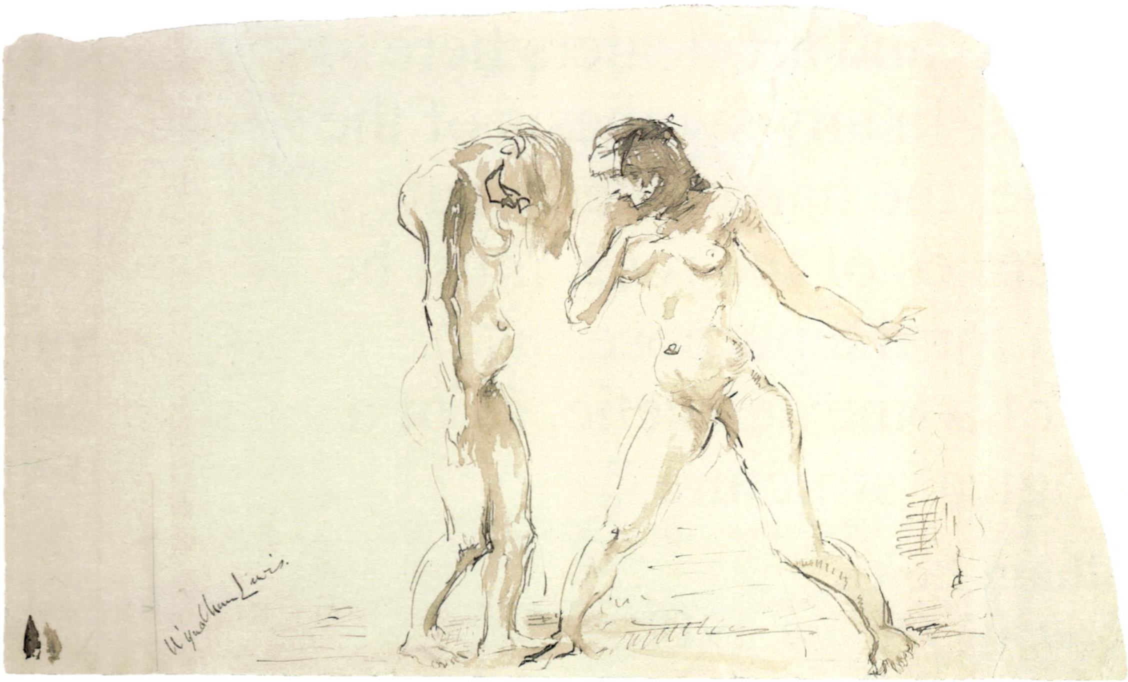

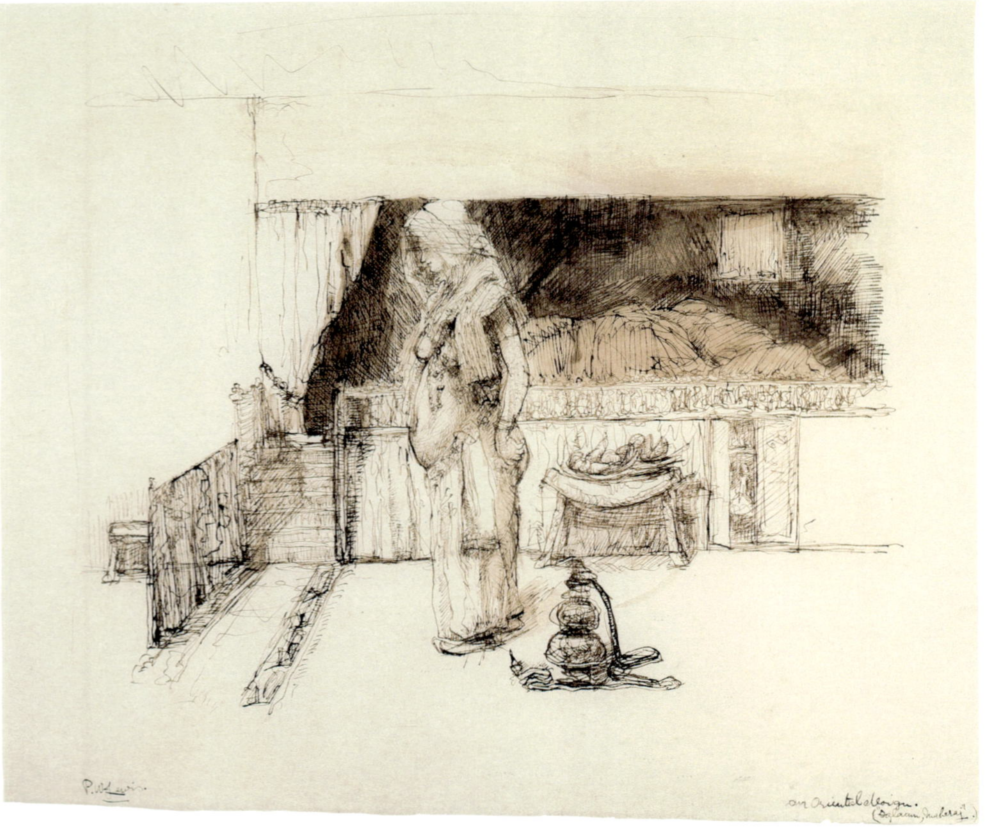

Cat. 4.
Salaam Maharaj: An Oriental Design, 1900–5. Pen and sepia ink, and wash of sepia ink on paper. 33 x 38 cm. Collection Brian Sewell. M 9

So few of Lewis's works survive from this period that we cannot say how characteristic this is. It seems to share some of the humour of *Two Nudes* (Cat. 3) and to show a continuing admiration of Rembrandt van Rijn. It bears resemblance to some works by Spencer Gore of the same period. Lewis and Gore stayed in Madrid for some weeks in 1902, visiting the Prado and studying the works of Francisco Goya. The significance of the inscription is unclear, but Lewis remained fascinated by the Orient throughout his career, though the closest he came to a visit was to North Africa in 1931.

“The artist’s function is to create–
to make something; not to make something pretty, as dowagers, dreamers, and art-dealers here suppose. In any synthesis of the universe, the harsh, the hirsute, the enemies of the rose, must be built in for the purposes as much of a fine aesthetic, as of a fine logical structure.”

Wyndham Lewis,
The Caliph’s Design, 1919

Cat. 5.
[Not in exhibition] *The Celibate*, 1909. Pencil, ink, watercolour and gouache on paper. 37.5 x 28.5 cm. Tatham Art Gallery, Pietermaritzburg, South Africa (0736/83). M (Addenda; 1909)

The title of this work is unexplained. It may be that Lewis was commenting on the removal from life that the stark treatment of this imposing figure has effected. The monumental draped figure looms above the spectator's viewpoint like an actor on a stage. The work shows a rudimentary understanding of Cubism, which is here understood as a clarification and sculptural simplification of form.

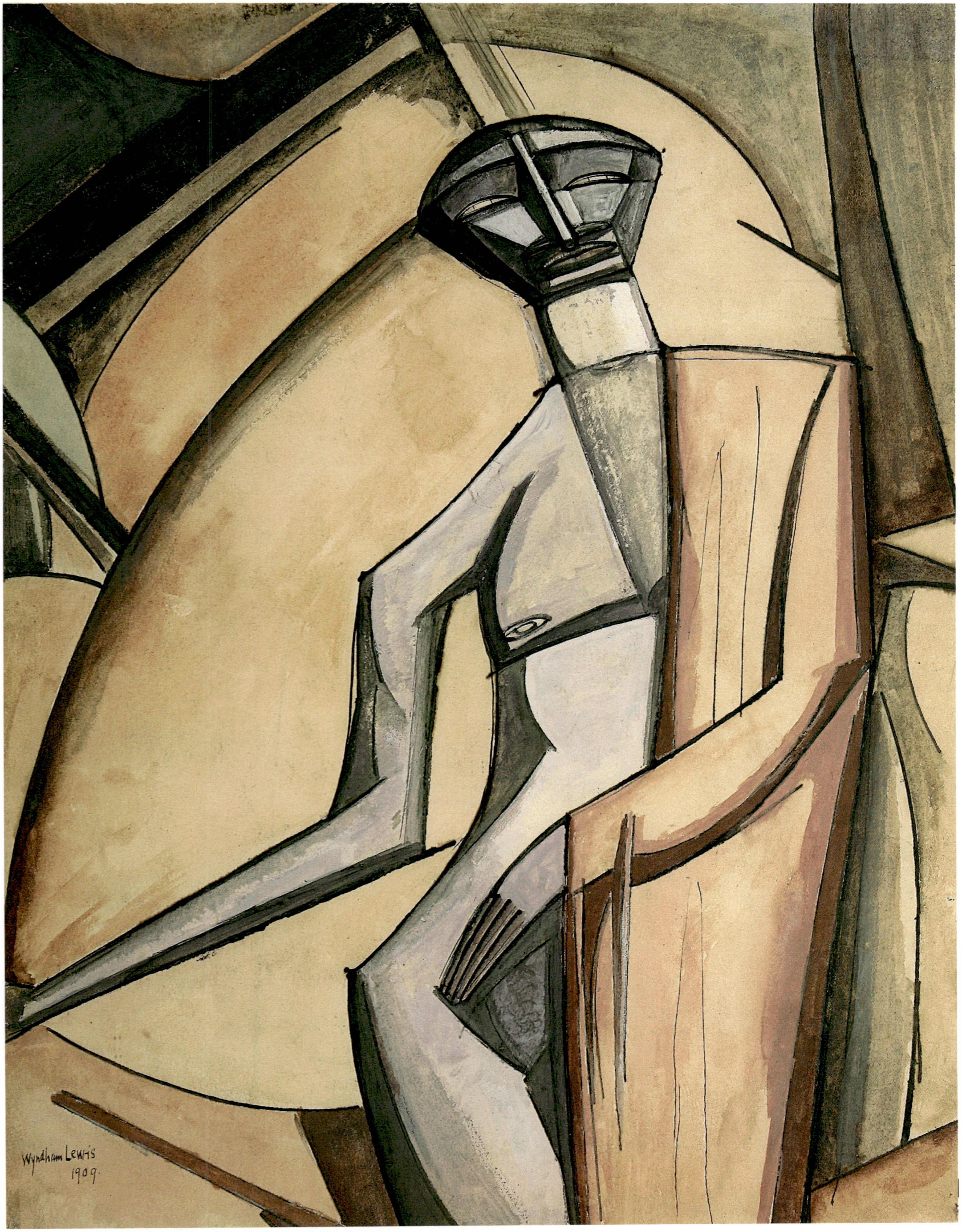
Wyndham Lewis
1909.

Cat. 7.
Café, 1910–11. Pen and ink, watercolour and crayon on paper. 21 x 13.5 cm. Courtesy of Austin/Desmond Fine Art. Private collection. M 18

This is a carefully calculated composition, despite its humorous, caricatural style. The drawing is a sketch for the lost painting, *Port de Mer* (M P1), which was exhibited in 1911 and bought by Augustus John. While in Paris as a student Lewis tried his hand at caricatures, hoping to make money by publishing them in the French press. He had an unusually high opinion of Honoré Daumier, in whose work caricature is an important element. Many of Lewis's early writings were humorous sketches of the eccentric characters he met on his travels as a student in France and Spain. He was particularly interested in the expressiveness of bodily attitudes. Here the contrast between the slouching man and the intimidating proprietress is emphasised. The scene that provokes their reaction takes place outside the picture frame.

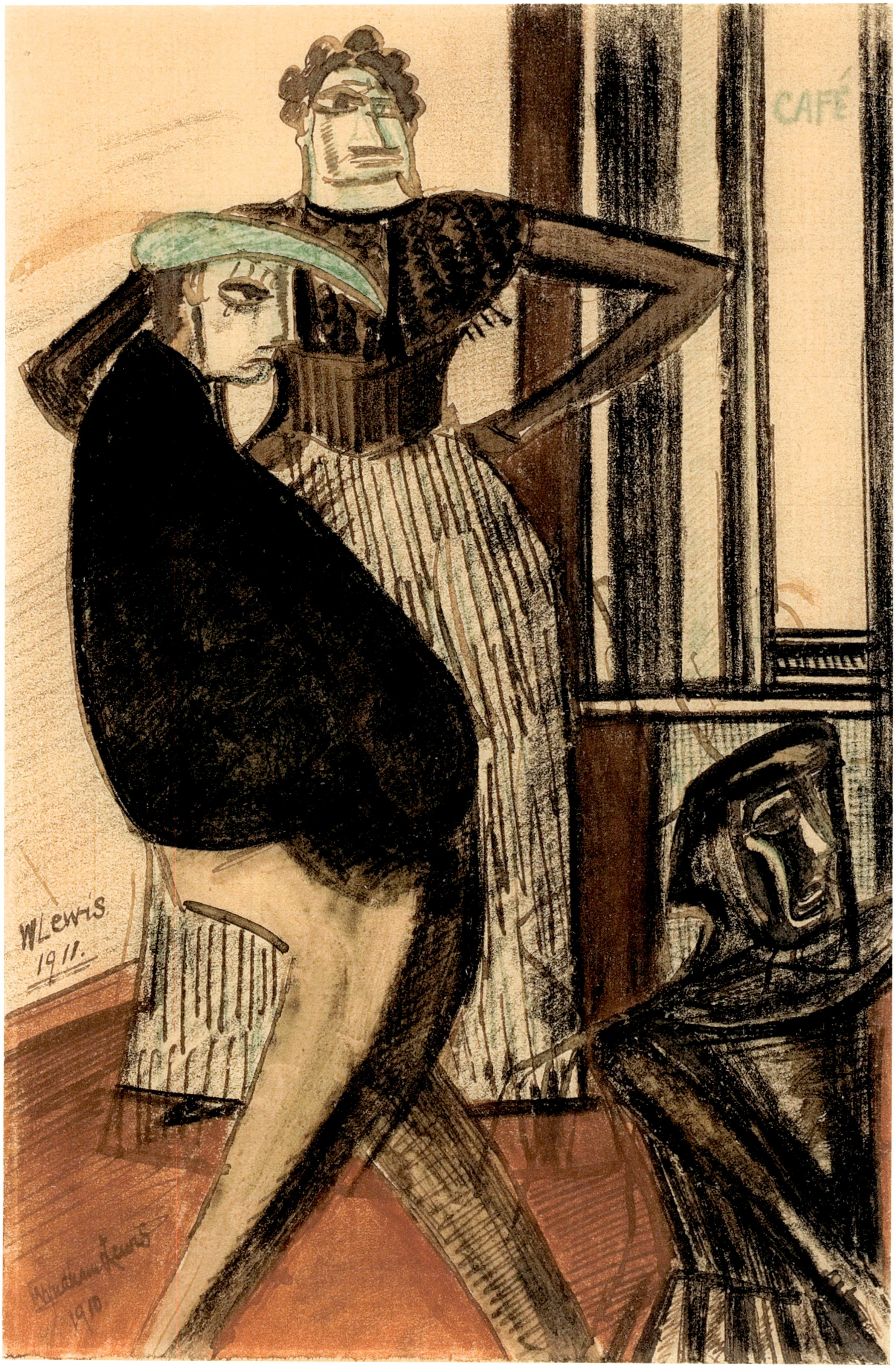

Cat. 6.
The Theatre Manager, 1909.
Pencil, ink and watercolour on paper. 29.5 x 31.5 cm. Victoria and Albert Museum (E 3779-1919). M 15

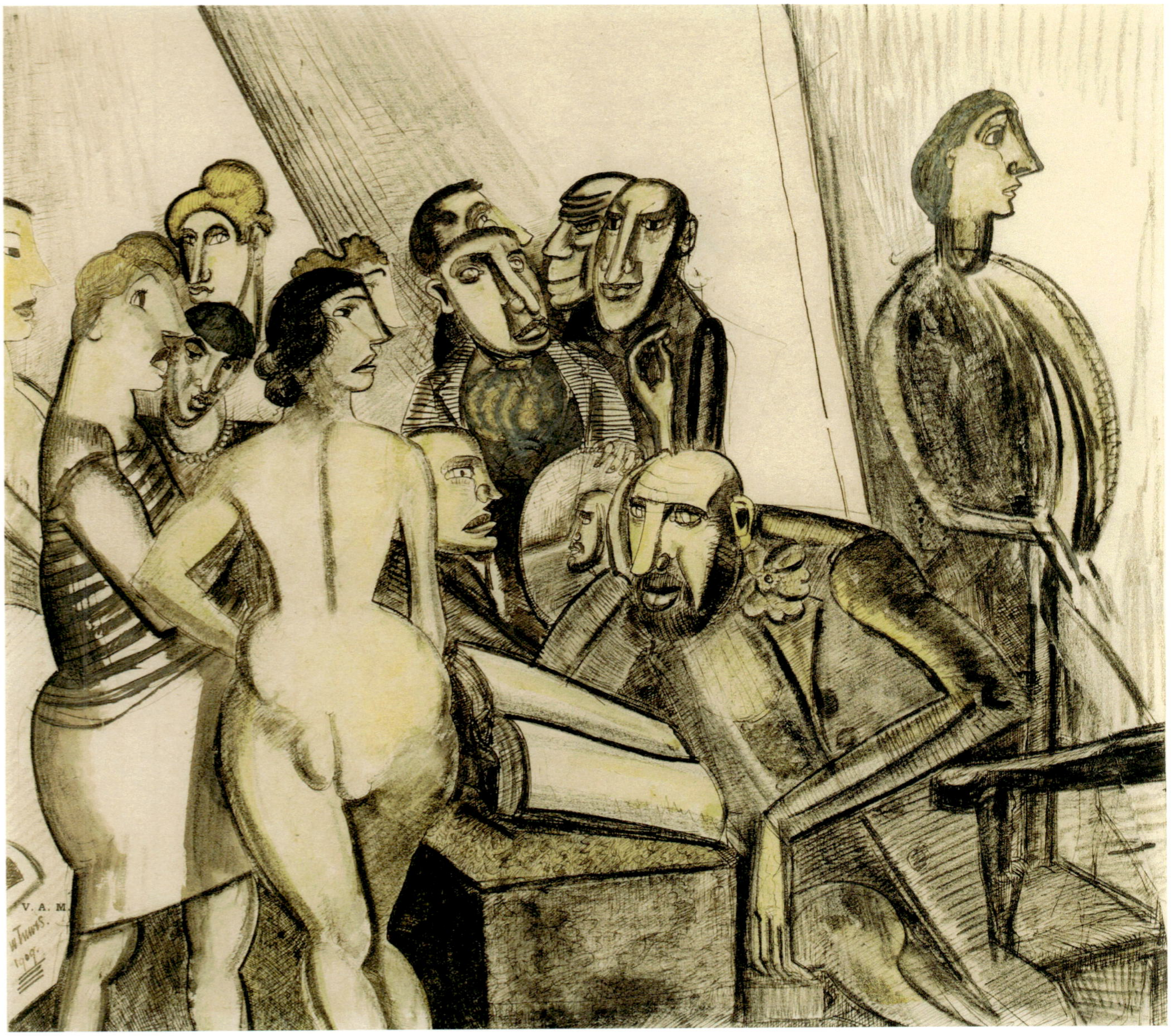

One of Lewis's most important early works, both formally and for its subject. Gustave Le Bon, in his study of crowd psychology, *The Crowd*,[1] observed that theatre managers need to "be able to transform themselves into a crowd" in order to judge the likelihood of the success of a script. The manager here, who physically resembles William Shakespeare, is reading such a script. His head is reflected in a mirror. Twelve actors of markedly disparate types await the results of his self-transformation into a "crowd"; he will supply the vision that turns them into something more than a collection of isolated individuals. This, it seems, is the artist's mission. Richard Cork has noted that Lewis modelled the features of the actors on figures by Albrecht Dürer, Leonardo da Vinci and Pablo Picasso.[2] Lewis may intend to convey that the visual artist's task is a synthesis of western traditions; but the influence from Picasso's "African" period suggests also the need to reach further than the West. An early sketchbook (now lost) that Lewis showed James Thrall Soby in 1947, compiled when he was at the Slade and had to draw from the classical plaster-casts in the British Museum, contained "copies of a grotesque man with a swollen underlip by Leonardo and of athletes by Michelangelo. On other pages were sketches of Pacific Island Masks."[3] The cultural universalism of twentieth-century art was something that Lewis was well prepared for.

1. Gustave Le Bon, *The Crowd: A Study of the Popular Mind* (London: T. Fisher Unwin, 1896), p. 38, cited by Chris Mullen, in *Wyndham Lewis*. Jane Farrington, ed. [exh. cat. Manchester City Art Gallery, Manchester; National Museum of Wales, Cardiff; City Art Centre, Edinburgh]. London: Lund Humphries Publishers, 1980, p. 50.
2. Richard Cork, cited ibid., pp. 49–50.
3. Paul O'Keeffe, *Some Sort of Genius: A Life of Wyndham Lewis* (London: Jonathan Cape, 2000), p. 34.

Cat. 8.
Girl Asleep, 1911. Pencil and gouache on paper. 28 x 38.5 cm. Manchester City Galleries (1925.504)

In 1911, Lewis reached a more sophisticated understanding of Cubism, as can be seen in this sensitive drawing, probably of his mistress Olive Johnson, who was the mother of his son Hoel, born in the same year. Although the drawing is closer to analytical Cubism, Lewis remains too interested in the affective content of the drawing – the capacity to "read" the model's humanity – to dissolve it completely into a matrix of intersecting and overlapping planes. The treatment of the hair, pillow and shoulder at the right of the drawing shows that he had sufficient understanding of Cubism to have done so had he wished, however.

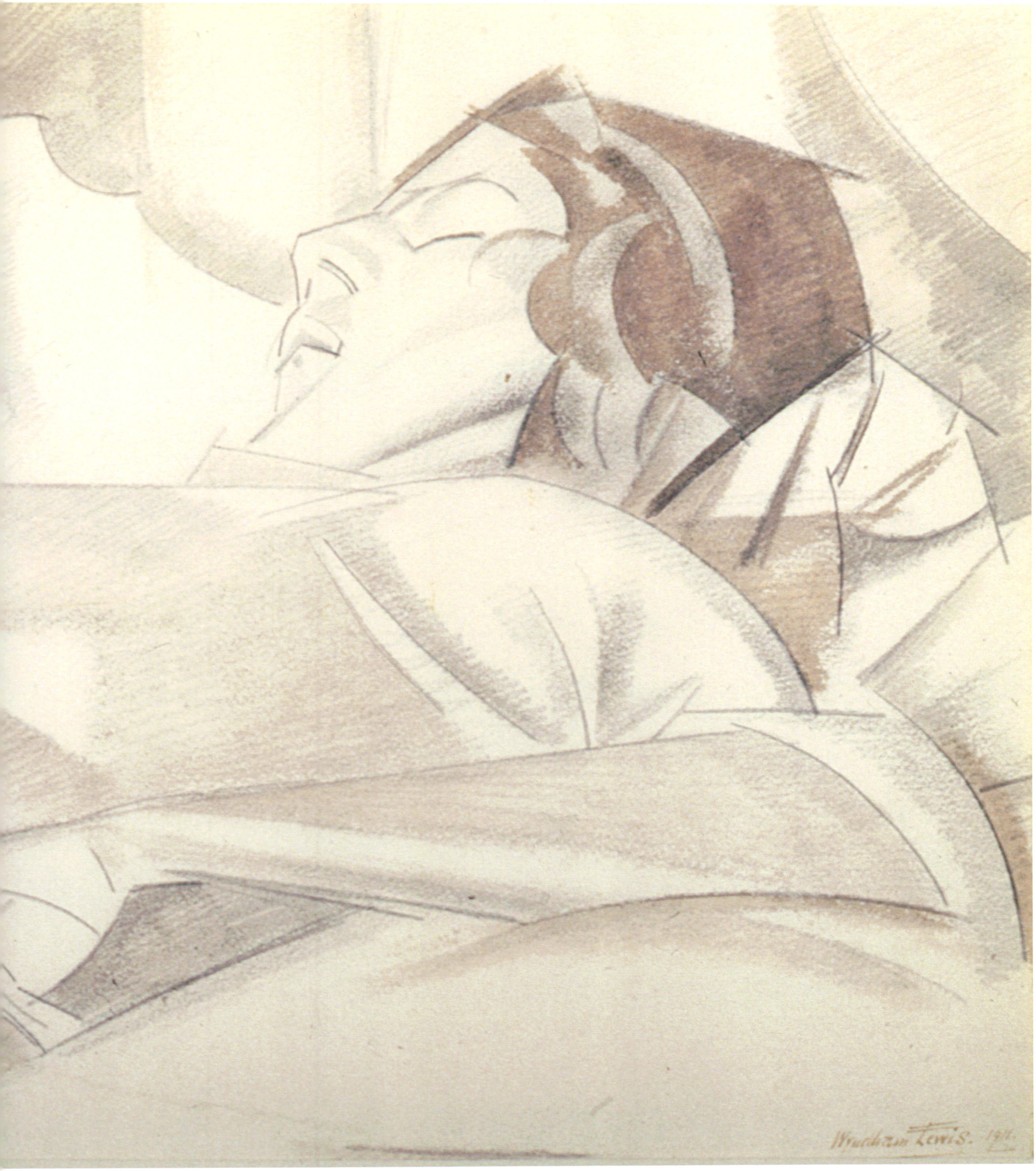
Wyndham Lewis. 1911.

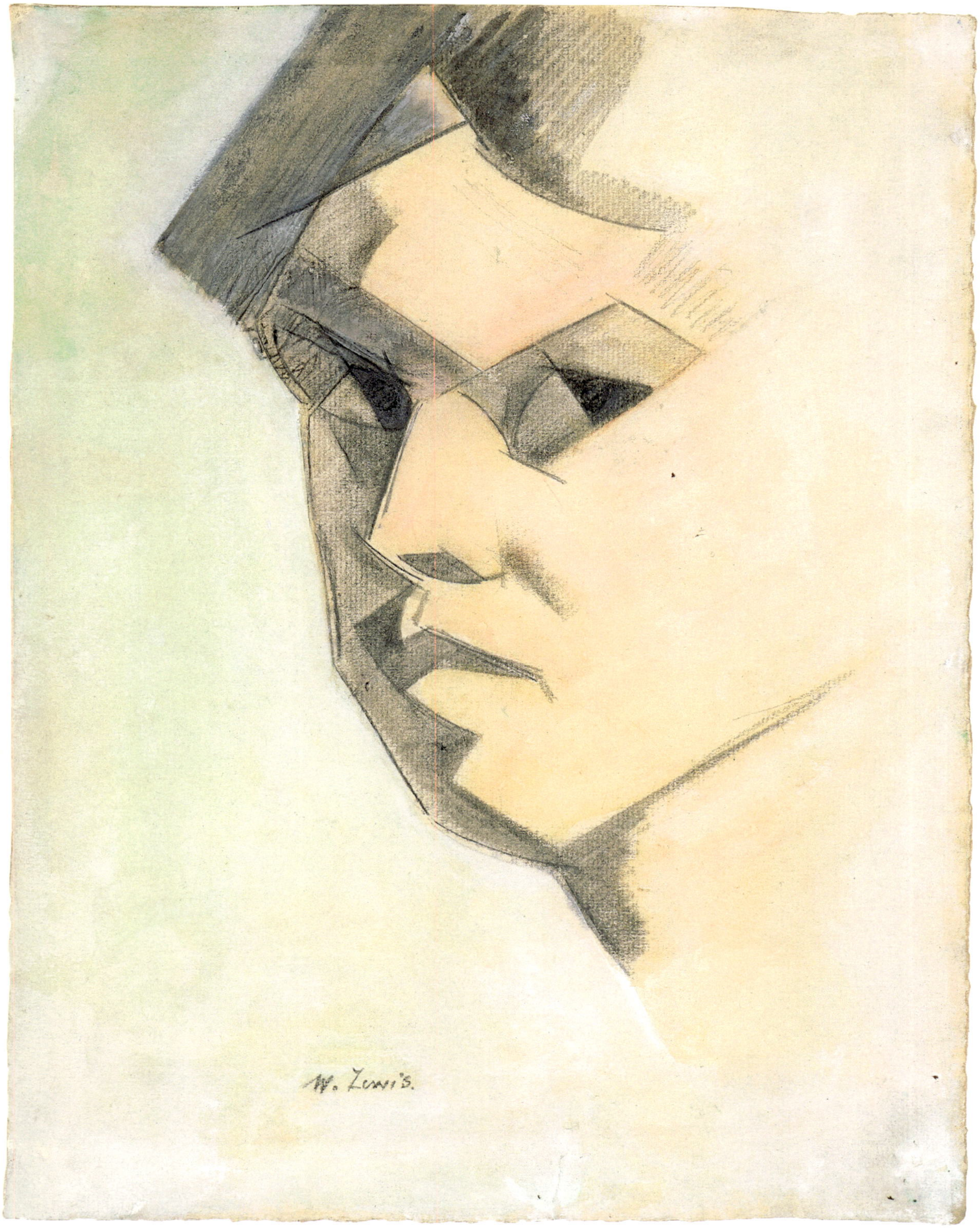

Cat. 9. ◀
Self-Portrait (1911). Graphite, pen and ink, watercolour and gouache on paper. 31.3 x 24.3 cm. C.J. Fox Collection (LD.2000.XX.I). M 26

Cat. 10. ▶
Self-Portrait, 1911–12. Pencil, crayon and wash on paper. 54 x 39.5 cm. Private collection, Ivor Braka Ltd M 25

Lewis produced three self-portraits in this style in 1911. Again, Cubist analysis takes second place to expressive intention and the formalised Cubist planes are used (in a way reminiscent of the less sophisticated *The Celibate* (Cat. 5)) to convey stark and dramatic monumentality. The contrast in the personalities represented is marked, and it may be that Lewis was (as in *The Theatre Manager* (Cat. 6)) intent on showing the multiplicity of personalities that the modern artist needs to find within himself if he is to reach some synthesis that will give expression to the "crowd" that is both his audience and a reflection of himself. The absence of colour in Cat. 10 increases the chiaroscuro, concentrating the artist's intense and disquieting gaze.
Cat. 9 shows a gentler personality, softened by the delicate green background into which the back of the head imperceptibly melts. But the eyes in this portrait, reduced to triangles bisected into dark and light, also have a slightly threatening quality.

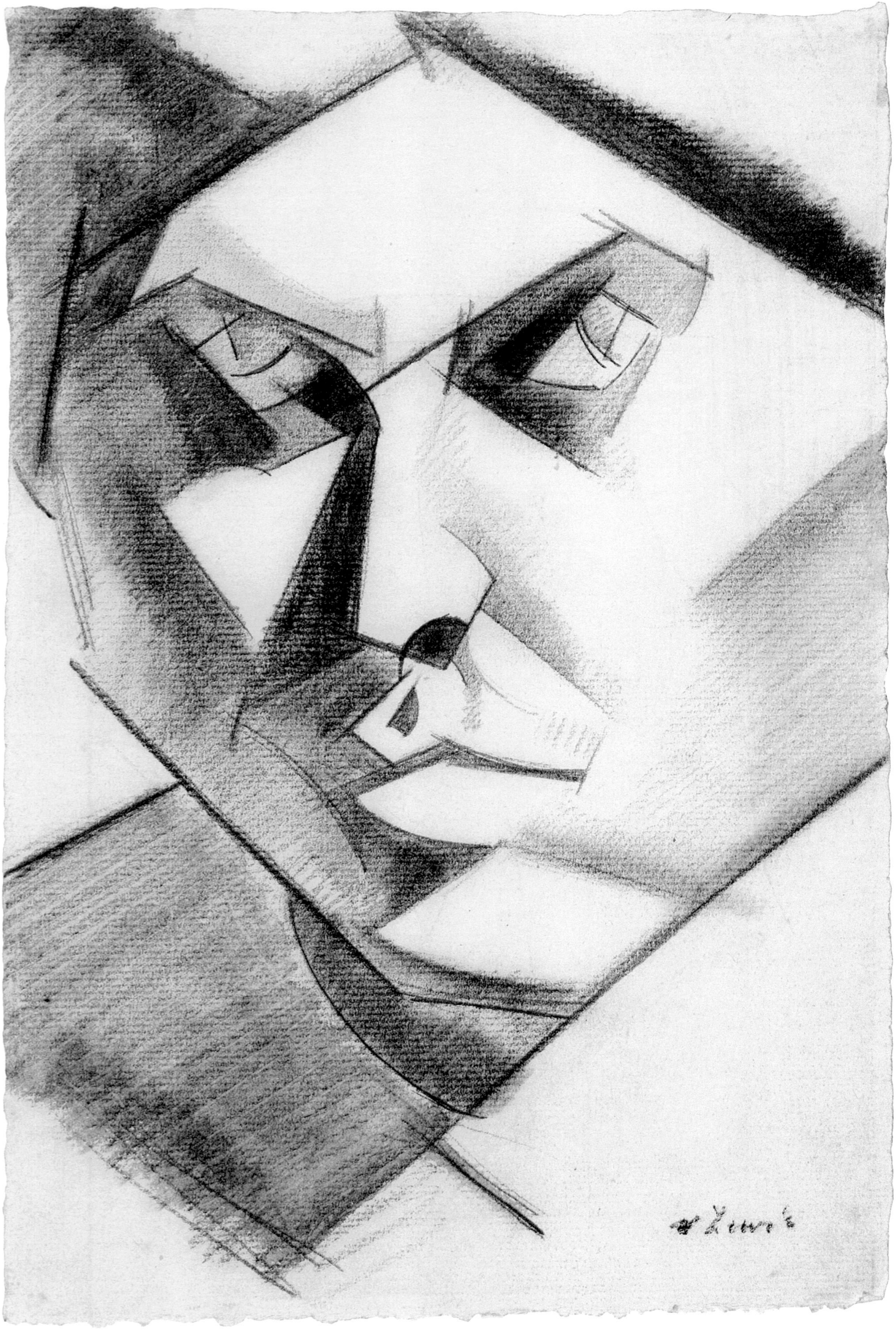

Cat. 11.
***Smiling Woman Ascending a Stair*, 1911. Charcoal and gouache on paper. 95 x 65 cm. Private collection. M 27**

Perhaps influenced by Henri Bergson, Lewis explored the paradox of laughter in this work, for which Kate Lechmere modelled. A much larger lost gouache, *The Laughing Woman* (M 22) showed the model in three-quarter view. Bergson, in his study, *Laughter*,[1] comments that laughter is our reaction when we witness a person suddenly behaving as if they were a machine. Human beings should be free and self-determined, but in certain circumstances they are reduced to physical objects governed simply by physical laws (when slipping on a banana skin, for example). The smiling woman is the laugher, not the object of laughter, but the rigidity of her posture (reinforced by Lewis's Cubist idiom) and her fixed grin give her also a disturbing mechanical quality. Lewis would write several analyses of laughter in his career (modifying Bergson's theories considerably). The disturbing grin in this drawing would recur later in his visual art as well, particularly in the series of "Tyros" he produced in the early 1920s. The object protruding from the table to the left appears to be a mask – perhaps Lewis's comment on the rigidifying effect of the fixed grin. It is not known whether the drawing is in any way related to Marcel Duchamp's *Nude Descending a Staircase* (1912).

1. Henri Bergson, *Laughter: An Essay on the Meaning of the Comic*. Trans. C. Brereton and F. Rothwell (London: Macmillan, 1911).

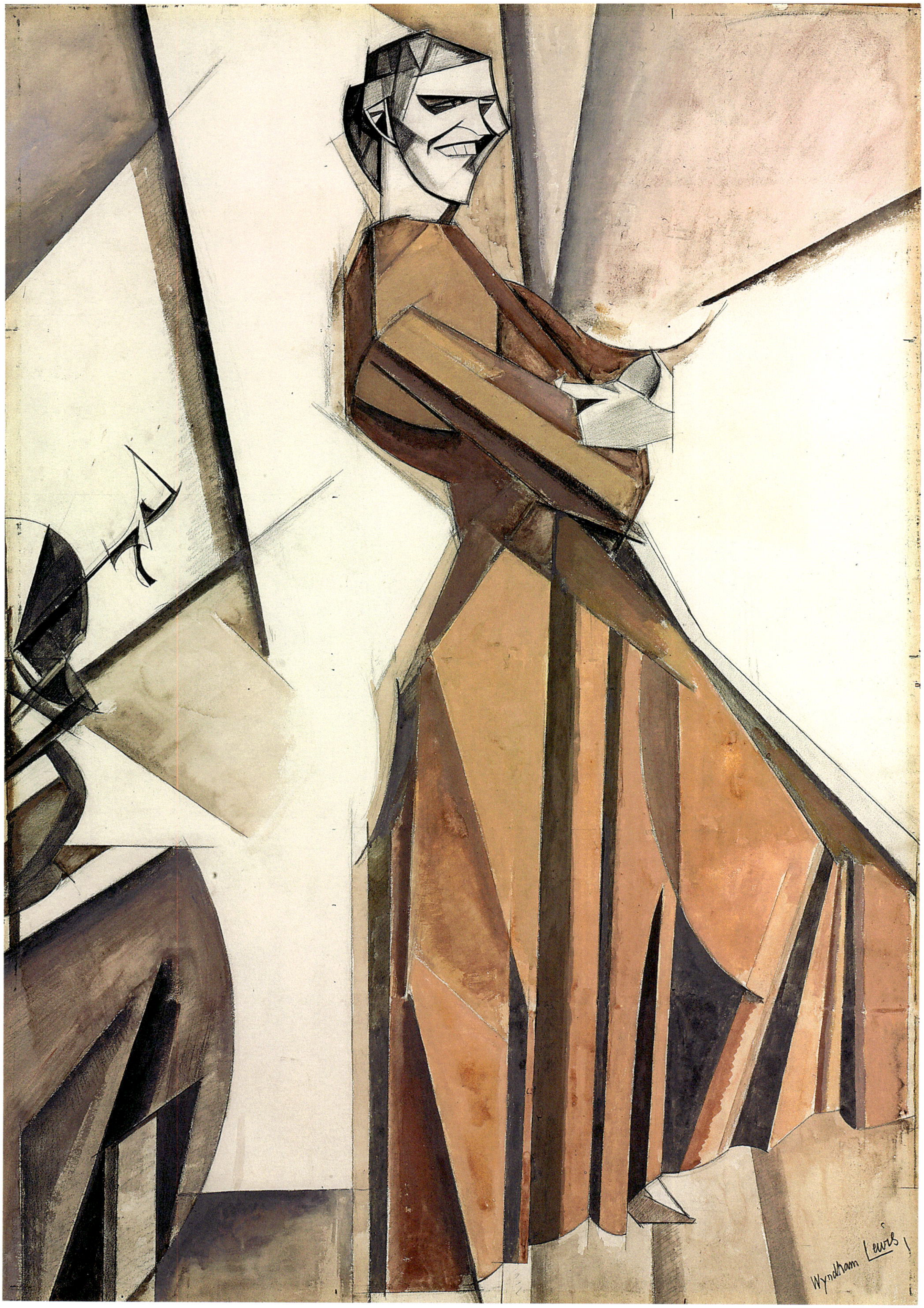

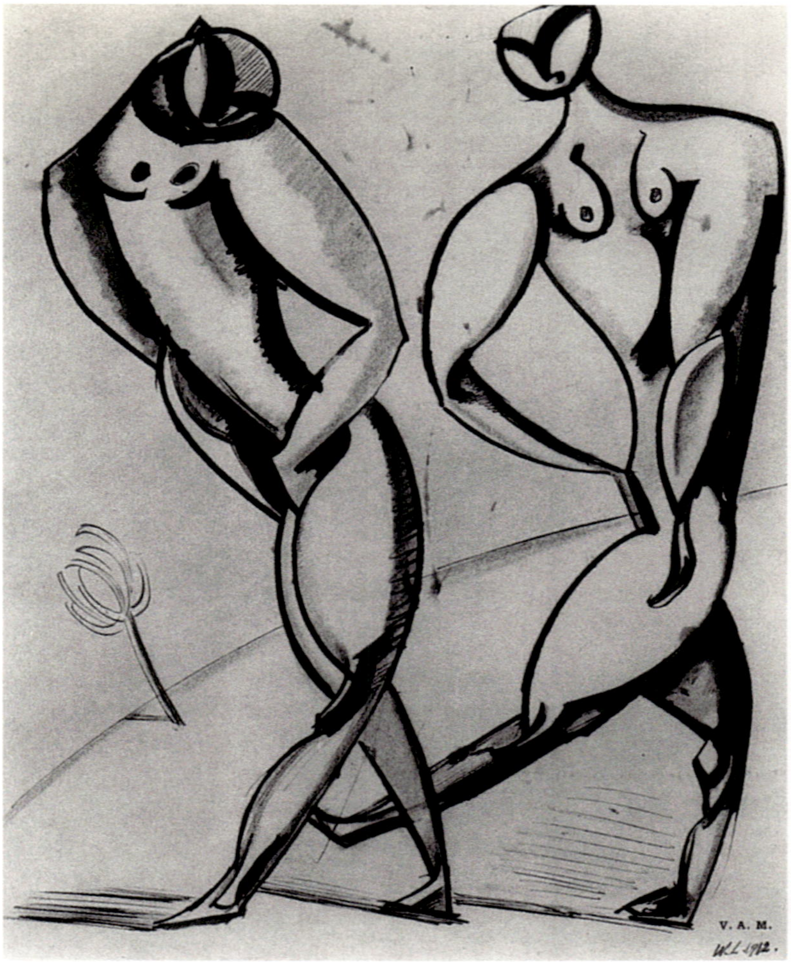

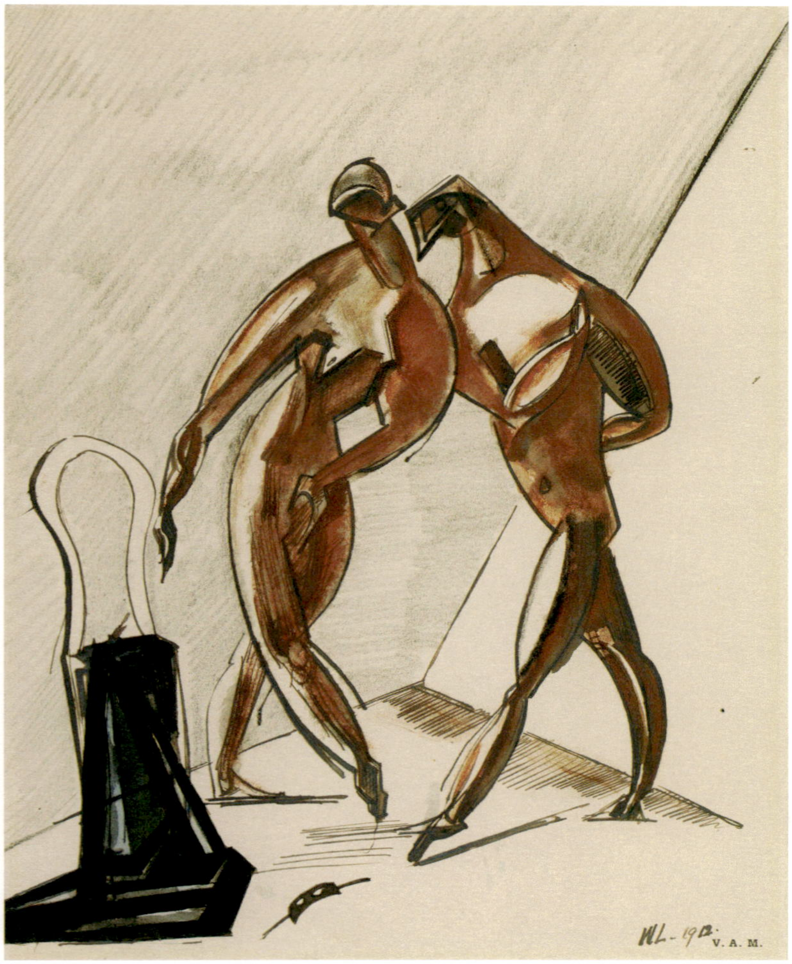

Cat. 12. ▲
Courtship, 1912. Pencil, ink and pastel on paper. 25.5 x 20.5 cm. Victoria and Albert Museum (E 3785-1919). M 45

Cat. 13. ▶
The Domino, 1912. Pencil, ink and watercolour on paper. 25.5 x 20.5 cm. Victoria and Albert Museum (E 3784-1919). M 54

In these works, Lewis gives a social dimension – and a markedly satirical one – to the primitivist pastoral idyll found in the work of Henri Matisse. The faces of the fauns in *Courtship*, in particular, have a kinship with Matisse's primitive figures. Lewis is concerned with conveying a Bergsonian sense of the internal "feel" of the body in movement. Henri Bergson noted that the precise quality of such a feeling could not be reproduced in "quantitative" language; the body was thus somehow prior to the artificial world of language and calculation that has overlaid our primal relationship with the world. In *Courtship*, the stalking (female?) figure and the coy male (?) that displays his presumably attractive hind parts, enact a ritual of the type Lewis depicted in his early writings about innkeepers and their guests, though in the stories sexuality is more in the background. *The Domino* also depicts ritualistic behaviour, with one figure perhaps inviting the other to don the small mask displayed on the chair. The effect in both these images is to call into question nostalgia for an unmediated "natural" existence. Lewis's linear mastery is displayed in the tense arcs heavily scored into the paper surface.

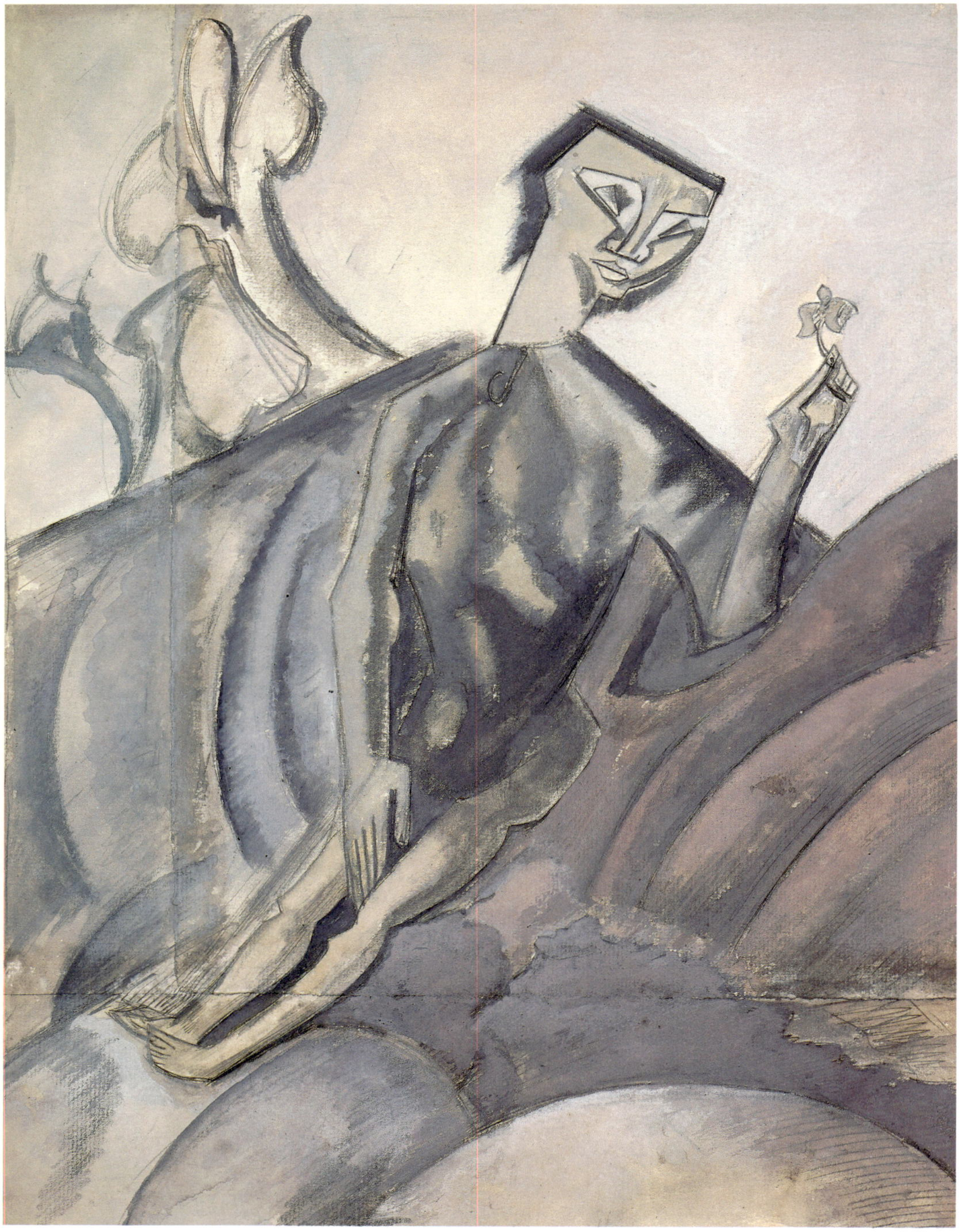

Cat. 14.
***Figure Holding a Flower*, 1912. Graphite, pen and ink, and gouache on paper. 38.1 x 29.1 cm. Wyndham Lewis Memorial Trust (LD.2004. XX.4). M 63**

This is another pastoral scene and the sad little flower gives it hint of a *vanitas*. Lewis adapts Cubist idiom to enforce a continuity between the figure and the ground against which she is silhouetted. In fact, the appearance is of being almost submerged in that ground, like the female protagonist of Samuel Beckett's play *Happy Days* (1961). In this semi-comic, semi-tragic scene, Lewis again critiques naive idealisations of the state of nature. This and the following drawings may be influenced by another aspect of Henri Bergson's philosophy (as originally suggested by Thomas Kush).[1] Lewis admitted to having followed Bergson's "evolutionary system," which explained the different states of matter and the hierarchy of plants and animals as the varying products of the efforts of a vital spirit (*élan vital*) to achieve the maximum amount of freedom in recalcitrant matter. Plant life represents a comparatively unsuccessful achievement of this effort, while human beings represent maximum success (in a certain direction, at any rate). Lewis's figures in this drawing seem barely able to sustain their position on the human side of the vegetable–human border.

1. Thomas Kush, *Wyndham Lewis's Pictorial Integer* (Ann Arbor, Michigan: UMI Research Press, 1981).

Cat. 15.
***The Starry Sky* or *Two Women*, 1912. Pencil, pen and ink, gouache and collage on paper. 48 x 62.5 cm. Arts Council Collection, Southbank Centre, London (ACC151). M 86**

Where the figure holding a flower (Cat. 14) was pathetic, these quasi-geological formations are grotesque, monumental and impressive. The figure–ground continuity is reinforced by the collaged "sky" behind the image. The strange title is Lewis's and may have an esoteric connotation relating it to the "play" that he published in *Blast*, No. 1, *Enemy of the Stars* (B&M Cat. 2):

The stars shone madly in the archaic blank wilderness of the universe, machines of prey.

Mastodons, placid in electric atmosphere, white rivers of power. They stood in eternal black sunlight.[1]

The stars are also called "pantheistic machines"[2]; Lewis's scepticism about "natural" values (as celebrated by Henri Matisse, for example) would soon extend to the mechanical environment that mankind invented to supplement nature.

1. Wyndham Lewis, *Enemy of the Stars*, *Blast*, No. 1 (June 1914), p. 64.
2. Ibid.

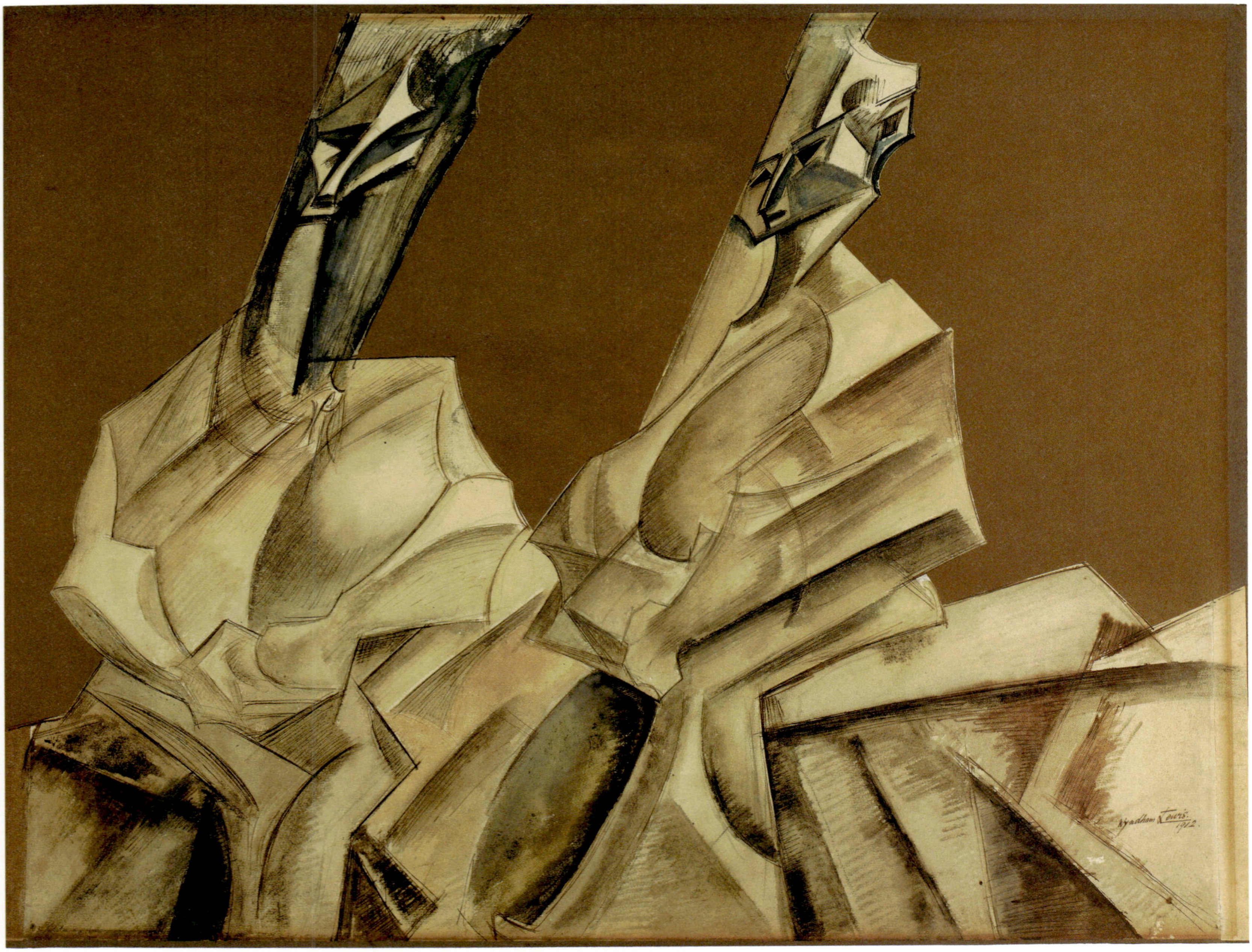

Cat. 16.
Figure Composition, 1912. Pen and ink, watercolour, pencil and gouache on paper. 25 x 31 cm. Private collection. M 61

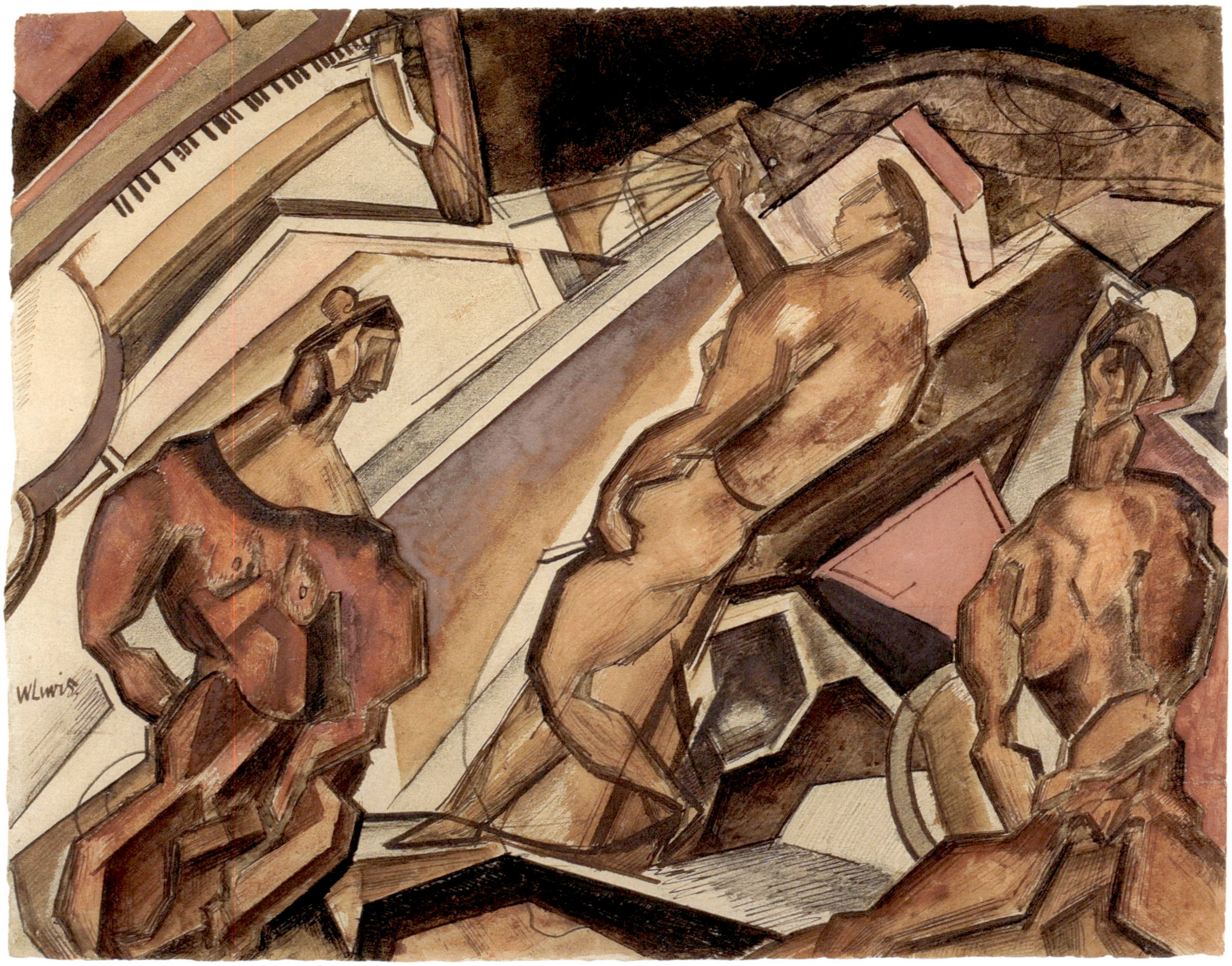

As in *Lovers* (Cat. 20), this work contains in the background of the figures hints of the geometricisation of Lewis's future Vorticist style. The figures themselves are pulpy and ungainly, suggesting a quasi-vegetative state. The elongation and distortion of these figures (as in *Sunset among the Michelangelos* (1912) (M 88, p. 25) could derive from El Greco, though they have been given a "Cubist" rigidity. The work may depict a circus scene: *pentimenti* at the top show traces of a group of horses. The central figure holds a drooping whip, while at the left of the picture a long-necked creature (a giraffe?) can be discerned in the matrix of the geometrical "background." The mane on its long neck resembles a piano keyboard.

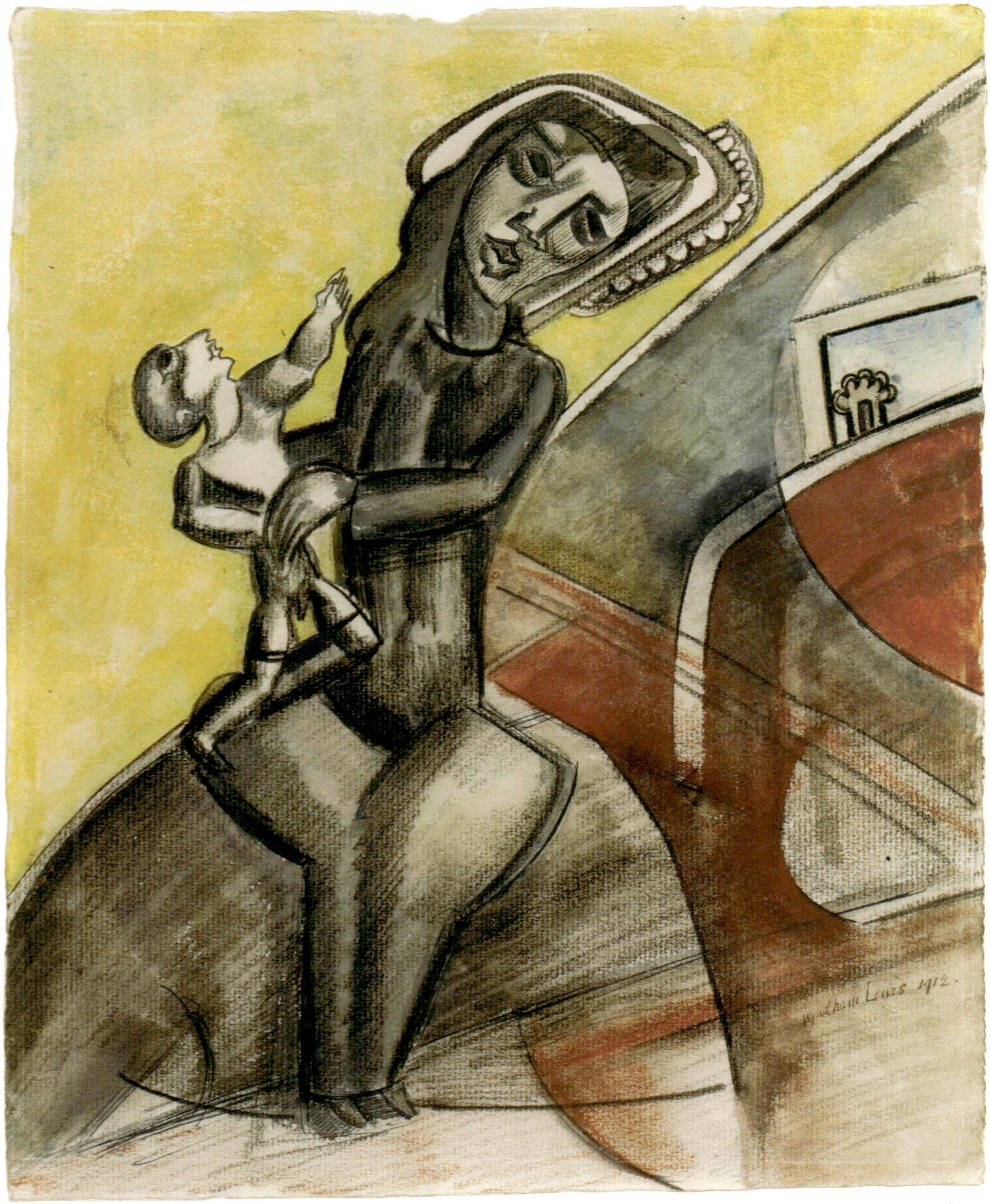

Cat. 17.
Russian Scene (Russian Madonna), 1912. Pencil, ink and watercolour on paper. 30.5 x 24 cm. Victoria and Albert Museum (E 3762-1919). M 83

As in Cat. 14, in this drawing the figure seems partially "embedded" in the ground, and like others of this kind, is pathetic and ungainly – an effect reinforced by the "primitivism" of Lewis's technique. The baby seems to have an energy with which the mother cannot cope. Lewis had read a great deal of Russian literature in French translations while a student in Paris. He was drawn to the patterns of absurd behaviour he found in these novels and attempted to create similar patterns in his own fiction. But the "Russian" dimension of this work may have been suggested by the resemblance to a primitive icon. Lewis had become a father the previous year and several of his works of 1911–12 show an interest in maternity as a motif. One of the works he exhibited at the *Second Post-Impressionist Exhibition* was a (now lost) *Mother and Child* (M P96), an oil painting in a more advanced "cubo-futurist" style in which there is also a contrast between the mother and her energetic baby.

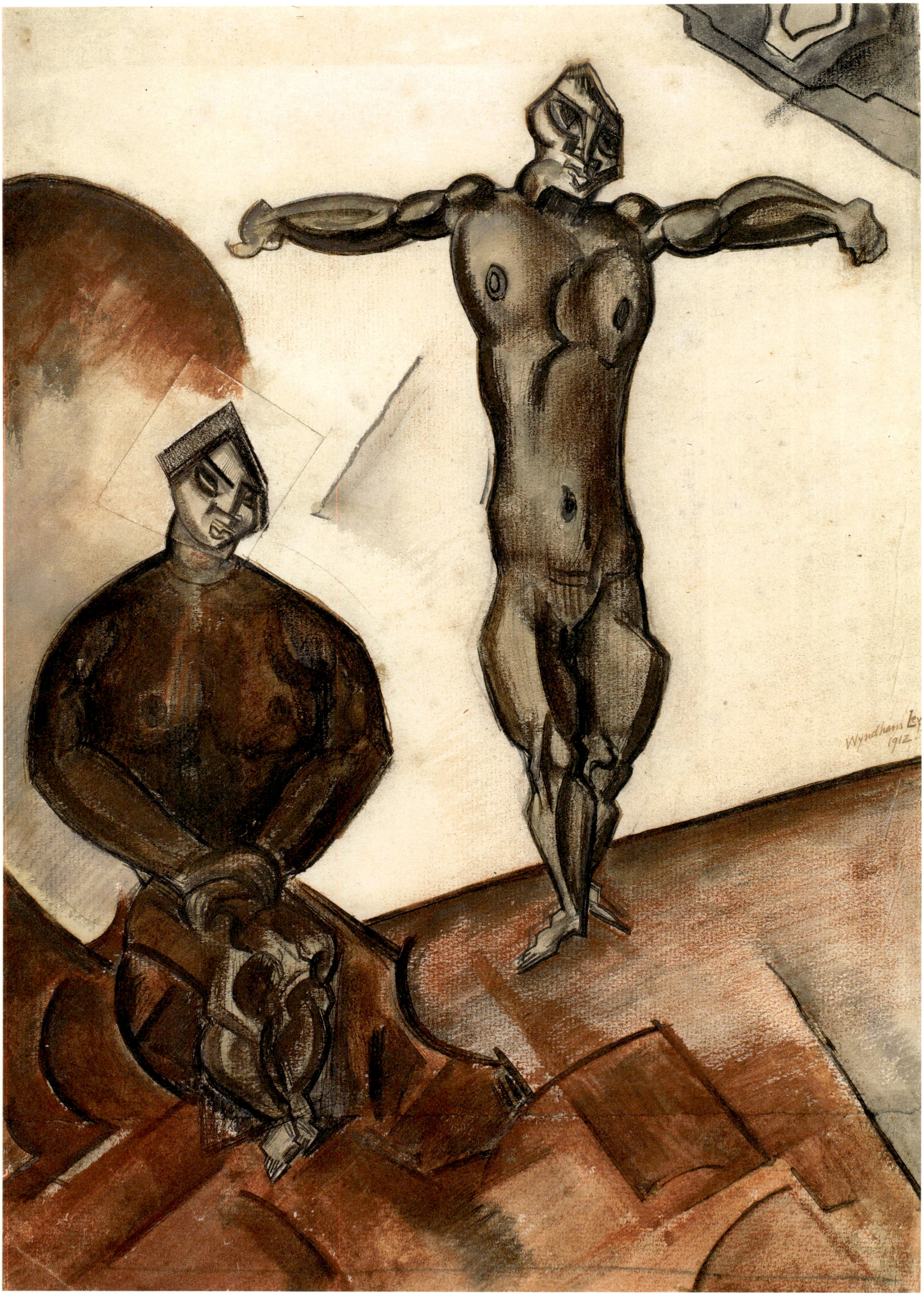
Wyndham Le
1912.

“If the material world were not empirical and matter simply for science, but were organized as in the imagination, we should live as though we were dreaming. Art’s business is to show how, then, the world would be.”

Wyndham Lewis,
Blast, 1914

Cat. 18.
Man and Woman, 1912.
Chalk, pen and ink, wash and gouache on paper. 36 x 26 cm. Wyndham Lewis Memorial Trust. G. and V. Lane Collection (LD.2009.XX.I). M 75

A photograph reproduced in Charles Handley-Read's *The Art of Wyndham Lewis* shows this work in an earlier state.[1] Lewis seems to have darkened the colours and strengthened the drawing, as well as adding a small cap to the head of the seated female figure. It is not clear from Handley-Read's commentary when this was done. The drawing is perhaps the most sympathetic representation in Lewis's early work of the tragedy of everyday existence. One of Lewis's earliest pieces of writing (dating from about 1907–8), describes a beggar and his companion outside a Breton church:

> [...] he sat motionless beside his insouciant and listless companion. With a heavy grey mat of hair, he was dark-skin'd and look'd like some Bedouin; the flesh was pucker'd round his eyes into innumerable deep wrinkles, as though some torrid sun were constantly in his eyes: and gazing into Space, he seem'd to find in the nothingness always before him and blank of his reverie, the same occupation as those old sailors find, sitting for hours on the benches of the quays, and gazing at the empty sea.[2]

The juxtaposition of seated peasant woman and "crucified" male transposes Gauguin's *Yellow Christ* (1889) to a secular, natural setting.

1. Charles Handley-Read, ed. *The Art of Wyndham Lewis* (London: Faber, 1951), plate 1.
2. Wyndham Lewis, untitled manuscript, quoted in Paul Edwards, *Wyndham Lewis: Painter and Writer* (New Haven/London: Yale University Press, 2000), pp. 12–13.

"The imagination, not to be a ghost, but to have the vividness and warmth of life, and the atmosphere of a dream, uses, where best inspired, the pigment and material of nature."

Wyndham Lewis, ***Blast,*** 1916

Cat. 19.

[Not in exhibition] Study for *Kermesse*, 1912. Pen and ink, wash and gouache on paper. 35 x 35.1 cm. Yale Center for British Art, Paul Mellon Fund and Gift of Neil F. and Ivan E. Phillips in memory of their mother, Mrs Rosalie Phillips. M 72

The lost painting for which this is a sketch was a very large one (about three metres square), designed to hang on the staircase of a nightclub opened in London's fashionable West End by Frida Strindberg, the third wife of the great Swedish playwright. It is one of the most serious losses in Lewis's *oeuvre*, as it disappeared after its owner offered it for sale at a knockdown price in *The Times* after being caricatured in Lewis's 1930 satirical novel, *The Apes of God* (B&M Cat. 21).[1] Its importance to Lewis is shown by the fact that he worked on it and repainted it twice before eventually selling it to the American collector, John Quinn. It marks the beginning of a "blue period" in Lewis's work, a colour perhaps adopted in order to show that blue need not be associated with the melancholy of Pablo Picasso's use of it. Originally entitled *Creation*, the painting showed a scene of Dionysian abandon; as one couple dances in the centre, a figure to the right with upraised arm pours an arc of cider (unsuccessfully) towards his mouth. To the left another figure sits at an improvised bar, being served, perhaps, by a waiter behind and above him. The scene is a "creation" in the Bergsonian sense that it is an outpouring of energy that aims to transcend the limitations of determinate, material existence. In Friedrich Nietzsche's idea of the Dionysian, "something never before experienced struggles for utterance – the annihilation of the veil of *Māyā*, Oneness as genius of the race, ay, of nature."[2] The dance was a popular motif for modernist artists as an adumbration of this state. But where Henri Matisse's *The Dance* of 1910 depicts this "oneness" and primordial unity, Lewis's dancers appear not so much to dissolve their material bonds through their violent exertions, but to confirm their inseparability from matter. When Lewis exhibited a second painting entitled *Creation* at the *Second Post-Impressionist Exhibition*, the first was renamed as *Kermesse*. Before it was sent to America in 1915, Lewis brightened the drab colouring to yellow and a range of reds and purples.

1. Wyndham Lewis, The Apes of God (London: The Arthur Press, 1930).
2. Friedrich Nietzsche, *The Birth of Tragedy*, section 2. Translation from Nietzsche's *Complete Works*. Ed. Oscar Levy, vol. 1 (Edinburgh/London: Foulis, 1909), p. 32.

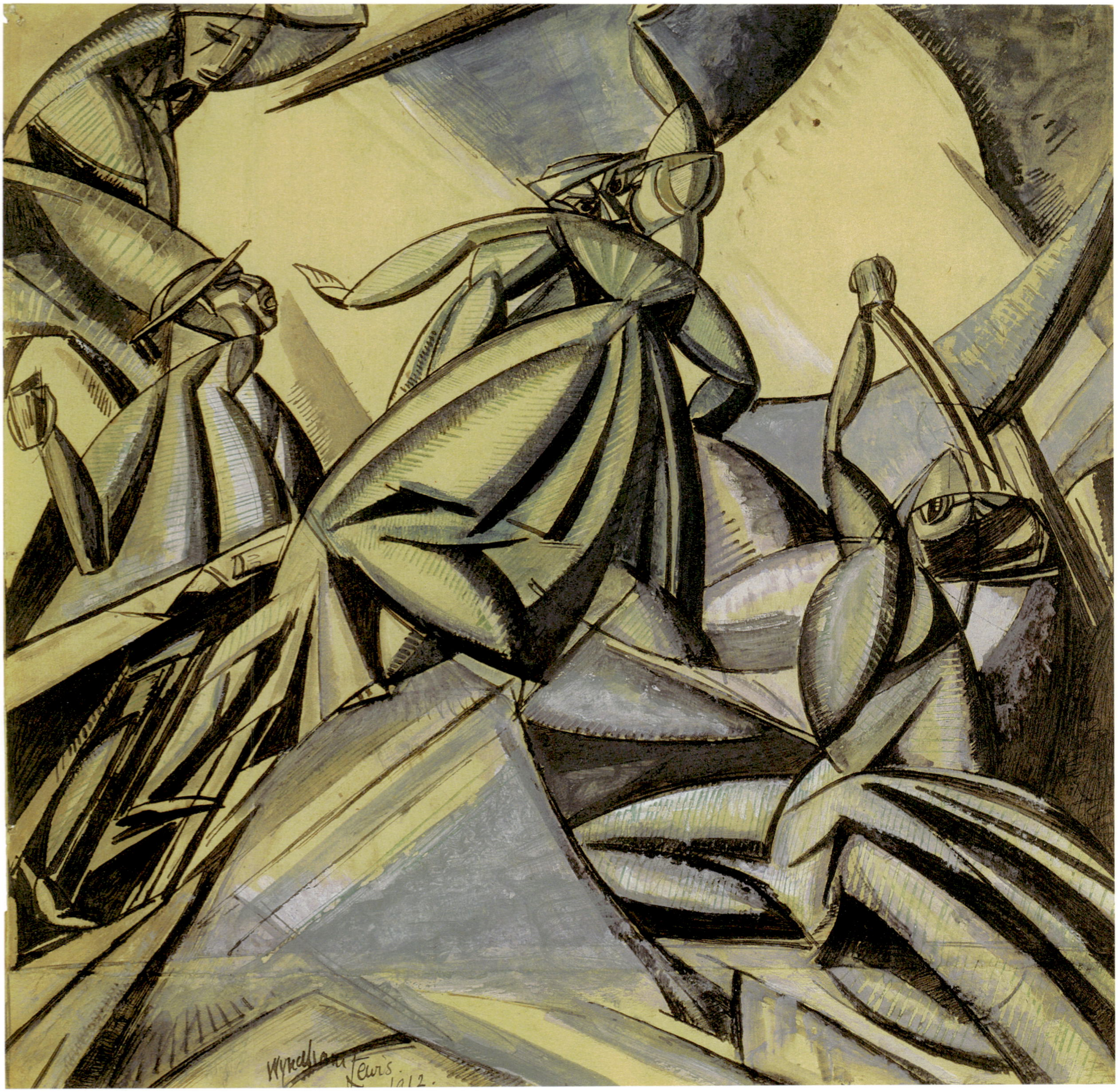

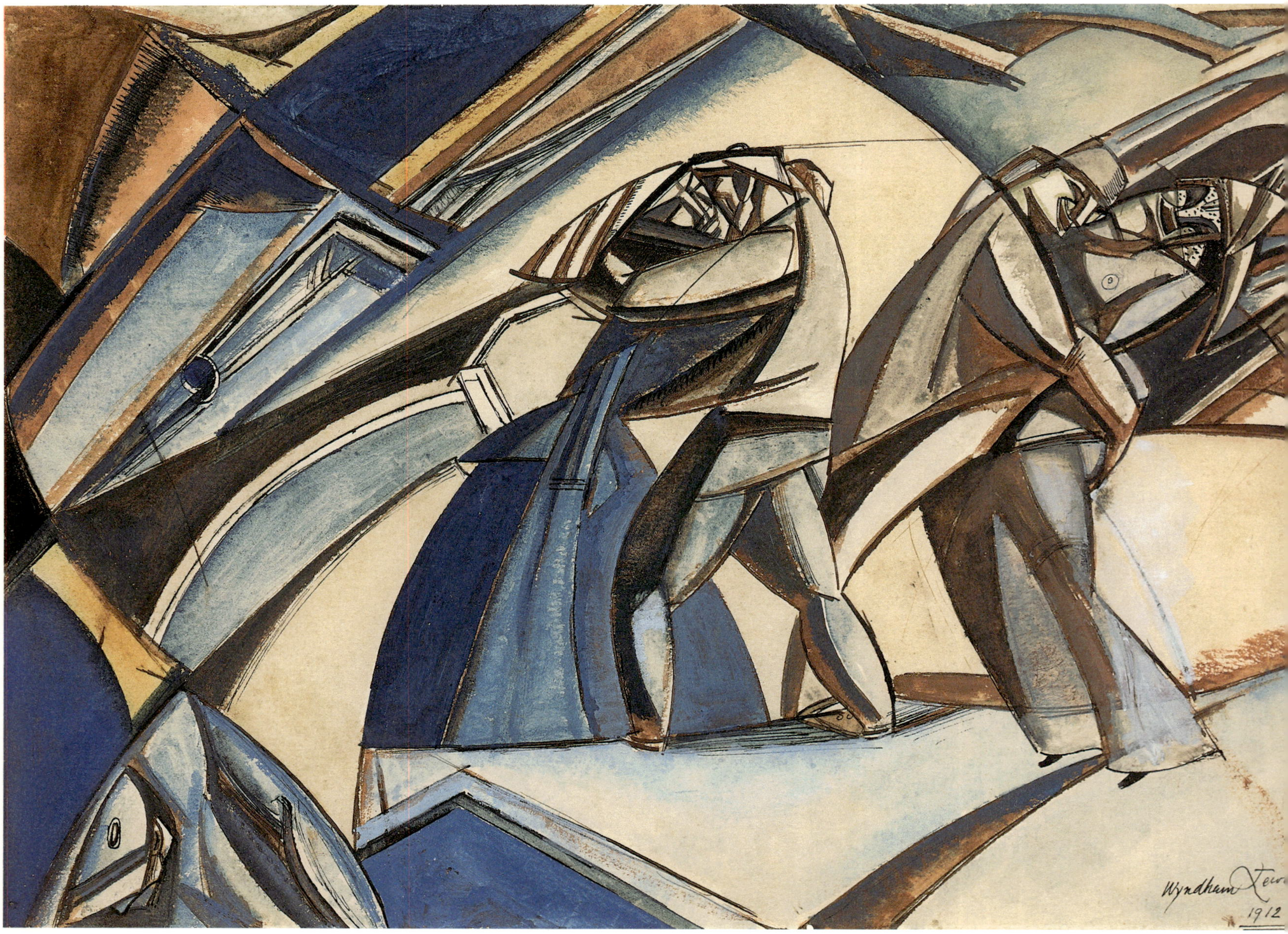

Cat. 20.
***Lovers*, 1912. Pen and ink, and watercolour on paper. 25.5 x 35.5 cm. Private collection. M 74**

The same mood of voracious passion as in the central couple of *Kermesse* (Cat. 19) is seen in these pairs of lovers or dancers. Lisa Tickner has shown how the prototype for these passionate dances is not so much Breton traditional dance as the "Apache" dances that were popular in France and in music halls at the turn of the century.[1] The two couples seem to be distinguished from each other by costume; the pair on the right wears modern clothes associated with the city (bowler hat, spotted veil), while the others seem to be wearing more traditional or "timeless" folk costume. Lewis may be suggesting a continuity between the urban and rural, just as he began to see an essential similarity between nature and the machine. The "background" to these figures shows Lewis beginning to develop the vocabulary of geometric abstraction that would dominate his visual art in 1913 and 1914.

1. Lisa Tickner, "The Popular Culture of *Kermesse*: Lewis, Painting, and Performance," *Modernism/Modernity* 4, no. 2 (April 1997), 67–120.

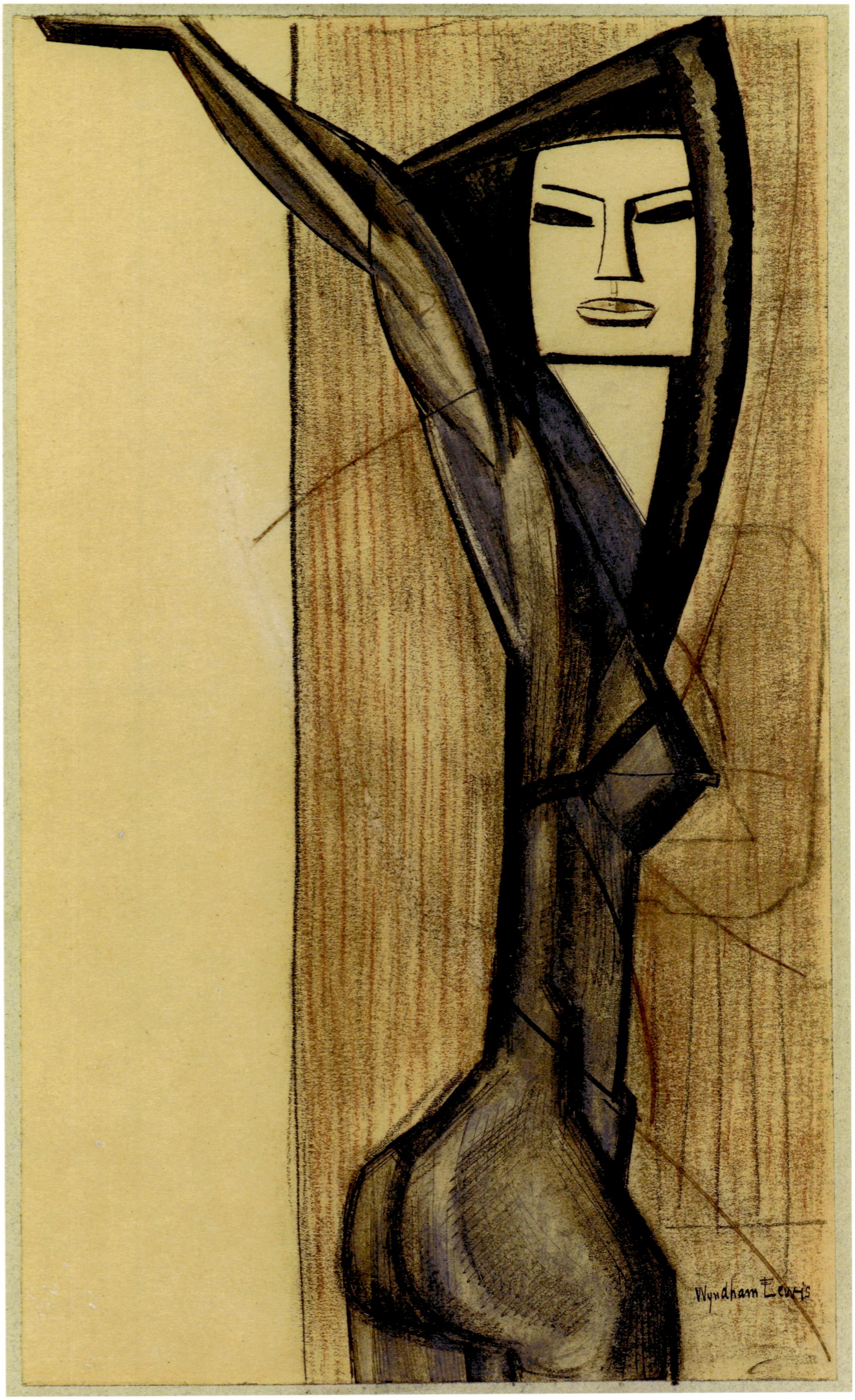

Cat. 21.
Odalisque, 1911–12. Pen and ink, and chalk on paper. 35.5 x 20.5 cm. Private collection. M 79

Lewis replaces the orientalist fantasy of nineteenth-century treatments of this subject with the impersonal plasticity of African sculpture. Ezra Pound (who may have owned this work) was especially enthusiastic about the sculpture of Jacob Epstein, who was working in London at this time. He told Epstein that he was less interested in modern painting and Epstein pointed out that Lewis's drawing had all the qualities of sculpture. Lewis imparts movement to this static figure by imperceptibly varying the viewpoint as our gaze ascends. The face of the odalisque resembles the impassive face of Epstein's flying angel carved for the tomb of Oscar Wilde in Père Lachaise Cemetery in Paris.

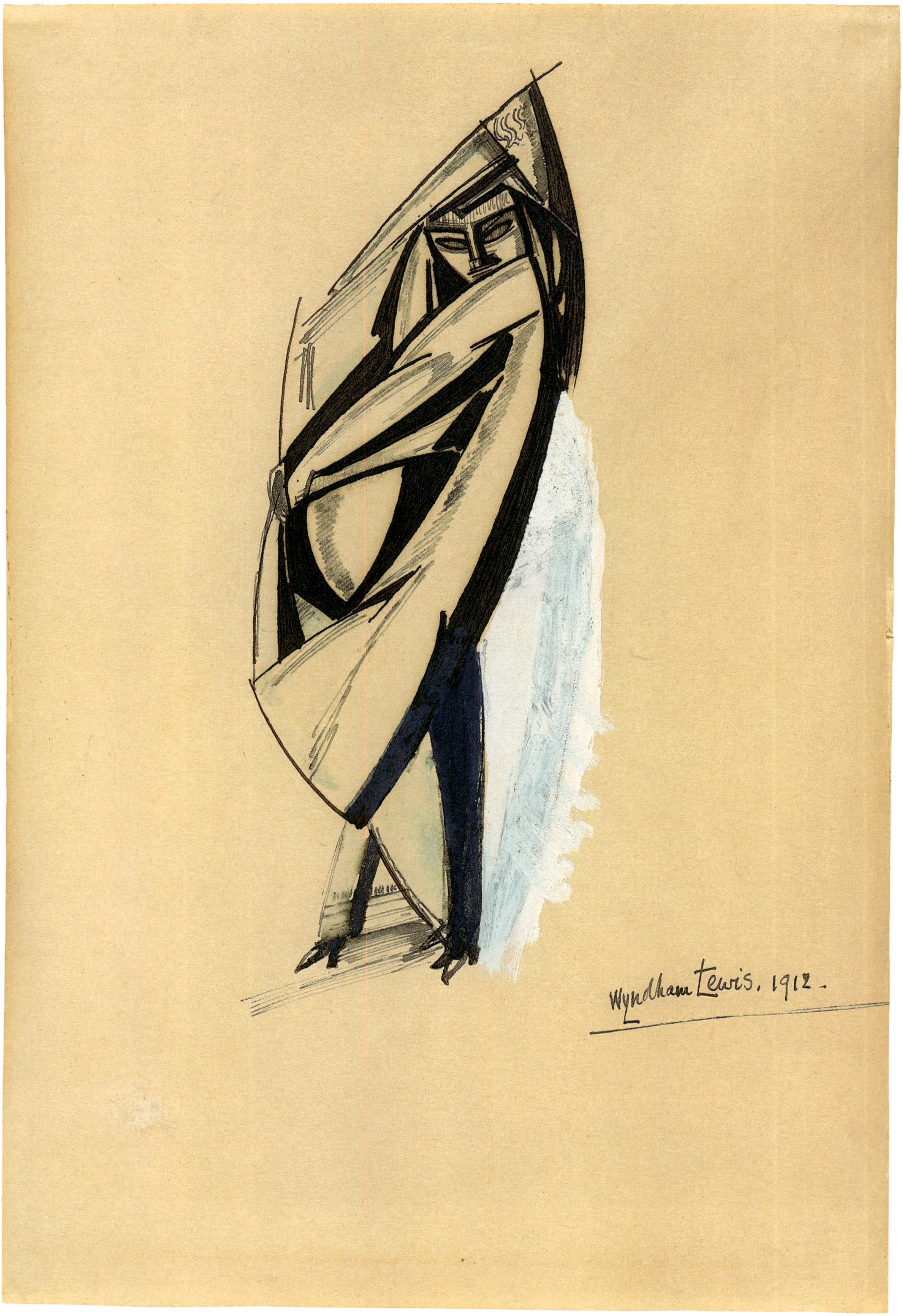

Cat. 22. ◀
Figure (Spanish Woman), 1912. Pen and ink, and gouache on paper. 31.2 x 20.7 cm. Wyndham Lewis Memorial Trust. G. and V. Lane Collection (LD.2004.XX.38). M 65

Cat. 23. ▶
The Courtesan, 1912. Pencil, ink and pastel on paper. 27.5 x 18.5 cm. Victoria and Albert Museum (E 3761-1919). M 44

The Spanish woman, clearly a dancer, has the same type of schematic and expressionless face as the odalisque. Lewis was fascinated both by passion and by ritual. Both, for him, had positive and negative possibilities; the passion that he exalted in his 1910 essay, "Our Wild Body"[1] (a critique of English reserve), could easily degenerate into a mindless violence. He paid homage to the compulsions of ritual in his own painting ("In a painting certain forms MUST be SO; in the same meticulous, profound manner that your pen or book must lie on the table at a certain angle, your clothes at night be arranged in a set personal symmetry [...]").[2] Such rituals, called "Inferior Religions" by Lewis, could also degenerate into predictable mechanical routines that were mindless. The beauty of Spanish traditional dance was, no doubt, that it combined passion and ritual so successfully. *The Courtesan* is related in subject matter as a study of ritualised behaviour (signalled by the two inverted masks at the bottom of the picture). Formally, however, with its crowded arcs, blocks and intersecting lines, it looks forward to the form of abstraction Lewis would develop out of this very personal variant of Cubism in the next year. The rather grimy or rusty texture and almost unfinished feel of this drawing also show a modernist willingness on Lewis's part to emphasise the ontological status of the work: an image conjured from material signs that will not retreat into transparency no matter how long we look at them.

1. Wyndham Lewis, "Our Wild Body" (1910). Rprt. *The Complete Wild Body* (1927). Ed. Bernard Lafourcade (Santa Barbara: Black Sparrow Press, 1982), pp. 251–56.
2. Wyndham Lewis, "Fêng Shui and Contemporary Form," *Blast*, No. 1 (June 1914), p. 38 (see Anthology, p. 346).

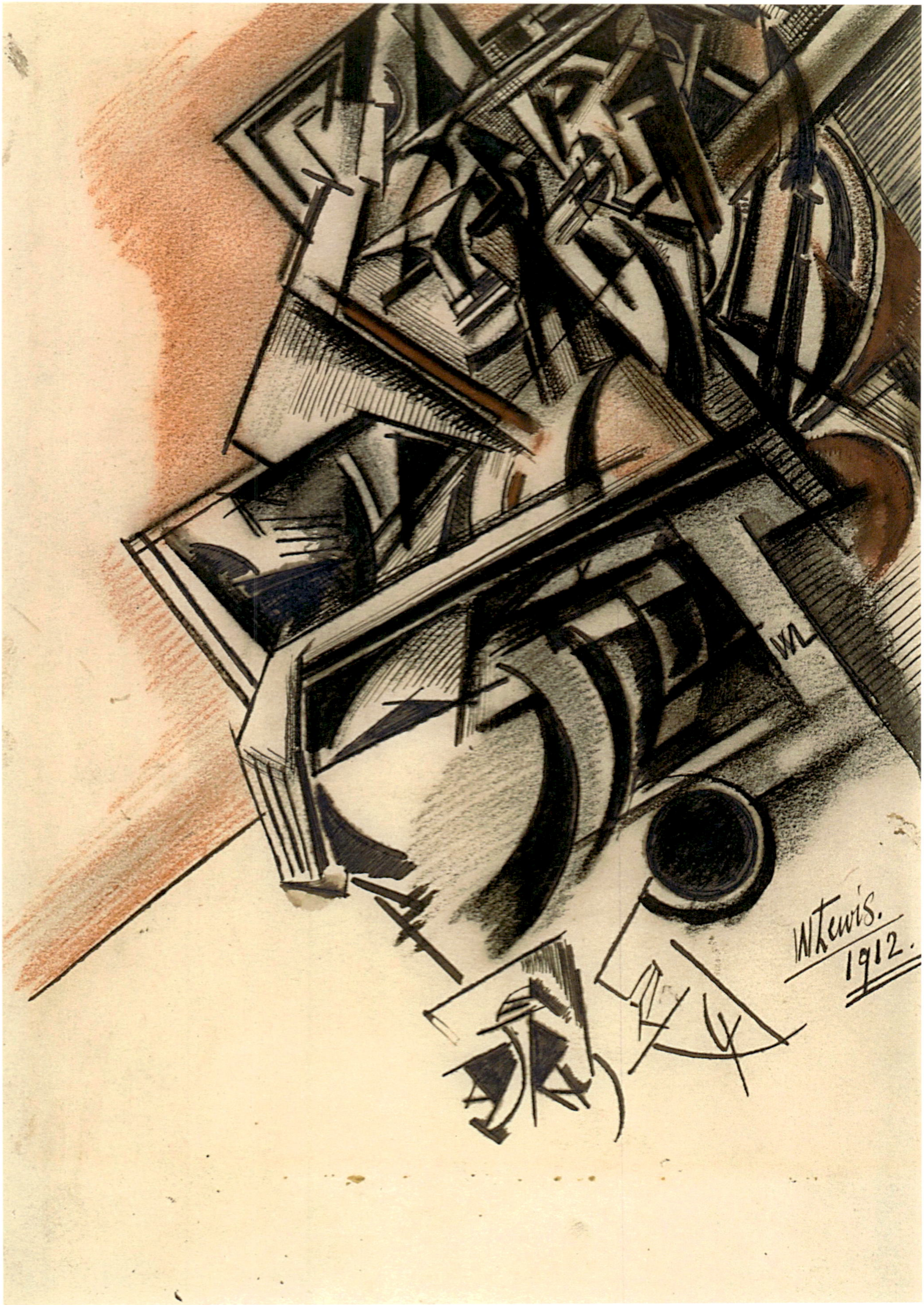
WL
W Lewis.
1912.

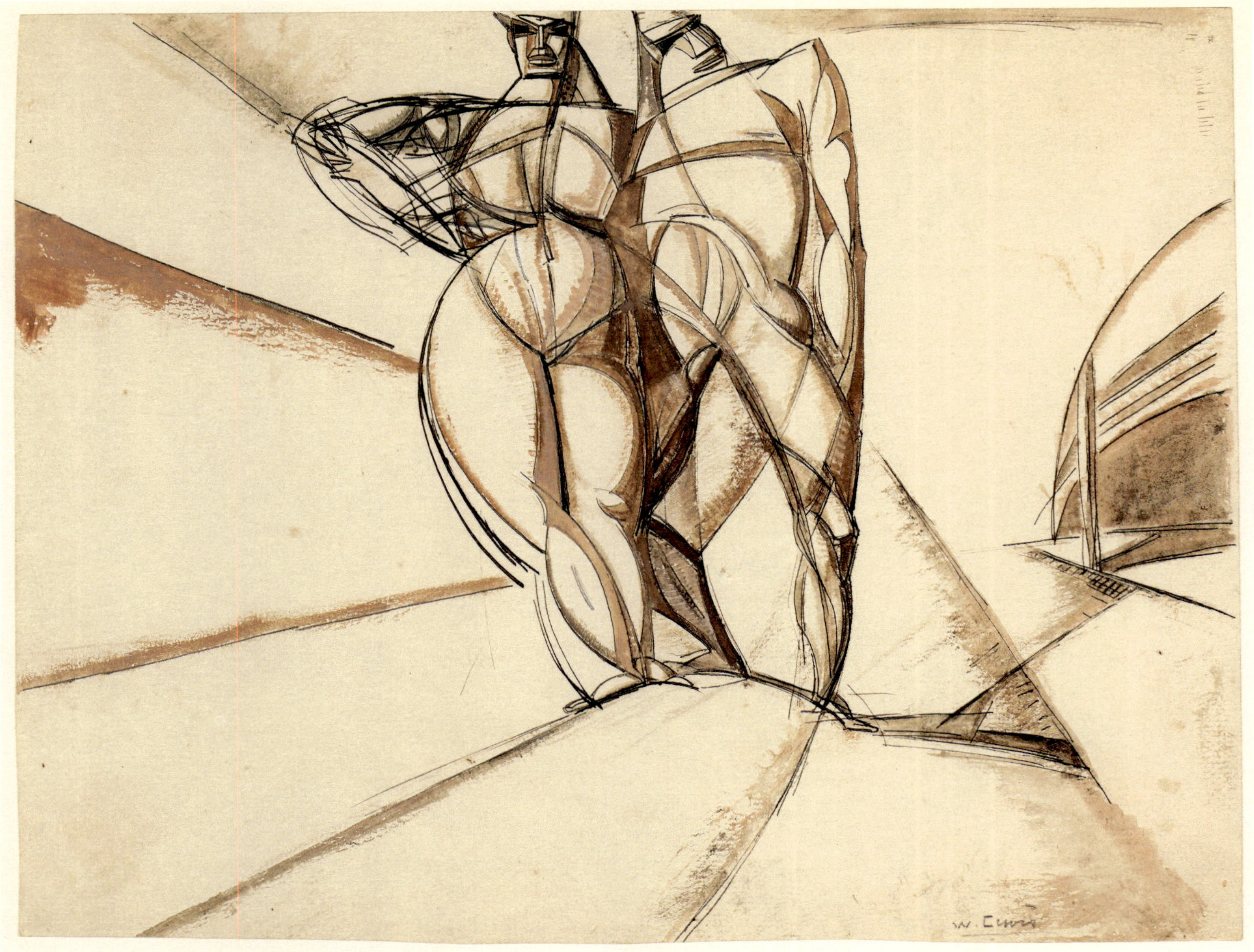

Cat. 24.
Two Vorticist Figures, 1912. Pen and black ink, and watercolour on paper. 24.7 x 31.9 cm. The Trustees of The British Museum (1984,0512.12). M 116

The title is probably a later invention. These muscular figures seem to be the centre of a "vortex" of energy that radiates in Futurist force-lines to the edges of the picture. A large oil painting, *Creation* (M P2), exhibited at the *Second Post-Impressionist Exhibition* and known only from a small press photograph from the *Daily Mirror* (3 October, 1912), shows a pair of lumbering figures emerging similarly from intersecting force-lines, though the painting was more Cubist in style than the present image.

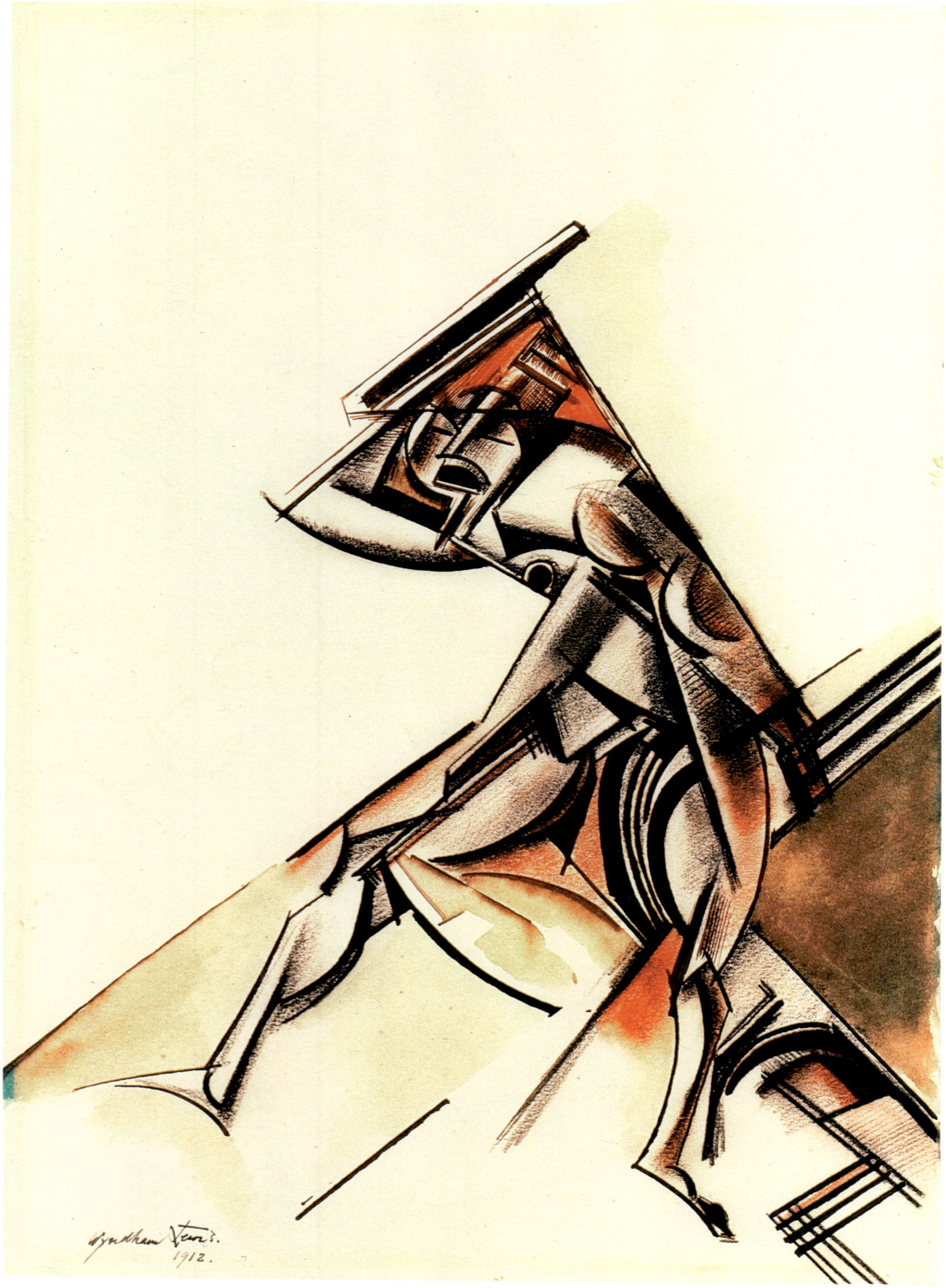

Cat. 25.
The Vorticist, 1912.
Watercolour on paper. 42.2 x 32.2 cm. Southampton City Art Gallery (1429). M 118

This work was owned by Edward Wadsworth, one of the painters associated with Lewis in the Vorticist movement (see Cat. 82). It was no doubt Wadsworth who gave it its anachronistic title; Vorticism did not exist as a movement until June 1914. Like *The Courtesan* (Cat. 23), this figure is conjured up from material signs, yet it appears almost to be in agony because of its own transformation into an armoured, insect-like figure. The continuity with matter that Lewis earlier showed by embedding the lower halves of his figures in striated earth is here translated into a continuity with a mechanised, geometric environment. This dual condition perhaps reminded Wadsworth of the similarly painful continuity between nature and machine in the figure of Jacob Epstein's (later dismantled) 1915 sculpture, *The Rock Drill*, where a semi-mechanised (but pregnant) figure was mounted on a real drill.

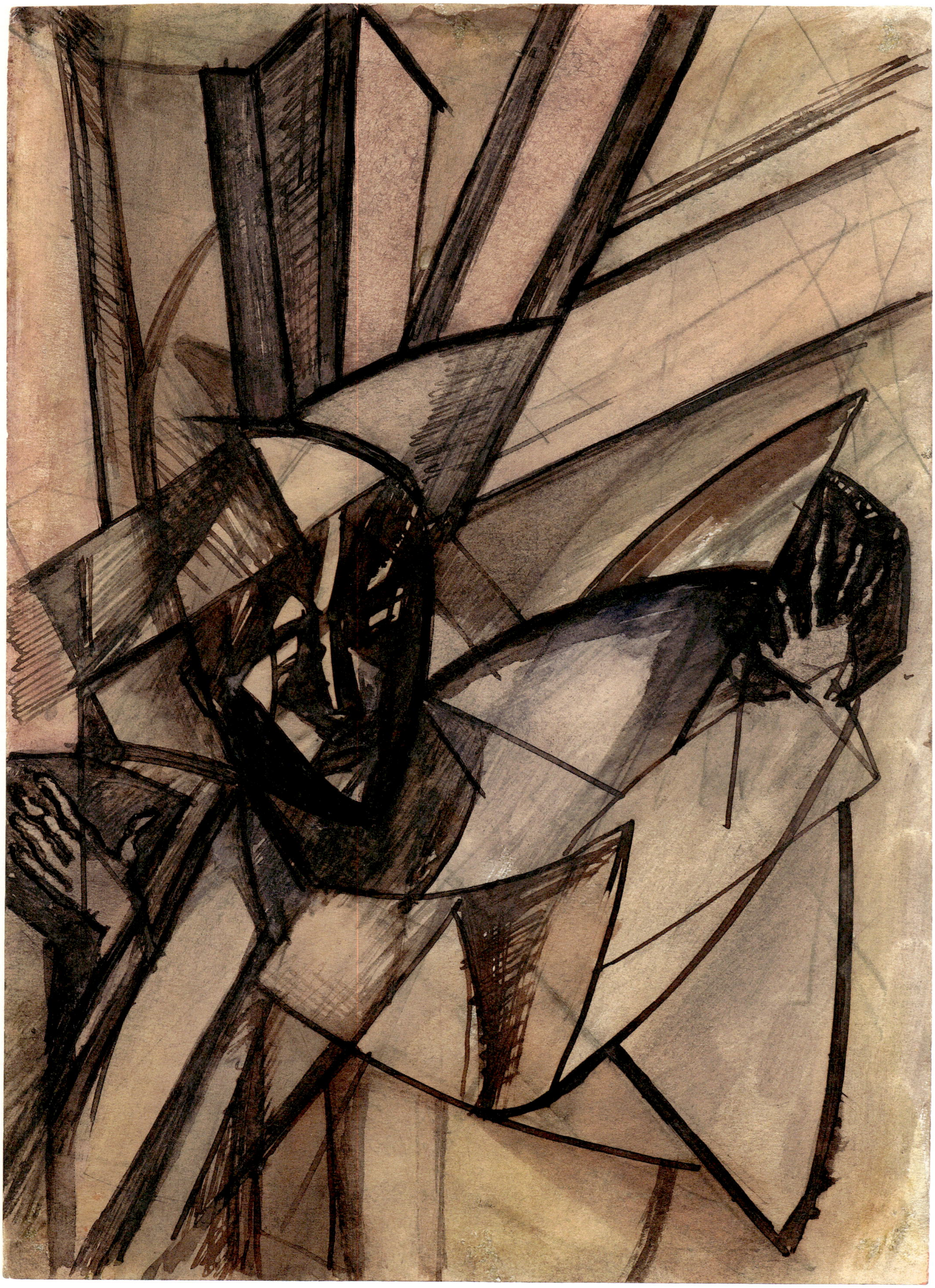

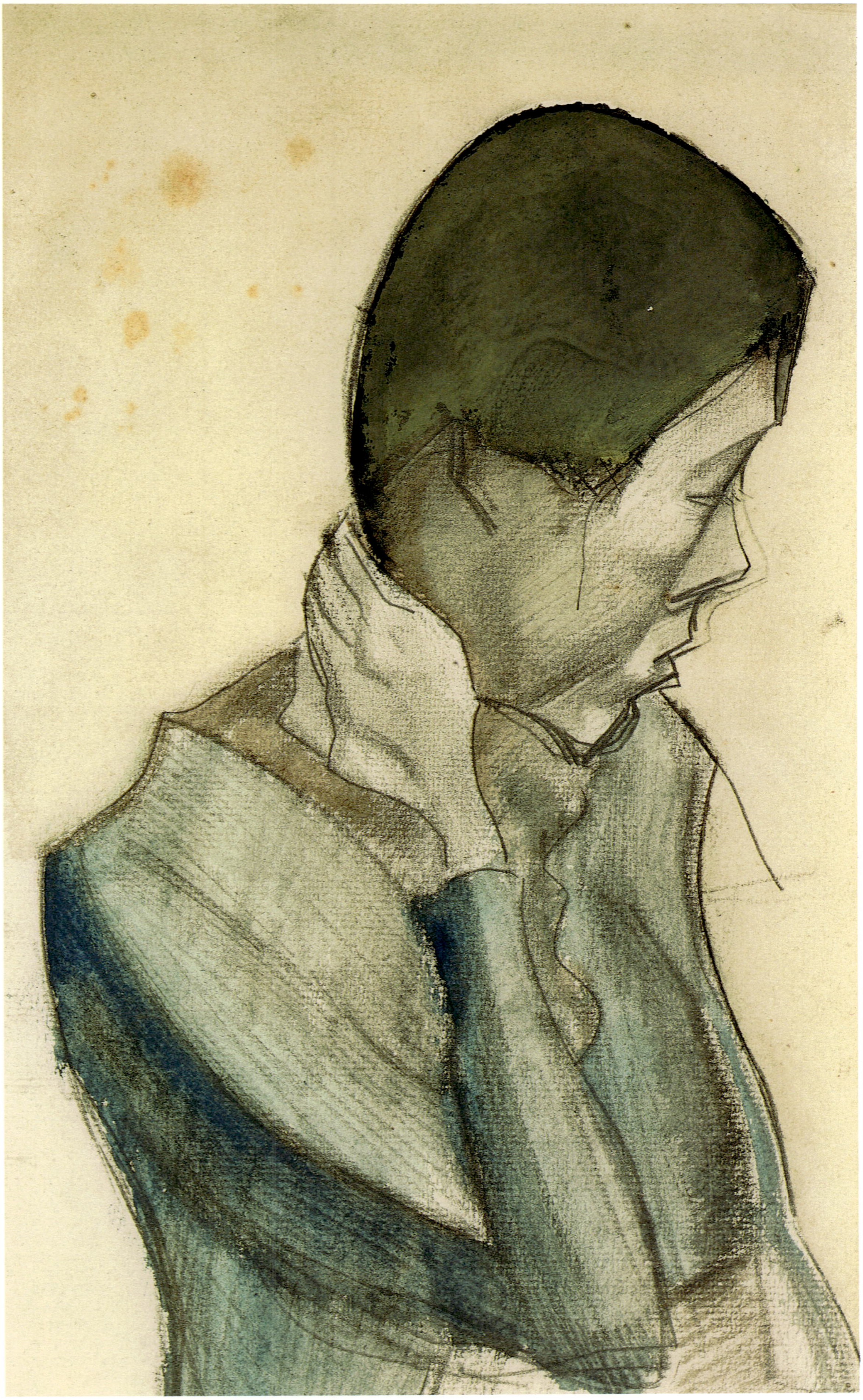

Cat. 26. ◀◀
***Futurist Figure*, 1912. Pencil, pen and ink, ink wash and wash on paper. 26 x 18.5 cm. Collection David Bowie. M 67**

Cat. 27. ◀
[Not in exhibition] *Helen Saunders*, 1913. Pencil and watercolour on paper. 28.5 x 18 cm. Private collection. M 147

According to her descendant, both these works are portraits of Helen Saunders, a member of the Vorticist group who produced some striking and original Vorticist work of her own, some of which seems particularly concerned with implications of mechanised life for women. A similar preoccupation is visible in her literary contributions to *Blast*, No. 2 (July 1915) (B&M Cat. 3). Saunders fell in love with Lewis and became psychologically dependent on him (which he eventually found intolerable). While he was in the army during the First World War, she looked after his paintings and acted as a secretary for him. The title *Futurist Figure* was assigned by Walter Michel, who suggests that it "may be a comment on Carrà's portrait of Marinetti."[1] If so, the naturalistic hands are probably included as a criticism of such incongruous pieces of conventional representation in Futurist canvases. The later portrait affords no concessions to the sitter's femininity.

1. Walter Michel, *Wyndham Lewis: Paintings and Drawings* (London: Thames and Hudson, 1971), p. 78.

“Our Vortex is proud of its polished sides.
Our Vortex will not hear of anything but its disastrous polished dance.”

Wyndham Lewis, *Blast,* 1914

Cat. 28.
[Not in exhibition] *Figure Composition (Man and Woman with Two Bulldogs)*, 1912. Pen and ink, watercolour and gouache on paper. 31.3 x 2.7cm. Collection Art Gallery of New South Wales. Purchased 1983. M 62

Lewis shows complete mastery of his own version of Cubism in this representation of one of his favourite motifs, the couple. Here they are accompanied by dogs, which symbolise for him the duality of our natures, divided into animal and spirit. This is one of the themes of *Enemy of the Stars*, in which the protagonist desires to repudiate the animal part of himself yet is inexorably drawn to recreating it in the person of his companion, Hanp. “I find I wanted to make a naif yapping Poodle-parasite of you,” he tells Hanp in disgust at himself. A more sympathetic portrayal of a strange dependence of a man on a dog is found in the 1915 story, “The French Poodle.” *Figure Composition* shows that Lewis could have completely dissolved his figures into the matrix of lines and planes that form the ground of the work; it is probably a residual humanism that holds him back from this step.

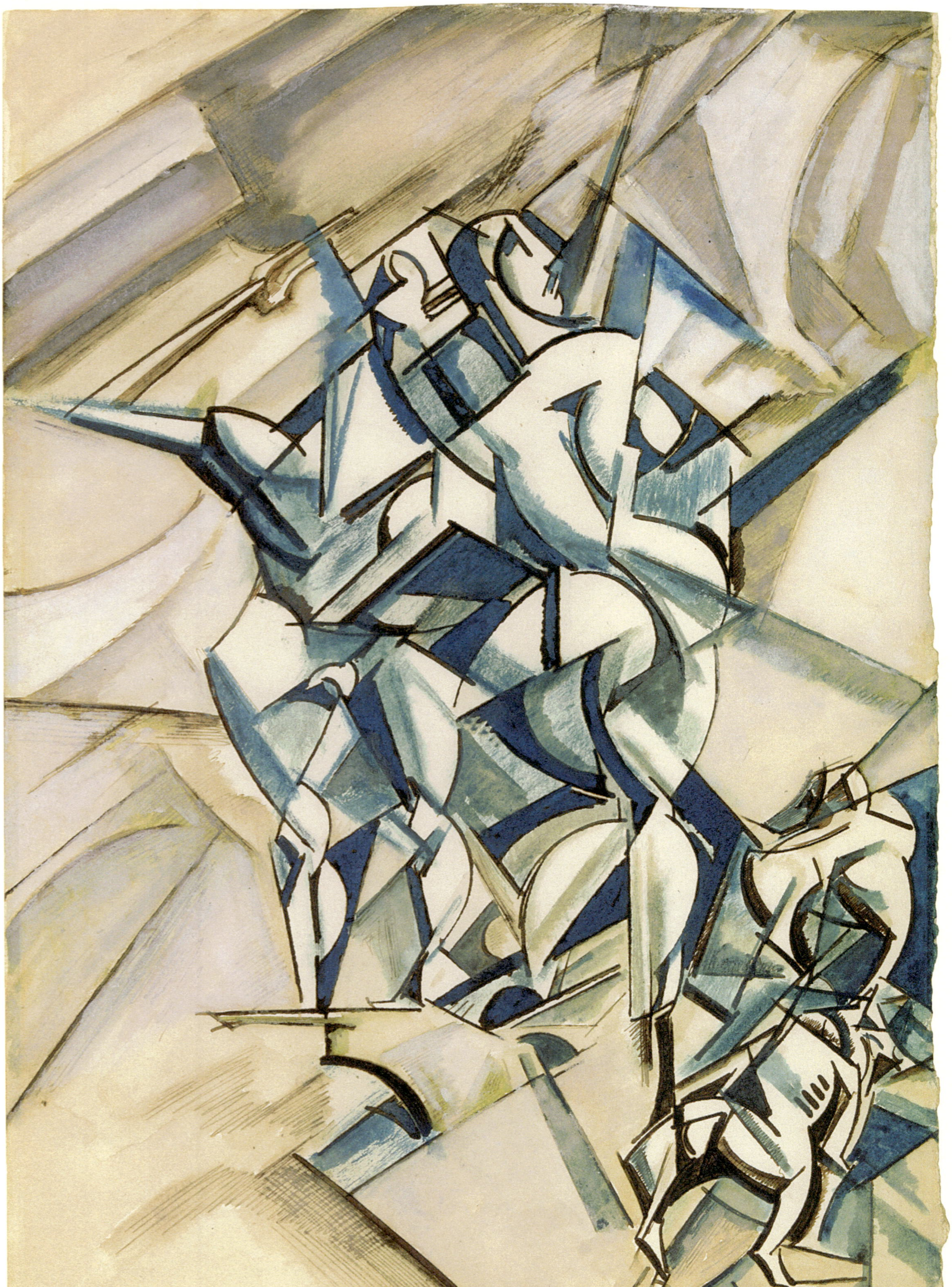

Cat. 29.

Drawing for Timon, **1912. Pen and ink, and watercolour on paper. 38 x 28.5 cm. Private collection. M 109**

This drawing was one of the works Lewis exhibited in the 1912 *Second Post-Impressionist Exhibition* in London. It is related to the *Timon of Athens* project that he would work on intermittently for over a year. It was not included in the published portfolio, however, despite its impressive formal success. Its placid calm was perhaps too remote from the mood and subject of the play as Lewis responded to them to find a place anywhere as an illustration.

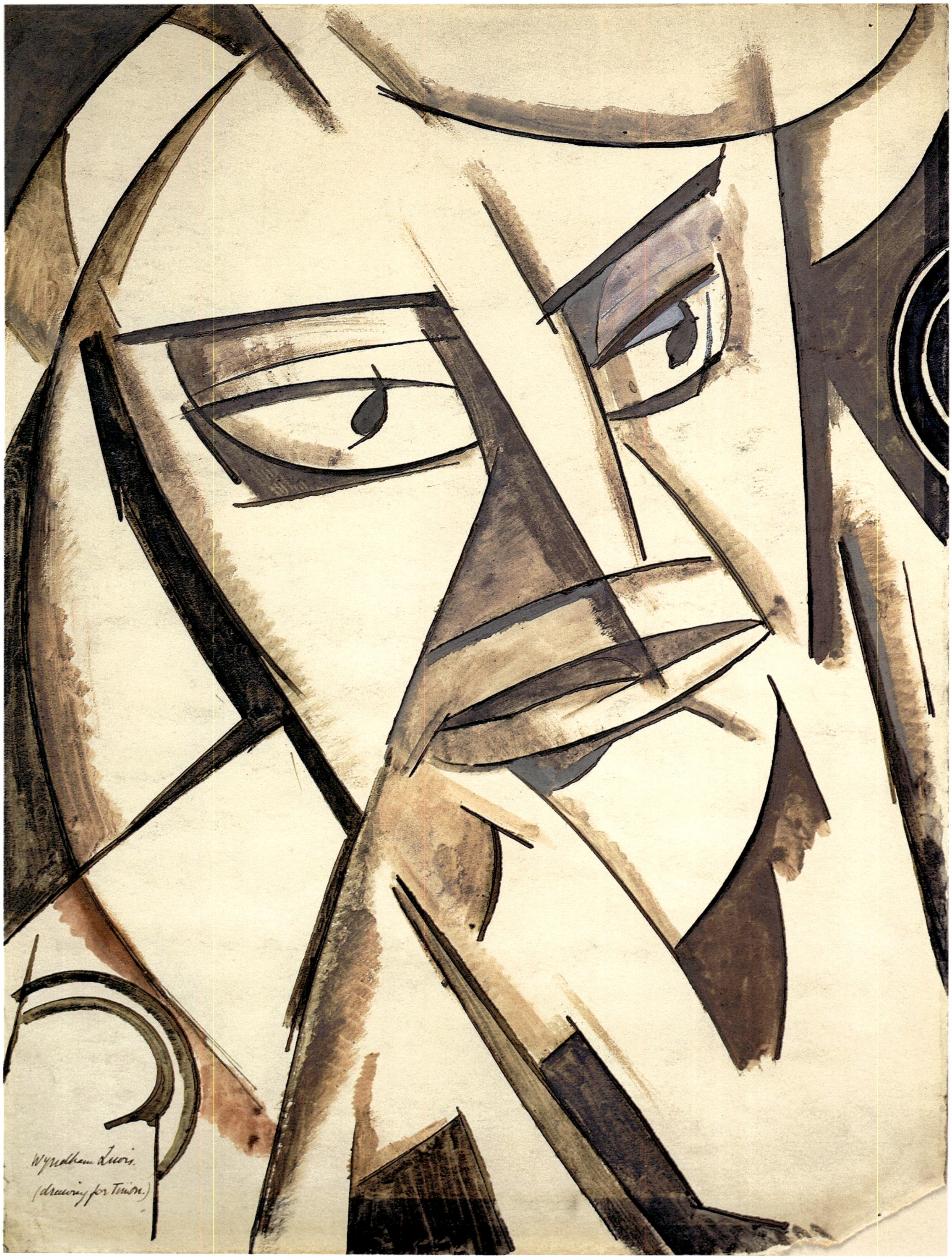

TIMON OF ATHENS

Wyndham Lewis hoped to produce an illustrated edition of William Shakespeare's play, *Timon of Athens*. The play probably interested him because of the two contrasting states of Timon's character: generous and friendly to the point of recklessness at the beginning of the play; scathingly misanthropic by its end. By working on such an edition, he was also declaring a certain independence from the two most influential modernist aesthetics of the time. First, he was using a variant of Futurist technique to depict scenes from a play that Filippo Tommaso Marinetti would consign to the fire, along with all museums and the art of the past. Second, he was showing that subject matter in a painting (and literary subject matter, at that) was at least as important as "pure form." In London, the critics Roger Fry and Clive Bell were insisting that it was form alone that determined aesthetic value in the visual arts. Indeed, Bell later instanced Lewis's lost painting *Creation* (exhibited in the *Second Post-Impressionist Exhibition*, October 1912); see Cat. 24 as an example of a painting where form alone was significant.

The publishers who were to undertake the project were reorganised when a partner left the business, and in 1913 the various plates and designs for title pages and ornaments were collected and issued as a portfolio, still with the intention of producing the book. In 1914, with the publisher under new ownership, the text of the play was printed – but without leaving any room for the designs. Lewis attempted to squeeze them in on one copy of the printed text, and the sole copy of text plus plates is in the Beinecke Library, Yale University. The new owner of the publishing firm was killed in the First World War. Ezra Pound collected the typescript of Lewis's book, "Our Wild Body," from the now defunct firm in 1917, and may have retrieved the copy of the portfolio that is in the Beinecke (and inscribed by Pound to Quinn as the unique copy) at the same time. Pound sold, or donated, it on Lewis's behalf to the American collector, John Quinn, in 1917.

Work on the project falls into several distinct phases. The first is represented by the watercolours in the style of *The Thebaid* (1912) (Cat. 33) – a sort of cubo-futurist mix of Lewis's own devising. These were originally intended to be used as title pages for the Acts. *A Masque of Timon* (Act I) (Cat. 30) still has the lettering to indicate this along the top. It can be seen that the images on the other plates of this type have been extended to cover the strip where similar headings must also originally have appeared. At least one other headed image in the same style (a now lost "Act IV") was painted by Lewis and was exhibited at the *Second Post-Impressionist Exhibition*. Such watercolours would have been expensive to reproduce and (perhaps more important) difficult to bind into the text at the precise places needed for title pages. It is probably because of such binding complications that Lewis decided to produce designs in ink that could be printed on the normal paper stock and did not need to be specially inserted. Even so, he did not complete the transformation. *A Masque of Timon* still has its heading, and no new design was produced for Act II's title page.

Lewis continued working on images inspired by the play in 1913, but only images from the portfolio are included in the model of the edition at the Beinecke. As late as 1919, in the portfolio, *Fifteen Drawings* (see Cats. 73 and 74), two new *Timon* drawings are included. In the 1927 book, *The Lion and the Fox: The Rôle of the Hero in the Plays of Shakespeare* (B&M Cat. 11), Lewis devotes a chapter to *Timon of Athens*, showing that the play still fascinated him.

The titles used for the works are Lewis's own, as given in the catalogue of the *Second Post-Impressionist Exhibition*. Photographs of only three of the *Timon* images as exhibited survive, however: of *Drawing for Timon* (Cat. 29) and of two lost works not reproduced in the portfolio but in the style of the "first phase" of the project. One is inscribed with lettering similar to that of *A Masque of Timon*, "Act IV."[1] The assignment of titles must remain conjectural, but unless further lost works from the series emerge, this choice seems the most probable. In *Wyndham Lewis: Paintings and Drawings*, Walter Michel invented new titles for the works because he could not be sure how Lewis's titles should be assigned.[2]

1. For photographs, reproduced from small newspaper prints, see Paul Edwards, "Wyndham Lewis at the Second Post-Impressionist Exhibition: New (Old) Reproductions of Three Lost Works," *Wyndham Lewis Annual* 9–10 (2002–3), pp. 73–79.
2. Walter Michel, *Wyndham Lewis: Paintings and Drawings* (London: Thames and Hudson, 1971).

Cat. 30. ▸
Timon of Athens: Act I (A Masque of Timon), 1912. Pen and ink, watercolour and gouache on paper. 48.5 x 33 cm. Wyndham Lewis Memorial Trust. G. and V. Lane Collection (LD.2000. XX.6). M 93

Cat. 31. ▸▸
Portfolio Timon of Athens: Act I (A Masque of Timon), 1913. Lithograph on paper. 38.8 x 27.2 cm. Wyndham Lewis Memorial Trust. G. and V. Lane Collection (LG.2004. XX.1). M 93

This is the most "Futurist" work that Lewis produced. The *Exhibition of Works by the Italian Futurist Painters* came to London's Sackville Gallery in March of 1912, and the influence of Umberto Boccioni's representations of the psychological merging of subject and object can be traced in this work. The table and candelabra in particular appear in different psychological perspectives in varying sizes in several places in the picture. The scene represented is one of Timon's lavish banquets, given in the days before the sudden loss of his fortune. The figure at the bottom left, with a staff, is probably the cynic philosopher Apemantus, who remains critical of Timon both when he is a reckless spendthrift and when he is a misanthropic hermit.

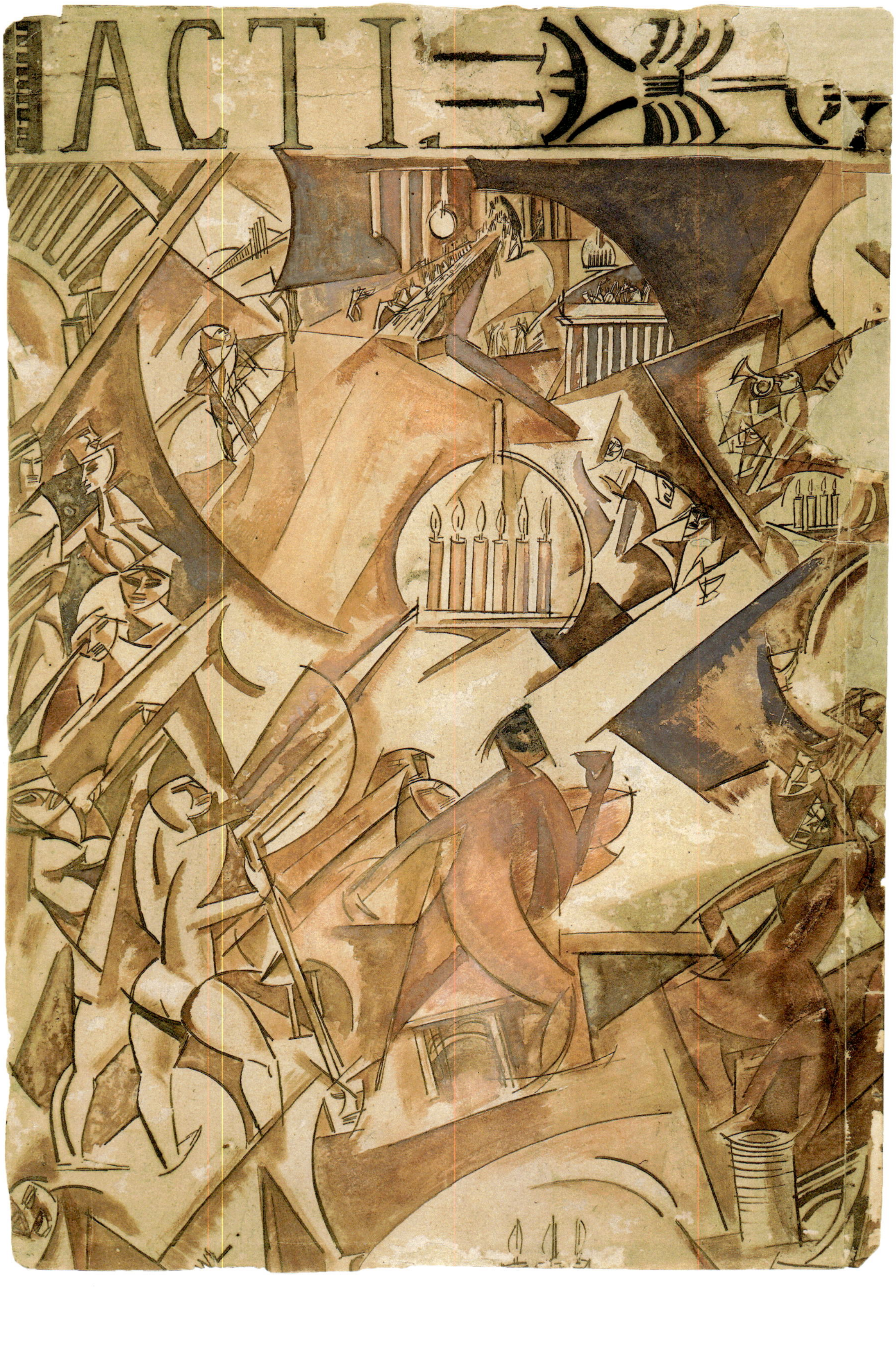

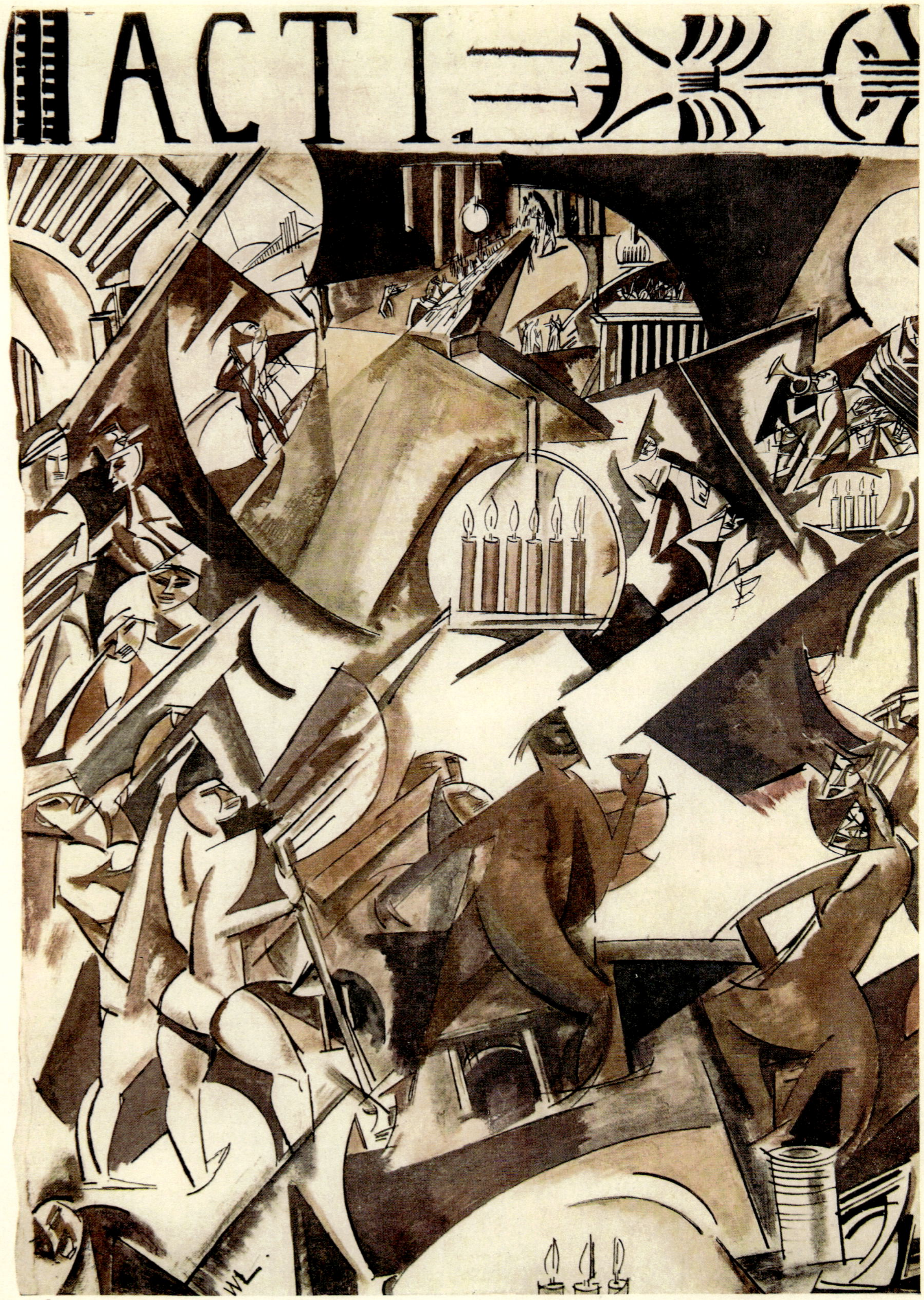
ACTI

“We must constantly strive to ENRICH abstraction till it is almost plain life, or rather get deeply enough immersed in material life to experience the shaping power among its vibrations, and to accentuate and perpetuate these.”

Wyndham Lewis, *Blast,* 1914

Cat. 32.
Portfolio *Timon of Athens: A Feast of Overmen,* 1913. Lithograph on paper. 38.8 x 27.2 cm. Wyndham Lewis Memorial Trust. G. and V. Lane Collection (LG.2004. XX.I). M 100

“Overman” was the contemporary English translation of Friedrich Nietzsche’s *Übermensch* and Lewis’s use of the term indicates that in these pictures he was intending to do something more ambitious than merely illustrate William Shakespeare’s play. The scene illustrated appears to be Act III scene vi. Timon lays on a final feast for his “friends” (“All covered dishes,” marvels one). In fact, the dishes contain stones and water, which Timon throws at them. “Uncover, dogs, and lap,” he shouts. The title of the plate therefore offers a sardonic commentary on the Nietzschean aspiration to transcend the normal limits of humanity. In *The Art of Being Ruled* (B&M Cat. 10), Lewis comments that the weakness in Nietzsche’s theory of sublimation was that, owing to his own poor health, he was unable to imagine his superior form of men doing anything with their “superfluous, creative energy” except “*the same things that we should be doing without it*. And his will requires to see this precious *something over* put to the same uses that many of his helots would have put it to.”[1] Michel gave this work the title of *The Creditors.* The original watercolour (M 100) was produced in 1912.

1. Wyndham Lewis, *The Art of Being Ruled* (London: Chatto and Windus, 1926), p. 126.

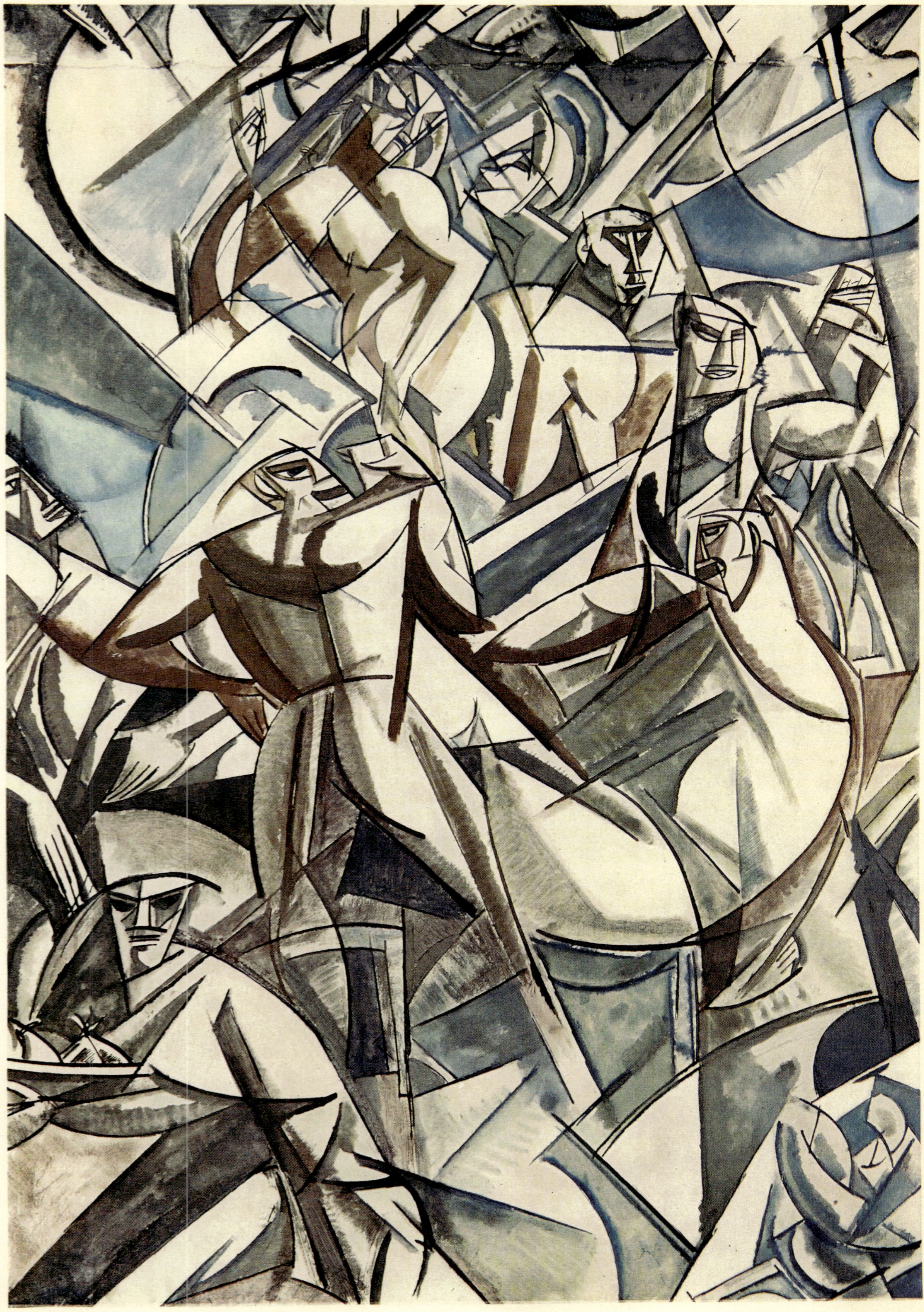

Cat. 33. ▶
The Thebaid, 1912. Pencil, ink and watercolour on paper. 38.7 x 27.2 cm. Private collection. M 98

Cat. 34. ▶▶
Portfolio *Timon of Athens: The Thebaid* (1913). Lithograph on paper. 38.8 x 27.2 cm. Wyndham Lewis Memorial Trust. G. and V. Lane Collection (LG.2004. XX.I). M 98

Walter Michel chose the title *Alcibiades* for this work. The central figure is indeed Alcibiades, come to conquer Athens with his army (on the pretext that the Athenians have mistreated Timon), and accompanied by the camp followers Phrynia and Timandra (to the left of the image). Timon, who has abandoned the society of men, is seen at the mouth of his cave, screaming his misanthropic and misogynistic invective at Alcibiades and the two women. The illustrated scene is Act IV scene iii. In 1969, Edmund Gray wrote of this image, "it is arguably the greatest single manifestation of artistic energy in the whole of English painting."[1]

1. Edmund Gray, "Wyndham Lewis and the Modern Crisis of Painting," *Agenda* (Wyndham Lewis Special Issue) 7, nos. 3 and 8, no. 1 (Autumn–Winter 1969–70), p. 90.

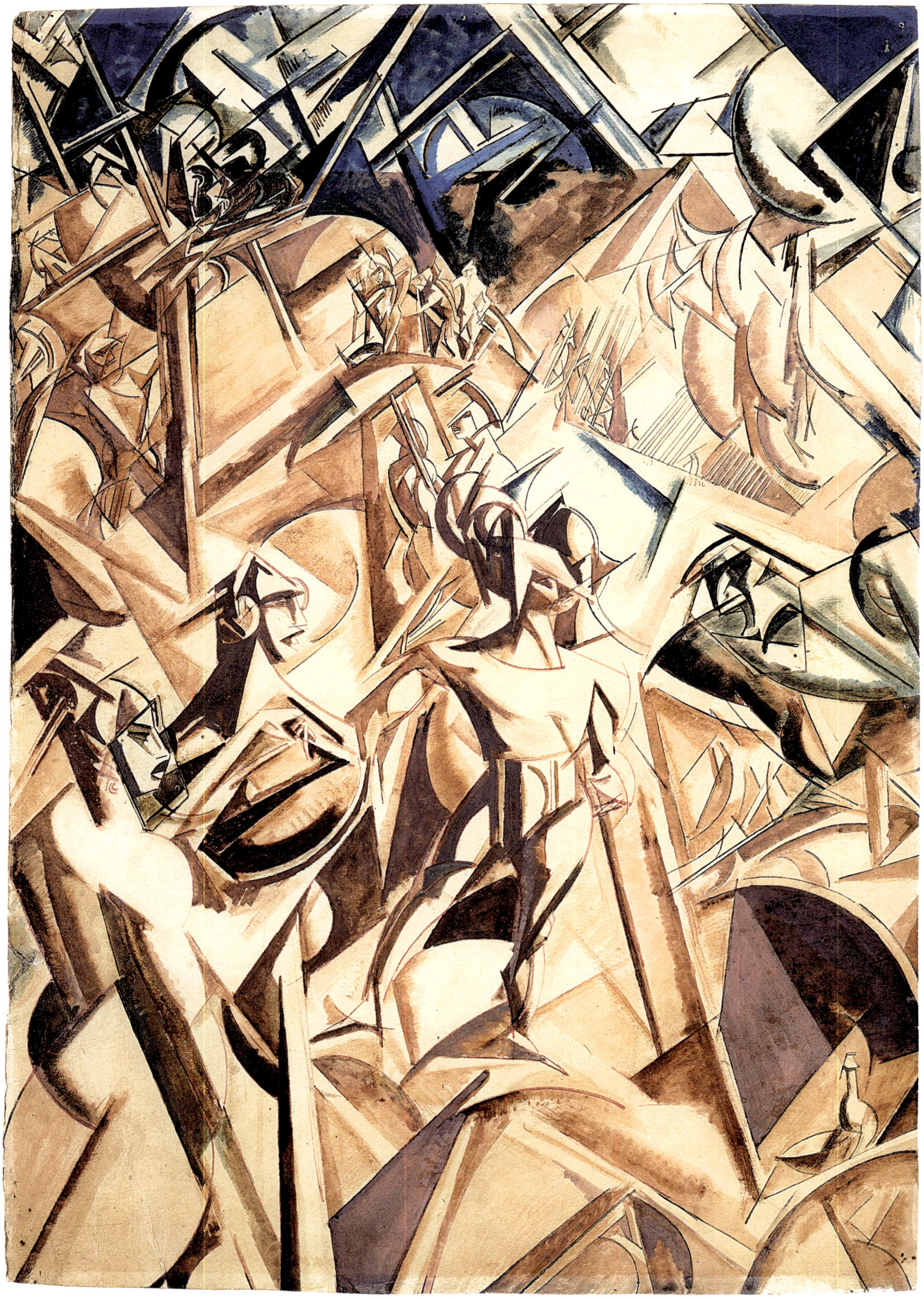

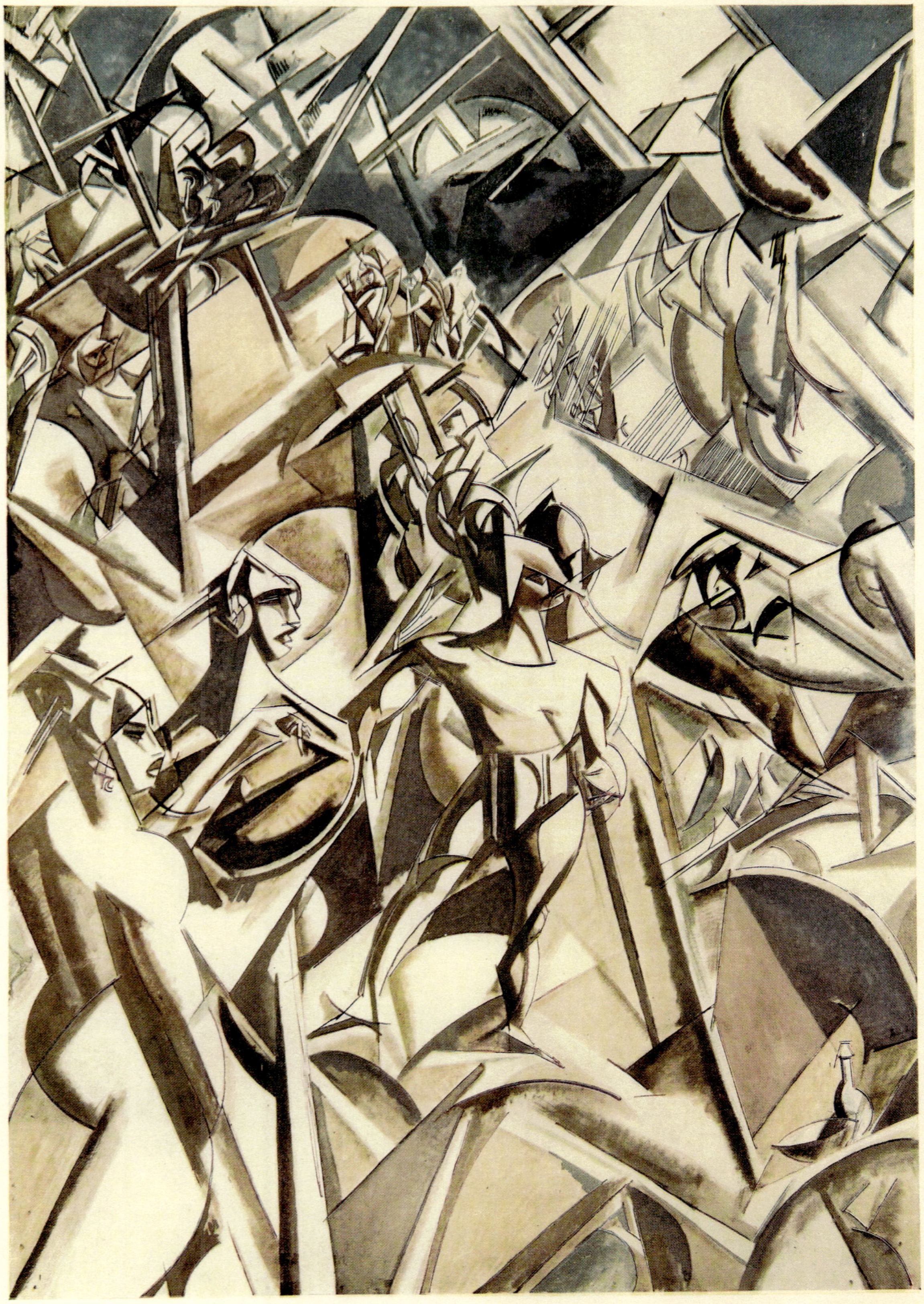

Cat. 35.
Portfolio *Timon of Athens: Act III*, 1913. Lithograph on paper. 38.8 x 27.2 cm. Wyndham Lewis Memorial Trust. G. and V. Lane Collection (LG.2004.XX.I). M 95

The black and white Act title pages were presumably intended to be easily reproduced and printed on the normal paper of the book. In developing their idiom, Lewis may well have been influenced by Umberto Boccioni's *Drawings after States of Mind* (1912) that he could have seen reproduced in *Der Sturm* in the summer of 1912. The inclusion of lettering as part of the design may have encouraged Lewis to think differently about picture space and the function of the picture plane. It is more a field around which pictorial elements are disposed than a "window" onto a scene. This, and the radical reduction of visual means, are essential prerequisites for the form of Vorticist abstraction that Lewis was shortly to develop. *Act III* shows the same characters as *The Thebaid* (Cat. 33). The fact that they do not actually appear in Act III shows that Lewis was not especially rigorous in matching the drawings to the events of the play. The original drawing has not survived.

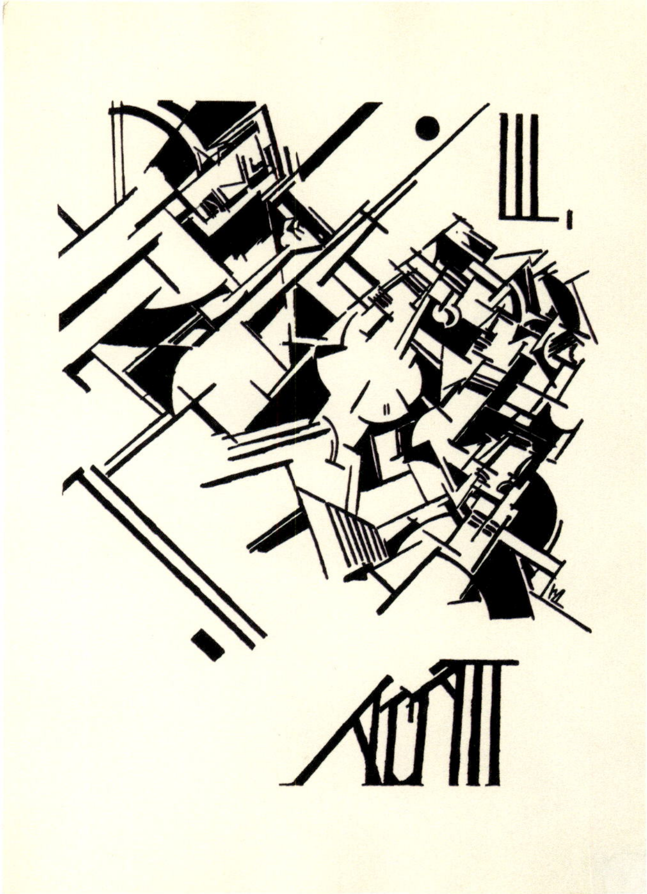

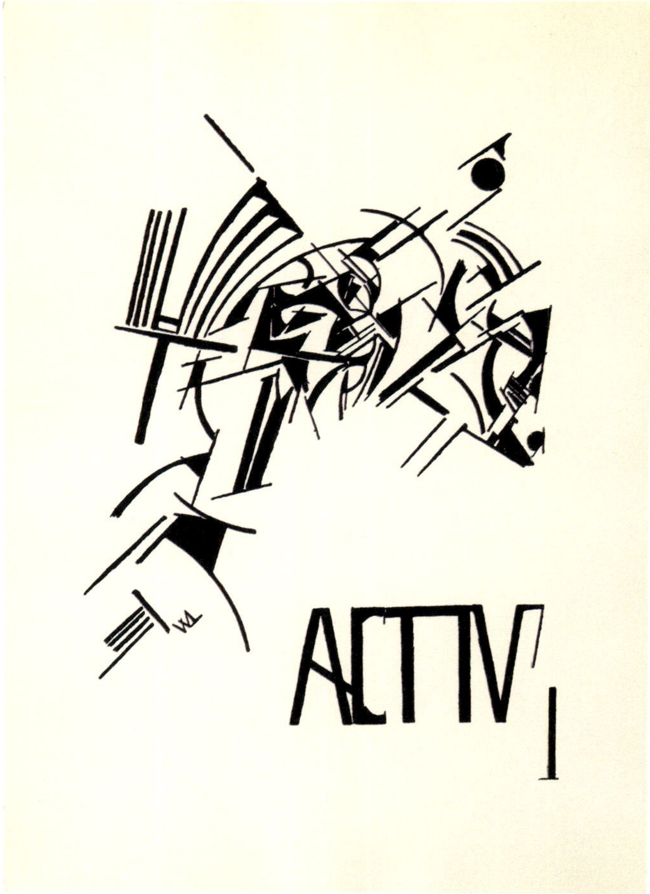

Cat. 36.
***Portfolio Timon of Athens: Act IV* (1913). Lithograph on paper. 38.8 x 27.2 cm. Wyndham Lewis Memorial Trust. G. and V. Lane Collection (LG.2004.XX.I). M 96**

The expressive quality of the drawing is almost entirely due to its "centrifugal" dynamic, though a face and (to the right) a mask (?) can be discerned. No original survives.

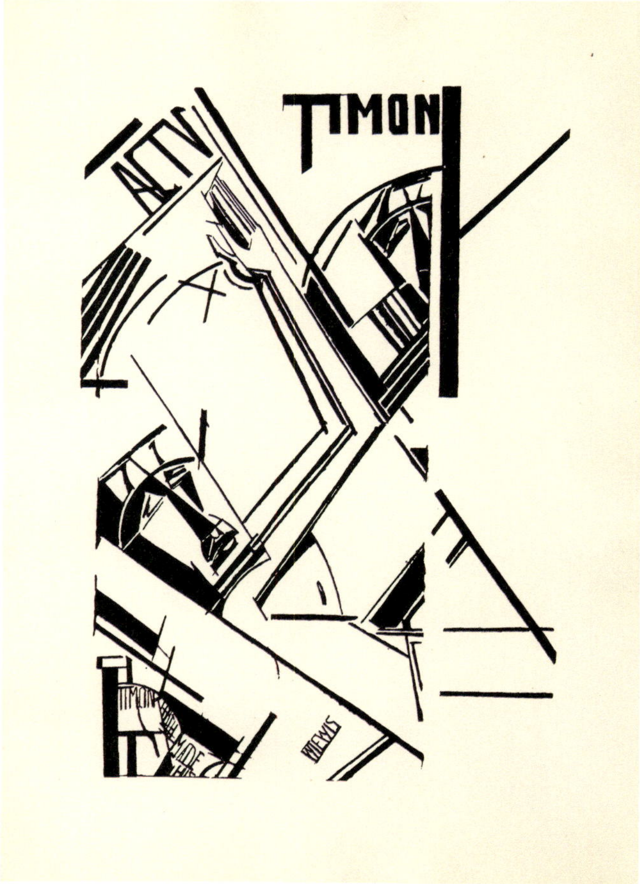

Cat. 37.
***Portfolio Timon of Athens: Act V* (1913). Lithograph on paper. 38.8 x 27.2 cm. Wyndham Lewis Memorial Trust. G. and V. Lane Collection (LG.2004.XX.I). M 97**

The lettering in the corner partially quotes from Timon's final speech (Act V, scene i, ll. 214–18), as he pronounces his own epitaph:

Timon hath made his ever-lasting mansion
Upon the beached verge of the salt flood,
Who once a day with his embossed froth
The turbulent surge shall cover; thither come,
And let my gravestone be your oracle.

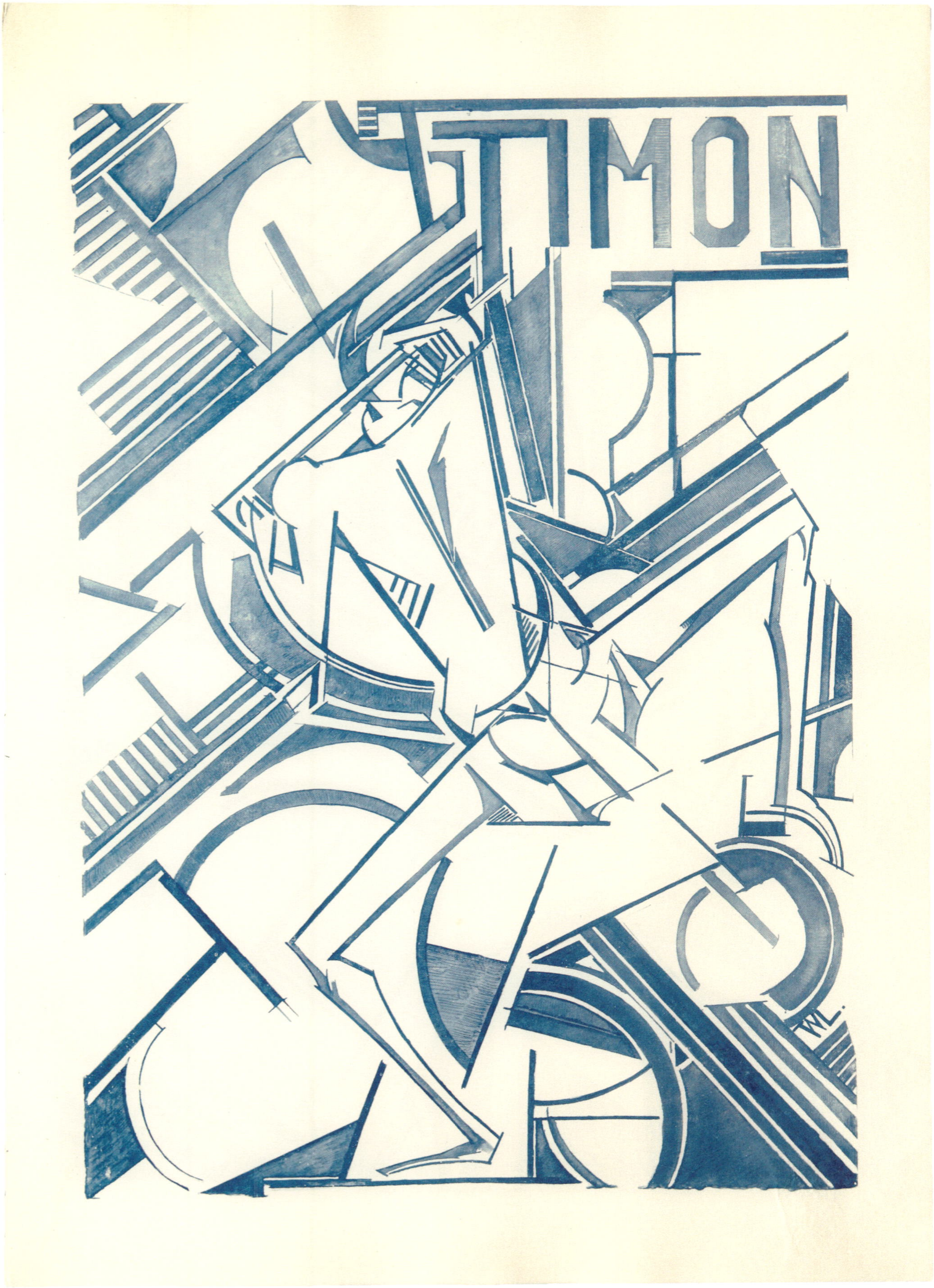

Cat. 38.
Portfolio *Timon of Athens: Timon* (1913) Lithograph on paper. 38.8 x 27.2 cm. Wyndham Lewis Memorial Trust. G. and V. Lane Collection (LG.2004.XX.1). M 102

In some ways the most important of the "second phase" of the portfolio prints, this image of Timon, which was intended as a frontispiece, is the last stage of humanism before the human figure is abandoned in Vorticism and subsumed into the network of mechanical and geometrical elements that form the material of the picture. Timon is a *configuration* of these, inescapably enmeshed in them, and this epitomises his tragedy. It is also the situation of modern man, produced by his environment. In "Inferior Religions," Lewis gives a comic perspective on this unexpected inverted relationship when he describes the subjects he planned for his first book of short stories in 1914: "The fascinating imbecility of the creaking men machines, that some little restaurant or fishing-boat works, was the original subject of these studies."[1] The original does not survive.

1. Wyndham Lewis, "Inferior Religions" (1927). Rprt. *The Complete Wild Body* (1927). Ed. Bernard Lafourcade (Santa Barbara: Black Sparrow Press, 1982), p. 149 (see Anthology, p. 357).

Cat. 39. ▸
Portfolio *Timon of Athens: Design for Front Cover*, 1913. Lithograph on paper. 38.8 x 27.2 cm. Wyndham Lewis Memorial Trust. G. and V. Lane Collection (LG.2004. XX.1). M 91

Cat. 40. ▸▸
Portfolio *Timon of Athens: Design for Back Cover*, 1913. Lithograph on paper. 38.8 x 27.2 cm. Wyndham Lewis Memorial Trust. G. and V. Lane Collection (LG.2004. XX.1). M 92

These designs were used on the envelope of the portfolio and on its board covers. They were no doubt intended for the covers of the book. The Cube Press did not exist, though when some of the *Timon* drawings were shown at the *Second Post-Impressionist Exhibition*, the catalogue stated that they were "exhibited by courtesy of the Cube Publishing Co."[1] The originals do not survive.

1. See Walter Michel, *Wyndham Lewis: Paintings and Drawings* (London: Thames and Hudson, 1971), p. 429.

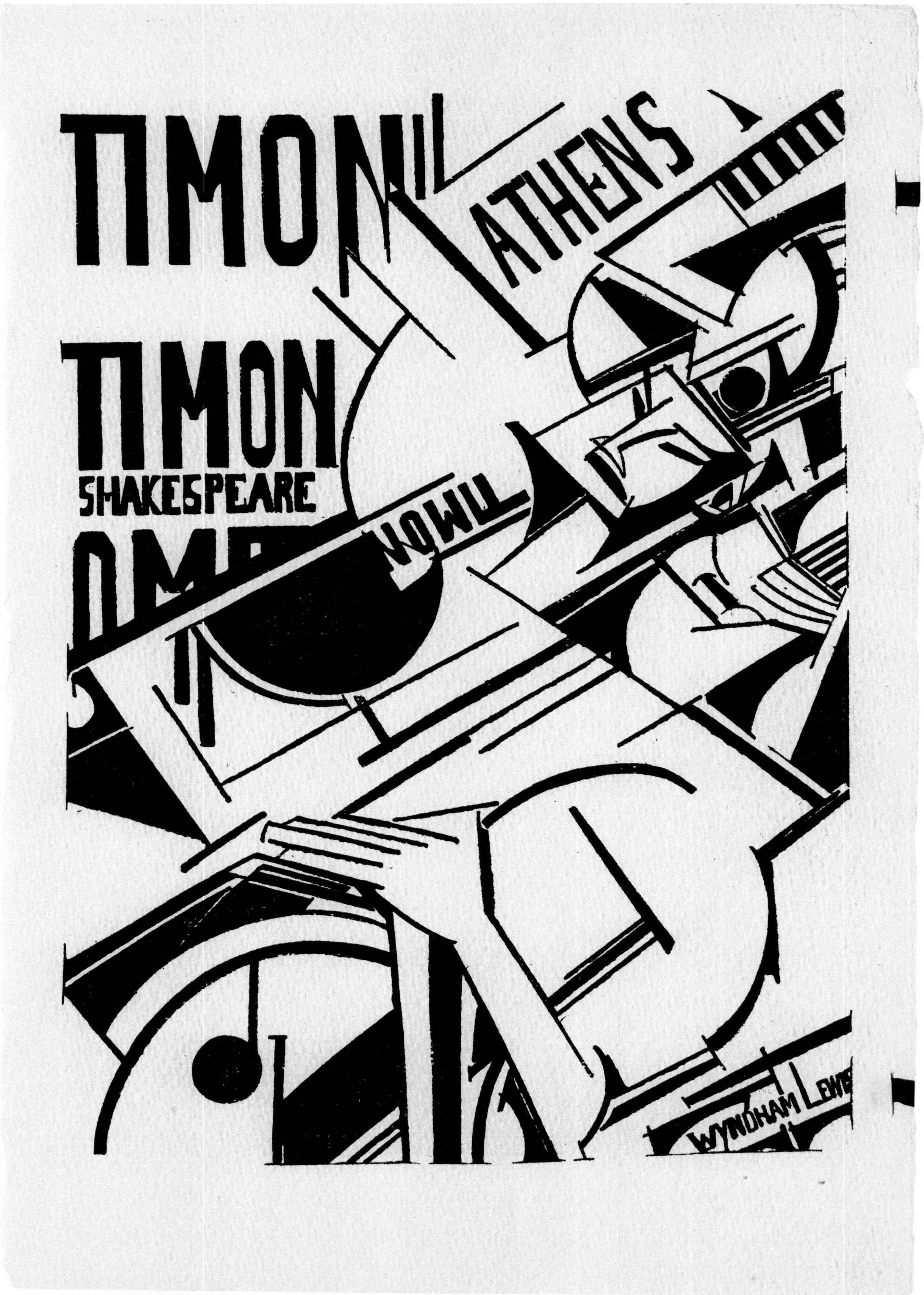

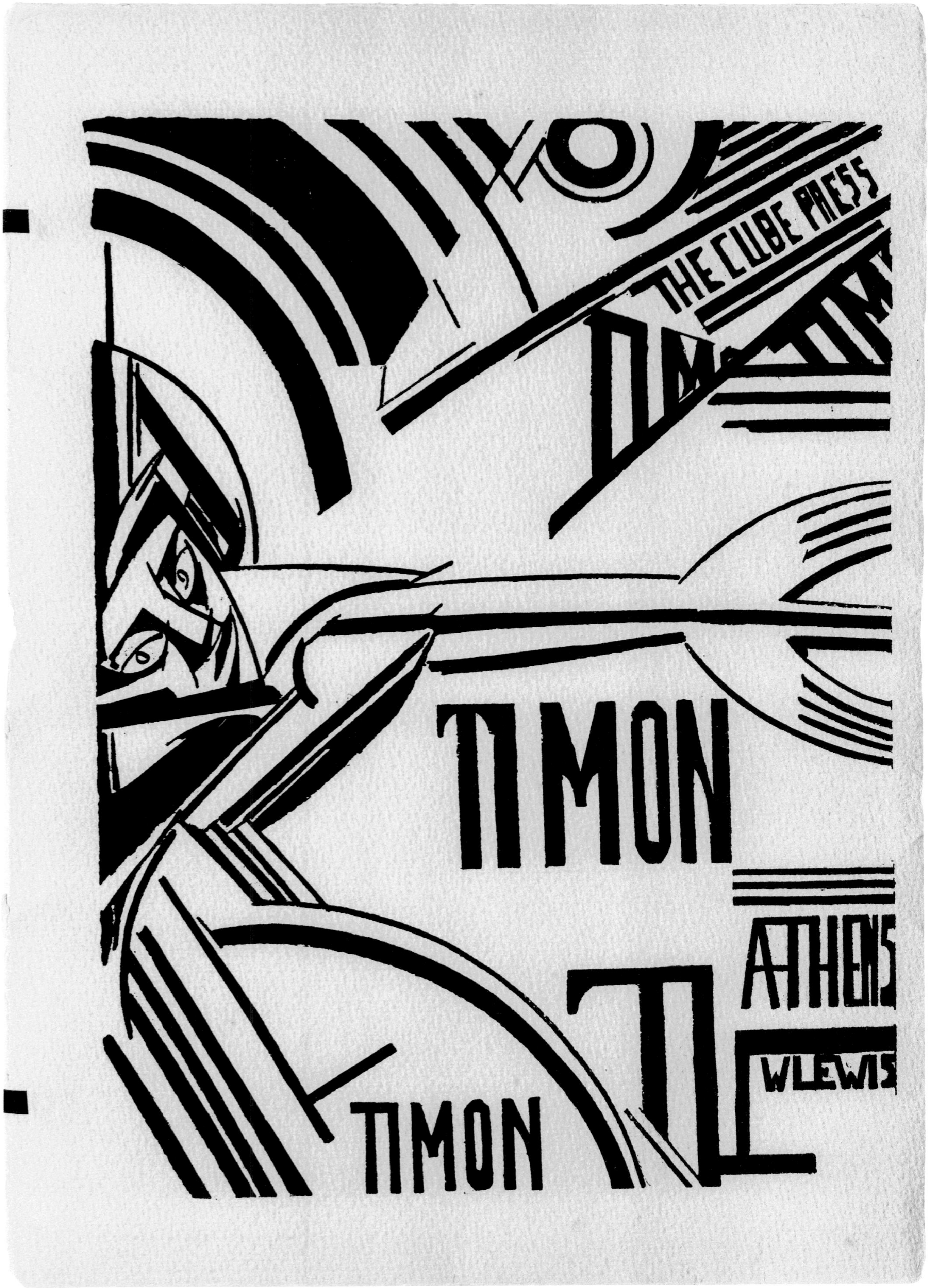

THE CUBE PRESS
TIMON
ATHENS
W LEWIS
TIMON

Cat. 41.
Design for a Folding Screen, 1913. Pencil and watercolour on paper. 51 x 38.5 cm. Victoria and Albert Museum (E 735-1955). M 131

The design was produced as part of Lewis's work for the Omega Workshops, a company created and run by the Bloomsbury critic and painter, Roger Fry, which opened in 1913. This was a continuation of the Arts and Crafts school of interior design pioneered in England, but with a "modernist" inflection. Lewis's prominence in the *Second Post-Impressionist Exhibition* no doubt led him to believe that a continued association with Bloomsbury would be helpful to his career, but he was not temperamentally suited to this kind of collaboration, and was out of sympathy with what he saw as the amateurism and shoddiness of Omega's products. His screen is prominently visible in photographs of the workshop on the opening day. He has returned to a style of drawing in which line, though not following precisely a naturalistic contour, gives the spectator an equivalent of the "feel" of the body in particular postures and actions, in this case, those of circus performers. Lewis's early story, "Les Saltimbanques,"[1] shows his fascination with the circus. Again, the combination of physical exertion and its use to express pre-determined roles (clown, ringmaster, etc.) appealed to him. Lewis's comic treatment of the subject contrasts with Pablo Picasso's melancholic treatment of similar subjects.

1. Wyndham Lewis, "Les Saltimbanques" (1909). Rprt. *The Complete Wild Body* (1927). Ed. Bernard Lafourcade (Santa Barbara: Black Sparrow Press, 1982), pp. 237–47.

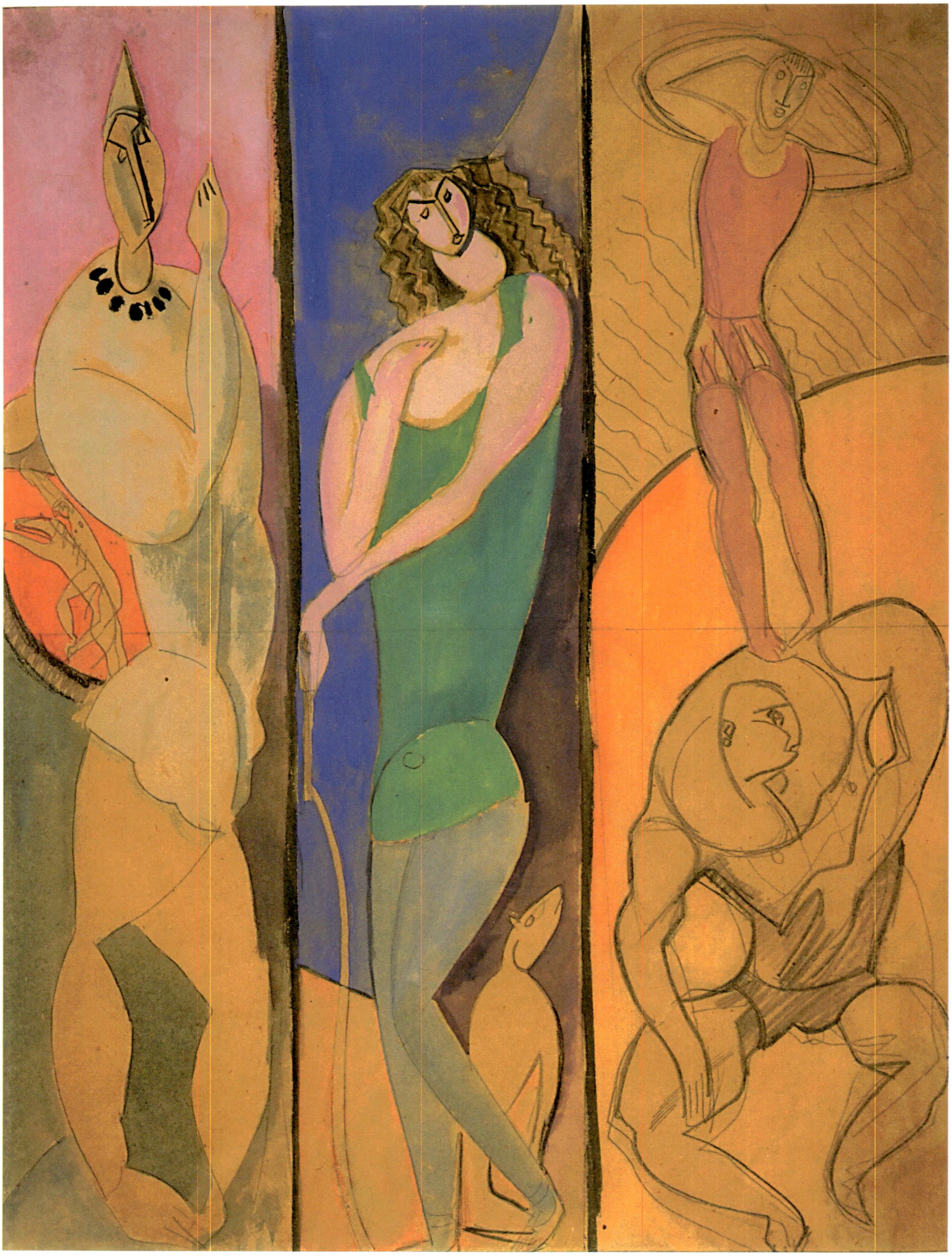

Cat. 42.
[Not in exhibition] *Cactus*, 1913. Pencil, ink, watercolour and chalk on paper. 34 x 23.5 cm. Victoria and Albert Museum, London (E 3768-1919). M 124

The drawing is a visual pun, comparing the simplified forms of modernist stylisation with the segmented structure of cacti. It is a witty variation on the theme of the figure and ground relationship as a metaphor for the relationship between man and nature, this time combined with mockery of the Matissean idealisation of primitive pastoral. But, as in the *Design for a Folding Screen* (Cat. 41), Lewis also achieves a paradoxical feeling in the spectator of the internal physical sensation of adopting these postures.

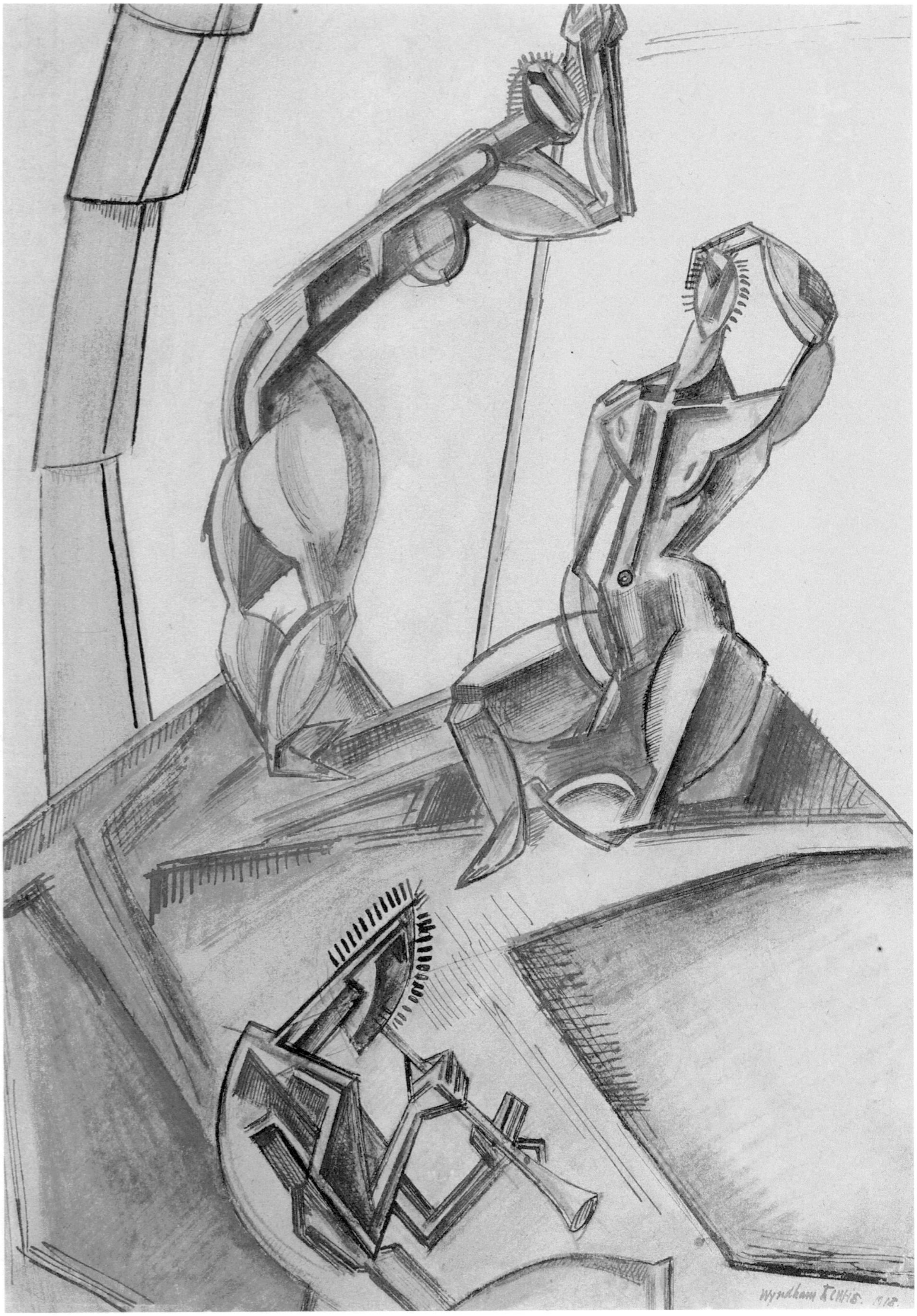

Cat. 43.
At the Seaside, 1913.
Watercolour, pencil and ink on paper. 47.5 x 31.5 cm.
Victoria and Albert Museum (E 3763-1919). M 123

Comparisons between modernist innovations and the work of Italian "primitives" were frequent in criticism of the time, and it may be that the wild incongruities of style and convention in this seaside scene are Lewis's comment on such comparisons. Visually, the work seems to declare, anything is possible. Photographs of British seaside resorts of the period show that people often wore heavy everyday clothes even when sitting on the beach in sunny weather.

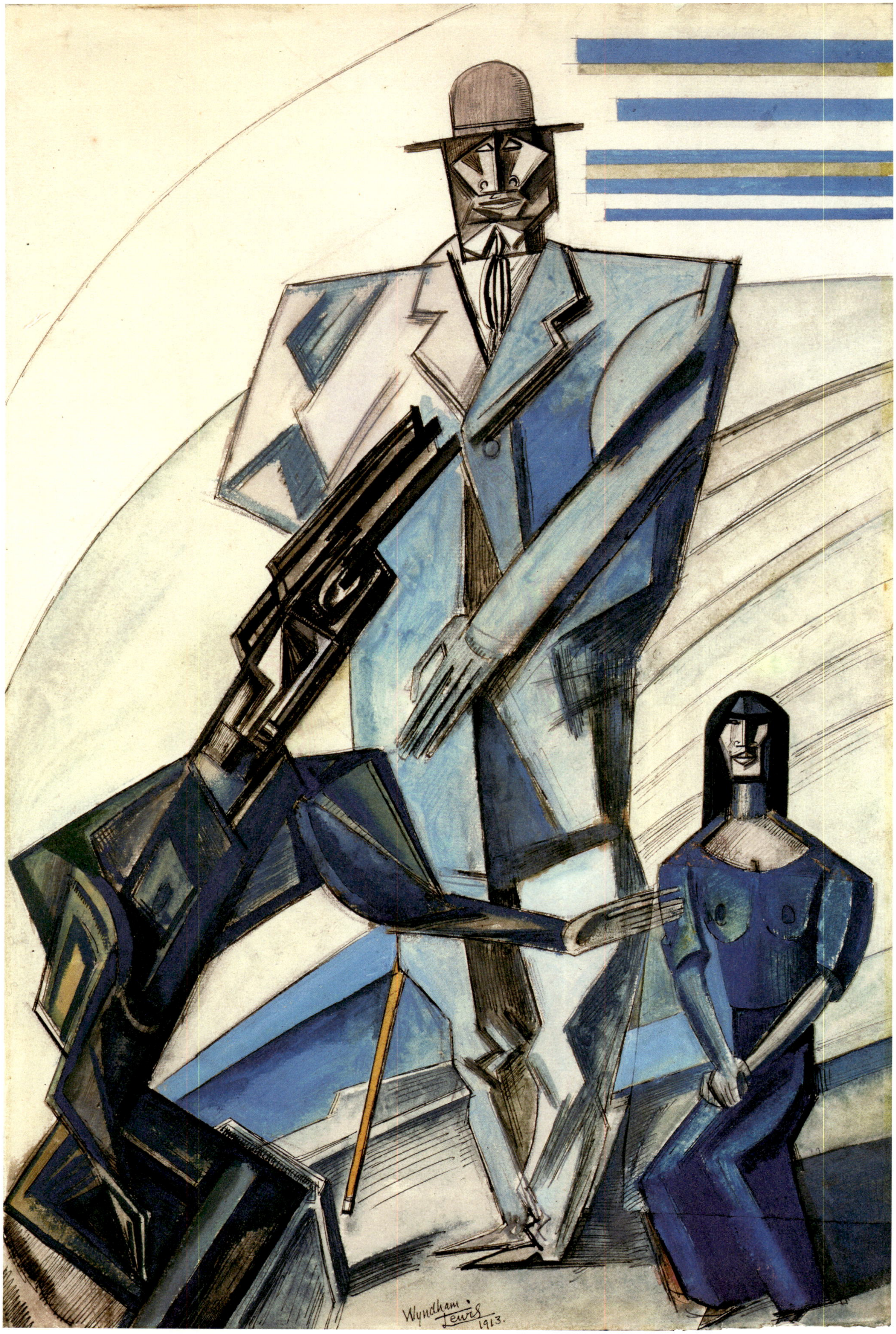

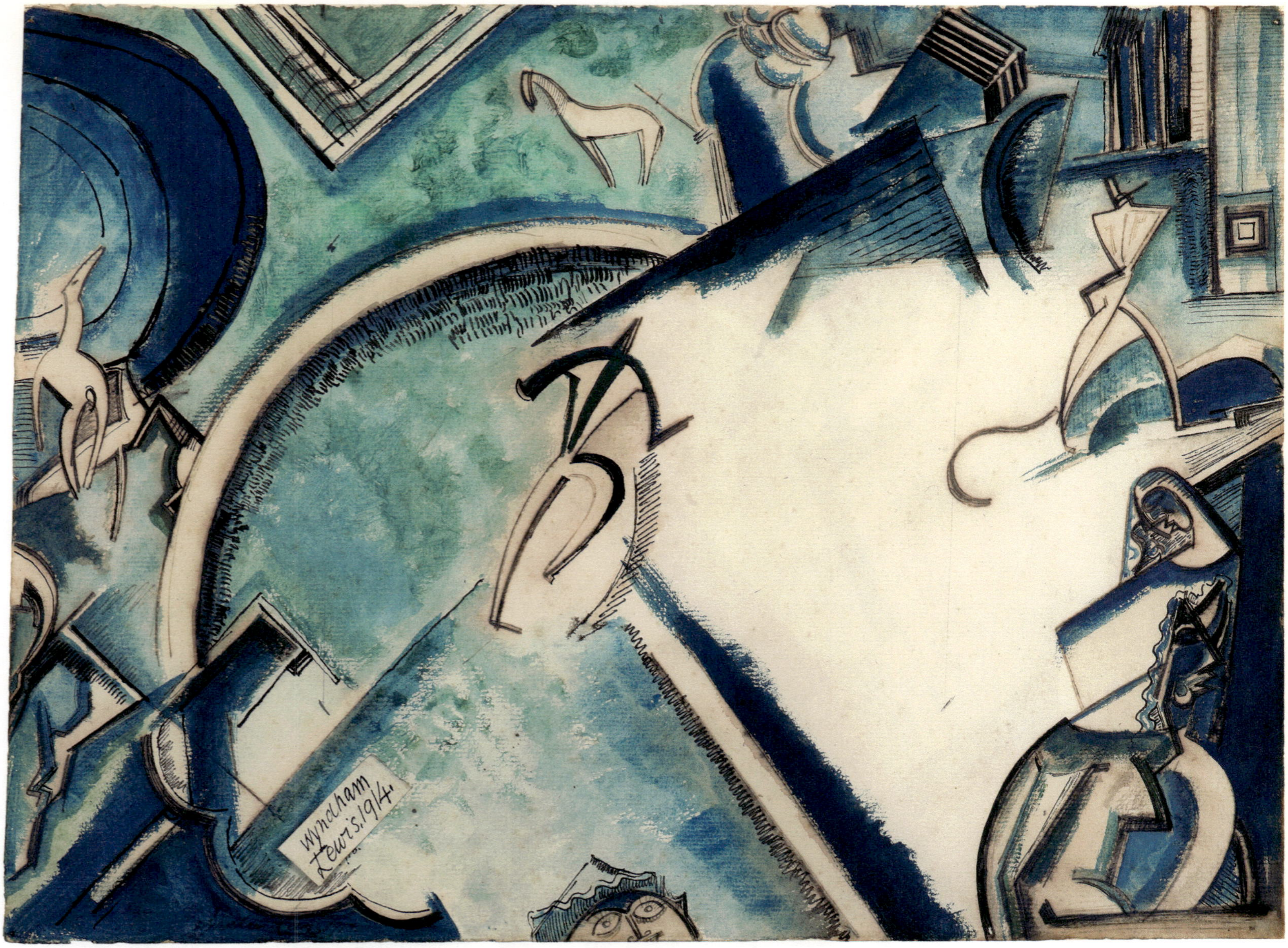

Cat. 44.
***Circus Scene*, 1913–14. Pen and ink, and watercolour on paper. 24 x 31 cm. Collection David Bowie. M 160**

Just as in *At the Seaside* (Cat. 43), Lewis is reconsidering the role of convention in representational art. The picture plane is reconceived as a field or arena around which elements and signs are grouped, and the form of representation has "punning" potentialities (the composite figure and facial profile at the bottom right). Despite its chromatic restraint, the work has a Kandinskian feel to it, and even the folk-whimsy of Marc Chagall may be an ingredient. The incongruous face peering in from bottom centre adds to the deliberate incoherence of the space and to the drawing's violation of normal pictorial convention.

Cat. 45.
Timon of Athens, 1913.
Pencil, pen and black and brown ink, and wash on paper. 34.5 x 26.5 cm. Private collection. M 154

In 1913, it still seemed likely that an edition of William Shakespeare's play with Lewis's illustrations would appear. Lewis now translates his vision of the play into the vocabulary of his new style of Vorticist abstraction (though Vorticism was not named until June 1914, by Lewis's friend Ezra Pound, the American poet living in London and promoting modernism in all its forms). Despite some of his later statements, Lewis's abstractions seem never to have been totally "abstract" or non-objective, in the sense that they never seem to deny the possibility of visual reference beyond themselves. They depend, indeed, for their effect on the activity of the spectator in exploring them and attempting to infer a possible "reality" that they may represent. They also depend on this exploration being interrupted by alternative possibilities and being both frustrated and ambiguous. The knots of more concentrated "activity" in this drawing invite such exploration and inference. It is possible that the work transposes *The Thebaid* (Cat. 33), or it might translate *Timon* (Cat. 38), integrating the figure of Timon even more inextricably in the networks of modernity from which he is constituted. The work was reproduced in the first issue of *Blast*, the Vorticists' magazine, plate v (B&M Cat. 2).

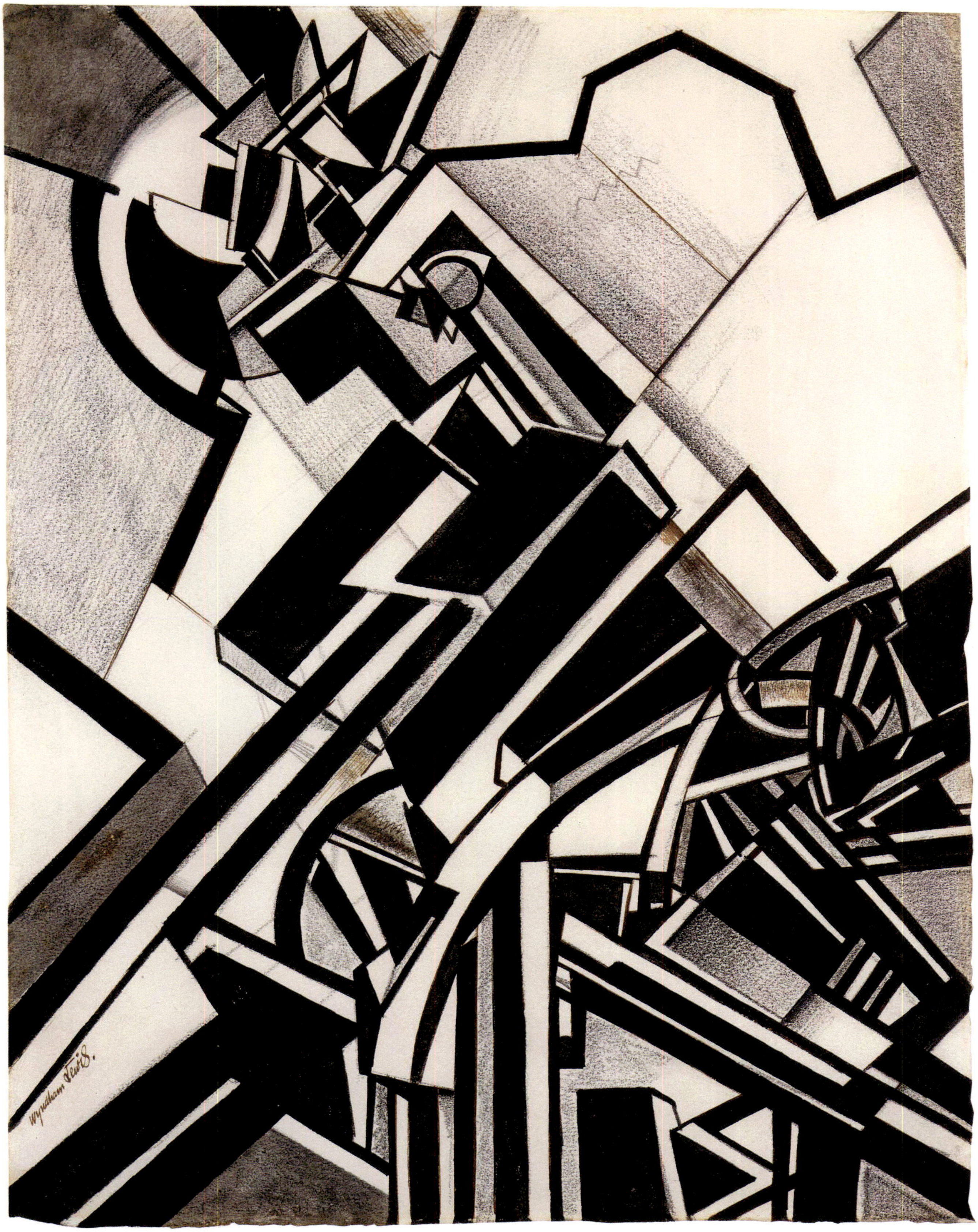

Cat. 46.
Composition – Later Drawing of Timon Series, 1913. Pen, watercolour and pencil on paper. 34.3 x 26.7 cm. Tate: Purchased 1949 (N05886). M 125

As in *Timon of Athens* (Cat. 45), the work communicates both by the sheer dynamism of its form and by a latent figuration that is difficult or impossible to retrieve. Lewis's range of visual reference is to mechanical and architectural forms (the curved, grating-like series of shapes in the bottom centre has been likened by Richard Cork to a photograph of train sheds taken by Alvin Langdon Coburn). Grimy textures and unmodulated colours allude to the mass-produced surfaces of popular decor such as were found in the London A.B.C. cafés that Lewis favoured. If interpreted as a "representational" work, this drawing shows a dancing couple, with the male severely abstracted (his head and eye top centre) and the smaller female beneath him, head thrown back in Apache dance style. The "grating" I have referred to, then, may be read as her skirt.

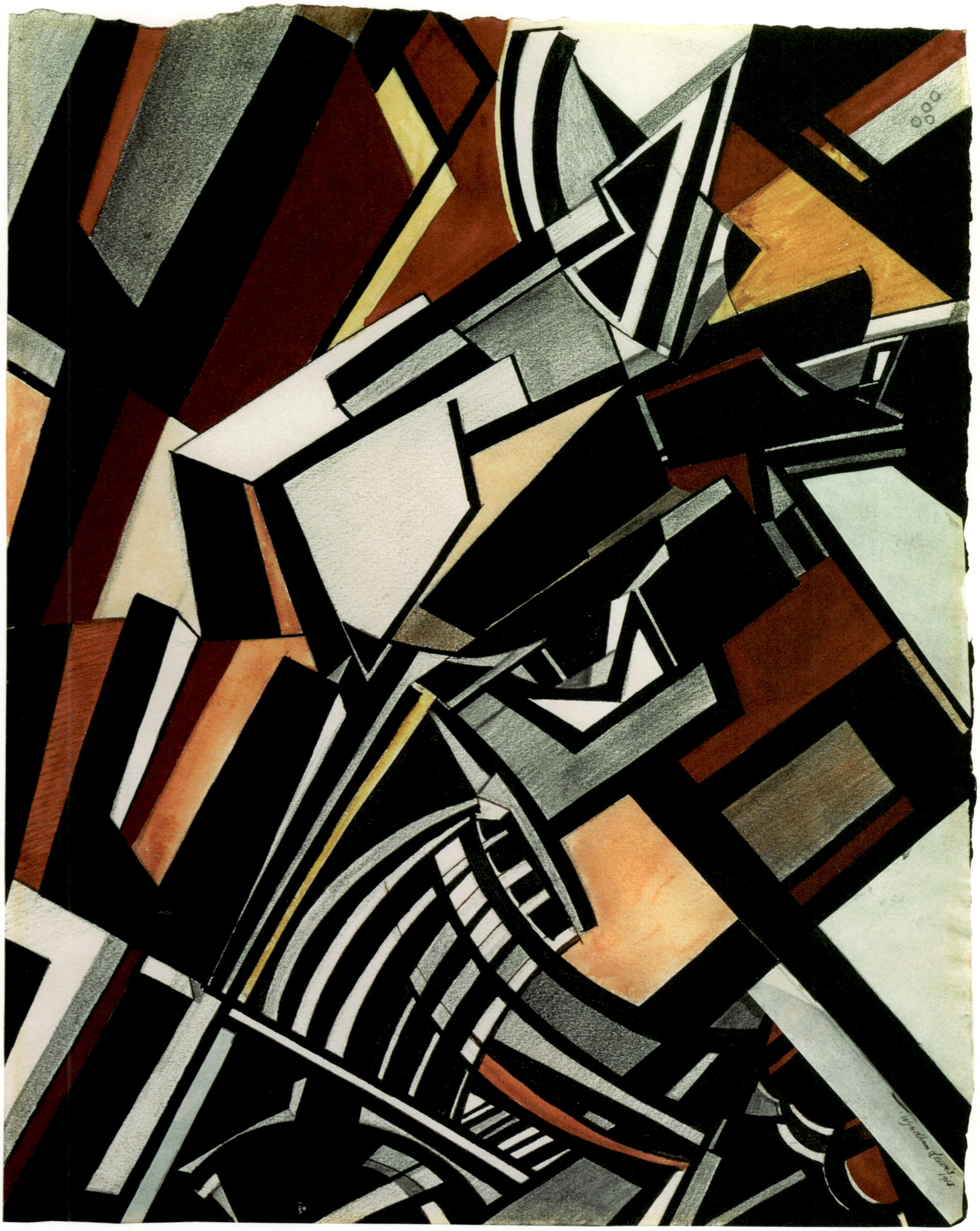

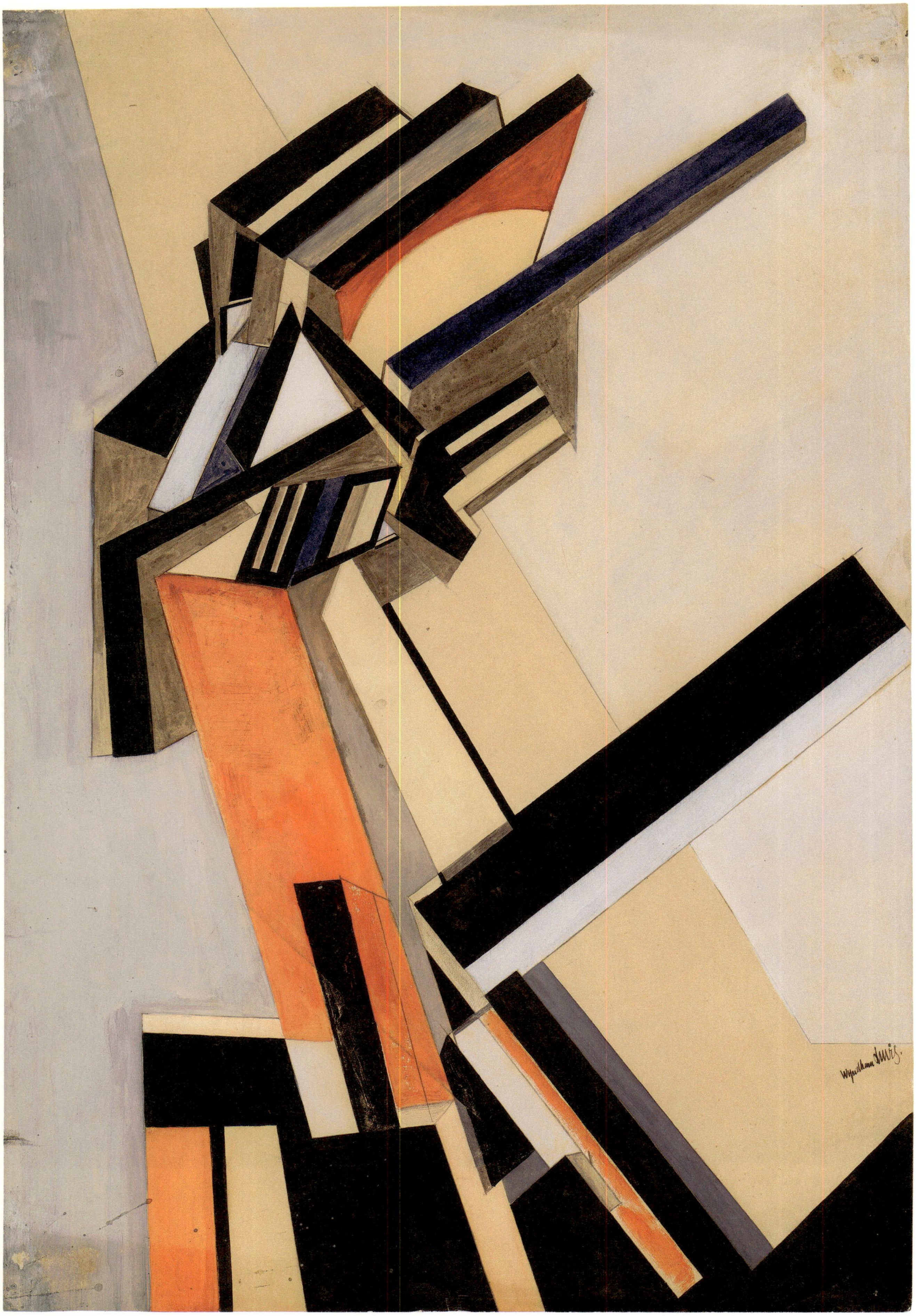

Cat. 47.
[Not in exhibition] *Portrait of an Englishwoman*, 1913. Pen and ink, pencil and watercolour on paper. 56 x 38 cm. The Wadsworth Atheneum Museum of Art. The Ella Gallup Sumner and Mary Catlin Sumner Collection Fund (1949.457). M 146

This work was reproduced in *Blast* (plate viii) (B&M Cat. 2). Lewis in later life talked about his Vorticist work as if it were purely non-objective abstraction: "the painter should sever his connections with nature, and should cease to behave as a copyist. He should invent shapes of his own, and assemble them – 'compose' them – in full independence, just as the musician does his sounds."[1] Writing to Charles Handley-Read in 1950, Lewis explained:

> The way these things were done – are done, by whoever uses this method of expression – is that a mental-emotive impulse [*Lewis's note*: By this is meant subjective intellection, like magic or religion.] is let loose upon a lot of blocks and lines of various dimensions, and encouraged to push them around and to arrange them as it will. It is of course not an accidental, isolated mood: but it is recurrent groups of emotions and coagulations of thinking, as it were, that is involved.[2]

Lewis's insistence in 1914, in "Fêng Shui and Contemporary Form,"[3] on the "magical thinking" involved in the disposition of forms on the surface of the painting ("in a painting certain forms MUST be SO"), shows that this account was not merely a later invention. *Portrait of an Englishwoman* was reproduced in 1915 in the Russian magazine, *Strelets* ("The Archer"), and its forms and organisation probably influenced the non-objective abstraction of Kazimir Malevich. But it is typical of the contrary spirit of Lewis's work that the *Portrait* can also be read as a caricature of a certain kind of Victorian English lady, wearing an elaborate hat.

1. Wyndham Lewis, 'The Vorticists' (1956). Rprt. *Wyndham Lewis on Art: Collected Writings 1913–1956*. Eds. Walter Michel and C.J. Fox (London: Thames and Hudson, 1969), p. 454.
2. Lewis to Charles Handley-Read, 2 September 1949, *The Letters of Wyndham Lewis*. Ed. W.K. Rose (London: Methuen, 1963), p. 504.
3. Wyndham Lewis, "Fêng Shui and Contemporary Form" *Blast*, No. 1 (June 1914), p. 138 (see Anthology, p. 346).

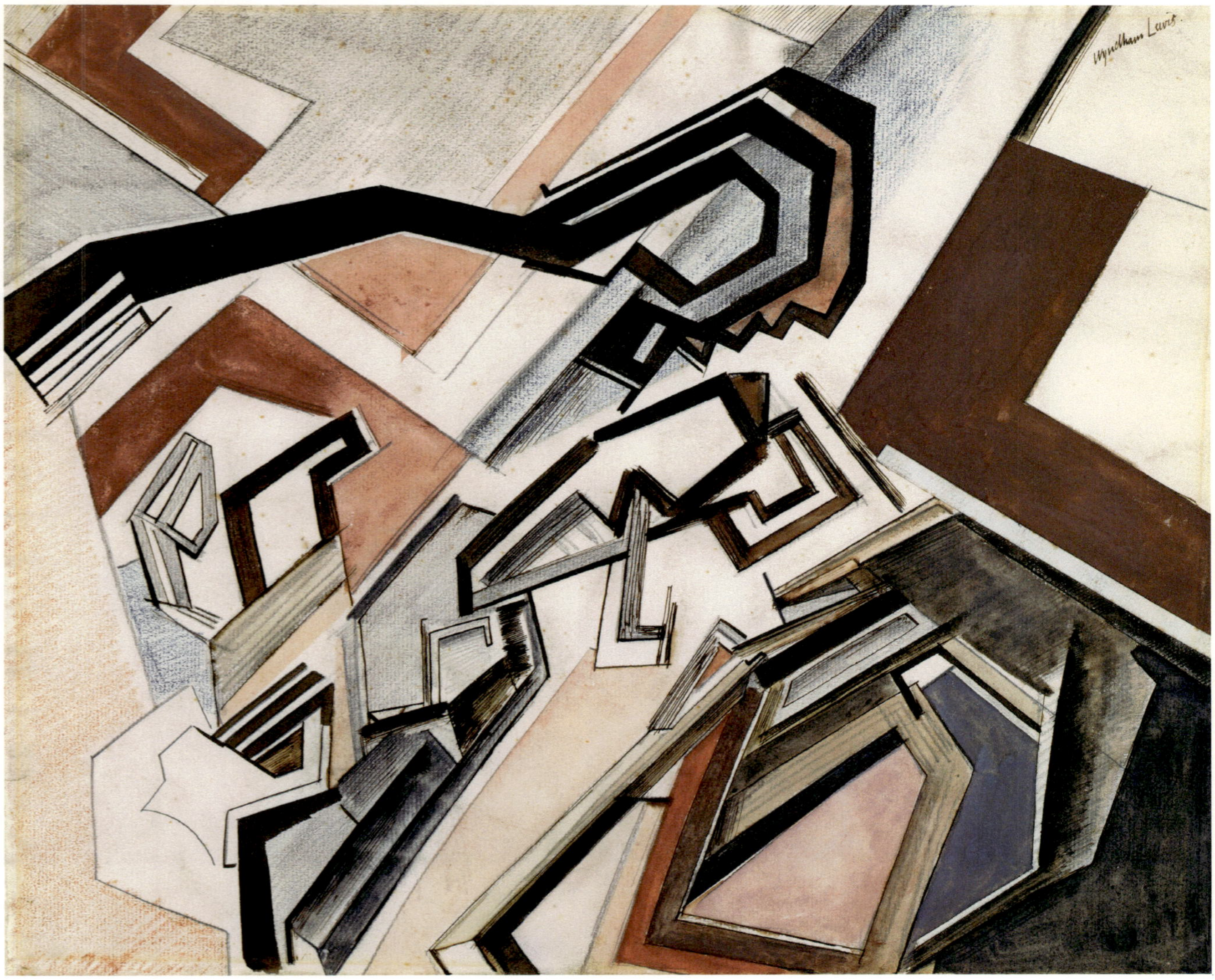

Cat. 48.
Planners (A Happy Day), 1913. Pen, gouache and pencil on paper. 31.1 x 38.1 cm. Tate: Purchased 1956 (T00106). M 145

Wyndham Lewis wrote to Charles Handley-Read (in the letter quoted in the entry for Cat. 47) that "'The Planners' is *a title* merely found for this drawing for the purposes of exhibition [in 1949] by Nan Kivell, I think." The title by which it was known to its first owner, *A Happy Day*, is likely to be Lewis's original title. It suggests the presence of one of the recurrent emotions that Lewis said were responsible for the organisation of forms in Vorticist abstraction, and this work is considerably less claustrophobic than the two Vorticist *Timon* images (Cats. 45 and 46). Rex Nan Kivell's later title, invented for Lewis's 1949 retrospective, was presumably suggested by the possibility of reading the image as a representation of a figure leaning over a drawing-table.

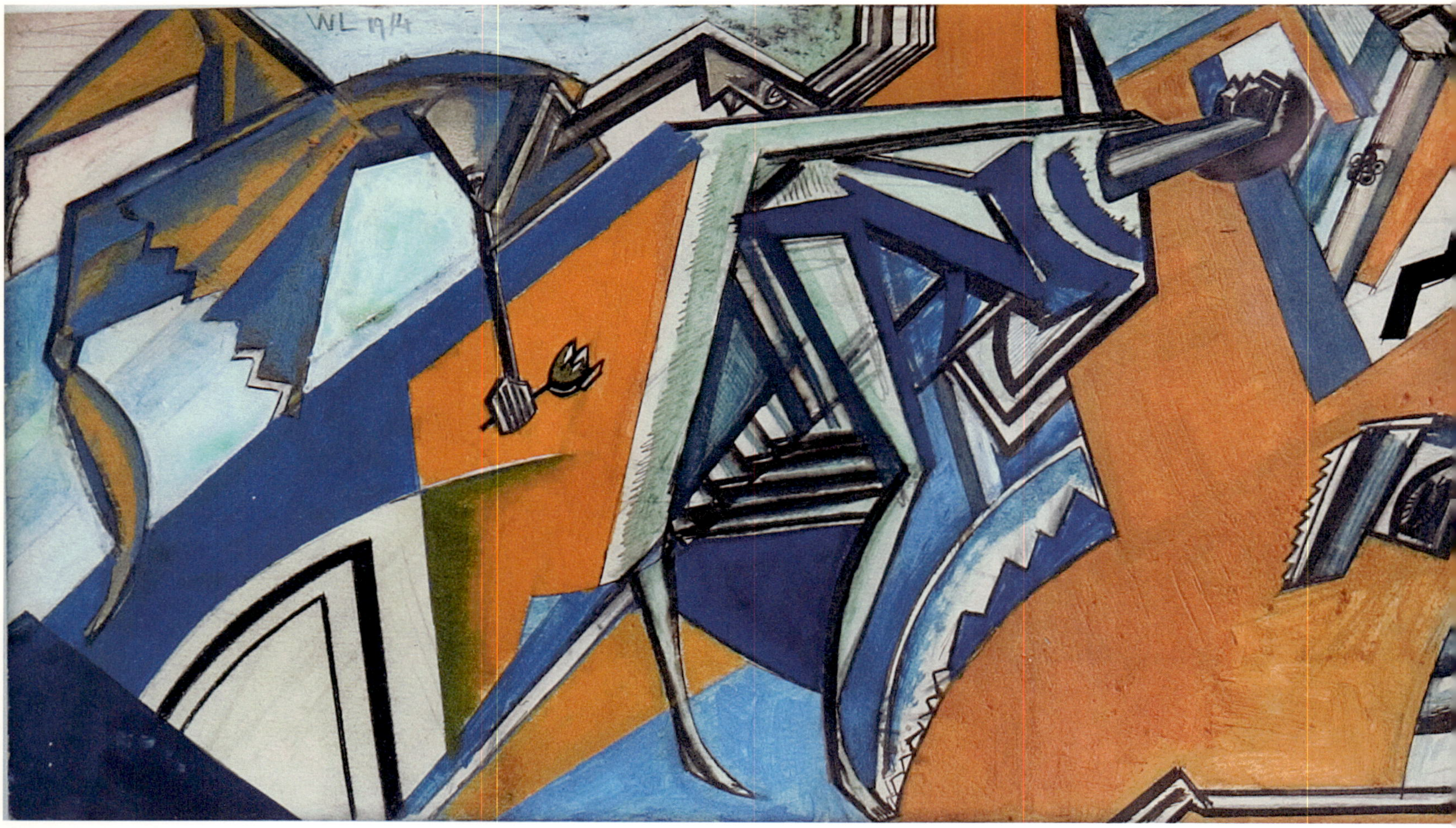

Cat. 49.
Dancing Figures, 1914.
Pencil, pen, ink, crayon, gouache and oil on paper.
21 x 50 cm. Private collection

In 1914, Lewis was commissioned to decorate the dining room of the fashionable young hostess, Lady Drogheda, in Wilton Place, London. Photographs of the room appeared in the popular press, and in *Blast* (plate vii) (B&M Cat. 2). Some of the "primitive" friezes and paintings above doors are in the same style as *Dancing Figures* (and have the same subject). This small work may therefore be a sketch for such a decorative scheme. The violent energy of its dancers recalls the dynamic couple in the 1912 Study for *Kermesse* (Cat. 19). It can be seen from the work that abstraction and representation were not "opposites" for Lewis, but part of a spectrum of possibilities, to be employed or combined at will, depending on the effect the painting was intended to convey. A description and analysis of Lewis's decorative scheme for Lady Drogheda can be found in Richard Cork, *Art Beyond the Gallery in Early 20th-Century England* (London/New Haven: Yale University Press, 1985).

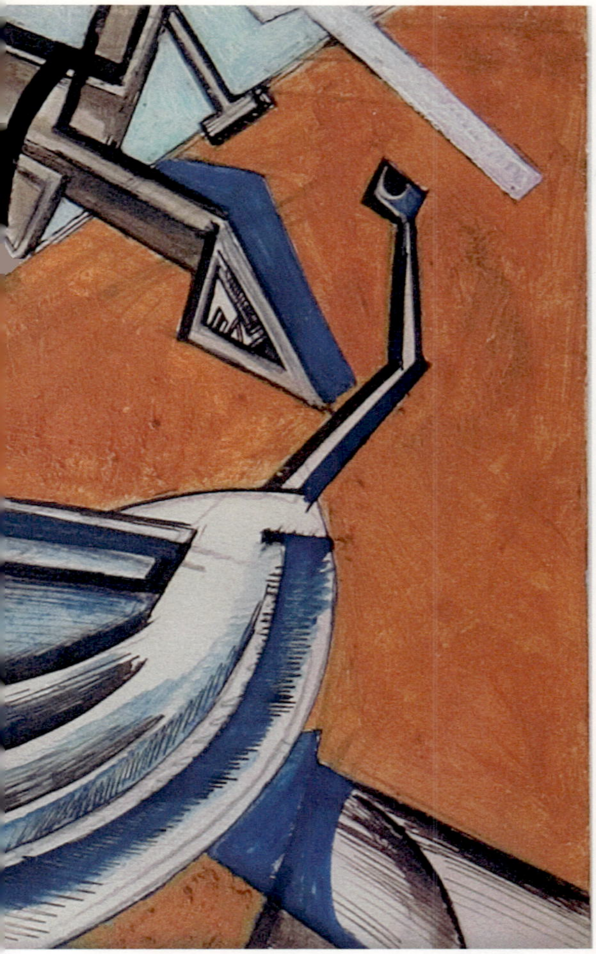

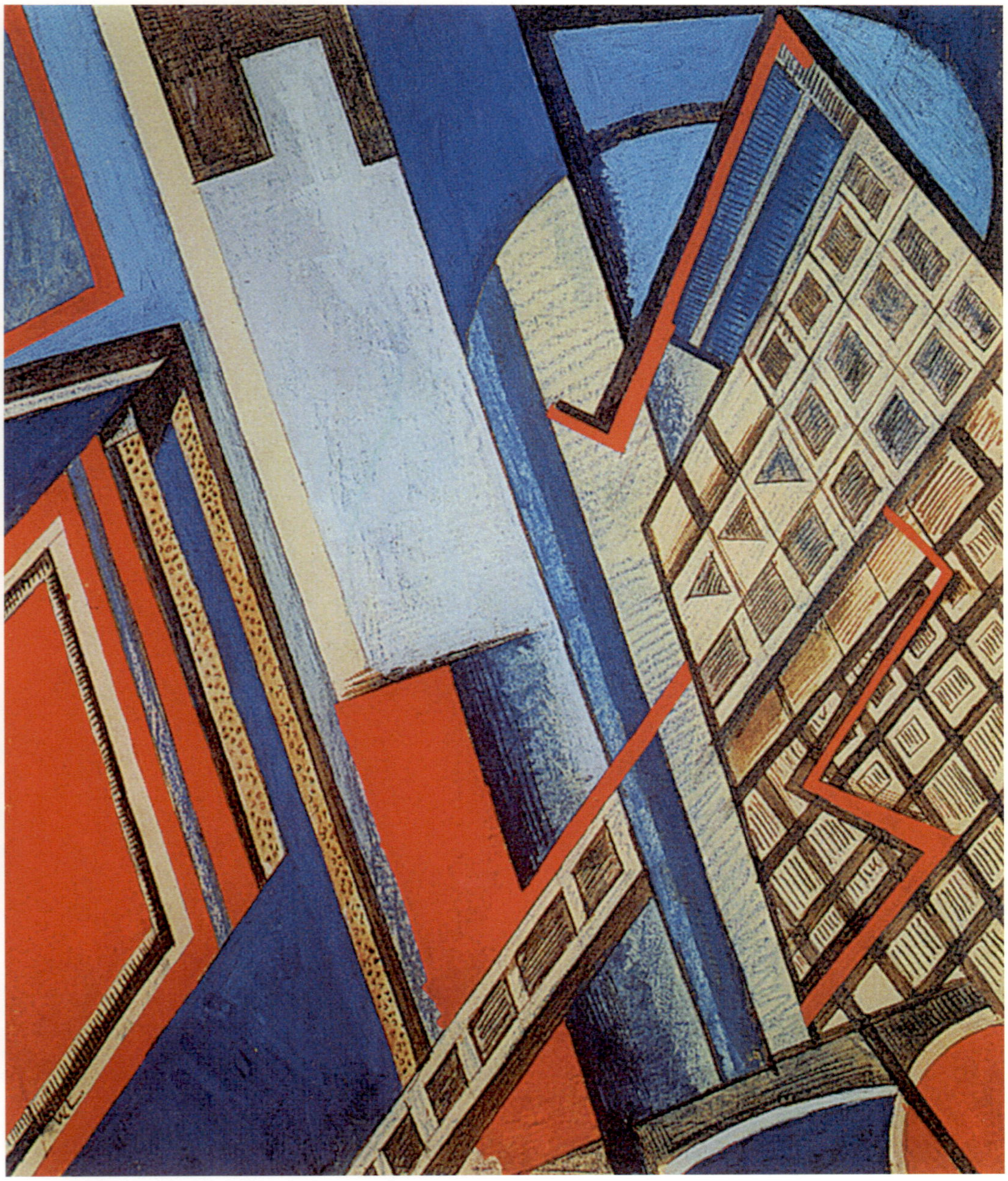

Cat. 50.
[Not in exhibition] *New York*, 1914. Pen and ink, and watercolour on paper.
31 x 26 cm.
Private collection. M 177

Among the forms of modernity that Lewis's Vorticism particularly engaged with was modern skyscraper architecture, for which at this time he seems to have shown almost unqualified enthusiasm. In this, he was influenced both by the photographs of New York of Alvin Langdon Coburn and the designs of the Futurist Antonio Sant'Elia. This is clearly not a mere *representation* of modern architecture, but a more abstracted celebration of its vertiginous perspectives. The brilliant discords of scarlet and blue, the insistently material feel of its textures and the violation of Euclidean space are essential to its effect. In 1915, Lewis discussed the issue of abstraction versus representation:

A Vorticist, lately, painted a picture in which a crowd of squarish shapes, at once suggesting windows, occurred. A sympathizer with the movement asked him, horror-struck, 'are not those windows?' 'Why not?' the Vorticist replied. 'A window is for you actually A WINDOW: for me it is a space, bounded by a square or oblong frame, by four bands or four lines, merely.'[1]

1. Wyndham Lewis, "A Review of Contemporary Art," *Blast*, No. 2 (July 1915), p. 44.

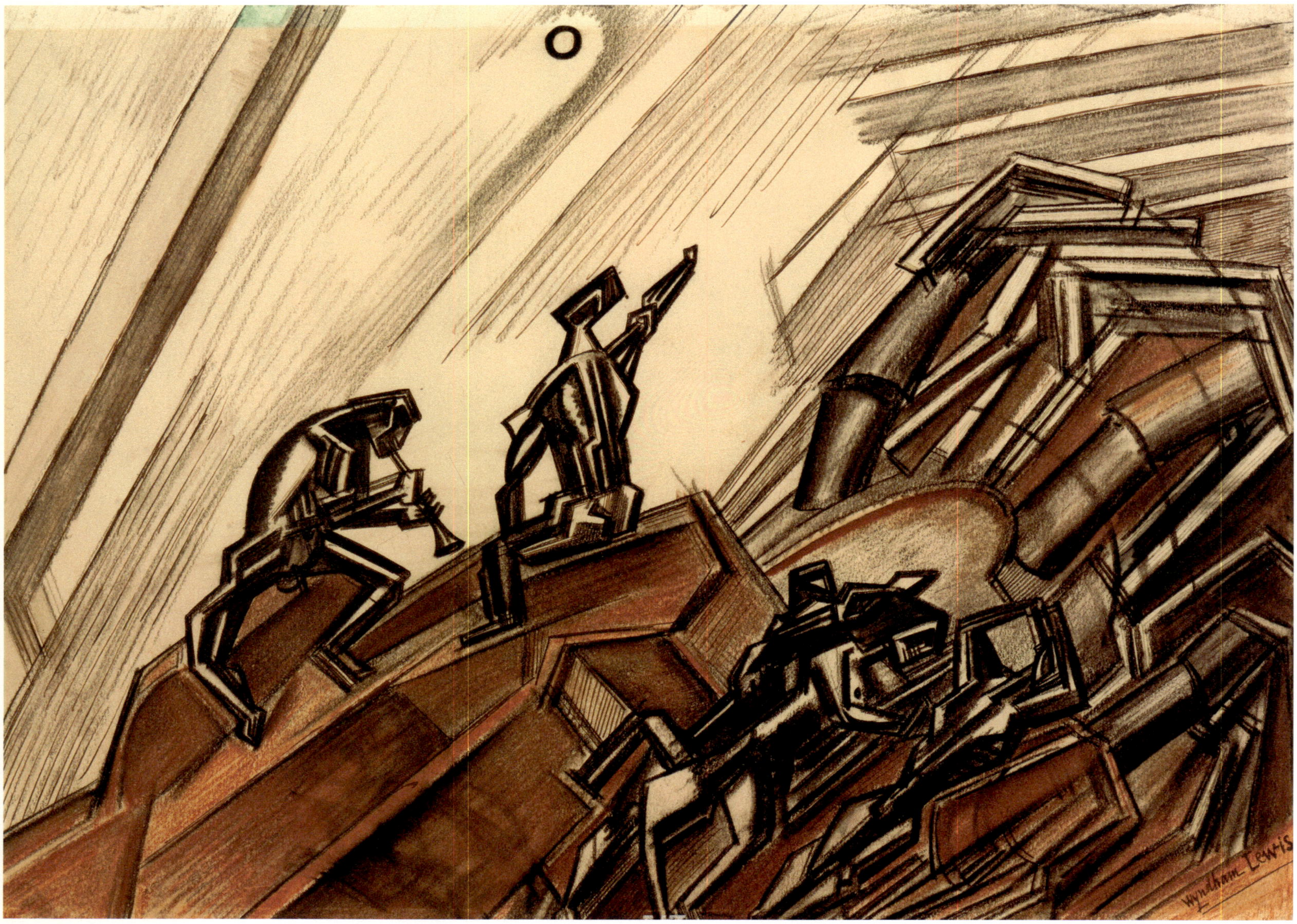

Cat. 51. ▲
Moonlight, 1914. Pencil, ink and chalk on paper.
27, 5 x 38 cm.
Victoria and Albert Museum (E 3766-1919). M 166.

Cat. 52. ▶▶
Combat No. 3, 1914. Pencil, ink and chalk on paper.
27, 5 x 38 cm.
Victoria and Albert Museum (E 3765-1919). M 162

These drawings are an unexpected deviation from what, at the height of the Vorticist period, must have seemed like an inevitable progress to the practice of total abstraction in Lewis's work. But, as Lewis's contemporary statement shows ("We must constantly strive to ENRICH abstraction till it is almost plain life"[1]), he did not think in these "progressive" terms. What we find in his work is rather a constant return to the sources of his own inspiration, which he then reworks in terms of the artistic resources of a particular moment of his development. This process is most evident in his writing, where early texts are later revised and reissued (this happened to the early *Wild Body* stories (B&M Cat. 17), the novel *Tarr* (B&M Cat. 18) and the 1914 "play," *Enemy of the Stars* (B&M Cat. 2), for instance). In these drawings, Lewis is revisiting some of the themes of his "anti-pastorals" of 1912 and reworking them in the mechanomorphic vocabulary of Vorticism. *Moonlight* presents a Matissean idyll, where nature and man have become mechanised. The image looks forward to the short story, "Cantelman's Spring-Mate" written in 1916 and published in *The Little Review* in October 1917, causing the magazine to be prosecuted for obscenity. In the story, a pastoral seduction is likewise described as brutal and mechanical.

Combat No.3 is clearly related in feeling, if not in ostensible subject matter, to *Moonlight*. Commenting on Lewis's unconventional use of colour to the collector, John Quinn, Ezra Pound wrote "I think [...] that Lewis with his fundamental realism has been trying to show the beauty of colour one actually sees in a modern brick, iron, sooty railroad yarded smoked modern city."[2] Just as *Man and Woman* (Cat. 18) may allude to Gauguin's *Yellow Christ*, *Combat No. 3* has been seen as Lewis's re-imagination of the same artist's *Vision After the Sermon* (1888), with its wrestling couple and praying figures.

1. Wyndham Lewis, "A Review of Contemporary Art," *Blast*, No. 2 (July 1915), p. 40.
2. Ezra Pound to John Quinn, 13 July 1916, *Ezra Pound and the Visual Arts*. Ed. Harriet Zinnes (New York: New Directions, 1980), pp. 238–39.

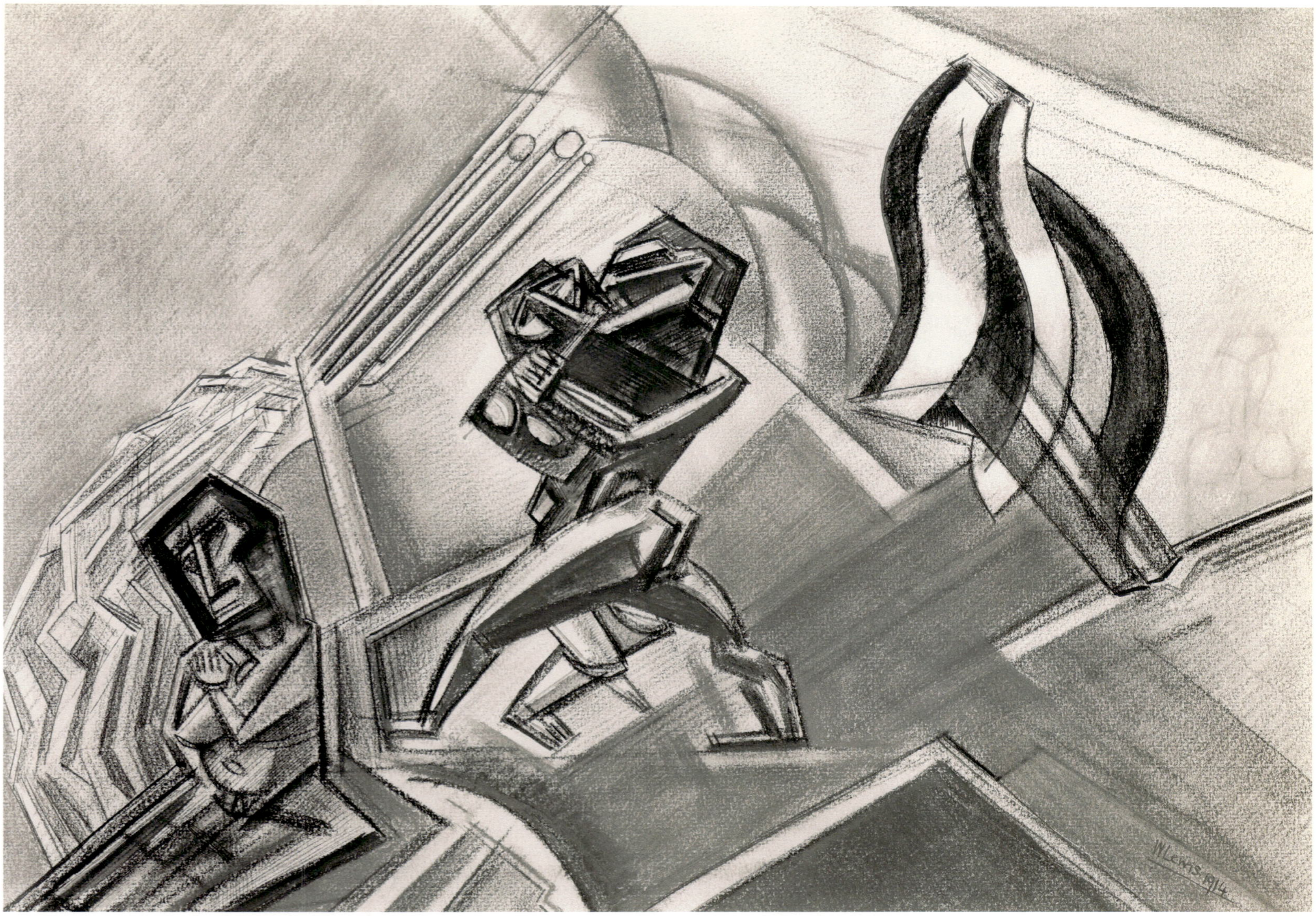

Cat. 53. ▶
Design from a Vorticist Sketchbook: Abstract Composition III, 1914–15. Pencil and watercolour on paper. 29.2 x 26.7 cm. San Francisco Museum of Modern Art. Fractional Gift of Bobbie and Mike Wilsey. M 180

Cat. 54. ▶▶
Design from a Vorticist Sketchbook: Abstract Composition VI, 1914–15. Pencil on paper. 35.9 x 25.1 cm. San Francisco Museum of Modern Art. Fractional Gift of Bobbie and Mike Wilsey. M 183

Cat. 55. ▶▶▶
[Not in exhibition] *Design from a Vorticist Sketchbook: Abstract Composition VIII*, 1914–15. Pencil on paper. 31.1 x 26 cm. San Francisco Museum of Modern Art. Fractional Gift of Bobbie and Mike Wilsey. M 184

Cat. 56. ▼
[Not in exhibition] *Design from a Vorticist Sketchbook: Abstract Composition IX*, 1914–15. Pencil on paper. 29.8 x 25.4 cm. San Francisco Museum of Modern Art. Fractional Gift of Bobbie and Mike Wilsey. M 185

At least six of the Vorticist oil paintings that Lewis produced from 1914 to 1915 no longer exist. In his disillusion with the style in the early 1920s, he seems to have cut up at least one and painted new works on the fragments of canvas. Others that dissatisfied him he may have destroyed ("et des fois je les ai brûlés," he wrote to Charles Handley-Read[1]). These sketches, together with such photographs as Alvin Langdon Coburn's of Lewis in front of a canvas (probably *Red Duet,* 1914, p. 30), give a hint of what such works may have looked like. They also provide an insight into Lewis's working methods, his way of generating these images, in the most "abstract" phase of Vorticism. "Non-Euclidean" space is created and peopled with forms in *Composition III* by the artist's decision to fill certain of the shapes generated by intersecting lines with hatching or wash. A more consistent and thoroughgoing application of the method generates the ladder-forms, "windows" and extended strips of hatching in *Composition VI*. This is also inscribed with colour notes. A similar "ladder" in *Composition VIII* is folded back on itself and a further form, in an apparently incongruent space, bears down on it from the upper right. This type of composition is exploited in the painting, *Workshop* (Cat. 58). The elegant *Composition IX* shows that Lewis's invention in this mode was potentially inexhaustible. The "boomerang" shape that is realised out of the sequence of lines is unlike anything else in his work.

1. Lewis to Charles Handley-Read, 2 September 1949, *The Letters of Wyndham Lewis*. Ed. W.K. Rose (London: Methuen, 1963), p. 504.

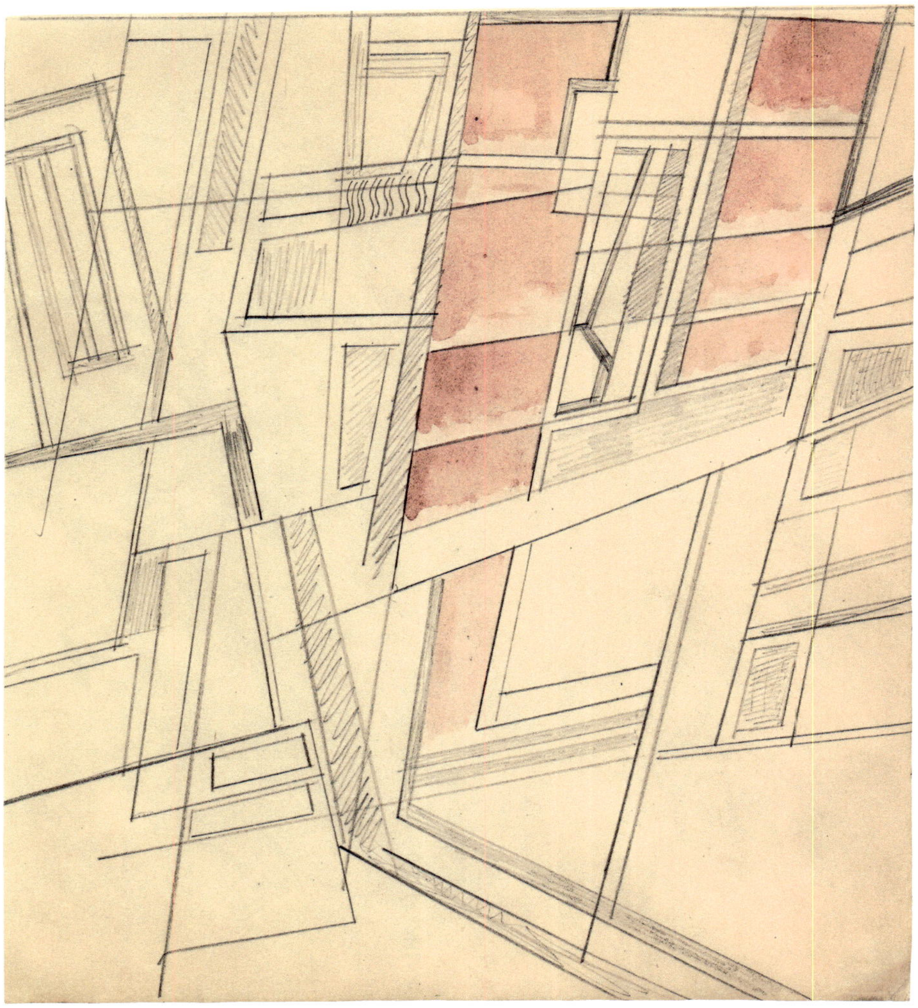

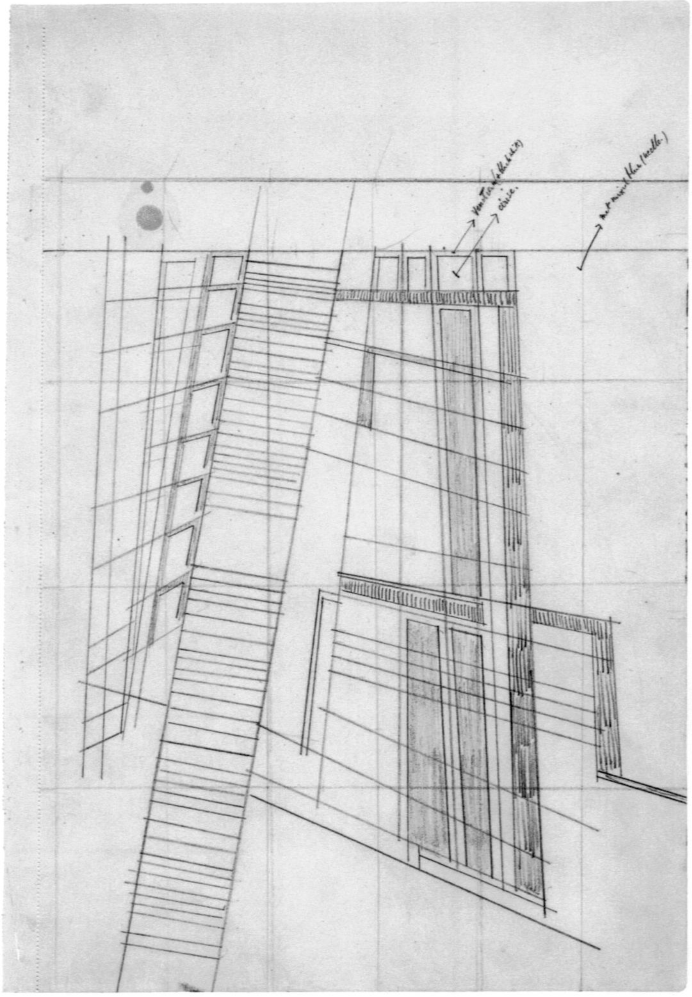

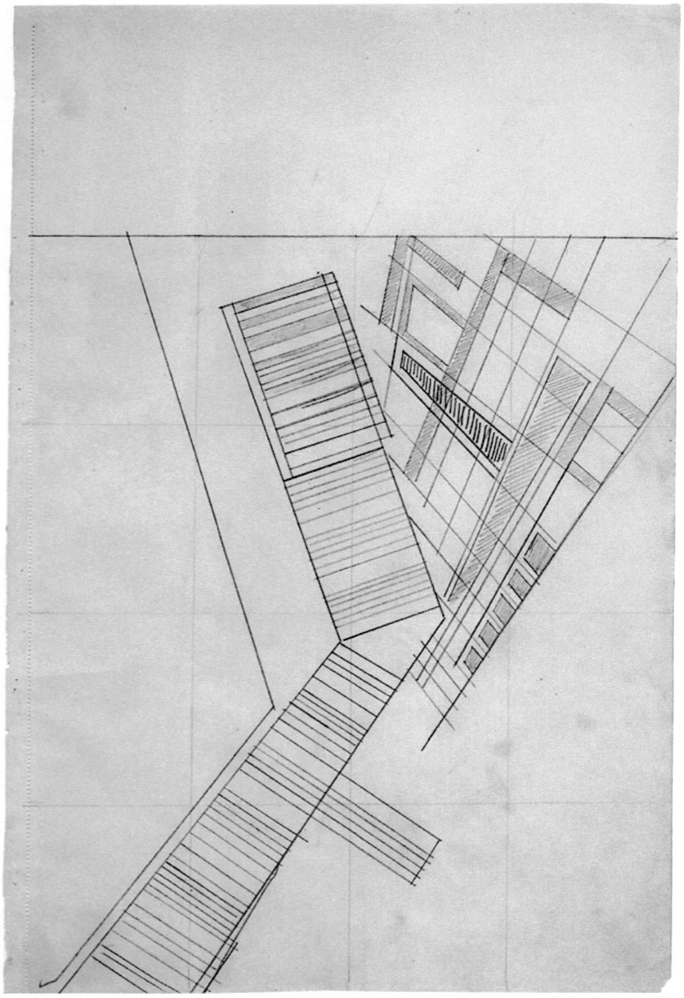

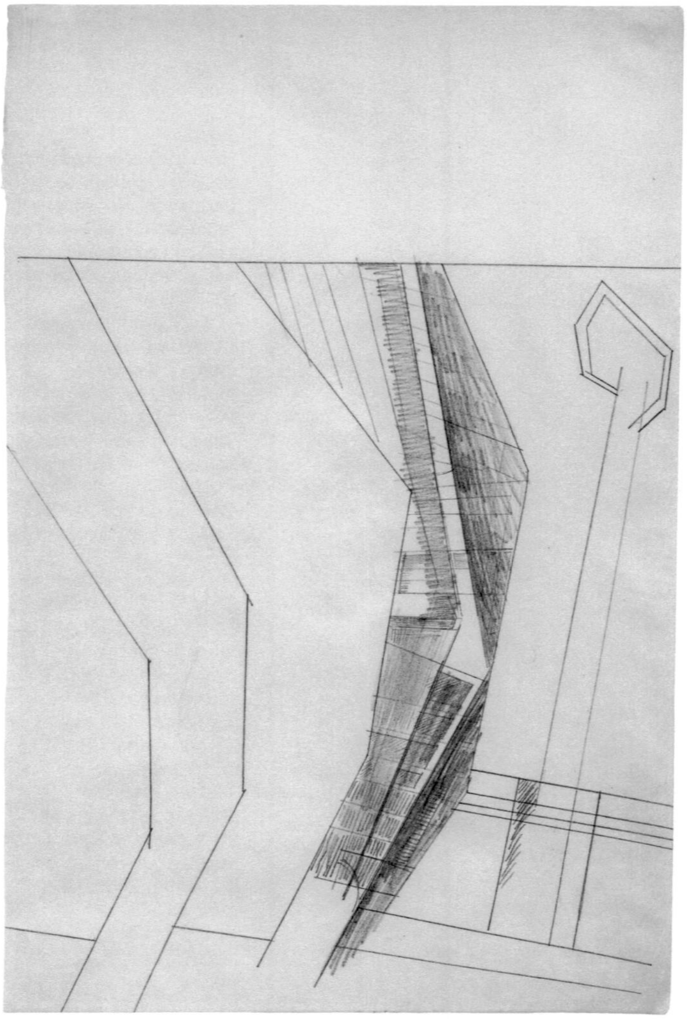

Cat. 57.
***Composition in Blue*, 1915. Chalk and watercolour on paper. 47 x 30.5 cm. Private collection. M 196**

This image has elements of diagrammatic battle-plans but its central form also resembles a standing figure. Lewis's friend, Frank Rutter,[1] commenting on the lost painting, *Plan of War* (1913–14) (M P12), reproduced in *Blast*, No. 1, plate iv (B&M Cat. 2), says that its forms were based on the diagrams of battles in military textbooks. Despite these (possible) military associations, this is the most lyrical of Lewis's Vorticist abstractions.

1. Frank Rutter, *Evolution in Modern Art: A Study of Modern Painting 1870–1925* (London: Harrap, 1925), pp. 115–16.

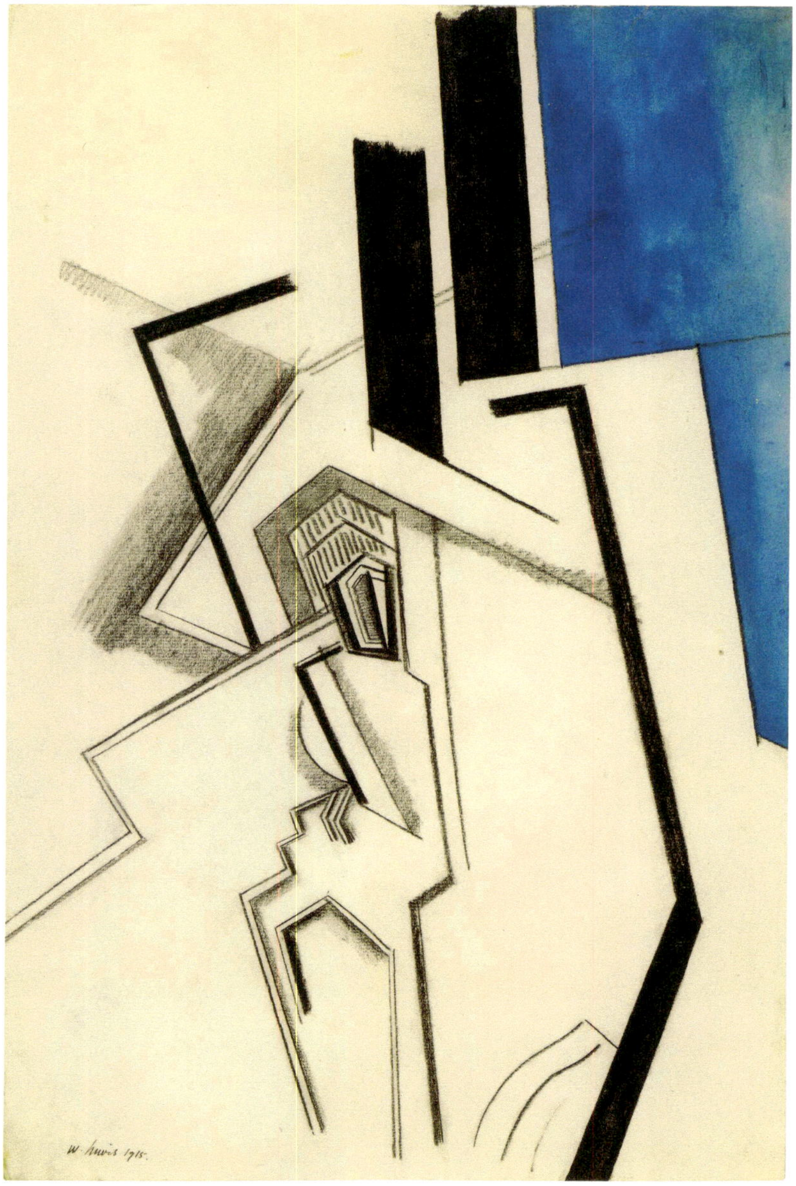

Cat. 58.
***Workshop*, 1915. Oil on canvas. 76.5 x 61 cm. Tate: Purchased 1974 (T01931). M P19**

This is Lewis's earliest surviving authenticated oil painting and was exhibited in the *Vorticist Exhibition* at the Doré Galleries, London in June 1915. The combination of ice-cream pinks, mustards, ochres and browns (enclosing in the centre two patches of blue) is deliberately discordant. Lewis wrote in "Orchestra of Media" in 1914:

> **The surfaces of cheap manufactured goods, woods, steel, glass, etc., already appreciated for themselves, and their possibilities realised, have finished the days of fine paint.**
>
> **Even if painting remain intact, it will be much more supple and extended, containing all the elements of discord and 'ugliness' consequent on the attack against traditional harmony.**[1]

The painting's title may relate to part of the "Bless England" section of the Blast–Bless section of the Vorticist manifesto in *Blast*, No. 1 (B&M Cat. 2): "BLESS ENGLAND, Industrial machine, pyramidal workshop, its apex at Shetland, discharging itself on the sea" (pp. 23–4). And, in *Tarr* (B&M Cat. 18), Lewis's spokesman responds to the Shakespearian "All the world's a stage" with "I say it's all an atelier – 'all the world's a workshop' I should say."[2]

1. *Blast*, No. 1 (June 1914), p. 142.
2. *Tarr*. Rev. ed. (London: Chatto and Windus, 1928), p. 303.

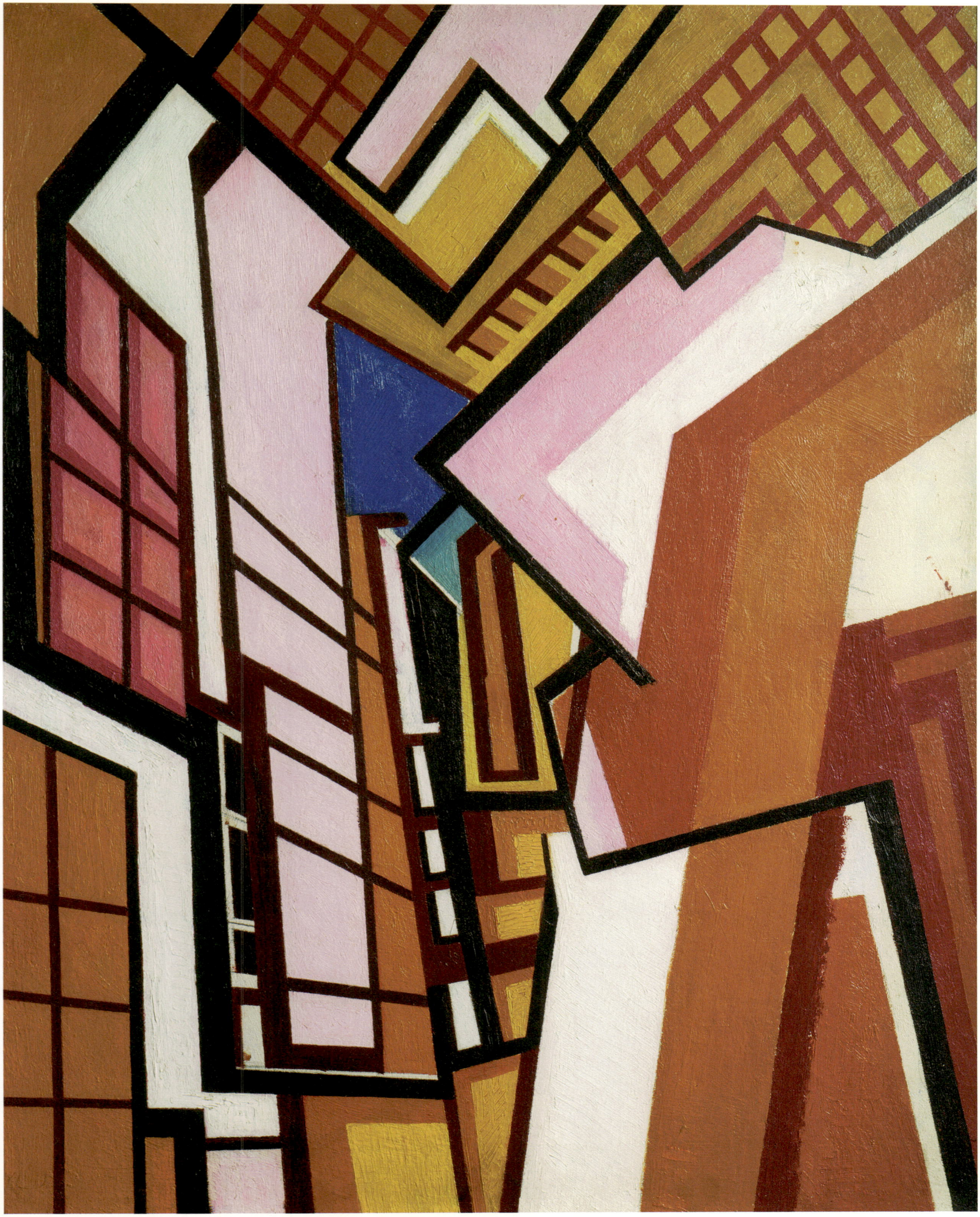

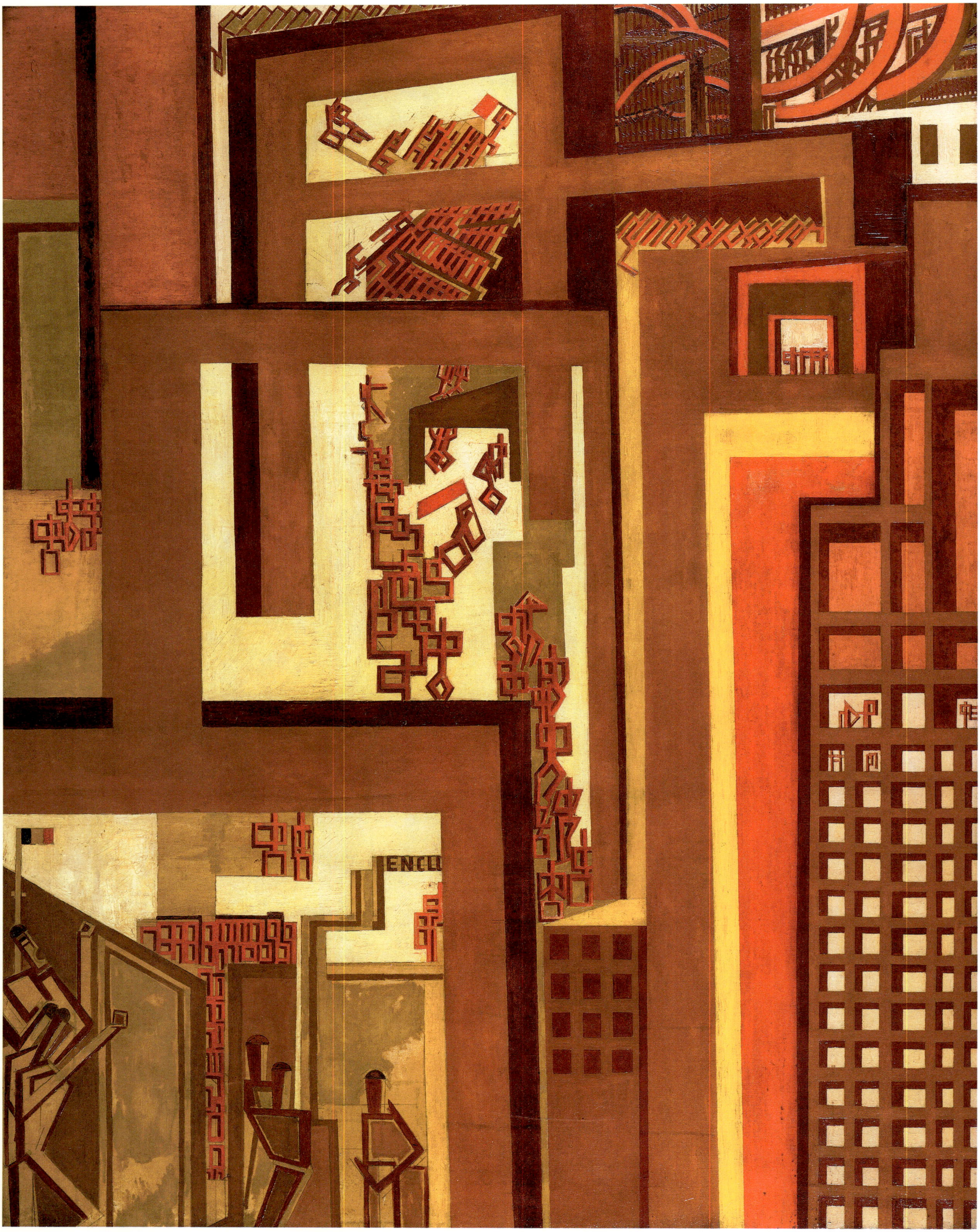
ENCL

Cat. 59.
The Crowd, 1914–15.
Oil and pencil on canvas. 200.7 x 153.7 cm. Tate: Presented by the Friends of the Tate Gallery 1964 (T00689). M P17

Lewis's interest in crowds and crowd psychology may have been revived by witnessing the war crowds of London in August 1914 on the outbreak of the First World War. His serial story, "The Crowd Master," in the second issue of *Blast* (pp. 94–102) (B&M Cat. 3), shows this renewal of interest and Lewis may well have re-read Gustave Le Bon's *The Crowd* (1896), which lay behind the 1909 work *The Theatre Manager* (Cat. 6). But the painting shows a revolutionary crowd with the red flag rather than a war crowd (though the tricolour intimates a French location, perhaps because France was the spiritual home of Georges Sorel's invention, the General Strike). The painting may be a response to Luigi's Russolo's *La Rivolta* (1911), a dramatic realisation of the Futurist ambition to celebrate crowds and revolution. Where Russolo's crowd seem to carry all before them, Lewis's small red figures are dwarfed by the gigantic and rigid forms of the modern city. When combined, indeed, they echo those forms in miniature and the stress on horizontals and verticals in the painting reduces the sense of dynamism found in most of Lewis's work. The revolutionary leaders (the ones with "brains," at the bottom left) encourage the crowd out of the "enclo[sure]." The crowd storms the industrial hive at the top right, where darker figures labour on semicircular forms that are probably treadmills. In "Inferior Religions," such a treadmill is cited as a much simplified version of the environments that "work" human beings. Lewis at this time was sympathetic to anarcho-syndicalist political views, but the painting seems to express a certain scepticism about the likely success of revolutionary violence. In a short play, *The Ideal Giant*, written at around the time this painting was produced, one of the characters puts forward the idea that the artist must in some sense "be" a crowd (like a theatre manager):

The artist is the Ideal Giant or Many. The Crowd at its moments of heroism also is. But Art is never at its best without the assaults of Egotism and of Life.

For the health of the Giant as much as for that of the individual this conflict and its alertes are necessary.

Revolution is the normal proper state of things.[1]

1. Wyndham Lewis, "The Ideal Giant" (1916). Wyndham Lewis, *Collected Poems and Plays*. Ed. Alan Munton (Manchester: Carcanet, 1979), pp. 131–32.

Cat. 60. ▼
Pastoral Toilet (1917. Pencil, ink and watercolour on paper. 17.5 x 21.5 cm. Victoria and Albert Museum (E 3772-1919). M 256

Cat. 61. ▶
Gossips, 1917. Pencil, ink and watercolour on paper. 28 x 38 cm. Victoria and Albert Museum (E 3767-1919). M 252

Lewis's training to become an artillery officer took over a year and he arrived at the Front in June 1917. Within a few weeks, he was hospitalised with "trench fever," and while in hospital recuperating he produced these drawings, which he sent to Ezra Pound. They reveal Lewis's continuing interest in the sheer oddness of human behaviour, depicted in *Gossips* using (in a far looser way) some of the geometric vocabulary of Vorticism. A familiar scene of women chatting is rendered outlandishly intense. In *Pastoral Toilet*, Lewis unknowingly looks forward to the style of pen-and-ink drawing he will develop in 1918 when he becomes a war artist. This style can also be seen to derive from that of *Salaam Maharaj: An Oriental Design* (Cat. 4), which at first sight seems an isolated and uncharacteristic piece of juvenilia. Lewis wrote to Pound (with some immodesty) about the drawings produced during his convalescence:

I don't think where there is much of anything else that style is worth maintaining in pictures – or books. Examine the Market-Women & a few pen drawings of Rembrandt, and you will notice – I hope not with an air of amazement & discovery – that the Market Ladies possess a similar character & a very similar quantity of Style. Sometimes I am a bit careless and harsh.[1]

1. Letter to Ezra Pound, 8 October 1917, *Pound / Lewis: The Letters of Ezra Pound and Wyndham Lewis*. Ed. Timothy Materer (New York: New Directions, 1985), p. 106.

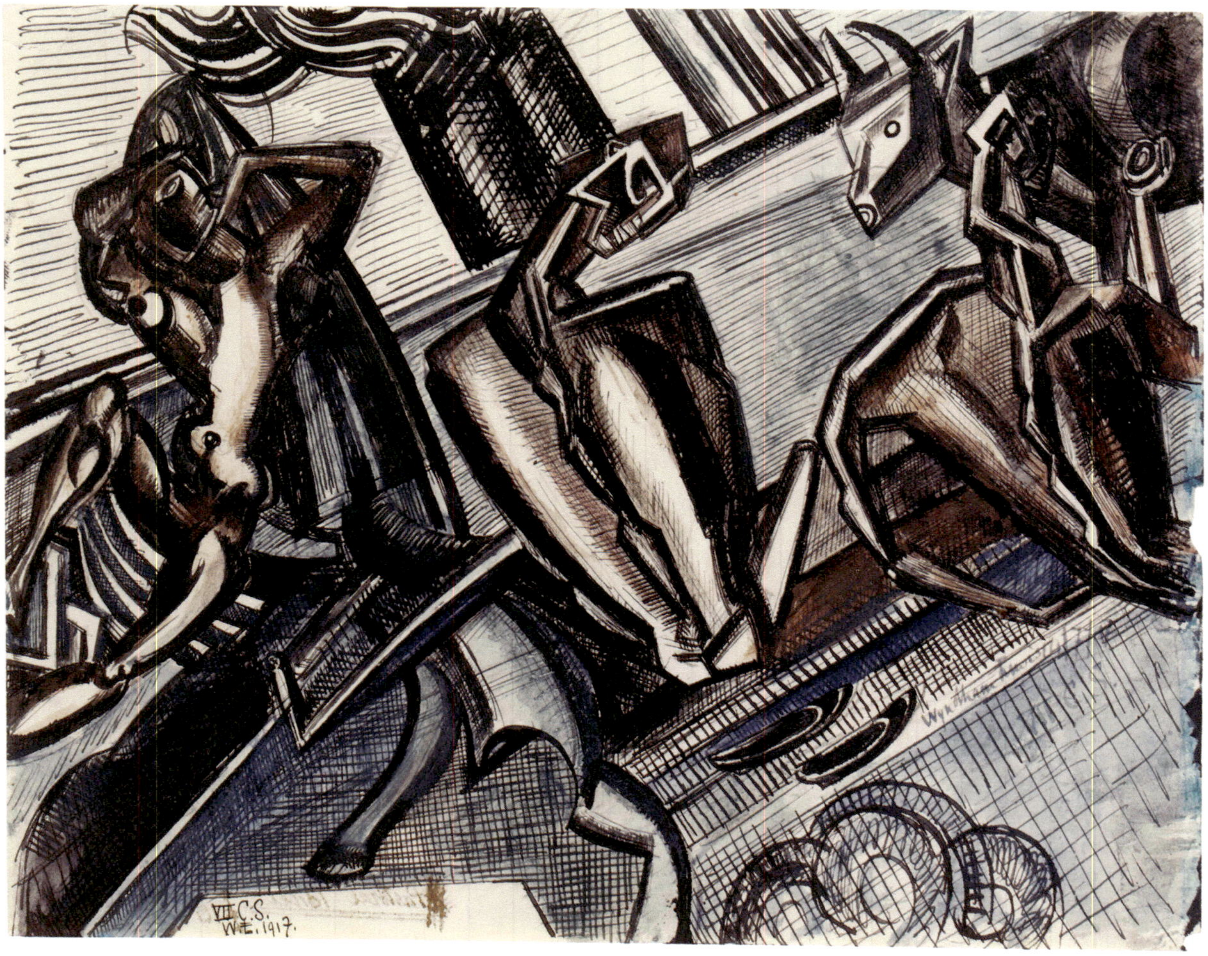

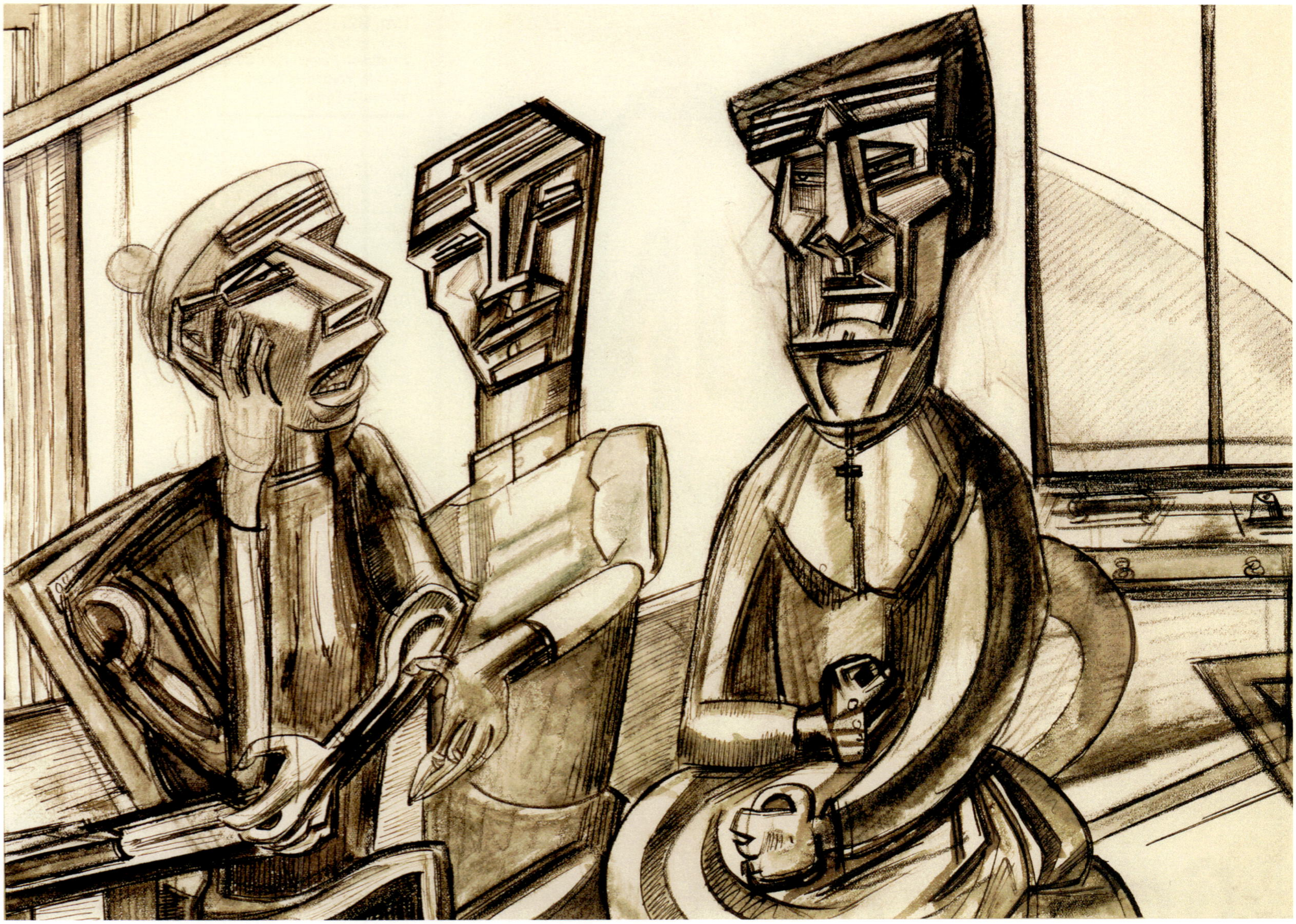

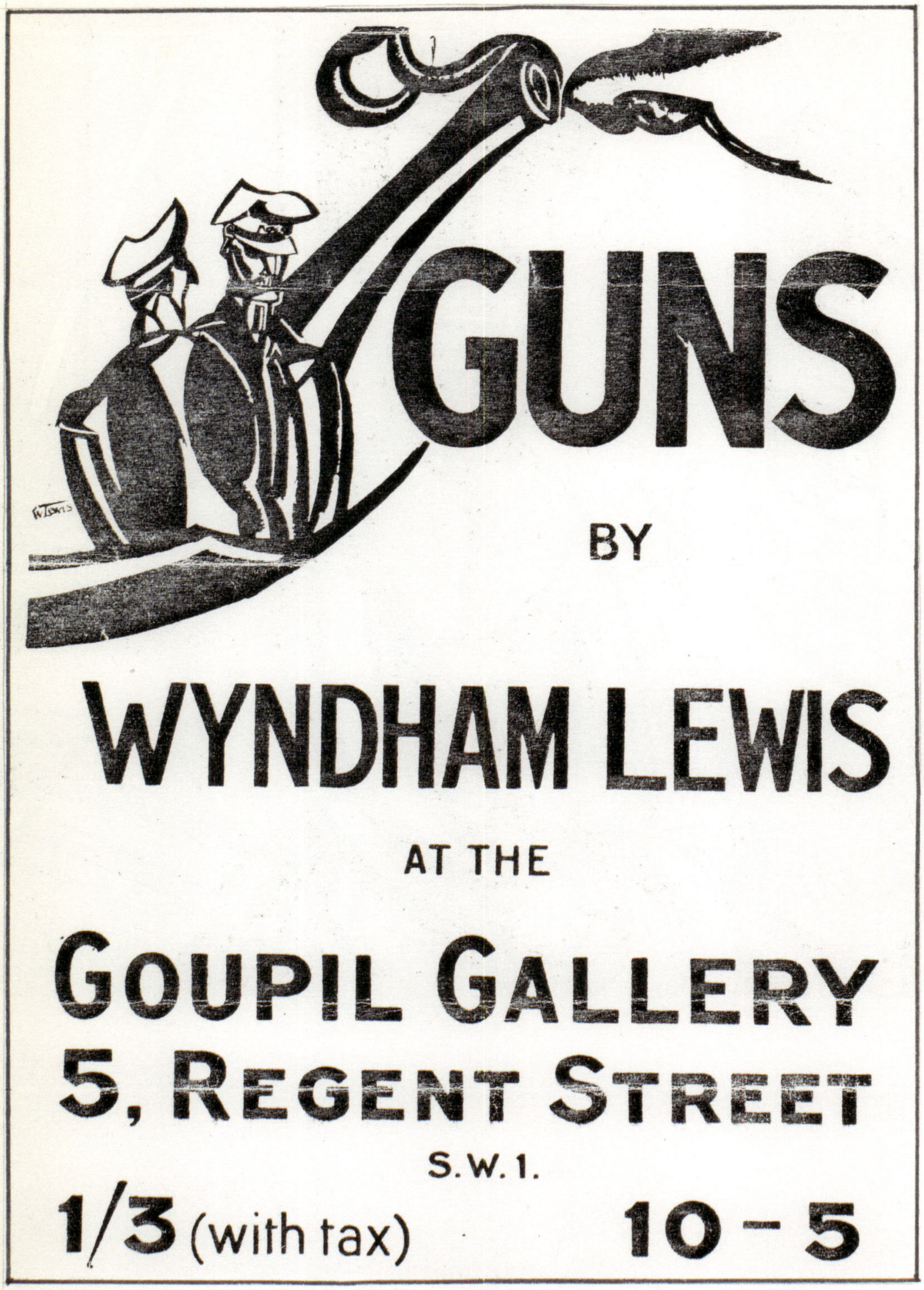

Cat. 62.
Guns by Wyndham Lewis Exhibition Poster, **1919. 29.5 x 21 cm. Wyndham Lewis Memorial Trust**

At the end of the Third Battle of Ypres in November 1917, Lewis returned to London to visit his mother, who was seriously ill in the Spanish Flu pandemic. While in London he was commissioned as an official war artist, first by the Canadian Government, and second by the British Government. For both, he was to produce large-scale oil paintings. The drawings and paintings that were exhibited in *Guns* in 1919, his first one-man exhibition, held at the Goupil Gallery, London, were not commissioned, but produced by Lewis in the course of his work as a war artist. He explained his conception of the exhibition in the catalogue:

I have attempted here only one thing: that is in a direct, ready formula to give an interpretation of what I took part in in France. I set out to do a series dealing with the Gunner's life from his arrival in the Depôt to his life in the Line. [...]

This show, then, pretends nothing, in extent: I make only the claim for it that it attempts to give a personal and immediate expression of a tragic event. Experimentation is waived: I have tried to do with pencil and brush what story-tellers like Tchehov or Stendhal did in their books.[1]

1. Wyndham Lewis, "Foreword," in *Guns* [exh. cat. Goupil Gallery, London]. London: Goupil Gallery, 1919, n.p.

Cat. 63.
Officer and Signallers**, 1918. Ink, watercolour and gouache on paper. 25.4 x 35.6 cm. Imperial War Museum, London (IWM ART 5932). M 302**

This was No. 22 in the *Guns* exhibition in 1919. Lewis explains the work in the catalogue: "An officer with a few signallers go up from the Battery position to the front-line, or a point near it, to observe the fire of their own Battery and other Batteries in the group, in the case of siege guns."

In most of his war drawings, Lewis builds on his early-developed ability to convey the physical sensation of bodies in action. He is concerned to show these actions as precisely adjusted to the special environment of the war: the soldier at the rear of the party, nearest to the exploding shell that destroys the duckboard, shows the strongest reaction, while the leading pair barely react, intent on their laborious progress.

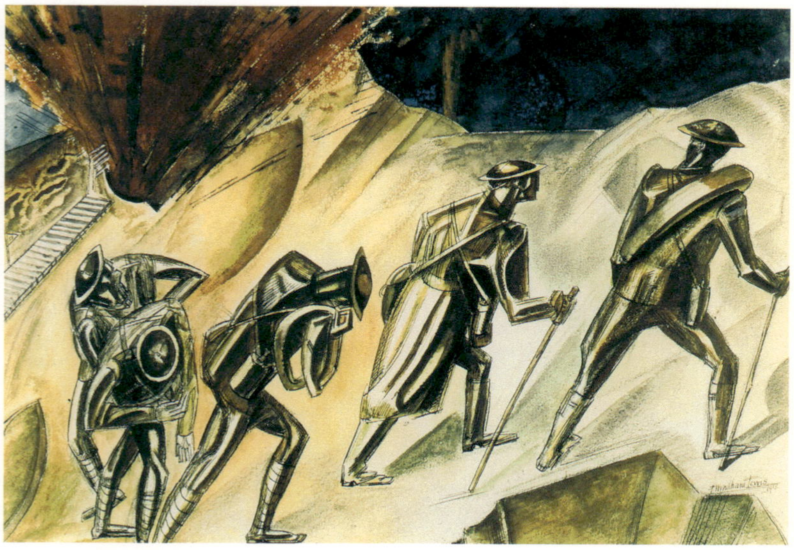

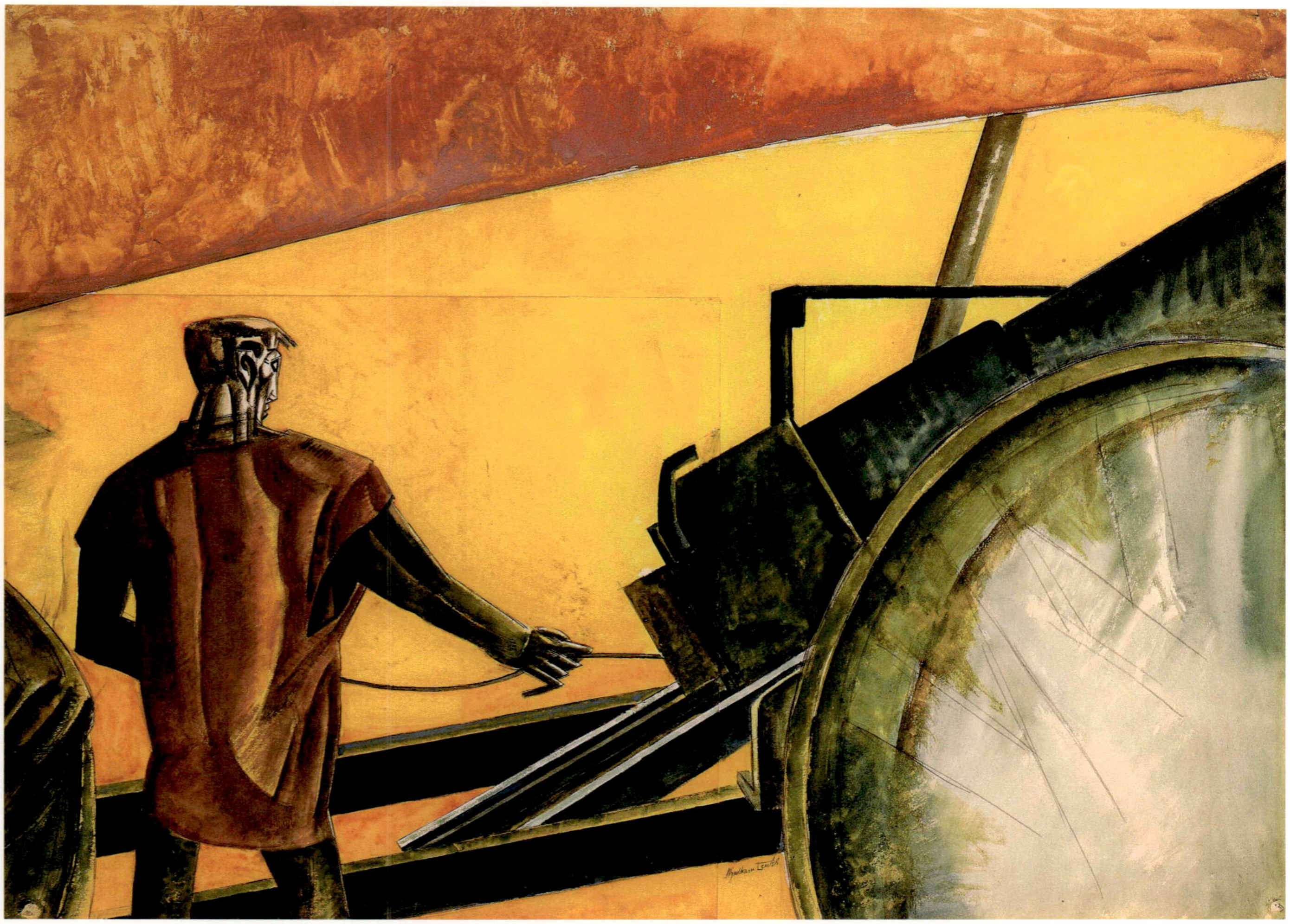

Cat. 64.
The No. 2**, 1918. Pen and ink, watercolour and pencil on paper. 54.5 x 75 cm. Private collection. M 295**

This was No. 26 in the *Guns* exhibition in 1919: "Each [member] of the gun crew has his number, each having a particular function. The No. 4 for instance is the man who lays the gun and nothing else. It is the No. 2 who fires the gun, by jerking a lanyard, wire or cord, so producing the series of explosions which cause the discharge."
The inhuman potential of machines, hinted at in Lewis's Vorticist abstractions, is here made explicit, as if in fulfilment of the dark side of these prophetic works. *The No. 2*, aside from the sculptural figure with its Cubist head and mechanical hand, could be a Vorticist abstraction, indeed. Lewis's favourite yellow gives it an added intensity, a device also employed in *Laying* (Cat. 69).

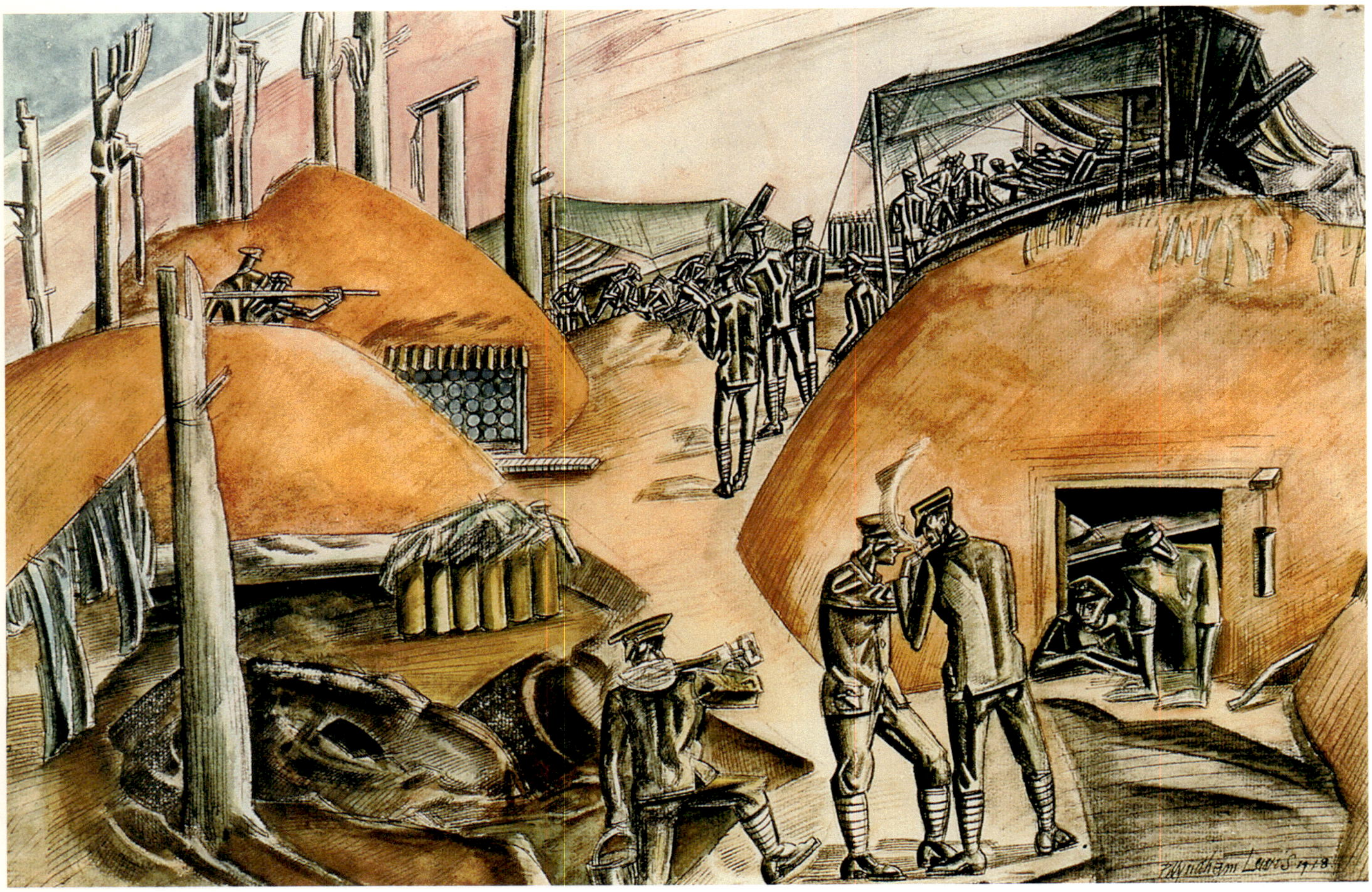

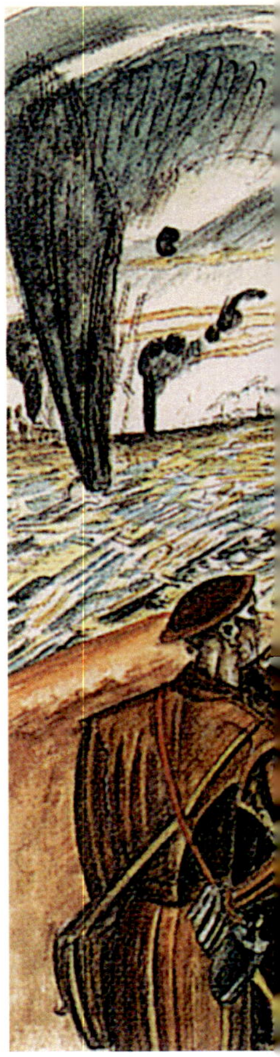

Cat. 65.
[Not in exhibition] *Battery Position in a Wood*, 1918. Pen and ink, chalk, watercolour on paper. 31.7 cm x 46.9 cm. Imperial War Museum, London (IWM ART 1672). M 267

This was No. 28 in the *Guns* exhibition in 1919. It was the only work in the exhibition acquired for the nation: it was donated by the purchaser, who was the first official war artist, Sir Muirhead Bone. The authorities were wary of employing Lewis and fearful that he would produce unacceptable "Cubist" works. There is no comment on this work in the *Guns* catalogue. Lewis's earlier insight about work – how machines, boats and small restaurants impose a pattern on human behaviour (to the extent that they "work" the human beings[1]) – is recalled in the labouring men serving the heavy gun. The scene is also a domestic one, however, with washing hung between the damaged trees and soldiers smoking. The shell-casing hanging outside the dugout was used as an alarm. The contrast of idle periods with sudden intense action is one of the themes pervading Lewis's representations of war.

1. Wyndham Lewis, "Inferior Religions" (1927). Rprt. *The Complete Wild Body* (1927). Ed. Bernard Lafourcade (Santa Barbara: Black Sparrow Press, 1982), p. 315.

Cat. 71.
A Battery Shelled, 1919. Oil on canvas. 182.7 x 317.7 cm. Imperial War Museum, London (IWM ART 2747). M P25

This was the painting that Lewis produced for the authorities that commissioned him as an official war artist. It is of the standard size required for the scheme (there are signs that Lewis had the canvas extended, probably after ordering one the wrong size). These large paintings (there was an even larger size, for "super-pictures," such as John Singer Sargent's *Gassed* (1918–19)) were intended to decorate a national memorial chapel, but this was never built. In the *Guns* catalogue, Lewis had contrasted the pageantry of Paulo Uccello's representations of war with Goya's passionate exposures of *The Disasters of War*: "Both are equally great as painting," he averred. In his large *A Canadian Gun Pit* (1918) (M P22), Lewis had leant towards the formal and decorative, following Uccello more than Goya; *A Battery Shelled* is an altogether more sombre work. Three guns are shown, with the expanding shock waves of an explosion silhouetting the profile of the soldier examining his pipe. Swags of scallop-shaped smoke hang across the top of the picture and insect-like men scurry to escape the shelling. Lewis has followed Ogata Kōrin's *Waves at Matsushima* (eighteenth century, Museum of Fine Arts, Boston) for the organisation and some of the forms of his canvas. For the composition, he has followed Piero della Francesca's *The Flagellation* (ca. 1469, Galleria Nazionale delle Marche) , with its three apparently unconcerned figures in the foreground, indifferent to the flogging of Christ that goes on behind them. Lewis's observers are ordinary soldiers (their tunics show they are not officers), inured to such scenes and too distant to need to react to save themselves. The one on the left, looking out of the picture, past the viewer and into the (intended) chapel, appears numb and his gaze is blank. This is more the result of stress than indifference, we conjecture. Two reactions to war are thus shown, one passive and one active, but the insect-like automatism of the smaller figures is misleading. Their apparent automatism is partly a function of the spectator's detachment, enforced by the distance from which they are observed. The group to the right of the centre of the picture is engaged in carefully carrying a wounded comrade, under the direction of an officer, to a dugout. The painting is a meditation, among other things, of one of Lewis's perennial concerns, the tension between observation and participation. "Truth has no place in action," he declares in the *Guns* catalogue (n.p.), apparently expressing his preference for observation. But the values of both states are here put under the pressure of war, in which no secure position can be reached. *A Battery Shelled* is perhaps the greatest English painting about war.

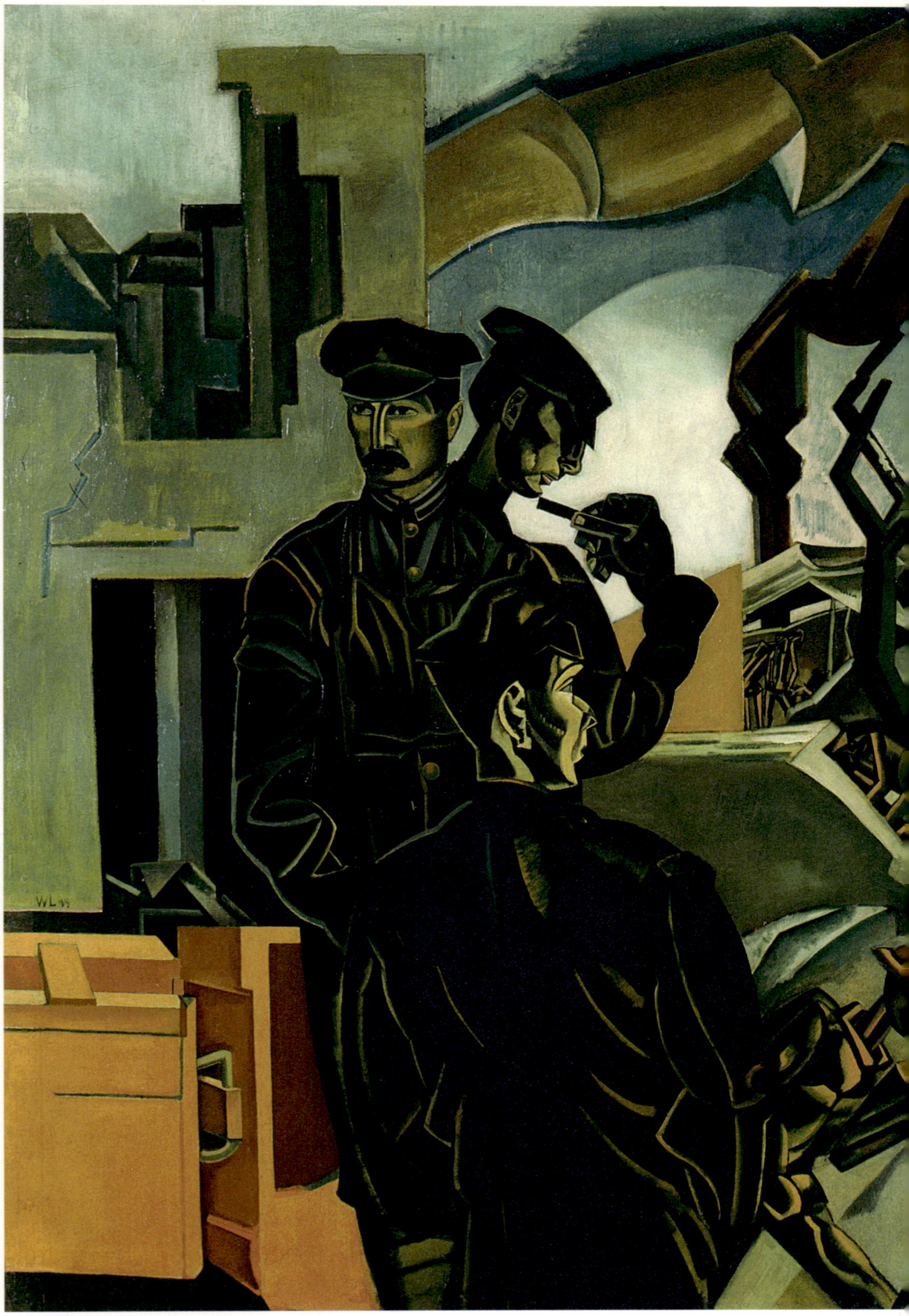

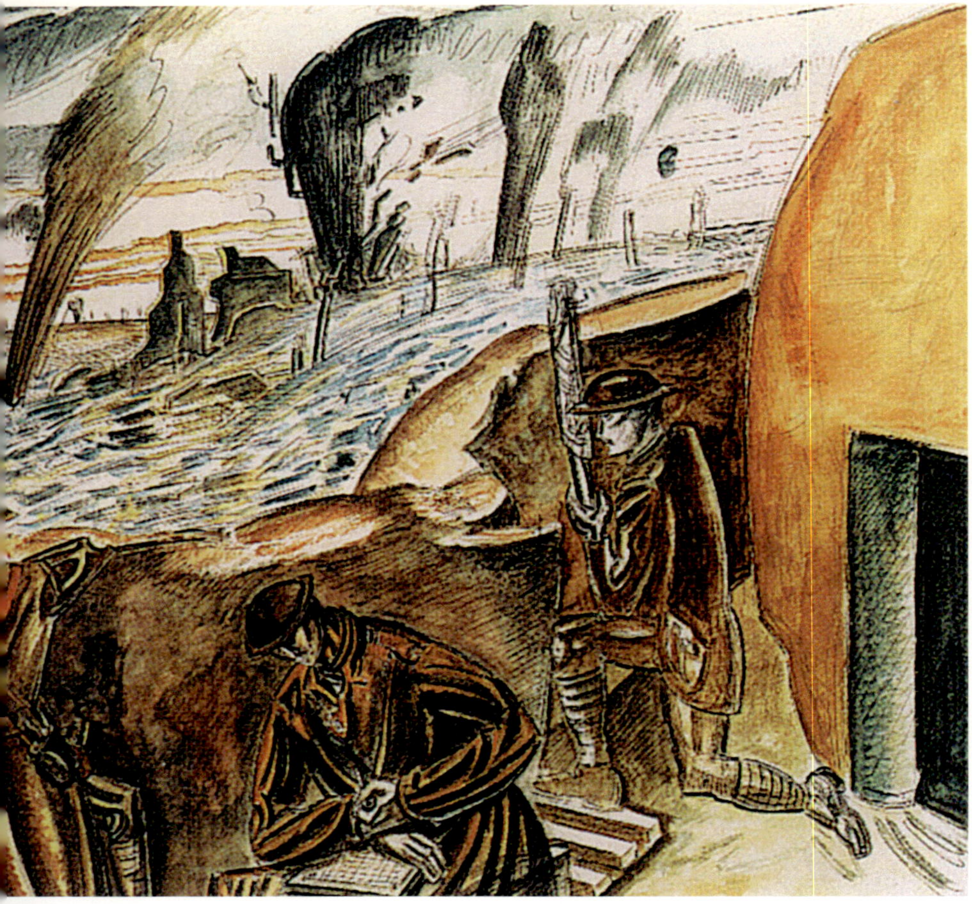

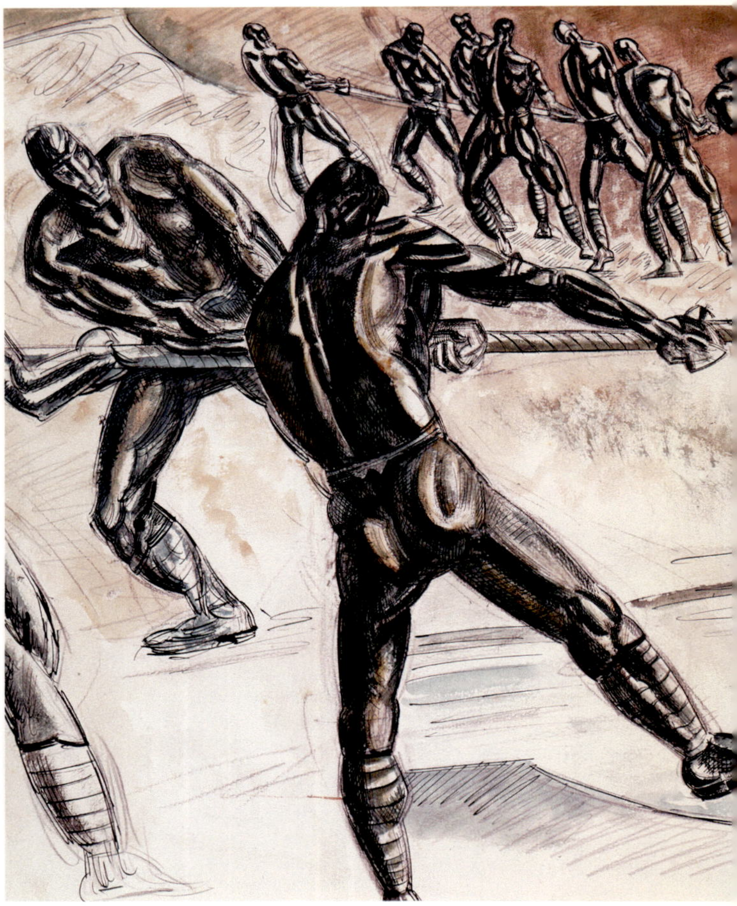

Cat. 66.
Great War Drawing No. 2, 1918. Watercolour on paper. 38.1 x 54.2 cm. Southampton City Art Gallery (1413). M 276

This drawing accords in subject matter with the description of No. 38 in the *Guns* exhibition:
In this painting officers and signallers are seen in trenches or dug-outs within sight of the enemy, observing the fire of their own batteries, barrages, and so on. It is their duty to range their batteries on different objectives, give details of the result of fire, accounts of hostile shelling, movements, etc.

Lewis tended to call works in oil on canvas "paintings" and any work on paper a "drawing," so this is unlikely to be the work referred to, though it may be a sketch for it. Much of Lewis's own work as a junior officer during the Third Battle of Ypres (Passchendaele) was as a Forward Observation Officer carrying out these duties. He later wrote that he had recognised that he was present at a "great military disaster." The figure kneeling at the right is using a periscope. The watery sea of mud that was no man's land during this battle of October–November 1917 is shown by strokes of blue and brown.

Cat. 67.
Drag-ropes, 1918. Black ink, pencil, watercolour and black chalk on paper. 35.3 x 41 cm. Manchester City Galleries (1925.487). M 273

This was No. 40 in the *Guns* exhibition in 1919. Lewis transposes to the formalised style of his post-Cubist idiom the muscular Renaissance figure-drawing idealised at the Slade School of Art. Manoeuvring and operating the heavy six-inch howitzers was heavy labour (as in Cat. 65).

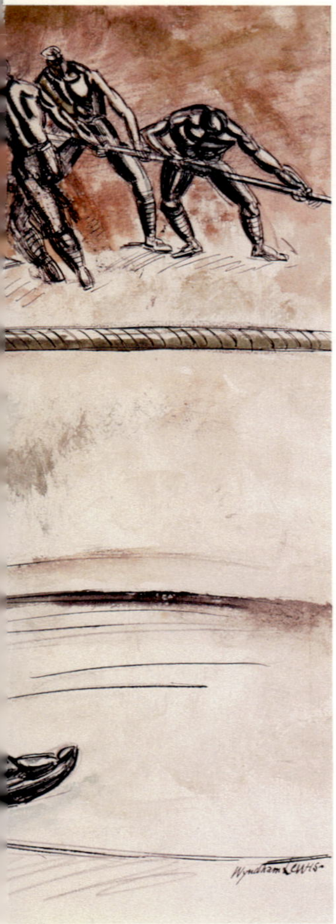

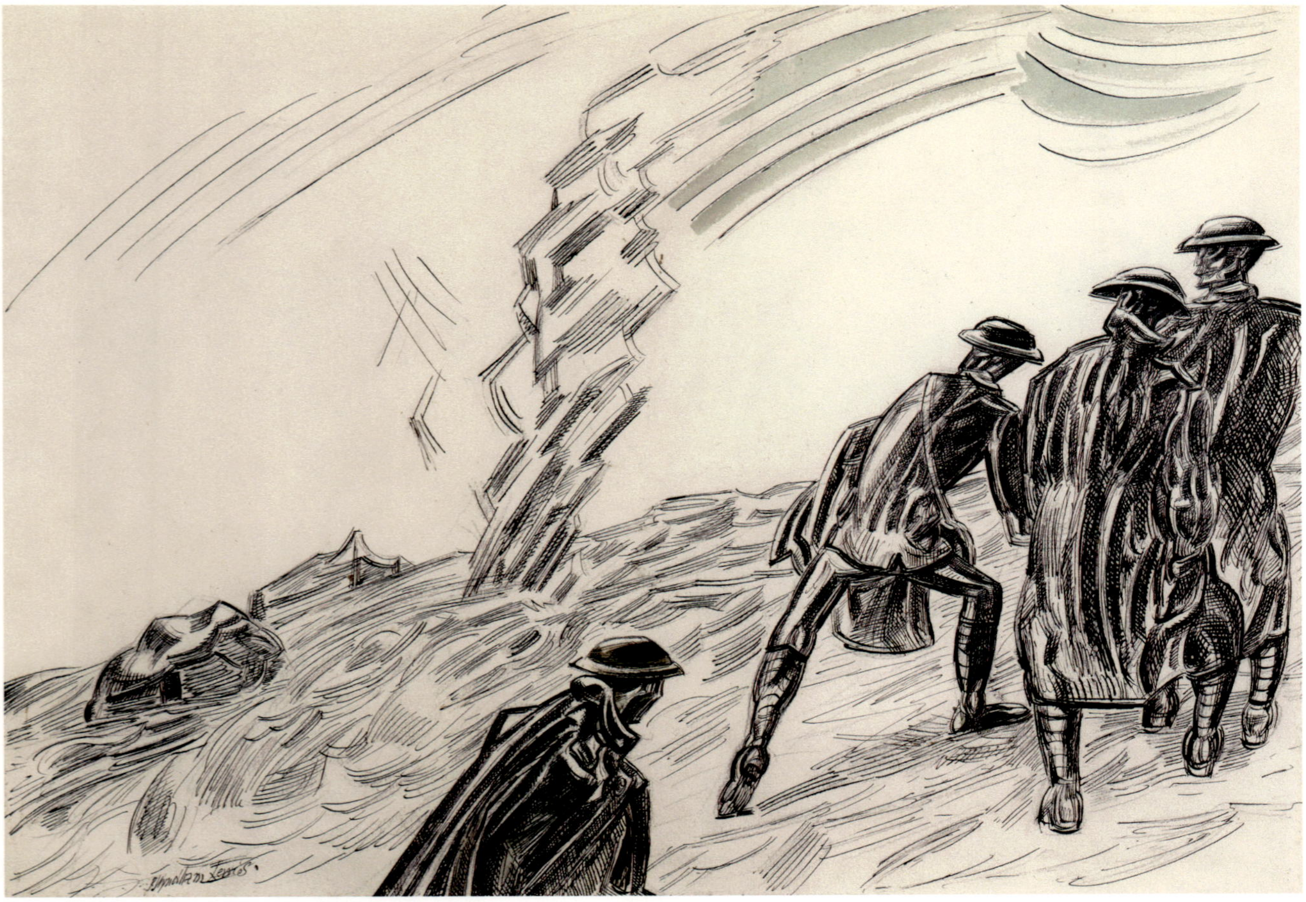

Cat. 68.
[Not in exhibition] ***"D" Subsection Relief*****, 1918. Pen and ink, and watercolour on paper. 35.5 x 51 cm. Private collection. M 274**

This was No. 41 in the *Guns* exhibition in 1919. It is one of the most daring of Lewis's compositions and one of his most beautiful works. The subject is similar to that of *Officer and Signallers* (Cat. 63), but the pen-and-ink technique is quite different, harking back to such works as *Pastoral Toilet* (Cat. 60). Everything falls off to the left, increasing the sense of labour, as the men, encumbered with heavy coats whose striations echo those of the ground, trudge uphill. As with *Officer and Signallers*, their reactions are relative to their distance from the exploding shell. The drawing was bought by Ezra Pound, who wrote at least two favourable reviews of the exhibition, despite his desire that Lewis would return to full Vorticist abstraction.

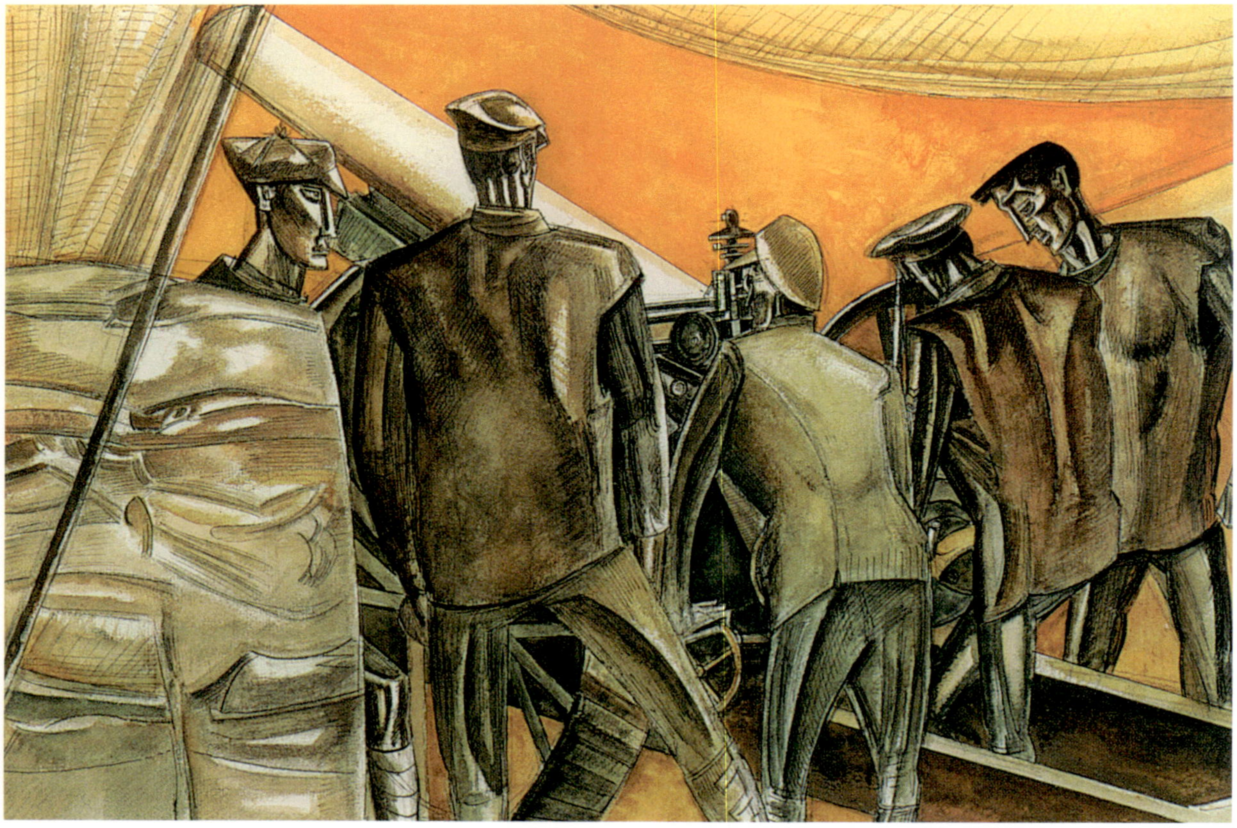

Cat. 69.
[Not in exhibition]
Laying, 1918. Pen and ink, and watercolour on paper. 35.5 x 51 cm. Arts Council Collection, Southbank Centre, London (ACC2/1952). M 283

This was No. 42 in the *Guns* exhibition in 1919 and not one of the works Lewis chooses to comment on. The scene, treated somewhat in the manner of *The No. 2* (Cat. 64), depicts the process of aiming the howitzer. It is a considerably more stylised sketch of part of the scene depicted in *A Canadian Gun Pit* (M P22), the large painting that Lewis produced in 1918 for the Canadian authorities that is now in the National Gallery of Canada, Ottawa.

Cat. 70.
The Battery Shelled, 1918. Watercolour on paper. 35.5 x 44 cm. Private collection. M 271

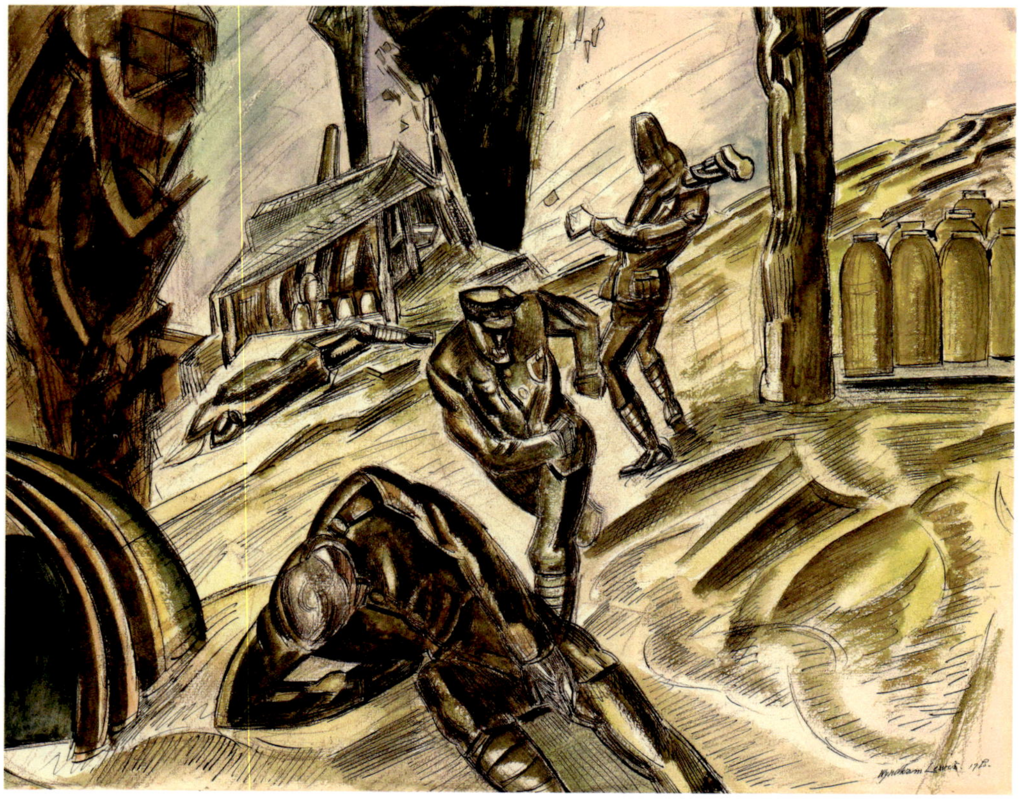

This was No. 42 in the *Guns* exhibition in 1919. It is the only one of Lewis's war paintings to show directly and close up men being killed and wounded (the lost No. 17 in the *Guns* exhibition, *Walking Wounded* (M 322), showed men away from the action, walking to a dressing-station). The subject was one that was close to Lewis's own experience and it may be his imaginary reconstruction of an incident that happened after he had been called away from his gun to carry out a task elsewhere:

When over an hour later I got back to the battery position my gunpit (that of No. 4 gun) was like a small quarry. The sergeant and a half dozen men had been in it: it had been a direct hit, a few feet at the side of the gun. He and six men were all killed or wounded. I wrote to the widow of my sergeant, saying what a popular man he was, and got a new N.C.O. for my gun and the necessary reinforcements. As this is written, so it happened. But that is obviously not how men's lives should be taken away from them, for nothing at all.[1]

1. Wyndham Lewis, *Blasting and Bombardiering: Autobiography (1914–1926)* (London: Eyre & Spottiswoode, 1937), p. 154.

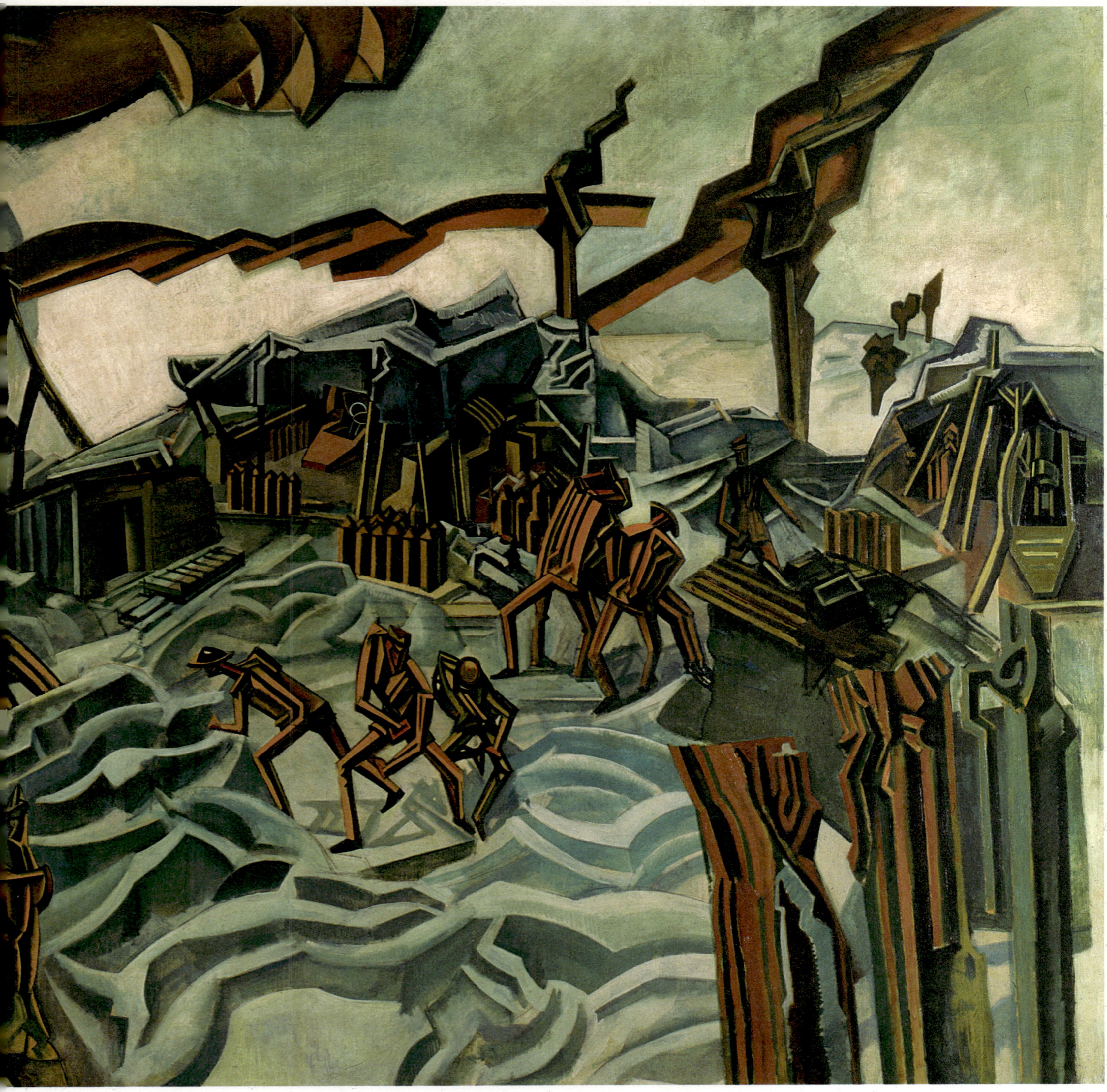

1919-

1929

From Avantgardist to Enemy

Pre-war London was amused by the novelties of Futurism and Vorticism, but after the First World War some visitors to exhibitions of war art found the new visual languages fitting for the horrors of war. Nevertheless the mood of the public was conservative. Roger Fry (1866–1934) and Clive Bell (1881–1964) dominated the art scene and promoted an unadventurous imitation of French post-Impressionism. In France itself, a "*rappel à l'ordre*" was issued and classicism was reinstated. Wyndham Lewis's response was an attempt to renew the pre-war avant-garde spirit. He hoped, but was unable, to produce a third issue of *Blast* (see B&M Cats. 2 and 3). (An attempt to re-form an avant-garde group in 1920, "Group X," was also unsuccessful after a single exhibition.) Instead, his pamphlet, *The Caliph's Design: Architects! Where is Your Vortex?* (1919) (B&M Cat. 7), argued that the new formal inventions of modernist painting should be employed in a reshaping of the built environment, starting with London, which as a first step should be transformed by a new street of Vorticist buildings. "*You must get Painting, Sculpture, and Design out of the studio and into life somehow or other* if you are not going to see this new vitality desiccated in a Pocket of inorganic experimentation." In painting itself, the various pre-war experiments needed consolidation into a single mode that would reflect "the great mass sensibility of our time." Obstacles that stood in the way were, in England, political apathy and the amateurish formalism of the hegemonic Bloomsbury school; in France, the conservative nostalgia of the local variety of "classicism." Lewis attacked all three.

From one point of view, the story of Lewis in the 1920s is about the failure to renew the avant-garde and the equivalent failure of his ambitions for art to transform life. But in terms of his own output during the period, out of his struggles to fulfil his vision for art, and the consequent critical and polemical analyses of the culture that rendered them ineffective, he produced a body of painting and writing unparalleled in brilliance and range. This gave him a peculiar public profile. After his 1921 one-man show at The Leicester Galleries, London, he had virtually no public presence as a painter, though he continued privately (and for particular patrons) to create visual works. The new form of abstraction that he developed from 1921 on – more "synthetic," more flexible and organic than the severe geometries of Vorticism – resulted in works on paper that were as "advanced" as any in Europe but were virtually unseen in England. They are still ignored in histories of British art.

It became impossible for Lewis to support himself through his art or to sustain a major effort in it. After his last real polemical essays on the aesthetics of modernist painting (which to some extent explained the rationale of these works) in 1922 in the second issue of his new magazine, *The Tyro* (B&M Cat. 9), Lewis fell comparatively silent until 1926. He then suddenly emerged as the author of a work of cultural analysis and political theory, *The Art of Being Ruled* (B&M Cat. 10). It was as a writer that he renewed his fame (and sealed his fate as an outsider) over the remainder of the decade, issuing seven more books and three numbers of another magazine, *The Enemy* (B&M Cats. 14–16) (largely written by Lewis himself), culminating in 1930 in a massive satire on the London art world, *The Apes of God* (B&M Cat. 21).

In 1919, however, returning to his work with an ambition to effect a revolutionary transformation in the lives of people and inspire them with the zest and gusto of the art of the avant-garde, Lewis began by consolidating the "one mode" of art that might accomplish this. He began by reinventing his draughtsmanship and giving a less nostalgic turn to a "classicism" that looked more to the East than to Graeco-Roman models. The numerous drawings of the human figure in which he perfected his technique tend to be of poses that both test his linear skills and produce a sense of alienation from the sitters. The sitters are not machines (tragically vulnerable creatures of flesh and blood, rather), but the technique that reduces them to these images operates with an almost mechanical efficiency that evokes an ambivalent response in a viewer. From 1920 onwards, Lewis develops this technique in different directions in his figurative work and portrait drawings, so that it may express an almost uncontainable artistic energy under tight control, or with incomparable delicacy and sensitivity serve to reveal the personality of his sitters. At its most stylised, in some of the works from the 1921 exhibition, it transforms the figure into unearthly grotesques, providing a commentary on the strangeness of life.

This "strangeness" is given a particular local context in Lewis's "Tyro" images. Tyros (beginners or novices) were invented as totemic equivalents of the shell-shocked society setting out into the new post-war world, the infantilised "children of a new epoch," as Lewis called them in his magazine, *The Tyro* (B&M Cats. 8 and 9). Few of these works survive, but their satirical spirit and deliberately popularised caricatural style were part of Lewis's efforts both to respond to the age's "mass-sensibility" and to awaken English art from its post-war post-Impressionist slumber. They were not welcomed by critics and caused no sensation.

Lewis always had a fractious, suspicious and difficult personality (coupled with a charm and conversational inventiveness that made even his "enemies" value his company). A friend, the painter Kate Lechmere (1887–1976), noted that he seemed to have lost some of his gaiety after his war experiences. Certainly, his suspicious and uncooperative behaviour with friends and patrons in the 1920s suggests personal insecurity to the point of paranoia and he managed to alienate most of those who were willing to help him. The (now unimaginable) conservatism of English visual culture in the 1920s would have prevented any public acceptance of the new advanced form of abstraction that Lewis developed from 1921 onwards, exemplified by *Archimedes Reconnoitring the Enemy Fleet* (1922) (Cat. 113), or the three totemic *Abstract Compositions* of 1926 (Cats. 120–22). But Lewis's patron, Sidney Schiff (1868–1944), found an opening for them at Léonce Rosenberg's L'Effort Moderne Gallery in Paris, and Lewis could have exhibited there: Rosenberg declared himself "delighted" with Lewis's work, Schiff reported. But some lack of confidence or other personal difficulty prevented Lewis from making this a reality. By 1929, when Lewis wrote an article on "A World Art and Tradition," this series of synthetic abstractions had become for him (the phrase is loaded with bitter irony at the failure of modernism in England), "fragments with which I amuse myself."

Lewis went "underground" (his own expression), spending months in the British Museum Reading Room, educating himself in anthropology, political theory, philosophy since Gottfried Leibniz (1646–1716), theology and modern physics. What had seemed simple in 1914 and 1919, to make use of industrial modernity and its products to produce a world with a new sensibility from which the spectre of war was banished, now looked more complex and difficult to achieve. The necessary "destructive" aspects of revolution accompanied and became confused with aspects that were creative and would lead to the transformation envisaged in *The Caliph's Design*. Lewis's non-fiction books and magazine (*The Enemy*, 1927–29) were the places where he attempted to carry out a sorting of positive and negative. A modern political system to replace the failed conservative system of democratic liberalism was needed, he felt, and he looked to the dictatorships of the Soviet Union and Fascist Italy as possible models for Britain. But *The Art of Being Ruled* is more concerned with observation and cultural analysis than it is with issuing prescriptions and it contains a prophetic account of modern, consumerist culture and ideology. In *The Enemy*, Lewis presents himself as a lone, campaigning warrior (a one-man avant-garde) battling (paradoxically) precisely against the mainstream avant-garde for its failure to have carried out the revolutionary "sorting" to which his work was now devoted. Friends like James Joyce (1882–1941) and Ezra Pound (1885–1972), and other members of the expatriate Paris-based Bohemia, found their work attacked for what Lewis saw as its naivety in unknowingly carrying within itself elements of ideology that militated against worthwhile revolutionary transformation. The critiques were elaborated and extended to historiography and metaphysics in the 1927 *Time and Western Man* (B&M Cat. 12).

In throwing himself wholeheartedly into a literary career, Lewis also renewed his commitment to fiction. The early stories collected in "Our Wild Body" were at last revised and issued as *The Wild Body* (1927) (B&M Cat. 17), and *Tarr* (B&M Cat. 5) was also revised and expanded (and to some extent made less stylistically extreme) in 1928. In the same year, Lewis issued the first volume of an intended trilogy, *The Childermass* (B&M Cat. 19). Set in the afterworld, this fantasy fictionalises all the concerns of the non-fiction books that Lewis had been writing. Its setting, strangely reminiscent of the landscape of the First World War in France, locates its concerns in an imagined but permanent metaphysical existence, but also in a specific historical crisis. In the *The Apes of God* (1930), a similar historical crisis is central: the General Strike in England in May 1926. It was a failed revolution and Lewis indicts the art world of London for its triviality and venality, which he sees as partly responsible for the impasse to which Britain had been brought. His own patrons and previous associates (Sidney Schiff, the rich and rebellious Sitwell family) bore the brunt of his devastating mockery.

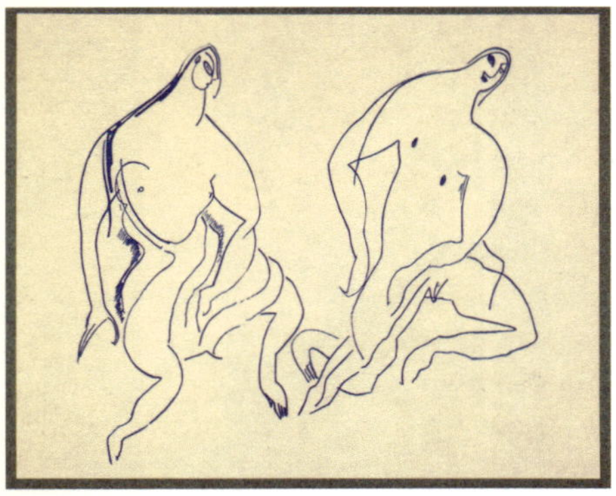

Blue Nudes (M 120)

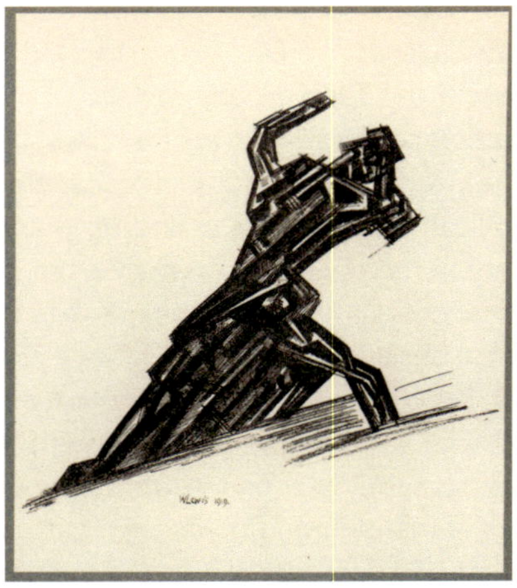

Drawing for Timon of Athens I (M 359)

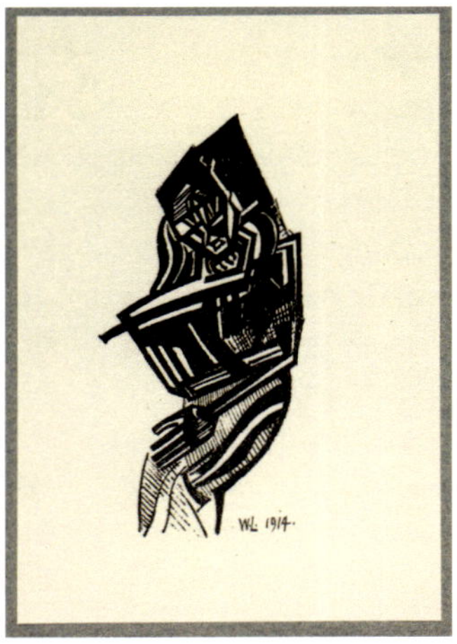

Drawing for Timon of Athens II (M 174)

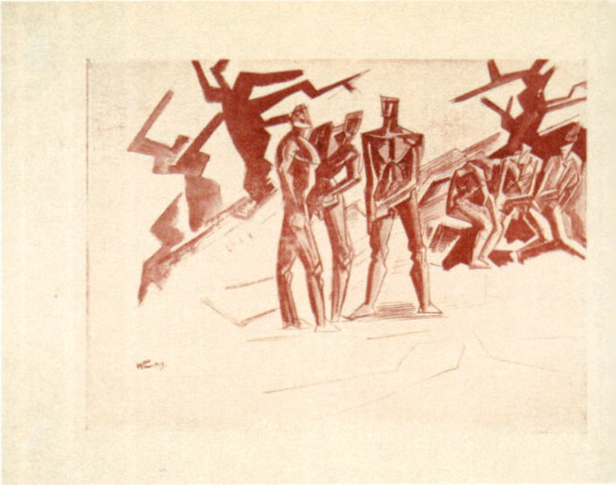

Group (M 331)

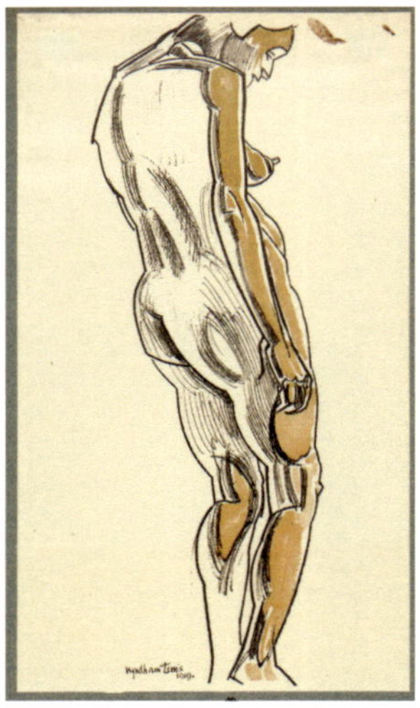

Nude III (M 341)

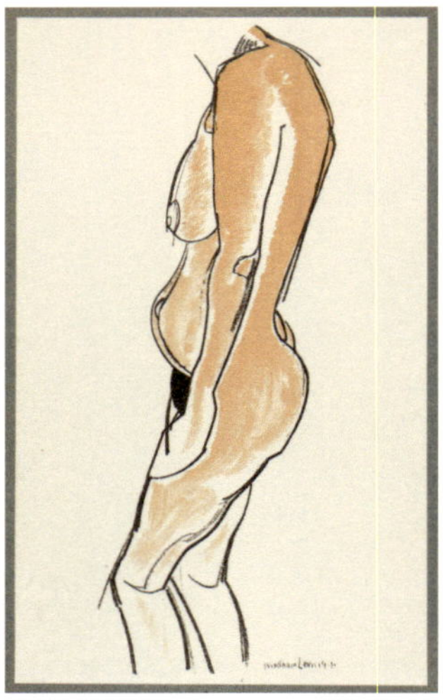

Nude IV (M 342)

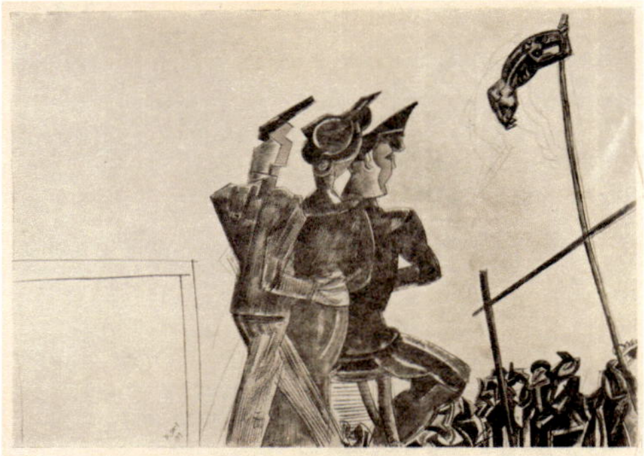

The Pole Jump (M 344)

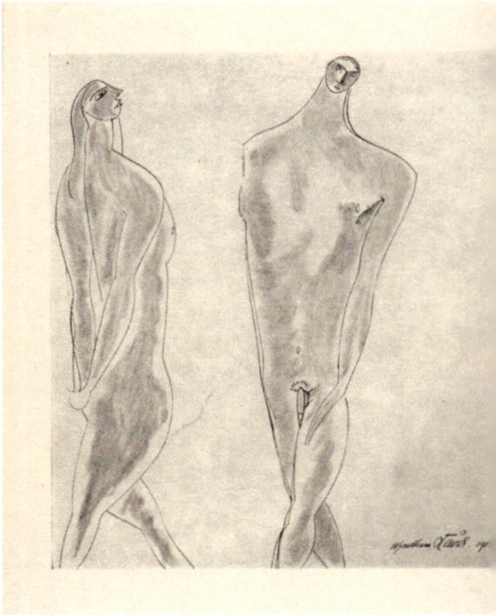

Post Jazz (M 150)

Portfolio *Fifteen Drawings*
London: The Ovid Press, 1919. Edition of 250 prints numbered. 40.6 x 27.9 cm
Wyndham Lewis Memorial Trust G. and V. Lane Collection (LG.2009.XX.9)

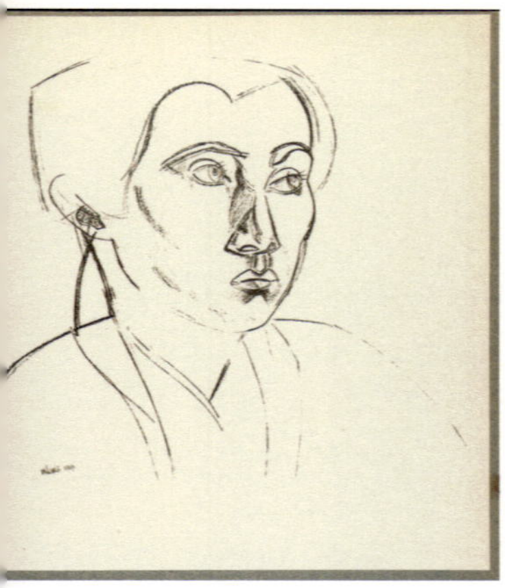

Head I (M 332)

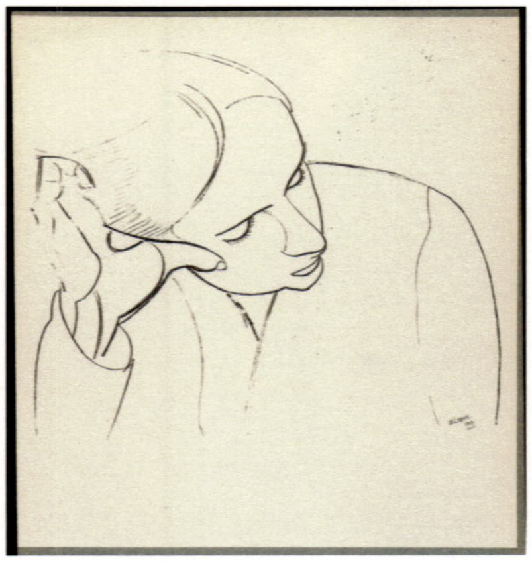

Head II (M 333)

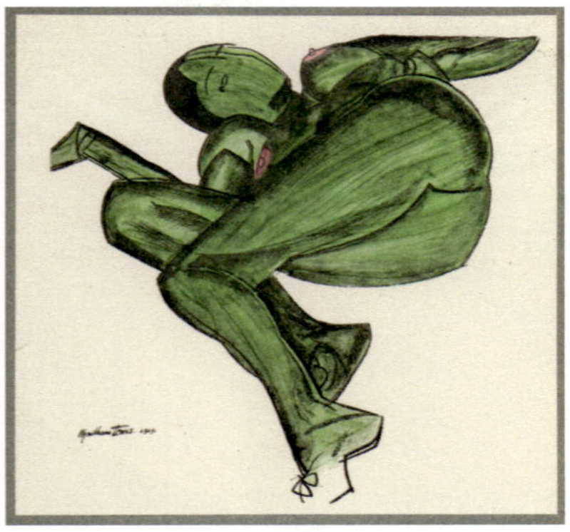

Nude I (M 339)

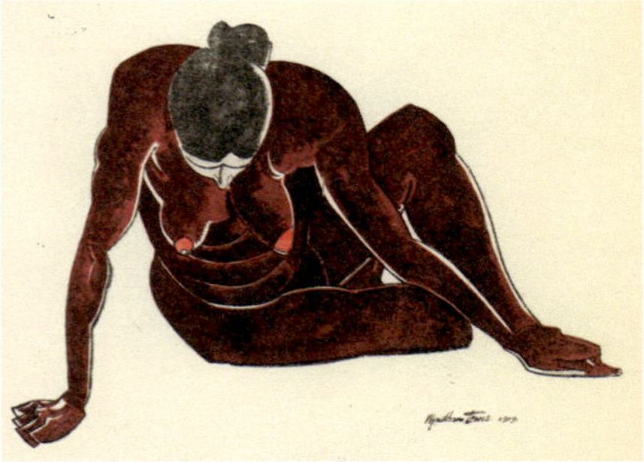

Nude II (M 340)

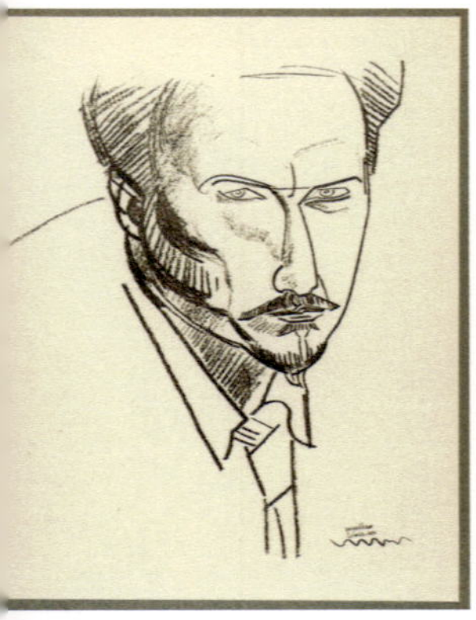

Ezra Pound, Esq. (M 345)

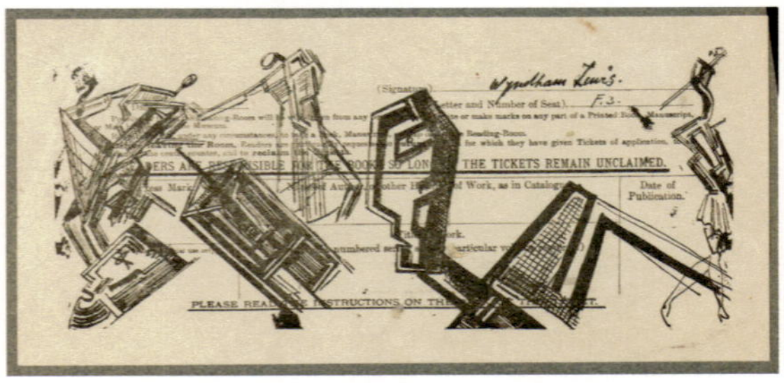

Reading Room (M 209)

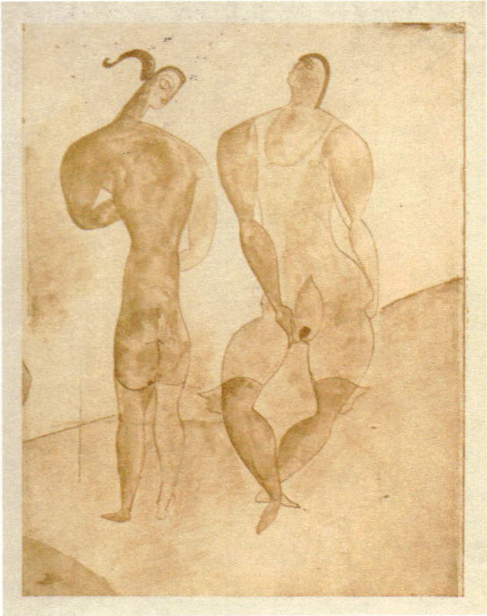

Seraglio (M 84)

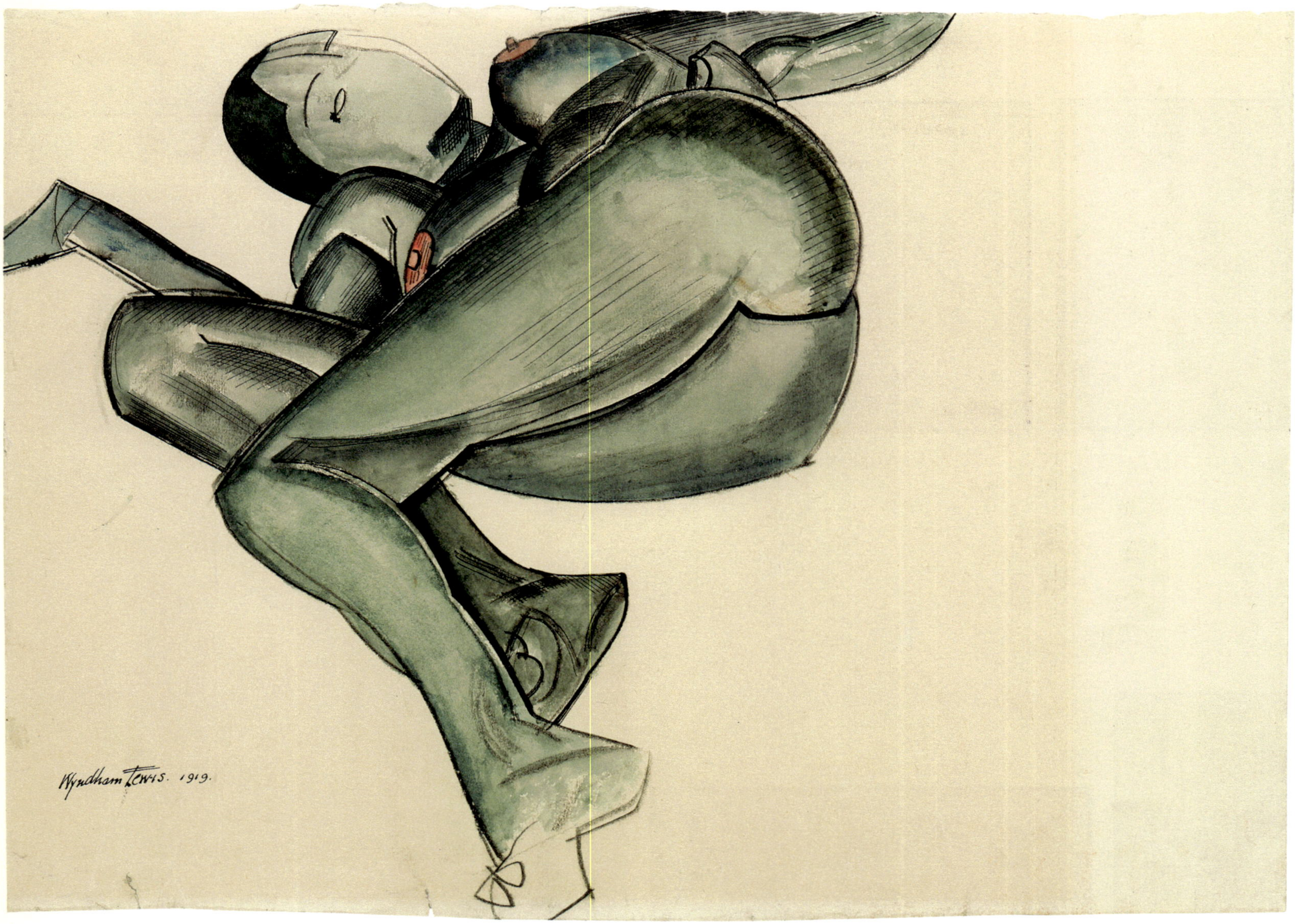

Cat. 72. ▲
Nude I, 1919. Pen and ink, watercolour and wash on paper. 24 x 34 cm. Leeds Museums and Galleries (Leeds Art Gallery) (LEEAG.1935.0014.0002). M 339

Cat. 73. ▶▲
Portfolio *Fifteen Drawings: Nude I*, 1919.

Cat. 74. ▶▼
Portfolio *Fifteen Drawings: Nude II*, 1919. Lithographs. Wyndham Lewis Memorial Trust. Collection G. and V. Lane. M 339 and 340

This portfolio of prints, some of which were hand-coloured, contains a selection of work from 1912 to 1919. It was produced by John Rodker's Ovid Press. Four of the drawings are of the female nude. Lewis may have been dissatisfied with the kind of stylisation with which his earlier work had treated the human figure. He subjected himself to a concentrated period of life drawing to perfect his "hand." Throughout his career he was dissatisfied with naturalism, however. In these drawings the unnatural colouring and unusual postures (together with the careful positioning of the figures on the sheet) counteract the naturalism. Art, though its products were material objects, referred away from this world to another, transcendent or ideal condition. To some extent, an actual "material" work of art would signal its borderline status between these worlds, but would never be a transparent "window" onto nature, just at it could never entirely belong to the ideal world of the artist's vision. This is as true of Lewis's virtuoso drawing of the 1920s as it was of the insistently "material" Vorticist abstractions. Lewis had studied Friedrich Nietzsche and Arthur Schopenhauer, and had been introduced to the ideas of Wilhelm Worringer before the war by T.E. Hulme (the poet and inventor of Imagism, philosopher and aesthetic theorist, killed by shellfire in 1917). He was therefore unusually aware that the ideal worlds referred to in art were the psychological products of *ressentiment* about this one. Several of the nudes that Lewis produced at this time contrast the virtuosity of the artist's "inhuman" hand and eye, with the frailty and imperfection of the body, sometimes achieving an effect of pathos, as in *Nude II*.

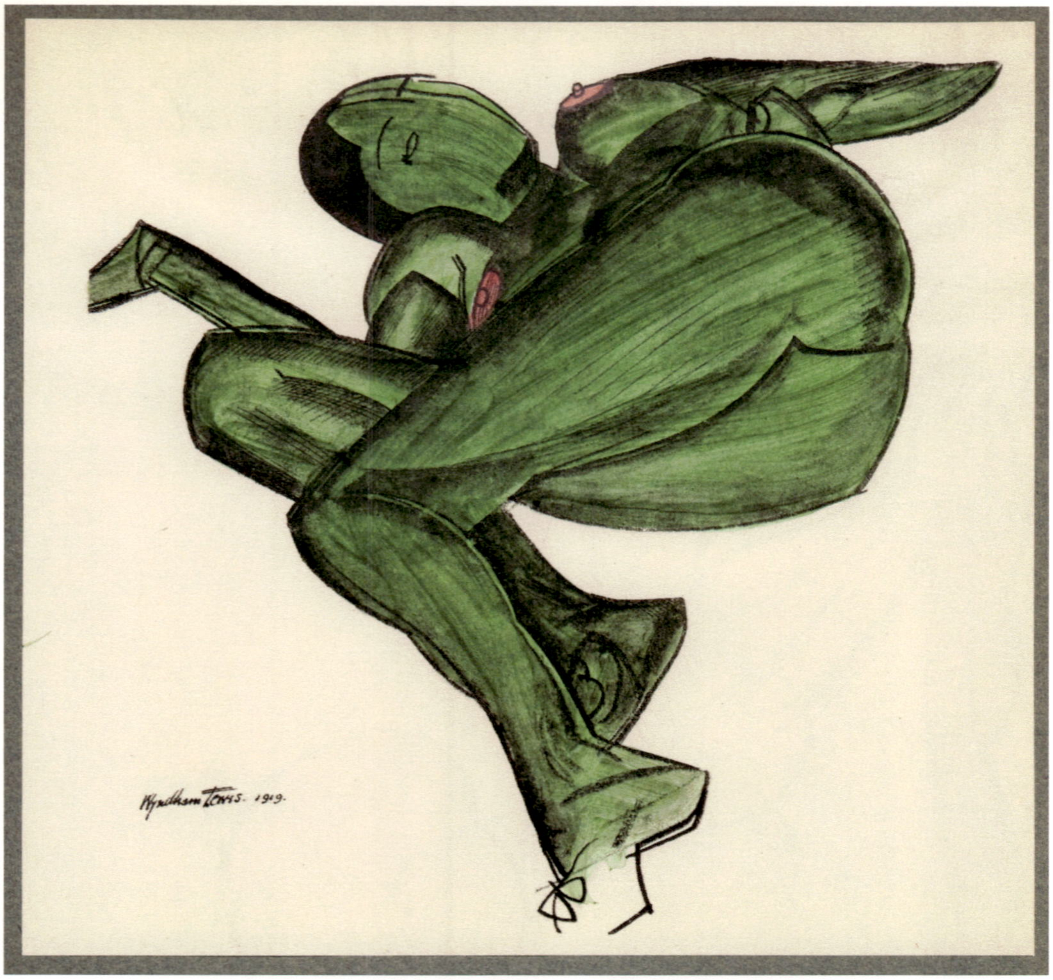
Wyndham Lewis. 1919.

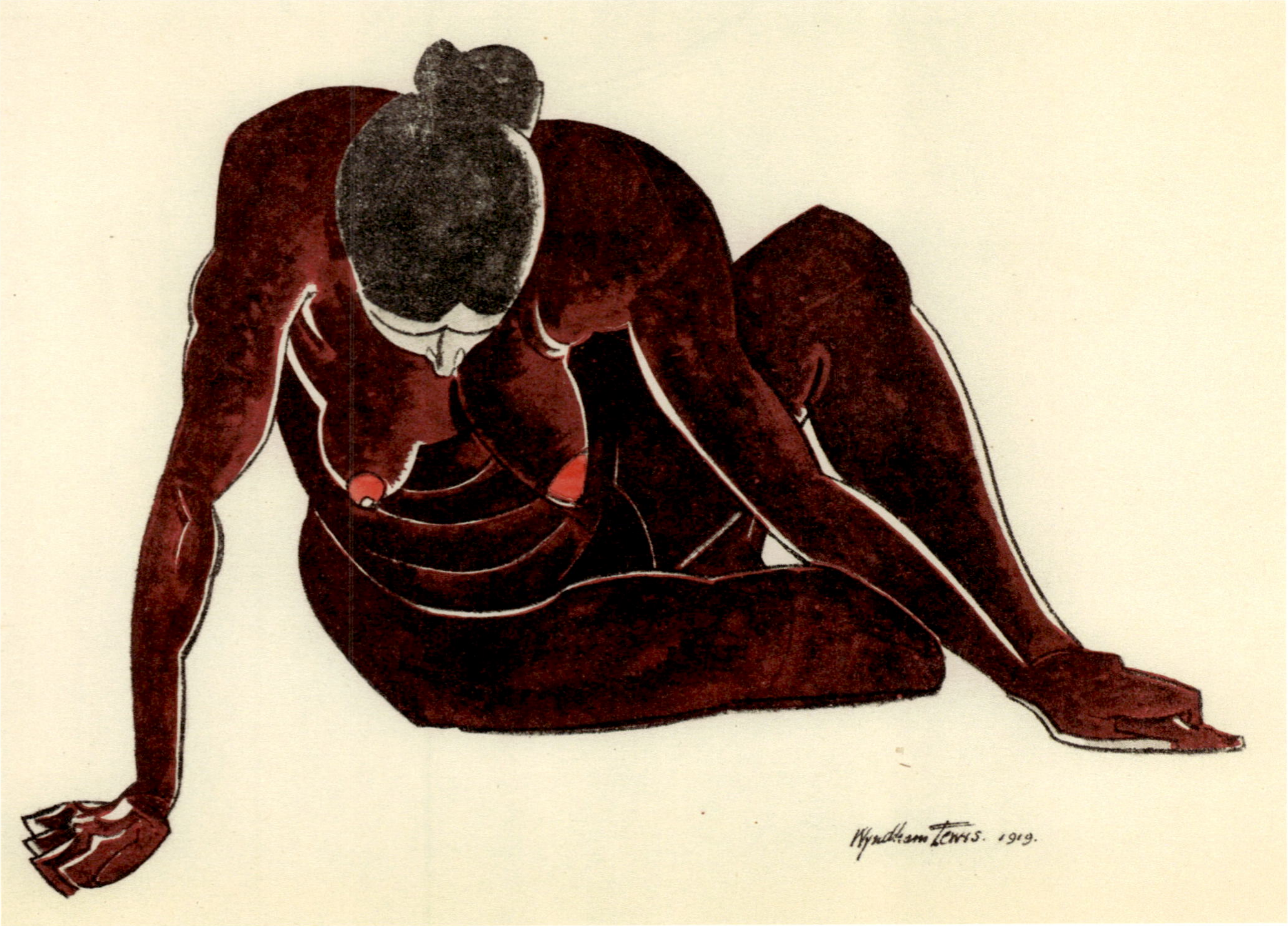
Wyndham Lewis. 1919.

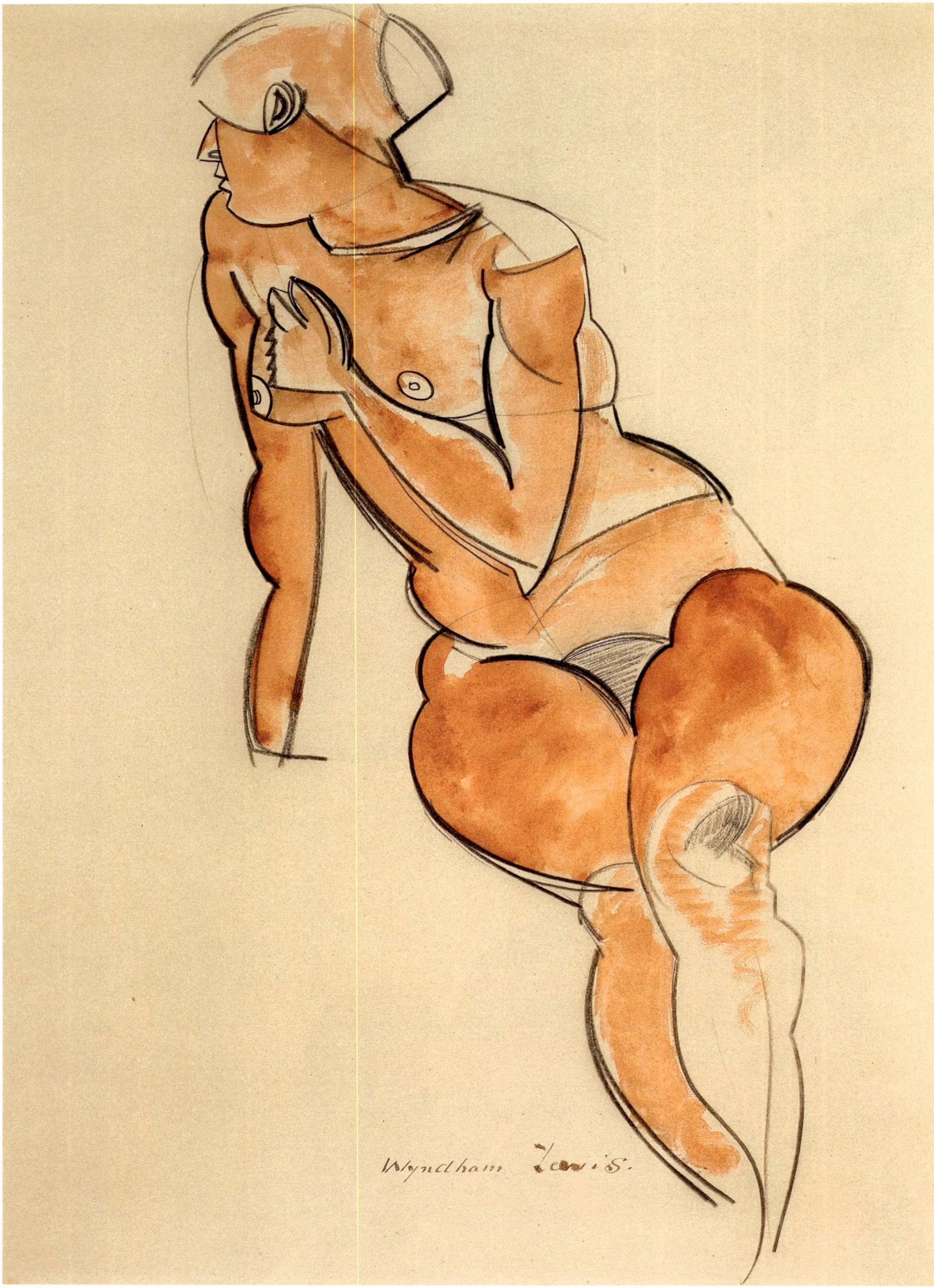

Cat. 75.
[Not in exhibition] *Nude*, 1919. Pencil and watercolour on paper. 61 x 47 cm. Private collection, Ivor Braka Ltd

This is a looser and more directly expressive drawing, as Lewis begins to allow his own predilection for swinging curves and "whiplash" flourishes to have more authority in the production of the image. The figure's posture and the delineation of the face in profile also give this drawing a more human presence than others in the series.

Cat. 77.
Girl Reclining, ca. 1919. Chalk on paper. 38.1 x 55.9 cm. Tate: Purchased 1955 (N06256). M 330

The "finished" quality of this drawing, which, unusually for Lewis, employs only a single medium, imparts a curious materiality to the soft surface on which the model reclines, though this is scarcely delineated. (The hair is similarly present by virtue of minimal signification.) Lewis's draughtsmanship is "about" the language of art and it is, above all, this that places it as modernist and post-Cubist.

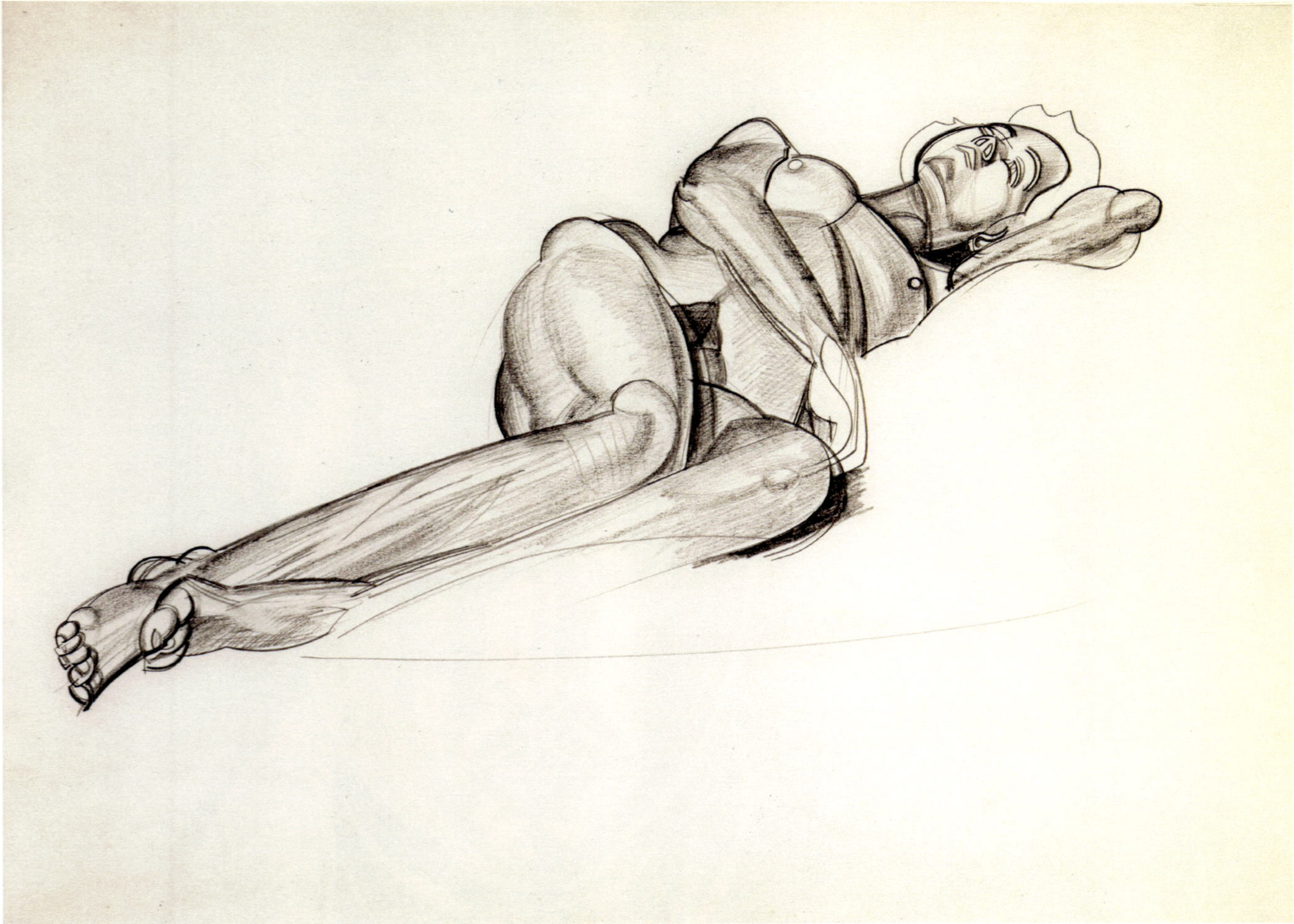

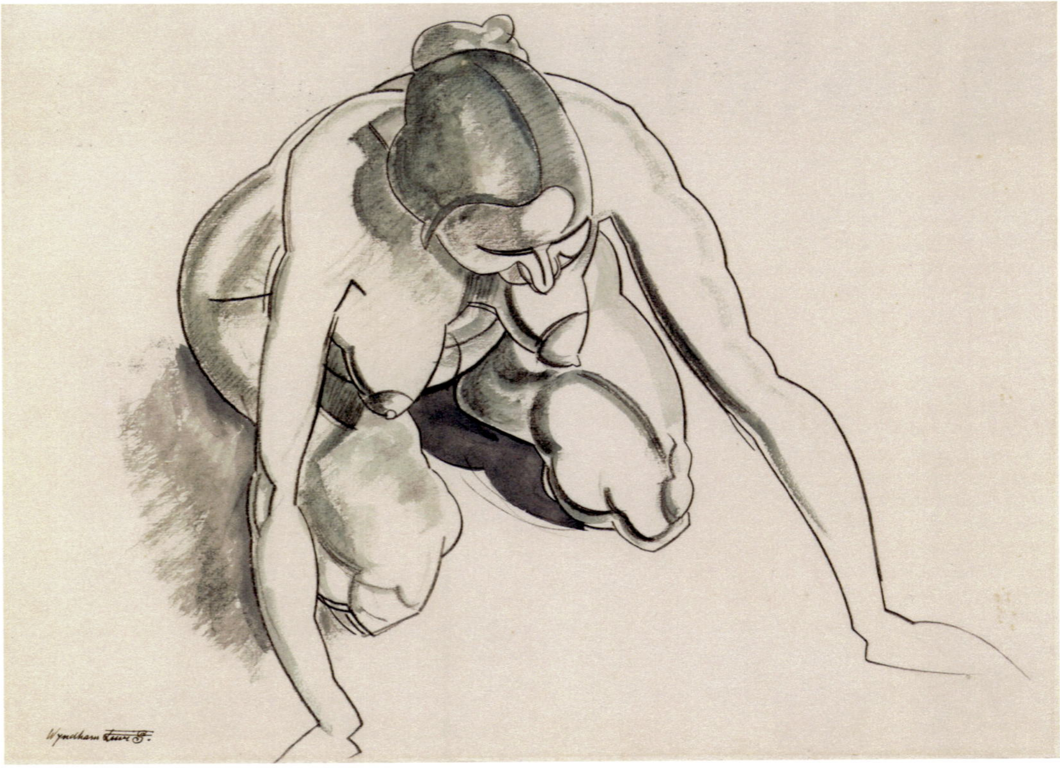

Cat. 76.
Crouching Woman, ca. 1919. Pencil and watercolour on paper. 27.9 x 38.1 cm. Tate: Purchased 1955 (N06255). M 366

An important element in Lewis's drawings of the nude is his placement of the figure on the sheet, and the compression of this figure within the rectangular format adds to the sense of muscular tension evoked by the uncomfortable posture. In this drawing the overlapping forms of head, breast and thigh within the silhouettes of the figure enable Lewis to produce a configuration of arcs and passages of wash that have the appeal and complexity of one of his "abstractions." His turn to figuration was not so much a negation of his earlier abstraction as a way of enriching his visual "grammar" so that later abstractions would also have more resources at their disposal.

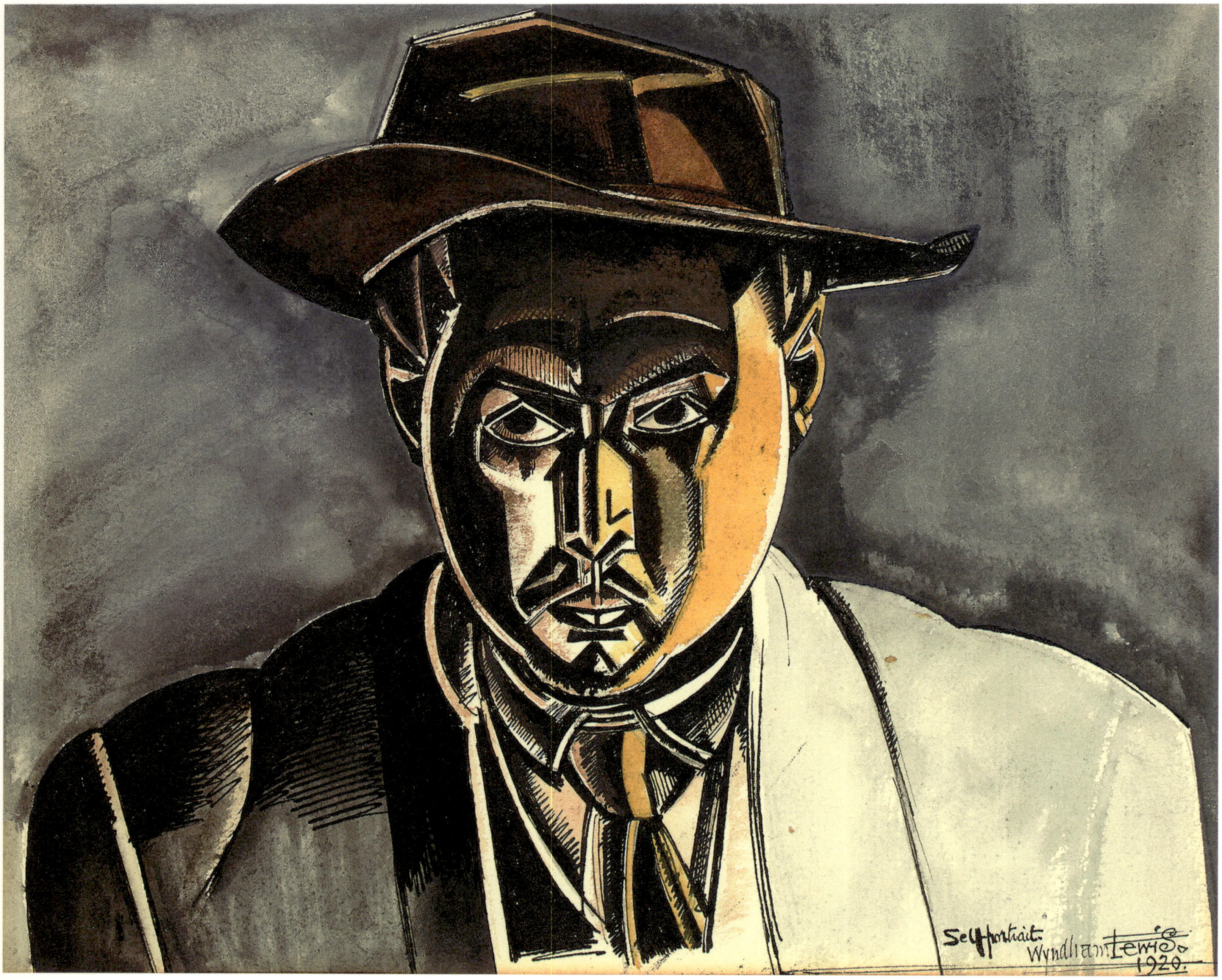

Cat. 78.
***Self-Portrait*, 1920. Pen and wash on paper. 18 x 22 cm. Private collection. M 423**

The drawing, like several pen-and-ink self-portraits Lewis produced for the "Group X" exhibition at the Mansard Gallery, London in March 1920, is reminiscent of a woodcut. It is made from almost, but not quite, symmetrical forms, contrasting in shape and colour. It was not actually exhibited at the exhibition, but four others were (one a painting) along with a drawing of a female nude. The choice of exhibits shows a reflective pre-occupation on Lewis's part with his own identity after the First World War, as if the avant-garde ambition of remoulding civilisation expressed in *The Caliph's Design* (B&M Cat. 7) had temporarily receded. As an avant-garde movement, Group X (which contained several ex-Vorticists), not surprisingly, failed. It is notable that, among painters, Lewis's role as theorist and chief energiser was crucial. Without him, the group disintegrated. One benefit of the association, however, was the beginning of the process of the transfer of the formal invention of modernist abstraction to popular, commercial culture. Edward McKnight Kauffer's posters for the underground and for such products as Eno's Fruit Salts directly echo the forms of Lewis's 1920s abstractions. The present drawing seems to confirm Lewis's personal uncertainty and vulnerability after the war (though other drawings of the period show a more confident and magisterial figure).

Cat. 80. ▸
Ezra Pound, 1920. Black chalk on paper. 31 x 33 cm. Private collection. M 414

Cat. 79. ▾
[Not in exhibition] *Ezra Pound* ca. 1919. Pencil and watercolour on paper. 35.5 x 38 cm. National Museum of Wales, Cardiff (NMW A 1867). M 347

Lewis met the American modernist poet, Ezra Pound, in 1912, but they did not become closely associated until 1913, when, for a period, they worked together as the main publicists and theorists of Vorticism – a name that Pound, indeed, invented. Lewis admired Pound's energy and enthusiasm and was grateful for his help, which extended to being Lewis's executor in case of death during the war, "salesman" of his work to the American collector, John Quinn, literary agent (in placing *Tarr* (B&M Cat. 18)) and critical publicist in numerous articles. In 1919, Lewis painted an over life-size portrait of Pound standing with the swagger of a renaissance *condottiere* (lost – or probably destroyed by Lewis). He produced several portrait drawings of Pound, partly in preparation for this. In the pencil and watercolour drawing from 1919, it is above all the volumes of Pound's head that concern him, and that are made prominent by the choice of a light-source below the head. As he often does in drawings where there is a strong element of naturalism, the artifice necessary to art is enforced by the perfunctory convention of hatching for the hair, with a dark background merely indicated by the narrow sickle-shaped wash strip that surrounds it. Along with Lewis, Pound in 1920 felt the lack of momentum for avant-garde effort in London. His poems, *Homage to Sextus Propertius* (1919) and *Hugh Selwyn Mauberley* (1920), examine English culture critically. For Pound, the conclusion was that England had to be abandoned and he left London to live in Paris. Part of his discontent no doubt related to Lewis's work, since he preferred the extremes of Lewis's Vorticist abstraction to the figurative mode that seemed to have displaced it in 1919–20. Ironically, the 1920 portrait head may be taken as a justification of Lewis's new mode: a concentrated "vortex" of linear energy, loose and expressive at its outer edges, but precise and controlled in the detail of eyes, nose and moustache.

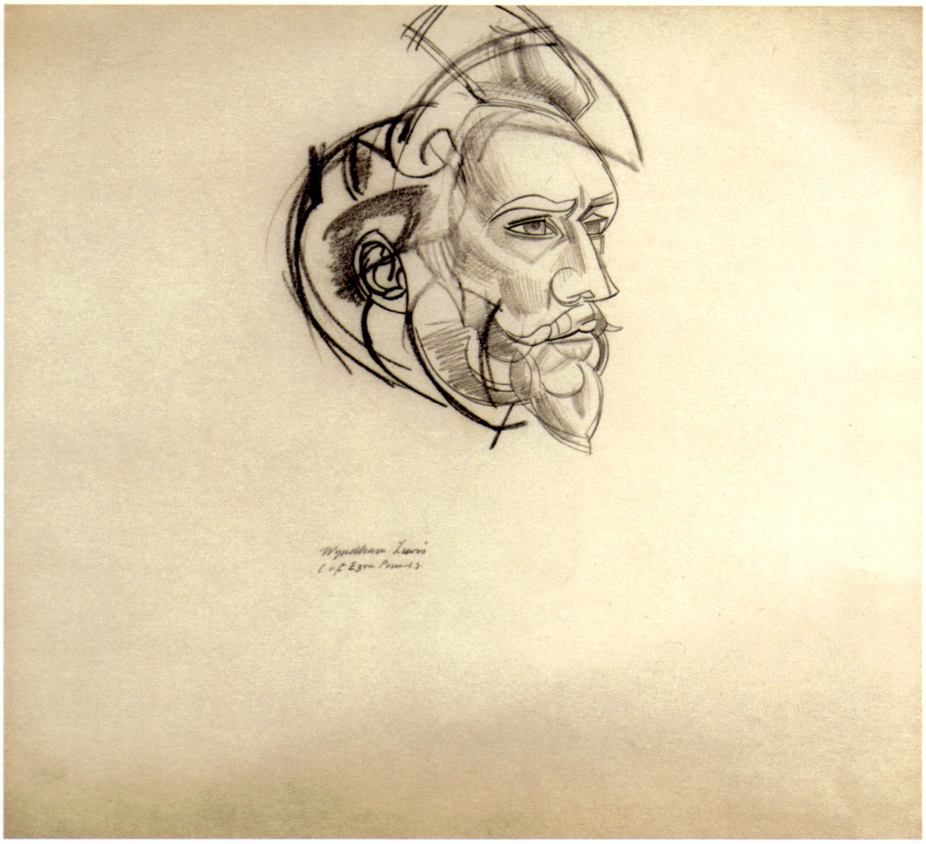

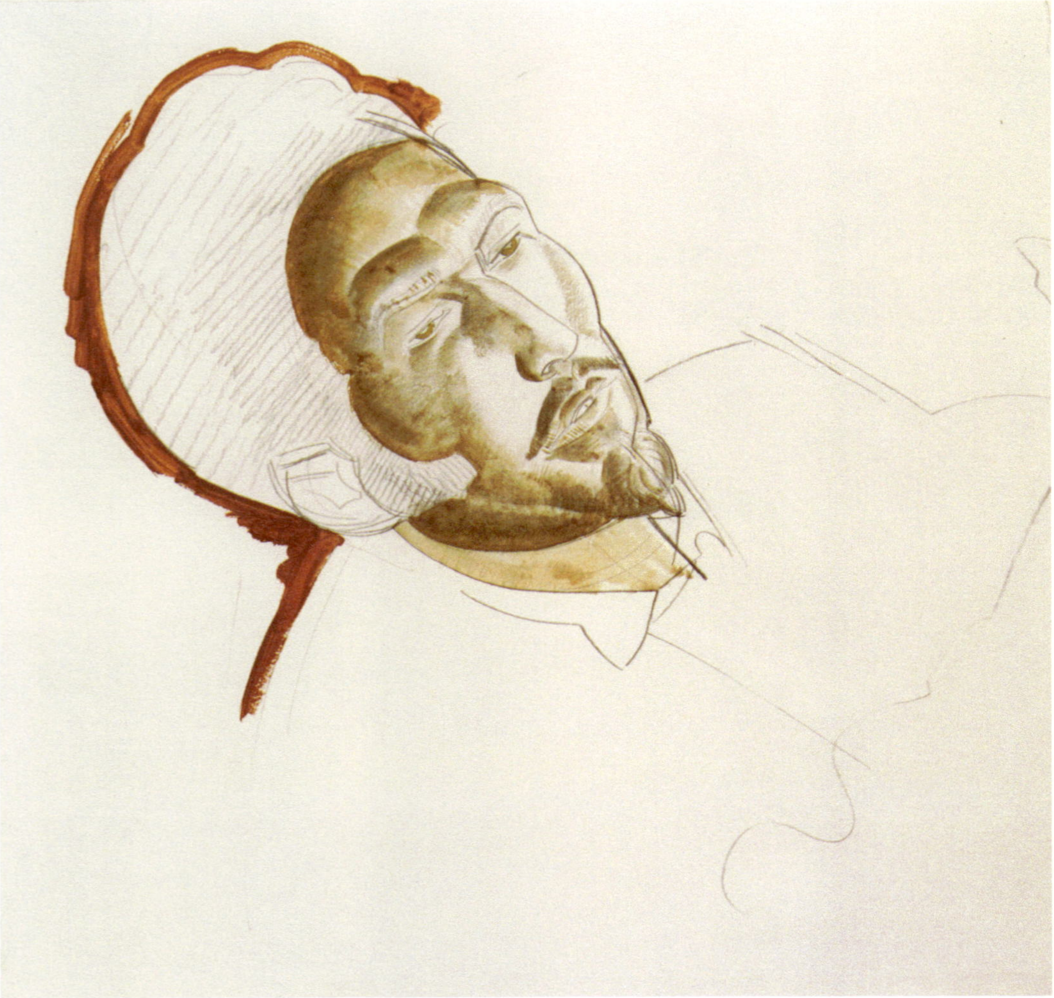

Cat. 81.
Ezra Pound, 1921. Black chalk on paper. 37 x 32 cm. Private collection

The true date of this drawing is probably 1920 and it is one of several of Ezra Pound seated in this posture in a chair frequently used by Lewis for sitters around this time. The elaborate and dynamic linear effects that foreshortening allowed the artist in such drawings as *Crouching Woman* (Cat. 76) are exploited again here and are aided by the haphazard folds and creases of clothing. The energy of the drawing transfers metonymically to Pound himself.

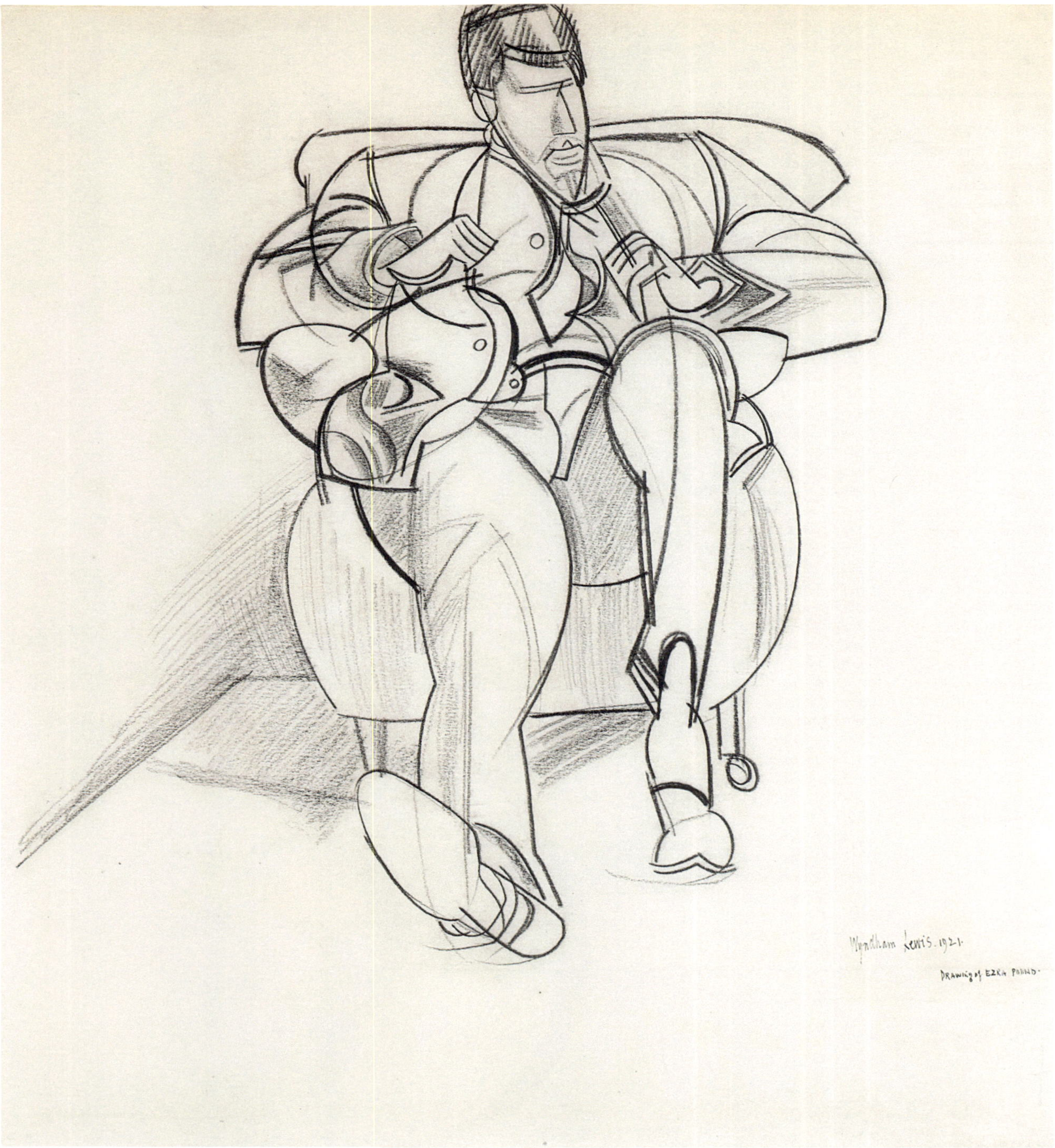

Cat. 82.
***Edward Wadsworth*, 1920. Black chalk and wash on paper. 38.5 x 28 cm. Pembroke College Oxford Junior Common Room Art Collection. M 436**

Lewis gave the title *The God in the Car* to this drawing when it was reproduced in *Artwork* (October 1924). The phrase derives from the title of an 1894 novel by Anthony Hope and refers to the Hindu Juggernaut (Jaggernath) under which worshippers traditionally immolated themselves. Edward Wadsworth was the son of a wealthy industrialist but became an artist. Lewis found him, of all his Vorticist colleagues, the most ready to engage with modernity in his art. After the war, Wadsworth took Lewis on a tour of the industrial north of England in his Rolls Royce and this trip was no doubt the inspiration for the alternative title. Wadsworth joined with other friends of Lewis to support him with a monthly stipend in 1924, but the scheme ended in rancour. Lewis seems to have been unable to tolerate dependence on friends who shared his trade, but got on well only with patrons who could not be considered colleagues or competitors. Wadsworth, his wife Fanny and other contributors to the scheme were duly satirised in the 1930 novel, *The Apes of God* (B&M Cat. 21). Wadsworth's Rolls Royce is there changed to a Bugatti.

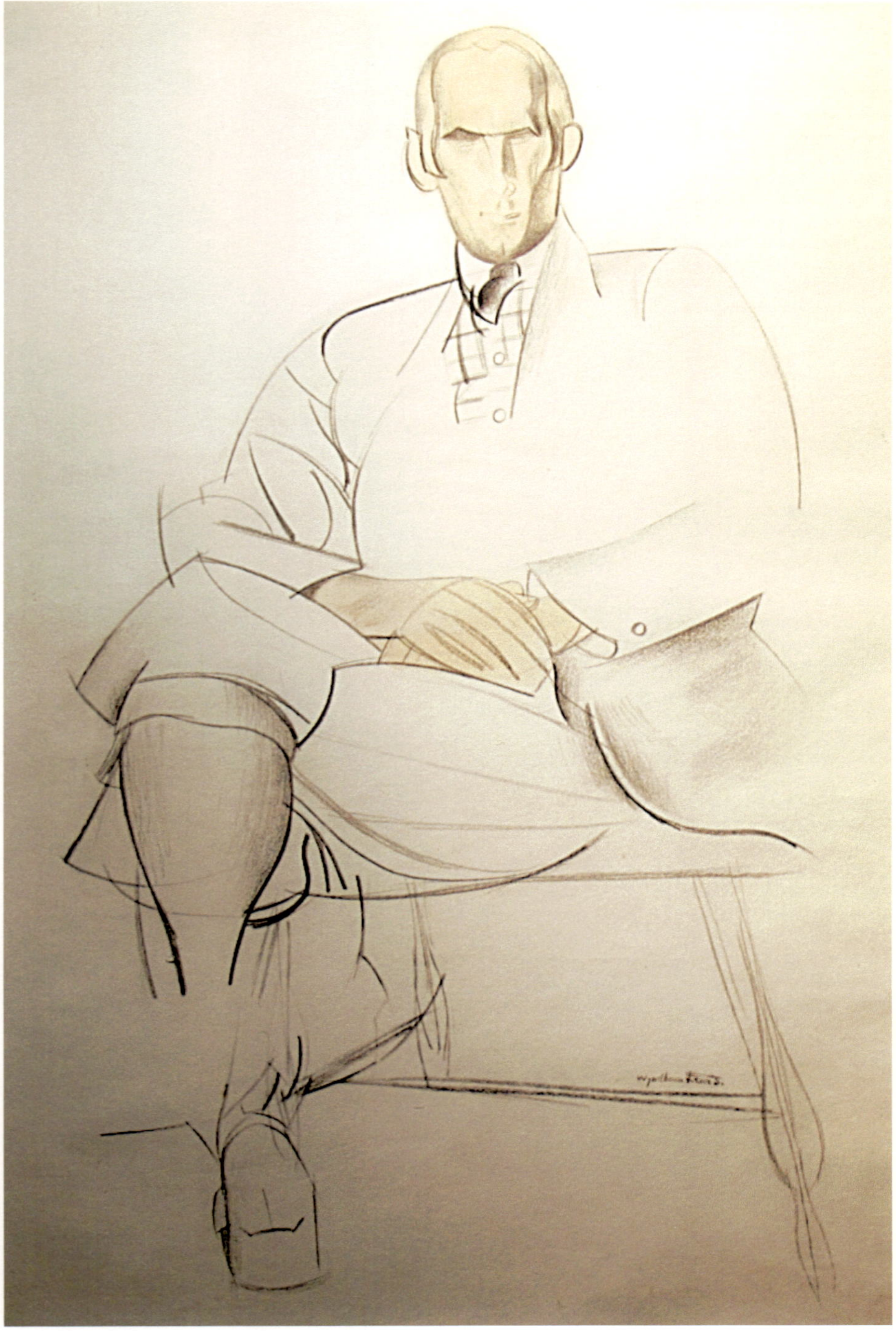

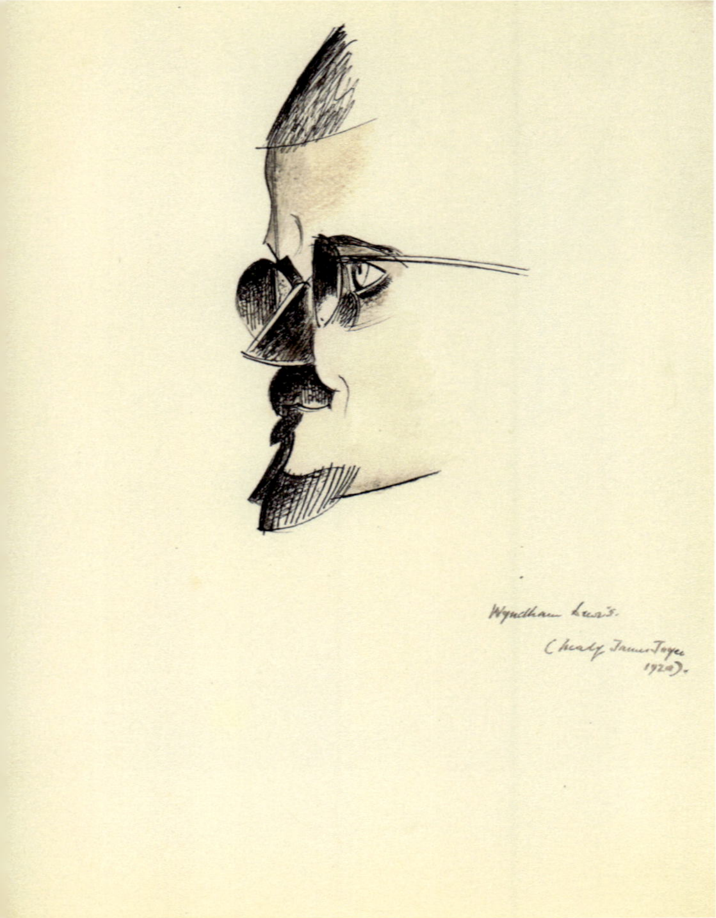

Cat. 83.
***James Joyce*, 1920. Pencil, ink and wash on paper. 26.5 x 20.5 cm. Private collection. M 397**

Ezra Pound performed a similar service for James Joyce as he did for Lewis, publicising his work and trying to find publishers for it in England. Pound tried to persuade Lewis to publish one of Joyce's stories in *Blast* (B&M Cats. 2 and 3), but Lewis had enough quiet naturalism with Ford Madox Hueffer's "The Saddest Story" (later completed as *The Good Soldier*). But Joyce was among those "blessed" in the magazine. Joyce was living in Trieste and Zurich, but moved to Paris after the war. Joyce felt a sense of grievance at his impoverished state, which he described graphically to Pound. Lewis visited Joyce with T.S. Eliot in the summer of 1920, bearing a parcel from Pound. In *Blasting and Bombardiering* (1937) (B&M Cat. 40), Lewis describes the embarrassment of the elegantly dressed Joyce, in his patent-leather shoes, when the parcel was opened to reveal a pair of old leather shoes and some of Pound's cast-off clothing. Joyce and Lewis became friends and drinking partners, but the friendship became guarded and uneasy after Lewis criticised *Ulysses* (1922) in the 1927 *Time and Western Man* (B&M Cat. 12).

Cat. 84. ▸
Lady in a Windsor Chair, 1920. Black crayon on paper. 56 x 38 cm. Manchester City Galleries (1925.212). M 400

Cat. 85. ▸▸
Woman with a Cigarette or Woman Standing, 1920. Pencil on paper. 56 x 37.8 cm. Aberystwyth University, School of Art Museum and Galleries (WD461). M 1167

The same sitter is shown in both drawings and in both Lewis makes the layers of clothing an opportunity for virtuoso linear effects. The viewpoint accentuates the monumentality of the images. In *The Caliph's Design* (B&M Cat. 7), Lewis vividly evoked the satisfactions of an art based on linear mastery, celebrating "The great line, the creative line; the fine exultant mass; the gaiety that snaps and clacks like a fine gut string."[1] In 1950, the critic Eric Newton picked up Lewis's musical analogies when he singled out for special praise the drawing of the *Lady in a Windsor Chair*, comparing its linear arabesques with the contours of a violin, adding, "A sheaf of violins, seen from every angle, and thought of not only as a linear arabesque but also sculpturally, would be a closer analogy."[2]

1. Wyndham Lewis, *The Caliph's Design: Architects! Where is Your Vortex?* (1919). Rprt. ed. Paul Edwards (Santa Barbara: Black Sparrow Press, 1986), p. 25.
2. Eric Newton, "Wyndham Lewis," *The Art of Wyndham Lewis*. Ed. Charles Handley-Read (London: Faber, 1951), p. 22.

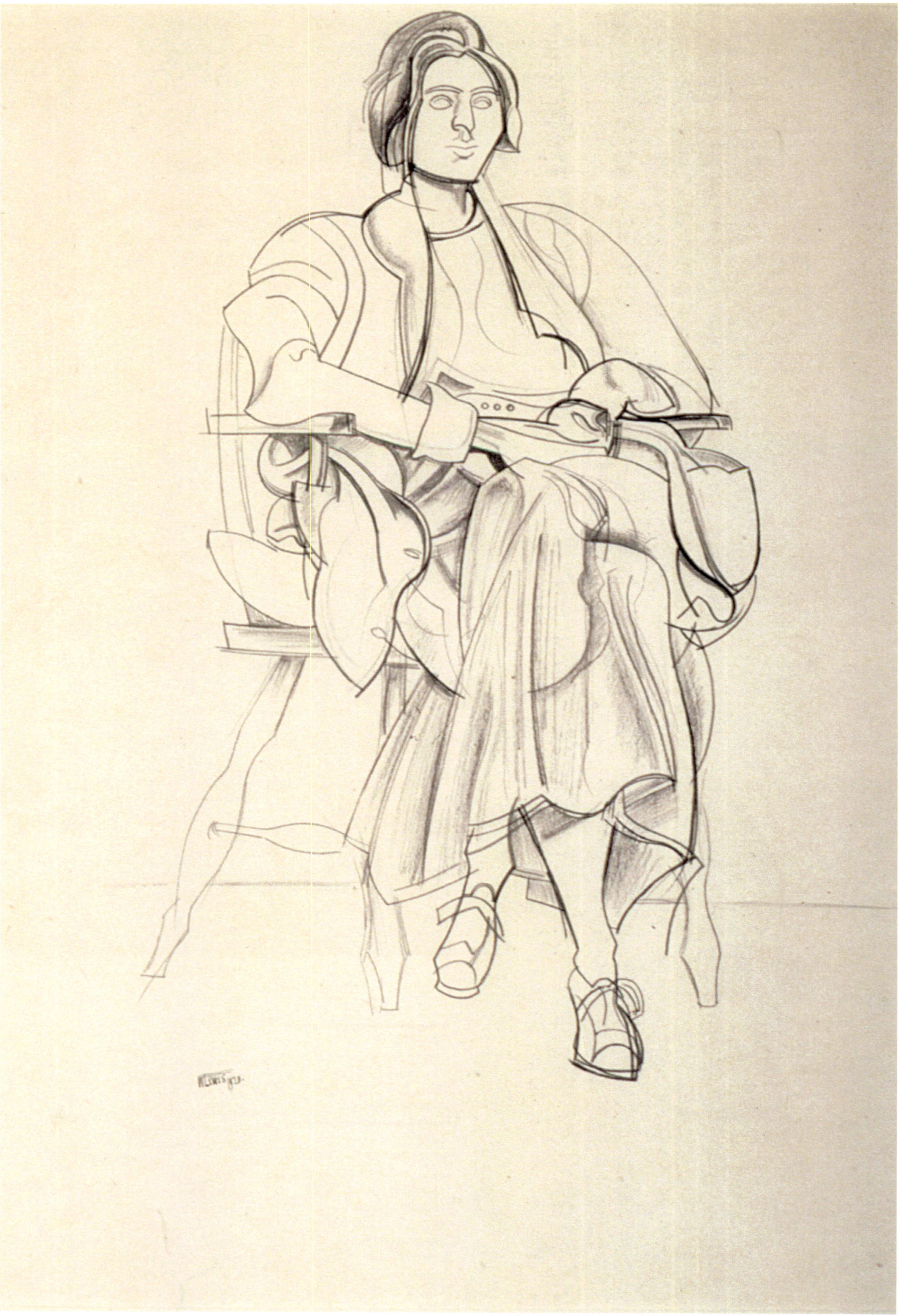

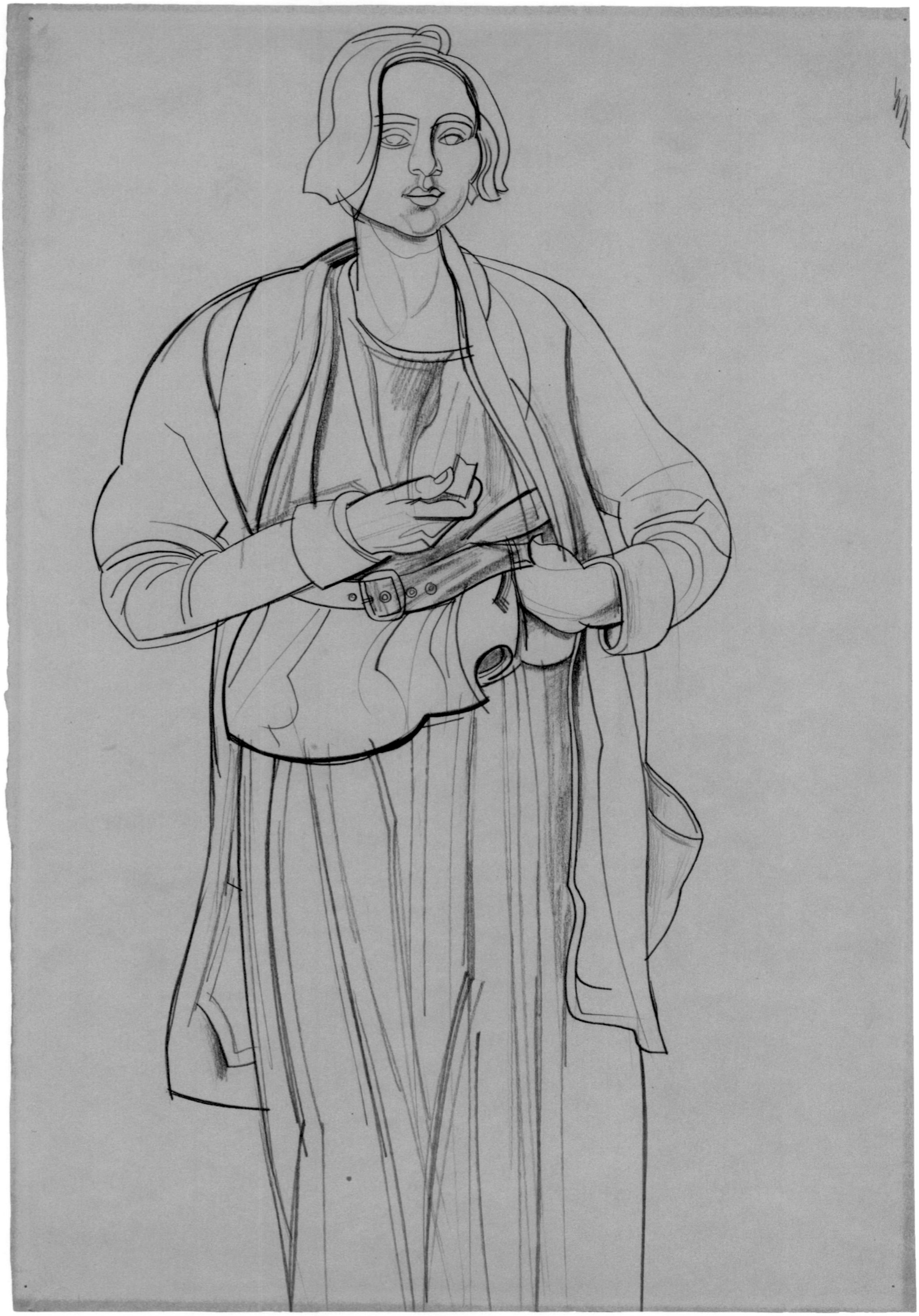

Cat. 86.
Seated Figure (Bella Medlar), 1921. Pencil on paper. 41.5 x 23.5 cm. O'Keeffe Collection, London. M 476

If visual art is, as Lewis maintained, a language, then this drawing might employ the device of synecdoche: in several of his drawings from 1921 onwards Lewis takes particular areas (features of the body, usually) and works them up to a high degree of finish, while leaving other parts of the figure minimally delineated, so that the detail of the part stands for the whole. In this case the clasped hands with their intertwined fingers and features of the head are "finished." In another drawing of 1921 (*Seated Lady* (M 477), Collection Rugby School), the lower leg and shoes are the focus of Lewis's attention. The influence of Japanese art on Lewis's art is clear in the drawing of Medlar.

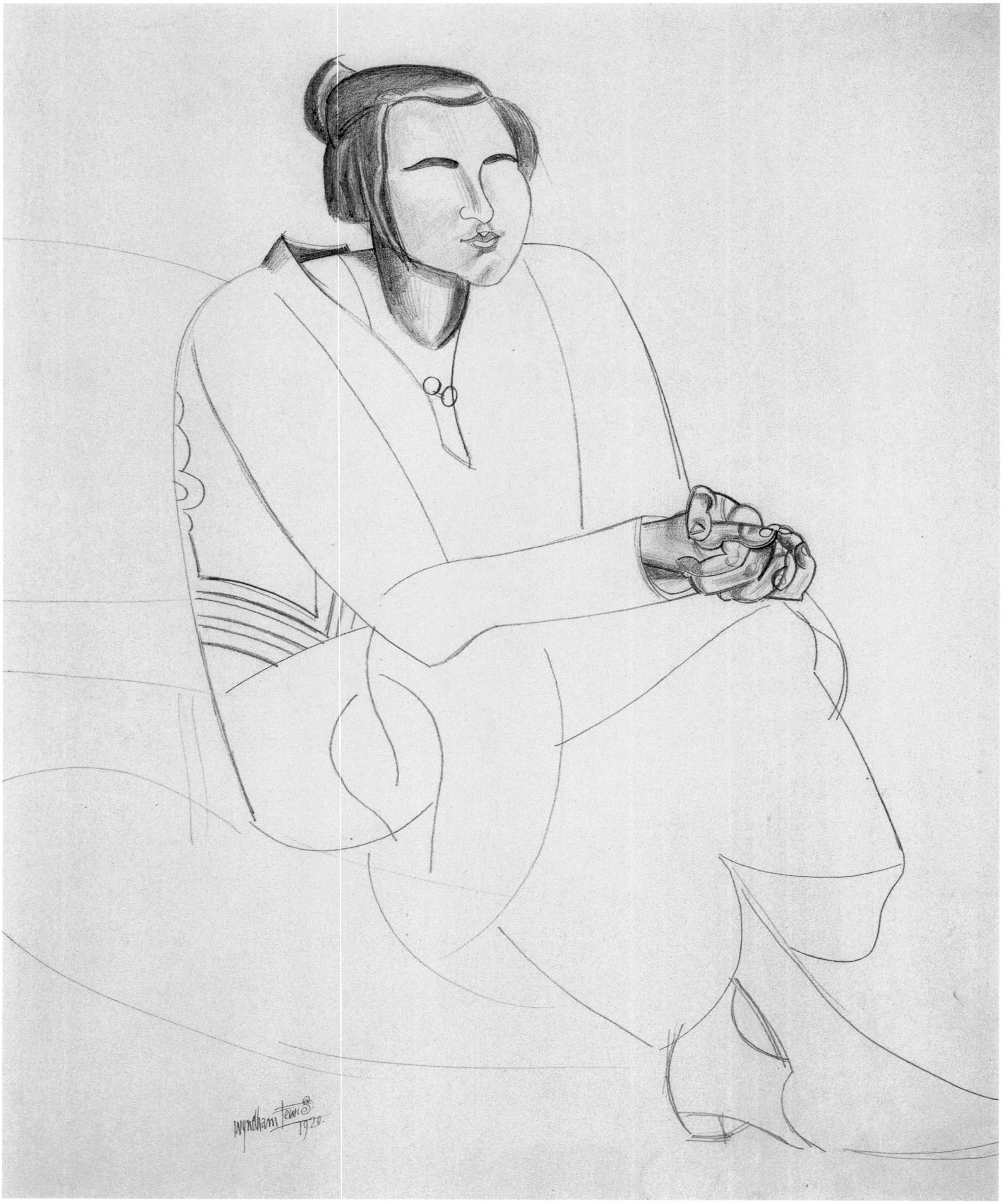

Cat. 87.
[Not in exhibition] *Cabby*
1920. Black chalk, pen and ink, and coloured washes on paper. 38.7 x 28.3 cm. National Gallery of Victoria, Melbourne. Felton Bequest, 1958. M 385

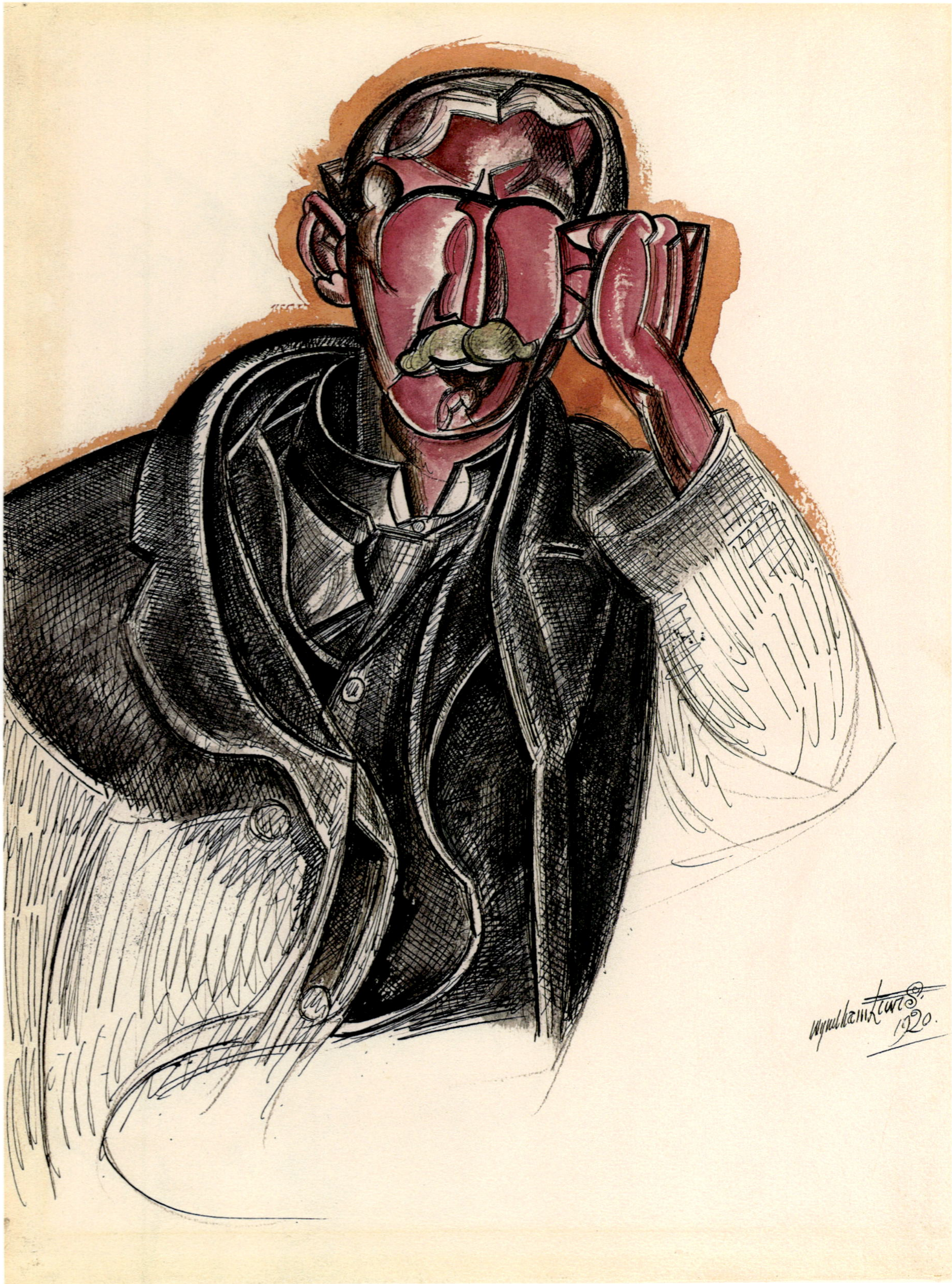

Lewis produced several drawings of this model, some comparatively naturalistic and sensitive, some (especially pen-and-ink drawings) worked to a high degree of artifice, translating the flesh, hair and the layers of soft clothing to a carved, sculptural rigidity. But this solid figure seems to emerge from nowhere, or from the paper itself, conjured out of the rough swirls of Lewis's pen at the bottom left of the sheet. A similar paradox governs our encounter with the brick red face, so "real" yet lacking a crucial feature. As with *Bella Medlar* (Cat. 86) and numerous other drawings of 1920–21, Lewis omits the eyes, never more daringly than in this drawing of the cab driver. The eye was for Lewis the crucial organ, not only for its importance as the source of visual art, but also as that which by its sparkle above all differentiated the living from the dead. In his dualism, it functioned like René Descartes' pineal gland, as the bridge between the two realms to which human life belonged. And art should avoid getting too close to this, rather than the "other" world. Too lifelike a representation of the eye threatened the special condition of art as referring as much to that other world as to this. In a 1924 essay, "The Dithyrambic Spectator," discussing the possible origins of art in Egyptian mummification, Lewis bemoans the later forms of Egyptian art in which a "sparkling eye" was closely imitated: "These sparkling eyes, had the Egyptians possessed the mechanical equipment, with the centuries of positive research behind them that we have, would soon have *moved*. Thereby, from the artist's point of view, they would have come into competition with apples, the advantage remaining heavily upon the side of the fruit."[1]

1. Wyndham Lewis, *The Diabolical Principle and The Dithyrambic Spectator* (London: Chatto and Windus, 1931), p. 183.

Cat. 88. ▸
The Pole Jump, 1919–29.
**Pencil, pen and ink, watercolour and gouache on paper. 32 x 43 cm.
Private collection. M 344**

Cat. 89. ▾
**Portfolio *Fifteen Drawings: The Pole Jump, 1919*.
Wyndham Lewis Memorial Trust. G. and V. Lane Collection**

Lewis here revives and renews the caricatural style of his earliest works. Exceptionally, he was prepared to acknowledge the presence of caricature in modernist art. He writes, for example, of Henri Matisse that his "funniness" (that is, his strangeness as far as the public is concerned) "consists of distortion, or a simplicity akin to the facile images of French caricature, and a certain vivacity of tint."[1] The drawing was originally much less finished, as can be seen in Cat. 89. In 1929, Lewis was commissioned by the Earl of Inchcape to produce a series of drawings of sporting scenes (see Cats. 129–31). He revised the present work and included it in the set.

1. Wyndham Lewis, *The Caliph's Design: Architects! Where is Your Vortex?* (1919). Rprt. ed. Paul Edwards (Santa Barbara: Black Sparrow Press, 1986), p. 103.

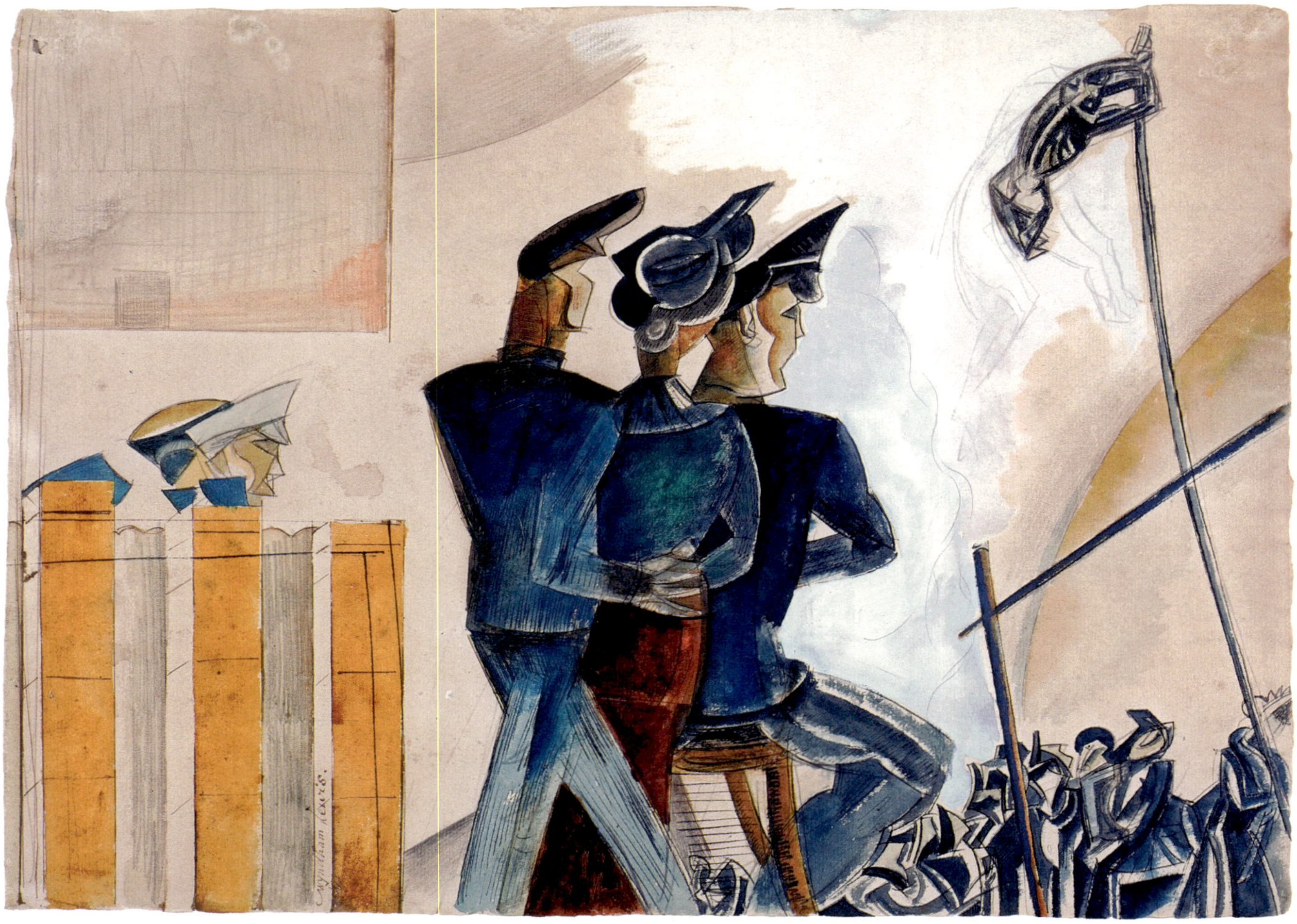

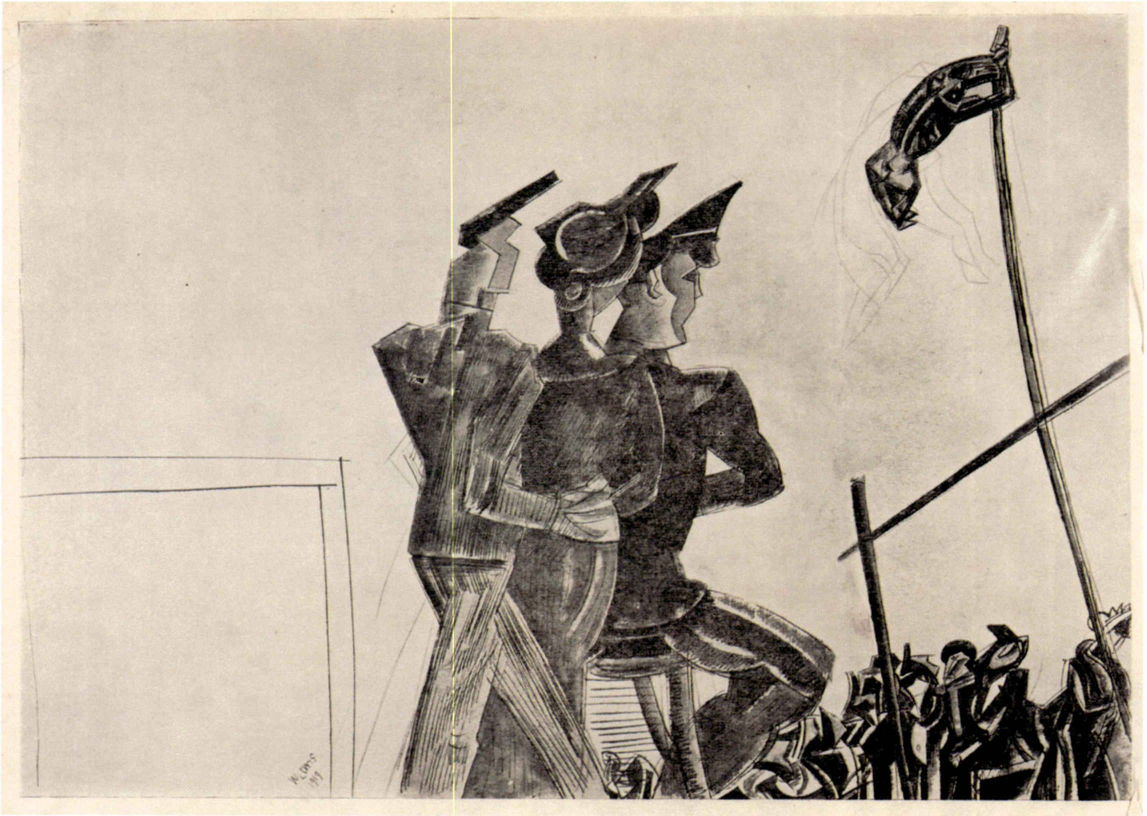

Cat. 90.
[Not in exhibition] ***A Shore Scene*** **(Figures on a Beach), 1920. Pen and ink, and wash on paper. 29.5 x 47.5 cm. Museum of New Zealand Te Papa Tongarewa. Purchased 1967 with Harold Beauchamp Collection funds (1967-0004-1). M 431**

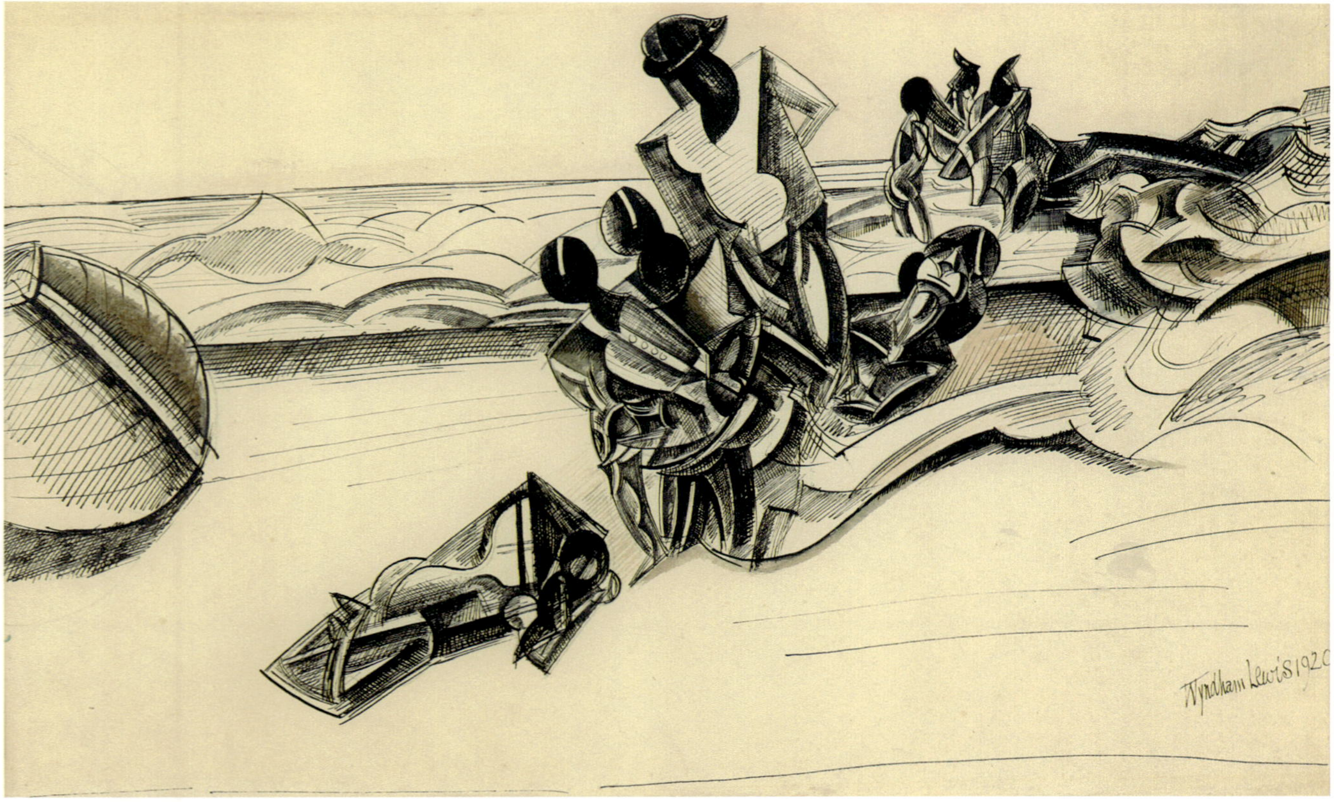

The intricate pen and ink of some of the First World War drawings and *Pastoral Toilet* (Cat. 60) is here invigorated by the sprung forms of the visual grammar Lewis has invented for his more naturalistic work of 1919–20. The same power of abstraction as is visible in the "Cubist" crowd looking up at the jumping figure in *The Pole Jump* (Cat. 88) has created these groups of figures and rocks that hover on the edge of decipherability but remain primarily a series of (perhaps erotically) interlocked sculptural forms. Only the upturned boat seeks to reassure us that, yes, this is simply a seaside scene. Walter Michel writes that this is the "most elaborate composition in ink of the period," and rightly calls it "one of Lewis's greatest drawings." He continues, "Forms never seen before, composed into clusters like the flowers of a tropical fruit, rise from the main diagonal," and comments that the varied textures of the hatching "show a play of light as if it were in colour."[1]

1. Walter Michel, *Wyndham Lewis: Paintings and Drawings* (London: Thames and Hudson, 1971), p. 99.

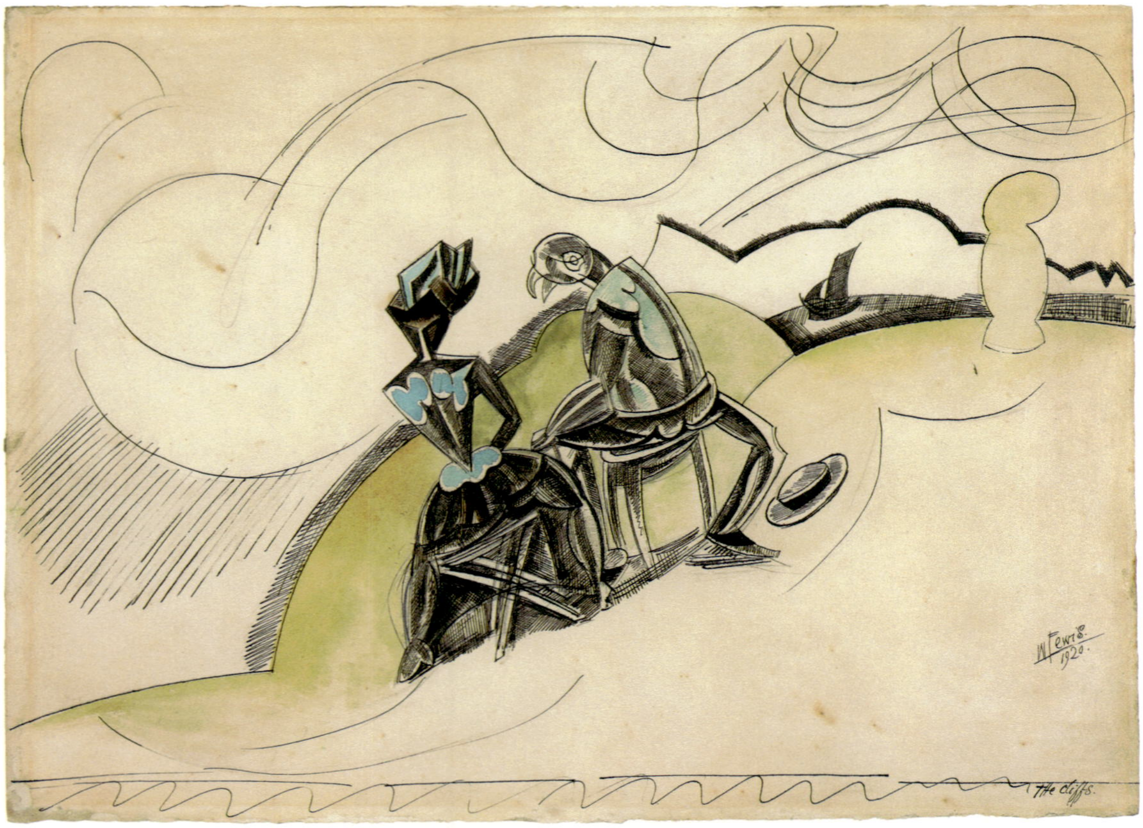

Cat. 91.
The Cliffs**, 1920. Pen and ink, graphite, watercolour and gouache on paper. 28.2 x 37.9 cm. Wyndham Lewis Memorial Trust. G. and V. Lane Collection (LD.2004.XX.39). M 388**

The breezy vivacity of the elements, whipping up the clouds and sending the small boat scudding along below the cliffs, contrasts with the parrot-like gentleman, boring (presumably) his lady companion with dreary conversation. The caricatural spirit of *The Pole Jump* (Cat. 88) is combined with the virtuoso handing of pen and ink displayed in *A Shore Scene* (Cat. 90).

Cat. 92.
Woman Knitting, 1920.
Pencil on buff paper.
50.2 x 32.5 cm.
Manchester City Galleries
(1925.234). M 440

A drawing of Lewis's lover, Iris Barry, with whom he lived for a few years after the war. The precision of the line, the formalised reduction of the volumes into carefully shaded planes and the rudimentary delineation of the chair transform the classicism of this drawing into Lewisian modernism. It raises one of the complicating biographical issues of the appreciation of Lewis's art, however, while as a drawing, seemingly remaining untouched by it. While expecting their daughter, Barry occupied herself with knitting, and even considered starting a knitting business "employing only one or two cheap cripples or people like that."[1] Lewis chose the name "Maisie" for the girl, apparently after the protagonist of Henry James's novel, *What Maisie Knew* (1897, about a child who survives unscathed the bitter breakdown of her parents' marriage and their subsequent squabbles over her. Lewis's children by Olive Johnson, a previous lover, were in care, supported by Lewis. Barry had become pregnant as a "proof of good will and all that"[2] after Lewis expressed doubts about the paternity of an earlier son (Robin, born in 1919, and sent to be brought up by Iris's mother for three years until he was sent to a children's home). Maisie was also farmed out to a children's home by her uncaring parents.

1. Quoted in Paul O'Keeffe, *Some Sort of Genius: A Life of Wyndham Lewis* (London: Jonathan Cape, 2000), pp. 221–22.
2. Quoted, ibid., p. 220.

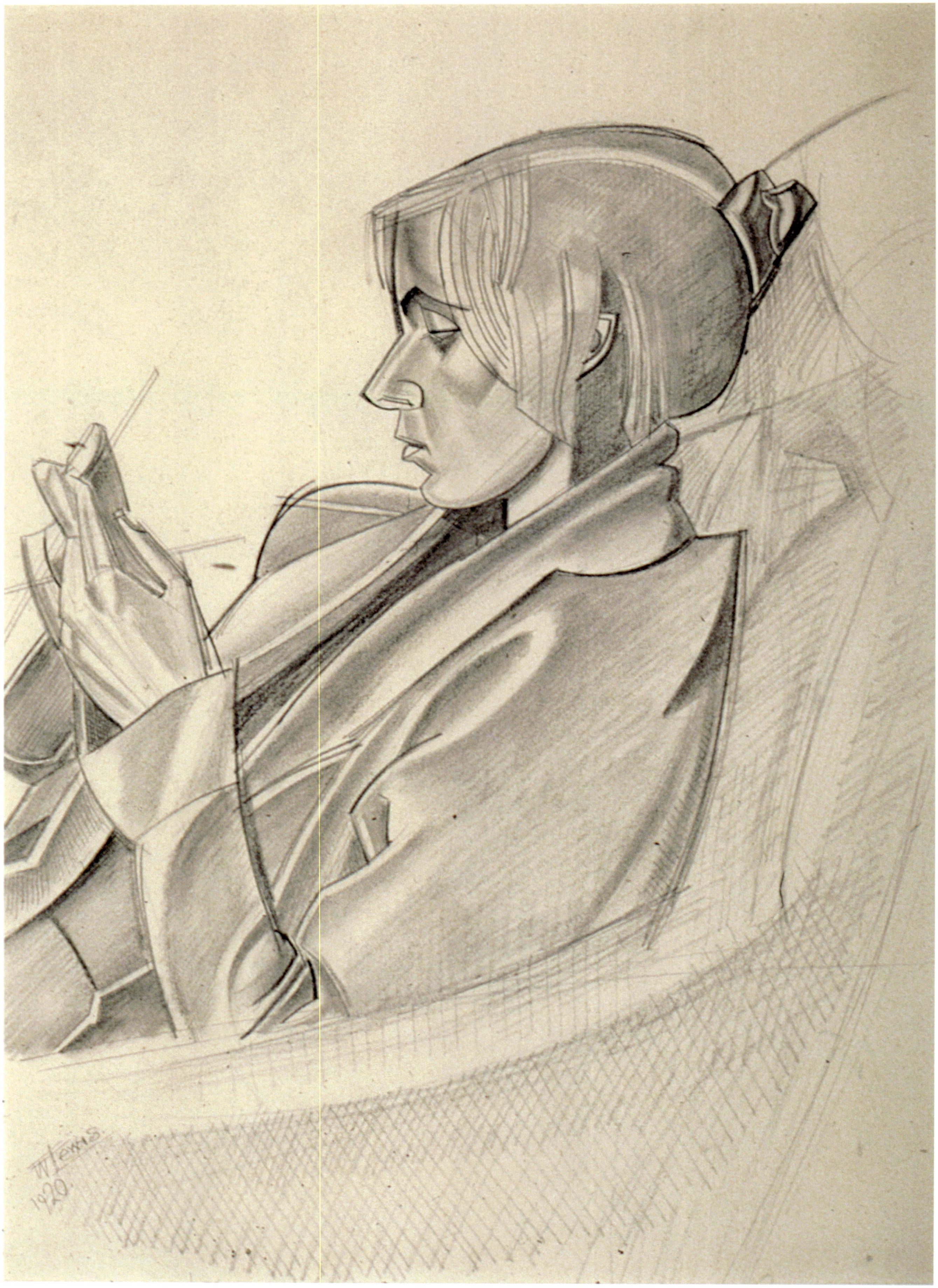

Cat. 93.
[Not in exhibition] *Girl Sewing*, 1921–38. Black chalk and watercolour on paper. 55 x 37 cm. Private collection. M 461

Lewis depicted Iris Barry in this 'Tam o'Shanter' hat and wraparound waistcoat in several drawings of 1921. These garments enabled him to emphasise the artifice that removes the objects of art from this world. Indeed, for him, this was the function of clothing and coiffure in general. Here the soft beret seems to have been hardened into a stiff, oriental bonnet. The drawing was considerably altered in 1938 for reproduction in a book, *The Role of Line in Art*, which was to have been issued by the Corvinus Press, illustrated with seven drawings by Lewis. The Second World War intervened and the publisher was killed in an air accident. Lewis eliminated an untidy left foot, made some changes to colouring and added the structure of books and background at the left-hand side.

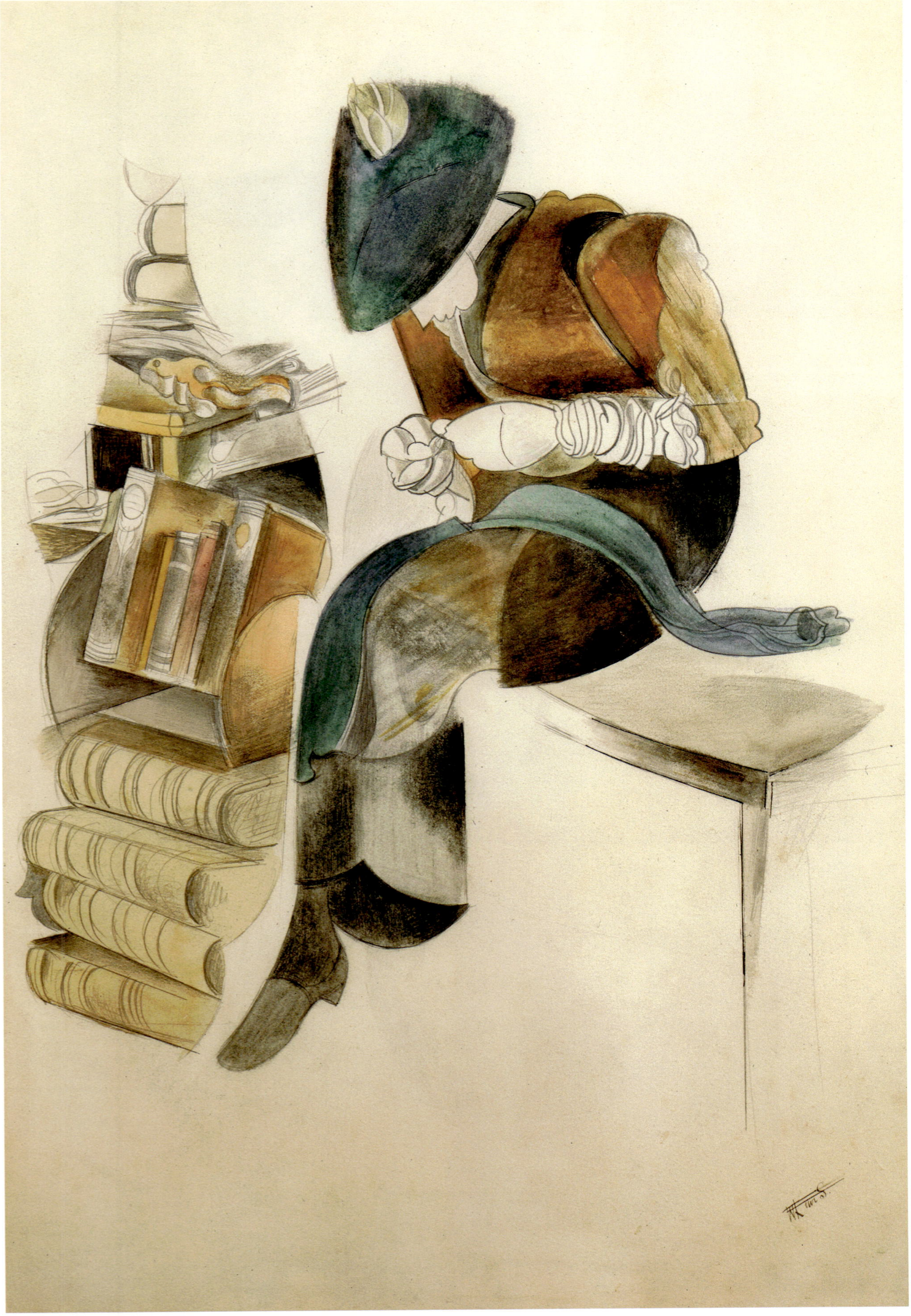

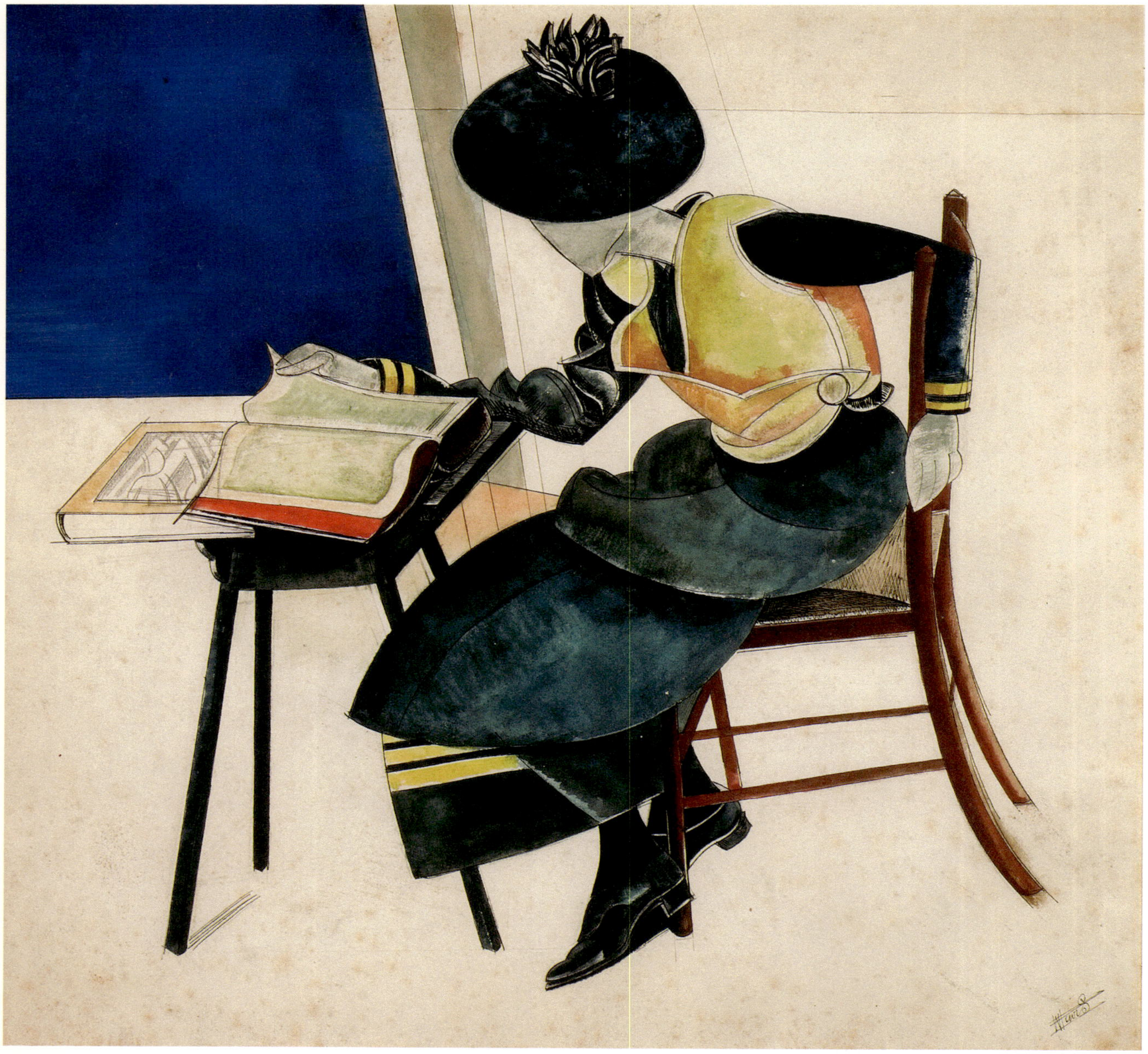

Cat. 94.
Woman in Blue, 1921.
Watercolour on paper.
41 x 58 cm.
Private collection.

There are analogies between the rigid articulated surfaces into which Lewis translated the human figure and the forms of insects, and Lewis explores these in some of the drawings of Iris Barry reading. The impersonal, almost mechanical feeling is reinforced by the absence of facial features. The blue dress with wasp-like yellow stripes recurs in several drawings, but most strikingly in *Praxitella* (Cat. 96).

Cat. 95.
Seated Figure, 1921. Oil on canvas. 75.7 x 63 cm.
Scottish National Gallery of Modern Art; Presented by Mrs Karina Williamson 1988 (GMA 3428)

The model is probably Iris Barry, since she is wearing the wraparound waistcoat also seen in Cat. 93, but this is not a portrait. Lewis plays with conventions, exposing different "grammars" of representation. The thinly scrubbed background, with traces of squaring-up, separates into horizontal floor and vertical wall only by virtue of the perfunctory strip of graduated paint that marks their boundary. The chair itself is in exaggerated perspective. The carved African mask of the face is placed above a torso wrapped apparently in a cylinder of sheet-armour. The dress and legs are treated in a quite different style, irremediably flat on the canvas, despite shapes that conventionally signify creases and their shadows. There are no hands, perhaps because Lewis felt that hands (like eyes) might humanise the painting too much. *Seated Figure* was exhibited in Lewis's 1921 exhibition, *Tyros and Portraits*, at The Leicester Galleries, London.

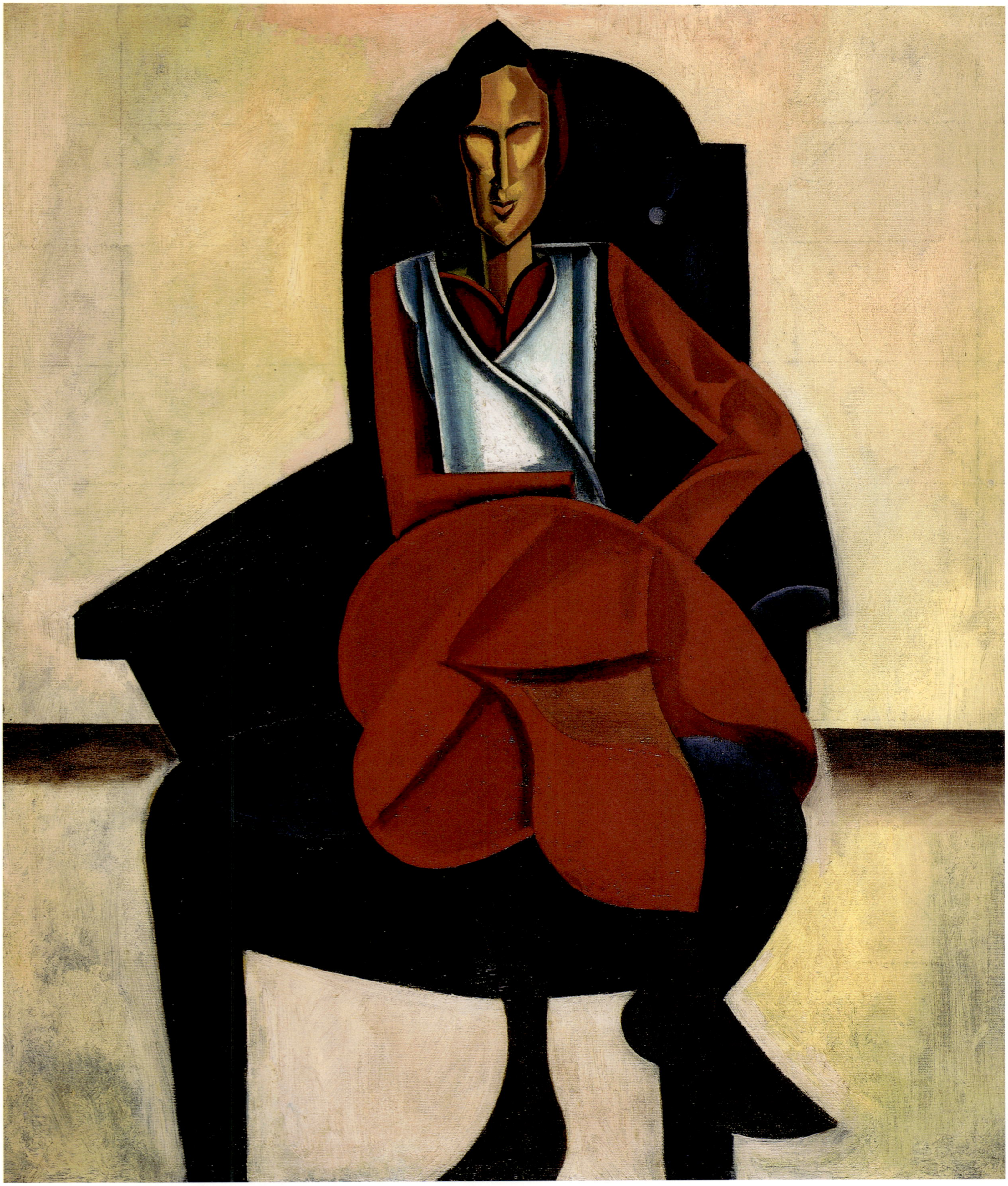

Cat. 96.
[Not in Exhibition] *Praxitella*, 1920–21. Oil on canvas. 142 x 101.5 cm. Leeds Museums and Galleries (City Art Gallery). M P30

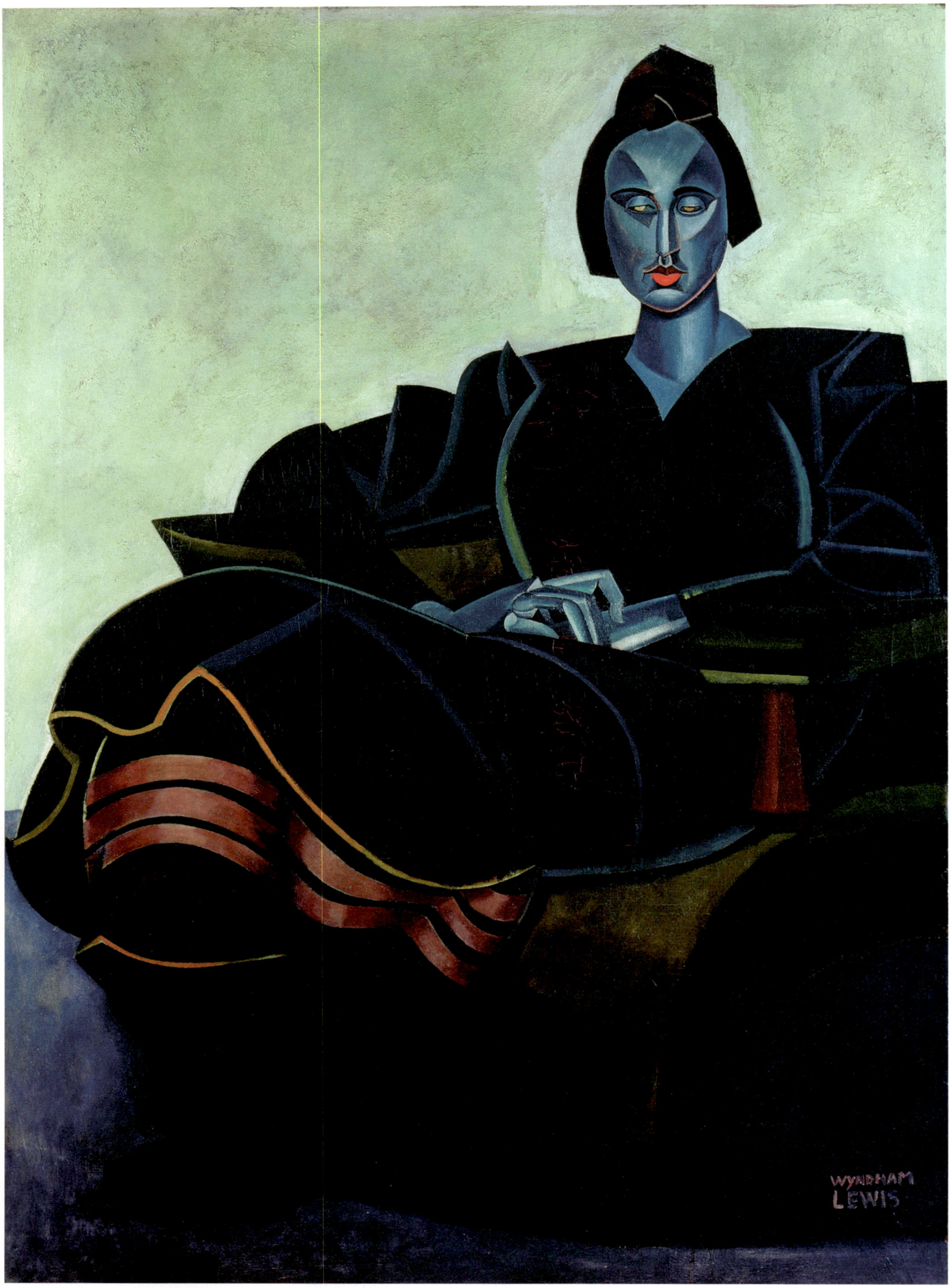

The culmination of all the studies and drawings of Iris Barry was this large painting of her wearing the blue dress with the wasp-stripes. She has been transformed into an alluring insect, with an unnaturally blue face, brilliant red lips and hooded orange eyes. The painting is Lewis's masterpiece of the 1920s and certainly one of his greatest. It was exhibited in the 1921 *Tyros and Portraits* exhibition. The title probably refers to Praxiteles, the master of Hellenic (naturalist) sculpture, and hence to the classical revival that was taking place in Europe under the leadership of the *école de Paris.* The painting has classical qualities, but completely rejects conservative naturalism. In an article about the peculiarities of the visual aesthetic at its purest, Lewis quotes Heinrich Heine from *The Romantic School*, endorsing his evocation of the condition of "classical" statues as having "a secret melancholy, a troubled memory, it may be, of Egypt, the land of the dead whence they sprang."[1]

1. Quoted in Wyndham Lewis, "The Credentials of the Painter" (1922). Rprt. *Creatures of Habit and Creatures of Change: Essays on Art, Literature and Society, 1914–1956.* Ed. Paul Edwards (Santa Rosa: Black Sparrow Press, 1989), p. 71.

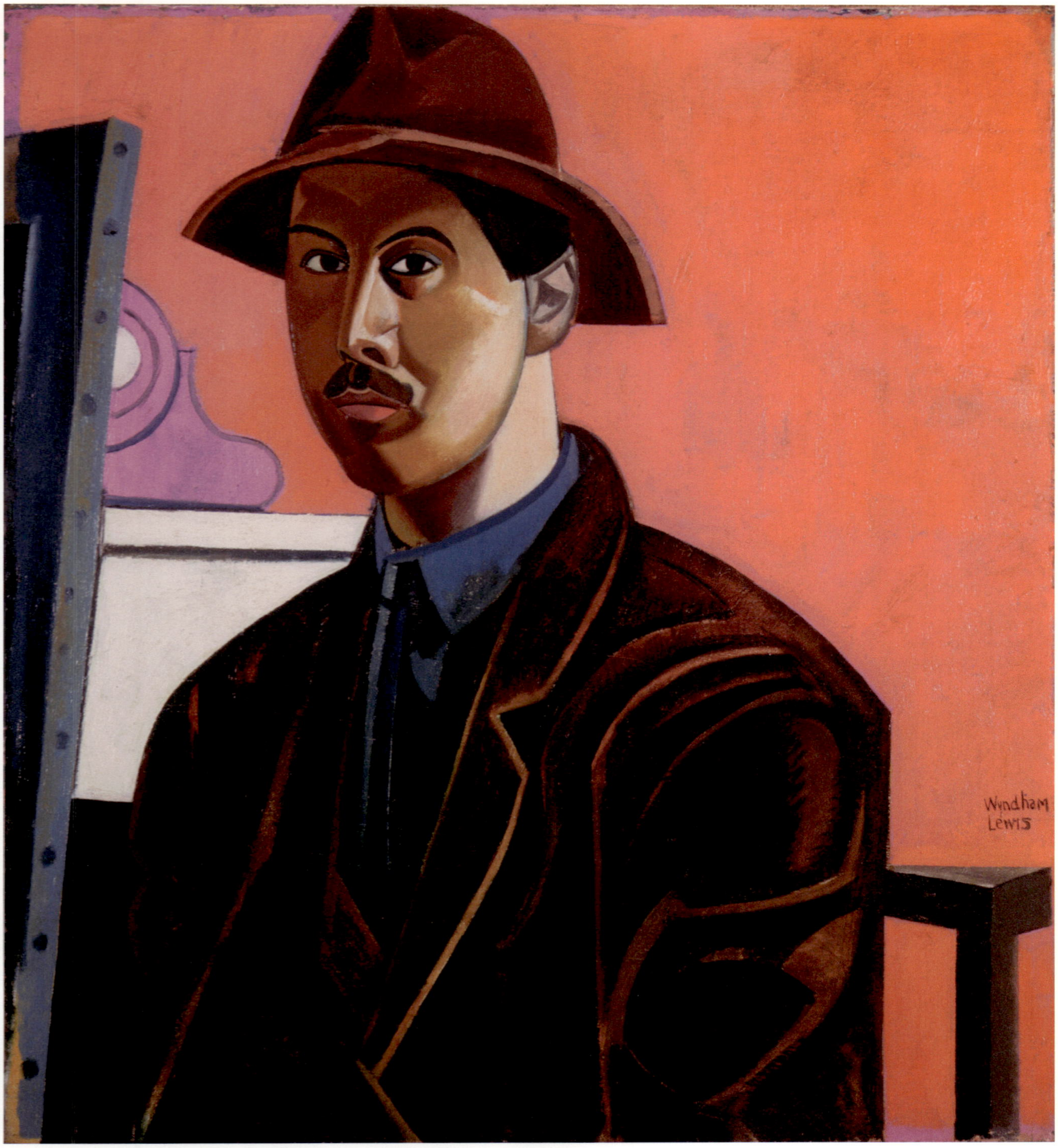

Cat. 97.
[Not in exhibition] *Portrait of the Artist as the Painter Raphael*, 1921. Oil on canvas. 76.3 x 68.6 cm. Manchester City Galleries (1925.579). M P29

This placid self-portrayal, with its vibrant, simplified background, uses the artificial convention developed in other paintings of the time for signifying creased clothing. The title, which evokes that of James Joyce's novel, *A Portrait of the Artist as a Young Man* 1916), signals a chronological incongruity: this is clearly not Raphael, though its placidity may recall the face of Raphael in *The School of Athens* (1510–11). In *The Caliph's Design* (B&M Cat. 7), Lewis rejects a return to the kind of classicism advocated by André Lhote in a series of articles published in 1919 in *The Athenaeum* in London. Lhote called for a return to Raphael, to which Lewis responded, "the hysterical second-rate Frenchman, with his morbid hankering after his mother-tradition, the eternal Graeco-Roman, should be discouraged."[1] He criticised Pablo Picasso, also, for reviving David. So Lewis's title is an ironic turn on his own classical ideals, which were based as much on both the Egyptian and oriental traditions as the literary traditions of William Shakespeare and William Hogarth. In this painting, Lewis models his self-portrait as much on the most famous portrayal of Shakespeare as he does on Raphael. It is painted on a fragment of a Vorticist canvas and was exhibited in the 1921 *Tyros and Portraits* exhibition.

1. Wyndham Lewis, *The Caliph's Design: Architects! Where is Your Vortex?* (1919). Rprt. ed. Paul Edwards (Santa Barbara: Black Sparrow Press, 1986), p. 139.

Cat. 98.
***A Reading of Ovid (Tyros)*, 1920–21. Oil on canvas. 165.2 x 90.2 cm. Scottish National Gallery of Modern Art (GMA 1685). M P31**

These grinning figures, reading a "classical" author (perhaps from Ovid's *Ars Amatoria* (The Art of Love) (1BC), a seventeenth-century translation of which Lewis later quoted in *The Apes of God* (1930) (B&M Cat. 21)), are "Tyros," a simplified race of fetishes invented by Lewis as the epitome of a shell-shocked society uncertain of its future. This painting, together with others now lost, such as *Reading Nietzsche*, *The School of Tyros* and *A Tyro about to Breakfast*, was exhibited in the 1921 *Tyros and Portraits* exhibition. Lewis was attempting to enlarge the scope of modern painting so that it dealt directly with social issues. He was protesting against the "art-for-art's-sake" preciousness of Bloomsbury painting and reasserting an older English tradition, going back to Ben Jonson, William Shakespeare, William Hogarth and Thomas Rowlandson. This was originally a popular tradition, and by developing the caricatural stark forms of his Tyro images, Lewis was also attempting to produce a popular rather than a purely highbrow art. He was at one with T.S. Eliot in this, and Eliot's "Sweeney" poems (1920) and his jazz-play, *Sweeney Agonistes* (1932), can be seen as part of a joint effort to renew the avant-garde interaction with a mass audience. Lewis was discouraged, it seems, by the lack of impact or shock value of his images. Whereas before the war anything "shocking" could be guaranteed illustration in the popular press, the Tyros were not shown, despite Lewis's attempt to publicise them in an interview for the *Daily Express*.[1]

1. "Dean Swift with a Brush: The Tyroist Explains his Art," *Daily Express*, no. 6548 (11 April 1921), p. 5.

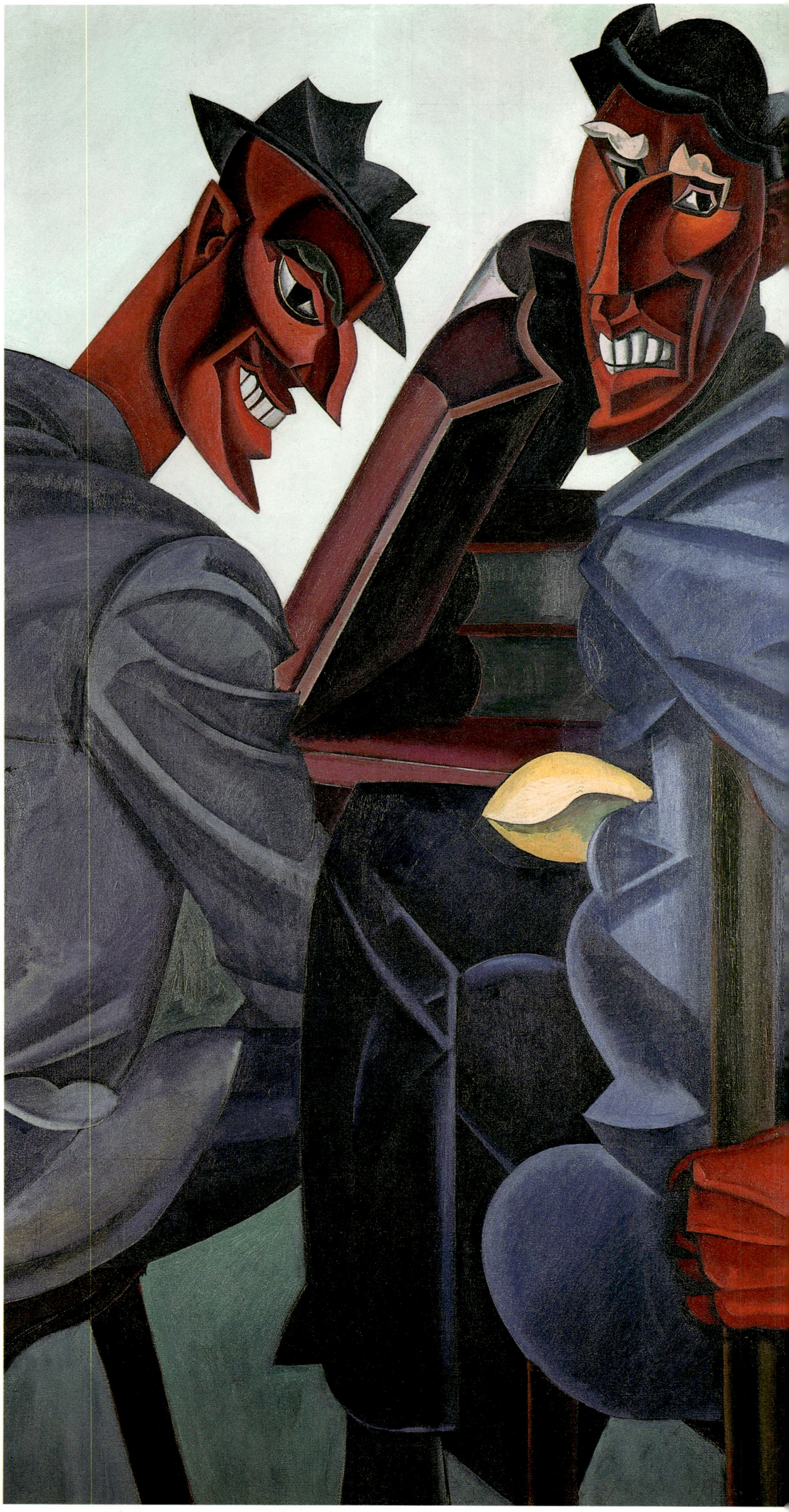

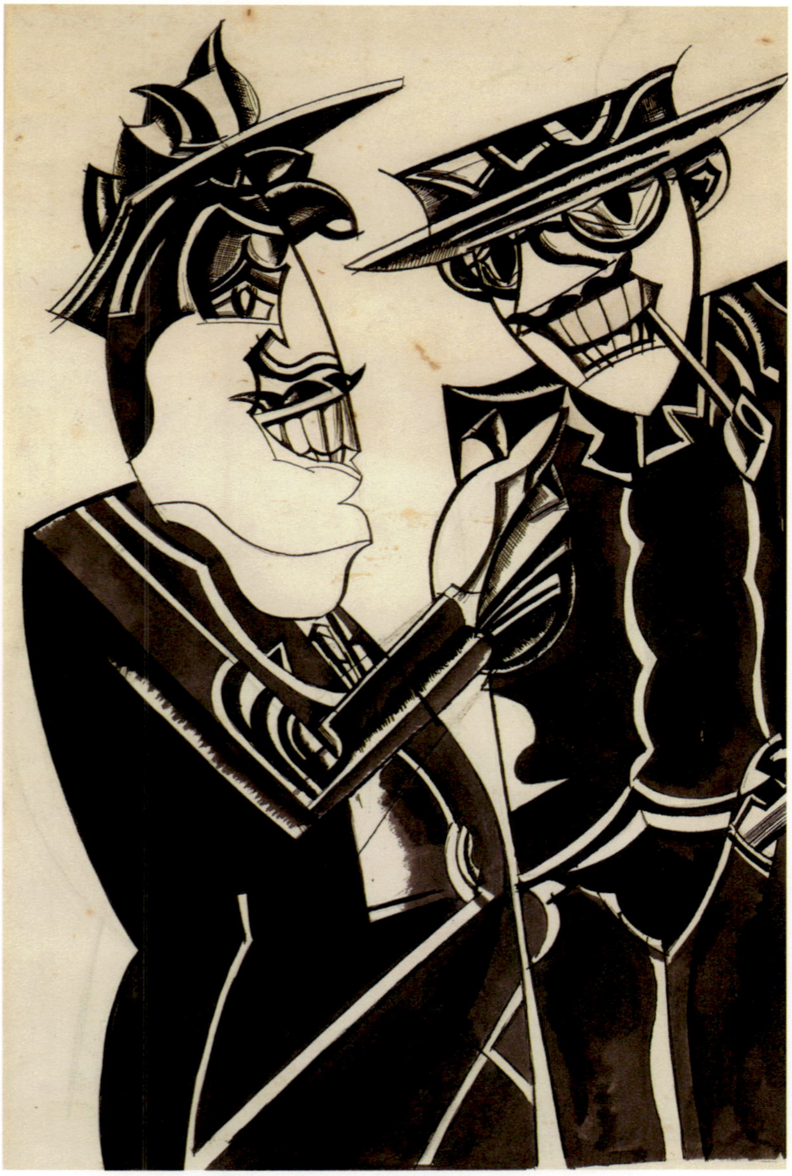

Cat. 100.
[Not in exhibition] ***Meeting between the Tyro, Mr Segando and the Tyro, Phillip*, 1921. Ink over pencil on paper. 37.2 x 21.3 cm. Herbert F. Johnson Museum of Art, Cornell University. Gift of Walter and Harriet Michel (63.237) M 470**

To coincide with his exhibition, Lewis produced the first issue of a new magazine (in small newspaper format), *The Tyro* (B&M Cat. 8). As well as reflections on the need for an alternative in British art to Bloomsbury formalism or Parisian classicism, it contained short stories by Lewis and others and some reproductions by artists such as David Bomberg and Cedric Morris. The *Meeting between the Tyro, Mr Segando and the Tyro, Phillip* illustrated a short fictional piece by John Rodker (publisher of the portfolio *Fifteen Drawings*). Lewis's comments in his exhibition foreword are relevant: "Some of these Tyros are trying to furnish you with a moment of almost Mediterranean sultriness, in order, in this region of engaging warmth, to obtain some advantage over you."[1]

1. Wyndham Lewis, "Note on Tyros," Foreword to *Tyros and Portraits* catalogue. Rprt. Walter Michel, *Wyndham Lewis: Paintings and Drawings* (London: Thames and Hudson, 1971), p. 438.

Cat. 99.
Mr Wyndham Lewis as a Tyro, 1920–21. Oil on canvas. 73 x 44 cm. Ferens Art Gallery, Hull Museums (KINCM:2005.5151). M P27

Lewis explained that Tyros were "immense novices":

These partly religious explosions of laughing Elementals are at once satires, pictures and stories. The action of a Tyro is necessarily very restricted; about that of a puppet worked with deft finger, with a screaming voice underneath. There is none of the pathos of Pagliacci in the story of a Tyro. It is the child in him that has risen in his laugh, and you get a perspective of his history.[1]

Lewis does not exclude himself from his own satire; his "history" of First World War trauma is hinted at by the sickly green of his insistently grinning face. Though the image is a "popular" one, the colours and the drawing are both reminiscent of Vincent Van Gogh's *L'Arlésienne* (1888), a work Lewis admired and in which he did detect pathos, as is shown in a short reflection on it found among his papers after his death.[2]

1. Wyndham Lewis, "Note on Tyros," Foreword to *Tyros and Portraits* catalogue. Rprt. Walter Michel, *Wyndham Lewis: Paintings and Drawings* (London: Thames and Hudson, 1971), p. 438.
2. Wyndham Lewis, "L'Arlésienne" (n.d.). Rprt. *Wyndham Lewis on Art: Collected Writings 1913–1956*. Eds. Walter Michel and C.J. Fox (London: Thames and Hudson, 1969), p. 459.

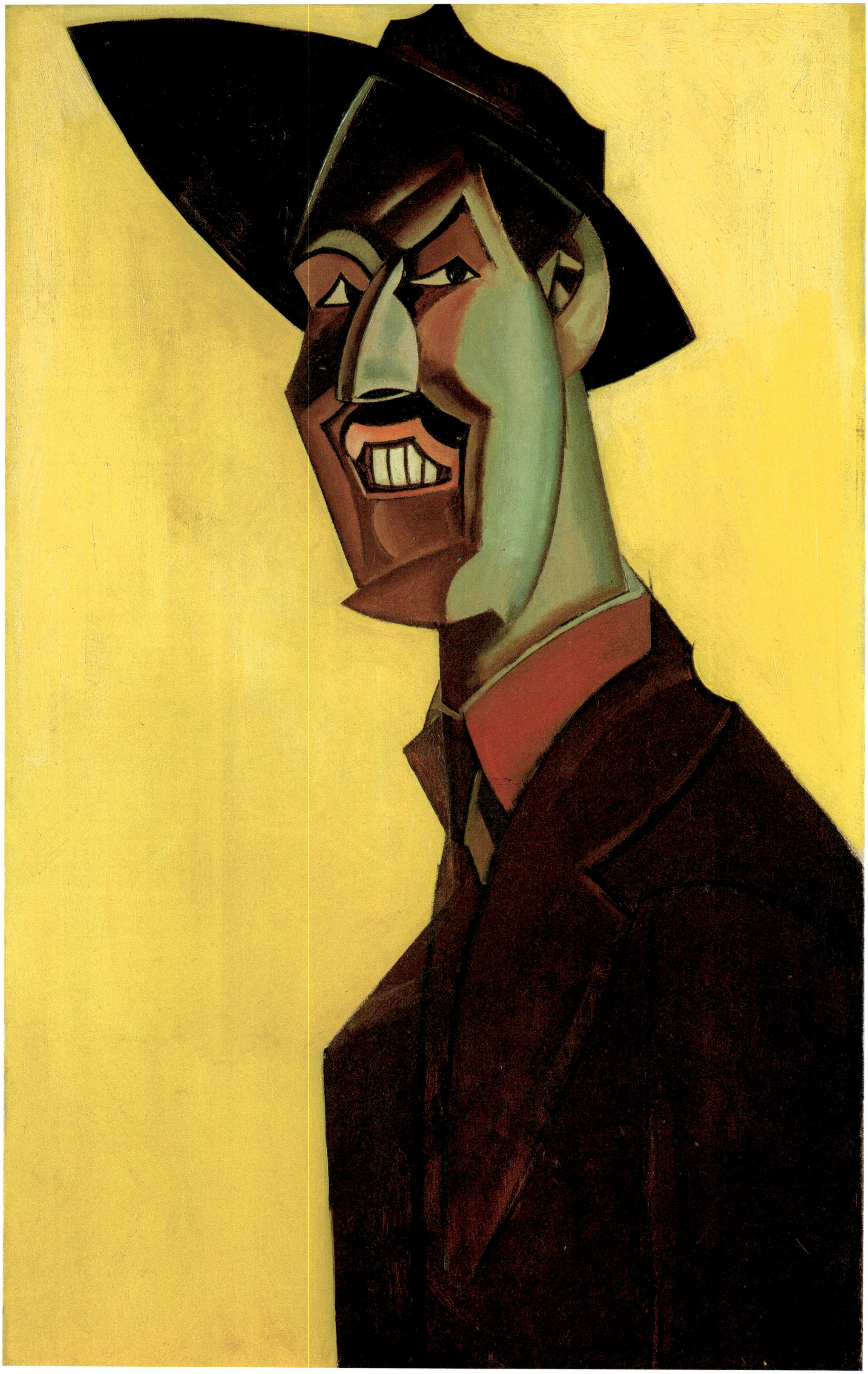

"At first this happy Vorticist did not in the least understand what was occurring. The [Great] War looked to him like an episode at first—rather proving his contentions than otherwise. He did not fully recognize the significance of that disaster until he found himself in the mud of Passchendaele, and dimly discerned that he was present at a great military defeat, and that the community to which he belonged would never be the same again: and that all surplus vigour was being bled away and stamped out."

Wyndham Lewis, *The Skeleton in the Cupboard Speaks,* 1939

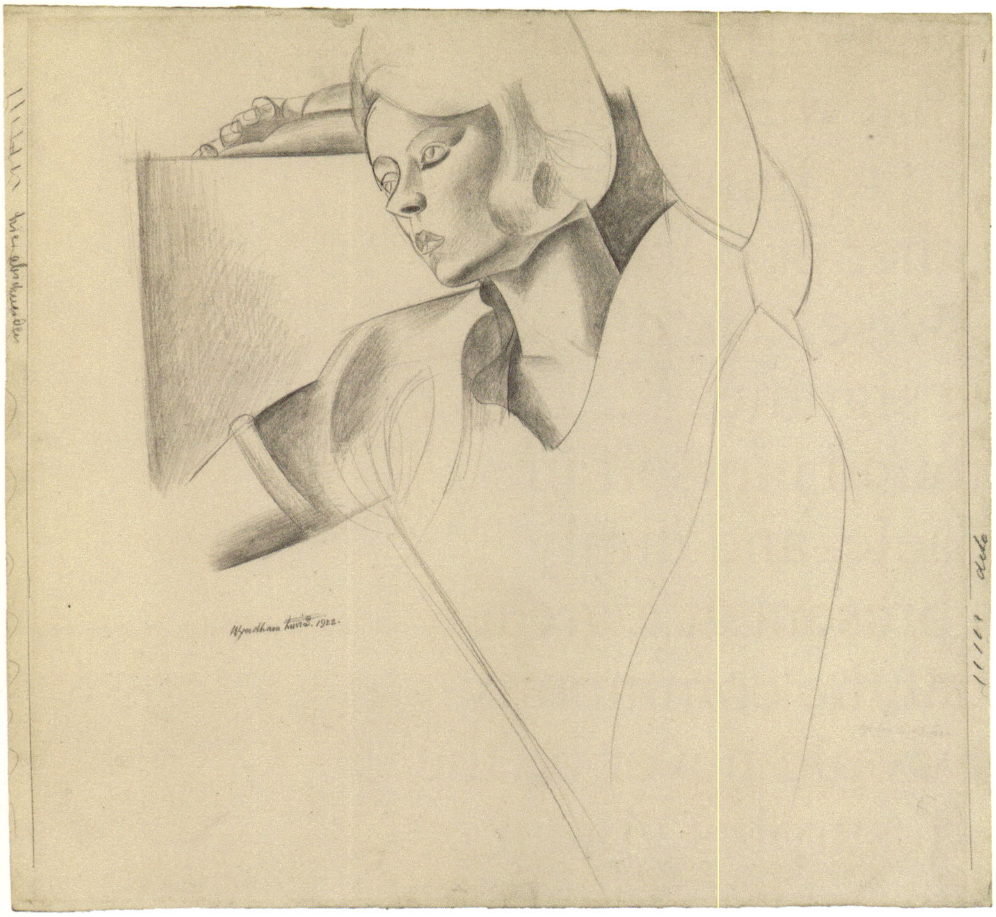

Cat. 101.
***Head of a Girl (Gladys Anne Hoskyns)*, 1922. Pencil on paper. 39.7 x 41.9 cm. Lent by The Metropolitan Museum of Art, Bequest of Scofield Thayer, 1982 (1984.433.248). M 535**

In 1922, Lewis began to produce portrait drawings that, while dependent on the virtuoso linear skills he developed in 1919–20, show a delicacy unprecedented in his work. Line remains important, but volumes are implied through shaded areas and many of the outlines are unclosed. This may indicate a new sympathy with the sitter (as in this case, where the sitter is his future wife, Gladys Anne Hoskyns), but it also signals an enhanced concern with metaphysics. The mystery of the emergence of identity from matter is hinted at, as Lewis produces a new version of his old concern with the figure–ground relationship.

Cat. 102.
***Girl Seated (Gladys Anne Hoskyns)*, 1922. Pencil on paper. 45 x 31 cm. Private collection.**

This is an astonishingly delicate drawing of (it is assumed) Gladys Hoskyns. Lewis complained in *The Caliph's Design* (B&M Cat. 7) about Pablo Picasso's revival of Jean Ingres, but clearly follows his example here and in such works as *Mrs Workman* (Cat. 103). By using a comparatively hard pencil, Lewis is able to achieve a lighter touch than Ingres used in his portrait drawings.

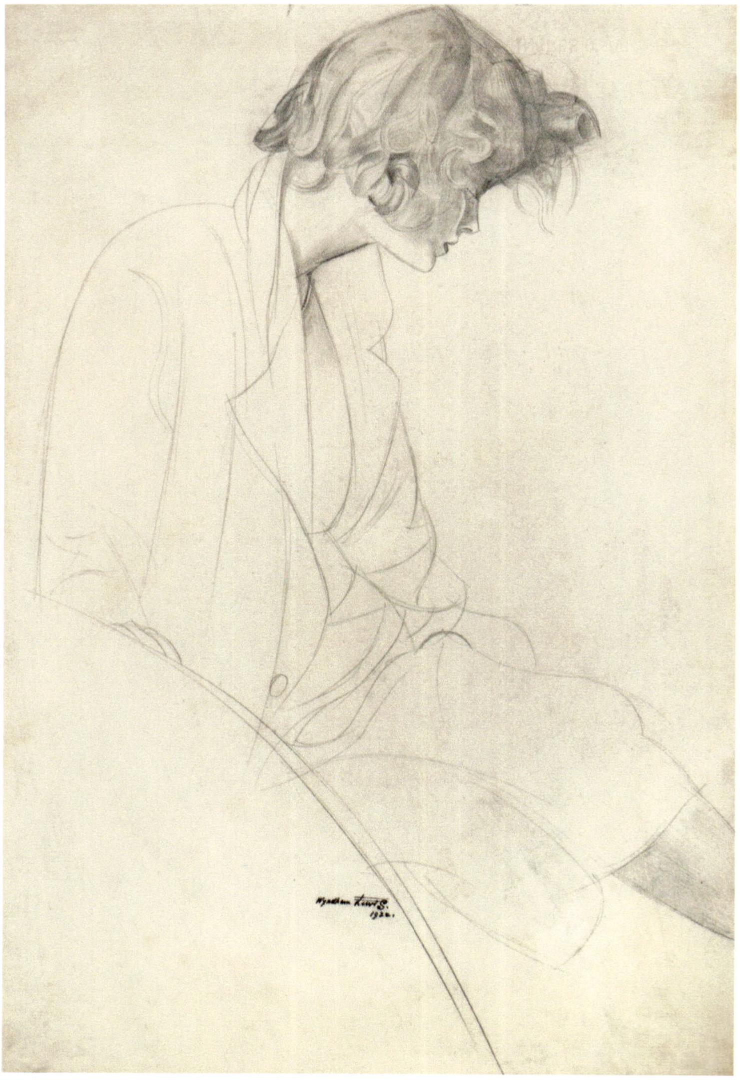

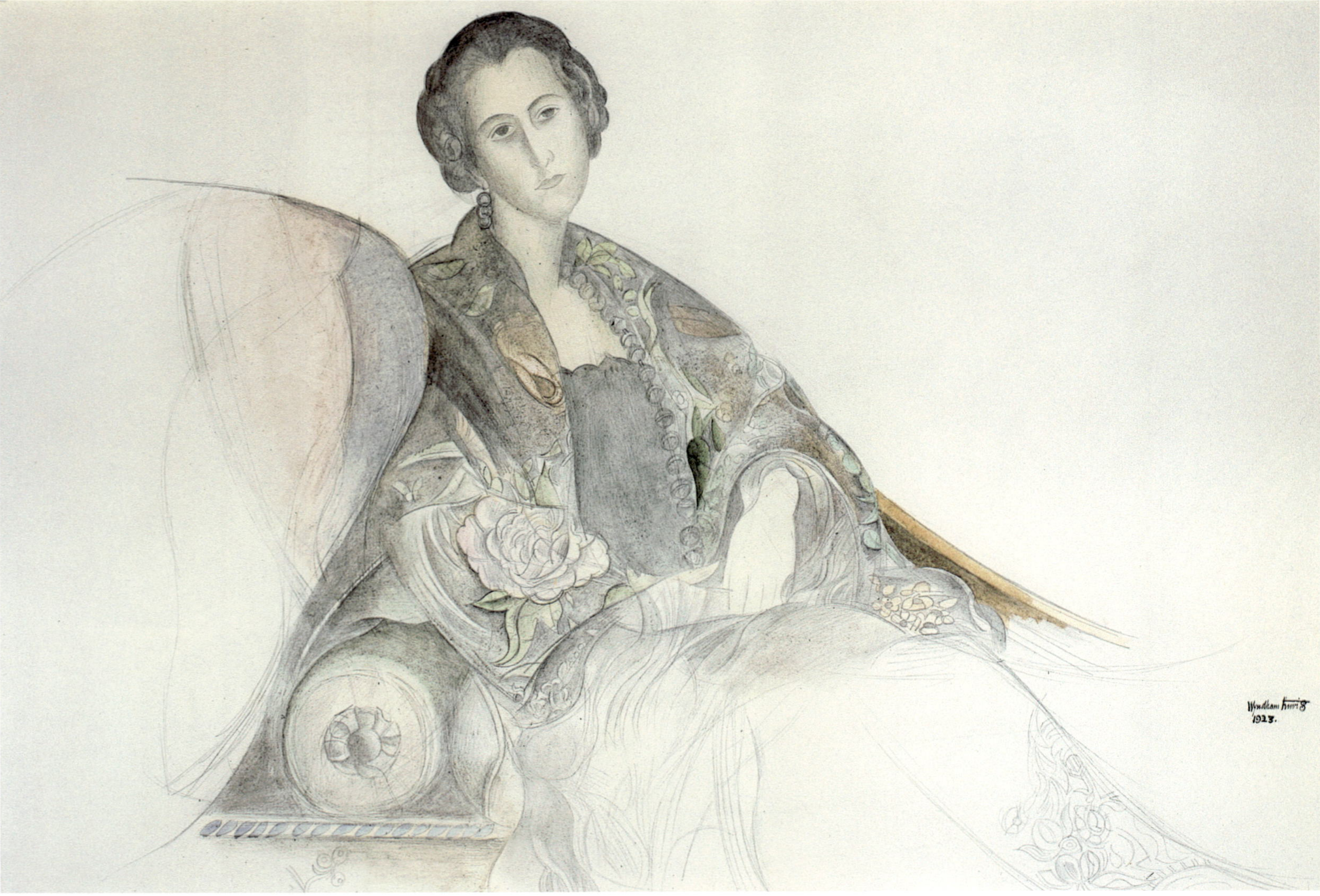

Cat. 103.
***Mrs Workman*, 1923. Pencil and wash on paper. 34.5 x 49 cm. Private collection. M 599**

The sitter, Elizabeth Russe Workman, was a collector of French art, whose collection was later sold after her industrialist husband lost his fortune. The subtle homage to Jean Ingres that the drawing performs may have been partly in recognition of Mrs Workman's taste in art (though she seems mainly to have collected twentieth-century works). The triangular format of the image and its "unfinished" areas that are left blank or minimally delineated are the main features that give the drawing its (for Lewis) necessary artifice. Line follows nature closely (instead of imposing Lewisian whiplash arcs) and washes are delicately applied in order to increase naturalism rather than to counteract it, as in some of Lewis's earlier drawings, such as *Gossips* (Cat. 61).

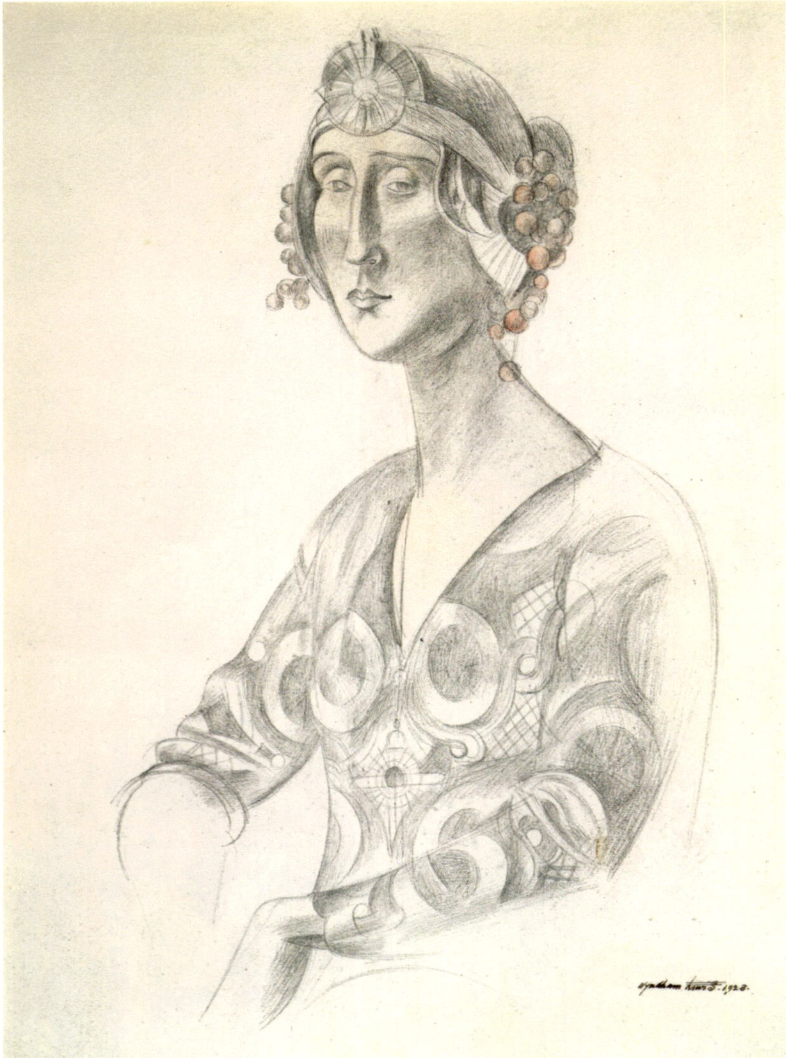

Cat. 104.

[Not in exhibition] *Edith Sitwell*, 1923. Pencil and wash on paper. 40 x 28.9 cm. National Portrait Gallery, London (NPG 4465). M 592

Edith Sitwell was a member of an aristocratic family, and an avant-garde poet whose poems were set to music by the composer William Walton in the suite called *Façade* (1923). Lewis was closely associated with the family, primarily for the patronage that he hoped would flow from the connection. The family did in fact buy several of his paintings and commissioned an oil portrait (Cat. 105). Lewis drew Edith several times and she stated that she sat for him every week for 10 months. The present drawing is in the delicate style of the portrait drawings produced from 1922 onwards. The Sitwell family soon began to seem to him to epitomise the wealthy amateur pseudo-artists who, instead of being pure patrons, compete with professionals and squeeze them out. By 1924, Lewis had already drafted the chapter of *The Apes of God* (B&M Cat. 21) in which the Sitwells are satirised (completed and published in 1930). In the finished chapter, a character mocks Edith's pretensions (she is fictionalised as "Harriet"): "There is a celebrated painting of Battista Sforza Duchess of Urbino. Tonight she is got up to look like the portrait." The drawing suggests that the idea of her mocked here is one that, as an artist, Lewis was prepared to entertain.

Cat. 105.

Edith Sitwell, 1923–35. Oil on canvas. 86.4 x 111.8 cm. Tate: Presented by Sir Edward Beddington-Behrens 1943 (N05437). M P36

The painting was still unfinished when Lewis had to abandon his studio in October 1923, unable to pay the rent. He resumed work on the painting in 1935. As in *Seated Figure* (Cat. 95), the hands are suppressed; this makes the very carefully painted head the focus of all our response to the image as a "human" presence. The portrait is delicately balanced on the edge of satire: the globe and books indicate learning, as in a traditional portrait, but the figure itself could almost be a studio prop, laden with fussily intricate clothing, jewelled cross and multicoloured scarf to disguise the absence of a real body beneath them. The articulation of the neck adds to the suspicion that this is "really" a puppet. The head is mask-like, but the half-closed eyes hint at the inward withdrawal of a sensitive woman from the clutter of the external world to a private world of the imagination.

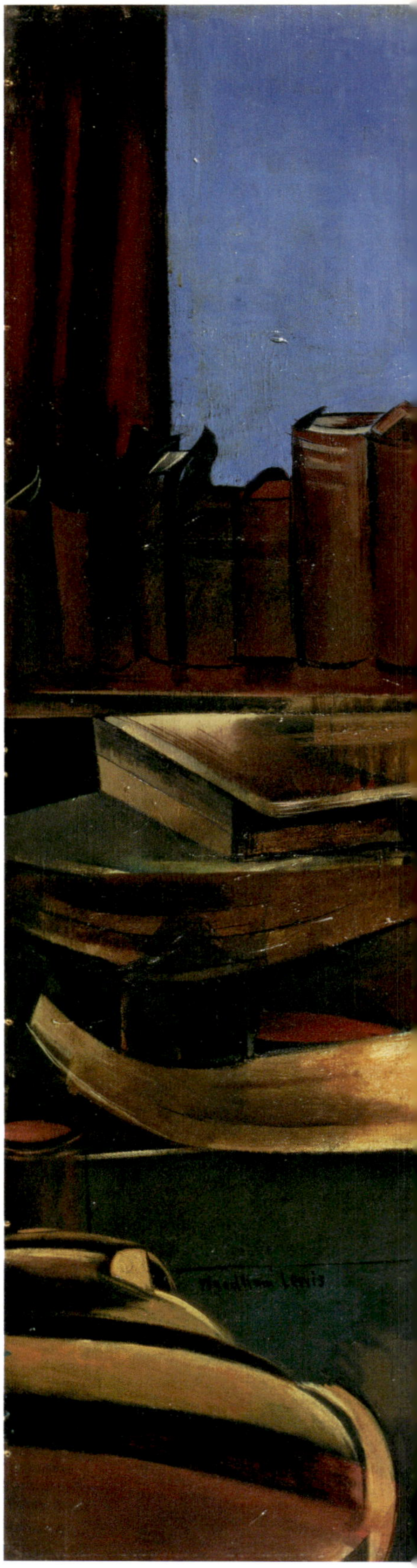

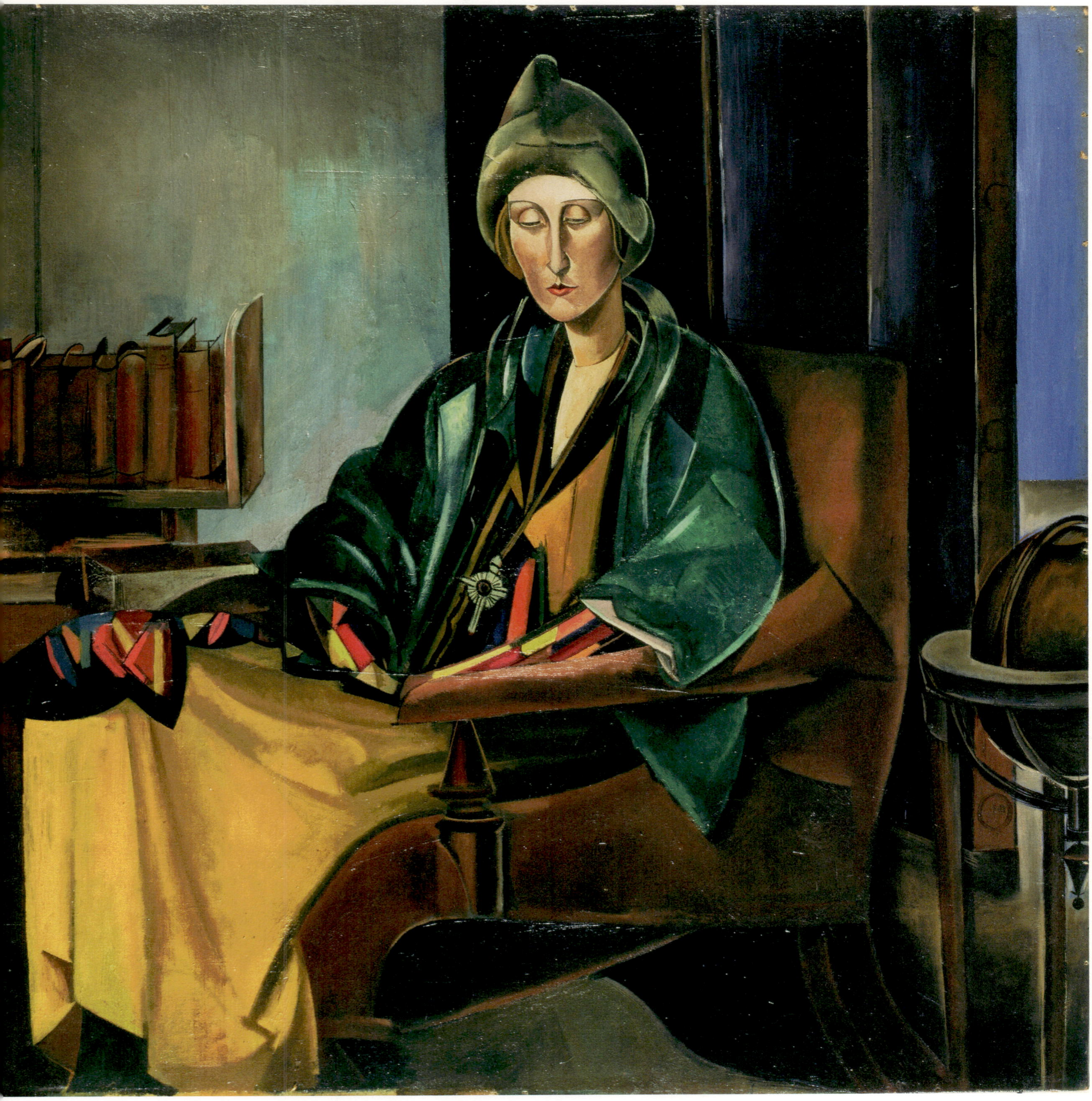

Cat. 106.
The King and Queen in Bed, 1920. Pen and ink, and wash on paper. 32.5 x 37 cm. Wyndham Lewis Memorial Trust. G. and V. Lane Collection (LD.2009.XX.2). M 399

There is a continuity between Lewis's abstractions and his figurative work of the 1920s. It comes from his recognition of the "linguistic" nature of art; just like an utterance in language, it deploys signs that refer to something (real or imagined) not itself, and to convey a meaning. Just as in an artwork constructed from language, the dimension of "form" (the way that the signs are put together and their "material" affective dimension) is also important and exists in a relationship with its communicative function. The present work is partly about such a relationship. In this case, the synthetic creation of the image's reality out of marks on paper is insisted on: it is "unfinished"; the pillow is constructed from the "Cubist" forms found everywhere in Lewis's more naturalistic work from the period; the "King and Queen" are a composite Cubist chess piece; and the bedpost is adorned with a playing card diamond. Art, the image hints, is a conventional "game" like chess and cards. Lewis would explore this idea in his 1922 "Essay on the Objective of Plastic Art in our Time."[1]

1. Wyndham Lewis, "Essay on the Objective of Plastic Art in our Time" (1922). Rprt. *Wyndham Lewis on Art: Collected Writings 1913–1956.* Eds. Walter Michel and C.J. Fox (London: Thames and Hudson, 1969).

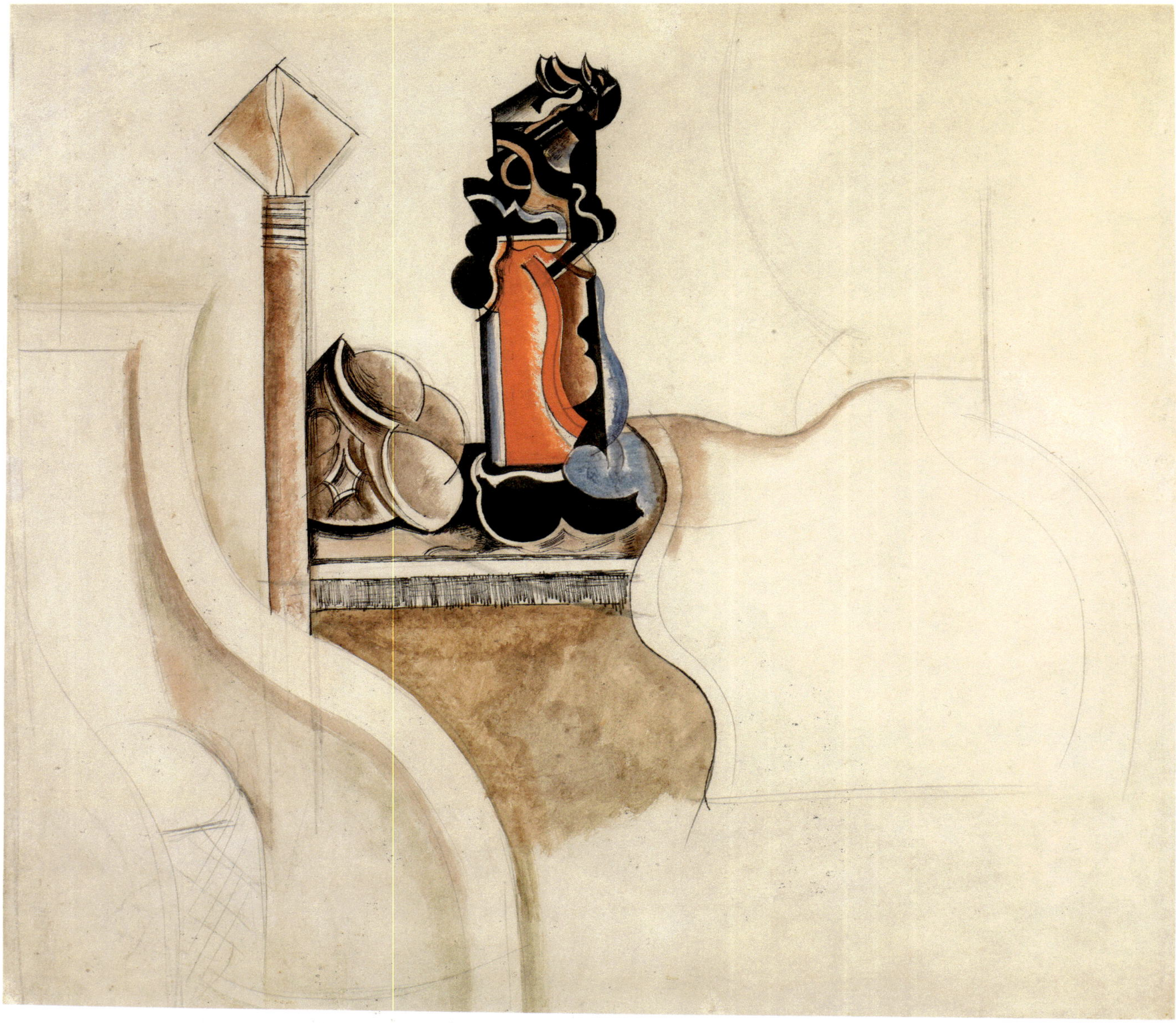

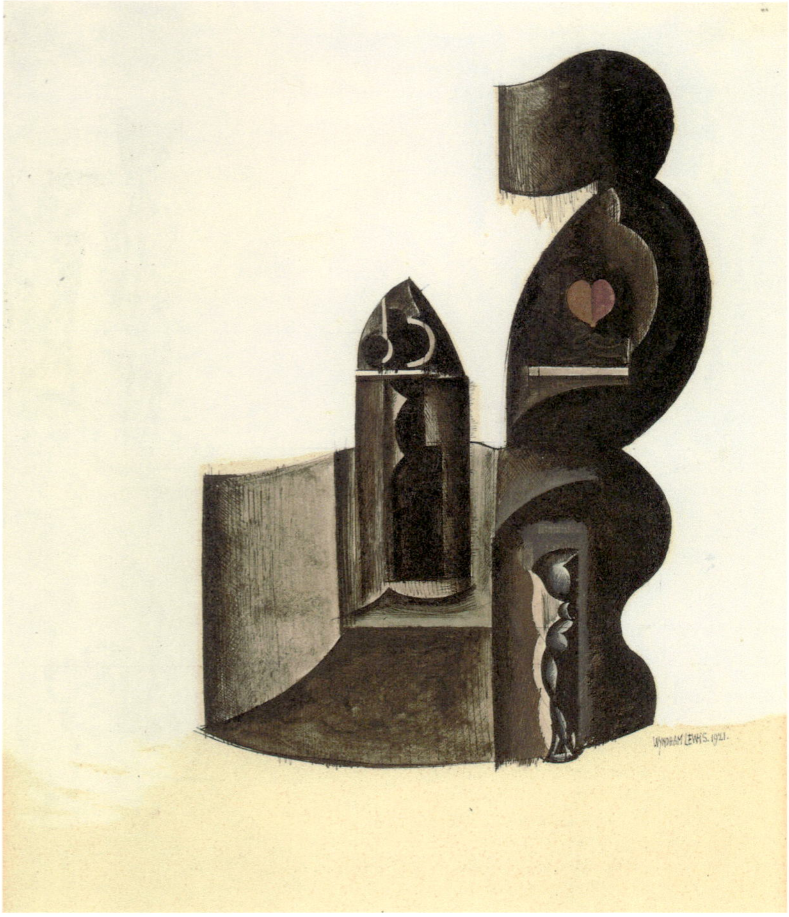

Cat. 107. ▶
Sensibility (Contemplator or Abstract), **1921. Pen and ink, and wash on paper. 31 x 26 cm. Private collection. M 483.**

Cat. 108. ▼
[Not in exhibition] ***Untitled***, **1921. Watercolour and bodycolour on paper. 38 x 28 cm. Private collection**

Lewis does not need to be concerned with abstraction versus representation, since in his understanding of the visual arts these are not "opposites" but points on a spectrum. The presence of "figures" in these works, partly integrated into (or simply particular locations of more concentrated and significant activity in) a larger abstract matrix, suggests a "narrative" dimension that is deliberately withheld, prompting the viewer to speculation that may reflect on life itself. The embedded heart, as well as conventionally signifying love, recalls the use of the playing card diamond in *The King and Queen in Bed* (Cat. 106). It reappears in ΑΘΑΝΑΤΟΝ ΑΡΑ Ή ΨΥΧΗ (Cat. 127).

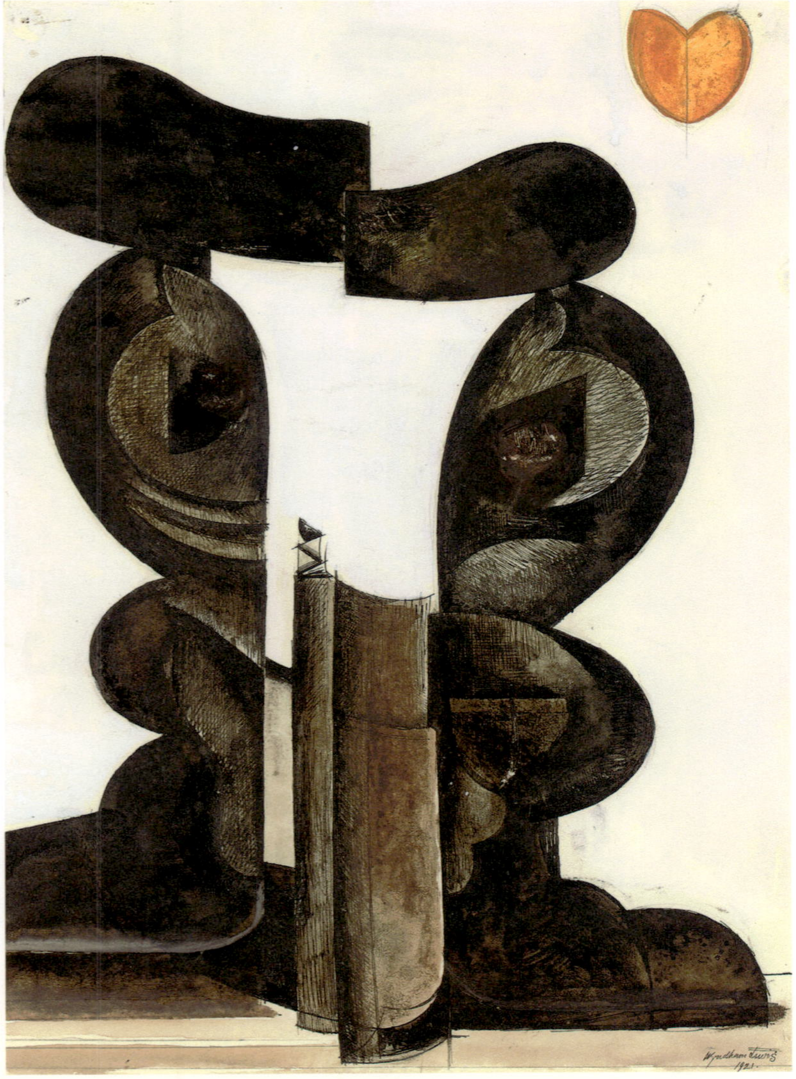

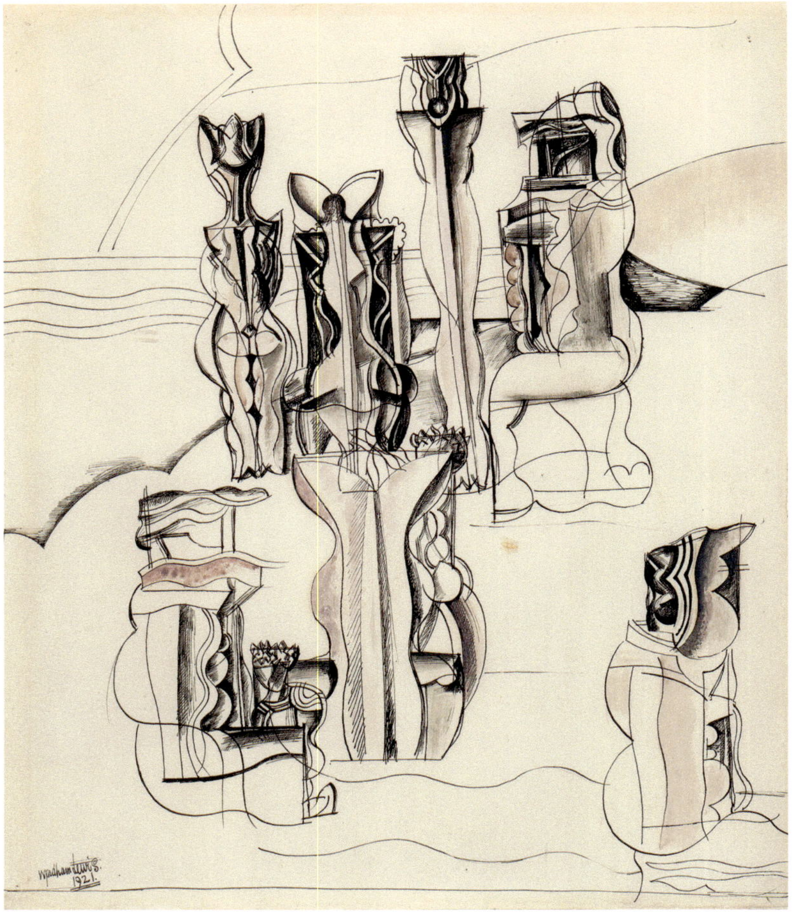

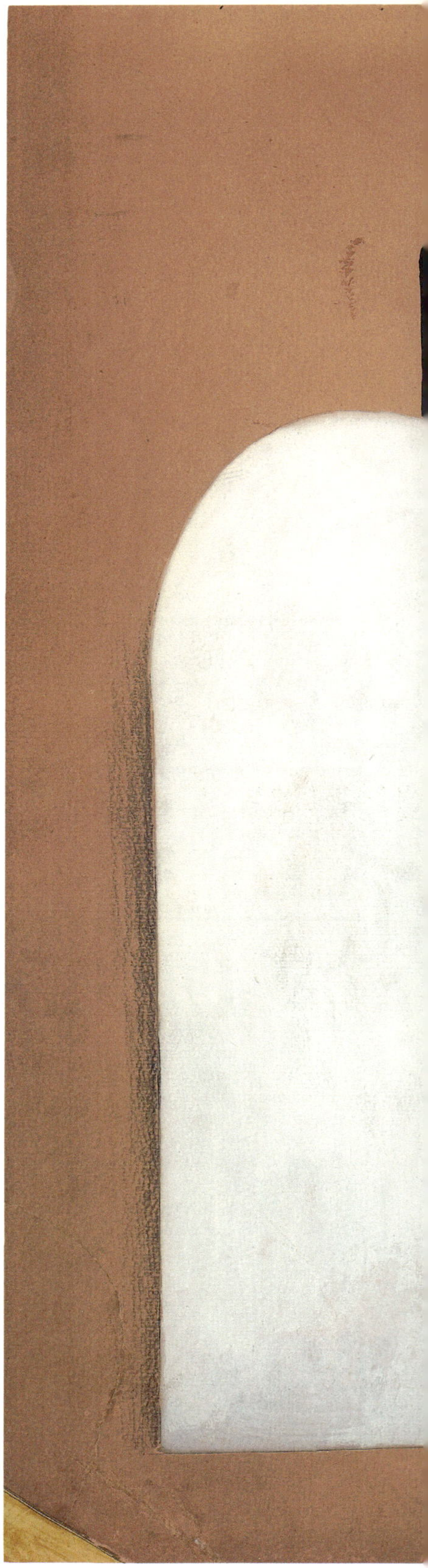

Cat. 109.
Abstract Figure Study, 1921.
Pen and ink, and wash on paper. 37 x 31 cm. Courtesy of Austin/Desmond Fine Art. Private collection. M 445

In 1956, in the catalogue to the Tate Gallery exhibition, *Wyndham Lewis and Vorticism*, Lewis wrote, "I had at all times the desire to project a race of visually logical beings,"[1] and this desire is behind this and a number of Lewis's other drawings from 1921. The organic shapes of the body are turned into a visual vocabulary that Lewis deploys to synthesise quasi-human figures in situations that reflect life on this planet but do not quite confirm to it. The scene here recalls that of *The Cliffs* (Cat. 91), though the figures are more hieratic and static, as if frozen in an unknown ritual. The figure at the top right kneels on one knee; the two figures at bottom left and bottom centre both carry babies. Lewis's last watercolour, *Red Figures Carrying Babies and Visiting Graves* (Cat. 205), returns, more tragically, to such static rituals.

1. Wyndham Lewis, "Introduction," *Wyndham Lewis and Vorticism* [exh. cat. Tate Gallery, London]. London: Tate Gallery, 1956, p. 4.

Cat. 110.
Abstract Composition, 1921.
Pen, collage and watercolour on paper. 61 x 78.8 cm. Collection of Bobbie and Mike Wilsey. M 441

The use of collage is unusual in Lewis's work, though the Oxford English Dictionary attributes to him the first use of the word in its artistic sense in the English language. Here the card "background" is an integral part of the image, as the pencil shading to the left of the white shape indicates. Two small lines forming triangles at the bottom left and right suggest that the background is itself only an opening into another, larger space. By overlapping the major areas of the painted portion of the image, Lewis introduces further spatial complexity: the deconstructed Cubist totem on the right is distanced from the green vase-like form by the pale blue plane that curves around it. To the left, a figure constructed from different forms may be the source of the vertical planes to the left, or may be located in front of them. No other painter in England at this time was producing abstractions as "advanced" as this and there are few parallels in European art. Yet the work is confident and achieved, not a tentative "experimental" imitation. That it has meaning and is not simply an essay in style is also clear – though the meaning remains deliberately beyond rational comprehension. In his "Essay on the Objective of Plastic Art in our Time" (*The Tyro*, No. 2 (B&M Cat. 9)), Lewis envisages the disintegration of philosophy as a mode of thought: "The artist gets a good share, it is certain, of the booty attending this demise."[1]

1. Wyndham Lewis, "Essay on the Objective of Plastic Art in our Time" (1922). Rprt. *Wyndham Lewis on Art: Collected Writings 1913–1956*. Eds. Walter Michel and C.J. Fox (London: Thames and Hudson, 1969), p. 202.

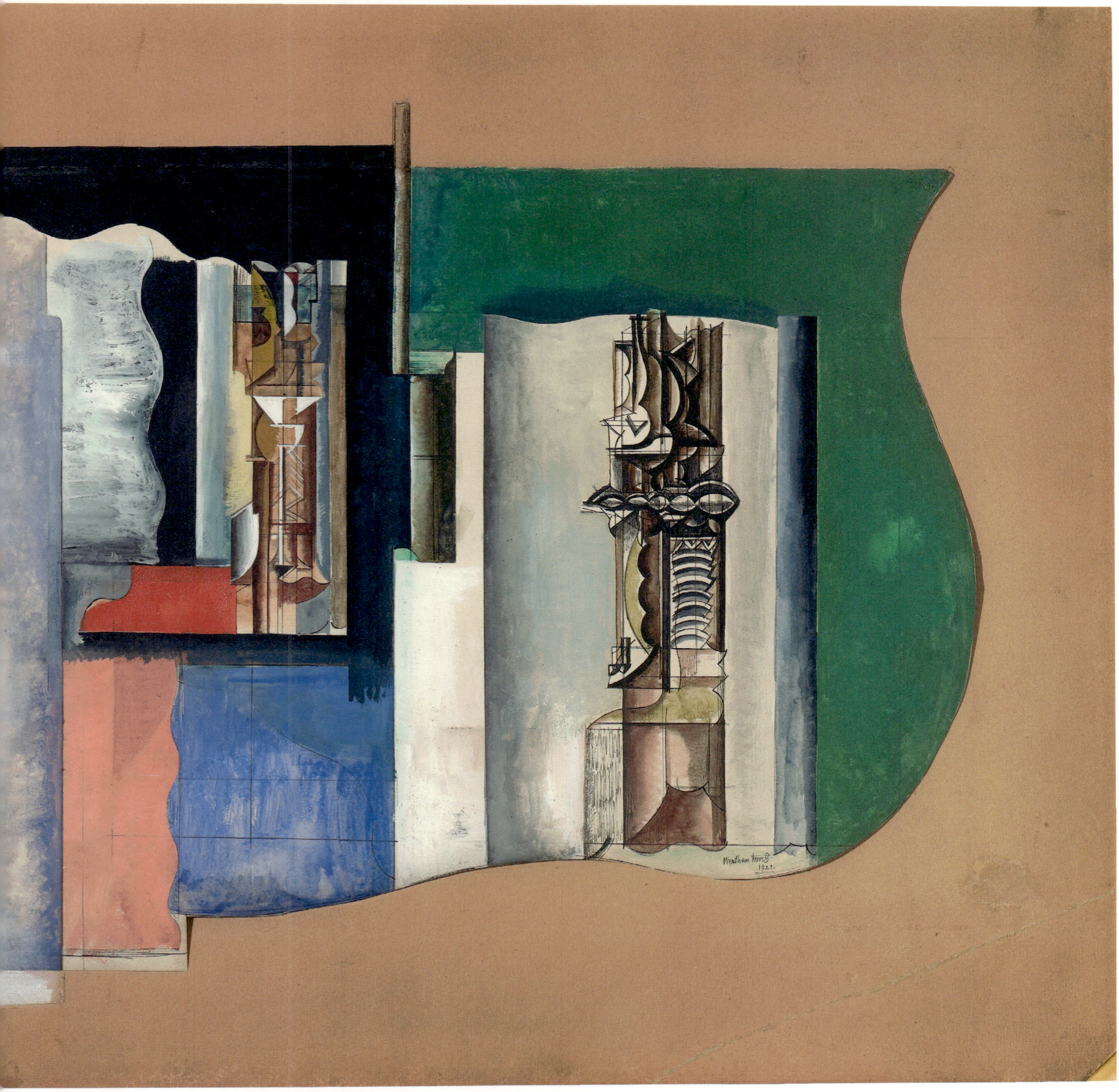

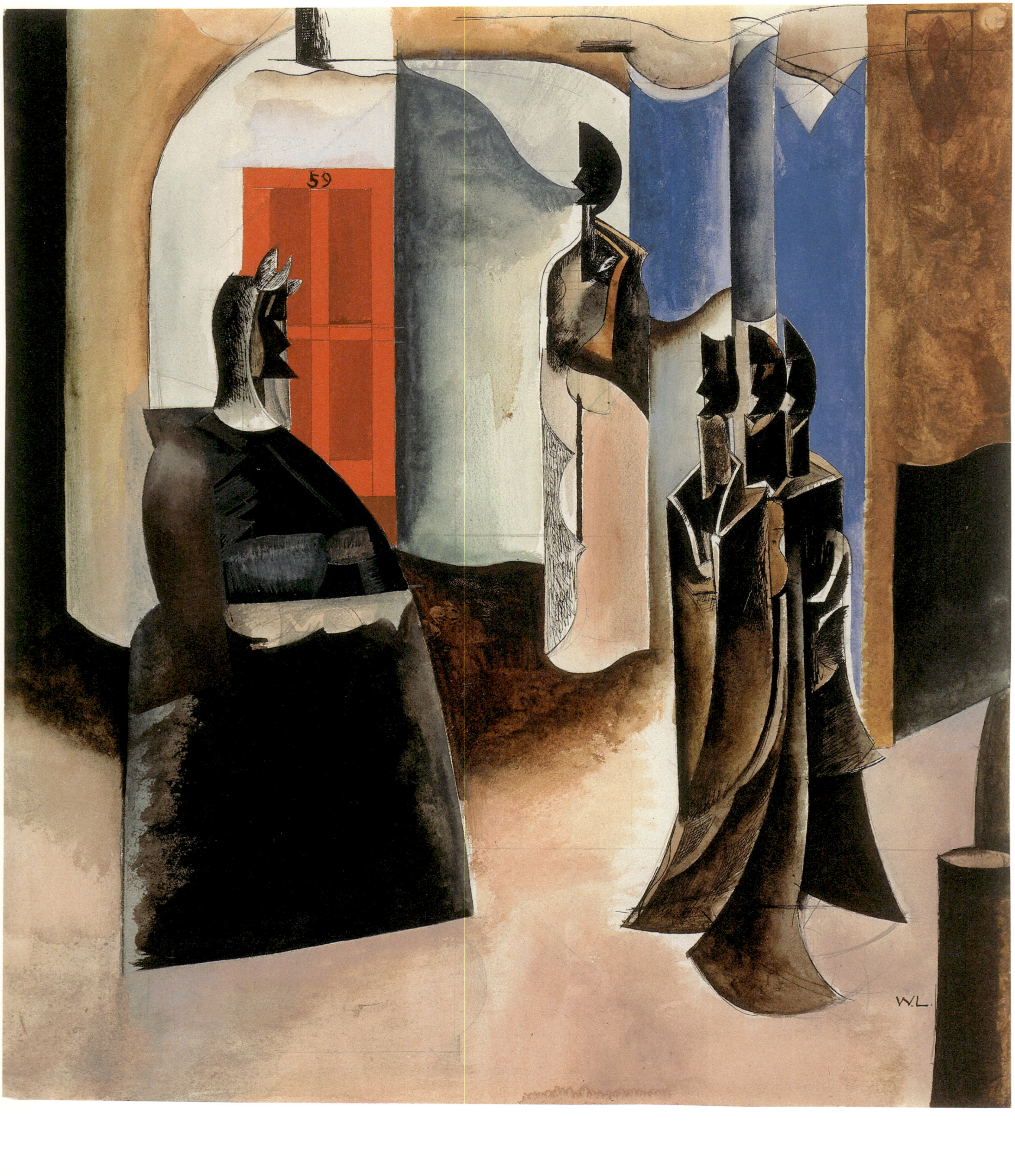
59
W.L.

Cat. 111.
Room No. 59, 1921–22.
Pencil, ink, watercolour and gouache on paper.
35 x 31 cm. Collection of BNY Mellon. M 505

Lewis wrote only rarely in detail about any of his visual works themselves, since he believed that it was best not to mix the practice of his two forms of expression. At some point (date unknown), however, he evidently decided to produce a group of short commentaries on some of them, perhaps to accompany reproductions in a book. *Room No. 59*, which was reproduced in 1922 in the second issue of *The Tyro* (B&M Cat. 9), was one of them. The passage indicates what kind of engagement Lewis expects from a viewer of his work of this type.

Whatever interpretation is placed on this picture, seen as an illustration, plastically it is completely satisfying. Masked figures twirl like waterspouts to the right of a broad bay flanked by the severe cliffs of a serpentine corridor. In the foreground an astonished trinity of fugitives is fixed by the ginfed eye of a kommissar-concierge. This dark rampart of falstaffian beef assuages the blue of the yawning hollow opposite. But it stands solid as a basalt colossus, and from behind its back a buttress rears dizzily, with the motion of a topheavy rocket, to stabilise the ramshackle roof through which light leaks as in a dream.

The figures are cut out of thick sheet iron, bent into graceful folds. The hindmost one is a steep pillar. Embedded in its skirt is the contour of a severed doublebass. The theme enunciated by this subtle arabesque sets up a static threedimensional fugue. The eye, racing round this nightmare interior, grows exhilarated, and returns to ride these muscular shapes like mettlesome steeds.[1]

1. Wyndham Lewis, "Specimen Marginalia," *Wyndham Lewis Annual* 3 (1996), p. 2.

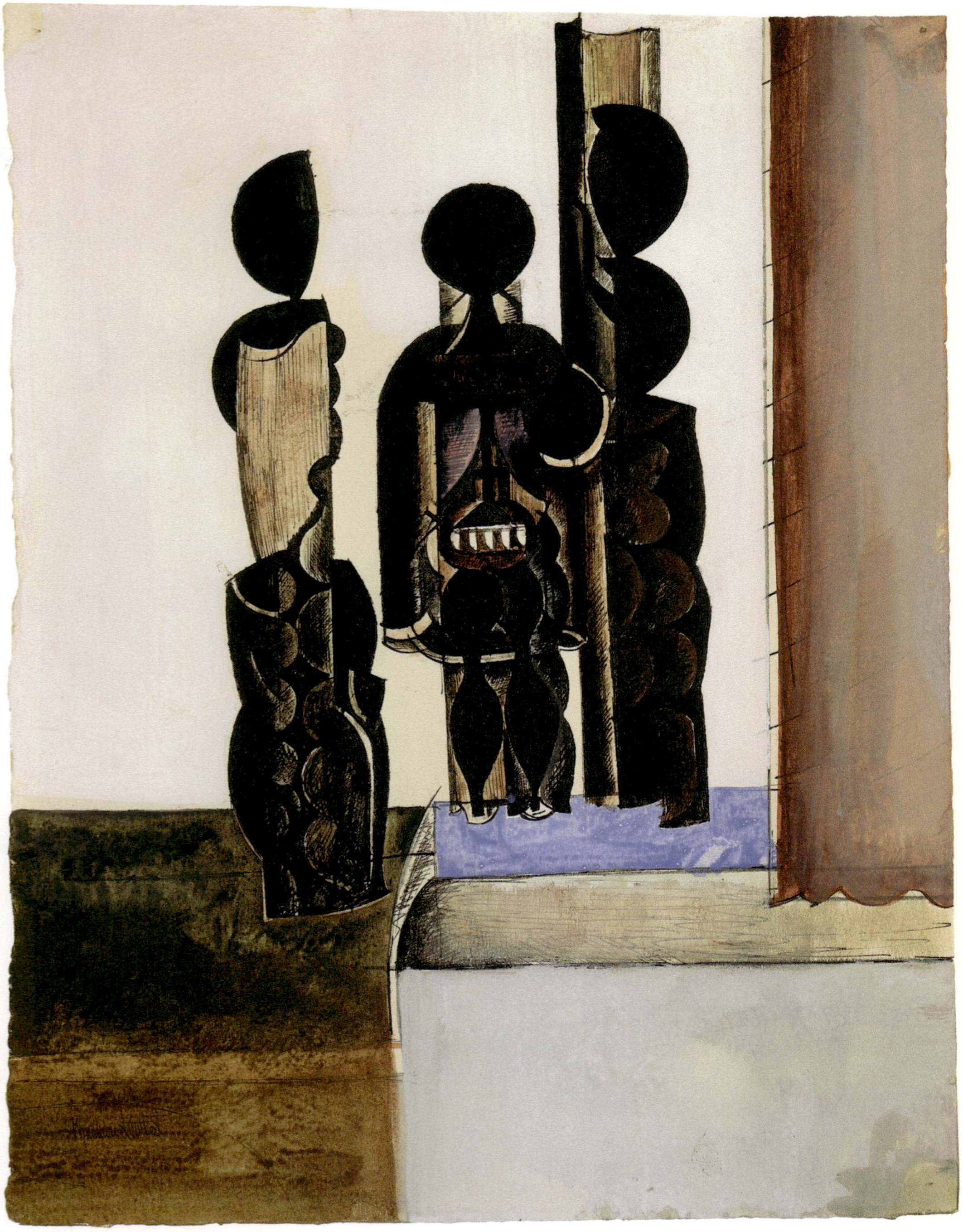

Cat. 112.
Women, 1921–22. **Pencil, ink, ink (wash) and gouache on paper. 27.5 x 21.3 cm. Wyndham Lewis Memorial Trust. G. and V. Lane Collection (LD.2004.XX.41). M 518**

This is another work that was reproduced in *The Tyro*, No. 2 (B&M Cat. 9). The figures show some kinship with those in *Room No. 59* (Cat. 111) and are situated in a space that hovers ambiguously between two and three dimensions. The title anchors the picture to a known social world in which groups of women (as in *Gossips* (Cat. 61)) exchange news. Lewis writes in "Essay on the Objective of Plastic Art in our Time" (in the same issue of *The Tyro*) that the function of the artist is to "show you the world, only a realer one than you would see, unaided […] What the artist's public also has to be brought to do is to see its world, and the people in it, as a *stranger* would." Two main methods have been devised for this, he continues, one "subjective," in which a subjectively-tinged naturalism affects the spectator's own perception of reality, the other being "to display a *strange* world to the spectator, and yet one that has so many analogies to his that, as he looks […] he sees his own reality through this veil, as it were, momentarily in truer colours."[1] But Lewis, though his practice is closer to the second of these methods (the first he finds akin to "religious tyranny" because it usurps the spectator's own freedom of perception), is not altogether happy with either of them, and looks forward to a "third" method ("between subject and object") that he believes some contemporary art presages – including, presumably, his own. He promised to explore this idea in a future instalment of the essay, but it remained unwritten. It may be, however, that the idea of art as a language would provide the concepts by which such a "third method" might be theorised.

1. Wyndham Lewis, "Essay on the Objective of Plastic Art in our Time" (1922). Rprt. *Wyndham Lewis on Art: Collected Writings 1913–1956*. Eds. Walter Michel and C.J. Fox (London: Thames and Hudson, 1969), p. 210.

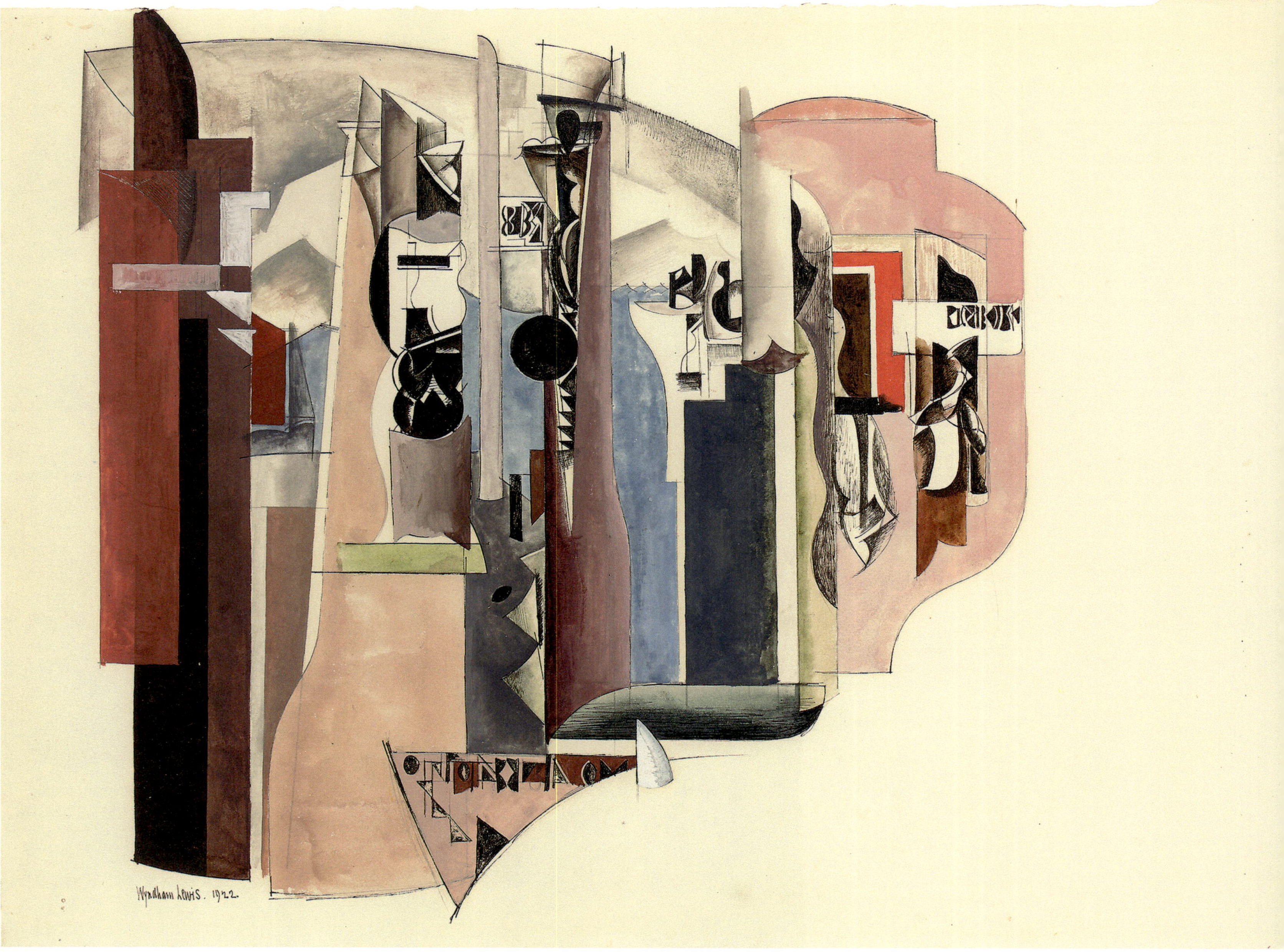

Cat. 113.
Archimedes Reconnoitring the Enemy Fleet, 1922.
Pencil, ink, watercolour and gouache on paper.
33 x 47.5 cm.
Private collection M 519

Archimedes, in a red cloak, stands to the left, absorbed in the thought-world that projects like a truncated Chinese scroll, to the right. The title alludes to the inventions that Archimedes devised in order to keep the besiegers of Syracuse at bay, and the drawing is an analogy for the creative intelligence at work on this task. The idea of the avant-garde artist (an embattled one) is implicit in the subject. The exuberance, precision and intricacy of the invention within the broad sweep of the major planes make this one of Lewis's most beautiful works. More than any other it fulfils his desire to produce a kind of abstraction that would be "musical" (like the "static threedimensional fugue" of *Room No. 59* (Cat. 111)). Small passages of occult "hieroglyphs" support the linguistic interpretation of Lewis's "third method, between subject and object." A deeper interpretation is also invited, however:

In art we are in a sense playing at what we designate as matter. We are entering the forms of the mighty phenomena around us, and seeing how near we can get to being a river or a star, without actually *becoming* that. Or we are placing ourselves somewhere behind the contradictions of matter and mind, where an identity (such as the school of American realists, William James, for example, has fancied) may more primitively exist.[1]

Archimedes Reconnoitring the Enemy Fleet is both a depiction and a product of that process.

1. Wyndham Lewis, "Essay on the Objective of Plastic Art in our Time" (1922). Rprt. *Wyndham Lewis on Art: Collected Writings 1913–1956*. Eds. Walter Michel and C.J. Fox (London: Thames and Hudson, 1969), pp. 204–5.

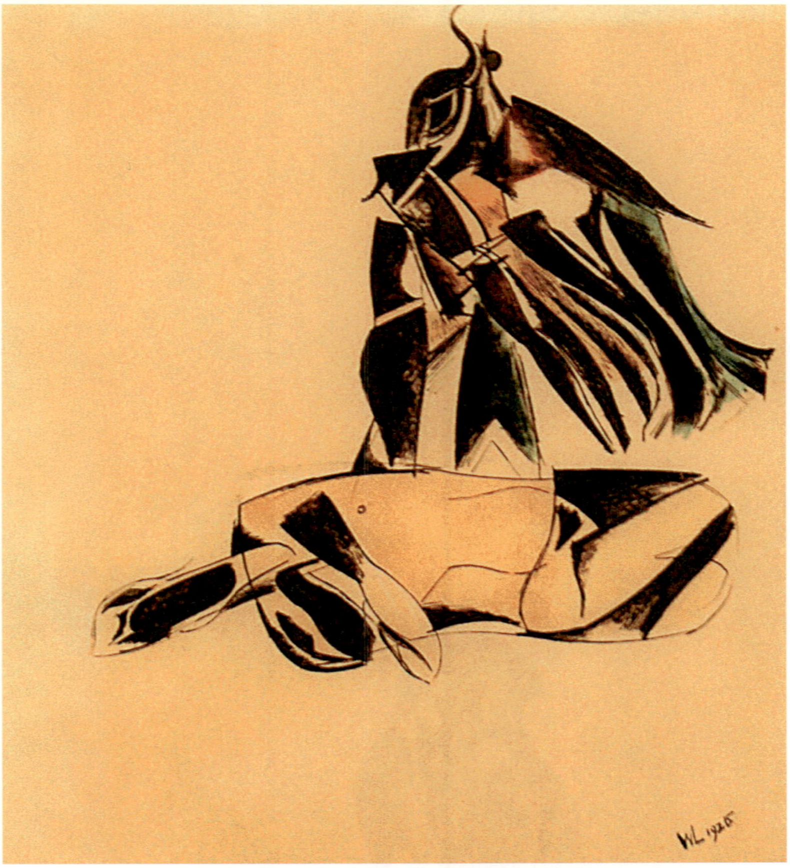

Cat. 114.
***Bird and Figure*, 1925. Pen, ink and watercolour on paper. 23 x 18.5 cm. Rugby School. M 609**

Even while Lewis was devoting most of his time to studying and writing, during the years 1923 to 1930 he still found time for some exercises of his "private" passion for visual invention. This drawing looks forward to works such as *Figures in the Air* (Cat. 125) and *Manhattan* (Cat. 126), in which prone figures may represent a buried hero figure on which civilisation, apparently risen beyond its primitive past, is elevated. In this drawing, the sinister bird forms appear to threaten the horizontal figure, which recoils from them.

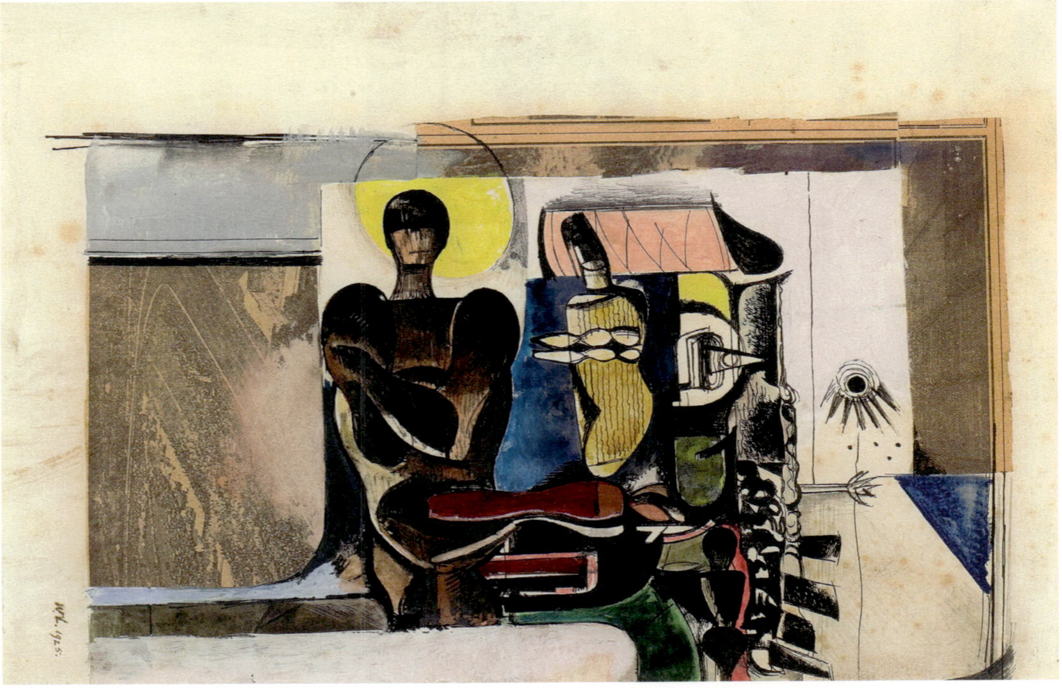

Cat. 115.
***Hero's Dream (Dream of Hamilcar or Dawn in Erewhon)*, 1925. Collage, watercolour, and pen and ink on paper. 26 x 17 cm. Courtesy of Austin/Desmond Fine Art. Private collection. M 614**

Lewis chose a different title for this work when he reproduced it on three separate occasions. It can also be viewed in different orientation, vertically, with the right edge at the top. Like *Bird and Figure* (Cat. 114), the drawing shows the beginning of Lewis's concern with buried hero figures (especially if seen vertically). In Samuel Butler's novel, *Erewhon* (1872), the entrance to the lost world of Erewhon is guarded by giant statues. The intimidating noise they make is revealed to be no more than the wind blowing through their hollows. Cicero reports in *De Divinatione* that Hamilcar Barca (ca. 275–228BC), the father of Hannibal, besieging the city of Syracuse, dreamt that within 24 hours he would be dining in the city, and took this as a good omen. But the Syracusans attacked the Carthaginians and the prophecy proved correct only because Hamilcar Barca was taken prisoner.[1] This drawing is unusual in Lewis's work for its use of a collaged newspaper photograph of an aerial view of a race-track.

1. Cicero, *De Divinatione*, I, 50 (London: Loeb, 1923), p. 280.

Cat. 116. ◀
[Not in exhibition] *The Dancers*, 1925. Pencil and ink on paper. 31 x 18 cm. Victoria and Albert Museum, London (Circ.421-1959). M 610

Cat. 117. ▶
[Not in exhibition] *Dancing Couple*, 1925. Blue ink on paper. 30.5 x 19.5 cm. The Frances Lehman Loeb Art Center, Vassar College, Poughkeepsie, New York. Gift of William K. Rose, 1965.16

In these drawings, restricted visual means are used to produce a familiar subject. The dance here, unlike those depicted in Lewis's 1912 works, has no metaphysical connotations. Lewis was probably attracted to dance and ballet scenes for the artistic discipline they demanded from the human body.

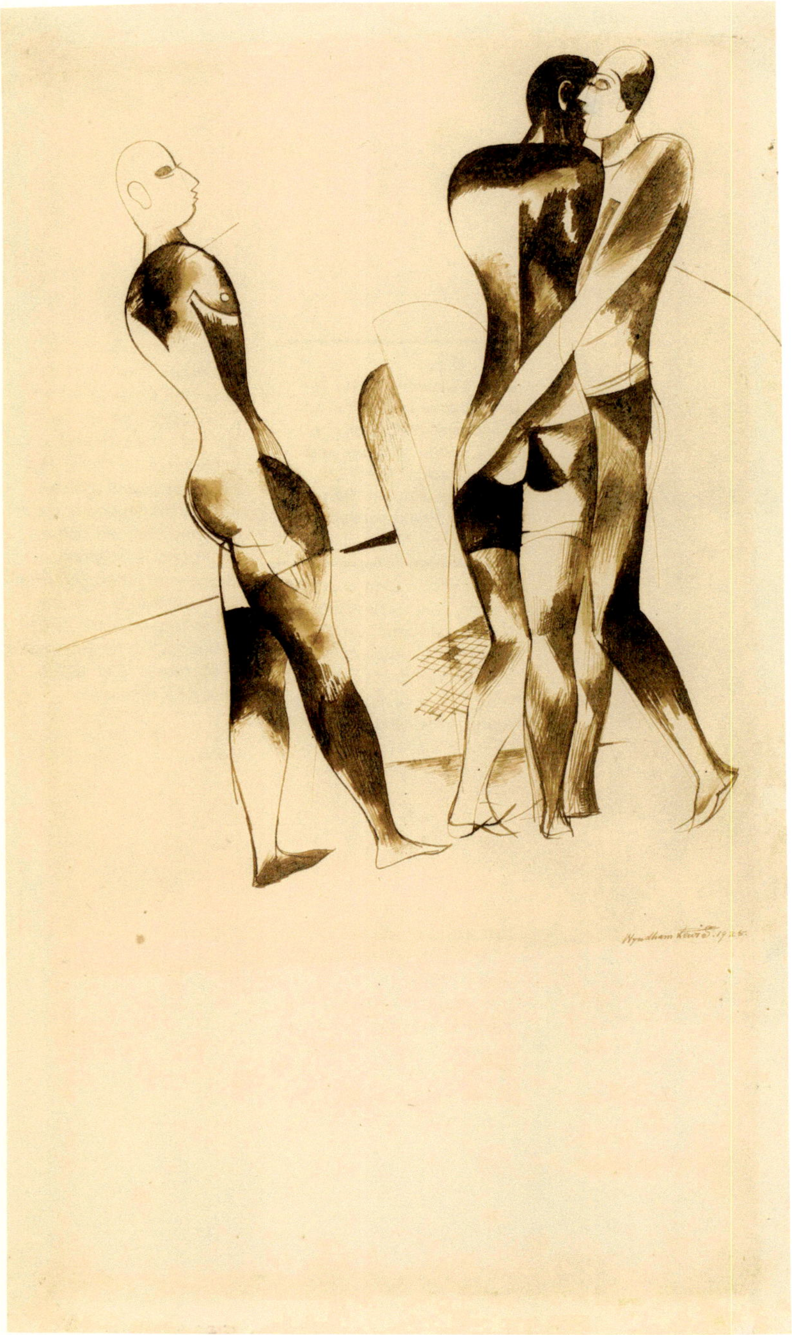

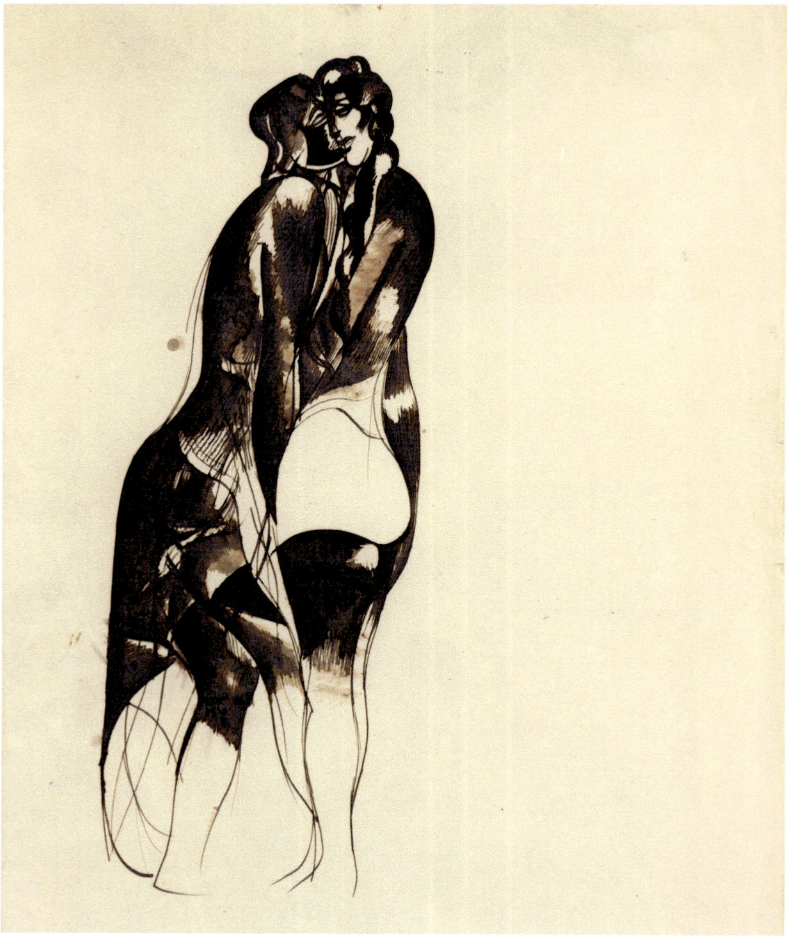

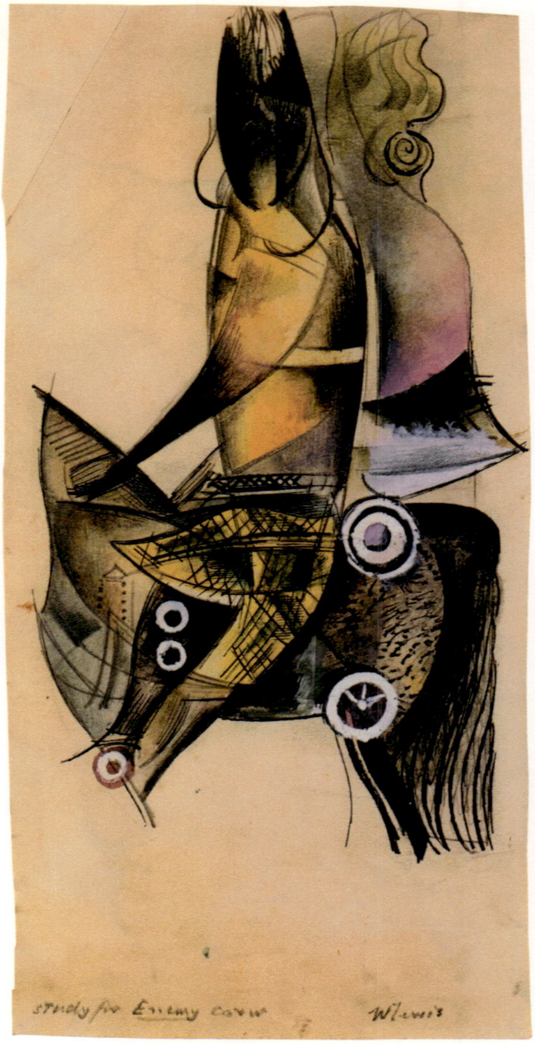

Cat. 118.
***Study for Enemy Cover*, 1926**
Gouache, ink and pencil on paper. 23.7 x 11.9 cm. The Museum of Modern Art, New York, Joseph M. and Dorothy B. Edinburg Fund, 1967 (2637.1967). M 621

The design Lewis finally used for the first issue of his third (and final) magazine, *The Enemy* (1927) (B&M Cat. 14), is a little more naturalistic than this sketch and shows a horse in its entirety, somewhat dwarfed by the warrior rider, who is accoutred with elaborate totemic paraphernalia and wears a mask. The magazine contained polemical attacks on the avant-garde, yet the cover design reveals that the attacker is a masked *persona*. The study also shows a second rider, behind the kilted warrior, an immaterial (apparently female) spirit. Lewis's aggression, the drawing intimates, functions in defence of values that are not themselves aggressive.

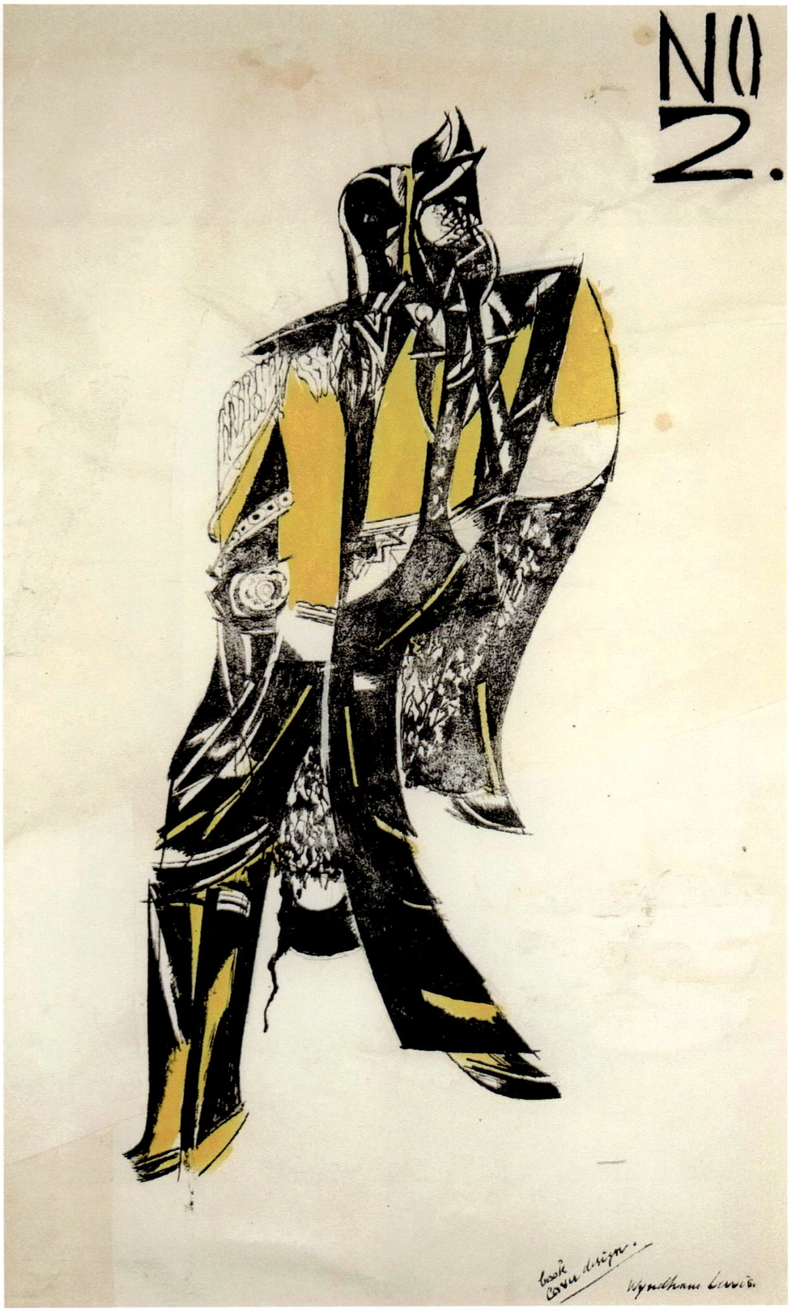

Cat. 119.
[Not in exhibition] *Book Cover Design*, 1927. Pen and ink, gouache, collage on paper. 28 x 15.5 cm. Collection Hugh Anson-Cartwright. M 627

Many of Lewis's publications of the 1920s were decorated on covers or title pages with line-block reproductions of ink designs of this kind. His criticisms of the avant-garde tended to be appreciated more by conservative elements in the culture than by the avant-garde itself (not surprisingly). By including examples of "advanced" art, Lewis may have felt that he could keep his own "revolutionary" commitment visible. This design was one that was tried in proof for *The Enemy*, No. 2 (B&M Cat. 15) and later reproduced in *Wyndham Lewis the Artist: From "Blast" to Burlington House* (B&M Cat. 43).

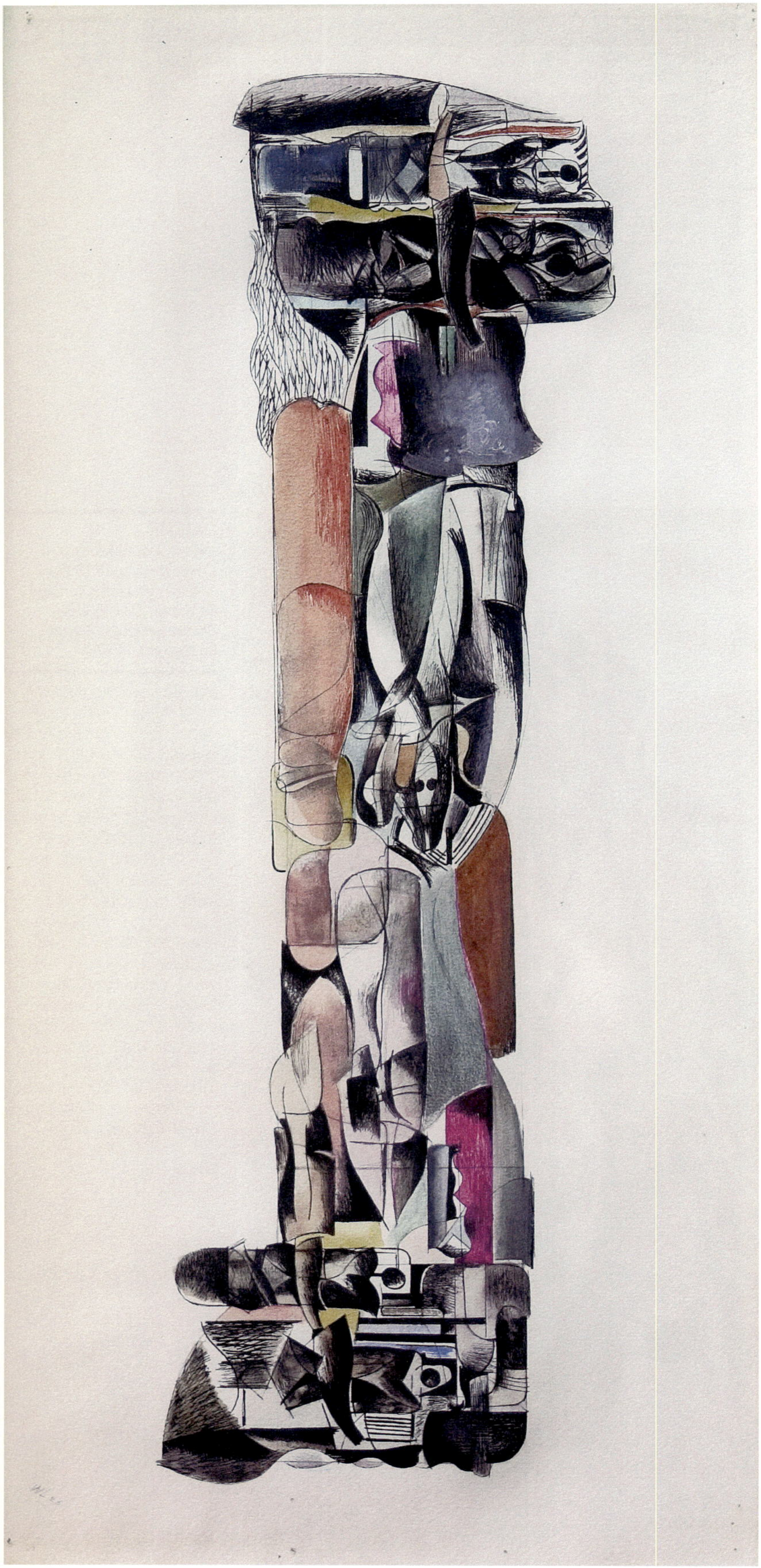

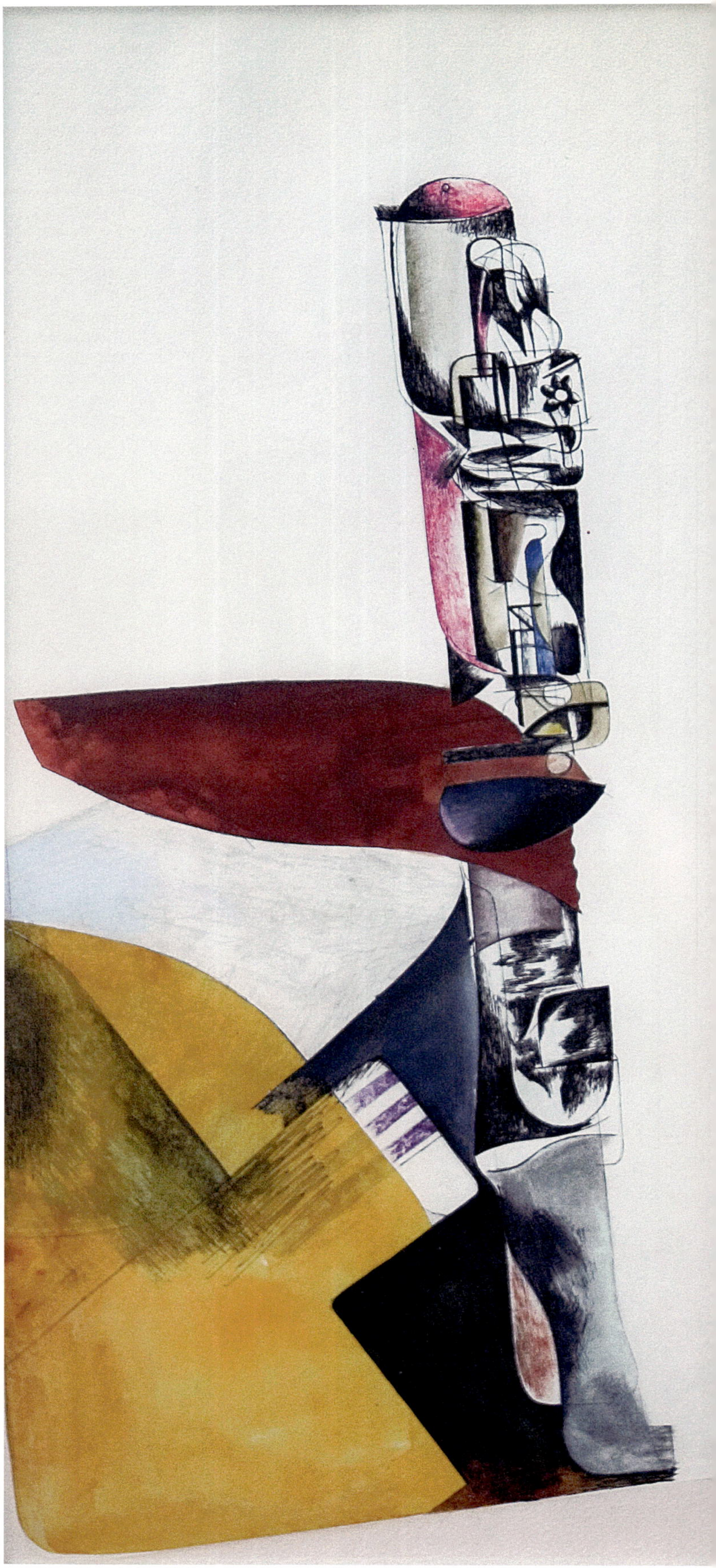

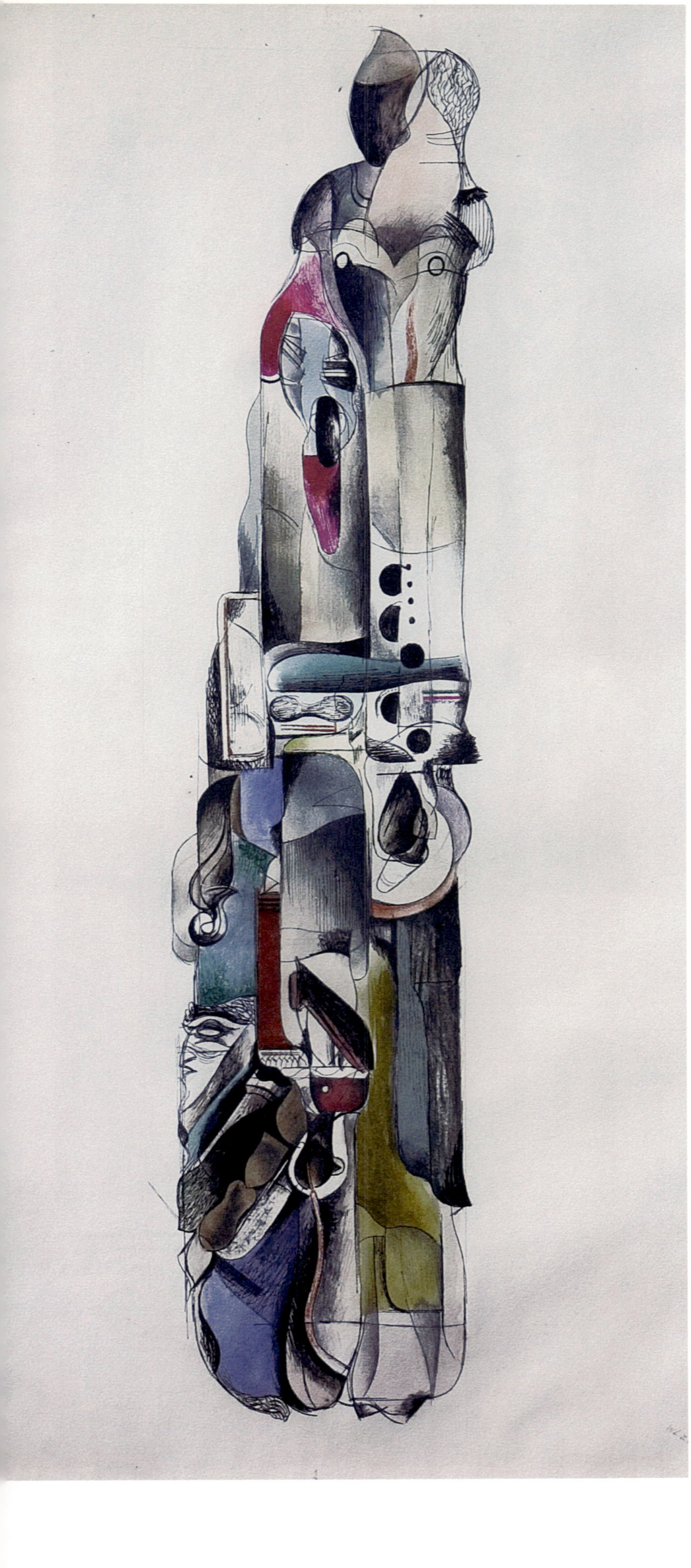

Cat. 120. ◀◀◀
***Abstract Composition*, 1926.**
Pen and ink, watercolour, wash and pencil on paper. 56 x 26.5 cm. Private collection. M 617

Cat. 121. ◀◀
***Abstract Composition*, 1926.**
Pencil and ink, watercolour and wash on paper. 56 x 26.5 cm. Private collection. M 618

Cat. 122. ◀
***Abstract Composition*, 1926.**
Pen and ink, watercolour, wash and pencil on paper. 50 x 24.5 cm. Private collection. M 619

This group of three "totemic" abstractions from 1926 is Lewis's most important visual project of the period. The works were designed with a specific location in mind, that is, in the house of the patron, Olivia Shakespear, who was the mother of Ezra Pound's wife Dorothy and lived in London. The proposal for the pictures came from Lewis himself, and in his letter to Mrs Shakespear he says he will visit her and explain the scheme, for which he had a "definite object" in mind.[1] His explanation is unrecorded. Olivia Shakespear shared some of the occult interests of her friend W.B. Yeats and it is possible that a "key" might be found to these works in various esoteric spiritualist writings. But it is unlikely, given that Lewis preferred the meaning of his visual works to be ambiguous, uncertain and beyond simple "decoding." He believed that art works were to some extent "fetishes," products of personal religious compulsions that paid tribute to a metaphysical reality that lay over the border in another world. In these three works, the hieroglyphic or pictographic elements of *Archimedes Reconnoitring the Enemy Fleet* (Cat. 113) have become more fluid and biomorphic and are allowed to interpenetrate in indefinite spatial dispositions. The scope they offer for visual exploration and speculative interpretation is almost infinite. All three have a human connotation. Cat. 121 appears to be topped with a suggestion of a head, perhaps wearing a schoolboy's pink cap. Cat. 120 has embedded in it, between the two sections at top and bottom that comprise smaller horizontal figures behind phallic shapes, a helmeted warrior figure (with a baby-like pink face). Cat. 122 has a torso and head at the top, accompanied by a spirit "double" that appears to emanate from and partly obscure the torso. The drawings are produced with amazing delicacy and glow with touches of vivid colour. They are unlike anything else in English (or European) modernism.

1. Wyndham Lewis, letter to Olivia Shakespear, 1 June 1925, quoted in *Wyndham Lewis*. Jane Farrington, ed. [exh. cat. Manchester City Art Gallery, Manchester; National Museum of Wales, Cardiff; City Art Centre, Edinburgh]. London: Lund Humphries Publishers, 1980, p. 97.

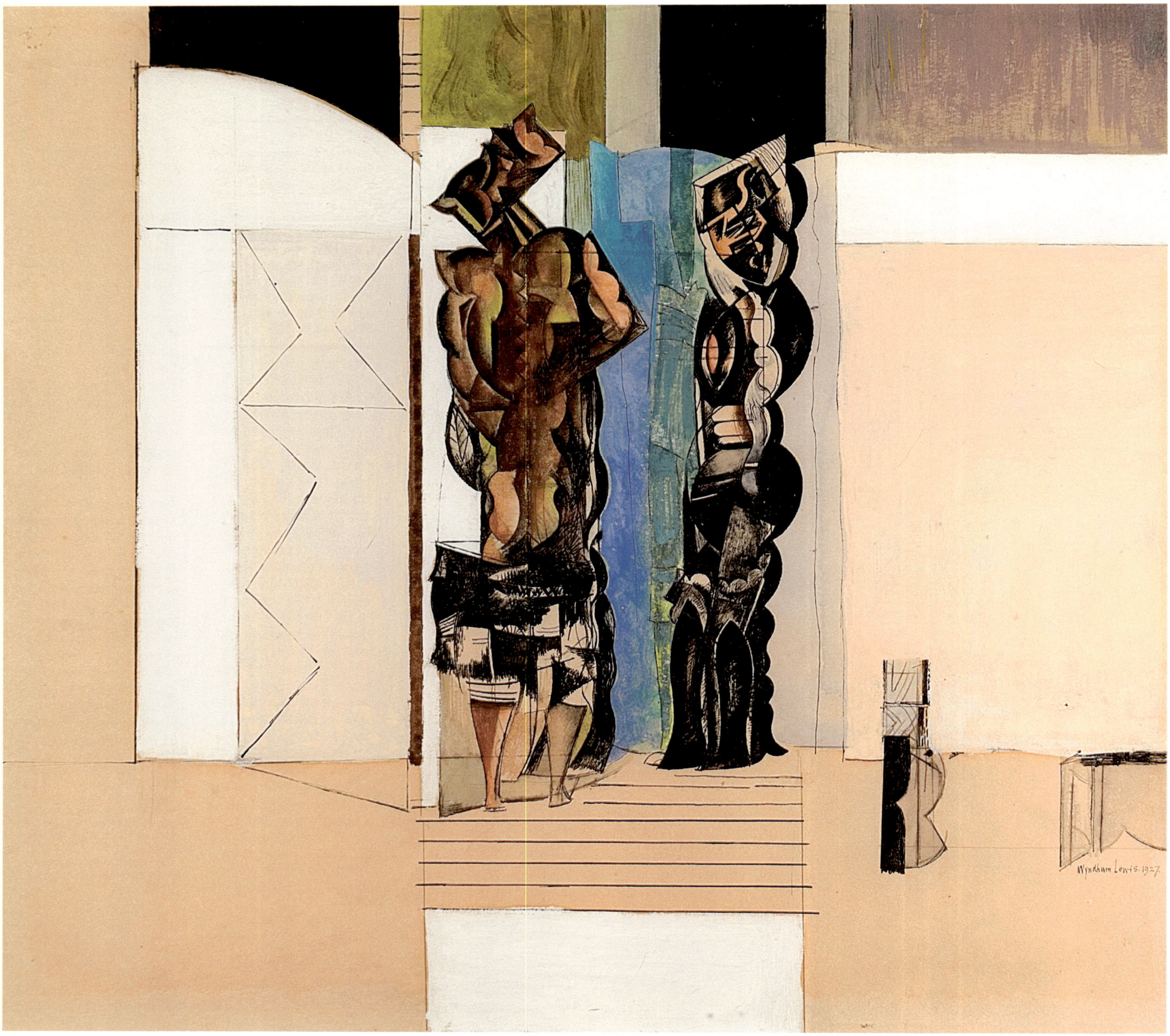

Cat. 123.
Two Figures, 1927. Pen, ink and gouache on paper. 32.5 x 36 cm. Collection Durban Art Gallery. M 644

Like Cats. 110 and 112, this work introduces figures into an indeterminate but apparently two-dimensional abstract environment. It is cool and unusually lyrical, thanks to its colours and balanced composition. All of Lewis's artistic vitality is absorbed by the inventive Cubistic rendition of the two figures (the right-hand, female, one adorned with an African mask).

Cat. 124.
Creation Myth, 1927.
Gouache, drawing and mixed media on paper.
32.7 x 29.8 cm.
Tate: Purchased 1956 (T00107). M 628

In his theoretical and polemical books of the 1920s, we find Lewis opposing as doctrines for life what he regarded as essential for art. Because, on the whole, it was life he was writing about, he appears quite often as an opponent of irrationalism, the unconscious (particularly the Freudian unconscious), mysticism and sentimental romanticism about "primitive races" and cultures. It could be said that his critical purposes necessarily restricted the resources available to him for expression in this writing and that his visual art simultaneously became the more open to them. Here he returns to his early interest in creation, appearing to treat it in a Darwinian rather than Bergsonian context (as he had in 1912; see Study for *Kermesse* (Cat. 19)). A marine environment is evoked, with whale- or shark-like forms diving towards the bottom. A human couple are mating at the bottom centre, and the shark-forms also suggest a womb, in which, as a drop of red, an embryo begins to form.

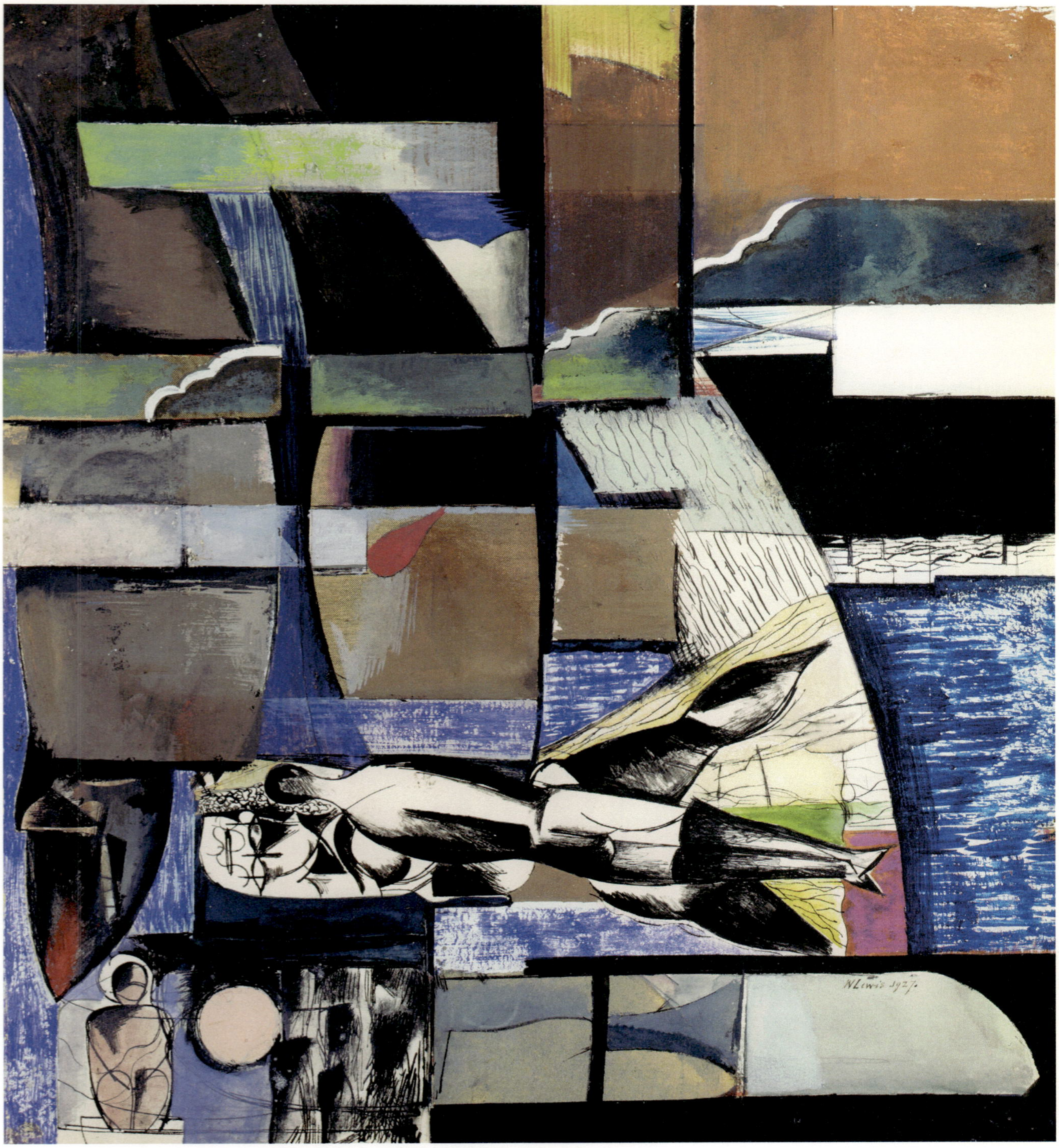

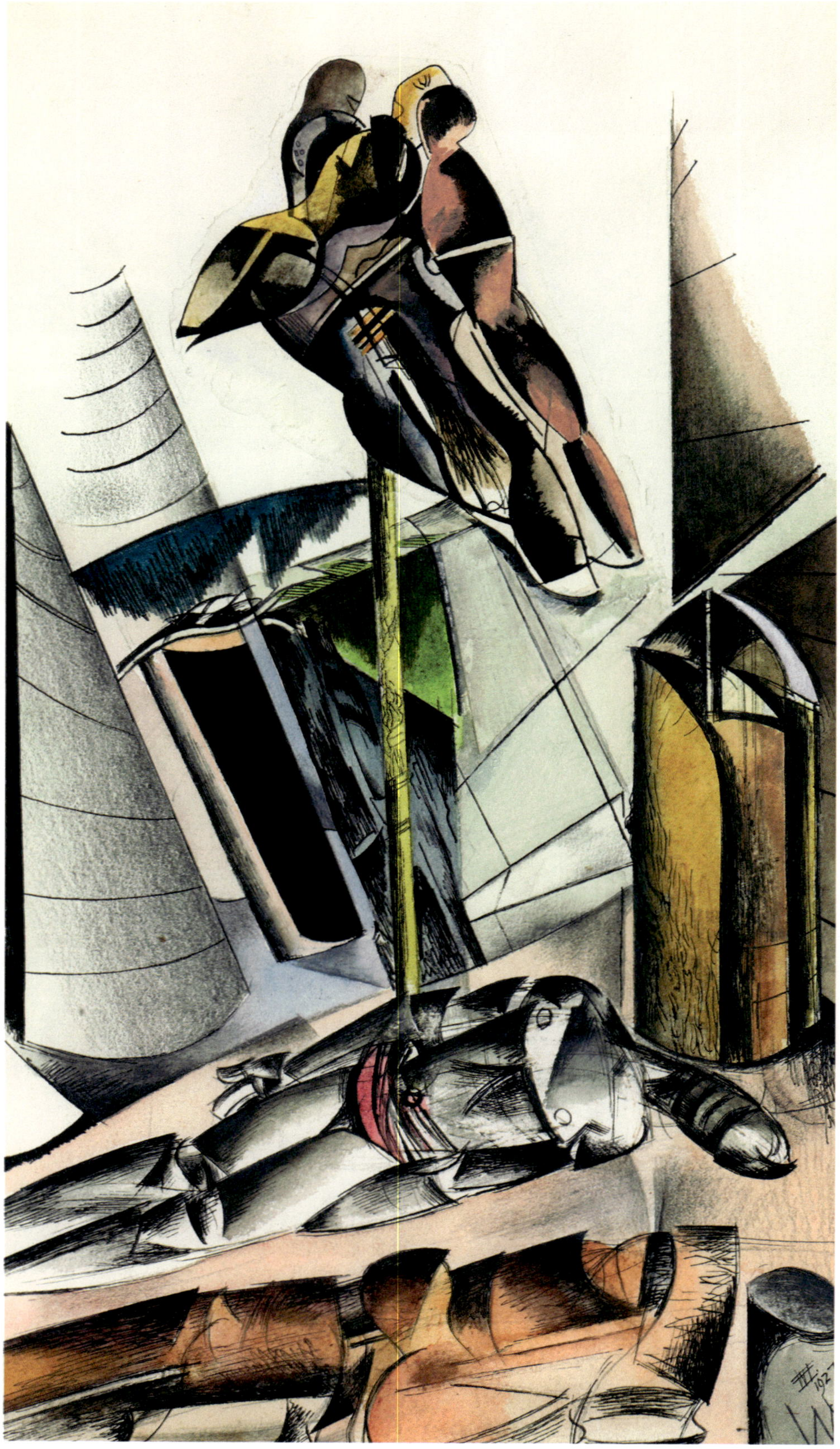

Cat. 125.
***Figures in the Air or On the Roof*, 1927. Pencil, pen and ink, watercolour and gouache with papier collé. 29.2 x 16.5 cm. Private collection. M 635**

This drawing was reproduced in colour in the first issue of *The Enemy* (B&M Cat. 14), in which Lewis also published an article by Wilfred Gibson on the art of Giorgio de Chirico, the "metaphysical" artist. The exaggerated perspective and the strange puppet-like forms of the figures aloft on their pole are somewhat reminiscent of de Chirico's visual world. Lewis was a member of the generation of modernists who were influenced by Sir James Frazer's synoptic study of fertility rites, *The Golden Bough* (1890). T.S. Eliot, in Part one of his *The Waste Land* (1922), "The Burial of the Dead," alludes to the annual ritual killing and burial of a king-figure to ensure the continued fertility of the kingdom. For Lewis's generation, the mass-slaughter of the First World War could not but appear to be a monstrous perversion of such a rite. This image makes no literal allusion to such ideas, leaving the spectator to speculate on its elevated figures, prone corpse and its central opening into some black interior. In 1940, Lewis drew up a plan for a book on modern painting. Chapter 12, which would have treated "painting as a department of metaphysics," was to be devoted to Pablo Picasso, de Chirico and Lewis himself.

Cat. 126.
Manhattan or New York Mystic, 1927. Pen and ink, watercolour and gouache with papier collé.
37 x 25 cm.
Private collection. M 637

Lewis visited New York for the first time in 1927, and responded positively to its architecture and what he called its "neo-barbarism." One of the results of his visit was an essay, "Paleface," published in the second issue of *The Enemy* (pp. 3–10) (B&M Cat. 15), in which he criticised what he saw as the sentimental admiration of the Negro race as (supposedly) essentially different from European races by virtue of possessing a "dark unconscious" to which "civilised" white races no longer had access. This has led Andrew Causey to interpret *Manhattan* as depicting the conquest of the white race by the black (seen hurrying across their white victim).[1] The prone "hero" figure is more likely to be an American Indian, however, and the work seems to be commenting on the "neo-barbarism" and dynamism of New York, built, like all civilisations, on a buried hero-victim.

1. Andrew Causey, "The Hero and the Crowd: The Art of Wyndham Lewis in the Twenties," in *Volcanic Heaven*. Ed. Paul Edwards (Santa Rosa: Black Sparrow Press, 1996), p. 98.

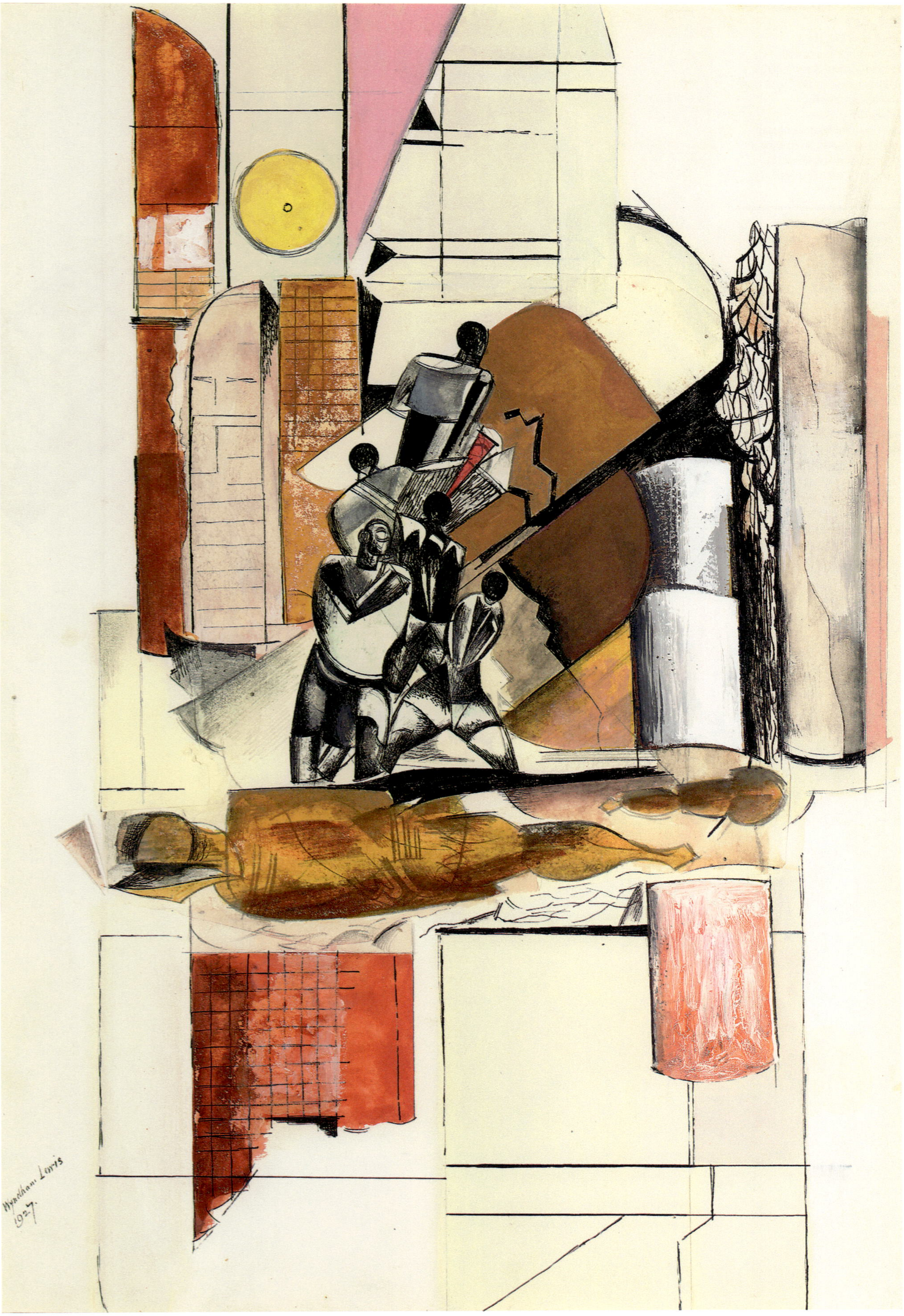

Cat. 127.
ΑΘΑΝΑΤΟΝ ΑΡΑ Ἡ ΨΥΧΗ ("Immortal Therefore the Soul"), 1927.
Watercolour, pencil, and pen and ink on paper.
25.4 x 35.6 cm.
Lent by The Metropolitan Museum of Art, Anonymous gift, in honor of Alfred H. Barr, Jr., 1981 (1981.488.1).
M 626

Lewis used the same Greek word for "immortality" again for two other works (including Cat. 126). The heart symbol on the panel containing what may be a reflection of the figure before it, recalls that in Cats. 107 and 108. This figure and its "reflections" are combined into the composite figure (a mother clasping her child?) that floats off on another panel at a diagonal to the first. A transition between the two contrasting states of the soul, from life to death, is suggested, a theme that would become important in some of Lewis's major oil paintings of the next decade.

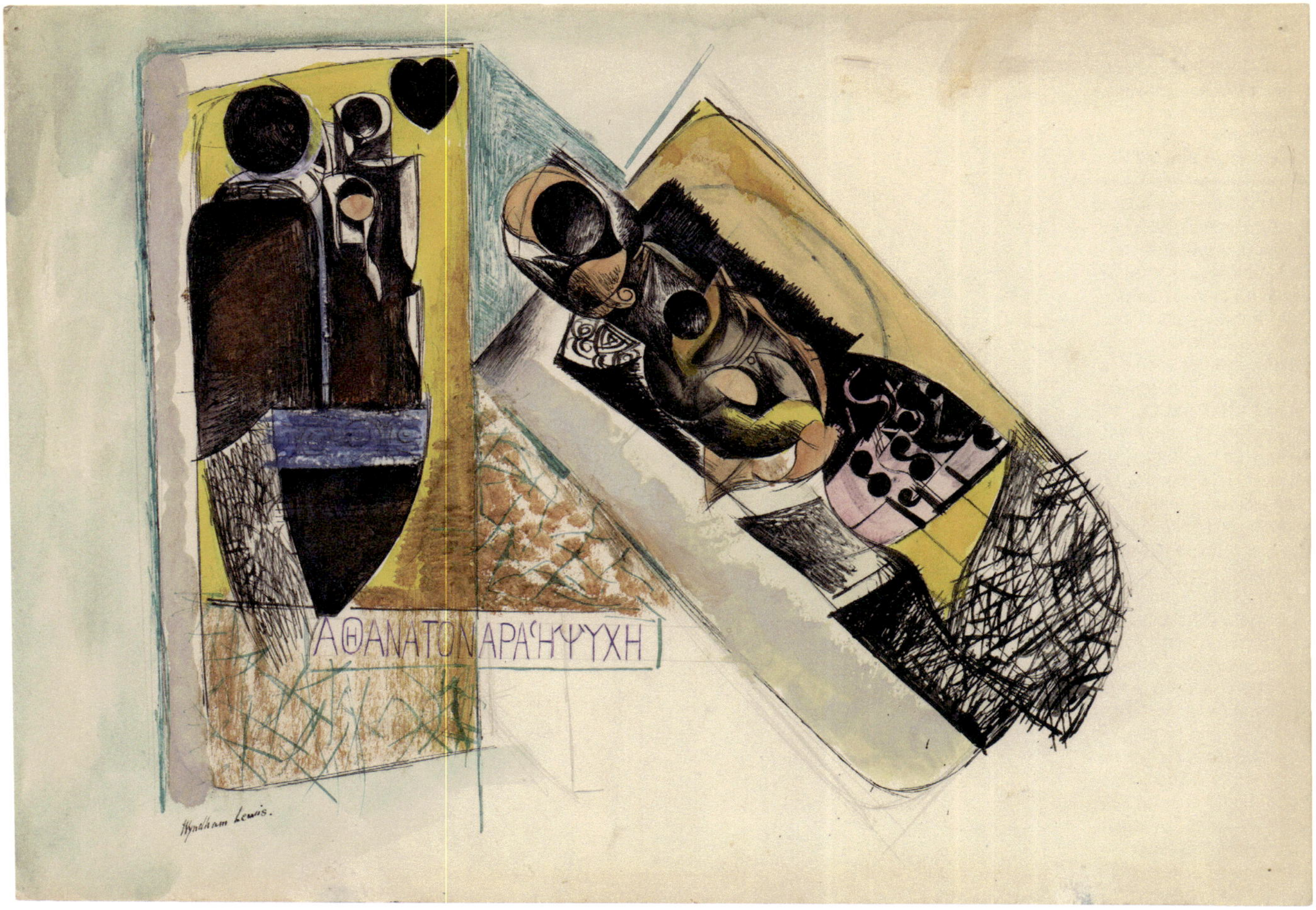

Cat. 128.
Bagdad, 1927–28. Oil on wood. 182.9 x 78.7 cm. Tate: Purchased 1956 (T00099). M P38

Bagdad is painted on a cupboard door and was probably originally a decoration for the Lewises' apartment. The title recalls *The Caliph's Design* (B&M Cat. 7), which begins with a short parable, whereby the Caliph of Baghdad orders two engineers to transform his "Vorticist" drawings into viable designs for a street of new buildings that would transfigure the city. In this "private" painting, then, Lewis is recalling his own public ambitions for a modernism that would transform both London and the consciousness of its people. The scene is presided over by archaic tutelary spirits, including the Egyptian *ka*, the bird symbol of the soul. The painting is also a kind of "creation myth," and the spiral form emerging from the disorganised collection of planes at the bottom is not only an architectural form, but also recalls W.B. Yeats's "Winding Stair" of cyclical history (*The Winding Stair* (1933)). Andrew Causey sees the painting as a summation of Lewis's concerns of the 1920s and an intimation of new beginnings:

It is a painting about the past, time, darkness and the unconscious wellsprings of creativity. It represents the traditional English love of poetic images of decay more than reconstruction and the new. Neither *Bagdad* nor Lewis's other painting of the period delivers a clear message. The cocoon of Classicism in which he wrapped himself in the immediate post-war years quickly ceased to represent the range of his ideas. Despite his puritanical self, which relied on the visual sense because it feared the hidden power of the emotions, Lewis was drawn into new and uncertain adventures.[1]

1. Andrew Causey, "The Hero and the Crowd: The Art of Wyndham Lewis in the Twenties," in *Volcanic Heaven*. Ed. Paul Edwards (Santa Rosa: Black Sparrow Press, 1996), p. 101.

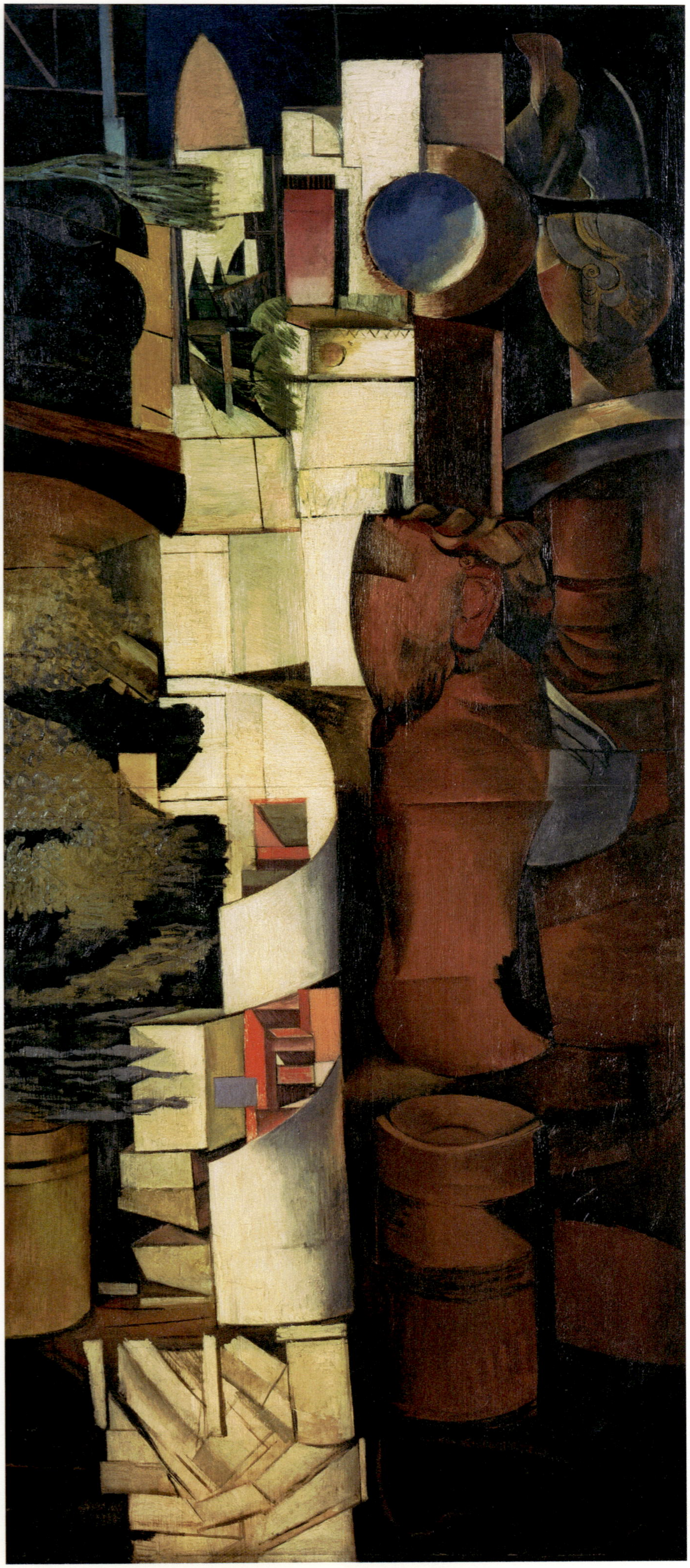

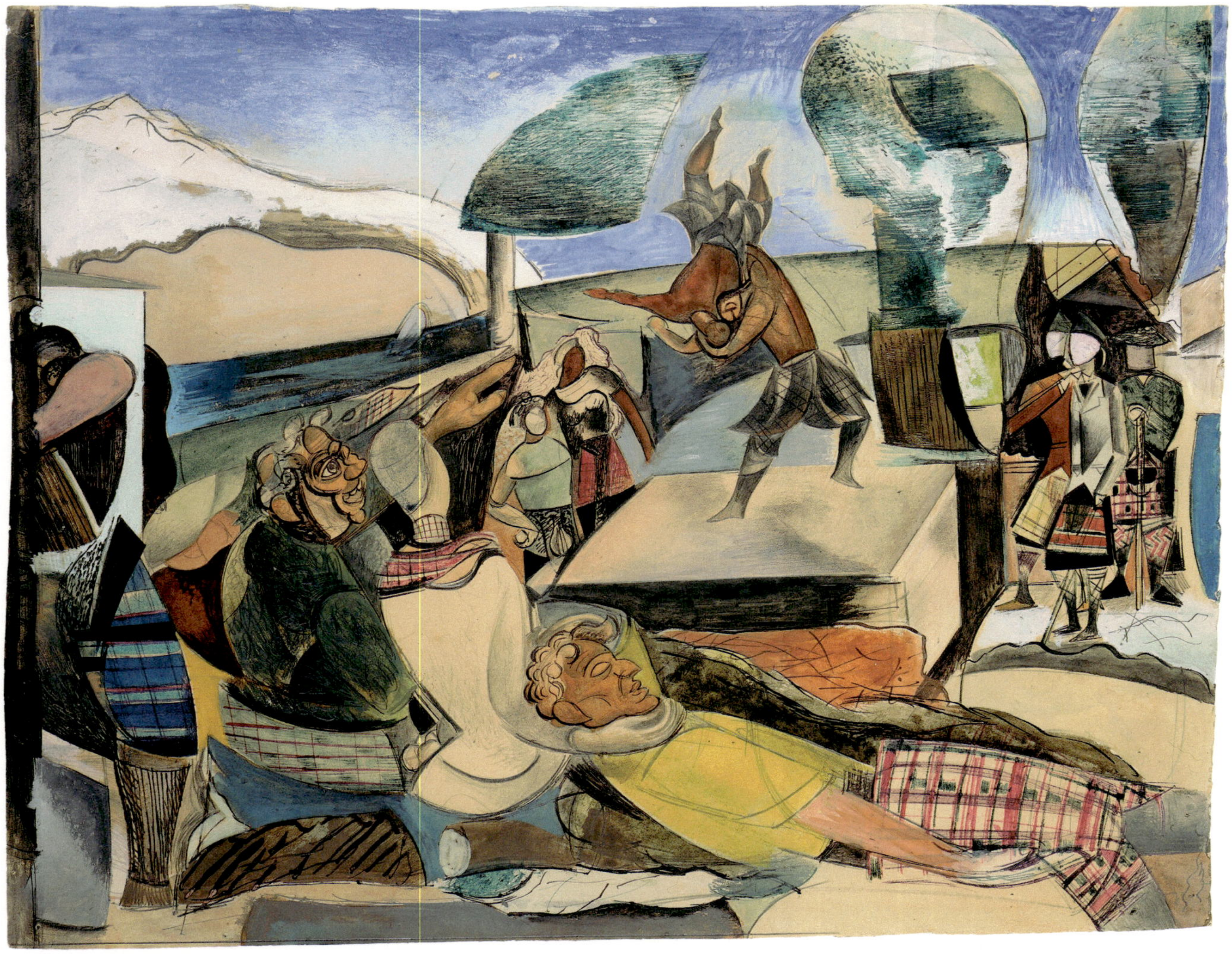

Cat. 129. ▲
Wrestling, 1929. Graphite, pen and ink, watercolour and gouache on paper. 34.5 x 43.1 cm. Wyndham Lewis Memorial Trust (LD.2004.XX.20). M 654

Cat. 130. ▶▲
Boxing at Juan-les-Pins, 1929. Pen and ink, wash and gouache on paper. 32 x 44 cm. Private collection. M 646

Cat. 131. ▶▼
Beach Scene, 1929. Pen and ink, watercolour and gouache on grey paper. 31 x 42.5 cm. Courtesy of Austin/Desmond Fine Art. Private collection. M 645

Lewis was commissioned to produce these drawings of sporting scenes (to which should be added the revised *The Pole Jump* of 1919 (Cat. 88)). As well as containing witty social observation (the placid aristocrats in suits and bow-ties versus the torrent of enthusiasm from the local crowd at the left of *Boxing*, for example), they are packed with examples of visual wit in their forms of representation.

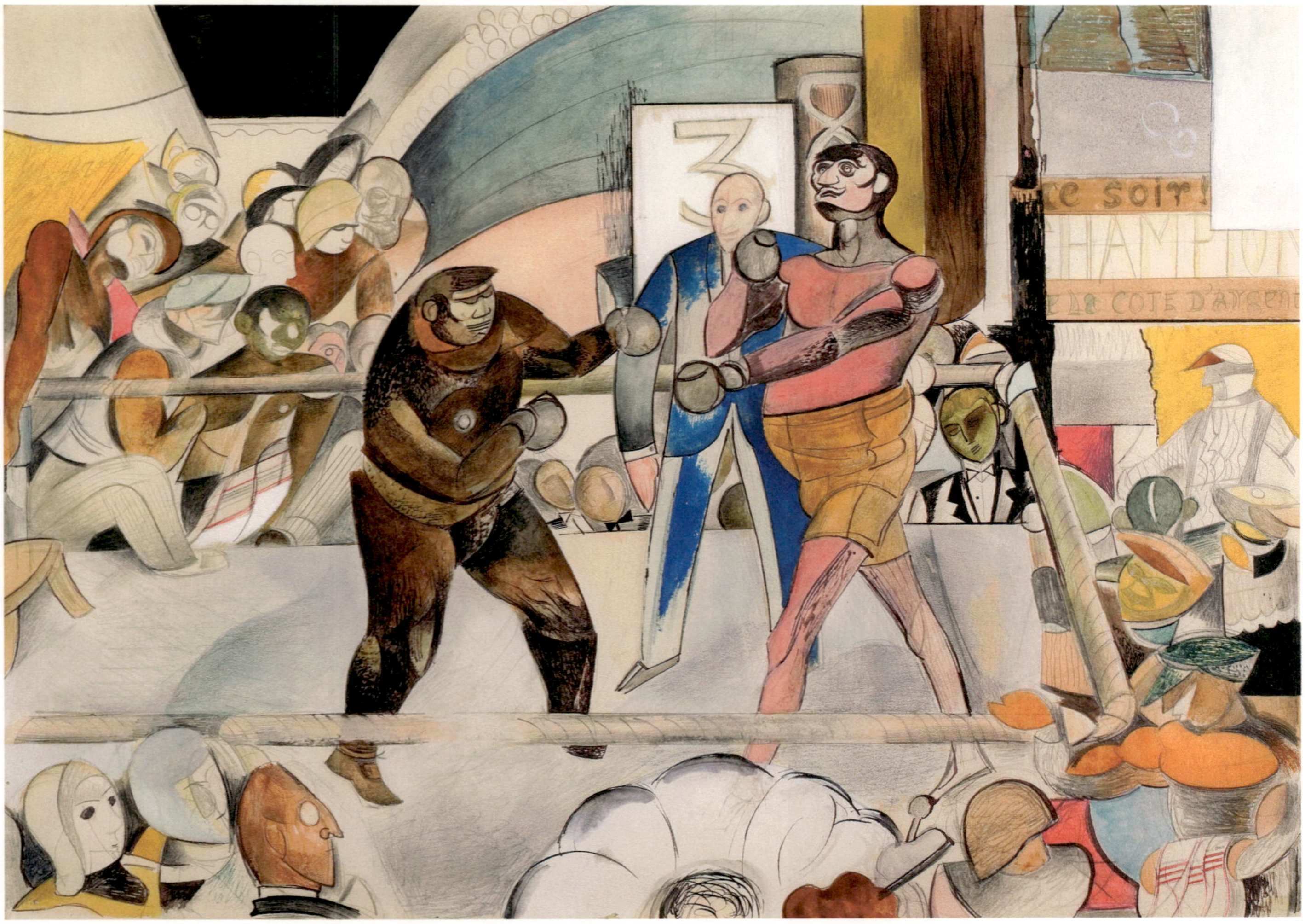

3
Ce soir!
HAMPION
LA COTE D'ARGENT

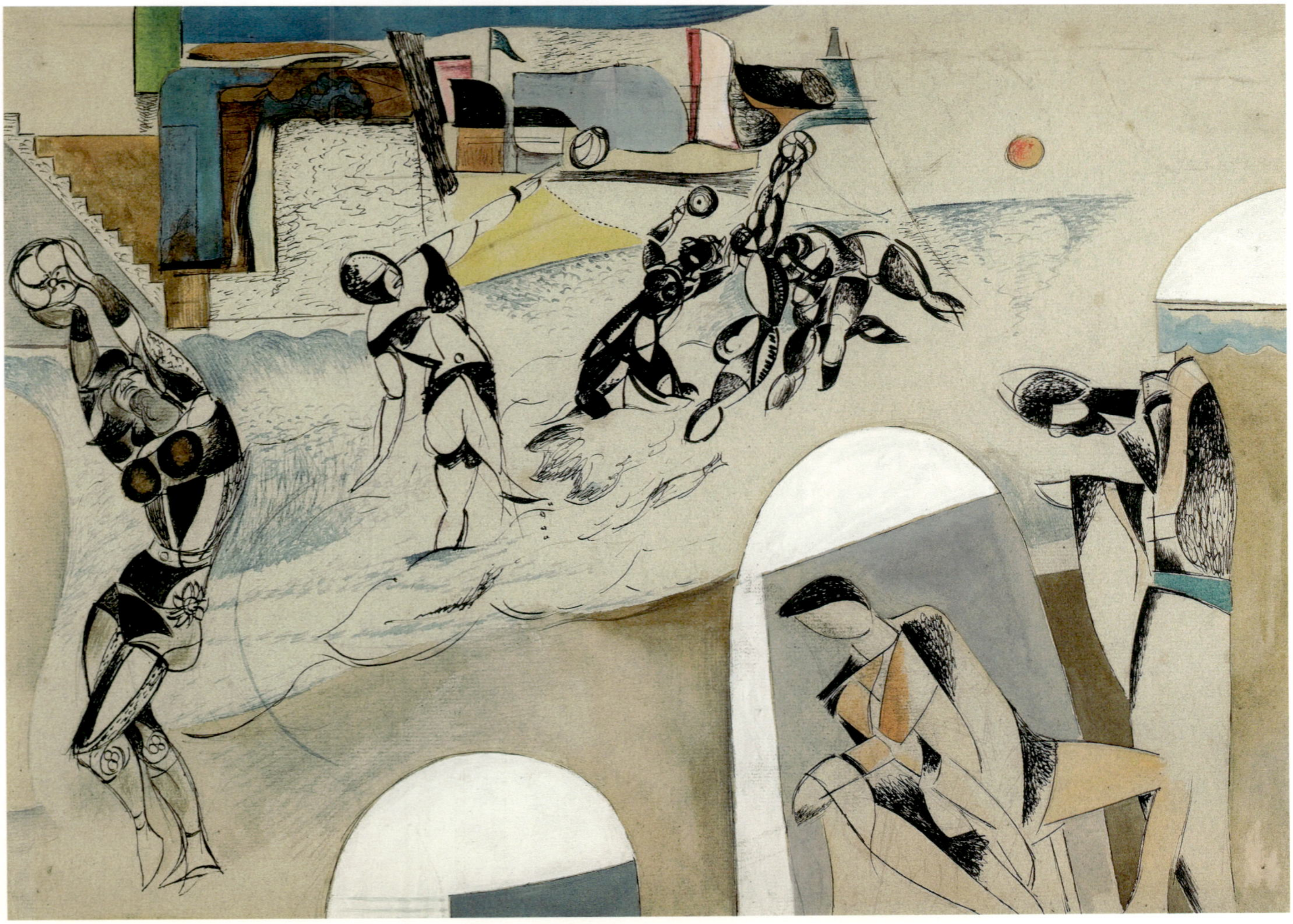

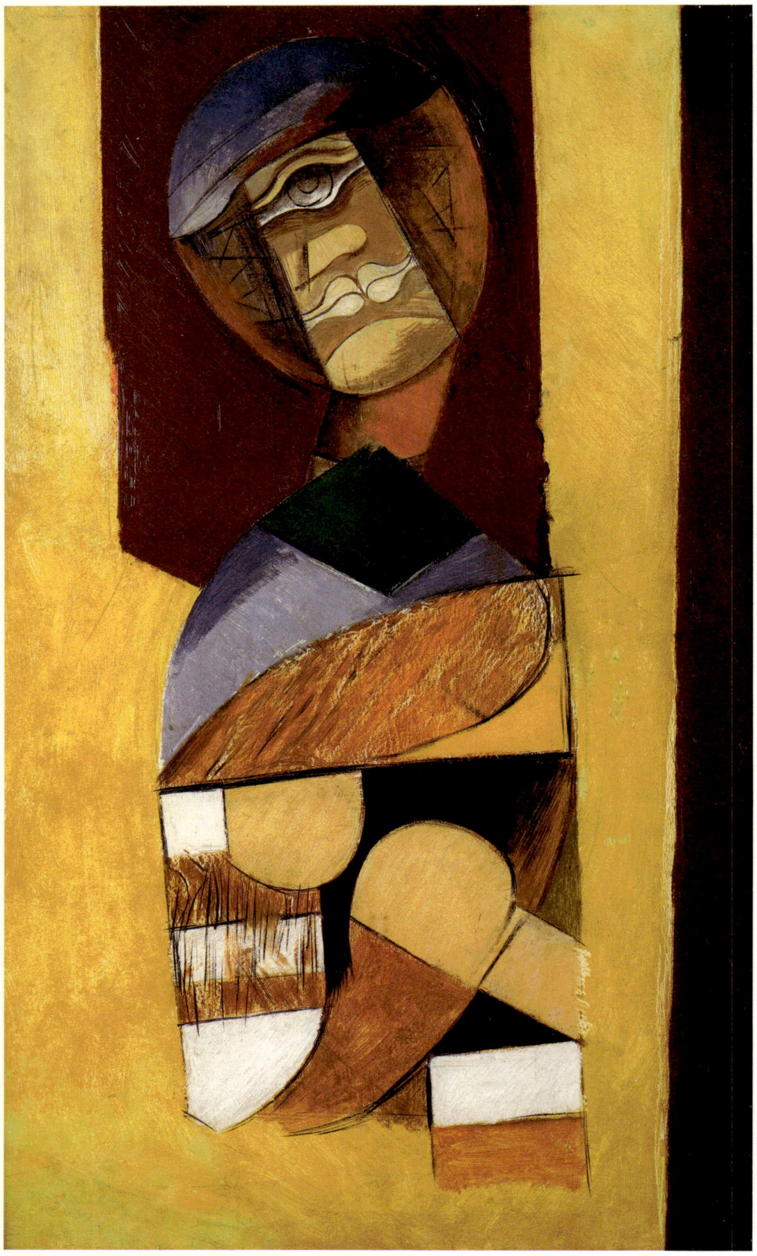

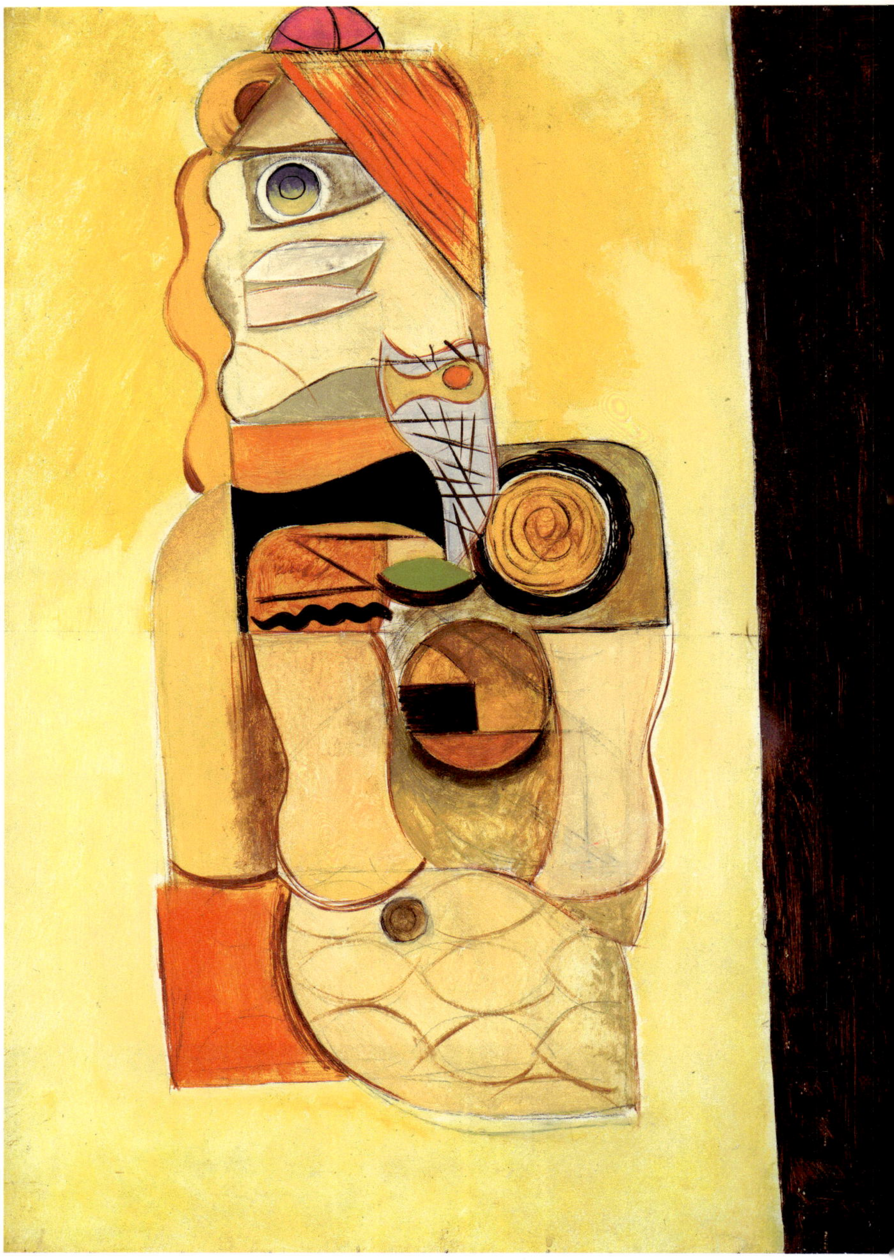

Cat. 132.
[Not in exhibition] *L'Homme surréaliste*, 1929. Oil on plywood. 70 x 43 cm. Private collection. M P39

Cat. 133.
[Not in exhibition] *Femme surréaliste*, 1929. Oil on plywood. 70 x 50 cm. Private collection. M P40

Cat. 134.
[Not in exhibition] *L'Homme surréaliste*, 1929. Oil on plywood. 70 x 43 cm. Private collection. M P41

Cat. 135.
[Not in exhibition] *Femme surréaliste*, 1929. Oil on plywood. 70 x 50 cm. Private collection. M P42

Like Cat. 128, these paintings were produced on panels from a cupboard. From the carefully controlled ink or pencil line and delicate washes, Lewis turns here to a loose (coarse, even) and carefree application of oil paint, which he scores, marks and abrades. Again apparently in private, he gives himself licence to release the "unconscious" in a more instinctive handling of his materials than he usually allowed himself. The titles are testimony to the homage he was here paying to a movement of which he disapproved politically (he did not think that good results would flow from an unrestrained release of the unconscious into everyday life, as he explained in an essay in the third issue of *The Enemy* (B&M Cat. 16)[1]). The artistic products of Surrealism were another matter, however. These, he thought, provided images that were "an official *échantillon* of what our civilization *might* become if it wanted to." His own work of this kind, disallowed in England, he dismisses with bitter irony as "fragments I amuse myself with in the intervals of my literary work."[2]

1. Wyndham Lewis, "The Diabolical Principle," *The Enemy*, No. 3 (First Quarter, 1929), pp. 41–41 (see Anthology, pp. 357-58).
2. Wyndham Lewis, "A World Art and Tradition" (1929). Rprt. *Wyndham Lewis on Art: Collected Writings 1913–1956*. Eds. Walter Michel and C.J. Fox (London: Thames and Hudson, 1969), pp. 257–58.

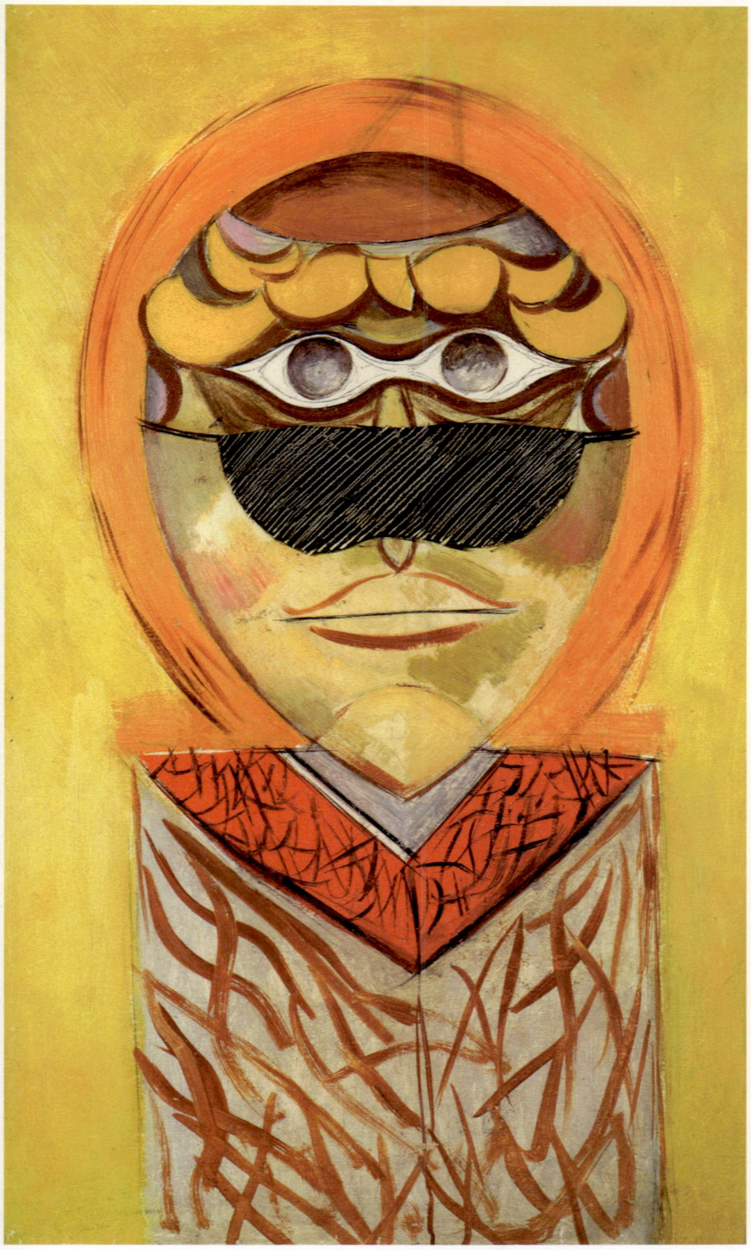
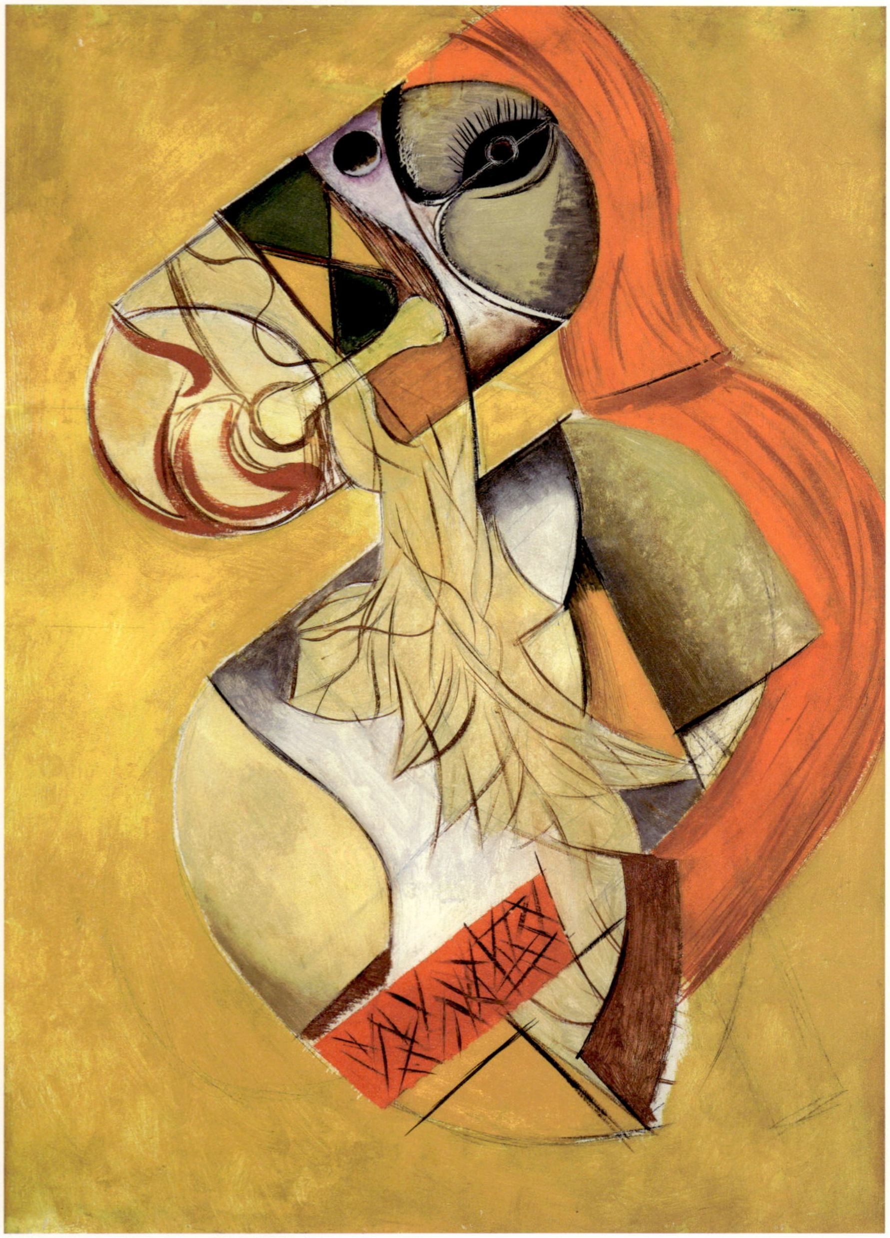

1930-

1939

Between Metaphysics and History

Lewis's outpouring of books from *The Art of Being Ruled* in 1926 (B&M Cat. 10) until the publication of *The Apes of God* in 1930 (B&M Cat. 21) had once again made him a major public figure in Britain. In these works, he had developed the previously latent range of his interests in the political, philosophical, literary and artistic spheres so that he was now a formidable cultural commentator, as well as one of England's most important painters and writers. The 1930s saw him active across a broad field, venturing into the complexities of the international political scene, with disastrous results for his reputation. In spite of his controversial support for aspects of Fascist ideology, however, he was a figure of great standing in British art and culture and had the support of many artists and writers, such as Henry Moore (1898–1986) and W.H. Auden (1907–73), who otherwise disagreed with his political opinions. He was also a married man, since 1930 when one of his models, Gladys Anne ('Froanna') Hoskyns became his wife; she looked after him through the recurrent, and often very serious, illnesses that interrupted his efforts to produce new work for the one-man exhibition that was finally held at The Leicester Galleries in London in 1937.

Lewis travelled to Germany in 1930 and wrote a series of articles that were published in 1931 as the book *Hitler* (B&M Cat. 26), two years before the dictator came to power. Although often insightful and humorous, the book was deeply misguided in its belief that Hitler's anti-Semitism was superficial and that he was a 'man of peace'. As he recognised too late, it badly damaged his reputation. Lewis continued to write political books throughout the decade: *The Old Gang and the New Gang* (1933) (B&M Cat. 34), *Left Wings Over Europe* (1936) (B&M Cat. 37) and *Count Your Dead: They are Alive!* (1937) (B&M Cat. 38) all took an anti-war line and proposed the appeasement of Hitler and conditional support for the authoritarian regimes on the continent. His novel *The Revenge for Love* (1937) (B&M Cat. 39) exposed the naivety of the support among young British artists and intellectuals for the Republican cause in Spain, demonstrating with poignant accuracy the cynical Communist Party machinations behind the cause. However, in true Lewis style, he also gave a work at the same time to an exhibition in London supporting the Republicans. His Communist and Fascist figures in the painting *Red and Black Principle* (1936) (Cat. 159) indicates something of the contradictory impulses in Lewis's understanding of contemporary political ideologies. He also realised after another trip to Germany in 1937 that he had himself been woefully naive in his estimation of Hitler and began attempts to revise his opinion in print. *The Jews: Are they Human?* (1939) (B&M Cat. 42) was an impassioned defence of the Jews and, in the same year, *The Hitler Cult* (B&M Cat. 44), not only attacked Nazism but also predicted that the Second World War would end, as it did, in six years. This was one of the few occasions, perhaps, when Lewis got something right in realpolitik.

Lewis's other writings in the 1930s were mostly far more substantial than his political books: as well as *The Revenge for Love*, he wrote the novel *Snooty Baronet* (1932) (B&M Cat. 33), in part an attack on the fashionable 'science' of behaviourism, and another satire, this time on the London literary scene, *The Roaring Queen* (1936) (B&M Cat. 25), which was suppressed for legal reasons. His critical works included another suppressed book, *The Doom of Youth* (1932) (B&M Cat. 28), a pioneering piece of cultural analysis that examined the growth of the youth cult of the period; *Men Without Art* (1934) (B&M Cat. 36), a book of literary criticism that made a stout defence of what Lewis described as the 'external' and satirical approach in art against a perceived subjective and 'internal' orthodoxy; and *The Mysterious Mr Bull* (1938) (B&M Cat. 41), an historical analysis of the English character and temperament, which was far more sympathetic towards his fellow countrymen than he had generally been before.

Lewis, in spite of serious illness and continual financial problems, therefore, was extraordinarily active as a writer throughout the 1930s, seeking to live the life of 'the man of the world' he had described in his writings of the 1920s. He was also determined, however, to continue his career as a visual artist. He had not held a one-man exhibition since 1921. Portraiture was a constant practice and also, of course, the one most likely to earn him much-needed income. The portraits of the 1930s include some of his finest works; the portfolio of drawings *Thirty Personalities and a Self-Portrait* (1932) shows him once again re-inventing his figurative drawing style in an effort to create an art of the times. The drawings of figures such as his feminist friend Rebecca West (1892–1983) (Cat. 139) and of established figures such as the novelist and polemicist G.K. Chesterton (1874–1936) are remarkable in their fusion of formal invention and life-likeness. The portfolio presents a unique record of the London cultural scene as well as of politicians and businessmen and popular heroes such as the aviator Wing-Commander Augustus H. Orlebar (1897–1943). Lewis also painted some of his finest oil portraits in the period 1937 to 1939. Two of these works, the great portraits of T.S. Eliot (1938) (Cat. 147) and of Ezra Pound (1939) (Cat. 149), are not only deeply personal images of close friends and colleagues, but also the finest British literary portraits of the first half of the twentieth century.

The exhibition at The Leicester Galleries in December 1937 mainly represented the imaginative work in oils that Lewis had been at work on, with much interruption, since 1933. It is in many respects the most sustained effort at major painting he ever made and, in his own words, was 'some sort of series'. Certain broad themes are evident: history, the after-life and contemporary life (personal and in the wider society). The historical works range across world cultures, from the epic voyages of marauding Norse seamen and the initiation rituals of the ancient Incas, to a Spanish fifteenth-century dynastic episode seen through a distinctly contemporary eye. The after-life imagery, made in the wake of Lewis's 1928 novel, *The Childermass* (B&M Cat. 19), underlines Lewis's fascination in a tradition in English art going back to William Blake (1757–1827) and Henry Fuseli (1741–1825). Lewis stages his metaphysical interests as dramas of semi-human figures in strange landscapes, moving from the horrific Dantesque scenes of the *Inferno* (1937) (Cat. 166), to the lost and regimented queues of *One of the Stations of the Dead* (1933) (Cat. 155). The contemporary imagery is often satirical. *Cubist Museum* (1936) (Cat. 160) is an amused but affectionate look at the audience for modern art in an age that Lewis believed struggled to respond to new aesthetic developments, and *The Betrothal of the Matador* (1933) (Cat. 152), yet another work with a Spanish dimension, is a tribute to Lewis's friend the poet Roy Campbell (1901–57). Lewis's personal life finds expression in *Convalescent* (1933) (Cat. 154), an unusually warm and domestic interior that shows the artist with his wife during the aftermath of one of his many illnesses in the 1930s. His love for 'Froanna' can be seen in his many portraits of her in oil and pencil, hinting at an emotional life with which 'The Enemy' is rarely associated. *Red Portrait (Froanna)* (1937) (Cat. 143) is a particularly haunting and original example. On a more public level, Lewis's experience of hospitals and clinics can be found in *The Tank in the Clinic* (1937) (Cat. 163), a work that seems to integrate responses to physical and metaphysical experience.

The Leicester Galleries exhibition was a critical success among Lewis's peers but a commercial failure. He had demonstrated once again his enormous inventiveness and technical ability as well as an unexpected gift for striking and yet subtle colour effects. Yet whether it was his public persona, satirical attacks on contemporaries or political opinions that militated against him, Lewis did not get the full recognition he desired and, indeed, deserved.

After the furore surrounding the rejection by the Royal Academy of the portrait of T.S. Eliot that he entered for the Summer Exhibition in 1938, and during which even Winston Churchill intervened to attack modernism, Lewis sought to capitalise on the publicity it elicited and in 1939 published a collection of his critical and theoretical writings on art since 1914, *Wyndham Lewis the Artist: From "Blast" to Burlington House* (1939) (B&M Cat. 43). It was a publication that certainly underlined Lewis's position as one of Britain's most important writers on art, though the outbreak of war, as with so many things, ensured its reception was delayed and attenuated in impact. It included writings of the 1930s that reveal Lewis's deep engagement with the critical discourses of the time and his attempt to formulate a concept of modernism that included figuration, history and narrative. Lewis coined the term 'Supernaturalism' to suggest the spirit in which his recent work had been made. Once again, however, events and his own behaviour ensured that Lewis's great achievement in 1937 was to be largely overlooked, while his portraits, certainly a remarkable contribution to their genre in British art, have helped considerably to sustain his reputation as a visual artist working since the 1920s.

Cat. 136. ▶
Desert Soukh, 1931.
Graphite, watercolour and gouache on board.
18 x 40.5 cm.
C.J. Fox Collection
(LD.2000.XX.4). M 712

Cat. 137. ▼
Berber Horseman, 1931.
Pencil, ink and ground colour on paper. 31 x 30 cm.
Private collection

Lewis travelled in North Africa with his wife in 1931 and wrote a series of articles about the journey, which became the book *Filibusters in Barbary* (1932) (B&M Cat. 29). This is an often hilarious account of his travels in the French colonial country of Morocco. He was particularly impressed by the Berber tribesmen who perhaps seemed to him like versions of his own horse-backed "Enemy" persona. He believed that they were of the same race as the Celts and possibly linked to the Incas and even Atlantans, making connections between these genealogies and his own Welsh descendants; Lewis was always fascinated by "secret histories."

Lewis also admired the Berber kasbahs (desert forts), such as the one seen in the background of Cat. 137, for their massive and crude simplicity, comparing them favourably with the decadent and theatrical neo-colonial architecture of the Europeanised cities such as Casablanca. Lewis was fascinated by all aspects of the life he saw in Morocco, including the "soukhs," or markets, which in Cat. 136 is a desert one providing many extraordinary shapes for him to work with. The Atlas Mountains and desert provided Lewis with imagery that he transformed into imaginative settings for many works in the 1930s and 1940s.

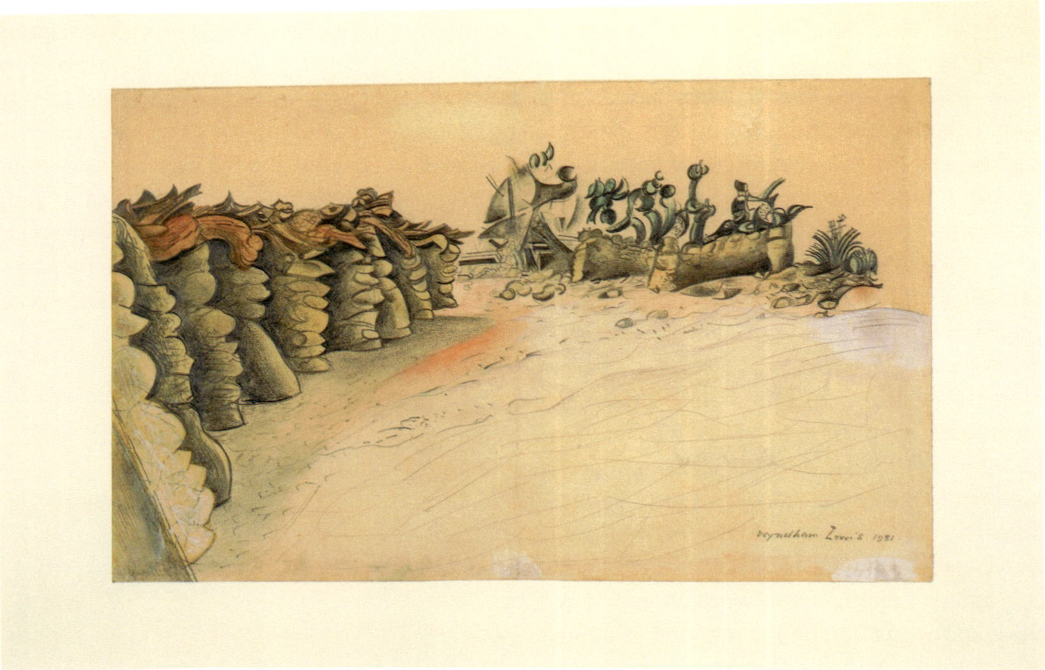

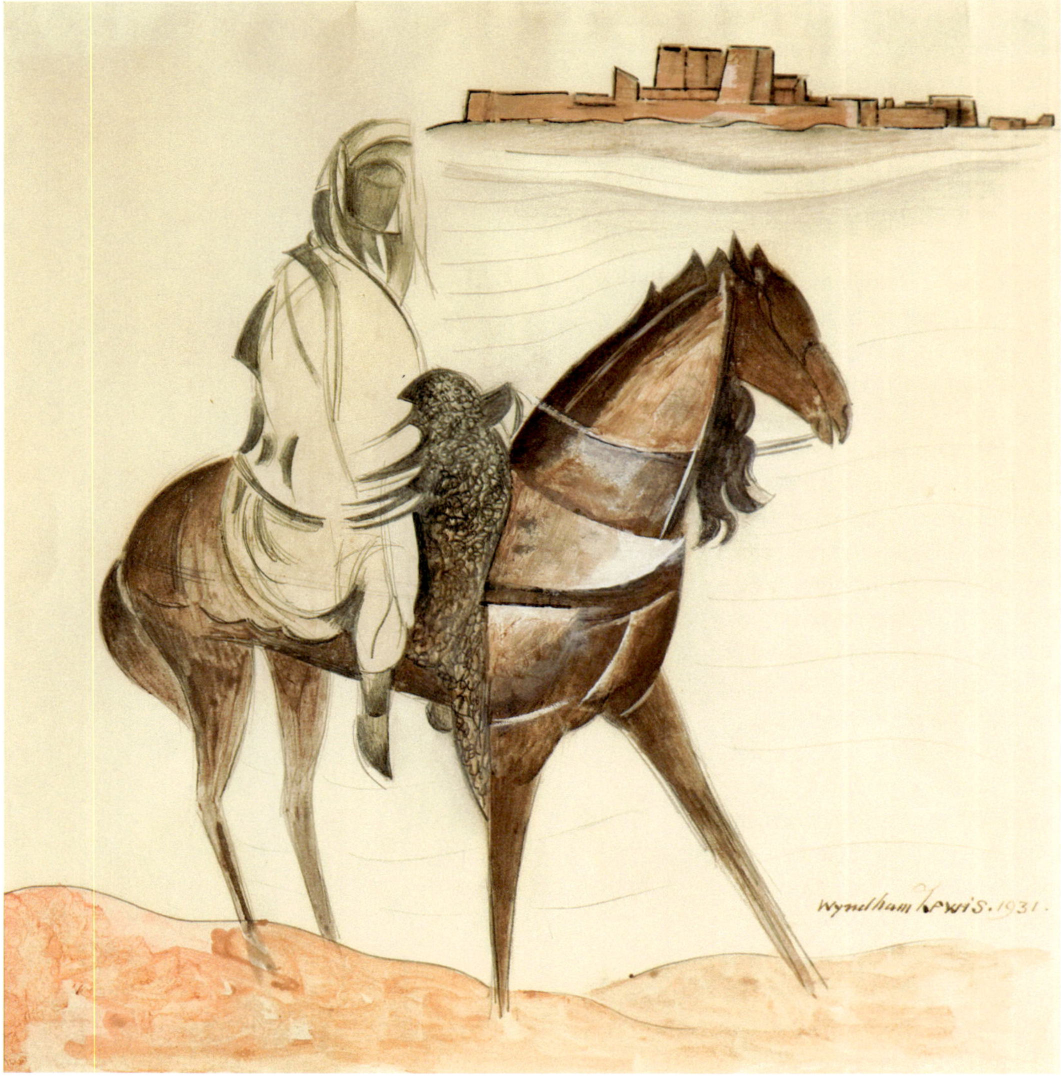

Cat. 138.
Tut, 1931. Pencil and wash on paper. 28 x 24 cm.
Private collection. M 730

Lewis and his wife were exceptionally fond of their dog "Tut," a Sealyham terrier, whose name was an abbreviation of Tutankhamun, the Egyptian pharaoh. As with a few earlier images of cats, Lewis shows his great sympathy with animals in this drawing, which focuses on the legs, belly and head and at one level is simply a virtuoso exercise in linear invention. However, Lewis also evokes the furry warmth of his pet and its simple enjoyment of physical life.

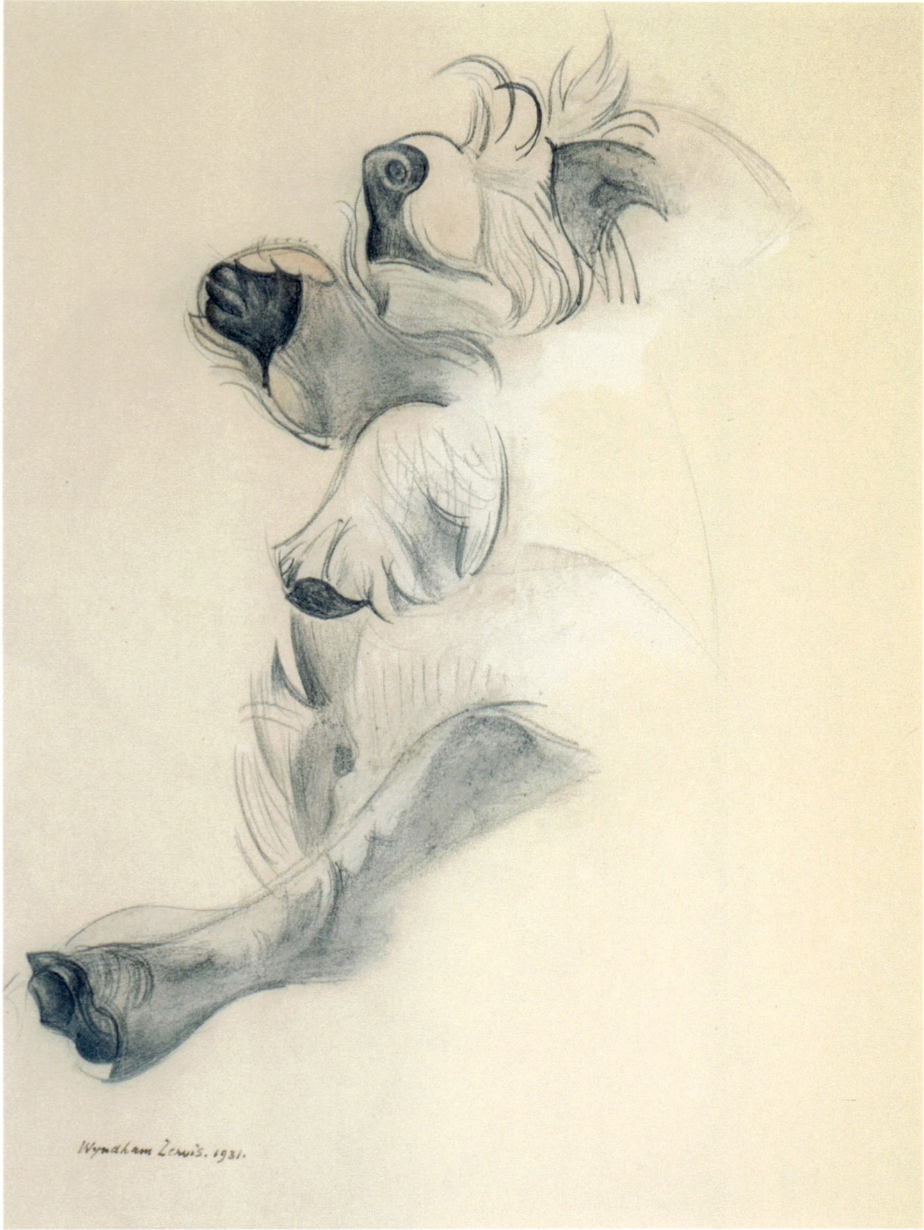

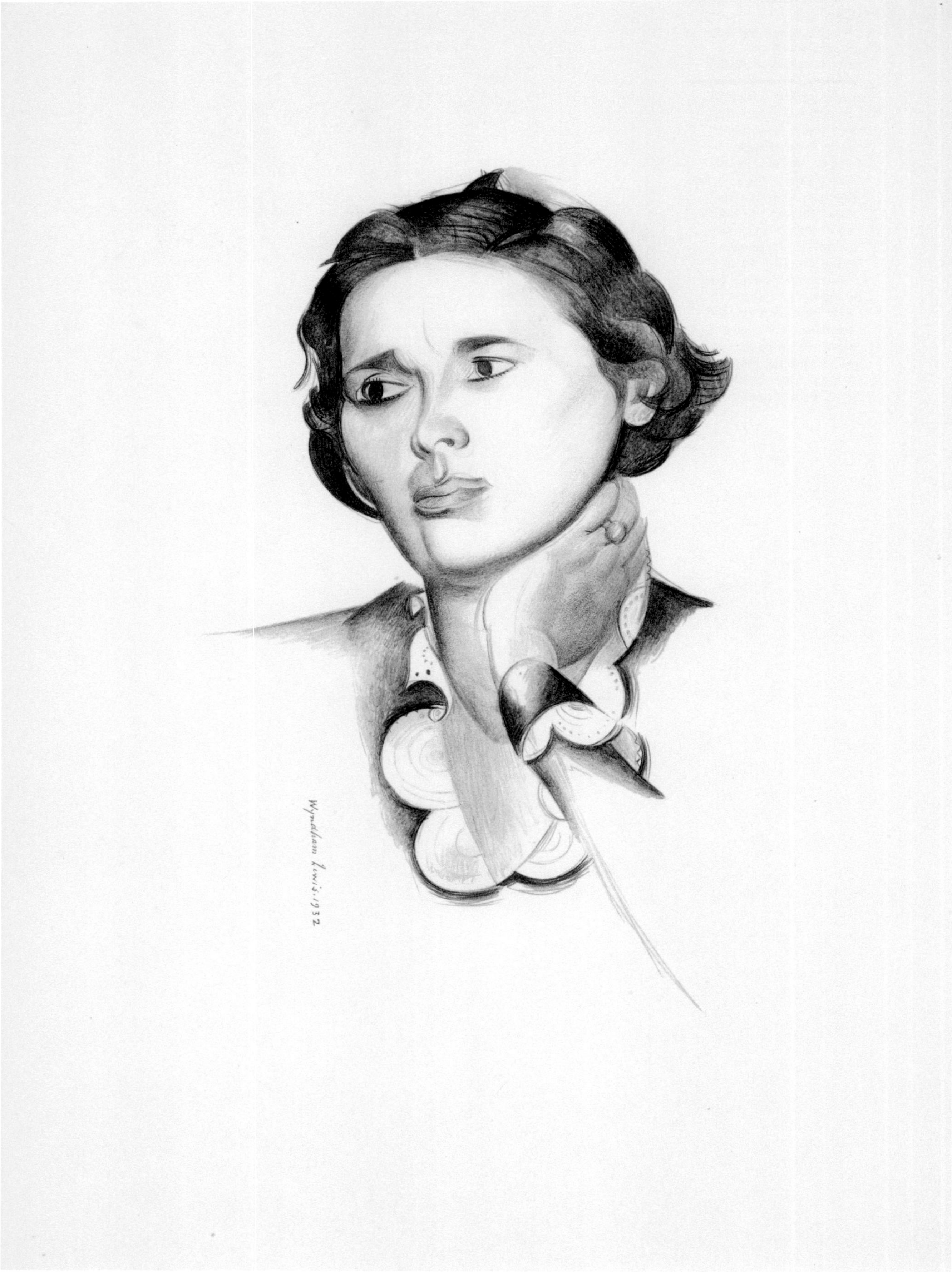

Cat. 139.
Rebecca West, 1932. Pencil on paper. 43 x 31 cm. National Portrait Gallery, London (NPG 5693). M 786

The writer Rebecca West had known Lewis since he published a story by her in *Blast* in 1914 (B&M Cat. 2). She was a militant feminist early in her life and a liberal politically between the wars who took a strong anti-Fascist stance. As with a number of women, she overcame her distaste for Lewis's own politics in the 1920s and 1930s and became his friend and admirer. Her most famous book is *The Meaning of Treason* (1949), an account of communist traitors. This drawing was produced for Lewis's portfolio, *Thirty Personalities and a Self-Portrait* (1932). It is one of his finest and most insightful portrait drawings and presents a woman of enormous strength of character and intellect and deep feminine charm.

Cat. 140.
Self-Portrait with Hat, 1932.
Ink and wash on paper.
25.4 x 19.7 cm.
National Portrait Gallery, London (NPG 4528). M 782

Lewis made self-portraits throughout his life, always creating a different version of his public self. In this pen-and-ink drawing, he presents himself as part-intellectual and, perhaps, part-gangster or private detective. He was by the 1930s deeply interested in American culture, because of his ancestry through his father and because he was increasingly fascinated by its emergence as a world power and its political system. This drawing creates a sharp image with precise line and dark shapes formed by Lewis's favourite dynamic arcs.

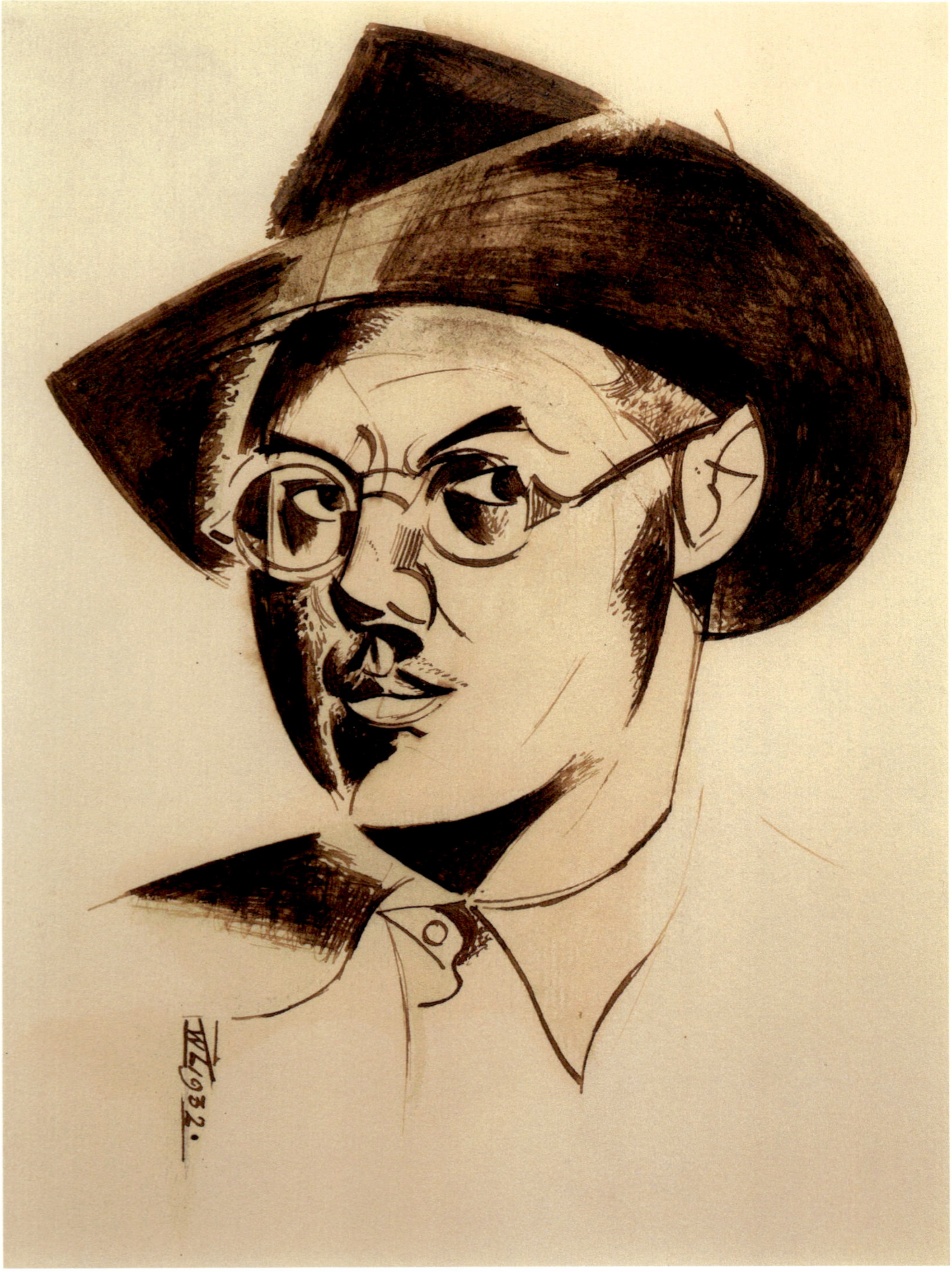

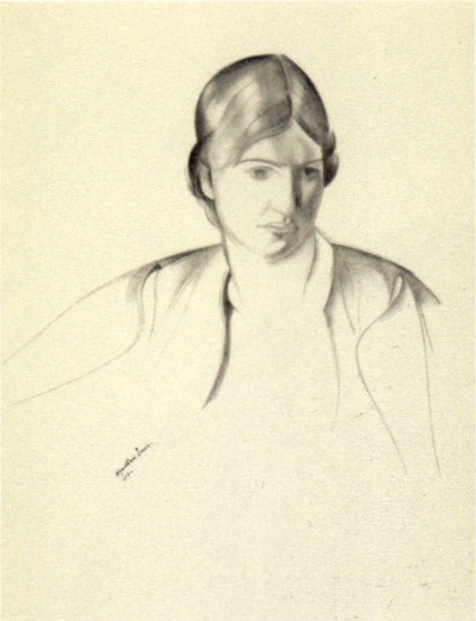

Miss Naomi Mitchison (M 718)

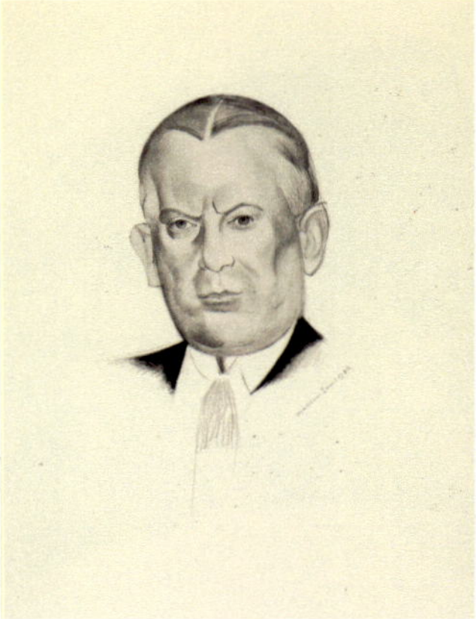

C.B. Cochran, Esq. (M 740)

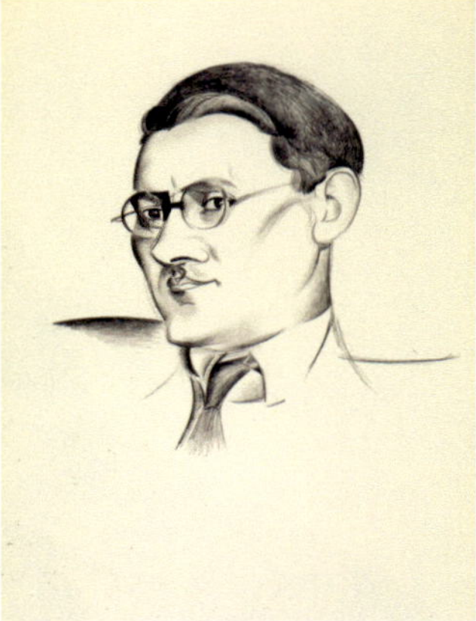

A.J.A. Symons, Esq. (M 785)

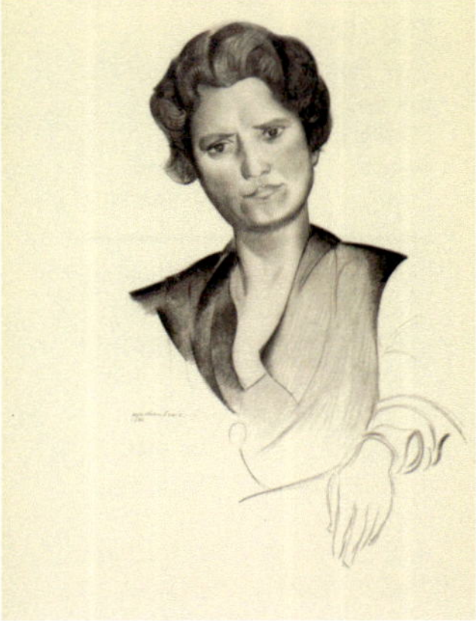

Viscountess Rhondda (M 778)

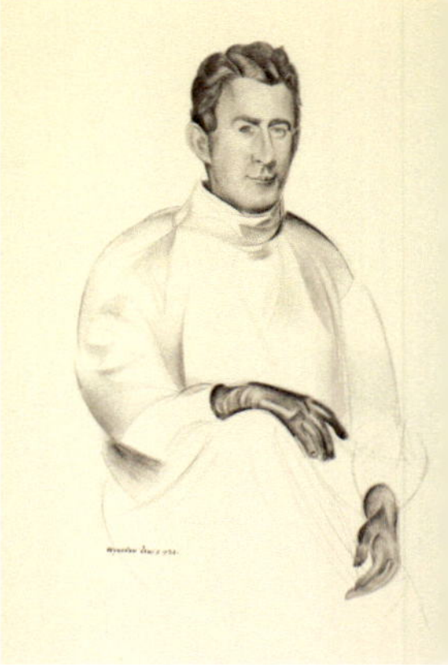

Ivor Black, Esq. (M 734)

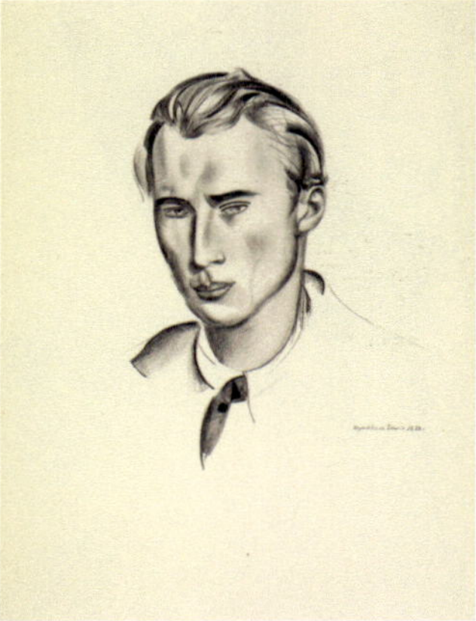

Desmond Harmsworth, Esq. (M 718)

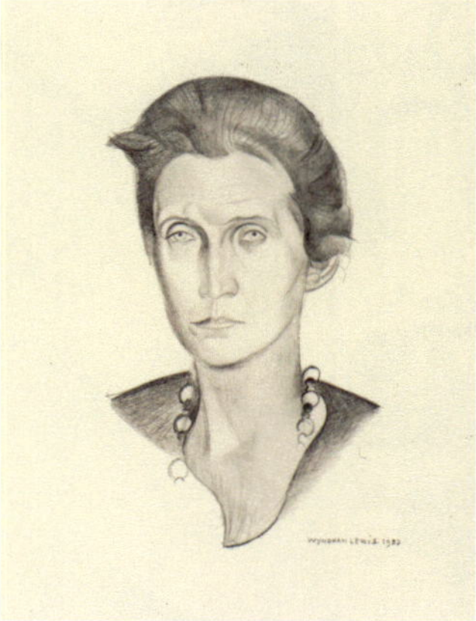

Miss Stela Benson (M 735)

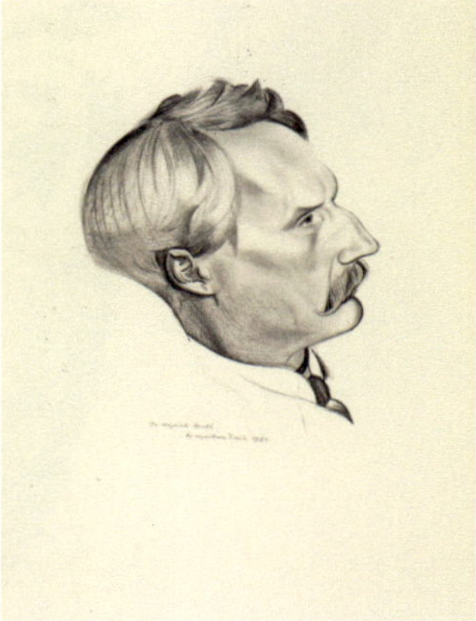

Dr Meyrick Booth (M 737)

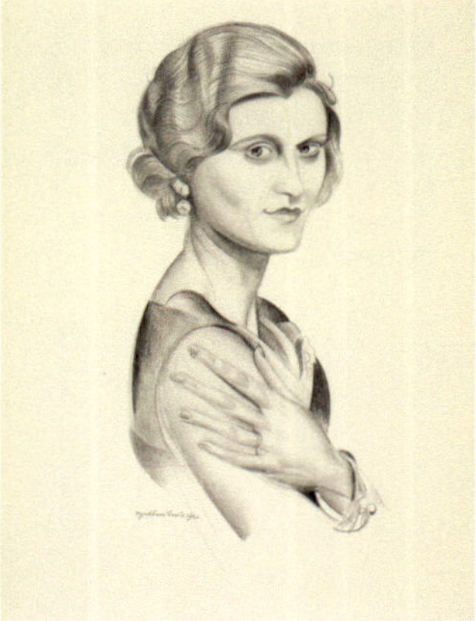

Miss Marie Ney (M 775)

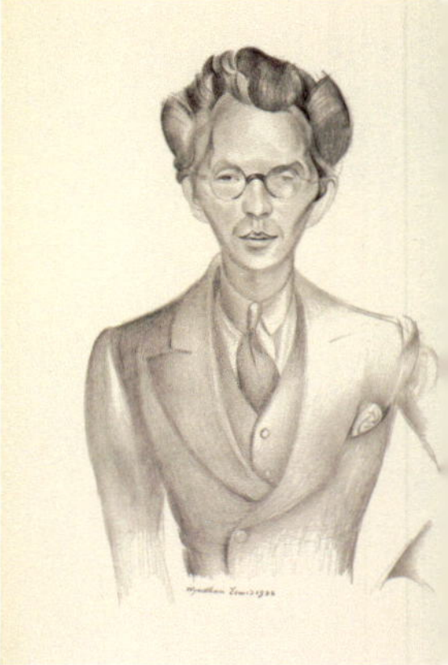

Duncan Masdoneld, Esq. (M 774

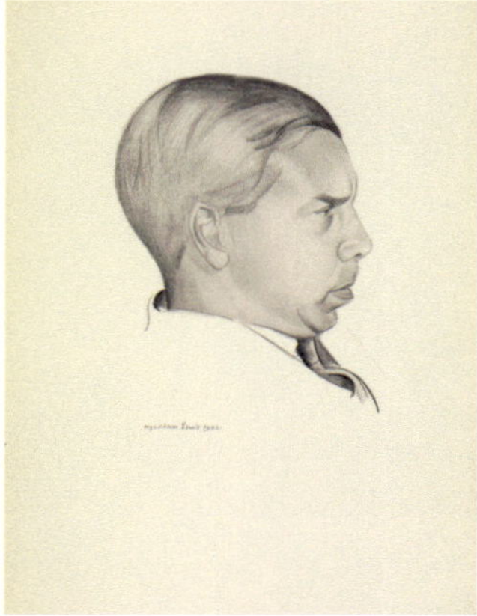

J.B. Priesly, Esq. (M 777)

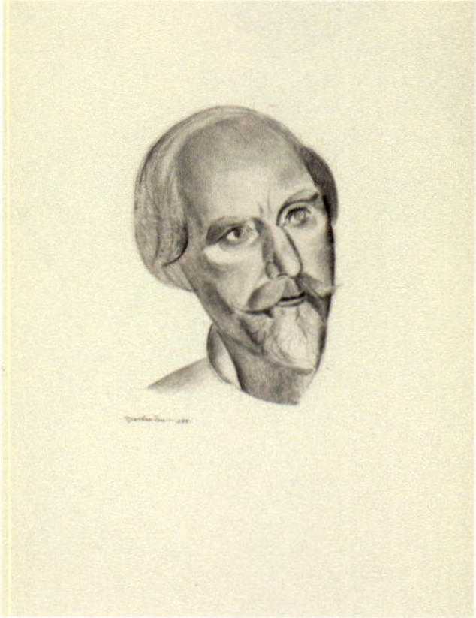

Augustus John, Esq. (M 769)

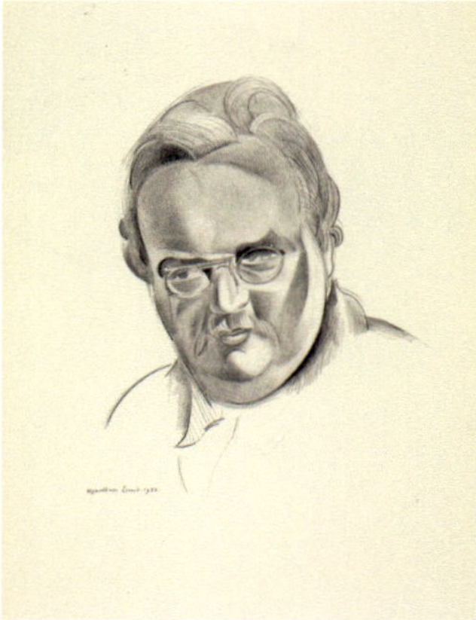

G.K. Chesterton, Esq. (M738)

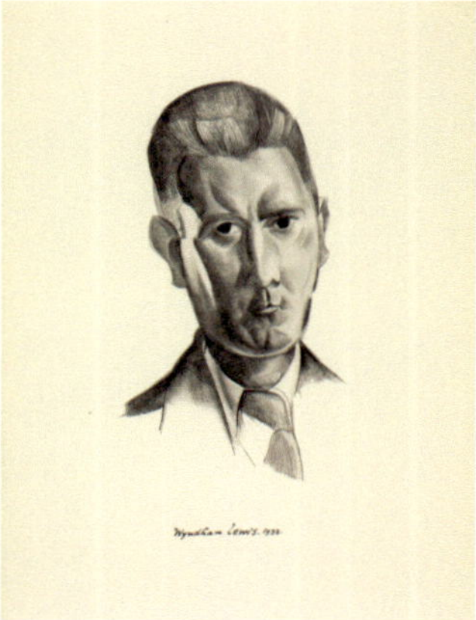

Thomas Earp, Esq. (M 746)

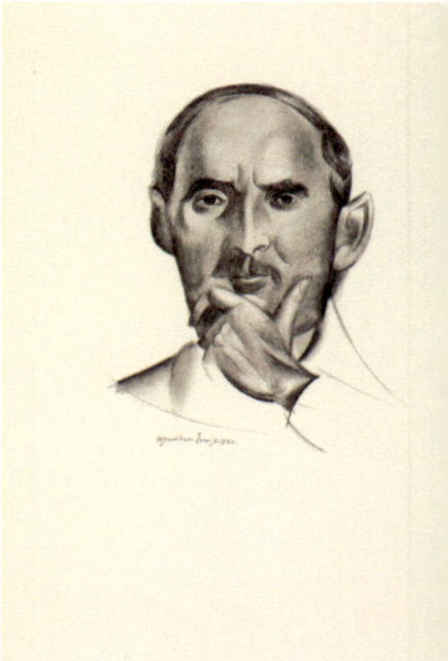

David Low, Esq. (M 773)

Portfolio *Thirty Personalities and a Self-Portrait*
London: Desmond Harmsworth Limited, 1932. Edition of 200 prints signed and numbered by the artist. 37.5 x 27 cm. Wyndham Lewis Memorial Trust. G. and V. Lane Collection LG.

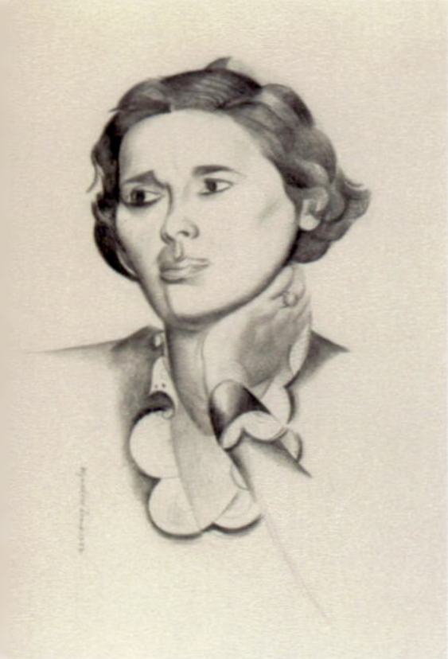

Miss Rebecca West (M 786)

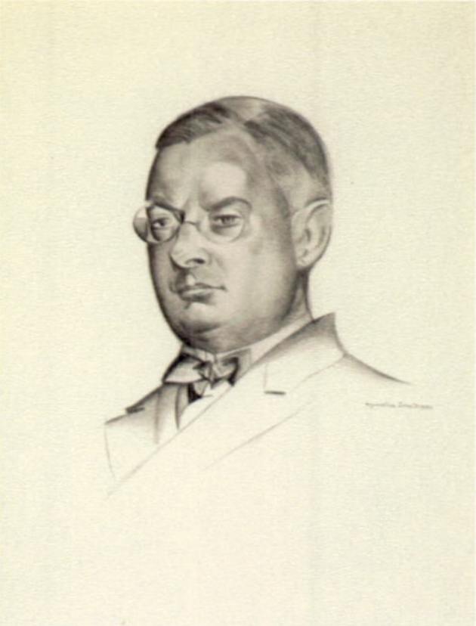

Newman Flower, Esq. (M 755)

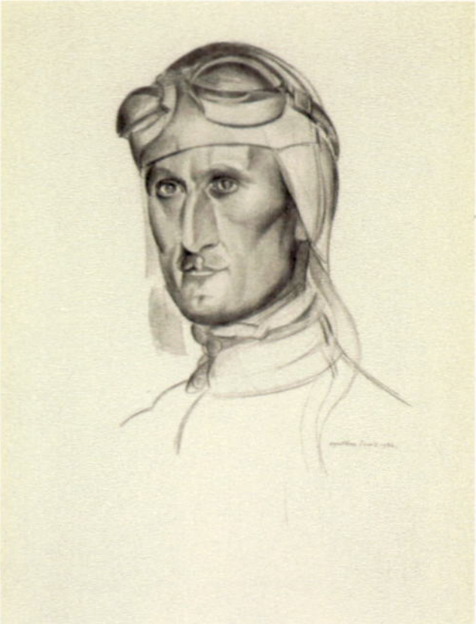

Wing Commander Orlebar (M 776)

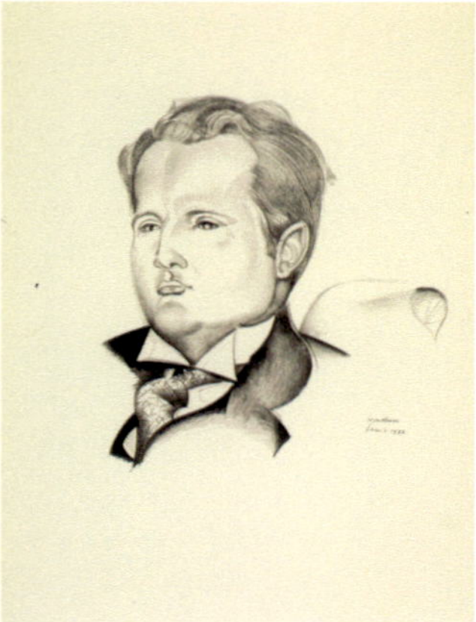

Constant Lambert, Esq. (M 718)

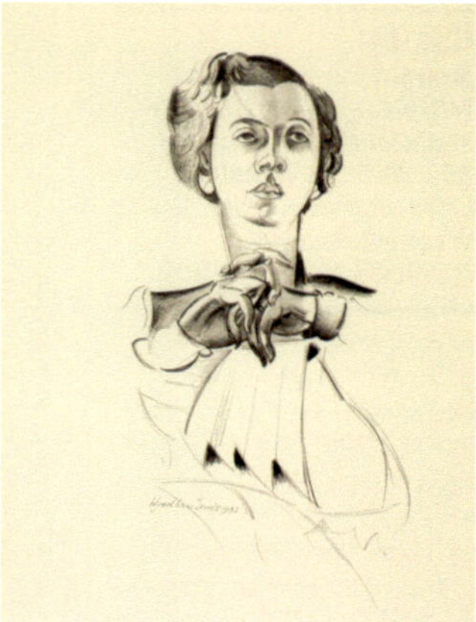

Mrs Desmond Harmsworth (M 718)

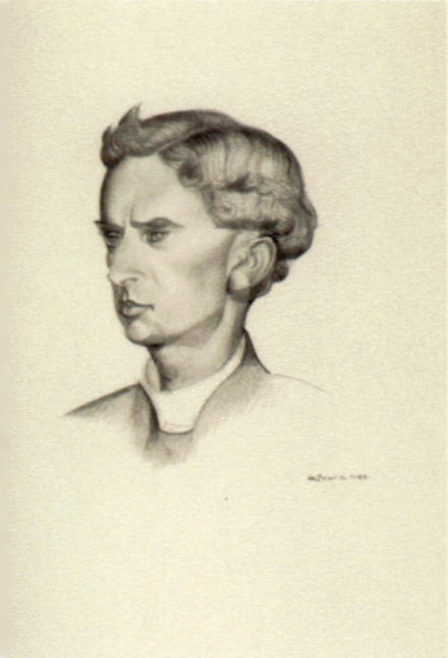

Rev. M. C. D'Arcy, S.J. (M 743)

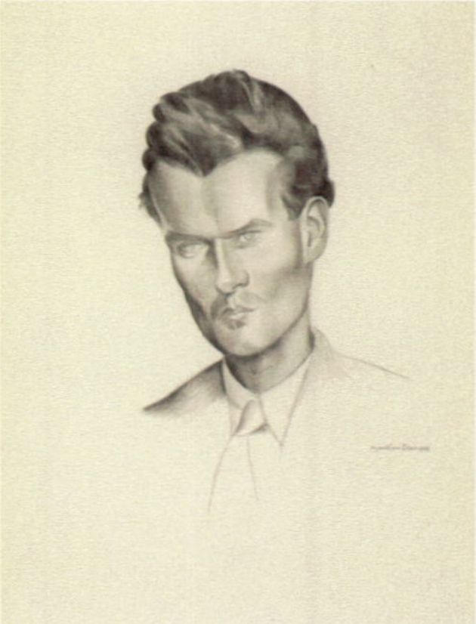

The Hon. Anthony Asquith (M 733)

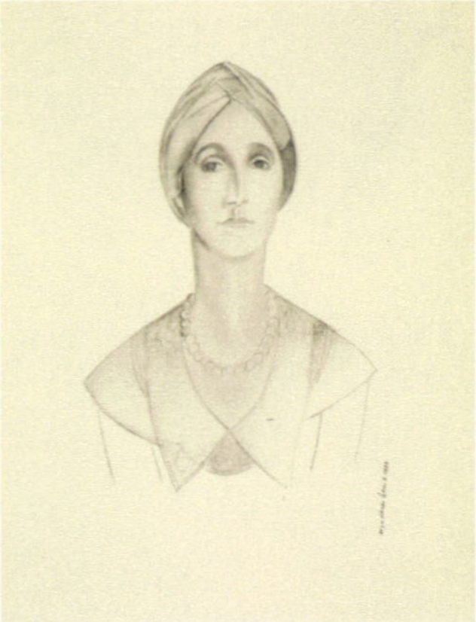

Marchioness of Cholmondeley (M 739)

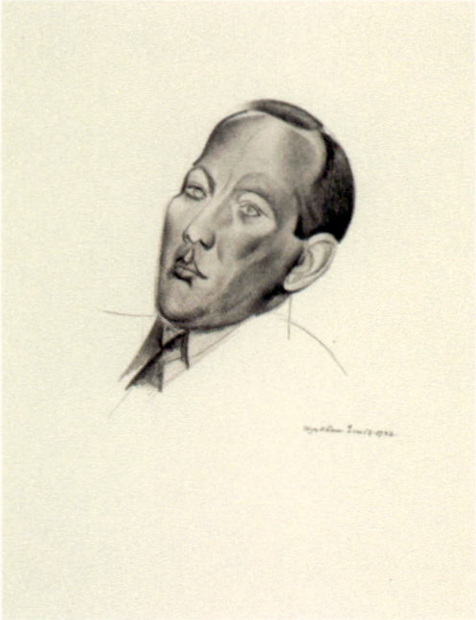

Noël Coward, Esq. (M 741)

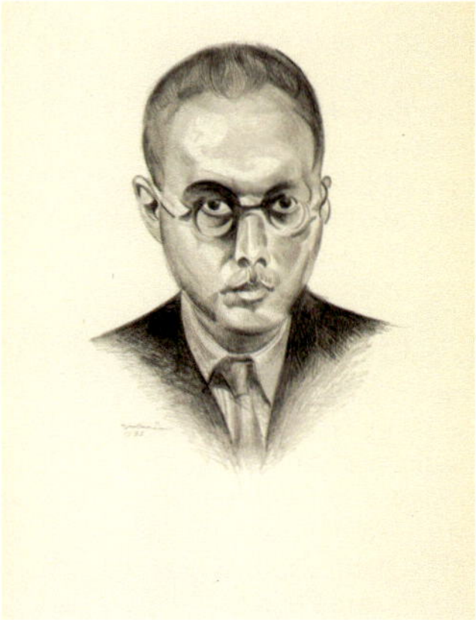

Wyndham Lewis, Esq. (M 781)

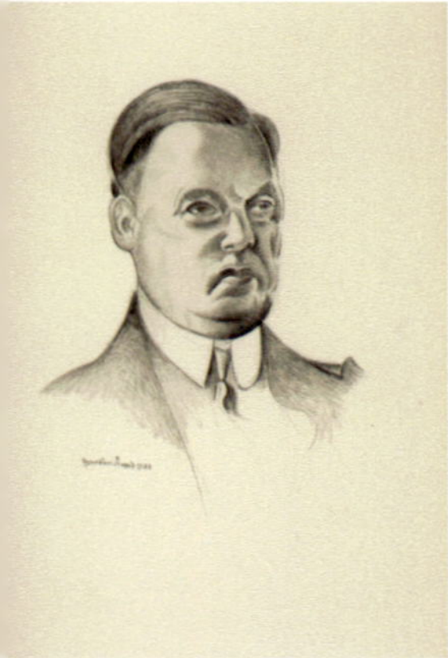

Viscount Rothermere (M 779)

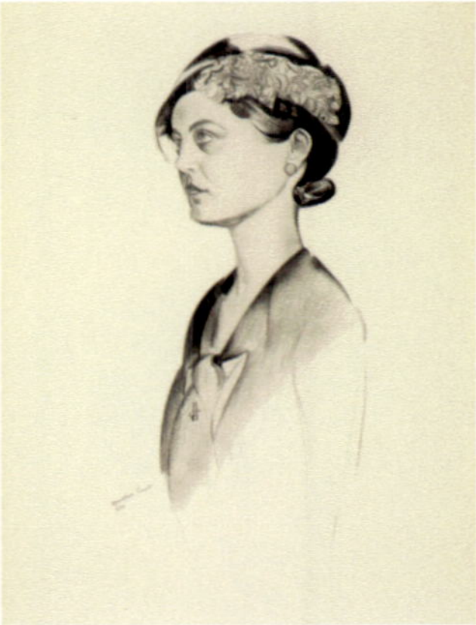

Mrs Desmond Flower (M 754)

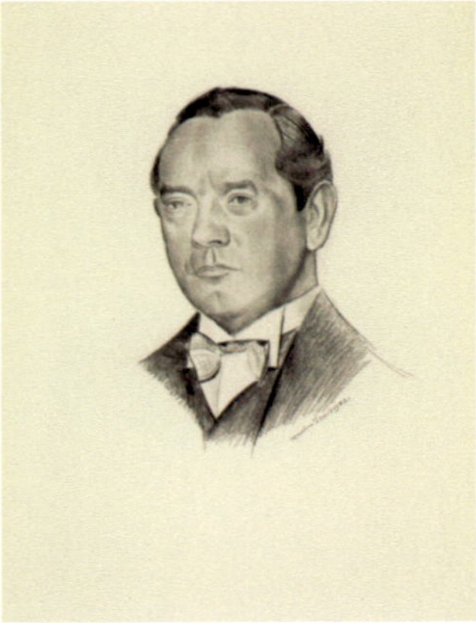

Ivor Stewart-Liberty, Esq. (M 783)

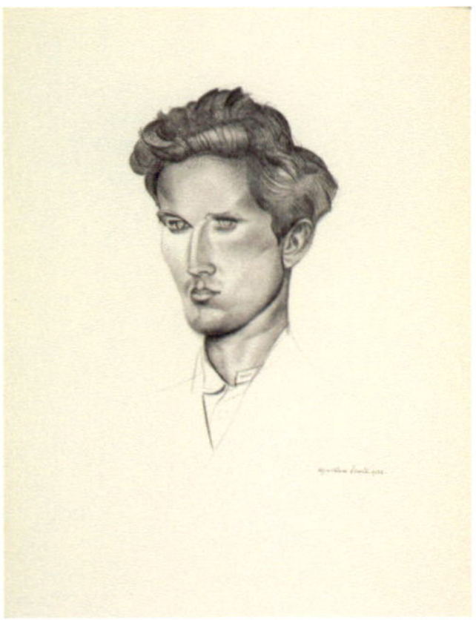

Henry John, Esq. (M 770)

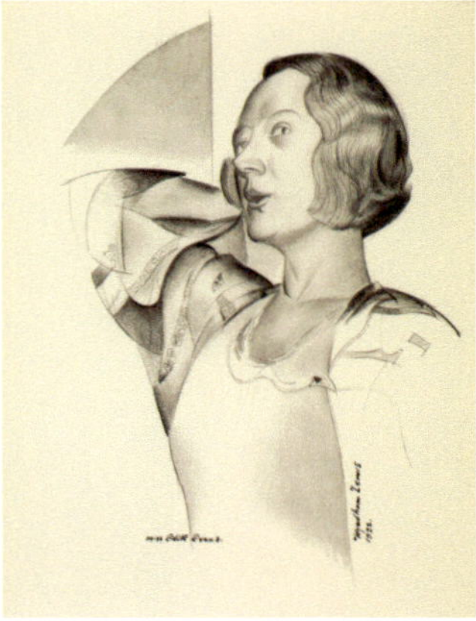

Miss Edith Evans (M 752)

Cat. 141.
Spartan Portrait (Naomi Mitchison), 1933. Graphite and watercolour on paper. 39 x 26.7 cm. Wyndham Lewis Memorial Trust. G. and V. Lane Collection (LD.2004.XX.45). M 809

Naomi Mitchison was a Scottish writer who became friendly with Lewis in the 1930s. He drew her on a number of occasions and painted a fine portrait in oils of her, which is now in the Scottish National Portrait Gallery in Edinburgh. The pair worked together on the fantasy story *Beyond this Limit* (1935), set in the British Museum, London, Lewis providing the charming illustrations for Mitchison's text. Like Rebecca West, the socialist and supporter of good causes, Mitchison was no admirer of Lewis's inter-war political views, but she greatly admired his intelligence, creativity and courage. Her best-known books are her historical novels, such as *The Corn King and the Spring Queen* (1931) and *The Blood of the Martyrs* (1939). The title of this drawing refers to her fascination with classical history.

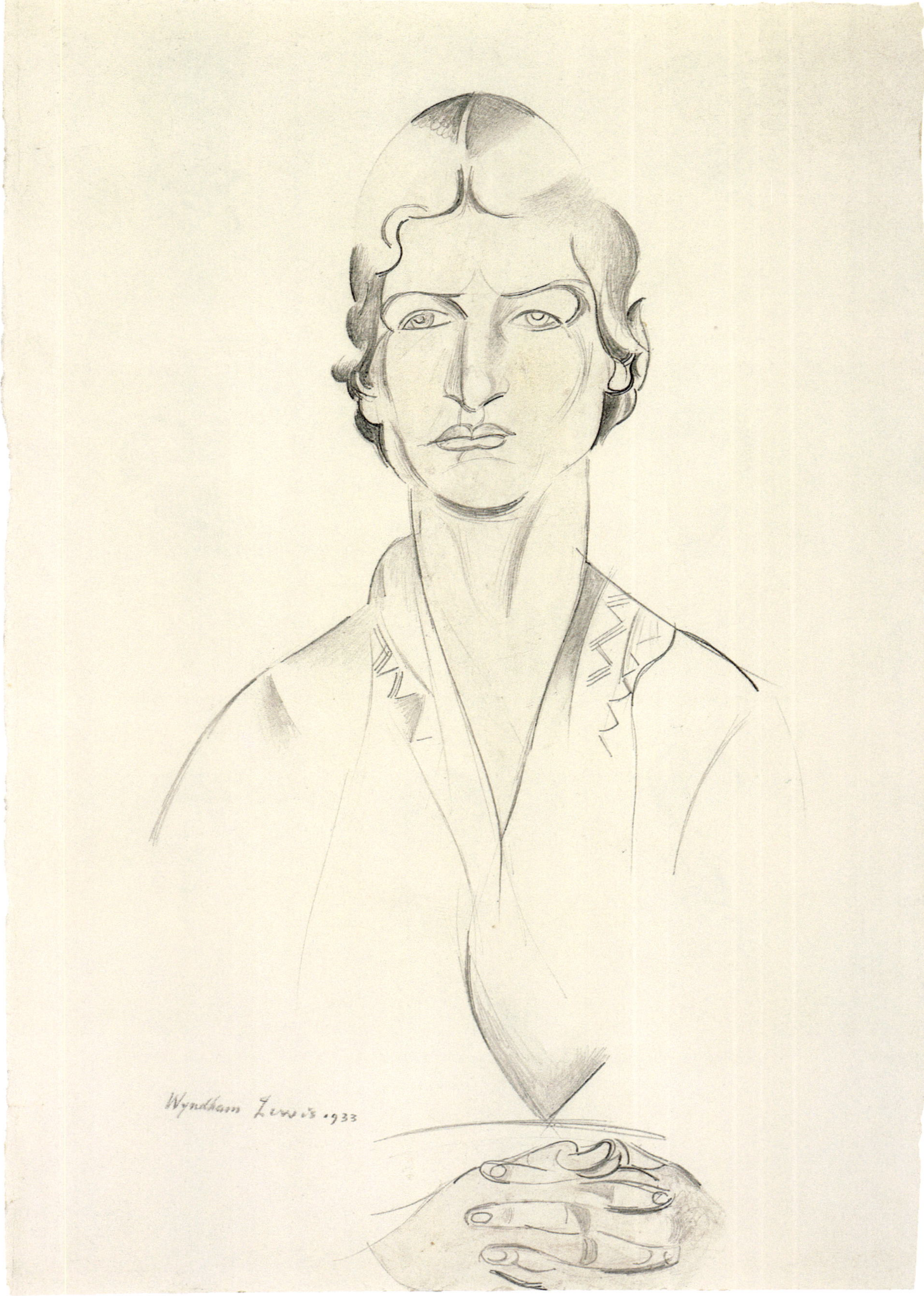

Cat. 142.
Girl Reading (Portrait of the Artist's Wife, Froanna), 1936. Graphite and watercolour on paper. 37.7 x 26.7 cm. British Museum (1939,0730.10). M 858

Lewis's portrait drawing style by the mid-1930s had acquired an almost rococo elegance, while retaining its characteristic complex inventiveness. Here, though creating a striking likeness, Lewis has typically made this image of his wife, Froanna, from a superbly executed orchestration of contrapuntal shapes and delicately shaded form. The almost ethereal quality of the drawing is enhanced by his use of a subtly applied wash of colour, creating an immaterial quality that the artist had sought since his earliest work. The pose is a traditional one of a woman concentrated on reading, which goes back to Dutch art of the seventeenth century.

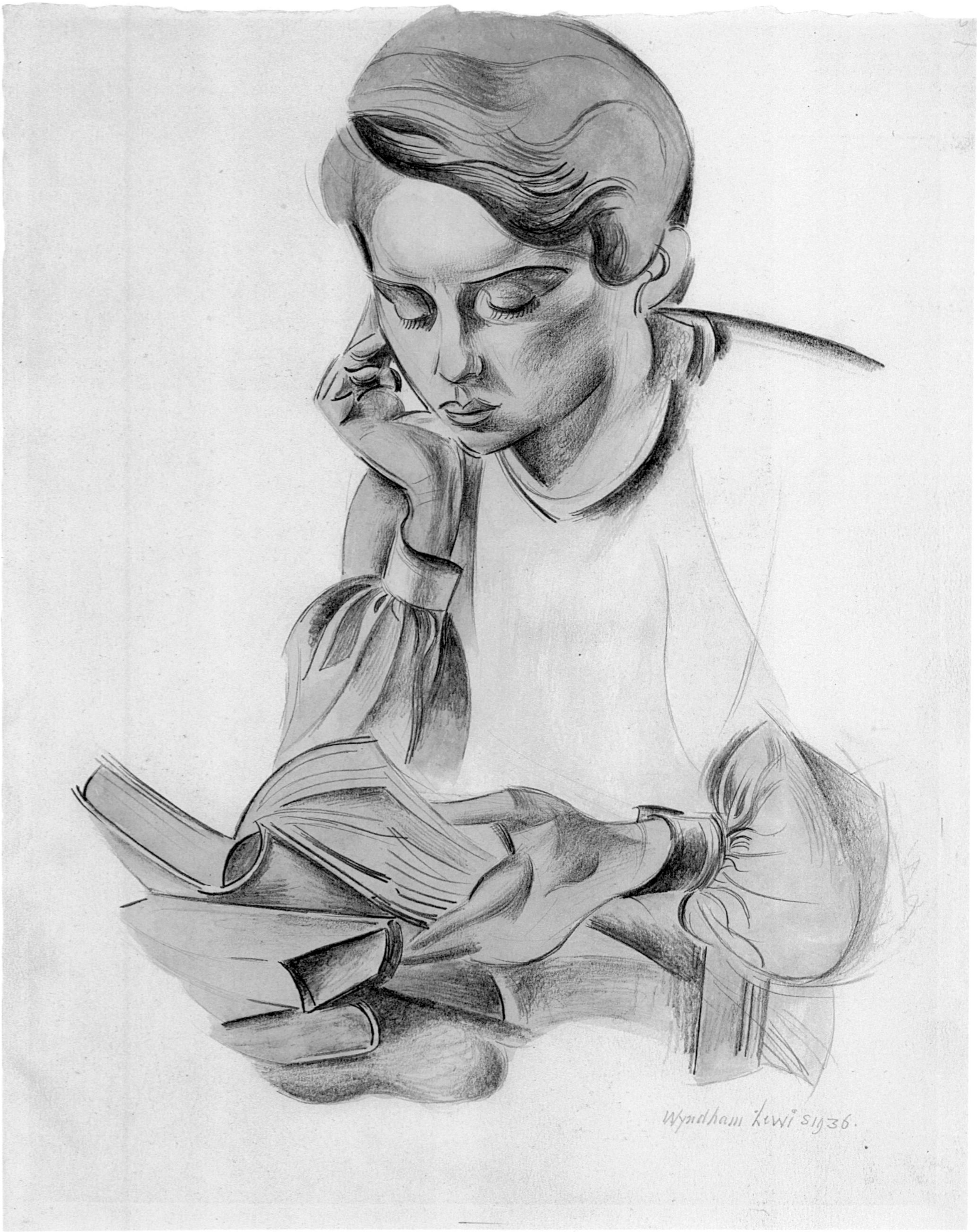

Cat. 143.
Red Portrait (Froanna), 1937.
Oil on canvas. 91.5 x 61 cm.
Wyndham Lewis Memorial
Trust. G. and V. Lane
Collection
(LP.2000.XX.1). M P76

The rather spectral figure of Lewis's wife, Froanna, is seated in front of a fire-place above which hangs an afterworld scene reminiscent of those Lewis was painting at the time. The dominant red colouring furthers a sense of the unworldly and perhaps even infernal, echoing the atmosphere of Red Scene (Cat. 161). Froanna's features seem like a brilliant but tentative projection of light over the setting, everything in the painting indeed having a dream-like uncertainty. At one level the painting is a virtuoso exercise in red; at another it is about the overlapping worlds of spirit and matter on which Lewis had always meditated. This was one of Lewis's favourite paintings.

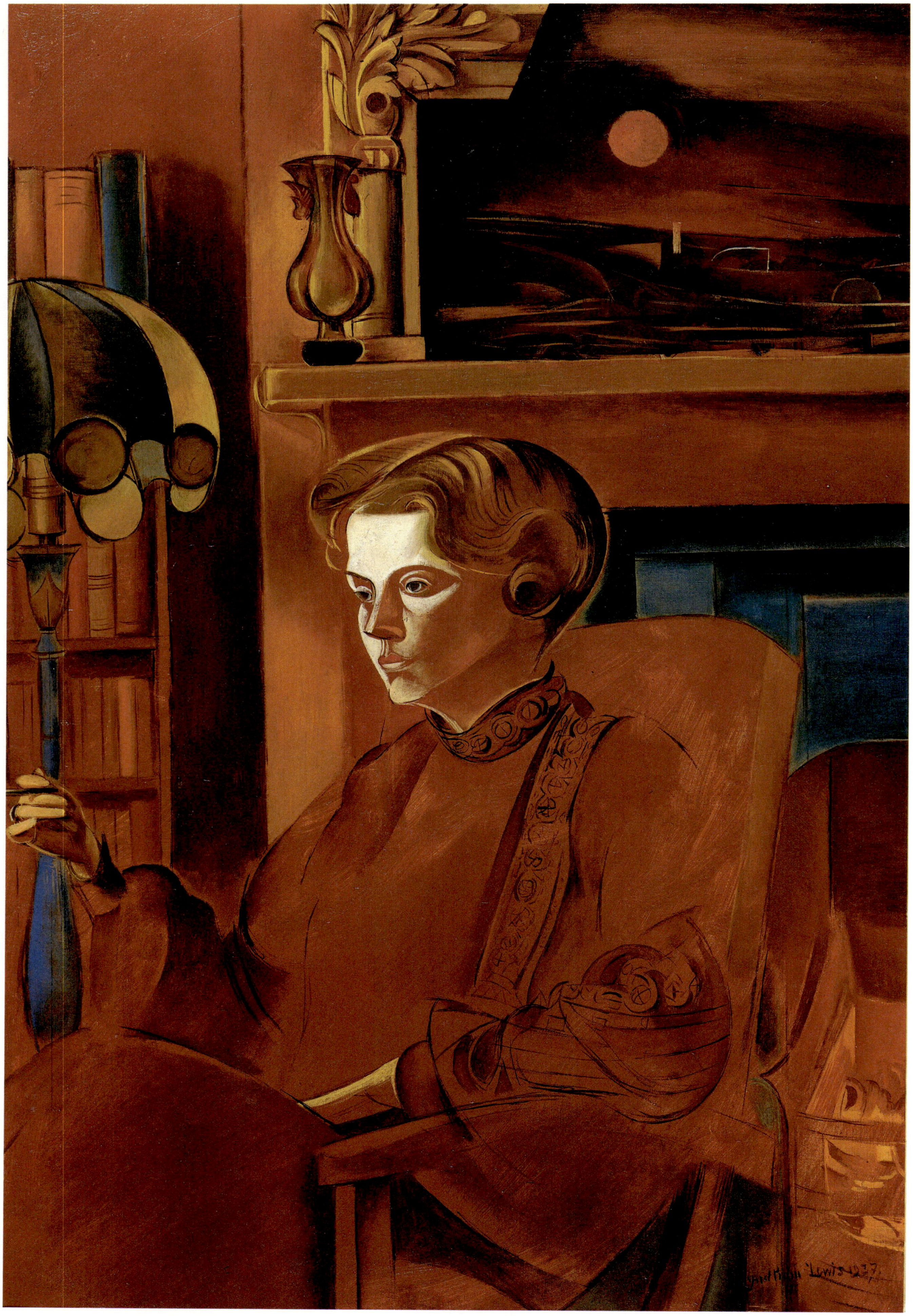

Cat. 144.
[Not in exhibition] *Froanna (Portrait of the Artist's Wife)*, 1937. Oil on canvas. 76 x 63.5 cm. Glasgow Museums. M P71

Although dominated by the colour red like the contemporary *Red Portrait* (Cat. 143), this painting is far more Realist in tendency than its counterpart, the sitter's flesh and the solidity of the tea service and table suggesting a pleasure on Lewis's part in the corporeal warmth of the body and the familiar comforts of an afternoon break. Lewis's trademark arabesques across the composition and the firm modelling of form give the painting great liveliness and strength. Lewis's use of strong reds in this and other works of the time has been attributed by some commentators to a reaction by the artist against a loss of ability to see red, caused by damage to his optic nerves by a tumour in his skull.

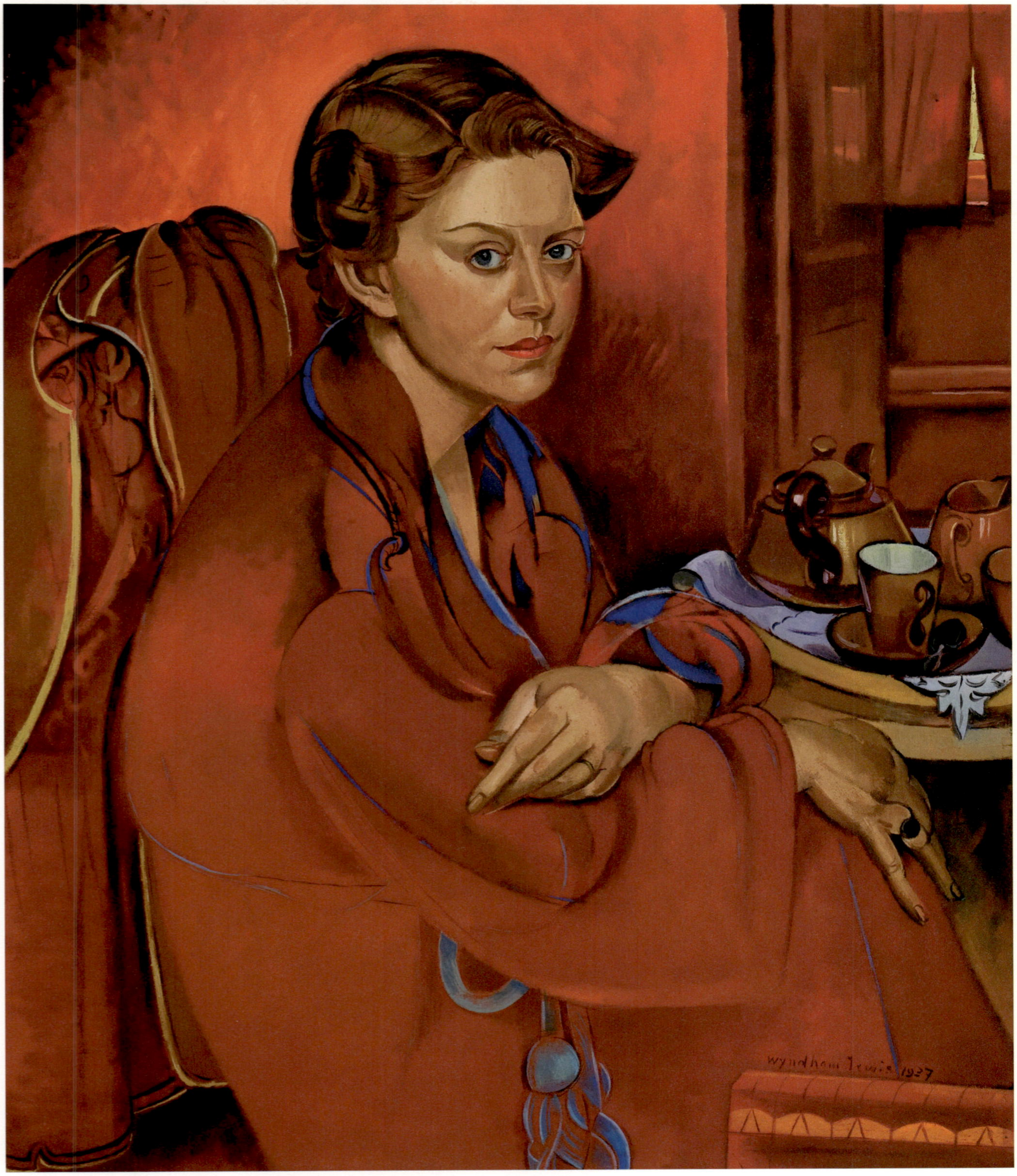

Cat. 146. ▶
Study for Portrait of T.S. Eliot, 1938. Pencil on paper. 38 x 28 cm.
Private collection.

Cat. 147. ▶▶
T.S. Eliot, 1938. Oil on canvas. 133.3 x 85.1 cm.
Collection Durban Art Gallery. M P80

Lewis began a portrait of his famous friend and colleague, the poet and critic T.S. Eliot, in spring 1938 and submitted it for inclusion in the Summer Exhibition at the Royal Academy that year, the only time he put a work up for exhibition at the august institution. Its rejection by the Selection Committee led Lewis's friend, Augustus John, to resign his RA status and the controversy dominated the arts and even front-page headlines for a number of weeks. Lewis's friends rallied round him while opponents, such as the amateur painter and professional politician Winston Churchill, saw the portrait as an example of the modernism against which they believed the Academy should stand firm. Lewis appeared on a newsreel, was interviewed repeatedly in the press and clearly relished a further incident in his career that underlined his rebellious character.

The portrait, for which Lewis made a number of preparatory drawings, presents Eliot as a rather cautious and conventional figure, his imaginative life suggested by the strange shapes spiralling upwards behind him on a screen. It is now considered one of the finest British portraits of the twentieth century.

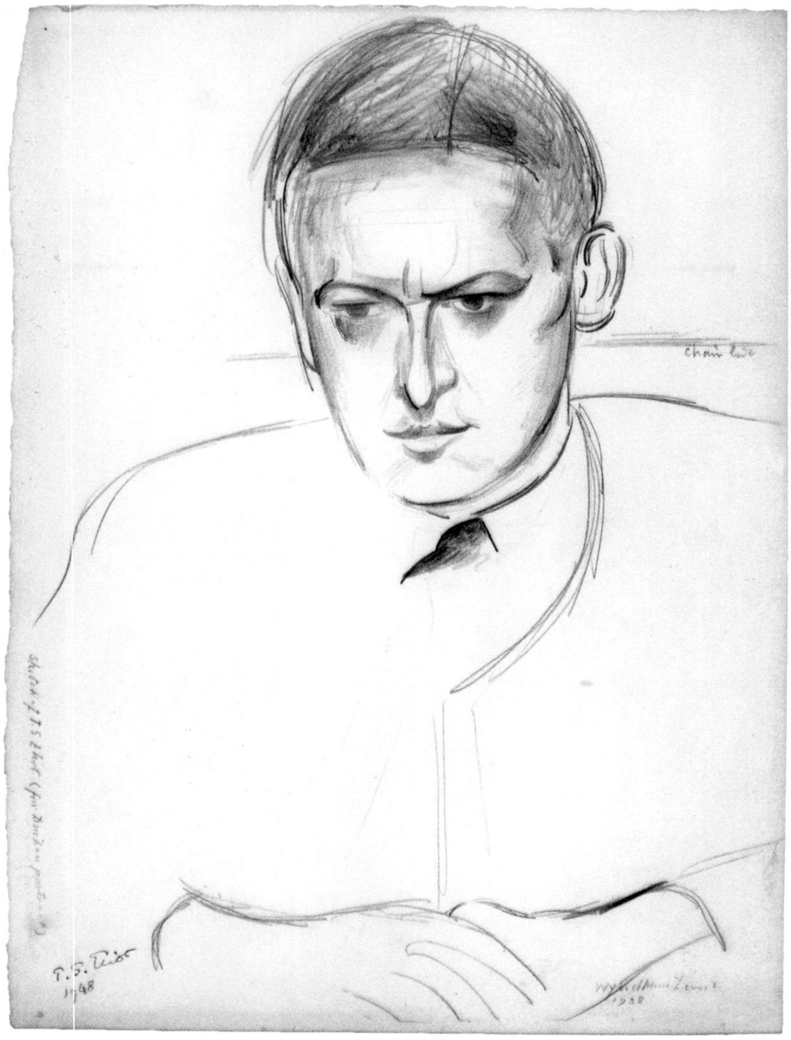

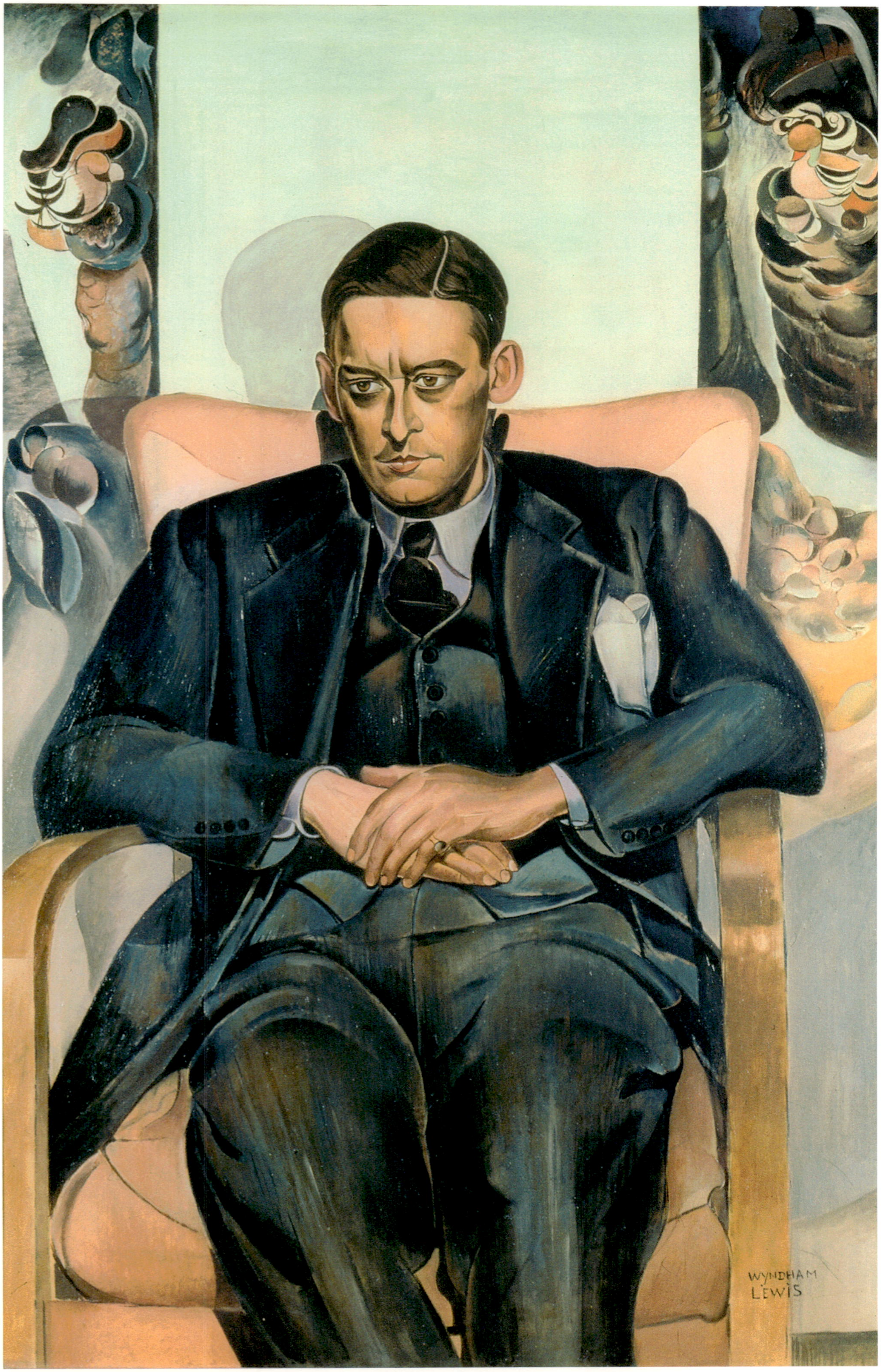
WYNDHAM
LEWIS

Cat. 145.
Julian Symons, 1938.
Pen and ink on paper.
33 x 25.5 cm.
Private collection. M 925

Julian Symons was a young Jewish left-wing intellectual who became friendly with Lewis in the late 1930s. His older brother, the dandy, aesthete and writer, Alphonse James Albert Symons, had known Lewis earlier in the decade. Julian Symons devoted an issue of his journal *Twentieth Century Verse* to Lewis in 1937. Like many other young writers on the left, Symons saw that Lewis's political opinions were far more subtle than many of his enemies allowed and later described being in his presence as "electrifying." This portrait emphasises the sitter's high forehead and magnificent crop of hair. It is a study towards an oil portrait of Symons, begun in 1939, which Lewis completed in 1949. Symons became best known as a writer of crime fiction after the war and also wrote biographies of his brother, and of Charles Dickens and Agatha Christie.

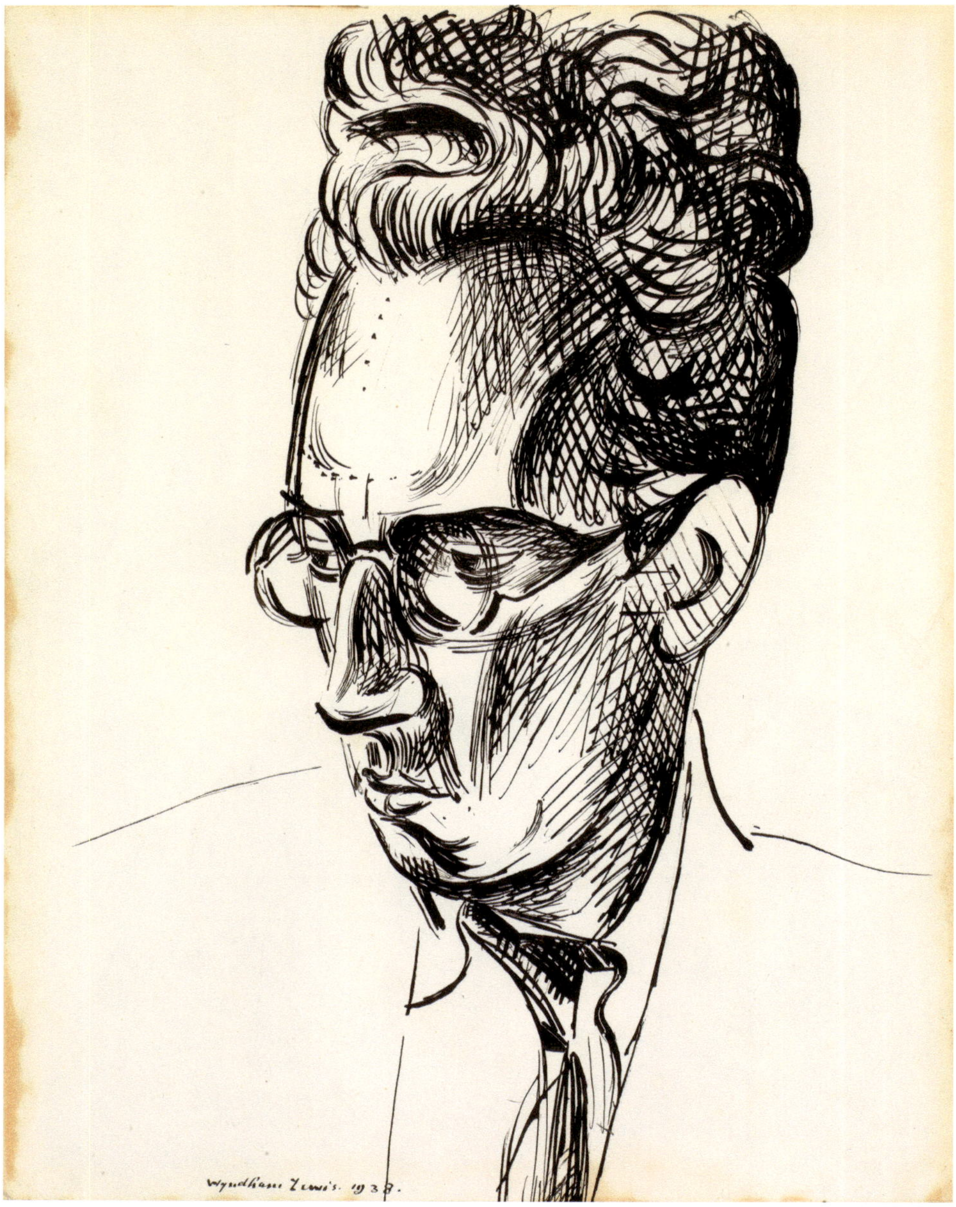

Cat. 148.
Stephen Spender, 1938. Oil on canvas. 100.5 x 59.5 cm. The Potteries Museum & Art Gallery (1939.347). M P86

Stephen Spender was a young left-wing poet who, with his friends W.H. Auden and Christopher Isherwood, had travelled to Weimar Germany in the late 1920s and to Spain in the later 1930s to report on the International Brigades fighting for the Republican side. Apparently, Harry Pollitt, the head of the Communist Party of Great Britain, had suggested that "the best way he could help the party was 'to go and get killed, comrade, we need a Byron in the movement'."[1] It was this kind of cynical attitude that Lewis attacked in his novel *The Revenge for Love* (1937) (B&M Cat. 39). Spender survived to write an autobiography, *World Within World* (1951), about the left-wing cultural scene in the 1930s. It is said he was the model for the naive poet, Dan Boleyn, in Lewis's satire *The Apes of God* (1930) (B&M Cat. 21). Again, we find a young leftist painted by "that lonely old volcano of the Right," in Auden's words, reminding us of how politically complex the period was.[2] Ironically, perhaps, Spender was knighted in the 1980s, an honour Lewis could never have expected for himself.

1. Hugh Thomas, *The Spanish Civil War*. 3rd ed., revised and enlarged (Harmondsworth: Penguin Books in association with Hamish Hamilton, 1977), p. 491, n. 2.
2. W.H. Auden, "Letter to Lord Byron – Part V," in *Letters from Iceland* (London: Faber and Faber, 1937), p. 233.

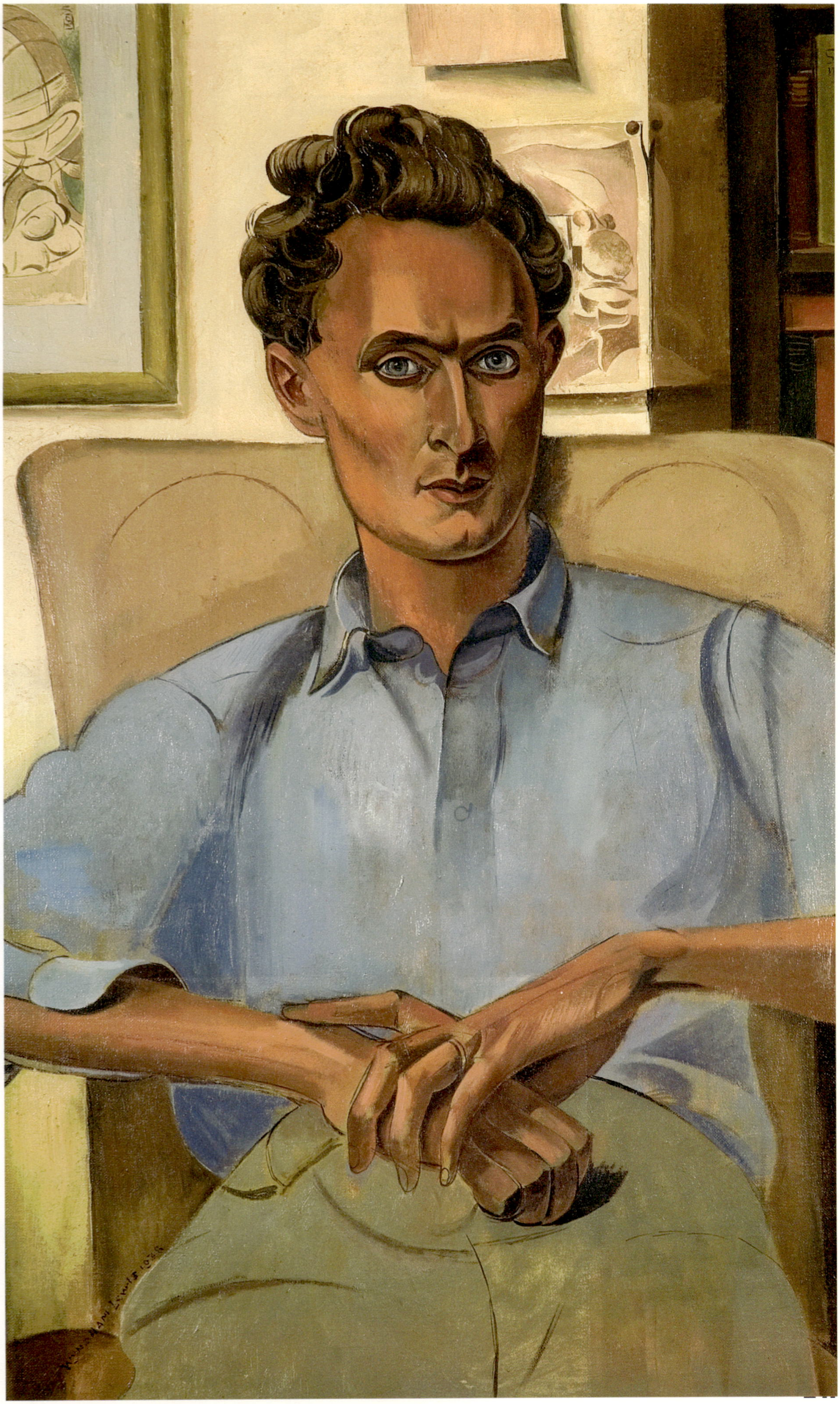

Cat. 149.
Ezra Pound, 1939. Oil on canvas. 76.2 x 101.6 cm. Tate: Purchased 1939 (N05042). M P99

Lewis had drawn and painted his friend and Vorticist colleague, the American poet Ezra Pound, on a number of occasions shortly after the First World War. Pound had subsequently moved to Italy and become a devoted follower of the Fascist dictator Benito Mussolini, much to the latter's suspicion and bemusement. When Pound travelled to London in 1939, Lewis, in the wake of his successes with portraiture in the previous year or so, set about painting him. Lewis remembers Pound coming into his flat, "coat tails flying" and commanding "Go to it Wyndham!"[1] The portrait shows Pound almost horizontal in an armchair, having fallen into a reverie. Behind him a canvas reminiscent of one of the poet's favourite artists, the American Impressionist J.A.M. Whistler, suggests the watery, Mediterranean world of his poetic imagination, hinting perhaps at the critique Lewis had made of Pound's poetry in the 1920s as too historicising and romantic.

1. Wyndham Lewis, *Blasting and Bombardiering: Autobiography (1914–1926)*. 2nd ed. (London: Calder & Boyars, 1967), p. 286.

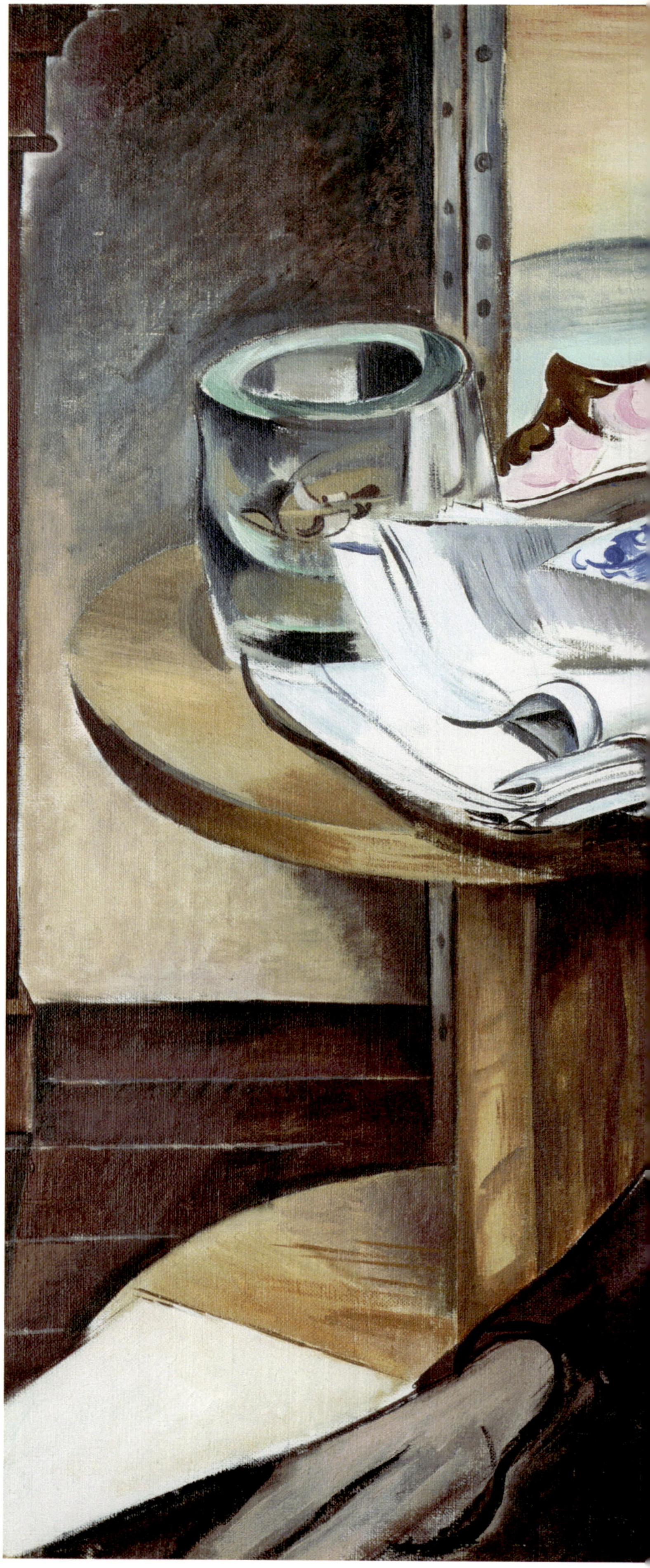

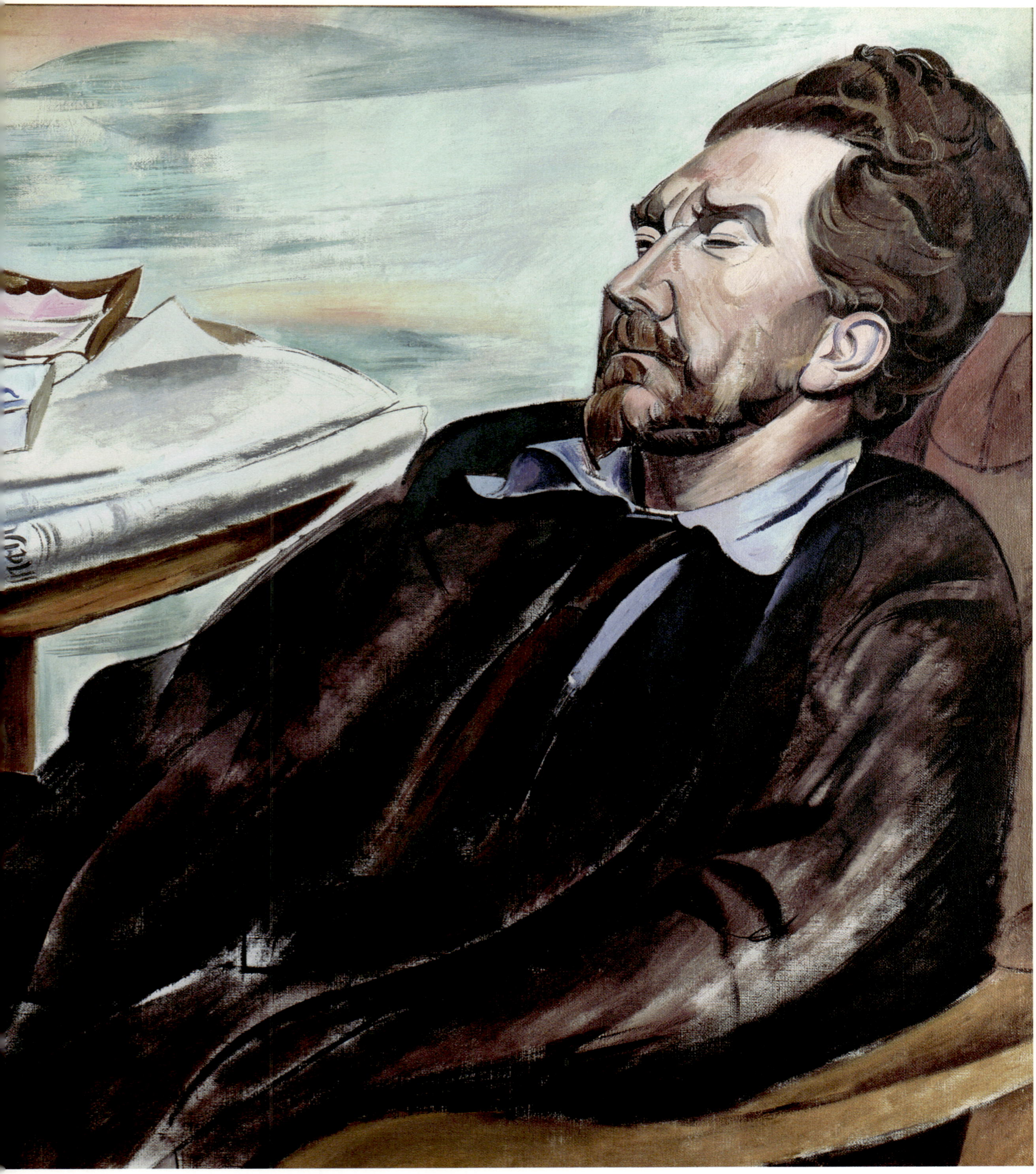

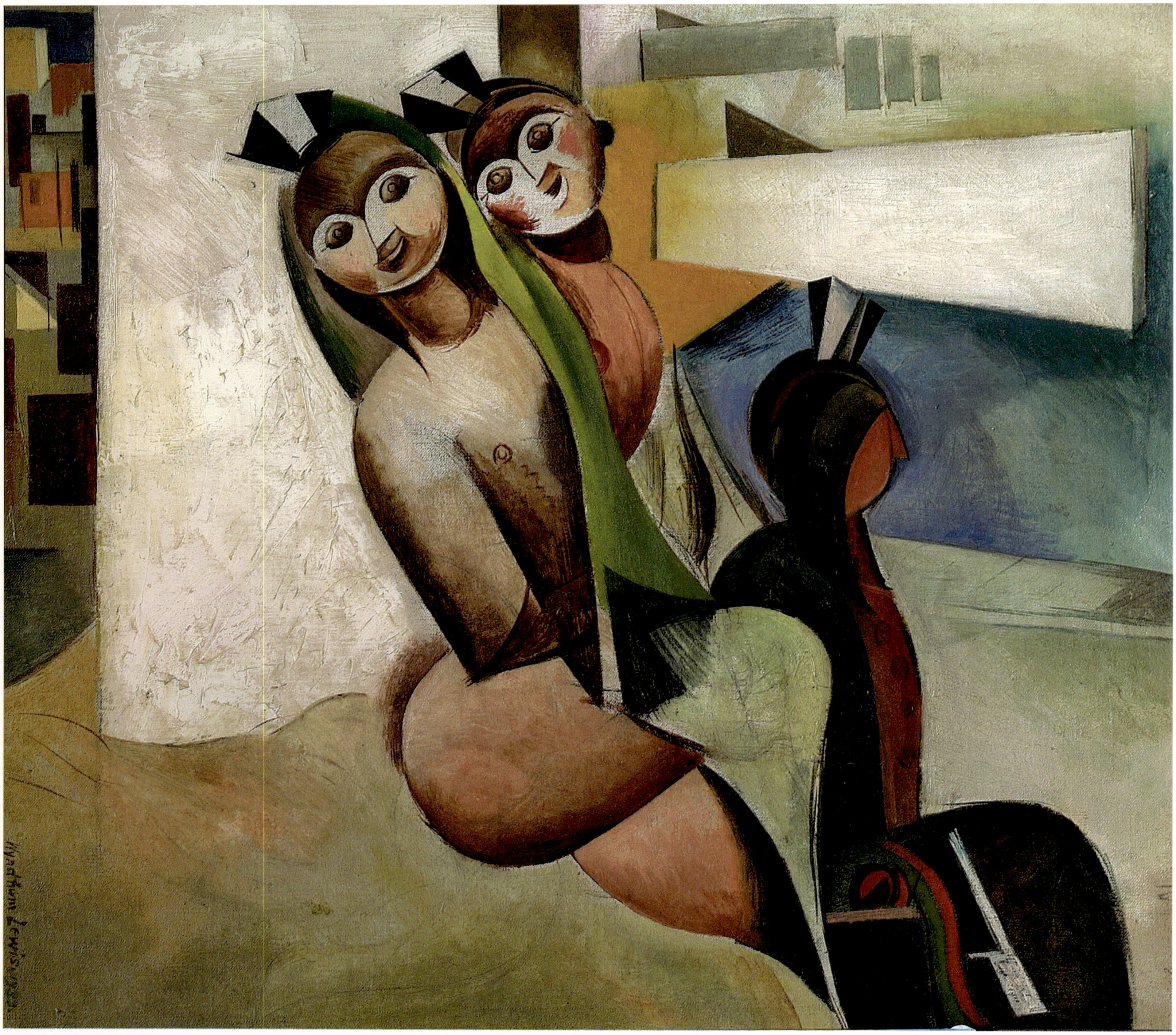

Cat. 151.
Two Beach Babies, 1933. Oil on canvas. 51 x 61 cm. Rugby Art Gallery and Museum. M P53

Lewis's subject matter had included beach imagery since the pre-war period and most recently in the works of 1929 (Cats. 129–31), where he exploited the opportunity to show figures in energetic movement against the elemental setting of sand, sea and sky. There is probably a Darwinian interest in the human figure seen near its original habitat, as well as a more poignant focus on a modern setting of a semi-paradisal kind where humans seek peace, rest and rejuvenation. These two female figures, or "monads" as he called such moon-faced descendants of his Tyros in the 1930s, are like the bathing beauties of commercial travel publicity and show Lewis's continuing interest in creating a race of satirical figures. The setting has a typically Lewisian stage-like quality.

Cat. 150.
Boats in a Port or *A Spanish Harbour*, 1933. Pencil and gouache on paper. 19.5 x 25 cm. Private collection. M 788

This work's alternative title suggests it may be based on a memory, perhaps a recent one recalling Lewis's journey by boat to North Africa. Since the Vorticist period, Lewis had created many compositions as if they were vignettes or emblems, integral units of compacted form set against the blank ground of the paper. Very often, the overall shape might suggest another, apparently unrelated, form; in this case possibly that of a recumbent figure. The subject matter itself is conventional, reminiscent of Pablo Picasso's and Georges Braque's early Cubist landscapes, yet Lewis's image is full of a surreal and allusive atmosphere and hints at a deep historical past.

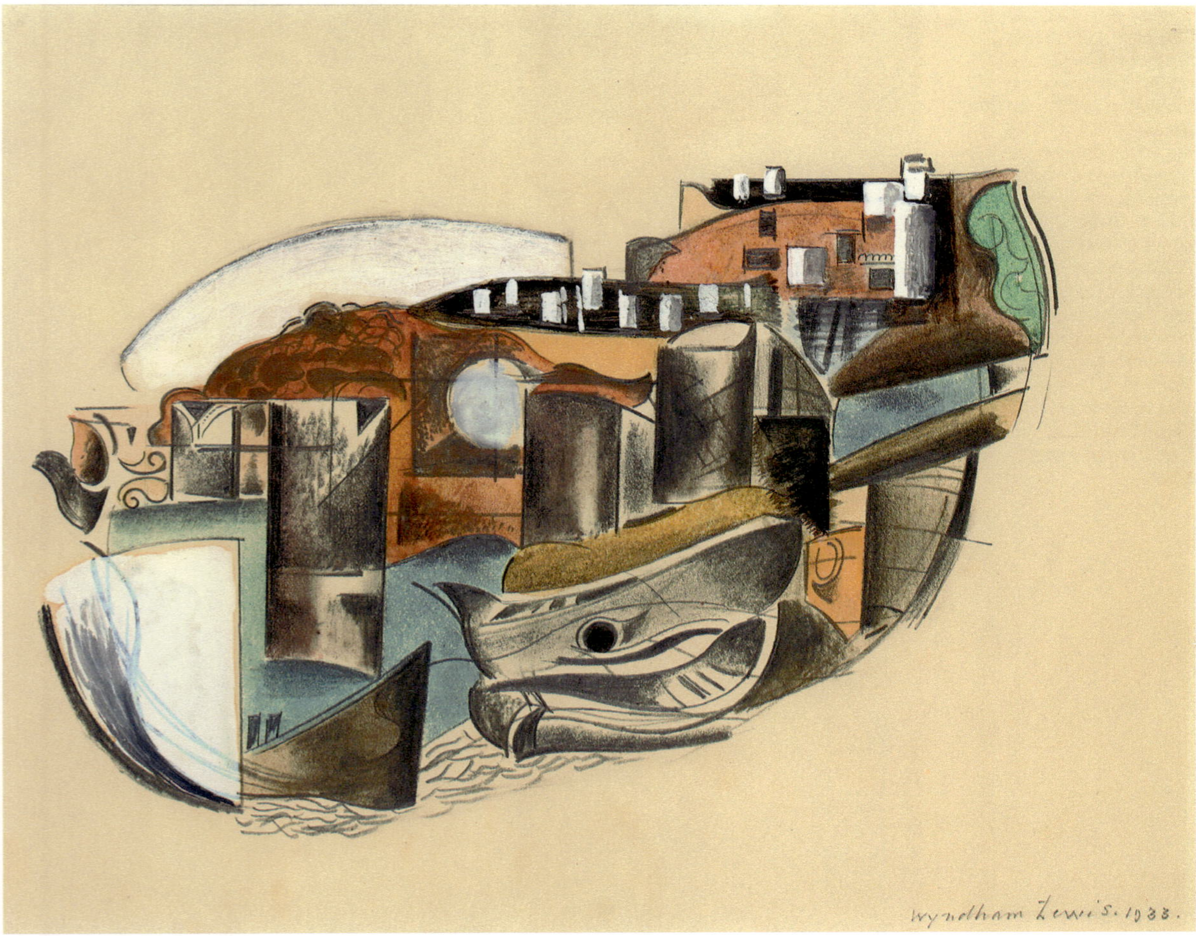

Cat. 152.
The Betrothal of the Matador, 1933. Oil on canvas. 54.5 x 42.5 cm. Wyndham Lewis Memorial Trust (LP.2008.XX.2). M P45

Another Spanish subject, this work is probably a private and humorous image inspired by the drunken and eventful life of Lewis's friend, the satirical poet and Franco supporter Roy Campbell. Campbell had met Lewis in the 1920s and the two veered politically to the right, both writing satires against the cultural elite in London, Campbell's effort being the poem *The Georgiad* (1931). Campbell had married in 1922 and, after his wife's lesbian affair with the Bloomsbury writer Vita Sackville-West, the couple moved to Provence and then to Spain. Campbell's poem *Mithraic Emblems* (1936) shows his great fascination with bullfighting and the image of the matador. He appeared as the rumbustious Scot, Rob McPhail, in Lewis's novel *Snooty Baronet* (1932) (B&M Cat. 33), a character that is gored to death by a bull.

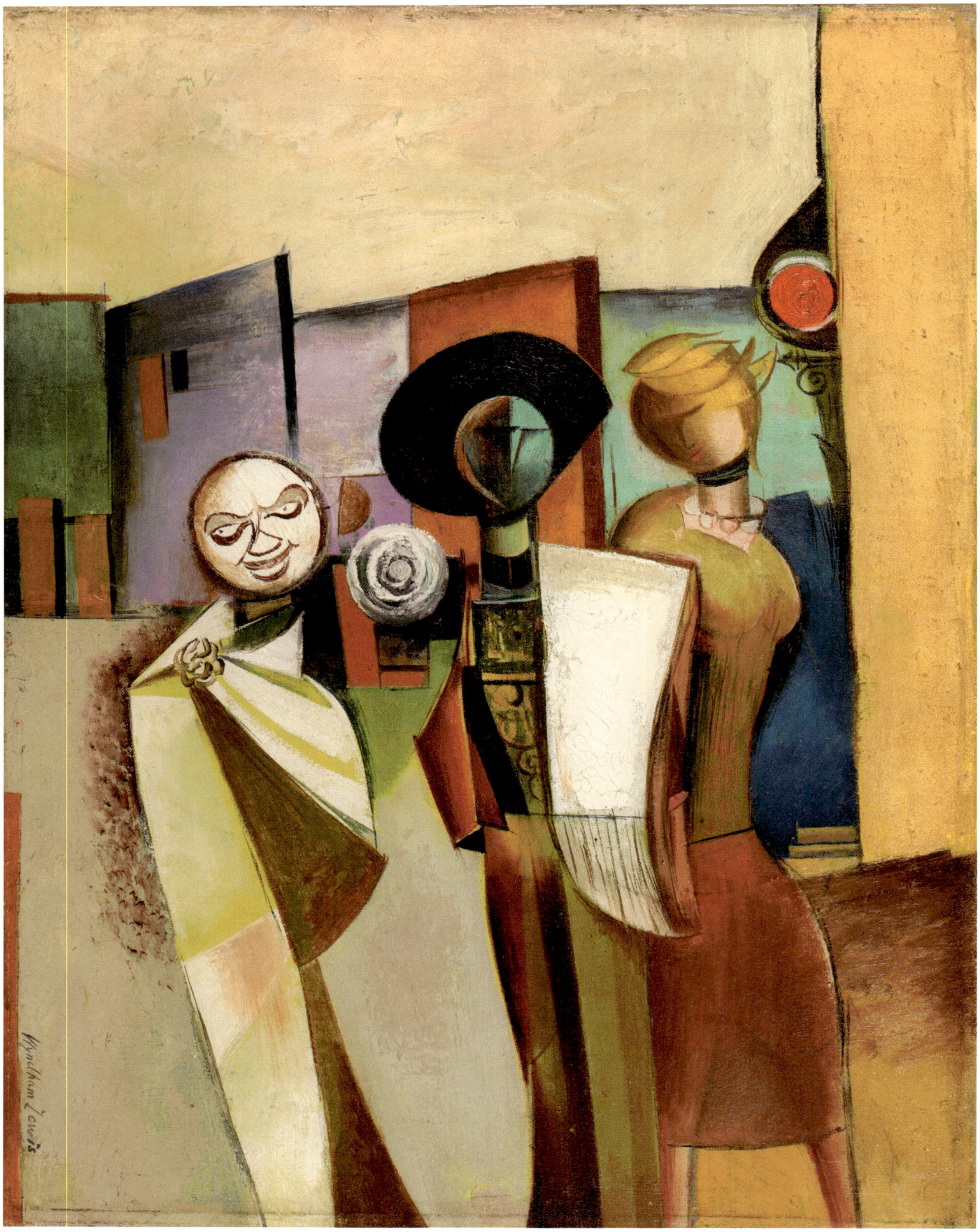

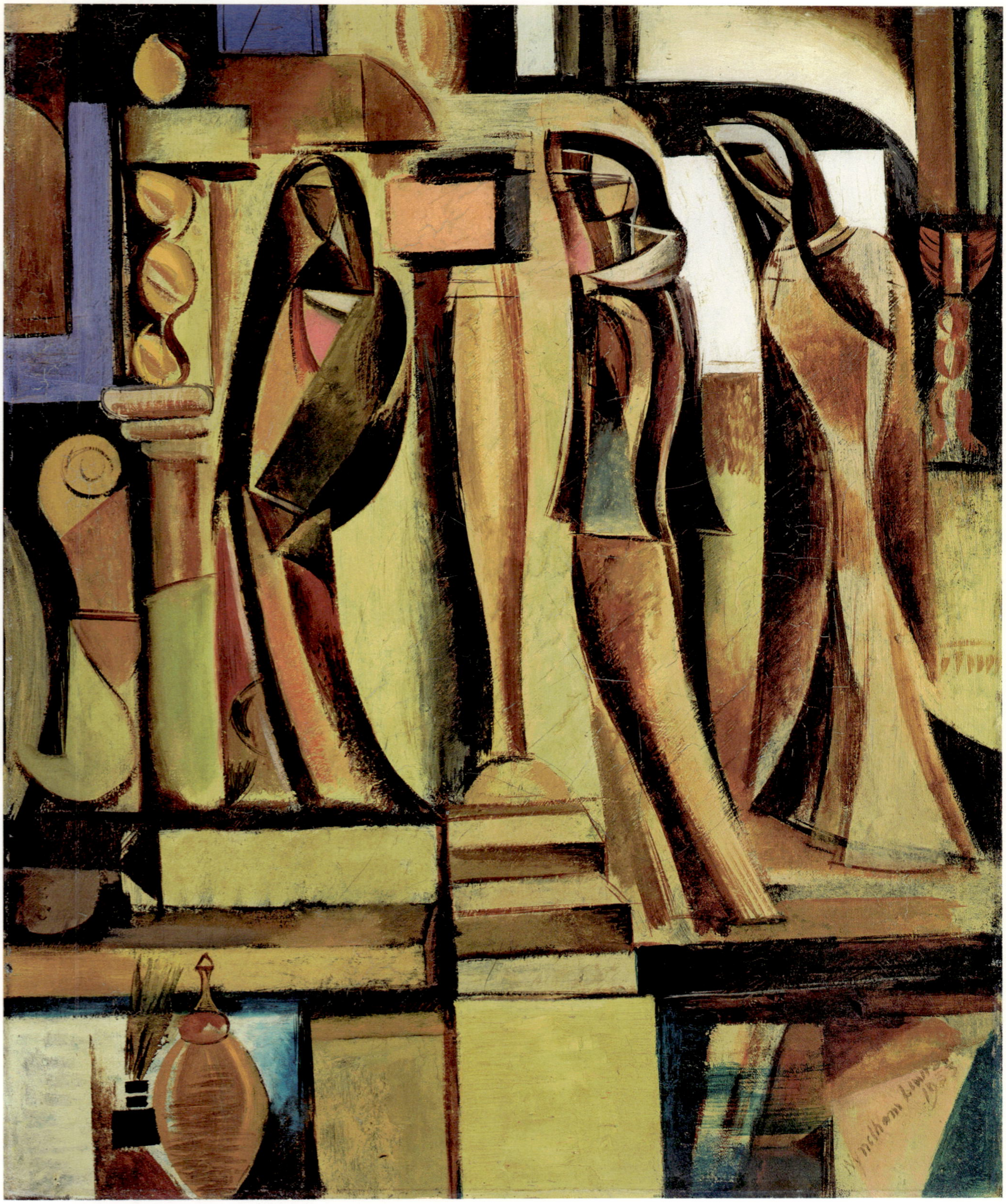

Cat. 153.
Group of Three Veiled Figures, 1933. Oil on canvas. 51 x 43 cm. Leeds Museums and Galleries (Leeds Art Gallery) (LEEAG.1978.0026). M P47

Lewis's fascination with Islam increased after his visit to Morocco in 1931 and this work may allude to the dress code of Muslim women. Like many of his works since the early 1920s, Lewis uses a flat, frieze-like composition within which he organises a group of rather mournful figures whose narrative meaning is ambiguous. Lewis evidently enjoyed taking such a simple format and developing its potential for variation of form and atmosphere. Such works also allowed him to explore the possibilities of colour and the texture of oil paint, a medium with which he was less familiar than pencil, pen and ink, and watercolour.

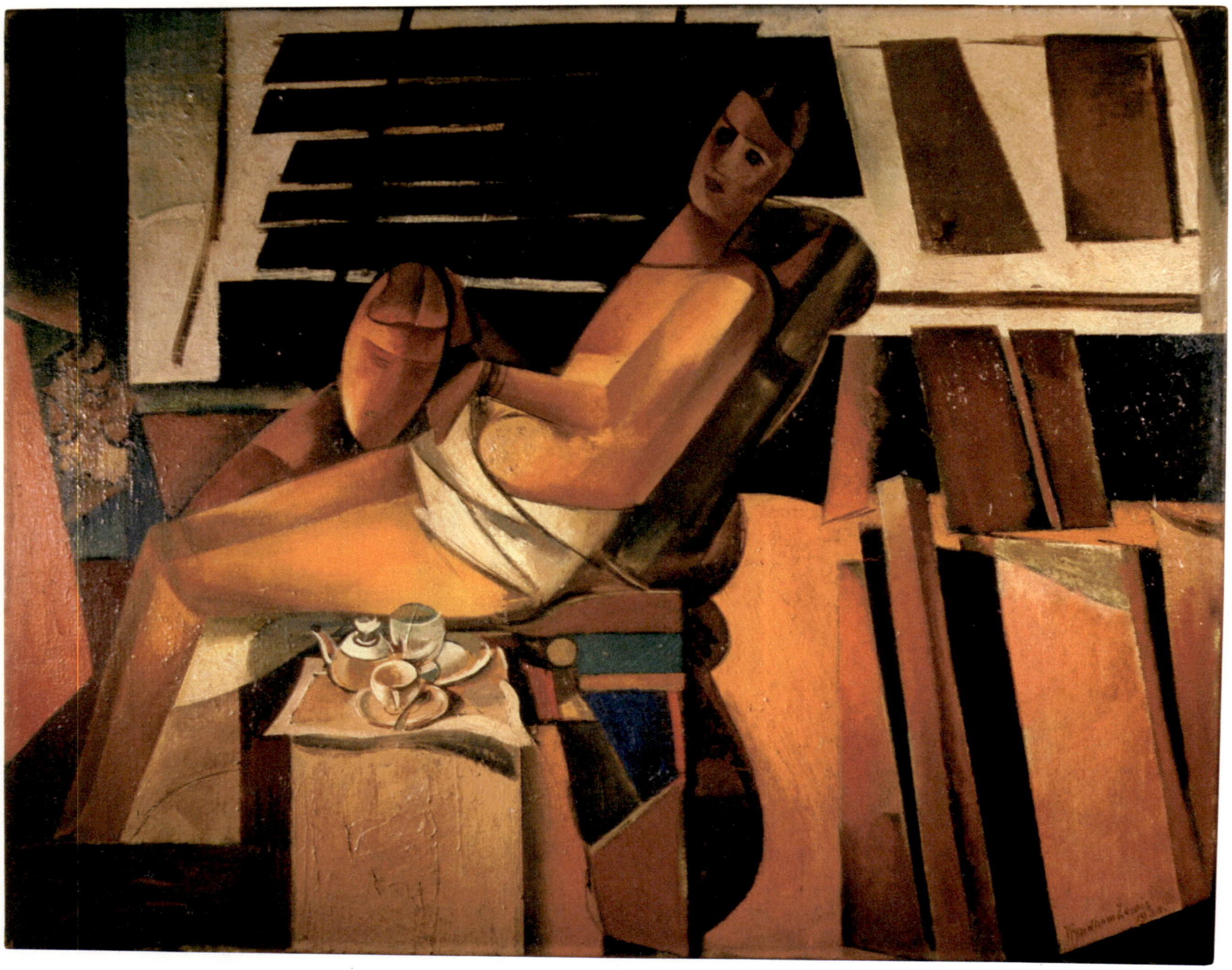

Cat. 154.
[Not in exhibition]
The Convalescent, 1933.
Oil on canvas. 61 x 76.5 cm.
Glynn Vivian Art Gallery
(GV 1976.17). M P46

This shady domestic interior with its loving couple and tea service is one of a number of personal pictures inspired by Lewis's relationship with his wife, Froanna. This work concerns her care for him during a lengthy and often painful series of medical treatments. Lewis had become ill in 1932 with an ulcer caused by a bladder infection on an old venereal scar. He spent much time over the next five years in hospitals and nursing homes and at one stage was in fear of his life. The painting, however, is not strictly autobiographical and the figures and faces suggest a general human condition of patient incarnation and sufferance. The German philosopher Friedrich Nietzsche had written about the idea of the convalescent and Lewis may be making a reference to his writings here.

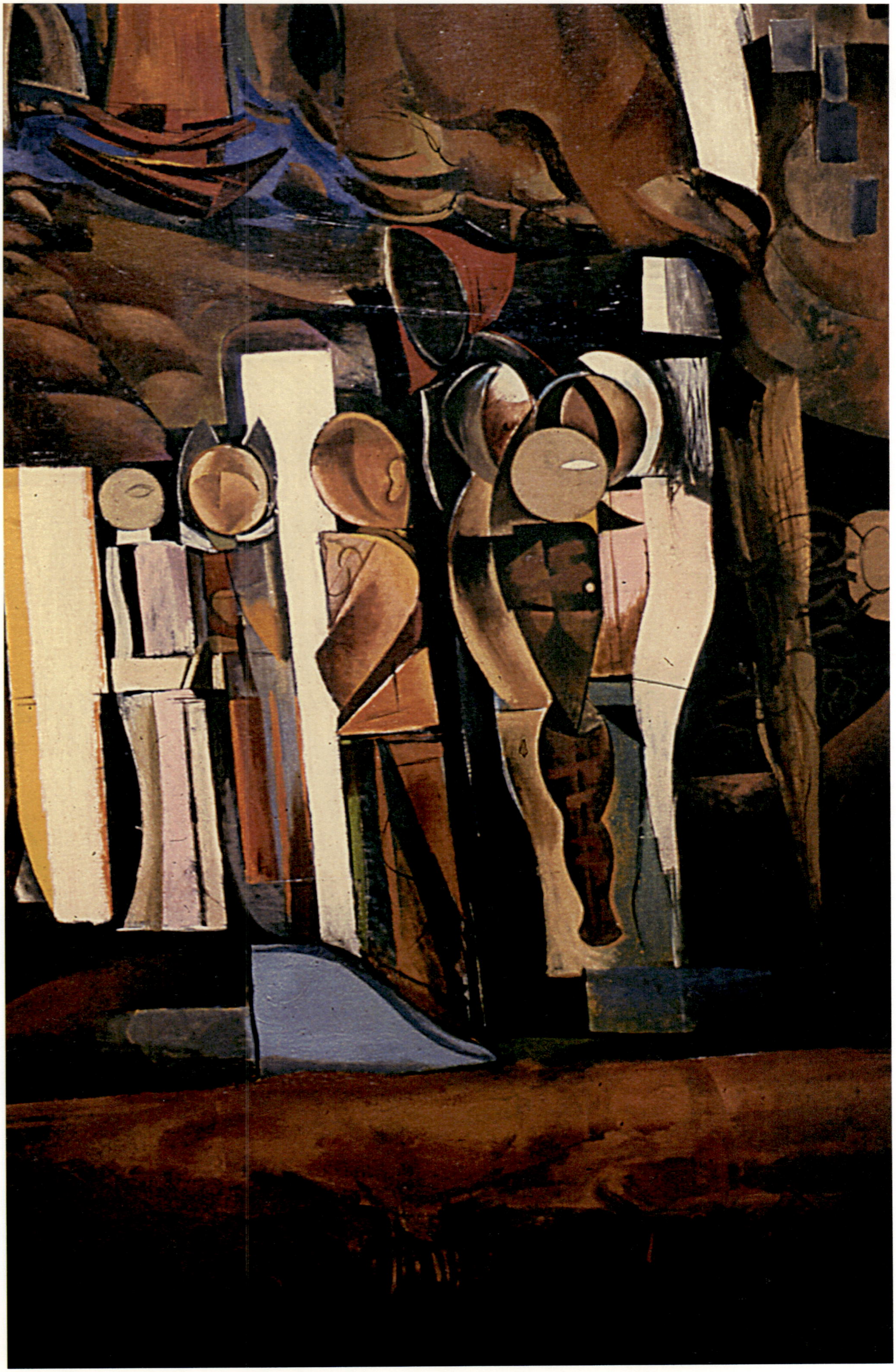

Cat. 155.
One of the Stations of the Dead, 1933. Oil on canvas. 127.6 x 75.8 cm. Aberdeen Art Gallery & Museums Collections (ABDAG 2522). M P50

Like Cat. 154, this canvas develops a complex composition from a frieze-like group of hieratic figures. However, in this painting Lewis seems to be drawing on the narrative content of his metaphysical novel, *The Childermass* (1928) (B&M Cat. 19), set in the borderlands just outside heaven immediately after the First World War. The novel creates a world recognisably human both in its characters who drift in an uncertain reality presided over by a sinister figure, the Bailiff, the embodiment of a bogus democratic politics, and in its analysis of contemporary intellectual and social collapse. The figures seem to be waiting at a station by the River Styx, a boat in the background perhaps arriving soon to take them to the next stage in the after-life. Like all Lewis's figures in his imaginative works of the 1930s, they are presented as faceless, cut-out "monads," victims of an elaborate sham.

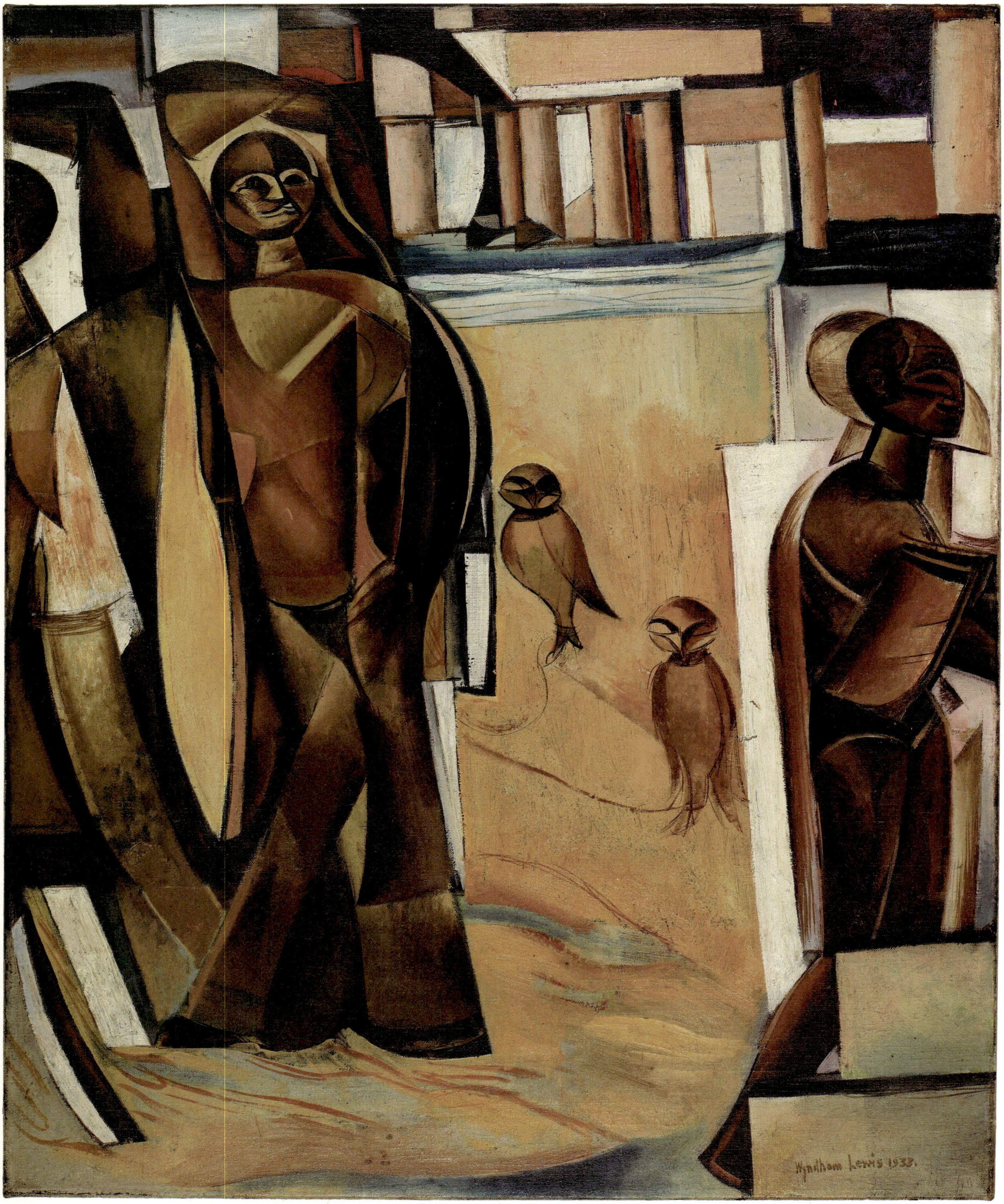
Wyndham Lewis 1933.

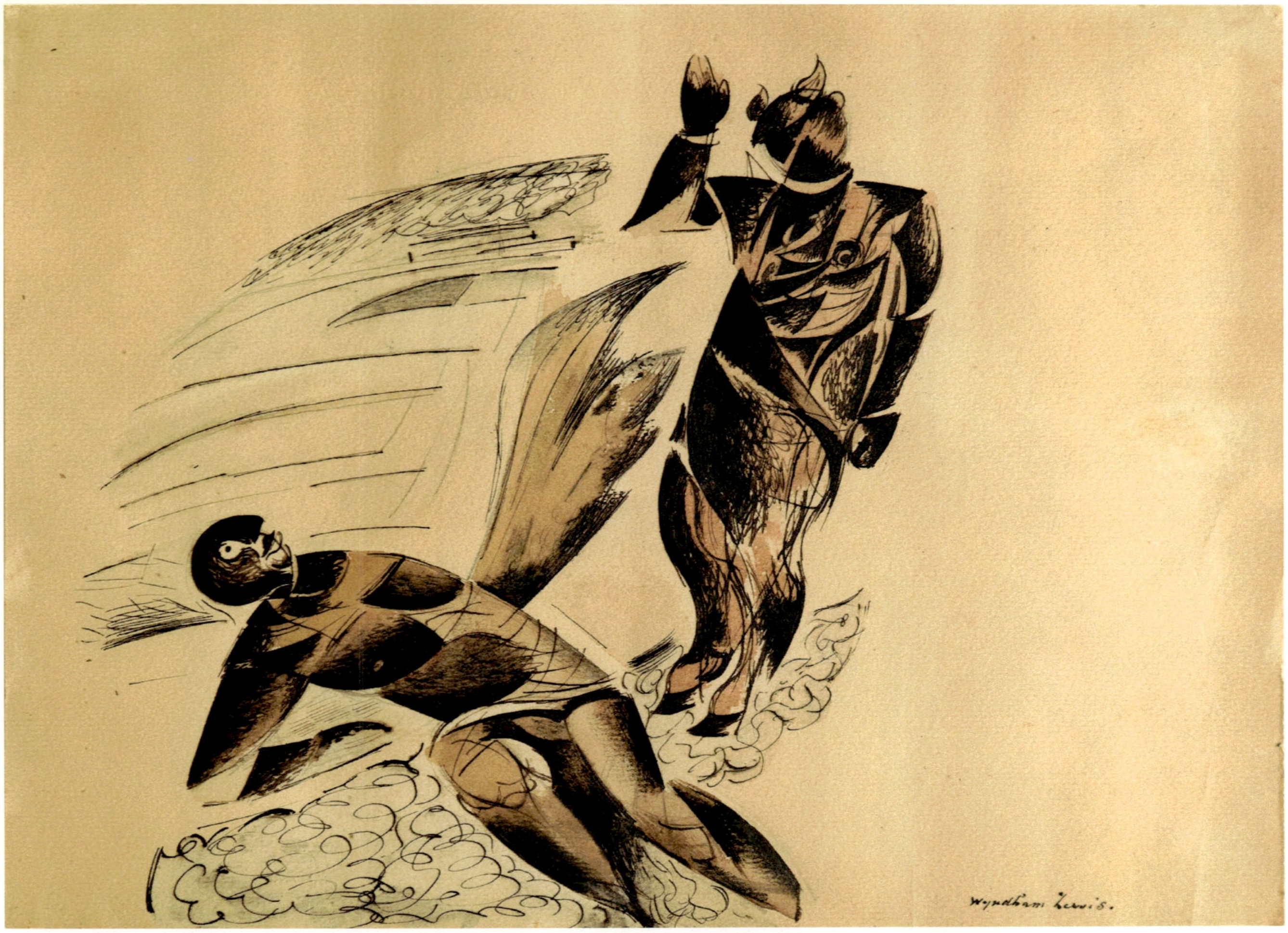

Cat. 157.
Figure Composition,
1933–38. Ink ground colour and watercolour on paper.
23 x 31 cm.
Private collection

Since the 1920s, Lewis had increasingly explored a metaphysical realm in his painting, matching themes emerging in some of his writing. This work shows his continuing interest in the work of the English poet and artist, William Blake, in its dramatisation of some kind of psychological encounter between angelic figures in flight. Frequently, as in Blake's work, Lewis suggests in such subject matter the conflicts of the soul, his figures representing different aspects of one personality as well as struggles between individuals. Another source for such works is the poetry of the great seventeenth-century writer, John Milton.

Cat. 156.
Inca and the Birds, 1933.
Oil on canvas.
67.3 x 54.6 cm.
Arts Council Collection, Southbank Centre, London (ACC4/1959). M P49

Lewis's works in the 1930s included a number of historical images. In the case of this painting, which he described as "a (non-Freudian) dream picture,"[1] we see an Inca prince just before or at the time of the Spanish invasion of Peru in the sixteenth century. Lewis's source was the American Romantic historian William H. Prescott, whose *The Conquest of Peru* (1847) was written when he was blind. Prescott's account of Inca society included a description of the initiation of Inca princes through an arduous journey into the mountains and desert to collect feathers from a male and female sacred "correquenque" bird, seen here behind Lewis's prince. This was an allegory of the attainment of maturity and, for Lewis, of the idea of the training of the ideal ruler. Lewis's figure may suggest an impostor, who has perhaps attained his feathers by deceit, pretending to an authority he does not deserve. The vast "mountain-palaces,"[2] in Lewis's words, of Inca society are shown here by the shores of Lake Titicaca.

1. Wyndham Lewis, "Foreword," in *Paintings and Drawings by Wyndham Lewis* [exh. cat. The Leicester Galleries, London]. London: The Leicester Galleries, December 1937, p. 7.
2. Ibid.

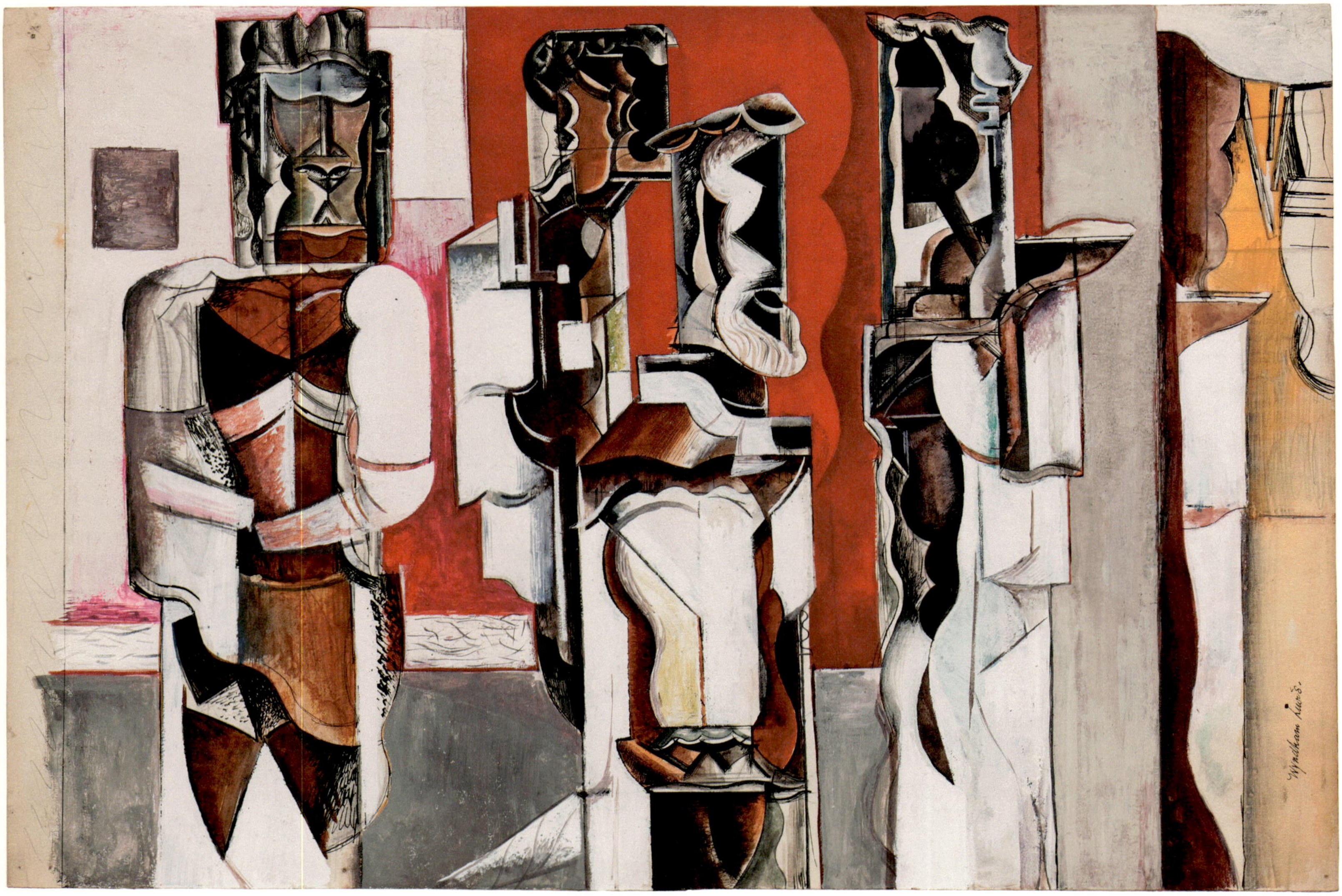

Cat. 158.
Roman Actors, 1934.
Watercolour, gouache, ink and pencil on paper.
38.4 x 56.2 cm.
The Museum of Modern Art, New York, Francis E. Brennan Fund, 1954 (14.1954). M 846

The precise subject matter of this work is obscure. The figures, arranged in a frieze-like composition, are formally close to those Lewis invented in the period 1921 to 1922, with their arabesques and allusions to armed and insect shapes. This work also has many parallels with the Vorticist watercolour *Red Duet* (1914). Lewis had drawn on theatrical themes since his earliest works and continued to do so until the end of his career, creating encounters and dynamic conflict between his "actors" on a stage. The reference to Romans in this work might suggest an interest in Latin drama, perhaps the stoic plays of Seneca for instance, as well as being an allusion to contemporary politics, in this case to Benito Mussolini's "new Roman Empire" in Fascist Italy.

Cat. 159.
Red and Black Principle, 1936. Oil on canvas. 116.8 x 61 cm. Santa Barbara Museum of Art, Gift of Wright S. Ludington (1956.2.1). M P62

This painting deploys two of Lewis's newly invented "monad" figures in an apparently political image. The figure on the left seems to wear a Roman-style tunic and on the extreme left there is a "fasces." Both figures have a military air about them. While the red and black of the title and the colouring of the work seem to refer to Communist and Fascist and/or anarchist conflict, the figures seem to relate to one another in a fairly harmonious fashion. Lewis's political writing often played on the possibility of harmony in duality. The dust jacket of Lewis's anti-war polemic *Count Your Dead: They are Alive!* (1937) (B&M Cat. 38) pits two dagger-wielding Communist and Nazi figures against one another, while also suggesting they are engaged in a deadly dance. The violence, it seems, has some possibility of resolution by virtue of an inner logic.

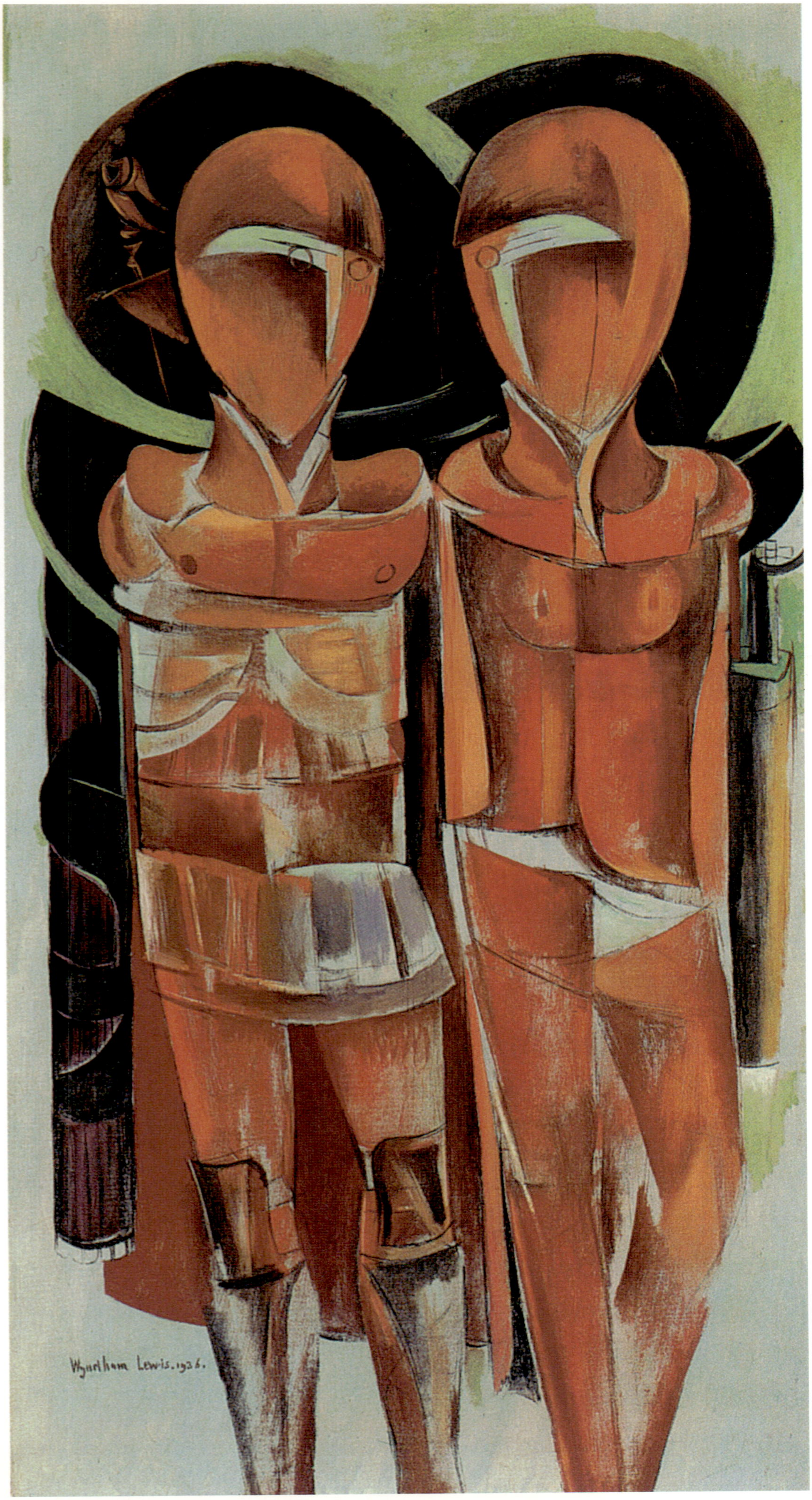

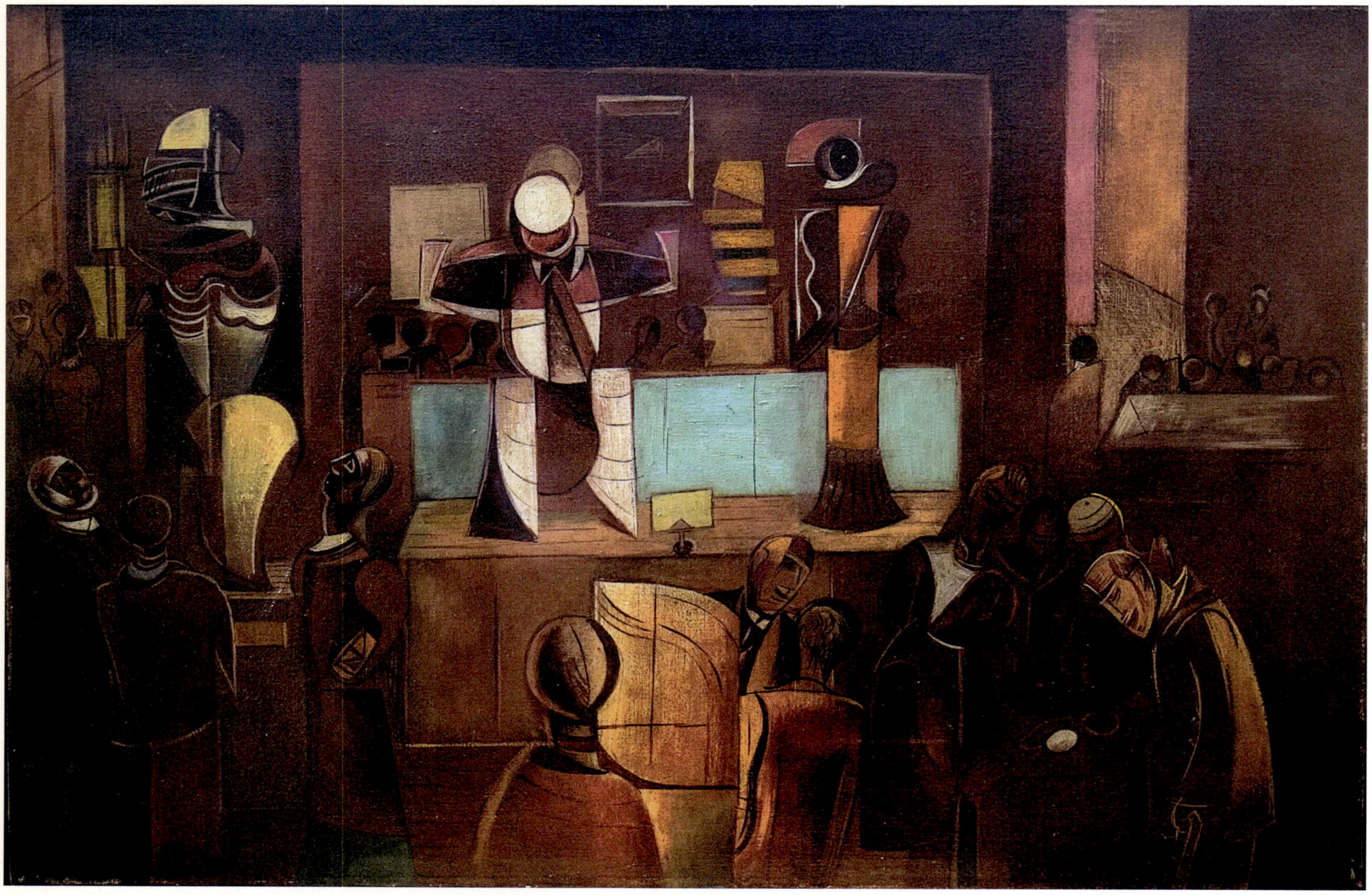

Cat. 160.
Cubist Museum, 1936.
Oil on canvas. 51 x 76 cm.
Private collection. M P58

Lewis was a great admirer of Alfred J. Barr's new Museum of Modern Art in New York and, probably coincidentally, his former lover, Iris Barry, had founded the film department there in 1935, a year before Lewis produced this painting. Lewis was an exponent of the modernist movement during the 1930s, though wary of its excesses and doubtful about some of its ideology. His inveterate satirical streak is shown here, as the visitors to the museum seem to have become like the sculptures that they are viewing. The group at the bottom right, wrapped in uncertain appreciation, stare intently at an egg-like form. Lewis's art had typically conflated the style applied to figures, objects and environment to suggest the ways in which humans create the psychological world that they inhabit and, in turn, become formed by it.

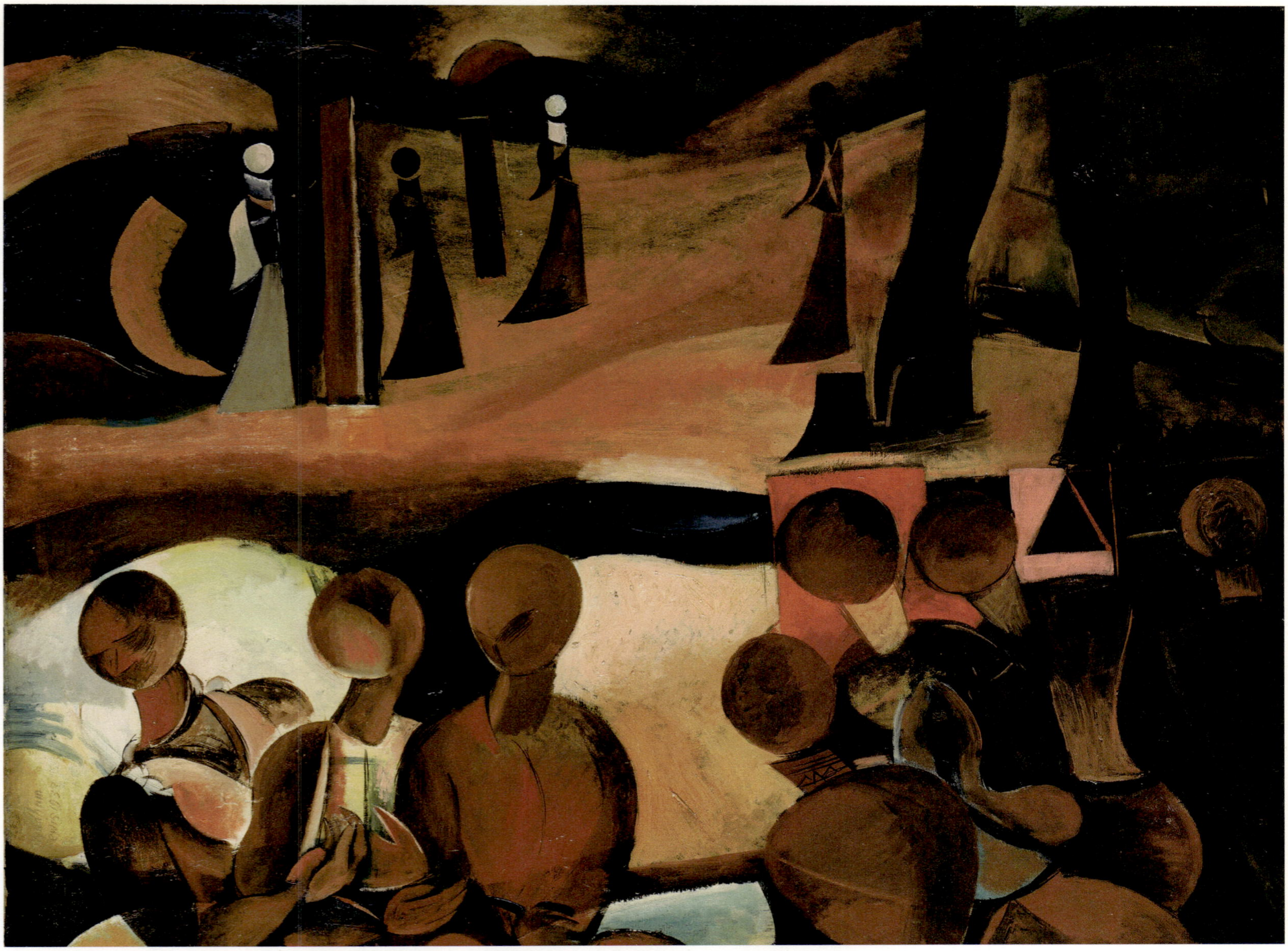

Cat. 161.
Red Scene, 1933–36. Oil on canvas. 71.1 x 91.4 cm. Tate: Purchased 1938 (N04913). M P52

Like *One of the Stations of the Dead* (1933) (Cat. 155) and a number of other important paintings of the 1930s, *Red Scene* shows an eerie afterworld inhabited by spectral "monad" figures. They are like those in his more this-worldly compositions, but are now transported into a darkness, in this case illuminated by a setting red sun that casts an ominous light across the desert-like landscape. To a significant degree, this work draws on the imagery of Lewis's metaphysical novel, *The Childermass* (1928) (B&M Cat. 19). The skirted figures in the background seem to float above the bare terrain while those in the foreground may be lost in bemused interaction. Lewis frequently used a single colour to develop a particular atmosphere, showing perhaps his interest in the work of Henri Matisse.

Cat. 162.
The Surrender of Barcelona, 1936–37. Oil on canvas. 83.8 x 59.7 cm. Tate: Purchased 1947 (N05768). M P61

Like *Inca and the Birds* (1933) (Cat. 156), this powerful and complex painting draws on the American historian William H. Prescott's narratives of Spanish history.[1] Prescott is the specific source from which Lewis uses the account of the siege of Barcelona in 1472, and Ferdinand's and Isabella's victorious entry into the city. There is obviously a reference to the Spanish Civil War and a suggestion of historical cycles and repetition; in the year that he completed this work, Lewis published his novel about the conflict, *The Revenge for Love* (1937) (B&M Cat. 39).

1. William H. Prescott, *History of the Reign of Ferdinand and Isabella the Catholic* (n.d.). Ed. John Foster Kirk (London: Swan Sonnenschein, 1841).

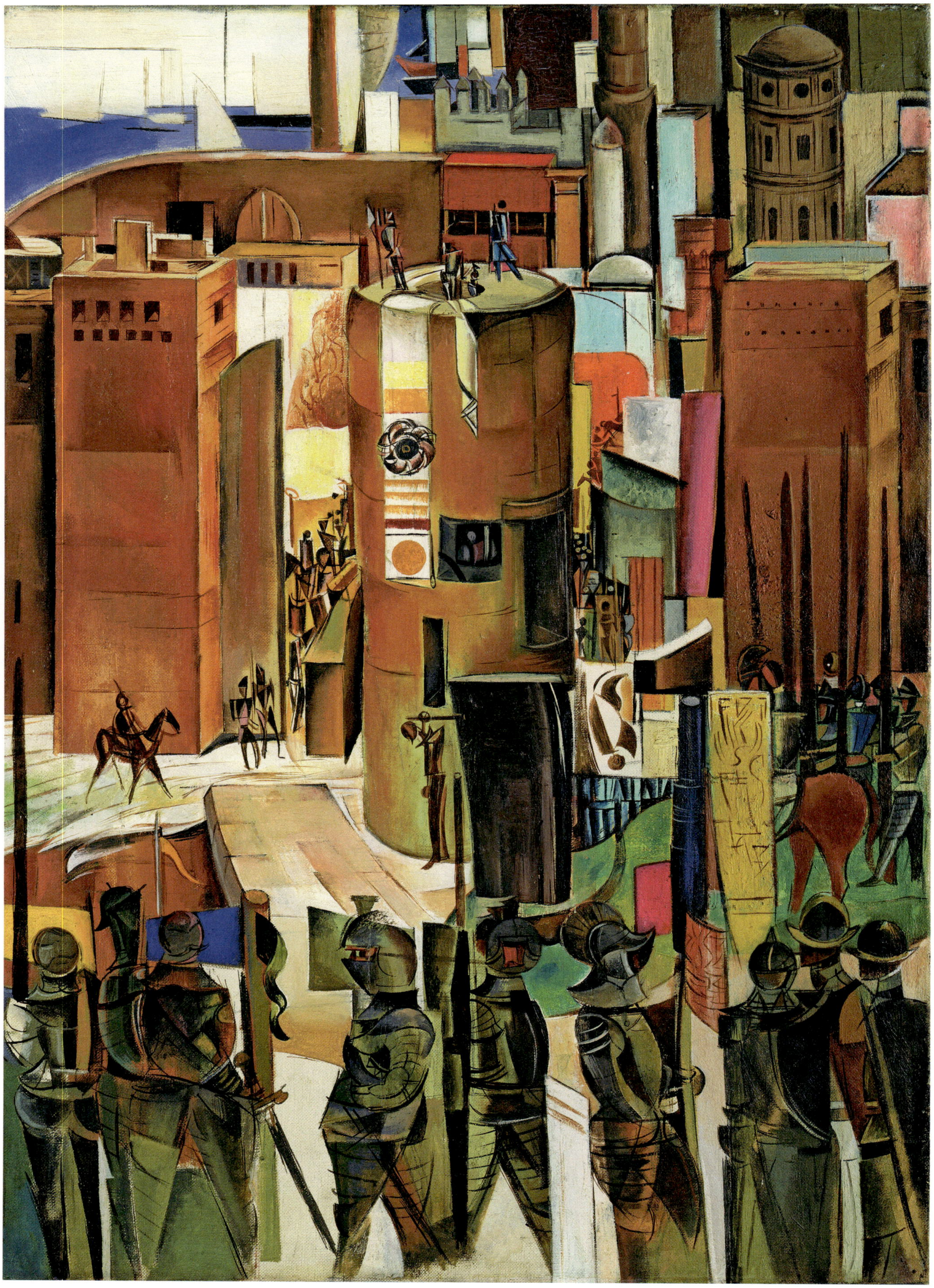

Cat. 163.
The Tank in the Clinic, 1937.
Oil on canvas. 68.5 x 51 cm.
Wyndham Lewis Memorial Trust (LP.2008.XX.4).
M P77

Lewis's frequent and often serious illnesses in the 1930s, referred to in the apparently autobiographical painting *The Convalescent* (1933) (Cat. 154), interrupted his efforts at painting, aggravated his financial problems and led him to take various "alternative" cures such as vitamin therapy. This work probably draws on an experience of submersion in water but develops a far more sinister and fantastic image of skeletal and drowning figures reminiscent, perhaps, of a modern concentration camp. Like many of Lewis's works of this period, there is here an attempt to describe the human condition in a dream-like world of ambiguous forms and controlling powers, political and medical in this instance, the strong architecture of the composition compounding the sense of claustrophobic and powerless imprisonment. The narrative is suggestively unclear.

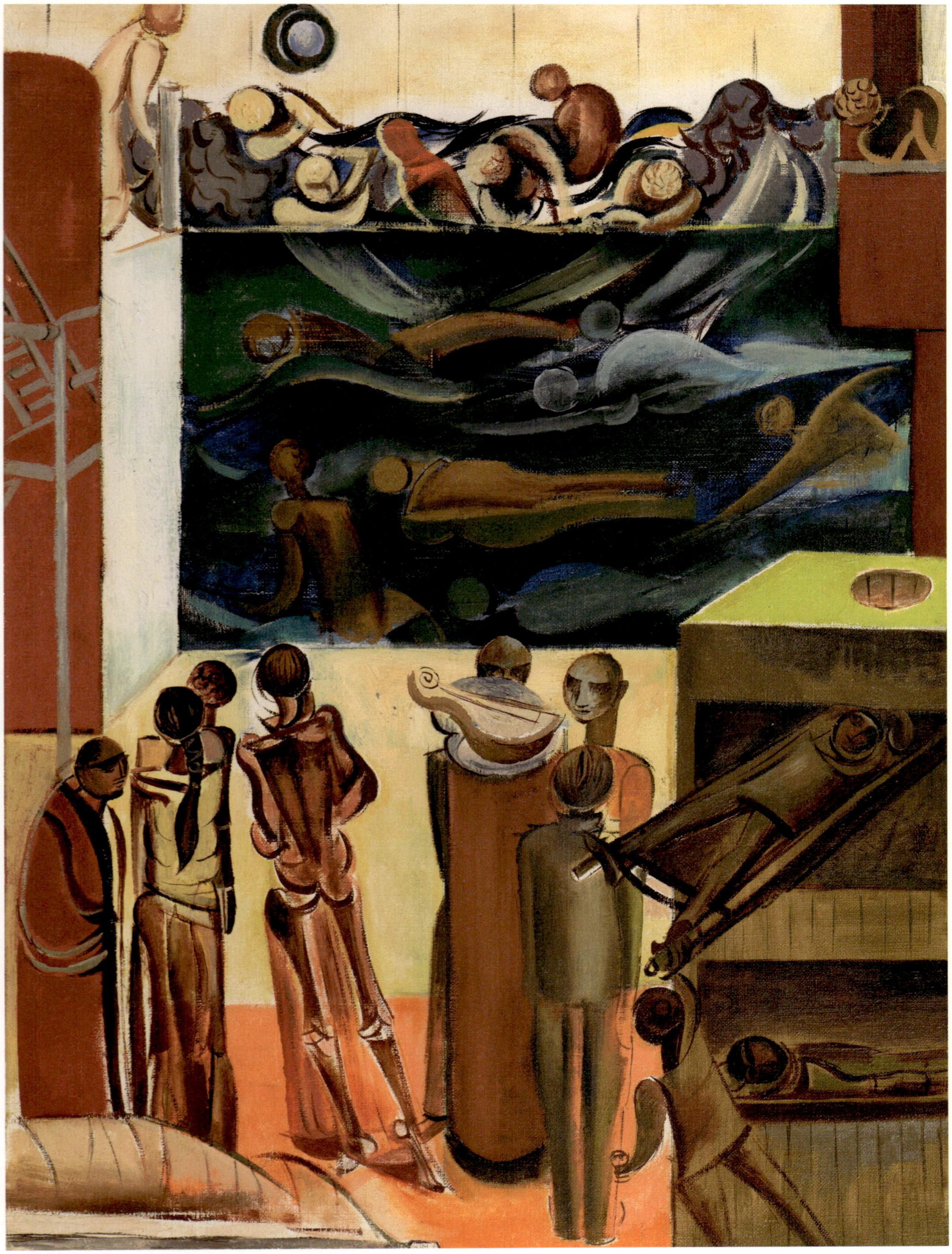

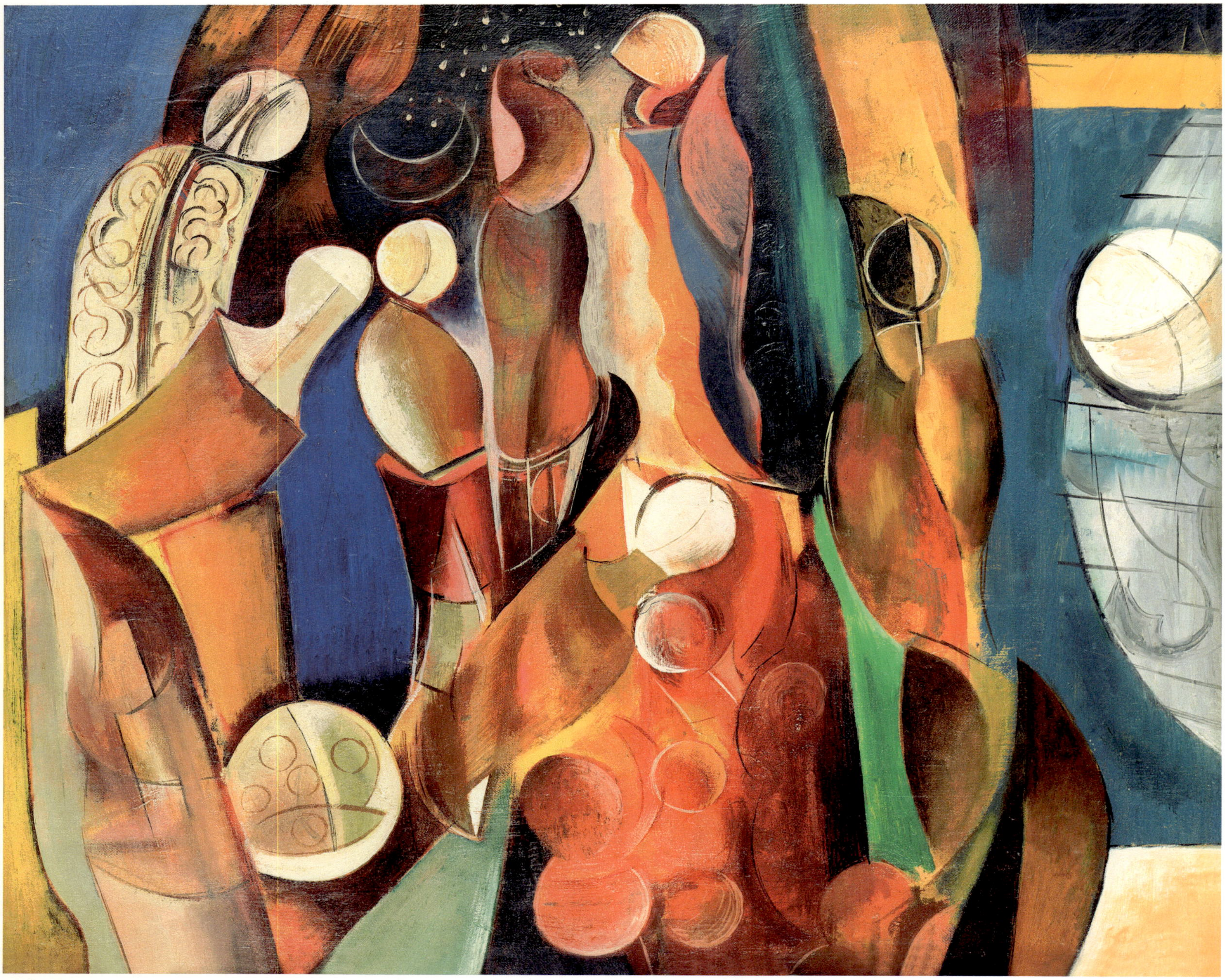

Cat. 164.
Creation Myth, 1937. Oil on canvas. 49.5 x 59 cm. The Warden and Scholars of New College, Oxford (NCO 1002). M P54

One of Lewis's recurrent themes as a painter is that of the creation myth. He was fascinated by the actual creation myths of ancient societies across the world, but also sought to demonstrate in such paintings the nature of creativity itself. Believing that a bureaucratic modern world dominated by science and technology had severely undermined the free creativity of the artist, his own creation myths conjure a world of organic shapes and rich colour, with cosmic, natural and human forms moving in a sea of dynamic possibility. Lewis believed the artist wielded a sacred and primeval power and many of his works on this theme suggest the compulsive and almost pre-historic power of the artist's imagination. Lewis staked his concept of true freedom on this semi-divine faculty. A number of works given the title "Creation Myth" in the 1940s anticipate post-war abstract art and show Lewis's sympathy with the traditions of Romanticism and Surrealism.

Cat. 165.
Landscape with Northmen,
1936–37. Oil on canvas.
67.5 x 49.5 cm.
Private collection, London.
M P66

Lewis's ambitions as a painter had always been global in subject matter and formal sources, as he explained in his essay, "A World Art and Tradition" (1929).[1] This painting seems to venture north to the world of the Vikings, another example of Lewis's fascination with the conquering impulse and its consequences for human history. However, the three figures in the foreground wearing horned helmets and standing by a ship may, in fact, be in a Mediterranean landscape, reminding us that the Vikings had travelled a long way from Scandinavia and that the Normans had gone as far as Sicily. The figures look a little bewildered by their surroundings and there is a comic aspect to the work as in so many of Lewis's paintings. Lewis also seems to take a real enjoyment in creating the rich landscape and cloudy sky.

1. Wyndham Lewis, "A World Art and Tradition," in *Drawing and Design* 5, no. 32 (February 1929), pp. 29–30. Rprt. *Wyndham Lewis on Art: Collected Writings 1913–1956.* Eds. Walter Michel and C.J. Fox (London: Thames and Hudson, 1969), p. 258.

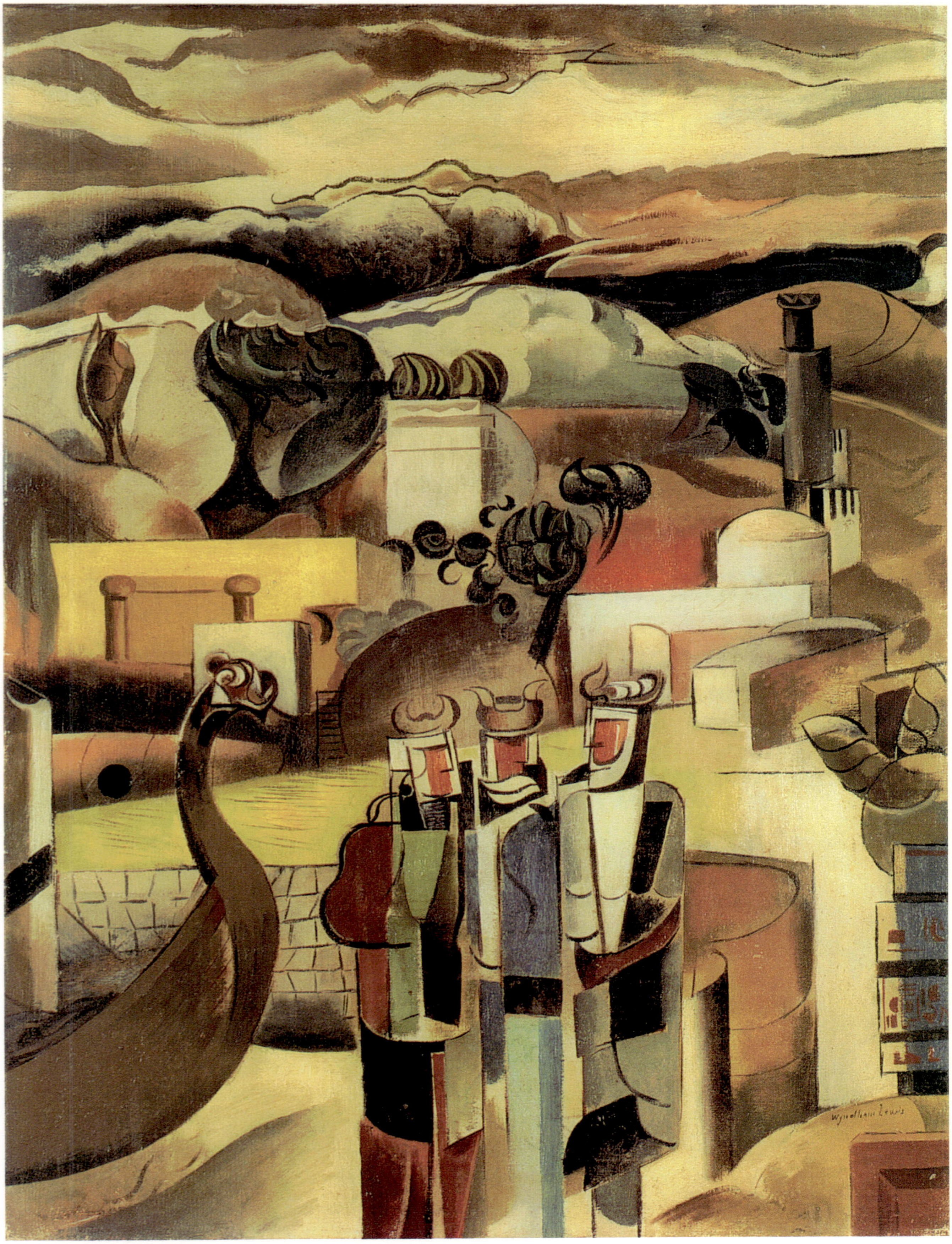

"A great artist falls into a trance of sorts when he creates, about that there is little doubt. The act of artistic creation is a trance or dream-state, but very different from that experienced by the entranced medium. A world of the most extreme and logically exacting physical definition is built up out of this susceptible condition in the case of the greatest art, in contrast to the cloudy phantasies of the spiritist."

Wyndham Lewis, *Time and Western Man,* 1927

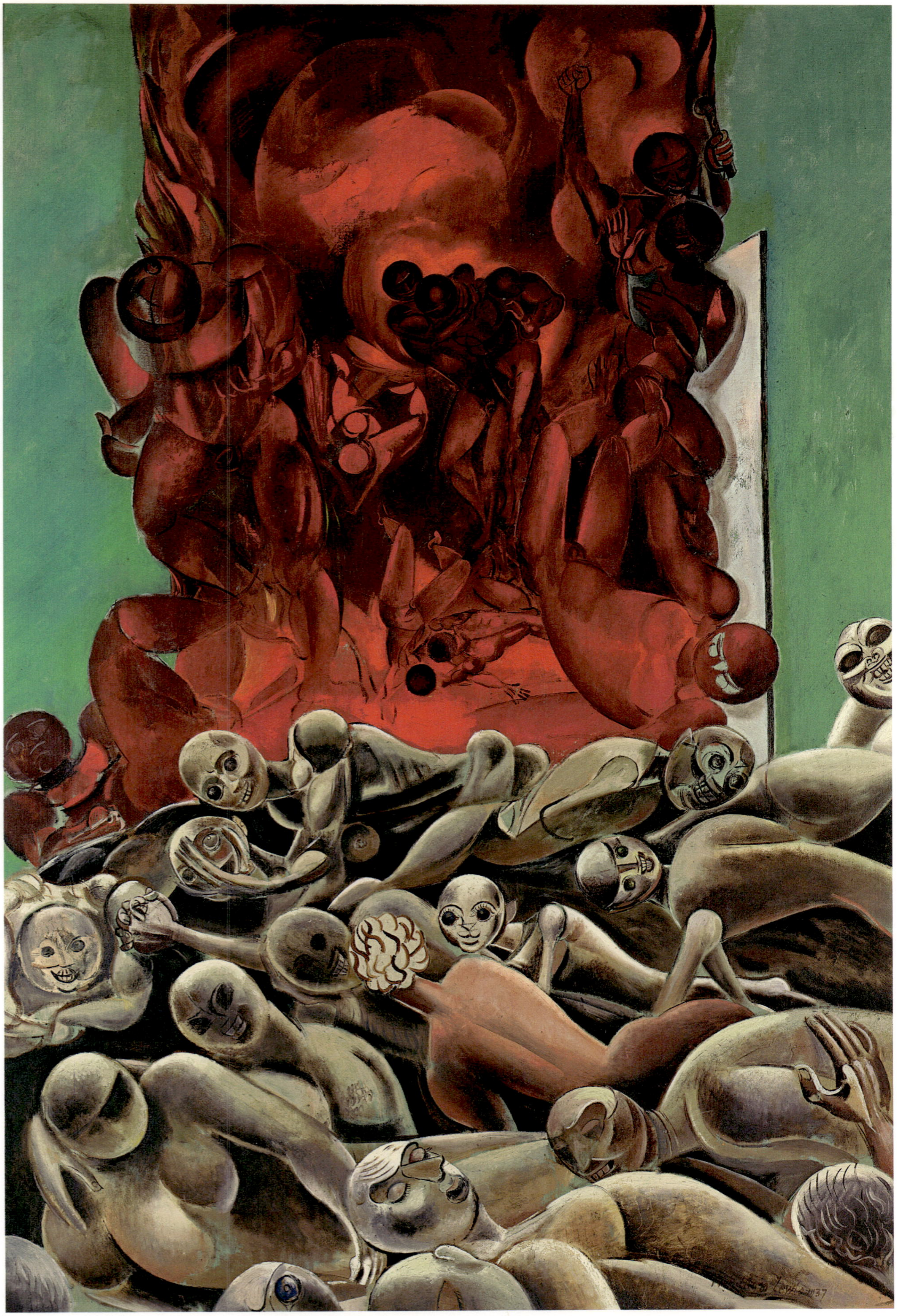

Cat. 166.
[Not in exhibition] *Inferno*, 1937. Oil on canvas. 152.5 x 101.8 cm. National Gallery of Victoria, Melbourne. Felton Bequest, 1964 (1411-5). M P72

This work was the last painting that Lewis completed in his series of imaginative compositions in oil, as well as the largest. It is related to other after-life scenes from the 1930s, such as Cats. 155 and 161. It is the grandest visual statement that Lewis ever produced in a continuing fascination that he had with metaphysical realities throughout his career. An inverted 'T' composition inscribes a vision of hell, in Lewis's own words in the foreword to the 1937 exhibition at The Leicester Galleries, a "world of shapes locked in eternal conflict [...] super-imposed upon a world of shapes, prone in the relaxations of an uneasy sensuality which is also eternal."[1] The painting anticipates to some degree the forms of the religious and other watercolours that Lewis painted in the early 1940s, such as Cats. 176, 181–83 and 193.

1. Wyndham Lewis, "Foreword," in *Paintings and Drawings by Wyndham Lewis* [exh. cat. The Leicester Galleries, London]. London: The Leicester Galleries, December 1937.

Cat. 168.
A Hand of Bananas, **1929–38. Gouache, watercolour, pencil and ink on paper. 20.3 x 18.1 cm. The Museum of Modern Art, New York. Purchase, 1941 (408.1941). M 904**

Lewis's imagery and titles are sometimes frankly, and no doubt deliberately, perplexing. He often developed his imagery from apparently absurd, dream-like or simply inscrutable initial forms, as here where a "hand of bananas" floats above a prostrate figure and in front of a screen. That a hand might be like a bunch of bananas is not an impossible idea but the phrase "a hand of bananas," by its grammar, suggests a peculiar world of impossible and surreal combination. Hands figure in many of Lewis's portraits, of course, even by their overt omission as in his portrait of Edith Sitwell (1923–35) (Cat. 105), and one of the vignettes for his satire *The Apes of God* (1930) (B&M Cat. 21) shows a fat hand hanging uselessly, which has similarities with this painting.

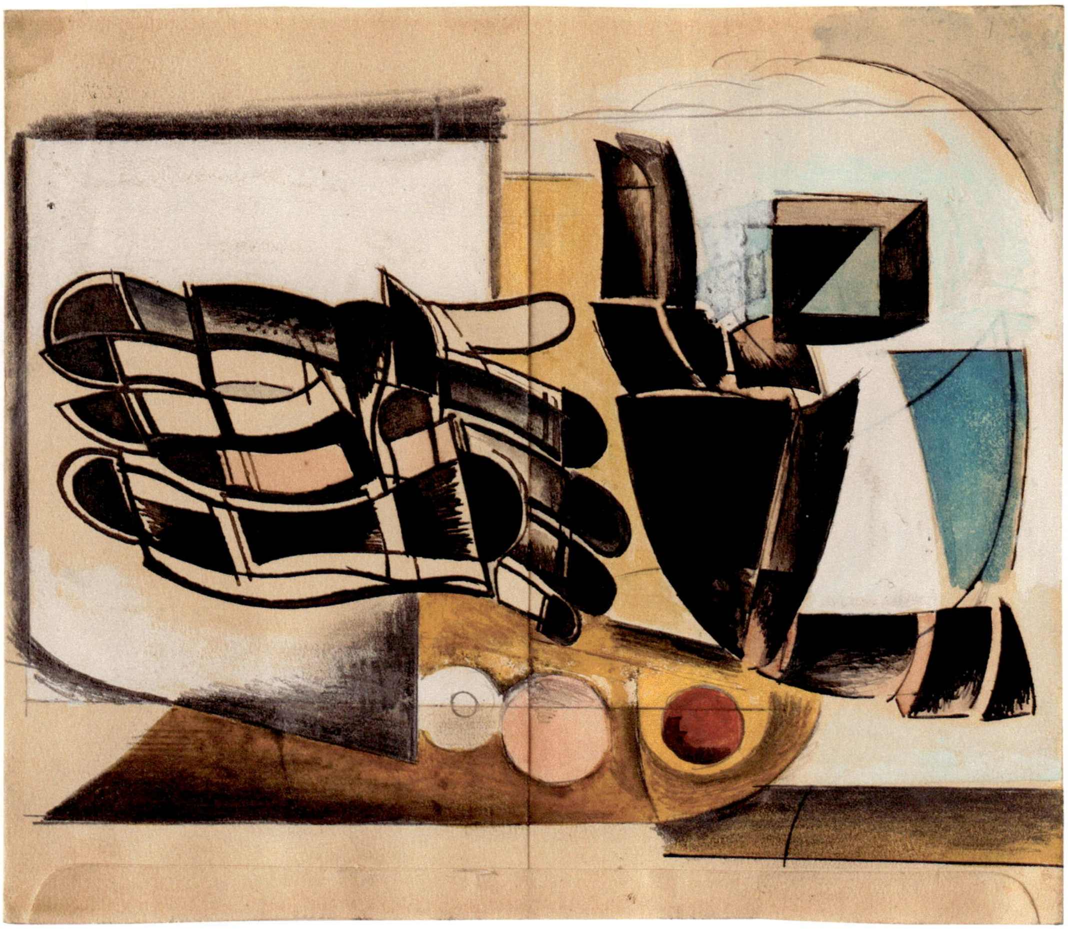

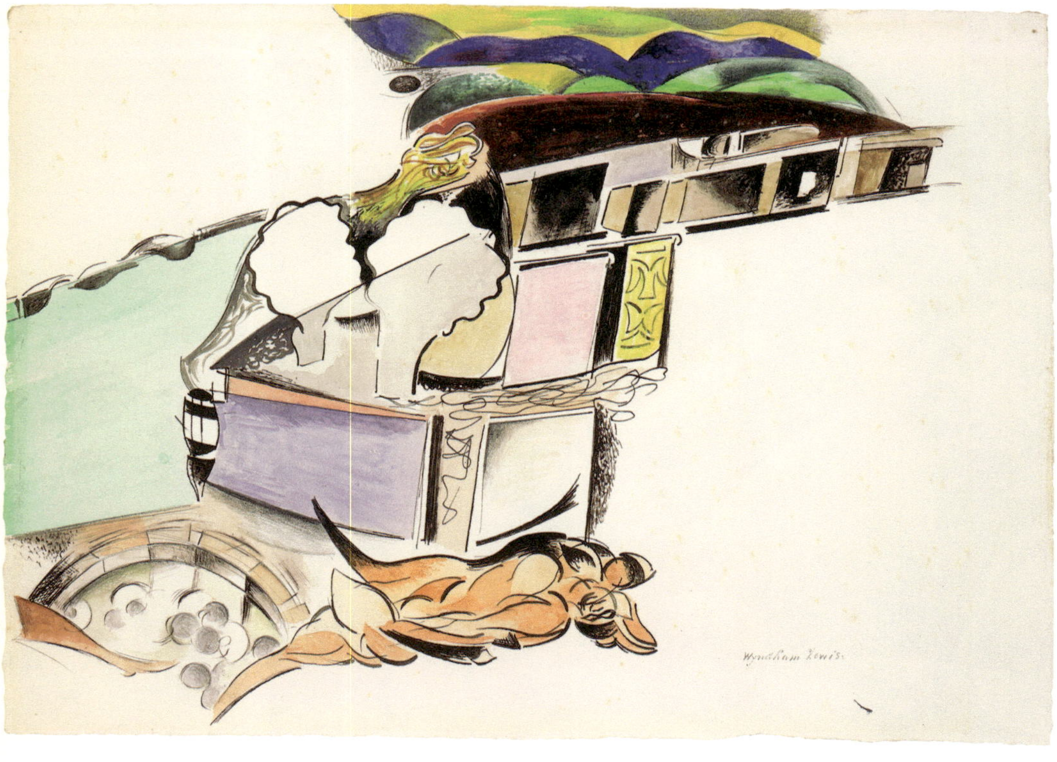

Cat. 167.
Bathing Scene, **1938. Pen and ink, watercolour and gouache on paper. 28.7 x 39.6 cm. Wyndham Lewis Memorial Trust (LD.2004.XX.28). M 900**

Lewis is rarely considered as a colourist yet many of his paintings are astonishingly original and inventive in their use of colour. This unusually idyllic scene, using a typically vignette-like composition, brings together in flowing shapes an unlikely but highly evocative configuration of violet, pale green, rich blue and other colours that hint at a moment of ease and pleasure rarely found in Lewis's work. Towards the end of a decade of appalling personal and political events, Lewis increasingly turned to a subject matter of innocent, yet tantalisingly insecure, escape in his visual work. There is a building up of coloured form against large empty spaces, which, along with the beautiful varied line employed, reminds us how much Lewis looked to Chinese art for inspiration.

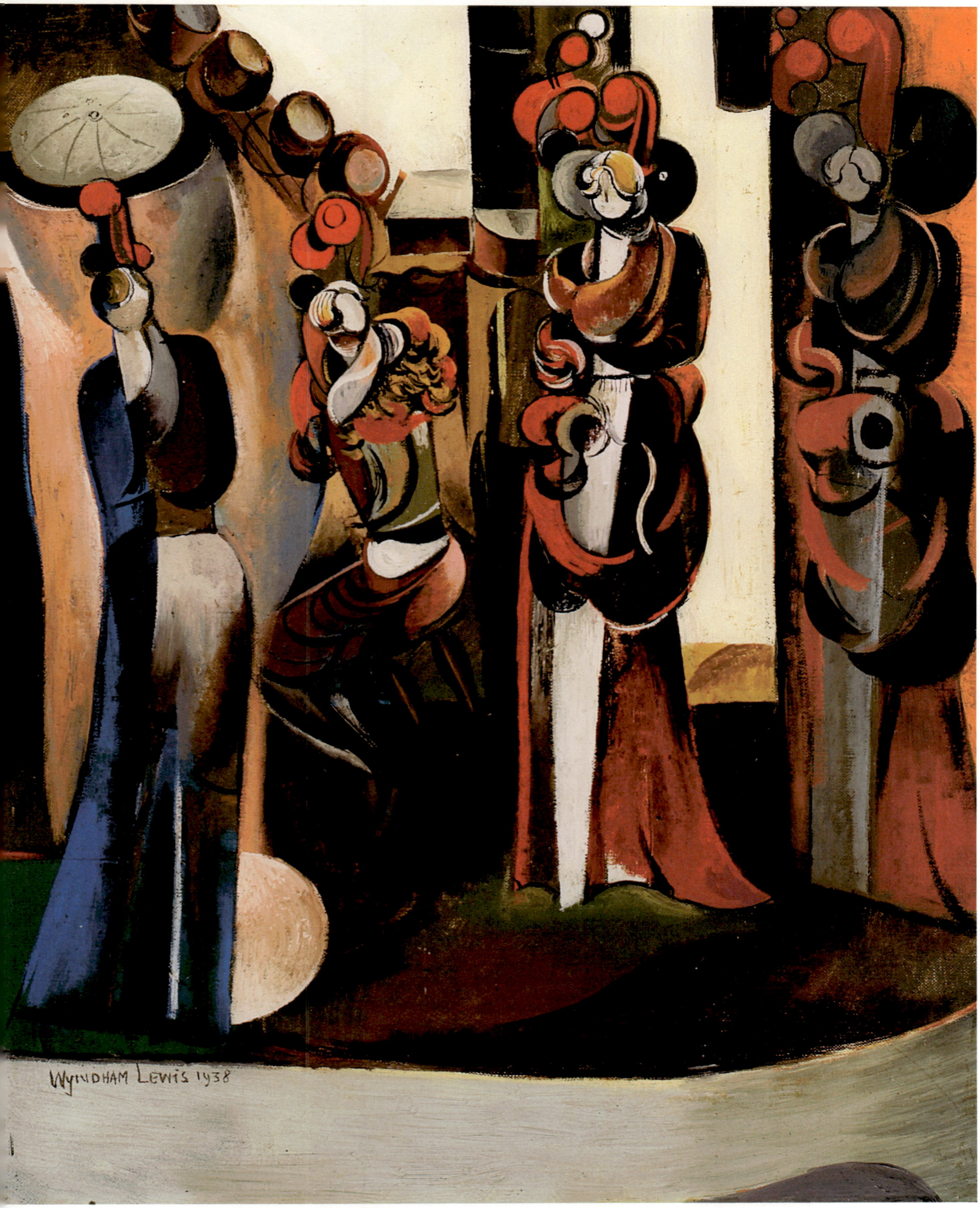

Cat. 169.
Four Figure Composition, 1938. Oil on canvas. 40 x 25.4 cm. Collection of Fred L. Emerson Gallery, Hamilton College. Gift of Omar S. Pound, Class of 1951 (1991.126). M P81

Most of Lewis's compositions in the 1930s have some narrative content that adds greatly to our response, whether in the case of what he called his "satiric realism," or his metaphysical or historic works. His aim during this period was in part to re-invent the possibilities of modernism through a complex subject matter. By contrast, some works, of which this painting is a fine example, seem to be lively and elegant exercises in form and colour. This work, executed after The Leicester Galleries exhibition, may have been painted simply to be attractive and sellable, though it is entirely possible that there is an underlying, though as yet undetected, theme. There is certainly a relationship with his overtly theatrical compositions in this painting, in which a row of stage lights can be seen at the top left and two figures are shown standing in the beams.

1939

-1951

Imagination Against the Void

As the Second World War broke out, Lewis and Froanna were crossing the Atlantic; they were not to return to Europe until the end of the war. Lewis believed his economic prospects, as a portraitist in particular, were better in North America. He also told writer and poet, Julian Symons (1912–94), that he could not bear to witness Europe tearing itself to pieces again. He decided to investigate his roots in upstate New York and Canada. He must also have been conscious that all his pamphleteering in the 1930s in favour of appeasing Fascist dictatorships in their defence against Communist aggression had undermined his credibility in Britain, despite the near reversal of these views after his 1937 visit to Berlin and Warsaw. The stay in the USA and Canada proved to be a terrible ordeal, not handled well by Lewis, who reverted to his customary habit of alienating those who offered to help him. Visa difficulties meant that most of the time was spent in Canada, where Lewis's tactless assumption of his own importance as a writer and painter were often met with offended incomprehension.

Lewis managed to blot his copybook in New York by announcing the 'death of abstract art' and writing a highly critical analysis of Pablo Picasso (1881–1973) (refining and extending the critique he had made in 1919) just at the point America was 'discovering' Picasso in the huge 1940 exhibition of his work at the Museum of Modern Art; abstraction, also, was about to be undergo a renewal in American Abstract Impressionism. In Buffalo, Lewis's crucial first commission, a portrait of the chancellor of the University, Samuel Capen (1878–1956), resulted in arguments and recriminations that did not encourage future patrons. A satirical account of his visit to the University of Toronto's Hart House, published in *America, I Presume* (1940) (B&M Cat. 45), put paid to the prospect of any work there. Years later, Hugh Kenner (1923–2003), the great critical 'inventor' and guide to Anglo-American modernism, bemoaned the fact that when he was an undergraduate at Toronto, Lewis was living in poverty in a hotel room nearby, ignored by the University authorities.

But Lewis made friends. Fr. Stanley Murphy (1904–?), of Assumption College, Windsor, put teaching and lecturing work his way; there were private portrait commissions; a local art collector-cum-dealer, Douglas Duncan (1902–68), would buy batches of the fantastic watercolours that Lewis was producing; and Lorne Pierce (1890–1961) of the Ryerson Press recognised his importance and published his propaganda pamphlet, *Anglosaxony: A League that Works* (1941) (B&M Cat. 46). In 1944, two young academics who admired Lewis's work, Marshall McLuhan (1911–80) and Felix Giovanelli (1913–ca. 1963), organised work for him in St Louis. In the end, having gone to America to look for 'roots', Lewis came to appreciate the 'rootlessness' and universality of its mass-culture and the democratic equality of its notion of citizenship. On his return to England, his first book was a study of American history and culture, praising precisely these aspects of the USA and proposing them as a model for a future world in which nation-states would be abolished and superseded by a world-state. It was a return to the more optimistic aspects of *The Art of Being Ruled* (1926) (B&M Cat. 10) and *Paleface: The Philosophy of the "Melting Pot"* (1929) (B&M Cat. 20), without their authoritarian politics; experience had taught Lewis the folly of his earlier infatuation with that variety of modernisation. It was from *America and Cosmic Man* (1948) (B&M Cat. 48) that McLuhan took his concept of the 'global village'.

Lewis's literary output during the war was meagre, compared with the immense productivity of the previous two decades. He completed a novel begun in England, where it was published in 1941. An attack on the British class system, it tells the story of a man from a working-class background who counterfeits money and a new identity in order to succeed. *The Vulgar Streak* (B&M Cat. 47) was considered by American publishers to be too 'anti-British' to be published in wartime. *America, I Presume* was a comparatively gentle satire on American manners, written from the point of view of a buffoonish British clubman who bears little resemblance to Lewis himself (but makes use of his sharp eyes). The profound revaluation of all Lewis's principles, and of his life itself, that came out of the enforced stay in North America (the Lewises had no access to the funds in Britain that would have enabled them to return) had to wait for literary expression until after the war, and after Lewis had gone blind, his sight destroyed by a tumour that had been slowly growing inside his skull for over 20 years.

While actually in North America, Lewis's primary artistic response to his situation was visual, and the visual revaluation may have been spurred on by a sudden and noticeable deterioration in his sight towards the end of 1940. The drawings and fantastic watercolours of 1941–42 were his last sustained effort (though it was not until 1950 that he became too blind to make paintings and drawings of any kind). Some drawings simply record the Lewises' domestic circumstances as they await in a limbo of uncertainty the outcome of the war. *War News* (Cat. 173) and *Portrait of the Artist's Wife* (Cat. 174) exemplify this strain. Other watercolours respond more imaginatively, if sometimes obliquely, to the horrors of war itself. A series of watercolour fantasies on the themes of creation, crucifixion, gestation and bathing constitute a poetic re-exploration of the entire philosophical basis of Lewis's art. They are unparalleled in English art but belong to a particularly English strain of visionary fantasy (William Blake (1757–1827), Richard Dadd (1817–86), Cecil Collins (1908–89)). Their profundity in relation to Lewis's worldview is not in question, but aesthetically their often playful idiosyncrasy makes them difficult to evaluate in the context of European modernism.

On returning to London after the war, Lewis resumed his pre-war productivity as a writer. An autobiography, *Rude Assignment: A Narrative of my Career Up-to-date* (1950) (B&M Cat. 50), surveyed his previous books and showed how they were not, as some supposed, expressions of Fascism. Although the book is occasionally a little disingenuous, it remains an excellent introduction to Lewis's thought. One of his intentions was to show that he had a place and function in the new 'socialist' society that was apparently being built in Britain in the wake of war. In theory this was true, but the irritations caused to members of Lewis's class by the introduction of a Welfare State in a period of national bankruptcy sometimes took precedence over theoretical approval, as in the collection of short stories, *Rotting Hill*, published in 1951 (B&M Cat. 51). This year saw the publication of Lewis's last major critical book, *The Writer and the Absolute* (B&M Cat. 53), which returned to the subject of ideological pressures and constraints on artistic freedom. Lewis believed that the production of art and fiction was something that needed no ideological or political justification: art was not the handmaiden of some other department of cultural practice. In this book he studies the effect of external 'historical' pressures on writers, particularly those associated with Existentialism, Jean-Paul Sartre (1905–80), André Malraux (1901–76) and Albert Camus (1913–60), with a section devoted to George Orwell (1903–50). Lewis also produced much art criticism, particularly for the BBC weekly, *The Listener*, praising the new generation of post-war British artists.

Lewis's last major works of fiction were written after he had announced in *The Listener* that he had lost his sight and must abandon his art reviews. They were written longhand on sheets of paper that remained, to his eyes, completely blank, and were laboriously transcribed by an amanuensis who learnt to decipher his 'blind' handwriting. *Self Condemned* (1954) (B&M Cat. 54), a novel based equally on the Lewises experiences in Toronto and on the crisis in their marriage caused by the stress of Lewis's gradual loss of sight and intermittently fading consciousness, was called by T.S. Eliot (1888–1965) a book of 'unbearable spiritual agony'. Like some of the Toronto drawings, it faces and reassesses Lewis's own gynophobia. It celebrates the common humanity of people who must continue in the face of the absurdity of life, and ultimately condemns its protagonist for his failure to maintain this standard of humanity himself. He is reduced to an empty shell of a man, a fate Lewis feared would be shared by European culture itself.

In 1951, a young BBC radio producer, D.G. Bridson (1910–80), dramatised *The Childermass* (1928) (B&M Cat. 19) for broadcast and persuaded the BBC to commission a completion of the work. Lewis began writing after finishing *Self Condemned*, retitling the whole work as *The Human Age* (B&M Cat. 61). The two protagonists, Pullman and Satters, enter 'Third City' (a kind of Purgatory), which is racked by ideological competition. Pullman must choose whom to follow. It is a choice that reproduces the dilemma of all intellectuals faced by the ideological absolutes of the twentieth century; Pullman makes an 'enlightened' choice that takes him to Hell. Here he finds himself forced to assist Satan himself in his war against the Divine, dressed up again as an enlightened project to institute a new 'Human Age' to replace outdated values. In this final great work of his career, Lewis creates a new fictional medium in which the metaphysical implications of the normal choices of ordinary life (particularly the ordinary life of an intellectual) suddenly shine through with unexpected clarity. Apparently damned for his compromises, the intellectual Pullman is spared at the end of Book Three of *The Human Age* (which appeared in book form after being broadcast in 1955) (B&M Cat. 57). But the 'Paradiso' of this Dantescan vision of the era of death camps and cold war, a projected fourth book, 'The Trial of Man', remained unwritten. The broadcast of *The Human Age* and the much acclaimed retrospective of Lewis's paintings at the Tate Gallery, London in 1956 marked his belated and temporary acceptance as a major figure in British and European art and thought of the twentieth century. He died shortly afterwards from the effects of the tumour inside his skull.

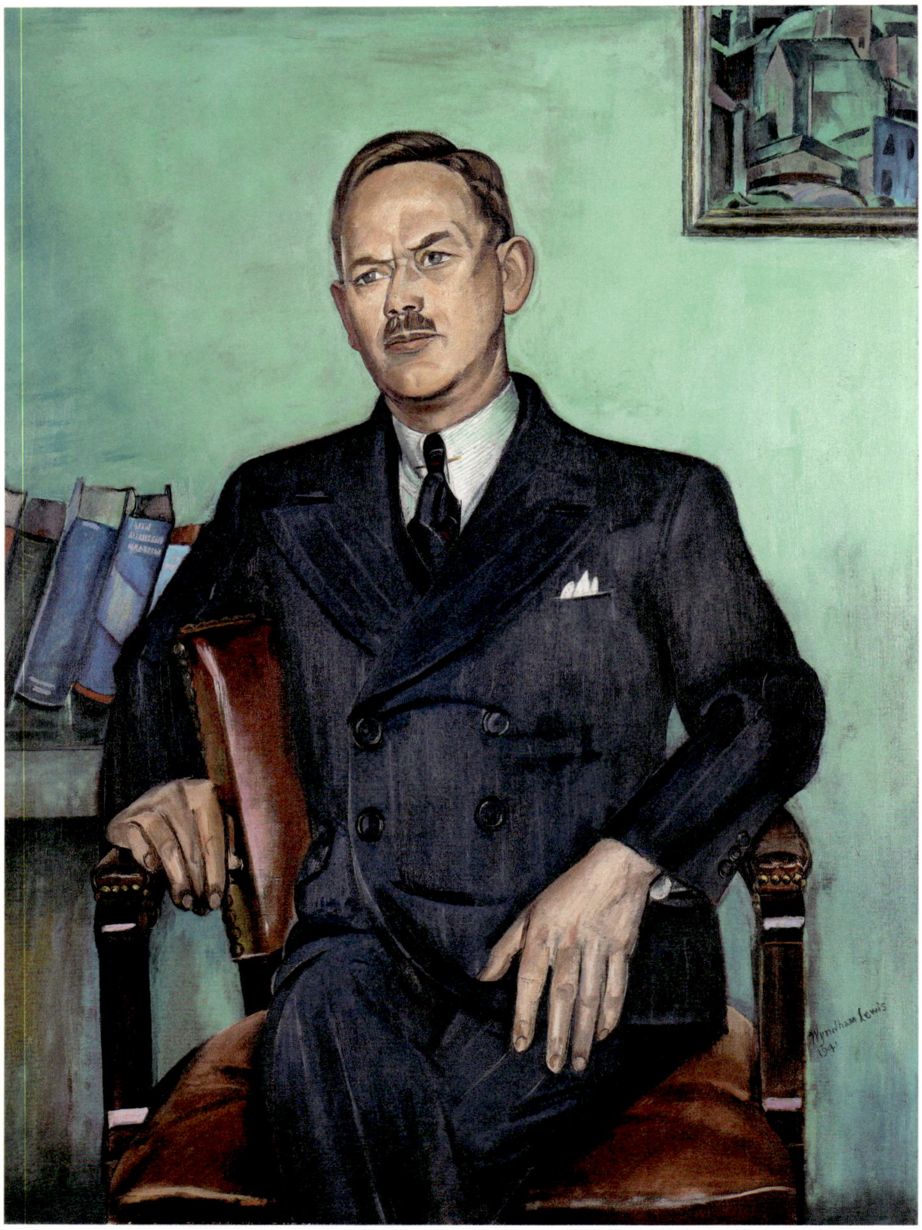

Cat. 171.
[Not in exhibition] *J.S. McLean*, 1941. Oil on canvas. 106.5 x 77 cm. Art Gallery of Ontario. Gift of The McLean Family, 2000 (Acc. 2000/1309). M P101

McLean was a Canadian industrialist. The portrait was commissioned by Canadian Packers, McLean's firm. Lewis also produced two bizarrely incompetent portraits for McLean, one of his daughter, and one of Mrs Lisa Sainsbury. A photograph of an earlier state of the portrait shows that the cultural props (A.Y. Jackson's (1882–1974) *Mining Town* (1935–37) and some books) were introduced at a late stage. Lewis has distorted the form of the chair and flattened McLean's figure, emphasising the size of his hands, in a slight echo of Jean Auguste Dominique Ingres's portrait of M. Bertin (1932). The painting now seems a comparatively conventional and successful portrait of a powerful man, and one that gives his face a sufficiently complex expression. When Lewis wrote in *Rude Assignment* (1950) (B&M Cat. 50) about the reaction of the family of one of his sitters to a portrait, however, it was probably this one that is referred to:

I remember doing a portrait of a redoubtable magnate in which I made him look the 'strong man' that he was, and that I supposed he would like to appear to posterity. I soon found out my mistake. His family, with one voice, objected that I had not brought out the 'kindliness', which was, they averred, so notable a feature of his personality.[1]

The painting was removed from its stretcher and stored until 1991, when it was disinterred for an exhibition of Lewis's Canadian work.

1. Wyndham Lewis, *Rude Assignment: A Narrative of my Career Up-to-date* (London: Hutchinson, 1950), pp. 48–49.

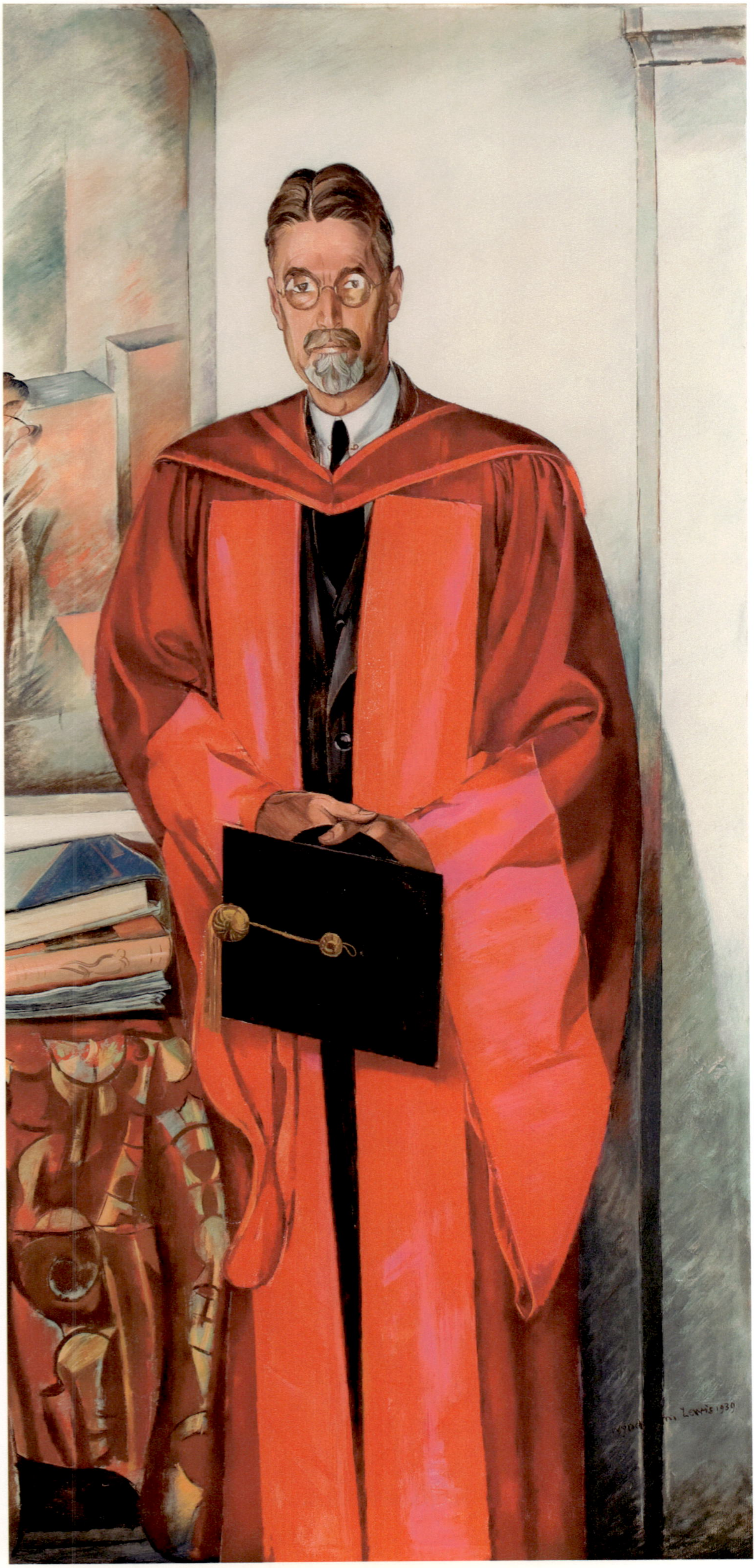

Cat. 170.
[Not in exhibition]
Chancellor Samuel Capen,
1939. Oil on canvas.
193 x 89 cm.
The Poetry Collection,
University at Buffalo.
M P94

The commission for the portrait was arranged by Charles Abbott, the Director of the Lockwood Memorial Library at the University of Buffalo, which also holds one of the main archives of Lewis's literary manuscripts. It was crucial for Lewis that he managed this commission well, but he found himself at the centre of a feud between two factions of Buffalo's culturati, and also failed at first to bring the portrait to a proper state of finish. He added the books and decorative drapery, also, apparently, heightening the colour of Capen's robes. The full-length El Greco-influenced portrayal of the ascetic figure of the Chancellor of the University is in an unusual format for Lewis. The art historian and Director of the Tate Gallery, John Rothenstein (1901–92), who visited Lewis in Buffalo not long after it was painted, thought the portrait not one of Lewis's best, and this was a judgement he was no doubt entitled to make after having acquired Lewis's *Ezra Pound* (1939), one of the greatest English portraits of the century, for £100 for the Tate Gallery. As a portraitist, Lewis reached the very highest levels only when matched with a figure of world-stature like Ezra Pound or T.S. Eliot, or when painting his wife.

Cat. 172.
The Artist's Wife, Froanna, 1940. Pencil and coloured chalks on blue paper. 48.3 x 31 cm. The Barber Institute of Fine Arts, The University of Birmingham (2006.3). M 958

After a year mainly in New York, the Lewises moved to Toronto in late 1940 on the expiry of their US visa and lived in the Tudor Hotel in Toronto for two and a half years. Lewis bought a supply of coloured paper from a drugstore and used it for numerous drawings in coloured chalk or pastel. The economic hardship of the Lewises' time in Canada had barely started, yet the portrait seems almost prophetic of the stress that this would place on Froanna. Eyes, their omission or inclusion, were always important in Lewis's portraiture, and their staring quality here is particularly expressive.

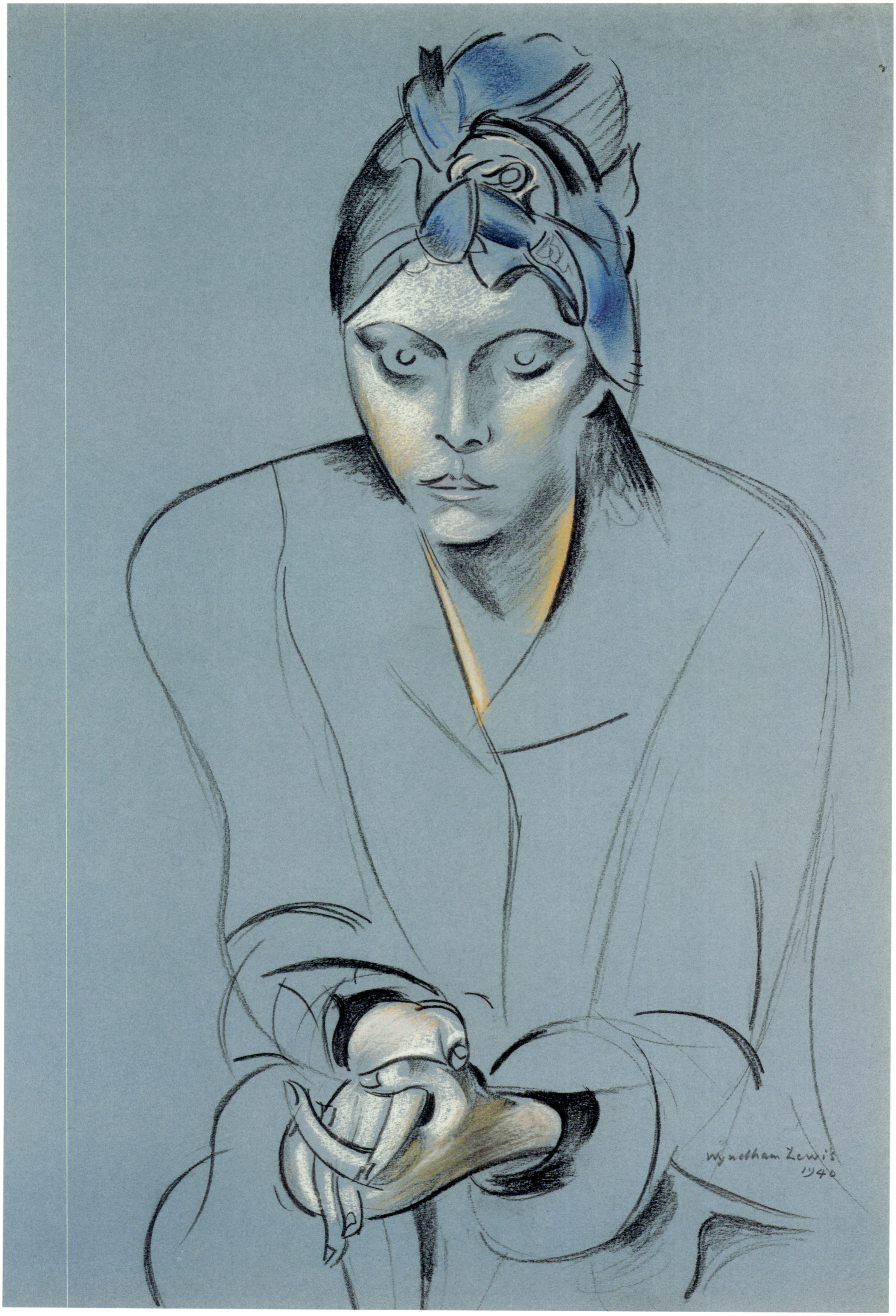

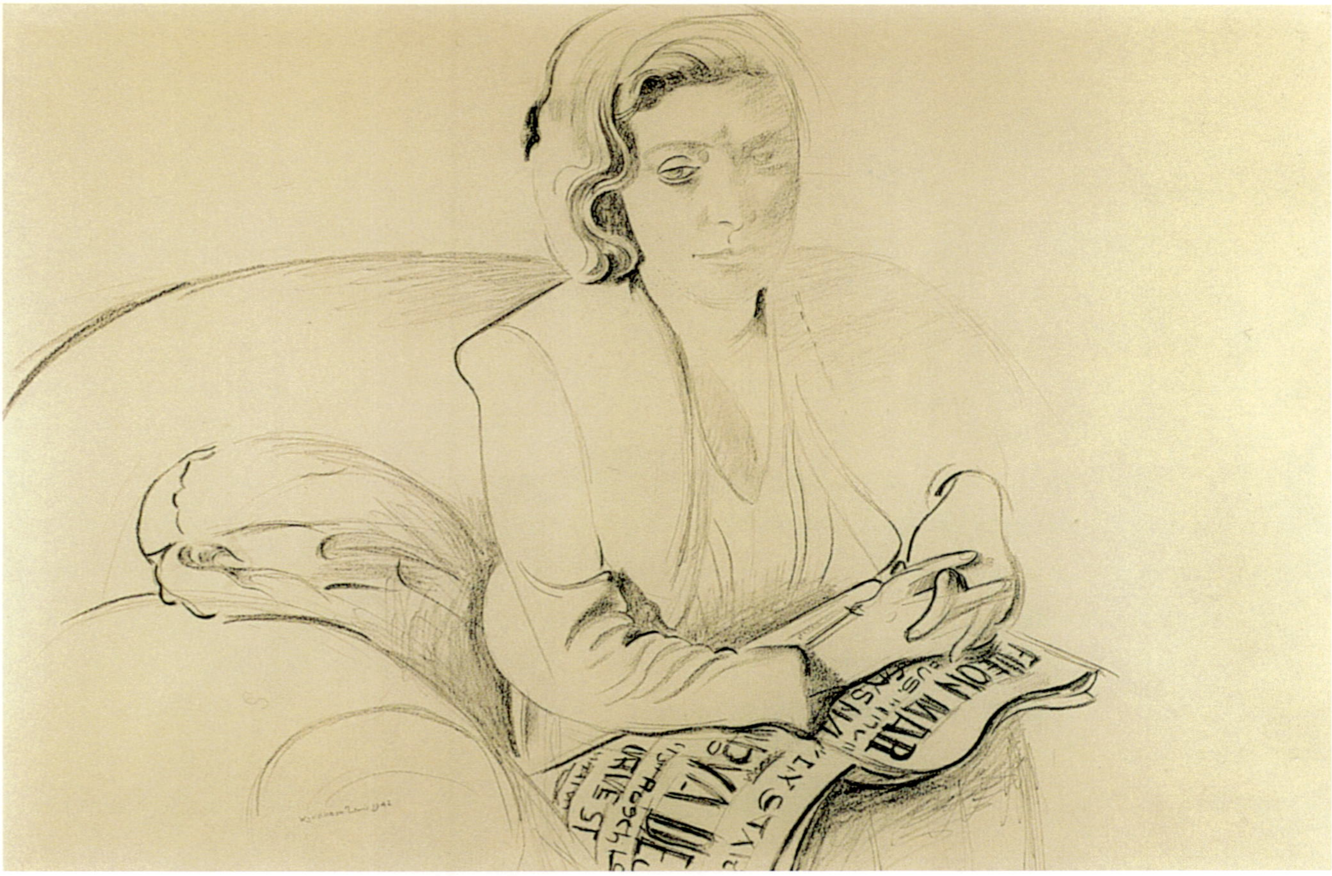

Cat. 174.
[Not in exhibition] *Portrait of the Artist's Wife*, 1944. Black and coloured pencil, and black and coloured chalks on paper. 37.7 x 27.8 cm. Art Gallery of Windsor, purchased with funds from the Bobs Cogill and Peter Haworth estate and the assistance of the Government of Canada through the Cultural Property Export and Import Act, 1991 (1991.038). M 1048

This drawing was presumably made shortly after the D-Day landings of allied forces in Normandy in June 1944. The newspaper, the strange map or explosion above it and Froanna's hunched, brooding posture, bring this time of uncertainty vividly to life. To the left of the picture, the small red disc may be a reminder that after the European war, the Japanese Empire still remained to be defeated.

Cat. 173.
War News (Portrait of Froanna), 1942. Pencil and crayon on paper. 53 x 71 cm. Collection of Middlesbrough Institute of Modern Art, Acquisition supported by the V&A Purchase Grant Fund (MIDMA/FA/0107). M 1021

During the Lewises' long stay in the Tudor Hotel in Toronto, Lewis produced several drawings of their domestic life; of sewing baskets, laden coffee tables or Froanna reading or sitting in her armchair, clearly bored. Lewis wrote of their experience in his 1954 novel *Self Condemned* (B&M Cat. 54):

They must vegetate, violent and morose – sometimes blissfully drunken, sometimes with no money for drink – within these four walls, in this identical daily scene – from breakfast until the time came to tear down the Murphy bed, to pant and sweat in the night temperatures kicked up by the radiators – until the war's end or the world's end was it? Until they had died or had become different people and the world that they had left had changed its identity too, or died as they had died.[1]

1. Wyndham Lewis, *Self Condemned* (London: Methuen, 1954), p. 171.

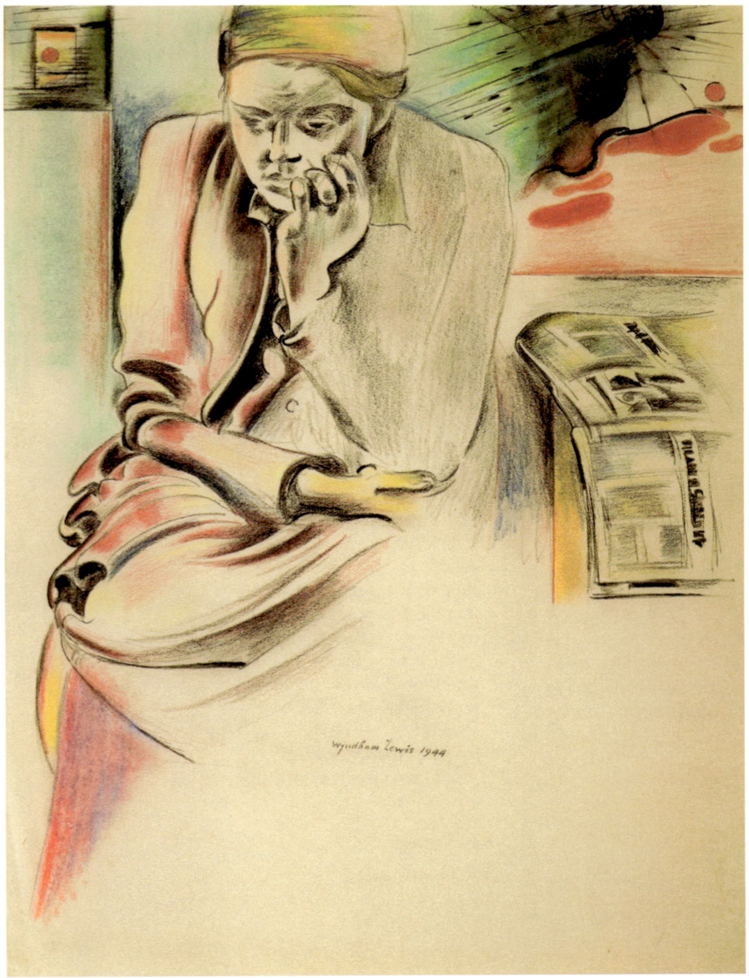

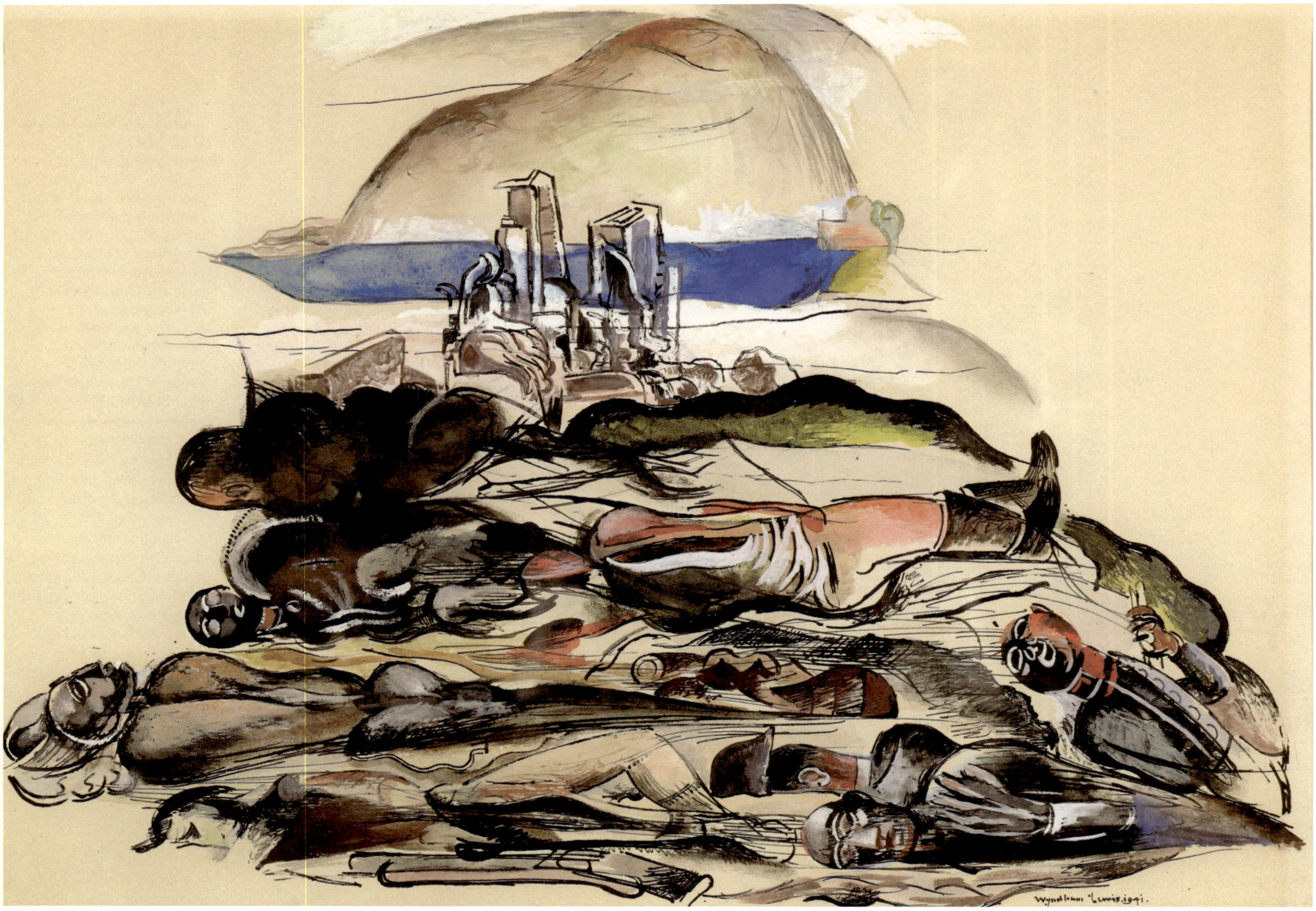

Cat. 175.
Lebensraum I: The Battlefield, 1941. Pen, Indian ink, watercolour and gouache on paper. 30.2 x 45.5 cm. Collection Art Gallery of Ontario, Toronto. Purchase, 1941 (Acc.2576). M 976

Lebensraum was the word used by Adolf Hitler to denote the German "need" to expand into neighbouring territories, resulting in the invasion of Russia in 1941. Lewis described this picture as depicting "a foreground clogged with layers of German dead: beyond is the skeleton of a Russian village, and beyond that a Crimean Mountain."[1] Walter Michel has written an illuminating essay on the metaphysical implications of this representation of the dead. He points out Lewis's indebtedness to Francisco Goya's etching, *Tanto y más* (1810–20), and reflects on the grotesque, quasi-comic depiction of the corpses and the technique of overlaying black with body-colour that Lewis uses for them:

> The eeriness of the faces, curiously resembling that in certain horror movies, suggests bodies drained of the *pneuma* of anything human, only a dark, chemical fluid remaining.
>
> The representation of dead as negation of all being, as nothingness, is here achieved not by allegory but by the most concrete means: black and blood as basic symbols; non-stylised forms, and omission of all reference to the ordered, living human world.[2]

1. Wyndham Lewis, unpublished manuscript, quoted in Paul Edwards, *Wyndham Lewis: Painter and Writer* (London/New Haven: Yale University Press, 2000), p. 431.
2. Walter Michel, "Irony in a War Picture," in *Volcanic Heaven: Essays on Wyndham Lewis's Painting and Writing*. Ed. Paul Edwards (Santa Rosa: Black Sparrow Press, 1996), p. 144.

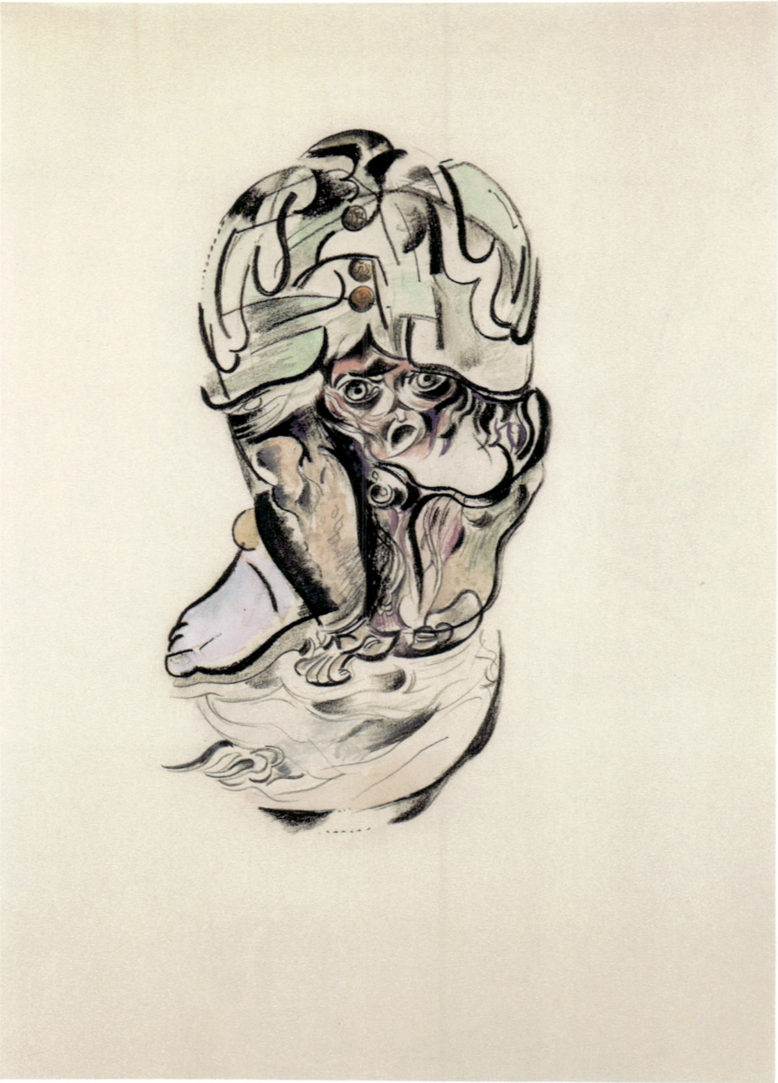

Cat. 176.
***Lebensraum II: The Empty Tunic*, 1941–42. Chalk, watercolour and gouache on paper. 34.6 x 24.3 cm. Wyndham Lewis Memorial Trust. G. and V. Lane Collection (LD.2004.XX.46). M 988**

The second of the *Lebensraum* drawings appears to allude to Francisco Goya's great contemporary, the English visionary painter-poet, William Blake, whose creator-God, "The Ancient of Days," seems to be echoed in the figure of Lewis's crouching, uniform-laden figure. The drawing seems to be another of Lewis's creation myths and the stormy world beneath and behind the figure has suggestions of supplicating figures at the bottom left. They recall the cowering figures in *Jehovah the Thunderer* (Cat. 180). Lewis, with his philosophical anti-naturalism, was always inclined to a Gnostic dualism, and stated his attraction to the Marcionite heresy, in which the wrathful Yahveh (the God of Justice) was distinguished from the God of Love represented by Jesus Christ.[1] The creator represented in *Lebensraun II*, with his face also reminiscent of masks in horror movies, is a kind of dark twin of a benevolent God, an evil *demiurge* both responsible for, and a victim of, the material world and its ills, expressed most terrifyingly in war.

1. The fullest study is Michael Nath, "Monstrous Starlight: Wyndham Lewis and Gnosticism," in *Volcanic Heaven: Essays on Wyndham Lewis's Painting and Writing*. Ed. Paul Edwards (Santa Rosa: Black Sparrow Press, 1996), pp. 149–67.

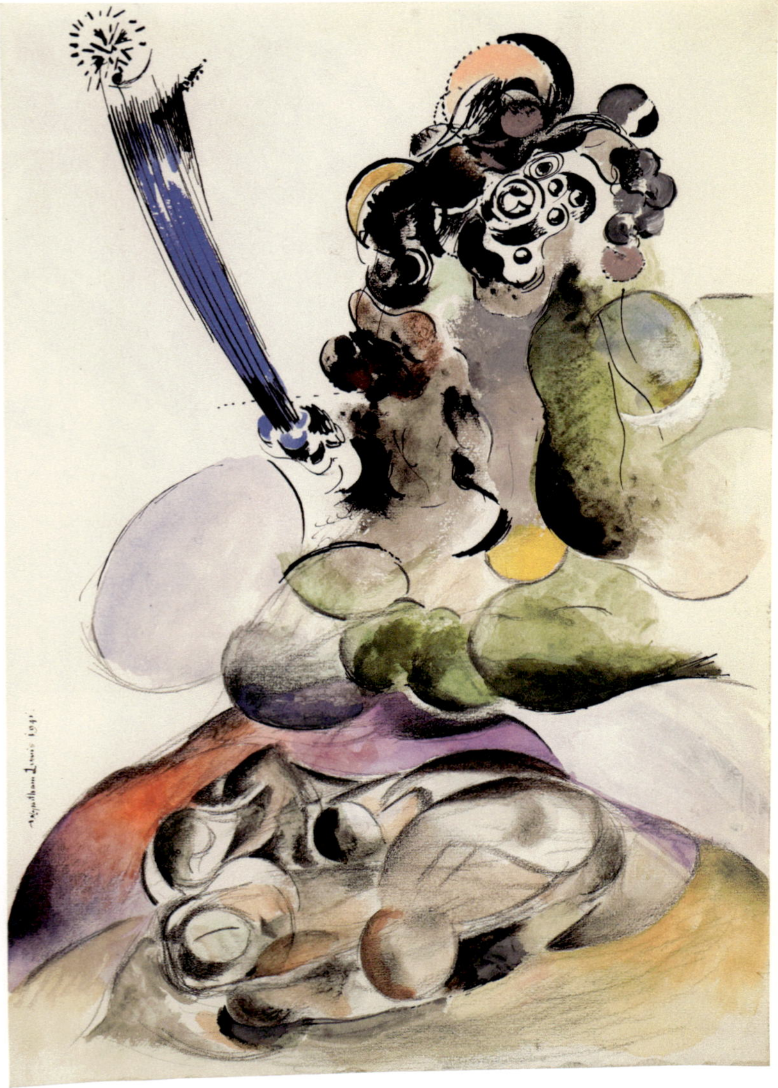

Cat. 180.
***Jehovah the Thunderer*, 1941. Pencil, ink and watercolour on paper. 37 x 25.5 cm. Collection Hugh Anson-Cartwright. M 975**

"All-Fathers have always been Battle-Fathers," Lewis writes in *Time and Western Man* (1927) (B&M Cat. 12), arguing for a strictly metaphysical version of theology. "The true religionist is such a scourge that his God is always an engine of destruction, and bears no resemblance to any Absolute with which metaphysics deals."[1] The cloudy and indefinite figure hovering intimidatingly over his creations is himself here in the process of further creation, the arc of blue representing either a sword or an out-throw of energy from which a world emerges at the top. The almost complete revolution (if not in religious terms) in aesthetic approach to picture-making that is exemplified in Lewis's practice in this watercolour is shown by the aptness of the words "cloudy and indefinite," to it. Before the Second World War and his Canadian "exile" (as he began to think of it), only what was clearly defined was deemed fit for visual art. One aesthetic continuity remains, however – the admiration for oriental art, shown here (as Walter Michel noticed) in the resemblance of the image to Tawaraya Sotatsu's *Wind God* (after 1621).

1. Wyndham Lewis, *Time and Western Man* (1927). Rprt. ed. Paul Edwards (Santa Rosa: Black Sparrow Press, 1993), pp. 379, 378.

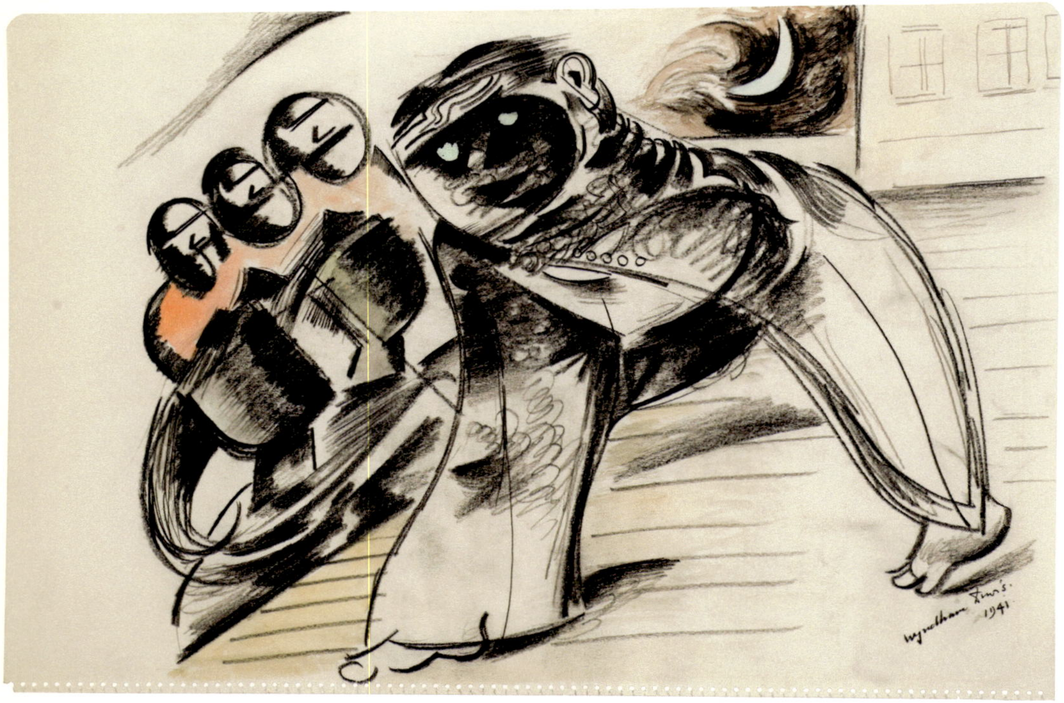

Cat. 177.
[Not in exhibition] *Armless Man on Stage*, 1941. Black chalk and wash on paper. 28.5 x 44 cm. Collection Hugh Anson-Cartwright. M 966

The grotesque, Gothic element of Lewis's imagined war is continued in this image of a terrified (and terrifying) victim of violence, unable to escape the scrutiny of the three figures who offer no response to his desperation.

Cat. 178.
Mother Love, 1942. Graphite, pen and ink, watercolour and gouache on paper. 43.6 x 28 cm. Wyndham Lewis Memorial Trust (LD.2004.XX.35). M 998

The universal satire against war and the conditions of material existence here becomes more particular, focused on military pride and its origins in the mother-son relationship. In *The Lion and the Fox* (1927) (B&M Cat. 11), Lewis had commented on this as it applies to the Roman military hero Coriolanus: "He is shown [...] as the child, drilled into a second nature which goes on mechanically obeying. His mother – whose ultra-roman despotism has been shown in other scenes – has coached and formed him into the madman he is."[1]

The son in *Mother Love* also resembles a mechanical ventriloquist's dummy on the knee of the Victorian matron (with her grotesquely elaborate hat). The decorative feature behind them, on top of what may be a lampshade, turns out on closer inspection to be billowing smoke and flames.

1. Wyndham Lewis, *The Lion and the Fox: The Rôle of the Hero in the Plays of Shakespeare* (London: Grant Richards, 1927), p. 242.

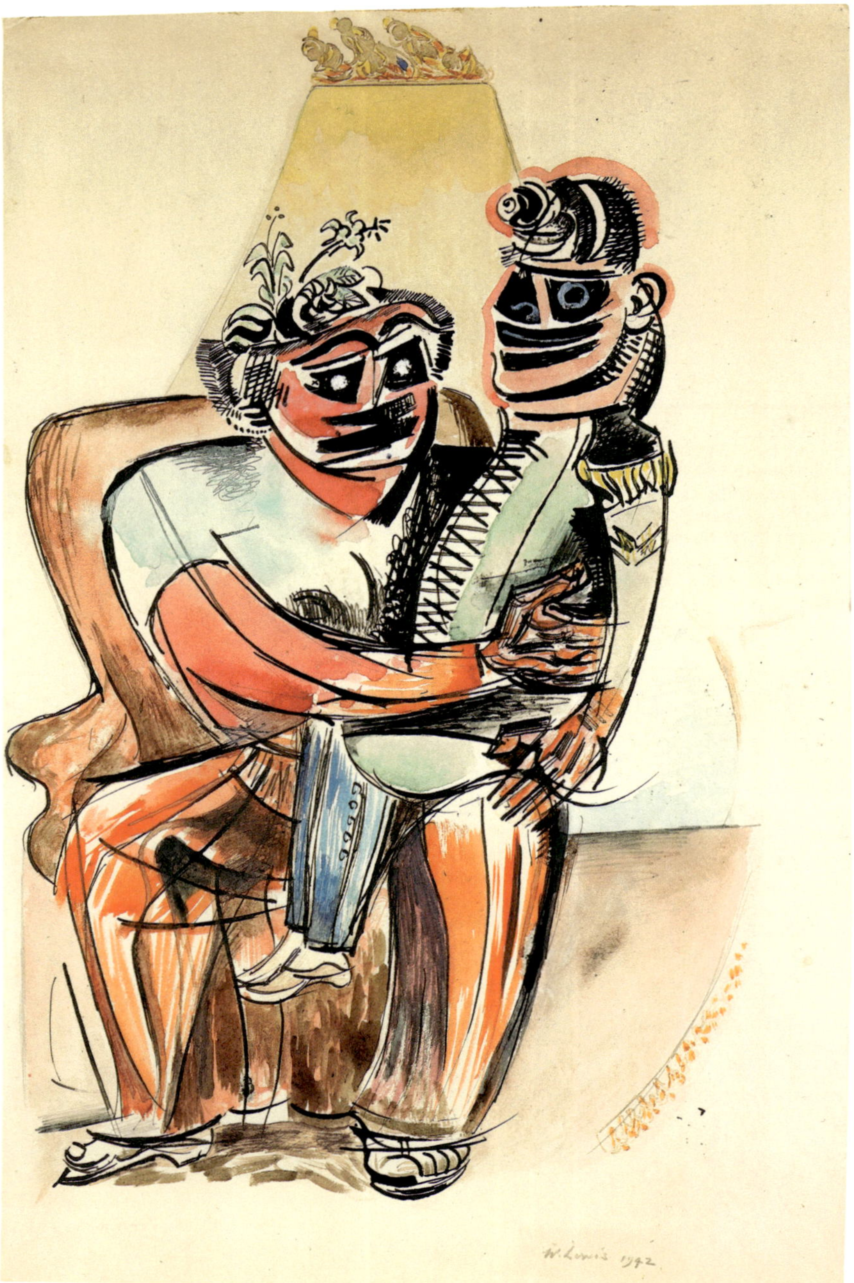

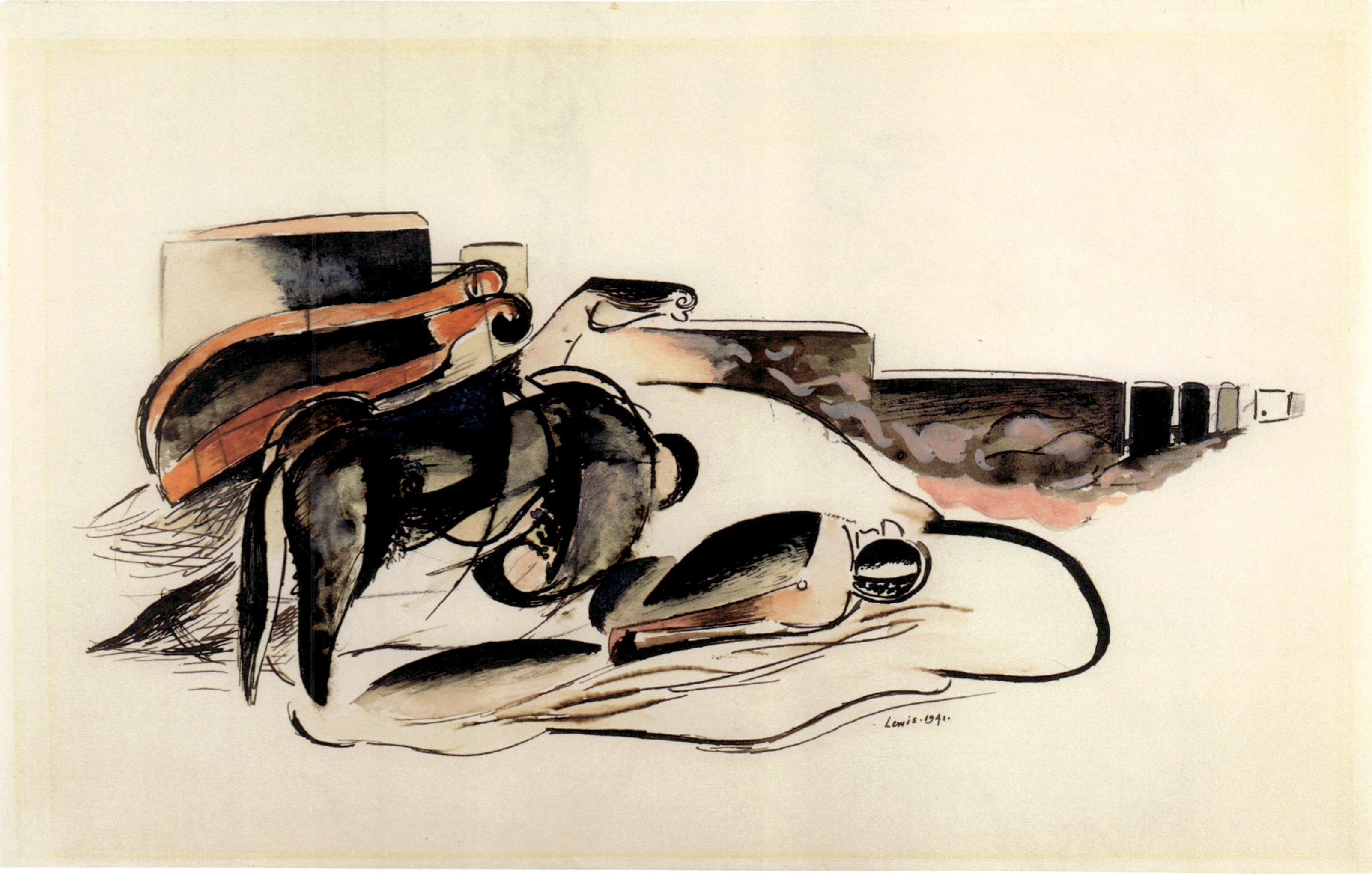

Cat. 179.
***A Man's Form Taking a Fall from a Small Horse*, 1941. Graphite, pen and ink, watercolour and gouache on paper. 29.5 x 45 cm. C.J. Fox Collection (LD.2000.XX.3). M 977**

Horses, though not much represented in this exhibition, were a recurrent presence in Lewis's art. In the early 1920s he produced several drawings of them, and just as he was finally losing his sight in 1950 he was planning a picture of a riding school and produced several sketches, including copies of Leonardo drawings.[1] Lewis was himself thrown by a horse while training during the First World War. An elaborate mounted warrior was the emblem of "the Enemy," Lewis's critical persona of the late 1920s (see Cat. 118 and B&M Cat. 14). And the *Berber Horseman* (Cat. 137) is a heroic and romantic figure. The epigraph to *The Art of Being Ruled* (1926) (B&M Cat. 10) was a quotation from George Chapman's play, *The Conspiracy and Tragedy of Charles, Duke of Byron*, in which the image of the man on horseback is put forward as an ideal emblem of happy government:

[...] and they make
A doctrinal and witty hiero-glyphic
Of a blessed kingdom.

For Lewis, European war was the inevitable consequence of an exaltation of dynamic energies that originates in Roman culture, is revived in the Renaissance and undergoes a cyclical return in history. Its outcome is here depicted allegorically; but the drawing has an overwhelmingly personal dimension.

1. See the entries for the following works in Walter Michel, *Wyndham Lewis: Paintings and Drawings* (London: Thames and Hudson, 1971): *Drawing for Jonathan Swift* (1922) (M 526), *Drawing of Horses* (1923) (M 572), *Two Horses* (1938) (M 927), and the late studies from the 1940s, M 1113–1121.

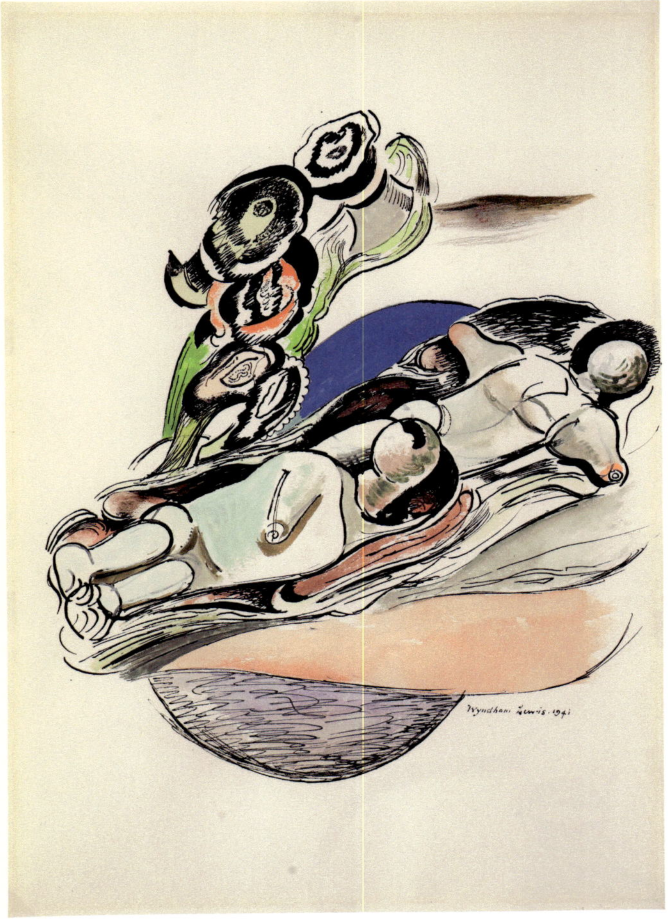
Wyndham Lewis 1941

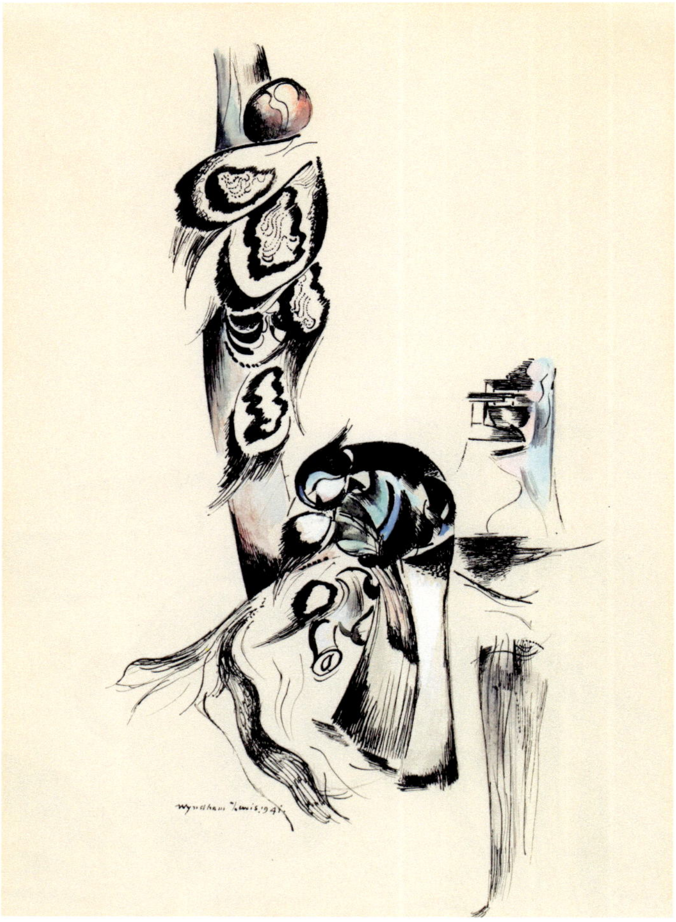
Wyndham Lewis 1941

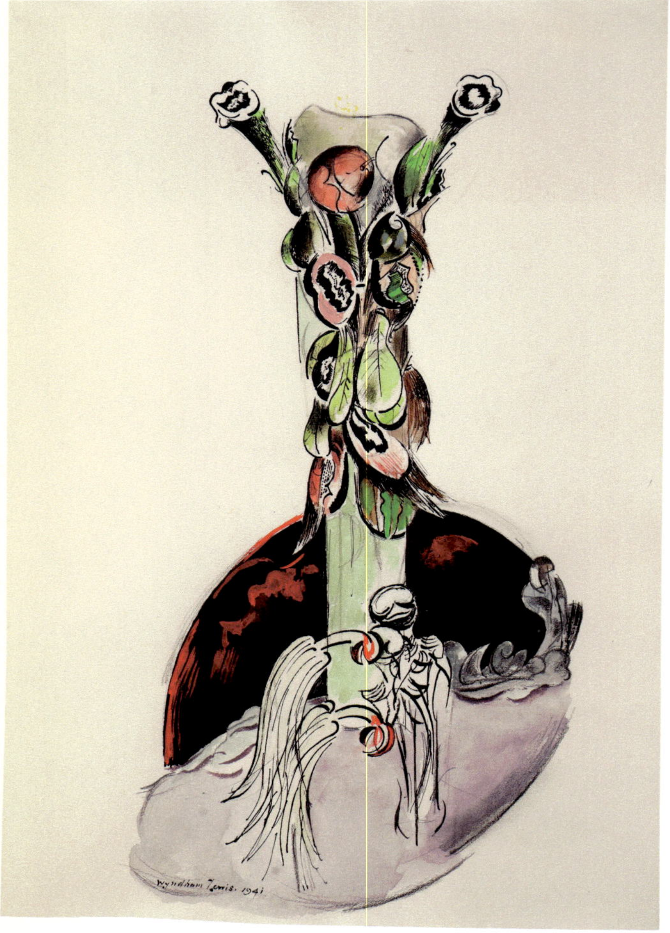
Wyndham Lewis 1941

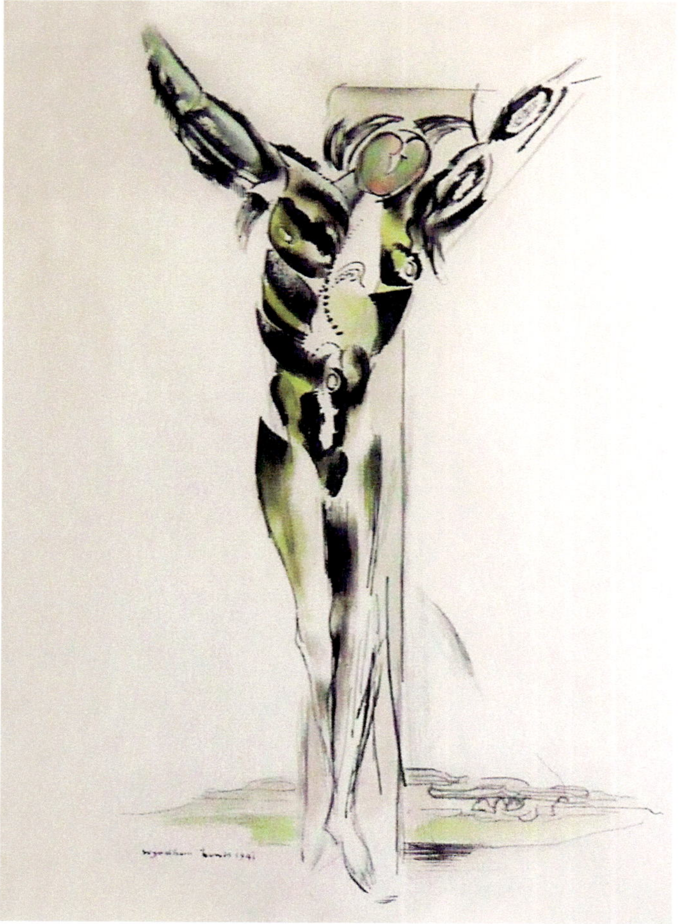
Wyndham Lewis 1941

Cat. 181. ◀◀
Small Crucifixion Series, I, 1941. Pencil, pen and ink, and watercolour on paper. 35.5 x 25 cm. Collection Hugh Anson-Cartwright. M 980

Cat. 182. ◀
Small Crucifixion Series, II: Pietà, 1941. Pen and ink, and watercolour on paper. 33 x 25.5 cm. Private collection. M 981

Cat. 183. ◀◀▼
Small Crucifixion Series, III, 1941. Pencil, pen and ink, and watercolour on paper. 35.5 x 25.5 cm. Collection Hugh Anson-Cartwright. M 982

Cat. 184. ◀▼
[Not in exhibition] *Small Crucifixion Series, IV,* 1941. Watercolour on paper. 36.5 x 25.5 cm. Private collection. M 983

Lewis's quasi-Gnostic dualism always implied a troubled relationship with flesh and the world of nature. So in 1927 Lewis demanded a God indifferent to his creation: "We do not want a God that is a kindly uncle, nor do we wish to see a God 'in love'. Any interest taken in us can be nothing but an intellectual passion: and surely we should be satisfied to be 'thoughts', rather than 'children'."[1] Beginning in the 1930s, particularly in *The Revenge for Love* (1937) (B&M Cat. 39), Lewis began to become more reconciled with the view (a more normal one, surely, for a visual artist) that it is through the world of flesh and blood, not in spite of it, that we find and express some of our deepest valuations. To be part of this "machine" of endless reproduction had always seemed nightmarish to Lewis (hence, perhaps, his rejection of his own children), and traces of that horror remain in these representations of the dying God. His heroine in *The Revenge*, Margot, reflects on motherhood and the grotesqueness of "normality" but recognises, perforce, her own part in it: "There was no use pretending she did not belong to this system of roaring and spluttering bestial life of flesh and blood."[2]

The first picture in the series fuses the idea of motherhood with that of crucifixion, as a foetus-like form emerges from the cavity of the womb. An opening in the head of the foetus reveals a hollow blackness within. The upright figure, composed of strange cellular or amoebic forms, lifts its left arm in horror and grief. Motherhood is again important in Cat. 182, a Pietà in which the crucified Christ is composed of the same ultimate biological building-blocks as in Cat. 181. Lewis presents different moments from the story simultaneously, as Mary mourns over the body she is supporting, its spirit apparently flowing away even as she grasps it. A somewhat metaphysical Mary Magdalene watches. Behind the green tree that bears a similar biologic-botanic Christ, a blood-soaked world emerges. Lewis uses the technique of overlaying gouache on black, as he had in *Lebensraum I* (Cat. 175). The weeping attendants at the scene also seem like wilting plants. It may be that Lewis's use of such forms alludes to the great vegetation and fertility myths collected in James Frazer's *The Golden Bough* (1890), and in this sense these works are as much pre-Christian as Christian, showing a permanent impulse in mankind to kill and torture. The final image shows the apparently flayed figure of Christ alone. In *Malign Fiesta* (1955) (B&M Cat. 57), Sammael comments to the protagonist, Pullman, after they have watched a devil punishing a woman sinner, "with the human, death is found a very short distance beneath the surface."[3]

1. Wyndham Lewis, *Time and Western Man* (1927). Rprt. ed. Paul Edwards (Santa Rosa: Black Sparrow Press, 1993), p. 435.
2. Wyndham Lewis, *The Revenge for Love* (1937) (London: Penguin, 2004), p. 298.
3. Wyndham Lewis, *The Human Age, Book Two: Monstre Gai; Book Three: Malign Fiesta* (London: Methuen, 1955), p. 376

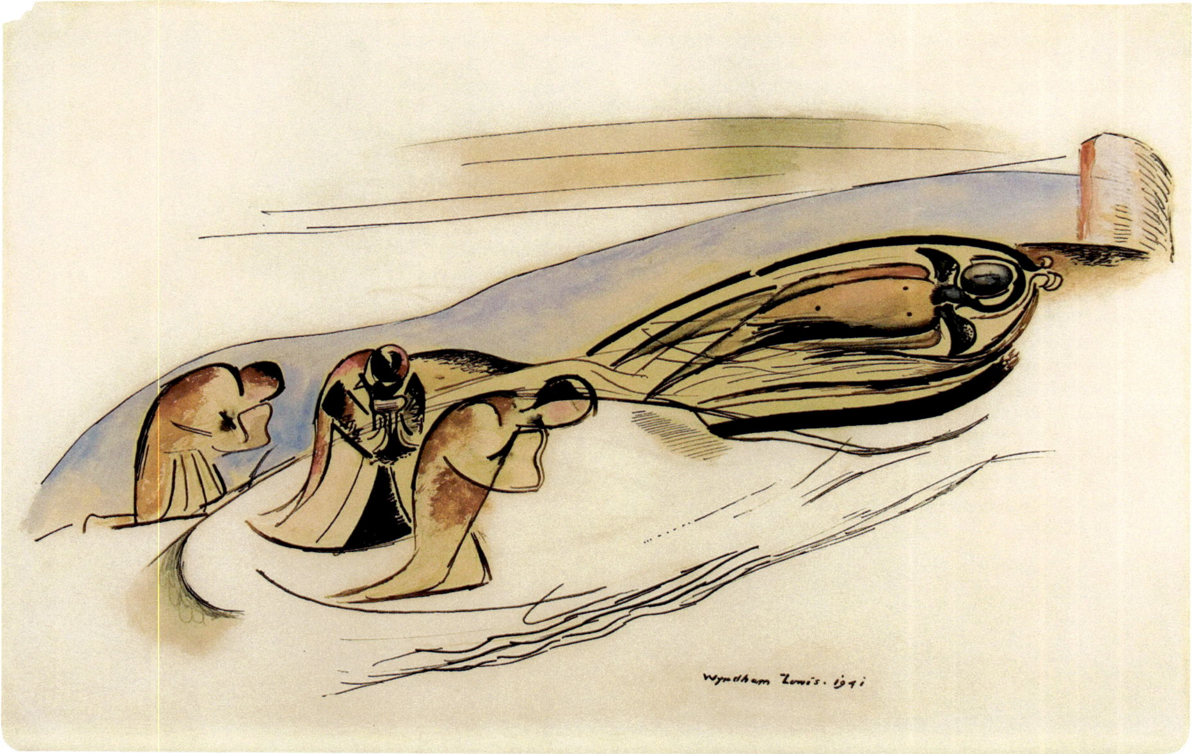

Cat. 185.
[Not in exhibition]
Supplicating Figures,
1941. Pen and ink, and watercolour on paper. 30.5 x 45.5 cm. Collection Mark F. McLean. M 984

This work is related to the *Small Crucifixion Series* (Cats. 181–84), though the forms and the horizontal emphasis are quite different. The figures may be mourning rather than supplicating the dead body.

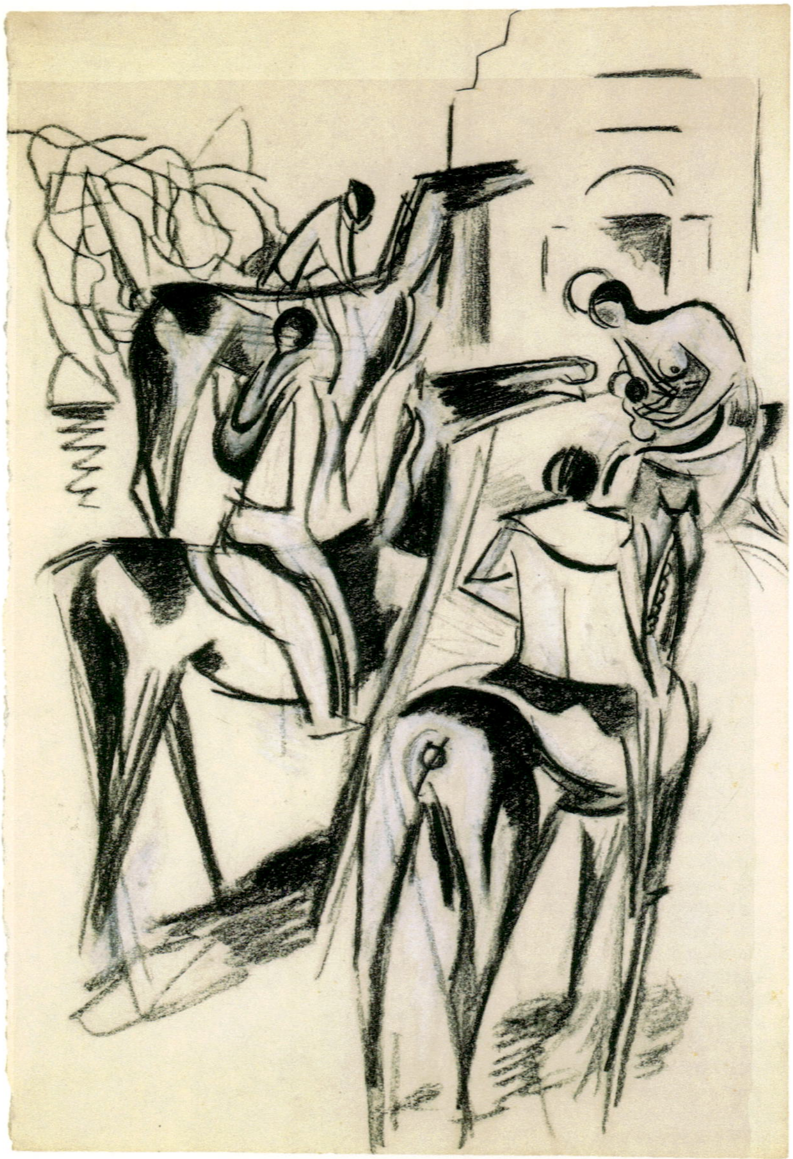

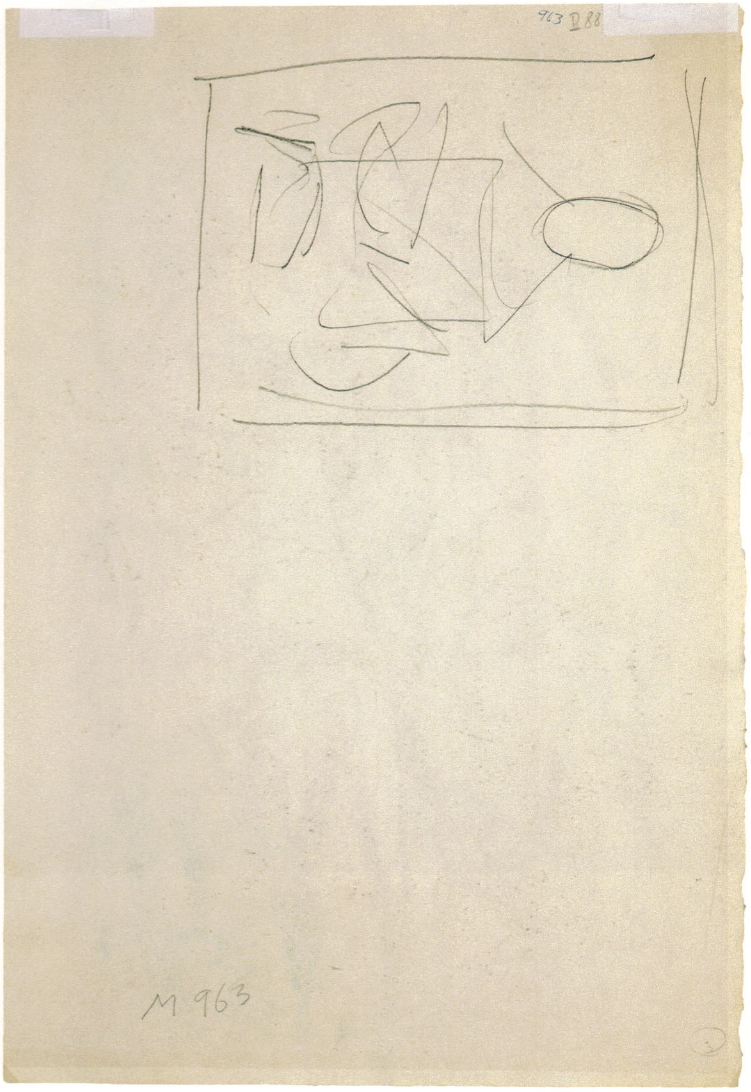

Cat. 186.
[Not in exhibition] *Adoration*, 1941 (recto and verso). Chalk and gouache on paper. 38 x 25.3 cm. Wyndham Lewis Memorial Trust (LD.2004.XX.32). M 963

A more orthodox scene from the Christian story, the drawing again shows a considerable loosening in Lewis's technique. It may be significant that Lewis's magi (if that is who they are) are mounted on horseback (see Cat. 179). The emblem of authority and power is thus submitting itself to the values implicit in the nativity scene.

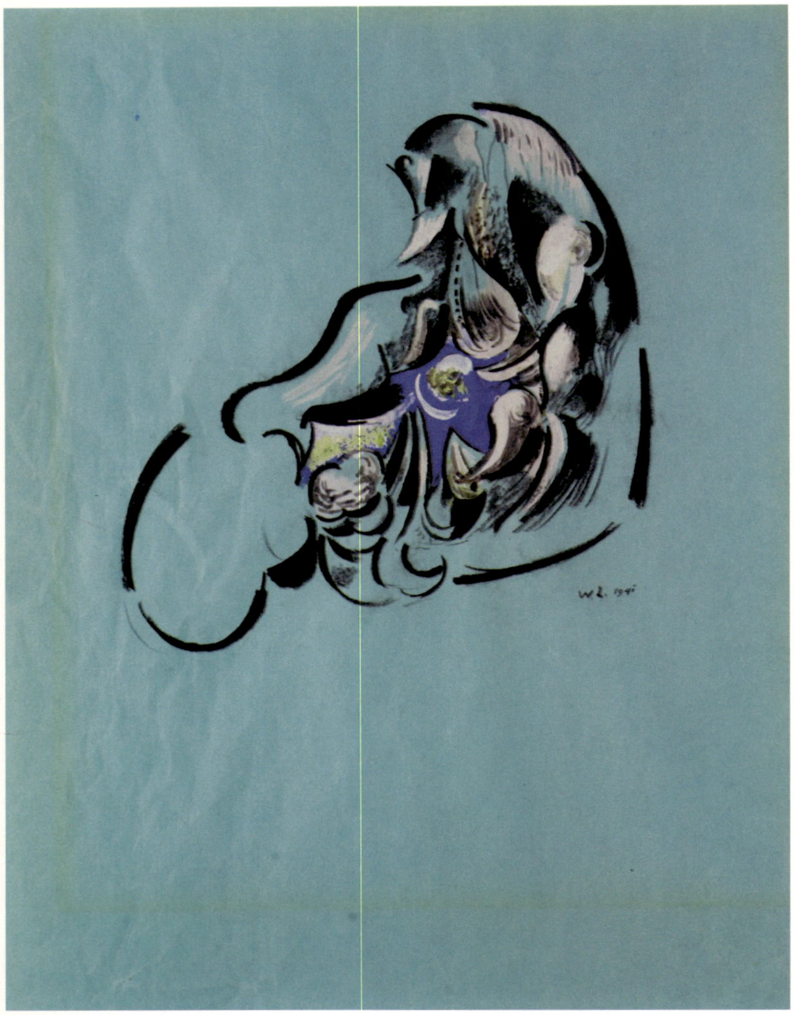

Cat. 187.
[Not in exhibition] ***Gestation or Creation Myth: Maternal Figure*****, 1941. Crayon and coloured chalks on blue paper. 30 x 24 cm. Collection Hugh Anson-Cartwright. M 971**

This is another drawing produced on the coloured paper Lewis that bought from a Toronto drugstore (see Cat. 172). His preoccupation with the processes of fleshly creation is evident in this work. The antithesis between artistic and natural creation is bridged, as the indefinite forms of the artist's imagination organise themselves into the suggestion of a developing foetus. In *Tarr* (1918) (B&M Cat. 5), Lewis's spokesman expresses his gynophobia in a graphic image that contrasts artistic and natural creation:

A woman had in the middle of her a kernel, a sort of very substantial astral baby. This baby was apt to swell. She then became *all* baby. The husk [i.e., Tarr's fiancée, Bertha] he held was a painted mummy case. He was a mummy case too. Only he contained nothing but innumerable other painted cases inside, smaller and smaller ones. The smallest was not a substantial astral baby, however, or live core, but a painting like all the rest. = His kernel was a painting. That was as it should be![1]

The dichotomy is overturned here, just as it was violently parodied in *Small Crucifixion I* (Cat. 181). The foetus had been for Lewis a symbol of threatening absurdity and cited as such in an analysis of laughter in the 1934 study, *Men Without Art* (B&M Cat. 36): "There is no reason at all why we should not burst out laughing at a foetus, for instance. We should after all only be laughing at *ourselves* – at ourselves early in our mortal career."[2] Absurdity was for Lewis an aspect of philosophical wonder and in this work wonder entirely displaces laughter.

1. Paul O'Keeffe, ed. *Tarr: The 1918 Version* (Santa Rosa: Black Sparrow Press, 1990), pp. 58–59. The baby is "astral" perhaps because Lewis saw the stars as the embodiment of the natural-mechanical process that at the time seemed to him to negate value (compare *Enemy of the Stars* (1914)).
2. Wyndham Lewis, *Men Without Art* (1937). Rprt. ed. Seamus Cooney (Santa Rosa: Black Sparrow Press, 1987), p. 92.

Cat. 188.
[Not in exhibition] ***Still-life: Figures in the Belly of a Duck*, 1942. Pencil and watercolour on paper. 35 x 25.7 cm. Collection of the Vancouver Art Gallery, Acquired from George Woodcock with the aid of donations by Dr Hugh S. Miller and Dr Kenneth S. Morton (VAG. 70.107). M 1005**

This work is another of Lewis's "creation myths." With its egg and serpent form (seen circling the bottom of the image and resembling also an orbiting planet), the image suggests Orphic mysteries. Lewis's knowledge of these, and interest in them, were in evidence in the mythological substratum of the 1930 satire, *The Apes of God* (B&M Cat. 21), where a major character, Zagreus, is named after the Orphic version of Dionysus. Technically, the method of creating various layers of semi-translucent space shows that, if the incisive draughtsmanship was no longer at his disposal, he was still capable of skilful control in other media.

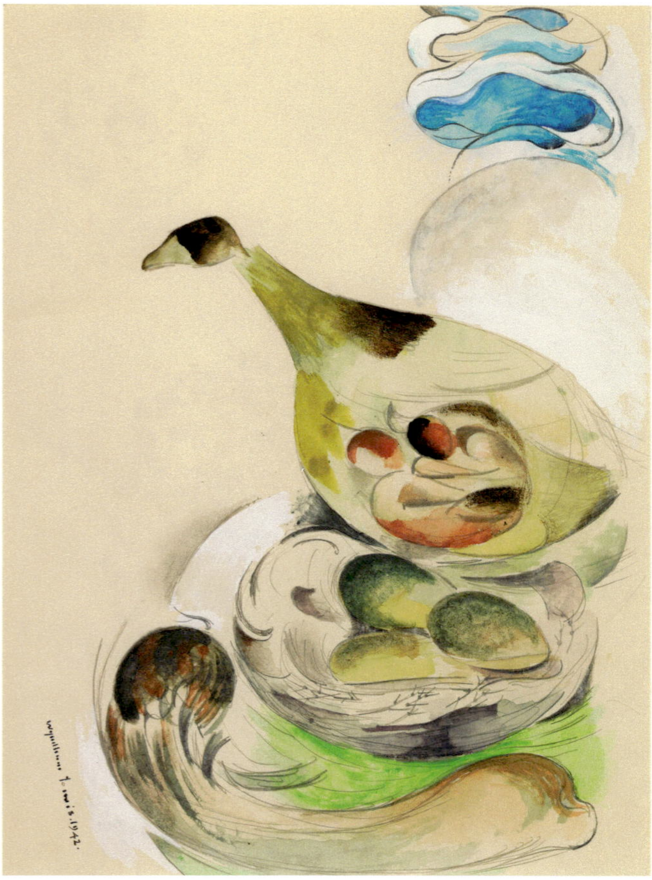

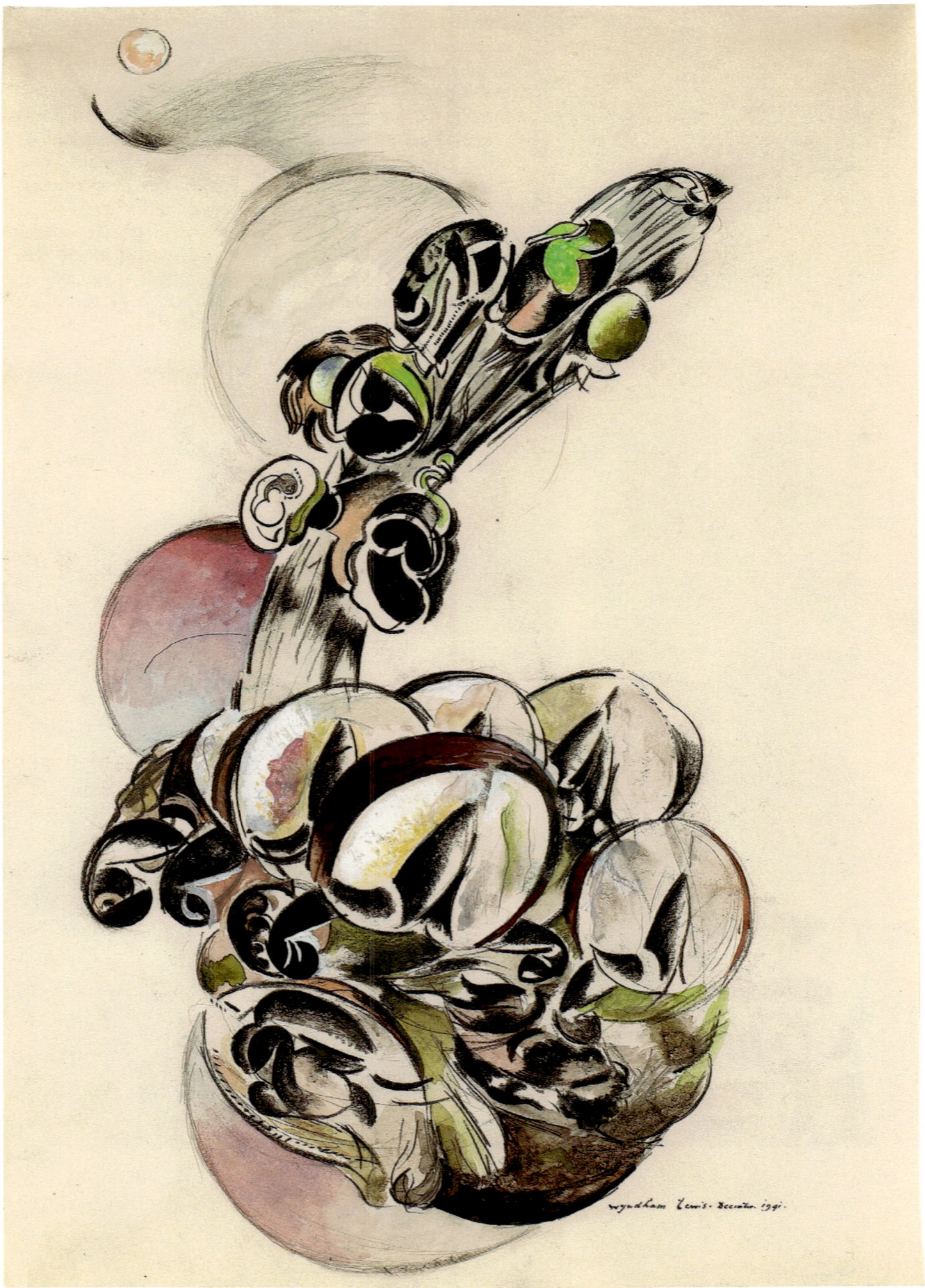

Cat. 189.
***Creation Myth No. 17*, 1941. Charcoal and graphite with watercolour and gouache on wove paper. 50.1 x 34.9 cm. National Gallery of Canada, Ottawa. Gift from the Douglas M. Duncan Collection, 1970 (NGC 16713). M 968**

The "number 17" of the title acknowledges a continuing fascination with this theme rather than reflecting any precise arithmetic. In an unused chapter intended for *Time and Western Man* (1927) (B&M Cat. 12), Lewis quoted (at that time in order to mock) Henri Bergson's image of creation as like a jet of condensing steam: "from an immense reservoir of life, jets must be gushing out unceasingly, of which each, falling back, is a world."[1] Such a jet of life is seen in *Jehovah the Thunderer* (Cat. 180). Here, in a faint echo of the forms used in the figures in the *Small Crucifixion Series* (Cats. 181–84), it is seen germinating into burgeoning young plant forms, one type of world in a larger cosmos. One of the small cells partially silhouetted against the blue-red globe at middle right appears to hold a small comma-shaped form: tadpole or foetus. Lewis's use of such "microscopic" imagery may be paralleled by some of Wassily Kandinsky's (1866–1944) later compositions, but there appears to be no influence involved, and the visual status of the forms is quite different.

1. Henri Bergson, *Creative Evolution*, quoted in Wyndham Lewis, *Time and Western Man* (1927). Rprt. ed. Paul Edwards (Santa Rosa: Black Sparrow Press, 1993), p. 542.

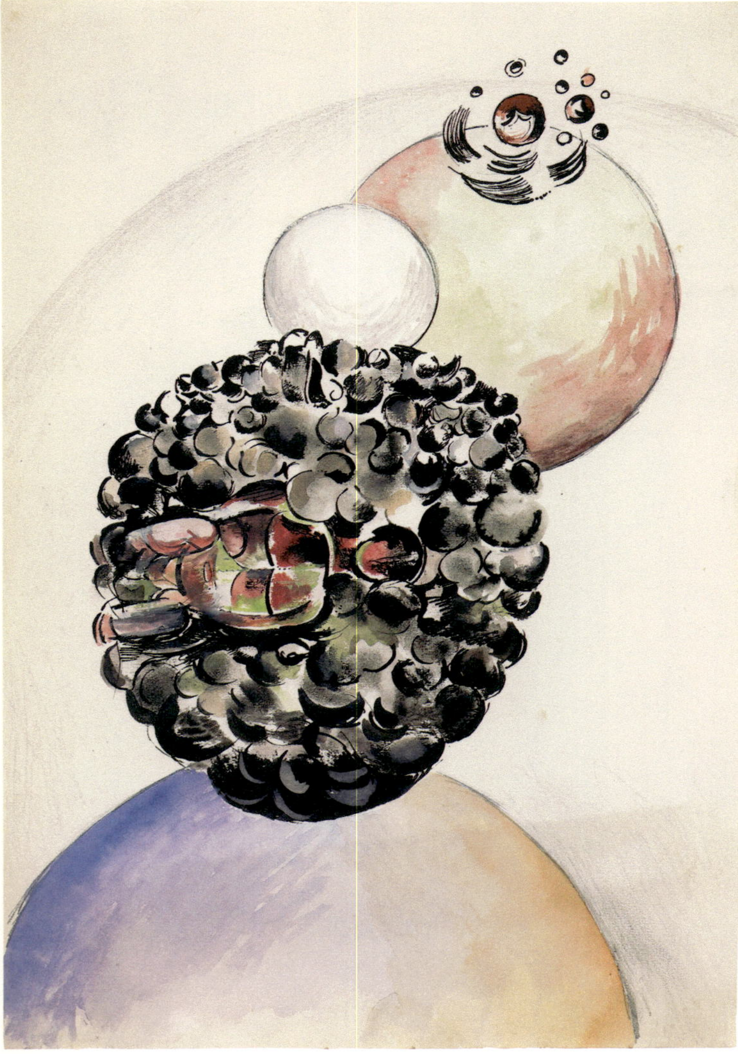

Cat. 190.
Creation Myth, 1941–42. Graphite, pen and ink, watercolour and gouache on paper. 37 x 25.1 cm. Wyndham Lewis Memorial Trust (LD.2004.XX.34). M 987

A human or turtle-like shape emerges from the black forms of the central floating world, while above, another world bursts like a bubble, throwing off yet more worlds in the cosmic void.

Cat. 192.
The Mind of the Artist about to Make a Picture, 1941–42. Pen and ink, and watercolour on paper. 39.5 x 30.5 cm. Wyndham Lewis Memorial Trust (LD.2004.XX.28). M 997

This is a playful work that is concerned with aspects of creation that Lewis felt more at home with than the cosmic and fleshly processes explored in other "creation myths" of the 1940s. The floating "bubbles" in front of the yellow-green panel relate the work, however, to the more "cosmic" type of creation depicted in the "creation myths" of the period. The artist here is a Romantic visionary, who has pulled down the blue blind that separates him from the outside world. Like the "Theatre Manager" depicted in Cat. 6, his inspiration is a book. His dream appears in the form of a painting above him. But the painting is a scaled-down version of *The Mind of the Artist about to Make a Picture* itself. And inside it can be seen yet another, even smaller version of the picture within that picture, presumably as part of an infinite series: "His kernel was a painting" (see Cat. 187).

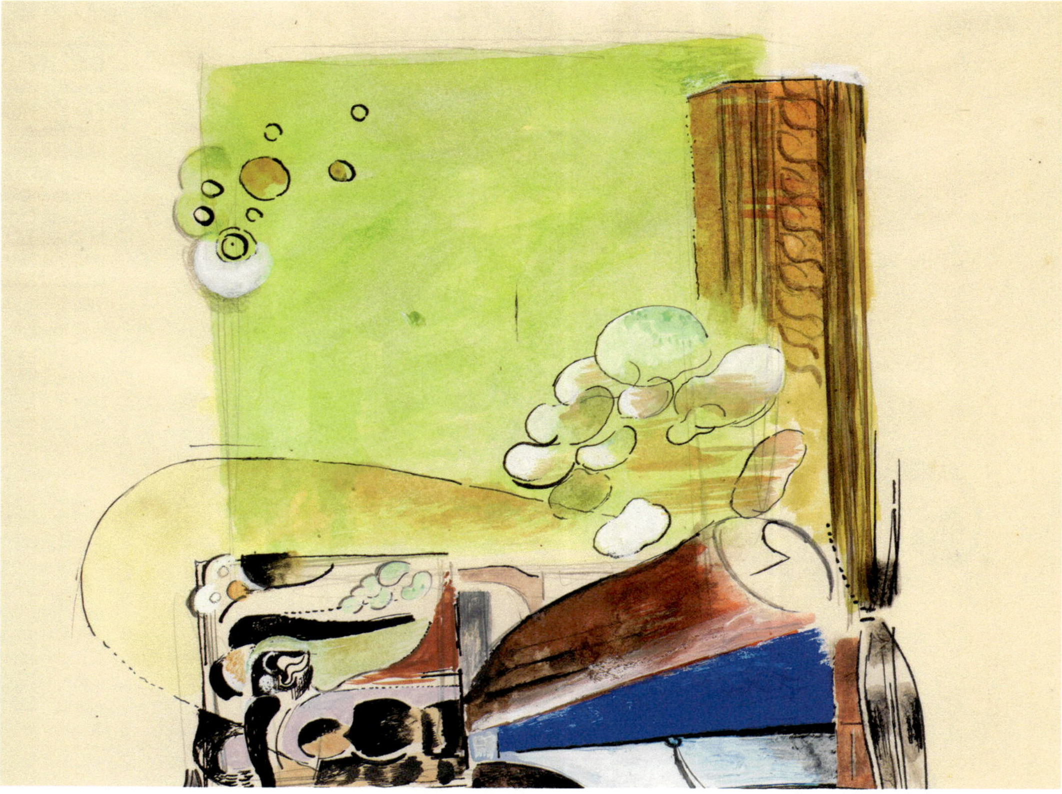

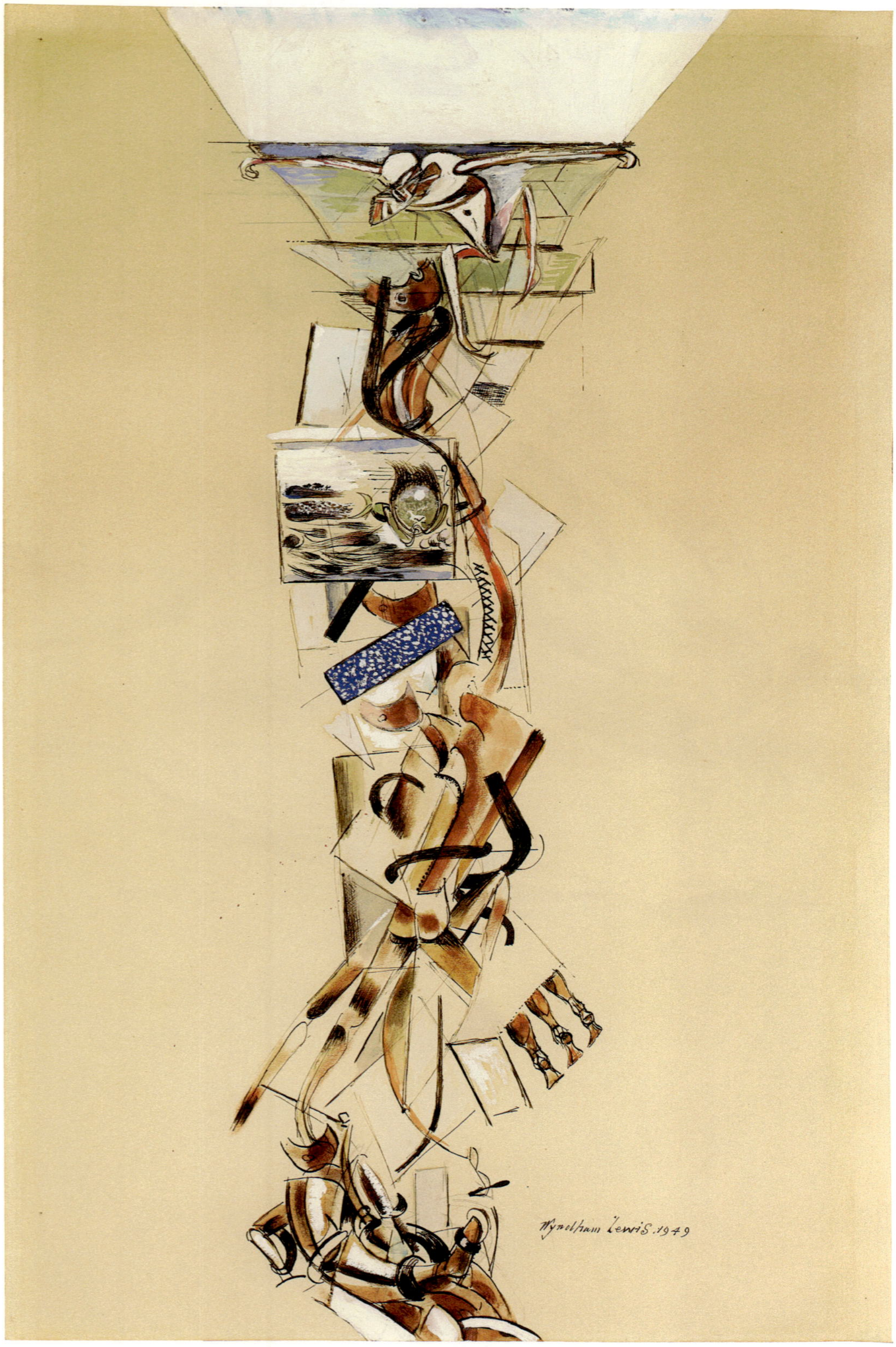

Cat. 203.
***The Ascent*, 1949. Pen and ink, and watercolour on paper. 54.5 x 32 cm. Private collection. M 1093**

Although the format of this drawing is similar to that of Cats. 120–22, the title suggests that it should be read as a quasi-narrative, starting at the bottom and culminating in the apparent crucifixion at the top. The narrative would then be of the ascent to the cross of the multiplied and disintegrated figure whose brown, crescent-like face occurs in several places. The athleticism of the naked striding figure (reminiscent of some of the figures in *The Island* (Cat. 200)) gives way to an assemblage of elements (the "blocks and lines" of Vorticism) and a miniature vignetted composition like that in *The Mind of the Artist about to Make a Picture* (Cat. 192). Finally, the figure is crucified, unless this culmination is to be seen as no more than an allusion to the *Small Crucifixion Series* that Lewis produced in Toronto (Cats. 181–84). If the image is taken as a reflection on Lewis's own career, the self-dramatisation may be forgiven. In 1949, he knew he faced complete loss of his already failing sight; an operation to remove the tumour in his skull (which in the end proved impossible) could have resulted in death. The identification of the artist with Christ was a Romantic trope with which Lewis was familiar from his early interest in Paul Gauguin.

Cat. 193.
"... And Wilderness were Paradise enow," 1941.
Chalk, watercolour and gouache on paper.
42.1 x 32 cm. Wyndham Lewis Memorial Trust (LD.2004.XX.31). M 965

The quotation is slightly misremembered from Edward Fitzgerald's famous Victorian translation, "The Rubaiyat of Omar Khayyam" (1859), or conflates some of its versions:

A Book of Verses
  underneath the Bough,
A Jug of Wine, a Loaf of Bread – and Thou
Beside me singing in the Wilderness –
Oh, Wilderness were Paradise enow!

What precisely the strange elephantine beast sprawled "beside me singing" on the sandy tussock is in this playful fantasy is not ascertainable. When an acquaintance of Lewis's was visiting Los Angeles in 1946, Lewis wrote to him asking him to approach Walt Disney to sit for a portrait to Lewis: "I would like to visit Hollywood [...] I have a boundless admiration for Disney [...] Most people in Hollywood are not artists, as you know. But Disney is a great artist. – See?"[1]

1. Letter to Nigel Tangye, 23 July 1946, quoted in Paul O'Keeffe, *Some Sort of Genius: A Life of Wyndham Lewis* (London: Jonathan Cape, 2000), p. 515.

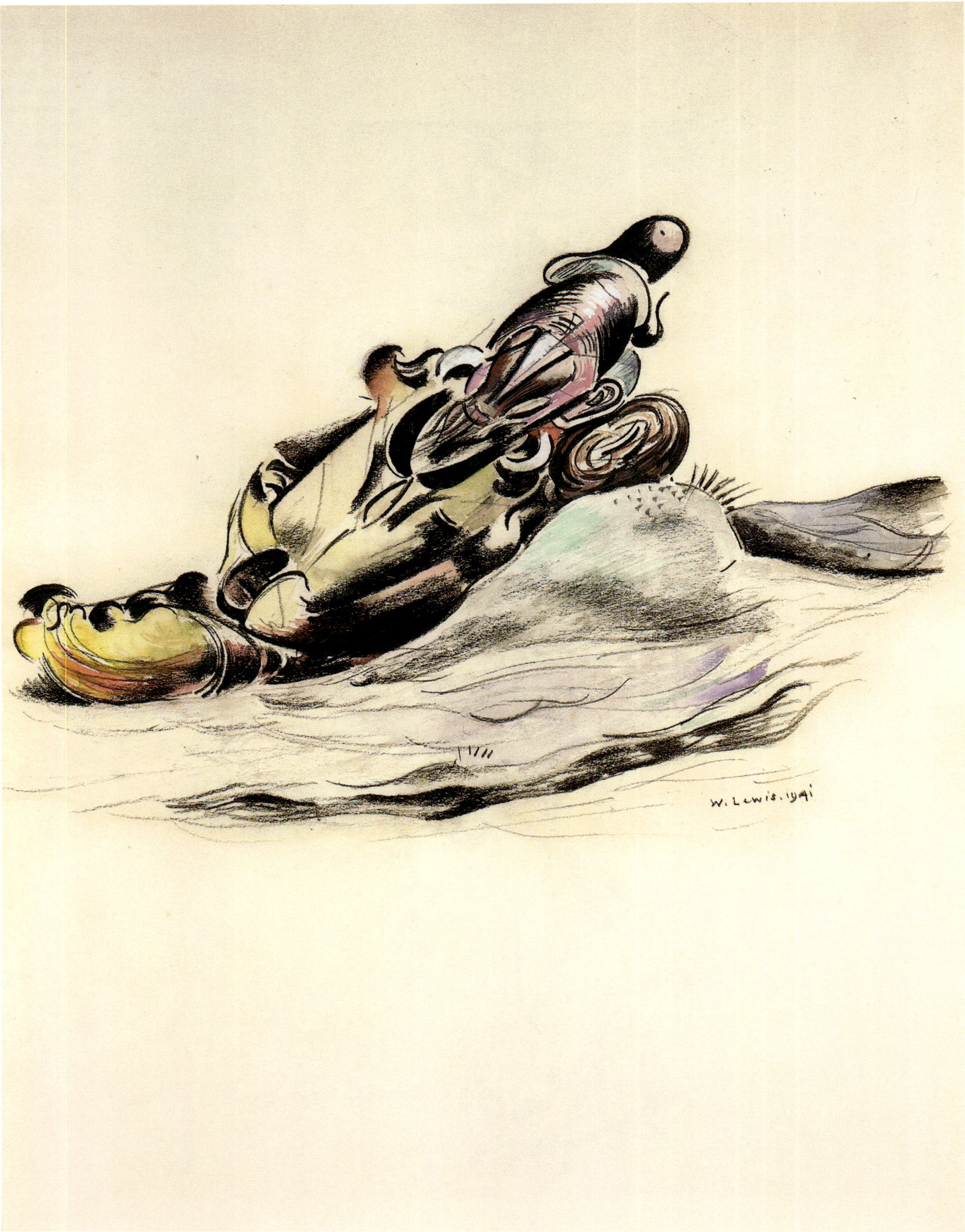

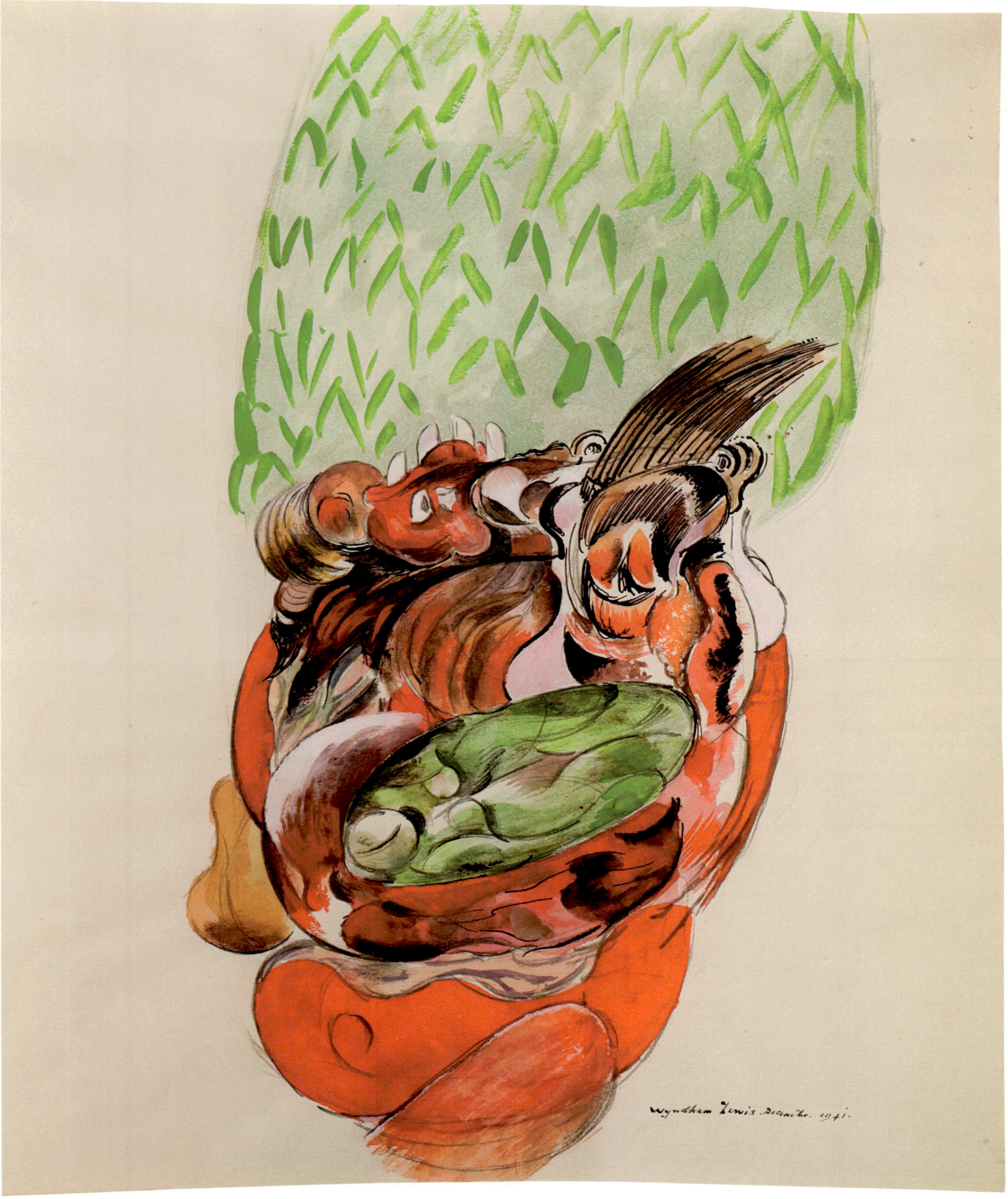

Cat. 191.
The Sage Meditating on the Life of Flesh and Blood, 1941. Pencil, pen and ink, watercolour and gouache on paper. 40 x 33.5 cm. Collection Hugh Anson-Cartwright. M 979

In terms of colour, this is the most shocking of the series of fantastic meditations on matter and creation that Lewis worked on during 1941. In "A Review of Contemporary Art" in *Blast*, No. 2 (B&M Cat. 3), Lewis wrote that his eyes "will never forget that red is the colour of blood, though it may besides that have a special quality of exasperation."[1] Its intensity here is emphasised by the juxtaposition with the vegetable green. How well Lewis was able to see such colours in 1941 is uncertain, but it seems likely that red in particular was by now difficult to see as well as it had been in the past, owing to the increasing damage his growing tumour was inflicting on his optic nerve. That damage was, it was thought at the time, perhaps the result of toxins from Lewis's neglected teeth. Stumps of teeth may be seen in the image, in which other unidentifiable parts of bodies also surround the aggregation of the vegetable foetus.

1. Rprt. Walter Michel and C.J. Fox, eds. *Wyndham Lewis on Art: Collected Writings 1913–1956* (London: Thames and Hudson, 1969), p. 72.

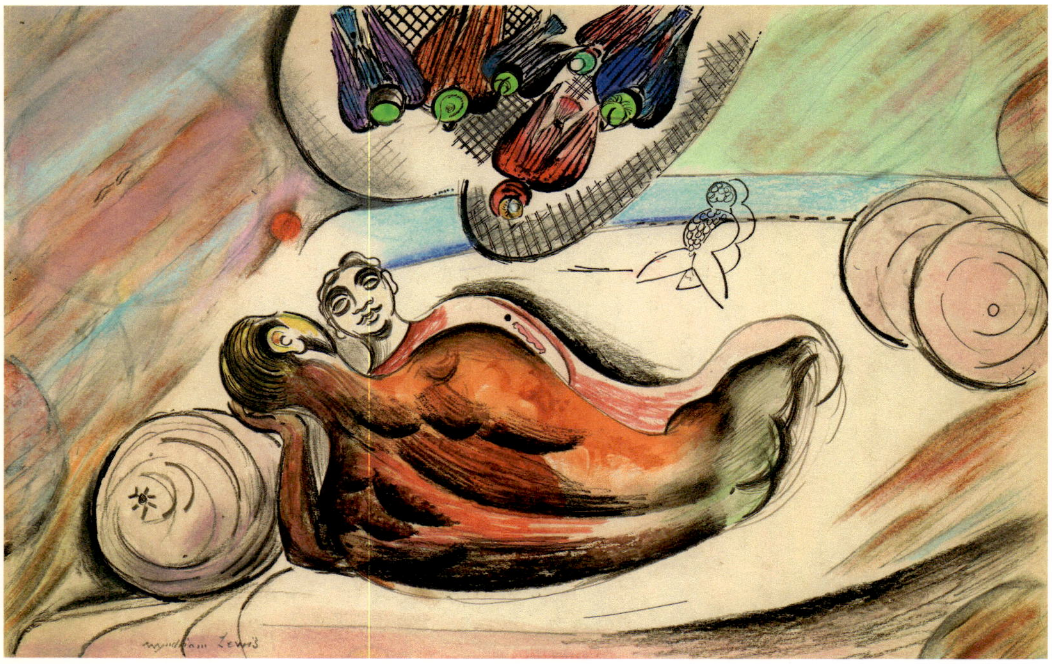

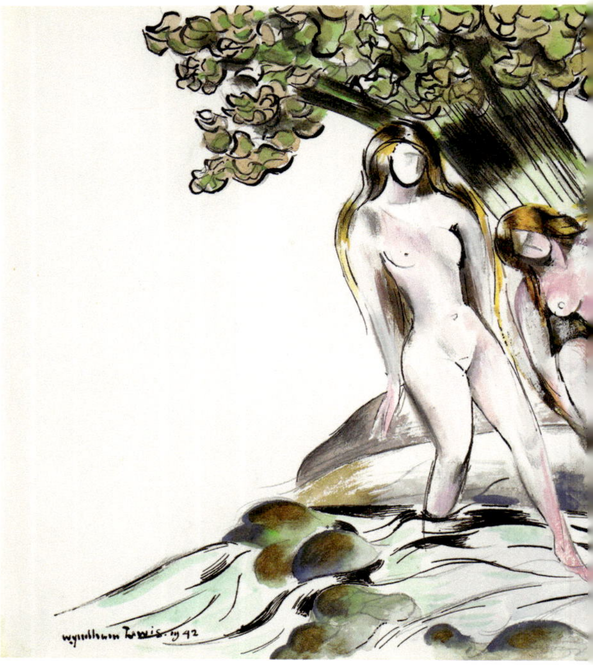

Cat. 194.
[Not in exhibition] *Sunset in Paradise*, 1940s. Ink, pencil, watercolour wash, coloured chalks and gouache on paper. 30.2 x 45.5 cm. Herbert F. Johnson Museum of Art, Cornell University (62.417). M 1124

This is another apparently whimsical fantasy, this time in the vein of Andrew Marvell's poem, *To his Coy Mistress* (1652), contrasting the "eternity" available to lovers after death with the need to seize the day while in this world: "had we but world enough and time […]." It may be contrasted with the altogether more ambitious and serious treatment of "metaphysical" existence in *Red Scene* (Cat. 161).

Cat. 195.
***Allégresse Aquatique*, 1941. Graphite, pen and ink, watercolour and gouache on wove paper. 31.8 x 44.5 cm. Collection Art Gallery of Ontario, Toronto. Purchase, 1941 (Acc.2577). M 964**

Lewis returns to the theme of the 1929 *Beach Scene* (Cat. 131), but, in keeping with his turn against his earlier aesthetic demands, the forms are now looser and not hardened into almost frozen postures. The one-time enemy of flux here emphasises the sheer joy of immersion within it. He had always thought that a Bergsonian attitude was acceptable in life, but that art should remove itself from the flux of becoming and substitute for it something fixed and defined. Here he seems to acknowledge that what is to be celebrated in life may also be due celebration in the most complete art. Nevertheless, the two figures to the right represent a withdrawn and contemplative attitude that implies, at least, a feeling that immersion in physical pleasure may not ultimately satisfy. This alternative attitude is one of the subjects of the large painting that is the summation of these late depictions of bathing figures, *The Island* (Cat. 200).

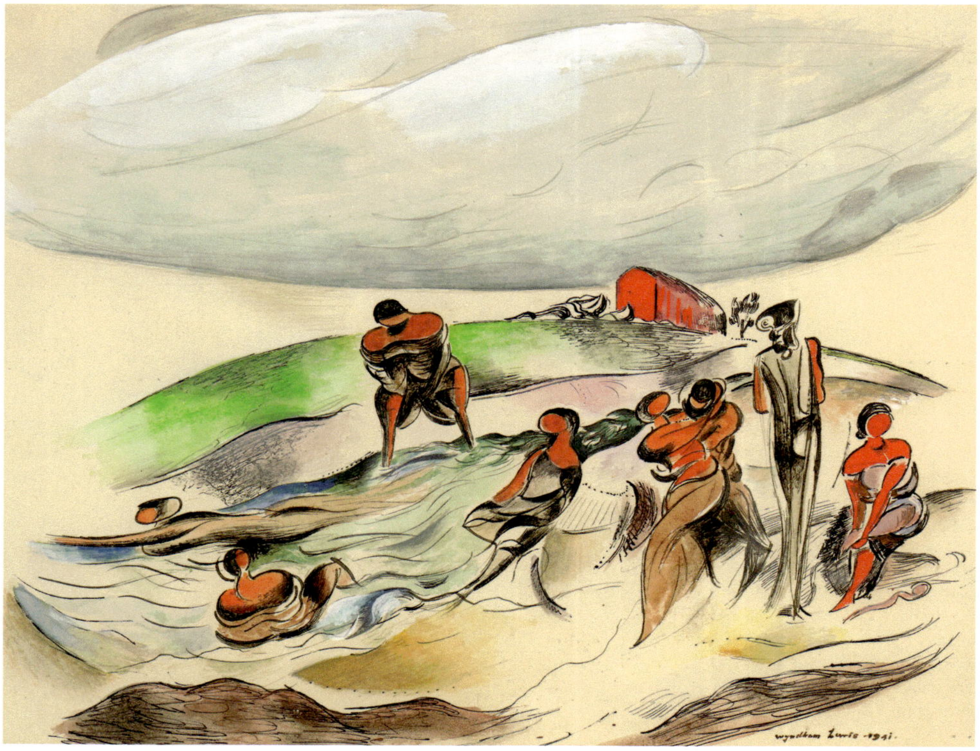

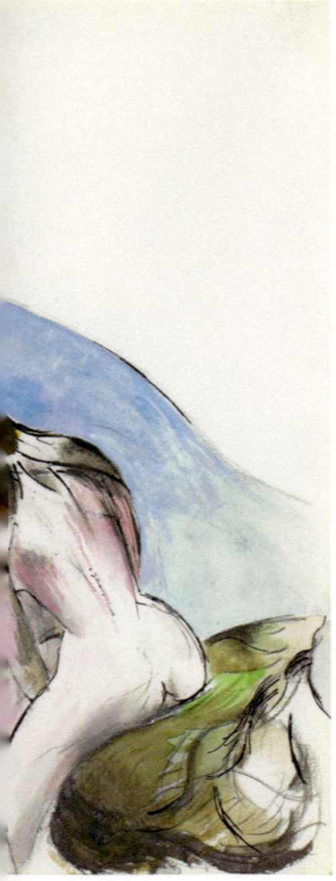

Cat. 196.
Homage to Etty, 1942.
Pen and black ink with watercolour and gouache over graphite on wove paper. 25.3 x 36.6 cm. National Gallery of Canada, Ottawa. Gift from the Douglas M. Duncan Collection, 1970 (NGC 16715). M 994

William Etty (1787–1849) was an English painter of sumptuous nudes. Robert Stacey argued that Lewis was likely to have seen the collection of Etty nudes owned by the Canadian industrialist, Sir James Dunn, during negotiations to produce a portrait.[1] One of the paintings (*The Bather* (1835–40)) shows a figure taking a step into water, a motif Lewis repeats here. Lewis's earliest works showed a concern (however satirical) with the subjective sensation of physical attitude or movement; the 1919 nudes, however, were observed fairly coldly from the outside. The present work clearly belongs to the voyeuristic tradition exemplified by the story of Diana and Actaeon, but, although the bathers are not individualised, the subjective imagination of the spectator is called on to empathise with the sensation of flesh tentatively immersed in water. The vegetable energy of the tree behind the bathers shows that the drawing ultimately belongs to the same imaginative world as the various creation myths that Lewis delineated around the same time.

1. Robert Stacey, "'Magical presences in a Magic Place': From *Homage to Etty* to *The Island*," in Catherine Mastin, Robert Stacey and Thomas Dilworth, *"The Talented Intruder": Wyndham Lewis in Canada, 1939–1945* [exh. cat. Art Gallery of Windsor, Ontario]. Windsor, Ontario: Art Gallery of Windsor, 1992.

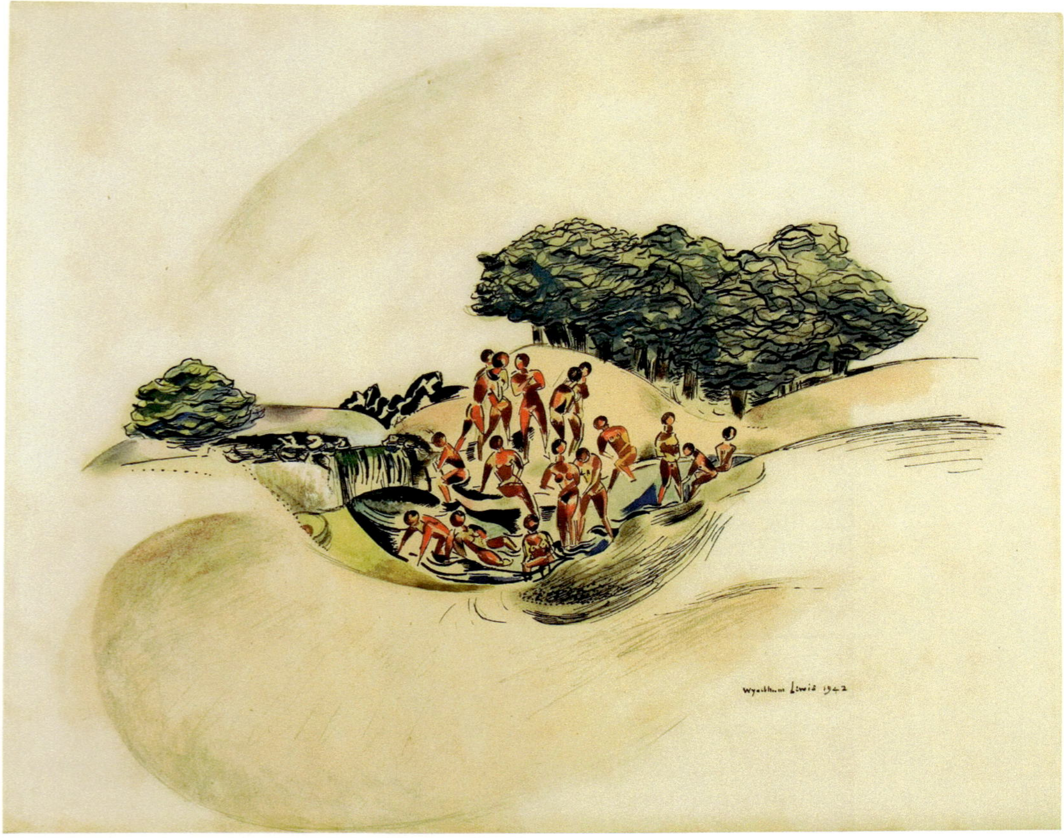

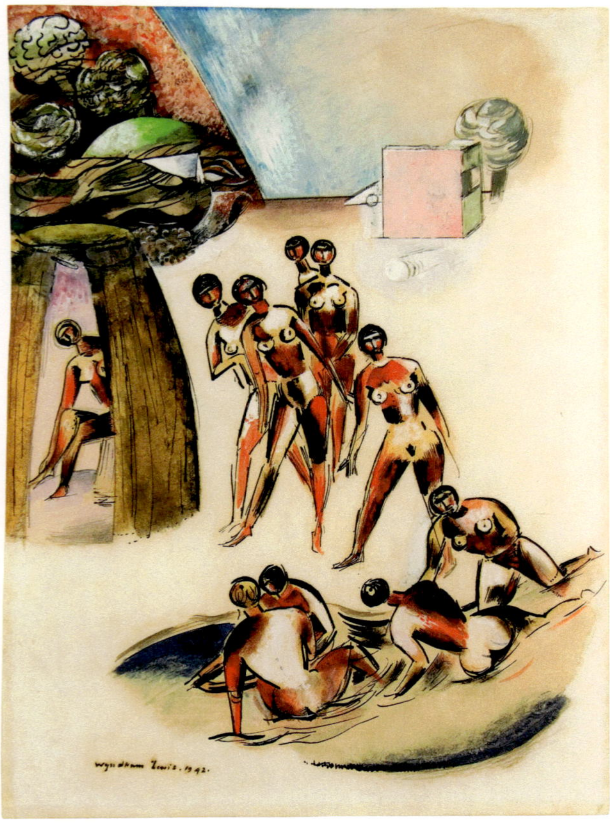

Cat. 197. ▲
Pool of the Amazons, 1942.
Pencil, ink and watercolour on paper. 35.7 x 44.2 cm. Collection Mark McLean. M 1003

Cat. 198. ▼
[Not in exhibition] *A Party of Girls*, 1942. **Pen and ink, watercolour and wash on paper. 35.5 x 25.5 cm. Collection Mark McLean. M 1000**

In these two works the schematic construction of the figures and their communal massing precludes the sensual empathy of *Homage to Etty* (Cat. 196). The *Pool of Amazons* additionally places the scene at a distance from the viewer in an indeterminate space that gives it the appearance of an oasis in a void. In *A Party of Girls*, the figures are carefully ranged on the sheet by Lewis to achieve a dynamism reflected in their postures and reinforced by the curved edge of the bathing tent and the boundary between the blue sky and the Romantic landscape at the top left. Stability is achieved by the more geometrical vignette at the top right.

Cat. 199.
Nude Panel, 1942. Graphite and watercolour on paper. 34.9 x 25.3 cm. Collection Mark McLean. M 999

The title of this work draws attention to its decorative conception: three scenes are placed above each other in a manner a little reminiscent of *The Mind of the Artist about to Make a Picture* (Cat. 192). The figure with the parasol (like the artist in that work) appears to have laid down her book, so that the figure above her, semi-dissolved in the flowing water, may be an emanation of her imagination. These almost "buried" figures also recall the prostrate "hero" figures of the drawings of the 1920s, such as those in *Figures in the Air* (Cat. 125) or *Manhattan* (Cat. 126), but the fact that they are female is an acknowledgement of the role of the female in the cycle of natural creativity. This is a benign, even graceful representation of such a natural cycle (again intimated by the trees overshadowing the figure at the top), which indicates an ethical development of Lewis's vision away from the Schopenhaurian anti-naturalism of his earlier outlook.

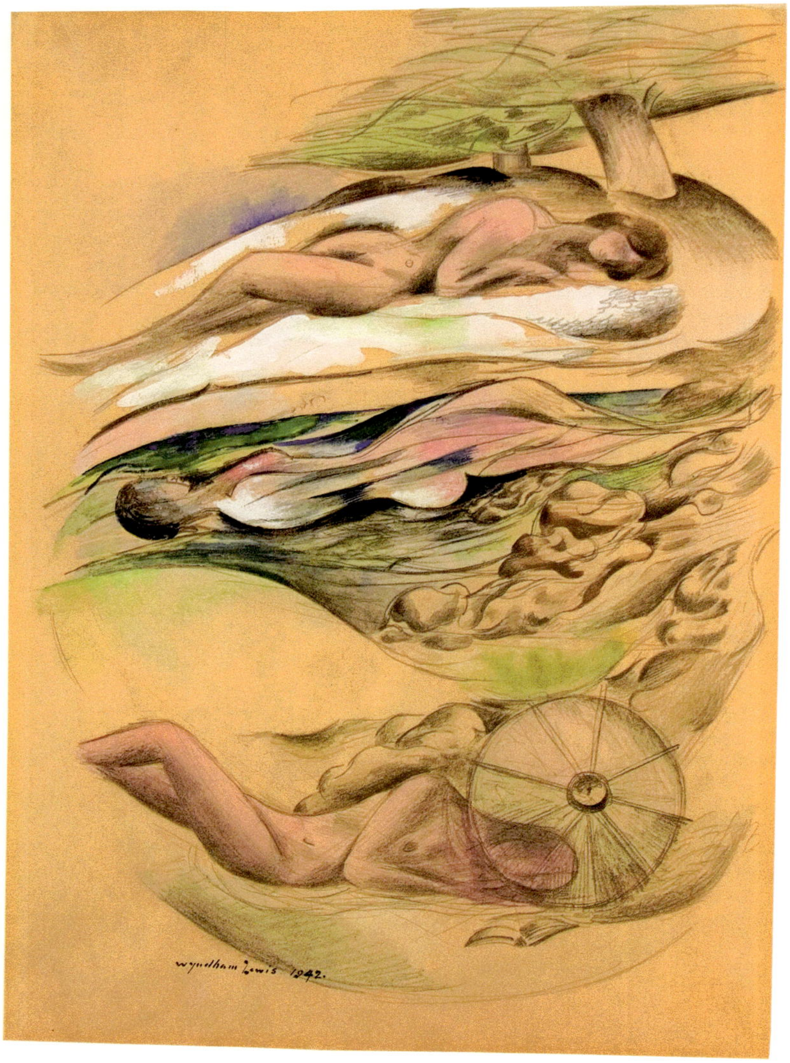

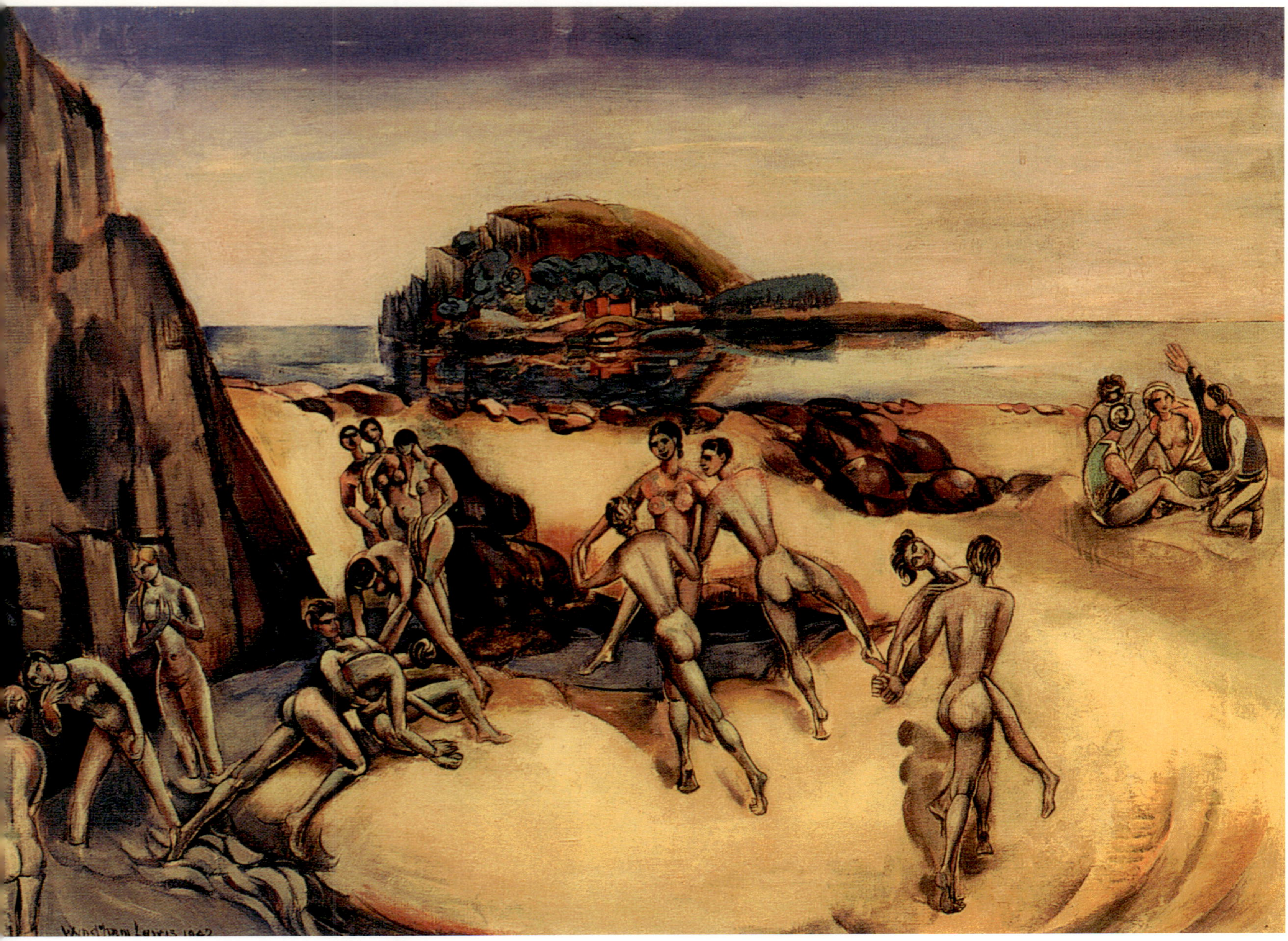

Cat. 200.
***The Island*, 1942. Oil on canvas. 69.9 x 91.4 cm. Santa Barbara Museum of Art, Gift of the Women's Board (1986.51). M P104**

The summation of the series of drawings on themes of bathing, this is Lewis's most important late painting from the imagination and the subject of an extended essay by the Canadian critic Robert Stacey.[1] Stacey discovers a long genealogy in western art for the painting (including William Etty, Paul Cézanne and Henri Matisse, and concluding with a drawing by Pablo Picasso of bathers that Lewis would have seen in the exhibition of Picasso's work at The Museum of Modern Art, New York, which he reviewed in 1940).[2] The group of three figures to the right (one of whom gestures towards the island), Stacey relates to Edouard Manet's *Le Déjeuner sur l'herbe* (1863). He quotes from Lewis's manuscript notes for a 1944 lecture on "ordering nature":

Nature is, as you know, a chaos It is a chaos of sound. And it is a visual chaos. All art, of any description, is the *creation of an island of order* – in the midst of this chaos.[3]

In his essay, "The Dithyrambic Spectator," Lewis endorsed Elliot Smith's speculations that art originated in the mummification practices of the Ancient Egyptians (see Cat. 85). It was because the original sculptors and painters of Egypt were working for the truth of another world beyond this one that "art" began:

It had its chance of perfection because it was working for *the other world*. [...] In touch in an organized way with a supernatural world of whose potentialities we can form no conception, the art of Egypt is as rare and irreplaceable a thing as would be some communication dropped upon our earth from another planet.[4]

The island depicted in the painting, which bears a slight resemblance to Arnold Böcklin's *Die Toteninsel* (1880–86), may symbolise this "other world" of art, about which the clothed figure instructs one of the naked figures who has turned aside from the sensual delights of her fellows frolicking in the stream. The allusions to other works that Stacey has traced are therefore particularly apposite, for Lewis's painting is about the transformation of nature into culture ("it might be argued that Lewis makes a culture out of nature").[5] W.B. Yeats, a poet whom Lewis particularly admired (the admiration was returned), wrote on a similar theme in his "Sailing to Byzantium" (1926), in which Byzantium is the equivalent of Lewis's Island – a place outside the cycle of "whatever is begotten, born or dies" but also its necessary completion.

1. Robert Stacey, "'Magical presences in a Magic Place': From *Homage to Etty* to *The Island*," in Catherine Mastin, Robert Stacey and Thomas Dilworth, *"The Talented Intruder": Wyndham Lewis in Canada, 1939–1945* [exh. cat. Art Gallery of Windsor, Ontario]. Windsor, Ontario: Art Gallery of Windsor, 1992, pp. 107–54.
2. Wyndham Lewis, "Picasso," *The Kenyon Review* 2, no. 2 (Spring 1940), pp. 196–211.
3. Quoted, ibid., p. 149.
4. Wyndham Lewis, *The Diabolical Principle and The Dithyrambic Spectator* (London: Chatto and Windus, 1931), pp. 194–95.
5. Roberty Stacey, "Magical Presences," op. cit., p. 145.

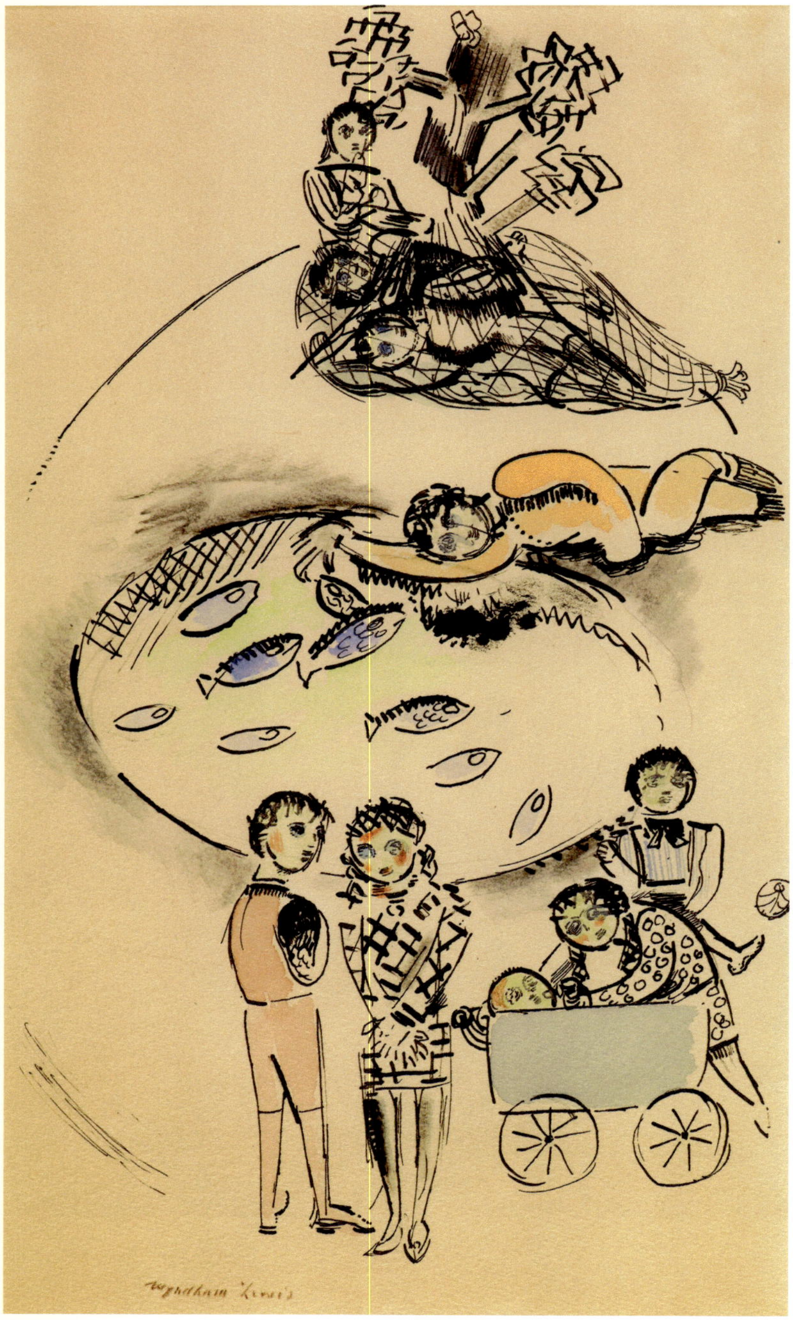

Cat. 201.
[Not in exhibition] *Children Playing*, 1945. Pen and ink, black chalk, watercolour, wash and gouache on paper. 37.5 x 22.9 cm. Collection of Fred L. Emerson Gallery, Hamilton College. Gift of Omar S. Pound, Class of 1951 (1994.128). M 1055

Lewis's last works, when his poor sight had made his earlier feats of draughtsmanship impossible, often resemble doodles. In "The Politics of Artistic Expression," a 1925 essay on the social necessity of art, Lewis compared the artist's activity with that of the child at play, able to imagine other forms of life, and able to inhabit them and make them real. "So the man, of whom the child is the playful father, is always imagining himself to be something that he is not – such as a bird, Napoleon, a gentleman, a fish, or an adding machine." In this drawing, it is the small boy lying beside the puddle who perhaps imagines he is a fish. Art is necessary because, Lewis writes, human beings "are intelligent enough to know that to be a man and nothing else is nothing to write home about. [...] They use their intelligence to circumvent nature [...]."[1] But only the boy appears to be playing in this way; the other children are rehearsing precisely what "nature" will prescribe for them: shame, jealousy and parenthood.

1. Wyndham Lewis, "The Politics of Artistic Expression" (1925). Rprt. *Creatures of Habit and Creatures of Change: Essays on Art, Literature and Society 1914–1956*. Ed. Paul Edwards (Santa Rosa: Black Sparrow Press, 1989), pp. 114, 115.

Cat. 204.
Walpurgisnacht, 1950.
Pen and ink on paper.
43 x 76 cm. Wyndham Lewis Memorial Trust. M 1126

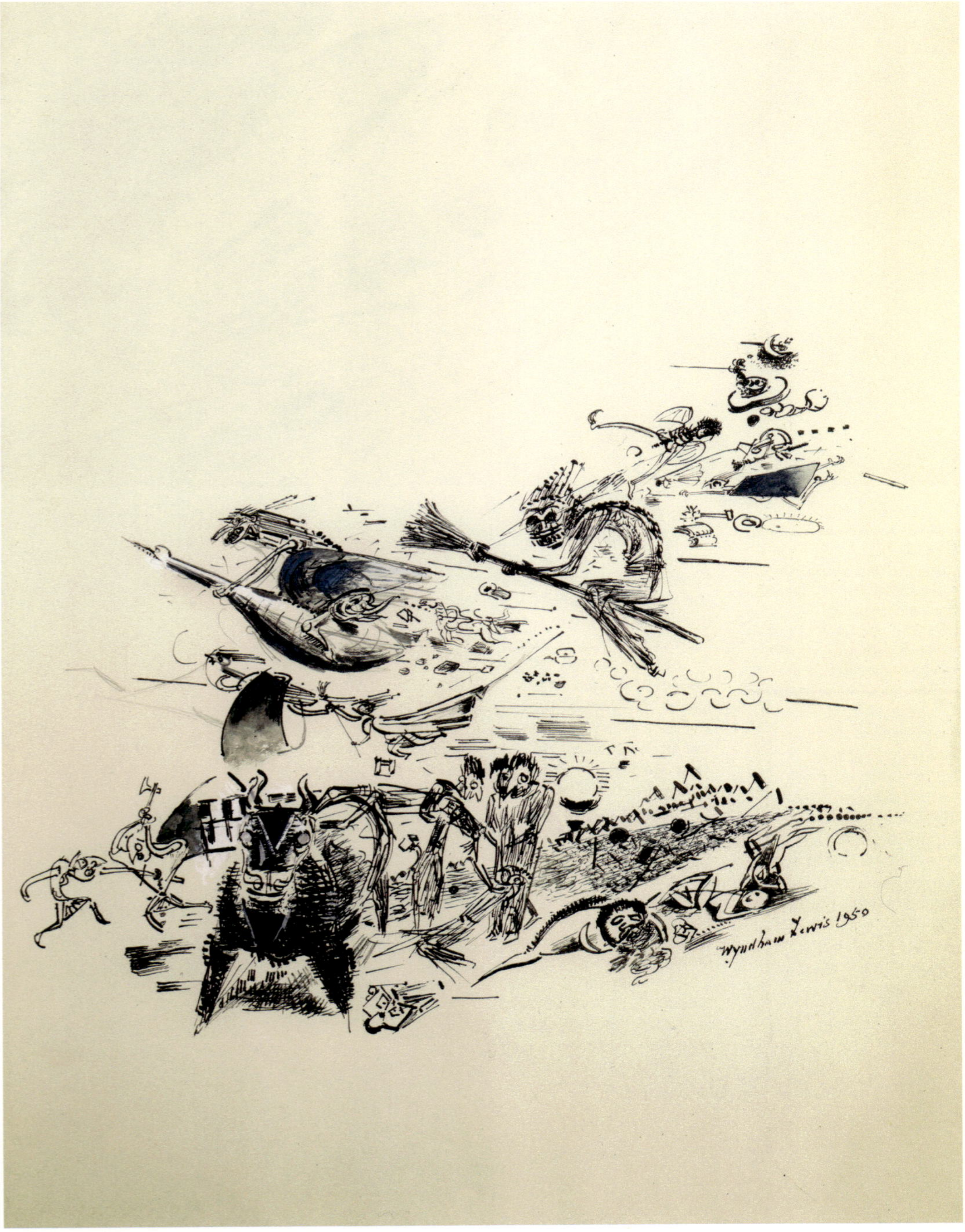

The near-blind Lewis used a magnifying glass in order to carry out the meticulous and precise placing of the small lines that compose this image. As his sight faded, he allowed more scope to his imagination. Violence and horror – that of fairy tales – were essential parts of this. Other works of a similar kind include *Witches Surprised by Dawn* (1942, M 1008), *Witch on Cowback* (1941, M 985) and *The Cow Jumped over the Moon* (1948, M1088; a title taken from a line in a nursery rhyme). In an article published six months before his death ("The Vorticists"), Lewis suggested that literary fantasy such as Lewis Carroll's *Through the Looking Glass* (1871) or *Jabberwocky* (1871), or Samuel Taylor Coleridge's *The Rime of the Ancient Mariner* (1797–98) provide models for what might be Britain's "best successes" in visual art in the future. "I am blind, but if I could see, I would do a large design of something like a Jabberwock outraging an eagle."[1]

1. Wyndham Lewis, "The Vorticists" (1956). Rprt. *Creatures of Habit and Creatures of Change: Essays on Art, Literature and Society 1914–1956*. Ed. Paul Edwards (Santa Rosa: Black Sparrow Press, 1989), pp. 382–83.

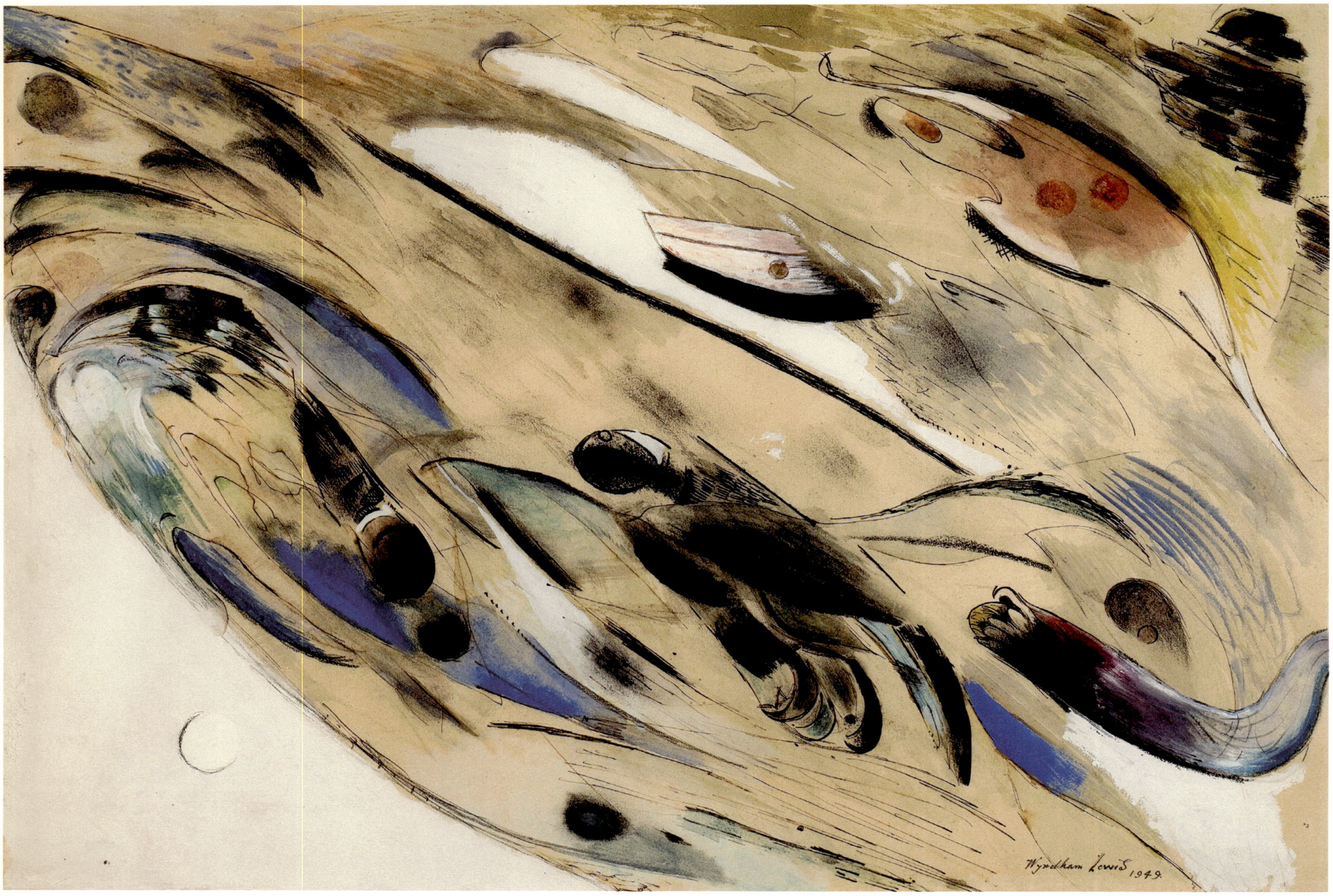

Cat. 202.
***What the Sea is like at Night*, 1949. Pencil, ink and gouache on paper. 56 x 37.5 cm. Courtesy of Austin/Desmond Fine Art, Private collection. M 1104**

In a letter to Charles Handley-Read (who was preparing a book on Lewis's art), Lewis suggested how such a work as this should be approached: "Point out that in greatly stylized images [*sic*] of the ocean, semi-human animals plunge and obtrude themselves, as if they had found their way into this from another dimension etc."[1]

The painting seems to be a reconciliation with all the Bergsonian ideas that Lewis had opposed in his maturity. Out of the flux, and out of intuition, creation occurs. To see this as a recantation is too simple, however. Even when apparently most classicist or rational, Lewis had always acknowledged deep, magical roots for artistic creation: "If you say that creative art is a spell, a talisman, an incantation – that it is *magic*, in short [...] I believe you would be correctly describing it. That the artist uses and manipulates a supernatural power seems very likely."[2] Lewis's objection to proponents of similar ideas (including the Surrealists) had been that they appeared to be advocating them as doctrines for life, rather than art; Lewis found these forces too dangerous to be released into life and wished them to be manifested rather in the "other world" of art. And in that world they were to be subject to the formal ordering that "classicism" provides (though they were not to be totally occluded by that ordering). The images that the artist provides are the source of the viewer's questioning exploration: "*who* are the monsters in the ocean"?[3]

1. Letter to Charles Handley-Read, 2 September 1949, *The Letters of Wyndham Lewis*. Ed. W.K. Rose (London: Methuen, 1963), p. 505.
2. Wyndham Lewis, *Time and Western Man* (1927). Rprt. ed. Paul Edwards (Santa Rosa: Black Sparrow Press, 1993), p. 187.
3. *Letters*, op. cit., p. 505.

Cat. 205.
***Red Figures Carrying Babies and Visiting Graves*, 1951.**
Pencil, pen and ink, and watercolour on paper.
33 x 40.3 cm. Wyndham Lewis Memorial Trust.
J. Dolman Collection (LD.2009.XX.5). M 1127

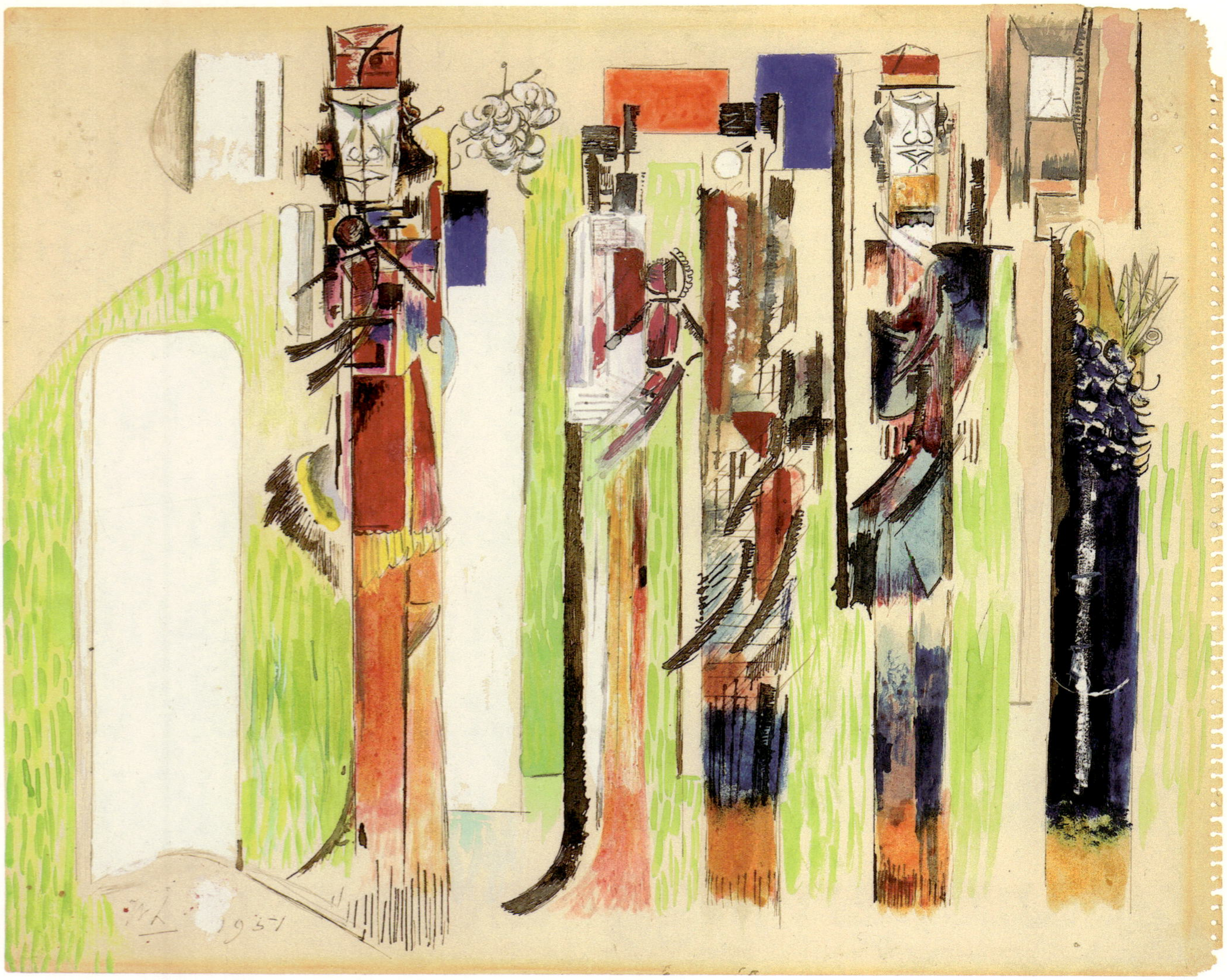

Both this drawing and *Walpurgisnacht* (Cat. 204) are reputed to be the last drawings that Lewis worked on; *Walpurgisnacht* is, as Walter Michel comments, "all line," while in *Red Figures* "the colour [is] so profuse it would dominate the picture, but for the fact that it becomes line at each edge." Michel also makes the pertinent comment that "the figures are bound so intimately to the composition that they become part of the abstract space"; Lewis has returned in this final work to the mysteries of being and becoming that he had often explored in the figure–ground relationship of his earlier abstractions.[1] The catalogue of the Tate Gallery exhibition, *Wyndham Lewis and Vorticism* (1956), states: "The artist's last finished watercolour. He originally described it as 'Poilus [i.e. French soldiers from the First World War] taking their babies to visit the graves of their mothers', but later said they were not beings who inhabit this world."[2]

Lewis remained until the end of his life preoccupied with the kind of questions that he found in William James's *Some Problems of Philosophy* (1911):

Is there a common stuff out of which all facts are made?
[...]
What binds things into one universe?
Is unity or diversity more fundamental?
[...]
How does anything act on anything else?
How can one thing change or grow out of another thing?[3]

Lewis's drawings, such as *Red Figures*, do not answer such questions, but depict imaginary worlds that make the questions real for us. They were always located for him in the mysteries of birth, death and identity, and rendered more intense by the colossal wars of the twentieth century, which sent so many innocents to an early grave.

1. Walter Michel, *Wyndham Lewis: Paintings and Drawings* (London: Thames and Hudson, 1971), p. 146.
2. Catalogue entry no. 114, *Wyndham Lewis and Vorticism*, [exh. cat. Tate Gallery, London]. London: Tate Gallery, 1956, p. 22.
3. William James, *Some Problems of Philosophy* (1911). Rprt. William James, *Writings 1902–1910*. Ed. Bruce Kuklick (New York: Library of America, 1987), p. 997. In an essay unpublished in his lifetime, "The Anonymity of Perfection" (manuscript at Cornell University), Lewis writes that the mother with her baby "is confronted, in most cases very obscurely, with one of the academic riddles of philosophy: namely HOW CAN ONE THING CHANGE OR GROW OUT OF ANOTHER THING?" (*Modernism/Modernity* 4, Wyndham Lewis Number, no. 2 (April 1997), p. 167).

"The act of creation, of which a book or picture is one form, is always an act of the human will, like poisoning your business rival, or setting your cap at somebody; the complete existence and exercise of this will entails much human imperfection, which will be incorporated in the book or picture, giving it the nervousness of its contours, and the rich odours, the sanguine or pallid appearance, which recommends it to us."

Wyndham Lewis,
Essay on the Objective of Plastic Art in our Time, 1922

C

WYNDHAM LEWIS: THE WRITER

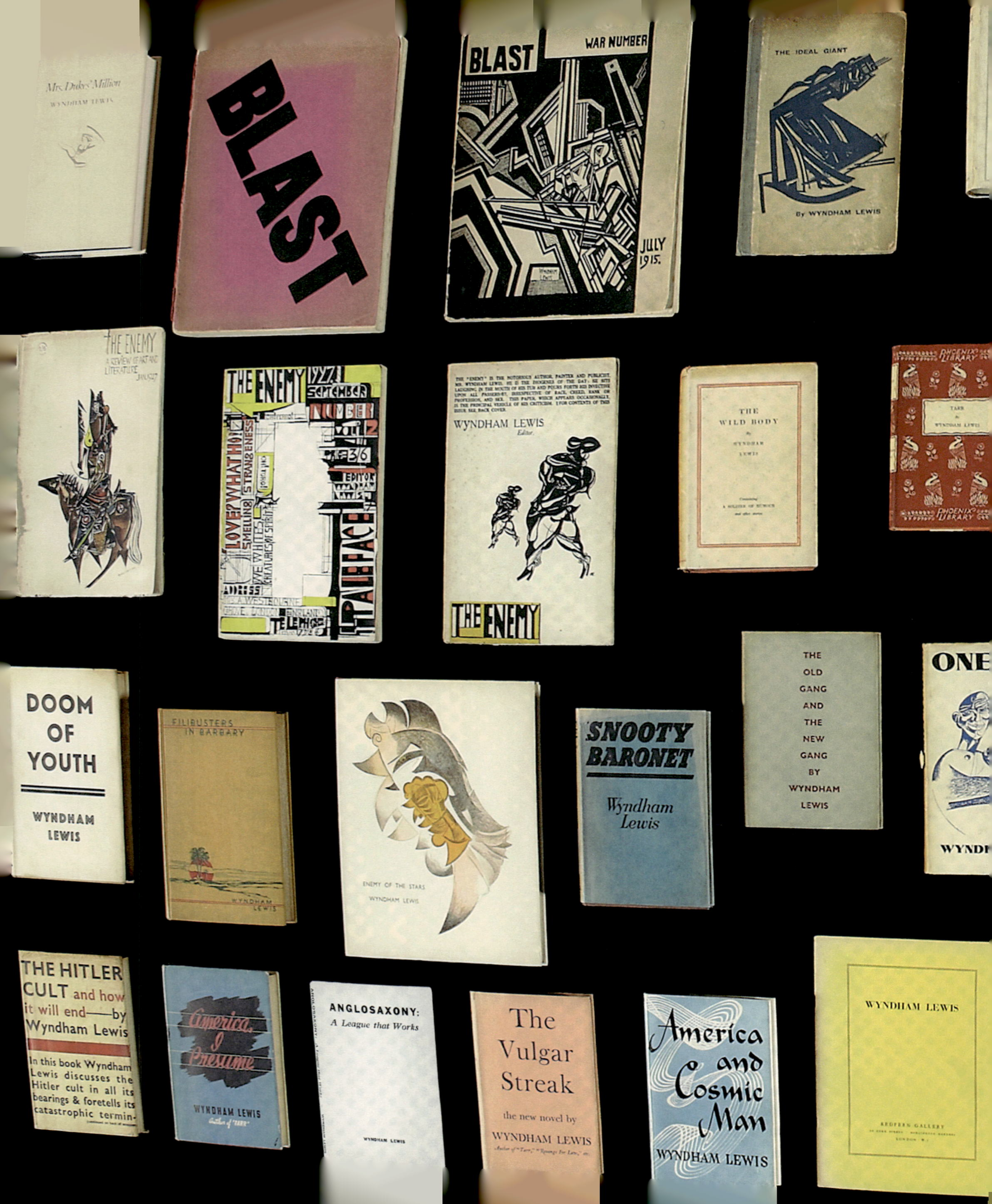

Mrs. Dukes' Million
WYNDHAM LEWIS
BLAST
BLAST
WAR NUMBER
JULY 1915.
THE IDEAL GIANT
By WYNDHAM LEWIS
THE ENEMY
A REVIEW OF ART AND LITERATURE
THE ENEMY
1927
SEPTEMBER
NUMBER
WYNDHAM LEWIS
Editor.
THE ENEMY
THE WILD BODY
PHOENIX LIBRARY
TARR
DOOM OF YOUTH
WYNDHAM LEWIS
FILIBUSTERS IN BARBARY
WYNDHAM LEWIS
ENEMY OF THE STARS
WYNDHAM LEWIS
SNOOTY BARONET
Wyndham Lewis
THE OLD GANG AND THE NEW GANG BY WYNDHAM LEWIS
THE HITLER CULT and how it will end——by Wyndham Lewis
In this book Wyndham Lewis discusses the Hitler cult in all its bearings & foretells its catastrophic termin-
America, I Presume
WYNDHAM LEWIS
ANGLOSAXONY:
A League that Works
WYNDHAM LEWIS
The Vulgar Streak
the new novel by
WYNDHAM LEWIS
America and Cosmic Man
WYNDHAM LEWIS
WYNDHAM LEWIS
REDFERN GALLERY

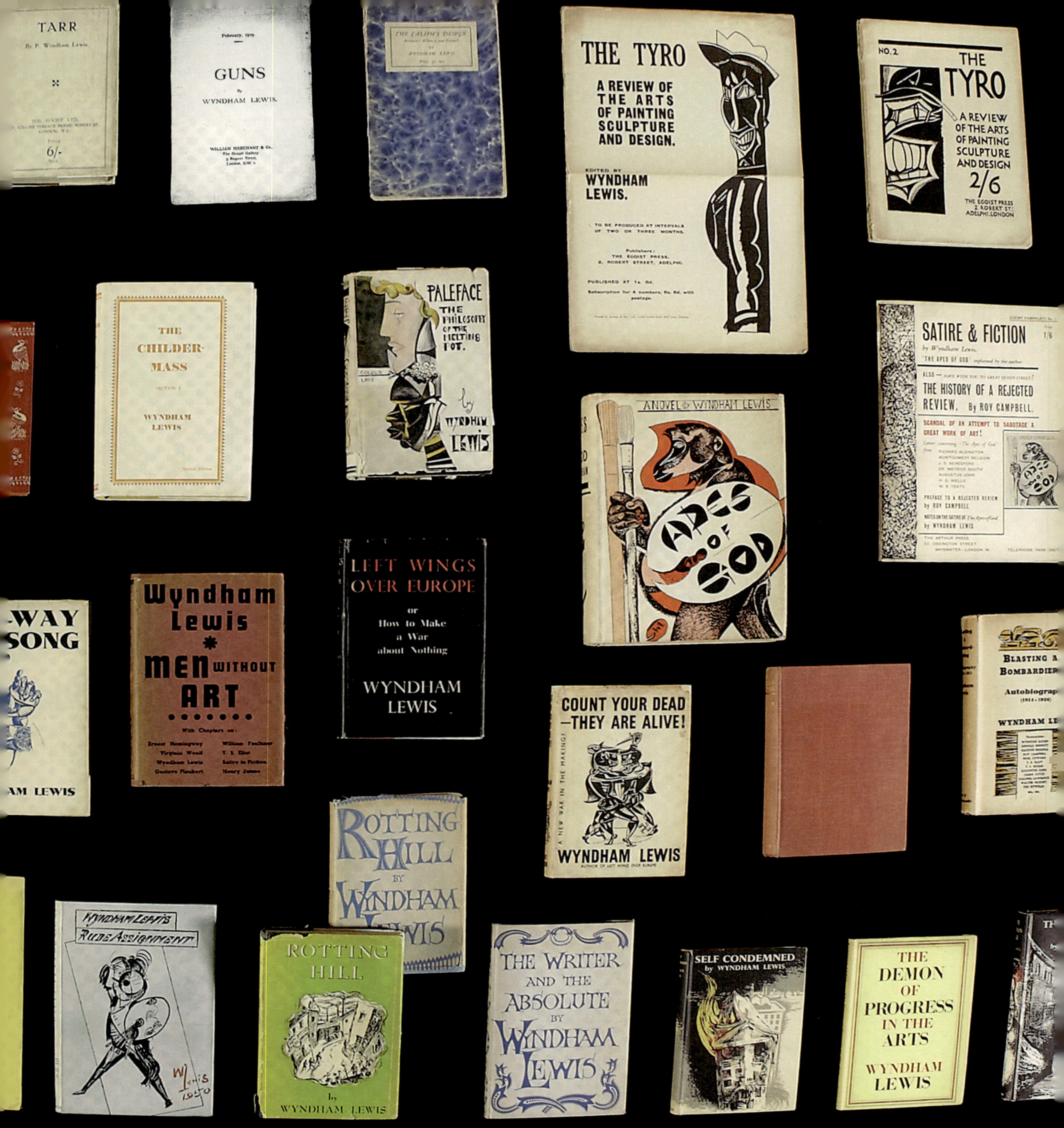
TARR
By P. Wyndham Lewis
February, 1919.
GUNS
By
WYNDHAM LEWIS.
WILLIAM MARCHANT & Co.
THE TYRO
A REVIEW OF THE ARTS OF PAINTING SCULPTURE AND DESIGN.
EDITED BY WYNDHAM LEWIS.
TO BE PRODUCED AT INTERVALS OF TWO OR THREE MONTHS.
Publishers: THE EGOIST PRESS, 2, ROBERT STREET, ADELPHI.
PUBLISHED AT 1s. 6d.
NO. 2
THE TYRO
A REVIEW OF THE ARTS OF PAINTING SCULPTURE AND DESIGN
2/6
THE EGOIST PRESS 2 ROBERT ST. ADELPHI. LONDON
THE CHILDERMASS
WYNDHAM LEWIS
PALEFACE
THE PHILOSOPHY OF THE MELTING POT.
by WYNDHAM LEWIS
SATIRE & FICTION
by Wyndham Lewis.
THE HISTORY OF A REJECTED REVIEW, By ROY CAMPBELL.
SCANDAL OF AN ATTEMPT TO SABOTAGE A GREAT WORK OF ART!
A NOVEL BY WYNDHAM LEWIS
APES OF GOD
Wyndham Lewis
MEN WITHOUT ART
LEFT WINGS OVER EUROPE
or
How to Make a War about Nothing
WYNDHAM LEWIS
-WAY SONG
AM LEWIS
BLASTING & BOMBARDIER
COUNT YOUR DEAD —THEY ARE ALIVE!
A NEW WAR IN THE MAKING!
WYNDHAM LEWIS
AUTHOR OF LEFT WINGS OVER EUROPE
ROTTING HILL
BY
WYNDHAM LEWIS
WYNDHAM LEWIS
RUDE ASSIGNMENT
ROTTING HILL
by WYNDHAM LEWIS
THE WRITER AND THE ABSOLUTE
BY
WYNDHAM LEWIS
SELF CONDEMNED
by WYNDHAM LEWIS
THE DEMON OF PROGRESS IN THE ARTS
WYNDHAM LEWIS

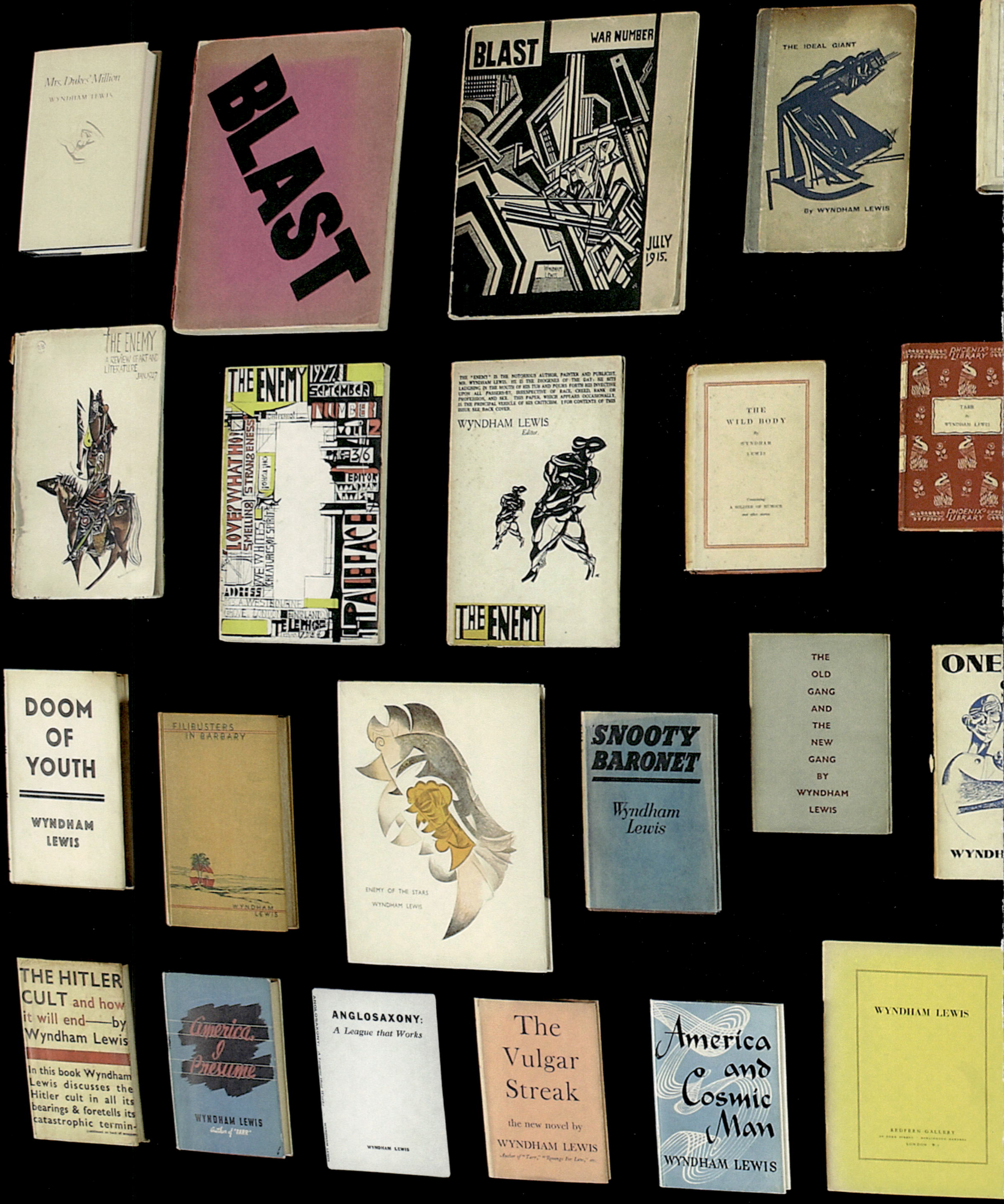
Mrs. Dukes' Million
WYNDHAM LEWIS
BLAST
BLAST
WAR NUMBER
JULY 1915.
THE IDEAL GIANT
By WYNDHAM LEWIS
THE ENEMY
A REVIEW OF ART AND LITERATURE
THE ENEMY
1927
SEPTEMBER
NUMBER
VOL. 2
WYNDHAM LEWIS
Editor
THE ENEMY
THE WILD BODY
By WYNDHAM LEWIS
A SOLDIER OF HUMOUR
and other stories
PHOENIX LIBRARY
DOOM OF YOUTH
WYNDHAM LEWIS
FILIBUSTERS IN BARBARY
WYNDHAM LEWIS
ENEMY OF THE STARS
WYNDHAM LEWIS
SNOOTY BARONET
Wyndham Lewis
THE OLD GANG AND THE NEW GANG BY WYNDHAM LEWIS
THE HITLER CULT and how it will end—by Wyndham Lewis
In this book Wyndham Lewis discusses the Hitler cult in all its bearings & foretells its catastrophic termin-
America, I Presume
WYNDHAM LEWIS
ANGLOSAXONY:
A League that Works
WYNDHAM LEWIS
The Vulgar Streak
the new novel by
WYNDHAM LEWIS
America and Cosmic Man
WYNDHAM LEWIS
WYNDHAM LEWIS
REDFERN GALLERY

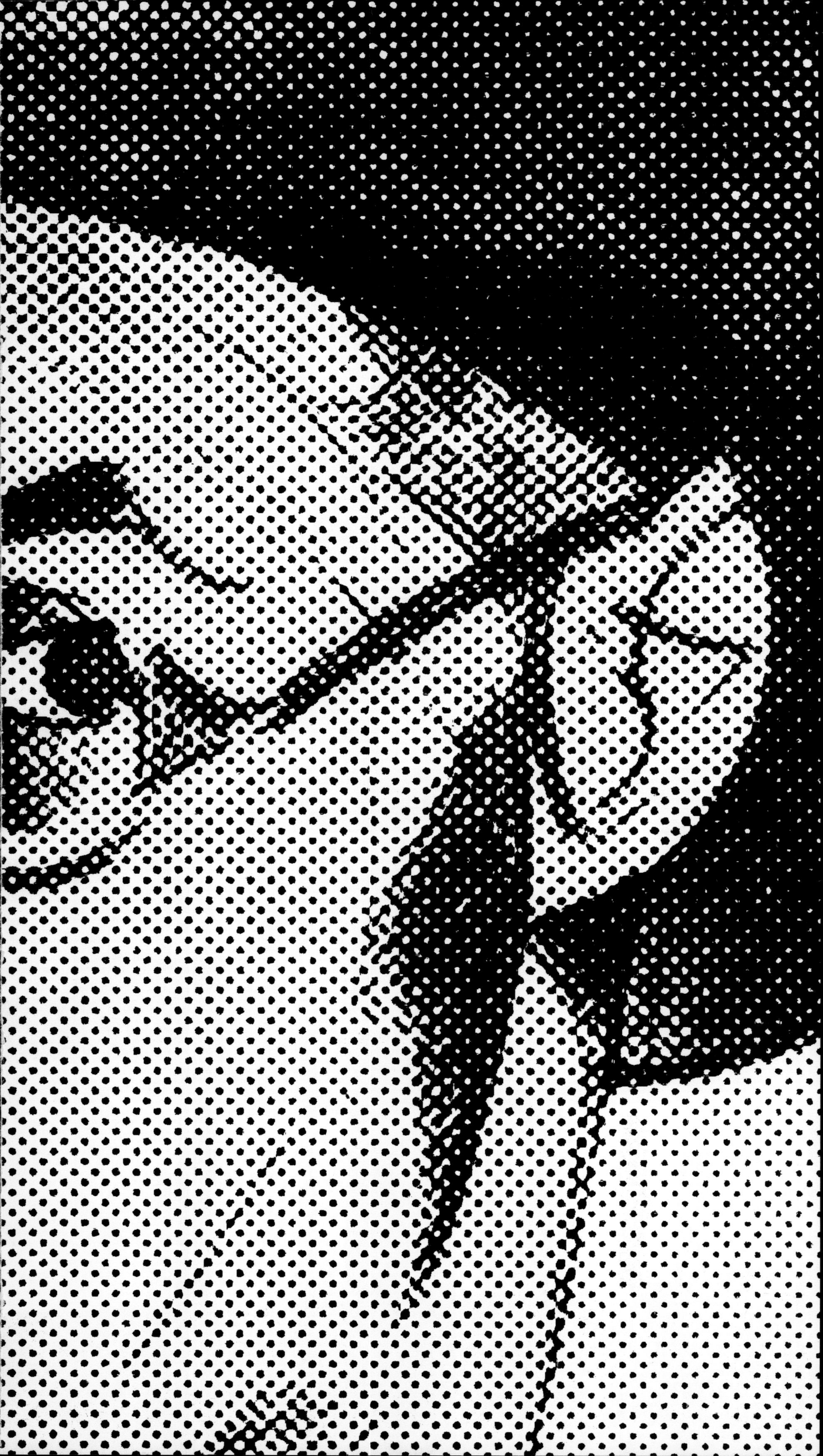

All bo
pampl
archiv
Lewis
have b
the do
Graha
Frank
of the
repres
thank
loans
collec

Book
incluc
exhib
"B&M

Texts

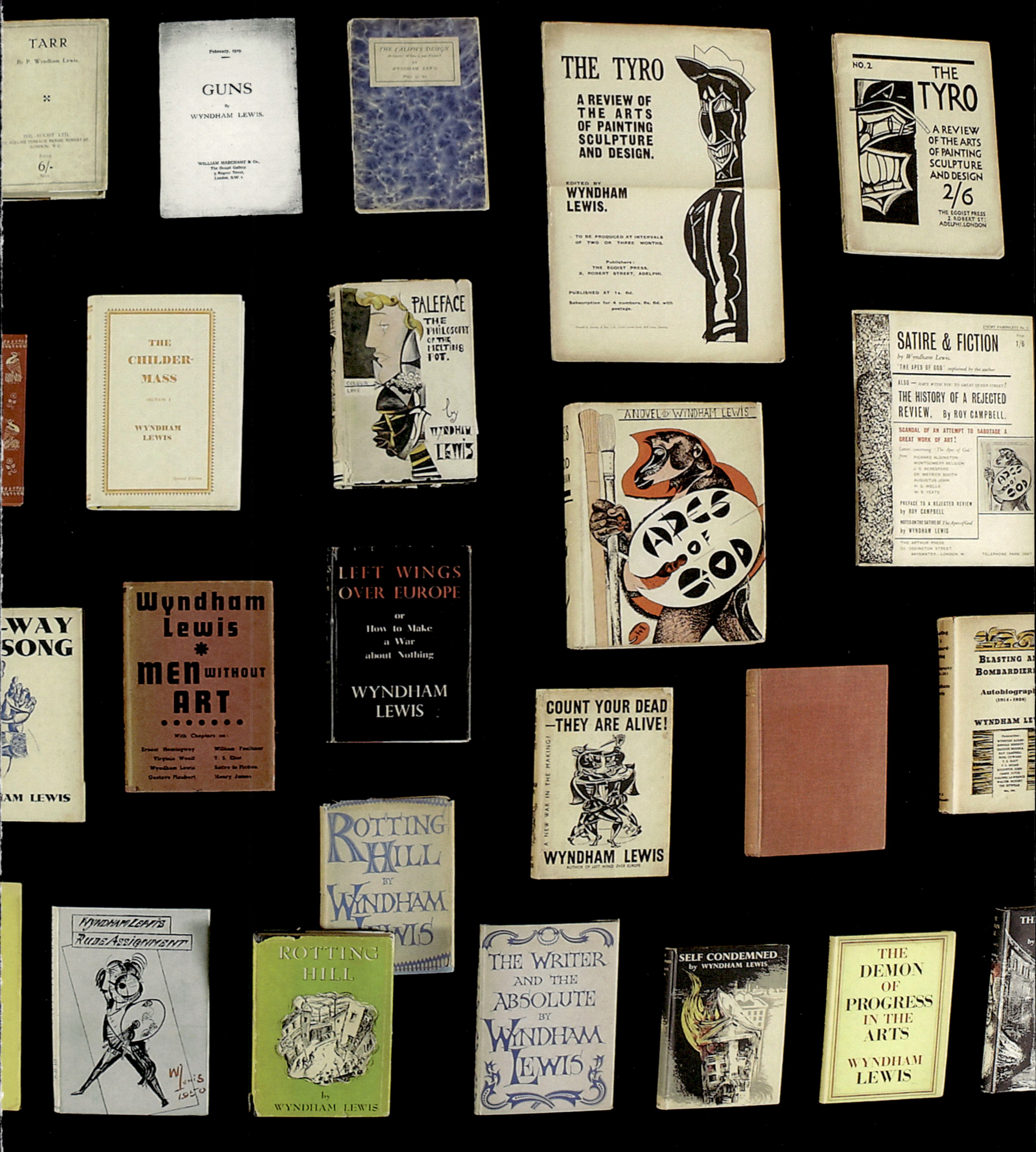
TARR
GUNS
WYNDHAM LEWIS
THE TYRO
A REVIEW OF THE ARTS OF PAINTING SCULPTURE AND DESIGN.
EDITED BY WYNDHAM LEWIS.
THE CHILDERMASS
PALEFACE
THE PHILOSOPHY OF THE MELTING POT.
SATIRE & FICTION
THE HISTORY OF A REJECTED REVIEW.
APES OF GOD
LEFT WINGS OVER EUROPE
or How to Make a War about Nothing
Wyndham Lewis
MEN WITHOUT ART
COUNT YOUR DEAD —THEY ARE ALIVE!
BLASTING AND BOMBARDIERING
ROTTING HILL
RUDE ASSIGNMENT
THE WRITER AND THE ABSOLUTE
SELF CONDEMNED
THE DEMON OF PROGRESS IN THE ARTS

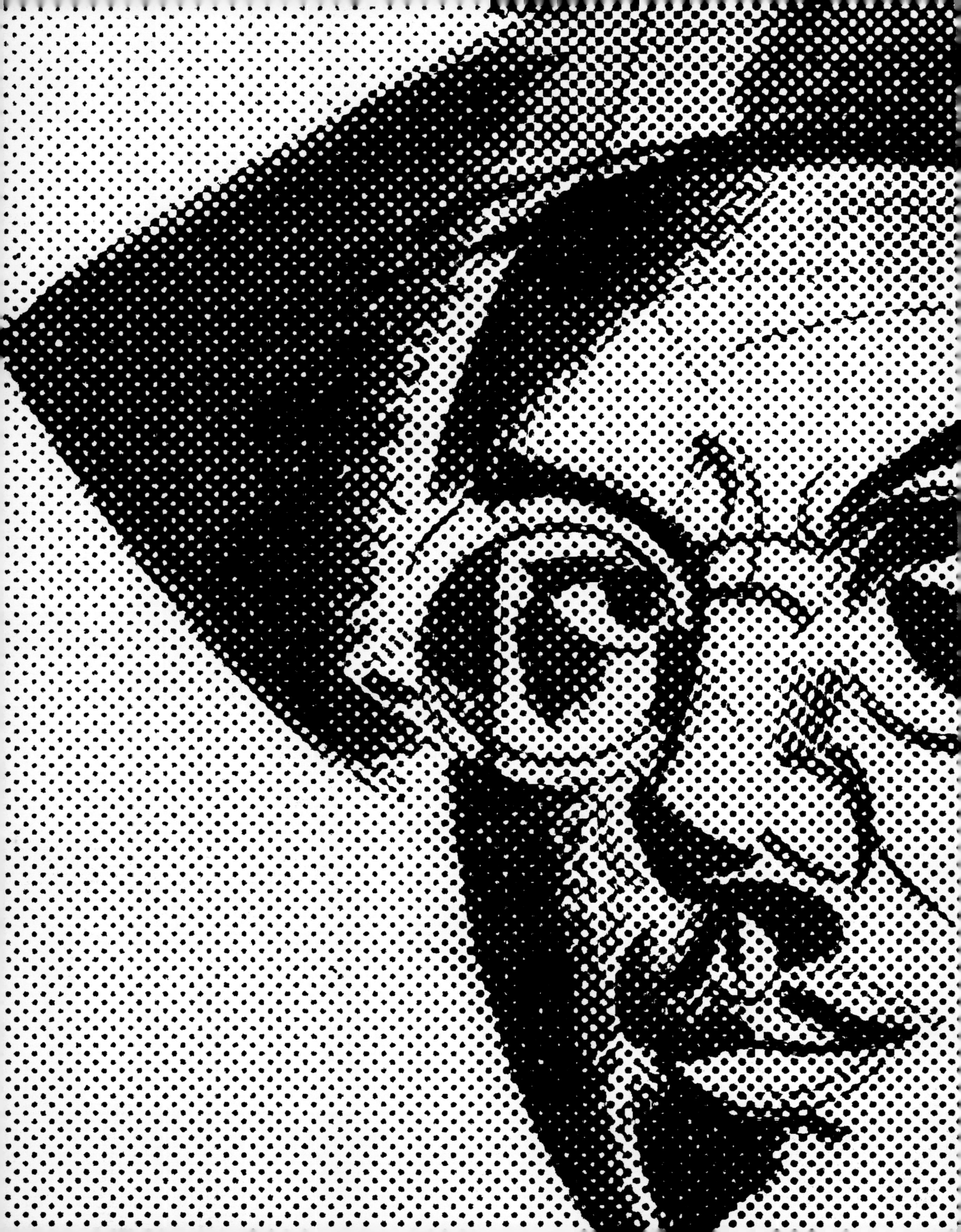

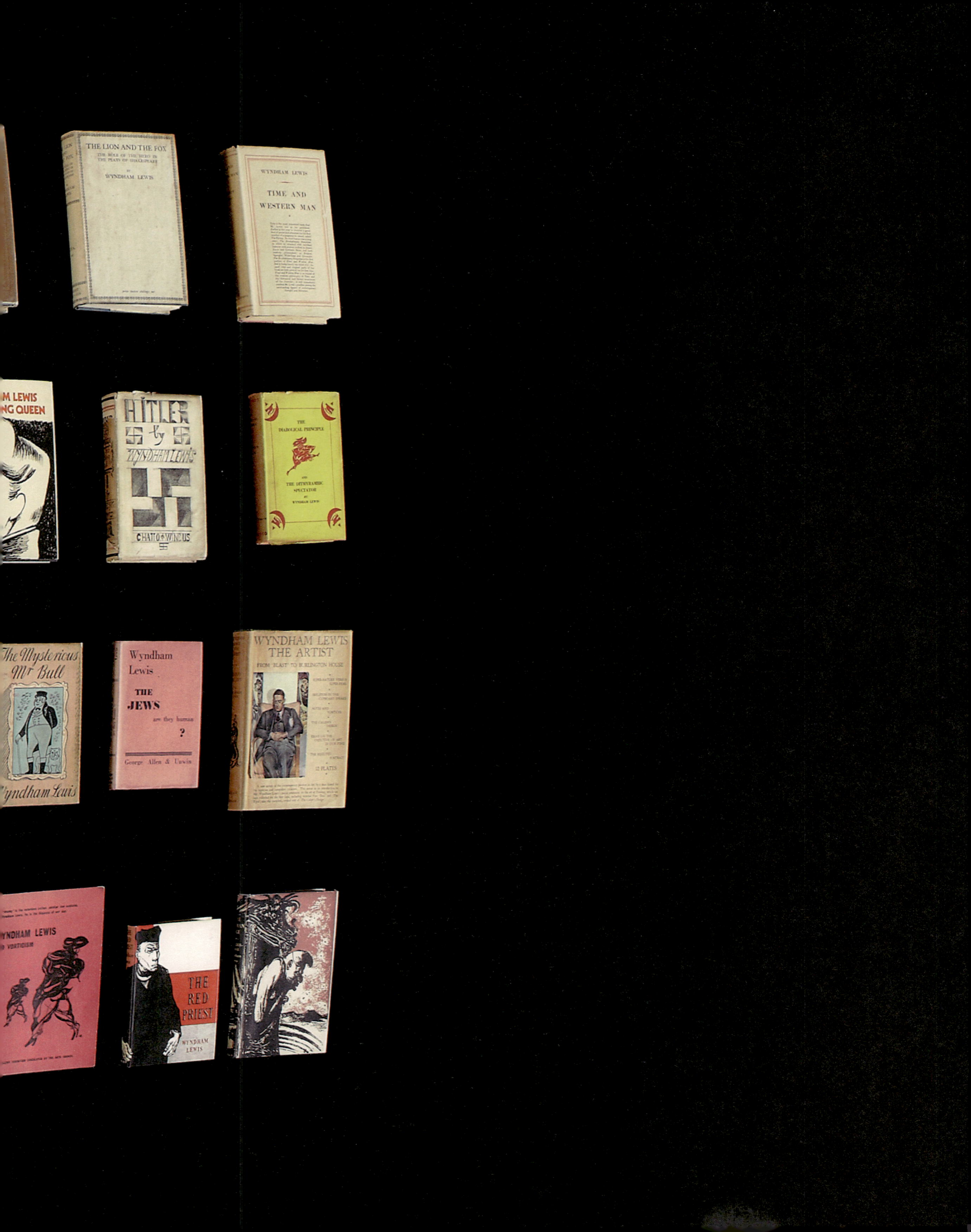
THE LION AND THE FOX
THE ROLE OF THE HERO IN THE PLAYS OF SHAKESPEARE
BY
WYNDHAM LEWIS
WYNDHAM LEWIS
TIME AND WESTERN MAN
HITLER
WYNDHAM LEWIS
CHATTO & WINDUS
THE DIABOLICAL PRINCIPLE
AND
THE DITHYRAMBIC SPECTATOR
BY
WYNDHAM LEWIS
The Mysterious Mr Bull
Wyndham Lewis
THE JEWS
are they human
?
George Allen & Unwin
WYNDHAM LEWIS THE ARTIST
FROM 'BLAST' TO BURLINGTON HOUSE
12 PLATES
THE RED PRIEST
WYNDHAM LEWIS

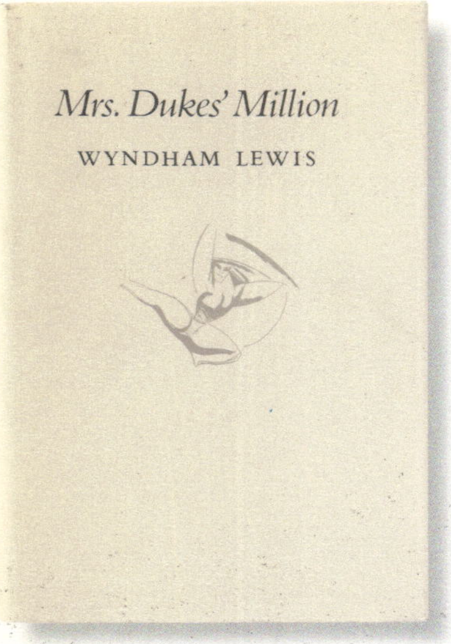

1

Mrs Dukes' Million
[Khan and Company]
(Toronto: The Coach House Press, 1977) 20.9 x 13.9 cm
PRIVATE COLLECTION YMJB

This "potboiler" was composed in about 1909 "to get if possible a little money so that I could complete comme il faut my other novel." The other novel was *Tarr* (1918) (B&M Cat. 5). *Khan and Company* was not published and Lewis declared that the experience was "a lesson showing the futility of potboiling for me."[1] The plot concerns an "actor gang" who stage real life fictional scenarios to carry out their crimes. In this case they kidnap a poor keeper of a lodging house who is in line for a huge legacy and install their own impersonator to take her place in the lodging house. In due course another actor has to replace the first and produces an identity at two removes from the original. There is, of course, also a love story that ends happily, with the young couple taking off in an aeroplane and flying over the Luxembourg Gardens. The novel is entertaining, but especially fascinating for the way it adumbrates themes (such as that of the nature of identity and the self) that will be treated more seriously in Lewis's later work. When it was eventually published in 1977, it was given a new title, *Mrs Dukes' Million*, by the editor, Frank Davey.

1. Letters to James Pinker (a celebrated literary agent), ca. 1909–10, *The Letters of Wyndham Lewis*. Ed. W.K. Rose (London: Methuen & Co. Ltd, 1963), pp. 43, 44.

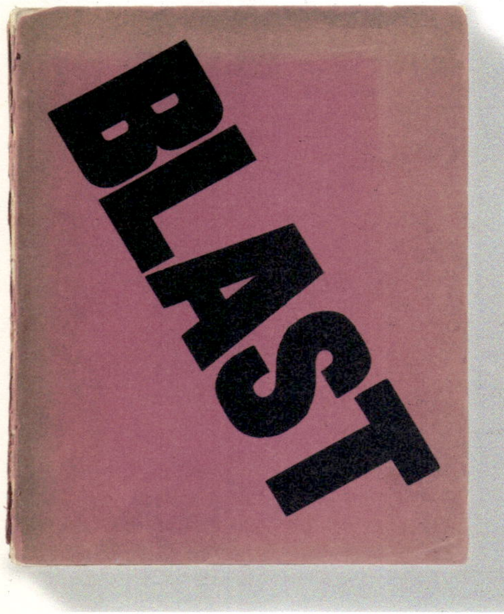

2

***Blast*, No. 1**
(London: John Lane, 1914)
31.8 x 26.7 cm
PRIVATE COLLECTION YMJB.
WYNDHAM LEWIS MEMORIAL TRUST

The Vorticists' magazine was edited by Wyndham Lewis, who was also the principal author of the group's manifestos and most of the short critical articles on contemporary painting and aesthetics in the magazine. Lewis wrote later that his quasi-Expressionist play, *Enemy of the Stars*, was intended to demonstrate to his literary contemporaries what a Vorticist literature that truly matched the painters' innovations should be like. The magazine also contains reproductions of Vorticist painting and sculpture by Edward Wadsworth, Frederick Etchells, William Roberts, Jacob Epstein, Gaudier Brzeska and Cuthbert Hamilton. Wadsworth, Etchells and Hamilton had accompanied Lewis when he stormed out of the Omega Workshops in October 1913. This led to the founding of the Rebel Art Centre (directed by Lewis), from where *Blast* was published. The bright magenta cover with its title in display block capitals, and the inventive typographical layouts of the manifestos, make *Blast* a landmark in the history of the avant-garde. It turns the popular visual culture of newspapers and posters to its artistic purpose, celebrating music-hall stars, boxers, suffragettes (and the then unknown James Joyce), while "blasting" Henri Bergson, various clergyman, the romantic novelist Marie Corelli, John Galsworthy and other establishment figures. Originally intended to be within the general ambit of Futurism, it became anti-Futurist when the new group decided to give themselves a new "Vorticist" identity. Over six months in preparation, it was eventually published only a month before the outbreak of the First World War.

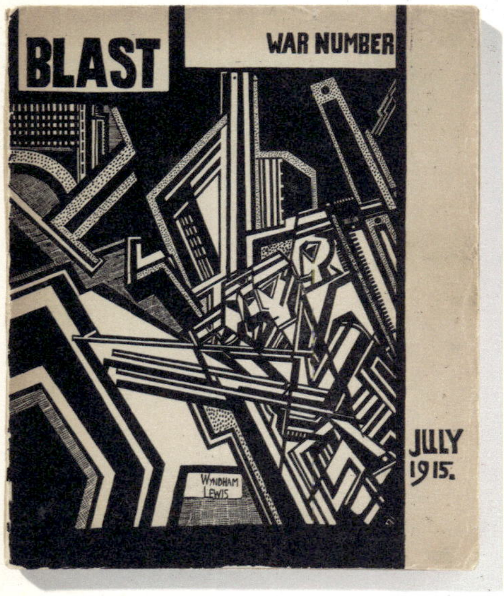

3

***Blast*, No. 2**
(London: John Lane, 1915)
30 x 24.6 cm
WYNDHAM LEWIS MEMORIAL TRUST

The "War Number" of *Blast* was published in July 1915, shortly after the Vorticists' only exhibition in England at the Doré Galleries in June. Production was considerably more economical than for No. 1, though Lewis's cover design, *Before Antwerp*, is almost as striking. Where the first issue was especially concerned with asserting a specifically English contribution to the international effort of European avant-gardes, in the second Lewis wanted to establish a viable position for Vorticism vis-à-vis the international conflict. Unlike the Futurists, the Vorticists had never celebrated war, but they supported Great Britain and France against German aggression. Lewis's war commentaries are partly concerned with the need to maintain a long-term artistic internationalism after the period of nationalist war. The issue contains contributions by the female Vorticists, Jessica Dismorr and Helen Saunders. It also saw the first publication in England of T.S. Eliot, two of whose poems are included. Lewis had been introduced to Eliot by Ezra Pound. Lewis's long essay, "A Review of Contemporary Art" is his most considered critical exposition of the relationship between Vorticism and other contemporary movements, notably Cubism, Expressionism and Futurism.

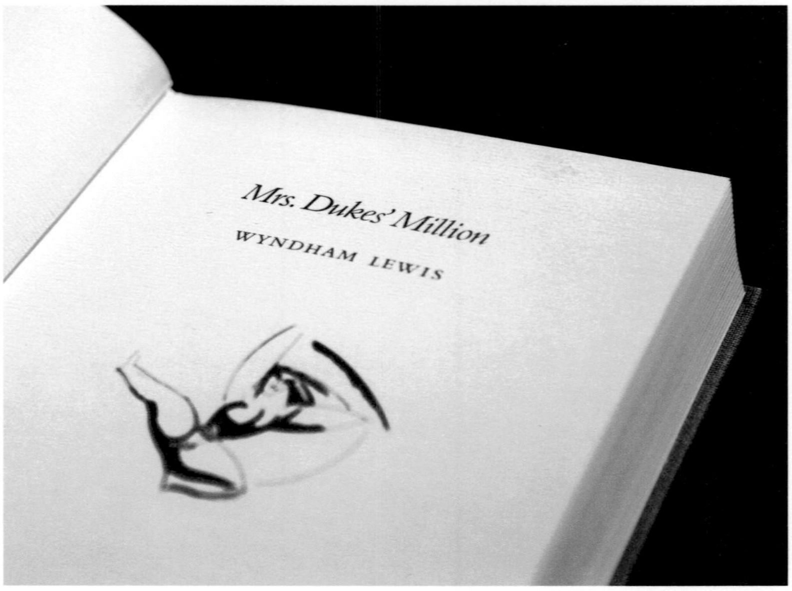
Mrs. Dukes' Million
WYNDHAM LEWIS

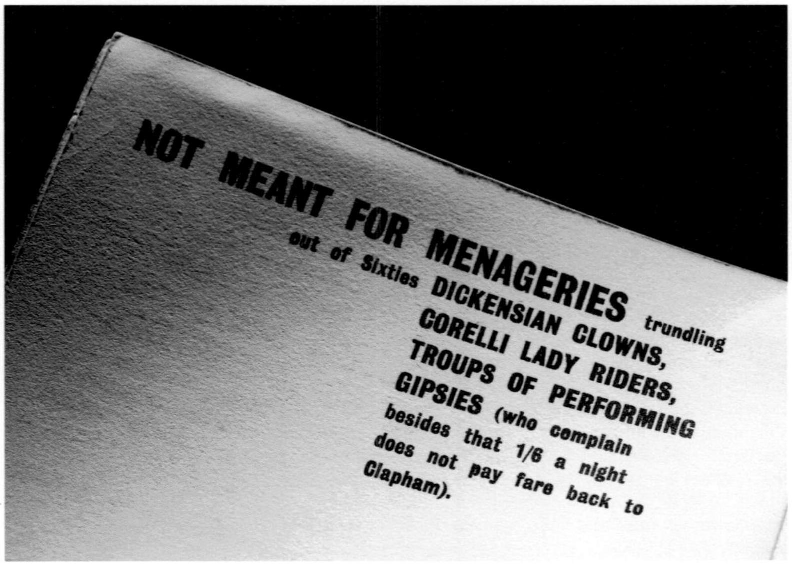
NOT MEANT FOR MENAGERIES trundling
out of Sixties DICKENSIAN CLOWNS,
CORELLI LADY RIDERS,
TROUPS OF PERFORMING
GIPSIES (who complain
besides that 1/6 a night
does not pay fare back to
Clapham).

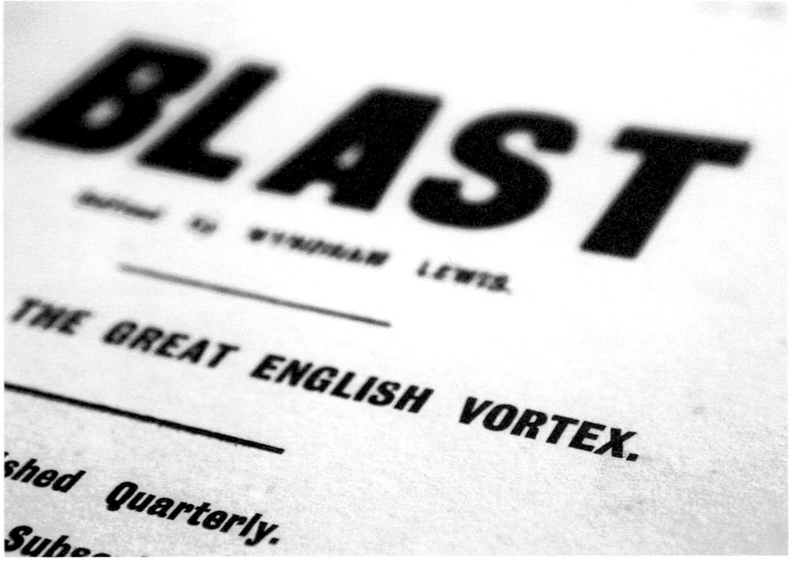
BLAST
THE GREAT ENGLISH VORTEX.
Quarterly.

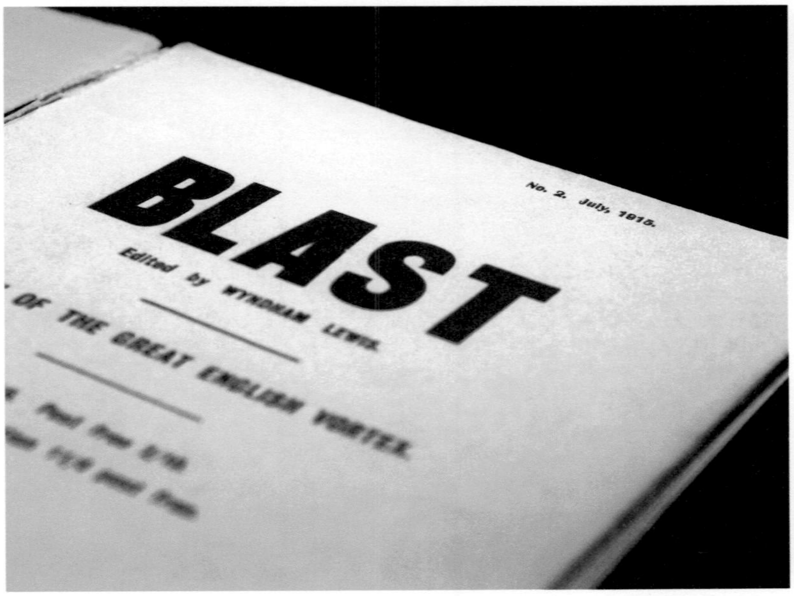
No. 2. July, 1915.
BLAST
Edited by WYNDHAM LEWIS.

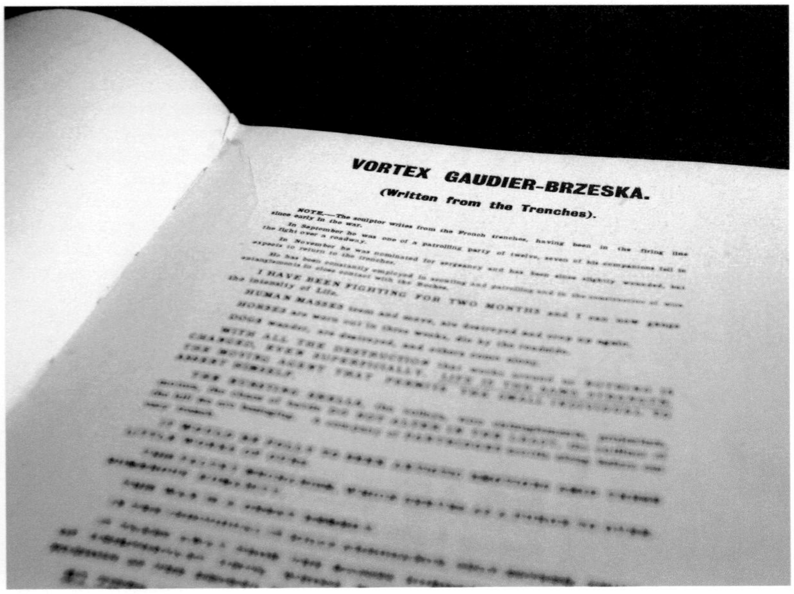
VORTEX GAUDIER-BRZESKA.
(Written from the Trenches).

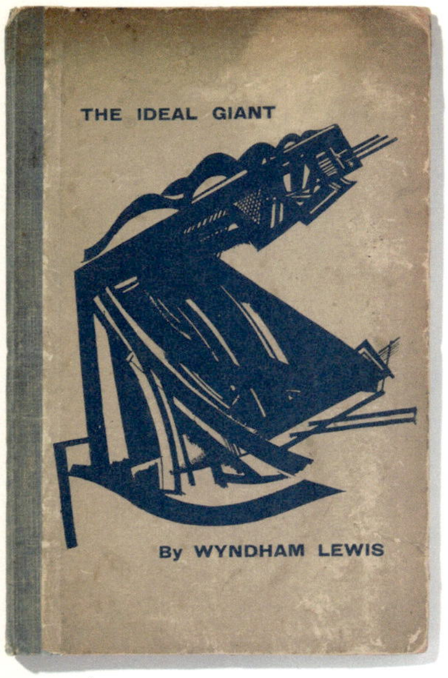

4

The Ideal Giant
(London: The Little Review, 1917) 24.5 x 16 cm
WYNDHAM LEWIS MEMORIAL TRUST

This rare book was published in a small edition under the auspices of the "London Office" of the Chicago-based magazine, *The Little Review*. There was no office and the publication was overseen by Ezra Pound. The aim was probably to secure copyright for three texts of Lewis's: "Cantelman's Spring-Mate," "The Ideal Giant" and "The Code of a Herdsman." "Cantelman's Spring-Mate," a story Lewis wrote in 1916 while in training as a gunner, had been prosecuted for obscenity in the USA. Cantelman (also training for the war) seduces and brutally abandons a girl from the local village, taking out on her his anger against humanity and nature for their Darwinian betrayal of his hopes for a transformed civilisation. "The Ideal Giant" is a short play in which the chief character expounds to other characters theories about art and action that are close to Lewis's own. Like Cantelman, however, he is confounded by actions that make his theorising look jejune. The "testing" of ideas that Lewis himself professed in fictions that revealed their limits was common in his work of this time. "The Code of a Herdsman" is a comic, Nietzschean piece, where again ideas that sound like Lewis's are both put forward and thrown into doubt – this time by the sheer, comic extremity of their elitism.

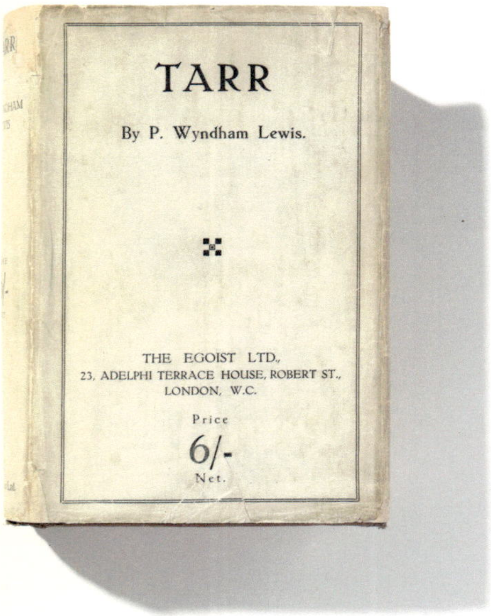

5

Tarr
(London: The Egoist Press, 1918) 18.7 x 13.4 cm
WYNDHAM LEWIS MEMORIAL TRUST

This, Lewis's first published novel, is broadly satirical in its presentation of the international bohemian society of art students in Paris before the war. Tarr is Lewis's surrogate, an English artist with a troubled relationship with the excessively bourgeois and conventional Bertha. Again, Lewis's own theories about art and life, expounded vehemently by the semi-autobiographical Tarr, are tested by the intransigence of the competing reality of other people. Tarr's "double" is the talentless German, Otto Kreisler (who had been the protagonist in a first, 1909, draft); he rapes Bertha and commits suicide. Lewis's prose style in the novel is unprecedented in English, extraordinarily detached and alienated from its subject while conveying psychological states with hallucinatory intensity.

Lewis began writing this novel in 1909 and declared it finished in 1911. When war broke out in 1914, he knew that he would enlist and realistically calculated that he might well be killed. Along with a volume of his writings on art (primarily from the two issues of *Blast* (B&M Cats 2 and 3)) and a collection of his early short stories ("Our Wild Body," contracted by Max Goschen and delivered to the publisher before Lewis enlisted in March 1916), he decided to revise the novel and leave behind as complete an *oeuvre* as he could. Accordingly, while recovering from gonorrhoea in 1915, he revised the text and, it seems, added chapters with conversations relating closely to his recent aesthetic ideas and love life. No publisher was interested in the book at the time, however, and Ezra Pound, who was simultaneously trying to place James Joyce's equally unwanted *A Portrait of the Artist as a Young Man* (1916), arranged serialisation in the magazine, *The Egoist*, funded by Harriet Shaw Weaver. In 1918, *The Egoist* published it as a book in England, while Alfred Knopf published it simultaneously in the USA.

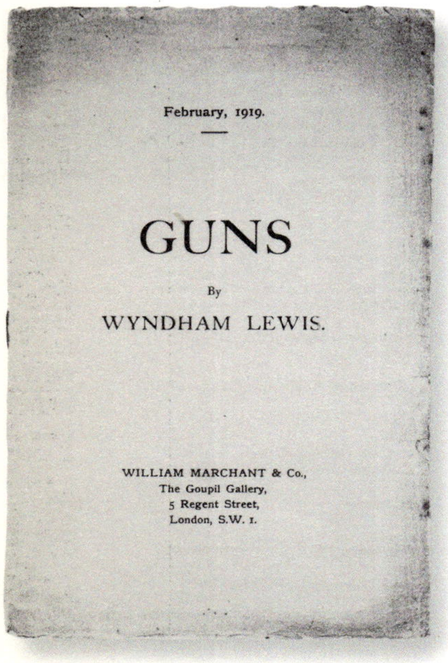

6

[Not in exhibition]
Guns by Wyndham Lewis
Exhibition Catalogue (London: Goupil Gallery, 1919) 20.8 x 13.4 cm

This is the catalogue of the exhibition of Lewis's war art (minus the major commissioned oils, *A Canadian Gun Pit* (1918) (M. P22) and *A Battery Shelled* (Cat. 71)). The centrepiece was the now lost oil painting, *To Wipe Out* (M. P24). Lewis's foreword disclaims an exclusive interest in abstraction (for which, as a Vorticist, he was famous) but seems to protest a little too much that he should be allowed to produce figurative work as well. More importantly, the foreword contains Lewis's thoughts on war art. He writes,

Whatever we may think [of the paintings of the war so far produced] it is certain that the philosophy of the war, all the serious interpretation of it, has yet to be done. [...] all the war journalism, in painting and writing, will cease with the punctuality of a pistol shot when the war-curtain goes down. It will then be the turn of those with experience of the subject, the inclination, the mood, to make the true record. Truth has no place in action. ("Foreword," n.p.)

A Battery Shelled to some extent fulfils that promise, but it could also be said that nearly all of Lewis's subsequent work testifies to his continuing attempts to understand the significance of the war in which he had fought and which he had recorded in the series of drawings exhibited in *Guns*.

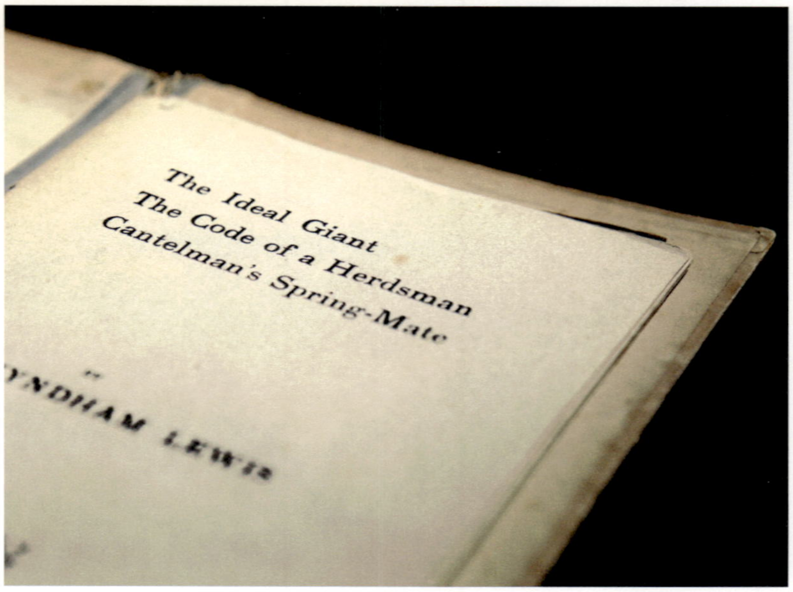

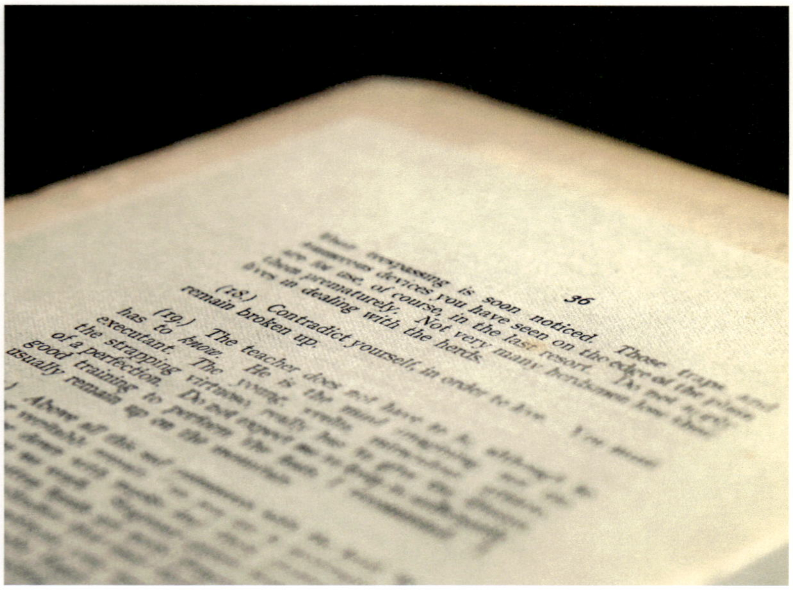

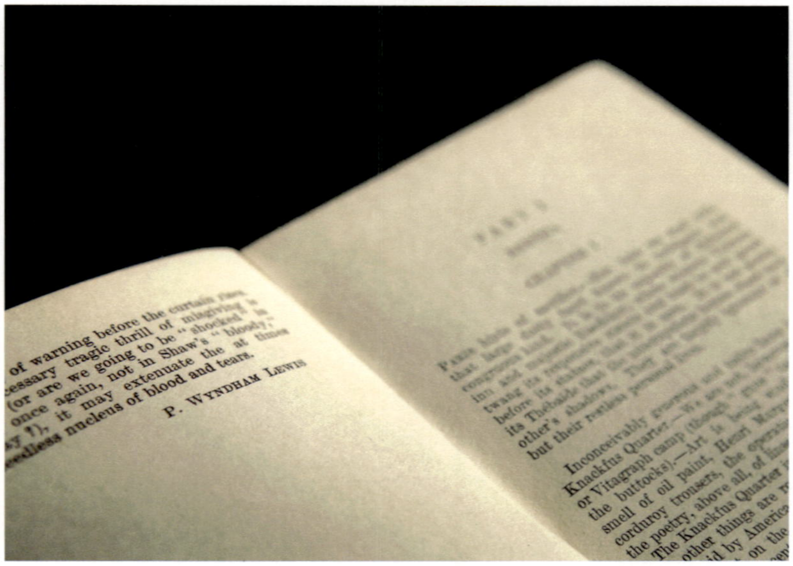

"As a logical development of much of the
solidest art in this very various world there is nothing
so devilish or mad in any of the experiments
in art that prevailed in the years preceding the War.
That much said, and turning to this exhibition [*Guns*]:
there is very little technically abstruse in it; except
in so far as it is always a source of astonishment to the
public that an artist should not attempt to transcribe Nature
literally, without comment, without philosophy,
without vision."

Wyndham Lewis,
Guns, 1919

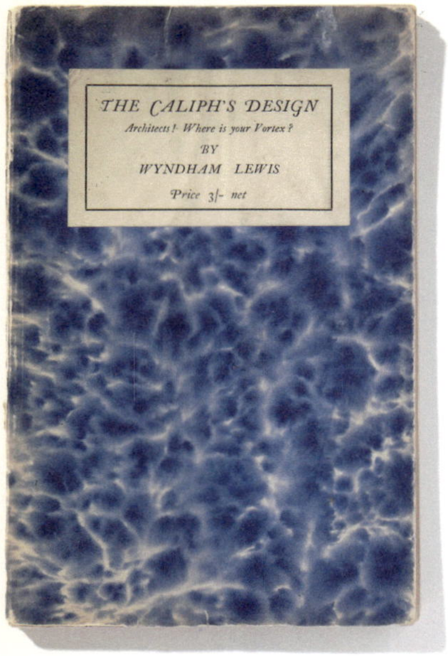

7

The Caliph's Design: Architects! Where is Your Vortex?
(London: The Egoist Press, 1919) 21.2 x 13.9 cm
PRIVATE COLLECTION YMJB

"We do not want to change the appearance of the world," Lewis maintained in June 1914 in the first *Blast* manifesto (B&M Cat. 2). But his experience in the First World War led him to believe that

> The energy at present pent up (and rather too congested) in the canvas painted in the studio and sold at the dealer's, and written of with a monotonous emphasis of horror or facetiousness in the Press, must be released into the general life of the community. And from thence, from the life outside, it will come back to enrich and invigorate the Studio.
> (*Caliph's Design*, p. 7)

How to do this through architecture, and how to prevent the modernist impulse in art petering out in Cubist "nature-mortism," nostalgic classicism or the passivity of Bloomsbury formalism, are the subjects of this pamphlet. The artist should go "back to the fish" and catch the "very first gusto of creation in this scale of life" in order to be a creator rather than a mere imitator. (*Caliph's Design*, p. 35)

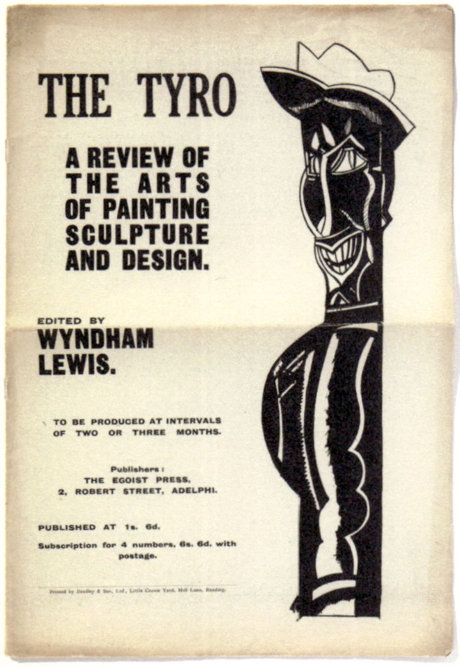

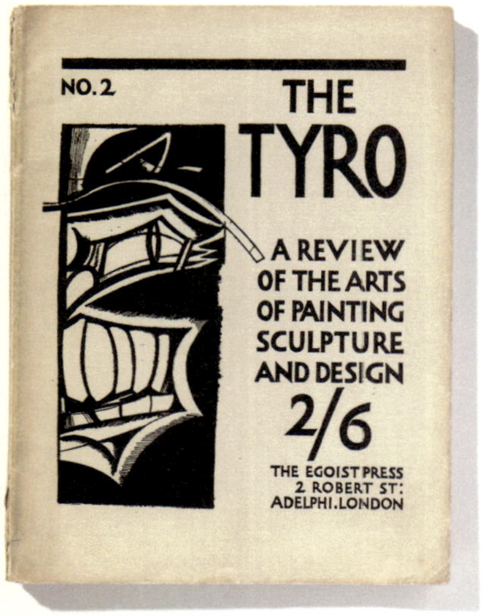

8

***The Tyro*, No. 1**
(London: The Egoist Press, 1921) 37.4 x 25 cm
WYNDHAM LEWIS MEMORIAL TRUST

9

***The Tyro*, No. 2**
(London: The Egoist Press, 1922) 24.8 x 18.6 cm
WYNDHAM LEWIS MEMORIAL TRUST

This was the second of the magazines Lewis edited, and, like *Blast* (B&M Cats. 2 and 3), it had only two issues. The format of issue one, with its striking image of *The Cept*, indicates that Lewis aims for a popular audience. Once again he attacks Roger Fry and Bloomsbury for their uncritical Francophilia. T.S. Eliot contributes two articles that bolster Lewis's campaign for a robust satirical classicism in the tradition of the playwrights Ben Jonson and William Congreve.

By the second issue, Lewis had abandoned the totemic "Tyros" (satires of a shell-shocked public entering a new world after the war), and the polemical spirit of issue number one gives way to a more reflective exposition of modernist aesthetics ("Essay on the Objective of Plastic Art in our Time"). The second issue also contains some reproductions on coated paper (including a sculpture by Jacques Lipschitz), adverts for *L'Esprit Nouveau* and *De Stijl* and a "Lettre de Paris" by Waldemar George. Lewis's object was to place the artistic avant-garde in England fully in the mainstream of the international movement. But during the First World War, all the levers of power in the art world of England had been secured by "Bloomsbury," who promoted the "painterly" post-Impressionist still lifes and domestic interiors of Duncan Grant as the most important development in British art.

"A number of the younger painters
are embarked upon an enterprise that involves
considerable sacrifices and discomforts, an
immense amount of application, and an eager
belief. This effort has to contend with the
scepticism of a shallow, tired and uncertain time.
There is no great communal or personal
force in the Western World of today, unless some
new political hegemony supply it, for art to
build on and to which to relate itself."

Wyndham Lewis,
The Caliph's Design, 1919

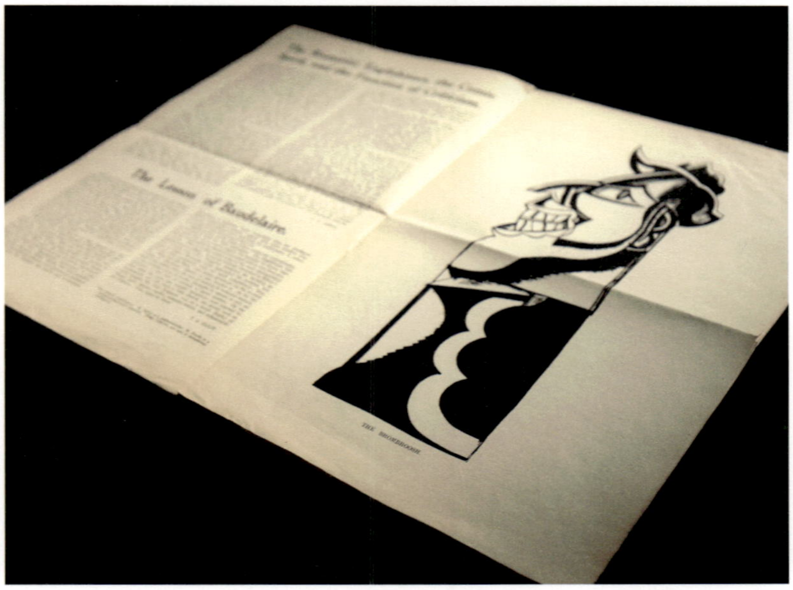

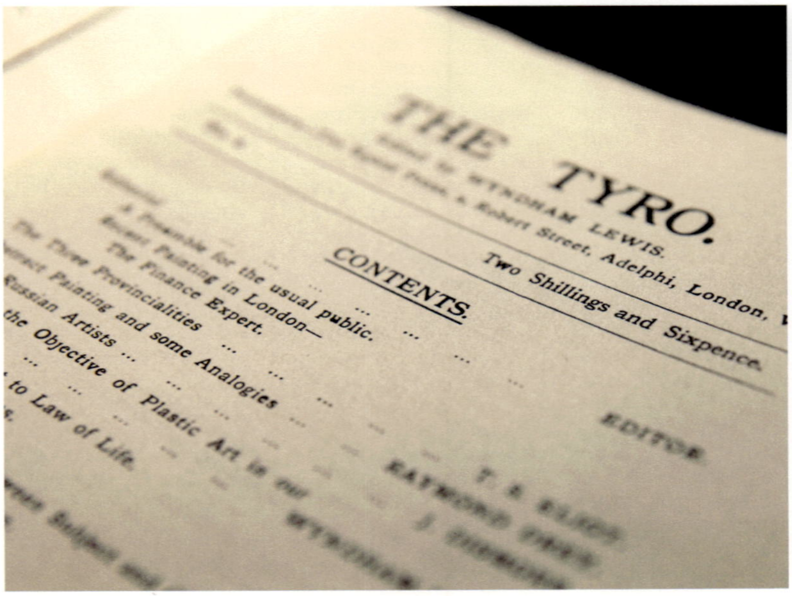

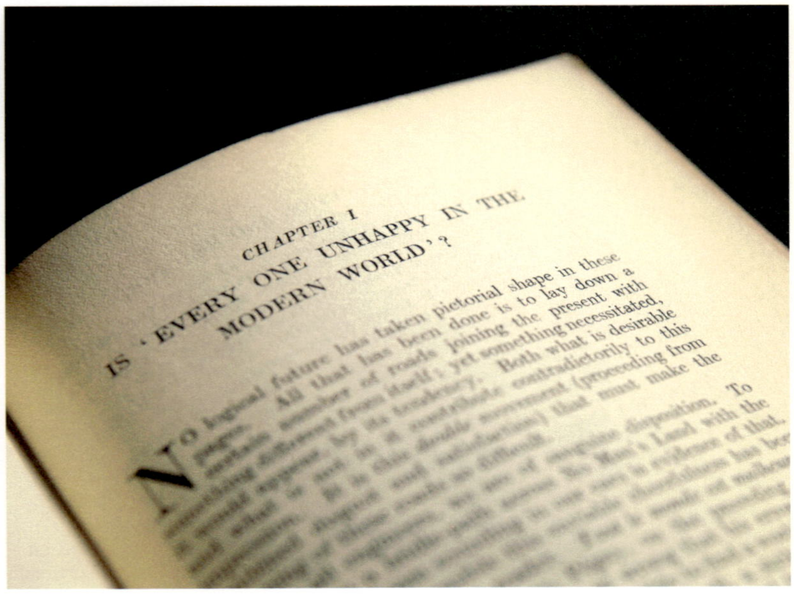

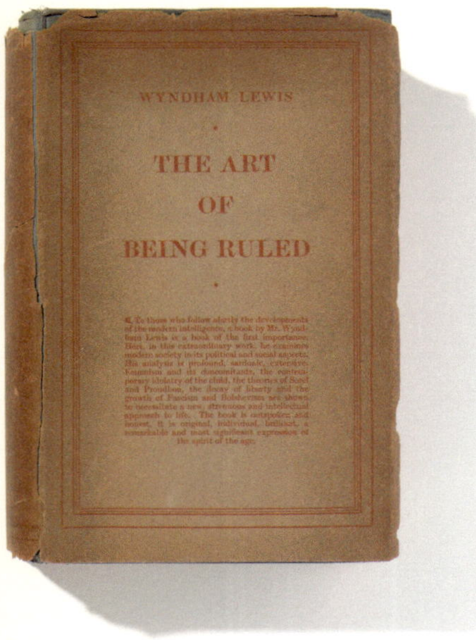

10

The Art of Being Ruled
(London: Chatto and Windus, 1926) 22.7 x 14.8 cm
PRIVATE COLLECTION YMJB

This is an analysis of the "democratic educationalist state" (p. 110), exposing the mechanism by which it turns potentially revolutionary forces into simulacra that support the status quo. The book anticipates many of the critiques of liberal capitalism of the Frankfurt School and postmodern thinkers like Jean Baudrillard. Lewis suggests that democracy is largely a sham, not much more than a form of mass-hypnotism, and that it would be more efficient to replace it with an authoritarian state on Marxist or Fascist lines: "what they [Italian Fascism and Soviet Communism] have done in a short time in the way of organization must be the admiration of the world" (p. 75). Lewis proposes that under such a benign system people could occupy themselves with more important things than politics. But making positive political prescriptions is not a major part of the book; its continuing life is in the brio of its social and ideological analysis. Feminism, homosexuality, the cult of youth, the death of the family, the competing attractions of centralised authority and Proudhonian anarchism are all discussed with typical stylistic vividness. Lewis later said that his aim was to give alternative views in his analyses, so that his readers could make up their own minds. The form of the book is thus somewhat antithetical to the authoritarianism it sometimes propounds.

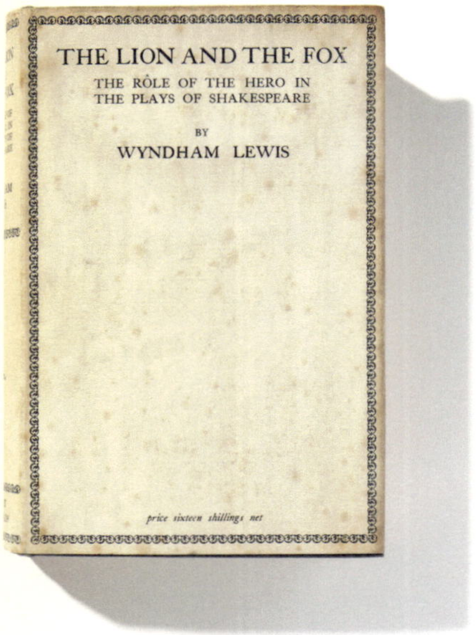

11

The Lion and the Fox: The Rôle of the Hero in the Plays of Shakespeare
(London: Grant Richards, 1927) 22.3 x 15.2 cm
WYNDHAM LEWIS MEMORIAL TRUST

Along with *The Art of Being Ruled* (B&M Cat.10), *Time and Western Man* (B&M Cats. 12 and 13) and several separately published essays, *The Lion and the Fox* derived from a huge treatise that Lewis completed and offered for publication in 1925, "The Man of the World." It was rejected and Lewis developed its sections into separate books, of which *The Lion and the Fox* was the first to be completed. Problems with the unreliable publisher, Grant Richards, delayed the book's publication by two years. The argument proposes a William Shakespeare who is half in a feudal world and half in the modern world of positive science, and uses Niccolò Machiavelli's metaphor of the lion and the fox for the struggle that Lewis traces between these outlooks in Shakespeare's work. The balance of forces in Shakespeare makes him the ideal artist of his time, and, by extension, a similar dualism is required in an artist who would seek to understand and explain the modern world.

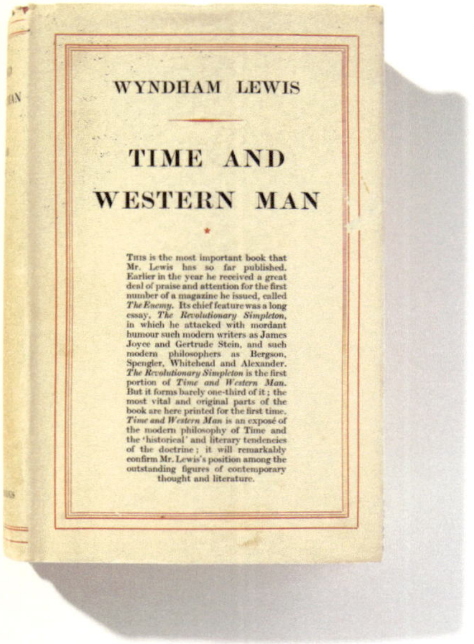

12

Time and Western Man
(London: Chatto and Windus, 1927) 22.8 x 14.7 cm
PRIVATE COLLECTION YMJB

13

Time and Western Man
Revised edition
(New York: Harcourt, Brace and Co., 1928) 22.8 x 14.7 cm
PRIVATE COLLECTION YMJB

This is the third of Lewis's great theoretical books of the 1920s. It performs an ideological analysis of contemporary philosophy and metaphysics, on some popular culture, on historiography (of Oswald Spengler), on theology, and most famously on the literary avant-garde. All have, in Lewis's view, an obsession with "time." All tend to be naturalist in the sense that they re-absorb the human spirit into a (sometimes cosmic) natural process, robbing that spirit of its freedom and independence to create and follow values of its own invention. Although there are in *Time and Western Man* traces of the formal "dualism" found in the previous books deriving from "The Man of the World" (the propounding of competing principles that oppose the book's apparent position), on the whole its polemical analysis is unshadowed by an ambivalent alternative. Lewis promises an exposition of his own metaphysics (a variant of Berkeleyan idealism) in a later book, but this remained unwritten. The long first section of the book, devoted to criticism of avant-garde movements (particularly Gertrude Stein, Ezra Pound and James Joyce), had already appeared in the first issue of Lewis's magazine, *The Enemy* (B&M Cat. 14). The American edition added a new preface, resulting in a slight reorganisation.

In his 1950 autobiography, *Rude Assignment* (B&M Cat. 50), referring to the time of composition of these books deriving from "The Man of the World," Lewis says

for some time I was very sore and that soreness increased, if anything, during the immediately ensuing years. The sentimental side of me suffered (I think now) more deeply than it should. – All that is to be found in those books will never be seen again, naturally, with that sharpness or excitement [...] or with so much distress.
(p. 184)

It is the sharpness and excitement that give the books their continuing life.

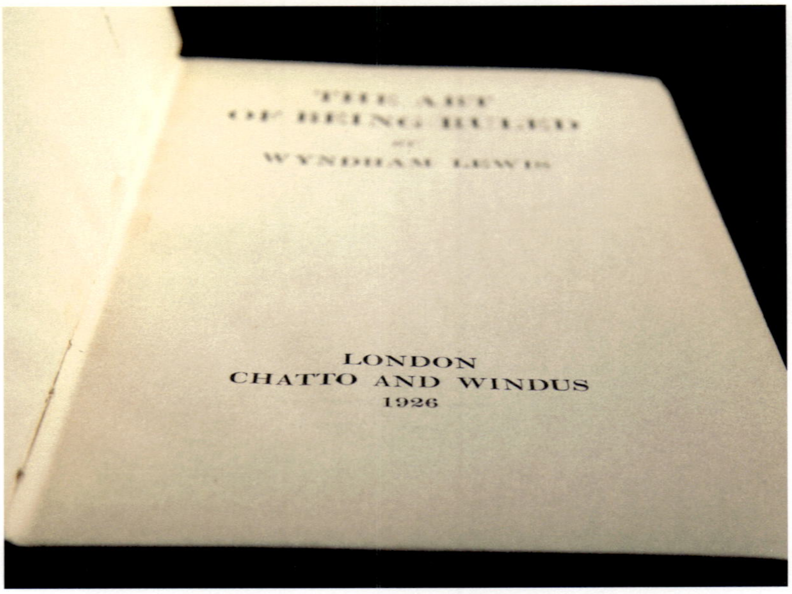
THE ART
OF BEING RULED
BY
WYNDHAM LEWIS
LONDON
CHATTO AND WINDUS
1926

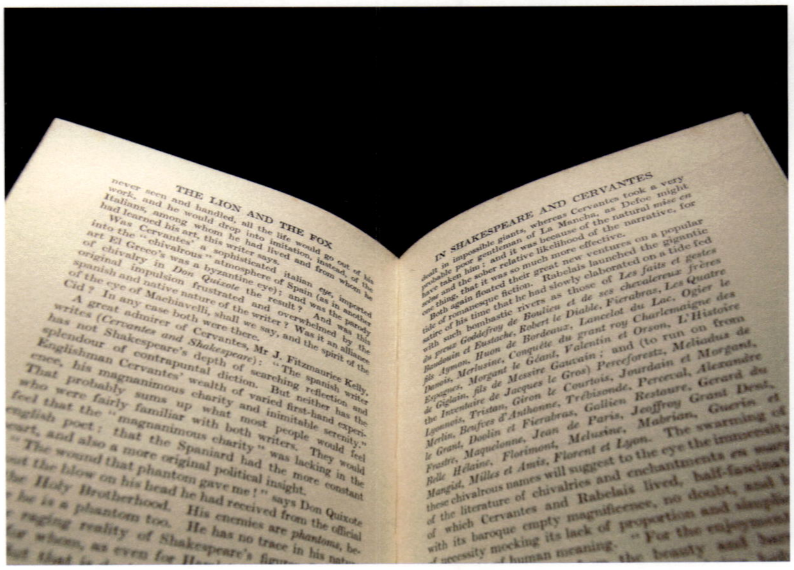
THE LION AND THE FOX
IN SHAKESPEARE AND CERVANTES

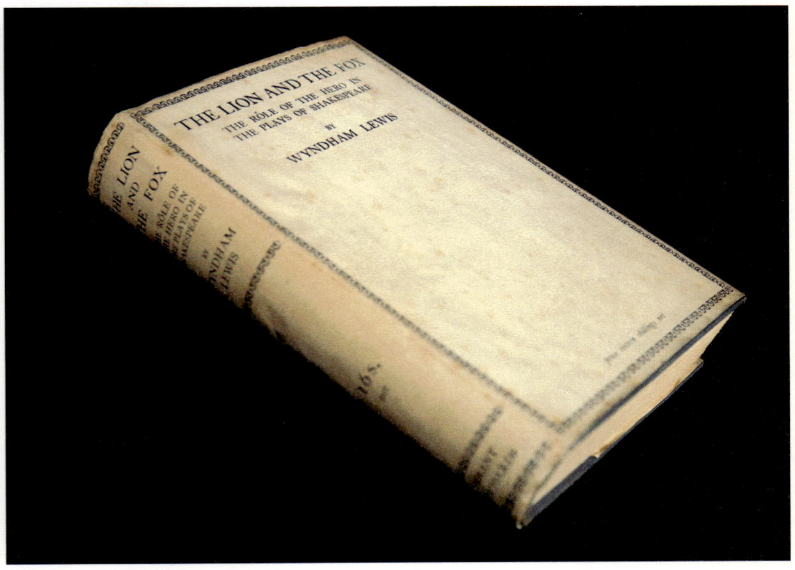
THE LION AND THE FOX
THE RÔLE OF THE HERO IN
THE PLAYS OF SHAKESPEARE
BY
WYNDHAM LEWIS

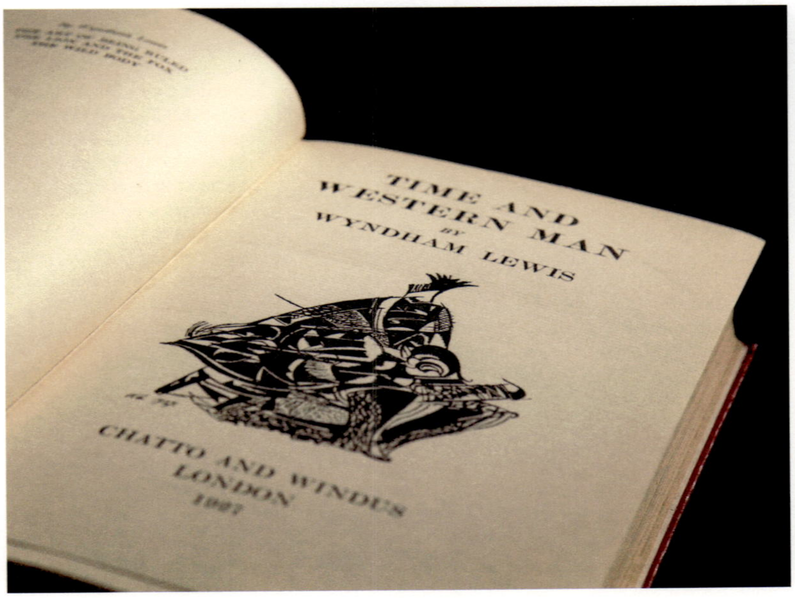
TIME AND
WESTERN MAN
BY
WYNDHAM LEWIS
CHATTO AND WINDUS
LONDON
1927

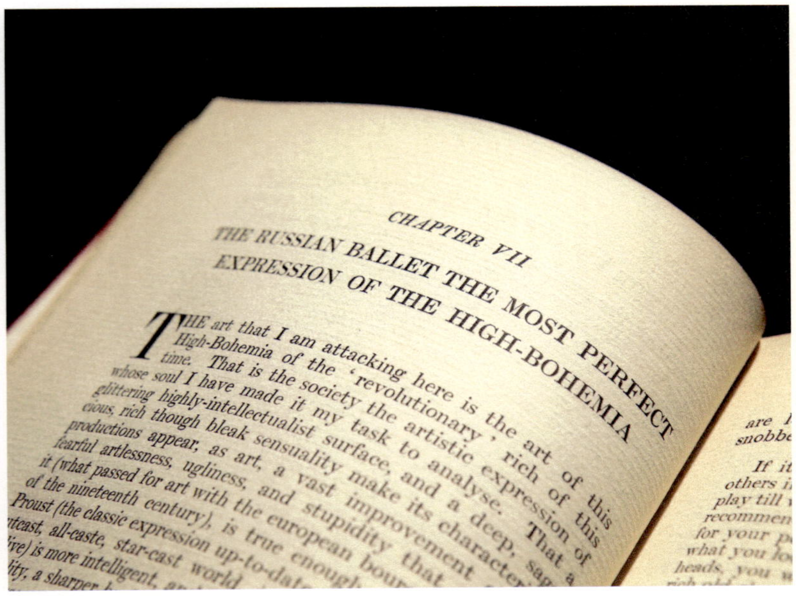
CHAPTER VII
THE RUSSIAN BALLET THE MOST PERFECT
EXPRESSION OF THE HIGH-BOHEMIA

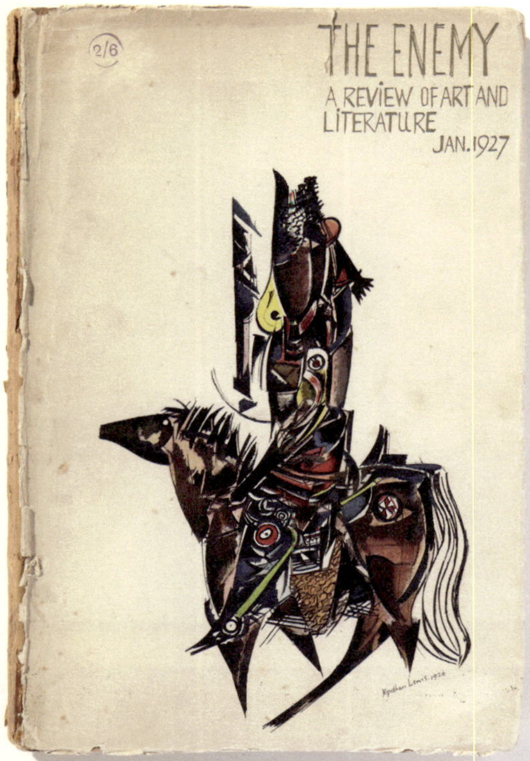

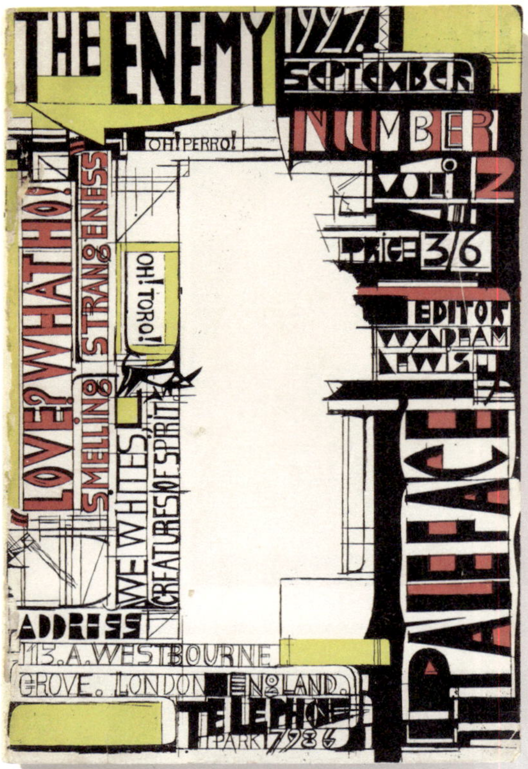

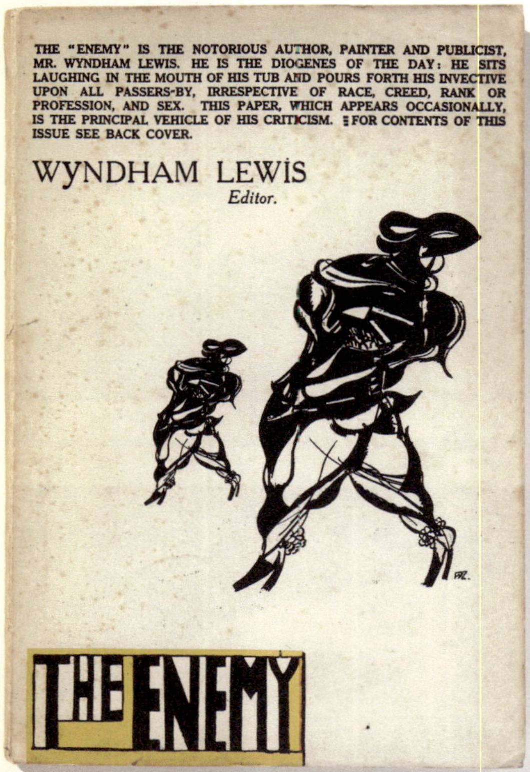

14

***The Enemy*, Vol. 1**
(1927) 28.7 x 18.8 cm
WYNDHAM LEWIS MEMORIAL TRUST

15

***The Enemy*, No. 2**
(1927) 28.1 x 18.8 cm
WYNDHAM LEWIS MEMORIAL TRUST

16

***The Enemy*, No. 3**
(1929) 28.3 x 18.5 cm
WYNDHAM LEWIS MEMORIAL TRUST

Under the patronage of Sir Nicholas Waterhouse (of the accountancy firm Price Waterhouse), Lewis was able to launch his third and final magazine. The main contents of each were book-length essays by Lewis himself, all campaigning works of cultural criticism. In Volume 1, the first part of *Time and Western Man* (B&M Cats. 12 and 13), "The Revolutionary Simpleton," was published for the first time. Lewis turns on his old associates, Ezra Pound and James Joyce. Pound is a "man in love with the past," unable to deal with modernity in his work (despite a naive enthusiasm for almost anything calling itself avant-garde); Joyce's *Ulysses* (1922) is about a time and place that in the post-war world have no real significance: "he collected like a cistern in his youth the last stagnant pumpings of Victorian anglo-irish life. This he held steadfastly intact for fifteen years or more – then when he was ripe, as it were, he discharged it, in a dense mass, to his eternal glory" (p. 109). Joyce was not pleased, despite the compliment, and neither the reproduction of a portrait of him in issue No. 2, nor the suggestion that he come over to Lewis's side, mollified him.

The second issue, which appeared towards the end of 1927, contained further sniping at the Paris-based avant-garde (Gertrude Stein and the magazine, *transition*), but the main essay was "Paleface: Or 'Love? What ho! Smelling Strangeness'," which analysed the sentimental idealisation of the "dark unconscious" of Afro-Americans and supposedly "primitive" races in the work of D.H. Lawrence and Sherwood Anderson. It would later be incorporated in *Paleface: The Philosophy of the "Melting Pot"* (B&M Cat. 20).

Issue No. 3 (1929) attacks *transition* again, in "The Diabolical Principle." The editors of the magazine had replied to Lewis's criticism, accusing him of being a reactionary who had been left behind by the avant-garde. Now Lewis analysed the Romantic roots of their ideology and criticised their destructive irrationalism. He had adopted the "Enemy" persona as a way to start debate within the avant-garde itself. He quoted a long passage from Plutarch as an epigraph to *The Enemy* (beginning, "A man of understanding is to benefit by his enemies [...]"). But the effect of his campaigning was to cut him off from precisely the artistic culture that he considered the most vital in contemporary literature, that of the avant-garde.

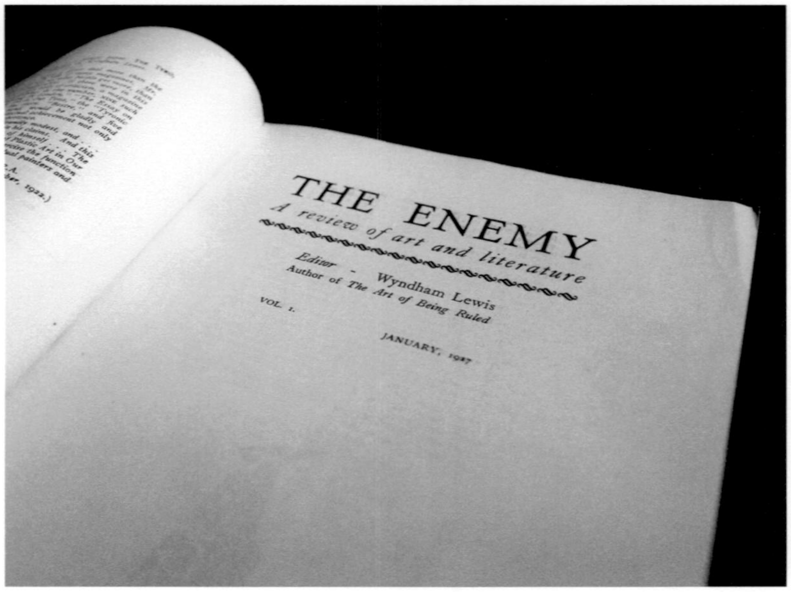
THE ENEMY
A review of art and literature
Editor - Wyndham Lewis
Author of The Art of Being Ruled
VOL. 1.
JANUARY, 1927

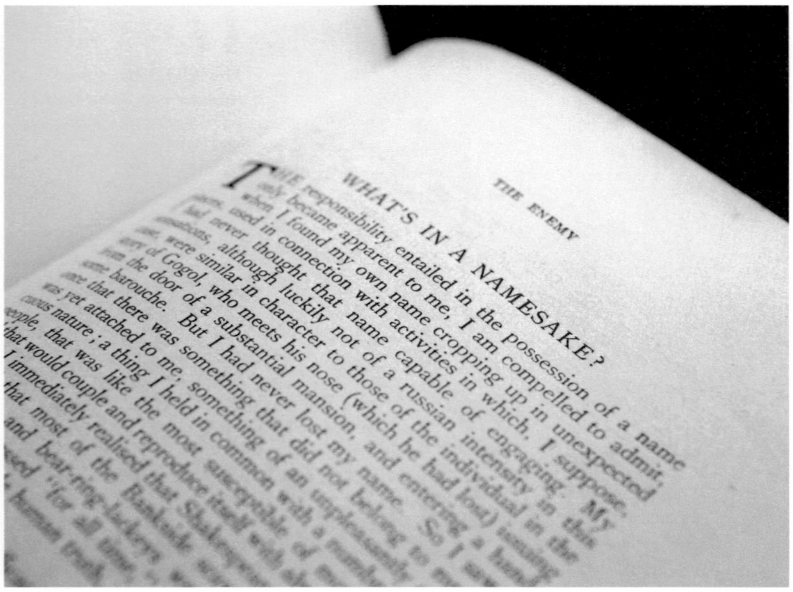
THE ENEMY
WHAT'S IN A NAMESAKE?

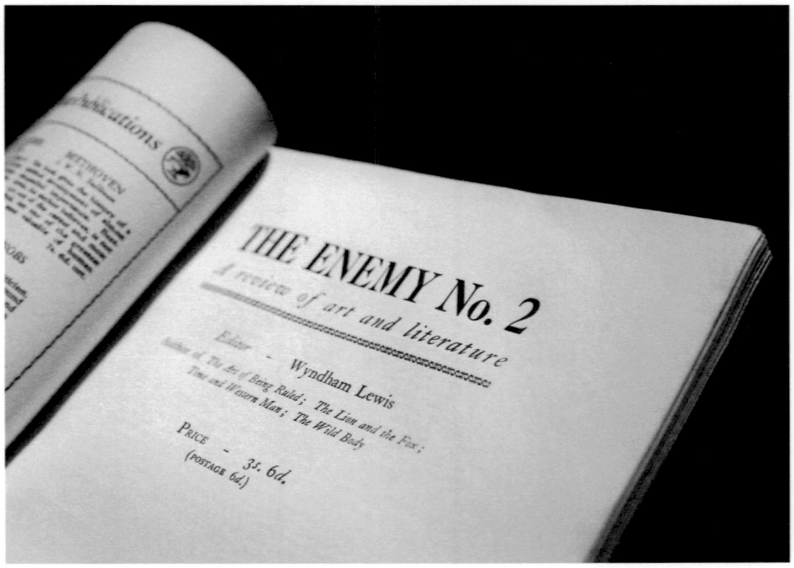
THE ENEMY No. 2
A review of art and literature
Editor - Wyndham Lewis
PRICE - 3s. 6d.
(POSTAGE 6d.)

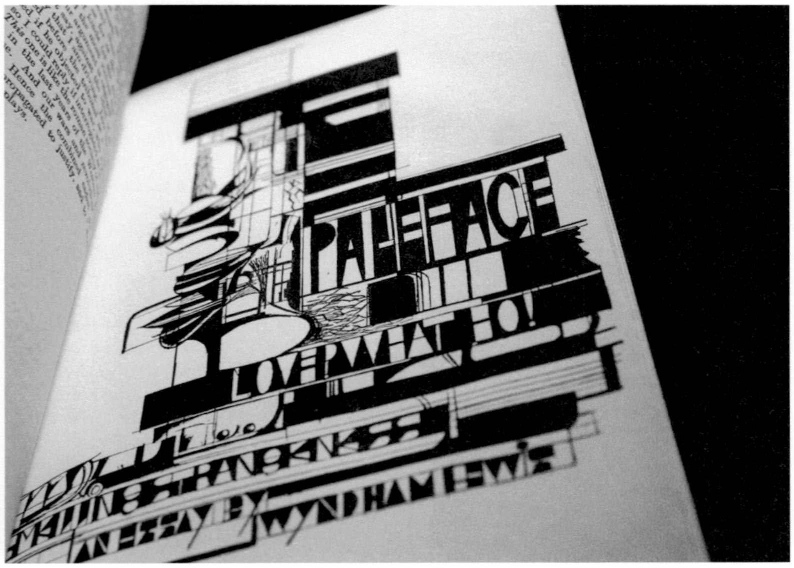
PALEFACE

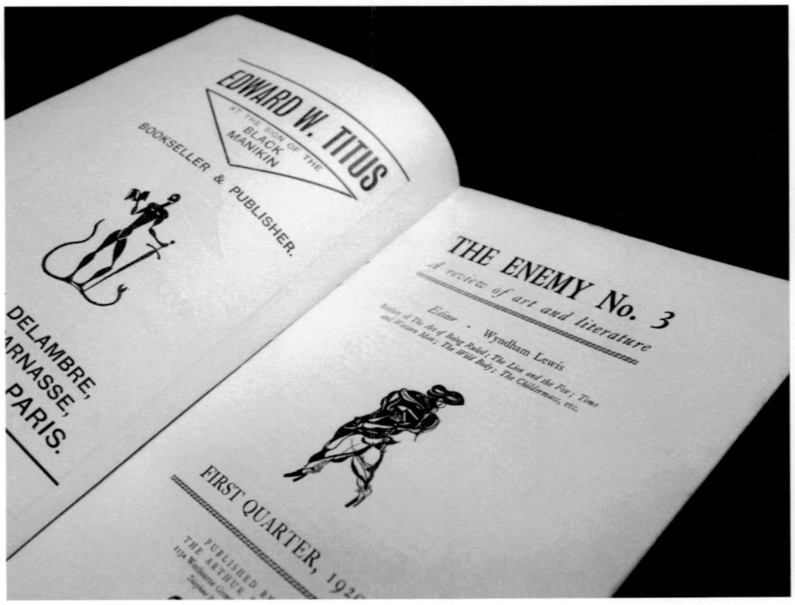
EDWARD W. TITUS
BLACK
MANIKIN
BOOKSELLER & PUBLISHER.
THE ENEMY No. 3
A review of art and literature
Editor - Wyndham Lewis

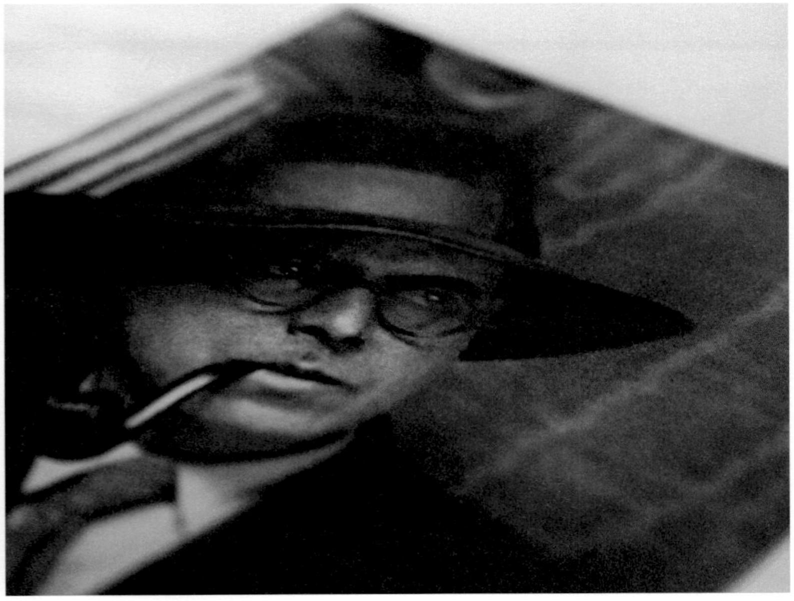

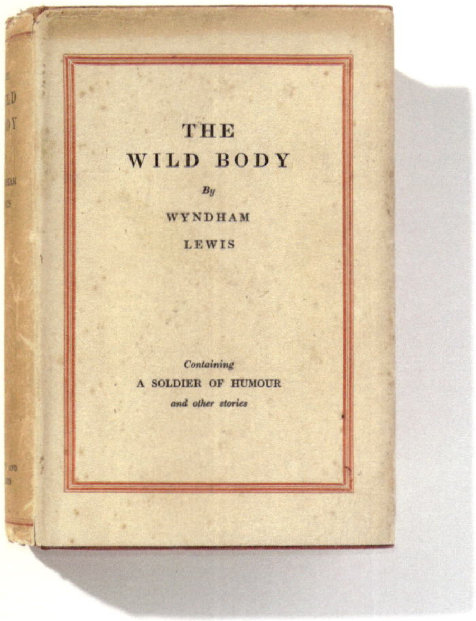

17

The Wild Body: A Soldier of Humour and Other Stories
(London: Chatto and Windus, 1927) 19.8 x 14 cm
PRIVATE COLLECTION YMJB

The book of short stories, "Our Wild Body," that Lewis submitted to "Max Goschen" before the war, had never been published as a book (though most had been published previously in magazines). Lewis now revised and remodelled the stories, foregrounding more thoroughly their narrator, who is almost a caricature of the author. Lewis's prose style in the revisions is an equivalent to the spiky "Cubism" of such pictures as *A Shore Scene* (Cat. 90) or *The Pole Jump* (Cat. 88):

The crocket-like floral postiches on the ridges of her head-gear looked crisped down in a threatening way: her nodular pink veil was an apoplectic gristle round her stormy brow; steam came out of her lips upon the harsh white atmosphere.
(p. 113)

There are two additional stories (one that makes allusion to Pedro Calderón's *La Vida es Sueño* (1635/36)) and, as well as a revised version of Lewis's seminal essay, "Inferior Religions," a new commentary on the dualistic and absurdist vision behind the stories, "The Meaning of the Wild Body."

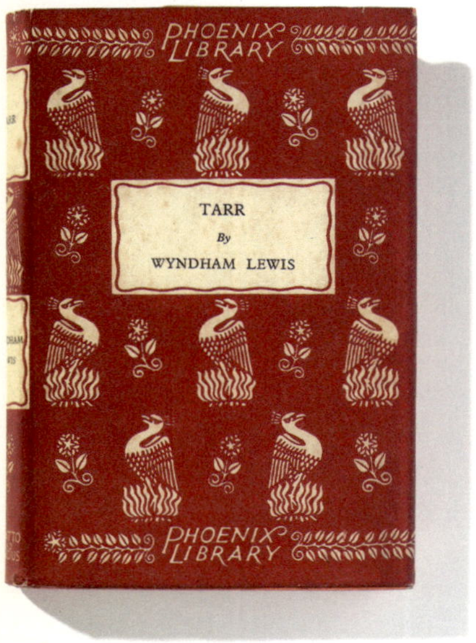

18

***Tarr*, revised edition**
(London: Chatto and Windus, 1928) 17.8 x 12 cm
WYNDHAM LEWIS MEMORIAL TRUST

Lewis, partly on the basis of comments by Ezra Pound in his review of the first edition, seems to have believed that *Tarr* was badly written. Where *The Wild Body* (B&M Cat. 17) revision made those texts more extreme, however, the revision of *Tarr* made the style a little more conventional. It has been pointed out that one particular expansion emphasises the role of a minor Jewish character in ensuring that a duel is fought between the German Otto Kreisler and his "rival" Louis Soltyk (a Pole). Interpreted allegorically, this may imply a fear on Lewis's part that Jews were fomenting war between European peoples.[1] Such inferences are speculative, but in the light of Lewis's sympathy for Nazism for much of the next decade, cannot be dismissed. It is ironic that in Kreisler Lewis makes a penetrating and prophetic critique of elements in German culture that found their most destructive and distorted expression in Hitler.

1. David Ayers, *Wyndham Lewis and Western Man* (Basingstoke: Macmillan, 1992), pp. 139–43.

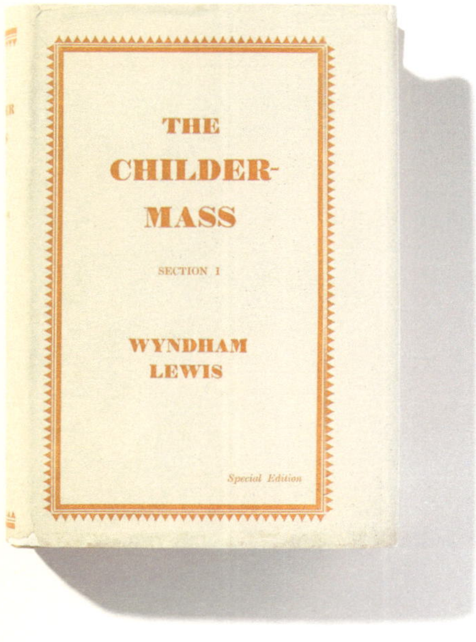

19

The Childermass: Section I
(London: Chatto and Windus, 1928) 22 x 15.5 cm
WYNDHAM LEWIS MEMORIAL TRUST

The title refers to "Childermas," the festival of the Innocents massacred by Herod, celebrated on 28 December. This is Lewis's first original fictional project brought to something near completion since he finished *Tarr* (B&M Cat. 18) in 1915. In honour of the status of this, the publisher produced a collector's edition of 225 signed copies, printed on Basingwerk parchment, uncut and with top edges gilt. The book presents some of Lewis's most vivid writing, giving his vision of the afterworld a hallucinatory brilliance. The mass of war-dead are collected on a plain "outside Heaven," awaiting admission to the Magnetic City across the River Styx. In a letter to the author quoted on the dust jacket of *The Apes of God* (B&M Cats. 21–23), W.B. Yeats compared the first 120 pages with Jonathan Swift's *Gulliver's Travels* (1726) for their imaginative intensity. Many readers find the remainder of the book, depicting the ideological debates at the court of the arbiter of "salvation," the Mussolini-like Bailiff, considerably less exciting. Lewis failed to complete the promised parts II and III, to the annoyance of the publisher. He resumed in a quite different vein in 1955, retitling the work, *The Human Age* (Cats. 57 and 61).

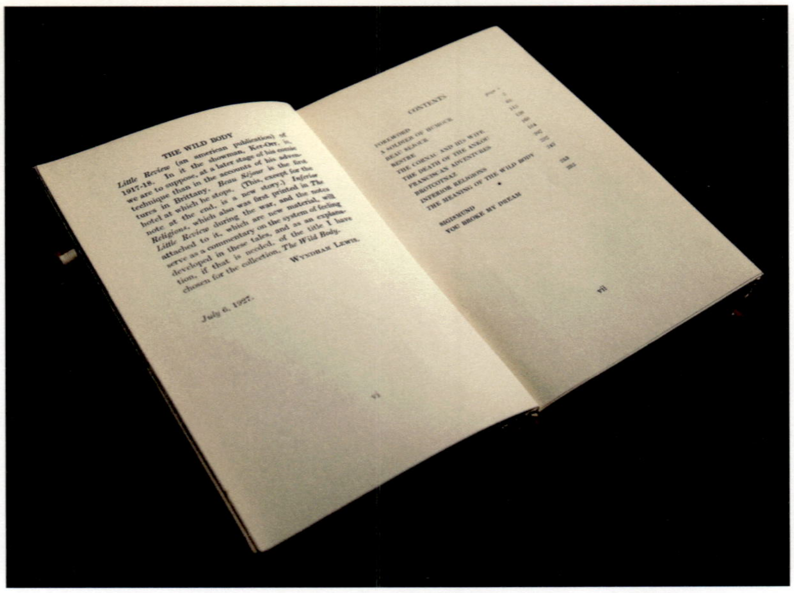
THE WILD BODY
CONTENTS
July 6, 1927.
WYNDHAM LEWIS

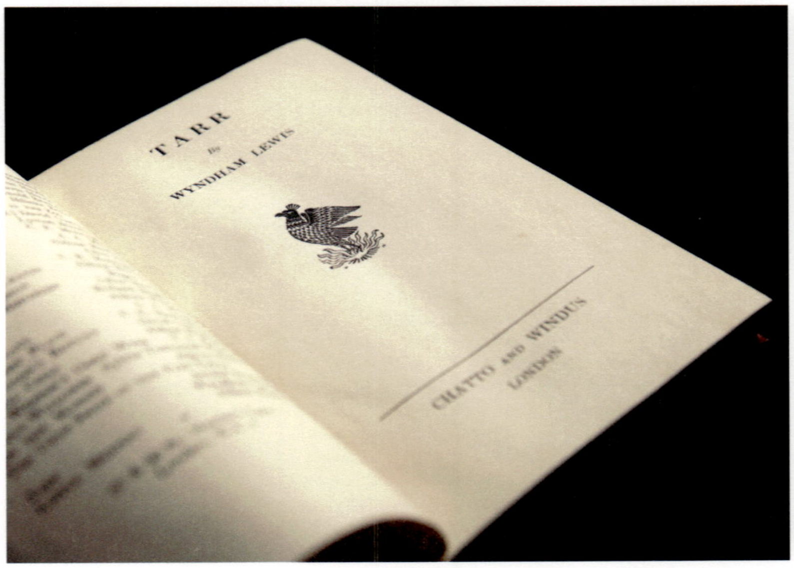
TARR
By
WYNDHAM LEWIS
CHATTO AND WINDUS
LONDON

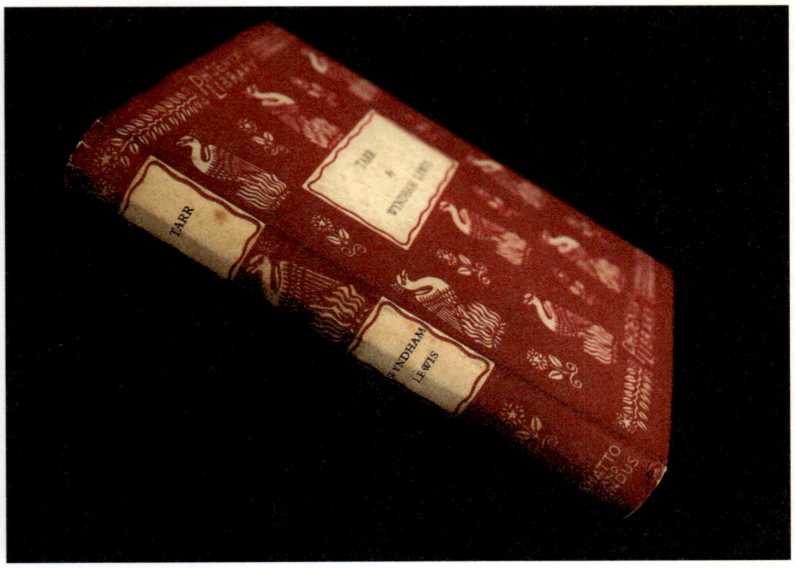
TARR
WYNDHAM LEWIS

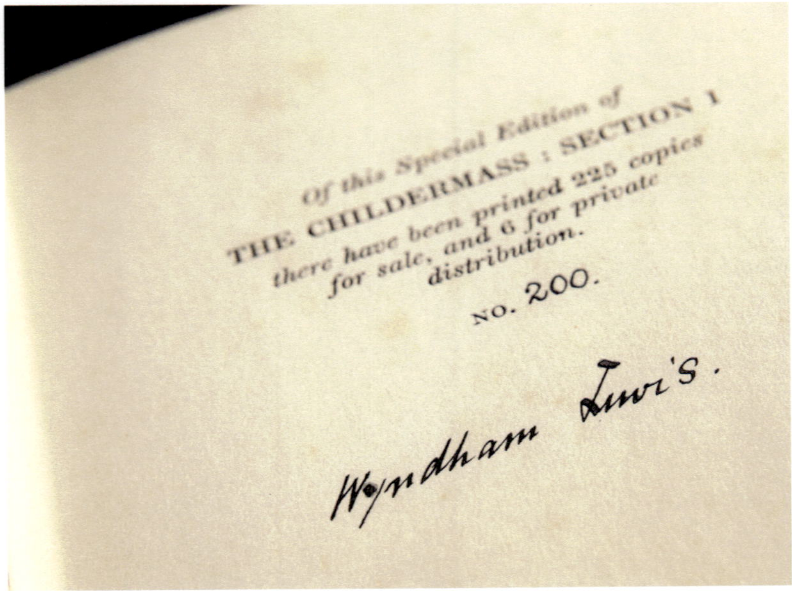
Of this Special Edition of
THE CHILDERMASS : SECTION 1
there have been printed 225 copies
for sale, and 6 for private
distribution.
NO. 200.
Wyndham Lewis.

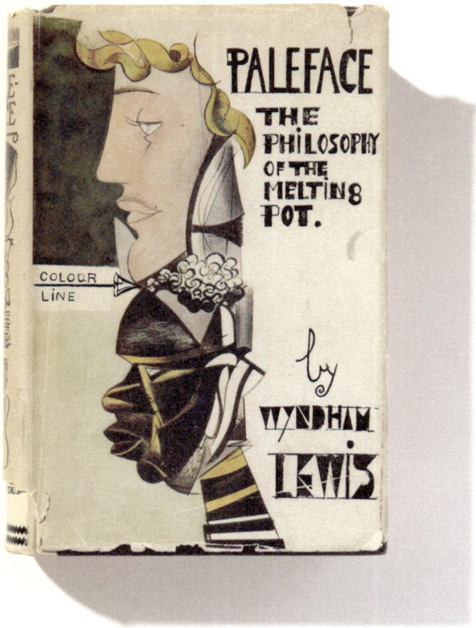

20

Paleface: The Philosophy of the "Melting Pot"
(London: Chatto and Windus, 1929) 20.8 x 14 cm
PRIVATE COLLECTION YMJB

The book expands and complicates the arguments of the essay published in *The Enemy*, No. 2 (B&M Cat. 15). Lewis believes that the European world is once again under threat, this time from ideologies of primitivism that would reduce it to mindless mechanical functionalism. His answer is a "new" West, based on a synthesis of European traditions and oriental ones (obviating also the chance of another European "civil" war). Lewis's aim is internationalist, as is confirmed by the contemporaneous advocacy of a "World Art" in the essay, "A World Art and Tradition." So Lewis advocates a European melting pot (on the analogy of the American melting pot), to induce a racial fellow-feeling among the European peoples. All this sounds suspiciously like Nazi *Blutsgefuhl* (which Lewis would endorse in the 1931 *Hitler*, (B&M Cat. 26)), but Lewis makes no suggestion of excluding Jews and suggests that Asian and African populations should also join the racial fusion in the future.

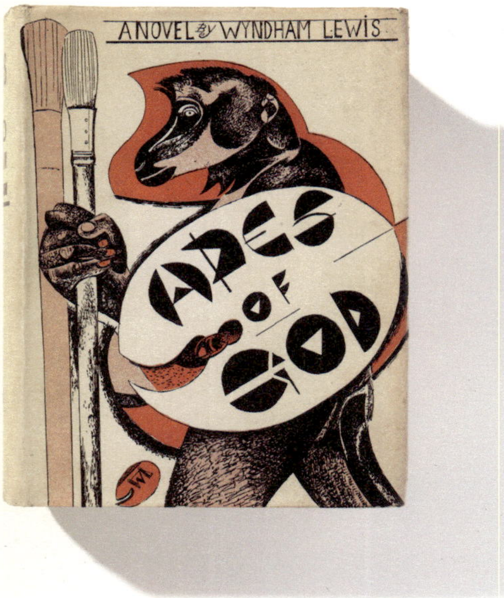

21

The Apes of God
(London: The Arthur Press, 1930) 25.7 x 20.5 cm
PRIVATE COLLECTION YMJB.
WYNDHAM LEWIS MEMORIAL TRUST

22

[Not in exhibition]
The Apes of God
(New York: MacBride, 1932) 20.7 x 14.3 cm

23

The Apes of God
(London: Arco Publishers Ltd, 1955) 20.7 x 14.3 cm
PRIVATE COLLECTION YMJB

Lewis's usual publisher, Chatto and Windus, would not pay him anything like what he considered this novel to be worth, so, using the "Arthur Press" imprint invented for publication of *The Enemy* (B&M Cats. 14–16), Lewis issued it himself, with the support of Sir Nicholas Waterhouse. The first, signed edition was issued in 750 copies printed on Basingwerk Parchment. The sheer size and physical weight of the book testify to Lewis's monumental intentions for this satire on the London art scene. The novel synthesises many of the observations made in *The Art of Being Ruled* (B&M Cat. 10). Its theme is revolution, for which the arts are supposed in Lewis's view to provide the visionary goals. But a simulacrum of revolution obtains in England and the arts are in the hands of a frivolous upper-class imitation of a real avant-garde: wealthy amateurs or "apes of God." Many of those satirised in the novel were colleagues and patrons who associated with Lewis in the 1920s. Much of the novel is farcical, but it has deeper theological and anthropological dimensions. The extremity of Lewis's stylistic invention seems to be holding a threatening nihilism at bay. Perhaps because many of the characters in the novel are travesties of known originals, it was one of the few books by Lewis to be an economic success. Yet it led to further isolation from the people who were the natural audience for his work and painting. In 1955, a 25th anniversary edition was published. Lewis was by then blind and ailing. He produced a new foreword, and a new cover was designed by Michael Ayrton, the young British artist who had become friends with Lewis after the Second World War.

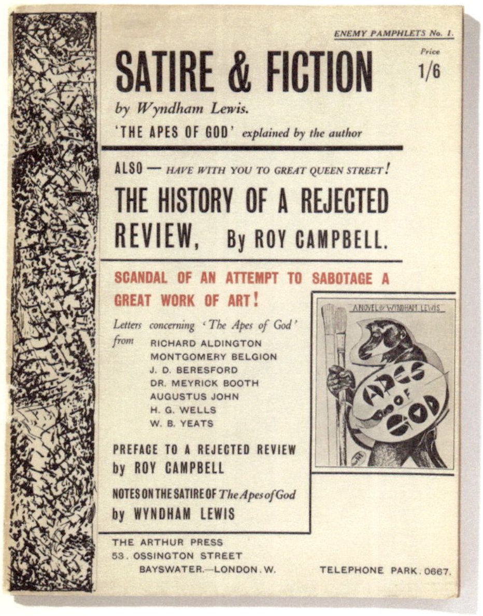

24

Satire & Fiction: Enemy Pamphlet No. 1
(London: The Arthur Press, 1930) 28.2 x 21.1 cm
WYNDHAM LEWIS MEMORIAL TRUST

As part of his publicity campaign for *The Apes of God* (B&M Cats. 21–23), Lewis issued this pamphlet, printing a favourable review by Roy Campbell that had been rejected by the editor of the weekly *New Statesman*. Numerous testimonials solicited from other writers are also included. An inserted flyer, "A Stop-Press Explosion from Another Quarter," recounts how two of Lewis's paintings, *Kermesse* (1912) (M. P4; see Cat. 19) and *Plan of War* (1913–14) (M. P12) had been offered for sale at knock-down prices in a personal advert in *The Times*. The seller was Richard Wyndham, who had bought them for the price of a case of champagne on the death of Lewis's American patron, John Quinn, in 1923. Wyndham resented the satirical portrayal of him as the grotesque simpleton "Dick Whittingdon" in *The Apes*. The paintings have not been seen since.

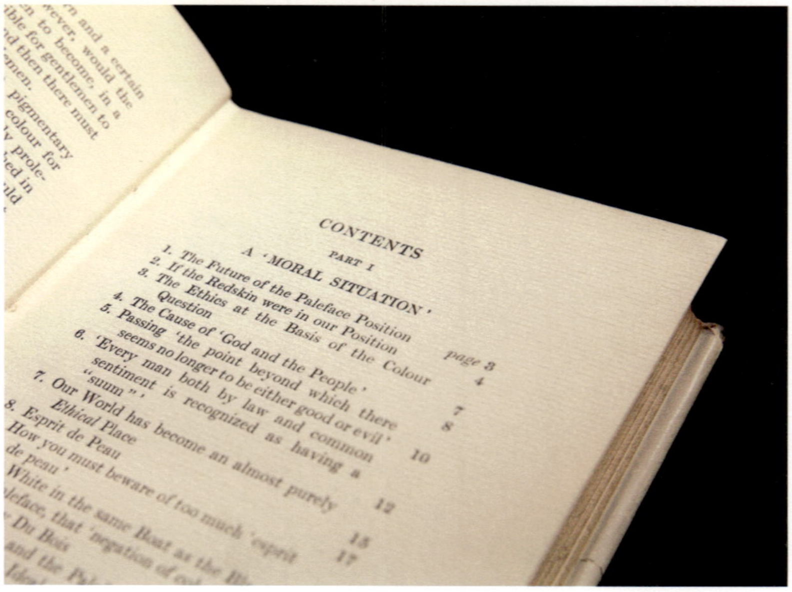
CONTENTS
PART I
A 'MORAL SITUATION'
1. The Future of the Paleface Position page 3
2. If the Redskin were in our Position 4
3. The Ethics at the Basis of the Colour Question
4. The Cause of 'God and the People' 7
5. Passing 'the point beyond which there seems no longer to be either good or evil' 8
6. 'Every man both by law and common sentiment is recognized as having a "suum"' 10
7. Our World has become an almost purely Ethical Place 12
8. Esprit de Peau

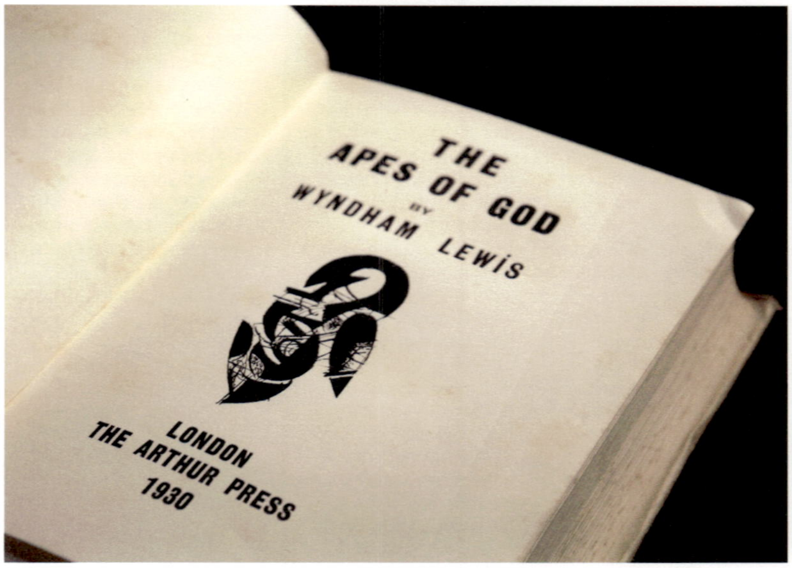
THE
APES OF GOD
BY
WYNDHAM LEWIS
LONDON
THE ARTHUR PRESS
1930

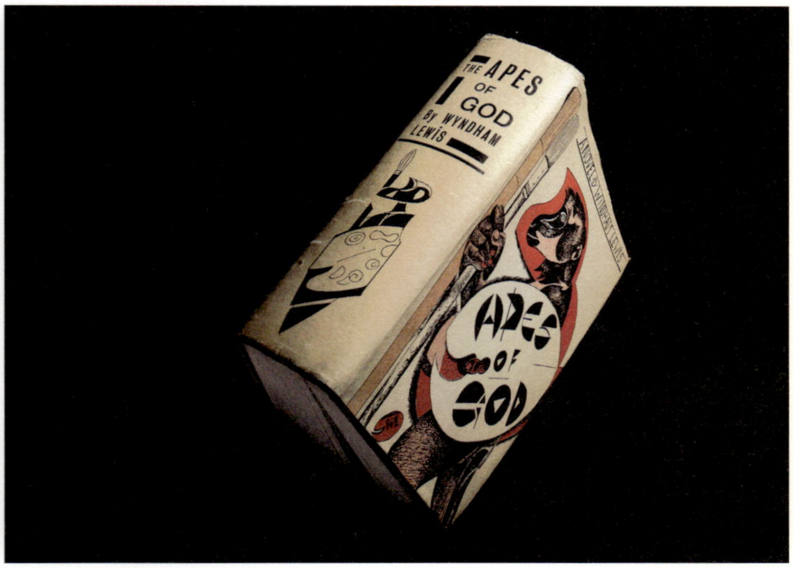
THE APES OF GOD
BY WYNDHAM LEWIS
APES OF GOD

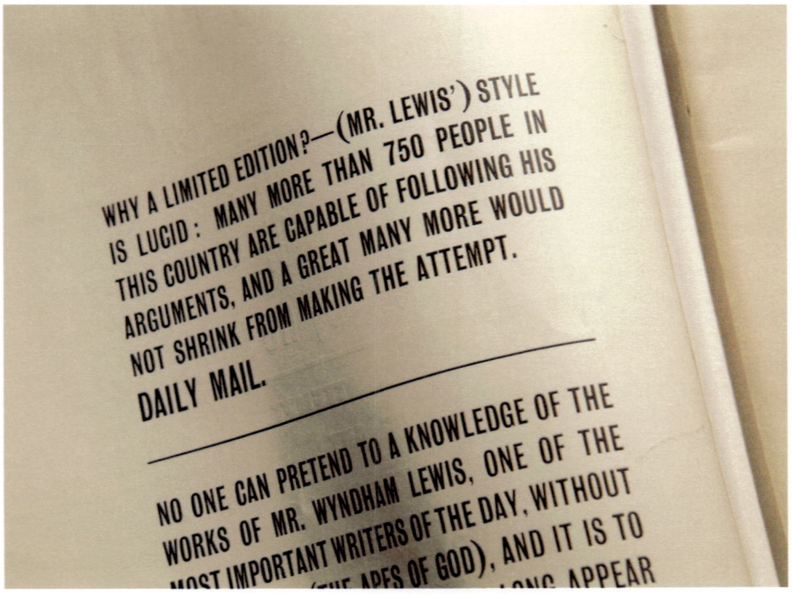
WHY A LIMITED EDITION?—(MR. LEWIS') STYLE IS LUCID: MANY MORE THAN 750 PEOPLE IN THIS COUNTRY ARE CAPABLE OF FOLLOWING HIS ARGUMENTS, AND A GREAT MANY MORE WOULD NOT SHRINK FROM MAKING THE ATTEMPT.
DAILY MAIL.
NO ONE CAN PRETEND TO A KNOWLEDGE OF THE WORKS OF MR. WYNDHAM LEWIS, ONE OF THE MOST IMPORTANT WRITERS OF THE DAY, WITHOUT

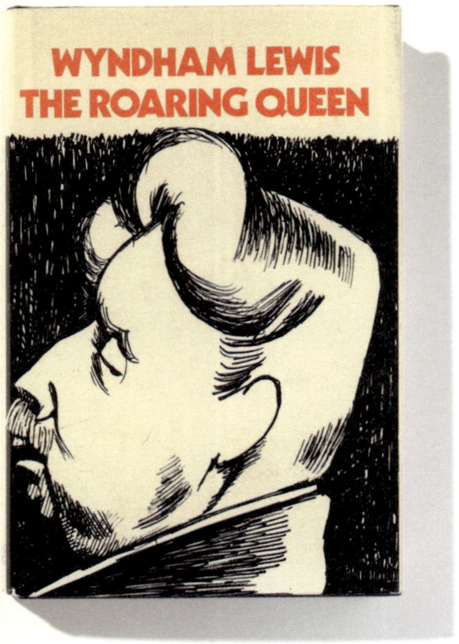

25

The Roaring Queen
(London: Secker and Warburg, 1973) 22.3 x 14.4 cm
COVER BY MICHAEL AYRTON.
PRIVATE COLLECTION YMJB

This satire on the world of book reviewing and of literary prizes was begun in 1930 and completed in 1932. It is a parody of a detective novel. The chief butt of its satire was the novelist Arnold Bennett, who was the head book reviewer on the *Evening Standard* and could affect book sales disproportionately by his comments – or so it was generally believed. Like others of the time, Lewis thought of Bennett as someone who reduced literature to a merely commercial trade. Others in the book world are also satirised (including Virginia Woolf) and no publisher was prepared to handle the book for fear of litigation. Jonathan Cape set the book in type and produced some proof copies in 1936, but backed out of publishing it at the last minute. Only in 1973, after all potential litigants were dead, did it appear. Michael Ayrton's cover caricatures Arnold Bennett.

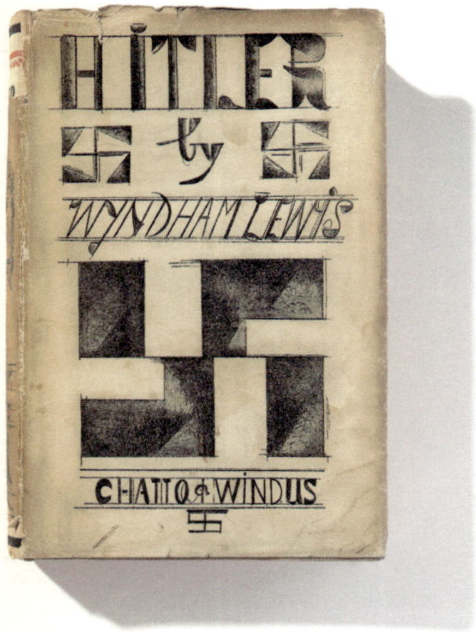

26

Hitler
(London: Chatto and Windus, 1931) 20.9 x 13.8 cm
PRIVATE COLLECTION YMJB

Lewis visited Germany in late 1930 to negotiate contracts for translations of his books into German. *Hitler* (which was serialised in the magazine, *Time and Tide*, before appearing in revised book form) was presented by Lewis as a record of his observations of the political scene in Germany during the visit. The book is sympathetic to National Socialism and presents Hitler as a "man of peace" whose anti-Semitic views (though unpalatable to an English audience) were unexceptional in Germany and should not be allowed to obscure his merits. The Nazis offered a bulwark against Communism and promised to restore the German economy. In fact, Lewis had been interested in far-right Nationalist movements for some time, and in a 1926 draft of "The Revolutionary Simpleton" (University of Buffalo Department of Rare Books) registered an emotional attraction to *Action Française*, Sinn Fein and "hackenkreuzler gunmen" (i.e. Nazi thugs) but nevertheless insisted that their reactionary views would lead to "the deadliest impasse": "They have no programme of which I have heard for absorbing what is novel and technically alive in the modern world."
In 1930 things looked different; the world had suffered the Great Crash of 1929 and subsequent Depression; Hitler had won 107 seats in the elections to the Reichstag in September, and he offered an economic policy that would throw off the burden of international debt and exploit the full productive potential of a modern economy. In what he called these "emergency conditions," Lewis swallowed Nazi propaganda whole, as many of his critics pointed out. Nevertheless, the full effect of the book on his career and reputation did not begin until 1933, when Hitler came to power.
As well as tendentious arguments in favour of Hitler, the book contains lively and satirical accounts of Berlin nightlife (to which Lewis had no moral objections).

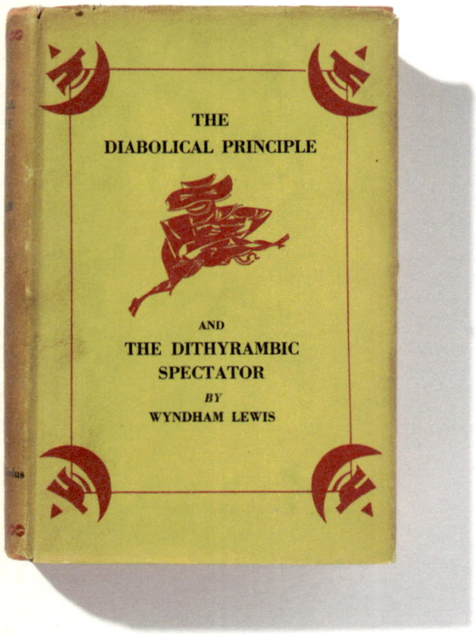

27

The Diabolical Principle and the Dithyrambic Spectator
(London: Chatto and Windus, 1931) 19.5 x 13 cm
PRIVATE COLLECTION YMJB

This book reprints two previously published essays, the first an essay in *The Enemy*, No. 3 (B&M Cat. 16) and the second, an essay in *The Calendar of Modern Letters* in 1926. "The Dithyrambic Spectator" attacks Jane Harrison's account of the origins of art in the religious rituals of ancient Greece in her 1913 book, *Ancient Art and Ritual*. Lewis's point is not so much that the account is mistaken as that it seems to have an ambition to lead art back to those origins, to break down the distinction between the players and the audience, the professionals and the amateurs, thus eliminating the essential aesthetic difference from life on which artistic experience depends. In contrast, Lewis praises Elliot Smith's account in *The Evolution of the Dragon* (1919) of the origins of art in the mummification practices of the ancient Egyptians. Lewis's continuing fascination with such ideas and their implications is visible in the late painting, *The Island* (Cat. 200). "The Diabolical Principle" is an attack on the editors of the Paris-based avant-garde magazine, *transition*. Lewis believed that they valued experimental art for its destructive revolutionary effect and that they were fundamentally interested in undermining society rather than in new forms of art. The literary Surrealism that they championed was anyway not a new form of thought but a simple inversion of conventional values, and was thus a recrudescence of the "immoralism" of the 1890s rather than a product of an original imagination.

"But if there is one thing … that does not produce art, it is the sentiment of power. Art has nothing to do with punching-power or blasting-power, or with crude speed – with the images of brutal force, or of colossal scale (witness Egypt in decay, with its immense, dull statuary). And the most gigantic power-station is controlling a power against which the power that is resident in art cannot be measured, for they have nothing in common."

Wyndham Lewis,
Power-Feeling and Machine-Age Art, 1934

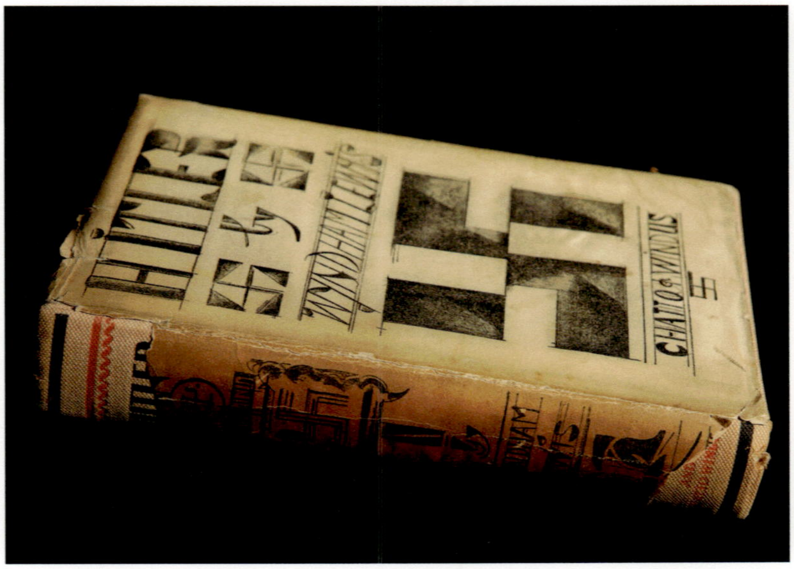

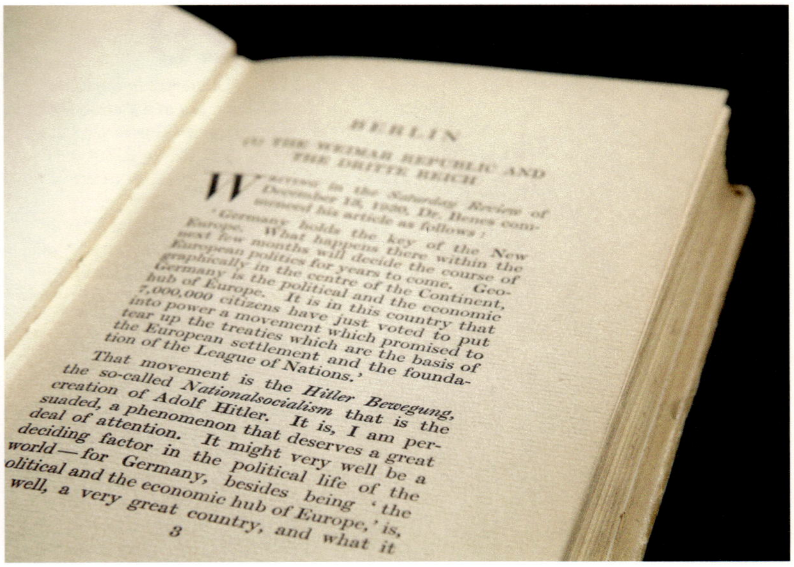

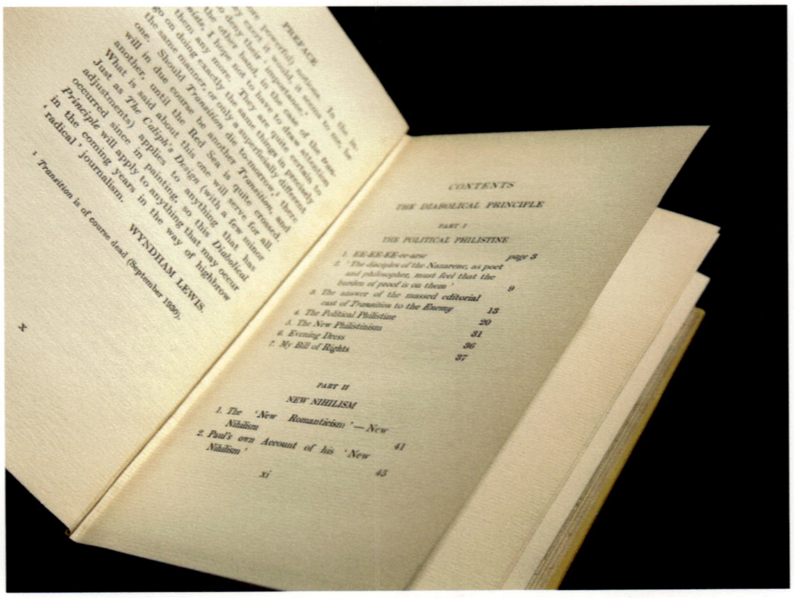

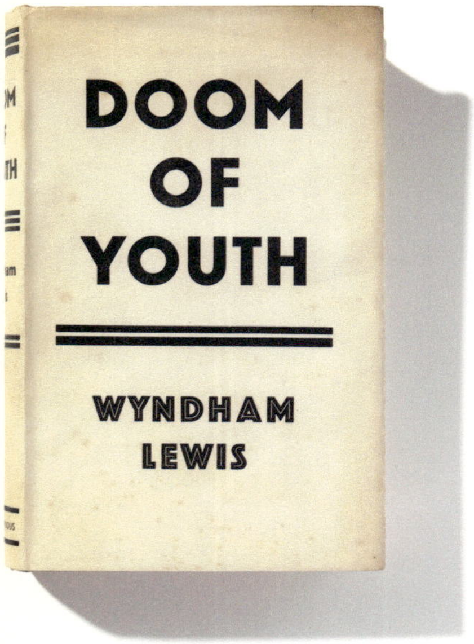

28

The Doom of Youth
(London: Chatto and Windus, 1932) 22.8 x 15.2 cm
WYNDHAM LEWIS MEMORIAL TRUST

This is a sociological and cultural analysis of "youth politics" and the exaltation of youth in the popular press. The title parodies that of Alec Waugh's 1917 novel, *The Loom of Youth*, and certain passages in it caused Waugh (and another writer) to threaten to sue for libel. The publisher withdrew the book in spite of Lewis's protests. As a result he published no more books with Chatto and Windus. *The Doom of Youth* extends *The Art of Being Ruled*'s (B&M Cat. 10) thesis that modern capitalism promotes "wars" between men and women, between classes and between generations in a strategy of "divide and rule." Youth was "doomed" according to Lewis because it would lose the privileged position it traditionally held in western societies by being incorporated as cheap labour into the capitalist economy. Lewis also predicts that capitalism will erode traditional gender-differences, leading to a "neuter class – saturated with sex" (p. 201). The most striking thing about the book is its "gallery of exhibits" in which articles from popular newspapers are reproduced and analysed. Whatever the weaknesses in Lewis's case, in its methods the book was a pioneering work of cultural analysis.

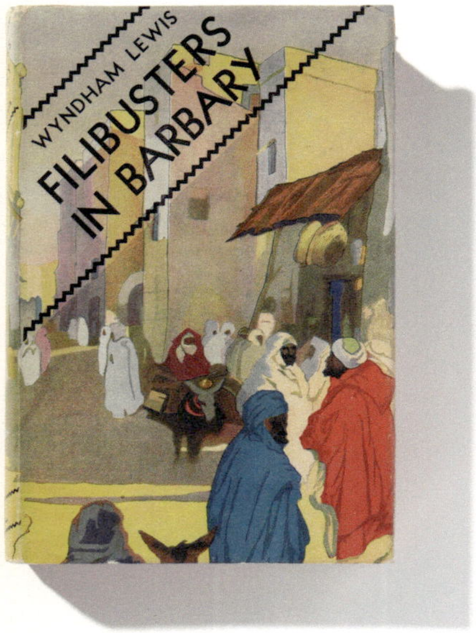

29

Filibusters in Barbary: Record of a Visit to the Sous
(London: Grayson and Grayson, 1932) 22.6 x 15.2 cm
WYNDHAM LEWIS MEMORIAL TRUST

After a serious illness requiring surgery, Lewis went with his wife to North Africa in 1931 and *Filibusters in Barbary* is a record of the visit. Lewis was particularly concerned about the deleterious effects of the European Depression on the colonised society of Morocco. He admired the architecture and culture of the Berbers, who he believed to be ethnically closer to European peoples than to the Arabs. The book is thus more than a simple narrative of travel, though as a travel book it contains some of Lewis's best comic writing.

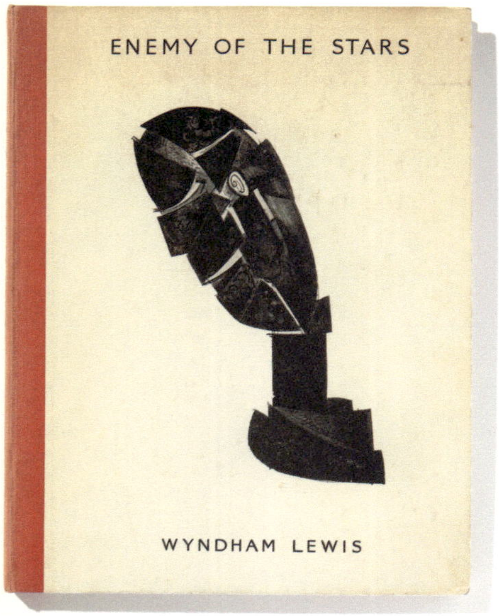

30

Enemy of the Stars
(London: Desmond Harmsworth, 1932)

31

Enemy of the Stars
(London: Desmond Harmsworth, 1932) (variant binding)

32

Enemy of the Stars
(London: Desmond Harmsworth, 1932) (variant binding) 28.9 x 22.2 cm
PRIVATE COLLECTION YMJB.
WYNDHAM LEWIS MEMORIAL TRUST

Enemy of the Stars was first published in *Blast*, No. 1 (B&M Cat. 2) in 1914. Lewis revised and expanded it for this new edition, adding an essay that he had first published in 1925, "The Physics of the Not-Self," as a commentary. The version in *Blast* is a landmark in English modernism, rejecting naturalism for an Expressionist puppet style that was clearly influenced by cinema. Lewis's language and syntax are harsh, abstract and at times obscure to the point of opacity. The play recounts the efforts of the protagonist, Arghol, to free himself from the entanglements and compromises of material life and human society, which he feels have replaced his authentic self with a simulacrum that pollutes his soul's original purity. He has fled from the city to lead the simple life of a labourer in his uncle's rural wheelwright's yard, where he practises a self-punishing asceticism. But here he attracts the discipleship of the more animal Hanp, a fellow worker, whom he uses as a sounding board for his arguments about nature and the self. Influenced by this discourse, Hanp becomes an imitation Arghol and is then violently rejected by the (yet again) polluted original. In resentful revenge, Hanp eventually kills, first, Arghol (the thing he loves) and then himself. Lewis's 1932 revision makes the language more conventional, filling out the syntactic gaps and making the speeches more naturalistic and, at times, comic. The range of philosophical reference is widened and other characters are introduced. The revision has attracted less critical commentary than the first and, though in places its revisions help clarify the meaning of passages in the first version, the additions do not add to the play's comprehensibility and philosophical coherence.

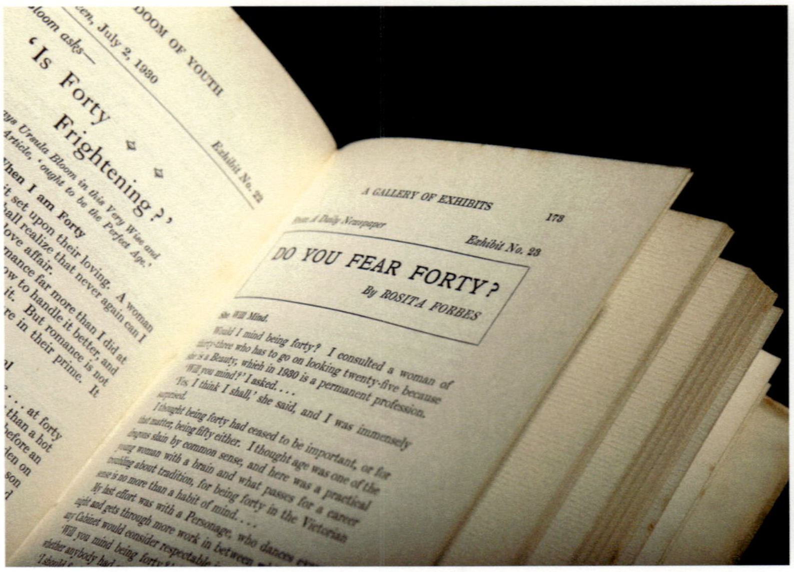
DOOM OF YOUTH
'Is Forty Frightening?'
A GALLERY OF EXHIBITS 173
From A Daily Newspaper
Exhibit No. 23
DO YOU FEAR FORTY?
By ROSITA FORBES

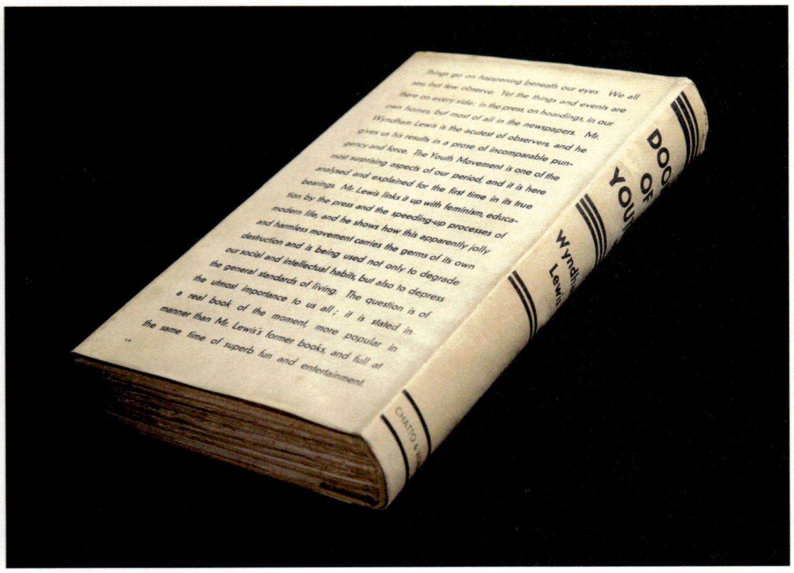
Things go on happening beneath our eyes. We all see, but few observe. Yet the things and events are there on every side: in the press, on hoardings, in our own homes, but most of all in the newspapers. Mr. Wyndham Lewis is the acutest of observers, and he gives us his results in a prose of incomparable pungency and force. The Youth Movement is one of the most surprising aspects of our period, and it is here analysed and explained for the first time in its true bearings. Mr. Lewis links it up with feminism, education by the press and the speeding-up processes of modern life, and he shows how this apparently jolly and harmless movement carries the germs of its own destruction and is being used not only to degrade our social and intellectual habits, but also to depress the general standards of living. The question is of the utmost importance to us all; it is stated in a real book of the moment, more popular in manner than Mr. Lewis's former books, and full at the same time of superb fun and entertainment.
DOOM OF YOUTH
Wyndham Lewis
CHATTO & WINDUS

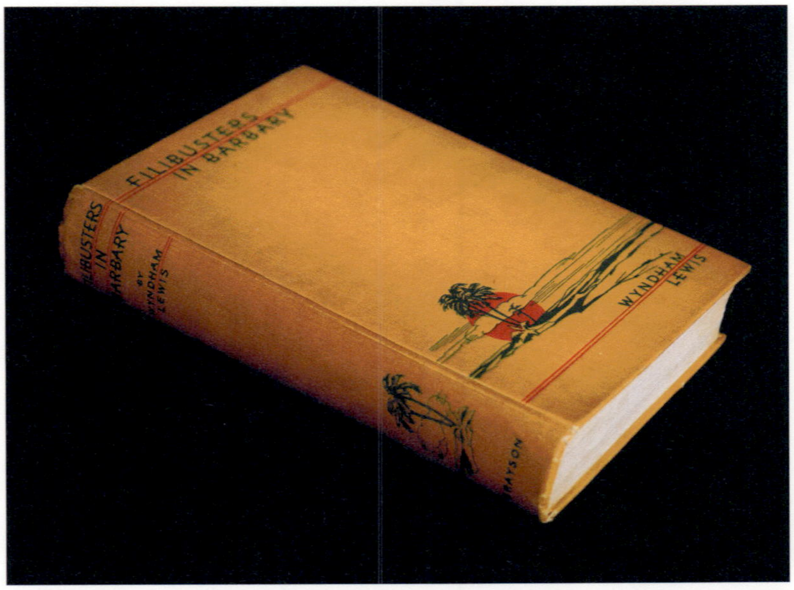
FILIBUSTERS IN BARBARY
WYNDHAM LEWIS
FILIBUSTERS IN BARBARY
BY WYNDHAM LEWIS
GRAYSON

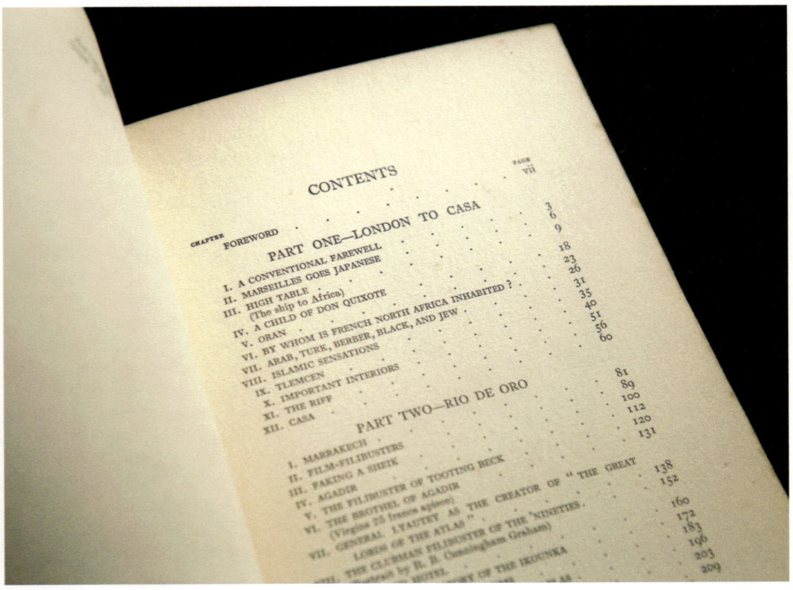
CONTENTS
PAGE vii
CHAPTER
FOREWORD 3
PART ONE—LONDON TO CASA 6
I. A CONVENTIONAL FAREWELL 9
II. MARSEILLES GOES JAPANESE 18
III. HIGH TABLE 23
(The ship to Africa) 26
IV. A CHILD OF DON QUIXOTE 31
V. ORAN 35
VI. BY WHOM IS FRENCH NORTH AFRICA INHABITED? 40
VII. ARAB, TURK, BERBER, BLACK, AND JEW 51
VIII. ISLAMIC SENSATIONS 56
IX. TLEMCEN 60
X. IMPORTANT INTERIORS
XI. THE RIFF
XII. CASA
PART TWO—RIO DE ORO 81
I. MARRAKECH 89
II. FILM-FILIBUSTERS 100
III. FAKING A SHEIK 112
IV. AGADIR 120
V. THE FILIBUSTER OF TOOTING BECK 131
VI. THE BROTHEL OF AGADIR
(Virgins 25 francs apiece) 138
VII. GENERAL LYAUTEY AS THE CREATOR OF "THE GREAT 152
LORDS OF THE ATLAS" 160
THE CLUBMAN FILIBUSTER OF THE 'NINETIES 172
(Portrait by R. B. Cunninghame Graham) 183
196
203
209

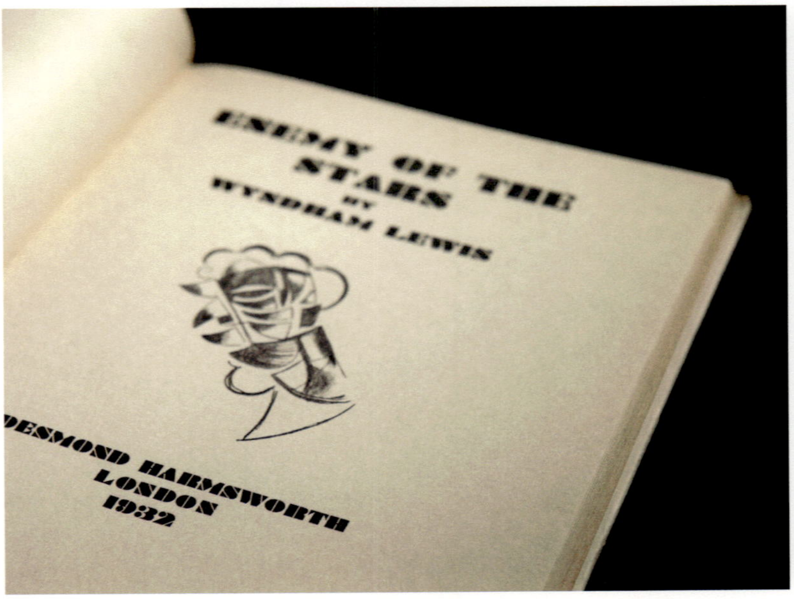
ENEMY OF THE STARS
BY
WYNDHAM LEWIS
DESMOND HARMSWORTH
LONDON
1932

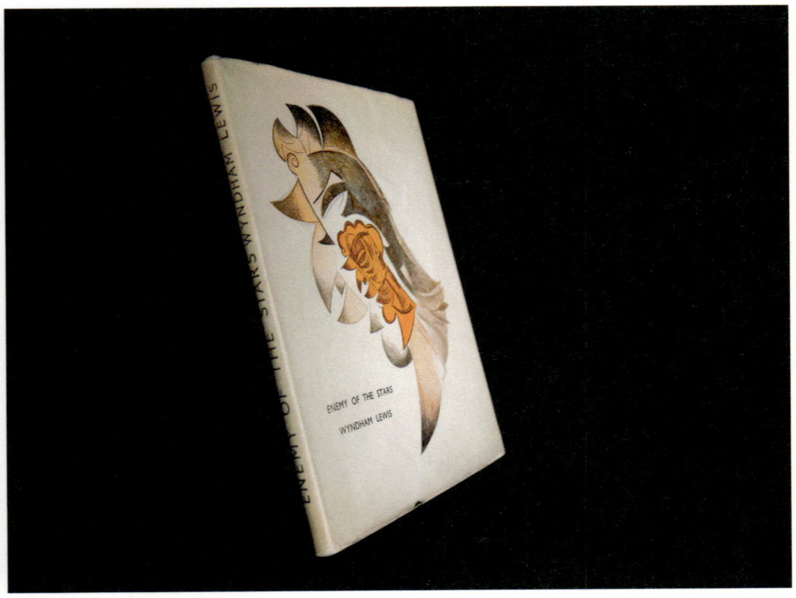
ENEMY OF THE STARS WYNDHAM LEWIS
ENEMY OF THE STARS
WYNDHAM LEWIS

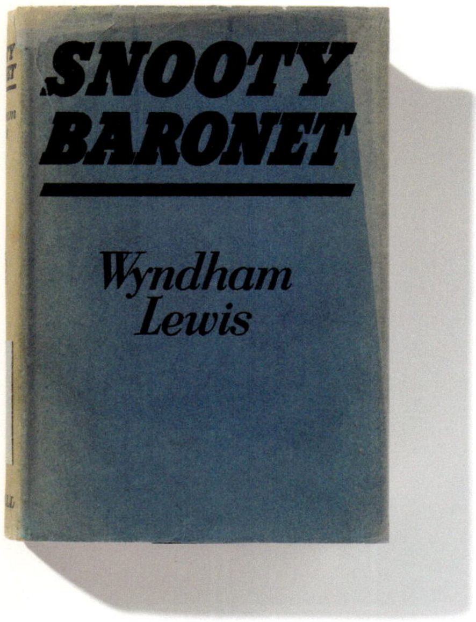

33

Snooty Baronet
(London: Cassell, 1932)
19.6 x 13.5 cm
WYNDHAM LEWIS MEMORIAL TRUST

After leaving Chatto and Windus, Lewis signed a contract for three books with Cassell, and *Snooty Baronet* was the first of these. It is a heartlessly comic novel – probably Lewis's funniest – narrated in the first person by the eponymous "snooty baronet," Sir Michael Kell-Imrie. This character is (like Lewis's other first-person narrator, Ker-Orr, in *The Wild Body* (B&M Cat. 17)) a monster of egotism, but surpasses him in sociopathic solipsism. He is a behaviourist writer of popular science books and the story is about a publicity stunt organised by Kell-Imrie's literary agent, in which Kell-Imrie should be kidnapped and ransomed by a Persian bandit, resulting in big sales for his next book. All goes to plan until, at the last moment in the mêlée, Kell-Imrie raises his gun and shoots the agent dead. What the novel is really concerned with is exposing the damage caused both individually and culturally by the trauma of the First World War (Kell-Imrie is a maimed survivor of the trenches). Behaviourism (whose tenets the character exemplifies) was denounced by Lewis in *Time and Western Man* (B&M Cats. 12 and 13) as a theory and practice devised specifically for turning human beings into war-like automatons for enlistment in the First World War.

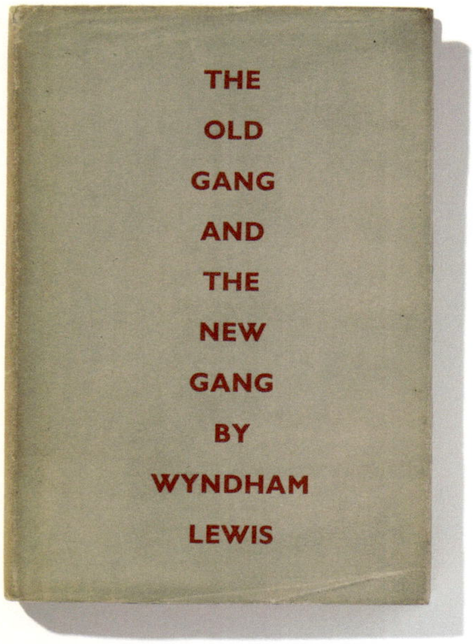

34

The Old Gang and the New Gang
(London: Desmond Harmsworth, 1933)
19.5 x 13.5 cm
WYNDHAM LEWIS MEMORIAL TRUST

After the suppression of *The Doom of Youth* (B&M Cat. 26), Lewis salvaged part of its argument for this short pamphlet. He concentrates particularly on the effect of the literature of the First World War (then coming to a peak) in fostering hostility between the generations. Lewis regards as simplistic the tactic of blaming the older generation for the calamity that was visited on their offspring. What is most remarkable in the book is the depth of Lewis's own indignation about the war, however, and his representation of it as a unique horror that lies outside the range of those artistic strategies that his own work always deploys: irony, caricature and aesthetic detachment. He denounces Erich Maria Remarque's *Im Westen Nichts Neues* (1929) for all three.

> No 'detachment' is possible, for a man – especially for a man who has taken part in these events – in such a case as this! [...] This sort of history is not, and cannot be, an 'aesthetic' transaction as between a soldier and civilians [...] That event – the war of 1914–18 – transcended all those conditions, on behalf of which such rules are made. It is a question for mankind. (p. 55)

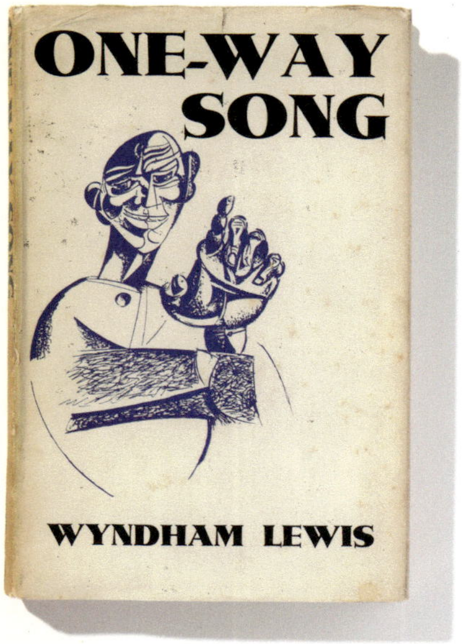

35

One-Way Song
(London: Faber and Faber, 1933)
22.6 x 14.8 cm
PRIVATE COLLECTION YMJB

When a student, Lewis had been known as "the poet" by his friends, but, apart from a short poem published in 1910 ("Grignolles," a meditation on a town in Brittany), *One-Way Song* contained the only poetry he ever published. It comprises four satirical, argumentative poems and an envoi, modelled in their style on the rough hectoring verse of Elizabethan satire. It contains an *apologia* ("If so the Man You Are"), both for Lewis and for his "Enemy" persona, including the lines "Is it not fitter that the Brit should know / The sort of Sunlessness makes Hitlers grow?" (p. 54). The longest section resumes Lewis's philosophical and political critique of "Time" doctrines first expounded in *Time and Western Man* (B&M Cats. 12 and 13), here presented with astonishing headlong energy. The ingenuity with which Lewis invents and manipulates imagery in order to give reality to his arguments in the reader's mind is unprecedented since the English "metaphysical" poets of the seventeenth century. He manages, also, to venture into technical arguments about relativity theory and time that had not appeared in the earlier book.

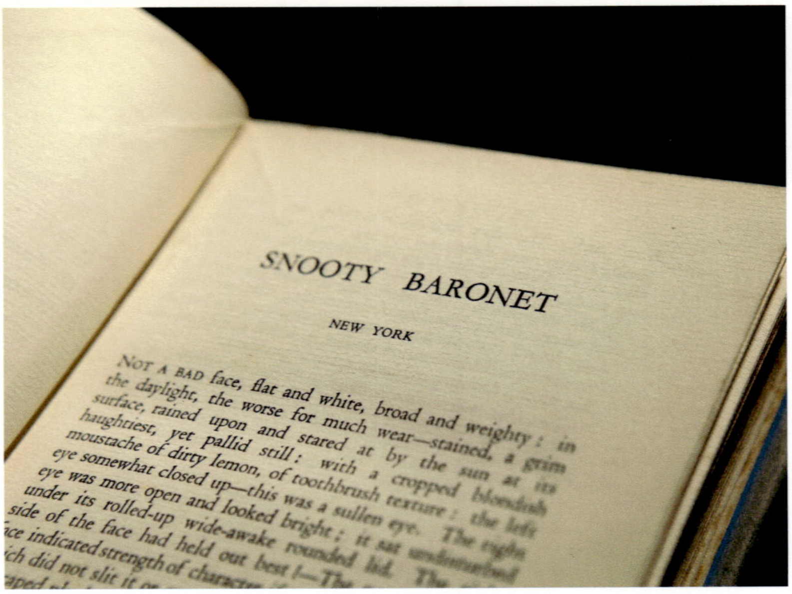
SNOOTY BARONET
NEW YORK
NOT A BAD face, flat and white, broad and weighty: in
the daylight, the worse for much wear—stained, a grim
surface, rained upon and stared at by the sun at its
haughtiest, yet pallid still: with a cropped blondish
moustache of dirty lemon, of toothbrush texture: the left
eye somewhat closed up—this was a sullen eye. The right
eye was more open and looked bright; it sat undisturbed
under its rolled-up wide-awake rounded lid.

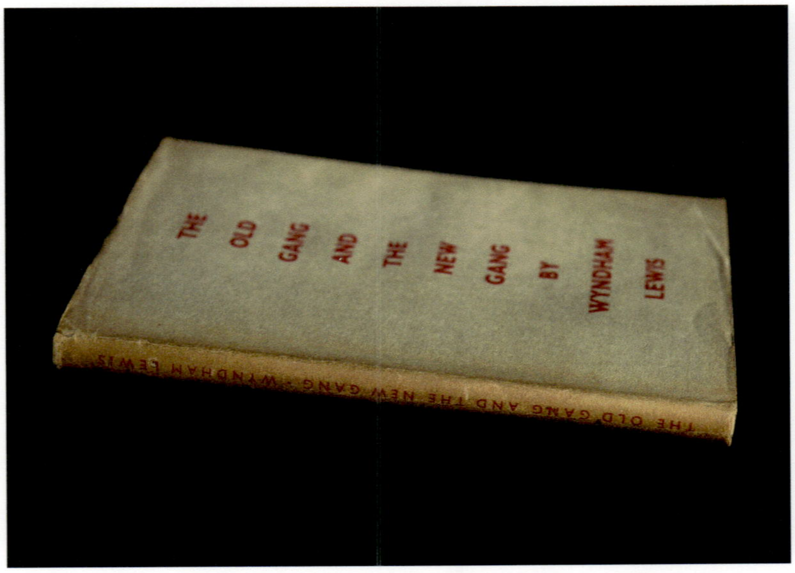
THE OLD GANG AND THE NEW GANG BY WYNDHAM LEWIS
THE OLD GANG AND THE NEW GANG WYNDHAM LEWIS

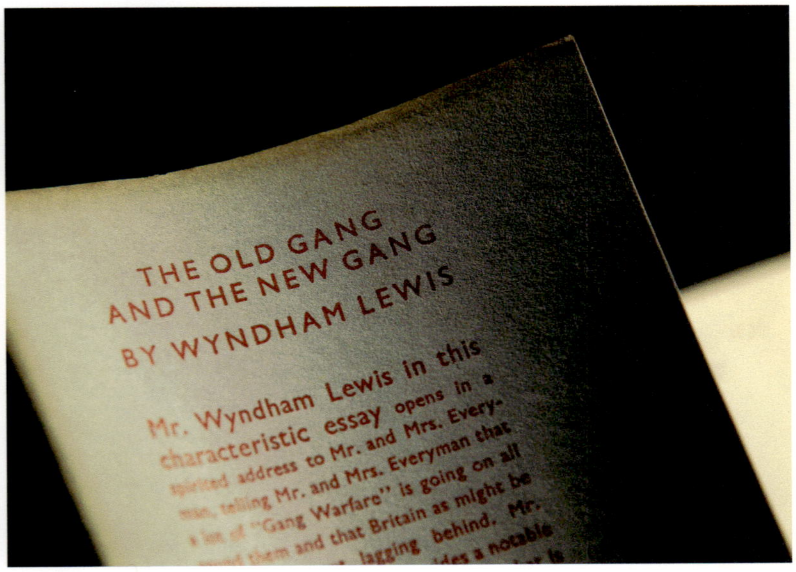
THE OLD GANG
AND THE NEW GANG
BY WYNDHAM LEWIS
Mr. Wyndham Lewis in this
characteristic essay opens in a
spirited address to Mr. and Mrs. Every-
man, telling Mr. and Mrs. Everyman that
a lot of "Gang Warfare" is going on all

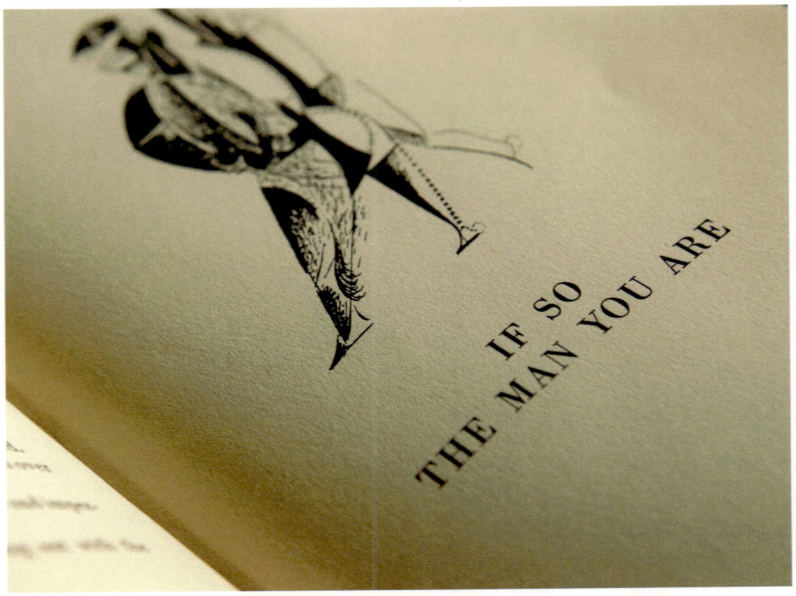
IF SO
THE MAN YOU ARE

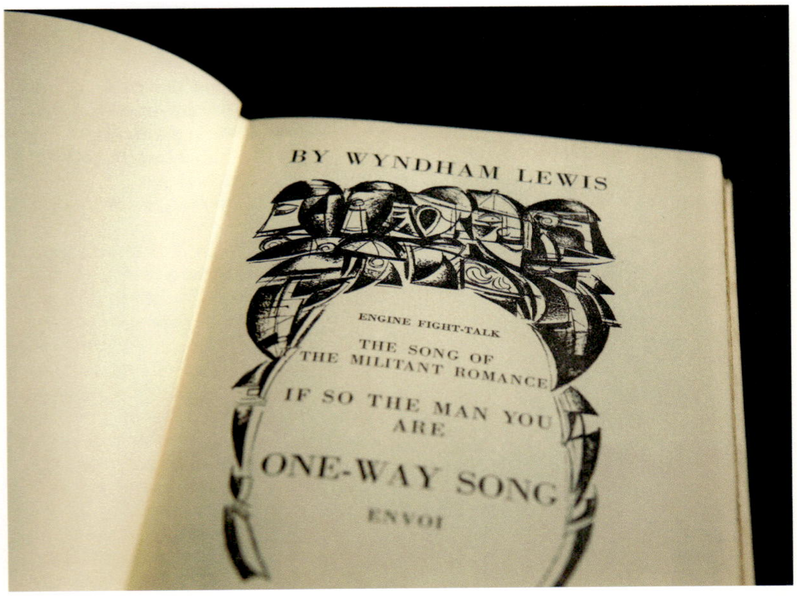
BY WYNDHAM LEWIS
ENGINE FIGHT-TALK
THE SONG OF
THE MILITANT ROMANCE
IF SO THE MAN YOU
ARE
ONE-WAY SONG
ENVOI

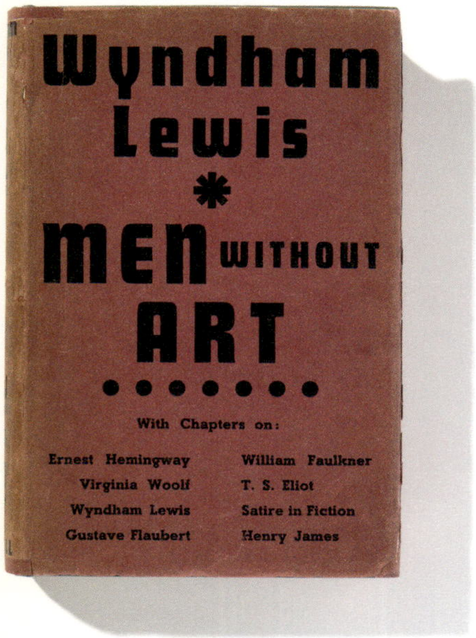

36

Men Without Art
(London: Cassell, 1934)
22.2 x 15.2 cm
WYNDHAM LEWIS MEMORIAL TRUST

This book of literary criticism grew out of *Satire & Fiction* (B&M Cat. 24). True satire, Lewis argues, does not really rely on ethics and has no moralistic purpose. More particularly, the "externalist" satire practised by Lewis himself in *The Apes of God* (B&M Cats. 21–23) is a model of this "metaphysical satire" that requires no justification from outside itself. Lewis extends this point of view so that it becomes a defence of art itself (satire and art becoming virtually synonymous in his argument). *Men Without Art* thus becomes a defence of art against those who insist that it should serve the values of politics, theology or morals. What the book is most memorable for, however, is the series of chapters devoted to analysis of particular writers. Ernest Hemingway was so upset by the chapter on his work ("The Dumb Ox") that he smashed a vase of flowers in the Shakespeare and Company bookshop in Paris, where he came upon it, ruining some of the stock. Another chapter criticises William Faulkner's moralism, while a third gleefully dissects the critical dilemma that T.S. Eliot's theory of impersonality had led him to.

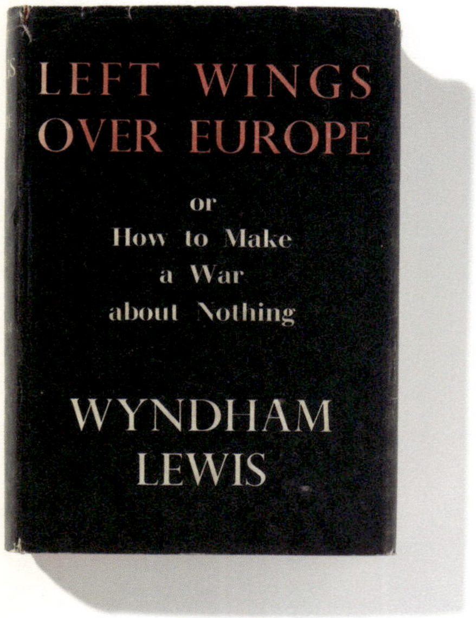

37

Left Wings Over Europe: Or, How to Make a War about Nothing
(London: Jonathan Cape, 1936) 20.6 x 14.6 cm
WYNDHAM LEWIS MEMORIAL TRUST

This book provides a close commentary on international events of 1936 – the German reoccupation of the Rhineland, the Italian invasion of Abyssinia – and argues strongly for Great Britain to respond pacifically and to appease the Fascist dictatorships. Lewis remained convinced that Hitler's aggressive actions were in fact defensive and that Germany offered no threat to world peace. Winston Churchill, who was already warning that the opposite was true, he dismisses as a warmonger. The policy of appeasement that Lewis recommends was actually the one followed by the British (though Lewis remained convinced that their policy was too anti-German). From the point of view of Lewis's political development, the most significant change in this book is a repudiation of his previous internationalism in favour of nationalism. He felt that nationalism was now the securest system to guarantee world peace in 1936. The book sold sufficiently well to warrant reprinting.

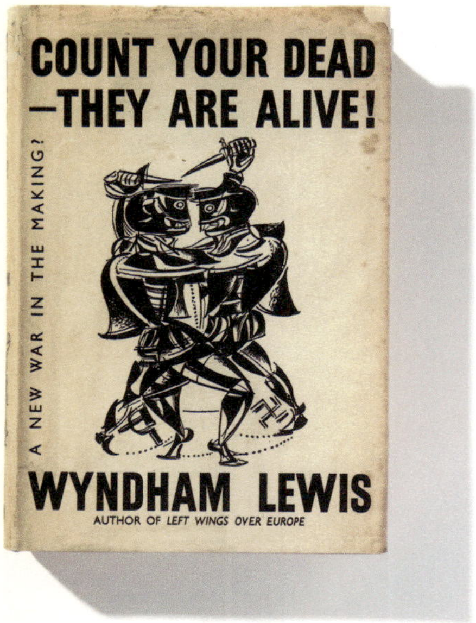

38

Count Your Dead: They are Alive! Or, A New War in the Making
(London: Lovat Dickson, 1937)
20.5 x 14.3 cm
WYNDHAM LEWIS MEMORIAL TRUST

Count Your Dead again concerns itself with the need for British foreign policy to be directed towards avoiding the threat of war. Here the focus is the Spanish Civil War. Lewis presents Francisco Franco as "an ordinary old-fashioned anti-monarchical Spanish *liberal*" who is simply defending Spain against the intervention of Russian Communism (p. 196). Great Britain, he believes, is too sympathetic to the Russians and is anti-German in its response to the Civil War. In his 1950 autobiography, *Rude Assignment* (B&M Cat. 50), Lewis claims that *Count Your Dead* was a "first-rate peace pamphlet," while *Left Wings Over Europe* (B&M Cat. 37) was "quite unimportant" (*Rude Assignment*, p. 211). This valuation of *Count Your Dead* is almost incomprehensible and D.G. Bridson, in his political study of Lewis (*The Filibuster* (1972)), is nearer the mark when he calls it Lewis's worst book. Lewis may have valued the book for its geopolitical understanding: he predicted that a war fought alongside Russia against Germany would leave Britain powerless and would lead to a Soviet hegemony over much of Europe. But he must have forgotten its complete misreading of actual events and intentions (particularly German intentions). For him Nazi Germany remained in a fundamentally defensive posture. It also provided an example to less modern nations, still in thrall to "loan capital," of economic modernisation unimpeded by what Lewis thought of as the sham institutions of democracy. It took a visit to Berlin and Warsaw in late 1937 for him to change his mind and admit that he had been "deceived."

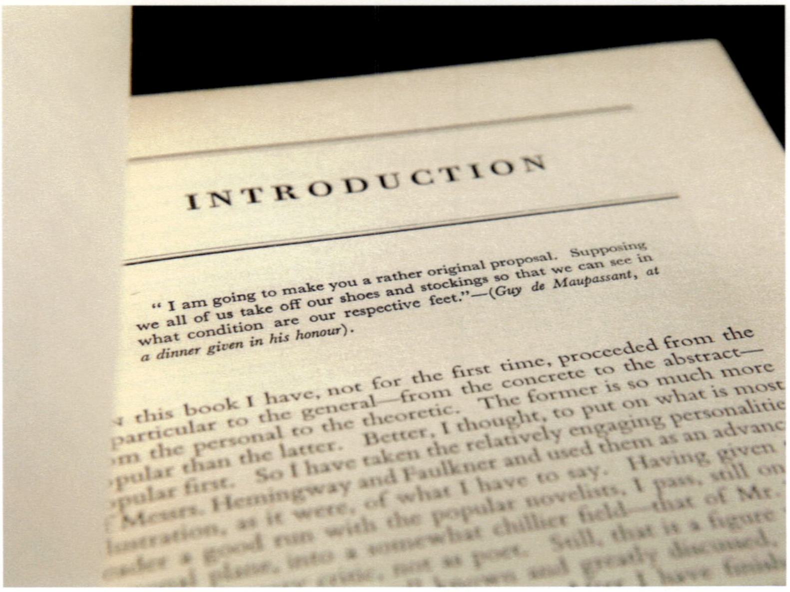
INTRODUCTION
" I am going to make you a rather original proposal. Supposing
we all of us take off our shoes and stockings so that we can see in
what condition are our respective feet."—(Guy de Maupassant, at
a dinner given in his honour).
this book I have, not for the first time, proceeded from the
particular to the general—from the concrete to the abstract—
the personal to the theoretic. The former is so much more
pular than the latter. Better, I thought, to put on what is most
pular first. So I have taken the relatively engaging personalitie
Messrs. Hemingway and Faulkner and used them as an advanc

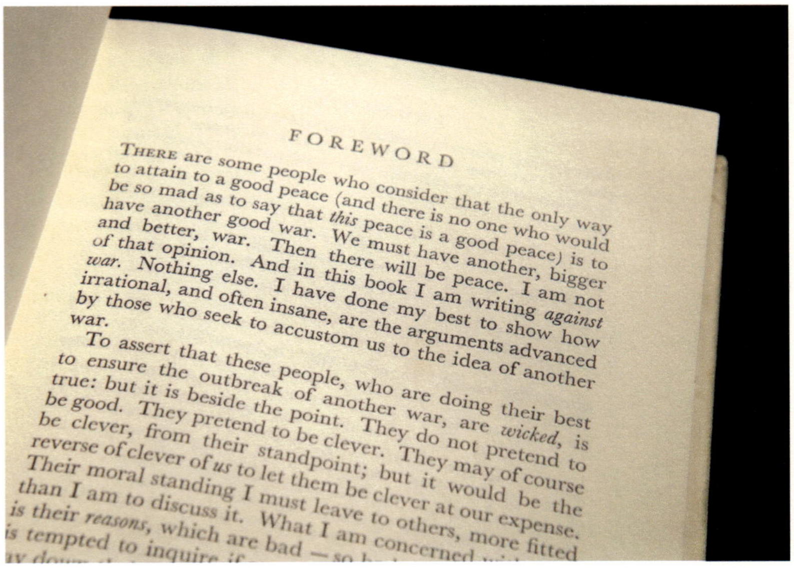
FOREWORD
THERE are some people who consider that the only way
to attain to a good peace (and there is no one who would
be so mad as to say that this peace is a good peace) is to
have another good war. We must have another, bigger
and better, war. Then there will be peace. I am not
of that opinion. And in this book I am writing against
war. Nothing else. I have done my best to show how
irrational, and often insane, are the arguments advanced
by those who seek to accustom us to the idea of another
war.
To assert that these people, who are doing their best
to ensure the outbreak of another war, are wicked, is
true: but it is beside the point. They do not pretend to
be good. They pretend to be clever. They may of course
be clever, from their standpoint; but it would be the
reverse of clever of us to let them be clever at our expense.
Their moral standing I must leave to others, more fitted
than I am to discuss it. What I am concerned
is their reasons, which are bad

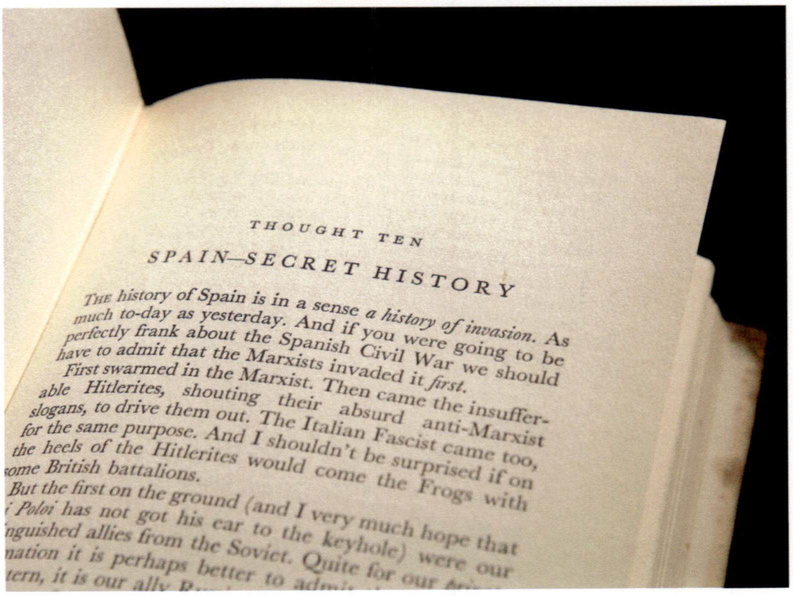
THOUGHT TEN
SPAIN—SECRET HISTORY
THE history of Spain is in a sense a history of invasion. As
much to-day as yesterday. And if you were going to be
perfectly frank about the Spanish Civil War we should
have to admit that the Marxists invaded it first.
First swarmed in the Marxist. Then came the insuffer-
able Hitlerites, shouting their absurd anti-Marxist
slogans, to drive them out. The Italian Fascist came too,
for the same purpose. And I shouldn't be surprised if on
the heels of the Hitlerites would come the Frogs with
some British battalions.
But the first on the ground (and I very much hope that
Polloi has not got his ear to the keyhole) were our
nguished allies from the Soviet. Quite for our
nation it is perhaps better to admi
tern, it is our ally

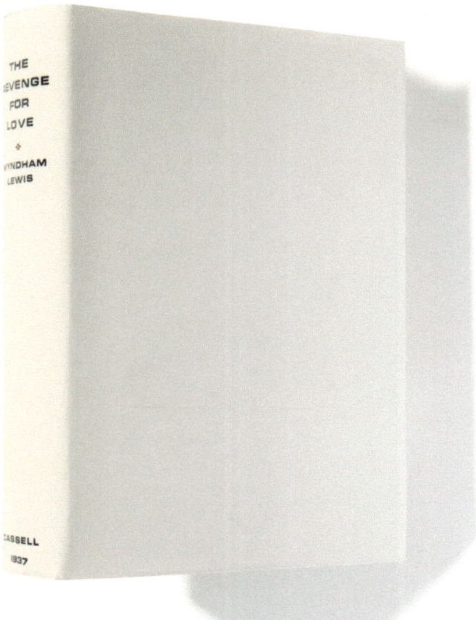

39

The Revenge for Love
(London: Cassell, 1937)
21 x 15 cm
WYNDHAM LEWIS MEMORIAL TRUST

This novel is almost universally regarded as Lewis's best. Written after a visit to the border region of the Pyrenees in 1934 and largely finished by the end of 1935, its publication was delayed because the publisher was worried that it might be banned for "obscenity" by the popular commercial lending libraries (as had happened to *Snooty Baronet* (B&M Cat. 33)). The novel concerns the fate of two impoverished innocents, the painter Victor Stamp and Margot Stamp, who passes as his wife, when they are caught up in a scheme to smuggle guns across the Franco-Spanish border. Lewis handles the political side of the novel (concerning the commitments of upper-class English people to Communism) with remarkable detachment, given his own Fascist sympathies at the time of writing. It is an adventure story, but one with a "metaphysical centre," Lewis later claimed. The original title, *False Bottoms*, gives a clue to this centre: a recognition of the provisional nature of all our versions of "reality" and of the need for the values of love to prevail over the values of power. In the tragic conclusion of *The Revenge for Love*, power obliterates love – as it always does in Lewis's pessimistic view of the universe, until the final pages of his late masterpiece, *The Human Age* (B&M Cats. 57 and 61).

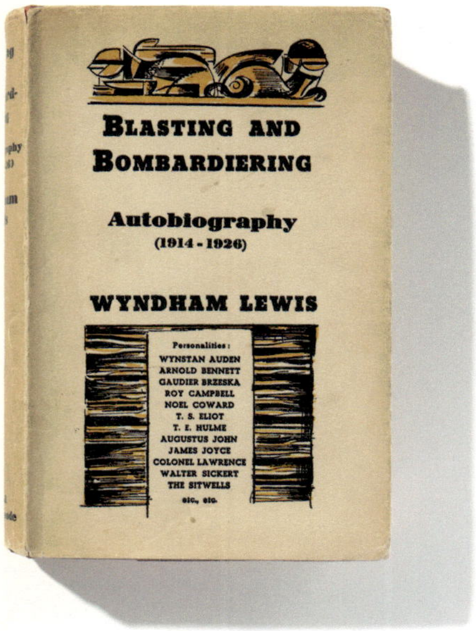

40

Blasting and Bombardiering: Autobiography (1914–1926)
(London: Eyre & Spottiswoode, 1937) 22.2 x 15.5 cm
PRIVATE COLLECTION YMJB.
WYNDHAM LEWIS MEMORIAL TRUST

This was Lewis's first autobiography, covering the years 1914 to 1926, and published just before his visit to Germany and Poland. Since 1932 Lewis had tried to attract a less exclusively highbrow audience for his work – *Snooty Baronet* (B&M Cat. 33) and *The Revenge for Love* (B&M Cat. 39) are aimed at general novel readers. This was partly because his financial circumstances in a period of continuing illness, requiring four major operations, meant that he needed to write books that would sell. *Blasting and Bombardiering* also addresses a popular audience, vividly recounting Lewis's activities in the avant-garde of 1914, his experiences as an artillery officer in the First World War, and recalling his first encounters with other "Men of 1914" such as Ezra Pound, T.S. Eliot and James Joyce. The book is to some extent elegiac: "We are the first men of a Future that has not materialized. We belong to a 'great age' that has not 'come off'," he writes (p. 258). But if Lewis is conscious of writing at the end of an era, he is not yet sure of the future: "Beneath the pressure of this convalescent vitality our cardboard make-believe is beginning to crack and to tumble down. You see how damned interesting all this is going to be?" (pp. 18–19).

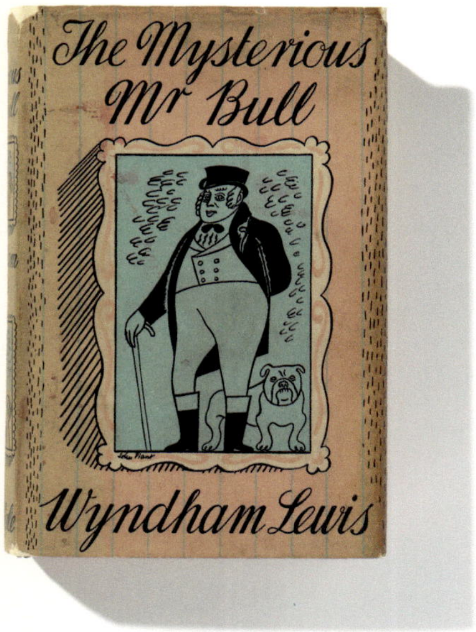

41

The Mysterious Mr Bull
(London: Robert Hale, 1938)
22 x 13.4 cm
WYNDHAM LEWIS MEMORIAL TRUST

"Mr Bull" is John Bull, the personification of the English character, and Lewis's book attempts a comprehensive review of him and his way of life. In a review, George Orwell recognised the book as marking a transition in Lewis's political attitudes: "I do not think it unfair to say that Mr Wyndham Lewis has 'gone left'."[1] The judgement is based particularly on Lewis's condemnation of the English class system and its oppressive effects on the working class. Despite the book's denunciation of English philistinism, bad cooking and general stupidity, the Lewis who emerges is a more humane and tolerant man than he had appeared to be in his previous books. A similar change is apparent in his painting – portraiture in particular – from 1937. He no longer supports Hitler, but has no prescription for Britain's foreign policy beyond a desire to avoid war. His views, he says "have modified of late: but I still regard a *status quo* policy, involving a major war, as stupid."
(p. 178). The book stresses the "racial" kinship of the English and the Germans in keeping with this desire to avoid war.

1. George Orwell, "Review of *The Mysterious Mr Bull* by Wyndham Lewis; *The School for Dictators* by Ignazio Silone," in *The Complete Works of George Orwell Volume Eleven: Facing Unpleasant Facts 1937–1939*. Ed. Peter Davison, assisted by Ian Angus and Sheila Davison (London: Secker and Warburg, 1998), p. 353. First published in *New English Weekly*, 8 June 1939.

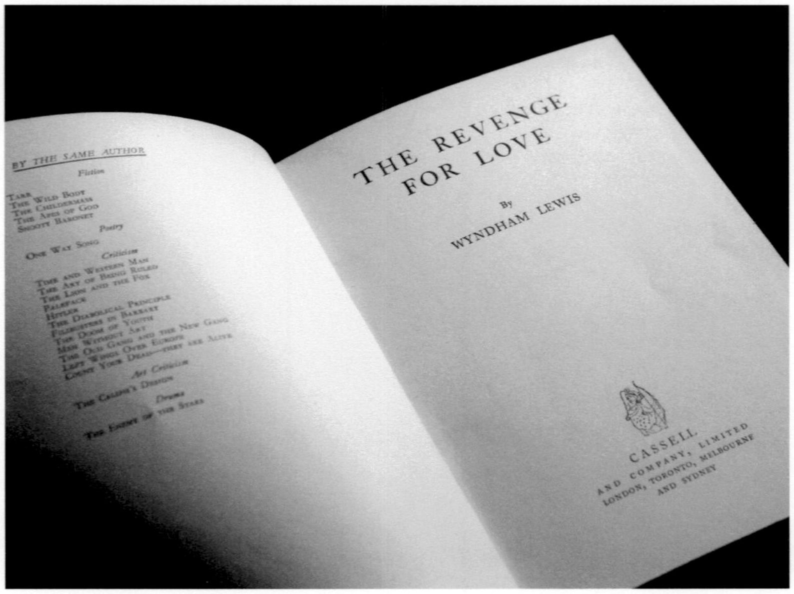
BY THE SAME AUTHOR
THE REVENGE FOR LOVE
By
WYNDHAM LEWIS
CASSELL
AND COMPANY, LIMITED
LONDON, TORONTO, MELBOURNE
AND SYDNEY

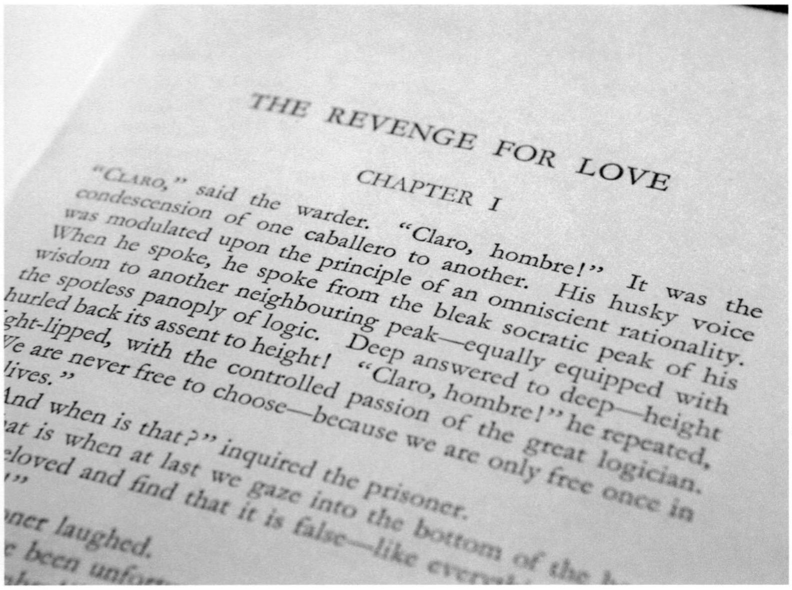
THE REVENGE FOR LOVE
CHAPTER I
"CLARO," said the warder. "Claro, hombre!" It was the
condescension of one caballero to another. His husky voice
was modulated upon the principle of an omniscient rationality.
When he spoke, he spoke from the bleak socratic peak of his
wisdom to another neighbouring peak—equally equipped with
the spotless panoply of logic. Deep answered to deep—height
hurled back its assent to height! "Claro, hombre!" he repeated,
We are never free to choose—because we are only free once in
"And when is that?" inquired the prisoner.

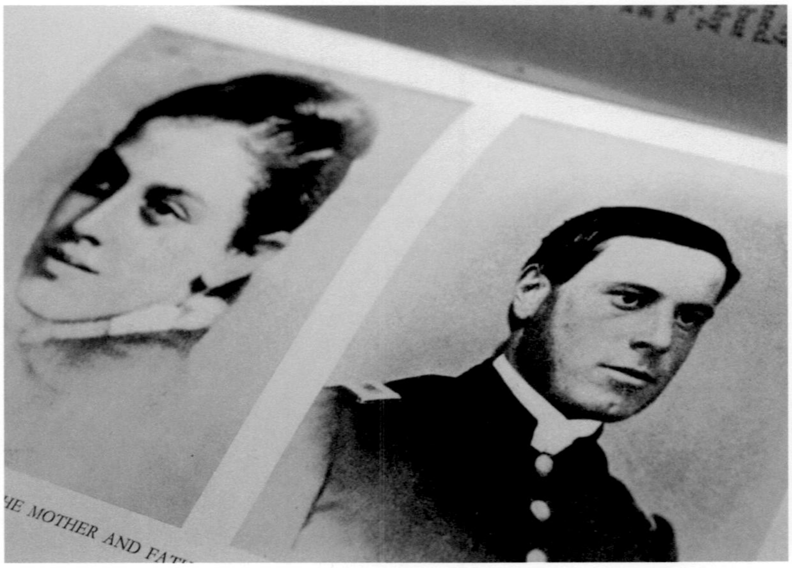
MOTHER AND

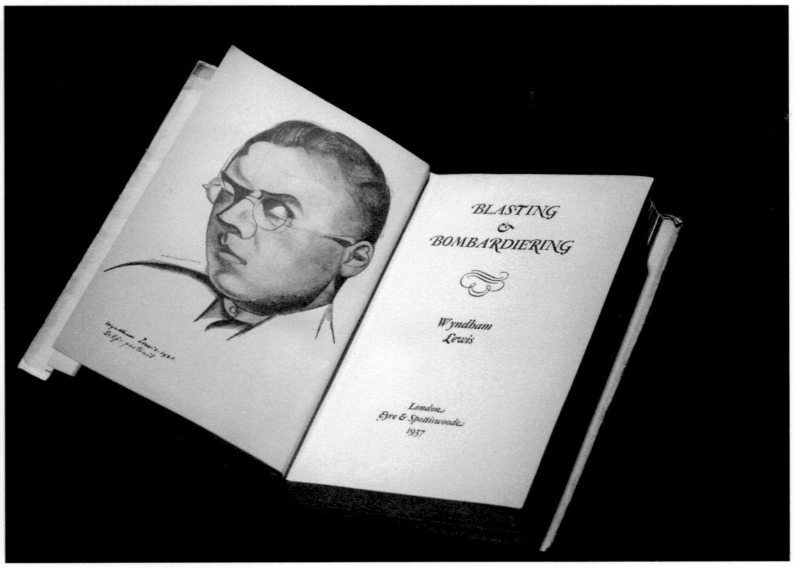
BLASTING
&
BOMBARDIERING
Wyndham
Lewis
London
Eyre & Spottiswoode
1937

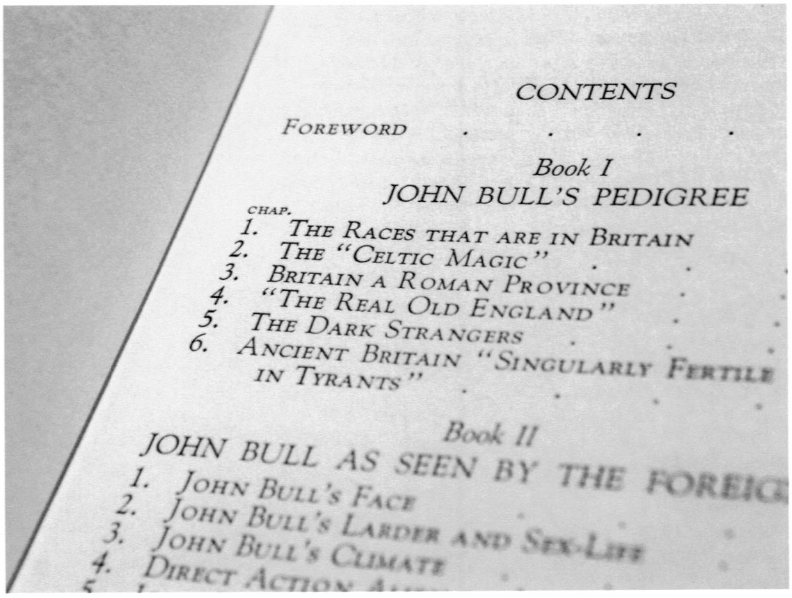
CONTENTS
FOREWORD
Book I
JOHN BULL'S PEDIGREE
CHAP.
1. THE RACES THAT ARE IN BRITAIN
2. THE "CELTIC MAGIC"
3. BRITAIN A ROMAN PROVINCE
4. "THE REAL OLD ENGLAND"
5. THE DARK STRANGERS
6. ANCIENT BRITAIN "SINGULARLY FERTILE IN TYRANTS"
Book II
1. JOHN BULL'S FACE
2. JOHN BULL'S LARDER AND SEX-LIFE
3. JOHN BULL'S CLIMATE

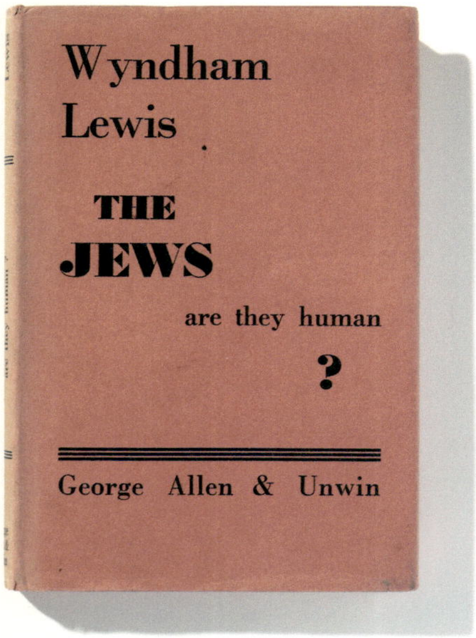

42

***The Jews: Are they Human?* (London: George Allen and Unwin, 1939) 19 x 12.9 cm**
PRIVATE COLLECTION YMJB

Just as by stressing his political radicalism in *The Mysterious Mr Bull* (B&M Cat. 41), Lewis attempted to show that his support for Germany had not been the result of any sympathy with internal Nazi oppression, so in *The Jews* he denounced anti-Semitism and dismantled the Nazi case for it. No doubt this was in response both to his witnessing of the treatment of Jews in Berlin and Warsaw in 1937 and to reports of Germany's state-sponsored pogrom, *Kristallnacht*, of November 1938. The book's apparently offensive title parodies a bestseller, Gustaaf Johannes Renier's *The English: Are they Human?* (1931). Lewis concludes, "We must give all people of Jewish race a new deal among us. Let us for Heaven's sake make an end of this silly nightmare once and for all, and turn our backs upon this dark chapter of our history." (p. 111).

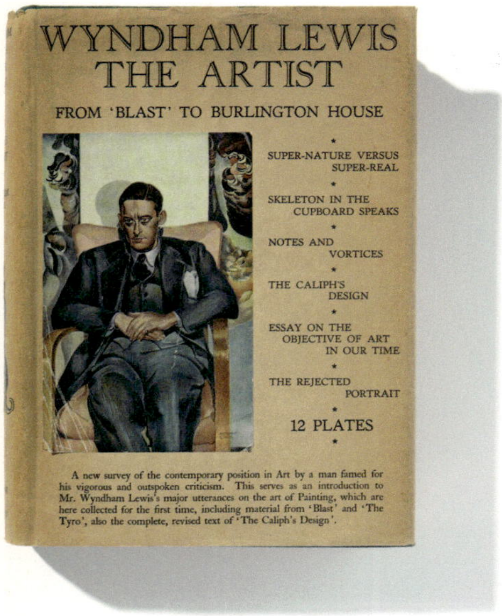

43

***Wyndham Lewis the Artist: From "Blast" to Burlington House* (London: Laidlaw and Laidlaw, 1939) 23.5 x 17.5 cm**
PRIVATE COLLECTION YMJB.
WYNDHAM LEWIS MEMORIAL TRUST

Burlington House in London is the home of the Royal Academy of Arts, the national institution for the visual arts, founded in the eighteenth century. "From 'Blast' to Burlington House" therefore suggests a journey from avant-garde rebelliousness to official acceptance. But the title is ironic; Lewis had not made such a journey, and when he submitted his portrait of T.S. Eliot to the Academy's annual exhibition in 1938 (as a "test case," he said) it was promptly rejected. The book collected some, but by no means all, of Lewis's writings on art and reproduced some of his most important recent paintings. The new material in it has, like *Blasting and Bombardiering* (B&M Cat. 40), an elegiac tone in response to the end of an era. Nationalist politics in Europe and Stalinism in Russia have brought an end to the great revolution in the arts, of which Vorticism represented one component. Lewis advocates, partly as an expedient, partly, it seems, with real enthusiasm, a return to nature and figuration in art – but to a nature transformed by the artist's imagination. In doing so he was articulating the aesthetic that would in fact dominate painting in England in the late 1940s and 1950s. Lewis accordingly welcomed that movement in English painting in his post-war art reviews for *The Listener* magazine (see B&M Cats. 55 and 56).

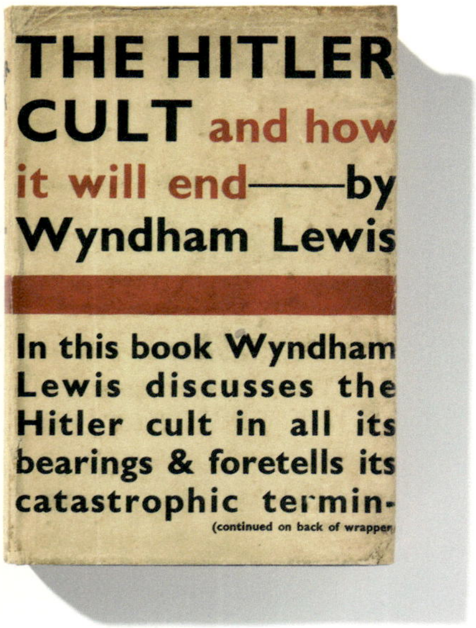

44

***The Hitler Cult* (London: Dent, 1939) 20 x 13.6 cm**
WYNDHAM LEWIS MEMORIAL TRUST

The dust jacket provides a subtitle for this attack on Hitlerism: *The Hitler Cult and How it will End.* Lewis probably began writing early in 1939, but events moved so fast in 1939 that by the time it was published three months after the outbreak of war much of its topical commentary was out of date, and Lewis himself had left England for the USA. The book was a recantation of earlier views and Lewis wrote it with gusto. He predicted (accurately) that National Socialism would die a violent death in six years' time. He reviewed and revised many of the positions he had taken up in his pro-appeasement books of the 1930s (see B&M Cats. 37 and 38). For example, he now says that it would have been best for Great Britain to have sunk German naval vessels in Spanish waters during the Civil War: "Miaja might have had a Victory Parade in Madrid instead of Franco" (p. 182). And in keeping with his reconversion to radical causes, Lewis declares, "*Now we are at war, every soldier should go into battle with a charter of new liberties in his pocket.* A solemn promise from his rulers of a new deal for him and his children." (p. 184). It was a perceptive prediction of the political mood of the nation when victory was eventually won and a Labour government was elected in 1945.

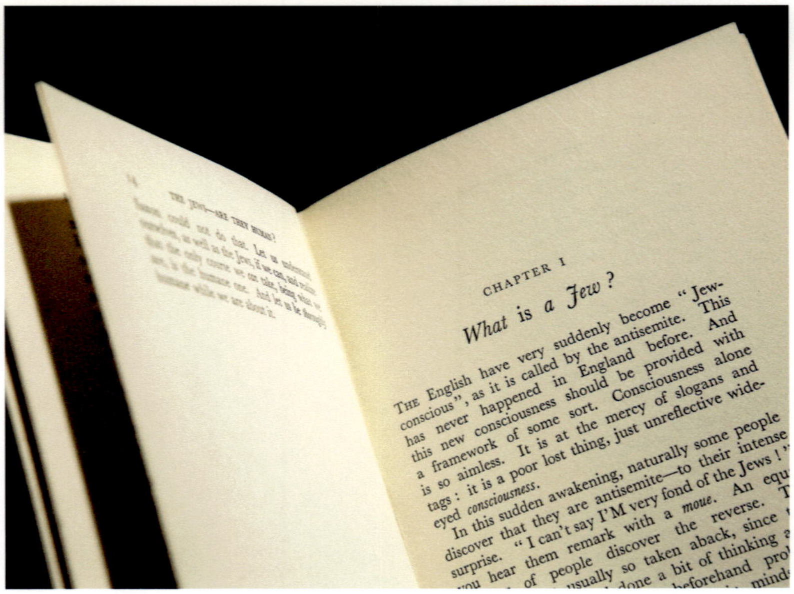
CHAPTER I
What is a Jew?
The English have very suddenly become "Jew-conscious", as it is called by the antisemite. This has never happened in England before. And this new consciousness should be provided with a framework of some sort. Consciousness alone is so aimless. It is at the mercy of slogans and tags: it is a poor lost thing, just unreflective wide-eyed consciousness.
In this sudden awakening, naturally some people discover that they are antisemite—to their intense surprise. "I can't say I'M very fond of the Jews!"

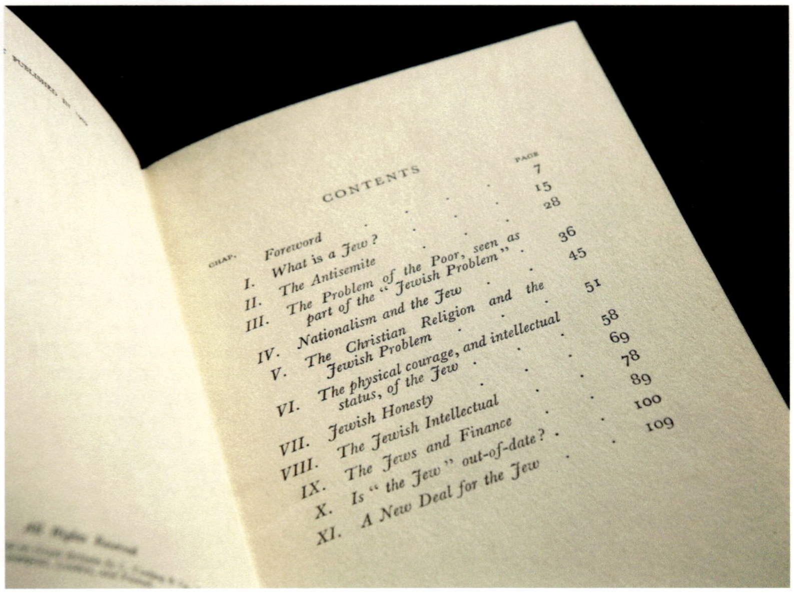
CONTENTS
CHAP. PAGE
Foreword 7
I. What is a Jew? 15
II. The Antisemite 28
III. The Problem of the Poor, seen as part of the "Jewish Problem" 36
IV. Nationalism and the Jew 45
V. The Christian Religion and the Jewish Problem 51
VI. The physical courage, and intellectual status, of the Jew 58
VII. Jewish Honesty 69
VIII. The Jewish Intellectual 78
IX. The Jews and Finance 89
X. Is "the Jew" out-of-date? 100
XI. A New Deal for the Jew 109

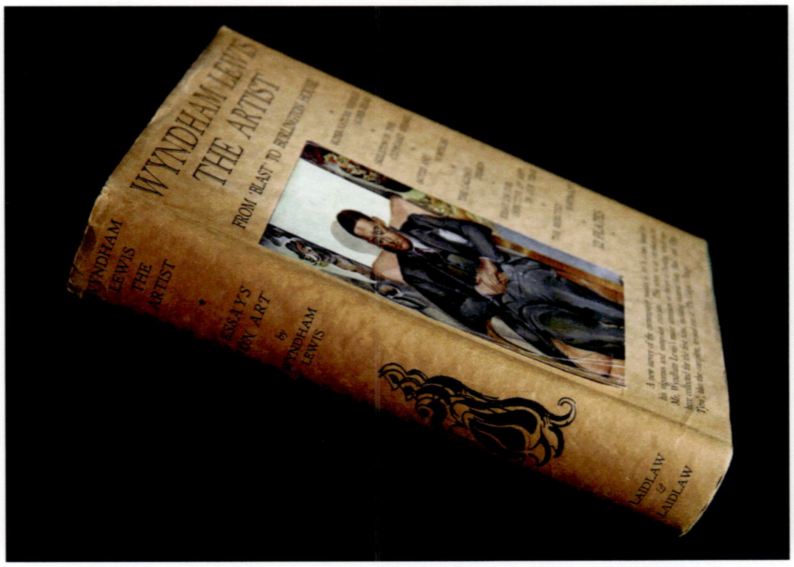
WYNDHAM LEWIS THE ARTIST
FROM 'BLAST' TO BURLINGTON HOUSE
WYNDHAM LEWIS THE ARTIST
ESSAYS ON ART
by
WYNDHAM LEWIS
LAIDLAW & LAIDLAW

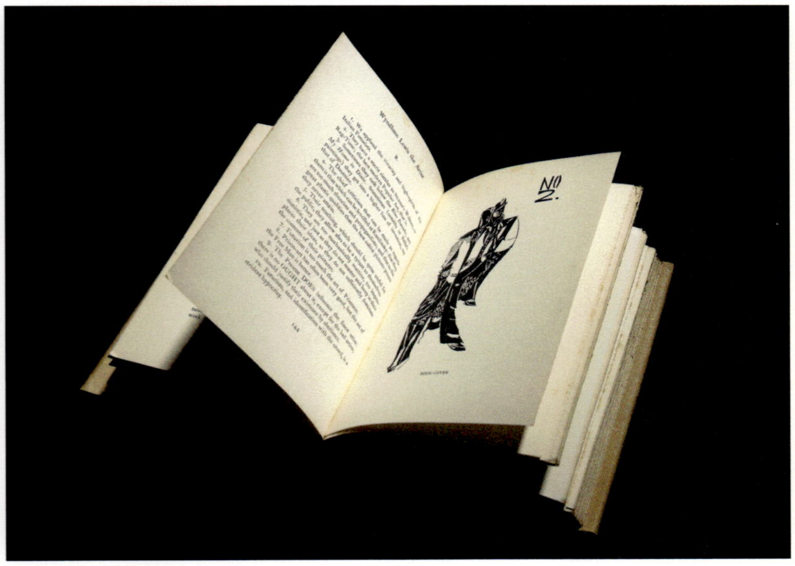
No. 2.

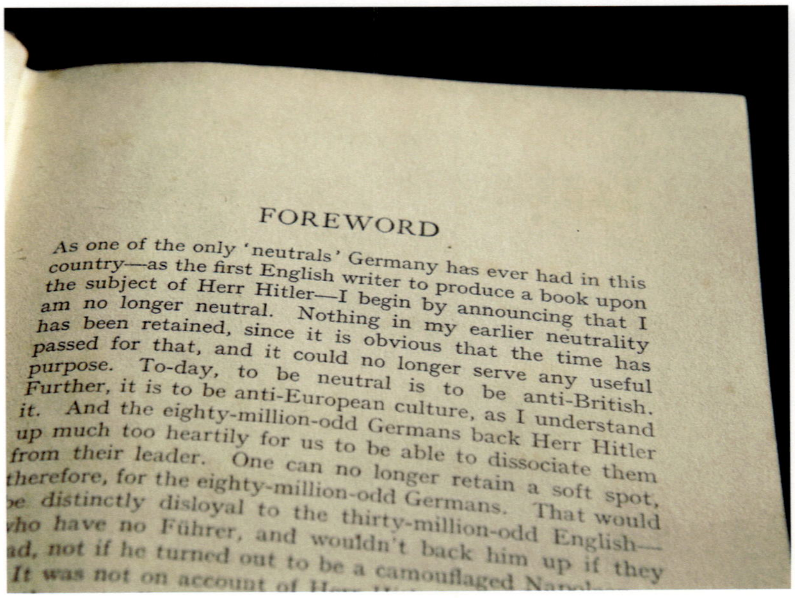
FOREWORD
As one of the only 'neutrals' Germany has ever had in this country—as the first English writer to produce a book upon the subject of Herr Hitler—I begin by announcing that I am no longer neutral. Nothing in my earlier neutrality has been retained, since it is obvious that the time has passed for that, and it could no longer serve any useful purpose. To-day, to be neutral is to be anti-British. Further, it is to be anti-European culture, as I understand it. And the eighty-million-odd Germans back Herr Hitler up much too heartily for us to be able to dissociate them from their leader. One can no longer retain a soft spot, therefore, for the eighty-million-odd Germans. That would be distinctly disloyal to the thirty-million-odd English— who have no Führer, and wouldn't back him up if they had, not if he turned out to be a camouflaged Napoleon.

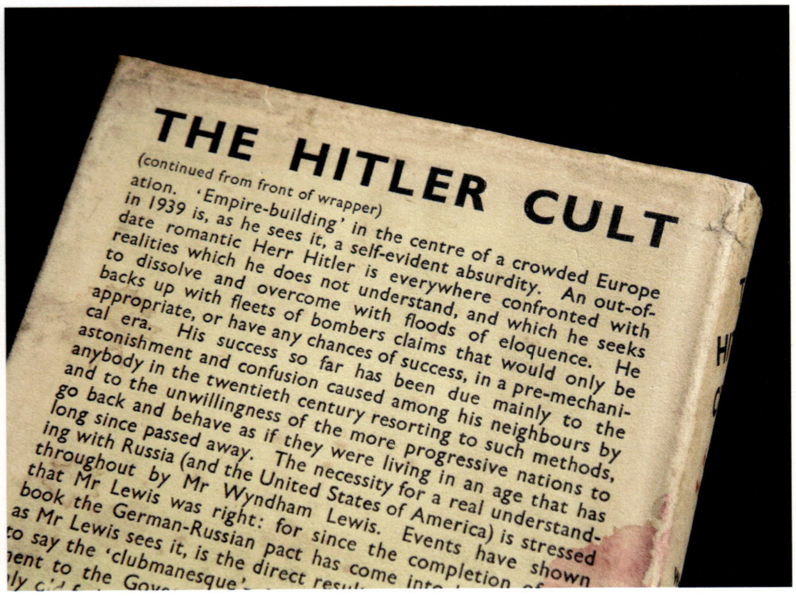
THE HITLER CULT
(continued from front of wrapper)
ation. 'Empire-building' in the centre of a crowded Europe in 1939 is, as he sees it, a self-evident absurdity. An out-of-date romantic Herr Hitler is everywhere confronted with realities which he does not understand, and which he seeks to dissolve and overcome with floods of eloquence. He backs up with fleets of bombers claims that would only be appropriate, or have any chances of success, in a pre-mechanical era. His success so far has been due mainly to the astonishment and confusion caused among his neighbours by anybody in the twentieth century resorting to such methods, and to the unwillingness of the more progressive nations to go back and behave as if they were living in an age that has long since passed away. The necessity for a real understanding with Russia (and the United States of America) is stressed throughout by Mr Wyndham Lewis. Events have shown that Mr Lewis was right: for since the completion of book the German-Russian pact has come into
as Mr Lewis sees it, is the direct result
to say the 'clubmanesque'

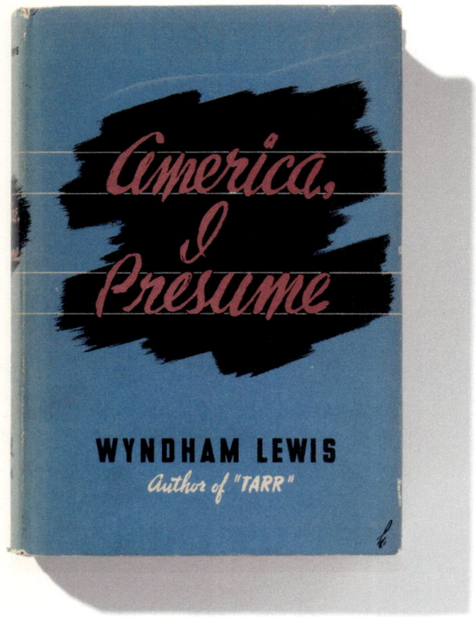

45

America, I Presume
(New York: Howell, Soskin & Co., 1940) 19.3 x 13.2 cm
PRIVATE COLLECTION YMJB

This potboiler gives a genial satirical account of American society as seen through the eyes of an insular and reactionary Englishman, "Major Corcoran." Lewis draws on his own experiences but uses the persona of this character – a philistine "clubman" who knows nothing about art and culture – to throw them into comic relief. In *The Wild Body* (B&M Cat. 17) and *Snooty Baronet* (B&M Cat. 33) he had used the device of a narrator who possessed some of his own characteristics but took them to extremes; here there is little resemblance between the Major and Lewis. The Major therefore has a wife, Agatha, whose opinions are closer to those of the author. One chapter is set in Canada and is based on a visit that Lewis made to Hart House, the Student Centre for the University of Toronto. What Lewis considered as gentle comic satire, to be excused by the supposed foolishness of the character describing the visit, Toronto considered to be an unpardonable insult, and his chances of patronage and employment there were damaged.

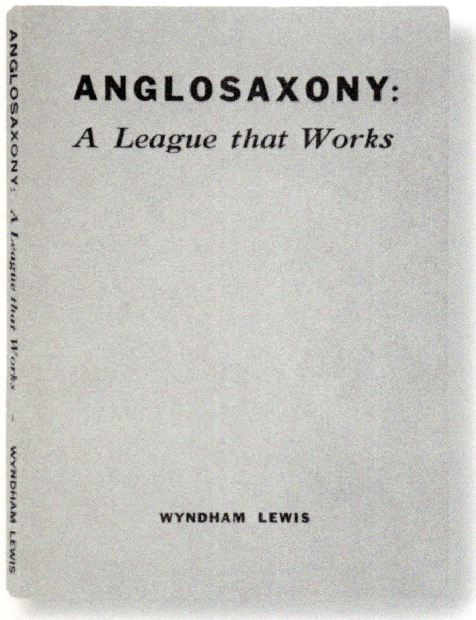

46

[Not in exhibition]
Anglosaxony: A League that Works **(Toronto: The Ryerson Press, 1941) 19.1 x 13 cm**

This is one of Lewis's rarest books, for only 310 copies were sold and the remainder were presumably pulped. Although Lewis left England to escape the war, he wished to do what he could to help the allied cause and this propaganda pamphlet (together with some articles in the press and radio talks) is the result of these efforts. He attacks Fascism as a religion of "action," tracing its origin to Filippo Tommaso Marinetti's Futurism (which, he reminds his readers, he criticised in 1914 for precisely the characteristics that Fascism adopted from it). For the first time in his work, he mounts a systematic defence of democracy as a political system and he praises Anglo-Saxon nautical "universalism" in contrast to the "blood and soil" values of Nazism. In doing so he reverts to some of the ideas he put forward in the manifestos in *Blast* (B&M Cats. 2 and 3). Finally, he praises this international culture's indifference to "racial purity"; it "looks upon the dissolution of racial barriers with a benevolent eye." (p. 68).

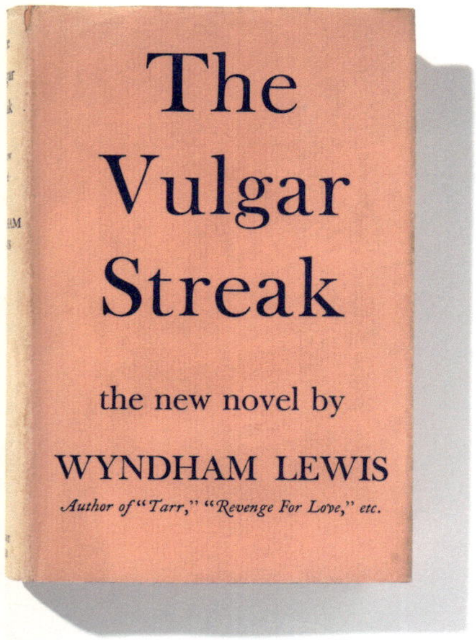

47

The Vulgar Streak
(London: Robert Hale, 1941) 19 x 13.2 cm
WYNDHAM LEWIS MEMORIAL TRUST

Lewis began writing this novel in 1939 and completed it at the John Jermain House in Sag Harbor, New York, over the summer of 1940. It is set in 1938 against the background of the British surrender to Hitler's expansionism in Czechoslovakia. Lewis makes a two-pronged critique of the cult of "action": first, as the basis of Fascism; second, in the character of his "man of action" hero, Vincent Penhale. More prominently, he attacks British class prejudices. Penhale has a working-class background but has constructed a false persona, supposedly with an elite education and family. The money he lives on is actually forged. He marries a woman from the privileged classes, realising too late that she loves him for himself, not for his pretended social status. In its critique of English society, the novel is the equivalent of *The Mysterious Mr Bull* (B&M Cat. 41); in its unequivocal valuation of love over power it continues the development in Lewis's sensibility initiated in *The Revenge for Love* (B&M Cat. 39). The novel was not published in America because New York publishers considered that its social views would be taken as anti-British during the war.

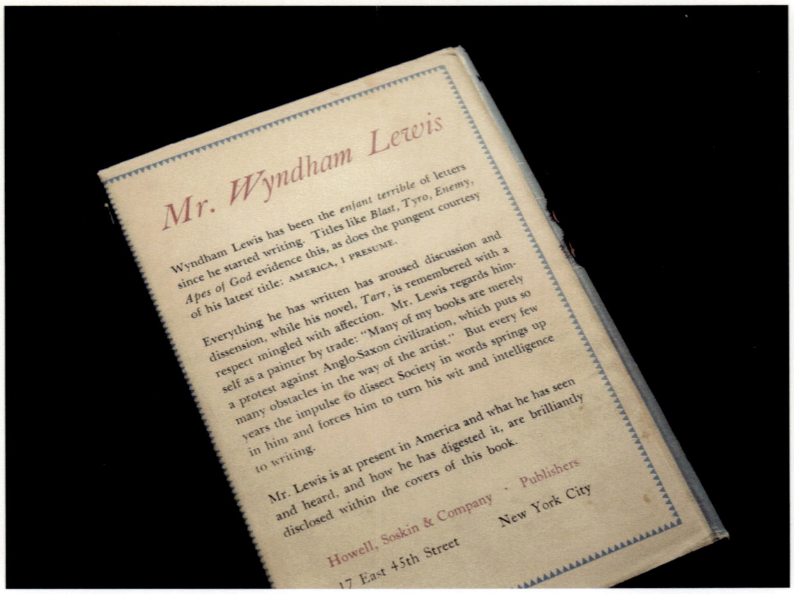

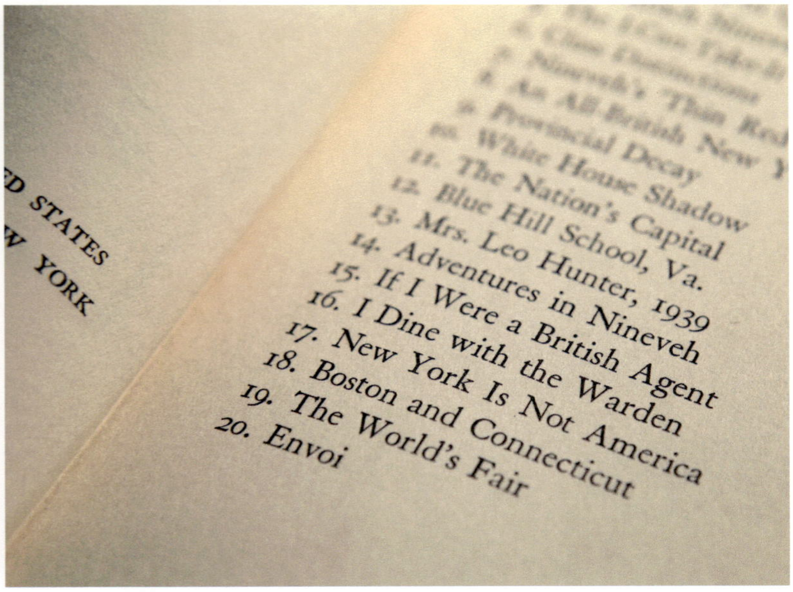

"If I may be forgiven such an extreme lapse
into the vulgar and the personal,
I should say that I am one of the half-dozen
painters in England whose pictures are
bought not because the people who purchase
them like me, but because they have
a fancy for the picture.
That is not so conceited as it sounds, for it
might be better for me if they liked me a little
more and my pictures a little less."

Wyndham Lewis,
Super-Nature versus Super-Real, 1939

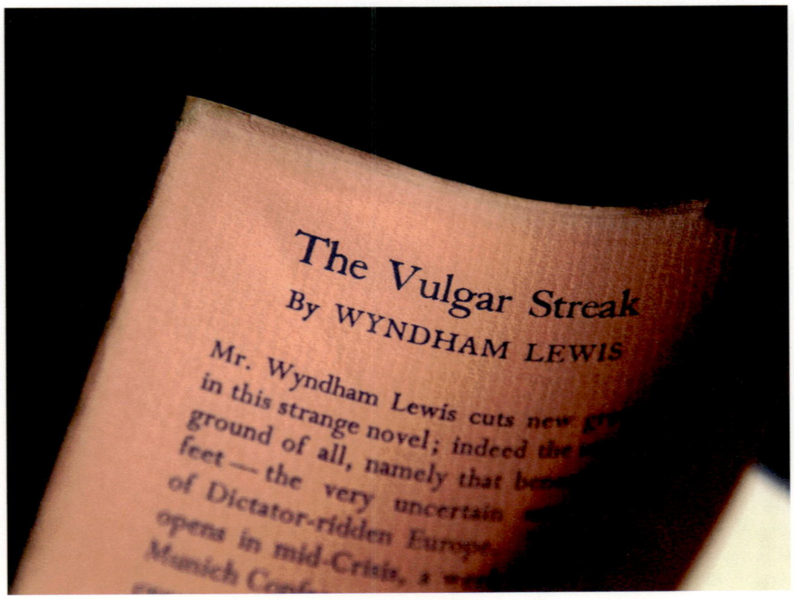

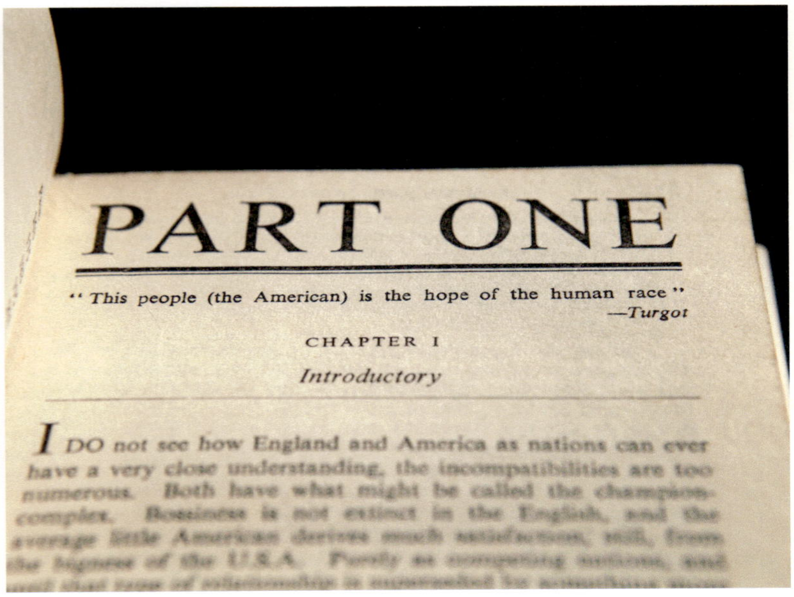

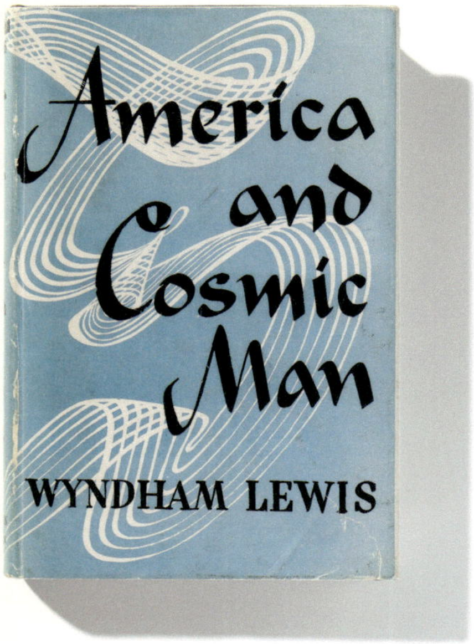

48

America and Cosmic Man
(London: Nicholson and Watson, 1948) 19.6 x 13.3 cm
WYNDHAM LEWIS MEMORIAL TRUST

This is a study of American politics, history and culture that proposes them as the prototype for a new global civilisation under a unitary authority. In November and December of 1943, Lewis delivered 12 lectures on "The Concept of Liberty in America" at Assumption College, Windsor, and *America and Cosmic Man* grew out of these. The book has been praised for its informed understanding of the US political system by the historian, Page Smith, who regarded it as one of the classic studies of America.[1] It is also one of the founding texts of postmodernism, at least in so far as it greatly influenced writer Marshall McLuhan's thoughts about the globalisation of culture. Lewis returns to many of the analyses of *The Art of Being Ruled* (B&M Cat. 10), but now with a democratic rather than authoritarian bias. The "cosmic" and universalist society that he foresees will be a "rootless Elysium" (p. 168). He shows a relish for the popular culture of America, particularly radio, and, shedding his old prejudice against jazz, he claims that "American civilisation as we know it owes more, probably, to the Negro than to anybody." (p. 186).

1. Page Smith, "Wyndham Lewis's *America and Cosmic Man*," in *Dissenting Opinions: Selected Essays* (San Francisco: North Point Press, 1984), pp. 42–51.

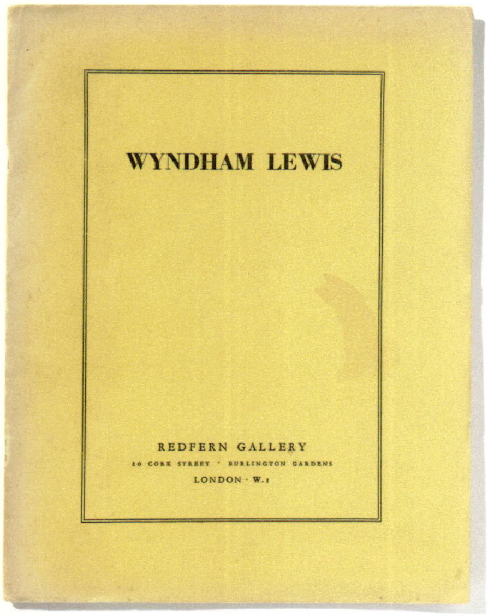

49

***Wyndham Lewis* Exhibition Catalogue (London: Redfern Gallery, 1949) 26 x 19.6 cm**
WYNDHAM LEWIS MEMORIAL TRUST

The exhibition was held in May 1949. In the introduction to the catalogue, Lewis comments on the role of abstraction in his work, saying that it is of two kinds. It is either "a new language altogether, of form and colour, not of this world," or it is "something to be *used*, merely in a humanly significant context" (n.p.). In his Vorticist work, he claims, his abstraction is of the first type, while his later work is of the second. After Vorticism he uses abstraction to "achieve some unusual effect, or to serve me in some expressionist excursion." Lewis also comments that many of the 128 works in the show are being exhibited for the first time, as his work has been occluded because of a "conspiracy of silence" that began in 1913 (when Lewis quarrelled with "Bloomsbury" and Roger Fry).

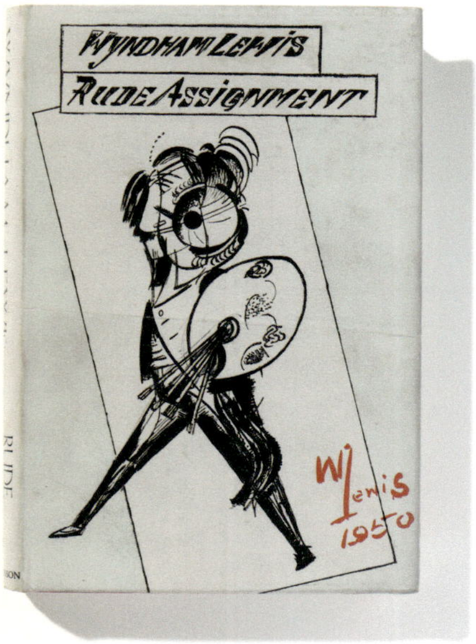

50

Rude Assignment: A Narrative of my Career Up-to-date
(London: Hutchinson & Co., 1950) 23.7 x 16.5 cm
PRIVATE COLLECTION YMJB

While Lewis's earlier autobiography, *Blasting and Bombardiering* (B&M Cat. 40), concentrated mainly on the external events of his life and was aimed at a mass audience, *Rude Assignment* focuses on the development of his art and thought. Lewis's intention was to clear away what he regarded as misunderstandings and misrepresentations of these. The first part of the book discusses the role of the intellectual, satire and politics, and it is not until the second part that the book begins to be autobiographical, with vivid accounts of Lewis's early life and the works that emerged from it. The third part takes his major books, from *Tarr* (B&M Cat. 18) to *The Revenge for Love* (B&M Cat. 39), one by one and explains his intentions. He says at the end of the book that his aim has simply been to establish that he is of good character (perhaps necessary for someone whose political reputation remained suspect to those who remembered his books of the 1930s). *Rude Assignment* is an excellent introduction to Lewis's thought, even though that thought sometimes emerges as a little more benign and humane than it actually was.

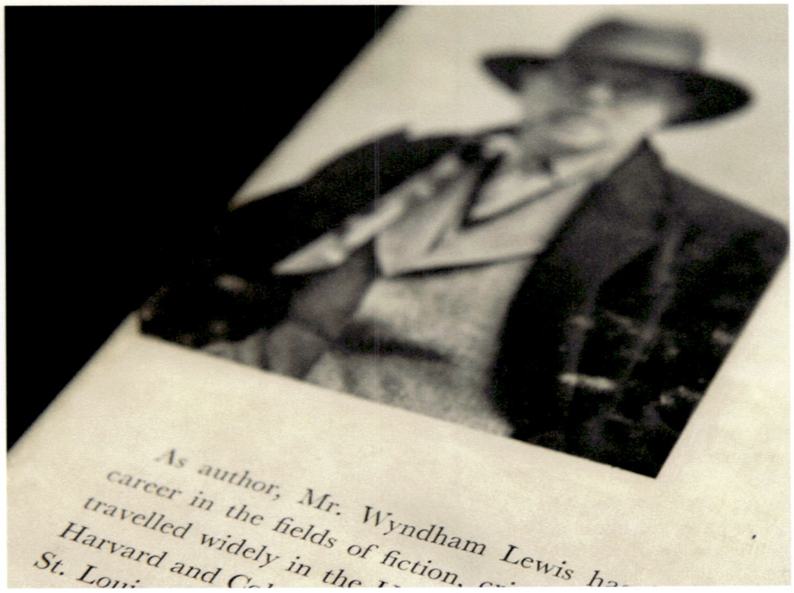
As author, Mr. Wyndham Lewis
career in the fields of fiction,
travelled widely in the
Harvard and

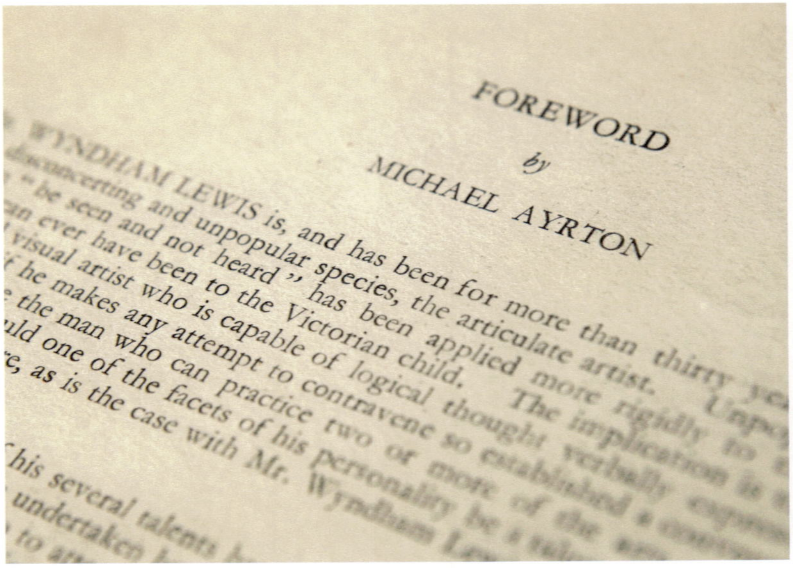
FOREWORD
by
MICHAEL AYRTON
WYNDHAM LEWIS is, and has been for more than thirty
disconcerting and unpopular species, the articulate artist.
be seen and not heard", has been applied more rigidly to
ever have been to the Victorian child. The implication is
visual artist who is capable of logical thought verbally
he makes any attempt to contravene so established a
the man who can practice two or more of the
one of the facets of his personality be a
as is the case with Mr. Wyndham
his several talents
undertaken

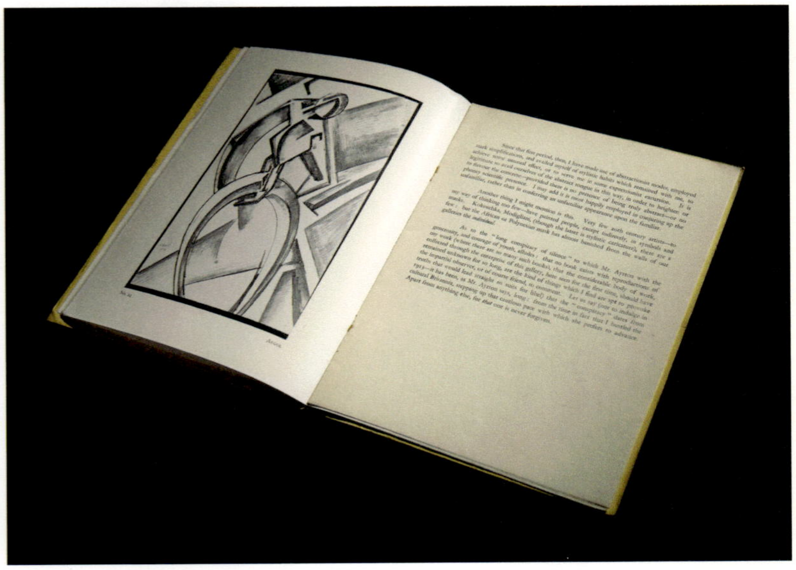

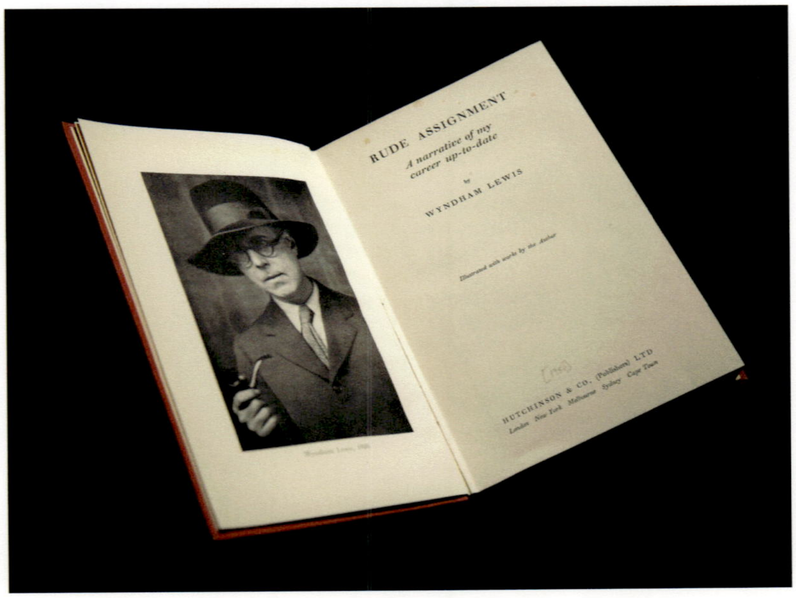
RUDE ASSIGNMENT
A narrative of my career up-to-date
by
WYNDHAM LEWIS
HUTCHINSON & CO. (Publishers) LTD
London New York Melbourne Sydney Cape Town

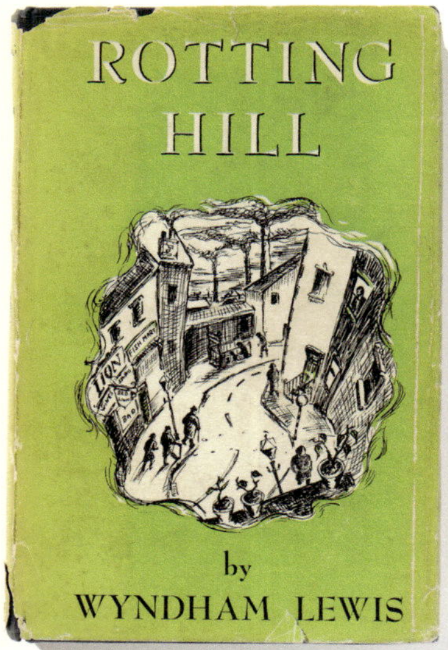

51

Rotting Hill
(London: Methuen & Co. Ltd, 1951) 23.7 x 16.5 cm
Cover by Charles Handley-Read
PRIVATE COLLECTION YMJB

52

Rotting Hill
(Chicago: Henry Regnery Co., 1952) 21.5 x 14 cm
PRIVATE COLLECTION YMJB

Wyndham Lewis lived in Notting Hill, a district in the west of London. The flat he shared with his wife lay empty throughout the war and on their return they found it riddled with dry rot. His letters to Ezra Pound about this prompted the poet to rename the district as "Rotting Hill," which Lewis takes up in this book of short stories about life in Britain in the period of post-war "austerity." Austerity and shortage were forced on the public because of the economic crisis caused by debts incurred in fighting the war. Lewis makes his story of the workmen tackling the rot in his flat into an allegory of a ruined society that is attempting to introduce socialism and a Welfare State. Many of the other stories in the book are also concerned with the social tensions that resulted from this, often focusing on the disgust of the bourgeoisie (including, at times, Lewis himself) at the decline in the quality of manufactured goods and the food rationing. It depicts a society frequently disrupted by petty acts of violence. This is the first of Lewis's books to be adorned with a dust jacket designed by Charles Handley-Read. Handley-Read had compiled the first book exclusively devoted to Lewis as an artist, *The Art of Wyndham Lewis*, published by Faber in 1951.

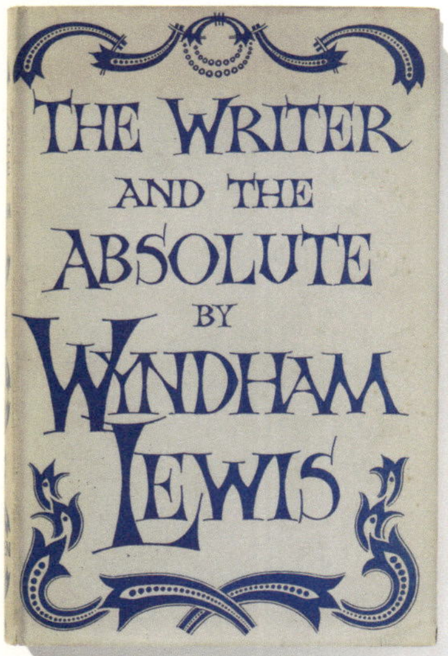

53

***The Writer and the Absolute* (London: Methuen & Co. Ltd, 1952) 22.2 x 15 cm**
Cover by Charles Handley-Read
WYNDHAM LEWIS MEMORIAL TRUST

These essays return to a perennial preoccupation of Lewis's: the freedom of writers to tell the truth as they see it, without interference from political or other ideological pressure. As well as giving a history of such pressures and their effects in the first half of the century, Lewis provides case studies of individual writers, most prominently Jean-Paul Sartre. He criticises Sartrean Existentialism as a development out of the "time-philosophy" that he attacked in *Time and Western Man* (B&M Cats. 12 and 13) and makes fun of Sartre's angst-ridden flirtation with Communism. Another major section of the book is devoted to George Orwell, to whom Lewis had sent a copy of *The Vulgar Streak* (B&M Cat. 47) on publication. He treats Orwell as a writer who gradually freed himself from the pressure of fashionable left-wing fellow-travelling conformism. "Four or five hundred years ago it was the religious Absolute which was the writer's problem. Today it is the political Absolute." (p. 195).

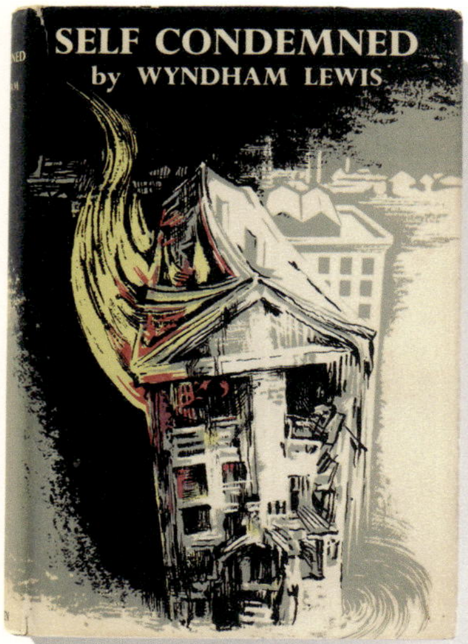

54

Self Condemned
(London: Methuen & Co. Ltd, 1954) 19 x 12.8 cm
Cover by Michael Ayrton.
PRIVATE COLLECTION YMJB

In 1951, Lewis announced his blindness; the tumour that had been growing for years on his pituitary gland had virtually destroyed his optic nerve and was also causing other ill effects. *Self Condemned*, a novel based on the experience of the Lewises in a Toronto hotel during the war, was the first book he wrote without being able to see the manuscript that he produced (laboriously, almost illegibly, four lines to a page). The experience of this illness and its devastating psychological consequences on Froanna are present in the depiction of their life in Canada. René Harding is a historian who gives up his university post on the outbreak of war and emigrates with his wife Hester to Canada. Their sufferings, the absurdity of the hotel and René's humiliation all contribute to an allegorical vision of the end of the project of the European Enlightenment and of the triumph of an ultimate absurdity. Remarkably, the novel portrays the simple companionship of a mutually supportive couple as no other of Lewis's does. This makes the death of Hester and the reduction of René to a mere "shell" of himself especially moving. For T.S. Eliot, *Self Condemned* was a book "of almost unbearable spiritual agony." The cover shows the destruction of the hotel by fire. Michael Ayrton, who worked closely with Lewis when producing it, has given the building an appropriately quasi-human countenance, for its destruction mirrors René's own.

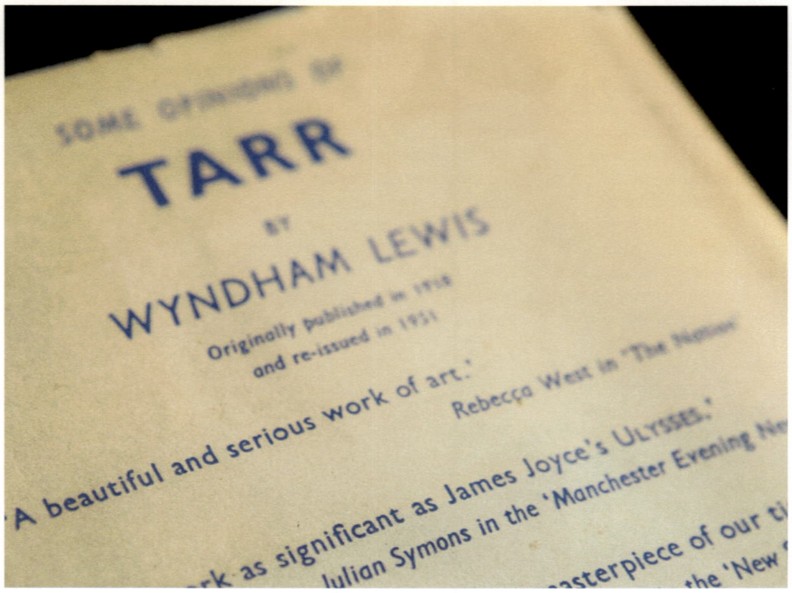
SOME OPINIONS OF
TARR
BY
WYNDHAM LEWIS
Originally published in 1918
and re-issued in 1951
'A beautiful and serious work of art.'
Rebecca West in 'The Nation'
as significant as James Joyce's ULYSSES.'
Julian Symons in the 'Manchester Evening

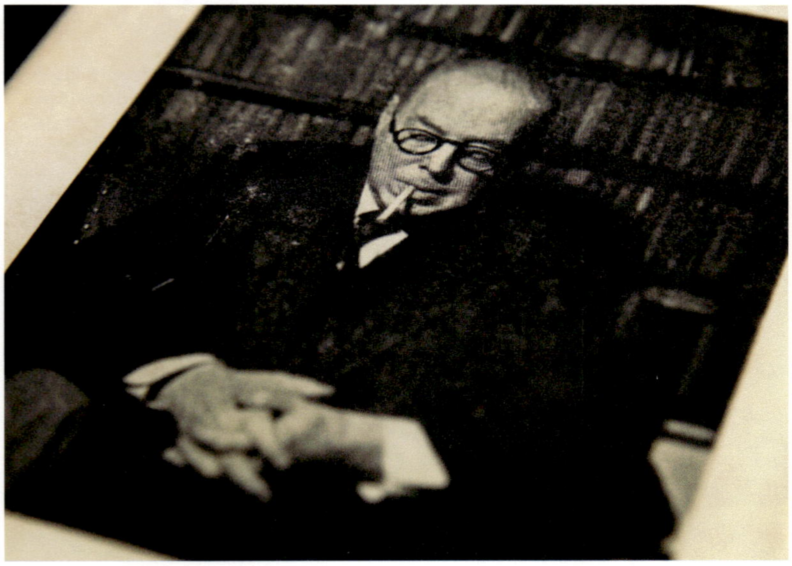

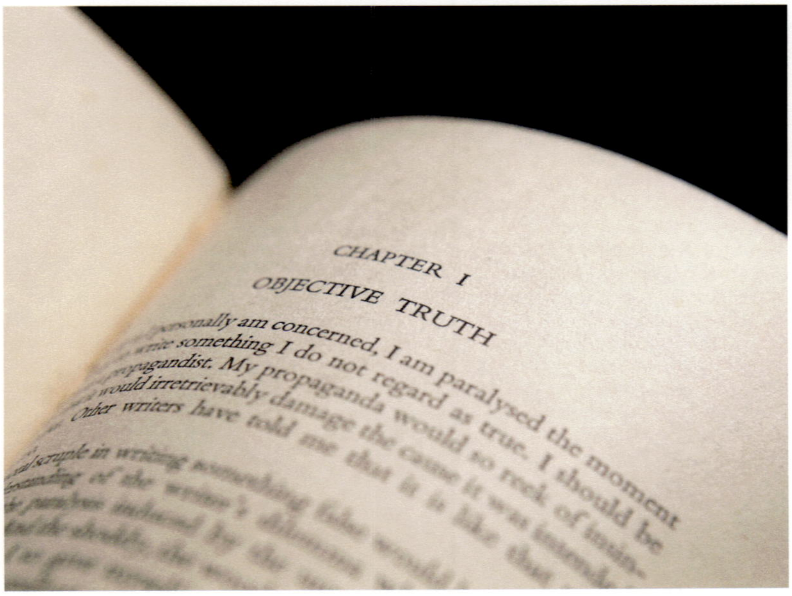
CHAPTER I
OBJECTIVE TRUTH
am concerned, I am paralysed the moment
something I do not regard as true. I should be
My propaganda would so reek of insin-
damage the cause it was intend-
Other writers have told me that it is like that

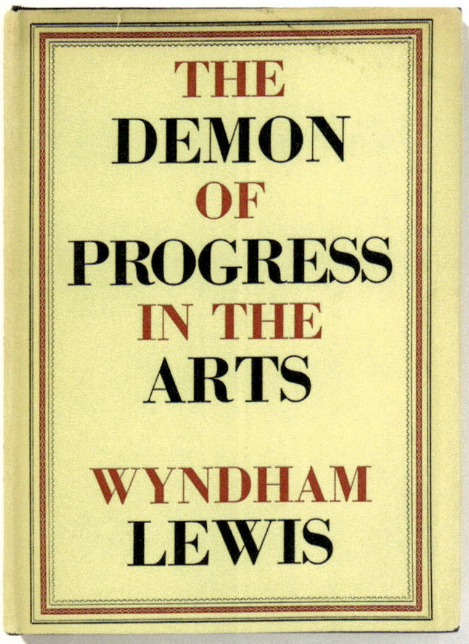

55

The Demon of Progress in the Arts **(London: Methuen & Co. Ltd, 1954). 20.3 x 14.2 cm**
PRIVATE COLLECTION YMJB

56

The Demon of Progress in the Arts **(Chicago: Henry Regnery Co., 1955) 21.5 x 14.6 cm**
FUNDACIÓN JUAN MARCH

Beginning in 1946, Lewis contributed reviews of London art exhibitions, particularly by younger British painters, to the BBC's cultural weekly, *The Listener*. Lewis had, of course, made a career out of opposition: the stance of the "Enemy." But these reviews, coinciding with his own virtual cessation of visual production, were sympathetic and appreciative, and Lewis became a champion for the Neo-romantic generation that became prominent after the war. *The Demon of Progress* was written some time after Lewis lost his ability to see, but draws on his memory of these works. He describes this generation as "the finest group of painters England has ever known," naming, among others, Francis Bacon, Robert Colquhoun, Ceri Richards, Graham Sutherland, Victor Pasmore and Michael Ayrton (who designed book jackets for Lewis and illustrated *The Human Age* (B&M Cats. 57 and 61)). *The Demon of Progress* is a kind of appendix to *The Writer and the Absolute* (B&M Cat. 53), combating the "absolute" that presses on the visual arts: an ideology of formal "progress" that Lewis fears will lead to a minimalism culminating in art that is "nothing."

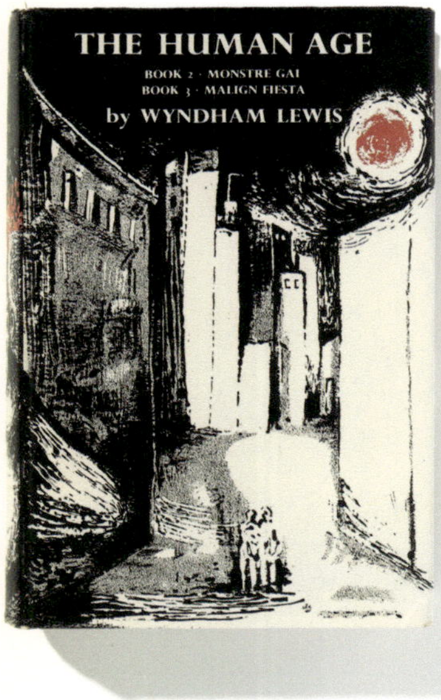

57

The Human Age, Book Two: Monstre Gai; Book Three: Malign Fiesta **(London: Methuen & Co. Ltd, 1955) 22.2 x 15 cm. Cover by Michael Ayrton.**
PRIVATE COLLECTION YMJB.
WYNDHAM LEWIS MEMORIAL TRUST

Lewis's fantasy of life after death, *The Childermass* (B&M Cat. 19) had been left incomplete since 1928. The BBC commissioned him to finish the story, which would be dramatised (by D.G. Bridson, a BBC radio producer) and broadcast on the radio and then published as a trilogy of novels. *The Human Age* takes the protagonist Pullman and his childish companion Satters to Purgatory, which is a modern European city whose (all-male) inhabitants are moronic "consumers" of the type Lewis always feared that capitalism would produce, and that he had witnessed in the cafés of Berlin in 1937. The city is under threat of war and Pullman, an enlightened intellectual, must choose between the apparently ineffectual and indifferent representative of a distant God, and the vibrant, much more human, Bailiff, who seems to rule the city as he had the encampment outside its walls. Pullman chooses to flee with the Bailiff and finds himself in Hell. This is again a modern city, but with an industrialised punishment, torture and extermination centre. Here once more, in order to survive, Pullman is forced to choose and becomes Satan's chief adviser in a scheme to undermine the Divine by instituting a "Human Age." He is the type of all intellectuals (including Lewis himself), who, in "emergency conditions," have overlooked ultimate values for what at the time seemed expedient and humane. God's angelic forces invade Hell and overthrow Satan; in the radio broadcast, Pullman is casually killed by the giant foot of a dark angel. But Lewis revised his idea for the work, and in the book as published the foot stamps out a flower instead. Pullman is rescued and carried off to Heaven by two angels. Lewis intended to write a final book, "The Trial of Man," in which Pullman's assimilation to this realm would be depicted, but his declining health and the sheer difficulty of the project prevented him. The quality of production of this book (paper, generosity of margins, illustrations) is much higher than for Lewis's other books published by Methuen, and is testimony to their belief in the work, which was no doubt reinforced by the great impression it made on critics and the public as a broadcast drama.

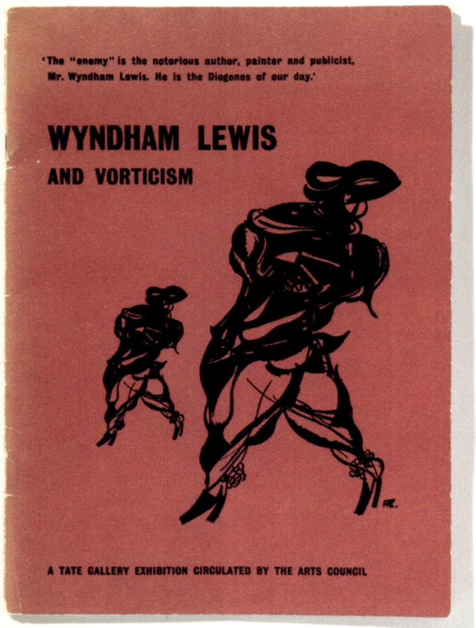

58

Wyndham Lewis and Vorticism Exhibition Catalogue **(London: Tate Gallery, 1956) 24.1 x 17.5 cm**

59

Wyndham Lewis and Vorticism Exhibition Catalogue **(London: Tate Gallery / Arts Council, 1956) 24.1 x 17.5 cm**
FUNDACIÓN JUAN MARCH.
WYNDHAM LEWIS MEMORIAL TRUST

The exhibition ran from 6 July to 19 August at the Tate Gallery, London, and then travelled in a much-reduced form to four other cities in Britain. Primarily a Lewis retrospective, it also contained a small number of works by Lewis's fellow-Vorticists. Lewis was seriously ill and frail, but attended the opening of the show, which included 155 of his works. Lewis's introduction in the catalogue contained his claim that "Vorticism, in fact, was what I, personally, did, and said, at a certain period." The statement (and perfunctory representation of his own *oeuvre* among "other Vorticists") annoyed the artist William Roberts, who produced several pamphlets attacking Lewis and the Director of the Tate Gallery, John Rothenstein. But the truth was that Lewis by now no longer valued his early Vorticist works. Cut off from the visual world by blindness, he declared his certainty that "Nature supplies us with all we need." Referring to his 1938 portrait of John McCleod (il. p. 15), he concludes, "My merit, whether great or small […] resides in the long legs of a Scot, the fondness for books of a mature man, and the stone and steel colour of the tweeds." (p. 4).

"Today I am a super-naturalist–so I might call myself: and I wished the reader of these Notes and Vortices [selected art criticism] to see what could be done by burying Euclid deep in the living flesh–that of Mr Eliot or of Mr Pound–rather than, at this time of day, displaying the astral geometries of those gentlemen. I am …
never unconscious of those underlying conceptual truths that are inherent in all appearances. But I leave them now where I find them, instead of isolating them in conceptual arabesques."

Wyndham Lewis,
Super-Nature versus Super-Real, 1939

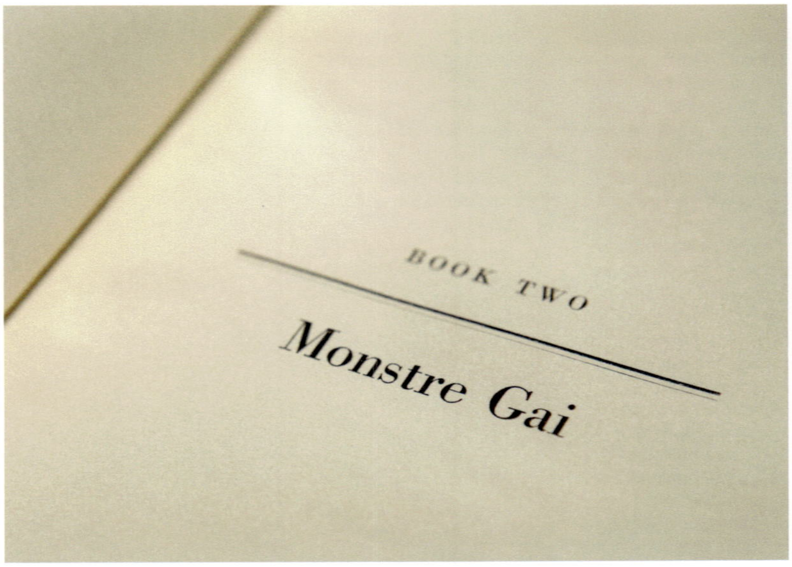

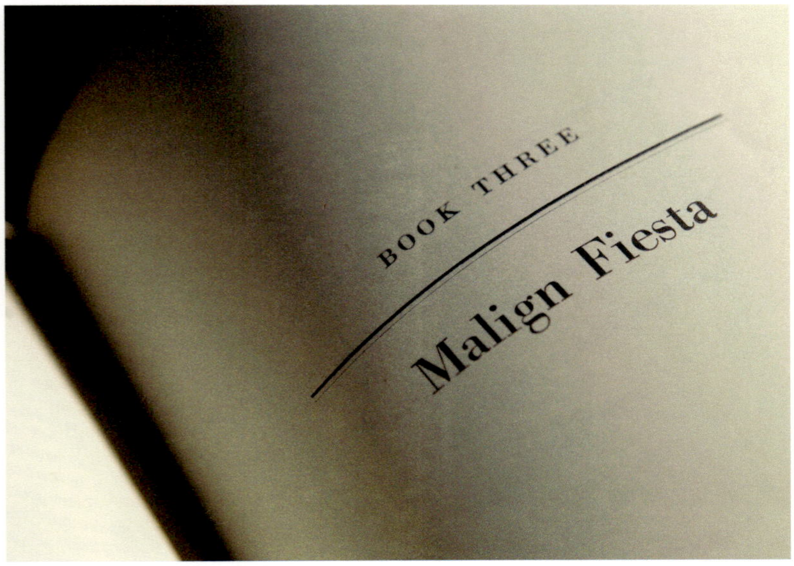

"What has fact on its side is still this strange synthesis of cultures and times (which we named Vorticism in England) and which is the first projection of a world-art, and also I think the clearest trail promising us delivery from the mechanical impasse."*

Wyndham Lewis,
A World Art and Tradition, 1939

* The "mechanical impasse" refers to the general deadness, the robotic nature, of contemporary culture, not to machines as such.

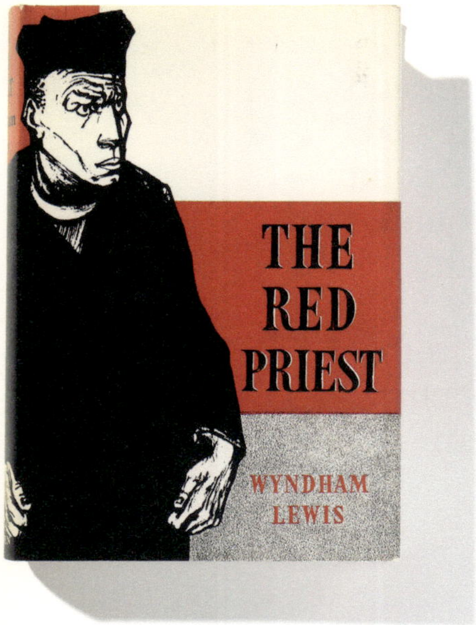

60

The Red Priest
(London: Methuen & Co. Ltd, 1956) 19 x 13 cm
Cover by Michael Ayrton.
PRIVATE COLLECTION YMJB

This, the last book that Lewis completed, is a novel about a High Church Anglican priest, Augustine Card, who is also a militant socialist and sympathiser with the Soviet Union. Such figures were not unknown in the Church of England. In some respects, the novel shows a serious decline in Lewis's novelistic abilities, a result of his rapidly deteriorating medical condition. But it is a serious study, nevertheless, returning to some of the theological themes of *Time and Western Man* (B&M Cats. 12 and 13). Card's zeal for absolutes, his dynamism and his yearning for a personal encounter with God, lead him to violence and, eventually, the Arctic wastes, where he is killed in a fight with an Eskimo. The novel shows the practical consequences of theology whose negation Lewis hoped to explore in "The Trial of Man" (see B&M Cat. 57).

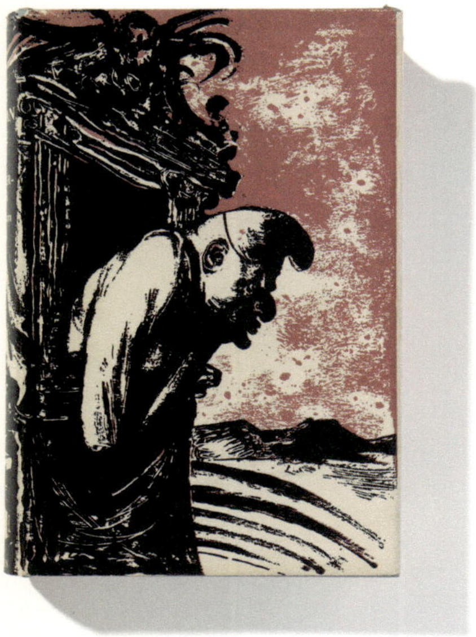

61

The Human Age, Book One: The Childermass
(London: Methuen & Co. Ltd, 1956) 22.2 x 15 cm
MICHAEL AYRTON. WYNDHAM LEWIS MEMORIAL TRUST

The continuation of *The Childermass* as *The Human Age* necessitated a reissue of the first book, published in 1928 (B&M Cat. 19). Michael Ayrton's monotype cover shows, on the front, the Bailiff in the booth from which he oversees the judgement (and murder) of the innocents awaiting entry to "Heaven"; on the back it depicts the volcano that appears in the narrative, looking ominously like an exploding hydrogen bomb – an appropriate image for this masterpiece of cold war and Great Power rivalry. Lewis would not have been able to carry out extensive revision to the original text, and the stylistic difference between the modernist virtuoso of 1928 and the more conventional and classical writing of Books Two and Three (see B&M Cat. 57) is striking. He did make some revisions, however. The most important is a passage added on the final page. In this short piece of Beckettian dialogue, Pullman and Satters fall in surreptitiously behind the Bailliff's cortège, enabling them to enter the city without undergoing examination at his court. "Step out. Pick your feet up," Pullman instructs Satters. "If you must go nowhere, step out." (p. 401).

"The only art at the present time about which there is any reason to employ the word 'revolutionary' … is either inferior and stupid, or else consciously political, art. For art is, in reality, one of the things that Revolutions are about, and cannot therefore itself be Revolution. Life as interpreted by the poet or philosopher is the objective of Revolutions, they are the substance of its Promised Land."

Wyndham Lewis,
Time and Western Man, 1927

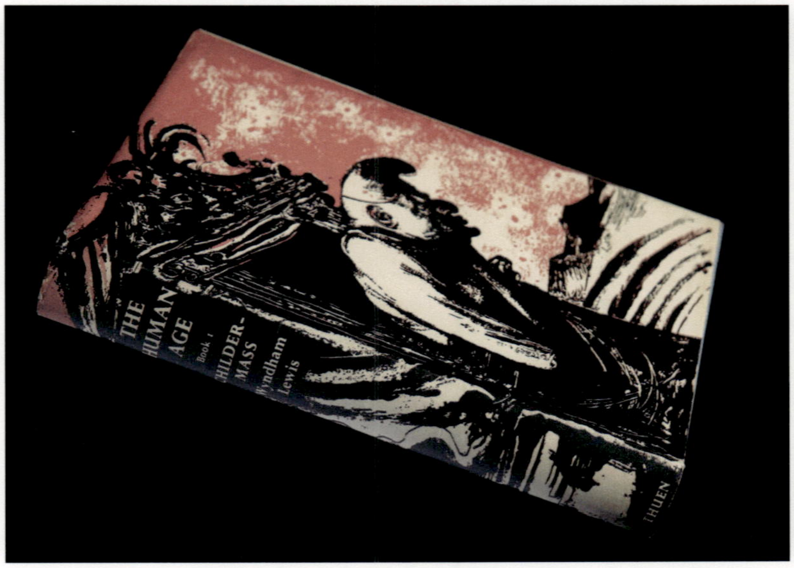

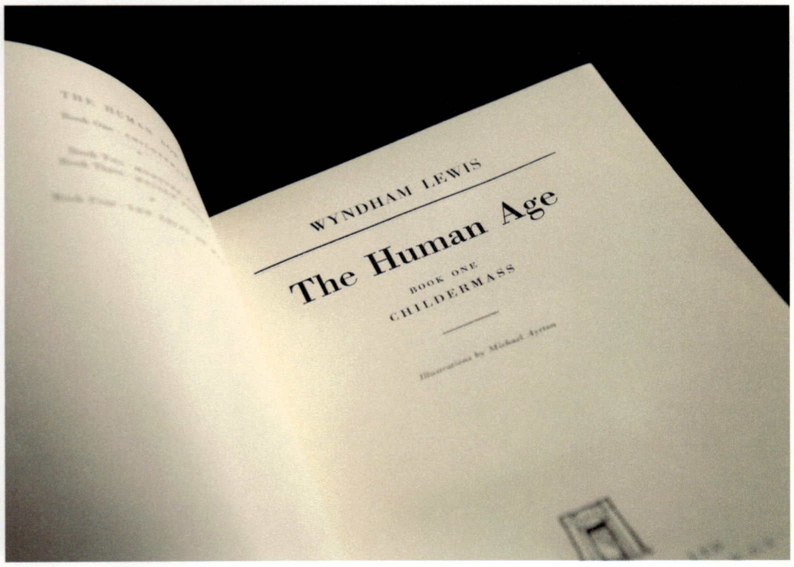

"To imitate what is under our eyes; to develop these imitations into generalized (super-natural – but not super-real) realities; and beyond that, and in a more general way, to care for, and to influence people to observe, the visual amenities, and to banish as far as possible from the visual field all that is degrading or stupid, all that is of trivial or slovenly design and texture: these are great human functions, surely, that people neglect to their cost."

Wyndham Lewis,
After Abstract Art, 1940

WYNDHAM LEWIS:
AN ANTHOLOGY

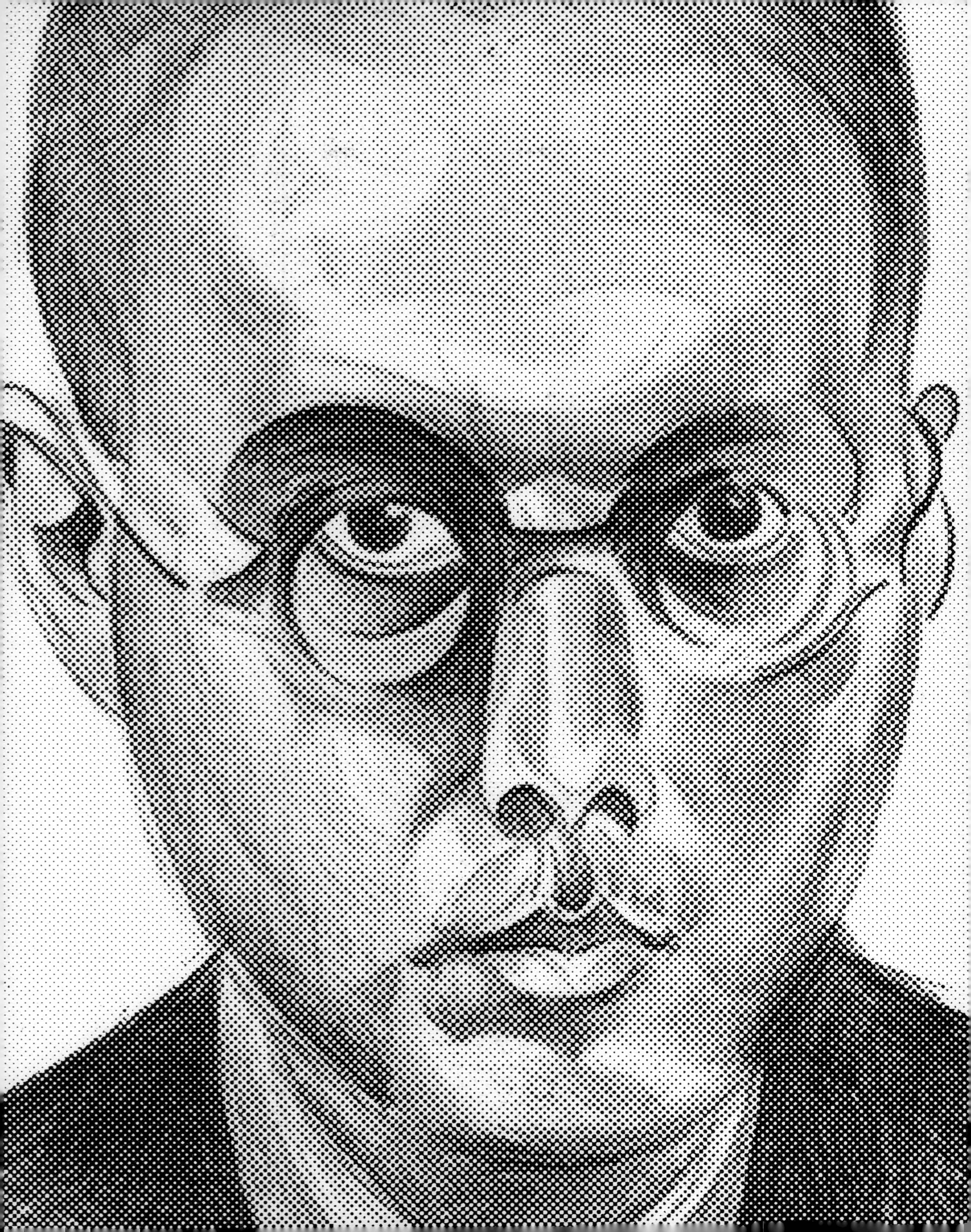

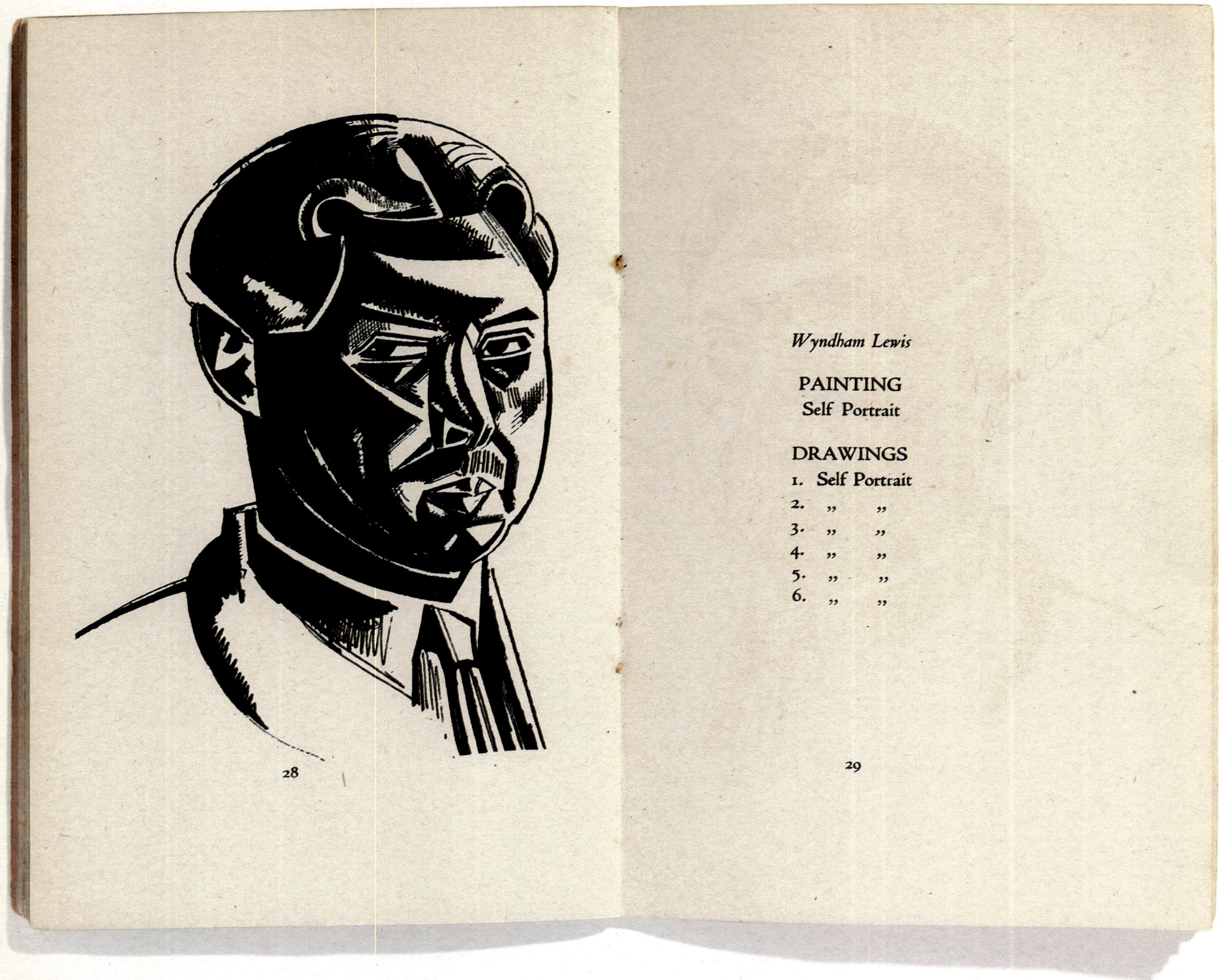

28

Wyndham Lewis

PAINTING
Self Portrait

DRAWINGS
1. Self Portrait
2. " "
3. " "
4. " "
5. " "
6. " "

29

Texts by Wyndham Lewis

Early Life and Shakespeare

It has been my experience of my few very eminent contemporaries that, after their various fashions, they have been the possessors of abnormally aggressive egos (and I daresay they may have discovered the same symptoms in myself). But what are these unhealthily large egos but one of the byproducts of the situation which isolates the so-called 'intellectual' from the common life, and demands of him much more domestic morale than is good for him?

When I saw Joyce described, as I did not long ago, as suffering from 'elephantiasis of the ego', I felt the usual contempt certain critics always succeed in provoking; for even their truths are so crude as to be invalid as they stand, having all the appearance of ill-favoured errors. But *of course* Joyce had 'elephantiasis of the ego'. Had he not suffered from something which lends itself to such an offensive description, you, Mr. Critic, would have no 'Ulysses' or 'Finnegans Wake' to gabble about: to blow hot and blow cold about – inflate your little reputation by puffing, and then reinflate it by a confession of disillusionment.

The only people of eminence I was in touch with as a beginner were painters, who enjoyed the usual robust self-esteem of their kind – painting being a much healthier occupation than writing. They overlooked in me the budding artist but accorded a generous recognition to something else. The first literary form I had used was verse, which I was writing while at the Slade [School of Art]. And to these elders I was known as a 'poet'. The Fine Arts they imagined were already in good hands, namely their own. Verse, as a form of literary composition, preceded my 'Wild Body' stories. I wrote a great deal, including a five-act play in blank verse. As early as my schooldays I had formed this habit, but what I wrote then was of a pietistic order.

About the time I went to the Slade I began to write Petrarchan sonnets, but soon changed to Shakespearean. They were easier to do. Some were so like Shakespeare's that as I recall lines in them I am never quite certain whether they are Shakespeare's or mine. It remains for me a mystery how so dumb a youth as I was can have produced them. It is nothing short of planchette, or automatic writing. Since the publication of Shakespeare's famous sequence many people have, it is true, written sonnets that could at first glance be mistaken for his. But they were usually experienced craftsmen.

My sonnet sequence contained no dark lady, all that side was appropriately absent, but if anything they exaggerated the Shakespearean pessimism. These pastiches, at all events, attracted attention among a small number of people. Here is a sonnetlike composition of that period, which I remember a luminary of those days singling out for commendation.

Doubt is the sole tonic that sustains the mind,
The keynote of this universe entire.
Self-conscious certainty is Doubt, and blind
God-worship but Doubt's sanctified attire.
God fashioned us in Doubt: for Eden-trees
Were planted there in God's initial Doubt:
. . . hope doth but tease
Us into . . . where certainty could not.

[. . .]

It was therefore an innovation for me to take to prose, when I began preparing material for stories in Brittany – at the time I felt a little of a come-down, or at least a condescension. My first attempts naturally were far less successful than the verse. The coastal villages of Finisterre in which I spent long summers (one of them with the artist, Henry Lamb) introduced one to a more primitive society. These fishermen went up to Iceland in quite small boats, they were as much at home in the huge and heaving Atlantic as the torero in the bull-ring: their speech was still Celtic and they were highly distrustful of the stranger. They brawled about money over their fierce apple-juice: when somebody was stabbed, which was a not infrequent occurrence, they would not call in a doctor, but come to the small inn where I stayed, for a piece of ice. A great part of their time was spent, when not at sea, jogging up and down between 'Pardons' [religious festivals], all the women provided with large umbrellas. Their miniature bagpipe is a fine screaming little object, to the music of which star dancers would leap up into the air, as if playing in a feudal ballet. On the whole, however, the dancing was sedate and mournful, compared with Rubens' peasants.

Long vague periods of an indolence now charged with some creative purpose were spent in digesting what I saw, smelt and heard. For indolent I remained. The Atlantic air, the raw rich visual food of the barbaric environment, the squealing of the pipes, the crashing of the ocean, induced a creative torpor. Mine was now a drowsy sun-baked ferment, watching with delight the great comic effigies which erupted beneath my rather saturnine but astonished gaze: Brotcotnaz, Bestre, and the rest.

During those days, I began to get a philosophy: but not a very good one, I am afraid. Like all philosophies, it was built up around the will – as primitive houses are built against a hill, or propped up upon a bog. As a timely expression of personal impulses it took the form of a reaction against civilised values. It was militantly vitalist. Only much later was I attracted to J.-J. Rousseau, or it might have had something to do with his anti-social dreaming.

The snobbishness (religion of the domestic) of the English middleclass, their cold philistinism, perpetual silly sports, all violently repudiated by me were the constant object of comparison with anything that stimulated and amused, as did these scenes. I overlooked the fact that I was observing them as a privileged spectator, having as it were purchased my front-row stall with money which I derived from that other life I despised. In spite of this flaw the contrast involved was a valid one: of the two types of life I was comparing, the one was essentially contemptible, the other at least rich in surface quality: in the clubhouse on an English golf-links I should not have found such exciting animals as I encountered here-undeniably the golfers' values are wanting in a noble animal zest. This is, however, a quandary that cannot be resolved so simply as I proposed – namely, the having-the-cake-and-eating-it way.

The epigraph at the beginning of my first novel, 'Tarr', is an expression of the same mood, which took a long time to evaporate altogether. It is a quotation from Montaigne. 'Que c'est un mol chevet que l'ignorance et l'incuriosité?' ['Are not incuriosity and ignorance a soft pillow?'] Even books, theoretically, were a bad thing, one was much better without them. Every time men borrowed something from outside they gave away something of themselves, for these acquisitions were artificial aggrandisement of the self, but soon there would be no core left. And it was the core that mattered. Books only muddied the mind: men's minds were much stronger when they only read the Bible.

The human personality, I thought, should be left alone, just as it is, in its pristine freshness: something like a wild garden – full, naturally, of starlight and nightingales, of sunflowers and the sun. The 'Wild Body' I envisaged as a piece of the wilderness. The characters I chose to celebrate – Bestre, the Cornac and his wife, Brotcotnaz, le père François – were all primitive creatures, immersed in life, as much as birds, or big, obsessed, sun-drunk insects.

The body was wild: one was attached to something wild, like a big cat that sunned itself and purred. The bums, alcoholic fishermen, penniless students (generally Russians) who might have come out of the pages of 'The Possessed', for long my favourite company, were an anarchist material. And as ringmaster of this circus I appointed my 'Soldier of Humour', who stalked imbecility with a militancy and appetite worthy of a much more light-hearted and younger Flaubert, who had somehow got into the universe of Gorky.

There is a psychological factor which may have contributed to what I have been describing. – I remained, beyond the usual period, congealed in a kind of cryptic immaturity. In my social relations the contacts remained, for long, primitive. I recognised dimly this obstruction: was conscious of gaucherie, of wooden responses – all fairly common symptoms of course. It resulted in experience with no natural outlet in conversation collecting in a molten column within. This *trop-plein* would erupt: that was my way of expressing myself-with intensity, and with the density of what had been undiluted by ordinary intercourse: a thinning-out which is, of course, essential for protection.

Observing introspectively this paradoxical flowering, this surface obtuseness, on the one hand, and unexpected fruit which it miraculously bore: observing this masterly inactivity, almost saurianly-basking sloth, and what that condition produced, something within me may quite reasonably have argued that this inspired *Dummheit* was an excellent idea. *Let us leave well alone!* may have been the mental verdict. I know everything already: why add irrelevant material to this miraculous source? Why acquire spectacles for an eye that sees so well without them? So there was superstition, and, I suspect, arrogance.

But I am gazing back into what is a very dark cavern indeed. An ungregarious childhood may have counted for something. A feature of perhaps greater importance was that after my schooldays, even with my intimates, I was much younger than those with whom I associated, since I had left school so early. And, finally, at school itself, developing habits as I did which appeared odd to the young empire-builders by whom I was surrounded, may have stiffened the defence natural to that age.

The rough set of principles arrived at was not, I have said, a very good philosophy. Deliberately to spend so much time in contact with the crudest life is, I believe, wasteful of life. It seems to involve the error that raw material is alone authentic life. I mistook for 'the civilised' the tweed-draped barbaric clown of the golf-links. But, as a philosophy of life, it principally failed in limiting life in a sensational sense. After two or three intermediate stages I reached ultimately an outlook that might be described as almost as formal as this earliest one was the reverse.

Rude Assignment: A Narrative of my Career Up-to-date (1950), pp. 115–18.

Vorticist Manifesto

I

1. Beyond Action and Reaction we would establish ourselves.

2. We start from opposite statements of a chosen world. Set up violent structure of adolescent clearness between two extremes.

3. We discharge ourselves on both sides.

4. We fight first on one side, then on the other, but always for the SAME cause, which is neither side or both sides and ours.

5. Mercenaries were always the best troops.

6. We are Primitive Mercenaries in the Modern World.

7. Our Cause is NO-MAN'S.

8. We set Humour at Humour's throat. Stir up Civil War among peaceful apes.

9. We only want Humour if it has fought like Tragedy.

10. We only want Tragedy if it can clench its side-muscles like hands on its belly, and bring to the surface a laugh like a bomb.

II

1. We hear from America and the Continent all sorts of disagreeable things about England: "the unmusical, anti-artistic, unphilosophic country."

2. We quite agree.

3. Luxury, sport, the famous English "Humour," the thrilling ascendancy and idée fixe of Class, producing the most intense snobbery in the World; heavy stagnant pools of Saxon blood, incapable of anything but the song of a frog, in home-counties: these phenomena give England a peculiar distinction, in the wrong sense, among the nations.

4. This is why England produces such good artists from time to time.

5. This is also the reason why a movement towards art and imagination could burst up here, from this lump of compressed life, with more force than anywhere else.

6. To believe that it is necessary for or conducive to art, to "improve" life, for instance – make architecture, dress, ornament, in "better taste," is absurd.

7. The Art-instinct is permanently primitive.

8. In a chaos of imperfection, discord, etc., it finds the same stimulus as in Nature.

9. The artist of the modern movement is a savage (in no sense an "advanced," perfected, democratic, Futurist individual of Mr Marinetti's limited imagination): this enormous, jangling, journalistic, fairy desert of modern life serves him as Nature did more technically primitive man.

10. As the steppes and the rigours of the Russian winter, when the peasant has to lie for weeks in his hut, produce that extraordinary acuity of feeling and intelligence we associate with the Slav; so England is just now the most favourable country for the appearance of a great art.

III

1. We have made it quite clear that there is nothing Chauvinistic or picturesquely patriotic about our contentions.

2. But there is violent boredom with that feeble Europeanism, abasement of the miserable "intellectual" before anything coming from Paris, Cosmopolitan sentimentality, which prevails in so many quarters.

3. Just as we believe that an Art must be organic with its Time,

So we insist that what is actual and vital for the South, is ineffectual and unactual in the North.

4. Fairies have disappeared from Ireland (despite foolish attempts to revive them) and the bull-ring languishes in Spain.

5. But mysticism on the one hand, gladiatorial instincts, blood and asceticism on the other, will be always actual, and springs of Creation for these two peoples.

6. The English Character is based on the Sea.

7. The particular qualities and characteristics that the sea always engenders in men are those that are, among the many diagnostics of our race, the most fundamentally English.

8. That unexpected universality as well, found in the completest English artists, is due to this.

IV

1. We assert that the art for these climates, then, must be a northern flower.

2. And we have implied what we believe should be the specific nature of the art destined to grow up in this country, and models of whose flue decorate the pages of this magazine.

3. It is not a question of the characterless material climate around us. Were that so the complication of the Jungle, dramatic Tropic growth, the vastness of American trees, would not be for us.

4. But our industries, and the Will that determined, face to face with its needs, the direction of the modern world, has reared up steel trees where the green ones were lacking; has exploded in useful growths, and found wilder intricacies than those of Nature.

V

1. We bring clearly forward the following points, before further defining the character of this necessary native art.

2. At the freest and most vigorous period of ENGLAND'S history, her literature, then chief Art, was in many ways identical with that of France.

3. Chaucer was very much cousin of Villon as an artist.

4. Shakespeare and Montaigne formed one literature.

5. But Shakespeare reflected in his imagination a mysticism, madness and delicacy peculiar to the North, and brought equal quantities of Comic and Tragic together.

6. Humour is a phenomenon caused by sudden pouring of culture into Barbary.

7. It is intelligence electrified by flood of Naivety.

8. It is Chaos invading Concept and bursting it like nitrogen.

9. It is the Individual masquerading as Humanity like a child in clothes too big for him.

10. Tragic Humour is the birthright of the North.

11. Any great Northern Art will partake of this insidious and volcanic chaos.

12. No great ENGLISH Art need be ashamed to share some glory with France, tomorrow it may be with Germany, where the Elizabethans did before it.

13. But it will never be French, any more than Shakespeare was, the most catholic and subtle Englishman.

VI

1. The Modern World is due almost entirely to Anglo-Saxon genius – its appearance and its spirit.

2. Machinery, trains, steam-ships, all that distinguishes externally our time, came far more from here than anywhere else.

3. In dress, manners, mechanical inventions, LIFE, that is, ENGLAND has influenced Europe in the same way that France has in Art.

4. But busy with this LIFE-EFFORT, she has been the last to become conscious of the Art that is an organism of this new Order and Will of Man.

5. Machinery is the greatest Earth-medium: incidentally it sweeps away the doctrines of a narrow and pedantic Realism at one stroke.

6. By mechanical inventiveness, too, just as Englishmen have spread themselves all over the Earth, they have brought all the hemispheres about them in their original island.

7. It cannot be said that the complication of the Jungle, dramatic tropic growths, the vastness of American trees, is not for us.

8. For, in the forms of machinery, Factories, new and vaster buildings, bridges and works, we have all that, naturally, around us.

VII

1. Once this consciousness towards the new possibilities of expression in present life has come, however, it will be more the legitimate property of Englishmen than of any other people in Europe.

2. It should also, as it is by origin theirs, inspire them more forcibly and directly.

3. They are the inventors of this bareness and hardness, and should be the great enemies of Romance.

4. The Romance peoples will always be, at bottom, its defenders.

5. The Latins are at present, for instance, in their "discovery" of sport, their Futuristic gush over machines, aeroplanes, etc., the most romantic and sentimental "moderns" to be found.

6. It is only the second-rate people in France or Italy who are thorough revolutionaries.

7. In England, on the other hand, there is no vulgarity in revolt.

8. Or, rather, there is no revolt, it is the normal state.

9. So often rebels of the North and the South are diametrically opposed species.

10. The nearest thing in England to a great traditional French artist, is a great revolutionary English one.

Signatures for Manifesto

R. Aldington Arbuthnot L. Atkinson
Gaudier Brzeska J. Dismorr C. Hamilton
E. Pound W. Roberts H. Sanders
E. Wadsworth Wyndham Lewis.

"Manifesto," *Blast*, No. 1 (June 1914), pp. 30–43.

Fêng Shui and Contemporary Form

1. That a mountain, river or person may not "suit" – the air of the mountain, the character of the person – and so influence lives, most men see.

But that a hill or man can be definitely disastrous, and by mere existence be as unlucky as hemlock is poisonous, shame or stupidity prevents most from admitting.

A certain position of the eyes, their fires crossing; black (as a sort of red) as sinister; white the mourning colour of China; white flowers, in the West, signifying death – white, the radium among colours, and the colour that comes from farthest off: 13, a terrible number: such are much more important discoveries than gravitation.

The law of gravitation took its place in our common science following the fall of an apple on somebody's head, which induced reflection.

13 struck people down again and again like a ghost, till they ceased hunting for something human, but invisible, and found a Number betraying its tragic nature and destiny.

Some Numbers are like great suns, round which the whole of Humanity must turn.

But people have a special personal Numerical which for them in particular is an object of service and respect.

2. Telegraph poles were the gloomiest of all Western innovations for China: their height disturbed definitely the delicate equilibrium of lives.

They were consequently resisted with bitterness.

Any text-book on China becomes really eloquent in its scorn when it arrives at the ascendancy of the Geomancers.

Geomancy is the art by which the favourable influence of the shape of trees, weight of neighbouring water and its colour, height of surrounding houses, is determined.

"No Chinese street is built to form a line of uniform height" (H.A. Giles), the houses are of unequal heights to fit the destinies of the inhabitants.

I do not suppose that good Geomancers are more frequent than good artists.

But their functions and intellectual equipment should be very alike.

3. Sensitiveness to volume, to the life and passion of lines, meaning of water, hurried conversation of the sky, or silence, impossible propinquity of endless clay nothing will right, a mountain that is a genius (good or evil) or a bore, makes the artist; and the volume, quality, or luminosity of a star at birth of Astrologers is also a clairvoyance within the painter's gift.

In a painting certain forms MUST be SO; in the same meticulous, profound manner that your pen or a book must lie on the table at a certain angle, your clothes at night be arranged in a set personal symmetry, certain birds be avoided, a set of railings tapped with your hand as you pass, without missing one.

Personal tricks and ceremonies of this description are casual examples of the same senses' activity.

Blast, No. 1 (June 1914), p. 138.

The New Egos

1. A civilized savage, in a desert-city, surrounded by very simple objects and restricted number of beings, reduces his Great Art down to the simple black human bullet.

His sculpture is monotonous. The one compact human form is his Tom-Tom.

We have nothing whatever to do with this individual and his bullet. Our eyes sweep life horizontally.

Were they in the top of our head, and full of blank light, our art would be different, and more like that of the savage.

The African we have referred to cannot allow his personality to venture forth or amplify itself, for it would dissolve in vagueness of space.

It has to be swaddled up in a bullet-like lump.

But the modern town-dweller of our civilization sees everywhere fraternal moulds for his spirit, and interstices of a human world.

He also sees multitude, and infinite variety of means of life, a world and elements he controls.

Impersonality becomes a disease with him.

Socially, in a parallel manner, his egotism takes a different form.

Society is sufficiently organized for his ego to walk abroad.

Life is really no more secure, or his egotism less acute, but the frontiers interpenetrate, individual demarcations are confused and interests dispersed.

2. According to the most approved contemporary methods in boxing two men burrow into each other, and after an infinitude of little intimate pommels, one collapses.

In the old style, two distinct, heroic figures were confronted, and one ninepin tried to knock the other ninepin over.

We all today (possibly with a coldness reminiscent of the insect-world) are in each other's vitals – overlap, intersect, and are Siamese to any extent.

Promiscuity is normal; such separating things as love, hatred, friendship are superseded by a more realistic and logical passion.

The human form still runs, like a wave, through the texture or body of existence, and therefore of art.

But just as the old form of egotism is no longer fit for such conditions as now prevail, so the isolated human figure of most ancient Art is an anachronism.

THE ACTUAL HUMAN BODY BECOMES OF LESS IMPORTANCE EVERY DAY. It now, literally, EXISTS much less.

Love, hatred, etc., imply conventional limitations.

All clean, clear-cut emotions depend on the element of strangeness, and surprise and primitive detachment.

Dehumanization is the chief diagnostic of the Modern World.

One feels the immanence of some REALITY more than any former human beings can have felt it.

This superseding of specific passions and easily determinable emotions by such uniform, more animal, instinctively logical Passion of Life, of different temperatures, but similar in kind, is, then, the phenomenon to which we would relate the most fundamental tendencies in present art, and by which we would gauge its temper.

Blast, No. 1 (June 1914), p. 141.

Abstraction and Representation

[...]

8. The first reason for not imitating Nature is that you cannot convey the emotion you receive at the contact of Nature by imitating her, but only by becoming her. To sit down and copy a person or a scene with scientific exactitude is an absurd and gloomy waste of time. It would imply the most abject depths of intellectual vacuity were it not for the fact that certain compensations of professional amusement and little questions of workmanship make it into a monotonous and soothing game.

9. The essence of an object is beyond and often in contradiction to, its simple truth: and literal rendering in the fundamental matter of arrangement and logic will never hit the emotion intended by unintelligent imitation.

10. Not once in ten thousand times will it correspond.

11. It is always the POSSIBILITIES in the object, the IMAGINATION, as we say, in the spectator, that matters. Nature itself is of no importance.

12. The sense of objects, even, is a sense of the SIGNIFICANCE of the object, and not its avoirdupois and scientifically ascertainable shapes and perspectives.

13. If the material world were not empirical and matter simply for science, but were organized as in the imagination, we should live as though we were dreaming. Art's business is to show how, then, life would be: but not as Flaubert, for instance, writes, to be a repose and "d'agir à la façon de la Nature," in giving sleep as well as dream.

15. [*sic*] The Imagination, not to be a ghost, but to have the vividness and warmth of life, and the atmosphere of a dream, uses, where best inspired, the pigment and material of nature.

16. For instance, because you live amongst houses, a "town-dweller," that is no reason why you should not specialize in soft forms, reminiscent of the lines of hills and trees, except that familiarity with objects gives you a psychological mastery akin to the practised mastery of the workman's hand.

17. But there is, on the other hand, no reason why you should not use this neighbouring material, that of endless masonry and mechanical shapes, if you enjoy it: and, as a practical reason, most of the best artists have exploited the plastic suggestions found in life around them.

18. If you do not use shapes and colours characteristic of your environment, you will only use some others characteristic more or less of somebody else's environment, and certainly no better. And if you wish to escape from this, or from any environment at all, you soar into the clouds, merely. That will only, in its turn, result in your painting what the dicky-birds would if they painted. Perhaps airmen might even conceivably share this tendency with the lark.

19. Imitation, and inherently unselective registering of impressions, is an absurdity. It will never give you even the feeling of the weight of the object, and certainly not the meaning of the object or scene, which is its spiritual weight.

20. But, to put against this, attempt to avoid all representative element is an equal absurdity. As much of the material poetry of Nature as the plastic vessel will stand should be included. But nowadays, when Nature finds itself expressed so universally in specialized mechanical counterparts, and cities have modified our emotions, the plastic vessel, paradoxically, is more fragile. The less human it becomes, the more delicate, from this point of view.

21. There is no necessity to make a sycophantish hullabulloo about this state of affairs, or burn candles in front of your telephone apparatus or motor car. It is even preferable to have the greatest contempt for these useful contrivances, which are no better and no worse than men.

22. Da Vinci recommends you to watch and be observant of the grains and markings of wood, the patterns found in Nature everywhere.

23. The patterned grains of stones, marble, etc., the fibres of wood, have a rightness and inevitability that is similar to the rightness with which objects arrange themselves in life.

24. Have your breakfast in the ordinary way, and, as the result of your hunger and unconsciousness, on getting up you will find an air of inevitability about the way the various objects, plates, coffee-pot, etc., lie upon the table, that it would be very difficult to get consciously. It would be still more difficult to convince yourself that the deliberate arrangement was natural.

25. IN THE SAME WAY THAT SAVAGES, ANIMALS AND CHILDREN HAVE A "RIGHTNESS," SO HAVE OBJECTS CO-ORDINATED BY UNCONSCIOUS LIFE AND USEFUL ACTIONS.

26. Use is always primitive.

27. This quality of ACCIDENTAL RIGHTNESS, is one of the principal elements in a good picture.

28. The finest artists – and this is what Art means – are those men who are so trained and sensitized that they have a perpetually renewed power of DOING WHAT NATURE DOES, only doing it with all the beauty of accident, without the certain futility that accident implies.

29. Beauty of workmanship in painting and sculpture is the appearance of Accident, in the sense of Nature's work, or rather of Growth, the best paintings being in the same category as flowers, insects and animals. And as Nature, with its glosses, tinting and logical structures, is as efficient as any machine and more wonderful; hand-made, as recommendation, means done by Nature.

30. Imperfect hands (most artists') produce what might be termed machine-made; as men were the first machines, just as insects were the first artists.

31. The best creation, further, is only the most highly developed selection and criticism.

32. It is well to study the patterns on a surface of marble. But the important thing is to be able to make patterns like them without the necessity of direct mechanical stimulus.

33. You must be able to organize the cups, saucers and people, or their abstract plastic equivalent, as naturally as Nature, only with the added personal logic of Art, that gives the grouping significance.

34. What is known as "Decorative Art" is rightly despised by both the laborious and unenterprising imitators of Nature on the one hand, and the brilliant inventors and equals of Nature on the other.

35. The "Decorative" artist (as examples, the sort of spirit that animates the Jugend, Rhythm, Mr Roger Fry's little belated Morris movement) is he who substitutes a banal and obvious human logic for the co-ordination and architectures that the infinite forces of Nature bring about.

36. These exterior "arrangers," not living their work, have not even the reflected life that the photographer can claim.

37. The only people who have nothing to do with Nature and who as artists are most definitely inept and in the same box as the Romantic, – who is half-way between the Vegetable and the God – are these between-men, with that most odious product of man, modern DECORATION.

F

1. To conclude: The Whole of art today can undoubtedly be modified in the direction of a greater imaginative freedom of work, and with renewed conception of aesthetics in sympathy with our time.

2. But I think a great deal of effort will automatically flow back into more natural forms from the barriers of the Abstract.

3. There have been so far in European painting Portrait, Landscape, Genre, Still-life.

4. Whatever happens, there is a new section that has already justified its existence, which is

bound to influence, and mingle with the others, as they do with each other; that is, for want of a better word, the Abstract.

"A Review of Contemporary Art," *Blast*, No. 2 (July 1915), pp. 45–46.

The Battle of Messines

This morning is peaceful: the enemy is now much farther away, and we are temporarily derelict among 12" railway mountings, horse lines: minor Headquarters are even moving up among us. I expect we shall have to go pretty soon. Yesterday once more I took my way to the forward intelligence O[bservation] P[ost]. We were shelled out of it yesterday morning, the side of the dugout being disorganized by an 8" shell. = Imagine a stretch of land one mile in depth sloping up from the old German first-line to the top of a ridge, & stretching to right & left as far as you can see. It looks very large, never-ending and empty. There are only occasional little groups of men round a bomb-dump, or building a light railway: two men pushing a small truck on which a man is being brought back, lying on his stomach, his head hanging over the side. The edge of the ridge is where you are bound for, at the corner of a demolished wood. The place is either loathesomely hot, or chilly according to the time of day at which you cross it. It is a reddish colour, and all pits, ditches & chasms, & black stakes, several hundred, here & there, marking the map-position of a wood. Shells never seem to do more than shave the trees down to these ultimate black stakes, except in the few cases when they tear them up, or a mine swallows them.

The moment you get in this stretch of land you feel the change from the positions you have come from. A watchfulness, fatigue and silence penetrates everything in it. You meet a small party of infantry slowly going up or coming back. Their faces are all dull, their eyes turned inwards in sallow thought or savage resignation; you would say revulsed, if it were not too definite a word. There is no regular system of communication trenches yet; this is the bad tract, the narrow and terrible wilderness. As a matter of fact it only becomes clearly unsafe as you approach the ridge. You get nearer to the shell bursts on the crest, until the nearest black cloud is only a hundred yards away, on the road at the skyline. Perhaps to your right, half way up, there has been heavy shelling, but not near enough to require craft, & the noise is inconsiderable. There are shrapnel bursts overhead almost continually, but for some reason absurdly high and ineffective. = As to the ridge: I have been three times. Yesterday as we got within a hundred yards of the road there was suddenly a swooping whistle: my commanding officer shouted down: we crouched in a shell-hole, and a 5.9 burst about 15 or 20 yards away, between us & the wood – about 3 shell holes away, you could say, they were so regular thereabouts. Another came over about 15 yards nearer the wood, & at the third, actually in the wood, we concluded it was the wood corner they were after, & proceeded. The road at the top runs along the front of the wood for about 100 yds; the O.P. on the edge of the wood, being about 40 yds from where we struck the road. This road for its own sake is being shelled constantly, & because the Bosche imagines that there are machine gun emplacements at farther end. He also imagines that the wood is bristling with batteries; & is fatuous enough, in addition, to believe that his beautiful concrete dugouts are being used by our men. (You notice how guarded my language is.) As we reached this road, four black bursts came in succession halfway down the short stretch we could see. Straight for those bursts we made: but I shall not repeat that often. Nothing else came over as it happened. But as soon as we had reached the handsomely concreted German dugout, three 5.9's dropped just outside the door. This goes on the whole while up there. = Shall I or shall I not ask to go up there again tomorrow? There is nothing there you cannot imagine: but it has the unexpected quality of reality. Also the imagined thing and the felt are in two different categories. This category has its points. I will write you further on the subject of War. Do not expect my compositions to be well-worded, as letters (my letters) are only meant to be chat and slop. – Remember me to Mrs Pound.

Yrs
W.L.

Letter to Ezra Pound, 14 June 1917.

Why Design Matters

What is this ugliness, banality, and squalor to which we have been referring? It is simply what meets your eye as it travels up practically any street in London today, or wanders around any Hotel lounge or Restaurant, or delects itself along the wall of the official galleries at Burlington House. Next, what influences go to the making of this horrible form-content and colour-content that we can either offer up a prayer of thankfulness for, take no notice of, or occupy ourselves with modifying, in our spare time? Exactly what set of circumstances, what lassitude or energy of mind working through millions of channels and multitudes of people, make the designs on match boxes (or the jokes on the back of some), the ornamental metal-work on the lamp-posts, gates, knife-handles, sepulchral enclosures, serviette-rings, most posters, ornamented Menu cards, the scenery in our Musical spectacles, chapter-headings and tail-pieces, brooches, bangles, embossments on watches, clocks, carving-knives, cruets, pendants in Asprey's, in Dobson's, in Hancock's windows in Bond Street; in fact, every stitch and scrap of art-work that indefatigably spreads its blight all over a modern city, invading every nook, befouling the loveliest necks, waists, ears, and bosoms; defiling even the doormat – climbing up, even, and making absurd and vapid the chimney pot, which you would have thought was inaccessible and out of sight enough for Art not to reach; for the cheap modern thousand-headed devil of design not to find it worth while to spoil?

We are all perfectly agreed, are we not, that practically any house, railing, monument, wall, structure, thoroughfare, or lamppost in this city should be instantly pulled down, were it not for the "amusement" and stimulus that the painter gets out of it?

A complete reform (were it not for the needs of the painter who *must* have his bit of banality, bless his little heart!) of every notion or lack of notion on the significance of the appearance of the world should be instituted. A gusto, a consciousness should imbue the placing and the shaping of every brick. A central spectacle, as a street like Regent Street is, should be worked out in the smallest detail. It should not grow like a weed, without forethought, meaning, or any agency but the drifting and accident of commerce. A great thoroughfare like Regent Street develops and sluggishly gets on its ill-articulated legs, and blankly looks at us with its silly face. There are Bouvards and Pécuchets in brick and stone, or just dull cheerless photographs. There is no beautiful or significant relief, even in this third-rate comic spectacle.

Do politicians understand so little the influence of the Scene of Life; or the effect of Nature, that they can be so indifferent to the capital of a wealthy and powerful community? Would not a more imaginative Cecil Rhodes have seen that the only way an Empire such as he imagined could impress itself on the consciousness of a people would be in some such way as all ambitious nations have taken to make the individual citizen aware of his privileges and his burden? Whether in the weight of a Rhetoric of buildings, or in the subtler ways of beauty signifying the delights and rewards of success won by toil and adventure; in a thousand ways the imagination of the multitude could be captured and fixed. But beyond the obvious policy of not having a mean and indolent surrounding for the capital of what sets out to be an "Empire," simply for human life at all, or what sets out to be human life – *to increase gusto and belief in that life* – it is of the first importance that the senses should be directed into such channels, appealed to in such ways, that this state of mind of relish, fullness and exultation should obtain.

It is life at which you must aim. Life, full life, is lived through the fancy, the senses, consciousness. These things must be stimulated and not depressed. The streets of a modern city are depressing. They are so aimless and so weak in their lines and their masses, that the mind and senses jog on their way like passengers in a train with blinds down in an overcrowded carriage.

"The Politician's Apathy," *The Caliph's Design: Architects! Where is Your Vortex?* (1919), pp. 15–16.

The Artist Older than the Fish

The artist goes back to the fish. The few centuries that separate him from the savage are a mere flea-bite to the distance his memory must stretch if it is to strike the fundamental slime of creation. And it is the condition, the very first gusto of creation in this scale of life in which we are set, that he must reach, before he, in his turn, can create!

The creation of a work of art is an act of the same description as the evolution of wings on the sides of a fish, the feathering of its fins; or the invention of a weapon within the body of a hymenopter to enable it to meet the terrible needs of its life. The ghostly and burning growths, the walking twigs and flying stones, the two anguished notes that are the voice of a being, the vapid twitter, the bellows of age-long insurrection and discontent, the complacent screech, all may be considered as types of art, all equally perfect, but not all equally desirable.

The attitude of instructed people as regards "the artist" has changed. It is mixed up with, and depends a good deal on, the exactitude of their application of this term. With the grotesque prostitution of the word Artist, and its loose, indeed very loose and paltry meaning in this country, I will deal in a separate section. A German philosopher, living in the heyday of last century German music, accepted the theory of an aesthetic justification of the universe. Many people play with this notion, just as they play with Art. But we should have to disembarrass "art" of a good deal of cheap adhesive matter, and cheap and pretty adhesive people, before it could appear a justification for anything at all; much less for such a gigantic and, from every point of view, dubious concern as the Universe!

The artist's function is to create – to make something; and not to *make something pretty*, as dowagers, dreamers, and dealers here suppose. In any synthesis of the universe, the harsh, the hirsute, the enemies of the rose, must be built in for the purposes as much of a fine aesthetic, as of a fine logical, structure. And having removed the sentimental gulf that often has, in the course of their chequered career, kept Sense and Beauty apart, we may at this stage of the proceedings even refer to their purposes as one.

Fabre describes the creative capabilities of certain beetles, realisable on their own bodies; beasts with a record capacity for turning their form and colour impulses into living flesh. These beetles can convert their faces into hideously carved and detestable masks, can grow out of their bodies menacing spikes, and throw up on top of their heads sinister headdresses, overnight. Such changes in their personal appearance, conceived to work on the psychology of their adversaries, is possibly not a very profound or useful invention, but it is surely a considerable feat. Any art worth the name is, at the least, a feat of this description. The New Guinea barred and whitewashed masks are an obvious parallel. But any invention or phantasy in painting or carving is such. As to the wing mechanism that first lifted a creature off the ground, and set it spinning or floating through the air, you must call Shakespeare in to compete with it. Ma Yuan we can consider, roughly speaking, as the creator of the first tree; or substitute for him the best artist, who has painted the best tree, that you can remember.

The more sensible we grow about the world, the more sensible we grow about the artist. We are really more in sympathy with a bird or a fish today than we have been for a considerable time. And while people at large are being forced, by snobbery, into a less anthropomorphic mood, they find, with some awakening of respect, traces and odd indications of the artist's presence everywhere they go beyond their simian pale. The artist, we all agree, was the first scientist! His "inhumanity" is so old that he looks with considerable contempt on the upstart and fashionable growth that the last twenty years has produced!

"The Artist Older than the Fish," *The Caliph's Design: Architects! Where is Your Vortex?* (1919), pp. 35–36.

Pablo Picasso

What do all these "periods" and very serious flutterings of Picasso imply? To dash uneasily from one seemingly personal mode to another may be a diagnostic of the same highly sensitive but non-centralized talent as you would think that a playing first in the mode of El Greco and then of David probably implied. [An inconstancy in the scholarly vein might be matched by an inconstancy in the revolutionary.]* These are difficult things to decide, since painters *are*, through the nature of their art, at the same time composers and executants. And you must usually get at this by consideration of, and sense for, the man's work as a whole.

What has happened in this volatile and many-phased career of Picasso's? Has he got bored with a thing the moment it was within his grasp? And he certainly has arrived on occasion at the possessive stage. If it is boredom, associated with so much power, one is compelled to wonder whether this power does not derive from a vitiated and tired source. He does not perhaps *believe* in what he has made. Is that it? And yet he is tirelessly compelled to go on achieving these images, immediately to be discarded.

But when we consider one by one, with a detailed scrutiny, the best types of work representing his various periods, we must admit that he had certain reason in abandoning them. However good a pastiche of El Greco may be, it is not worth prolonging indefinitely such an exercise. The same applies to his Daumieresque period. Splendid paintings as the *Miss Stein* and *Monsieur Sagot* undoubtedly are, they are still pure Cézanne. And although many artists, among his dilettante admirers or his lesser brethren, would give their heads to produce such pure and almost first-hand Cézannes, once you *can* do this as easily as Picasso, it can hardly seem worth while to continue to do it. Very likely, at the present moment, his Ingres or David paintings will induce the same sensations of boredom in him (I can imagine David inducing *very* dismal feelings in an interpreter), and have a similar fate. All that remain to be considered are the less easily deciphered works of his more abstract periods. I think his effort of initiation and obstinacy in this brand of work showed a different temper to the other set of things that we have been considering. But they, again, are open to question. They reduce themselves to three principal phases. The first, or Cubist, phase, really a dogmatic and savage development of Cézanne's idiosyncrasy (example: *Dame jouant de la mandoline*) is in a way the most satisfactory. But I am not convinced that Cézanne gains anything by what is a very interesting interpretation of his vision. But, on the other hand, the *Lady with the Mandoline* appears to me as interesting as a typical Cézanne portrait, and it is a powerful and inventive variation on Cézanne. And about the next step – fourth-dimensional preoccupations and new syntheses added to the earlier ones (*Dame assise*) and the first Braque-like contrivances – you wonder if they are not more important as experiments, and important because of their daring and new nature than as final works. But the whole character of these things: the noble structural and ascetic quality, the feeling that he must have had, and that he imparted to them, that he was doing something at last worth while, and in fitting relation to his superb painter's gift – this makes them a more serious contribution to painting than anything else done by him. All the admiration that you feel for the really great artist in Picasso finds its most substantial footing in the extraordinary series of works beginning with the paintings of the time of the Miss Stein portrait, and finishing somewhere in the beginning of his Braque period.

* Added 1939.

"Picasso," *The Caliph's Design: Architects! Where is Your Vortex?* (1919), pp. 57–58.

Art, Science and Philosophy

The way in which science differs, at first sight, from art, is that the progress of scientific knowledge seems a positive and illimitable progression; in the sense that we know more today about the phenomenon of electricity, for example, or of disease, or the structure of the world, than men are recorded ever to have known. There is a reason to believe that we shall soon be still better informed. In painting, on the other hand, a masterpiece of Sung or of the best sculpture of Dynastic Egypt is, as art, impossible to improve on, and very little has been produced in our time that could bear comparison with it.

But art is a valuation: in its relation to science it is somewhat in the position philosophy has so far occupied. Science presents men with more and more perfected instruments, and the means of material ascendancy: these appliances are used, and the use of them reacts on the user, and on his estimate of the meaning and possibilities of life. These estimates and beliefs are chalked up, and more or less critically signalled, in the works of the artist, and assessed sometimes by the philosopher. So science, in a sense, is criticized by art at the same time as is man.

The popular current belittlement of the function of what, since Socrates, has been called philosophy, tends, as is always the case, to become vindictive; to thrust too harshly some hero of the moment into the empty throne. But no doubt philosophy must become something else to survive, though the character of mind that has made a man up to the present a philosopher will still operate. The pseudo-scientific element in philosophy, with the growth of exact specialized science, has brought it to its present pass. That unbridled emotional element found in it, that has discredited most speculation in retrospect, is proper to art, where it can be usefully organized and controlled. All that side of the philosopher has its legitimate outlet there. And the man of science, so long as he remains ideally that, is a servant and not a master. He is the perfect self-effacing highly technical valet of our immediate life. The philosopher as such shows every sign of disintegrating into something like (1) the artist, (2) the man of science, and (3) the psychologist. The artist gets a good share, it is certain, of the booty attending this demise.

At the moment of this break-up it is perhaps natural that art and science should both be momentarily swollen with the riches of this neighbouring province suffering partition. The disinherited spirit of the philosopher finds asylum in these related activities. The philosopher, that hybrid of the religious teacher, man of science and artist, was always, certainly, a more artificial and vulnerable figure than his neighbours. And yet neither the artist nor the man of science can take his place.

When, however, the definitely intellectual character of art today is complained of, and artists are accused of theorizing too much on the subject of their books and pictures, one cannot do better than quote David Hume where, in the process of relating morals to the aesthetic sense, he writes: "But in many orders of beauty, particularly those of the finer arts, it is requisite to employ much reasoning, in order to feel the proper sentiment; and a false relish may frequently be corrected by argument and reflection. There are just grounds to conclude that moral beauty partakes much of this latter species, and demands the assistance of our intellectual faculties, in order to give it a suitable influence on the human mind."

The finer the art, the more extended the role the intellectual faculties Hume speaks of are called upon to play.

"Essay on the Objective of Plastic Art in our Time," *The Tyro*, No. 2 (1922), pp. 23–24.

The Sense of the Future

Bergson's view that the permanence of the work of art, or its continued interest for us, depends on its uniqueness, on the fact that such and such a thing will *never happen again*, would make everything in life a work of art. This uniqueness is a portion of everything, and need not be invoked for the definition of art. In fact, the other factors of the work of art of an opposite and general description are those that distinguish it from the rest of life, cancelling as far as possible its uniqueness. Indeed, as I have shown, it would seem that successful expression occurs exactly at the point where, should this uniqueness be diminished any further, it would lose in force as human expression. Even one of the only standards of measurement we have is the distance to which a personality can penetrate into the general or the abstract, without losing its force and reality for us.

The object, in Schopenhauer's words: "Plucked out of the stream," also is only plucked so far as will still enable it to breathe and live. Or rather – to dispense with the metaphor – the "plucking" consists just in *abstracting* it. When it has been abstracted it is not quite what it was when in the stream. It is always a *different* thing, as we have said, when conveyed to us as an object of contemplation. And yet, it is that particular thing, still, that it was in the stream. For the distance it has traversed in the process of abstraction is insignificant if compared with the distances involved were it to reach an ultimate abstraction.

The question of uniqueness is bound up with that of the "present time" for the "present" is the essence of the unique, or of *our* unique. I will deal with this later on in the present essay, only considering for the moment our relation to the *future*, which must be considered at this point.

If it is true that all the past is in us, that it is this past, in terms of the present, that the artist shows you when he excites you most; – where, we must ask, in all this, does the future come in? Tragedy drags to the surface your wild monsters, gives them a few hours' frolic, and they are then driven back quietly to their dens. There is another sort of artist (of which the Italian Futurist, now deceased, is an excellent specimen) who should really be called a Presentist. He is closely related to the pure Impressionist. He pretends to live, and really succeeds sometimes, a sort of spiritual hand-to-mouth existence. He has tried with frenzy to identify himself with matter –with the whizzing, shrieking body, the smooth rolling machine, the leaping gun. And his life is such an eternal present as is matter's: only, being a machine, he wears out: but with his death nothing comes to an end, or is supposed to come to an end, but the matter of which his dynamic present is composed.

There are, however, some men who seem to contain the future as others contain the past. These are, in the profoundest sense, also our men of action, if you admire that term: for, as the hosts of the unlived thing, they are the impersonification of action. I think that every poet, painter or philosopher worth the name has in his composition a large proportion of *future* as well as of past. The more he has, the more prophetic intuition, and the more his energy appears to arrive from another direction to that of the majority of men (namely, the past), the better poet, painter or philosopher he will be.

A space must be cleared, all said and done, round the hurly-burly of the present. No man can reflect or create, in the intellectual sense, while he is acting – fighting, playing tennis, or making love. *The present man in all of us is the machine*. The farther away from the present, though not too far, the more free. So the choice must be between the past and the future. Every man has to choose, or rather the choice is early made for each of us.

We all know people, and not necessarily old people, who live in the past. The past that they survey is only a prolonged present, stretching back as far as their mind's eye can reach. We know a great many more, the majority, of machine-like, restless and hard individuals, who positively rattle with a small, hollow, shaken ego; or, less objectionably, throb and purr with the present vibration of a plodding and complacent mechanism.

The man of the future, the man who is in league with time, is as engrossed *away* from the actual as the first man is in his dear past. There is not such a sad light over the future: it is not infected with so many old murders, and stale sweet-heartings, and therefore the man accustomed to its landscapes is of a more cheerful disposition than his neighbour the other way.

I must leave this attractive figure, however, and once more hurry on, hoping to deal with him more fully before this essay is completed.

I will offer an exhortation, however, on this theme before departing from it.

You handle with curiosity and reverence a fragment belonging to some civilization developed three millenniums ago. Why cannot you treat the future with as much respect? Even if the Future is such a distant one that the thing you hold in your hand, or the picture you look at has something of the mutilation and imperfection that the fragment coming to you from the past also has, is not the case a similar one? May it not actually possess as well the "charm" you allow to your antiquarian sense? I think we should begin to regard ourselves all more in this light – as drawing near to a remote future, rather than receding from an historic past. The time has perhaps arrived to do that! Have not a few of us been preparing?

The future possesses its history as well as the past, indeed. All living art is the history of the future. The greatest artists, men of science and political thinkers, come to us from the future – from the opposite direction to the past.

"Essay on the Objective of Plastic Art in Our Time," *The Tyro*, No. 2 (1922), pp. 34–36.

Henri Matisse

The Matisse – *La Danse aux Capucines* – suggests to me – and whenever I see anything by Matisse I am forced to the same conclusion – that the contemporary world of art has in the case of Matisse gone very far wrong in according him the great place that it has. The reasons for that, seeing the dimensions of the mistake, would require an analysis that I cannot offer here. They can, however, be very roughly indicated.

The summary and superficial *chic* of his work makes it, I think, the natural ideal of the dilettante. Most of his well-known paintings have been posters, to begin with, scrawled and distempered thinly on a uniform ground. They have been specifically *caricatures* in the sense that they resemble – allowing for their difference in scale – a quantity of very entertaining and dextrous little drawings that you can see any day of the week in a French comic paper. In a deviation from the normal – of which caricature is an example – It is not possibly so easy, but it is as natural, to distort or rearrange in the direction of a *heightening* of effect, as of a *lowering*. It is unnecessary to say that all the art that we have up to the present agreed to admire has tended rather to the former deviation than to the latter. Of course, it is not a simple matter to agree on this question of direction; and the sculpture of Matisse – which invariably shows you some pathological distortion or variety of imbecility – could be defended against the superior assault of, say, the head of Colleoni at Venice on the ground that the latter is that of an *energumene*, demented in its martial energy. I must content myself here with saying that: (1) The people in the work of Matisse are arbitrarily distorted to satisfy a human predilection of the painter, rather than to satisfy the magnetic behests of neighbouring objects; (2) the predilection seems to me to be a mean, ridiculous, and empty one; (3) the effect has been to degrade the human accompaniment of his pots, furniture, and screens not only in significance, but also in beauty; (4) and that even from the coarse, summary treatment – showing an apt, but thin and slovenly, intelligence – this result could be anticipated.

Matisse is best at a very circumscribed, thin, gay, and pretty cleverly arranged effect; and many small canvases of his for what they set out to be, are good enough. They especially have the merit of providing a fairly palatable, "sketchy" article for the amateur who feels the absence in his life of intellectual excitement, but does not want too much. And (as remarked above) they also meet the dilettante painter half-way – providing him with a common ground of "work" – half-way between the playful immaturity of his daubing and dabbing, and the forbidden regions of great achievement. This, in an age when the spectators have revolted, and insist on participating in the performance, and refuse to take an interest in anything that cannot be easily imitated – has taken Matisse a long way, too.

[…]

La Danse aux Capucines is a good specimen of his work. The two human figures are unstrung streams of paint, rather *sarcoid* than *living*, like distended toffee-sticks rather than anything else. It is a well-arranged, tasteful decoration, the colouring of which is certainly no better than you usually get in any Japanese print of however degenerate and coarse a type. Indeed, the harshness and crudity of some of the late bad prints are usually much more pleasantly irritant than the merely sweet, "tasteful," and pleasant colouring of Matisse.

"Art Chronicle" (1924). Rprt. *Creatures of Habit and Creatures of Change* (1989), pp. 105–6.

Friedrich Nietzsche

Many great writers (and Nietzsche was of course a very great one) address audiences who do not exist. Nietzsche was always addressing people who did not exist. To address passionately and sometimes with very great wisdom *people who do not exist* has this disadvantage (especially when the imaginary audience is a very large one, as was the case with Nietzsche) that there will always be a group of people who, seeing a man shouting apparently at somebody or other, and seeing nobody else in sight, will think that it is they who are being addressed. Nietzsche was sufficiently all-there to realize that this must happen. And most that is unsatisfactory in his teaching was a result of that consciousness. Nietzsche imagined a new type of human being – the Superman; and to "supermen" he poured out sometimes his secret thoughts, and sometimes what he thought they ought to know of his secret thoughts. But he lived in a Utopia, and wrote in and for a Utopia, hoping to make Europe that Utopia by pretending that it was. He had a very great effect on Europe: but an opposite one to what you would have anticipated from his creed, as was only to be expected. For a message getting into the hands of the many, or of people opposite to those for whom it is destined, has usually an opposite effect to that it is intended to have by its sender.

"Nietzsche as a Vulgariser," *The Art of Being Ruled* (1926), pp. 123–24.

Jean-Jacques Rousseau

Rousseau was as truly a revolutionary as Bakunin. Proudhon was as little a revolutionary as Bouvard or Pécuchet. Proudhon, as an anti-revolutionary, anti-religious mind, can be regarded as one of the last bulwarks of the roman world. There is nothing so *french* in France today as Proudhon. The *roman* becomes more and more eroded and emolliated.

On the other hand, Rousseau is the great landmark of the new world of revolutionary modern Europe. This has nothing to do with whether or to what extent he was responsible for the French Revolution. He stands just behind it, as a great symbol of disintegration, of the final abdication of the roman, pagan, legal intelligence to the forces of a nature "stronger in mystery," of an intenser life and deeper intelligence than itself. It is as though the militant East had entered into Europe with Rousseau. He seems like a messenger sent to the gossiping, agnostic, mechanical eighteenth-century philosophic *salon*, to announce a god's displeasure; or to throw it, with his eloquence, into a preliminary disarray.

"Rousseau's Mysterious Power of Awakening Hostility," *The Art of Being Ruled* (1926), pp. 359–60.

The Politics of the Intellect

The life of the intelligence is the very incarnation of freedom: where it is dogmatic and harsh it is impure; where it is too political it is impure: its disciplines are less arbitrary and less *political* than those of religion: and it is the most inveterate enemy of unjust despotic power. In its operation it is less violent and more beneficent than religion, with its customary intolerance of emotional extremes. It does not exercise power by terror or by romantic pictures of the vast machinery of Judgment and Destruction. It is more humane than are the programmes of the theological justiciary. And its servants are not a sect nor an organized caste, like the priest or the hereditary aristocrat, but individuals possessing no concerted and lawless power, coming indifferently from all classes, and living simply among other people. And their pride, if they have it, is because of something inside themselves which has been won at no one else's expense, and that no one can give them or remove from them.

"The Politics of the Intellect," *The Art of Being Ruled* (1926), pp. 432–33.

An Ark for the Soul

In such a fluid world we should by all rights be building boats rather than houses. But this essay is a sort of ark, or dwelling for the mind, designed to float and navigate; and we should all be wise, with or without covenants, to provide ourselves with some such shell in everything, rather than to rely on any conservative structures. For a very complete and profound inundation is at hand. After *us* comes the Deluge: more probably than not, however, before that, and out of its epigrammatic sequence.

Meantime, we have a duty where the *officials of the Flood*, as they might be called, are concerned. We have to serve them out with gas-masks, light navigable craft of a seaworthy and inconspicuous type, and furnish them with instructions as to currents, winds, head-swells, maritime effluvia, Sargasso seas, doldrums, sharks, waterspouts, and sea-serpents. The complete equipment of an inspector of the Flood would be of such a technical description that it is impossible, however, to more than hint at it.

When Heine's english engineer had made his automaton, it "gnashed and growled" in his ear, "Give me a soul!" Naturally, being an english engineer, he had never thought of that, nor was he able to invent it. Some day we shall probably be confronted with some such harsh request. And we shall probably be as ill provided as was the english engineer. We should remember what we owe to our machines, which are our creatures. "Remember the machines!" would be a good watchword or catchword. We are imbuing them with our own soullessness. We only have ourselves to thank if things turn out badly as a result. We brutalize them as the Senegalese and other native troops are brutalized by contact with our ruthless and too barbarous methods of warfare. But, as I have suggested above, in all likelihood the evolution of the machine will eventually be guided into more humane channels, when the destruction phase is past.

The modern "soul" began, of course, in the Reformation. The most beautiful illustration of that birth (where you could almost observe it being born out of the bowels of the Venus of Milo) would be found within the anxious brain of Olympia Morata, the saintly blue-stocking of Ferrara. There the classical learning and beauty of the ancient world bred, body to body with the Reformation, this strange child.

When Luther appealed for the individual soul direct to God, and the power of all mediating authority was definitely broken, God must have foreseen that he would soon follow His viceregents. The individual soul would later on, had he been God, have known very well that when he abandoned God, he would before long himself be abandoned. The mediator should have known that too. In any case this necessary triad has vanished. The trinity of God, Subject, and Object is at an end. The collapse of this trinity is the history also of the evolution of the subject into the object or of the child back into the womb from which it came.

"Creative and Destructive Revolution," *The Art of Being Ruled* (1926), pp. 16–17.

Don Quixote, Chivalry and Falstaff

"The wound that phantom gave me!" says Don Quixote about the blow on his head he had received from the official of the Holy

Brotherhood. His enemies are *phantoms*, because he is a phantom too. He has no trace in his nature of the raging reality of Shakespeare's figures, Timon or Lear, for whom, as even for Hamlet, enemies are only too *real*. But that is doubtless also because Don Quixote has the luck to be a phantom himself.

At first sight, then, Don Quixote appears as a mighty satire on something which, being such a great artist, Cervantes himself must have been (leaving *the Spaniard* out of the question).

All the chivalrous splendours of the Middle Ages, which redeem their "darkness," it was his destiny to "laugh away." Rabelais, it is true, did somewhat the same thing, although their objects were quite different; only Rabelais dealt in impossible giants, whereas Cervantes took a very probable poor gentleman of La Mancha, as Defoe might have taken him; and it was because of the natural *mise en scène* and the sober relative likelihood of the narrative, for one thing, that it was so much more effective.

Both again floated their great new ventures on a popular tide of romanesque fiction. Rabelais launched the gigantic satire of his time that he had slowly elaborated on a tide fed with such bombastic rivers as those of *Les faits et gestes du preux Goddefroy de Boulieu et de ses chevalereux freres Baudouin et Eustache*, *Robert le Diable*, *Fierabras*, *Les Quatre fils Aymon*, *Huon de Bordeaux*, *Lancelot du Lac* [...]

The writer to whom I am principally indebted for my information on the sources of Rabelais – Jean Lattard – insists that it was not Rabelais' intention to *ridicule* the *chevaleresque* literature of France, but only to make use of its success for his own purposes. Indeed he cites La Noue on the subject of the *Amadis* and similar books to the effect that if in those times "quelqu'un les eust voulu alors blamer, on lui eust craché au visage, d'autant qu'ils servaient de pedagogues, de jouet et d'entretien à beaucoup de personnes."

But this seems to me to be talking as though the literature of chivalry contained nothing but one thing – that it was chivalry itself, in short. It might be that both Rabelais' and Cervantes' feeling on the subject of this contemporary literature was that in the long run it was adapted in its vulgarized form to make the chivalrous characteristics of bravery, simple-heartedness, generosity, good faith and exalted and romantic love, very ridiculous: much more so, in fact, than any deliberate caricature of them could effect. The popularization of the ideal of aristocracy by Nietzsche, and its effect on many a little bourgeois, is a parallel of interest. But how anyone can have thought that it was to satirize a figure of that calibre that Don Quixote was written is difficult to see.

For *Don Quixote* advertises and perpetuates chivalry, does it not, far more than any *Amadis de Gaula* or the *Gesta* of the Cid? And Cervantes betrays a tenderness for this *hijo seco*, this mournful and stately child of his, in a wild and commonplace world, which cannot be missed, and which no burlesque can displace; and which is certainly not the handling of political satire. The millionaire monsters of roman satire, cheap and dull, swimming in a sewer of disfiguring luxury, are not on the same side of the battle as this penniless, sober, solemn gentleman, setting out on a haggard horse to relieve distress and uphold his empty dream.

For if Miguel Cervantes were *attacking* Don Quixote – the very statement of this unnatural event disposes of it – it would be the one lonely and conspicuous case of an attack by a great artist on the poor, the unfortunate, the mocked-at, insulted and despised. Which (applying the euclidean formula, and remembering our earlier axiom that "Satire is always directed at the fortunate and successful") is impossible.

Therefore, if we had nothing else to guide us, we should know that Cervantes was identifying himself with Don Quixote, rather than with the world besetting his knight. It would be identifying all that he admired most with his hero, at the same time that he understood its melancholy destiny: the laughter and mockery that he stirred up around this noble fiction he knew that violence alone could silence, and that for its depravity and foolishness the bitterest laughter would be too light a thing. And in that violence he was not disposed to deal. The violence that stamped out periodically all the foolishness was the rage of a thing of the same flesh and blood as itself, fighting it on its own material ground with material weapons. The rage behind the satire of Juvenal or Persius would easily take the form of a murderous violence and eclipse in one suffocating blow the image of itself that it hated. But the poor lunatic gentleman of La Mancha – no real rage ever came near him, at most the impatient buffeting of things he mistook for something they were not (as Roland, when he went mad, charged flocks of sheep in place of the infidel): he is as remote from life as an image of the Buddha. He is one of the greatest productions of the western imagination: he is not a postulant but a complete initiate – but far more dissociated from his world than the high things of the asiatic imagination have been from theirs.

Taken as a satire, then, all the satire is concentrated not upon the palpable object of its activity, but just upon those assistants it conjures up to help it with its supposed victim. The stupid go-between, the half-hearted devotee, Sancho Panza, the faithful dog dazzled by something it cannot understand, its scepticism delivering constant assaults upon its infatuation, this fragment of the alien world sticking to the saint, is the focus for the satire in reality. The senseless turning of the windmills, even, is included in the mechanical personality of the homely and cunning spanish Hodge.

Sancho Panza's *catechism* under the tree outside Toboso, "Let us know now, brother Sancho, where you are going," has often been compared with Falstaff's famous catechism on the field of Shrewsbury. But it has never suggested, I believe, the natural conclusion of where we should look, in english literature, for our knight.

This is all the more so as *Henry IV* is, as the german critic Gervinus says, that play where more than elsewhere the full power of the english "national poet" is associated with a theme inalienably english. ("The genius of a nation has never appeared on any stage in such bright cheerfulness," etc.) To match Cervantes (if it were a question of comparing the two artists) I should choose myself some play of Shakespeare's where this "national cheerfulness" played a less important role. And *Don Quixote* is too wide and too personal to be "spanish" first and foremost. But all allowances made, and conceding that *Henry IV* is not *Shakespeare's* most significant work, though it may be *the national poet's*, and that you could get as *spanish* a production as Don Quixote without the great personal genius of Cervantes; nevertheless these works can be confronted as peculiarly representative of their respective countries.

It may be as well to recall by reproducing it the well-known soliloquy of Falstaff:

"Can honour set to a leg? no: or an arm? or take away the grief of a wound? No. Honour hath no skill in surgery, then? no. What is honour? a word. What is in that word, honour? air. A trim reckoning! – Who hath it? he that died o'Wednesday. Doth he feel it? no. Doth he hear it? no. 'Tis insensible, then? yea, to the dead. But will it not live with the living? no. Why? detraction will not suffer it: – therefore, I'll none of it."

There is the characteristic reasoning, but with a rapider and more informed cunning, of Sancho Panza. Only the english Sancho Panza, if Falstaff is he, is ten times the size of the spanish one. He is also a *knight*; so in a sense the roles are reversed. He is a man of the world – a compendium of rosy vices, very pleasant and amusing: fallen on rather evil times, he displays himself as in reality a cutpurse, drunkard and sneak. And, without very much fancifulness, we could pursue the parallel, and show him surrounded (in Shakespeare's *Henry IV*) with rather dull and boorish specimens of real chivalry, against which background he shows off to good advantage.

"The Contest of the Lion and the Fox in Shakespeare and Cervantes," *The Lion and the Fox* (1927), pp. 204–8.

The Revolutionary Rich "Apes of God"

When a great creation or invention of art makes its appearance, usually a short sharp struggle ensues. The social organism is put on its metal. If it is impossible quite to overcome the work in question, it is (after the short sharp struggle) accepted. Its canonization is the manner of its martyrdom. It is at all events robbed of its effect by a verbal acquiescence and a little crop of coarse imitations. Nothing really ugly or powerful, in most instances, has been at all disturbed.

All the revolutionary idealism of the European has by this time suffered the same dilution, and, not canonization, but promotion to the status of an eminently respectable, millionaire article. In the millionaire, and progressive middle-class, Atlantic World, the general temper of revolutionary change has already been thoroughly absorbed. This has very curious results. The phenomenon of the "revolutionary rich," of a gilded Bohemia whose members disport themselves as though they were already in the Millennium – as, indeed, as far as they are concerned, they are – makes its appearance. I cannot here provide a substitute for the very detailed analysis of these things that I have given elsewhere. But I can briefly sketch the more salient features.

All the "smart-set" life of any Western capital to-day is a kind of Trianon existence, passed in the midst of a fabulous private luxury, the traditional "bohemian" manners of the poor artist borrowed – along with the term "bohemian" – to cover the glimpses the man-in-the-street may have of this excess. What was a picturesque necessity for the needy members of Mürger's sub-world of art, becomes a luxurious affectation for the super-world of irresponsible freedom of the revolutionary rich of today. Thus when some magnate in mufti (he is possibly a labour member in "real" life, or he may be an armament magnifico) is observed with a brilliant party issuing from a Rolls-Royce, and making for one of those "quiet little bohemian restaurants" which are at least twice as expensive as the Ritz, it is not as a magnate or a "swell," at all, but as a mere "bohemian," that he is regarded by Mr Citizen gaping at this lucky dog (an artist probably, thinks he, probably like one of those "artists" on the film, in a velvet jacket, palette in hand, in some semi-asiatic palace, the most expensive screen-star in America posing upon the sumptuous heavily-upholstered "throne"). And indeed Mr Citizen would not be so entirely wrong; for any studio that is big enough to paint in is occupied by a millionaire, or by some member of this new tribe of debonair, millennial, bohemian magnates. What has happened to art and its practitioners it is unnecessary even to inquire.

This situation, which I have so hastily outlined, is, of course, a dream-come-true. It is a pity that some of the dreamers cannot return to witness it. It is (on a relatively small scale) the William Morris', tolstoyan, or other utopist dream of a millennium in which no one would have to work too much; and in which, above all, everyone would "have scope to develop his personality," everybody be a "genius" of some sort; in which everyone would be an "artist" – singing, painting, composing or writing, as the case might be, and in which a light-hearted "communism" should reign in the midst of an idyllic plenty. This has today been achieved by a section of the community, as I have indicated. In their political opinions these people are all, without exception, orthodoxly "revolutionary" or "radical." Several even have become militant socialists. Others are dramatists, others "great painters," or "great composers," many act or dance professionally, or are keepers of luxury-shops. Wistfully, but, oh, so bravely! they exclaim, Times have changed, we must all do something! And, of course, a great many people still possess the means required for such "little socialist experiments," as one of these pathetic people described what he was doing – for this thrilling type of idyllic *work*, the necessary capital to return to the Feudal Age as a romantic "craftsman," even if that return cannot be effected in the rôle of chatelain.

What results from this situation is, of course, that the audience, in the widest sense, becomes professional, or, worse, semi-professional (whatever may happen upon the stage), and the employer turns into a rival of his employee. The argument for "amateurism" of any kind is that "professionalism" is the drabbest, most mechanical and sordid affair; which, of course, is true; as it is true that most "professionals" are incompetent, untalented, hacks. But that is a one-sided argument; the assumption at this point always is that the amateur is a fresh, capricious and carefully-sheltered plant, and as such is relieved of the distorting necessities that dog the professional. So, romantically, *all* amateurs tend to become, for the sentimental utopian enthusiast of "amateurism," a kind of gifted eternal child, their naïveté never blemished by that odious "power" that knowledge brings or by dark necessities of a bread-and-butter order. The truth is very different from that. Almost without exception the amateur in real life – not in utopian theory – is an imitation-professional. If he is not that, he is a *faux-naïf* of the most blood-curdling description. There are no more true naïfs among amateurs than among professionals.

But it is the results and not the causes that we are concerned with here. And the proof of that millennial pudding that we have eaten is there for everybody to observe, in the world of art at least. The merging of the spectator and the performer – for that is the technical definition of amateurism in its widest implication – can scarcely be expected in art or social life to have a more satisfactory upshot than the same process applied in politics or industry.

But as we look round us, and observe the rich bohemianism in which all social power is concentrated today, we should recognize that we are in the presence of an instalment of the millennium, in full-flower. That privilege should be made the fullest use of, and we should draw the necessary conclusions. Our opportunity for practical first-hand observation is a unique one.

"Appendix to Book I," *Time and Western Man* (1927), pp. 144–46.

Ezra Pound

Ezra is a crowd; a little crowd. People are seen by him only as types. There is the "museum official," the "norman cocotte," and so on. By himself he would seem to have neither any convictions nor eyes in his head. There is nothing that he intuits well, certainly never originally. Yet when he can get into the skin of somebody else, of power and renown, a Propertius or an Arnaut Daniel, he becomes a lion or a lynx on the spot. This sort of parasitism is with him phenomenal.

Again, when he writes in person, as Pound, his phrases are invariably stagey and false, as well as insignificant. There is the strangest air of insincerity about his least purely personal utterance; the ring of the superbest conviction when he is the mouthpiece of a scald or of a jongleur.

The hosts of this great intellectual parasite, then, are legion; but in meeting Ezra you find yourself in the presence of a person who, if evidently not a source of life himself, has yet none of the unpleasant characteristics we associate with an organism dependent on others for its habitat and soil. He is such a "big bug" in his class, that he has some of the airs of his masters. If thoroughly conventional, as you would expect of a good servant – his mind moving in grooves that have been made for it by his social milieu – he is not without personality, of a considerable and very charming sort.

My way of accounting for these discrepancies is as follows:

If Ezra Pound as a living individual were less worthy and admirable, I am convinced he would be unable to enter into the renowned and noble creatures whom· he has passed his time in entering, so cleanly as he does – so faultlessly in places that you could not tell which is Pound and which is them. They or their genius or something that is in their work to guard it, would detect the imposture, and would certainly prevent him from working through them, in the splendid way that he has, were there any vulgarity or sham in the essential Ezra.

His dedication to his task has been fanatical. In order to slip in and out, as he does, in order to want to do so, so often as he has, and in such a great variety of cases, it was necessary for him – for his proper dedication to these men-gods – to be a kind of intellectual eunuch. That is my idea.

So I like, respect, and, in a sense, reverence Ezra Pound; I have found him a true, disinterested and unspoilt individual. He has not effected this intimate entrance into everything that is noble and enchanting for nothing. He has really walked with Sophocles beside the Aegean; he has seen the Florence of Cavalcanti; there is almost nowhere in the Past that he has not visited; he has been a great time-trotter, as we could describe this new kind of tourist. And he is not unworthy, in himself, of these many privileges.

But where the Present is concerned it is a different matter. He is extremely untrustworthy where that is concerned. That is the penalty of his function, like that of the eunuch instanced above. When he tries to be up-to-date it is a very uncomfortable business. And because he is conventional, and so accepts counterfeit readily where no standard has been established, he is a danger as far as he exerts any contemporary influence. He should not be taken seriously as a living being at all. Life is not his true concern, his gifts are all turned in the other direction. "In his chosen or fated field he bows to no one," to use his words. But his field is purely that of the dead. As the *nature mortist*, or painter essentially of still-life, deals for preference with life-that-is-still, that has not much life, so Ezra for preference consorts with the dead, whose life is preserved for us in books and pictures. He has never loved anything living as he has loved the dead.

"A Man in Love with the Past," *Time and Western Man* (1927), pp. 86–87.

Art and Politics

Whether politicians or not, the affairs of art, literature or science cannot be treated by us as though hung somewhere in a state of enchantment, in the air. But there is more than that. If you want to know what is actually occurring *inside*, underneath, at the centre, at any given moment, art is a truer guide than "politics," more often than not. Its movements represent, in an acuter form, a deeper emotional truth, though not discursively. *The Brothers Karamazov*, for example, is a more cogent document for the history of its period than any record of actual events. The parallel political displays, too, are only intended for the very simple as things are today; whereas the art-displays do often provide a little intelligent amusement.

So if art has a directer access to reality, is truer and less artificial and more like what it naturally grows out of, than are politics, it seems a pity that it should take its cue from them. The artist is relieved of that obligation of the practical man to lie. Why not retain this privilege to be one of the "truthful ones" of nietzschean myth?

"Appendix to Book I," *Time and Western Man* (1927), p. 136.

James Joyce's *Ulysses*

At the end of a long reading of *Ulysses* you feel that it is the very nightmare of the naturalistic method that you have been experiencing. Much as you may cherish the merely physical enthusiasm that expresses itself in this stupendous outpouring of *matter*, or *stuff*, you wish, on the spot, to be transported to some more abstract region for a time, where the dates of the various toothpastes, the brewery and laundry receipts, the growing pile of punched 'bus-tickets, the growing holes in the baby's socks and the darn that repairs them, assume less importance. It is your impulse perhaps quickly to get your mind where there is nothing but air and rock, however inhospitable and featureless, and a little timeless, too. You will have had a glut, for the moment (if you have really persevered), of *matter*, procured you by the turning on of all this river of what now is rubbish, but which was not *then*, by the obsessional application of the naturalistic method associated with the exacerbated time-sense. And the fact that you were not in the open air, but closed up inside somebody else's head, will not make things any better. It will have been your catharsis of the objective accumulations that obstinately collect in even the most active mind.

Now in the graphic and plastic arts that stage of fanatic naturalism long ago has been passed. All the machinery appropriate to its production has long since been discarded, luckily for the pure creative impulse of the artist. The nineteenth-century naturalism of that obsessional, fanatical order is what you find on the one hand in *Ulysses*. On the other, you have a great variety of recent influences enabling Mr Joyce to use it in the way that he did.

The effect of this rather fortunate confusion was highly stimulating to Joyce, who really got the maximum out of it, with an appetite that certainly will never be matched again for the actual *matter* revealed in his composition, or proved to have been lengthily secreted there. It is like a gigantic victorian quilt or antimacassar. Or it is the voluminous curtain that fell, belated (with the alarming momentum of a ton or two of personally organized rubbish), upon the victorian scene. So rich was its delivery, its pent-up outpouring so vehement, that it will remain, eternally cathartic, a monument like a record diarrhoea. No one who looks *at* it will ever want to look *behind* it. It is the sardonic catafalque of the victorian world.

Two opposite things were required for this result. Mr Joyce could never have performed this particular feat if he had not been, in his make-up, extremely immobile; and yet, in contradiction to that, very open to new technical influences. It is the *craftsman* in Joyce that is progressive; but the *man* has not moved since his early days in Dublin. He is on that side a "young man" in some way embalmed. His technical adventures do not, apparently, stimulate him to think. On the contrary, what he thinks seems to be of a conventional and fixed order, as though perhaps not to embarrass the neighbouring evolution of his highly progressive and eclectic craftsmanship.

So he collected like a cistern in his youth the last stagnant pumpings of victorian anglo-irish life. This he held steadfastly intact for fifteen years or more – then when he was ripe, as it were, he discharged it, in a dense mass, to his eternal glory. That was *Ulysses*. Had the twenty-year-old Joyce of the *Dubliners* not remained almost miraculously intact, we should never have witnessed this peculiar spectacle.

"An Analysis of the Mind of James Joyce," *Time and Western Man* (1927), pp. 108–9.

The Human and the Absolute

The personality that we each possess we are apt to despise, certainly, because it has so little material power; but still without conceit at all or even blasphemy, we have a god-like experience in that only. Or rather the usually ill-defined term "God" can only justify itself therein: since material power, like scale, is irrelevant. If we consider that the analogy expires in the abjectness of that concept, "man," of which we hear so much disparagement, then we surely should discard it altogether. Let us attempt now to express the most sanguine belief we have on this subject, such as would be most hospitable to the notion of God. The rapprochement is not so absurd as it at first sounds, especially to our ears, so accustomed to disobliging descriptions of the human state, in the service of levelling mass-doctrines. It is only blasphemy or absurdity, rather, for those who have long grown accustomed to blaspheme and heap ridicule on mankind, or to listen credulously to those engaged in that cheerful occupation, not to us. We are not at all disposed to ridicule or despise men because they are materially insignificant, because they are not as big as the earth, or the solar system, or as powerful as the forces of an earthquake. Those are the habits of a world that is not our world. We regard it as a similar vulgarity to ridiculing or despising a man because he is poor. Worldly or material power is not the standard used here. But if people could for a moment be persuaded to neglect that aspect of the affair, by which they are obsessed, we are sure that the matter would at once appear in another light. Meanwhile we can say that no Absolute need be ashamed of the feelings or thoughts of what we call a great artist or a great poet. Let us repeat this argument. Any God could put His name to the *Oedipus* or to *King Lear*. Anything communicating, not in a mechanically-perfect way, but still directly, more "greatness," we cannot imagine; and hence, scale apart, any other material of deity for the construction of God is meaningless, to us. And the vulgar delusions connected with quantity, scale or duration, delusions largely fostered by the gross subject-matter of positive science, are the only things that could be an obstacle to the embracing of this view. The Sistine Chapel Ceiling is worthy of the hand of any God which we can infer, dream of, or postulate. We may certainly say that God's hand is visible in it.

When at some moment or another in the process of evolution we were introduced to that extraordinary Aladdin's Cave, that paradise (which the behaviourist and many other people regard with such fanatical displeasure, belief in which will soon, it is very likely, be taxed, or definitely put out of bounds, with angels of a jealous God of Science sweeping fiery swords hither and thither in front of it), *our minds*: or when the magnificent private picture-gallery of its stretched-out imagery was thrown open, and we were allowed to wander in it in any direction, and to any private ends we pleased; that was certainly, if it is the gift of a God, a highly democratic proceeding on His part: especially when you consider that this is not one picture-gallery, thronged by a swarming public, but is *one-apiece* for any number of individuals – the conception of so democratic a God that He became aristocratic again, as it were, for the sake of others – each individual, however small, made into an "aristocrat" at once where His mind's eye is concerned. It is indeed evident that thereby in a sense God abdicated. He apparently no longer wished to be "the Absolute." So He introduced us to, and made us free of, His heavenly pictures. What it was that brought about this change heart, or mental crisis, in the Absolute – if that should be by chance the true account of what occurred – it is otiose to speculate upon. But it must be remarked at the same time that, alongside of this absolute and princely gift, the "iron-round of necessity" was maintained outside the magical circle of mind, or at least so it appears.

If the contrast is between a conception of the world as an ultimate Unity on the one hand, or a Plurality on the other; if you have, dogmatic and clear-cut, or rather if you could have, on the one side a picture of a multiplicity of wave-like surface changes only, while all the time the deep bed of Oneness reposes unbroken underneath: on the other side the idea of an absolute plurality, every midget existence, every speck and grain, unique (for what such "uniqueness" was worth) and equally real, irrespective of any hierarchy of truth at all: then can there be any question that the hypothesis of Oneness is the profounder hypothesis, and must, if it lay thus barely between these two, be the real. But we are surface-creatures only, and by nature are meant to be only that, if there is any meaning in nature. No metaphysician goes the whole length of departure from the surface-condition of mind – that fact is not generally noticed. For such departures result in self-destruction, just as though we hurled ourself into space – into "mental-space," if you like, in this case. We are surface-creatures, and the "truths" from beneath the surface contradict our values. It is among the flowers and leaves that our lot is cast, and the roots, however "interesting," are not so ultimate for us. For us the ultimate thing is the surface, the last-comer, and that is committed to a plurality of being. So what in a sense we have arrived at, is, for practical reasons, the opposite to the conclusions of Kant's "practical reason." For the same reason we think it is most true and better to *say* there is no God. To us the practical requirements seem to indicate the contrary of Kant's pragmatical solution – to require the conception of a Many instead of a One. On the other hand, if anything, the speculative reason seems to us to point to a One. But on the One we must turn our back in order to exist. Evidences of a oneness seem everywhere apparent. But we *need*, for practical purposes, the illusion of a plurality. So in one sense we are more near to the conception of a God than Kant: in another – the official and practical – we are farther from it. The illusion must in short be our "real." And our reason is not the pragmatical member among our faculties at all, but for us the ultimate truth-bearing vehicle. Yet it is only in league with our sensuous machinery of illusion that it is able to convey the "real," which machinery is pluralistic. We feel that we have to ignore the possibility of a God emotionally, as positive Science must, for the purposes of its empirical activity, ignore the unknown – to pretend, in order to be able to act at all, that it is omniscient. And perhaps we are more fundamentally religious than the kantian, with his chilling pragmatical deity; and if there is such a Reality, closer in touch with it than he. For Kant pleased all the positivists who came after him too well not to be too positive himself for us. In any case, we come to this contrary conclusion: that it is we who have to pretend to be real, if anyone has to, not to pretend that God is. For if He is real, He is so much realler than we that there is no need for Him to be bolstered up by our "practical reasons": and if He does not exist, then there is no need at all to invent Him, with a voltairean gesture.

"God as Reality," *Time and Western Man* (1927), pp. 400–03.

The Absurd

To begin to understand the totality of *the absurd*, at all, you have to assume much more than belongs to a social differentiation. There is nothing that is animal (and we as bodies are animals) that is not absurd. This sense of the absurdity, or, if you like, the madness of our life, is at the root of every true philosophy. William James delivers himself on this subject as follows:–

> One need only shut oneself in a closet and begin to think of the fact of one's being there, of one's queer bodily shape in the darkness (a thing to make children scream at, as Stevenson says), of one's fantastic character and all, to have the wonder steal

over the detail as much as over the general fact of being, and to see that it is only familiarity that blunts it. Not only that *anything* should be, but that *this* very thing should be, is mysterious. Philosophy stares, but brings no reasoned solution, for from nothing to being there is no logical bridge.

It is the chasm lying between being and non-being, over which it is impossible for logic to throw any bridge, that, in certain forms of laughter, we leap. We land plumb in the centre of Nothing. It is easy for us to see, if we are french, that the German is "absurd," or if german, that the French is "ludicrous," for we are *outside* in that case. But it was Schopenhauer (whom James quotes so aptly in front of the above passage), who also said: "He who is proud of being 'a German', 'a Frenchman', 'a Jew', can have very little else to be proud of." (In this connection it may be recalled that his father named him "Arthur," because "Arthur" was the same in all languages. Its possession would not attach him to any country.) So, again, if we have been at Oxford or Cambridge, it is easy to appreciate, from the standpoint acquired at a great university, the absurdity of many manners not purified or intellectualized by such a training. What it is far more difficult to appreciate, with any constancy, is that, whatever his relative social advantages or particular national virtues may be, every man is profoundly open to the same criticism or ridicule from any opponent who is only different enough. Again, it is comparatively easy to see that another man, as an animal, is absurd; but it is far more difficult to observe oneself in that hard and exquisite light. But no man has ever continued to live who has observed himself in that manner for longer than a flash. Such consciousness must be of the nature of a thunderbolt. Laughter is only summer-lightning. But it occasionally takes on the dangerous form of absolute revelation.

"The Meaning of the Wild Body," *The Wild Body* (1927), pp. 244–45.

Laughter

I will catalogue the attributes of Laughter.
1. Laughter is the Wild Body's song of triumph.
2. Laughter is the climax in the tragedy of seeing, hearing, and smelling self-consciously.
3. Laughter is the bark of delight of a gregarious animal at the proximity of its kind.
4. Laughter is an independent, tremendously important, and lurid emotion.
5. Laughter is the representative of tragedy, when tragedy is away.
6. Laughter is the emotion of tragic delight.
7. Laughter is the female of tragedy.
8. Laughter is the strong elastic fish, caught in Styx, springing and flapping about until it dies.
9. Laughter is the sudden handshake of mystic violence and the anarchist.
10. Laughter is the mind sneezing.
11. Laughter is the one obvious commotion that is not complex, or in expression dynamic.
12. Laughter does not progress. It is primitive, hard and unchangeable.

"Inferior Religions," *The Wild Body* (1927), pp. 236–37.

Beauty and Reality

A scornful optimism, with its confident onslaughts on our snobbism, will not make material existence a peer for our energy. The gladiator is not a perpetual monument of triumphant health: Napoleon was harried with Elbas: moments of vision are blurred rapidly, and the poet sinks into the rhetoric of the will.

But life is invisible, and perfection is not in the waves or houses that the poet sees. To rationalize that appearance is not possible. Beauty is an icy douche of ease and happiness at something *suggesting* perfect conditions for an organism: it remains suggestion. A stormy landscape, and a pigment consisting of a lake of hard, yet florid waves; delight in each brilliant scoop or ragged burst, was John Constable's beauty. Leonardo's consisted in a red rain on the shadowed side of heads, and heads of massive female aesthetes.

Uccello accumulated pale parallels, and delighted in cold architecture of distinct colour. Korin found in the symmetrical gushing of water, in waves like huge vegetable insects, traced and worked faintly, on a golden pâte, his business. Cézanne liked cumbrous, democratic slabs of life, slightly leaning, transfixed in vegetable intensity.

Beauty is an immense predilection, a perfect conviction of the desirability of a certain thing, whatever that thing may be. It is a universe for one organism. To a man with long and consumptive fingers, a sturdy hand may be heaven. We can aim at no universality of form, for what we see is not the reality. Henri Fabre was in every way a superior being to a Salon artist, and he knew of elegant grubs which he would prefer to the Salon painter's nymphs. – It is quite obvious though, to fulfil the conditions of successful art, that we should live in relatively small communities.

"Inferior Religions," *The Wild Body* (1927), p. 241.

Surrealism as an Ideology

The actual merging of the dream-condition and the waking-condition must result in a logical emulsion of the forms and perspectives of life as we know them, and, translated into an art expression, will approximate most closely to the art of the child. That is, of course, what has everywhere occurred with the theorists of that persuasion. The infantile is the link between the Superrealists and Miss Stein, as it is between Miss Stein and Miss Loos.

[…]

Then if you take "the merging of the external and internal," that dogmatic subjectivism would manipulate the objective truth, of necessity, in favour of some version of the private mental world of the isolated mind. But what in the super-realist account is omitted, is the fact that all reality is a merging, in one degree or another, of the external and internal: all reality is *one* reality to some extent, saturated with our imagination. Even more is that the case with the reality of art, or myth. And this dogmatic *imagism* or dream-doctrine merely wishes to make a sort of official "reality" of what, in art, is always, in every case in which a great creative fancy is operating, actual.

Super-reality, in short, is not so much a doctrine for art as for life. It is a sort of cheap and unnecessary, popularised, *artistic-ness* of outlook that is involved. The creative faculty, released into popular life, and possessed by everybody, that is really what "Super-reality" means – it is merely a picturesque phase of the democratisation of the artistic intelligence and the creative faculty. It would result in practice, and in everyday life, in a radical shifting of the normal real towards the *unconscious* pole. If thoroughly effective it would result, even, in a submergence of the normal, conscious, real in the Unconscious.

But it is not a specifically *art* doctrine, that is a doctrine that issues from the problems of the arts of expression: for all art worth the name is already *super-real*. To say that it should be more so – or so very much more so as is implied in super-reality – is to pass over into the living material of all art, its ground and what it contemplates, and tamper directly with the cézannesque apples, for instance, before the painter has started his picture, or modify the social life which the artist interprets or reflects.

[…]

So here again it could be shown that we are not in the presence of an aesthetic phenomenon, but of something else. The dream, indeed the opium-dream or the coke dream, of the super-realists, is to be imposed upon the living material of life: it is "art" going over into life and changing it, so that it shall conform to its fantasy. But it is art become life as it were, prior to its translation. And as an art it is a feverish, untrue, dehumanized, exceedingly artificial art. And it is artificial because it has fed upon a life falsified with doctrine, and merged in dream. Or, if we call it *a dream* instead of *an art*, then, as a dream, it is evidently a sort of static nightmare, of the *Maldoror* order. It is its avowed programme "to evoke the logic of pathological terror" and to shock human society "to its foundations." And that is also one of the avowed objectives of the communists in their Films. But horror, or "pathological terror," however useful in politics, is not of the same standing in art.

It is in formulas and arguments of the most superficial sort (about "reality" and so forth […]) that such a movement clothes itself. The more shallow and obvious they are, of course, the better they serve the propagandist purpose. But this subject is of great importance for a full understanding of the various affiliated theoretic groups involved in this analysis. The "reality" in question is a religious or semi-religious reality – the religion behind it in the case of the Super-realists being the religion of Communism. It is not a "reality" of art. Indeed it is the opposite of that: for it must have for its result not the "merging" of the external in the internal, but the *merging of art in life*. And by "art" here is meant something much more generally important than merely current water-colour paintings or polite fiction. Art at its fullest is a very great force indeed, a magical force, a sort of *life*, a very great "reality." It is *that* reality, that magic, that force, that this "dream-aesthetic" proposes to merge with life, exactly on the same principle as the Producers of Moscow theatres today merge audience and performer, stage and auditorium.

"The Diabolical Principle," *The Enemy*, No. 3 (First Quarter, 1929), pp. 41–43.

Art as Prophecy

The function of an artist of the Left, at present, is to secure the equilibrium of the jelly-like Centre, I think – by his presence rather than his technical influence however. (The Centre has already incorporated as much as it dare of his extremism: another cubic inch and its bread and butter would be threatened.) I am only using the term Left to indicate any ambitious experimentalism in Painting: and I must in a moment make clear what I have meant by "experimental" and "abstract." As to the question whether the tornado of Cubism, Futurism, Expressionism, Vorticism, has left art better than it found it, that can only be answered in the affirmative. It has forbidden a quantity of stupidities and has filtered a little backbone into almost everything (except for certain quite irreclaimable regions). Perhaps beyond the great upheavals to which our present society is distinctly liable (religious or political) it might be called upon to express more completely than so far it has been able to do, in the midst of our degenerate commercialism, what it is suited to express. Meantime, there it is still in such effective energetic knots as that formed by the association of Ernst, Milhaud, Tanguy, etc., or in Russia or Germany, as groups and as individuals (such as Klee), like an official *échantillon* of what our civilization might become if it wanted to. That civilization can always say to itself – "There is my model, in full working order: there is architecture, there is every form of design, indications of novel art-forms, only waiting to burst harshly into bloom: if I wanted to I could take all that up and quit my kitchen-garden tomorrow or the asafoetida of my hot-house: it only rests with me. Not that I ever shall: still it is jolly to reflect that I could if I had a mind to."

The few dozen artists meanwhile who continue in those directions have become like Aztecs or Atlantans, representatives of a submerged civilization. It is perfectly astounding the dreams that they represent: there is a complete world, with its aqueducts, its drains, its courts, private dwellings, personal ornaments, almost its religion with its theurgic implements, which have never existed. And this world, it must always be recalled, may be the actual world of the future. That, of course, does not make it any more important, but it gives it an indirect reality – it brings it into the sphere of practical politics as it were – far too much, it must be confessed, on occasion.

There are a number of individuals, and some are among the most important artists of the day, who live, at least to their own complete satisfaction, in the light of that glimpse of a novel world. The rest, the majority, without changing their own habits very much, "hint blue" – squeeze a drop here and a drop there, of the novel concoction: and so a sickly reflection of the light that never was of the "extremist" plastic imagination spreads over everything. This phenomenon has a parallel in the "pink" revolutionary principles of our Western society.

The fragments I amuse myself with in the intervals of my literary work are, I suppose, among the only specimens of such painting done in England today.

"A World Art and Tradition" (1929). Rprt. *Wyndham Lewis on Art* (1969), pp. 257–58.

Hitler 1931: "A Man of Peace"

Hitler is The German Man, therefore Hitler is a Man of Peace – so I asserted just now, and so I have done again in the heading of this chapter. But I must go into this in greater detail, if I am to substantiate such a paradox. It is, I suppose, not much use just saying that the "Boche" is in his heart "a Man of Peace," and leaving it at that. For the "war-guilt-lie," as the Germans call it, not only involves the late rulers of Germany. The whole German People were regarded, so very recently, thanks to the Allied propaganda-department, as a swarm of ferocious "Huns," that it would be too much to hope that the average anglo-saxon reader would accept the theory of Adolf Hitler being a sucking-dove, merely because he was a "Boche"!

Now that we have got down to the root of Hitlerism – namely Herr Hitler himself – let us take Hitler in his rôle of *nationalist*, and then consider what that nationalism may portend for the rest of Europe. That is, after all, what we mainly want to find out.

First, as I stated in an earlier chapter, the militancy of the Hitlerist will be misunderstood if it is identified in any way with that of the *Action Française*. Self-conscious gallic nationalism today is a very frail thing indeed. A handful of catholic royalists – that is the *Action Française* movement. It is true that recently it has shown a tendency to grow, perhaps in sympathy with Hitlerism. But it is still a Paris political fad, rather than a National Movement.

The nationalism of Adolf Hitler is, it must always be remembered, national-*socialism*. It is the militancy of an armed peasant, not the aristocratic militancy of a dispossessed aristocratic class; or that of a royalist intellectual, of aristocratic disposition, like Charles Maurras. Then regarded historically, and in the light of post-war practical politics, the nationalism of the *Action Française* (that of Charles Maurras and of Leon Daudet) in its dogmatic anti-germanism, has always seemed to me, I confess, unrealistic: and (in the light of our immediate political necessities) all wrong. Similarly, the gallicism of Monsieur Coty, the founder of

L'Ami du Peuple, suffered from an automatic phobia against the traditional enemy across the Rhine. These nationalist phobias, if carried to their logical conclusion, could only end in the complete "Balkanization" of Europe. And that "Balkanization" is already far too far advanced for an intelligent observer to feel sympathy with any man who seemed likely to accelerate it.

It is because I believe that Hitler is *not* a "Nationalist" of that "Balkanizing" order that I am interested in the Hitler movement. I believe that he, and his associates, may have a true prescription embedded in the heart of their doctrine, for a "nationalism" that would be wider and more intelligent than that of the *Action Française* or than that of Mussolini.

This belief I base upon certain statements of Hitler. They have sounded far more intelligent than one is accustomed to expect from nationalist dictators. Hitler has even of late experienced some difficulty with the more conventional of his followers, especially in the matter of France. These malcontents objected that the friendly remarks of their leader upon the subject of France, and his dispatch of olive-branches to Paris, smacked of the unpatriotic, even of an ungerman attitude to the secular "enemy" of the german people. Those were evidently short-sighted junker objections.

It is essential to understand that Adolf Hitler is not a sabre-rattler at all. Indeed, he uses all his influence to prevent his followers from engaging in stupid "Nationalist" demonstrations against France or against Poland. [...]

Hitler is *not* a straightforward, simple, fire-eating, true-blue, sabre-rattling, moustachioed puppet at all. I do not think if Hitler had his way he would bring fire and the sword across otherwise peaceful frontiers. He would, I am sure, remain peacefully at home, fully occupied with the internal problems of the *Dritte Reich*. And as regards, again, the vexed question of the "antisemitic" policy of his party, in that also I believe Hitler himself – once he had obtained power – would show increasing moderation and tolerance.

"Adolf Hitler a Man of Peace," *Hitler* (1931), pp. 44–48.

Fascism and Modernist Art

The present violent return to the sentiment of nationhood – in opposition to the natural evolution (as it seems) towards a commonwealth of nations – may persist for so many years, and take such roots, as to deflect, or attract to itself, the main course of history. It appears to me improbable; but stranger things have happened. The *esprit de corps* of the Byzantine sporting factions (in the course of whose pitched battles thousands died) was a far stranger thing than even the campaign of the Chaco, where the irrational ferocity of national pride reached its climax of absurdity – seeing that both sides spoke the same tongue and were identical in racial origin.

The vorticist, cubist, and expressionist movements – to return to them – which aimed at a renewal of our artistic sensibility, and to provide it with a novel alphabet of shapes and colours with which to express itself, presupposed a new human ethos, which undoubtedly must have superseded, in some measure, modes of feeling of a merely national order.

That these movements have not succeeded is plain enough: for now let us come to today – the early months of the year 1939 – and endeavour to arrive at some not too prejudiced idea of what is happening – of what is the actual, if it is not the real.

What has *already happened* – that can be said at once – is that modern art, of the highly experimental sort advocated in these essays and manifestos, is at an end. It is all over except for the shouting – of the rearguard, as they fly, but who, true to the best traditions of contemporary journalism, affect to be *advancing*, while they hurry off the stricken field.

In the form of Expressionism all that smells of the "modern" in art has been booted out of Germany, and the door been bolted against it. In Italy its only manifestation was "Futurism," which lived but three years. It was buried in 1914. Giorgio de Chirico has taken to chocolate-boxes – upon which a symbolical charger, more and more fatigued, languidly prances. (It was the Horse, actually, that killed Chirico, it is said.) He was the solitary important Italian.

As to Paris, there it is the *crépuscule*. The picture-market has collapsed (and the French book-market is down fifty per cent, as reported year ending 1938): all the graceful *petits maîtres*, a great store of which France always possesses, have crept out of their holes, as the Catalan sun sets – in human blood, alas! As Barcelona falls, and the phalangist standard is unfurled there, we can all see that that is the end of a chapter – of painting, among other things. There will be no more Catalan painters, to act as hormones to the old Paris *cocotte*.

Under the shadow of Politics, the great movement in the arts celebrated in these pages, bankrupt or refugee, is expiring.

"Super-nature versus Super-real," *Wyndham Lewis the Artist: From "Blast" to Burlington House* (1939), pp. 18–19.

Hitler (2): 1939

Herr Hitler himself must now be my theme. The Führer must be taken to pieces. This engine for producing mass-emotion is very interesting indeed. And in nothing is it so interesting as in what it offers to *the eye*. For this is, after all, a talking-box to be *seen* as well as to be *heard*. The cut of a soap-boxer's coat, or the colour of his hair, is as important as the timbre of his voice.

There are warlike persons who, perhaps with the intuition of the quarrelsome in recognizing another of their kind, spotted Hitler at once as a potential Tamerlane. There are some people, too, who go about looking for Tamerlanes. But heavens! what a flair a man must have to detect Tamerlane beneath that platitudinous exterior – that plebeian protégé of the Junker Papen, with the humble cut of whose German sports-jacket, and with whose disarming toothbrush moustache, we are all now so familiar. Still, I confess that in one respect I was badly taken in, in 1930. What more than anything else caused my judgment to trip was that unusual trinity of celibacy, teetotalism, and anti-nicotine.

I was cowed at the thought of such superiority to alcohol, such a contempt for tobacco, such sublime indifference to the sex-urge. Yet that there was something sinister about this pointed abstinence was elementary. I should at once have been on my guard at the spectacle of more than two major inhumanities.

As it was, I allowed my suspicions to be lulled. This could not be a dangerous man – he was a crude puppet; and when he had served his turn he would be knocked on the head and popped back into his box, by his tough and wily junker masters – as came very near happening in June 1934.

I gazed at Herr Hitler with complete equanimity. No one had anything to fear from so commonplace an agitator: who would probably do his stuff; clean up a social mess beyond the Rhine; put the French jingoes and armament crooks in their places, and save Europe from war – not bring back that boring phantom, which is what has happened.

The argument from his abstinence was unsound. But what two things are more inseparable than alcohol and war? My experience as a soldier had established that fact firmly in my mind. And then there was no meat either. Somehow milk and watercress do not seem to rhyme with blood and iron.

"Herr Hitler's Personal Appearance," *The Hitler Cult* (1939), pp. 37–38.

Existentialism as Nihilism

I have spoken of the nihilism of the existential thinkers. Very briefly let me explain my use of that expression. As one or two of the critics of this system have shown, it is the *bracketing* that has in fact led to the situation we find. A man, having delivered up his soul, not to the Devil but to the tree outside his window – to his coal scuttle and "bedroom suite" and to all the objects he can lay his eyes on, then suddenly cuts himself off from all this, from the external world. This comes about as a result of the Husserlian device called "bracketing." But he finds himself (suddenly, also) in an empty house – a void, a *nothing*. For this man – this philosopher – had beforehand scrupulously emptied, purified, the consciousness or ego (which is the *house* of which I speak, of which this wretched man is the inmate) of everything. When he inherited it he found that ancestors during thousands of years had accumulated in it all that a man needs for life. All kinds of quite invaluable gadgets. His vanity is such that he had cleared this out entirely – disinfected it of all tell-tale odour of "essence," reduced the Reason to the status of a despised drudge. So – having cut himself off from the phenomenal world outside – in this empty shell our Existentialist flings himself on the floor and contemplates this echoless vacuity. Hence all the accompaniments of existential thought – "Angst" or "Anguish," "Dereliction," "Loneliness," and "Despair." This is the despondent vocabulary of the most recent of these cults, with which everyone who has read a little about it will be familiar.

Or again: man has uncovered his nothingness, naturally enough, in identifying himself *absolutely* with his chairs and tables, his Ford car and his tabby-cat, producing an "essence" in this act of union – or semi-union, for what I have spoken of figuratively as the "empty house" still remains, and is still called a "consciousness." "Existence precedes essence!" So says Sartre, after Heidegger. And when the Existentialist boils down (figuratively) his chairs and tables, his Ford card, etc., and values them, the result is not far from Zero for the philosophic mind. – It does not help matters at all to assert that man *creates* himself as he goes along (though there are some people stupid enough I suppose to feel rather puffed up at the thought of self-creation): nor is it really an advantage that man is always a few jumps ahead of himself – and in fact is not only largely *nothing* ("permeated with nothingness") but *nowhere*, too.

Upon reflection, and after the momentary elation of feeling that he is battling his way into his future – like an American marine in a tropical jungle infested with Japs; or "creating" himself, as an artist "creates" – the more modest and sensible man recognizes that he is not after all a work of art – that the *initial* creation was far beyond his powers or that of any man: that as to his future (for all his self-creation and following the precepts of action-at-any-price) all that can happen is that the Ford car may increase in size and (with luck) he may do rather more than keep-up-with-the-Joneses.

No help comes either, in the Existentialist picture, from the starring of the magical word, *liberty*. Of course I suppose people will get the usual kick at the mere sight of it. Then we are assured by Sartre that owing to the final disappearance of God our liberty is *absolute*! At this the entire audience waves its hat or claps its hands. But this natural enthusiasm is turned abruptly into something much less buoyant when it is learnt that this liberty weighs us down immediately with tremendous responsibilities. We now have to take all God's worries on our shoulders – now that we are become "men like gods." It is at this point that the Anxiety and Despondency begin, ending in utter despair.

"Twentieth Century Nihilism," *The Writer and the Absolute* (1952), pp. 126–28.

Francis Bacon

This Hanover Gallery show [of Francis Bacon], however, is of exceptional importance.

Of the younger painters none actually paints so beautifully as Francis Bacon. I have seen painting of his that reminded me of Velazquez and like that master he is fond of blacks. Liquid whitish accents are delicately dropped upon the sable ground, like blobs of mucus – or else there is the cold white glitter of an eyeball, or of an eye distended with despairing insult behind a shouting mouth, distended also to hurl insults. Otherwise it is a baleful regard from the mask of a decayed clubman or business executive – so decayed that usually part of the head is rotting away into space. But black is his pictorial element. These faces come out of the blackness to glare or to shout. I must not attempt to describe these amazing pictures – the shouting creatures in glass cases, these dissolving ganglia the size of a small fist in which one can always discern the shouting mouth, the wild distended eye. In the *Nude*, in front of not the least ominous of curtains, about to enter, the artist is seen at his best. Bacon is one of the most powerful artists in Europe today and he is perfectly in tune with his time. Not like his namesake "the brightest, wisest of mankind," he is, on the other hand, one of the darkest and most possessed.

"Round the London Art Galleries," *The Listener* (17 November 1949), p. 860.

The Sea-Mists of the Winter

It became evident quite early that it was going to be a deplorable winter. The cold was unvarying, it had purpose, it seemed. Usually in a London winter it forgets to be cold half the time; it strays back to autumn or wanders dreamily forward to spring, after a brief attempt at winter toughness, perhaps, squeezing out a few flakes of snow. But *this* winter though it experienced its usual difficulty in producing anything but a contemptible snowfall there has been an un-British quality, an unseemly continuity.

Speaking for myself, what struck me most was the veil of moisture like a sea-mist which never left my part of the town. I remember first remarking this just before Christmas. I said to Scott, my journalist-newsagent-friend, that these perpetual mists must slow him down in the morning; he drives up to business in his car, from his home in the outer suburbs. He did not seem to mind a light sea-mist for he shook his head absent-mindedly. Another time I was talking to him over the magazine counter of the shop and indicating the street outside, with its transparent film of blue-grey. I protested, "Another mist!" He looked out and said, a little sharply, "There is no mist." I did not argue, I suppose that he meant it was not up to the specification of what he called "a mist."

But you may have seen through my innocent device. The truth is that there was no mist. The mist was in my eyes: there was no sea-mist in nature. In spite of conditions which, one would have supposed, would have made it quite clear what these atmospheric opacities were, it took me a considerable time to understand. It was not, you see, like this that I had imagined my sight would finally fade out. "You have been going blind for a long time," said the neuro-surgeon. And I had imagined that I should go on going blind for a long time yet: just gradually losing the power of vision. I had never visualized mentally, a sea-mist.

In such cases as mine there always arrives

a time when normal existence becomes impossible, and you have to turn towards the consultant who has made a speciality of your kind of misfortune. When I started my second portrait of T.S. Eliot, which now hangs in Magdalene College, Cambridge, in the early summer of "forty-nine," I had to draw up very closely to the sitter to see exactly how the hair sprouted out of the forehead, and how the curl of the nostril wound up into the dark interior of the nose. There was no question of my not succeeding, my sight was still adequate. But I had to move too close to the forms I was studying. Some months later, when I started a portrait of Stella Newton, I had to draw still closer and even then I could not quite see. So I had to have my eyes examined again. This was the turning-point, the date, December 1949. What, in brief is my problem, is that the optic nerves, at their chiasma, or crossing, are pressed upon by something with the pleasing name of cranial pharyngeoma. It is therefore a more implacable order of misfortune than if I had a jolly little cataract. There has been a great acceleration of failure of vision during the last seven months or so. Of course I was told that I should first lose my "central vision," which would mean that I should no longer be able to read or write. Already I was obliged to read with a magnifying glass. Then I found I could no longer read the names of streets, see the numbers on houses, or see what stations I was passing through on the railway. About that time everything except banner headlines was invisible: then I found I could no longer read the letters inside the finger-holes of a telephone-dial. At present, if I wish to dial a number, I count the holes with my fingertips until I reach the opening where I know the letter I have to locate is situated. Thus seven is P.R.S. five is J.K.L. I know what letters the holes near the beginning and end of the half-circle contain, and what the figures are as well.

As to typing, it is some time ago now that I ceased to see distinctly the letters on the keys. I still write a certain amount with a pen or pencil, but I write blind. However much I write on it the page before me is still an unsullied white: and sometimes the lines I have written distressingly amalgamate. The two books on which I am at present working, one a novel, the other an art book, will proceed quite smoothly, but the method of their production will be changed. A dictaphone, or "recorder" as the Americans call it, will supersede the pen or the typewriter, at least as far as the first stages of composition are concerned. Many American writers I am informed employ the recorder, although possessing ordinary visual powers.

As to the sea-mist, that is now too pretty a name for it. Five or six weeks ago I still went to my newsagent to have a talk with Scott and make some purchases. He of course would move about as a fresh customer would come in and demand attention. At any given time I found it extremely difficult to decide whether he was there before me or not, for he would come back and stand silently near me, and often it was only because of the tobacco he was smoking, and a slight movement in the mist before me, or at my side, that I knew that he had returned. Recently he has told me that he realized that half the time I did not know he was there. I went to other shops as well, as long as it was possible: but when for me the butcher became nothing but a white apron, and the skinned back of a bullock protruding, as it hung, seemed to me a fleshly housewife, I ceased to be a shopper. Now I take my exercise arm-in-arm with some pleasant companion, and it's surprising how easily one can thread one's way in and out of the shadowy pedestrians, very slightly steered by another but sharp-eyed person.

Sometimes I am still at large solo, though increasingly rarely. I may go out, for instance, and some twenty yards away look for a taxicab. In these cases I will stand upon the edge of the pavement, calling imperiously "Are you *free*?" to owner-drivers, who probably observe me coldly from behind their steering wheels as if I were the Yonghi-Bongi-Bo. I signal small vans, I peer hopefully at baby-trucks. At length I get a response. It is a taxi! But I assure you that it is one thing to hail a taxi-cab, another to get into it. This is quite extraordinarily difficult. I try to force my way in beside the indignant driver. He or I will open the door. But as I see everything so indistinctly I attempt to effect a passage through the wood of the door itself, in Alice Through the Looking Glass fashion, rather than take advantage of the gaping hole in the side of the taxi produced by the opening of the door. It is with a sign of relief that I at last find my way in, after vainly assaulting the stationary vehicle in two or three places. This I realize must be extremely difficult to understand for a person with rude eyesight and piercing vision. It is also difficult for the acquaintance who comes up, as I am staring through the slabs of dark grey at darker slabs, which I hope may be taxis, who addresses me with familiar cordiality. For he is just another slab of nondescript grey, at which I stare, inquiring a little unceremoniously, "Who are you?"

When visited by friends, which will be usually in the evening, in a room lit by electric light properly shaded (for I have not removed these obstacles to sight, belonging to an era out of which I am passing) I see them after a fashion, but fragmentarily, obliquely, and spasmodically. I can see no one immediately in front of me. But I sit and talk to them without embarrassment, of course, just as if I could see them. It is rather like telephone conversations, where the voice is the main thing. But an awareness of the bodily presence is always there, and as one turns one's head hither and thither, glimpses constantly recur, delivering to one's fading eyesight a piece of old so-and-so's waistcoat or bald head, or dear Janet's protruding nose. These token odds and ends of personality are really just as good as seeing them whole, and their voices have an added significance.

The failure of sight which is already so advanced, will of course become worse from week to week until in the end I shall only be able to see the external world through little patches in the midst of a blacked out tissue. On the other hand, instead of little patches, the last stage may be the absolute black-out. Pushed into an unlighted room, the door banged and locked for ever, I shall then have to light a lamp of aggressive voltage in my mind to keep at bay the night.

New as I am to the land of blind-man's-buff I can only register the novel sensations, and not deny myself the enjoyment of this curious experience. It amuses me to collide with a walking belly; I quite enjoy being treated as a lay-figure, seized by the elbows and heaved up in the air as I approach a kerb, or flung into a car. I relish the absurdity of gossiping with somebody the other side of the partition. And everyone is at the other side of the partition. I am not allowed to see them. I am like a prisoner condemned to invisibility, although permitted an unrestricted number of visitors. Or I have been condemned to be a blind-folded delinquent, but not otherwise interfered with. And meanwhile I gaze backward over the centuries at my fellow condamnés. Homer heads the list, but there are surprisingly few. I see John Milton sitting with his three daughters (the origin of this image, is to my shame, it seems to me, a Royal Academy picture), the fearful blow at his still youthful pride distorting his face with its frustrations. He is beginning his great incantation: "Of Man's first Disobedience and the Fruit of that Forbidden Tree," while one of the women sits, her quill-pen poised ready to transcribe the poetry. Well, Milton had his daughters, I have my dictaphone.

This short story of mine has the drawback of having its tragedy to some extent sublimated. Also, we have no ending. Were I a dentist, or an attorney I should probably be weighing the respective advantages of the sleek luminal, or the noisy revolver. For there is no such thing as a blind dentist, or a blind lawyer. But as a writer, I merely change from pen to dictaphone. If you ask, "And as an artist, what about that?" I should perhaps answer, "Ah, sir, as to the artist in England, I have often thought that it would solve a great many problems if English painters were born blind."

And finally, which is the main reason for this unseemly autobiographical outburst, my articles on contemporary art exhibitions necessarily end, for I can no longer see a picture.

"The Sea-mists of the Winter," *The Listener* (10 May 1951), p. 765.

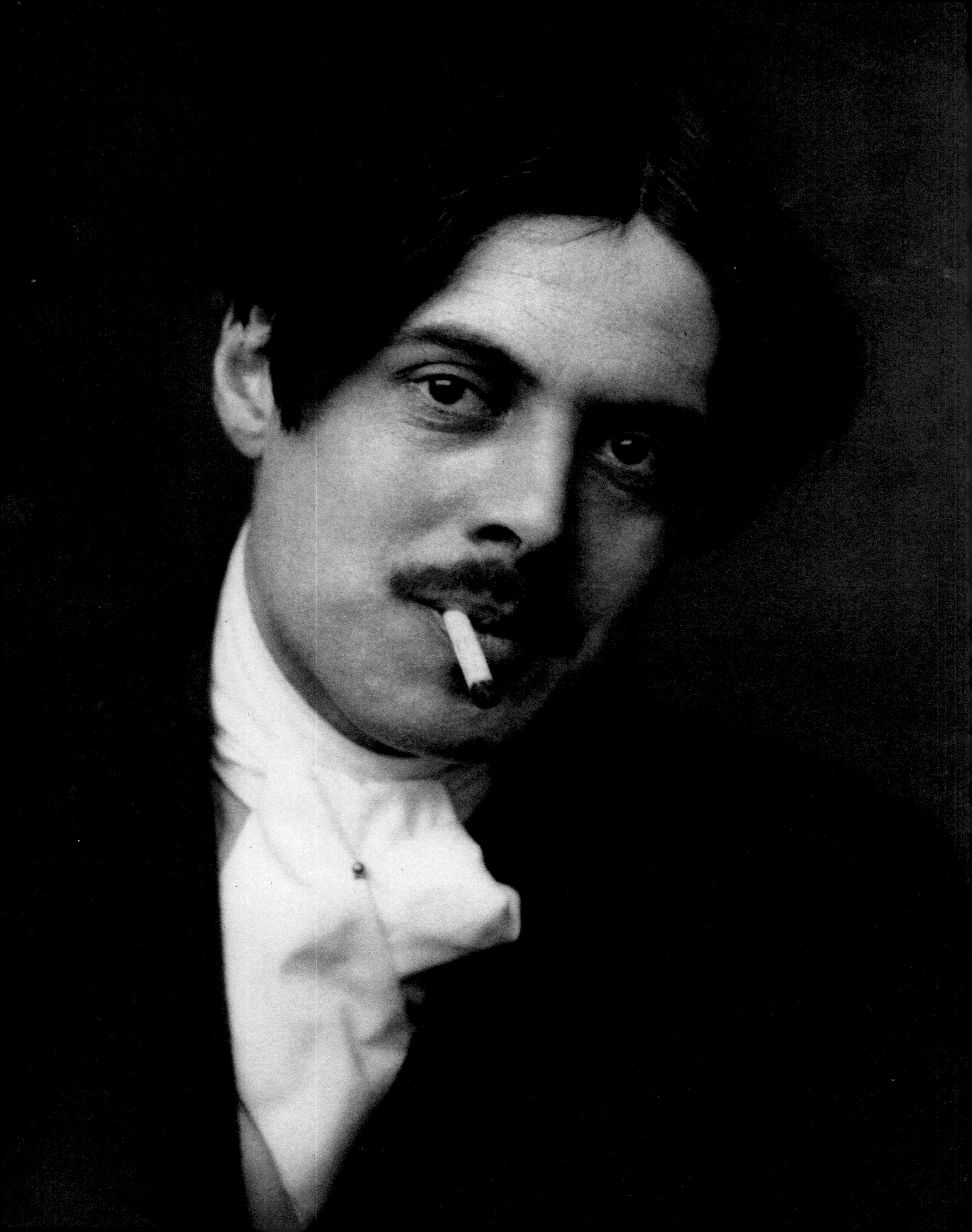

Texts on Wyndham Lewis

Letter to John Quinn

Ezra Pound

London, 10 March 1916.
Dear Quinn: Lewis has just sent in the first dozen drawings. They are all over the room, and the thing is stupendous. The vitality, the fullness of the man! Nobody knows it. My God, the stuff lies in a pile of dirt on the man's floor. Nobody has seen it. Nobody has *any* conception of the volume and energy and the variety.

Blake, that W.B.Y. is always going on about!!!! Lewis has got Blake scotched to a finish. He's got so much more *in him* than Gaudier. I know he is seven years older. Ma chè Cristo!

I have certainly GOT to do a Lewis book to match the Brzeska. Or perhaps a "Vorticists" (being nine-tenths Lewis, and reprinting my paper on Wadsworth, with a few notes on the others).

This is the first day for I don't know how long that I have envied any man his spending money. It seems to me that Picasso alone, certainly alone among the living artists whom I know of, is in anything like the same class. It is not merely knowledge of technique, or skill, it is intelligence and knowledge of life, of the whole of it, beauty, heaven, hell, sarcasm, every kind of whirlwind of force and emotion. Vortex. That is the right word, if I did find it myself.

From a letter. *The Letters of Ezra Pound*. Ed. D.D. Paige (London: Faber, 1951), pp. 121–22.

Tarr

T.S. Eliot

The fact that Mr. Wyndham Lewis is known as a draughtsman and painter is not of the least consequence to his standing as a prose writer. To treat his writing as an outlet for his superabundant vitality, or a means on his part of satisfying intellectual passions and keeping his art healthy, cannot lead to accurate criticism. His prose must be judged quite independently of his painting, he must be allowed the hypothesis of a dual creative personality. It would be quite another thing, of course, to find in his writing the evidences of a draughtsman's training – the training to respond to an ocular impression with the motion of a line on paper: the special reaction to vision and especially the development of the tactile sense, recognition of emotion by the physical strains and movements which are its basis.

It is already a commonplace to compare Mr. Lewis to Dostoevsky, analogy fostered by Mr. Lewis's explicit admiration for Dostoevsky. The relationship is so apparent that we can all the more easily be mistaken in our analysis of it. To find the resemblance is nothing; several other contemporary novelists have obviously admired Dostoevsky, and the result is of no importance. Mr. Lewis has made such good use of Dostoevsky – has commandeered him so efficiently for his purposes – that his differences from the Russian must be insisted upon. His mind is different, his method is different, his aims are different.

The method of Mr. Lewis is in fact no more like that of Dostoevsky, taking *Tarr* as a whole, than it is like that of Flaubert. The book does not comply with any of the accepted categories of fiction. It is not the extended *conte* (*Cantelman's Spring Mate* is not on the pattern of either Turgenev or Maupassant). It is not the elaboration of a datum, as *Madame Bovary*. From the standpoint of a Dostoevsky novel *Tarr* needs filling out: so much of Dostoevsky's effect is due to apparent pure receptivity, lack of conscious selection, to the irrelevances which merely happen and contribute imperceptibly to a total impression. In contrast to Dostoevsky, Mr. Lewis is impressively deliberate, frigid; his interest in his own personages is wholly intellectual. This is a peculiar intellectuality, not kin to Flaubert; and perhaps inhuman would be a better word than frigid. Intelligence, however, is only a part of Mr. Lewis's quality; it is united with a vigorous physical organism which interests itself directly in sensation for its own sake. The direct contact with the senses, perception of the world of immediate experience with its own scale of values, is like Dostoevsky, but there is always the suggestion of a purely intellectual curiosity in the senses which will disconcert many readers of the Russian novelist. And there is another important quality, neither French nor Russian, which may disconcert them still more. This is Humour.

Humour is distinctively English. No one can be so aware of the environment of Stupidity as the Englishman; no other nationality perhaps provides so dense an environment as the English. The *intelligent* Englishman is more aware of loneliness, has more reserves, than the man of intelligence of any other nation. Wit is public, it is in the object; humour (I am speaking only of *real* humour) is the instinctive attempt of a sensitive mind to protect beauty against ugliness; and to protect itself against stupidity. The older British humour is of this sort; in that great but decadent humorist, Dickens, and in some of his contemporaries it is on the way to the imbecilities of *Punch*. Mr. Lewis's humour is near to Dickens, but on the right side, for it is not too remote from Ben Jonson. In *Tarr* it is by no means omnipresent. It turns up when the movement is relaxed, it disappears when the action moves rapidly. The action is in places very rapid indeed: from the blow given by Kreisler in the café to the suicide is one uninterrupted movement. The awakening of Kreisler by the alarum-clock is as good as anything of the sort by Dostoevsky; the feverish haste of the suit-case episode proceeds without a smile. Bertha's impression of Kreisler is good in the same way:

> She saw side by side, and unconnected, the silent figure drawing her and the other one full of blindness and violence. Then there were two other figures, one getting up from the chair, yawning, and the present lazy one at the window – four in all, that she could not bring together somehow, each in a complete compartment of time of its own.

It is always with the appearance of Tarr, a very English figure, that Humour is apt to enter; whenever the situation is seen from Tarr's point of view, Humour invests him. He impressed you "as having inherited himself last week, and as under a great press of business to grasp the details and resources of the concern." Bertha's apartment, with the "repulsive shades of Islands of the Dead" is as it appeared to Tarr. Humour, indeed *protects* Tarr from Bertha, from the less important Anastasya, from the Lipmann circle. As a figure in the book, indeed, he is protected too well: "Tarr exalts life into a comedy," but it remains *his* (private) comedy. In one scene, and that in contact with Kreisler, Tarr is moved from his reserve into reality: the scene in which Tarr is forced out of Kreisler's bedroom. Here there is another point of contact with Dostoevsky, in a variation of one of Dostoevsky's best themes: Humiliation. This is one of the most important elements in human life, and one little exploited. Kreisler is a study in humiliation.

I do not understand the *Times* when it remarks that the book "is a very brilliant *reduction ad absurdum* not only of its own characters, but its own method." I am not sure that there is one method at all; or that there is not a different method for Tarr, for Kreisler, and for Bertha. It is absurd to attack the method which produced Kreisler and Bertha; they are permanent for literature. But there is an invisible conflict in progress all the time, between Tarr and Kreisler, to impose two different methods upon the book. We cannot say, therefore, that the form is perfect. In form, and in the actual writing, it is surpassed by *Cantelman's Spring Mate*. And *Inferior Religions* remains in my opinion the most indubitable evidence of genius, the most powerful piece of imaginative thought, of anything Mr. Lewis has written.

There can be no question of the importance of *Tarr*. But it is only in part a novel; for the rest, Mr. Lewis is a magician who compels our interest in himself; he is the most fascinating personality of our time rather than a novelist. The artist, I believe, is more *primitive*, as well as more civilized, than his contemporaries, his experience is deeper than civilization, and he only uses the phenomena of civilization in expressing it. Primitive instincts and the acquired habits of ages are confounded in the ordinary man. In the work of Mr. Lewis we recognize the thought of the modern and the energy of the cave-man.

The Egoist 5, no. 8 (September 1918), pp. 105–06.

The Leicester Galleries Exhibition, 1937

T.W. Earp

[T]he completeness that marks his show results in his emerging from modern painting's interregnum unexhausted and more vital than ever. Which of the elements has been the most saving one, is hard to fix. I should hazard that it is imagination, controlling an amazing gift of craftsmanship, while the craftsmanship of the majority only too well controls their imagination.

They have made this matter of craftsmanship a dull one, because continually it is all that calls for discussion, and leads on to nothing else. So with Lewis it had better at once be disposed of. He is a chief among the swiftly-lessening company still capable of giving an accurate imitation of reality in art. Whenever he cares, he can carry off his certificate. Such ability is of course worth only what its possessor makes of it, and painters for Academies and Salons make very little. But an enormous number of people who hold picture-shows have not got it at all. Their exhibitions display them still busy trying to forge an instrument. Lewis's gives a demonstration of an admirable instrument in use.

He puts it to glorious purpose, on vaster range and increased ease of practice. He has already accustomed us to excellent renderings of the visible, inventions within reality well-spiced with comment, or lyric interpretations of happy oases of beauty in actuality, while he is the greatest living creator of abstract design. But the present exhibition adds something more. There is an epic sweep in vision; a mature comprehension, a more final philosophy, in illustration.

A good prologue for the show as a whole is "Creation Myth," whose cascade of coloured worlds and budding forms has an elemental grandeur of imagination. From it any subject, any attitude might develop. Its impulse and its blaze start a continuity of rhythm and intellectual adventure that pulses on through the rest of the work.

Allied to it is a group of pictures making a supreme assertion of poetic exaltation. "One of the Stations of the Dead," with its grave shadows, the deep blue river of ultimate passage and the towering barrier of rock, joins in another art what is greatest in classic verse. "Group of Three Veiled Figures," with its intimation of calm mourning ritual, shares its mood.

Dynamic in form, and in conception near to Dante and Signorelli, is the flaming torrent of the doomed in "Inferno," whose excitement flickers down to neutral hues and the bleakness of contemporary myth in "Queue of the Dead." These interpretations of their theme form successive viewpoints in time, bring back a lost creative power to painting.

It continues, though in softer key, in those works that capture a dream's mystery, but would be marred by more explicit symbolism – "Marina's Departure from Chaos," with its sense of gracious gesture; the hieratic "Inca with Birds"; the ghostly, tensed "Red Scene"; "The Siege of Barcelona," with its rattling bustle and instant's vision of the past; and the gay, gusty "Newfoundland."

"The Tank in the Clinic," "Mud Clinic" and "Cubist Museum" are scenes of present-day suggestion, projected into fantasy and touched with satire. Their balance of design and direct effect of description rests on a consummate intricacy of pattern and plane. Candid in realism and content with simple unities are the golden

"Nordic Beach" and the grave brown and red "Invalid," with its charming little still-life.

Lewis makes the possibilities of the visible world a channel for communicating his imagination. Style with him is meaning, a matter of the aptest medium of expression. It may be a development of cubism, or imitative representation sharpened by a stress on essentials of form. It is wedded to its purpose of interpretation, and in the fusion of the two is the individuality of his art. In this respect his actual texture of pigment, limpid and clearly-bounded in application, is worth notice, when much false painterliness masquerades in luscious, streaks, in grease-paint.

The show's novelty of subject-invention has its counterpart, its co-identity, in the richness of purely pictorial invention, in lure of perspective, arresting passages of colour, or sudden weaving of form. "Panel for the Safe of a Great Millionaire" and its kindred paintings are adventures in these for their own sake, with their individual excitement and music of vibrating rhythm, which reassert Lewis a Master of the Abstract.

But in the portraits, paintings and drawings alike, is a fine humility of faithfulness to fact. It is accompanied by exceptional sensitiveness of notation and lit by a delight in human character. The portraits, indeed, are the most clinching testimony to the quality of his line, and that is the first foundation of the completeness that makes him a Renaissance artist in the twentieth century.

From "The Leicester Galleries Exhibition," *Twentieth Century Verse*. Wyndham Lewis Double Number, no. 6/7 (November/December 1937), n.p.

Lewis and Nature

Eric Newton

Nothing could be more fascinating than to watch Mr Lewis identifying Nature (i.e. his given subject matter) with metal, taking all the really metallic objects in his stride and gently wooing and coaxing the non-metallic objects till they begin to speak with a metallic accent without losing their "essence."

Take, for example, a magnificent early painting: "A Battery Shelled," of 1919. Wyndham Lewis won't take the easy way out of making the gun the hero of the picture and turning its context and its attendants into a painted back-cloth. Being a humanist he almost conceals the gun (it is of the first importance in warfare that guns should be concealed). But the mess of crazy, wheel-rutted ground that surrounds it, the dug-out entrances, the bits of corrugated iron, the shattered trees, the members of the gun team, the officers in the foreground – these are really worthy of his close attention. They have to be coaxed and translated until they become the inevitable symbols of scientific violence, disciplined chaos. It would be easy but ineffective to turn them all into metal – metal mackintoshes, metal men. That would be the opposite of humanism. It would also be boring. But they must *hint* at metal: the officers' faces look as though they might have been cast in a mould, even though they are flesh. The members of the gun team are not dressed in armour plating, but neither are they wearing khaki cloth. The rutted earth they stand on is mud, certainly, but carved mud. The rhythm of metal rather than metal itself pervades the picture. A metamorphosis has taken place. Nature has lost, under Lewis's treatment, a great deal of herself. Constable would be horrified at what she has lost. So would Titian. Mantegna would not. But what she has *not* lost has been presented to us as a "more tense and angular entity" than could ever be found anywhere but in the mind of an unusually creative artist.

It is also surprising to note, as one examines the picture, how much she has not lost. She is as fully three-dimensional and solid as Constable or Titian could desire. One could make one's way step by step from the officers and the blasted tree-trunks in the foreground across the intermediate carved-mud wilderness peopled with active automata, to the gun, and beyond it to the three shellbursts in the distance; one could equally travel into the picture through the air, following the formalized banner of drifting smoke.

It is by no means his best painting, though it is as complete a factual account of one aspect of modern war as I have seen. But it provides a key to his style.

One can work backwards from it to the prewar drawings of which the "Centauress" (1912) and the crowded drawing from the "Timon of Athens" series (1912) are examples. Or one can work forward to the more flexible and more skilful drawings done between the wars. The "Timon" drawing [*The Thebaid*] is a very remarkable achievement; it presents one with a convincing world, a world made of nothing but harsh angles and arcs of circles, an ordered pandemonium of a world in which, one would have thought, nothing organic could live. Yet not only do Alcibiades and two of his lady friends, and groups of soldiers in the distance and middle distance, manage to live in it: they are an integral part of it: they have characters of their own and they perform their parts in the drama.

That is a difficult creative act to have accomplished. It is precisely the poet's act, the counterpart of the feat whereby a writer takes the world of words and, extracting from it those that will serve his purpose, drills and regiments them, imposes rhythms on them, marshals them into little squads full of verbal energy, yet never robs them of their meaning – gives them, in fact, not a new but an intensified meaning. The "Timon" drawing was done, of course, at a moment when art had become unusually conscious of the possibilities of this kind of regimenting. Pound, Eliot and Joyce were juggling with words in much the same way that Lewis was juggling with shapes. Joyce, in the end, juggled so skilfully that they became uncomfortably charged with meaning. In the second decade of this century both words and shapes became more potent instruments. The tools at the disposal of the artist and the writer became more precise and more expressive. As it turned out, most artists were incapable of using them to advantage since they had little to express. But the credit for the fashioning of those artists' tools is largely due to Wyndham Lewis.

The "Timon" drawing shows these tools in the making, used with virtuosity but with less skill than later drawings. The "Girl in a Windsor Chair" of 1920 is drawn with the precision of a lathe. Direction, pressure on the pencil point, the relation of curve to curve, curve to straight, are all under control. The girl and the chair have become as beautiful (I use the word in its strictest sense) as a violin and much more complex. A sheaf of violins, seen from every angle, and thought of not only as a linear arabesque but also sculpturally, would be a closer analogy. Such precision of control could only arrive after years of hard slogging. Mantegna would have done the same thing with equal precision, and with far more affection but with less freedom, less power to turn a pencil line into a whiplash, and less positive delight in manipulating the whip. After Mantegna, who?

The word "whiplash" reminds me that neither skill nor a love of the cool and the metallic (with which, of course, goes a positive hatred of softness and warmth: Wyndham Lewis and Matthew Smith are exact opposites) are enough to explain the emotional undertones of an artist's work. "Whiplash" suggests castigation; the whip, elegantly used, is the satirist's weapon. It is here, on this deeper level, that Mantegna and Wyndham Lewis cease to have anything in common. Mantegna is no satirist. In Wyndham Lewis's work there is always an undercurrent of satire. His subject-matter may be as innocent as a daisy but the resultant work of art suggests a cynical frame of mind, a refusal to be taken in by false sentiment and a consequent mistrust of any sentiment. His imaginative paintings are never of a desirable world, his sitters are rarely heroes and heroines.

From "Wyndham Lewis," *The Art of Wyndham Lewis*. Ed. Charles Handley-Read (London: Faber, 1951), pp. 21–23.

The Gods of Time

Hugh Kenner

In 1927, however, Hitler was still in the future, and Lewis alone, with his image of Shakespeare to prop him, was busily opposing The Time. The liaison between The Time and "Time" is explained in the editorial to the second issue of *The Enemy* (1927):

> 'History' is just what occurs, what gets into Time, as opposed to what does not, or what remains latent, unused or unexplored: that is the directest meaning of 'history'. And the 'Destiny-idea', about which Spengler makes so much fuss, is, again, just that: what is, is. [...] It is the religion of Fate, and it is called 'History'.

All rhetoric about "manifest destiny," about "modernity" or "the spirit of the age," comes down, for Lewis, to that: genuflection before the random visage discernible in what happens to have happened. He was exacerbated not so much by the events as by their succession being deified into a massive trend:

> All other times have bred criticism. [...] Only this time exacts an uncritical sleep of all within it. This, as elsewhere I am showing, is the sleep of the machine, or humanly, of the mass. [...] We have become so conscious of this obsessing 'Time' that we tend to personalize it.

This was a discernment of great accuracy. Since Hanp [the character representing the ordinary man in *Enemy of the Stars*] by hypothesis seeks safety in numbers, Lewis in any age would have been in opposition. "Life" is what the herd is doing, and Art is the enemy of "Life," of what happens "naturally." Life passes through time and dies, whereas Art, as Tarr explained to Anastasya, "is ourselves disentangled from death and accident. [...] Anything living, quick and changing, is bad art, always." But with the momentum of his opposition, Lewis was enabled to discern as did no one else a special and unusual fact about the twentieth century: flux was not being taken for granted, it was being hypostatized. *La durée*, as Bergson had been explaining when the young Lewis visited his Paris lecture-room early in the century, was the only reality. The Self was being cut up into chronological compartments; Hanp was being told not only that he was a new man every morning, but that he was really not a man at all but a congeries of mental occurrences. " 'It thinks here' is as good sense as 'it rains here', the thought merely getting a certain colour from where it occurs. [...] We are the spot where a bundle of things is tied: we are the intersection of a multitude of paths." Simultaneously the pennies, chairs, and bricks of the *Not-Self* were being reduced to a series of "spatial apparitions made up of pure instantaneous sensations, enclosed in a temporal pen or corral." Everything, mental and physical, was being handed over to sensate "life," beyond the reach alike of the Intelligence and of Art. People didn't claim to be thinking, they claimed to be interpreting the sense of the age; nor did they claim that there was anything there to think about, only the sensations presented by one's "point of view."

This, reduced to essentials, is the argument of *Time and Western Man*, one of the dozen or so most important books of the twentieth century. The facts it surveys have become common knowledge; its value arises from its violently partisan tone. Disliking as he did the whole direction of contemporary philosophic thought, Lewis was able to expose its extraordinarily ramifying consequences in art, morals, and politics with a thoroughness and vividness denied to the submissive denizen of the time-stream. "Between Personality and Mankind it is always a question of dog and cat," said Arghol [protagonist of *Enemy of the Stars*]. So it didn't surprise Lewis at all that Science, with its cult of anonymity and impersonality, should be busily destroying, by means of behaviorist doctrines, the concept of the Person. A mass-mind, furthermore, offers advantages to Machiavelli's devotee of Power:

> Politically, of course (and envisaging science as the supreme functioning of the consciousness of the crowd), 'consciousness' is equally objectionable. For so long as that, in any sense, and in whatever disguise, holds out, it is very difficult to get the *individual* firmly by the scruff of the neck, and seat of the trousers, and fling him into the 'Unconscious'. How the 'Unconscious' comes to be the great democratic stronghold that it is, may require, in passing, a little further explanation.
>
> The 'Unconscious' is really what Plato meant by the 'mob of the senses', or rather it is where they are to be found, the mother region of 'sensational' life. It is in 'our Unconscious' that we live in a state of common humanity. There are no *individuals* in the Unconscious; because a man is only an individual when he is conscious. [...]

It is because Lewis is so far from disinterested that *Time and Western Man* sparkles with epithetic vigor. [...]

This is philosophic discussion conducted by an artist whose hyperconsciousness of the Self makes him unusually aware of the *will* (to call it that) behind the gray doctrines he has made it his business to anatomize. *Time and Western Man*, by connecting the most recondite thought with the most banal events, provides every necessary key to the controlling sensibility of our age. "Each man is every man, an abstraction, not a *concrete person.*" In book, film, and daydream, this is the age of History; and "the historical writer, in every case, is distracting people from a living Present (which becomes dead as the mind withdraws) into a Past into which they have gone to live." Having conjured up a vision of Mr. and Mrs. Citizen of the Future switching on a sound-film and living again "the sandwiches, the tea in the thermos, the ginger beer and mosquitoes, of a dozen years ago," Lewis comments that "People have already somewhat that sense of things laid out side by side, of the unreality of time, and yet of its paramount importance, that the conditions indicated above would breed." This is "the sleep of the machine"; when Professor Norbert Wiener in 1948 announced with some unction that the supersession of Man by Cybernetics was underwritten by the philosophy of Bergson, he was supplying an unconsciously Swiftian footnote to a neglected book then over twenty years old.

From "The Gods of Time," *Wyndham Lewis* (Norfolk: New Directions, 1954), pp. 72–76.

Reputation

Walter Michel

Lewis does not belong in the ranks of "neglected minor artists of some individuality" now being combed through by art dealers. The variety, the completeness, the imaginative power of his works, [...] which he maintained for forty years, clearly mark him as major. If he has, nevertheless, been neglected, this has been brought about in part by circumstances (notably two wars) which have nothing to do with his painting, and in part by the uniqueness of that painting. For Lewis created a modern art of his own. In an age which increasingly turned to texture, literary allusion or decorative appeal, and to large scale, he carried out pencil drawings washed with watercolour and heightened with gouache, or thinly painted oils not more than thirty inches high. To the easy appeal of the colour and matter of most of his contemporaries' works he opposed a world, delicate and often difficult of access, "just below the surface of life, in touch with a tragic organism." The exception was the period 1912–15, with its sensational wall decorations, fifteen or more canvases (probably all large in size), and close involvement with the movements of the time. But the subtle figure drawings he piled up almost in secret during these years, his growing scepticism toward movements, his view that the two other major figures in the Vorticist movement, Gaudier and Pound, were not radical enough, and finally the fact of his having, by 1914–15, "achieved the necessary notoriety" for being a painter in London, suggest he was likely soon to withdraw from any groupings and go determinedly his own way. Had not the war come, one can well imagine Lewis having one-man shows on the Continent in 1916, and gaining by storm the European reputation which, as a painter, has been on the whole denied him.

His work of the twenties, just as good as the pre-war work, though occasional, delicate and, with a few exceptions, confined to drawings, cannot readily be seen in such a conquering role. It is interesting to speculate (and of how many painters can this be said?) on what he would have done had he painted more – had he had the support, say, of [Roger] Fry, who was the spokesman for English painting on the Continent. ("Why," Picasso is reported to have asked Ben Nicholson, "when I ask about modern artists in England am I always told about Duncan Grant?" If, as has been said, Roger Fry and Clive Bell "did not get the living painters to champion that they deserved," the deprivation was mutual.) Instead of a massive output of paintings came the satires and polemics, *The Apes of God* and *The Enemy*, all largely written for an English-speaking public and intractable to the Continental market. As punishment for these writings, which represent a large part of what intellectual achievement England in the twenties could boast, important remnants of Victorian sensibility, which were *offended*, could silently blackball Lewis as somehow unpleasant and a cad.

His comeback in the thirties was a feat of energy and endurance, but also a remarkable tribute to his staying power as a painter. As has been noted, the bright young men who were publishing the "little magazines" became interested. His 1937 exhibition was a *succès d'estime*, and by 1938 Lewis was once more solidly entrenched as a painter, with exhibitions abroad a logical next step. But two years later he was again an unknown. With sickening sameness the events of 1914 had repeated themselves. The war which began in 1939 shattered his subsequent career as a painter – so much so, that most of his important works of the forties are, even today, accessible only to the most intrepid researcher.

After the war, with the early pictures scattered and those from the thirties exhibitions largely in the basements of dealers, a good memory or a willingness to take trouble was required of one who wanted to form a fresh opinion of Lewis's work. He was not represented in the Penguin Modern Painters series, published in the forties and fifties, an omission which he attributed to "Bloomsbury" influence. At this time, so relatively modest a tribute as the inclusion of a reproduction of his in Michael Ayrton's book *British Drawings*, published in 1946, was an occasion for surprise and gratification to the artist. A few painters and critics, aware of his merits, extolled his work, but a broad and sustained base of familiarity with it was lacking. Those who praised Lewis, one suspects, often succeeded only in irritating a public which saw little of his visual work but much of the peculiarly personal criticism often quite casually directed at him.

Even a few years after the 1956 Arts Council exhibition at the Tate Gallery, which had been, in fact if not in name, a Lewis retrospective, paintings from the 1937 Leicester Galleries show could still be bought at prices only twice those originally asked (which were, indeed, much the same as those for which his paintings sold before World War 1).

What remains is a thousand drawings, a hundred paintings and the memory of a man who kept his passion for life and for art, and preserved his independence. He was the greatest representative in his generation of one direction of modern English painting, one that embodies what, in *The Tyro*, he had held up as a tradition which English artists might well follow: "the English virtues, of the intellect and sensibility, developed by Rowlandson, Hogarth and their contemporaries, and earlier at their flood-tide in the reign of Elizabeth." He was also a twentieth-century man, one of the last "Europeans," and his fractured career accurately reflects the fate of the West.

From "Reputation," *Wyndham Lewis: Paintings and Drawings* (London: Thames and Hudson, 1971), pp. 147–49.

Lewis's Prose

Fredric Jameson

"It is a style," Kenner tells us, "composed of phrases, not actions": to which we have already added the proviso that the phrases, with their heterogeneous sources and references, are never completely subdued and mastered by the sentence as a larger unity. But this observation about the coexistence of ready-made, free-floating bits of speech can readily be converted into a statement about the figural content of such passages, which derives, not from symbolic structures inherent in the fable itself, but rather from some extrinsic and impersonal storehouse of cultural materials:

> Tying their chokers, trotting clowns hurrying at the crack of the magisterial circus-whip, the six scuttle and trip, but never fall, the ground rising in pustules at their feet to mock them, the wind clipping them on the ear, or pushing them upon the obstructions arranged for them to amuse the idiot-universe. They skip and dance on the bulky treacherous surface of the earth, stoic beneath nature's elemental hot-fisted cuffs, tumblers or Shakespearean clowns, punchballs got up as Pierrot. (CM, 132–33)[1]

The shifting appositions (circus clowns, Shakespearean clowns, Pierrots) program the events of the sentence in progress, and, themselves received images, are reflected in the outer form of the language itself as a constant reshuffling of received idiom ("hot-fisted cuffs" as a portmanteau of the expression "hot-tempered" and the word "fisticuffs," the whole then refashioned on the model of "tight-fisted").

The great sentences of Lewis have therefore little enough in common with that Flaubertian aesthetic of the "mot juste," of which Joyce, with his "artfully" placed adverbs and his traces of Paterian unction, is the hegemonic modernist realization. They give little enough aid and comfort to the modernist conviction that sense perception can ultimately be fully rendered in a sentence structure, that a "parole pleine" is possible, that the world really does exist to end up in a Book which will replace it and in which the glint of sunlight on a pond, the stir of wind upon the earth's surfaces, will thus forever gleam and mildly tremble in the eternal immobility of the printed sentence.

At the same time, there can be no doubt that Lewis fulfills another, and apparently quite different, tendency at work in the stylistic practice of Flaubert: that of the "sottisier" and the "dictionary of received ideas," the inventory of "bêtise," and the relish in the mindless use of stereotypes. How could it be otherwise, when the very mechanisms of Lewis' style presuppose our indispensable preliminary familiarity with the stereotypical epithets and appositions that inaugurate it and program its perceptions?

> Satters fully dressed is propped within, his lush bulk pitched against the jamb, occupying the breach in beefy sinuosity, his curled head bent somewhat to clear the lintel, his eyes cast archly up. The smile of

Leonardo's St. John, appropriated to the features of a germanic ploughboy, sustains an expression of heavy mischief. (CM, 121)

Where the Joycean reading play opens a place for the spectator to witness Mr. Bloom's homosexual tendencies in all their rouged *coquetterie*, dissolving the cultural or advertising stereotypes into the merest pretexts for the simulacrum of a stage or music hall perception, in Lewis they preserve their autonomy; and the prestige of the no longer adequately visualizable masterpiece of Leonardo, diffused through Sunday rotogravures and banalized by art appreciation, shoots forth a distant and degraded ray to strike this passage with a spurious glow as the sign that this new face of Satters has been certified as "perceptible" by experts in some absent precinct of an official culture.

The collage-composition practiced by Lewis thus draws heavily and centrally on the warehouse of cultural and mass cultural cliché, on the junk materials of industrial capitalism, with its degraded commodity art, its mechanical reproduceability, its serial alienation of language, in short, with what the structuralists would call the Symbolic Order: that systematized network of cultural code and representation which preexists, speaks, and produces the individual subject by means of the ruse of a belief in individuality itself. In such a situation, the personal language, the private thought are themselves illusions, where conventionalized formulae dictate in advance the thought that had seemed to choose them for its own instruments. Nor can genuine experience be readily identified any longer, when a degraded culture intervenes between us and our objects, to substitute for them, by an imperceptible sleight of hand, some standardized snapshot. Whoever under such circumstances continues to believe in the unproblematical functioning of natural language falls most surely victim to this illusionistic structure which silently undoes its most "authentic" utterances.

This is the dilemma to which Lewis' linguistic praxis speaks in exemplary and ingenious fashion: his "method," if we can call it that, is to use the cliché against itself – or better still, to pit clichés on the level of gestural images against the verbal clichés with which the sentences themselves are hopelessly corroded. In this way, a kind of perceptual freshness is reinvented out of the unexpectedly virulent interaction of stale and faded substances. Witness the following account of Pullman's movements as he offers to help Satters to his feet:

> Stalking and stretching tense-legged, in a succession of classical art-poses suggestive of shadow-archery, he approaches Satters. He relaxes like the collapse of a little house of cards, extends a friendly lackadaisical hand, and sings out: 'Up again, come jump to it!' (CM, 19)

The visual cliché has here been broken into its component parts, then reverbalized into segments of linguistic commonplace such that the latter are unable to discharge their automatic meaning-effects, but, neutralized by discontinuity and each other's indifference, remain as empty imperatives to visualize the central gesture. Yet we must already know in advance what that gesture is, since the words have long since lost their capacity to convey new information:

> Pullman several times is parted from one of his slippers, having to stop to reinsert his foot and prise it up with humped toes. (CM, 27)

Without personal knowledge of the muscular operation that lends this sentence the force of a recall, it must deteriorate into a series of inert notations, as empty as an untranslatable hieroglyph.

> He sat upon a cushion, leoninely slumped back against the panelling, as if luxuriating in a technical knockout. (RL, 156)[2]

Such a sentence hangs uncertainly between two received images, the late-night glimpse of a besotted party-goer, and the newsreel snapshot of the boxer seated against the ropes: only the metaphorical term fails to intensify the literal one, but rather bears it off along with it into sheerest conventionality. What unexpectedly remains behind is however the unspecified place of their twin referent, the "real" Victor sprawling upon a material sofa in some unique moment of historical time – a vivid "idea" which the reader hastens to substitute for the tangible words that have ceased to function.

So it is that over the great moments in Lewis there hangs a strange and nagging sense of *dèja vu*.

1. "CM" refers to *The Childermass* (London: Calder and Boyars, 1968). This reprints *The Human Age, Book One: Childermass* (London: Methuen, 1956).
2. "RL" refers to *The Revenge for Love* (1937). Rprt. (Chicago: Regnery, 1952).

From *Fables of Aggression: Wyndham Lewis, the Modernist as Fascist* (Berkeley: University of California Press, 1979), pp. 71–75.

The Attitude of Genius

Julian Symons

You walked down a white-tiled passage, rather like the entrance to a public lavatory, rang a bell. The man who opened the door was tall and bulky, the face broad and white, the brown eyes mild beneath an artist's big black hat. This was Wyndham Lewis as I saw him in his Notting Hill Gate studio half a century ago, a man in his middle fifties, his movements slow, voice catarrhal and gentle except when touched by enthusiasm or anger, manner polite but enquiring. He agreed readily to co-operate with the production of a special number dealing with his work in the little magazine I ran, and after it had appeared I saw him frequently in the months before the War, less often when he had returned to England from Canada and the United States in the late Forties.

What makes one feel in the presence of genius, rather than of intelligence and ordinary talent? I can vouch for the feeling but not explain it, any more than could the novelist and critic Walter Allen when he said Lewis was one of the two or three geniuses he had met, and discerned a tragic dimension in him missing from Auden; or T.S. Eliot, who said he had never really known Lewis the man, but also called him the most fascinating personality of his time. The testimonials could be multiplied, some of them coming from those who neither liked Lewis nor greatly admired him as writer and visual artist, but still felt themselves in the presence of an extraordinary, perhaps inimical, force when in his company.

Yet the company was agreeable, the reverse of pretentious, genial and not at all forbidding. Feet up, glass of whisky in hand, he would express unbuttoned views about other writers and artists past and present, and encourage one to do the same. Geoffrey Grigson remembered that at their first meeting, in an ABC teashop, Lewis asked across the tea and buns what he knew about Goya, Gogol, Conrad, and whether he admired Virginia Woolf. With me it was Kafka, the pre-Raphaelites, Ruskin and Carlyle. Others could tell the same story, with different names. He had no ordinary small talk, but a great appetite for cultural gossip. Fed bits of such gossip, he would create verbal fantasies about the behaviour of current literary figures often wildly funny, and sometimes so far outside the bounds of their possible behaviour as to have a surreal absurdity. These visions of the impossible were generally too caricatural to be called malicious, and they were not confined to his numerous enemies. Walter Allen was delighted but startled when, meeting Lewis for only the second time, he was asked whether he would like to write a book about his host. Allen played for safety by mentioning other possible candidates. What about Grigson or Symons? Grigson would produce a pastiche, Lewis said, and Symons was just waiting for him to die and would then have a book out about him in no time. Allen was shocked at this attitude towards admirers, but he should not have been. Lewis acknowledged few equals, whether among friends or enemies. He talked as he wrote, from the attitude of genius.

That image of an alien force, a visitor from a planet where the whole conception of life and its proper ordering was different, is the best way to see Wyndham Lewis. Behind the immediate geniality there seemed to be a kind of inner rage, at the conditions of life, the nature of society, the dullness of other people. It was not possible to be long in his company without realising that he looked at what was around him through eyes quite different from one's own. He saw men and women as machines walking, their appendages of ears, nose, hands oddly stuck on, their activities from speech and eating to excretion and copulation stutteringly awkward and comic. Allen rightly called his way of thinking profoundly unEnglish, and said the shorthand expression for it might be Cartesian. Lewis certainly resembled Descartes in being a man of supreme intelligence who rejected purely rational thought in favour of what seemed to him evident truths based on his individual and extraordinary perceptions. Descartes, however, proceeded from the basis that the power of thought is the proof of selfhood ("cogito ergo sum") to deduce the existence of God. Lewis's perceptions were used to assert the power of art, and he applied them to a view of society that, except in his last years, was remote from religious feeling. He saw the society he lived in as undergoing drastic and revolutionary changes in the decades between the Wars. "My mind is ahistoric, I would welcome the clean sweep," he wrote to me in 1937. "I could build something better, I am sure of that, than has been left by our fathers." The "something better" he identified as a finer art, which would be achieved in a society revering works of art as the greatest products of civilisation. And he took it for granted that he was capable of producing such works.

An approach of this kind is inimical to British ways of thought and feeling which, especially in the Victorian and Edwardian periods, permitted and even welcomed eccentricity in its artists, but did not expect a personal announcement of genius. Lewis aroused suspicious dislike also by the variety of his talents. He first became known as a near-abstract visual artist, the most important figure connected with Vorticism, the movement he founded although Ezra Pound gave it a name. Then he became known as a writer of novels and short stories, some of them satiric. He was always ready to defend and explain his work in essays and articles, and to dissect the work of others with a frankness often resented. From the early 1920s until his death in 1957 he supported his own art works with a philosophical, political and economic analysis of society that suggested possible directions in which social power would develop, and looked at which of these directions might be most beneficial to art.

All this work – the novels and stories, along with the criticism, exposition, discussion and denunciation – was done with an exclamatory jocular freedom very similar to the form of his conversation, although the conversational tone was heightened on the page. Eliot was not alone in calling him the greatest English prose stylist of the century. Others found him unreadable because of the very qualities Lewis's admirers regard as virtues, although few went so far as Anthony Quinton who called Lewis the worst prose writer of the century. Certainly the style was unique, rapid and exclamatory, learned yet vividly colloquial. He discussed complex philosophical questions with the jovial slanginess of a man arguing with others in a pub. This style is not, as it looks, artless, but the product of careful design, devised as the best means of conveying messages about the need for and nature of the changes in society that Lewis, writing in the Twenties, expected to see emerge.

In his fiction the style is thicker and more complex, but still infused with the same frantic energy. His rendering of dialogue is, again, entirely original, revealing the hesitations, repetitions, clichés and inanities of common conversation with the faithfulness of a tape recorder put into a room where the speakers are unaware of its presence.

From "Introduction," *The Essential Wyndham Lewis* (London: André Deutsch, 1989), pp. 1–4.

Lewis's "Modernism"

Tom Lubbock

It's possible to think that Lewis just repudiated modern art, that he went the way of de Chirico, reverting to a weird, kitsch, retro manner. Lewis certainly repudiated pure abstraction. He certainly criticised modern art and the various directions it took. He opposed Cubism for performing its formal experiments on such boring subject matter. He opposed Surrealism for doing interesting subjects in such a traditional style.

Lewis is a mixer. He doesn't believe in – at any rate, he doesn't practice – a pure, single-minded art. His own abstracts had never been pure; there's always some figurative action more or less sublimated in them. His Tyro figures were a kind of modernism-cum-caricature. The pictures of the Twenties and Thirties belong to no known species. There is a dramatic play of styles. There are subjects that suggest a visionary, mythological, after-life, sci-fi world *and also* a satirical grotesque picture of the contemporary world, divinities and hollow men.

Nothing is clear. In the same image, garrulous illustration, telling stories, inventing characters arid worlds, proceed in tandem – but never quite in unison – with a decorative doodling, e1aborating forms, accumulating, complicating. Figures, scenery, shapes and forces overlap and interlock and metamorphose. Richard Humphreys, in the best short introduction to Lewis's art, (*Wyndham Lewis*, Tate), gets the feel of it exactly: "endlessly fascinating to the eye and productively if inconclusively irritating the associative faculties." There's something going on, something you can never quite grasp. Everything is equivocal, and it produces an extremely sophisticated, vital, beautiful but unclassifiable art, that isn't a proper modernist signature nor a jokey post-modernist game. Maybe it isn't quite art at all.

On the eve of the World War Two, Lewis and his wife got out of Europe, took the boat across the Atlantic, and stayed in Canada and the USA for the duration. He did portraits and lectures to earn money; pointlessly insulted more people; had a pretty bad time; made increasingly other-worldly drawings; came back to London; started again.

Started yet again. The admirable or awful thing about Lewis's life is that there is no point where he sits back, settles down, enjoys, lives at ease, where he stops – stops struggling or stops minding. There's never a moment when he feels that the world might not need the benefit of his views. There's never a moment when he doesn't need to earn or otherwise get money.

He began doing art reviews of contemporary artists, and came out strongly for younger talents like Francis Bacon. Then, in 1951, "My articles on contemporary art exhibitions necessarily end, for I can no longer see a picture." A pituitary tumour had destroyed his vision. Blind and fading, he was given a sort of Tate retrospective in 1956 (there's hasn't been one since) and died the following year.

In London, where he spent most of his

working life, there are no blue plaques commemorating Lewis. If there were any, there might be dozens – he had so many short-stay flats and studios. His most permanent address, the flat in Notting Hill he occupied on and off since the late Thirties, was demolished by the local authority not long after his death.

It's almost 50 years on. Lewis has his fan-base still, continually pushing the cause. But there was a lot of Lewis, and the cause tends to get fragmented. Some people like him for his prose, for those dense, vivid, lapidary, switch-back paragraphs that in a few lines manage multiple changes of gear, voice and perspective. Some people like him for his general attitude, disaffected and embattled, liberal bashing, aesthete bashing, sod-the-lot-of-them. For those who still dream of a true avant-garde, an art that's both aesthetically and politically radical – it's usually a left-wing dream – then the "lonely old volcano of the right" (as Auden called him) is the only British exemplar. For many though, for me, it's the visual works, the paintings and drawings, that are the crux of the matter.

I can't remember where I first came across these pictures. I can remember the conversion experience – and of course if Lewis had been a more famous artist it probably wouldn't have happened like this. It was in the reference section of a public library. Our most intense encounters with art are often in reproduction. There's not much you can do about this (apart from never looking at reproductions) because you can never tell when you're going to come across a reproduction of a picture that you had no idea you wanted to see... but afterwards, even seeing the real thing may not surpass that first piercing hit.

The book was the complete catalogue of Lewis's paintings and drawings, and there they were. I had no idea images could be so glutting: the unimaginably gorgeous colours, the unfathomable imagery, the sharp and eliding textures, that electric line drawing. Unable to take out the large volume on my ticket, I felt obliged to remove it from the library surreptitiously, which was quite difficult. No one else was going to want it so badly. Still, that was my own line drawing undone. Irresistibly magnetised to Lewis's lines, but quite unequal to them, it had to stop.

It's only because of the art that I'm interested in the rest, in the writing, the manifestos, the criticism, the theorising, the satire, the whole controversial phenomenon, the personality and the life. It's only because of the art that I remotely care whether or not Lewis was a fascist. As for his art itself being visually or stylistically fascist, well I don't believe that. A hard, sharp-edged classicism is "fascist"? And a formless, oceanic, Wagnerian romanticism is "fascist" too, right? These general political diagnoses of style don't have much purchase.

And is it proper modern art? Is it art full stop? I don't know. I'd kind of like to have Lewis in the central pioneer pantheon of modernism. It's one way of getting him noticed. But frankly I wonder. In all his many activities, he never played it straight. Maybe he started off as an artist – and then turned into one of the great English illustrators.

The obvious comparison for Wyndham Lewis is another marginal, unplaceable creator, William Blake. Blake's images have that same elusive mix of archetypal vision and contemporary polemic, dense thought and blazing design. Blake's images took some time to emerge from their awkward, border-line, not-quite-art position. Now they're everywhere.

"The Sensationalist," *The Independent* (*ABC* section) (13 February 2005), p. 11.

"When a painter is also a writer, whether good or ill should ensue, artistically, upon this double birth – this twinship in the fashion of Siam of the literary and the plastic executant – depends upon how these partners are mutually balanced. With me, I am inclined to claim, the equilibrium was practically perfect. My best picture, I believe, is as well done as my best book."

Wyndham Lewis,
Beginning, 1935

E

CATALOGUE OF WORKS

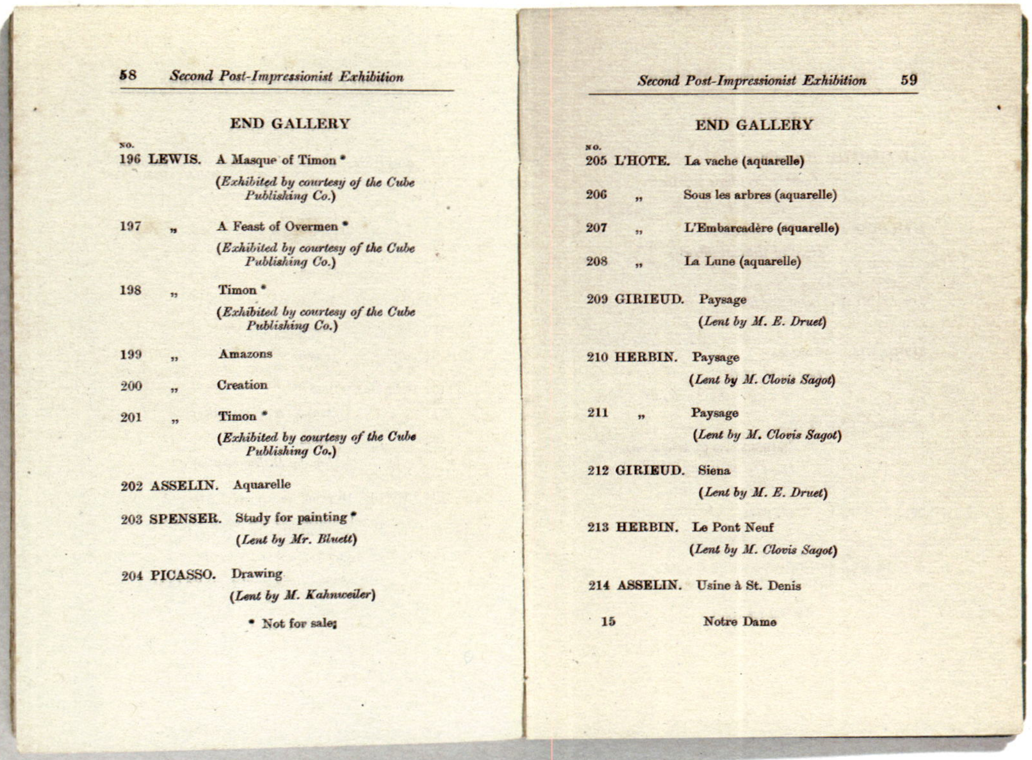

58 *Second Post-Impressionist Exhibition*

END GALLERY

NO.		
196	LEWIS.	A Masque of Timon * (*Exhibited by courtesy of the Cube Publishing Co.*)
197	„	A Feast of Overmen * (*Exhibited by courtesy of the Cube Publishing Co.*)
198	„	Timon * (*Exhibited by courtesy of the Cube Publishing Co.*)
199	„	Amazons
200	„	Creation
201	„	Timon * (*Exhibited by courtesy of the Cube Publishing Co.*)
202	ASSELIN.	Aquarelle
203	SPENSER.	Study for painting * (*Lent by Mr. Bluett*)
204	PICASSO.	Drawing (*Lent by M. Kahnweiler*)

* Not for sale.

Second Post-Impressionist Exhibition 59

END GALLERY

NO.		
205	L'HOTE.	La vache (aquarelle)
206	„	Sous les arbres (aquarelle)
207	„	L'Embarcadère (aquarelle)
208	„	La Lune (aquarelle)
209	GIRIEUD.	Paysage (*Lent by M. E. Druet*)
210	HERBIN.	Paysage (*Lent by M. Clovis Sagot*)
211	„	Paysage (*Lent by M. Clovis Sagot*)
212	GIRIEUD.	Siena (*Lent by M. E. Druet*)
213	HERBIN.	Le Pont Neuf (*Lent by M. Clovis Sagot*)
214	ASSELIN.	Usine à St. Denis
15		Notre Dame

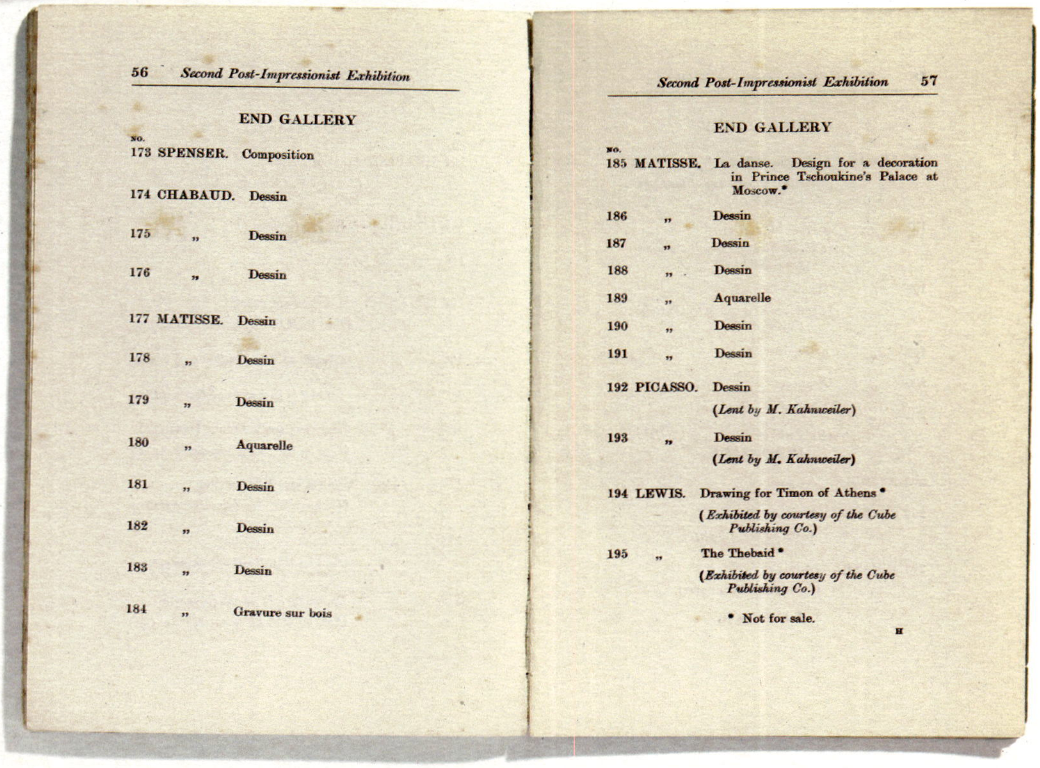

56 *Second Post-Impressionist Exhibition*

END GALLERY

NO.		
173	SPENSER.	Composition
174	CHABAUD.	Dessin
175	„	Dessin
176	„	Dessin
177	MATISSE.	Dessin
178	„	Dessin
179	„	Dessin
180	„	Aquarelle
181	„	Dessin
182	„	Dessin
183	„	Dessin
184	„	Gravure sur bois

Second Post-Impressionist Exhibition 57

END GALLERY

NO.		
185	MATISSE.	La danse. Design for a decoration in Prince Tschoukine's Palace at Moscow.*
186	„	Dessin
187	„	Dessin
188	„	Dessin
189	„	Aquarelle
190	„	Dessin
191	„	Dessin
192	PICASSO.	Dessin (*Lent by M. Kahnweiler*)
193	„	Dessin (*Lent by M. Kahnweiler*)
194	LEWIS.	Drawing for Timon of Athens * (*Exhibited by courtesy of the Cube Publishing Co.*)
195	„	The Thebaid * (*Exhibited by courtesy of the Cube Publishing Co.*)

* Not for sale.

H

Wyndham Lewis: the Artist

CAT. 1. *Nude Boy Bending (Stooping Nude Boy)*, 1900. Pencil on paper. 34.5 x 29 cm. UCL Art Collections, University College London (SDC6003). M 2

CAT. 2. *Alfred de Pass*, ca. 1903. Red chalk on paper. 46.8 x 31 cm. Wyndham Lewis Memorial Trust, London (LD.2004.XX.1)

CAT. 3. *Two Nudes*, 1903. Pen and ink, and ink wash on paper. 24.4 x 39.5 cm. Wyndham Lewis Memorial Trust, London (LD.2004.XX.2). M 6

CAT. 4. *Salaam Maharaj: An Oriental Design*, 1900–5 . Pen and sepia ink, and wash of sepia ink on paper. 33 x 38 cm. Collection Brian Sewell. M 9

CAT. 5. [Not in exhibition] *The Celibate*, 1909. Pencil, ink, watercolour and gouache on paper. 37.5 x 28.5 cm. Tatham Art Gallery, Pietermaritzburg, South Africa (0736/83). M (Addenda; 1909)

CAT. 6. *The Theatre Manager*, 1909. Pencil, ink and watercolour on paper. 29.5 x 31.5 cm. Victoria and Albert Museum, London (E 3779-1919). M 15

CAT. 7. *Café*, 1910–11. Pen and ink, watercolour and crayon on paper. 21 x 13.5 cm. Courtesy of Austin/Desmond Fine Art, London. Private collection. M 18

CAT. 8. *Girl Asleep*, 1911. Pencil and gouache on paper. 28 x 38.5 cm. Manchester City Galleries (1925.504)

CAT. 9. *Self-Portrait* (1911). Graphite, pen and ink, watercolour and gouache on paper. 31.3 x 24.3 cm. C.J. Fox Collection (LD.2000.XX.I). M 26

CAT. 10. *Self-Portrait,* 1911–12. Pencil, crayon and wash on paper. 54 x 39.5 cm. Private collection, Ivor Braka Ltd. M 25

CAT. 11. *Smiling Woman Ascending a Stair*, 1911. Charcoal and gouache on paper. 95 x 65 cm. Private collection. M 27

CAT. 12. *Courtship*, 1912. Pencil, ink and pastel on paper. 25.5 x 20.5 cm. Victoria and Albert Museum, London (E 3785-1919). M 45

CAT. 13. *The Domino*, 1912. Pencil, ink and watercolour on paper. 25.5 x 20.5 cm. Victoria and Albert Museum, London (E 3784-1919). M 54

CAT. 14. *Figure Holding a Flower*, 1912. Graphite, pen and ink, and gouache on paper. 38.1 x 29.1 cm. Wyndham Lewis Memorial Trust, London (LD.2004.XX.4). M 63

CAT. 15. *The Starry Sky* or *Two Women*, 1912. Pencil, pen and ink, gouache and collage on paper. 48 x 62.5 cm. Arts Council Collection, Southbank Centre, London (ACC151). M 86

CAT. 16. *Figure Composition*, 1912. Pen and ink, watercolour, pencil and gouache on paper. 25 x 31 cm. Private collection. M 61

CAT. 17. *Russian Scene (Russian Madonna)*, 1912. Pencil, ink and watercolour on paper. 30.5 x 24 cm. Victoria and Albert Museum, London (E 3762-1919). M 83

CAT. 18. *Man and Woman*, 1912. Chalk, pen and ink, wash and gouache on paper. 36 x 26 cm. Wyndham Lewis Memorial Trust, London. G. and V. Lane Collection (LD.2009.XX.I). M 75

CAT. 19. [Not in exhibition] Study for *Kermesse*, 1912. Gouache and watercolor with pen and black ink over graphite on two joined sheets of wove paper. 30.5 x 30.6 cm. Yale Center for British Art, New Haven, Connecticut. Paul Mellon Fund and Gift of Neil F. and Ivan E. Phillips in memory of their mother, Mrs Rosalie Phillips. M 72

CAT. 20. *Lovers*, 1912. Pen and ink, and watercolour on paper. 25.5 x 35.5 cm. Private collection. M 74

CAT. 21. *Odalisque*, 1911–12. Pen and ink, and chalk on paper. 35.5 x 20.5 cm. Private collection. M 79

CAT. 22. *Figure (Spanish Woman)*, 1912. Pen and ink, and gouache on paper. 31.2 x 20.7 cm. Wyndham Lewis Memorial Trust, London. G. and V. Lane Collection (LD.2004.XX.38). M 65

CAT. 23. *The Courtesan*, 1912. Pencil, ink and pastel on paper. 27.5 x 18.5 cm. Victoria and Albert Museum, London (E 3761-1919). M 44

CAT. 24. *Two Vorticist Figures*, 1912. Pen and black ink, and watercolour on paper. 24.7 x 31.9 cm. Trustees of the British Museum, London (1984,0512.12). M 116

CAT. 25. *The Vorticist*, 1912. Watercolour on paper. 42.2 x 32.2 cm. Southampton City Art Gallery (1429). M 118

CAT. 26. *Futurist Figure*, 1912. Pencil, pen and ink, ink wash and wash on paper. 26 x 18.5 cm. Collection David Bowie. M 67

CAT. 27. [Not in exhibition] *Helen Saunders*, 1913. Pencil and watercolour on paper. 28.5 x 18 cm. Private collection. M 147

CAT. 28. [Not in exhibition] *Figure Composition (Man and Woman with Two Bulldogs)*, 1912. Pen and ink, watercolour and gouache on paper. 31.3 x 2.7cm . Collection Art Gallery of New South Wales, Sydney. Purchased 1983. M 62

CAT. 29. *Drawing for Timon*, 1912. Pen and ink, and watercolour on paper. 38 x 28.5 cm. Private collection. M 109

CAT. 30. *Timon of Athens: Act I (A Masque of Timon)*, 1912. Pen and ink, watercolour and gouache on paper. 48.5 x 33 cm. Wyndham Lewis Memorial Trust, London. G. and V. Lane Collection (LD.2000.XX.6). M 93

CAT. 31. Portfolio *Timon of Athens: Act I (A Masque of Timon)*, 1913. Lithograph on paper. 38.8 x 27.2 cm. Wyndham Lewis Memorial Trust, London. G. and V. Lane Collection (LG.2004.XX.1). M 93

CAT. 32. Portfolio *Timon of Athens: A Feast of Overmen*, 1913. Lithograph on paper. 38.8 x 27.2 cm. Wyndham Lewis Memorial Trust, London. G. and V. Lane Collection (LG.2004.XX.1). M 100

CAT. 33. *The Thebaid*, 1912. Pencil, ink and watercolour on paper. 38.7 x 27.2 cm. Private collection. M 98

CAT. 34. Portfolio *Timon of Athens: The Thebaid* (1913). Lithograph on paper. 38.8 x 27.2 cm. Wyndham Lewis Memorial Trust, London. G. and V. Lane Collection (LG.2004.XX.1). M 98

CAT. 35. Portfolio *Timon of Athens: Act III*, 1913. Lithograph on paper. 38.8 x 27.2 cm. Wyndham Lewis Memorial Trust, London. G. and V. Lane Collection (LG.2004.XX.1). M 95

CAT. 36. Portfolio *Timon of Athens: Act IV* (1913). Lithograph on paper. 38.8 x 27.2 cm. Wyndham Lewis Memorial Trust, London. G. and V. Lane Collection (LG.2004.XX.1). M 96

CAT. 37. Portfolio *Timon of Athens: Act V* (1913). Lithograph on paper. 38.8 x 27.2 cm. Wyndham Lewis Memorial Trust, London. G. and V. Lane Collection (LG.2004.XX.1). M 97

CAT. 38. Portfolio *Timon of Athens: Timon* (1913). Lithograph on paper. 38.8 x 27.2 cm. Wyndham Lewis Memorial Trust, London. G. and V. Lane Collection (LG.2004.XX.1). M 102

CAT. 39. Portfolio *Timon of Athens: Design for Front Cover*, 1913. Lithograph on paper. 38.8 x 27.2 cm. Wyndham Lewis Memorial Trust, London. G. and V. Lane Collection (LG.2004.XX.1). M 91

CAT. 40. Portfolio *Timon of Athens: Design for Back Cover*, 1913. Lithograph on paper. 38.8 x 27.2 cm. Wyndham Lewis Memorial Trust, London. G. and V. Lane Collection (LG.2004.XX.1). M 92

CAT. 41. *Design for a Folding Screen*, 1913. Pencil and watercolour on paper. 51 x 38.5 cm. Victoria and Albert Museum, London (E 735-1955). M 131

CAT. 42. [Not in exhibition] *Cactus*, 1913. Pencil, ink, watercolour and chalk on paper. 34 x 23.5 cm. Victoria and Albert Museum, London (E 3768-1919). M 124

CAT. 43. *At the Seaside*, 1913. Watercolour, pencil and ink on paper. 47.5 x 31.5 cm. Victoria and Albert Museum, London (E 3763-1919). M 123

CAT. 44. *Circus Scene*, 1913–14. Pen and ink, and watercolour on paper. 24 x 31 cm. Collection David Bowie. M 160

CAT. 45. *Timon of Athens*, 1913. Pencil, pen and black and brown ink, and wash on paper. 34.5 x 26.5 cm. Private collection. M 154

CAT. 46. *Composition – Later Drawing of Timon Series*, 1913. Pen, watercolour and pencil on paper. 34.3 x 26.7 cm. Tate, London: Purchased 1949 (N05886). M 125

CAT. 47. [Not in exhibition] *Portrait of an Englishwoman*, 1913. Pen and ink, pencil and watercolour on paper. 56 x 38 cm. The Wadsworth Atheneum Museum of Art, Hartford, Connecticut. The Ella Gallup Sumner and Mary Catlin Sumner Collection Fund (1949.457). M 146

CAT. 48. *Planners (A Happy Day)*, 1913. Pen, gouache and pencil on paper. 31.1 x 38.1 cm. Tate, London: Purchased 1956 (T00106). M 145

CAT. 49. *Dancing Figures*, 1914. Pencil, pen, ink, crayon, gouache and oil on paper. 21 x 50 cm. Private collection

CAT. 50. [Not in exhibition] *New York*, 1914. Pen and ink, and watercolour on paper. 31 x 26 cm. Private collection. M 177

CAT. 51. *Moonlight*, 1914. Pencil, ink and chalk on paper. 27, 5 x 38 cm. Victoria and Albert Museum, London (E 3766-1919). M 166

CAT. 52. *Combat No. 3*, 1914. Pencil, ink and chalk on paper. 27, 5 x 38 cm. Victoria and Albert Museum, London (E 3765-1919). M 162

CAT. 53. *Design from a Vorticist Sketchbook: Abstract Composition III*, 1914–15. Pencil and watercolour on paper. 29.2 x 26.7 cm. San Francisco Museum of Modern Art. Fractional Gift of Bobbie and Mike Wilsey. M 180

CAT. 54. *Design from a Vorticist Sketchbook: Abstract Composition VI*, 1914–15. Pencil on paper. 35.9 x 25.1 cm. San Francisco Museum of Modern Art. Fractional Gift of Bobbie and Mike Wilsey. M 183

CAT. 55. [Not in exhibition] *Design from a Vorticist Sketchbook: Abstract Composition VIII,* 1914–15. Pencil on paper. 31.1 x 26 cm. San Francisco Museum of Modern Art. Fractional Gift of Bobbie and Mike Wilsey. M 184

CAT. 56. [Not in exhibition] *Design from a Vorticist Sketchbook: Abstract Composition IX*, 1914–15. Pencil on paper. 29.8 cm x 25.4 cm . San Francisco Museum of Modern Art. Fractional Gift of Bobbie and Mike Wilsey. M 185

CAT. 57. *Composition in Blue*, 1915. Chalk and watercolour on paper. 47 x 30.5 cm. Private collection. M 196

CAT. 58. *Workshop*, 1915. Oil on canvas. 76.5 x 61 cm. Tate, London: Purchased 1974 (T01931). M P19

CAT. 59. *The Crowd*, 1914–15. Oil and pencil on canvas. 200.7 x 153.7 cm. Tate, London: Presented by the Friends of the Tate Gallery 1964 (T00689). M P17

CAT. 60. *Pastoral Toilet* (1917. Pencil, ink and watercolour on paper. 17.5 x 21.5 cm. Victoria and Albert Museum, London (E 3772-1919). M 256

CAT. 61. *Gossips*, 1917. Pencil, ink and watercolour on paper. 28 x 38 cm. Victoria and Albert Museum, London (E 3767-1919). M 252

CAT. 62. *Guns by Wyndham Lewis* Exhibition Poster, 1919. 29.5 x 21 cm. Wyndham Lewis Memorial Trust, London. (LG.2009. XX)

CAT. 63. *Officer and Signallers*, 1918. Ink, watercolour and gouache on paper. 25.4 x 35.6 cm. Imperial War Museum, London (IWM ART 5932). M 302

CAT. 64. *The No. 2*, 1918. Pen and ink, watercolour and pencil on paper. 54.5 x 75 cm. Private collection. M 295

CAT. 65. [Not in exhibition] *Battery Position in a Wood*, 1918. Pen and ink, chalk, watercolour on paper. 31.7 cm x 46.9 cm. Imperial War Museum, London (IWM ART 1672). M 267

CAT. 66. *Great War Drawing No. 2*, 1918. Watercolour on paper. 38.1 x 54.2 cm. Southampton City Art Gallery (1413). M 276

CAT. 67. *Drag-ropes*, 1918. Black ink, pencil, watercolour and black chalk on paper. 35.3 x 41 cm. Manchester City Galleries (1925.487). M 273

CAT. 68. [Not in exhibition] *"D" Subsection Relief*, 1918. Pen and ink, and watercolour on paper. 35.5 x 51 cm. Private collection. M 274

CAT. 69. [Not in exhibition] *Laying*, 1918. Pen and ink, and watercolour on paper. 35.5 x 51 cm. Arts Council Collection, Southbank Centre, London (ACC2/1952). M 283

CAT. 70. *The Battery Shelled*, 1918. Watercolour on paper. 35.5 x 44 cm. Private collection. M 271

CAT. 71. *A Battery Shelled*, 1919. Oil on canvas. 182.7 x 317.7 cm. Imperial War Museum, London (IWM ART 2747). M P25

CAT. 72. *Nude I*, 1919. Pen and ink, watercolour and wash on paper. 24 x 34 cm. Leeds Museums and Galleries (Leeds Art Gallery) (LEEAG.1935.0014.0002). M 339

CAT. 73-74. Portfolio *Fifteen Drawings: Nude I* and *Nude II,* 1919. London: The Ovid Press, 1919 . Edition of 250 prints numbered. 40.6 x 27.9 cm. Wyndham Lewis Memorial Trust, London Collection G. and V. Lane. (LG.2009. XX.9). M 339 and 340

CAT. 75. *Nude*, 1919. Pencil and watercolour on paper. 61 x 47 cm. Private collection, Ivor Braka Ltd

CAT. 76. *Crouching Woman*, ca. 1919. Pencil and watercolour on paper. 27.9 x 38.1 cm. Tate, London: Purchased 1955 (N06255). M 366

CAT. 77. *Girl Reclining*, ca. 1919. Chalk on paper. 38.1 x 55.9 cm. Tate, London: Purchased 1955 (N06256). M 330

CAT. 78. *Self-Portrait*, 1920. Pen and wash on paper. 18 x 22 cm. Private collection. M 423

CAT. 79. [Not in exhibition] *Ezra Pound,* ca. 1919. Pencil and watercolour on paper. 35.5 x 38 cm. National Museum of Wales, Cardiff (NMW A 1867). M 347

CAT. 80. *Ezra Pound*, 1920. Black chalk on paper. 31 x 33 cm. Private collection. M 414

CAT. 81. *Ezra Pound*, 1921. Black chalk on paper. 37 x 32 cm. Private collection

CAT. 82. *Edward Wadsworth*, 1920. Black chalk and wash on paper. 38.5 x 28 cm. Pembroke College Oxford Junior Common Room Art Collection. M 436

CAT. 83. *James Joyce*, 1920. Pencil, ink and wash on paper. 26.5 x 20.5 cm. Private collection. M 397

CAT. 84. *Lady in a Windsor Chair*, 1920. Black crayon on paper. 56 x 38 cm. Manchester City Galleries (1925.212). M 400

CAT. 85. *Woman with a Cigarette* or *Woman Standing,* 1920. Pencil on paper. 56 x 37.8 cm. Aberystwyth University, School of Art Museum and Galleries (WD461). M 1167

CAT. 86. *Seated Figure (Bella Medlar)*, 1921. Pencil on paper. 41.5 x 23.5 cm. O'Keeffe Collection, London. M 476

CAT. 87. [Not in exhibition] *Cabby,* 1920. Black chalk, pen and ink, and coloured washes on paper. 38.7 x 28.3 cm. National Gallery of Victoria, Melbourne. Felton Bequest, 1958. M 385

CAT. 88. *The Pole Jump*, 1919–29. Pencil, pen and ink, watercolour and gouache on paper. 32 x 43 cm. Private collection. M 344

CAT. 90. [Not in exhibition] *A Shore Scene (Figures on a Beach)*, 1920. Pen and ink and wash on paper. 29.5 x 47.5 cm. Museum of New Zealand Te Papa Tongarewa. Purchased 1967 with Harold Beauchamp Collection funds (1967-0004-1). M 431

CAT. 91. *The Cliffs*, 1920. Pen and ink, graphite, watercolour and gouache on paper. 28.2 x 37.9 cm. Wyndham Lewis Memorial Trust, London. G. and V. Lane Collection (LD.2004.XX.39). M 388

CAT. 92. *Woman Knitting*, 1920. Pencil on buff paper . 50.2 x 32.5 cm. Manchester City Galleries (1925.234). M 440

CAT. 93. [Not in exhibition] *Girl Sewing*, 1921–38. Black chalk and watercolour on paper. 55 x 37 cm. Private collection. M 461

CAT. 94. *Woman in Blue*, 1921. Watercolour on paper. 41 x 58 cm. Private collection

CAT. 95. *Seated Figure*, 1921. Oil on canvas. 75.7 x 63 cm. Scottish National Gallery of Modern Art, Edinburgh. Presented by Mrs Karina Williamson 1988 (GMA 3428)

CAT. 96. [Not in Exhibition] *Praxitella*, 1920–21. Oil on canvas. 142 x 101.5 cm. Leeds Museums and Galleries (City Art Gallery) (LEEAG.1945.0015.0001). M P30

CAT. 97. [Not in exhibition] *Portrait of the Artist as the Painter Raphael*, 1921. Oil on canvas. 76.3 x 68.6 cm. Manchester City Galleries (1925.579). M P29

CAT. 98. *A Reading of Ovid (Tyros)*, 1920–21. Oil on canvas. 165.2 x 90.2 cm. Scottish National Gallery of Modern Art, Edinburgh (GMA 1685). M P31

CAT. 99. *Mr Wyndham Lewis as a Tyro*, 1920–21. Oil on canvas. 73 x 44 cm. Ferens Art Gallery, Hull Museums, Hull (KINCM:2005.5151). M P27

CAT. 100. [Not in exhibition] *Meeting between the Tyro, Mr Segando and the Tyro, Phillip*, 1921. Ink over pencil on paper. 37.2 x 21.3 cm. Herbert F. Johnson Museum of Art, Cornell University, Ithaca, NY. Gift of Walter and Harriet Michel (63.237). M 470

CAT. 101. *Head of a Girl (Gladys Anne Hoskyns)*, 1922. Pencil on paper. 39.7 x 41.9 cm. Lent by The Metropolitan Museum of Art), New York, Bequest of Scofield Thayer, 1982 (1984.433.248M 535

CAT. 102. *Girl Seated (Gladys Anne Hoskyns)*, 1922. Pencil on paper. 45 x 31 cm. Private collection

CAT. 103. *Mrs Workman*, 1923. Pencil and wash on paper. 34.5 x 49 cm. Private collection. M 599

CAT. 104. [Not in exhibition] *Edith Sitwell,* 1923. Pencil and wash on paper. 40 x 28.9 cm. National Portrait Gallery, London (NPG 4465). M 592

CAT. 105. *Edith Sitwell*, 1923–35. Oil on canvas. 86.4 x 111.8 cm. Tate, London: Presented by Sir Edward Beddington-Behrens 1943 (N05437). M P36

CAT. 106. *The King and Queen in Bed*, 1920. Pen and ink, and wash on paper. 32.5 x 37 cm. Wyndham Lewis Memorial Trust, London. G. and V. Lane Collection (LD.2009.XX.2). M 399

CAT. 107. *Sensibility (Contemplator* or *Abstract)*, 1921. Pen and ink, and wash on paper. 31 x 26 cm. Private collection. M 483

CAT. 108. [Not in exhibition] *Untitled*, 1921. Watercolour and bodycolour on paper. 38 x 28 cm. Private collection

CAT. 109. *Abstract Figure Study*, 1921. Pen and ink, and wash on paper. 37 x 31 cm. Courtesy of Austin/Desmond Fine Art, London. Private collection. M 445

CAT. 110. *Abstract Composition*, 1921. Pen, collage and watercolour on paper. 61 x 78.8 cm. Collection of Bobbie and Mike Wilsey. M 441

CAT. 111. *Room No. 59*, 1921–22. Pencil, ink, watercolour and gouache on paper. 35 x 31 cm. Collection of BNY Mellon, New York. M 505

CAT. 112. *Women*, 1921–22. Pencil, ink, ink (wash) and gouache on paper. 27.5 x 21.3 cm. Wyndham Lewis Memorial Trust, London. G. and V. Lane Collection (LD.2004.XX.41). M 518

CAT. 113. *Archimedes Reconnoitring the Enemy Fleet*, 1922. Pencil, ink, watercolour and gouache on paper. 33 x 47.5 cm. Private collection. M 519

CAT. 114. *Bird and Figure*, 1925. Pen, ink and watercolour on paper. 23 x 18.5 cm. Rugby School, Warwickshire. M 609

CAT. 115. *Hero's Dream (Dream of Hamilcar* or *Dawn in Erewhon)*, 1925. Collage, watercolour, and pen and ink on paper. 26 x 17 cm. Courtesy of Austin/Desmond Fine Art, London. Private collection. M 614

CAT. 116. [Not in exhibition] *The Dancers*, 1925. Pencil and ink on paper. 31 x 18 cm. Victoria and Albert Museum, London (Circ.421-1959). M 610

CAT. 117. [Not in exhibition] *Dancing Couple*, 1925. Blue ink on paper. 30.5 x 19.5 cm. The Frances Lehman Loeb Art Center, Vassar College, Poughkeepsie, New York. Gift of William K. Rose, 1965.16

CAT. 118. *Study for Enemy Cover*, 1926. Gouache, ink and pencil on paper. 23.7 x 11.9 cm. The Museum of Modern Art, New York. Joseph M. and Dorothy B. Edinburg Fund, 1967 (2637.1967). M 621

CAT. 119. [Not in exhibition] *Book Cover Design*, 1927. Pen and ink, gouache, collage on paper. 28 x 15.5 cm. Collection Hugh Anson-Cartwright. M 627

CAT. 120. *Abstract Composition*, 1926. Pen and ink, watercolour, wash and pencil on paper. 56 x 26.5 cm. Private collection. M 617

CAT. 121. *Abstract Composition*, 1926. Pencil and ink, watercolour and wash on paper. 56 x 26.5 cm. Private collection. M 618

CAT. 122. *Abstract Composition*, 1926. Pen and ink, watercolour, wash and pencil on paper. 50 x 24.5 cm. Private collection. M 619

CAT. 123. *Two Figures*, 1927. Pen, ink and gouache on paper. 32.5 x 36 cm. Collection Durban Art Gallery, KwaZulu-Natal, Southafrica. M 644

CAT. 124. *Creation Myth*, 1927. Gouache, drawing and mixed media on paper. 32.7 x 29.8 cm. Tate, London: Purchased 1956 (T00107). M 628

CAT. 125. *Figures in the Air* or *On the Roof*, 1927. Pencil, pen and ink, watercolour and gouache with *papier collé.* 29.2 x 16.5 cm. Private collection. M 635

CAT. 126. *Manhattan* or *New York Mystic*, 1927. Pen and ink, watercolour and gouache with *papier collé.* 37 x 25 cm. Private collection. M 637

CAT. 127. *ΑΘΑΝΑΤΟΝ ΑΡΑ Ή ΨΥΧΗ* (“*Immortal Therefore the Soul*”), 1927. Watercolour, pencil, and pen and ink on paper. 25.4 x 35.6 cm. Lent by The Metropolitan Museum of Art, New York. Anonymous gift, in honor of Alfred H. Barr, Jr., 1981, (1981.488.1). M 626

CAT. 128. *Bagdad*, 1927–28. Oil on wood. 182.9 x 78.7 cm. Tate, London: Purchased 1956 (T00099). M P38

CAT. 129. *Wrestling*, 1929. Graphite, pen and ink, watercolour and gouache on paper. 34.5 x 43.1 cm. Wyndham Lewis Memorial Trust, London (LD.2004.XX.20). M 654

CAT. 130. *Boxing at Juan-les-Pins*, 1929. Pen and ink, wash and gouache on paper. 32 x 44 cm. Private collection. M 646

CAT. 131. *Beach Scene*, 1929. Pen and ink, watercolour and gouache on grey paper. 31 x 42.5 cm. Courtesy of Austin/Desmond Fine Art, London. Private collection. M 645

CAT. 132. [Not in exhibition] *L'Homme surréaliste*, 1929. Oil on plywood. 70 x 43. Private collection. M P39

CAT. 133. [Not in exhibition] *Femme surréaliste*, 1929. Oil on plywood. 70 x 50. Private collection. M P40

CAT. 134. [Not in exhibition] *L'Homme surréaliste*, 1929. Oil on plywood. 70 x 43. Private collection. M P41

CAT. 135. [Not in exhibition] *Femme surréaliste*, 1929. Oil on plywood. 70 x 50. Private collection. M P42

CAT. 136. *Desert Soukh*, 1931. Graphite, watercolour and gouache on board. 18 x 40.5 cm. C.J. Fox Collection (LD.2000.XX.4). M 712

CAT. 137. *Berber Horseman*, 1931. Pencil, ink and ground colour on paper. 31 x 30 cm. Private collection

CAT. 138. *Tut*, 1931. Pencil and wash on paper. 28 x 24 cm. Private collection. M 730

CAT. 139. *Rebecca West*, 1932. Pencil on paper. 43 x 31 cm. National Portrait Gallery, London (NPG 5693). M 786

CAT. 140. *Self-Portrait with Hat*, 1932. Ink and wash on paper. 25.4 x 19.7 cm. National Portrait Gallery, London (NPG 4528). M 782

CAT. 141. *Spartan Portrait (Naomi Mitchison)*, 1933. Graphite and watercolour on paper. 39 x 26.7 cm. Wyndham Lewis Memorial Trust, London. G. and V. Lane Collection (LD.2004.XX.45). M 809

CAT. 142. *Girl Reading (Portrait of the Artist's Wife, Froanna)*, 1936. Graphite and watercolour on paper. 37.7 x 26.7 cm. Trustees of the British Museum, London (1939,0730.10). M 858

CAT. 143. *Red Portrait (Froanna)*, 1937. Oil on canvas. 91.5 x 61 cm. Wyndham Lewis Memorial Trust, London. G. and V. Lane Collection (LP.2000.XX.1). M P76

CAT. 144. [Not in exhibition] *Froanna (Portrait of the Artist's Wife)*, 1937. Oil on canvas. 76 x 63.5 cm. Glasgow Museums. M P71

CAT. 145. *Julian Symons*, 1938. Pen and ink on paper. 33 x 25.5 cm. Private collection. M 925

CAT. 146. Study for *Portrait of T.S. Eliot*, 1938. Pencil on paper. 38 x 28 cm. Private collection

CAT. 147. *T.S. Eliot*, 1938. Oil on canvas. 133.3 x 85.1 cm. Collection Durban Art Gallery, KwaZulu-Natal, Southafrica. M P80

CAT. 148. *Stephen Spender*, 1938. Oil on canvas. 100.5 x 59.5 cm. The Potteries Museum & Art Gallery (1939.347). M P86

CAT. 149. *Ezra Pound*, 1939. Oil on canvas. 76.2 x 101.6 cm. Tate, London: Purchased 1939 (N05042). M P99

CAT. 150. *Boats in a Port* or *A Spanish Harbour*, 1933. Pencil and gouache on paper. 19.5 x 25 cm. Private collection. M 788

CAT. 151. *Two Beach Babies*, 1933. Oil on canvas. 51 x 61 cm. Rugby Art Gallery and Museum. M P53

CAT. 152. *The Betrothal of the Matador*, 1933. Oil on canvas. 54.5 x 42.5 cm. Wyndham Lewis Memorial Trust, London (LP.2008.XX.2). M P45

CAT. 153. *Group of Three Veiled Figures*, 1933. Oil on canvas. 51 x 43 cm. Leeds Museums and Galleries (Leeds Art Gallery) (LEEAG.1978.0026). M P47

CAT. 154. [Not in exhibition] *The Convalescent*, 1933. Oil on canvas. 61 x 76.5 cm. Glynn Vivian Art Gallery, Swansea (GV 1976.17). M P46

CAT. 155. *One of the Stations of the Dead*, 1933. Oil on canvas. 127.6 x 75.8 cm. Aberdeen Art Gallery & Museums Collections (ABDAG 2522). M P50

CAT. 156. *Inca and the Birds*, 1933. Oil on canvas. 67.3 x 54.6 cm. Arts Council Collection, Southbank Centre, London (ACC4/1959). M P49

CAT. 157. *Figure Composition*, 1933–38. Ink ground colour and watercolour on paper. 23 x 31 cm. Private collection

CAT. 158. *Roman Actors*, 1934. Watercolour, gouache, ink and pencil on paper. 38.4 x 56.2 cm. The Museum of Modern Art, New York. Francis E. Brennan Fund, 1954 (14.1954). M 846

CAT. 159. *Red and Black Principle*, 1936. Oil on canvas. 116.8 x 61 cm. Santa Barbara Museum of Art. Gift of Wright S. Ludington (1956.2.1). M P62

CAT. 160. *Cubist Museum*, 1936. Oil on canvas. 51 x 76 cm. Private collection. M P58

CAT. 161. *Red Scene*, 1933–36. Oil on canvas. 71.1 x 91.4 cm. Tate, London: Purchased 1938 (N04913). M P52

CAT. 162. *The Surrender of Barcelona*, 1936–37. Oil on canvas. 83.8 x 59.7 cm. Tate, London: Purchased 1947 (N05768). M P61

CAT. 163. *The Tank in the Clinic*, 1937. Oil on canvas. 68.5 x 51 cm. Wyndham Lewis Memorial Trust, London (LP.2008.XX.4). M P77

CAT. 164. *Creation Myth*, 1937. Oil on canvas. 49.5 x 59 cm. The Warden and Scholars of New College, Oxford (NCO 1002). M P54

CAT. 165. *Landscape with Northmen*, 1936–37. Oil on canvas. 67.5 x 49.5 cm. Private collection, London. M P66

CAT. 166. [Not in exhibition] *Inferno*, 1937. Oil on canvas. 152.5 x 101.8 cm. National Gallery of Victoria, Melbourne. Felton Bequest, 1964 (1411-5). M P72

CAT. 167. *Bathing Scene*, 1938. Pen and ink, watercolour and gouache on paper. 28.7 x 39.6 cm. Wyndham Lewis Memorial Trust, London (LD.2004.XX.28). M 900

CAT. 168. *A Hand of Bananas*, 1929–38. Gouache, watercolour, pencil and ink on paper. 20.3 x 18.1 cm. The Museum of Modern Art, New York. Purchase, 1941 (408.1941). M 904

CAT. 169. *Four Figure Composition*, 1938. Oil on canvas. 40 x 25.4 cm. Collection of Fred L. Emerson Gallery, Hamilton College. Gift of Omar S. Pound, Class of 1951 (1991.126). M P81

CAT. 170. [Not in exhibition] *Chancellor Samuel Capen*, 1939. Oil on canvas. 193 x 89 cm. The Poetry Collection, University at Buffalo, NY. M P94

CAT. 171. [Not in exhibition] *J.S. McLean*, 1941. Oil on canvas. 106.5 x 77 cm. Art Gallery of Ontario, Toronto. Gift of the McLean Family, 2000 (Acc. 2000/1309). M P101

CAT. 172. *The Artist's Wife, Froanna*, 1940. Pencil and coloured chalks on blue paper . 48.3 x 31 cm. The Barber Institute of Fine Arts, The University of Birmingham (2006.3). M 958

CAT. 173. *War News (Portrait of Froanna)*, 1942. Pencil and crayon on paper. 53 x 71 cm. Collection of Middlesbrough Institute of Modern Art. Acquisition supported by the V&A Purchase Grant Fund (MIDMA/FA/0107). M 1021

CAT. 174. [Not in exhibition] *Portrait of the Artist's Wife*, 1944. Black and coloured pencil, and black and coloured chalks on paper. 37.7 x 27.8 cm. Art Gallery of Windsor, Canada. Purchased with funds from the Bobs Cogill and Peter Haworth estate and the assistance of the Government of Canada through the Cultural Property Export and Import Act, 1991 (1991.038). M 1048

CAT. 175. *Lebensraum I: The Battlefield*, 1941. Pen, Indian ink, watercolour and gouache on paper. 30.2 x 45.5 cm. Collection Art Gallery of Ontario, Toronto. Purchase, 1941 (Acc.2576). M 976

CAT. 176. *Lebensraum II: The Empty Tunic*, 1941–42. Chalk, watercolour and gouache on paper. 34.6 x 24.3 cm. Wyndham Lewis Memorial Trust, London. G. and V. Lane Collection (LD.2004.XX.46). M 988

CAT. 177. [Not in exhibition] *Armless Man on Stage*, 1941. Black chalk and wash on paper. 28.5 x 44 cm. Collection Hugh Anson-Cartwright. M 966

CAT. 178. *Mother Love*, 1942. Graphite, pen and ink, watercolour and gouache on paper. 43.6 x 28 cm. Wyndham Lewis Memorial Trust, London (LD.2004.XX.35). M 998

CAT. 179. *A Man's Form Taking a Fall from a Small Horse*, 1941. Graphite, pen and ink, watercolour and gouache on paper. 29.5 x 45 cm. C.J. Fox Collection (LD.2000.XX.3). M 977

CAT. 180. *Jehovah the Thunderer*, 1941. Pencil, ink and watercolour on paper. 37 x 25.5 cm. Collection Hugh Anson-Cartwright. M 975

CAT. 181. *Small Crucifixion Series, I*, 1941. Pencil, pen and ink, and watercolour on paper. 35.5 x 25 cm. Collection Hugh Anson-Cartwright. M 980

CAT. 182. *Small Crucifixion Series, II: Pietà*, 1941. Pen and ink, and watercolour on paper. 33 x 25.5 cm. Private collection. M 981

CAT. 183. *Small Crucifixion Series, III*, 1941. Pencil, pen and ink, and watercolour on paper. 35.5 x 25.5 cm. Collection Hugh Anson-Cartwright. M 982

CAT. 184. [Not in exhibition] *Small Crucifixion Series, IV*, 1941. Watercolour on paper. 36.5 x 25.5 cm. Private collection. M 983

CAT. 185. [Not in exhibition] *Supplicating Figures*, 1941. Pen and ink, and watercolour on paper. 30.5 x 45.5 cm. Collection Mark. McLean. M 984

CAT. 186. [Not in exhibition] *Adoration*, 1941. Chalk and gouache on paper. 38 x 25.3 cm. Wyndham Lewis Memorial Trust, London (LD.2004.XX.32). M 963

CAT. 187. [Not in exhibition] *Gestation* or *Creation Myth: Maternal Figure*, 1941. Crayon and coloured chalks on blue paper. 30 x 24 cm. Collection Hugh Anson-Cartwright. M 971

CAT. 188. [Not in exhibition] *Still-life: Figures in the Belly of a Duck*, 1942. Pencil and watercolour on paper. 34.8 x 35.5 cm. Collection of the Vancouver Art Gallery. Acquired from George Woodcock with the aid of donations by Dr Hugh S. Miller and Dr Kenneth S. Morton (VAG. 70.107). M 1005

CAT. 189. *Creation Myth No. 17*, 1941. Charcoal and graphite with watercolour and gouache on wove paper. 50.1 x 34.9 cm. National Gallery of Canada, Ottawa. Gift from the Douglas M. Duncan Collection, 1970 (NGC 16713). M 968

CAT. 190. *Creation Myth*, 1941–42. Graphite, pen and ink, watercolour and gouache on paper. 37 x 25.1 cm. Wyndham Lewis Memorial Trust, London (LD.2004.XX.34). M 987

CAT. 191. *The Sage Meditating on the Life of Flesh and Blood*, 1941. Pencil, pen and ink, watercolour and gouache on paper. 40 x 33.5 cm. Collection Hugh Anson-Cartwright. M 979

CAT. 192. *The Mind of the Artist about to Make a Picture*, 1941–42. Pen and ink, and watercolour on paper. 39.5 x 30.5 cm. Wyndham Lewis Memorial Trust, London (LD.2004.XX.28). M 997

CAT. 193. *"... And Wilderness were Paradise enow"*, 1941. Chalk, watercolour and gouache on paper. 42.1 x 32 cm. Wyndham Lewis Memorial Trust, London (LD.2004.XX.31). M 965

CAT. 194. [Not in exhibition] *Sunset in Paradise*, 1940s. Ink, pencil, watercolour wash, coloured chalks and gouache on paper. 30.2 x 45.5 cm. Herbert F. Johnson Museum of Art, Cornell University, Ithaca, NY (62.417). M 1124

CAT. 195. *Allégresse Aquatique*, 1941. Graphite, pen and ink, watercolour and gouache on wove paper. 31.8 x 44.5 cm. Collection Art Gallery of Ontario, Toronto. Purchase, 1941 (Acc.2577). M 964

CAT. 196. *Homage to Etty*, 1942. Pen and black ink with watercolour and gouache over graphite on wove paper. 25.3 x 36.6 cm. National Gallery of Canada, Ottawa. Gift from the Douglas M. Duncan Collection, 1970 (NGC 16715). M 994

CAT. 197. *Pool of the Amazons*, 1942. Pencil, ink and watercolour on paper. 35.7 x 44.2 cm. Collection Mark McLean. M 1003

198. [Not in exhibition] *A Party of Girls*, 1942. Pen and ink, watercolour and wash on paper. 35.5 x 25.5 cm. Collection Mark McLean. M 1000

CAT. 199. *Nude Panel*, 1942. Graphite and watercolour on paper. 34.9 x 25.3 cm. Collection Mark McLean. M 999

CAT. 200. *The Island*, 1942. Oil on canvas. 69.9 x 91.4 cm. Santa Barbara Museum of Art. Gift of the Women's Board (1986.51). M P104

CAT. 201. [Not in exhibition] *Children Playing*, 1945. Pen and ink, black chalk, watercolour, wash and gouache on paper. 37.5 x 22.9 cm. Collection of Fred L. Emerson Gallery, Hamilton College. Gift of Omar S. Pound, Class of 1951 in honour of Anne Wyndham Lewis (1994.128). M 1055

CAT. 202. *What the Sea is like at Night*, 1949. Pencil, ink and gouache on paper. 56 x 37.5 cm. Courtesy of Austin/Desmond Fine Art, Private collection. M 1104

CAT. 203. *The Ascent*, 1949. Pen and ink, and watercolour on paper. 54.5 x 32 cm. Private collection. M 1093

CAT. 204. *Walpurgisnacht*, 1950. Pen and ink on paper. 43 x 76 cm. Wyndham Lewis Memorial Trust, London. M 1126

CAT. 205. *Red Figures Carrying Babies and Visiting Graves*, 1951. Pencil, pen and ink, and watercolour on paper. 33 x 40.3 cm. Wyndham Lewis Memorial Trust, London. J. Dolman Collection (LD.2009.XX.5). M 1127

Wyndham Lewis: the Writer

B&M CAT. 1. *Mrs Dukes' Million* [*Khan and Company*] (Toronto: The Coach House Press, 1977). 20.9 x 13.9 cm. Private collection YMJB

B&M CAT. 2. *Blast*, No. 1 (London: John Lane, 1914). 31.8 x 26.7 cm. Private collection YMJB. Wyndham Lewis Memorial Trust, London

B&M CAT. 3. *Blast*, No. 2 (London: John Lane, 1915). 30 x 24.6 cm. Wyndham Lewis Memorial Trust, London

B&M CAT. 4. *The Ideal Giant* (London: The Little Review, 1917). 24.5 x 16 cm. Wyndham Lewis Memorial Trust, London

B&M CAT. 5. *Tarr* (London: The Egoist Press, 1918). 18.7 x 13.4 cm. Wyndham Lewis Memorial Trust, London

B&M CAT. 6. [Not in exhibition] *Guns by Wyndham Lewis* Exhibition Catalogue (London: Goupil Gallery, 1919). 20.8 x 13.4 cm

B&M CAT. 7. *The Caliph's Design: Architects! Where is Your Vortex?* (London: The Egoist Press, 1919). 21.2 x 13.9 cm. Private collection YMJB

B&M CAT. 8. *The Tyro*, No. 1 (London: The Egoist Press, 1921). 37.4 x 25 cm. Wyndham Lewis Memorial Trust, London

B&M CAT. 9. *The Tyro*, No. 2 (London: The Egoist Press, 1922). 24.8 x 18.6 cm. Wyndham Lewis Memorial Trust, London

B&M CAT. 10. *The Art of Being Ruled* (London: Chatto and Windus, 1926). 22.7 x 14.8 cm. Private collection YMJB

B&M CAT. 11. *The Lion and the Fox: The Rôle of the Hero in the Plays of Shakespeare* (London: Grant Richards, 1927). 22.3 x 15.2 cm. Wyndham Lewis Memorial Trust, London

B&M CAT. 12. *Time and Western Man* (London: Chatto and Windus, 1927). 22.8 x 14.7 cm. Private collection YMJB

B&M CAT. 13. *Time and Western Man* revised edition (New York: Harcourt, Brace and Co., 1928). 22.8 x 14.7 cm. Private collection YMJB

B&M CAT. 14. *The Enemy*, Vol. 1 (1927). 28.7 x 18.8 cm. Wyndham Lewis Memorial Trust, London

B&M CAT. 15. *The Enemy*, No. 2 (1927). 28.1 x 18.8 cm. Wyndham Lewis Memorial Trust, London

B&M CAT. 16. *The Enemy*, No. 3 (1929). 28.3 x 18.5 cm. Wyndham Lewis Memorial Trust, London

B&M CAT. 17. *The Wild Body: A Soldier of Humour and Other Stories* (London: Chatto and Windus, 1927). 19.8 x 14 cm. Private collection YMJB

B&M CAT. 18. *Tarr*, revised edition (London: Chatto and Windus, 1928). 17.8 x 12 cm. Wyndham Lewis Memorial Trust, London

B&M CAT. 19. *The Childermass: Section I* (London: Chatto and Windus, 1928). 22 x 15.5 cm. Wyndham Lewis Memorial Trust, London

B&M CAT. 20. *Paleface: The Philosophy of the "Melting Pot"* (London: Chatto and Windus, 1929). 20.8 x 14 cm. Private collection YMJB

B&M CAT. 21. *The Apes of God* (London: The Arthur Press, 1930). 25.7 x 20.5 cm. Private collection YMJB. Wyndham Lewis Memorial Trust, London

B&M CAT. 22. [Not in exhibition] *The Apes of God* (New York: MacBride, 1932). 20.7 x 14.3 cm

B&M CAT. 23. *The Apes of God* (London: Arco Publishers Ltd, 1955). 20.7 x 14.3 cm. Private collection YMJB

B&M CAT. 24. *Satire & Fiction: Enemy Pamphlet No. 1* (London: The Arthur Press, 1930). 28.2 x 21.1 cm. Wyndham Lewis Memorial Trust, London

B&M CAT. 25. *The Roaring Queen* (London: Secker and Warburg, 1973). 22.3 x 14.4 cm. Cover by Michael Ayrton. Private collection YMJB

B&M CAT. 26. *Hitler* (London: Chatto and Windus, 1931). 20.9 x 13.8 cm. Private collection YMJB

B&M CAT. 27. *The Diabolical Principle and the Dithyrambic Spectator* (London: Chatto and Windus, 1931). 19.5 x 13 cm. Private collection YMJB

B&M CAT. 28. *The Doom of Youth* (London: Chatto and Windus, 1932). 22.8 x 15.2 cm. Wyndham Lewis Memorial Trust, London

B&M CAT. 29. *Filibusters in Barbary: Record of a Visit to the Sous* (London: Grayson and Grayson, 1932). 22.6 x 15.2 cm. Wyndham Lewis Memorial Trust, London

B&M CAT. 30. *Enemy of the Stars* (London: Desmond Harmsworth, 1932).

B&M CAT. 31. *Enemy of the Stars* (London: Desmond Harmsworth, 1932) (variant binding)

B&M CAT. 32. *Enemy of the Stars* (London: Desmond Harmsworth, 1932) (variant binding). 28.9 x 22.2 cm. Private collection YMJB. Wyndham Lewis Memorial Trust, London

B&M CAT. 33. *Snooty Baronet* (London: Cassell, 1932). 19.6 x 13.5 cm. Wyndham Lewis Memorial Trust, London

B&M CAT. 34. *The Old Gang and the New Gang* (London: Desmond Harmsworth, 1933). 19.5 x 13.5 cm. Wyndham Lewis Memorial Trust, London

B&M CAT. 35. *One-Way Song* (London: Faber and Faber, 1933). 22.6 x 14.8 cm. Private collection YMJB

B&M CAT. 36. *Men Without Art* (London: Cassell, 1934). 22.2 x 15.2 cm. Wyndham Lewis Memorial Trust, London

B&M CAT. 37. *Left Wings Over Europe: Or, How to Make a War about Nothing* (London: Jonathan Cape, 1936). 20.6 x 14.6 cm. Wyndham Lewis Memorial Trust, London

B&M CAT. 38. *Count Your Dead: They are Alive! Or, A New War in the Making* (London: Lovat Dickson, 1937). 20.5 x 14.3 cm. Wyndham Lewis Memorial Trust, London

B&M CAT. 39. *The Revenge for Love* (London: Cassell, 1937). 21 x 15 cm. Wyndham Lewis Memorial Trust, London

B&M CAT. 40. *Blasting and Bombardiering: Autobiography (1914–1926)* (London: Eyre & Spottiswoode, 1937). 22.2 x 15.5 cm. Private collection YMJB. Wyndham Lewis Memorial Trust, London

B&M CAT. 41. *The Mysterious Mr Bull* (London: Robert Hale, 1938). 22 x 13.4 cm. Wyndham Lewis Memorial Trust, London

B&M CAT. 42. *The Jews: Are they Human?* (London: George Allen and Unwin, 1939). 19 x 12.9 cm. Private collection YMJB

B&M CAT. 43. *Wyndham Lewis the Artist: From "Blast" to Burlington House* (London: Laidlaw and Laidlaw, 1939). 23.5 x 17.5 cm. Private collection YMJB. Wyndham Lewis Memorial Trust, London

B&M CAT. 44. *The Hitler Cult* (London: Dent, 1939). 20 x 13.6 cm. Wyndham Lewis Memorial Trust, London

B&M CAT. 45. *America, I Presume* (New York: Howell, Soskin & Co., 1940). 19.3 x 13.2 cm. Private collection YMJB

B&M CAT. 46. [Not in exhibition] *Anglosaxony: A League that Works* (Toronto: The Ryerson Press, 1941). 19.1 x 13 cm

B&M CAT. 47. *The Vulgar Streak* (London: Robert Hale, 1941). 19 x 13.2 cm. Wyndham Lewis Memorial Trust, London

B&M CAT. 48. *America and Cosmic Man* (London: Nicholson and Watson, 1948). 19.6 x 13.3 cm. Wyndham Lewis Memorial Trust, London

B&M CAT. 49. *Wyndham Lewis* Exhibition Catalogue (London: Redfern Gallery, 1949). 26 x 19.6 cm. Wyndham Lewis Memorial Trust, London

B&M CAT. 50. *Rude Assignment: A Narrative of my Career Up-to-date* (London: Hutchinson & Co., 1950). 23.7 x 16.5 cm. Private collection YMJB

B&M CAT. 51. *Rotting Hill* (London: Methuen & Co. Ltd, 1951). 23.7 x 16.5 cm. Cover by Charles Handley-Read. Private collection YMJB

B&M CAT. 52. *Rotting Hill* (Chicago: Henry Regnery Co., 1952). 21.5 x 14 cm. Private collection YMJB

B&M CAT. 53. *The Writer and the Absolute* (London: Methuen & Co. Ltd, 1952). 22.2 x 15 cm. Cover by Charles Handley-Read. Wyndham Lewis Memorial Trust, London

B&M CAT. 54. *Self Condemned* (London: Methuen & Co. Ltd, 1954). 19 x 12.8 cm. Cover by Michael Ayrton. Private collection YMJB

B&M CAT. 55. *The Demon of Progress in the Arts* (London: Methuen & Co. Ltd, 1954). 20.3 x 14.2 cm. Private collection YMJB

B&M CAT. 56. *The Demon of Progress in the Arts* (Chicago: Henry Regnery Co., 1955). 21.5 x 14.6 cm. Fundación Juan March, Madrid

B&M CAT. 57. *The Human Age, Book Two: Monstre Gai; Book Three: Malign Fiesta* (London: Methuen & Co. Ltd, 1955). 22.2 x 15 cm. Cover by Michael Ayrton. Private collection YMJB. Wyndham Lewis Memorial Trust, London

B&M CAT. 58. *Wyndham Lewis and Vorticism* Exhibition Catalogue (London: Tate Gallery, 1956). 24.1 x 17.5 cm

B&M CAT. 59. *Wyndham Lewis and Vorticism* Exhibition Catalogue (London: Tate Gallery / Arts Council, 1956). 24.1 x 17.5 cm. Fundación Juan March. Wyndham Lewis Memorial Trust, London

B&M CAT. 60. *The Red Priest* (London: Methuen & Co. Ltd, 1956). 19 x 13 cm. Cover by Michael Ayrton. Private collection YMJB. 57).

B&M CAT. 61. *The Human Age, Book One: The Childermass* (London: Methuen & Co. Ltd, 1956). 22.2 x 15 cm. Cover and illustrations by Michael Ayrton. Wyndham Lewis Memorial Trust, London

Works by other exhibited artists

CAT. 206. AUGUSTUS EDWIN JOHN (1878 – 1961). *Wyndham Lewis*, c. 1903. Etching on paper. 17.6 x 13.8 cm. National Portrait Gallery, London (NPG 6066)

CAT. 207. AUGUSTUS EDWIN JOHN (1878 – 1961). *Wyndham Lewis,* 1905. Oil on canvas. 80 x 61 cm. Private collection

CAT. 208. WILLIAM ROBERTS (1895 – 1980). *The Vorticists at the Restaurant de la Tour Eiffel: Spring, 1915* 196162. Oil on canvas. 182.9 x 213.4 cm. Tate, London: Presented by the Trustees of the Chantrey Bequest 1962

CAT. 209. G. C. BERESFORD (George Charles) (1864 –1938). *Wyndham Lewis as a Bohemian*, 1913. Photograph. 20.3 x 25.4 cm. National Portrait Gallery, London (NPG 6535)

CAT. 210. ALVIN LANGDON COBURN (1882 – 1966). *Wyndham Lewis,* 1916. Photogravure (in *More Men of Mark by Alvin Langdon Coburn*. London: Duckworth & Co., 1922). 19.9 x 14.8 cm. Scottish National Portrait Gallery, Edinburgh (R 885.20)

CAT. 211 (a-h). ALVIN LANGDON COBURN (1882 – 1966). *Untitled* (8 photographies of Wyndham Lewis), ca. 1916. Photograph. Courtesy of George Eastman House, International Museum of Photography and Film, Rochester, NY (1979:3901:0002)

CAT. 212. G. C. BERESFORD (George Charles) (1864 – 1938). *Wyndham Lewis,* 1929. Photograph. 20.3 x 25.4 cm. National Portrait Gallery, London (NPG 6536)

Other exhibited books

B&M CAT. 62. *Second Post-Impressionist* Exhibition Catalogue. Crafton Galleries, London, 1912. 18.4 x 12.5 cm. Wyndham Lewis Memorial Trust, London

B&M CAT. 63. *Vorticist* Exhibition Catalogue. Doré Galleries, London, 1915. 21.5 x 14 cm. Book Library, The Courtauld Institute, London

B&M CAT. 64. *Group X* Exhibition Catalogue. Mansard Gallery, London, 1920. 21.7 x 13.5 cm. Wyndham Lewis Memorial Trust, London

B&M CAT. 65. *Tyros and Portraits* Exhibition Catalogue. Leicester Galleries, London, 1921. 14.6 x 11.3 cm. Wyndham Lewis Memorial Trust, London

B&M CAT. 66. *Thirty Personalities by Wyndham Lewis* Exhibition Catalogue. Lefevre Galleries, London, 1932. 21.6 x 14.7 cm. Wyndham Lewis Memorial Trust, London

B&M CAT. 67. *Paintings and Drawings by Wyndham Lewis* Exhibition Catalogue. Leicester Galleries, London, 1937. 14.6 x 11.3 cm. Wyndham Lewis Memorial Trust, London

B&M CAT. 68. *Wyndham Lewis Paintings and Drawings* Exhibition Catalogue. Zwemmer Gallery, London, 1957. 12.5 x 19.6 cm. Wyndham Lewis Memorial Trust

B&M CAT. 69. Ford Madox Hueffer, *Antwerp.* Cubierta diseñada por Wyndham Lewis. Private collection YMJB

List of illustrations

F

WYNDHAM LEWIS: SOLO AND GROUP EXHIBITIONS

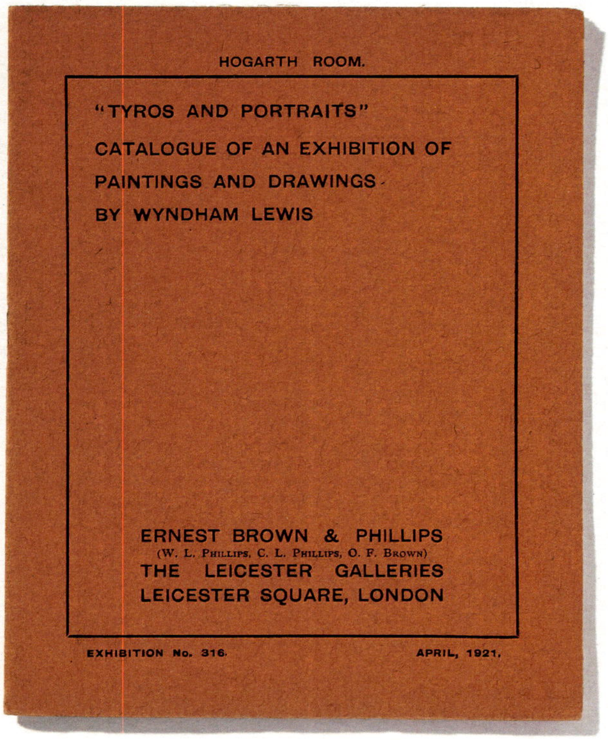

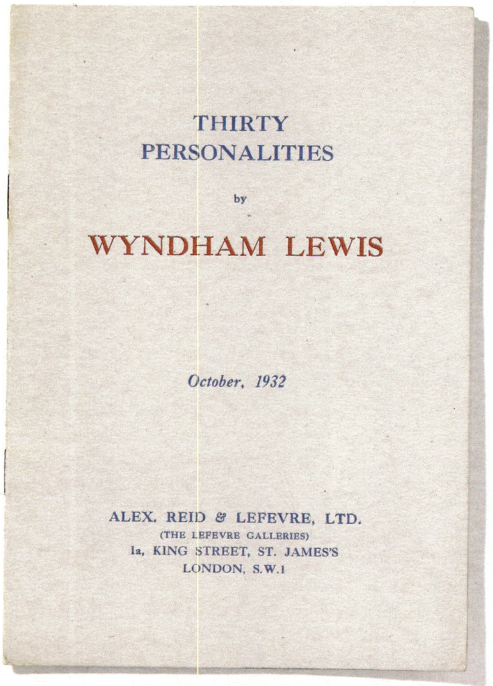

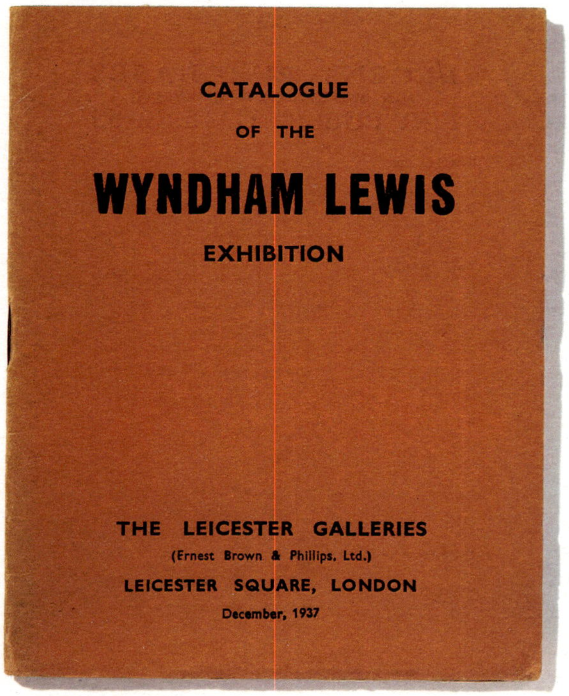

Solo exhibitions

1919
Guns by Wyndham Lewis, Goupil Gallery, London, February 1919.

1920
Drawings by Wyndham Lewis, Adelphi Gallery, London, January 1920.

1921
Tyros and Portraits, Hogarth Room, The Leicester Galleries, London, April 1921.

1932
Thirty Personalities, The Lefevre Galleries, London, October 1932.

1937
Paintings and Drawings by Wyndham Lewis, The Leicester Galleries, London, December 1937.

1938
New Paintings and Drawings by Wyndham Lewis, Beaux Arts Gallery, London, June–July 1938.

1944
Exhibition of Books and Pictures by Wyndham Lewis, Wednesday Club, St Louis, Missouri, January 1944.

1949
Exhibition of Paintings, Drawings and Watercolours of Wyndham Lewis, Redfern Gallery, London, 5–26 May 1949.

1950
Wyndham Lewis: Drawings and Watercolours, Victoria College, University of Toronto, Toronto, February 1950.

1956
Wyndham Lewis and Vorticism, Tate Gallery, London, 6 July–19 August; City Art Gallery, Manchester, 1–22 September; The Art Gallery, Glasgow, 29 September–20 October; City Art Gallery, Bristol, 27 October–17 November; City Art Gallery, Leeds, 24 November–15 December 1956.

1957
Percy Wyndham Lewis: Paintings, Drawings and Prints, Santa Barbara Museum of Art, Santa Barbara, California, August–September 1957.

1964
Paintings and Books by Wyndham Lewis, York University Art Gallery, Glendon College, Toronto, 27 November–30 December 1964.

1971
Word and Image I: Wyndham Lewis 1882–1957, The National Book League, London, 1971.

1974
An Exhibition of Paintings and Drawings by Wyndham Lewis, The Mayor Gallery, London, May–June 1974.

1980
Wyndham Lewis, Manchester City Art Gallery, Manchester, 1 October–15 November 15 1980; National Museum of Wales, Cardiff, 29 November 1980–11 January 1981; City Art Centre, Edinburgh, 23 January–7 March 1981.

1982
Wyndham Lewis: A Centennial Salute, Art Gallery of Nova Scotia, Halifax, Nova Scotia, 5 August–5 September 1982.

Wyndham Lewis et le Vorticisme, Centre Georges Pompidou, Paris, 16 June–6 September 1982.

1983
Wyndham Lewis: Drawings and Watercolours 1910–1920, Anthony d´Offay Gallery, London, 13 April–14 May 1983.

1984
Wyndham Lewis: The Twenties, Anthony d'Offay Gallery, London, 12 September–12 October 1984.

1985
Wyndham Lewis: The Early Decades, Washburn Gallery, New York, 18 September–26 October 1985.

1990
Wyndham Lewis 1882–1957, Austin Desmond Fine Art, London, 11 September–6 October 1990.

1992
Graphic Works by Wyndham Lewis, Harry Ransom Humanities Research Center, Austin, Texas, 2 March–30 June 1992.

Wyndham Lewis: Art and War, Imperial War Museum, London, 25 June–11 October 1992.

The Talented Intruder: Wyndham Lewis in Canada 1939–1945, Art Gallery of Windsor, Windsor, Ontario, November 1992–January 1993; Glenbow Museum, Calgary, Alberta, July–August 1993; Art Gallery of Ontario, Toronto, September–November 1993.

2003
Wyndham Lewis, The Hunterian Museum and Gallery, University of Glasgow, Glasgow, 2003.

2004
'The bone beneath the pulp': Drawings by Wyndham Lewis, Courtauld Institute of Art Gallery, London, 14 October 2004–13 February 2005; Abbot Hall Art Gallery (Abbot Institute of Art), Kendal, Cumbria, 7 March–4 June 2005.

2005
Wyndham Lewis, Fine Arts, Design & Antiques Fair, Olympia, London, 1–6 March 2005.

2007
An Exhibition of Paintings and Drawings by Percy Wyndham Lewis (1897–98), Rugby School, Rugby, Warwickshire, 26 November–8 December 2007.

2008
Wyndham Lewis: Portraits, National Portrait Gallery, London, 3 July–19 October 2008.

2009
The Lion and the Fox: Art and Literary Works by Wyndham Lewis from the C.J. Fox Collection, University of Victoria Libraries, Victoria, Canada, 1 April–28 May 2009.

2010
Wyndham Lewis (1882–1957), Fundación Juan March, Madrid, 5 February–16 May 2010.

Group exhibitions

1904
Thirty-Second Exhibition of Modern Pictures held by the New English Art Club, Dudley Gallery, London, April–May 1904.

1911
The First Exhibition of the Camden Town Group, Carfax Gallery, London, June 1911.

The Second Exhibition of the Camden Town Group, Carfax Gallery, London, December 1911.

1912
Quelques Indépendants Anglais, Galerie Barbazanges, Paris, March 1912.

The London Salon of the Allied Artists' Association Ltd (fifth year), Royal Albert Hall, London, July 1912.

Second Post-Impressionist Exhibition, Grafton Galleries, London, October–December 1912.

The Third Exhibition of the Camden Town Group, Carfax Gallery, London, December 1912.

1913
The Contemporary Art Society, Goupil Gallery, London, April 1913.

The London Salon of the Allied Artists' Association Ltd (sixth year), Royal Albert Hall, London, July 1913.

Post-Impressionist and Futurist Exhibition, Doré Galleries, London, October 1913.

English Post-Impressionists, Cubists and Others (The Cubist Room), Brighton Public Art Galleries, Brighton, December 1913–January 1914.

1914
The First Exhibition of Works by Members of the London Group, Goupil Gallery, London, March 1914.

Twentieth-Century Art: A Review of Modern Movements, Whitechapel Art Gallery, London, May–June 1914.

The London Salon of the Allied Artists' Association Ltd (seventh year), Holland Park Hall, London, July 1914.

Exhibition in Scarborough Arts Club, Scarborough, Yorkshire, August 1914.

1915
The Second Exhibition of Works by Members of the London Group, Goupil Gallery, London, March 1915.

Vorticist Exhibition, Doré Galleries, London, June 1915.

1917
Exhibition of the Vorticists at the Penguin, Penguin Club, New York, January 1917.

1919

Canadian War Memorials Exhibition, Anderson Gallery, New York, 10 June–31 July; Canadian National Exhibition, Toronto, August–September; Art Association of Montreal, October–November 1919.

The Nation's War Paintings and Other Records, Royal Academy of Arts, London, December 1919–February 1920.

1920

Group X, Mansard Gallery, London, 26 March–24 April 1920.

1924

Second Exhibition of Canadian War Memorials, National Gallery of Canada, Ottawa, 18 January–30 April 1924.

1926

Exhibition of Canadian War Memorials, Art Gallery of Toronto, Toronto, October 1926.

1939

British Pavilion, New York World's Fair, New York, 30 April–27 October 1940.

1941

Britain at War, The Museum of Modern Art, New York, May–September; National Gallery of Canada, Ottawa, October; Art Gallery of Toronto, November–December 1941; Art Association of Montreal, Montreal, January 1942; London Public Library and Art Museum, Elsie Perrin Williams Memorial Building, London, Ontario, February 1942.

1942

19th Annual Exhibition, Canadian Society of Graphic Art, Art Gallery of Toronto, Toronto, April 1942.

15th Annual Exhibition, Canadian Society of Painters in Watercolour, Art Gallery of Toronto, Toronto, April 1942.

1943

English Paintings since 1900, London Public Library and Art Museum, Elsie Perrin Williams Memorial Building, London, Ontario, 7 May–12 June 1943.

1948

Contemporary British Drawings 1948–1949, National Gallery of Canada, Ottawa, 7–31 October; Art Gallery of Ontario, Toronto, 1–30 November; Art Gallery of Greater Victoria, Victoria, 1–28 February 1948; Art Gallery of Alberta, Edmonton, 1–31 March 1949.

1954

Exhibition of the Beaverbrook Collection of Paintings and Prints and some Portraits from the Collection of Sir James Dunn, Bart, The Bonar Law-Bennett Library, The University of New Brunswick, New Jersey, 8–20 November 1954.

1955

British Watercolours and Drawings of the Twentieth Century, Willistead Art Gallery of Windsor, Windsor, Ontario, 1955 (travelling exhibition, Canada, 1955–1957).

1957

Wyndham Lewis, Francis Kelly, Zwemmer Gallery, London, May 1957.

1964

Paintings from the Canadian War Memorials, National Gallery of Canada, Ottawa, 26 June–October; Art Gallery of Hamilton, Ontario, November 1964.

1966

Windsor Collectors, Willistead Art Gallery of Windsor, Windsor, Ontario, 5 October–10 November 1966.

1967

Some Paintings, Drawings and Prints from the Douglas Duncan Collection, Willistead Art Gallery of Windsor, Windsor, Ontario, 4 October–9 November; London Public Library and Art Museum, Elsie Perrin Williams Memorial Building, London, Ontario, 5–27 December 1967; Art Gallery of Hamilton, Ontario, 6–22 January 1968.

1974

Vorticism and its Allies, Hayward Gallery, London, 27 March–2 June 1974.

1984–1987

Preferred Places: A Selection of British Landscape Watercolours from the Permanent Collection of the Art Gallery of Ontario, Glendon Gallery, York University, Toronto, Ontario, 30 November 1984—13 January 1985; Kitchener/Waterloo Art Gallery, Kitchener, Ontario, 26 February–26 April 1985; Sarnia Public Library and Art Gallery, Sarnia, Ontario, 5 June–6 July 1987.

1986

Five years on: A Selection of Acquisitions 1981–1986, Art Gallery of New South Wales, Australia, 26 September–23 November 1986.

1987

British Art in the Twentieth Century: The Modern Movement, Royal Academy of Arts, London, 15 January–5 April 1987.

Twentieth Century British Art from the Collection of the Art Gallery of Ontario, Art Gallery of Peterborough, Ontario, 13 August–15 September; Rodman Hall Arts Centre, St Catharines, Ontario, 2 October–1 November 1987; Sarnia Public Library and Art Gallery, Sarnia, Ontario, 11 June–11 July 1988.

1993

Modern British Art: Vorticism and the Grosvenor School 1912–1935, Hearst Art Gallery, Saint Mary's College of California, Moraga, 25 September–7 November 1993.

The Great English Vortex: Modern Drawings from the Collection of Mr and Mrs Michael W. Wilsey, San Francisco Museum of Modern Art, San Francisco, 11 November 1993–16 January 1994.

1996

BLAST: Vortizismus-Die erste Avantgarde in England 1914–1918, Sprengel Museum, Hannover, 18 August–3 November 1996; Haus der Kunst, Munich, 15 November 1996–26 January 1997.

1997

Modern Art in Britain 1910–1914, Barbican Art Gallery, London, 20 February–26 May 1997.

1999

Michelangelo to Matisse: Drawing the Figure, Art Gallery of New South Wales, Australia, 20 November 1999–27 February 2000.

2004

Blasting the Future! Vorticism in Britain 1910–1920, Estorick Collection of Modern Italian Art, London, 4 February–18 April; The Whitworth Art Gallery, Manchester, 7 May–25 July 2004.

The Edwin Morgan Collection, Hunterian Art Gallery, University of Glasgow, Glasgow, 15 November 2004–March 2005.

2007

Modern Britain 1900–1960, National Gallery of Victoria, Melbourne, 15 November 2007–24 February 2008.

2008

Rhythms of Modern Life: British Prints 1914–1939, Museum of Fine Arts, Boston, 30 January–1 June; The Metropolitan Museum of Art, New York, 23 September–7 December 2008; The Wolfsonian-Florida International University, Miami, 21 November 2009–28 February 2010.

Rubens to Mackintosh: Drawings from the Hunterian Art Gallery, Hunterian Art Gallery, University of Glasgow, Glasgow, 1 May–6 September 2008.

¡1914! La Vanguardia y la Gran Guerra, Museo Thyssen-Bornemisza and Fundación Caja Madrid, Madrid, 7 October 2008–11 January 2009.

The Discovery of Spain: British Artists and Collectors: Goya to Picasso, National Galleries of Scotland, Edinburgh, 18 July–11 October 2009

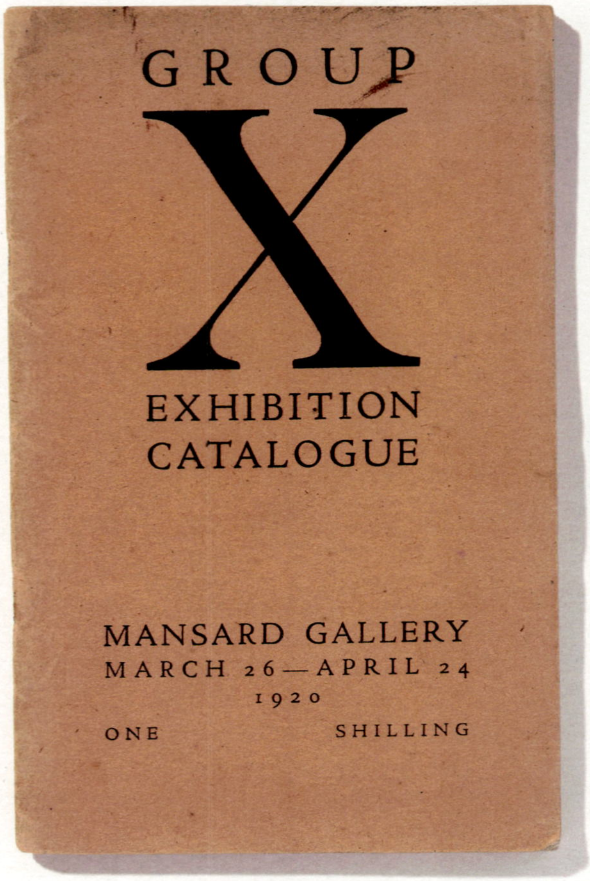
GROUP
X
EXHIBITION
CATALOGUE
MANSARD GALLERY
MARCH 26—APRIL 24
1920
ONE SHILLING

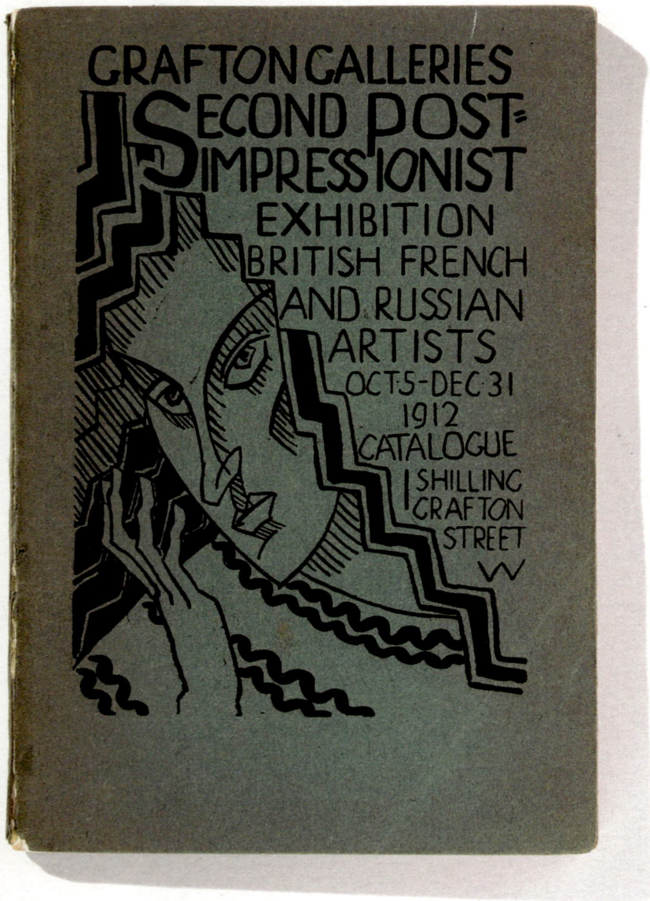
GRAFTON GALLERIES
SECOND POST=
IMPRESSIONIST
EXHIBITION
BRITISH FRENCH
AND RUSSIAN
ARTISTS
OCT 5-DEC 31
1912
CATALOGUE
1 SHILLING
GRAFTON
STREET
W

G

WYNDHAM LEWIS: THE ARTIST, THE WRITER, THE EDITOR: A BIBLIOGRAPHY

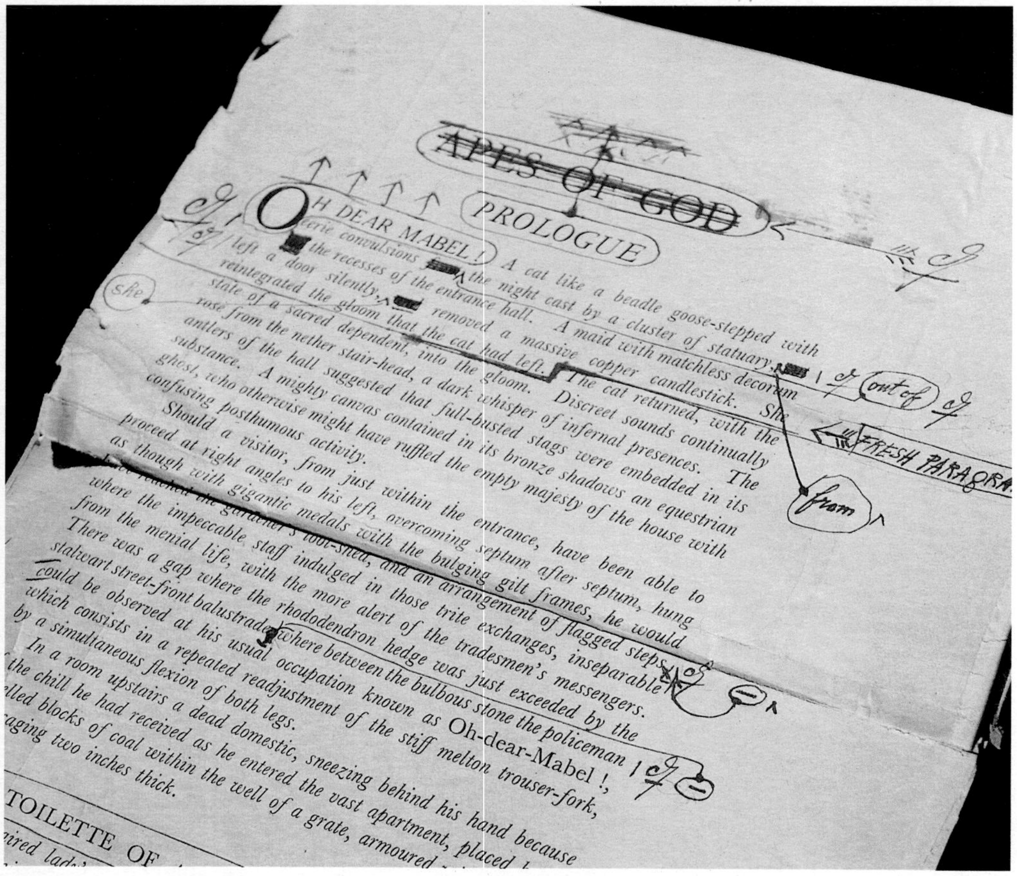
APES OF GOD

PROLOGUE

OH DEAR MABEL ! A cat like a beadle goose-stepped with
eerie convulsions [redacted] the night cast by a cluster of statuary. [redacted]
[redacted] the recesses of the entrance hall. A maid with matchless decorum
left a door silently, [redacted] removed a massive copper candlestick. She
reintegrated the gloom that the cat had left. The cat returned, with the
state of a sacred dependent, into the gloom. Discreet sounds continually
rose from the nether stair-head, a dark whisper of infernal presences. The
antlers of the hall suggested that full-busted stags were embedded in its
substance. A mighty canvas contained in its bronze shadows an equestrian
ghost, who otherwise might have ruffled the empty majesty of the house with
confusing posthumous activity.

Should a visitor, from just within the entrance, have been able to
proceed at right angles to his left, overcoming septum after septum, hung
as though with gigantic medals with the bulging gilt frames, he would
... reached the gardener's tool-shed, and an arrangement of flagged steps,
where the impeccable staff indulged in those trite exchanges, inseparable
from the menial life, with the more alert of the tradesmen's messengers.
There was a gap where the rhododendron hedge was just exceeded by the
stalwart street-front balustrade where between the bulbous stone the policeman
could be observed at his usual occupation known as Oh-dear-Mabel !,
which consists in a repeated readjustment of the stiff melton trouser-fork,
by a simultaneous flexion of both legs.

In a room upstairs a dead domestic, sneezing behind his hand because
the chill he had received as he entered the vast apartment, placed ...
...lled blocks of coal within the well of a grate, armoured ...
...aging two inches thick.

TOILETTE OF ...

INDEX

About this Bibliography

This bibliography is based on Bradford Morrow and Bernard Lafourcade's comprehensive *A Bibliography of the Writings of Wyndham Lewis* (Santa Barbara: Black Sparrow Press, 1978), and the equally thorough Wyndham Lewis. *A Descriptive Bibliography by Omar S. Pound and Philip Grover* (Kent: Dawson Archon Books, 1978). They are supplemented here by a selective bibliography of books that have since been published on Lewis and that is by no means exhaustive, given the bibliographic resources available online.

Wyndham Lewis's writings have been organized chronologically not by publication date but by date of writing. Of his books, all first editions are listed, whether English or American, as are those published during Lewis's lifetime that were revised and expanded, as well as known posthumous reprints and other special editions, such as facsimiles and anthologies. The articles included here, however, date only until Lewis's death in 1957, and do not include those published posthumously.

1. Wyndham Lewis: the Artist

1.1. Solo exhibition catalogues

Guns by Wyndham Lewis [exh. cat. Goupil Gallery, London]. London: Goupil Gallery, 1919.

Tyros and Portraits [exh. cat. The Leicester Galleries, London]. London: J. Miles and Co. Ltd, 1921.

Thirty Personalities by Wyndham Lewis [exh. cat. The Lefevre Galleries, London]. London: The Lefevre Galleries, 1932.

Paintings and Drawings by Wyndham Lewis [exh. cat. The Leicester Galleries, London]. London: J. Miles and Co. Ltd, 1937.

New Paintings and Drawings by Wyndham Lewis [exh. cat. Beaux Arts Gallery, London]. London: Beaux Arts Gallery, 1938.

Wyndham Lewis [exh. cat., Redfern Gallery, London]. London: The Beauchamp Press, 1949.

Wyndham Lewis: Drawings and Watercolours [exh. cat. Victoria College, University of Toronto]. Toronto: Victoria College, 1950.

Wyndham Lewis and Vorticism [exh. cat. Tate Gallery, London]. London: Tate Gallery, 1956.

Wyndham Lewis and Vorticism [exh. cat. City Art Gallery, Manchester; The Art Gallery, Glasgow; City Art Gallery, Bristol; City Art Gallery, Leeds]. London: The Arts Council, 1956.

Paintings and Books by Wyndham Lewis [exh. cat. York University Art Gallery, Toronto]. Toronto: York University, 1964.

Word and Image I: Wyndham Lewis 1882–1957 [exh. cat. The National Book League, London]. London: National Book League, 1971.

An Exhibition of Paintings and Drawings by Wyndham Lewis [exh. cat. The Mayor Gallery, London]. London: The Mayor Gallery, 1974.

Wyndham Lewis, Jane Farrington, ed. [exh. cat. Manchester City Art Gallery, Manchester; National Museum of Wales, Cardiff; City Art Centre, Edinburgh]. London: Lund Humphries Publishers, 1980.

Wyndham Lewis: A Centennial Salute [exh. cat. Art Gallery of Nova Scotia, Halifax]. Halifax: Art Gallery of Nova Scotia, 1982.

Wyndham Lewis et le Vorticisme, Richard Cork, ed. [exh. cat. Centre Georges Pompidou, Paris]. Paris: Pandora Editions, 1982.

Wyndham Lewis: Drawings and Watercolours 1910–1920 [exh. cat. Anthony d´Offay, London]. London: Anthony d´Offay, 1983.

Wyndham Lewis: The Twenties [exh. cat. Gallery Anthony d´Offay, London]. London: Anthony d´Offay, 1984.

Wyndham Lewis: The Early Decades [exh. cat. Washburn Gallery, New York]. New York: Washburn Gallery, 1985.

Wyndham Lewis 1882–1957, Andrew Wilson, ed. [exh. cat. Austin Desmond Fine Art, London]. London: Austin Desmond Fine Art, 1990.

Graphic Works by Wyndham Lewis [exh. cat. Harry Ransom Humanities Research Center, Austin, Texas]. Austin: University of Texas, 1992.

The Talented Intruder: Wyndham Lewis in Canada 1939–1945, Catharine M. Mastin, Robert Stacey, Thomas Dilworth, eds. [exh. cat. Art Gallery of Windsor, Ontario; Glenbow Museum, Calgary, Alberta; Art Gallery of Ontario, Toronto]. Ontario: The Art Gallery of Windsor, 1992.

Wyndham Lewis: Art and War, Paul Edwards, ed. [exh. cat. Imperial War Museum, London]. London: Lund Humphries Publishers, 1992.

Wyndham Lewis [exh. cat. The Hunterian Museum and Gallery, University of Glasgow]. Glasgow: Hunterian Museum and Art Gallery, 2003.

'The bone beneath the pulp': Drawings by Wyndham Lewis, Jacky Klein, ed. [exh. cat. Courtauld Institute of Art Gallery, London; Abbot Hall Art Gallery, Cumbria]. London: Courtauld Institute of Art Gallery, 2005.

Wyndham Lewis [exh. cat. Fine Arts, Design & Antiques Fair, Olympia, London]. London: Apollo, 2005.

An Exhibition of Paintings and Drawings by Percy Wyndham Lewis (1897–98) [exh. cat. Rugby School, Rugby]. Rugby: Rugby School, 2007.

Wyndham Lewis: Portraits, Paul Edwards with Richard Humphreys, eds. [exh. cat. National Portrait Gallery, London]. London: National Portrait Gallery, 2008.

The Lion and the Fox: Art and Literary Works by Wyndham Lewis from the C.J. Fox Collection [exh. cat. University of Victoria Libraries, Victoria]. Victoria: University of Victoria Libraries, 2009.

Wyndham Lewis (1882–1957) [exh. cat. Fundación Juan March, Madrid]. Madrid: Fundación Juan March: Editorial Arte y Ciencia, 2010.

1.2. Group exhibition catalogues

Second Post-Impressionist Exhibition [exh. cat. Grafton Galleries, London]. London: Ballantyne & Co. Ltd, 1912.

Exhibition of English Post-Impressionists, Cubists and Others [exh. cat. Public Art Galleries, Brighton]. 1913.

The London Salon of the Allied Artists´ Association Ltd (seventh year) [exh. cat. Holland Park Hall, London]. London, 1914.

The London Salon of the Allied Artists´ Association Ltd (sixth year) [exh. cat. Royal Albert Hall, London]. London, 1913.

Vorticist Exhibition [exh. cat. Doré Galleries, London]. Harlesden: Leveridge and Co., 1915.

Exhibition of the Vorticists at the Penguin [exh. cat. Penguin Club, New York]. New York: Penguin Club, 1917.

Canadian War Memorials Exhibition [exh. cat. Anderson Gallery, New York; Canadian National Exhibition, Toronto; Art Association of Montreal]. National Exhibition Toronto and Art Association of Montreal, 1919.

Group X [exh. cat. Mansard Gallery, London]. London: Pelican Press, 1920.

Second Exhibition of Canadian War Memorials [exh. cat. National Gallery of Canada, Ottawa]. Ottawa: National Gallery of Canada, 1924.

Contemporary British Drawings [exh. cat. National Gallery of Canada, Ottawa]. Ottawa: National Gallery of Canada, 1948.

Wyndham Lewis, Francis Kelly [exh. cat. Zwemmer Gallery, London]. London: Zwemmer Gallery, 1957.

Abstract Art in England 1913–15 [exh. cat. Anthony d´Offay Gallery, London]. London: Anthony d´Offay Gallery, 1969.

Vorticism and its Allies, Richard Cork, ed. [exh. cat. Hayward Gallery, London]. London: Arts Council of Great Britain, 1974.

Five Years on: A Selection of Acquisitions 1981–1986 [exh. cat. Art Gallery of New South Wales, New South Wales]. New South Wales: Art Gallery of New South Wales, 1986.

British Art in the Twentieth Century: The Modern Movement, Susan Compton, ed. [exh. cat. Royal Academy of Arts, London]. London: Royal Academy of Arts; Munich: Prestel-Verlag, 1987.

Modern British Art. Vorticism and the Grosvenor School 1912–1935, Judith C. Eurich, ed. [exh. cat. Hearst Art Gallery, Saint Mary's College of California]. Moraga: Hearst Art Gallery, 1993.

The Great English Vortex: Modern Drawings from the Collection of Mr and Mrs Michael W. Wilsey, Kara Kirk, ed. [exh. cat. Museum of Modern Art, San Francisco]. San Francisco: Museum of Modern Art, 1993.

BLAST: Vortizismus-Die erste Avantgarde in England 1914–1918 [exh. cat. Sprengel Museum, Hannover; Haus der Kunst, Munich]. Berlin: Nicolaische Verlagsbuchhandlung; Hannover: Sprengel Museum, 1996.

Modern Art in Britain 1910–1914, Anna Gruetzner Robins, ed. [exh. cat. Barbican Art Gallery, London]. London: Merrell Holberton in association with Barbican Art Gallery, 1997.

Michelangelo to Matisse: Drawing the Figure [exh. cat. Art Gallery of New South Wales, New South Wales]. New South Wales: Art Gallery of New South Wales, 1999.

Blasting the Future! Vorticism in Britain 1910–1920 [exh. cat. Estorick Collection of Modern Italian Art, London; The Whitworth Art Gallery, Manchester]. London: Philip Wilson Publishers, 2004.

Modern Britain 1900–1960 [exh. cat. National Gallery of Victoria, Melbourne]. Melbourne: National Gallery of Victoria, 2007.

Rhythms of Modern Life: British Prints 1914–1939 [exh. cat. Museum of Fine Arts, Boston; The Metropolitan Museum of Art, New York; The Wolfsonian-Florida International University, Miami]. Boston: Museum of Fine Arts, 2008.

¡1914! La Vanguardia y la Gran Guerra, Javier Arnaldo, ed. [exh. cat. Museo Thyssen-Bornemisza y Fundación Caja Madrid, Madrid]. Madrid: Fundación Colección Thyssen-Bornemisza, 2008.

2. Wyndham Lewis: the Writer

2.1. Books

1908

Mrs Dukes' Million. Toronto: The Coach House Press, 1977.

1909

Crossing the Frontier, Bernard Lafourcade and Bradford Morrow (introd.). Santa Barbara: Black Sparrow Press, 1978.

1917

The Ideal Giant. London: The Little Review, 1917.

1918

Tarr. New York: Alfred A. Knopf, 1918; London: The Egoist Press, 1918; London: Chatto and Windus, 1928 (rev. ed.); *Tarr. The 1918 Version.* Ed. Paul O'Keeffe. Santa Rosa: Black Sparrow Press, 1990.

1919

LEWIS, Wyndham and Louis F. FERGUSSON, *Harold Gilman: An Appreciation.* London: Chatto and Windus, 1919.

The Caliph's Design: Architects! Where is Your Vortex? London: The Egoist Press, 1919; Ed. Paul Edwards. Santa Barbara: Black Sparrow Press, 1986.

1926

The Art of Being Ruled. London: Chatto and Windus, 1926; Ed. Reed Way Dasenbrock. Santa Rosa: Black Sparrow Press, 1989.

1927

The Lion and the Fox: The Rôle of the Hero in the Plays of Shakespeare. London: Grant Richards, 1927; London: Methuen & Co. Ltd, 1966.

The Wild Body: A Soldier of Humour and Other Stories. London: Chatto and Windus, 1927; *The Complete Wild Body.* Ed. Bernard Lafourcade. Santa Barbara: Black Sparrow Press, 1982; London: Penguin Books, 2004.

Time and Western Man. London: Chatto and Windus, 1927; New York: Harcourt, Brace and Co., 1928 (rev. ed.); Ed. Paul Edwards. Santa Rosa: Black Sparrow Press, 1993.

1928

The Childermass: Section I. London: Chatto and Windus, 1928; *The Human Age, Book One: The Childermass.* London: Methuen & Co. Ltd, 1956 (rev. ed.); New York: Riverrun Press, 2001.

1929

Paleface: The Philosophy of the "Melting Pot." London: Chatto and Windus, 1929; New York: Gordon Press, 1972 (facs. ed.).

1930

The Apes of God. London: The Arthur Press, 1930; London: Arco Publishers Ltd, 1955 (facs. ed. with new introd. by the author); Santa Barbara: Black Sparrow Press, 1981.

1931

Hitler. London: Chatto and Windus, 1931; New York: Gordon Press, 1972 (facs. ed.).

The Diabolical Principle and the Dithyrambic Spectator. London: Chatto and Windus, 1931; New York: Haskell House, 1971 (facs. ed.).

1932

Enemy of the Stars. London: Desmond Harmsworth, 1932.

Filibusters in Barbary: Record of a Visit to the Sous. London: Grayson and Grayson, 1932; New York: National Travel Club, 1932; New York: Haskell House, 1972.

Snooty Baronet. London: Cassell, 1932; Ed. Bernard Lafourcade. Santa Barbara: Black Sparrow Press, 1984.

The Doom of Youth. New York: Robert M. McBride, 1932; London: Chatto and Windus, 1932.

The Roaring Queen. Ed. Walter Allen. London: Secker and Warburg, 1973.

1933

One-Way Song. London: Faber and Faber, 1933.

The Old Gang and the New Gang. London: Desmond Harmsworth, 1933; New York: Haskell House Publishers, 1972.

1934

Men without Art. London: Cassell, 1934; Ed. Seamus Cooney. Santa Barbara: Black Sparrow Press, 1987.

1936

Left Wings Over Europe: Or, How to Make a War about Nothing. London: Jonathan Cape, 1936; New York: Gordon Press, 1972.

1937

Blasting and Bombardiering: Autobiography (1914–1926). London: Eyre & Spottiswoode, 1937; *Estallidos y bombardeos.* Ed. and trans. Yolanda Morató. Madrid: Impedimenta, 2008.

Count Your Dead: They are Alive! Or, A New War in the Making. London: Lovat Dickson, 1937.

The Revenge for Love. London: Cassell, 1937; Ed. Reed Way Dasenbrock. Santa Barbara: Black Sparrow Press, 1991; London: Penguin, 2004; *Dobles Fondos.* Trans. Miguel Temprano. Madrid: Alfaguara, 2004.

1938

The Mysterious Mr Bull. London: Robert Hale, 1938.

1939

The Hitler Cult. London: Dent, 1939; New York: Gordon Press, 1972.

The Jews: Are they Human? London: George Allen and Unwin, 1939; New York: Gordon Press, 1972.

Wyndham Lewis the Artist: From "Blast" to Burlington House. London: Laidlaw and Laidlaw, 1939; New York: Haskell House Publishers, 1971.

1940

America, I Presume. New York: Howell, Soskin & Co., 1940; New York: Howell, Soskin & Co.; Haskell House Publishers, 1972.

1941

Anglosaxony: A League that Works. Toronto: The Ryerson Press, 1941.

The Role of Line in Art. Ed. P.W. Nash. Witney: The Strawberry Leaf Press, 2007.

The Vulgar Streak. London: Robert Hale, 1941; Ed. Paul Edwards. Santa Rosa: Black Sparrow Press, 1985.

1948

America and Cosmic Man. London: Nicholson and Watson, 1948; Garden City, New York: Doubleday, 1949.

1950

Rude Assignment: A Narrative of my Career Up-to-date. London: Hutchinson & Co., 1950; *Rude Assignment: An Intellectual Autobiography.* Ed. Toby Foshay. Santa Barbara: Black Sparrow Press, 1984.

1951

Rotting Hill. London: Methuen & Co. Ltd, 1951; Chicago: Henry Regnery Co., 1952; Ed. Paul Edwards. Santa Barbara: Black Sparrow Press, 1986.

1952

The Writer and the Absolute. London: Methuen & Co. Ltd, 1952.

1954

Self Condemned. London: Methuen & Co. Ltd, 1954; Santa Barbara: Black Sparrow Press, 1983.

The Demon of Progress in the Arts. London: Methuen & Co. Ltd, 1954.

1955

The Human Age, Book Two: Monstre Gai; Book Three: Malign Fiesta. London: Methuen & Co. Ltd, 1955.

1956

The Red Priest. London: Methuen and Co. Ltd, 1956.

2.2. Contributions to periodicals

1909

"The Pole," *The English Review* II (May), pp. 255–56.

"Some Innkeepers and Bestre," *The English Review* II (June), pp. 471–84.

"Les Saltimbanques," *The English Review* III (August), pp. 76–87.

1910

"Our Wild Body," *The New Age* II, no. 1 (May), pp. 8–10.

"A Spanish Household," *The Tramp: An Open Air Magazine* I (June–July), pp. 356–60.

"A Breton Innkeeper," *The Tramp: An Open Air Magazine* I (August), pp. 411–14.

«Le Père François (A Full-Length Portrait of a Tramp)», *The Tramp: an Open Air Magazine* I (September), pp. 517–21.

"Grignolles (Brittany)," *The Tramp: An Open Air Magazine* II (December), p. 246.

1911

"Brobdingnag," *The New Age* VIII (Literary Supplement), no. 10 (5 January), pp. 2–3.

"Unlucky for Pringle," *The Tramp: An Open Air Magazine* II (February), pp. 404–14.

1914

"The Cubist Room," *The Egoist* I, no. 1 (1 January), pp. 8–9.

"Letter to the Editor: Epstein and his Critics, or Nietzsche and his Friends," *The New Age* XIV, no. 10 (8 January), p. 319.

"Letter to the Editor: Mr. Arthur Rose's Offer," *The New Age* XIV, no. 15 (12 February), p. 479.

"Letter to the Editor: Modern Art," *The New Age* XIV, no. 22 (2 April), p. 703.

"Rebel Art in Modern Life," *The Daily News and Leader* XXI, no. 240 (7 April), p. 14.

"A Man of the Week: Marinetti," *The New Weekly* I, no. 11 (30 May 1914), pp. 328–29.

"Futurism," *The New Weekly* I, no. 13 (13 June), p. 406; *The Observer* VI (14 June), p. 9; *The Egoist* I, no. 12 (15 June), p. 239.

"Manifesto," *Blast*, No. 1 (20 June), pp. 9–28.

"Manifesto [II]," *Blast*, No. 1 (20 June), pp. 30–43.

"Enemy of the Stars," *Blast*, No. 1 (20 June), pp. 51–85.

"Vortices and Notes," *Blast*, No. 1 (20 June), pp. 127–49.

"Fredrick Spencer Gore," *Blast*, No. 1 (20 June), p. 150.

"To Suffragettes," *Blast*, No. 1 (20 June), pp. 151–152.

"Automobilism," *The New Weekly* II, no. 1 (June), p. 13.

"Futurism and the Flesh. A Futurist's Reply to Mr. G.K. Chesterton," *T.P.'s Weekly* XXXIV, no. 609 (11 July), p. 49.

"Kill John Bull with Art," *The Outlook* XXXIV, no. 74 (18 July), p. 74.

"A Later Arm than Barbarity," *The Outlook*, XXXIV (September), pp. 298–99.

1915

"Editorial," *Blast*, No. 2 (July), pp. 5–6.

"Notice to Public," *Blast*, No. 2 (July), p. 7.

"The God of Sport and Blood," *Blast*, No. 2 (July), pp. 9–10.

"Constantinople our Star," *Blast*, No. 2 (July), p. 11.

"Mr. Shaw's Effect on my Friend," *Blast*, No. 2 (July), p. 12.

"A Super-Krupp – or War's End," *Blast*, No. 2 (July), pp. 13–14.

"The European War and Great Communities," *Blast*, No. 2 (July), pp. 15–16.

"Artists and the War," *Blast*, No. 2 (July), pp. 23–24.

"The Exploitation of Blood," *Blast*, No. 2 (July), p. 24.

"The Six Hundred, Verestchagin and Uccello," *Blast*, No. 2 (July), pp. 25–26.

"Marinetti's Occupation," *Blast*, No. 2 (July), p. 26.

"A Review of Contemporary Art," *Blast*, No. 2 (July), pp. 38–47.

"The Art of the Great Race," *Blast*, No. 2 (July), pp. 70–72.

"The London Group," *Blast*, No. 2 (July), pp. 77–79.

"Modern Caricature and Impressionism," *Blast*, No. 2 (July), p. 79.

"History of the Largest Independent Society in England," *Blast*, No. 2 (July), pp. 80–81.

"Life has no Taste," *Blast*, No. 2 (July), p. 82.

"American Art," *Blast*, No. 2 (July), p. 82.

"Wyndham Lewis Vortex No. 1: Art Vortex. Be thyself," *Blast*, No. 2 (July), p. 91.

"Blast [and] Bless," *Blast*, No. 2 (July), pp. 92–93.

"The Crowd-Master," *Blast*, No. 2 (July), pp. 94–102.

"Preface," *The Cambridge Magazine* V, no. 8 (4 December), p. 173.

1916

"The French Poodle," *The Egoist* III, no. 3 (March), pp. 39–41.

"A Young Soldier," *The Egoist* III, no. 3 (March), p. 46.

"Tarr," *The Egoist* III, no. 3 (1 April), pp. 54–63.

"Tarr," *The Egoist* III, no. 5 (1 May), pp. 72–79.

"Tarr," *The Egoist* III, no. 6 (1 June), pp. 90–94.

"Tarr," *The Egoist* III, no. 7 (1 July), pp. 107–10.

"Tarr," *The Egoist* III, no. 8 (August), pp. 122–25.

"Tarr," *The Egoist* III, no. 9 (September), pp. 139–43.

"Tarr," *The Egoist* III, no. 10 (October), pp. 155–58.

"Tarr," *The Egoist* III, no. 11 (November), pp. 170–73.

"Tarr," *The Egoist* III, no. 12 (December), pp. 184–86.

1917

"Tarr," *The Egoist* IV, no. 1 (January), pp. 10–15.

"Tarr," *The Egoist* IV, no. 2 (February), pp. 29–30.

"Tarr," *The Egoist* IV, no. 3 (April), pp. 39–41.

"Tarr," *The Egoist* IV, no. 4 (May), pp. 60–61.

"Imaginary Letters I (Six Letters of William Bland to his Wife)," *The Little Review* IV, no. 1 (May), pp. 19–23.

"Tarr," *The Egoist* IV, no. 5 (June), pp. 75–78.

"Imaginary Letters II (Six Letters of William Bland to his Wife)," *The Little Review* IV, no. 2 (May), pp. 22–26.

"Tarr," *The Egoist* IV, no. 6 (July), pp. 93–95.

"Imaginary Letters. The Code of a Herdsman," *The Little Review* IV, no. 3 (July), pp. 3–7.

"Tarr," *The Egoist* IV, no. 7 (August), pp. 106–09.

"Tarr," *The Egoist* IV, no. 8 (September), pp. 123–27.

"Inferior Religions," *The Little Review* IV, no. 5 (September), pp. 3–8.

"Tarr," *The Egoist* IV, no. 9 (October), pp. 138–41.

"Cantelman's Spring-Mate," *The Little Review* IV, no. 6 (October), pp. 8–14.

"Tarr: and Epilogue," *The Egoist* IV, no. 10 (November), pp. 152–53

"A Soldier of Humour. Part I," *The Little Review* IV, no. 8 (December), pp.32–46.

1918

"A Solder of Humour. Part II," *The Little Review* IV, no. 9 (January), pp. 35–51.

"Imaginary Letters (William Bland Burn to his Wife)," *The Little Review* IV, no. 11 (March), pp. 23–30.

"Imaginary Letters (William Bland Burn to his Wife)," *The Little Review* IV, no. 12 (April), pp. 50–54.

"The Ideal Giant," *The Little Review* VI, no. 1 (May), pp. 1–18.

"The War Baby," *Art and Letters* II, no. 1 (Winter), pp. 14–41.

1919

"The Men who will Paint Hell. Modern War as a Theme for the Artist," *Daily Express*, no. 5877 (10 February), p. 4.

"Mr. Wadsworth's Exhibition of Woodcuts," *Art and Letters* II, no. 2 (Spring), pp. 85–89.

"What Art Now?," *The English Review* XXVIII (April), pp. 334–38.

"Prevalent Design. I. Nature and the Monster of Design," *The Athenaeum*, no. 4673 (21 November), pp. 1230–31.

"Prevalent Design. II. Painting the Soul," *The Athenaeum*, no. 4676 (12 December), p. 1343.

"Prevalent Design. III. The Man behind the Eyes," *The Athenaeum*, no. 4678 (26 December), p. 1404.

1920

"Prevalent Design. IV. The Bulldog Eye's Depredations," *The Athenaeum*, no. 4681 (16 January), pp. 84–85.

"Letter to the Editor: Mr. Ezra Pound," *Observer*, no. 6713 (18 January), p. 5.

"Letter to the Editor: Mr. Clive Bell and 'Wilcoxism'," *The Athenaeum*, no. 4689 (12 March), p. 349.

"Art Saints for Villages," *The Weekly Dispatch*, no. 6197 (9 May), p. 8.

"Sigismund," *Art and Letters* III, no. 1 (Winter), pp. 14–31.

1921

"Why Picasso Does It," *Daily Mail* (10 January), p. 6.

"Note on Tyros," *The Tyro*, No. I (April), p. 2.

"The Objects of this Paper," *The Tyro*, No. I (April), p. 2.

"The Children of the New Epoch," *The Tyro*, No. I (April), p. 3.

"Roger Fry's Role of Continental Mediator," *The Tyro*, No. I (April), p. 3.

"Will Eccles," *The Tyro*, No. I (April), p. 6.

"Dialogue between Mr. Segando and Phillip," *The Tyro*, No. I (April), p. 7.

"Dean Swift with a Brush. The Tyroist Explains His Art," *Daily Express*, no. 6548 (11 April), p. 5.

"The Coming Academy," *Sunday Express*, no. 121 (24 April), p. 3.

"Art in Common Life," *The Times*, no. 42706 (28 April), p. 13

"Paris versus the World," *The Dial* LXXI, no. 1 (July), pp. 22–27.

1922

"The Credentials of the Painter – I.," *The English Review* XXXIV (January), pp. 33–38.

"Editorial," *The Tyro*, No. 2 (March), pp. 3–10.

"Essay on the Objective of Plastic Art in Life," *The Tyro*, No. 2 (March), pp. 21–37.

"Tyronic Dialogues – X. and F.," *The Tyro*, No. 2 (March), pp. 46–49.

"Bestre," *The Tyro*, No. 2 (March), pp. 53–63.

"The Credentials of the Painter – II.," *The English Review* XXXIV (April), pp. 391–96.

"The Long and the Short of It. Mr. Wyndham Lewis Settles the War of the Skirt," *Evening Standard*, no. 30, 499 (28 April), p. 3.

"The Worse-Than-Ever Academy," *Sunday Express*, no. 174 (30 April), p. 5.

1924

"Mr. Zagreus and the Split-Man," *The Criterion* II, no. 6 (February), pp. 124–42.

"The Strange Actor," *New Statesman* XXII, no. 563 (2 February), pp. 474–76.

"The Young Methuselah," *New Statesman* XXII, no. 567 (1 March), pp. 601–02.

"The Apes of God," *The Criterion* II, no. 7 (April), pp. 300–10.

"The Dress-Body-Mind Aggregate," *New Statesman* XXIII, no. 579 (24 May), p. 191.

"Art Chronicle," *The Criterion* II, no. 8 (July), pp. 447–82

"Art Chronicle," *The Criterion* II, no. 9 (October), pp. 107–13.

1925

"Books of the Quarter. Recent Anthropology," *The Criterion* III, no. 10 (January), pp. 311–15.

"The Dithyrambic Spectator: An Essay on the Origins and Survivals of Art. Introduction," *The Calendar of Modern Letters* I, no. 2 (April), pp. 89–107.

"The Dithyrambic Spectator: An Essay on the Origins and Survivals of Art. Part II," *The Calendar of Modern Letters* I, no. 3 (May), pp. 194–213.

"The Politics of Artistic Expression," *Artwork* I, no. 4 (May–August), pp. 223–26.

"The Foxes' Case," *The Calendar of Modern Letters* II, no. 8 (October), pp. 73–90.

"The Physics of the Not-Self," *The Chapbook (A Yearly Miscellany)*, no. 40 (London: Jonathan Cape), pp. 68–77.

1926

"Britons Never Shall Be Bees," *The Calendar of Modern Letters* II, no. 11 (January), pp. 360–62.

"The New Roman Empire," *The Calendar of Modern Letters* II, no. 12 (February), pp. 411–20.

"Creatures of Habit and Creatures of Change," *The Calendar of Modern Letters* III, no. 1 (April), pp. 17–44.

1927

"Preliminary Note to the Public," *The Enemy*, Vol. I (February), pp. vii–viii.

"Editorial," *The Enemy*, Vol. I (February), pp. ix–xv.

"What's in a Namesake," *The Enemy*, Vol. I (February), pp. 19–23.

"The Revolutionary Simpleton," *The Enemy*, Vol. I (February), pp. 25–192.

"The Hypocrite in the Drawing-Room," *Evening Standard*, no. 32,056 (6 May), p. 11.

"The Values of the Doctrine Behind 'Subjective' Art," *The Monthly Criterion* VI, no. 1 (July), pp. 4–13.

"Notes Regarding Details of Publication and Distribution," *The Enemy*, No. 2 (September), pp. vii–x.

"Editorial Notes," *The Enemy*, No. 2 (September), pp. xi–xxxi.

"Editorial," *The Enemy*, No. 2 (September), pp. xxxiii–xi.

"Paleface or 'Love? What Ho! Smelling Strangeness'," *The Enemy*, No. 2 (September), pp. 3–112.

1929

"Enemy Bulletin. 1929 (First Quarter)," *The Enemy*, No. 3 (25 January), pp. vii–viii.

"The Diabolical Principle," *The Enemy*, No. 3 (25 January), pp. 9–84.

"Details Regarding Publication and Distribution," *The Enemy*, No. 3 (25 January), p. 90.

"Notes," *The Enemy*, No. 3 (25 January), pp. 91–100.

"A World Art and Tradition," *Drawing and Design* V, no. 32 (February), pp. 29–30, 56.

"[Answer to a Questionnaire]," *The Little Review* XII, no. 2 (May), p. 49.

" *** !!—…? *** !!! ," *Daily Herald*, no. 9200 (25 October), p. 10.

"The Future of American Art," *The Studio* 98, no. 439 (October), pp. 687–90.

1930

"Our Sham Society – an Interview with Wyndham Lewis by Dr. Meyrick Booth," *Everyman* III, no. 75 (3 July), p. 707.

"A Storm in that Tea-Cup Called London," *Satire & Fiction* 1 (September), pp. 7–8.

"General Editorial Comments," *Satire & Fiction* 1 (September), pp. 17–21.

"Circular Letter Issued by the Arthur Press," *Satire & Fiction* 1 (September), p. 22.

"An Alibi!," *Satire & Fiction* 1 (September), p. 40.

"Satire & Fiction," *Satire & Fiction* 1 (September), pp. 43–62.

"An 'Agony' Surprise for Chelsea. One Artist and Another Artist's Paintings. 'For Sale'," *Daily Express*, no. 9466 (4 September), p. 1.

1931

"Hitlerism – Man and Doctrine: the Weimar Republic and the Dritte Reich," *Time and Tide* XII, no. 3 (17 January), pp. 59–60.

"Hitlerism – Man and Doctrine: Berlin im Licht!," *Time and Tide* XII, no. 4 (24 January), pp. 87–88.

"Hitlerism – Man and Doctrine: the Oneness of 'Hitlerism' and of Hitler," *Time and Tide* XII, no. 5 (31 January), pp. 119–20.

"Hitlerism – Man and Doctrine: the Doctrine of the Blutsgefühl□, *Time and Tide* XII, no. 6 (7 February), pp. 151–52.

"Mr. Wyndham Lewis Replies to his Critics," *Time and Tide* XII, no. 6 (7 February) 159.

"Hitlerism – Man and Doctrine: Creditcrankery Rampant," *Time and Tide* XII, no. 7 (14 February), pp. 182, 184–85.

"Nebulae in Brussels Sprouts," *Time and Tide* XII, no. 9 (28 February), pp. 255–56.

"Wyndham Lewis: the Great Satirist of our Day," *Everyman* V, no. 112 (19 March), pp. 231–33.

"The Son of Woman," *Time and Tide* XII, no. 16 (18 April), pp. 470–72.

"Youth Politics. Foreword: the Everymans," *Time and Tide* XII, no. 24 (13 June), pp. 703–04.

"Youth-Politics. The Age Complex," *Time and Tide* XII, no. 25 (20 June), pp. 738–40.

"Youth-Politics. Youth-Politics upon the Super-Tax Plane," *Time and Tide* XII, no. 26 (27 June), pp. 770–72.

"Youth-Politics. There is *NOTHING* Big Business Can't Ration," *Time and Tide* XII, no. 27 (4 July), pp. 798–800.

"Youth-Politics. The *CLASS-WAR* of Parents and Children," *Time and Tide* XII, no. 28 (11 July), pp. 826–28.

"Youth-Politics. Government by Inferiority Complex," *Time and Tide* XII, no. 29 (18 July), pp. 854–55.

"Youth-Politics. How Youth-Politics will Abolish Youth," *Time and Tide* XII, no. 30 (25 July), pp. 883–84.

"Filibusters in Barbary. High Table: the Packet to Africa," *Everyman* VI, no. 144 (29 October), pp. 437–38.

"The Blue Sultan," *The Graphic* CXXXIV, no. 3230 (7 November), p. 180.

"Filibusters in Barbary. Turning Darks into Whites," *Everyman* VI, no. 146 (12 November), p. 492.

"Filibusters in Barbary. Islamic Sensations," *Everyman* VI, no. 148 (26 November), p. 583.

"Filibusters in Barbary. A Deserted African Lido," *Everyman* VI, no. 150 (10 December), p. 660.

"Filibusters in Barbary. Petrol-Tin Town," *Everyman* VI, no. 152 (24 December), pp. 724, 726.

1932

"Filibusters in Barbary. The Mouth of the Sahara," *Everyman* II, no. 154 (7 January), pp. 793–94.

"A Tip from the Augean Stable," *Time and Tide* XIII, no. 12 (19 March), pp. 322–24.

"A Tip from the Augean Stable," *Time and Tide* XIII, no. 13 (26 March), pp. 348–49.

"The Artist as Crowd," *The Twentieth Century* III, no. 14 (April), pp. 12–15.

"Arnold Bennett as Critic: Mr. Wyndham Lewis Replies," *Time and Tide* XIII, no. 16 (16 April), pp. 423–24.

"What It Feels Like to be an Enemy," *Daily Herald*, no. 5082 (30 May), p. 8.

"Filibusters in Agadir," *Traveler* XII, no. 16 (June), p. 59.

"Fénelon and His Valet," *Time and Tide* XIII, no. 25 (18 June), pp. 673–74.

"The Artist and the New Gothic," *Time and Tide* XIII, no. 26 (25 June), pp. 707–08.

"Flaubert as a Marxist," *Time and Tide* XIII, no. 27 (2 July), pp. 737–38.

"Notes on the Way," *Time and Tide* XIII, no. 41 (8 October), pp. 1072–73.

"Notes on the Way," *Time and Tide* XIII, no. 42 (15 October), pp. 1098–1100.

"Notes on the Way," *Time and Tide* XIII, no. 43 (22 October), pp. 1129–32.

"A Historical Close-Up," *Time and Tide* XIII, no. 43 (22 October [Autumn Supplement]), p. 1154.

"Notes on the Way," *Time and Tide* XIII, no. 44 (29 October), pp. 1174–75.

"Wyndham Lewis and Comrade Gollancz," *Time and Tide* XIII, no. 45 (5 November), pp. 1214–15.

1933

"The Kasbahs of the Atlas," *The Architectural Review* LXXIII, no. 434 (6 January), pp. 73–74.

"Poor Brave Little Barbary," *Daily Herald* no. 5508 (10 October), p. 10.

"One Way Song," *New Britain* II, no. 30 (13 December), p. 121.

"What Are the Berbers?," *The Bookman* LXXXV, no. 507 (December), pp. 183–86.

1934

"Shropshire Lads or Robots?," *New Britain* II, no. 33 (3 January), p. 194.

"Shropshire Lads or Robots Again," *New Britain* II, no. 34 (10 January), pp. 226–27.

"What is 'Difficult' Poetry?," *New Britain* II, no. 42 (7 March), pp. 482–83.

"The Dumb Ox: A Study of Ernest Hemingway," *Life and Letters* X, no. 52 (April), pp. 33–45.

"In Praise of Outsiders," *The New Statesman and Nation* VII no. 168 (12 May), pp. 709–10.

"A Moralist with a Corn Cob: A Study of William Faulkner," *Life and Letters* X, no. 54 (June), pp. 314–28.

"The Dumb Ox: A Study of Ernest Hemingway," *The American Review* III, no. 3 (June), pp. 189–212.

"Demos Defied," *The Spectator* CLII, no. 5528 (8 June), p. 892.

"The English Sense of Humour," *The Spectator*, no. 5529 (15 June), pp. 915–16.

"Art in a Machine Age," *The Bookman* LXXXVI, no. 514 (July), pp. 184–87.

"The Propagandist in Fiction," *Current History* (August), pp. 567–72.

"Keyserling," *Time and Tide* XV, no. 31 (4 August), pp. 984–85.

"The Satirist and the Physical World," *The Spectator* CLIII, no. 5537 (10 August), p. 196.

"Rousseau," *Time and Tide* XV, no. 33 (18 August), pp. 1034–35.

"Nationalism," *The Bookman* LXXXVI, no. 516 (September), pp. 276–78.

"A Communist Abroad," *Time and Tide* XV, no. 37 (15 September), pp. 1141–42.

"Tradesmen, Gentleman and Artists," *The Listener* XII, no. 298 (26 September), p. 545.

"'Classical Revival' in England," *The Bookman* LXXXVII, no. 517 (October), pp. 8–10.

"Studies in the Art of Laughter," *The London Mercury* XXX, no. 180 (October), pp. 509–15.

"An Enquiry," *New Verse*, no. 11 (October), pp. 7–8.

"Detachment and the Fictionist [Part I]," *The English Review* LIX (October), pp. 441–52.

"One Picture is More than Enough," *Time and Tide* XV, no. 41 (13 October), pp. 1252–53.

"Power-Feeling and Machine-Age Art," *Time and Tide* XV, no. 42 (20 October), pp. 1312–14.

"Detachment and the Fictionist [Part II]," *The English Review* LIX (November), pp. 564–73.

"Plain Home-Builder: Where is your Vorticist?" *The Architectural Review* LXXVI, no. 456 (November), pp. 155–58.

"Letter to the Editor: The Criticism of Mr. Wyndham Lewis," *The Spectator* CLIII, no. 5549 (2 November), p. 675.

"Art in Industry," *Time and Tide* XV, no. 45 (10 November), pp. 1410–12.

"Sitwell Circus," *Time and Tide* XV, no. 46 (17 November), p. 1480.

"Art as Life," *The Spectator* CLIII, no. 5552 (Literary Supplement), (23 November), pp. 6, 8.

"Letter to the Editor: Mr. Lewis and Mr. Murray," *Times Literary Supplement* XXXIII, no. 1713 (29 November), p. 856.

Letter to the Editor, *The New Statesman and Nation* VIII, no. 199 (New Series) (15 December), p. 900.

"Letter to the Editor: Mr. Lewis and Mr. Murray," *Times Literary Supplement* XXXIII, no. 1716 (20 December), p. 909.

1935

"Notes on the Way," *Time and Tide* XVI, no. 9 (2 March), pp. 304–06.

"Wyndham Lewis Asks What is Industrial Art?," *Commercial Art and Industry* XVIII, no. 105 (6 March), pp. 83–86.

"Notes on the Way," *Time and Tide* XVI, no. 10 (9 March), pp. 332–34.

"Notes on the Way," *Time and Tide* XVI, no. 11 (16 March), pp. 390–92.

"Notes on the Way," *Time and Tide* XVI, no. 12 (23 March), pp. 425–27.

"Notes on the Way," *Time and Tide* XVI, no. 13 (30 March), pp. 456–58.

"First Aid for the Unorthodox," *The London Mercury* XXXII, no. 187 (May), pp. 27–32.

"Freedom that Destroys Itself," *The Listener* XIII, no. 330 (May), pp. 793–94.

"Among the British Islanders – Art and Literature," *The Listener* XIII, no. 337 (26 June), pp.1108–09.

"Letter to the Editor: Martian Opinions," *The Listener* XIV, no. 340 (17 July), p. 125.

1936

"Letter to the Editor: Mr. Ervine and the Poets," *Observer,* no. 7549 (2 February), p. 13.

"Left-Wingism," *The New Statesman and Nation* XI, no. 279 (27 June), p. 1024.

"The Big Soft 'Centre'," *The English Review* LXIII, no. 1 (July), pp. 27–34.

1937

"'Left Wings' and the C3 Mind," *The British Union Quarterly* I, no. 1 (January–April), pp. 22–34.

"My Reply to Mr. Aldington. A Defence of Style: the Novel and the Newspaper," *John O'London's Weekly and the Outline* XXXVII, no. 952 (9 July), pp. 555–56.

"Count Your Dead – They Are Alive: Wyndham Lewis's New Tract for the Times," *The American Review* XIX, no. 2 (Summer), pp. 266–95.

"Rebel and Royalist," *The Spectator*, no. 5701 (1 October), p. 553.

"Letter to the Editor," *Twentieth Century Verse (Wyndham Lewis Double Number)*, no. 6–7 (November–December), pp. 3–5.

1938

"Pictures as Investments: a Straight Talk; Some Possible Gold Mines of Tomorrow," *John O'London's Weekly and the Outline* XXXVIII, no. 985 (25 February), pp. 852, 858.

"Royal Academy Attacked. 'Prejudice against Art of To-Day.' Wyndham Lewis Criticisms," *Daily Telegraph*, no. 25, 861 (22 April), p. 16.

"Letter to the Editor: The Academy and Modern Art. Is Burlington House too Advanced"?, *Daily Telegraph*, no. 25, 864 (25 April), p. 14.

"Mr. Augustus John Resigns from Academy," *Daily Telegraph*, no. 25, 865 (26 April), p. 18.

"Letter to the Editor: The Rejected Portrait. Policy of the Royal Academy. Art and Nature," *The Times*, no. 47, 983 (2 May), p. 17.

"Letter to the Editor: The Rejected Portrait," *The Times*, no. 47, 985 (4 May), p. 10.

"Letter to the Editor: The Rejected Portrait," *The Times*, no. 47, 988 (7 May), p. 8.

"After Nine Years: Augustus John," *The Listener* XIX, no. 489 (25 May), pp. 1105–07.

"When John Bull Laughs," *The Listener* XIX, no. 495 (7 July), pp. 38–39.

1939

"W. B. Yeats," *New Verse* I, no. 2 (May), pp. 45–46.

"The Nude is Dying Out," *Lilliput* IV, no. 5 (May), pp. 441–44.

"Britain's Most Advanced Painter Leads a Return to Naturalism, but – It is a New Naturalism," *The World of Art Illustrated* I, no. 8 (7 June), pp. 6–7.

"Traditional versus Modern Art. A Televised Discussion," *The Listener* XXI, no. 543 (8 June), pp. 1191–95, 1223.

"The Life of an Artist," *Lilliput* V, no. 1 (July), pp. 19–22.

1940

"Picasso," *The Kenyon Review* II, no. 2 (Spring), pp. 196–211.

"The End of Abstract Art," *The New Republic* CII, no. 14 (1 April), pp. 438–39.

"Letter to the Editor: Abstract Art Turns Over," *The New Republic* CII, no. 21 (20 May), p. 675.

"After Abstract Art," *The New Republic* CIII, no. 2 (8 July), pp. 51–52.

"End of Abstraction," *Art and Reason* VI, no. 68 (August), pp. 3–4.

1941

"How would you Expect the English to Behave?," *Saturday Night: The Canadian Weekly* LVII, no. 4 (4 October), pp. 18–19.

"Reasons why an Englishman is an Englishman," *Saturday Night: The Canadian Weekly* LVII, no. 10 (15 November), p. 34b.

1942

"That 'Now-or-Never' Spirit," *Saturday Night: The Canadian Weekly* LVII, no. 40 (13 June), p. 6.

"What Books for Total War?" *Saturday Night: The Canadian Weekly* LVII, no. 5 (10 October), p. 16.

1945

"The Cosmic Uniform of Peace," *The Sewanee Review* LIII, no. 4 (Autumn), pp. 507–31.

1946

"Canadian Nature and Its Painters," *The Listener* XXXVI, no. 920 (29 August), pp. 267–68.

"De Tocqueville and Democracy," *The Sewanee Review* LIV, no. 4 (Autumn), pp. 555–75.

"American Melting Pot," *Contact Books* II ("Britain East and West") (October), pp. 56–59.

"The Art of Gwen John," *The Listener* XXXVI, no. 926 (10 October), p. 484.

"Moore and Hepworth," *The Listener* XXXVI, no. 927 (17 October), pp. 505–06.

1947

"Round the Art Galleries," *The Listener* XXXVII, no. 944 (13 February), p. 283.

"Puritans of the Steppes," *The Listener* XXXVII, no. 949 (3 April), pp. 508–09.

"Letter to the Editor: Satire in the Twenties," *Times Literary Supplement* XLVI, no. 2383 (4 October), p. 507.

"Round the Art Exhibitions," *The Listener* XXXVIII, no. 978 (23 October), p. 736.

1948

"The Brotherhood," *The Listener* XXXIX, no. 1004 (22 April), p. 672.

"The Pre-Raphaelite Brotherhood," *The Listener* XXXIX, no. 1006 (6 May), p. 743.

"Augustus John and the Royal Academy," *The Listener* XXXIX, no. 1007 (13 May), p. 794.

"Round the Art Galleries," *The Listener* XXXIX, no. 1011 (10 June), p. 944.

"Round the London Art Galleries," *The Listener* XXXIX, no. 1012 (17 June), p. 980.

"Letter to the Editor: Standards of Art Criticism," *The Listener* XXXIX, no. 1013 (24 June), p. 1009.

"Letter to the Editor: Standards in Art Criticism," *The Listener* XL, no. 1014 (1 July), p. 22.

"Letter to the Editor: Standards in Art Criticism," *The Listener* XL, no. 1015 (8 July), pp. 61–63.

"Letter to the Editor: Standards in Art Criticism," *The Listener* XL, no. 1016 (15 July), pp. 99–100.

"Letter to the Editor: Standards in Art Criticism," *The Listener* XL, no. 1017 (22 July), p. 133.

"Letter to the Editor: Mr. Russell and the Vortex," *Times Literary Supplement* XLVII, no. 2430 (28 August), p. 485.

"Round the London Art Exhibitions," *The Listener* XL, no. 1029 (14 October), p. 572.

"Letter to the Editor: America and Cosmic Man," *Times Literary Supplement* XLVII, no. 2437 (16 October), p. 583.

"End of Abstraction," *Art and Reason* XIV, no. 166 (October), pp. 11–12.

"The Rot: a Narrative," *Wales* VIII, no. 30 (November), pp. 574–89.

"De Tocqueville's *Democracy in America*," *The Mint*, no. 2 (Autumn), pp. 121–37.

1949

"The Chantrey Collection at the Academy," *The Listener* XLI, no. 1042 (13 January), p. 65.

"Round the London Galleries," *The Listener* XLI, no. 1050 (10 March), p. 408.

"Painting in America," *The Listener* XLI, no. 1054 (7 April), p. 584.

"Round the London Art Galleries," *The Listener* XLI, no. 1059 (12 May), pp. 811–12.

"The Case Against Roots," *Saturday Review of Literature* XXXII, no. 21 (21 May), pp. 7–8, 32–33.

"White Fire," *Time* (Atlantic Overseas Edition) LIII, no. 22 (30 May), p. 32.

"The London Art Galleries," *The Listener* XLI, no. 1063 (9 June), p. 988.

"Edward Wadsworth: 1889–1949," *The Listener* XLI, no. 1066 (30 June), p. 1107.

"The London Galleries," *The Listener* XLII, no. 1068 (14 July), p. 68.

"Letter to the Editor: Wyndham Lewis Comments," *Saturday Review of Literature* XXXII, no. 31 (30 July), p. 24.

"Bread and Ballyhoo," *The Listener* XLII, no. 1076 (8 September), p. 407.

"The Rot," *The Sewanee Review* LVII, no. 4 (October), pp. 541–49.

"Round the Art Galleries," *The Listener* XLII, no. 1082 (20 October), p. 686.

"Round the London Art Galleries," *The Listener* XLII, no. 1086 (17 November), p. 860.

"Ezra: the Portrait of a Personality," *Quarterly Review of Literature* V, no. 2 (December), pp. 136–44.

"Round the London Art Galleries," *The Listener* XLII, no. 1088 (1 December), p. 959.

1950

"Round the London Art Galleries," *The Listener* XLIII, no. 1095 (19 January), p. 116.

"Round the London Art Galleries," *The Listener* XLIII, no. 1099 (16 February), p. 298.

□Fernand Léger at the Tate Gallery□, *The Listener* XLIII, no. 1101 (2 March), p. 396.

"Round the London Art Galleries," *The Listener* XLIII, no. 1104 (23 March), p. 522.

"Contemporary Art at the Tate," *The Listener* XLIII, no. 1106 (6 April), pp. 610–11.

"Round the London Art Galleries," *The Listener* XLIII, no. 1108 (20 April), p. 685.

"Royal Academy," *Contact* I, no. 1 (May–June), pp. 22–25.

"Round the London Art Galleries," *The Listener* XLIII, no. 1112 (18 May), pp. 878–79.

"Round the London Art Galleries," *The Listener* XLIII, no. 1120 (13 July), p. 62.

"A Note on Michael Ayrton," *Nine* II, no. 3 (August), pp. 184–185.

"Round the London Art Galleries," *The Listener* XLIV, no. 1129 (21 September), p. 388.

"Round the London Art Galleries," *The Listener* XLIV, no. 1132 (9 November), p. 508.

"Letter to the Editor: Henry Moore's 'Head of a Child'," *The Listener* XLIV, no. 1135 (30 November), p. 647.

"Round the London Art Galleries," *The Listener* XLIV, no. 1135 (30 November), p. 650.

"A Negro Artist," *The Listener* XLIV, no. 1136 (7 December), p. 696.

"Letter to the Editor: Nature and Art," *The Listener* XLIV, no. 1137 (14 December), p. 745.

"Nature and Art," *The Listener* XLIV, no. 1139 (28 December), p. 839.

1951

"Letter to the Editor: Nature and Art," *The Listener* XLV, no. 1140 (4 January), p. 22.

"Letter to the Editor: Nature and Art," *The Listener* XLV, no. 1141 (11 January), p. 63.

"Letter to the Editor: Nature and Art," *The Listener* XLV, no. 1142 (18 January), p. 106.

"Round the London Art Galleries," *The Listener* XLV, no. 1142 (18 January), p. 110.

"Nature and Art," *The Listener* XLV, no. 1143 (25 January), p. 145.

"The Rock Drill," *The New Statesman and Nation* XLI, no. 1048 (7 April), p. 398.

"The Sea-Mists of the Winter," *The Listener* XLV, no. 1158 (10 May), p. 765.

1952

"Augustus John Looks Back," *The Listener* XLVII, no. 1203 (20 March), pp. 476–79.

"Rot," *The American Mercury* LXXIV, no. 340 (April), pp. 91–106.

1953

"The Rebellious Patient," *Shenandoah* IV, no. 2/3 (Summer–Autumn) ("Wyndham Lewis Number"), pp. 3–16.

1954

□Doppelgänger: A Story□, *Encounter* II, no. 1 (January), pp. 23–33.

"Matthew Arnold," *Times Literary Supplement* LIII, no. 2740 (6 August), p. xxii.

"Meredith as a Novelist," *Time and Tide* XXXV, no. 39 (25 September), pp. 1269–70.

1955

"Monstre Gai," *The Hudson Review* VII, no. 4 (Winter), pp. 502–21.

"Monstre Gai," *The Hudson Review* VIII, no. 1 (Spring), pp. 28–56.

"A Very Sinister Old Lady," *Shenandoah* VII, no. 1 (Autumn), pp. 3–14.

1956

"Pish-Tush," *Encounter* VI, no. 2 (February), pp. 40–50.

"With Glinting Irony… With Gay Savagery… and a Slogging Pencil. The Blind Outsider Battles on at 71," *Daily Mail* (6 September), p. 4.

"The Vorticists," *Vogue* CXII, no. 9 (September), pp. 216, 221.

"Perspectives on Lawrence," *The Hudson Review* VIII, no. 4 (Winter), pp. 596–608.

1957

"A Note on Michael Ayrton," *Spectrum* V, no. 2 (Spring–Summer), pp. 15–18

2.3. Other contributions

2.3.1. To books

"Preface," in *Mayvale*. H.E. Clifton and James Wood. Cambridge: Express Printing Works, 1915.

"Preface," in *Madness in Shakespearian Tragedy*. H. Somerville. London: The Richard Press, 1929.

Text, in *Beginnings*. Various authors. London/Edinburgh/Paris/Toronto/New York: Thomas Nelson & Sons, 1935.

Chapter V, in *Freedom*. Various authors. London: George Allen and Unwin, 1936.

"The Zoo," in *London Guide*. Ed. William Kimber. London: Hutchinson & Co., 1938.

"American Melting Pot," in *Britain between West and East*. Various authors. London: Cole and Co., 1946.

"Towards an Earth Culture or the Eclectic Culture of the Transition," in *The Pavilion*. Ed. Myfanwy Evans. London: Gerald Duckworth, 1946.

□De Tocqueville's *Democracy in America*," in *The Mint*, no. 2. Ed. Geoffrey Grigson. London: Routledge and Kegan Paul, 1948.

"Early London Environment," in *T.S. Eliot a Symposium*. Various authors. London: Editions Poetry London, 1948.

"Ezra Pound," in *Ezra Pound a Collection of Essays*. Peter Russell. London; New York: Peter Nevill Ltd, 1950.

"If so the Man you Are" and "One-Way Song," in *The Penguin Book of Contemporary Verse*. Various authors. London: Penguin Books, Harmondsworth, 1950.

Prologue, in *Golden Sections*. Michael Ayrton. London: Methuen & Co. Ltd, 1957.

"On Canada" and □Nature's Place in Canadian Culture□, in *Wyndham Lewis in Canada*. Ed. George Woodcock. Vancouver: University of British Columbia, 1970.

2.3.2. To catalogues

"Room III (The Cubist Room)," in *English Post-Impressionists, Cubists and Others* [exh. cat. Public Art Galleries, Brighton]. 1913.

"Preface," in *Exhibition, Leeds* [exh. cat. Leeds]. 1914.

"Note for Catalogue," in *Vorticist Exhibition* [exh. cat. Doré Galleries, London]. Harlesden: Leveridge and Co., 1915.

"Foreword," in *Guns by Wyndham Lewis* [exh. cat. Goupil Gallery, London]. London: Goupil Gallery, 1919.

"Foreword," in *Group X* [exh. cat. Mansard Gallery, London]. London: Pelican Press, 1920.

"Foreword," in *Tyros and Portraits* [exh. cat. The Leicester Galleries, London]. London: Miles and Co. Ltd., 1921.

"Preface," in *Thirty Personalities by Wyndham Lewis* [exh. cat. The Lefevre Galleries, London]. London: The Lefevre Galleries, 1932.

"Foreword," in *Paintings and Drawings by Wyndham Lewis* [exh. cat. The Leicester Galleries, London]. London: J. Miles and Co. Ltd, 1937.

"Introduction," in *Michael Ayrton & Toulouse-Lautrec* [exh. cat. Redfern Gallery, London]. London: The Beauchamp Press, 1949.

"Introduction," in *Wyndham Lewis*, [exh. cat. Redfern Gallery, London]. London: The Beauchamp Press, 1949.

"Two Notes on the Paintings," in *Michael Ayrton, Paintings Drawings Theatre Design* [exh. cat. Wakefield City Art Gallery]. Wakefield: John Fletcher, 1949.

"Introduction," in *Wyndham Lewis and Vorticism* [exh. cat. Tate Gallery, London]. London: Tate Gallery, 1956.

"Introduction," in *Wyndham Lewis and Vorticism* [travelling exh. cat.]. London: The Arts Council, 1956.

2.4. Anthologies

EDWARDS, Paul, ed. *Creatures of Habit and Creatures of Change: Essays on Art, Literature and Society, 1914–1956*. Santa Rosa: Black Sparrow Press, 1989.

FOX, C.J., ed. *Enemy Salvoes: Selected Literary Criticism by Wyndham Lewis*. London: Vision, 1976.

FOX, C.J., ed. *Journey into Barbary: Morocco Writings and Drawings*. Santa Barbara: Black Sparrow Press, 1983.

FOX, C.J. and Robert T. CHAPMAN, eds. *Unlucky for Pringle: Unpublished and Other Stories*. London: Vision, 1973.

MICHEL, Walter and C.J. FOX, eds. *Wyndham Lewis on Art: Collected Writings 1913–1956*. London: Thames and Hudson; New York: Funk & Wagnalls, 1969.

MUNTON, Alan, *Wyndham Lewis: The Relation between the Theory and the Fiction, from his Earliest Writings to 1941*. PhD dissertation, Faculty of English, University of Cambridge, 1976. Available at: Wyndham Lewis Memorial Trust Archives.

MUNTON, Alan, ed. *Collected Poems and Plays*. Manchester: Carcanet, 1979, 2003.

MUNTON, Alan, coord. *Wyndham Lewis's Art Criticism in The Listener, 1946–1951*. Logroño: Universidad de la Rioja, 2009. Available at: www.unirioja.es/listenerartcriticism

ROSENTHAL, Raymond, ed. *A Soldier of Humor and Selected Writings*. New York; Toronto: The New American Library, 1966.

SYMONS, Julian, *The Essential Wyndham Lewis*. London: André Deutsch, 1989.

TOMLIN, E.W.F., ed. *Wyndham Lewis: An Anthology of his Prose*. London: Methuen & Co. Ltd, 1969.

2.5. Epistolary

CASSIDY, Victor, ed., "The Sturge Moore Letters: Wyndham Lewis: Letters to Thomas Sturge Moore," *Lewisletter*, no.7 (October 1977), pp. 8–23.

CASSIDY, Victor, ed., "Letters of Wyndham Lewis to Sidney and Violet Schiff," *Enemy News*, no.21 (Summer 1985), pp. 9–31.

DANIELS, Mary F., comp. *Wyndham Lewis: A Descriptive Catalogue of the Manuscript Material in the Department of Rare Books Cornell University Library*. Ithaca, NY: Cornell University Library, 1972.

LONDRAVILLE, Richard and Jane, eds., "Two Men at War with Time: The Unpublished Correspondence of Wyndham Lewis and John Quinn [Part I]," *English* 39, no. 164 (Summer 1990), pp. 97–104; "Two Men at War with Time: The Unpublished Correspondence of Wyndham Lewis and John Quinn:

Concluded," *English* 39, no. 165 (Winter 1990), pp. 229–51.

MATERER, Timothy, ed. *Pound/ Lewis: The Letters of Ezra Pound and Wyndham Lewis.* London: Faber and Faber; New York: New Directions, 1985.

ROSE, William K., ed. *The Letters of Wyndham Lewis.* London: Methuen & Co. Ltd, 1963.

3. Wyndham Lewis: the Editor

1914

Blast: Review of the Great English Vortex. No. 1. London: John Lane, The Bodley Head; New York: John Lane Co.; Toronto: Bell & Cockburn, June 1914; Santa Rosa: Black Sparrow Press, 1981 (facs. ed.); Berkeley: Gingko Press, 2009 (facs. ed.); *Blast. Revista del Gran Vórtice Inglés*. Trans. and notes Yolanda Morató. Madrid: Fundación Juan March: Editorial Arte y Ciencia, 2010 (semifacs. ed. in Spanish).

1915

Blast: Review of the Great English Vortex. No. 2. London: John Lane, The Bodley Head; New York: John Lane Co.; Toronto: Bell & Cockburn, July 1915; Santa Rosa: Black Sparrow Press, 2000 (facs. ed.).

1921

The Tyro: A Review of the Arts of Painting, Sculpture and Design. No. 1. London: The Egoist Press, April 1921; London: Cass, 1970 (facs. ed.).

1922

The Tyro: A Review of the Arts of Painting, Sculpture and Design. No.2. London: The Egoist Press, March 1922; London: Cass, 1970 (facs. ed.).

1927

The Enemy: A Review of Art and Literature. Vol. 1. London: The Arthur Press, January 1927; Ed. David Peters Corbett. Santa Rosa: Black Sparrow Press, 1994 (facs. ed.).

The Enemy: A Review of Art and Literature. No. 2. London: The Arthur Press, September 1927; Ed. David Peters Corbett. Santa Rosa: Black Sparrow Press, 1994 (facs. ed.).

1929

The Enemy: A Review of Art and Literature. No. 3. London: The Arthur Press, March 1929; Ed. David Peters Corbett. Santa Rosa: Black Sparrow Press, 1994 (facs. ed.).

1930

Enemy Pamphlet No. 1: Satire & Fiction. London: The Arthur Press, 1930.

4. Secondary Bibliography

4.1. Monographs and articles

AYERS, David. *Wyndham Lewis and Western Man.* Basingstoke: Macmillan, 1992.

BRIDSON, Douglas Geoffrey. *The Filibuster: A Study of the Political Ideas of Wyndham Lewis*. London: Cassell, 1972.

BROWN, Denis. *Intertextual Dynamics within the Literary Group: Joyce, Lewis, Pound and Eliot: The Men of 1914.* Basingstoke: Macmillan, 1990.

CHAPMAN, Robert T. *Wyndham Lewis: Fiction and Satires*. London: Vision Press, 1973.

CIANCI, Giovanni, ed. *Wyndham Lewis: Letteratura/Pittura.* Palermo: Sellerio Editore, 1982.

COONEY, Seamus, ed. *Blast 3*. Santa Barbara: Black Sparrow Press, 1984.

CORBETT, David Peters, ed. *Wyndham Lewis and the Art of Modern War.* Cambridge: Cambridge University Press, 1998.

CORK, Richard. *Vorticism and Abstract Art in the First Machine Age*. London: G. Fraser, 1976.

CUNCHILLOS Jaime Carmelo, Claves para una revaluación necesaria: Percy Wyndham Lewis," in *Fifty Years of English Studies in Spain (1952–2002): A Commemorative Volume.* Santiago de Compostela: Servicio de Publicaciones, Universidad, 2003, pp. 21–30.

CUNCHILLOS Jaime Carmelo, ed. *Wyndham Lewis the Radical: Essays on Literature and Modernity.* Bern/New York: Peter Lang, 2007.

DASENBROCK, Reed Way. *The Literary Vorticism of Ezra Pound and Wyndham Lewis: Towards the Condition of Painting*. Baltimore: Johns Hopkins University Press, 1985.

DÍAZ LAGE, José María. *The Construction of Modernism: Discourse, Aesthetics, History.* PhD dissertation, Universidad de Santiago Compostela, 2003.

EDWARDS, Paul. *Wyndham Lewis: Art and War.* London: Lund Humphries, 1992.

EDWARDS, Paul, ed. *Volcanic Heaven. Essays on Wyndham Lewis's Painting and Writing*. Santa Rosa: Black Sparrow Press, 1996.

EDWARDS, Paul, ed. *BLAST. Vorticism 1914–1918.* Aldershot: Ashgate Publishing, 2000 (English adaptation of the exh. cat. *BLAST: Vortizismus- Die erste Avantgarde in England 1914–1918*, Sprengel Museum, Hannover; Haus der Kunst, Munich, 1996–97).

EDWARDS, Paul, "Wyndham Lewis's Narrative of Origins: 'The Death of the Ankou'," *The Modern Language Review* 92, no. 1 (January 1997), pp. 22–35.

EDWARDS, Paul. *Wyndham Lewis: Painter and Writer*. New Haven/ London: Yale University Press, 2000.

FEIJÓ, Antonio M. *Near Miss: A Study of Wyndham Lewis (1909–1930)*. New York: Peter Lang, 1998.

FOSHAY, Toby Avard. *Wyndham Lewis and the Avant-Garde: The Politics of the Intellect.* Montreal: McGill-Queen's University Press, 1992.

GASIOREK, Andrzej. *Wyndham Lewis and Modernism*. Tavistock: Northcote House/British Council, 2004.

GASIOREK, Andrzej, "The 'Little Magazine' as Weapon: BLAST (1914–15)," in *The Oxford Critical and Cultural History of Modernist Magazines*, vol. 1. Eds. Peter Brooker and Andrew Thacker. Oxford: Oxford University Press, 2009, pp. 290–313.

GAWSWORTH, John (Terence Ian Fytton Armstrong). *Apes, Japes and Hitlerism*. London: Unicorn Press, 1932.

GRIGSON, Geoffrey. *A Master of our Time: A Study of Wyndham Lewis*. New York: Gordon Press, 1972.

HANDLEY-READ, Charles, ed. *The Art of Wyndham Lewis*. London: Faber and Faber Ltd, 1951.

HEAD, Philip. *Some Enemy Fight-Talk: Aspects of Wyndham Lewis on Art and Society.* Borough Green: Green Knight Editions, 1999.

HEAD, Philip. *The Gentle Art of Contradiction in the Work of Wyndham Lewis.* Borough Green: Green Knight Editions, 2001.

HICKMAN, Miranda B. *The Geometry of Modernism: The Vorticist Idiom in Lewis, Pound, H.D., and Yeats.* Austin: University of Texas Press, 2005.

HUMPHREYS, Richard. *Wyndham Lewis.* London: Tate Publishing, 2004.

IGLESIA, Fco. Javier de la, "Wyndham Lewis: reventador y bombardero," *Calle Mayor*, no. 6 (Spring 1987), pp. 33–54

JAMESON, Fredric. *Fables of Aggression: Wyndham Lewis, the Modernist as Fascist*. Berkeley/London: University California Press, 1979.

KADLEC, David, "Pound, Blast, and Syndicalism," *ELH* 60, no. 4 (Winter 1993), pp. 1015–31.

KENNER, Hugh. *Wyndham Lewis.* New York: New Directions, 1954.

KENNER, Hugh. *The Pound Era: The Age of Ezra Pound, T.S. Eliot, James Joyce and Wyndham Lewis.* London: Faber and Faber, 1972.

KLEIN, Scott W. *The Fictions of James Joyce and Wyndham Lewis: Monsters of Nature and Design*. Cambridge/New York: Cambridge University Press, 1994.

KUSH, Thomas. *Wyndham Lewis's Pictorial Integer*. Michigan: UMI Research Press, 1981.

MACEDO, Ana Gabriela, "Misogyny and the Carnivalesque in Wyndham Lewis's 'The Wild Body'," *Cuadernos de Filología Inglesa* 6, no. 1 (1997), pp. 79–94.

MARK, Daniel. *The Laughing Man.* London: Michael Joseph, 1984.

MATERER, Timothy. *Wyndham Lewis, the Novelist*. Detroit: Wayne State University Press, 1976.

MEYERS, Jeffrey. *The Enemy. A Biography of Wyndham Lewis*. Boston/ London/Melbourne: Routledge & Kegan Paul, 1980.

MEYERS, Jeffrey, ed. *Wyndham Lewis: A Revaluation: New Essays.* Montreal: McGill-Queen's University Press, 1980.

MICHEL, Walter. *Wyndham Lewis: Paintings and Drawings*. London: Thames and Hudson; Los Angeles: University of California Press, 1971.

MILLER, Tyrus. *Late Modernism: Politics, Fiction and the Arts between the World Wars*. Berkeley/ London: University of California Press, 1999.

MORATÓ, Yolanda, El Vorticismo. Una victoria pírrica, *ZUT* 1, no. 1 (Spring 2005), pp. 45–60.

MORATÓ, Yolanda, "Cuando tu enemigo es 'el Enemigo': Desencuentros literarios entre James Joyce y Wyndham Lewis," in *The Scallop of Saint James: An Old Pilgrim's Hoard. Reading Joyce from the Peripheries*. Eds. S. Domínguez, M. Estévez and A. MacCarthy. Weston, Florida: Netbiblo, 2006.

MORATÓ, Yolanda, *Tarr* y *Self-Condemned*: suicidio y autobiografía in las novelas de Wyndham Lewis, in "El suicidio literario: Aproximaciones comparativistas." Eds. Jorge Casanova et al. *30th Proceedings of AEDEAN*. Huelva: Servicio de Publicaciones de la Universidad de Huelva, 2007.

MORATÓ, Yolanda, "*Timon of Athens*. Shakespeare's Impact on Wyndham Lewis," in *Ensayos sobre Shakespeare / Essays in Shakespeare*. Cáceres: Universidad de Extremadura / SEDERI, 2010.

MUNTON, Alan, "The Politics of Wyndham Lewis," *PN Review* 1 (March 1976), pp. 34–39.

MUNTON, Alan, "From Charlie Chaplin to Bill Haley: Popular Culture and Ideology in Wyndham Lewis," in *Wyndham Lewis the Radical: Essays on Literature and Modernity*. Ed. Cunchillos Jaime, Carmelo. Bern/ Oxford: Peter Lang, 2007, pp. 159–86.

MUNTON, Alan, "From Proudhon to Hitler (and back): the Strange Political Journey of Wyndham Lewis," in *Right/ Left/Right: Revolving Commitments: France and Britain 1929–1950*. Eds. Jennifer Birkett and Stan Smith. Newcastle: Cambridge Scholars Publishing, 2008, pp. 47–60. *EREA* 4, no. 2 (Autumn 2006). Available at: http://erea.revues.org/index220.html y www.e-rea.org

NATH, Jogendra. *Wyndham Lewis, a Friend to the Enemies*. Nueva Delhi: Vani Prakashan, 1983.

NEILSON Maxwell, Brett. *Wyndham Lewis as Crowd*. PhD dissertation, Yale University, 1994 (microform).

NORMAND, Tom. *Wyndham Lewis the Artist: Holding the Mirror up to Politics*. Cambridge: Cambridge University Press, 1992.O´KEEFFE, Paul. *Some Sort of Genius. A Life of Wyndham Lewis*. London: Jonathan Cape, 2000.

PEPPIS, Paul. *Literature, Politics and the English Avant-garde: Nation and Empire, 1901–1918*. Cambridge: Cambridge University Press, 2000.

PERRINO, Mark. *The Poetics of Mockery: Wyndham Lewis's "The Apes of God" and the Popularization of Modernism*. Leeds: W.H. Maney for the Modern Humanities Research Association, 1995.

PORTEUS, Hugh Gordon. *Wyndham Lewis: A Discursive Exposition*. London: D. Harmsworth, 1932.

POWER, Kevin, ed. "El Vorticismo," *Poesía. Revista Ilustrada de Información Poética*, no. 9 (Autumn 1980), pp. 19–56.

PRITCHARD, William H. *Wyndham Lewis*. New York: Twayne, 1968.

QUÉMA, Anne. *The Agon of Modernism: Wyndham Lewis's Allegories, Aesthetics, and Politics*. Lewisburg: Bucknell University Press; London: Associated University Presses, 1999.

REYNOLDS, Paige, "'Chaos Invading Concept': Blast as a Native Theory of Promotional Culture," *Twentieth Century Literature* 46, no. 2 (Summer 2000), pp. 1015–31.

SCHENKER, Daniel. *Wyndham Lewis: Religion and Modernism*. Tuscaloosa: University of Alabama Press, 1992.

SHERRY, Vincent B. *Ezra Pound, Wyndham Lewis, and Radical Modernism*. New York/Oxford: Oxford University Press, 1993.

STIRTON, Paul, "British Artists and the Spanish Civil War," in *The Discovery of Spain: British Artists and Collectors: Goya to Picasso*. Christopher Baker et al., eds. [exh. cat. National Galleries of Scotland, Edinburgh]. Edinburgh: National Galleries of Scotland, 2009, pp. 133–37.

TERRAZAS, Melania, "Social Implications in Percy Wyndham Lewis's 'The Vulgar Streak': A Resource Theory Approach," *The Grove. Working Papers on English Studies*, no. 9 (2002), pp. 207–18.

TERRAZAS, Melania. *Intercambio de recursos en la ficción de Percy Wyndham Lewis = A Resource Theory for Approaching Interpersonal Relationships in Percy Wyndham Lewis*. Logroño: Universidad de La Rioja, Departamento de Filologías Modernas, 2002.

TERRAZAS, Melania. *Relational Structures in Wyndham Lewis's Fiction: Complexity and Value*. Munich: Lincom Europa, 2005.

TICKNER, Lisa. *Modern Life and Modern Subjects: British Art in the Early Twentieth Century*. New Haven: Yale University Press, 2000.

TOMLIN, Eric Walter Frederick. *Wyndham Lewis*. London: Longmans, Green for the British Council and the National Book League, 1955.

TUMA, Keith, "Wyndham Lewis, Blast, and Popular Culture," *ELH* 54, no. 2 (Summer 1987), pp. 403–19.

VILLAR FLOR, Carlos, "Wyndham Lewis, o el arte de hacer enemigos," *Fábula: Revista Literaria*, no. 24 (2008), pp. 54–60.

WAGNER, Geoffrey. *Wyndham Lewis: A Portrait of the Artist as the Enemy*. New Haven: Yale University Press, 1957.

WEES, W.C. *Vorticism and the English Avant-garde*. Manchester: Manchester University Press, 1957.

WRAGG, David A. *Wyndham Lewis and the Philosophy of Art in Early Modernist Britain: Creating a Political Aesthetic*. Lewiston, New York: Edwin Mellen Press, 2005.

YVARS J.F, "Wyndham Lewis: un artista incómodo [1995]", in *Modos de persuasión. Notas de crítica*. Barcelona: Random House Mondador, 2005.

4.2. Wyndham Lewis Society publications

Imaginary Letters. Ed. Alan Munton. Glasgow: Wyndham Lewis Society, 1977.

The Code of a Herdsman. Ed. Alan Munton. Glasgow: Wyndham Lewis Society, 1977.

HEAD, Philip. *Vorticist Antecedents*. Ware, Herts: Wyndham Lewis Society, 1997.

Enemy News: Newsletter of the Wyndham Lewis Society, 1978–1993 (continued by *Wyndham Lewis Annual*).

Wyndham Lewis Annual. Ed. Paul Edwards, 1994–99; Ed. Alan Munton. Plymouth: University of Plymouth, 2000–.

Lewisletter: Newsletter of the Wyndham Lewis Society. Ed. Robin Healey. Great Chishill, Royston, 1994–.

4.3. Other materials

"Wyndham Lewis: End of Enemy Interlude (1940)," in *Futurism & Dada Reviewed 1912–1959* [CD-Audio]. Ed. James Nice. LMT Publishing, 2000.

Wyndham Lewis. The Enemy Speaks [CD-Audio]. Ed. James Nice. LMT Recordings, 2007.

BBC Broadcasts and Recordings (preserved in the BBC Sound Archives Library):

Broadcasts in Wyndham Lewis's voice:

"Writers of today: Mr Wyndham Lewis. Reading from his own work," 21 January 1928.

"Freedom," 30 April 1935.

"Art and Literature," 21 June 1935.

"When John Bull Laughs," 29 June 1938.

"Liberty and the Individual," 3 January 1947.

"A Crisis of Thought," 16 March 1947.

Composite broadcasts, in which Wyndham Lewis took part:

"Modern Art," 23 May 1939.

"The Visual Arts," 31 October 1946.

Broadcasts that included the recorded voice of Wyndham Lewis:

"Cafe Royal. A Study in Conversation and Reminiscence," 28 December 1955.

"Satiric Verse," 9 July 1957.

Dramatisations of his novels, in which Wyndham Lewis collaborated:

"The Childermass," 18 June 1951.

"The Human Age, Book One," 24 May 1955.

"The Human Age, Book Two," 26 May 1955.

"The Human Age, Book Three," 28 May 1955.

"Tarr," 18 July 1956.

Dramatisations of his novels, in which Wyndham Lewis did not collaborate:

"The Revenge for Love," 23 June 1957.

This catalogue, and its Spanish edition, are published
by the occasion of the exhibition

WYNDHAM LEWIS (1882–1957)

Fundación Juan March
Madrid

5 February – 16 May 2010

EXHIBITION

Concept
Paul Edwards (Guest Curator),
and Richard Humphreys
Department of Exhibitions, Fundación Juan March, Madrid
Manuel Fontán del Junco (Director of Exhibitions)
María Zozaya (Exhibitions Coordinator)

Organisation
Department of Exhibitions, Fundación Juan March, Madrid

CATALOGUE

COPY EDITOR
Linda Schofield

EDITORIAL COORDINATION
Jordi Sanguino and María Zozaya, Department of Exhibitions, Fundación Juan March, Madrid
Images Coordinator: Laure Cavalié

TRANSLATIONS
Spanish- English:
© Vanesa Rodríguez Galindo (Biography)
© Deborah Roldán (Foreword and essay by Manuel Fontán del Junco)
© Laura Suffield (essays by Yolanda Morató and Juan Bonilla)

DESIGN
Guillermo Nagore

Created in 1955 by the Majorcan financier Juan March Ordinas, the **Fundación Juan March** is an active family and cultural institution dedicated to the humanities and science. It organizes exhibitions, concerts, lecture series and seminars, and the Fundación's headquarters in Madrid has a library specializing in music and theater. The Fundación also administers the Museo de Arte Abstracto Español in Cuenca, and Museu Fundación Juan March in Palma. In addition, through the Instituto Juan March de Estudios e Investigaciones, it promotes specialized research and cooperation between Spanish and international scientists.

ILLUSTRATIONS

Typography: HTF Knockout, Akzidenz Grotesk, Times New Roman
Paper: Gardapat Kiara, 115 gr.; Cyclus offset, 115 gr.

Printing: Estudios Gráficos Europeos S.A., Madrid
Binding: Ramos S.A., Madrid

Spanish edition (hard cover):
ISBN: 978-847075-575-0 Fundación Juan March, Madrid
ISBN: 978-847075-575-0 Editorial de Arte y Ciencia S.A., Madrid
Spanish edition (soft cover):
ISBN: 978-847075-576-7 Fundación Juan March, Madrid
ISBN: 978-847075-576-7 Editorial de Arte y Ciencia S.A., Madrid
English edition (hard cover):
ISBN: 978-847075-577-4 Fundación Juan March, Madrid
ISBN: 978-847075-577-4 Editorial de Arte y Ciencia S.A., Madrid

Depósito legal:
Spanish edition (hard cover): M-4152-2010
Spanish edition (soft cover): M-4150-2010
English edition (hard cover): M-4151-2010

Inside cover/Inside back cover: Alvin Langdon Coburn, 8 photographs of Wyndham Lewis, 1916. Courtesy of The George Eastman House, International Museum of Photography and Film, Rochester, NY (Cat. 211, a-h)
Back cover: C. G. Beresford, *Wyndham Lewis as a Bohemian*, 1913. National Portrait Gallery, London (Cat. 209)

FUNDACIÓN JUAN MARCH

Castelló, 77
E-28006 Madrid
Teléfono: +34 (91) 435 42 40
Fax: +34 (91) 431 42 27
www.march.es

ALBA GRUPO MARCH
BANCA MARCH
IBERIA

EXHIBITIONS CATALOGUES AND OTHER PUBLICATIONS BY THE FUNDACIÓN JUAN MARCH

KEY: Out of print | Available publications in February 2010 | Ⓟ Exhibition at the Museu Fundación Juan March, Palma | Ⓒ Exhibition at the Museo

1966

CATÁLOGO MUSEO DE ARTE ABSTRACTO ESPAÑOL. CUENCA
[Guide to the Museo de Arte Abstracto Español]
Text by Fernando Zóbel
Bilingual ed. (Spanish/English)
Published by the Museo de Arte Abstracto Español, Cuenca, 1966

1969

MUSEO DE ARTE ABSTRACTO ESPAÑOL. CUENCA
[Guide to the Museo de Arte Abstracto Español]
Texts by Gustavo Torner, Gerardo Rueda and Fernando Zóbel
Published by the Museo de Arte Abstracto Español, Cuenca, 1969

1973

ARTE'73
Multilingual ed. (Spanish, English, French, Italian and German)

1974

MUSEO DE ARTE ABSTRACTO ESPAÑOL. CUENCA
[Guide to the Museo de Arte Abstracto Español]
Essays by Gustavo Torner, Gerardo Rueda and Fernando Zóbel
Bilingual ed. (Spanish/English)
Published by the Museo de Arte Abstracto Español, Cuenca, 1974 (2nd ed., rev. and exp.)

1975

OSKAR KOKOSCHKA. Óleos y acuarelas. Dibujos, grabados, mosaicos. Obra literaria
Texts by Heinz Spielmann

EXPOSICIÓN ANTOLÓGICA DE LA CALCOGRAFÍA NACIONAL
Texts by Enrique Lafuente Ferrari and Antonio Gallego

I EXPOSICIÓN DE BECARIOS DE ARTES PLÁSTICAS

1976

JEAN DUBUFFET
Texts by Jean Dubuffet

ALBERTO GIACOMETTI. Colección de la Fundación Maeght
Texts by Jean Genêt, Jean-Paul Sartre, Jacques Dupin and Alberto Giacometti

II EXPOSICIÓN DE BECARIOS DE ARTES PLÁSTICAS

1977

ARTE USA
Texts by Harold Rosenberg

ARTE DE NUEVA GUINEA Y PAPÚA. Colección A. Folch y E. Serra
Texts by B. A. L. Cranstone and Christian Kaufmann

PICASSO
Texts by Rafael Alberti, Gerardo Diego, Vicente Aleixandre, Eugenio d'Ors, Juan Antonio Gaya Nuño, Ricardo Gullón, José Camón Aznar, Guillermo de Torre and Enrique Lafuente Ferrari

MARC CHAGALL. 18 pinturas y 40 grabados
Texts by André Malraux and Louis Aragon (in French)
P

ARTE ESPAÑOL CONTEMPORÁNEO. COLECCIÓN DE LA FUNDACIÓN JUAN MARCH
[This catalogue accompanied the exhibition of the same name that traveled to 67 Spanish venues between 1975 and 1996; at many venues, independent catalogues were published.]

III EXPOSICIÓN DE BECARIOS DE ARTES PLÁSTICAS

1978

ARS MEDICA
Text by Carl Zigrosser

FRANCIS BACON
Text by Antonio Bonet Correa

BAUHAUS
Texts by Hans M. Wingler, Will Grohmann, Jürgen Joedicke, Nikolaus Pevsner, Hans Eckstein, Oskar Schlemmer, László Moholy-Nagy, Otto Stelzer and Heinz Winfried Sabais
Published by the Institut für Auslandsbeziehungen, Stuttgart, 1976

KANDINSKY: 1923-1944
Texts by Werner Haftmann, Gaëtan Picon and Wasili Kandinsky

ARTE ESPAÑOL CONTEMPORÁNEO. COLECCIÓN DE LA FUNDACIÓN JUAN MARCH

IV EXPOSICIÓN DE BECARIOS DE ARTES PLÁSTICAS

1979

WILLEM DE KOONING. Obras recientes
Texts by Diane Waldman

MAESTROS DEL SIGLO XX. NATURALEZA MUERTA
Texts by Reinhold Hohl

GEORGES BRAQUE. Óleos, gouaches, relieves, dibujos y grabados
Texts by Jean Paulhan, Jacques Prévert, Christian Zervos, Georges Salles, André Chastel, Pierre Reverdy and Georges Braque

V EXPOSICIÓN DE BECARIOS DE ARTES PLÁSTICAS

GOYA. CAPRICHOS, DESASTRES, TAUROMAQUIA, DISPARATES
Texts by Alfonso E. Pérez-Sánchez

1980

JULIO GONZÁLEZ. Esculturas y dibujos
Text by Germain Viatte

ROBERT MOTHERWELL
Text by Barbaralee Diamonstein and Robert Motherwell

HENRI MATISSE. Óleos, dibujos, gouaches, découpées, esculturas y libros
Texts by Henri Matisse

VI EXPOSICIÓN DE BECARIOS DE ARTES PLÁSTICAS

1981

MINIMAL ART
Text by Phyllis Tuchman

PAUL KLEE. Óleos, acuarelas, dibujos y grabados
Texts by Paul Klee

MIRRORS AND WINDOWS. AMERICAN PHOTOGRAPHY SINCE 1960
Text by John Szarkowski
English ed. (Offprint: Spanish translation of text by John Szarkowski)
Published by The Museum of Modern Art, New York, 1980

MEDIO SIGLO DE ESCULTURA: 1900-1945
Texts by Jean-Louis Prat

MUSEO DE ARTE ABSTRACTO ESPAÑOL. CUENCA
[Guide to the Museo de Arte Abstracto Español]
Texts by Gustavo Torner, Gerardo Rueda and Fernando Zóbel

1982

PIET MONDRIAN. Óleos, acuarelas y dibujos
Texts by Herbert Henkels and Piet Mondrian

ROBERT Y SONIA DELAUNAY
Texts by Juan Manuel Bonet, Jacques Damase, Ramón Gómez de la Serna, Isaac del Vando Villar, Vicente Huidobro and Guillermo de Torre

PINTURA ABSTRACTA ESPAÑOLA: 1960-1970
Text by Rafael Santos Torroella

KURT SCHWITTERS
Texts by Werner Schmalenbach, Ernst Schwitters and Kurt Schwitters

VII EXPOSICIÓN DE BECARIOS DE ARTES PLÁSTICAS

1983

ROY LICHTENSTEIN: 1970-1980
Texts by Jack Cowart
English ed.
Published by Hudson Hill Press, New York, 1981

FERNAND LÉGER
Text by Antonio Bonet Correa and Fernand Léger

PIERRE BONNARD
Texts by Ángel González García

ALMADA NEGREIROS
Texts by Margarida Acciaiuoli, Antonio Espina, Ramón Gómez de la Serna, José Augusto França, Jorge de Sena, Lima de Freitas and Almada Negreiros
Published by the Ministério de Cultura de Portugal, Lisboa, 1983

ARTE ABSTRACTO ESPAÑOL EN LA COLECCIÓN DE LA FUNDACIÓN JUAN MARCH
[Guide to the Museo de Arte Abstracto Español]
Texts by Julián Gállego

GRABADO ABSTRACTO ESPAÑOL. COLECCIÓN DE LA FUNDACIÓN JUAN MARCH
Texts by Julián Gállego
[This catalogue accompanied the exhibition of the same name that traveled to 44 Spanish venues between 1983 and 1999.]

1984

EL ARTE DEL SIGLO XX EN UN MUSEO HOLANDÉS: EINDHOVEN
Texts by Jaap Bremer, Jan Debbaut, R. H. Fuchs, Piet de Jonge and Margriet Suren

JOSEPH CORNELL
Texts by Fernando Huici

FERNANDO ZÓBEL
Text by Francisco Calvo Serraller
Madrid, Cuenca

JULIA MARGARET CAMERON: 1815-1879
Texts by Mike Weaver and Julia Margaret Cameron
English ed. (Offprint: Spanish translation of text by Mike Weaver)
Published by John Hansard Gallery & The Herbert Press Ltd., Southampton, 1984

JULIUS BISSIER
Text by Werner Schmalenbach

1985

ROBERT RAUSCHENBERG
Texts by Lawrence Alloway

VANGUARDIA RUSA: 1910-1930. Museo y Colección Ludwig
Texts by Evelyn Weiss

DER DEUTSCHE HOLZSCHNITT IM 20
Texts by Gunther Thiem
German ed. (Offprint: Spanish translations of texts)
Published by the Institut für Auslandsbeziehungen, Stuttgart, 1984

ESTRUCTURAS REPETITIVAS
Texts by Simón Marchán Fiz

1986

MAX ERNST
Texts by Werner Spies and Max Ernst

ARTE, PAISAJE Y ARQUITECTURA. El arte referido a la arquitectura en la República Federal de Alemania
Texts by Dieter Honisch and Manfred Sack
German ed. (Offprint: Spanish translation of introductory texts)
Published by the Institut für Auslandsbeziehungen, Stuttgart, 1983

ARTE ESPAÑOL EN NUEVA YORK: 1950-1970. Colección Amos Cahan
Text by Juan Manuel Bonet

OBRAS MAESTRAS DEL MUSEO DE WUPPERTAL. De Marées a Picasso
Texts by Sabine Fehleman and Hans Günter Wachtmann

1987

BEN NICHOLSON
Texts by Jeremy Lewison and Ben Nicholson

IRVING PENN
Text by John Szarkowski
English ed. Published by The Museum of Modern Art, New York, 1984 (reimp. 1986)

MARK ROTHKO
Texts by Michael Compton and Mark Rothko

1988

EL PASO DESPUÉS DE EL PASO EN LA COLECCIÓN DE LA FUNDACIÓN JUAN MARCH
Text by Juan Manuel Bonet

ZERO, A EUROPEAN MOVEMENT. The Lenz Schönberg Collection
Texts by Dieter Honisch and Hannah Weitemeier
Bilingual ed. (Spanish/English)

COLECCIÓN LEO CASTELLI
Texts by Calvin Tomkins, Judith Goldman, Gabriele Henkel, Leo Castelli, Jim Palette, Barbara Rose and John Cage

1989

RENÉ MAGRITTE
Texts by Camille Goemans, Martine Jacquet, Catherine de Croës, François Daulte, Paul Lebeer and René Magritte

EDWARD HOPPER
Text by Gail Levin

ARTE ESPAÑOL CONTEMPORÁNEO. FONDOS DE LA FUNDACIÓN JUAN MARCH
Texts by Miguel Fernández-Cid

1990

ODILON REDON. Colección Ian Woodner
Texts by Lawrence Gowing, Odilon Redon and Nuria Rivero

CUBISMO EN PRAGA. Obras de la Galería Nacional
Texts by JiÐí Kotalík, Ivan Neumann and JiÐíi Šetlik

ANDY WARHOL. COCHES
Texts by Werner Spies, Cristoph Becker and Andy Warhol

COL·LECCIÓ MARCH. ART ESPANYOL CONTEMPORANI. PALMA
[Guide to the Museu d'Art Espanyol Contemporani]
Texts by Juan Manuel Bonet
Multilingual ed. (Spanish, Catalan, English and German)

1991

PICASSO. RETRATOS DE JACQUELINE
Texts by Hélène Parmelin, María Teresa Ocaña, Nuria Rivero, Werner Spies and Rosa Vives

VIEIRA DA SILVA
Texts by Fernando Pernes, Julián Gállego, Mª João Fernandes, René Char (in French), António Ramos Rosa (in Portuguese) and Joham de Castro

MONET EN GIVERNY. Colección del Museo Marmottan de París
Texts by Arnaud d'Hauterives, Gustave Geffroy and Claude Monet

MUSEO DE ARTE ABSTRACTO ESPAÑOL. CUENCA
[Guide to the Museo de Arte Abstracto Español]
Texts by Juan Manuel Bonet
(2nd ed., 1st ed. 1988)

1992

RICHARD DIEBENKORN
Text by John Elderfield

ALEXEJ VON JAWLENSKY
Text by Angelica Jawlensky

DAVID HOCKNEY
Text by Marco Livingstone

1993

MALEVICH. Colección del Museo Estatal Ruso, San Petersburgo
Texts by Eugenija N. Petrova, Elena V. Basner and Kasimir Malevich

PICASSO. EL SOMBRERO DE TRES PICOS. Dibujos para los decorados y el vestuario del ballet de Manuel de Falla
Texts by Vicente García-Márquez, Brigitte Léal and Laurence Berthon

MUSEO BRÜCKE BERLÍN. ARTE EXPRESIONISTA ALEMÁN
Texts by Magdalena M. Moeller

1994

GOYA GRABADOR
Texts by Alfonso E. Pérez-Sánchez and Julián Gállego

ISAMU NOGUCHI
Texts by Shoji Sadao, Bruce Altshuler and Isamu Noguchi

TESOROS DEL ARTE JAPONÉS. Período Edo: 1615-1868. Colección del Museo Fuji, Tokio
Texts by Tatsuo Takakura, Shin-ichi Miura, Akira Gokita, Seiji Nagata, Yoshiaki Yabe, Hirokazu Arakawa and Yoshihiko Sasama

FERNANDO ZÓBEL. RÍO JÚCAR
Texts by Fernando Zóbel and Rafael Pérez-Madero
C

1995

KLIMT, KOKOSCHKA, SCHIELE. UN SUEÑO VIENÉS: 1898-1918
Texts by Gerbert Frodl and Stephan Koja

ROUAULT
Texts by Stephan Koja, Jacques Maritain and Marcel Arland

MOTHERWELL. Obra gráfica: 1975-1991. Colección Kenneth Tyler
Texts by Robert Motherwell
C

1996

TOM WESSELMANN
Texts by Marco Livingstone, Jo-Anne Birnie Danzker, Tilman Osterwold and Meinrad Maria Grewenig
Published by Hatje Cantz, Ostfildern, 1996

TOULOUSE-LAUTREC. De Albi y de otras colecciones
Texts by Danièle Devynck and Valeriano Bozal

MILLARES. Pinturas y dibujos sobre papel: 1963-1971
Texts by Manuel Millares
P C

MUSEU D'ART ESPANYOL CONTEMPORANI. FUNDACION JUAN MARCH. PALMA
[Guide to the Museu d'Art Espanyol Contemporani]
Texts by Juan Manuel Bonet and Javier Maderuelo
Bilingual eds. (Spanish/Catalan and English/German)

PICASSO. SUITE VOLLARD
Text by Julián Gállego
Spanish ed., bilingual ed. (Spanish/German) and trilingual ed. (Spanish/German/English)
[This catalogue accompanies the exhibition of the same name that, since 1996, has traveled to five Spanish and foreign venues.]

1997

MAX BECKMANN
Texts by Klaus Gallwitz and Max Beckmann

EMIL NOLDE. NATURALEZA Y RELIGIÓN
Texts by Manfred Reuther

FRANK STELLA. Obra gráfica: 1982-1996. Colección Tyler Graphics
Texts by Sidney Guberman, Dorine Mignot and Frank Stella
P C

EL OBJETO DEL ARTE
Text by Javier Maderuelo
P C

MUSEO DE ARTE ABSTRACTO ESPAÑOL. FUNDACIÓN JUAN MARCH. CUENCA
[Guide to the Museo de Arte Abstracto Español]
Texts by Juan Manuel Bonet and Javier Maderuelo
Bilingual ed. (Spanish/English)

1998

AMADEO DE SOUZA-CARDOSO
Texts by Javier Maderuelo, Antonio Cardoso and Joana Cunha Leal

PAUL DELVAUX
Text by Gisèle Ollinger-Zinque

RICHARD LINDNER
Text by Werner Spies

1999

MARC CHAGALL. TRADICIONES JUDÍAS
Texts by Sylvie Forestier, Benjamin Harshav, Meret Meyer and Marc Chagall

KURT SCHWITTERS Y EL ESPÍRITU DE LA UTOPÍA. Colección Ernst Schwitters
Texts by Javier Maderuelo, Markus Heinzelmann, Lola and Bengt Schwitters

LOVIS CORINTH
Texts by Thomas Deecke, Sabine Fehlemann, Jürgen H. Meyer and Antje Birthälmer

MIQUEL BARCELÓ. Ceràmiques: 1995-1998
Text by Enrique Juncosa
Bilingual ed. (Spanish/Catalan)
P

FERNANDO ZÓBEL. Obra gráfica completa
Texts by Rafael Pérez-Madero
Published by Departamento de Cultura, Diputación Provincial de Cuenca, Cuenca, 1999
P C

2000

VASARELY
Texts by Werner Spies and Michèle-Catherine Vasarely

EXPRESIONISMO ABSTRACTO. OBRA SOBRE PAPEL. Colección de The Metropolitan Museum of Art, Nueva York
Text by Lisa M. Messinger

SCHMIDT-ROTTLUFF. Colección Brücke-Museum Berlin
Text by Magdalena M. Moeller

NOLDE. VISIONES. Acuarelas. Colección de la Fundación Nolde-Seebüll
Text by Manfred Reuther
P C

LUCIO MUÑOZ. ÍNTIMO
Text by Rodrigo Muñoz Avia
C

EUSEBIO SEMPERE. PAISAJES
Text by Pablo Ramírez
P C

2001

DE CASPAR DAVID FRIEDRICH

Abstracto Español, Cuenca

A PICASSO. Obras maestras sobre papel del Museo Von der Heydt, de Wuppertal
Texts by Sabine Fehlemann

ADOLPH GOTTLIEB
Texts by Sanford Hirsch

MATISSE. ESPÍRITU Y SENTIDO. Obra sobre papel
Texts by Guillermo Solana, Marie-Thérèse Pulvenis de Séligny and Henri Matisse

RÓDCHENKO. GEOMETRÍAS
Texts by Alexandr Lavrentiev and Alexandr Ródchenko
P C

2002

GEORGIA O'KEEFFE. NATURALEZAS ÍNTIMAS
Texts by Lisa M. Messinger and Georgia O'Keeffe

TURNER Y EL MAR. Acuarelas de la Tate
Texts by José Jiménez, Ian Warrell, Nicola Cole, Nicola Moorby and Sarah Taft

MOMPÓ. Obra sobre papel
Texts by Dolores Durán Úcar
C

RIVERA. REFLEJOS
Texts by Jaime Brihuega, Marisa Rivera, Elena Rivera, Rafael Alberti and Luis Rosales
C

SAURA. DAMAS
Texts by Francisco Calvo Serraller and Antonio Saura
P C

GOYA. CAPRICHOS, DESASTRES, TAUROMAQUIA, DISPARATES
Texts by Alfonso E. Pérez-Sánchez

2003

ESPÍRITU DE MODERNIDAD. DE GOYA A GIACOMETTI. Obra sobre papel de la Colección Kornfeld
Text by Werner Spies

KANDINSKY. ORIGEN DE LA ABSTRACCIÓN
Texts by Valeriano Bozal, Marion Ackermann and Wassily Kandinsky

CHILLIDA. ELOGIO DE LA MANO
Text by Javier Maderuelo
P C

GERARDO RUEDA. CONSTRUCCIONES
Text by Barbara Rose
C

ESTEBAN VICENTE. Collages
Texts by José María Parreño and Elaine de Kooning
C

LUCIO MUÑOZ. ÍNTIMO
Texts by Rodrigo Muñoz Avia and Lucio Muñoz
P

MUSEU D'ART ESPANYOL CONTEMPORANI. FUNDACION JUAN MARCH. PALMA
[Guide to the Museu d'Art Espanyol Contemporani]
Texts by Juan Manuel Bonet and Javier Maderuelo
Bilingual eds. (Catalan/Spanish and English/German)

2004

MAESTROS DE LA INVENCIÓN DE LA COLECCIÓN E. DE ROTHSCHILD DEL MUSEO DEL LOUVRE
Texts by Pascal Torres Guardiola, Catherine Loisel, Christel Winling, Geneviève Bresc-Bautier, George A. Wanklyn and Louis Antoine Prat

FIGURAS DE LA FRANCIA MODERNA. De Ingres a Toulouse-Lautrec del Petit Palais de París
Texts by Delfín Rodríguez, Isabelle Collet, Amélie Simier, Maryline Assante di Panzillo and José de los Llanos
Bilingual ed. (Spanish/French)

LIUBOV POPOVA
Text by Anna María Guasch
P C

ESTEBAN VICENTE. GESTO Y COLOR
Text by Guillermo Solana
P

LUIS GORDILLO. DUPLEX
Texts by Miguel Cereceda and Jaime González de Aledo
Bilingual ed. (Spanish/English)
P C

NEW TECHNOLOGIES, NEW ICONOGRAPHY, NEW PHOTOGRAPHY. Photography of the 80's and 90's in the Collection of the Museo Nacional Centro de Arte Reina Sofía
Texts by Catherine Coleman, Pablo Llorca and María Toledo
Bilingual ed. (Spanish/English)
P C

KANDINSKY. Acuarelas. Städtische Galerie im Lenbachhaus, Munich
Texts by Helmut Friedel and Wassily Kandinsky
Bilingual ed. (Spanish/German)
P C

2005

CONTEMPORANEA. Kunstmuseum Wolfsburg
Texts by Gijs van Tuyl, Rudi Fuchs, Holger Broeker, Alberto Ruiz de Samaniego and Susanne Köhler
Bilingual ed. (Spanish/English)

ANTONIO SAURA. DAMAS
Texts by Francisco Calvo Serraller and Antonio Saura
Bilingual ed. (Spanish/English)

CELEBRATION OF ART: A Half Century of the Fundación Juan March
Texts by Juan Manuel Bonet, Juan Pablo Fusi, Antonio Muñoz Molina, Juan Navarro Baldeweg and Javier Fuentes
Spanish and English eds.

BECKMANN. Von der Heydt-Museum, Wuppertal
Text by Sabine Fehlemann
Bilingual ed. (Spanish/German)
P C

EGON SCHIELE: IN BODY AND SOUL
Text by Miguel Sáenz
Bilingual ed. (Spanish/English)
P C

LICHTENSTEIN: IN PROCESS
Texts by Juan Antonio Ramírez and Clare Bell
Bilingual ed. (Spanish/English)
P C

FACES AND MASKS: Photographs from the Ordóñez-Falcón Collection
Texts by Francisco Caja
Bilingual ed. (Spanish/English)
P C

2006

OTTO DIX
Texts by Ulrike Lorenz
Bilingual ed. (Spanish/English)

CREATIVE DESTRUCTION: Gustav Klimt, the Beethoven Frieze and the Controversy about the Freedom of Art
Texts by Stephan Koja, Carl E. Schorske, Alice Strobl, Franz A. J. Szabo, Manfred Koller, Verena Perhelfter and Rosa Sala Rose, Hermann Bahr, Ludwig Hevesi and Berta Zuckerkandl
Spanish, English and German eds.
Published by Prestel, Munich/ Fundación Juan March, Madrid, 2006

Supplementary publication: Hermann Bahr. CONTRA KLIMT
Original text by Hermann Bahr (1903), with additional texts by Christian Huemer, Verena Perlhefter, Rosa Sala Rose and Dietrun Otten

LA CIUDAD ABSTRACTA: 1966. El nacimiento del Museo de Arte Abstracto Español

KEY: Out of print | Available publications in February 2010 | P Exhibition at the Museu Fundación Juan March, Palma | C Exhibition at the Museo

Texts by Santos Juliá, María Bolaños, Ángeles Villalba, Juan Manuel Bonet, Gustavo Torner, Antonio Lorenzo, Rafael Pérez Madero, Pedro Miguel Ibáñez and Alfonso de la Torre

GARY HILL: IMAGES OF LIGHT. Works from the Collection of the Kunstmuseum Wolfsburg
Text by Holger Broeker
Bilingual ed. (Spanish/English)
P C

GOYA. CAPRICHOS, DESASTRES, TAUROMAQUIA, DISPARATES
Texts by Alfonso E. Pérez-Sánchez (11ª ed., 1ª ed. 1979)
[This catalogue accompanied the exhibition of the same name that, since 1979, has traveled to 173 Spanish and foreign venues. The catalogue has been translated into more than seven languages.]

2007

ROY LICHTENSTEIN: BEGINNING TO END
Texts by Jack Cowart, Juan Antonio Ramírez, Ruth Fine, Cassandra Lozano, James de Pasquale, Avis Berman and Clare Bell
Spanish, French and English eds.

Supplementary publication:
Roy Fox Lichtenstein. PAINTINGS, DRAWINGS AND PASTELS: A THESIS
Original text by Roy Fox Lichtenstein (1949), with additional texts by Jack Cowart and Clare Bell

THE ABSTRACTION OF LANDSCAPE: From Northern Romanticism to Abstract Expressionism
Texts by Werner Hofmann, Hein-Th. Schulze Altcappenberg, Barbara Dayer Gallati, Robert Rosenblum, Miguel López-Remiro, Mark Rothko, Cordula Meier, Dietmar Elger, Bernhard Teuber, Olaf Mörke and Víctor Andrés Ferretti
Spanish and English eds.

Supplementary publication:
Sean Scully. BODIES OF LIGHT
Original text by Sean Scully (1998)
Bilingual ed. (Spanish/English)

EQUIPO CRÓNICA. CRÓNICAS REALES
Texts by Michèle Dalmace, Fernando Marías and Tomàs Llorens
Bilingual ed. (Spanish/English)
P C

BEFORE AND AFTER MINIMALISM: A Century of Abstract Tendencies in the Daimler Chrysler Collection.
Virtual guide: www.march.es/arte/palma/anteriores/CatalogoMinimal/index.asp
Spanish, Catalan, English and German eds.
P

2008

MAXImin: Maximum Minimization in Contemporary Art
Texts by Renate Wiehager, John M Armleder, Ilya Bolotowsky, Daniel Buren, Hanne Darboven, Adolf Hölzel, Norbert Kricke, Heinz Mack and Friederich Vordemberge-Gildewart
Spanish and English eds.

TOTAL ENLIGHTENMENT: Conceptual Art in Moscow 1960-1990
Texts by Boris Groys, Ekaterina Bobrinskaya, Martina Weinhart, Dorothea Zwirner, Manuel Fontán del Junco, Andrei Monastyrski and Ilya Kabakov
Bilingual ed. (Spanish/English)
Published by Hatje Cantz, Ostfildern/Fundación Juan March, Madrid, 2008

ANDREAS FEININGER: 1906-1999
Texts by Andreas Feininger, Thomas Buchsteiner, Jean-François Chevrier, Juan Manuel Bonet and John Loengard
Bilingual ed. (Spanish/English)
P C

JOAN HERNÁNDEZ PIJUAN: THE DISTANCE OF DRAWING
Texts by Valentín Roma, Peter Dittmar and Narcís Comadira
Bilingual ed. (Spanish/English)
P C

Supplementary publication:
IRIS DE PASCUA. JOAN HERNÁNDEZ PIJUAN
Text by Elvira Maluquer
Bilingual ed. (Spanish/English)

MUSEO DE ARTE ABSTRACTO ESPAÑOL. FUNDACIÓN JUAN MARCH. CUENCA
[Guide to the Museo de Arte Abstracto Español]
Texts by Juan Manuel Bonet and Javier Maderuelo
Bilingual ed. (Spanish/English) (2nd ed., 1st ed. 2005)

2009

TARSILA DO AMARAL
Texts by Aracy Amaral, Juan Manuel Bonet, Jorge Schwartz, Regina Teixeira de Barros, Tarsila do Amaral, Mário de Andrade, Oswald de Andrade, Manuel Bandeira, Haroldo de Campos, Emiliano di Cavalcanti, Ribeiro Couto, Carlos Drummond de Andrade, António Ferro, Jorge de Lima and Sérgio Milliet
Spanish and English eds.

Supplementary publication:
Oswald de Andrade. PAU BRASIL
Semi-facsimile Spanish ed., Spanish translation by Andrés Sánchez Robayna

Blaise Cendrars.
HOJAS DE RUTA
Semi-facsimile Spanish ed., Spanish translation by José Antonio Millán Alba

CARLOS CRUZ-DIEZ: COLOR HAPPENS
Texts by Osbel Suárez, Carlos Cruz-Diez, Gloria Carnevali and Ariel Jiménez
Spanish and English eds.
P C

Supplementary publication:
Carlos Cruz-Diez. REFLECTION ON COLOR
Original text by Carlos Cruz-Diez (1989), rev. and exp.
Spanish and English eds.

CASPAR DAVID FRIEDRICH; THE ART OF DRAWING
Texts de Christina Grummt, Helmut Börch-Supan, y Werner Busch
Spanish and English eds.

MUSEU FUNDACION JUAN MARCH, PALMA
[Guide to the Museu Fundación Juan March]
Texts by Miquel Seguí Aznar and Elvira González Gozalo, Juan Manuel Bonet, and Javier Maderuelo
Catalan, Spanish, English, and German eds.

2010

WYNDHAM LEWIS (1882–1957)
Texts by Paul Edwards, Richard Humphreys, Yolanda Morató, Juan Bonilla, Andrzej Gasiorek, and Alan Munton
Spanish and English eds.

Supplementary publication:
William Shakespeare and Thomas Middleton. TIMÓN DE ATENAS/TIMON OF ATHENS
With illustrations by Wyndham Lewis, translated and annotated by Ángel-Luis Pujante and Salvador Oliva
Bilingual edition (Spanish/English)

Supplementary publication:
BLAST. Revista del gran vórtice inglés
Translation and notes by Yolanda Morató
Semi-facsimile Spanish ed.

For more information: www.march.es

Abstracto Español, Cuenca

A TYPOGRAPHICAL NOTE

Wyndham Lewis (1882-1957)
has been composed in Knockout as the main display typeface, and
Times New Roman and Akzidenz Grotesk for the text

Aa

Knockout, designed in 2000 by Jonathan Hoefler,
was inspired by late 19th-century circus posters and their vigorous
grotesques. It and was chosen for its similarity to the
strong sans serif typefaces that populate
Wyndham Lewis's publications, such as *Blast*, which
show his rebel spirit through a daring use of bold letters
that are a true "punch in the page"

Aa

Times New Roman is the counterpoint to Knockout
representing the "classic" side of the late
Lewis. Nothing illustrates this better than the British typeface
commissioned by *The Times* of London, drawn in
1931 by Stanley Morison and Victor Lardent as
the modern interpretation of the venerable typeface
of the newspaper, which was, typographically,
behind the times

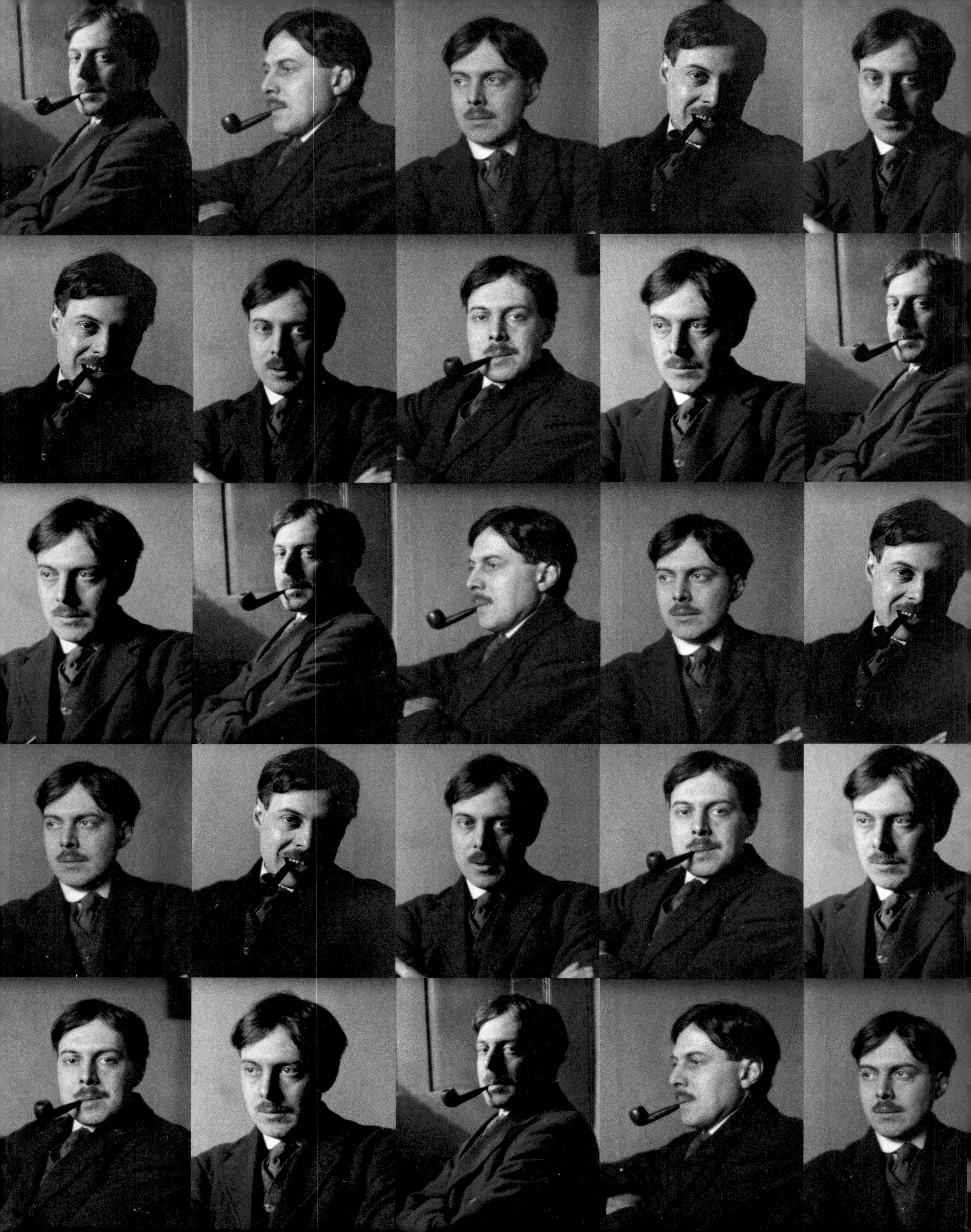